CCNA®
Routing and Switching Complete Deluxe
Study Guide
Second Edition

Todd Lammle

SYBEX®
A Wiley Brand

Senior Acquisitions Editor: Kenyon Brown
Development Editor: Kim Wimpsett
Technical Editor: Todd Montgomery
Production Editor: Christine O'Connor
Copy Editor: Judy Flynn
Editorial Manager: Mary Beth Wakefield
Production Manager: Kathleen Wisor
Executive Publisher: Jim Minatel
Book Designers: Judy Fung and Bill Gibson
Proofreader: Josh Chase, Word One New York
Indexer: Johnna vanHoose Dinse
Project Coordinator, Cover: Brent Savage
Cover Designer: Wiley
Cover Image: Getty Images Inc./Jeremy Woodhouse

Acknowledgments

There are many people who work to put a book together, and as an author, I dedicated an enormous amount of time to write this book, but it would have never been published without the dedicated, hard work of many other people.

Kenyon Brown, my acquisitions editor, is instrumental to my success in the world of Cisco certification. Ken, I look forward to our continued progress together in both the print and video markets! My technical editor, Todd Montgomery, was absolutely amazing to work with and he was always there to check my work and make suggestions. Thank you! Also, I've worked with Kim Wimpsett, the development editor, for years now and she coordinated all the pages you hold in your hands as they flew from thoughts in my head to the production process.

Christine O'Connor, my production editor, and Judy Flynn, my copyeditor, were my rock and foundation for formatting and intense editing of every page in this book. This amazing team gives me the confidence to help keep me moving during the difficult and very long days, week after week. How Christine stays so organized with all my changes as well as making sure every figure is in the right place in the book is still a mystery to me! You're amazing, Christine! Thank you! Judy understands my writing style so well now, after doing at least a dozen books with me, that she even sometimes finds a technical error that may have slipped through as I was going through the material. Thank you, Judy, for doing such a great job! I truly thank you both.

About the Author

Todd Lammle is the authority on Cisco certification and internetworking and is Cisco certified in most Cisco certification categories. He is a world-renowned author, speaker, trainer, and consultant. Todd has three decades of experience working with LANs, WANs, and large enterprise licensed and unlicensed wireless networks, and lately he's been implementing large Cisco Firepower networks. His years of real-world experience are evident in his writing; he is not just an author but an experienced networking engineer with very practical experience working on the largest networks in the world, at such companies as Xerox, Hughes Aircraft, Texaco, AAA, Cisco, and Toshiba, among many others. Todd has published over 60 books, including the very popular *CCNA: Cisco Certified Network Associate Study Guide, CCNA Wireless Study Guide, CCNA Data Center Study Guide,* and *SSFIPS (Firepower),* all from Sybex. He runs an international consulting and training company based in Colorado, Texas, and San Francisco.

You can reach Todd through his forum and blog at www.lammle.com/ccna.

Contents at a Glance

Introduction   *xxv*

Assessment Test   *1*

Part I	**ICND1**	**1**
Chapter 1	Internetworking	3
Chapter 2	Ethernet Networking and Data Encapsulation	41
Chapter 3	Introduction to TCP/IP	85
Chapter 4	Easy Subnetting	135
Chapter 5	VLSMs, Summarization, and Troubleshooting TCP/IP	175
Chapter 6	Cisco's Internetworking Operating System (IOS)	205
Chapter 7	Managing a Cisco Internetwork	273
Chapter 8	Managing Cisco Devices	323
Chapter 9	IP Routing	357
Chapter 10	Layer 2 Switching	411
Chapter 11	VLANs and Inter-VLAN Routing	443
Chapter 12	Security	483
Chapter 13	Network Address Translation (NAT)	521
Chapter 14	Internet Protocol Version 6 (IPv6)	547
Part II	**ICND2**	**581**
Chapter 15	Enhanced Switched Technologies	583
Chapter 16	Network Device Management and Security	649
Chapter 17	Enhanced IGRP	681
Chapter 18	Open Shortest Path First (OSPF)	745
Chapter 19	Multi-Area OSPF	783
Chapter 20	Troubleshooting IP, IPv6, and VLANs	831
Chapter 21	Wide Area Networks	881
Chapter 22	Evolution of Intelligent Networks	947

Appendix A   Answers to Written Labs   977

Appendix B   Answers to Review Questions   997

Appendix C   Disabling and Configuring Network Services   1037

Index   *1047*

Contents

Introduction   *xxv*

Assessment Test   *l*

Part I	**ICND1**	**1**
Chapter 1	**Internetworking**	**3**

Internetworking Basics   4
Internetworking Models   13
    The Layered Approach   13
    Advantages of Reference Models   14
The OSI Reference Model   15
    The Application Layer   17
    The Presentation Layer   18
    The Session Layer   18
    The Transport Layer   18
    The Network Layer   24
    The Data Link Layer   26
    The Physical Layer   29
Summary   31
Exam Essentials   31
Written Labs   32
    Written Lab 1.1: OSI Questions   32
    Written Lab 1.2: Defining the OSI Layers and Devices   34
    Written Lab 1.3: Identifying Collision and Broadcast
        Domains   34
Review Questions   36

Chapter 2	**Ethernet Networking and Data Encapsulation**	**41**

Ethernet Networks in Review   42
    Collision Domain   43
    Broadcast Domain   44
    CSMA/CD   45
    Half- and Full-Duplex Ethernet   47
    Ethernet at the Data Link Layer   49
    Ethernet at the Physical Layer   55
Ethernet Cabling   59
    Straight-Through Cable   59
    Crossover Cable   60
    Rolled Cable   62
    Fiber Optic   64

Data Encapsulation   66
The Cisco Three-Layer Hierarchical Model   69
    The Core Layer   71
    The Distribution Layer   71
    The Access Layer   72
Summary   72
Exam Essentials   73
Written Labs   74
    Written Lab 2.1: Binary/Decimal/Hexadecimal Conversion   74
    Written Lab 2.2: CSMA/CD Operations   77
    Written Lab 2.3: Cabling   78
    Written Lab 2.4: Encapsulation   78
Review Questions   79

Chapter 3   Introduction to TCP/IP   85

Introducing TCP/IP   86
    A Brief History of TCP/IP   87
TCP/IP and the DoD Model   87
    The Process/Application Layer Protocols   89
    The Host-to-Host or Transport Layer Protocols   99
    The Internet Layer Protocols   108
IP Addressing   116
    IP Terminology   116
    The Hierarchical IP Addressing Scheme   117
    Private IP Addresses (RFC 1918)   122
IPv4 Address Types   123
    Layer 2 Broadcasts   124
    Layer 3 Broadcasts   124
    Unicast Address   125
    Multicast Address   126
Summary   127
Exam Essentials   127
Written Labs   129
    Written Lab 3.1: TCP/IP   129
    Written Lab 3.2: Mapping Applications to the DoD Model   129
Review Questions   131

Chapter 4   Easy Subnetting   135

Subnetting Basics   136
    How to Create Subnets   138
    Subnet Masks   138
    Classless Inter-Domain Routing (CIDR)   140
    IP Subnet-Zero   142

Subnetting Class C Addresses   142
Subnetting Class B Addresses   154
Subnetting Class A Addresses   163
Summary   166
Exam Essentials   166
Written Labs   167
Written Lab 4.1: Written Subnet Practice #1   167
Written Lab 4.2: Written Subnet Practice #2   168
Written Lab 4.3: Written Subnet Practice #3   169
Review Questions   170

Chapter   5   VLSMs, Summarization, and Troubleshooting TCP/IP   175

Variable Length Subnet Masks (VLSMs)   176
VLSM Design   178
Implementing VLSM Networks   179
Summarization   186
Troubleshooting IP Addressing   189
Determining IP Address Problems   192
Summary   196
Exam Essentials   197
Written Lab 5   198
Lab 5.1: Summarization Practice   198
Review Questions   199

Chapter   6   Cisco's Internetworking Operating System (IOS)   205

The IOS User Interface   206
Cisco IOS   206
Connecting to a Cisco IOS Device   207
Bringing Up a Switch   209
Command-Line Interface (CLI)   209
Entering the CLI   210
Overview of Router Modes   210
CLI Prompts   211
Editing and Help Features   213
Administrative Configurations   218
Hostnames   219
Banners   219
Setting Passwords   221
Encrypting Your Passwords   227
Descriptions   229
Router and Switch Interfaces   231
Bringing Up an Interface   234

Viewing, Saving, and Erasing Configurations   240
   Deleting the Configuration and Reloading the Device   242
   Verifying Your Configuration   242
Summary   255
Exam Essentials   256
Written Lab 6: IOS Understanding   259
Hands-on Labs   259
   Hands-on Lab 6.1: Erasing an Existing Configuration   260
   Hands-on Lab 6.2: Exploring User, Privileged,
     and Configuration Modes   260
   Hands-on Lab 6.3: Using the Help and Editing Features   261
   Hands-on Lab 6.4: Saving a Configuration   262
   Hands-on Lab 6.5: Setting Passwords   263
   Hands-on Lab 6.6: Setting the Hostname, Descriptions, IP
     Address, and Clock Rate   265
Review Questions   267

Chapter   7   Managing a Cisco Internetwork   273

The Internal Components of a Cisco Router and Switch   274
   The Router and Switch Boot Sequence   275
Backing Up and Restoring the Cisco Configuration   276
   Backing Up the Cisco Configuration   277
   Restoring the Cisco Configuration   279
   Erasing the Configuration   279
Configuring DHCP   280
   DHCP Relay   281
   Verifying DHCP on Cisco IOS   282
Syslog   283
   Configuring and Verifying Syslog   285
Network Time Protocol (NTP)   288
Exploring Connected Devices Using CDP and LLDP   289
   Getting CDP Timers and Holdtime Information   290
   Gathering Neighbor Information   291
   Documenting a Network Topology Using CDP   295
Using Telnet   298
   Telnetting into Multiple Devices Simultaneously   300
   Checking Telnet Connections   300
   Checking Telnet Users   301
   Closing Telnet Sessions   301
Resolving Hostnames   302
   Building a Host Table   302
   Using DNS to Resolve Names   304
Checking Network Connectivity and Troubleshooting   306
   Using the *ping* Command   306
   Using the *traceroute* Command   307

Debugging 308
Using the *show processes* Command 310
Summary 311
Exam Essentials 311
Written Labs 7 313
Written Lab 7.1: IOS Management 313
Written Lab 7.2: Router Memory 314
Hands-on Labs 314
Hands-on Lab 7.1: Backing Up the Router Configuration 315
Hands-on Lab 7.2: Using the Cisco Discovery
Protocol (CDP) 315
Hands-on Lab 7.3: Using Telnet 316
Hands-on Lab 7.4: Resolving Hostnames 317
Review Questions 319

Chapter 8 Managing Cisco Devices 323

Managing the Configuration Register 324
Understanding the Configuration Register Bits 324
Checking the Current Configuration Register Value 326
Boot System Commands 327
Recovering Passwords 328
Backing Up and Restoring the Cisco IOS 331
Verifying Flash Memory 332
Backing Up the Cisco IOS 333
Restoring or Upgrading the Cisco Router IOS 334
Using the Cisco IOS File System (Cisco IFS) 337
Licensing 341
Right-To-Use Licenses (Evaluation Licenses) 344
Backing Up and Uninstalling the License 347
Summary 348
Exam Essentials 348
Written Lab 8 349
Written Lab 8.1: IOS Management 350
Hands-on Labs 350
Hands-on Lab 8.1: Backing Up Your Router IOS 350
Hands-on Lab 8.2: Upgrading or Restoring Your Router IOS 351
Review Questions 352

Chapter 9 IP Routing 357

Routing Basics 359
The IP Routing Process 361
The Cisco Router Internal Process 366
Testing Your IP Routing Understanding 367
Configuring IP Routing 372
Corp Configuration 373

SF Configuration   375
LA Configuration   379
Configuring IP Routing in Our Network   381
Static Routing   382
Default Routing   387
Dynamic Routing   390
Routing Protocol Basics   390
Routing Information Protocol (RIP)   392
Configuring RIP Routing   393
Holding Down RIP Propagations   396
Summary   399
Exam Essentials   399
Written Lab 9   400
Hands-on Labs   401
Hands-on Lab 9.1: Creating Static Routes   402
Hands-on Lab 9.2: Configuring RIP Routing   403
Review Questions   405

Chapter 10   Layer 2 Switching   411

Switching Services   412
Three Switch Functions at Layer 2   413
Port Security   417
Configuring Catalyst Switches   422
Catalyst Switch Configuration   423
Verifying Cisco Catalyst Switches   430
Summary   433
Exam Essentials   433
Written Lab 10   434
Hands-on Labs   434
Lab 10.1: Configuring Layer 2 Switches   435
Lab 10.2: Verifying Layer 2 Switches   436
Lab 10.3: Configuring Port Security   437
Review Questions   438

Chapter 11   VLANs and Inter-VLAN Routing   443

VLAN Basics   444
Broadcast Control   447
Security   448
Flexibility and Scalability   448
Identifying VLANs   449
Frame Tagging   451
VLAN Identification Methods   452
Routing between VLANs   454
Configuring VLANs   456

Assigning Switch Ports to VLANs   459
Configuring Trunk Ports   461
Configuring Inter-VLAN Routing   465
Summary   472
Exam Essentials   472
Written Lab 11   473
Hands-on Labs   473
Hands-on Lab 11.1: Configuring and Verifying VLANs   474
Hands-on Lab 11.2: Configuring and Verifying Trunk Links   474
Hands-on Lab 11.3: Configuring Router on a Stick Routing   475
Hands-on Lab 11.4: Configuring IVR with a Layer 3 Switch   476
Review Questions   477

Chapter   12   Security   483

Perimeter, Firewall, and Internal Routers   484
Introduction to Access Lists   485
Mitigating Security Issues with ACLs   488
Standard Access Lists   489
Wildcard Masking   490
Standard Access List Example   492
Controlling VTY (Telnet/SSH) Access   496
Extended Access Lists   497
Extended Access List Example 1   501
Extended Access List Example 2   503
Extended Access List Example 3   504
Named ACLs   505
Remarks   507
Monitoring Access Lists   508
Summary   510
Exam Essentials   511
Written Lab 12   511
Hands-on Labs   512
Hands-on Lab 12.1: Standard IP Access Lists   513
Hands-on Lab 12.2: Extended IP Access Lists   514
Review Questions   517

Chapter   13   Network Address Translation (NAT)   521

When Do We Use NAT?   522
Types of Network Address Translation   524
NAT Names   524
How NAT Works   525
Static NAT Configuration   527
Dynamic NAT Configuration   527
PAT (Overloading) Configuration   528
Simple Verification of NAT   529

Testing and Troubleshooting NAT   529
Summary   535
Exam Essentials   535
Written Lab 13   535
Hands-on Labs   536
    Lab 13.1: Preparing for NAT   537
    Lab 13.2: Configuring Dynamic NAT   538
    Lab 13.3: Configuring PAT   540
Review Questions   542

Chapter   14   Internet Protocol Version 6 (IPv6)   547

Why Do We Need IPv6?   549
The Benefits and Uses of IPv6   549
IPv6 Addressing and Expressions   551
    Shortened Expression   551
    Address Types   552
    Special Addresses   554
How IPv6 Works in an Internetwork   555
    Manual Address Assignment   555
    Stateless Autoconfiguration (eui-64)   556
    DHCPv6 (Stateful)   559
    IPv6 Header   559
    ICMPv6   561
IPv6 Routing Protocols   565
    Static Routing with IPv6   565
Configuring IPv6 on Our Internetwork   566
Configuring Routing on Our Internetwork   569
Summary   572
Exam Essentials   573
Written Labs 14   573
    Written Lab 14.1   573
    Written Lab 14.2   574
Hands-on Labs   574
    Hands-on Lab 14.1: Manual and Stateful Autoconfiguration   574
    Hands-on Lab 14.2: Static and Default Routing   576
Review Questions   577

Part   II   ICND2   581

Chapter   15   Enhanced Switched Technologies   583

VLAN Review   584
    Assigning Switch Ports to VLANs   587
    Configuring Trunk Ports   589

VLAN Trunking Protocol (VTP)   593
   VTP Modes of Operation   594
   VTP Pruning   596
Configuring VTP   597
   Troubleshooting VTP   598
Spanning Tree Protocol (STP)   602
   Spanning-Tree Terms   603
   Spanning-Tree Operations   607
Types of Spanning-tree Protocols   610
   Common Spanning Tree   610
   Per-VLAN Spanning Tree+   611
Modifying and Verifying the Bridge ID   618
Spanning-Tree Failure Consequences   623
PortFast and BPDU Guard   625
   BPDU Guard   627
EtherChannel   629
   Configuring and Verifying Port Channels   630
Summary   634
Exam Essentials   635
Written Lab 15   635
Hands-on Labs   636
   Hands-on Lab 15.1: Verifying STP and Finding
      Your Root Bridge   637
   Hands-on Lab 15.2: Configuring and Verifying
      Your Root Bridge   638
   Hands-on Lab 15.3: Configuring PortFast and BPDU
      Guard   640
   Hands-on Lab 15.4: Configuring and Verifying
      EtherChannel   641
Review Questions   643

Chapter   16   Network Device Management and Security   649

Mitigating Threats at the Access Layer   650
External Authentication Options   653
   RADIUS   653
   TACACS+   654
SNMP   655
   Management Information Base (MIB)   656
   Configuring SNMP   657
Client Redundancy Issues   659
Introducing First Hop Redundancy Protocols (FHRPs)   661
Hot Standby Router Protocol (HSRP)   662
   Virtual MAC Address   664

	HSRP Timers	665
	Group Roles	667
	Configuring and Verifying HSRP	669
	Summary	675
	Exam Essentials	675
	Written Lab 16	676
	Review Questions	677

Chapter   17   Enhanced IGRP   681

	EIGRP Features and Operations	682
	Neighbor Discovery	683
	Reliable Transport Protocol (RTP)	688
	Diffusing Update Algorithm (DUAL)	689
	Route Discovery and Maintenance	689
	Configuring EIGRP	690
	VLSM Support and Summarization	693
	Controlling EIGRP Traffic	696
	Split Horizon	707
	Verifying and Troubleshooting EIGRP	709
	Troubleshooting Example with EIGRP	715
	Simple Troubleshooting EIGRP for the CCNA	725
	EIGRPv6	727
	Summary	732
	Exam Essentials	733
	Written Lab 17	733
	Hands-on Labs	734
	Hands-on Lab 17.1: Configuring and Verifying EIGRP	734
	Hands-on Lab 17.2: Configuring and Verifying EIGRPv6	735
	Review Questions	737

Chapter   18   Open Shortest Path First (OSPF)   745

	Open Shortest Path First (OSPF) Basics	746
	OSPF Terminology	749
	OSPF Operation	751
	Configuring OSPF	753
	Enabling OSPF	753
	Configuring OSPF Areas	754
	Configuring Our Network with OSPF	757
	OSPF and Loopback Interfaces	762
	Configuring Loopback Interfaces	763
	Verifying OSPF Configuration	765
	The *show ip ospf* Command	766
	The *show ip ospf database* Command	767
	The *show ip ospf interface* Command	768

The *show ip ospf neighbor* Command   769
The *show ip protocols* Command   770
Summary   771
Exam Essentials   771
Written Lab 18   772
Hands-on Labs   772
    Hands-on Lab 18.1: Enabling the OSPF Process   773
    Hands-on Lab 18.2: Configuring OSPF Interfaces   774
    Hands-on Lab 18.3: Verifying OSPF Operation   775
Review Questions   776

Chapter 19   Multi-Area OSPF   783

OSPF Scalability   784
Categories of Multi-area Components   786
    Adjacency Requirements   786
    OSPF Router Roles   787
    Link-State Advertisements   788
    OSPF Hello Protocol   790
    Neighbor States   791
Basic Multi-area Configuration   793
Verifying and Troubleshooting Multi-area OSPF Networks   796
    The *show ip ospf* Command   797
    The *show ip ospf interface* Command   798
    The *show ip protocols* Command   801
    The *show ip route* Command   801
    The *show ip ospf database* Command   802
Troubleshooting OSPF Scenario   804
    Simple Troubleshooting OSPF for the CCNA   812
OSPFv3   814
    Verifying OSPFv3   816
Summary   819
Exam Essentials   819
Written Lab 19   820
Hands-on Labs   820
    Hands-on Lab 19.1: Configuring and Verifying OSPF
      Multi-Area   821
    Hands-on Lab 19.2: Configuring and Verifying OSPFv3 824
Review Questions   826

Chapter 20   Troubleshooting IP, IPv6, and VLANs   831

Troubleshooting IP Network Connectivity   832
    Using IP SLA for Troubleshooting   843
    Using SPAN for Troubleshooting   845
    Configuring and Verifying Extended Access Lists   847

Troubleshooting IPv6 Network Connectivity   850
   ICMPv6   850
   Troubleshooting IPv6 Extended Access Lists   858
Troubleshooting VLAN Connectivity   862
   VLAN Troubleshooting   862
   Trunk Troubleshooting   867
Summary   874
Exam Essentials   875
Written Lab 20   875
Review Questions   877

Chapter 21   Wide Area Networks   881

Introduction to Wide Area Networks   882
   WAN Topology Options   883
   Defining WAN Terms   885
   WAN Connection Bandwidth   886
   WAN Connection Types   887
   WAN Support   888
   Cisco Intelligent WAN (IWAN)   891
Cabling the Serial Wide Area Network   894
   Serial Transmission   894
   Data Terminal Equipment and Data Communication
      Equipment   895
High-Level Data-Link Control (HDLC) Protocol   896
Point-to-Point Protocol (PPP)   898
   Link Control Protocol (LCP) Configuration Options 899
   PPP Session Establishment   900
   PPP Authentication Methods   901
   Configuring PPP on Cisco Routers   901
   Configuring PPP Authentication   901
   Verifying and Troubleshooting Serial Links 902
   Multilink PPP (MLP)   907
   PPP Client (PPPoE)   911
   Configuring a PPPoE Client   912
Virtual Private Networks   913
   Benefits of VPNs   914
   Enterprise- and Provider-Managed VPNs   915
   Introduction to Cisco IOS IPsec   917
   IPsec Transforms   918
GRE Tunnels   919
   GRE over IPsec   920
   Configuring GRE Tunnels   921
   Verifying GRP Tunnels   923

Single-Homed EBGP 925
  Protocol Comparison and Overview 926
  Configuring and Verifying EBGP 929
  Verifying EBGP 931
Summary 934
Exam Essentials 934
Written Lab 21 935
Hands-on Labs 935
  Hands-on Lab 21.1: Configuring PPP Encapsulation
    and Authentication 936
  Hands-on Lab 21.2: Configuring and Monitoring HDLC 937
  Hands-on Lab 21.3: Configuring a GRE Tunnel 938
Review Questions 941

Chapter 22 Evolution of Intelligent Networks 947

Switch Stacking 948
Cloud Computing and Its Effect on the Enterprise Network 950
  Service Models 952
Overview of Network Programmability in Enterprise
  Network 953
Application Programming Interfaces (APIs) 954
  Southbound APIs 955
  Northbound APIs 956
Cisco APIC-EM 957
  Using APIC-EM for Path Tracing 959
Cisco Intelligent WAN 960
Quality of Service 962
  Traffic Characteristics 962
Trust Boundary 964
QoS Mechanisms 965
  Classification and Marking 965
  Policing, Shaping, and Re-Marking 966
  Tools for Managing Congestion 967
  Tools for Congestion Avoidance 970
Summary 971
Exam Essentials 971
Written Lab 22 971
Review Questions 973

Appendix A Answers to Written Labs 977

Chapter 1: Internetworking 978
  Written Lab 1.1: OSI Questions 978
  Written Lab 1.2: Defining the OSI Layers and Devices 979

Written Lab 1.3: Identifying Collision and Broadcast
  Domains   979
Chapter 2: Ethernet Networking and Data Encapsulation   980
  Written Lab 2.1: Binary/Decimal/Hexadecimal Conversion   980
  Written Lab 2.2: CSMA/CD Operations   982
  Written Lab 2.3: Cabling   982
  Written Lab 2.4: Encapsulation   982
Chapter 3: Introduction to TCP/IP   983
  Written Lab 3.1: TCP/IP   983
  Written Lab 3.2: Mapping Applications to the DoD Model   983
Chapter 4: Easy Subnetting   984
  Written Lab 4.1: Written Subnet Practice #1   984
  Written Lab 4.2: Written Subnet Practice #2   985
  Written Lab 4.3: Written Subnet Practice #3   985
Chapter 5: VLSMs, Summarization and Troubleshooting
  TCP/IP   986
Chapter 6: Cisco's Internetworking Operating System (IOS)   986
  Written Lab 6: Cisco IOS   986
Chapter 7: Managing a Cisco Internetwork   987
  Written Lab 7.1: IOS Management   987
  Written Lab 7.2: Router Memory   987
Chapter 8: Managing Cisco Devices   988
  Written Lab 8.1: IOS Management   988
Chapter 9: IP Routing   988
Chapter 10: Layer 2 Switching   989
Chapter 11: VLANs and InterVLAN Routing   989
Chapter 12: Security   990
Chapter 13: Network Address Translation (NAT)   991
Chapter 14: Internet Protocol Version 6 (IPv6)   991
  Written Lab 14.1: IPv6 Foundation   991
  Written Lab 14.2: EUI-64 Format   992
Chapter 15: Enhanced Switched Technologies   992
  Written Lab 15   992
Chapter 16: Network Device Management and Security   993
  Written Lab 16   993
Chapter 17: Enhanced IGRP   993
  Written Lab 17   993
Chapter 18: Open Shortest Path First (OSPF)   994
  Written Lab 18   994
Chapter 19: Multi-Area OSPF   994
  Written Lab 19   994
Chapter 20: Troubleshooting IP, IPv6, and VLANs   995
  Written Lab 20   995

Chapter 21: Wide Area Networks   995
    Written Lab 21   995
Chapter 22: Evolution of Intelligent Networks   996
    Written Lab 22   996

Appendix   B   Answers to Review Questions   997

Chapter 1: Internetworking   998
Chapter 2: Ethernet Networking and Data Encapsulation   1000
Chapter 3: Introduction to TCP/IP   1002
Chapter 4: Easy Subnetting   1003
Chapter 5: VLSMs, Summarization, and Troubleshooting
    TCP/IP   1005
Chapter 6: Cisco's Internetworking Operating System (IOS)   1007
Chapter 7: Managing a Cisco Internetwork   1009
Chapter 8: Managing Cisco Devices   1010
Chapter 9: IP Routing   1012
Chapter 10: Layer 2 Switching   1013
Chapter 11: VLANs and InterVLAN Routing   1015
Chapter 12: Security   1017
Chapter 13: Network Address Translation (NAT)   1019
Chapter 14: Internet Protocol Version 6 (IPv6)   1020
Chapter 15: Enhanced Switched Technologies   1022
Chapter 16: Network Device Management and Security   1024
Chapter 17: Enhanced IGRP   1025
Chapter 18: Open Shortest Path First (OSPF)   1027
Chapter 19: Multi-Area OSPF   1029
Chapter 20: Troubleshooting IP, IPv6, and VLANs   1031
Chapter 21: Wide Area Networks   1032
Chapter 22: Evolution of Intelligent Networks   1033

Appendix   C   Disabling and Configuring Network Services   1037

Blocking SNMP Packets   1038
Disabling Echo   1038
Turning off BootP and Auto-Config   1039
Disabling the HTTP Interface   1040
Disabling IP Source Routing   1040
Disabling Proxy ARP   1040
Disabling Redirect Messages   1040
Disabling the Generation of ICMP Unreachable Messages   1041
Disabling Multicast Route Caching   1041
Disabling the Maintenance Operation Protocol (MOP)   1041
Turning Off the X.25 PAD Service   1042

Enabling the Nagle TCP Congestion Algorithm   1042
Logging Every Event   1042
Disabling Cisco Discovery Protocol   1043
Disabling the Default Forwarded UDP Protocols   1043
Cisco's *auto secure*   1044

Index   *1047*

Introduction

Welcome to the exciting world of Cisco certification! If you've picked up this book because you want to improve yourself and your life with a better, more satisfying, and secure job, you've done the right thing. Whether you're striving to enter the thriving, dynamic IT sector or seeking to enhance your skill set and advance your position within it, being Cisco certified can seriously stack the odds in your favor to help you attain your goals!

Cisco certifications are powerful instruments of success that also markedly improve your grasp of all things internetworking. As you progress through this book, you'll gain a complete understanding of networking that reaches far beyond Cisco devices. By the end of this book, you'll comprehensively know how disparate network topologies and technologies work together to form the fully operational networks that are vital to today's very way of life in the developed world. The knowledge and expertise you'll gain here is essential for and relevant to every networking job and is why Cisco certifications are in such high demand—even at companies with few Cisco devices!

Although it's now common knowledge that Cisco rules routing and switching, the fact that it also rocks the security, collaboration, data center, wireless and service provider worlds is also well recognized. And Cisco certifications reach way beyond the popular but less extensive certifications like those offered by CompTIA and Microsoft to equip you with indispensable insight into today's vastly complex networking realm. Essentially, by deciding to become Cisco certified, you're proudly announcing that you want to become an unrivaled networking expert—a goal that this book will get you well on your way to achieving. Congratulations in advance on the beginning of your brilliant future!

For up-to-the-minute updates covering additions or modifications to the Cisco certification exams, as well as additional study tools, review questions, videos, and bonus materials, be sure to visit the Todd Lammle websites and forum at www.lammle.com/ccna.

Cisco's Network Certifications

It used to be that to secure the holy grail of Cisco certifications—the CCIE—you passed only one written test before being faced with a grueling, formidable hands-on lab. This intensely daunting, all-or-nothing approach made it nearly impossible to succeed and predictably didn't work out too well for most people. Cisco responded to this issue by creating a series of new certifications, which not only made it easier to eventually win the highly coveted CCIE prize, it gave employers a way to accurately rate and measure the skill levels of prospective and current employees. This exciting paradigm shift in Cisco's certification path truly opened doors that few were allowed through before!

Beginning in 1998, obtaining the Cisco Certified Network Associate (CCNA) certification was the first milestone in the Cisco certification climb, as well as the official prerequisite to each of the more advanced levels. But that changed in 2007, when Cisco announced the Cisco Certified Entry Network Technician (CCENT) certification. And then in May 2016, Cisco once again proclaimed updates to the CCENT and CCNA Routing and Switching (R/S) tests. Now the Cisco certification process looks like Figure I.1.

FIGURE I.1   The Cisco certification path

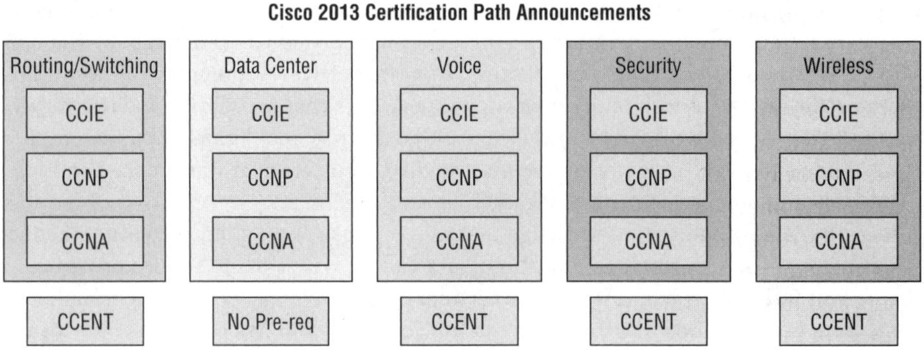

Cisco 2013 Certification Path Announcements

Routing/Switching	Data Center	Voice	Security	Wireless
CCIE	CCIE	CCIE	CCIE	CCIE
CCNP	CCNP	CCNP	CCNP	CCNP
CCNA	CCNA	CCNA	CCNA	CCNA
CCENT	No Pre-req	CCENT	CCENT	CCENT

> **NOTE**   I have included only the most popular tracks in Figure I.1. In addition to the ones in this image, there are also tracks for Design, Service Provider, Service Provider Operations, and Video.

The Cisco R/S path is by far the most popular and could very well remain so, but soon you'll see the Data Center path become more and more of a focus as companies migrate to data center technologies. The Security and Collaboration tracks also actually does provide a good job opportunity, and an even newer one that is becoming more popular is the Industrial CCNA. Still, understanding the foundation of R/S before attempting any other certification track is something I highly recommend.

Even so, and as the figure shows, you only need your CCENT certification to get underway for most of the tracks. Also, note that there are a few other certification tracks you can go down that are not shown in the figure, although they're not as popular as the ones shown.

Cisco Certified Entry Network Technician (CCENT)

Don't be fooled by the oh-so-misleading name of this first certification because it absolutely isn't entry level! Okay—maybe entry level for Cisco's certification path, but definitely not for someone without experience trying to break into the highly lucrative yet challenging IT job market! For the uninitiated, the CompTIA A+ and Network+ certifications aren't official prerequisites, but know that Cisco does expect you to have that type and level of experience before embarking on your Cisco certification journey.

All of this gets us to 2016, when the climb to Cisco supremacy just got much harder again. The innocuous-sounding siren's call of the CCENT can lure you to some serious trouble if you're not prepared, because it's actually much harder than the old CCNA ever was. This will rapidly become apparent once you start studying, but be encouraged! The fact that the certification process is getting harder really works better for you in the long run, because that which is harder to obtain only becomes that much more valuable when you finally do, right? Yes, indeed!

Another important factor to keep in mind is that the Interconnection Cisco Network Devices Part 1 (ICND1) exam, which is the required exam for the CCENT certification, costs $150 per attempt and it's anything but easy to pass! The good news is that Part 1 of this book (Chapters 1-14) will guide you step-by-step in building a strong foundation in routing and switching technologies. You really need to build on a strong technical foundation and stay away from exam cram type books, suspicious online material, and the like. They can help somewhat, but understand that you'll pass the Cisco certification exams only if you have a strong foundation and that you'll get that solid foundation only by reading as much as you can, performing the written labs and review questions in this book, and practicing lots and lots of hands-on labs. Additional practice exam questions, videos, and labs are offered on my website, and what seems like a million other sites offer additional material that can help you study.

However, there is one way to skip the CCENT exam and still meet the prerequisite before moving on to any other certification track, and that path is through the CCNA R/S Composite exam. First, I'll discuss the Interconnecting Cisco Network Devices Part 2 (ICND2) exam, and then I'll tell you about the CCNA Composite exam, which will provide you, when successful, with both the CCENT and the CCNA R/S certification.

Cisco Certified Network Associate Routing and Switching (CCNA R/S)

Once you have achieved your CCENT certification, you can take the ICND2 (200-105) exam in order to achieve your CCNA R/S certification, which is the most popular certification Cisco has by far because it's the most sought-after certification of all employers.

As with the CCENT, the ICND2 exam is also $150 per attempt—although thinking you can just skim a book and pass any of these exams would probably be a really expensive mistake! The CCENT/CCNA exams are extremely hard and cover a lot of material, so you have to really know your stuff. Taking a Cisco class or spending months with hands-on experience is definitely a requirement to succeed when faced with this monster!

And once you have your CCNA, you don't have to stop there—you can choose to continue and achieve an even higher certification, called the Cisco Certified Network Professional (CCNP). There are various ones, as shown in Figure NaN.1. The CCNP R/S is still the most popular, with Voice certifications coming in at a close second. And I've got to tell you that the Data Center certification will be catching up fast. Also good to know is that anyone with a CCNP R/S has all the skills and knowledge needed to attempt the notoriously dreaded but coveted CCIE R/S lab. But just becoming a CCNA R/S can land you that job you've dreamed about and that's what this book is all about: helping you to get and keep a great job!

Still, why take two exams to get your CCNA if you don't have to? Cisco still has the CCNA Composite (200-125) exam that, if passed, will land you with your CCENT and your CCNA R/S via only one test priced at only $250. Some people like the one-test approach, and some people like the two-test approach. Part 2 of this book (Chapters 15-22) covers the ICND2 exam topics.

Why Become a CCENT and CCNA R/S?

Cisco, like Microsoft and other vendors that provide certification, has created the certification process to give administrators a set of skills and to equip prospective employers with a way to measure those skills or match certain criteria. And as you probably know, becoming a CCNA R/S is certainly the initial, key step on a successful journey toward a new, highly rewarding, and sustainable networking career.

The CCNA program was created to provide a solid introduction not only to the Cisco Internetwork Operating System (IOS) and Cisco hardware but also to internetworking in general, making it helpful to you in areas that are not exclusively Cisco's. And regarding today's certification process, it's not unrealistic that network managers—even those without Cisco equipment—require Cisco certifications for their job applicants.

Rest assured that if you make it through the CCNA and are still interested in Cisco and internetworking, you're headed down a path to certain success!

What Skills Do You Need to Become a CCNA R/S?

This ICND1 exam (100-105) tests a candidate for the knowledge and skills required to successfully install, operate, and troubleshoot a small branch office network. The exam includes questions on the operation of IP data networks, LAN switching technologies, IPv6, IP routing technologies, IP services, network device security, and basic troubleshooting. The ICND2 exam (exam 200-105) tests a candidate for the knowledge and skills required to successfully install, operate, and troubleshoot a small- to medium-size enterprise branch network. The exam includes questions on LAN switching technologies, IP routing technologies, security, troubleshooting, and WAN technologies.

How Do You Become a CCNA R/S

If you want to go straight for our CCNA R/S and take only one exam, all you have to do is pass the CCNA Composite exam (200-125). Oh, but don't you wish it were that easy? True, it's just one test, but it's a whopper, and to pass it you must possess enough knowledge to understand what the test writers are saying, and you need to know everything I mentioned previously, in the sections on the ICND1 and ICND2 exams! Hey, it's hard, but it can be done!

What does the CCNA Composite exam (200-125) cover? Pretty much the same topics covered in the ICND1 and ICND2 exams. Candidates can prepare for this exam by taking the Todd Lammle authorized Cisco boot camps. 200-125 tests a candidate's knowledge and skills required to install, operate, and troubleshoot a small- to medium-size enterprise branch network.

While you can take the Composite exam to get your CCNA, it's good to know that Cisco offers the two-step process I discussed earlier in this Introduction. And this book covers both those exams too! It may be easier than taking that one ginormous exam for you, but don't think the two-test method is easy. It takes work! However, it can be done; you just need to stick with your studies.

The two-test method involves passing the following:

- Exam 100-105: Interconnecting Cisco Networking Devices Part 1 (ICND1)
- Exam 200-105: Interconnecting Cisco Networking Devices Part 2 (ICND2)

I can't stress this point enough: It's critical that you have some hands-on experience with Cisco routers. If you can get a hold of some basic routers and switches, you're set, but if you can't, I've worked hard to provide hundreds of configuration examples throughout this book to help network administrators, or people who want to become network administrators, learn the skills they need to pass the CCENT and CCNA R/S exams.

> For Cisco certification hands-on training with CCSI Todd Lammle, please see: www.lammle.com/ccna. Each student will get hands-on experience by configuring at least three routers and two switches—no sharing of equipment!

What Does This Book Cover?

This book covers everything you need to know to pass the ICND1 (100-105) and ICND2 (200-105) exams, as well as the CCNA Composite (200-125) exam. But regardless of which path you choose, as I've said, taking plenty of time to study and practice with routers or a router simulator is the real key to success.

You will learn the following information in this book:

Chapter 1: Internetworking Chapters 1–14 map to the ICND1 exam. In Chapter 1, you will learn the basics of the Open Systems Interconnection (OSI) model the way Cisco wants you to learn it. There are written labs and plenty of review questions to help you. Do not even think of skipping the fundamental written labs in this chapter!

Chapter 2: Ethernet Networking and Data Encapsulation This chapter will provide you with the Ethernet foundation you need in order to pass both the CCENT and CCNA exams. Data encapsulation is discussed in detail in this chapter as well. And as with the other chapters, this chapter includes written labs and review questions to help you.

Chapter 3: Introduction to TCP/IP   This chapter provides you with the background necessary for success on the exam, as well as in the real world with a thorough presentation of TCP/IP. This in-depth chapter covers the very beginnings of the Internet Protocol stack and goes all the way to IP addressing and understanding the difference between a network address and a broadcast address before finally ending with network troubleshooting.

Chapter 4: Easy Subnetting   You'll actually be able to subnet a network in your head after reading this chapter if you really want to! And you'll find plenty of help in this chapter as long as you don't skip the written labs and review questions at the end.

Chapter 5: VLSMs, Summarization, and Troubleshooting TCP/IP   Here, you'll find out all about variable length subnet masks (VLSMs) and how to design a network using VLSMs. This chapter will finish with summarization techniques and configurations. As with Chapter 4, plenty of help is there for you if you don't skip the written lab and review questions.

Chapter 6: Cisco's Internetworking Operating System (IOS)   This chapter introduces you to the Cisco Internetworking Operating System (IOS) and command-line interface (CLI). In this chapter you'll learn how to turn on a router and configure the basics of the IOS, including setting passwords, banners, and more. Hands-on labs will help you gain a firm grasp of the concepts taught in the chapter. Before you go through the hands-on labs, be sure to complete the written lab and review questions.

Chapter 7: Managing a Cisco Internetwork   This chapter provides you with the management skills needed to run a Cisco IOS network. Backing up and restoring the IOS, as well as router configuration, are covered, as are the troubleshooting tools necessary to keep a network up and running. As always, before tackling the hands-on labs in this chapter, complete the written labs and review questions.

Chapter 8: Managing Cisco Devices   This chapter describes the boot process of Cisco routers, the configuration register, and how to manage Cisco IOS files. The chapter finishes with a section on Cisco's new licensing strategy for IOS. Hands-on and written labs, along with review questions, will help you build a strong foundation for the objectives covered in this chapter.

Chapter 9: IP Routing   This is a fun chapter because we will begin to build our network, add IP addresses, and route data between routers. You will also learn about static, default, and dynamic routing using RIP and RIPv2. Hands-on labs, a written lab, and the review questions will help you fully nail down IP routing.

Chapter 10: Layer 2 Switching   This chapter sets you up with the solid background you need on layer 2 switching, how switches perform address learning and make forwarding and filtering decisions. In addition, switch port security with MAC addresses is covered in detail. As always, go through the hands-on labs, written lab, and review questions to make sure you've really got layer 2 switching down!

Chapter 11: VLANs and Inter-VLAN Routing   Here I cover virtual VLANs and how to use them in your internetwork. This chapter covers the nitty-gritty of VLANs and the different concepts and protocols used with VLANs. I'll also guide you through troubleshooting techniques in this all-important chapter. The hands-on labs, written lab, and review questions are there to reinforce the VLAN material.

Chapter 12: Security   This chapter covers security and access lists, which are created on routers to filter the network. IP standard, extended, and named access lists are covered in detail. Written and hands-on labs, along with review questions, will help you study for the security and access-list portion of the Cisco exams.

Chapter 13: Network Address Translation (NAT)   New information, commands, troubleshooting, and detailed hands-on labs will help you nail the NAT CCENT objectives.

Chapter 14: Internet Protocol Version 6 (IPv6)   This is a fun chapter chock-full of some great information. IPv6 is not the big, bad scary creature that most people think it is, and it's a really important objective on the latest exam, so study this chapter carefully—don't just skim it. And make sure you hit those hands-on labs hard!

Chapter 15: Enhanced Switched Technologies   Chapter 15 is the first chapter of Part 2 of this book, which maps to the ICND2 exam. This chapter will start off with STP protocols and dive into the fundamentals, covering the modes, as well as the various flavors of STP. VLANs, trunks, and troubleshooting are covered as well. EtherChannel technologies, configuration, and verification are also covered. There are hands-on labs, a written lab, and plenty of review questions to help you. Do not even think of skipping the fundamental written and hands-on labs in this chapter!

Chapter 16: Network Device Management and Security Managing Cisco Devices   This chapter describes the boot process of Cisco routers, the configuration register, and how to manage Cisco IOS files. The chapter finishes with a section on Cisco's new licensing strategy for its IOS. Hands-on and written labs, along with review questions, will help you build a strong foundation for the objectives covered in this chapterhow to mitigate threats at the access layer using various security techniques. AAA with RADIUIS and TACACS+, SNMP and HSRP are also covered in this chapter. Don't skip the hands-on labs that are included, as well as a written lab and review questions at the end of the chapter.

Chapter 17: Enhanced IGRP   EIGRP was not covered in the ICND1 (CCENT) chapters, so this is a full chapter on nothing but EIGRP and EIGRPv6. There are lots of examples, including configuration, verification, and troubleshooting labs, with both IP and with IPv6. Great hands-on labs are included, as well as a written lab and review questions.

Chapter 18: Open Shortest Path First (OSPF)   Chapter 9 dives into more complex dynamic routing by covering OSPF routing. The written lab, hands-on labs, and review questions will help you master this vital routing protocol.

Chapter 19: Multi-Area OSPF   The ICND1 (CCENT) portion of this book had a large chapter on OSPF, so before reading this chapter, be sure you have the CCENT objectives down pat with a strong OSPF foundation. This chapter will take off where that ICND1 chapter left off and add multi-area networks along with advanced configurations and then finish with OSPv3. Hands-on labs, a written lab, and challenging review questions await you at the end of the chapter.

Chapter 20: Troubleshooting IP, IPv6, and VLANs   I want to say this is the most important chapter in the book, but that's hard to say. You can decide that yourself when you take the exam! Be sure to go through all the troubleshooting steps for IP, IPv6, and VLANs. The hands-on labs for this chapter will be included in the free bonus material and dynamic labs that I'll write and change as needed. Don't skip the written lab and review questions.

Chapter 21: Wide Area Networks   This is the longest, and last, chapter in the book. It covers multiple protocols in depth, especially HDLC, PPP, and Frame Relay, along with a discussion on many other technologies. Good troubleshooting examples are provided in the PPP and Frame Relay configuration sections, and these cannot be skipped! Hands-on labs meant to focus squarely on the objectives are included at the end of the chapter, as well as a written lab and challenging review questions.

Chapter 22: Evolution of Intelligent Networks   I saved the hardest chapter for last. What makes this chapter challenging is that there is no configuration section to you really need to dive deep into the cloud, APIC-EM and QoS sections with an open and ready mind. I stuck as close to the objectives as possible in order to help you ace the exam. The written lab and review questions are spot on for the objectives.

Appendix A: Answers to Written Labs   This appendix contains the answers to the book's written labs.

Appendix B: Answers to Chapter Review Questions   This appendix provides the answers to the end-of-chapter review questions.

Appendix C: Disabling and Configuring Network Services   Appendix C takes a look at the basic services you should disable on your routers to make your network less of a target for denial of service (DoS) attacks and break-in attempts.

Be sure to check the announcements section of my forum to find out how to download bonus material I created specifically for this book.

What's Available Online?

I have worked hard to provide some really great tools to help you with your certification process. All of the following tools, most of them available at www.wiley.com/go/sybextestprep, should be loaded on your workstation when you're studying for the test. As a fantastic bonus, I was able to add to the download link a preview section from my CCNA video series! Please understand that these are not the full versions, but they're still a great value for you included free with this book.

Test Preparation Software   The test preparation software prepares you to pass the ICND1 and ICND2 exams and the CCNA R/S Composite exam. You'll find all the review and assessment questions from the book *plus* additional practice exam questions that appear exclusively from the downloadable study tools.

Electronic Flashcards   The companion study tools include over 200 flashcards specifically written to hit you hard, so don't get discouraged if you don't ace your way through them at first! They're there to ensure that you're really ready for the exam. And no worries—armed with the review questions, practice exams, and flashcards, you'll be more than prepared when exam day comes!

Glossary   A complete glossary of CCENT, ICND2, CCNA R/S and Cisco routing terms is available at www.wiley.com/go/sybextestprep.

Todd Lammle Bonus Material and Labs   Be sure to check the announcement section of my forum at www.lammle.com/ccna for directions on how to download all the latest bonus material created specifically to help you study for your ICND1, ICND2, and CCNA R/S exams.

Todd Lammle Videos   I have created a full CCNA series of videos that can be purchased at www.lammle.com/ccna

How to Use This Book

If you want a solid foundation for the serious effort of preparing for the Interconnecting Cisco Network Devices Part 1 and 2 exams, or the CCNA R/S Composite exam, then look no further. I've spent hundreds of hours putting together this book with the sole intention of helping you to pass the Cisco exams, as well as really learn how to correctly configure Cisco routers and switches!

This book is loaded with valuable information, and you will get the most out of your study time if you understand why the book is organized the way it is.

So to maximize your benefit from this book, I recommend the following study method:

1. Take the assessment test that's provided at the end of this introduction. (The answers are at the end of the test.) It's okay if you don't know any of the answers; that's why you bought this book! Carefully read over the explanations for any questions you get wrong and note the chapters in which the material relevant to them is covered. This information should help you plan your study strategy.

2. Study each chapter carefully, making sure you fully understand the information and the test objectives listed at the beginning of each one. Pay extra-close attention to any chapter that includes material covered in questions you missed.

3. Complete the written labs at the end of each chapter. (Answers to these appear in Appendix A.) Do *not* skip these written exercises because they directly relate to the Cisco exams and what you must glean from the chapters in which they appear. Do not just skim these labs! Make sure you completely understand the reason for each correct answer.

4. Complete all hands-on labs in each chapter, referring to the text of the chapter so that you understand the reason for each step you take. Try to get your hands on some real equipment, but if you don't have Cisco equipment available, try the LammleSim IOS version, which you can use for the hands-on labs found only in this book. These labs will equip you with everything you need for all your Cisco certification goals.

5. Answer all of the review questions related to each chapter. (The answers appear in Appendix B.) Note the questions that confuse you, and study the topics they cover again until the concepts are crystal clear. And again—do not just skim these questions! Make sure you fully comprehend the reason for each correct answer. Remember that these will not be the exact questions you will find on the exam, but they're written to help you understand the chapter material and ultimately pass the exam!

6. Try your hand at the practice questions that are exclusive to this book. The questions can be found only at www.wiley.com/go/sybextestprep. And be sure to check out www.lammle.com/ccna for the most up-to-date Cisco exam prep questions, videos, Todd Lammle boot camps, and more.

7. Test yourself using all the flashcards, which are also found on the download link. These are brand-new and updated flashcards to help you prepare for the CCNA R/S exam and a wonderful study tool!

To learn every bit of the material covered in this book, you'll have to apply yourself regularly, and with discipline. Try to set aside the same time period every day to study, and select a comfortable and quiet place to do so. I'm confident that if you work hard, you'll be surprised at how quickly you learn this material!

If you follow these steps and really study—*doing hands-on labs every single day* in addition to using the review questions, the practice exams, the Todd Lammle video sections, and the electronic flashcards, as well as all the written labs—it would actually be hard to fail the Cisco exams. But understand that studying for the Cisco exams is a lot like getting in shape—if you do not go to the gym every day, it's not going to happen!

Where Do You Take the Exams?

You may take the ICND1, ICND2, or CCNA R/S Composite or any Cisco exam at any of the Pearson VUE authorized testing centers. For information, check www.vue.com or call 877-404-EXAM (3926).

To register for a Cisco exam, follow these steps:

1. Determine the number of the exam you want to take. (The ICND1 exam number is 100-105, ICND2 is 100-205, and CCNA R/S Composite is 200-125.)

2. Register with the nearest Pearson VUE testing center. At this point, you will be asked to pay in advance for the exam. At the time of this writing, the ICND1 and ICND2 exams are $150, and the CCNA R/S Composite exam is $250. The exams must be taken within one year of payment. You can schedule exams up to six weeks in advance or as late as the day you want to take it—but if you fail a Cisco exam, you must wait five days before you will be allowed to retake it. If something comes up and you need to cancel or reschedule your exam appointment, contact Pearson VUE at least 24 hours in advance.

3. When you schedule the exam, you'll get instructions regarding all appointment and cancellation procedures, the ID requirements, and information about the testing-center location.

Tips for Taking Your Cisco Exams

The Cisco exams contain about 40-50 questions and must be completed in about 90 minutes or less. This information can change per exam. You must get a score of about 85 percent to pass this exam, but again, each exam can be different.

Many questions on the exam have answer choices that at first glance look identical—especially the syntax questions! So remember to read through the choices carefully because close just doesn't cut it. If you get commands in the wrong order or forget one measly character, you'll get the question wrong. So, to practice, do the hands-on exercises at the end of this book's chapters over and over again until they feel natural to you.

Also, never forget that the right answer is the Cisco answer. In many cases, more than one appropriate answer is presented, but the *correct* answer is the one that Cisco recommends. On the exam, you will always be told to pick one, two, or three options, never "choose all that apply." The Cisco exam may include the following test formats:

- Multiple-choice single answer
- Multiple-choice multiple answer
- Drag-and-drop
- Router simulations

Cisco proctored exams will not show the steps to follow in completing a router interface configuration, but they do allow partial command responses. For example, show run, sho running, or sh running-config would be acceptable.

Here are some general tips for exam success:

- Arrive early at the exam center so you can relax and review your study materials.

- Read the questions *carefully*. Don't jump to conclusions. Make sure you're clear about *exactly* what each question asks. "Read twice, answer once," is what I always tell my students.

- When answering multiple-choice questions that you're not sure about, use the process of elimination to get rid of the obviously incorrect answers first. Doing this greatly improves your odds if you need to make an educated guess.

- You can no longer move forward and backward through the Cisco exams, so double-check your answer before clicking Next since you can't change your mind.

After you complete an exam, you'll get immediate, online notification of your pass or fail status, a printed examination score report that indicates your pass or fail status, and your exam results by section. (The test administrator will give you the printed score report.) Test scores are automatically forwarded to Cisco within five working days after you take the test, so you don't need to send your score to them. If you pass the exam, you'll receive confirmation from Cisco, typically within two to four weeks, sometimes a bit longer.

Objective Map for CCNA Routing and Switching Certification Exam

We've provided this objective map to help you locate where objectives for the CCNA Routing and Switching certification exams are covered in each chapter. Please refer to it when you want to find an objective quickly.

ICND1 Exam Objectives

Exam objectives are subject to change at any time without prior notice and at Cisco's sole discretion. Please visit Cisco's certification website (www.cisco.com/web/learning) for the latest information on the ICND1 Exam 100-105.

TABLE I.1   20% 1.0 Network Fundamentals

Objective	Chapter(s)
1.1 Compare and contrast OSI and TCP/IP models	3
1.2 Compare and contrast TCP and UDP protocols	3
1.3 Describe the impact of infrastructure components in an enterprise network	1
1.3.a Firewalls	1
1.3.b Access points	1
1.3.c Wireless controllers	1
1.4 Compare and contrast collapsed core and three-tier architectures	2
1.5 Compare and contrast network topologies	1
1.5.a Star	1
1.5.b Mesh	1
1.5.c Hybrid	1
1.6 Select the appropriate cabling type based on implementation requirements	2
1.7 Apply troubleshooting methodologies to resolve problems	3, 5
1.7.a Perform fault isolation and document	3, 5
1.7.b Resolve or escalate	3, 5
1.7.c Verify and monitor resolution	3, 5
1.8 Configure, verify, and troubleshoot IPv4 addressing and subnetting	4, 5
1.9 Compare and contrast IPv4 address types	3
1.9.a Unicast	3
1.9.b Broadcast	3
1.9.c Multicast	3

Objective	Chapter(s)
1.10 Describe the need for private IPv4 addressing	3
1.11 Identify the appropriate IPv6 addressing scheme to satisfy addressing requirements in a LAN/WAN environment	14
1.12 Configure, verify, and troubleshoot IPv6 addressing	14
1.13 Configure and verify IPv6 Stateless Address Auto Configuration	14
1.14 Compare and contrast IPv6 address types	14
1.14.a Global unicast	14
1.14.b Unique local	14
1.14.c Link local	14
1.14.d Multicast	14
1.14.e Modified EUI 64	14
1.14.f Autoconfiguration	14
1.14.g Anycast	14

TABLE I.2   26% 2.0 LAN Switching Fundamentals

Objective	Chapter(s)
2.1 Describe and verify switching concepts	10
2.1.a MAC learning and aging	10
2.1.b Frame switching	10
2.1.c Frame flooding	10
2.1.d MAC address table	10
2.2 Interpret Ethernet frame format	2
2.3 Troubleshoot interface and cable issues (collisions, errors, duplex, speed)	6
2.4 Configure, verify, and troubleshoot VLANs (normal range) spanning multiple switches	11
2.4.a Access ports (data and voice)	11
2.4.b Default VLAN	11
2.5 Configure, verify, and troubleshoot interswitch connectivity	11
2.5.a Trunk ports	11
2.5.b 802.1Q	11
2.5.c Native VLAN	11
2.6 Configure and verify Layer 2 protocols	7
2.6.a Cisco Discovery Protocol	7
2.6.b LLDP	7
2.7 Configure, verify, and troubleshoot port security	10

Objective	Chapter(s)
2.7.a Static	10
2.7.b Dynamic	10
2.7.c Sticky	10
2.7.d Max MAC addresses	10
2.7.e Violation actions	10
2.7.f Err-disable recovery	10

TABLE I.3   25% 3.0 Routing Fundamentals

Objective	Chapter(s)
3.1 Describe the routing concepts	9
3.1.a Packet handling along the path through a network	9
3.1.b Forwarding decision based on route lookup	9
3.1.c Frame rewrite	9
3.2 Interpret the components of routing table	9
3.2.a Prefix	9
3.2.b Network mask	9
3.2.c Next hop	9
3.2.d Routing protocol code	9
3.2.e Administrative distance	9
3.2.f Metric	9
3.2.g Gateway of last resort	9
3.3 Describe how a routing table is populated by different routing information sources	9
3.3.a Admin distance	9
3.4 Configure, verify, and troubleshoot inter-VLAN routing	11
3.4.a Router on a stick	11
3.5 Compare and contrast static routing and dynamic routing	9
3.6 Configure, verify, and troubleshoot IPv4 and IPv6 static routing	9
3.6.a Default route	9, 14
3.6.b Network route	9
3.6.c Host route	9
3.6.d Floating static	9
3.7 Configure, verify, and troubleshoot RIPv2 for IPv4 (excluding authentication, filtering, manual summarization, redistribution)	9

TABLE I.4   15% 4.0 Infrastructure Services

Objective	Chapter(s)
4.1 Describe DNS lookup operation	7
4.2 Troubleshoot client connectivity issues involving DNS	7
4.3 Configure and verify DHCP on a router (excluding static reservations)	7
4.3.a Server	7
4.3.b Relay	7
4.3.c Client	7
4.3.d TFTP, DNS, and gateway options	7
4.4 Troubleshoot client- and router-based DHCP connectivity issues	7
4.5 Configure and verify NTP operating in client/server mode	7
4.6 Configure, verify, and troubleshoot IPv4 standard numbered and named access list for routed interfaces	12
4.7 Configure, verify, and troubleshoot inside source NAT	13
4.7.a Static	13
4.7.b Pool	13
4.7.c PAT	13

TABLE I.5   14% 5.0 Infrastructure Maintenance

Objective	Chapter(s)
5.1 Configure and verify device-monitoring using syslog	7
5.2 Configure and verify device management	7, 8
5.2.a Backup and restore device configuration	7
5.2.b Using Cisco Discovery Protocol and LLDP for device discovery	7
5.2.c Licensing	8
5.2.d Logging	7
5.2.e Timezone	7
5.2.f Loopback	7
5.3 Configure and verify initial device configuration	6
5.4 Configure, verify, and troubleshoot basic device hardening	6
5.4.a Local authentication	6
5.4.b Secure password	6
5.4.c Access to device	6
5.4.c. (i) Source address	6
5.4.c. (ii) Telnet/SSH	6
5.4.d Login banner	6

Objective	Chapter(s)
5.5 Perform device maintenance	6, 8
5.5.a Cisco IOS upgrades and recovery (SCP, FTP, TFTP, and MD5 verify)	8
5.5.b Password recovery and configuration register	8
5.5.c File system management	8
5.6 Use Cisco IOS tools to troubleshoot and resolve problems	6
5.6.a Ping and traceroute with extended option	6
5.6.b Terminal monitor	6
5.6.c Log events	6

ICND2 Exam Objectives

Exam objectives are subject to change at any time without prior notice and at Cisco's sole discretion. Please visit Cisco's certification website (www.cisco.com/web/learning) for the latest information on the ICND2 Exam 200-105.

TABLE I.6   26% 1.0 LAN Switching Technologies

Objective	Chapter(s)
1.1 Configure, verify, and troubleshoot VLANs (normal/extended range) spanning multiple switches	15
1.1.a Access ports (data and voice)	15
1.1.b Default VLAN	15
1.2 Configure, verify, and troubleshoot interswitch connectivity	15
1.2.a Add and remove VLANs on a trunk	15
1.2.b DTP and VTP (v1&v2)	15
1.3 Configure, verify, and troubleshoot STP protocols	15
1.3.a STP mode (PVST+ and RPVST+)	15
1.3.b STP root bridge selection	15
1.4 Configure, verify, and troubleshoot STP-related optional features	15
1.4.a PortFast	15
1.4.b BPDU guard	15
1.5 Configure, verify, and troubleshoot (Layer 2/Layer 3) EtherChannel	15
1.5.a Static	15
1.5.b PAGP	15
1.5.c LACP	15
1.6 Describe the benefits of switch stacking and chassis aggregation	22
1.7 Describe common access layer threat mitigation techniques	15, 16, 20

Objective	Chapter(s)
1.7.a 802.1x	16
1.7.b DHCP snooping	16
1.7.c Nondefault native VLAN	15, 20

TABLE I.7   29% 2.0 Routing Technologies

Objective	Chapter(s)
2.1 Configure, verify, and troubleshoot Inter-VLAN routing 1	15
2.1.a Router on a stick 1	15
2.1.b SVI 1	15
2.2 Compare and contrast distance vector and link-state routing protocols	17, 18, 19
2.3 Compare and contrast interior and exterior routing protocols	17, 18, 19
2.4 Configure, verify, and troubleshoot single area and multiarea OSPFv2 for IPv4 (excluding authentication, filtering, manual summarization, redistribution, stub, virtual-link, and LSAs)	18, 19
2.5 Configure, verify, and troubleshoot single area and multiarea OSPFv3 for IPv6 (excluding authentication, filtering, manual summarization, redistribution, stub, virtual-link, and LSAs)	18, 19
2.6 Configure, verify, and troubleshoot EIGRP for IPv4 (excluding authentication, filtering, manual summarization, redistribution, stub)	17
2.7 Configure, verify, and troubleshoot EIGRP for IPv6 (excluding authentication, filtering, manual summarization, redistribution, stub)	17

TABLE I.8   16% 3.0 WAN Technologies

Objective	Chapter(s)
3.1 Configure and verify PPP and MLPPP on WAN interfaces using local authentication	21
3.2 Configure, verify, and troubleshoot PPPoE client-side interfaces using local authentication	21
3.3 Configure, verify, and troubleshoot GRE tunnel connectivity	21
3.4 Describe WAN topology options	21
3.4.a Point-to-point	21
3.4.b Hub and spoke	21
3.4.c Full mesh	21
3.4.d Single vs dual-homed	21
3.5 Describe WAN access connectivity options	21
3.5.a MPLS	21

Objective	Chapter(s)
3.5.b MetroEthernet	21
3.5.c Broadband PPPoE	21
3.5.d Internet VPN (DMVPN, site-to-site VPN, client VPN)	21
3.6 Configure and verify single-homed branch connectivity using eBGP IPv4 (limited to peering and route advertisement using Network command only)	21

TABLE I.9   14% 4.0 Infrastructure Services

Objective	Chapter(s)
4.1 Configure, verify, and troubleshoot basic HSRP	16
4.1.a Priority	16
4.1.b Preemption	16
4.1.c Version	16
4.2 Describe the effects of cloud resources on enterprise network architecture	22
4.2.a Traffic path to internal and external cloud services	22
4.2.b Virtual services	22
4.2.c Basic virtual network infrastructure	22
4.3 Describe basic QoS concepts	22
4.3.a Marking	22
4.3.b Device trust	22
4.3.c Prioritization	22
4.3.c. (i) Voice 4.3.c. (ii) Video 4.3.c. (iii) Data	22
4.3.d Shaping	22
4.3.e Policing	22
4.3.f Congestion management	22
4.4 Configure, verify, and troubleshoot IPv4 and IPv6 access list for traffic filtering	20
4.4.a Standard	20
4.4.b Extended	20
4.4.c Named	20
4.5 Verify ACLs using the APIC-EM Path Trace ACL analysis tool	22

TABLE I.10   15% 5.0 Infrastructure Maintenance

Objective	Chapter(s)
5.1 Configure and verify device-monitoring protocols	16
5.1.a SNMPv2	16
5.1.b SNMPv3	16
5.2 Troubleshoot network connectivity issues using ICMP echo-based IP SLA	20
5.3 Use local SPAN to troubleshoot and resolve problems	20
5.4 Describe device management using AAA with TACACS+ and RADIUS	16
5.5 Describe network programmability in enterprise network architecture	22
5.5.a Function of a controller	22
5.5.b Separation of control plane and data plane	22
5.5.c Northbound and southbound APIs	22
5.6 Troubleshoot basic Layer 3 end-to-end connectivity issues	22

CCNA Exam Objectives (Composite Exam)

Exam objectives are subject to change at any time without prior notice and at Cisco's sole discretion. Please visit Cisco's certification website (www.cisco.com/web/learning) for the latest information on the CCNA Exam 200-125.

TABLE I.11   15% 1.0 Network Fundamentals

Objective	Chapter(s)
1.1 Compare and contrast OSI and TCP/IP models	3
1.2 Compare and contrast TCP and UDP protocols	3
1.3 Describe the impact of infrastructure components in an enterprise network	1
1.3.a Firewalls	1
1.3.b Access points	1
1.3.c Wireless controllers	1
1.4 Describe the effects of cloud resources on enterprise network architecture	22
1.4.a Traffic path to internal and external cloud services	22
1.4.b Virtual services	22
1.4.c Basic virtual network infrastructure	22
1.5 Compare and contrast collapsed core and three-tier architectures	2
1.6 Compare and contrast network topologies	1
1.6.a Star	1
1.6.b Mesh	1

Objective	Chapter(s)
1.6.c Hybrid	1
1.7 Select the appropriate cabling type based on implementation requirements	2
1.8 Apply troubleshooting methodologies to resolve problems	3, 5
1.8.a Perform and document fault isolation	3, 5
1.8.b Resolve or escalate	3, 5
1.8.c Verify and monitor resolution	3, 5
1.9 Configure, verify, and troubleshoot IPv4 addressing and subnetting	4, 5
1.10 Compare and contrast IPv4 address types	3
1.10.a Unicast	3
1.10.b Broadcast	3
1.10.c Multicast	3
1.11 Describe the need for private IPv4 addressing	3
1.12 Identify the appropriate IPv6 addressing scheme to satisfy addressing requirements in a LAN/WAN environment	14
1.13 Configure, verify, and troubleshoot IPv6 addressing	14
1.14 Configure and verify IPv6 Stateless Address Auto Configuration	14
1.15 Compare and contrast IPv6 address types	14
1.15.a Global unicast	14
1.15.b Unique local	14
1.15.c Link local	14
1.15.d Multicast	14
1.15.e Modified EUI 64	14
1.15.f Autoconfiguration	14
1.15.g Anycast	14

TABLE I.12   21% 2.0 LAN Switching Technologies

Objective	Chapter(s)
2.1 Describe and verify switching concepts	10
2.1.a MAC learning and aging	10
2.1.b Frame switching	10
2.1.c Frame flooding	10
2.1.d MAC address table	10
2.2 Interpret Ethernet frame format	2
2.3 Troubleshoot interface and cable issues (collisions, errors, duplex, speed)	6
2.4 Configure, verify, and troubleshoot VLANs (normal/extended range) spanning multiple switches	11

Objective	Chapter(s)
2.4.a Access ports (data and voice)	11
2.4.b Default VLAN	11
2.5 Configure, verify, and troubleshoot interswitch connectivity	11
2.5.a Trunk ports	11
2.5.b Add and remove VLANs on a trunk	15
2.5.c DTP, VTP (v1&v2), and 802.1Q	15
2.5.d Native VLAN	11
2.6 Configure, verify, and troubleshoot STP protocols	15
2.6.a STP mode (PVST+ and RPVST+)	15
2.6.b STP root bridge selection	15
2.7 Configure, verify and troubleshoot STP related optional features	15
2.7.a PortFast	15
2.7.b BPDU guard	15
2.8 Configure and verify Layer 2 protocols	7
2.8.a Cisco Discovery Protocol	7
2.8.b LLDP	7
2.9 Configure, verify, and troubleshoot (Layer 2/Layer 3) EtherChannel	15
2.9.a Static	15
2.9.b PAGP	15
2.9.c LACP	15
2.10 Describe the benefits of switch stacking and chassis aggregation	22

TABLE I.13   23% 3.0 Routing Technologies

Objective	Chapter(s)
3.1 Describe the routing concepts	9
3.1.a Packet handling along the path through a network	9
3.1.b Forwarding decision based on route lookup	9
3.1.c Frame rewrite	9
3.2 Interpret the components of a routing table	9
3.2.a Prefix	9
3.2.b Network mask	9
3.2.c Next hop	9
3.2.d Routing protocol code	9
3.2.e Administrative distance	9
3.2.f Metric	9

Objective	Chapter(s)
3.2.g Gateway of last resort	9
3.3 Describe how a routing table is populated by different routing information sources	9
3.3.a Admin distance	9
3.4 Configure, verify, and troubleshoot inter-VLAN routing	11, 15
3.4.a Router on a stick	11, 15
3.4.b SVI	15
3.5 Compare and contrast static routing and dynamic routing	9
3.6 Compare and contrast distance vector and link state routing protocols	17, 18, 19
3.7 Compare and contrast interior and exterior routing protocols	18, 19
3.8 Configure, verify, and troubleshoot IPv4 and IPv6 static routing	9
3.8.a Default route	9, 14
3.8.b Network route	9
3.8.c Host route	9
3.8.d Floating static	9
3.9 Configure, verify, and troubleshoot single area and multi-area OSPFv2 for IPv4 (excluding authentication, filtering, manual summarization, redistribution, stub, virtual-link, and LSAs)	4, 5
3.10 Configure, verify, and troubleshoot single area and multi-area OSPFv3 for IPv6 (excluding authentication, filtering, manual summarization, redistribution, stub, virtual-link, and LSAs)	4, 5
3.11 Configure, verify, and troubleshoot EIGRP for IPv4 (excluding authentication, filtering, manual summarization, redistribution, stub)	3
3.12 Configure, verify, and troubleshoot EIGRP for IPv6 (excluding authentication, filtering, manual summarization, redistribution, stub)	3
3.13 Configure, verify, and troubleshoot RIPv2 for IPv4 (excluding authentication, filtering, manual summarization, redistribution)	9
3.14 Troubleshoot basic Layer 3 end-to-end connectivity issues	7

TABLE I.14 10% 4.0 WAN Technologies

Objective	Chapter(s)
4.1 Configure and verify PPP and MLPPP on WAN interfaces using local authentication	21
4.2 Configure, verify, and troubleshoot PPPoE client-side interfaces using local authentication	21
4.3 Configure, verify, and troubleshoot GRE tunnel connectivity	21
4.4 Describe WAN topology options	21
4.4.a Point-to-point	21

Objective	Chapter(s)
4.4.b Hub and spoke	21
4.4.c Full mesh	21
4.4.d Single vs dual-homed	21
4.5 Describe WAN access connectivity options	21
4.5.a MPLS	21
4.5.b Metro Ethernet	21
4.5.c Broadband PPPoE	21
4.5.d Internet VPN (DMVPN, site-to-site VPN, client VPN)	21
4.6 Configure and verify single-homed branch connectivity using eBGP IPv4 (limited to peering and route advertisement using Network command only)	21
4.7 Describe basic QoS concepts	22
4.7.a Marking	22
4.7.b Device trust	22
4.7.c Prioritization	22
4.7.c. (i) Voice	22
4.7.c. (ii) Video	22
4.7.c. (iii) Data	22
4.7.d Shaping	22
4.7.e Policing	22
4.7.f Congestion management	22

TABLE I.15   10% 5.0 Infrastructure Services

Objective	Chapter(s)
5.1 Describe DNS lookup operation	7
5.2 Troubleshoot client connectivity issues involving DNS	7
5.3 Configure and verify DHCP on a router (excluding static reservations)	7
5.3.a Server	7
5.3.b Relay	7
5.3.c Client	7
5.3.d TFTP, DNS, and gateway options	7
5.4 Troubleshoot client- and router-based DHCP connectivity issues	7
5.5 Configure, verify, and troubleshoot basic HSRP	16
5.5.a Priority	16
5.5.b Preemption	16
5.5.c Version	16

Objective	Chapter(s)
5.6 Configure, verify, and troubleshoot inside source NAT	13
5.6.a Static	13
5.6.b Pool	13
5.6.c PAT	13
5.7 Configure and verify NTP operating in a client/server mode	7

TABLE I.16   11% 6.0 Infrastructure Security

Objective	Chapter(s)
6.1 Configure, verify, and troubleshoot port security	10
6.1.a Static	10
6.1.b Dynamic	10
6.1.c Sticky	10
6.1.d Max MAC addresses	10
6.1.e Violation actions	10
6.1.f Err-disable recovery	10
6.2 Describe common access layer threat mitigation techniques	15, 16, 20
6.2.a 802.1x	16
6.2.b DHCP snooping	16
6.2.c Nondefault native VLAN	15, 20
6.3 Configure, verify, and troubleshoot IPv4 and IPv6 access list for traffic filtering	20
6.3.a Standard	20
6.3.b Extended	20
6.3.c Named	20
6.4 Verify ACLs using the APIC-EM Path Trace ACL Analysis tool	22
6.5 Configure, verify, and troubleshoot basic device hardening	6
6.5.a Local authentication	6
6.5.b Secure password	6
6.5.c Access to device	6
6.5.c. (i) Source address	6
6.5.c. (ii) Telnet/SSH	6
6.5.d Login banner	6
6.6 Describe device security using AAA with TACACS+ and RADIUS	16

TABLE I.17   10% 7.0 Infrastructure Management

Objective	Chapter(s)
7.1 Configure and verify device-monitoring protocols	16
7.1.a SNMPv2	16
7.1.b SNMPv3	16
7.1.c Syslog	7, 16
7.2 Troubleshoot network connectivity issues using ICMP echo-based IP SLA	20
7.3 Configure and verify device management	7, 8
7.3.a Backup and restore device configuration	7
7.3.b Using Cisco Discovery Protocol or LLDP for device discovery	7
7.3.c Licensing	8
7.3.d Logging	7
7.3.e Timezone	7
7.3.f Loopback	7
7.4 Configure and verify initial device configuration	6
7.5 Perform device maintenance	6, 8
7.5.a Cisco IOS upgrades and recovery (SCP, FTP, TFTP, and MD5 verify)	8
7.5.b Password recovery and configuration register	8
7.5.c File system management	8
7.6 Use Cisco IOS tools to troubleshoot and resolve problems	6
7.6.a Ping and traceroute with extended option	6
7.6.b Terminal monitor	6
7.6.c Log events	6
7.6.d Local SPAN	6, 20
7.7 Describe network programmability in enterprise network architecture	22
7.7.a Function of a controller	22
7.7.b Separation of control plane and data plane	22
7.7.c Northbound and southbound APIs	22

Assessment Test

1. What is the sys-id-ext field in a BPDU used for?

   A. It is a 4-bit field inserted into an Ethernet frame to define trunking information between switches.

   B. It is a 12-bit field inserted into an Ethernet frame to define VLANs in an STP instance.

   C. It is a 4-bit field inserted into an non-Ethernet frame to define EtherChannel options.

   D. It is a 12-bit field inserted into an Ethernet frame to define STP root bridges.

2. You have four RSTP PVST+ links between switches and want to aggregate the bandwidth. What solution will you use?

   A. EtherChannel

   B. PortFast

   C. BPDU Channel

   D. VLANs

   E. EtherBundle

3. What configuration parameters must be configured the same between switches for LACP to form a channel? (Choose three.)

   A. Virtual MAC address

   B. Port speeds

   C. Duplex

   D. PortFast enabled

   E. Allowed VLAN information

4. You reload a router with a configuration register setting of 0x2101. What will the router do when it reloads?

   A. The router enters setup mode.

   B. The router enters ROM monitor mode.

   C. The router boots the mini-IOS in ROM.

   D. The router expands the first IOS in flash memory into RAM.

5. Which of the following commands provides the product ID and serial number of a router?

   A. `show license`

   B. `show license feature`

   C. `show version`

   D. `show license udi`

6. Which command allows you to view the technology options and licenses that are supported on your router along with several status variables?

   A. `show license`

   B. `show license feature`

   C. `show license udi`

   D. `show version`

7. Which of the following services provide the operating system and the network?

   A. IaaS

   B. PaaS

   C. SaaS

   D. none of the above

8. You want to send a console message to a syslog server, but you only want to send status messages of 3 and lower. Which of the following commands will you use?

   A. `logging trap emergencies`

   B. `logging trap errors`

   C. `logging trap debugging`

   D. `logging trap notifications`

   E. `logging trap critical`

   F. `logging trap warnings`

   G. `logging trap alerts`

9. When stacking switches, which is true? (Choose 2)

   A. The stack is managed as multiple objects, and has a single management IP address

   B. The stack is managed as a single object, and has a single management IP address

   C. The master switch is chosen when you configure the first switches master algorithm to on

   D. The master switch is elected form one of the stack member switches

10. You need to connect to a remote IPv6 server in your virtual server farm. You can connect to the IPv4 servers, but not the critical IPv6 server you desperately need. Based on the following output, what could your problem be?

```
C:\>ipconfig
   Connection-specific DNS Suffix  . : localdomain
   IPv6 Address. . . . . . . . . . . : 2001:db8:3c4d:3:ac3b:2ef:1823:8938
   Temporary IPv6 Address. . . . . . : 2001:db8:3c4d:3:2f33:44dd:211:1c3d
   Link-local IPv6 Address . . . . . : fe80::ac3b:2ef:1823:8938%11
   IPv4 Address. . . . . . . . . . . : 10.1.1.10
   Subnet Mask . . . . . . . . . . . : 255.255.255.0
   Default Gateway . . . . . . . . . : 10.1.1.1
```

   A. The global address is in the wrong subnet.

   B. The IPv6 default gateway has not been configured or received from the router.

C. The link-local address has not been resolved so the host cannot communicate to the router.

D. There are two IPv6 global addresses configured. One must be removed from the configuration.

11. What command is used to view the IPv6-to-MAC-address resolution table on a Cisco router?

A. show ip arp

B. show ipv6 arp

C. show ip neighbors

D. show ipv6 neighbors

E. show arp

12. An IPv6 ARP entry is listed as with a status of REACH. What can you conclude about the IPv6-to-MAC-address mapping?

A. The interface has communicated with the neighbor address and the mapping is current.

B. The interface has not communicated within the neighbor reachable time frame.

C. The ARP entry has timed out.

D. IPv6 can reach the neighbor address but the addresses has not yet been resolved.

13. Serial0/1 goes down. How will EIGRP send packets to the 10.1.1.0 network?

```
Corp#show ip eigrp topology
[output cut]
P 10.1.1.0/24, 2 successors, FD is 2681842
        via 10.1.2.2 (2681842/2169856), Serial0/0
        via 10.1.3.1 (2973467/2579243), Serial0/2
        via 10.1.3.3 (2681842/2169856), Serial0/1
```

A. EIGRP will put the 10.1.1.0 network into active mode.

B. EIGRP will drop all packets destined for 10.1.1.0.

C. EIGRP will just keep sending packets out s0/0.

D. EIGRP will use s0/2 as the successor and keep routing to 10.1.1.0.

14. What command produced the following output?

```
via FE80::201:C9FF:FED0:3301 (29110112/33316), Serial0/0/0
via FE80::209:7CFF:FE51:B401 (4470112/42216), Serial0/0/1
via FE80::209:7CFF:FE51:B401 (2170112/2816), Serial0/0/2
```

A. show ip protocols

B. show ipv6 protocols

C. show ip eigrp neighbors

D. show ipv6 eigrp neighbors

E. show ip eigrp topology

F. show ipv6 eigrp topology

15. You need to troubleshoot an adjacency between two EIGRP configured routers? What should you look for? (Choose four.)

   A. Verify the AS numbers.

   B. Verify that you have the proper interfaces enabled for EIGRP.

   C. Make sure there are no mismatched K-values.

   D. Check your passive interface settings.

   E. Make sure your remote routers are not connected to the Internet.

   F. If authentication is configured, make sure all routers use different passwords.

16. You have two OSPF directly configured routers that are not forming an adjacency. What should you check? (Choose three.)

   A. Process ID

   B. Hello and dead timers

   C. Link cost

   D. Area

   E. IP address/subnet mask

17. When do two adjacent routers-enter the 2WAY state?

   A. After both routers have received Hello information

   B. After they have exchanged topology databases

   C. When they connect only to a DR or BDR

   D. When they need to exchange RID information

18. Which type of LSAs are generated by ABRs and referred to summary link advertisements (SLAs)?

   A. Type 1

   B. Type 2

   C. Type 3

   D. Type 4

   E. Type 5

19. Which of the following is *not* provided by the AH portion of IPsec?

   A. Integrity

   B. Confidentiality

   C. Authenticity

   D. Anti-reply

20. Which statement about GRE is not true?

   A. GRE is stateless and has no flow control.

   B. GRE has security.

   C. GRE has additional overhead for tunneled packets, at least 24 bytes.

   D. GRE uses a protocol-type field in the GRE header so any layer 3 protocol can be used through the tunnel.

21. Which QoS mechanism will drop traffic if a session uses more than the allotted bandwidth?

   A. Congestion management

   B. Shaping

   C. Policing

   D. Marking

22. IPv6 unicast routing is running on the Corp router. Which of the following addresses would show up with the show ipv6 int brief command?

```
Corp#sh int f0/0
FastEthernet0/0 is up, line protocol is up
  Hardware is AmdFE, address is 000d.bd3b.0d80 (bia 000d.bd3b.0d80)
[output cut]
```

   A. FF02::3c3d:0d:bdff:fe3b:0d80

   B. FE80::3c3d:2d:bdff:fe3b:0d80

   C. FE80::3c3d:0d:bdff:fe3b:0d80

   D. FE80::3c3d:2d:ffbd:3bfe:0d80

23. A host sends a type of NDP message providing the MAC address that was requested. Which type of NDP was sent?

   A. NA

   B. RS

   C. RA

   D. NS

24. Each field in an IPv6 address is how many bits long?

   A. 4

   B. 16

   C. 32

   D. 128

25. To enable OSPFv3, which of the following would you use?

   A. Router(config-if)#**ipv6 ospf 10 area 0.0.0.0**

   B. Router(config-if)#**ipv6 router rip 1**

   C. Router(config)#**ipv6 router eigrp 10**

   D. Router(config-rtr)#**no shutdown**

   E. Router(config-if)#**ospf ipv6 10 area 0**

26. What does the command routerA(config)#**line cons 0** allow you to perform next?

    A. Set the Telnet password.

    B. Shut down the router.

    C. Set your console password.

    D. Disable console connections.

27. Which two statements describe the IP address 10.16.3.65/23? (Choose two.)

    A. The subnet address is 10.16.3.0 255.255.254.0.

    B. The lowest host address in the subnet is 10.16.2.1 255.255.254.0.

    C. The last valid host address in the subnet is 10.16.2.254 255.255.254.0.

    D. The broadcast address of the subnet is 10.16.3.255 255.255.254.0.

    E. The network is not subnetted.

28. On which interface do you configure an IP address for a switch?

    A. int fa0/0

    B. int vty 0 15

    C. int vlan 1

    D. int s/0/0

29. Which of the following is the valid host range for the subnet on which the IP address 192.168.168.188 255.255.255.192 resides?

    A. 192.168.168.129–190

    B. 192.168.168.129–191

    C. 192.168.168.128–190

    D. 192.168.168.128–192

30. Which of the following is considered to be the inside host's address after translation?

    A. Inside local

    B. Outside local

    C. Inside global

    D. Outside global

31. Your inside locals are not being translated to the inside global addresses. Which of the following commands will show you if your inside globals are allowed to use the NAT pool?

```
ip nat pool Corp 198.18.41.129 198.18.41.134 netmask 255.255.255.248
ip nat inside source list 100 int pool Corp overload
```

    A. debug ip nat

    B. show access-list

    C. show ip nat translation

    D. show ip nat statistics

32. How many collision domains are created when you segment a network with a 12-port switch?

A. 1

B. 2

C. 5

D. 12

33. Which of the following commands will allow you to set your Telnet password on a Cisco router?

A. `line telnet 0 4`

B. `line aux 0 4`

C. `line vty 0 4`

D. `line con 0`

34. Which router command allows you to view the entire contents of all access lists?

A. `show all access-lists`

B. `show access-lists`

C. `show ip interface`

D. `show interface`

35. What does a VLAN do?

A. Acts as the fastest port to all servers

B. Provides multiple collision domains on one switch port

C. Breaks up broadcast domains in a layer 2 switch internetwork

D. Provides multiple broadcast domains within a single collision domain

36. If you wanted to delete the configuration stored in NVRAM, choose the best answer for the Cisco objectives.

A. `erase startup`

B. `delete running`

C. `erase flash`

D. `erase running`

37. Which protocol is used to send a destination network unknown message back to originating hosts?

A. TCP

B. ARP

C. ICMP

D. BootP

38. Which class of IP address provides 15 bits for subnetting?

    A. A

    B. B

    C. C

    D. D

39. There are three possible routes for a router to reach a destination network. The first route is from OSPF with a metric of 782. The second route is from RIPv2 with a metric of 4. The third is from EIGRP with a composite metric of 20514560. Which route will be installed by the router in its routing table?

    A. RIPv2

    B. EIGRP

    C. OSPF

    D. All three

40. Which one of the following is true regarding VLANs?

    A. Two VLANs are configured by default on all Cisco switches.

    B. VLANs only work if you have a complete Cisco switched internetwork. No off-brand switches are allowed.

    C. You should not have more than 10 switches in the same VTP domain.

    D. You need to have a trunk link configured between switches in order to send information about more than one VLAN down the link.

41. Which two of the following commands will place network 10.2.3.0/24 into area 0? (Choose two.)

    A. `router eigrp 10`

    B. `router ospf 10`

    C. `router rip`

    D. `network 10.0.0.0`

    E. `network 10.2.3.0 255.255.255.0 area 0`

    F. `network 10.2.3.0 0.0.0.255 area0`

    G. `network 10.2.3.0 0.0.0.255 area 0`

42. How many broadcast domains are created when you segment a network with a 12-port switch?

    A. 1

    B. 2

    C. 5

    D. 12

43. If routers in a single area are configured with the same priority value, what value does a router use for the OSPF router ID in the absence of a loopback interface?

   A. The lowest IP address of any physical interface

   B. The highest IP address of any physical interface

   C. The lowest IP address of any logical interface

   D. The highest IP address of any logical interface

44. What protocols are used to configure trunking on a switch? (Choose two.)

   A. VLAN Trunking Protocol

   B. VLAN

   C. 802.1q

   D. ISL

45. What is a stub network?

   A. A network with more than one exit point

   B. A network with more than one exit and entry point

   C. A network with only one entry and no exit point

   D. A network that has only one entry and exit point

46. Where is a hub specified in the OSI model?

   A. Session layer

   B. Physical layer

   C. Data Link layer

   D. Application layer

47. What are the two main types of access control lists (ACLs)? (Choose two.)

   A. Standard

   B. IEEE

   C. Extended

   D. Specialized

48. Which of the following is the best summarization of the following networks: 192.168.128.0 through 192.168.159.0?

   A. 192.168.0.0/24

   B. 192.168.128.0/16

   C. 192.168.128.0/19

   D. 192.168.128.0/20

49. What command is used to create a backup configuration?

   A. `copy running backup`

   B. `copy running-config startup-config`

   C. `config mem`

   D. `wr net`

50. 1000Base-T is which IEEE standard?

   A. 802.3f

   B. 802.3z

   C. 802.3ab

   D. 802.3ae

51. Which protocol does DHCP use at the Transport layer?

   A. IP

   B. TCP

   C. UDP

   D. ARP

52. If your router is facilitating a CSU/DSU, which of the following commands do you need to use to provide the router with a 64000 bps serial link?

   A. `RouterA(config)#`**`bandwidth 64`**

   B. `RouterA(config-if)#`**`bandwidth 64000`**

   C. `RouterA(config)#`**`clockrate 64000`**

   D. `RouterA(config-if)#`**`clock rate 64`**

   E. `RouterA(config-if)#`**`clock rate 64000`**

53. Which command is used to determine if an access list is enabled on a particular interface?

   A. `show access-lists`

   B. `show interface`

   C. `show ip interface`

   D. `show interface access-lists`

54. Which of the following statements is true with regard to ISL and 802.1q?

   A. 802.1q encapsulates the frame with control information; ISL inserts an ISL field along with tag control information.

   B. 802.1q is Cisco proprietary.

   C. ISL encapsulates the frame with control information; 802.1q inserts an 802.1q field along with tag control information.

   D. ISL is a standard.

55. The protocol data unit (PDU) encapsulation is completed in which order?

   A. Bits, frames, packets, segments, data

   B. Data, bits, segments, frames, packets

   C. Data, segments, packets, frames, bits

   D. Packets, frames, bits, segments, data

56. Based on the configuration shown below, what statement is true?

```
S1(config)#ip routing
S1(config)#int vlan 10
S1(config-if)#ip address 192.168.10.1 255.255.255.0
S1(config-if)#int vlan 20
S1(config-if)#ip address 192.168.20.1 255.255.255.0
```

   A. This is a multilayer switch.

   B. The two VLANs are in the same subnet.

   C. Encapsulation must be configured.

   D. VLAN 10 is the management VLAN.

Answers to Assessment Test

1. B. To allow for the PVST+ to operate, there's a field inserted into the BPDU to accommodate the extended system ID so that PVST+ can have a root bridge configured on a per-STP instance. The extended system ID (VLAN ID) is a 12-bit field, and we can even see what this field is carrying via show spanning-tree command output. See Chapter 15 for more information.

2. A. Cisco's EtherChannel can bundle up to eight ports between switches to provide resiliency and more bandwidth between switches. See Chapter 15 for more information.

3. B, C, E. All the ports on both sides of every link must be configured exactly the same between switches or it will not work. Speed, duplex, and allowed VLANs must match. See Chapter 15 for more information.

4. C. 2100 boots the router into ROM monitor mode, 2101 loads the mini-IOS from ROM, and 2102 is the default and loads the IOS from flash. See Chapter 8 for more information.

5. D. The show license udi command displays the unique device identifier (UDI) of the router, which comprises the product ID (PID) and serial number of the router. See Chapter 8 for more information.

6. B. The show license feature command allows you to view the technology package licenses and feature licenses that are supported on your router along with several status variables related to software activation and licensing, both licensed and unlicensed features. See Chapter 8 for more information.

7. C, D, F. The SDN architecture slightly differs from the architecture of traditional networks. It comprises three stacked layers: Data, Control and Application. See Chapter 8 for more information.

8. B. There are eight different trap levels. If you choose, for example level 3, level 0 through level 3 messages will be displayed. See Chapter 8 for more information.

9. B, D. Each stack of switches has a single IP address and is managed as a single object. This single IP management applies to activities such as fault detection, VLAN creation and modification, security, and QoS controls. Each stack has only one configuration file, which is distributed to each member in the stack. When you add a new switch to the stack, the master switch automatically configures the unit with the currently running IOS image and the configuration of the stack. You do not have to do anything to bring up the switch before it is ready to operate. See chapter 22 for more information.

10. B. There is no IPv6 default gateway listed in the output, which will be the link-local address of the router interface, sent to the host as a router advertisement. Until this host receives the router address, the host will communicate with IPv6 only on the local subnet. See Chapter 20 for more information.

11. D. The command show ipv6 neighbors provides the ARP cache for on a router. See Chapter 20 for more information.

12. A. If the state is STALE when the interface has not communicated within the neighbor reachable time frame. The next time the neighbor communicates, the state will be REACH. See Chapter 20 for more information.

13. C. There are two successor routes, so by default, EIGRP was load-balancing out s0/0 and s0/1. When s0/1 goes down, EIGRP will just keep forwarding traffic out the second link s0/0. s0/1 will be removed from the routing table. See Chapter 17 for more information.

14. F. There isn't a lot to go on from with the output, but the only commands that provide the FD and AD are show ip eigrp topology and show ipv6 eigrp topology. The addresses in the output are link-local IPv6 addresses, so our answer is the latter. See Chapter 17 for more information.

15. A, B, C, D. Cisco has documented steps, according to the objectives, that you must go through when troubleshooting an adjacency. See Chapter 18 for more information.

16. B, D, E. In order for two OSPF routers to create an adjacency, the Hello and dead timers must match, and they must both be configured into the same area, as well as being in the same subnet. See Chapter 18 for more information.

17. A. The process starts by sending out Hello packets. Every listening router will then add the originating router to the neighbor database. The responding routers will reply with all of their Hello information so that the originating router can add them to its own neighbor table. At this point, we will have reached the 2WAY state—only certain routers will advance beyond to this. See Chapter 19 for more information.

18. C. Referred to as summary link advertisements (SLAs), Type 3 LSAs are generated by area border routers. These ABRs send Type 3 LSAs toward the area external to the one where they were generated. See Chapter 19 for more information.

19. B. Authentication Header (AH) provides authentication of either all or part of the IP packet through the addition of a header that is calculated based on the values in the packet, but it doesn't offer any encryption services. See Chapter 21 for more information.

20. B. Generic Routing Encapsulation (GRE) has no built-in security mechanisms. See Chapter 21 for more information.

21. C. When traffic exceeds the allocated rate, the policer can take one of two actions. It can either drop traffic or re-mark it to another class of service. The new class usually has a higher drop probability. See Chapter 21 for more information.

22. B. This can be a hard question if you don't remember to invert the 7th bit of the first octet in the MAC address! Always look for the 7th bit when studying for the Cisco R/S, and when using eui-64, invert it. The eui-64 autoconfiguration then inserts an FF:FE in the middle of the 48-bit MAC address to create a unique IPv6 address. See Chapter 14 for more information.

23. A. The NDP neighbor advertisement (NA) contains the MAC address. A neighbor solicitation (NS) was initially sent asking for the MAC address. See Chapter 14 for more information.

24. B. Each field in an IPv6 address is 16 bits long. An IPv6 address is a total of 128 bits. See Chapter 14 for more information.

25. A. To enable OSPFv3, you enable the protocol at the interface level, as with RIPng. The command string is area-id. It's important to understand that area 0 and area 0.0.0.0 both describe area 0. See Chapter 19 for more information.

26. C. The command line console 0 places you at a prompt where you can then set your console user-mode password. See Chapter 6 for more information.

27. B, D. The mask 255.255.254.0 (/23) used with a Class A address means that there are 15 subnet bits and 9 host bits. The block size in the third octet is 2 (256−254). So this makes the subnets in the interesting octet 0, 2, 4, 6, etc., all the way to 254. The host 10.16.3.65 is in the 2.0 subnet. The next subnet is 4.0, so the broadcast address for the 2.0 subnet is 3.255. The valid host addresses are 2.1 through 3.254. See Chapter 4 for more information.

28. C. The IP address is configured under a logical interface, called a management domain or VLAN 1, by default. See Chapter 10 for more information.

29. A. 256 − 192 = 64, so 64 is our block size. Just count in increments of 64 to find our subnet: 64 + 64 = 128. 128 + 64 = 192. The subnet is 128, the broadcast address is 191, and the valid host range is the numbers in between, or 129–190. See Chapter 4 for more information.

30. C. An inside global address is considered to be the IP address of the host on the private network after translation. See Chapter 13 for more information.

31. B. Once you create your pool, the command ip nat inside source must be used to say which inside locals are allowed to use the pool. In this question, we need to see if access list 100 is configured correctly, if at all, so show access-list is the best answer. See Chapter 13 for more information.

32. D. Layer 2 switching creates individual collision domains per port. See Chapter 1 for more information.

33. C. The command line vty 0 4 places you in a prompt that will allow you to set or change your Telnet password. See Chapter 6 for more information.

34. B. To see the contents of all access lists, use the show access-lists command. See Chapter 12 for more information.

35. C. VLANs break up broadcast domains at layer 2. See Chapter 11 for more information.

36. A. The command erase startup-config deletes the configuration stored in NVRAM. See Chapter 6 for more information.

37. C. ICMP is the protocol at the Network layer that is used to send messages back to an originating router. See Chapter 3 for more information.

38. A. Class A addressing provides 22 bits for host subnetting. Class B provides 16 bits, but only 14 are available for subnetting. Class C provides only 6 bits for subnetting. See Chapter 3 for more information.

39. B. Only the EIGRP route will be placed in the routing table because EIGRP has the lowest administrative distance (AD), and that is always used before metrics. See Chapter 8 for more information.

40. D. Switches send information about only one VLAN down a link unless it is configured as a trunk link. See Chapter 11 for more information.

41. B, G. To enable OSPF, you must first start OSPF using a process ID. The number is irrelevant; just choose a number from 1 to 65,535 and you're good to go. After you start the OSPF process, you must configure interfaces on which to activate OSPF using the network command with wildcards and specification of an area. Option F is wrong because there must be a space after the parameter area and before you list the area number. See Chapter 9 for more information.

42. A. By default, switches break up collision domains on a per-port basis but are one large broadcast domain. See Chapter 1 for more information.

43. B. At the moment of OSPF process startup, the highest IP address on any active interface will be the router ID (RID) of the router. If you have a loopback interface configured (logical interface), then that will override the interface IP address and become the RID of the router automatically. See Chapter 18 for more information.

44. C, D. VLAN Trunking Protocol (VTP) is not right because it has nothing to do with trunking except that it sends VLAN information across a trunk link. 802.1q and ISL encapsulations are used to configure trunking on a port. See Chapter 11 for more information.

45. D. Stub networks have only one connection to an internetwork. Default routes should be set on a stub network or network loops may occur; however, there are exceptions to this rule. See Chapter 9 for more information.

46. B. Hubs regenerate electrical signals, which are specified at the Physical layer. See Chapter 1 for more information.

47. A, C. Standard and extended access control lists (ACLs) are used to configure security on a router. See Chapter 12 for more information.

48. C. If you start at 192.168.128.0 and go through 192.168.159.0, you can see that this is a block of 32 in the third octet. Since the network address is always the first one in the range, the summary address is 192.168.128.0. What mask provides a block of 32 in the third octet? The answer is 255.255.224.0, or /19. See Chapter 5 for more information.

49. B. The command to back up the configuration on a router is copy running-config startup-config. See Chapter 7 for more information.

50. C. IEEE 802.3ab is the standard for 1 Gbps on twisted-pair. See Chapter 2 for more information.

51. C. User Datagram Protocol is a connection network service at the Transport layer, and DHCP uses this connectionless service. See Chapter 3 for more information.

52. E. The clock rate command is two words, and the speed of the line is in bits per second (bps). See Chapter 6 for more information.

53. C. The show ip interface command will show you if any interfaces have an outbound or inbound access list set. See Chapter 12 for more information.

54. C. Unlike ISL, which encapsulates the frame with control information, 802.1q inserts an 802.1q field along with tag control information. See Chapter 11 for more information.

55. C. The PDU encapsulation method defines how data is encoded as it goes through each layer of the TCP/IP model. Data is segmented at the Transport later, packets created at the Network layer, frames at the Data Link layer, and finally, the Physical layer encodes the 1s and 0s into a digital signal. See Chapter 2 for more information.

56. A. With a multilayer switch, enable IP routing and create one logical interface for each VLAN using the interface vlan number command and you're now doing inter-VLAN routing on the backplane of the switch! See Chapter 11 for more information.

ICND1

PART
I

Chapter

1

Internetworking

THE FOLLOWING ICND1 EXAM TOPICS ARE COVERED IN THIS CHAPTER:

✓ **Network Fundamentals**

- 1.3 Describe the impact of infrastructure components in an enterprise network

  - 1.3.a Firewalls

  - 1.3.b Access points

  - 1.3.c Wireless controllers

- 1.5 Compare and contrast network topologies

  - 1.5.a Star

  - 1.5.b Mesh

  - 1.5.c Hybrid

Welcome to the exciting world of internetworking. This first chapter will serve as an internetworking review by focusing on how to connect networks together using Cisco routers and switches, and I've written it with the assumption that you have some simple basic networking knowledge. The emphasis of this review will be on the Cisco CCENT and/or CCNA Routing and Switching (CCNA R/S) objectives, on which you'll need a solid grasp in order to succeed in getting your certifications.

Let's start by defining exactly what an internetwork is: You create an internetwork when you connect two or more networks via a router and configure a logical network addressing scheme with a protocol such as IP or IPv6.

We'll also dissect the Open Systems Interconnection (OSI) model, and I'll describe each part of it to you in detail because you really need complete, reliable knowledge of it. Understanding the OSI model is key for the solid foundation you'll need to build upon with the more advanced Cisco networking knowledge gained as you become increasingly more skilled.

The OSI model has seven hierarchical layers that were developed to enable different networks to communicate reliably between disparate systems. Since this book is centering upon all things CCNA, it's crucial for you to understand the OSI model as Cisco sees it, so that's how I'll be presenting the seven layers to you.

After you finish reading this chapter, you'll encounter review questions and written labs. These are given to you to really lock the information from this chapter into your memory. So don't skip them!

To find up-to-the-minute updates for this chapter, please see www.lammle.com/ccna or the book's web page via www.sybex.com/go/ccna.

Internetworking Basics

Before exploring internetworking models and the OSI model's specifications, you need to grasp the big picture and the answer to this burning question: Why is it so important to learn Cisco internetworking anyway?

Networks and networking have grown exponentially over the past 20 years, and understandably so. They've had to evolve at light speed just to keep up with huge increases in basic, mission-critical user needs (e.g., the simple sharing of data and printers) as well as greater burdens like multimedia remote presentations and conferencing. Unless everyone who needs to share network resources is located in the same office space—an increasingly uncommon situation—the challenge is to connect relevant networks so all users can share the wealth of whatever services and resources are required.

Figure 1.1 shows a basic *local area network (LAN)* that's connected using a *hub*, which is basically just an antiquated device that connects wires together. Keep in mind that a simple network like this would be considered one collision domain and one broadcast domain. No worries if you have no idea what I mean by that because coming up soon, I'm going to talk about collision and broadcast domains enough to make you dream about them!

FIGURE 1.1   A very basic network

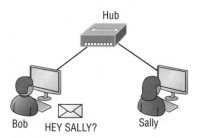

Things really can't get much simpler than this. And yes, though you can still find this configuration in some home networks, even many of those as well as the smallest business networks are more complicated today. As we move through this book, I'll just keep building upon this tiny network a bit at a time until we arrive at some really nice, robust, and current network designs—the types that will help you get your certification and a job!

But as I said, we'll get there one step at a time, so let's get back to the network shown in Figure 1.1 with this scenario: Bob wants to send Sally a file, and to complete that goal in this kind of network, he'll simply broadcast that he's looking for her, which is basically just shouting out over the network. Think of it like this: Bob walks out of his house and yells down a street called Chaos Court in order to contact Sally. This might work if Bob and Sally were the only ones living there, but not so much if it's crammed with homes and all the others living there are always hollering up and down the street to their neighbors just like Bob. Nope, Chaos Court would absolutely live up to its name, with all those residents going off whenever they felt like it—and believe it or not, our networks actually still work this way to a degree! So, given a choice, would you stay in Chaos Court, or would you pull up stakes and move on over to a nice new modern community called Broadway Lanes, which offers plenty of amenities and room for your home plus future additions all on nice, wide streets that can easily handle all present and future traffic? If you chose the latter, good choice... so did Sally, and she now lives a much quieter life, getting letters (packets) from Bob instead of a headache!

The scenario I just described brings me to the basic point of what this book and the Cisco certification objectives are really all about. My goal of showing you how to create efficient networks and segment them correctly in order to minimize all the chaotic yelling and screaming going on in them is a universal theme throughout my CCENT and CCNA series books. It's just inevitable that you'll have to break up a large network into a bunch of smaller ones at some point to match a network's equally inevitable growth, and as that expansion occurs, user response time simultaneously dwindles to a frustrating crawl. But if you master the vital technology and skills I have in store for you in this series, you'll be well equipped to rescue your network and its users by creating an efficient new network neighborhood to give them key amenities like the bandwidth they need to meet their evolving demands.

And this is no joke; most of us think of growth as good—and it can be—but as many of us experience daily when commuting to work, school, etc., it can also mean your LAN's traffic congestion can reach critical mass and grind to a complete halt! Again, the solution to this problem begins with breaking up a massive network into a number of smaller ones—something called *network segmentation*. This concept is a lot like planning a new community or modernizing an existing one. More streets are added, complete with new intersections and traffic signals, plus post offices are built with official maps documenting all those street names and directions on how to get to each. You'll need to effect new laws to keep order to it all and provide a police station to protect this nice new neighborhood as well. In a networking neighborhood environment, all of this is carried out using devices like *routers*, *switches*, and *bridges*.

So let's take a look at our new neighborhood now, because the word has gotten out; many more hosts have moved into it, so it's time to upgrade that new high-capacity infrastructure that we promised to handle the increase in population. Figure 1.2 shows a network that's been segmented with a switch, making each network segment that connects to the switch its own separate collision domain. Doing this results in a lot less yelling!

FIGURE 1.2   A switch can break up collision domains.

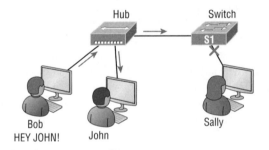

This is a great start, but I really want you to make note of the fact that this network is still one, single broadcast domain, meaning that we've really only decreased our screaming and yelling, not eliminated it. For example, if there's some sort of vital announcement that everyone in our neighborhood needs to hear about, it will definitely still get loud! You can see that the hub used in Figure 1.2 just extended the one collision domain from the switch port. The result is that John received the data from Bob but, happily, Sally did not. This is good because Bob intended to talk with John directly, and if he had needed to send a broadcast instead, everyone, including Sally, would have received it, possibly causing unnecessary congestion.

Here's a list of some of the things that commonly cause LAN traffic congestion:

- Too many hosts in a collision or broadcast domain
- Broadcast storms

- Too much multicast traffic

- Low bandwidth

- Adding hubs for connectivity to the network

- A bunch of ARP broadcasts

Take another look at Figure 1.2 and make sure you see that I extended the main hub from Figure 1.1 to a switch in Figure 1.2. I did that because hubs don't segment a network; they just connect network segments. Basically, it's an inexpensive way to connect a couple of PCs, and again, that's great for home use and troubleshooting, but that's about it!

As our planned community starts to grow, we'll need to add more streets with traffic control, and even some basic security. We'll achieve this by adding routers because these convenient devices are used to connect networks and route packets of data from one network to another. Cisco became the de facto standard for routers because of its unparalleled selection of high-quality router products and fantastic service. So never forget that by default, routers are basically employed to efficiently break up a *broadcast domain*—the set of all devices on a network segment, which are allowed to "hear" all broadcasts sent out on that specific segment.

Figure 1.3 depicts a router in our growing network, creating an internetwork and breaking up broadcast domains.

FIGURE 1.3   Routers create an internetwork.

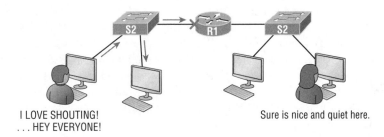

I LOVE SHOUTING!
. . . HEY EVERYONE!   Sure is nice and quiet here.

The network in Figure 1.3 is actually a pretty cool little network. Each host is connected to its own collision domain because of the switch, and the router has created two broadcast domains. So now our Sally is happily living in peace in a completely different neighborhood, no longer subjected to Bob's incessant shouting! If Bob wants to talk with Sally, he has to send a packet with a destination address using her IP address—he cannot broadcast for her!

But there's more... routers provide connections to *wide area network (WAN)* services as well via a serial interface for WAN connections—specifically, a V.35 physical interface on a Cisco router.

Let me make sure you understand why breaking up a broadcast domain is so important. When a host or server sends a network broadcast, every device on the network must read and process that broadcast—unless you have a router. When the router's interface receives this broadcast, it can respond by basically saying, "Thanks, but no thanks," and discard the broadcast without forwarding it on to other networks. Even though routers are known for breaking up broadcast domains by default, it's important to remember that they break up collision domains as well.

There are two advantages to using routers in your network:

▪ They don't forward broadcasts by default.

▪ They can filter the network based on layer 3 (Network layer) information such as an IP address.

Here are four ways a router functions in your network:

▪ Packet switching

▪ Packet filtering

▪ Internetwork communication

▪ Path selection

I'll tell you all about the various layers later in this chapter, but for now, it's helpful to think of routers as layer 3 switches. Unlike plain-vanilla layer 2 switches, which forward or filter frames, routers (layer 3 switches) use logical addressing and provide an important capacity called *packet switching*. Routers can also provide packet filtering via access lists, and when routers connect two or more networks together and use logical addressing (IP or IPv6), you then have an *internetwork*. Finally, routers use a routing table, which is essentially a map of the internetwork, to make best path selections for getting data to its proper destination and properly forward packets to remote networks.

Conversely, we don't use layer 2 switches to create internetworks because they don't break up broadcast domains by default. Instead, they're employed to add functionality to a network LAN. The main purpose of these switches is to make a LAN work better—to optimize its performance—providing more bandwidth for the LAN's users. Also, these switches don't forward packets to other networks like routers do. Instead, they only "switch" frames from one port to another within the switched network. And don't worry, even though you're probably thinking, "Wait—what are frames and packets?" I promise to completely fill you in later in this chapter. For now, think of a packet as a package containing data.

Okay, so by default, switches break up collision domains, but what are these things? *Collision domain* is an Ethernet term used to describe a network scenario in which one device sends a packet out on a network segment and every other device on that same segment is forced to pay attention no matter what. This isn't very efficient because if a different device tries to transmit at the same time, a collision will occur, requiring both devices to retransmit, one at a time—not good! This happens a lot in a hub environment, where each host segment connects to a hub that represents only one collision domain and a single broadcast domain. By contrast, each and every port on a switch represents its own collision domain, allowing network traffic to flow much more smoothly.

 Switches create separate collision domains within a single broadcast domain. Routers provide a separate broadcast domain for each interface. Don't let this ever confuse you!

The term *bridging* was introduced before routers and switches were implemented, so it's pretty common to hear people referring to switches as bridges. That's because bridges and switches basically do the same thing—break up collision domains on a LAN. Note to self that you cannot buy a physical bridge these days, only LAN switches, which use bridging technologies. This does not mean that you won't still hear Cisco and others refer to LAN switches as multiport bridges now and then.

But does it mean that a switch is just a multiple-port bridge with more brainpower? Well, pretty much, only there are still some key differences. Switches do provide a bridging function, but they do that with greatly enhanced management ability and features. Plus, most bridges had only 2 or 4 ports, which is severely limiting. Of course, it was possible to get your hands on a bridge with up to 16 ports, but that's nothing compared to the hundreds of ports available on some switches!

> You would use a bridge in a network to reduce collisions within broadcast domains and to increase the number of collision domains in your network. Doing this provides more bandwidth for users. And never forget that using hubs in your Ethernet network can contribute to congestion. As always, plan your network design carefully!

Figure 1.4 shows how a network would look with all these internetwork devices in place. Remember, a router doesn't just break up broadcast domains for every LAN interface, it breaks up collision domains too.

FIGURE 1.4 Internetworking devices

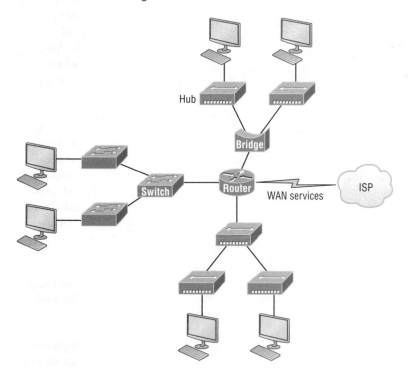

Looking at Figure 1.4, did you notice that the router has the center stage position and connects each physical network together? I'm stuck with using this layout because of the ancient bridges and hubs involved. I really hope you don't run across a network like this, but it's still really important to understand the strategic ideas that this figure represents!

See that bridge up at the top of our internetwork shown in Figure 1.4? It's there to connect the hubs to a router. The bridge breaks up collision domains, but all the hosts connected to both hubs are still crammed into the same broadcast domain. That bridge also created only three collision domains, one for each port, which means that each device connected to a hub is in the same collision domain as every other device connected to that same hub. This is really lame and to be avoided if possible, but it's still better than having one collision domain for all hosts! So don't do this at home; it's a great museum piece and a wonderful example of what not to do, but this inefficient design would be terrible for use in today's networks! It does show us how far we've come though, and again, the foundational concepts it illustrates are really important for you to get.

And I want you to notice something else: The three interconnected hubs at the bottom of the figure also connect to the router. This setup creates one collision domain and one broadcast domain and makes that bridged network, with its two collision domains, look majorly better by contrast!

Don't misunderstand... bridges/switches are used to segment networks, but they will not isolate broadcast or multicast packets.

The best network connected to the router is the LAN switched network on the left. Why? Because each port on that switch breaks up collision domains. But it's not all good—all devices are still in the same broadcast domain. Do you remember why this can be really bad? Because all devices must listen to all broadcasts transmitted, that's why! And if your broadcast domains are too large, the users have less bandwidth and are required to process more broadcasts. Network response time eventually will slow to a level that could cause riots and strikes, so it's important to keep your broadcast domains small in the vast majority of networks today.

Once there are only switches in our example network, things really change a lot! Figure 1.5 demonstrates a network you'll typically stumble upon today.

FIGURE 1.5 Switched networks creating an internetwork

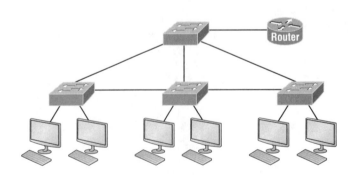

Here I've placed the LAN switches at the center of this network world, with the router connecting the logical networks. If I went ahead and implemented this design, I'll have created something called virtual LANs, or VLANs, which are used when you logically break up broadcast domains in a layer 2, switched network. It's really important to understand that even in a switched network environment, you still need a router to provide communication between VLANs. Don't forget that!

Still, clearly the best network design is the one that's perfectly configured to meet the business requirements of the specific company or client it serves, and it's usually one in which LAN switches exist in harmony with routers strategically placed in the network. It's my hope that this book will help you understand the basics of routers and switches so you can make solid, informed decisions on a case-by-case basis and be able to achieve that goal! But I digress...

So let's go back to Figure 1.4 now for a minute and really scrutinize it because I want to ask you this question: How many collision domains and broadcast domains are really there in this internetwork? I hope you answered nine collision domains and three broadcast domains! The broadcast domains are definitely the easiest to spot because only routers break up broadcast domains by default, and since there are three interface connections, that gives you three broadcast domains. But do you see the nine collision domains? Just in case that's a no, I'll explain. The all-hub network at the bottom is one collision domain; the bridge network on top equals three collision domains. Add in the switch network of five collision domains—one for each switch port—and you get a total of nine!

While we're at this, in Figure 1.5, each port on the switch is a separate collision domain, and each VLAN would be a separate broadcast domain. So how many collision domains do you see here? I'm counting 12—remember that connections between the switches are considered a collision domain! Since the figure doesn't show any VLAN information, we can assume the default of one broadcast domain is in place.

Before we move on to Internetworking Models, let's take a look at a few more network devices that we'll find in pretty much every network today as shown in Figure 1.6.

FIGURE 1.6   Other devices typically found in our internetworks today.

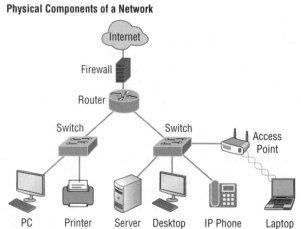

Taking off from the switched network in Figure 1.5, you'll find WLAN devices, including AP's and wireless controllers, and firewalls. You'd be hard pressed not to find these devices in your networks today.

Let's look closer at these devices:

- WLAN devices: These devices connect wireless devices such as computers, printers, and tablets to the network. Since pretty much every device manufactured today has a wireless NIC, you just need to configure a basic access point (AP) to connect to a traditional wired network.

- Access Points or APs: These devices allow wireless devices to connect to a wired network and extend a collision domain from a switch, and are typically in their own broadcast domain or what we'll refer to as a Virtual LAN (VLAN). An AP can be a simple standalone device, but today they are usually managed by wireless controllers either in house or through the internet.

- WLAN Controllers: These are the devices that network administrators or network operations centers use to manage access points in medium to large to extremely large quantities. The WLAN controller automatically handles the configuration of wireless access points and was typically used only in larger enterprise systems. However, with Cisco's acquisition of Meraki systems, you can easily manage a small to medium sized wireless network via the cloud using their simple to configure web controller system.

- Firewalls: These devices are network security systems that monitor and control the incoming and outgoing network traffic based on predetermined security rules, and is usually an Intrusion Protection System (IPS). Cisco Adaptive Security Appliance (ASA) firewall typically establishes a barrier between a trusted, secure internal network and the Internet, which is not secure or trusted. Cisco's new acquisition of Sourcefire put them in the top of the market with Next Generation Firewalls (NGFW) and Next Generation IPS (NGIPS), which Cisco now just calls Firepower. Cisco new Firepower runs on dedicated appliances, Cisco's ASA's, ISR routers and even on Meraki products.

 Real World Scenario

Should I Replace My Existing 10/100 Mbps Switches?

Let's say you're a network administrator at a large company. The boss comes to you and says that he got your requisition to buy a bunch of new switches but he's really freaking out about the price tag! Should you push it—do you really need to go this far?

Absolutely! Make your case and go for it because the newest switches add really huge capacity to a network that older 10/100 Mbps switches just can't touch. And yes, five-year-old switches are considered pretty Pleistocene these days. But in reality, most of us just don't have an unlimited budget to buy all new gigabit switches; however, 10/100 switches are just not good enough in today's networks.

Another good question: Do you really need low-latency 1 Gbps or better switch ports for all your users, servers, and other devices? Yes, you *absolutely* need new higher-end switches! This is because servers and hosts are no longer the bottlenecks of our internetworks, our routers and switches are—especially legacy ones. We now need gigabit on the desktop and on every router interface; 10 Gbps is now the minimum between switch uplinks, so go to 40 or even 100 Gbps as uplinks if you can afford it.

Go ahead. Put in that requisition for all new switches. You'll be a hero before long!

Okay, so now that you've gotten a pretty thorough introduction to internetworking and the various devices that populate an internetwork, it's time to head into exploring the internetworking models.

Internetworking Models

First a little history: When networks first came into being, computers could typically communicate only with computers from the same manufacturer. For example, companies ran either a complete DECnet solution or an IBM solution, never both together. In the late 1970s, the *Open Systems Interconnection (OSI) reference model* was created by the International Organization for Standardization (ISO) to break through this barrier.

The OSI model was meant to help vendors create interoperable network devices and software in the form of protocols so that different vendor networks could work in peaceable accord with each other. Like world peace, it'll probably never happen completely, but it's still a great goal!

Anyway the OSI model is the primary architectural model for networks. It describes how data and network information are communicated from an application on one computer through the network media to an application on another computer. The OSI reference model breaks this approach into layers.

Coming up, I'll explain the layered approach to you plus how we can use it to help us troubleshoot our internetworks.

Goodness! ISO, OSI, and soon you'll hear about IOS! Just remember that the ISO created the OSI and that Cisco created the Internetworking Operating System (IOS), which is what this book is all-so-about.

The Layered Approach

Understand that a *reference model* is a conceptual blueprint of how communications should take place. It addresses all the processes required for effective communication and divides them into logical groupings called *layers*. When a communication system is designed in this manner, it's known as a hierarchical or *layered architecture*.

Think of it like this: You and some friends want to start a company. One of the first things you'll do is sort out every task that must be done and decide who will do what. You would move on to determine the order in which you would like everything to be done with careful consideration of how all your specific operations relate to each other. You would then organize everything into departments (e.g., sales, inventory, and shipping), with each department dealing with its specific responsibilities and keeping its own staff busy enough to focus on their own particular area of the enterprise.

In this scenario, departments are a metaphor for the layers in a communication system. For things to run smoothly, the staff of each department has to trust in and rely heavily upon those in the others to do their jobs well. During planning sessions, you would take notes, recording the entire process to guide later discussions and clarify standards of operation, thereby creating your business blueprint—your own reference model.

And once your business is launched, your department heads, each armed with the part of the blueprint relevant to their own department, will develop practical ways to implement their distinct tasks. These practical methods, or protocols, will then be compiled into a standard operating procedures manual and followed closely because each procedure will have been included for different reasons, delimiting their various degrees of importance and implementation. All of this will become vital if you form a partnership or acquire another company because then it will be really important that the new company's business model is compatible with yours!

Models happen to be really important to software developers too. They often use a reference model to understand computer communication processes so they can determine which functions should be accomplished on a given layer. This means that if someone is creating a protocol for a certain layer, they only need to be concerned with their target layer's function. Software that maps to another layer's protocols and is specifically designed to be deployed there will handle additional functions. The technical term for this idea is *binding*. The communication processes that are related to each other are bound, or grouped together, at a particular layer.

Advantages of Reference Models

The OSI model is hierarchical, and there are many advantages that can be applied to any layered model, but as I said, the OSI model's primary purpose is to allow different vendors' networks to interoperate.

Here's a list of some of the more important benefits of using the OSI layered model:

- It divides the network communication process into smaller and simpler components, facilitating component development, design, and troubleshooting.

- It allows multiple-vendor development through the standardization of network components.

- It encourages industry standardization by clearly defining what functions occur at each layer of the model.

- It allows various types of network hardware and software to communicate.

- It prevents changes in one layer from affecting other layers to expedite development.

The OSI Reference Model

One of best gifts the OSI specifications gives us is paving the way for the data transfer between disparate hosts running different operating systems, like Unix hosts, Windows machines, Macs, smartphones, and so on.

And remember, the OSI is a logical model, not a physical one. It's essentially a set of guidelines that developers can use to create and implement applications to run on a network. It also provides a framework for creating and implementing networking standards, devices, and internetworking schemes.

The OSI has seven different layers, divided into two groups. The top three layers define how the applications within the end stations will communicate with each other as well as with users. The bottom four layers define how data is transmitted end to end.

Figure 1.7 shows the three upper layers and their functions.

FIGURE 1.7   The upper layers

Application	• Provides a user interface
Presentation	• Presents data • Handles processing such as encryption
Session	• Keeps different applications' data separate

When looking at Figure 1.6, understand that users interact with the computer at the Application layer and also that the upper layers are responsible for applications communicating between hosts. None of the upper layers knows anything about networking or network addresses because that's the responsibility of the four bottom layers.

In Figure 1.8, which shows the four lower layers and their functions, you can see that it's these four bottom layers that define how data is transferred through physical media like wire, cable, fiber optics, switches, and routers. These bottom layers also determine how to rebuild a data stream from a transmitting host to a destination host's application.

FIGURE 1.8   The lower layers

Transport	• Provides reliable or unreliable delivery • Performs error correction before retransmit
Network	• Provides logical addressing, which routers use for path determination
Data Link	• Combines packets into bytes and bytes into frames • Provides access to media using MAC address • Performs error detection not correction
Physical	• Moves bits between devices • Specifies voltage, wire speed, and pinout of cables

The following network devices operate at all seven layers of the OSI model:

- *Network management stations (NMSs)*
- Web and application servers
- Gateways (not default gateways)
- Servers
- Network hosts

Basically, the ISO is pretty much the Emily Post of the network protocol world. Just as Ms. Post wrote the book setting the standards—or protocols—for human social interaction, the ISO developed the OSI reference model as the precedent and guide for an open network protocol set. Defining the etiquette of communication models, it remains the most popular means of comparison for protocol suites today.

The OSI reference model has the following seven layers:

- Application layer (layer 7)
- Presentation layer (layer 6)
- Session layer (layer 5)
- Transport layer (layer 4)
- Network layer (layer 3)
- Data Link layer (layer 2)
- Physical layer (layer 1)

Some people like to use a mnemonic to remember the seven layers, such as **A**ll **P**eople **S**eem **T**o **N**eed **D**ata **P**rocessing. Figure 1.9 shows a summary of the functions defined at each layer of the OSI model.

FIGURE 1.9   OSI layer functions

Application	• File, print, message, database, and application services
Presentation	• Data encryption, compression, and translation services
Session	• Dialog control

Transport	• End-to-end connection
Network	• Routing

Data Link	• Framing
Physical	• Physical topology

I've separated the seven-layer model into three different functions: the upper layers, the middle layers, and the bottom layers. The upper layers communicate with the user interface and application, the middle layers do reliable communication and routing to a remote network, and the bottom layers communicate to the local network.

With this in hand, you're now ready to explore each layer's function in detail!

The Application Layer

The *Application layer* of the OSI model marks the spot where users actually communicate to the computer and comes into play only when it's clear that access to the network will be needed soon. Take the case of Internet Explorer (IE). You could actually uninstall every trace of networking components like TCP/IP, the NIC card, and so on and still use IE to view a local HTML document. But things would get ugly if you tried to do things like view a remote HTML document that must be retrieved because IE and other browsers act on these types of requests by attempting to access the Application layer. So basically, the Application layer is working as the interface between the actual application program and the next layer down by providing ways for the application to send information down through the protocol stack. This isn't actually part of the layered structure, because browsers don't live in the Application layer, but they interface with it as well as the relevant protocols when asked to access remote resources.

Identifying and confirming the communication partner's availability and verifying the required resources to permit the specified type of communication to take place also occurs at the Application layer. This is important because, like the lion's share of browser functions, computer applications sometimes need more than desktop resources. It's more typical than you would think for the communicating components of several network applications to come together to carry out a requested function. Here are a few good examples of these kinds of events:

- File transfers
- Email
- Enabling remote access
- Network management activities
- Client/server processes
- Information location

Many network applications provide services for communication over enterprise networks, but for present and future internetworking, the need is fast developing to reach beyond the limits of current physical networking.

The Application layer works as the interface between actual application programs. This means end-user programs like Microsoft Word don't reside at the Application layer, they interface with the Application layer protocols. Later, in Chapter 3, "Introduction to TCP/IP," I'll talk in detail about a few important programs that actually reside at the Application layer, like Telnet, FTP, and TFTP.

The Presentation Layer

The *Presentation layer* gets its name from its purpose: It presents data to the Application layer and is responsible for data translation and code formatting. Think of it as the OSI model's translator, providing coding and conversion services. One very effective way of ensuring a successful data transfer is to convert the data into a standard format before transmission. Computers are configured to receive this generically formatted data and then reformat it back into its native state to read it. An example of this type of translation service occurs when translating old Extended Binary Coded Decimal Interchange Code (EBCDIC) data to ASCII, the American Standard Code for Information Interchange (often pronounced "askee"). So just remember that by providing translation services, the Presentation layer ensures that data transferred from the Application layer of one system can be read by the Application layer of another one.

With this in mind, it follows that the OSI would include protocols that define how standard data should be formatted, so key functions like data compression, decompression, encryption, and decryption are also associated with this layer. Some Presentation layer standards are involved in multimedia operations as well.

The Session Layer

The *Session layer* is responsible for setting up, managing, and dismantling sessions between Presentation layer entities and keeping user data separate. Dialog control between devices also occurs at this layer.

Communication between hosts' various applications at the Session layer, as from a client to a server, is coordinated and organized via three different modes: *simplex*, *half-duplex*, and *full-duplex*. Simplex is simple one-way communication, kind of like saying something and not getting a reply. Half-duplex is actual two-way communication, but it can take place in only one direction at a time, preventing the interruption of the transmitting device. It's like when pilots and ship captains communicate over their radios, or even a walkie-talkie. But full-duplex is exactly like a real conversation where devices can transmit and receive at the same time, much like two people arguing or interrupting each other during a telephone conversation.

The Transport Layer

The *Transport layer* segments and reassembles data into a single data stream. Services located at this layer take all the various data received from upper-layer applications, then combine it into the same, concise data stream. These protocols provide end-to-end data transport services and can establish a logical connection between the sending host and destination host on an internetwork.

A pair of well-known protocols called TCP and UDP are integral to this layer, but no worries if you're not already familiar with them because I'll bring you up to speed later, in Chapter 3. For now, understand that although both work at the Transport layer, TCP is known as a reliable service but UDP is not. This distinction gives application developers more options because they have a choice between the two protocols when they are designing products for this layer.

The Transport layer is responsible for providing mechanisms for multiplexing upper-layer applications, establishing sessions, and tearing down virtual circuits. It can also hide the details of network-dependent information from the higher layers as well as provide transparent data transfer.

> The term *reliable networking* can be used at the Transport layer. Reliable networking requires that acknowledgments, sequencing, and flow control will all be used.

The Transport layer can be either connectionless or connection-oriented, but because Cisco really wants you to understand the connection-oriented function of the Transport layer, I'm going to go into that in more detail here.

Connection-Oriented Communication

For reliable transport to occur, a device that wants to transmit must first establish a connection-oriented communication session with a remote device—its peer system—known as a *call setup* or a *three-way handshake*. Once this process is complete, the data transfer occurs, and when it's finished, a call termination takes place to tear down the virtual circuit.

Figure 1.10 depicts a typical reliable session taking place between sending and receiving systems. In it, you can see that both hosts' application programs begin by notifying their individual operating systems that a connection is about to be initiated. The two operating systems communicate by sending messages over the network confirming that the transfer is approved and that both sides are ready for it to take place. After all of this required synchronization takes place, a connection is fully established and the data transfer begins. And by the way, it's really helpful to understand that this virtual circuit setup is often referred to as overhead!

FIGURE 1.10   Establishing a connection-oriented session

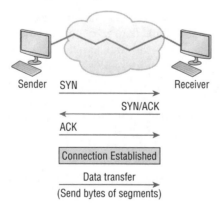

Okay, now while the information is being transferred between hosts, the two machines periodically check in with each other, communicating through their protocol software to ensure that all is going well and that the data is being received properly.

Here's a summary of the steps in the connection-oriented session—that three-way handshake—pictured in Figure 1.9:

- The first "connection agreement" segment is a request for *synchronization (SYN)*.

- The next segments *acknowledge (ACK)* the request and establish connection parameters—the rules—between hosts. These segments request that the receiver's sequencing is synchronized here as well so that a bidirectional connection can be formed.

- The final segment is also an acknowledgment, which notifies the destination host that the connection agreement has been accepted and that the actual connection has been established. Data transfer can now begin.

Sounds pretty simple, but things don't always flow so smoothly. Sometimes during a transfer, congestion can occur because a high-speed computer is generating data traffic a lot faster than the network itself can process it! And a whole bunch of computers simultaneously sending datagrams through a single gateway or destination can also jam things up pretty badly. In the latter case, a gateway or destination can become congested even though no single source caused the problem. Either way, the problem is basically akin to a freeway bottleneck—too much traffic for too small a capacity. It's not usually one car that's the problem; it's just that there are way too many cars on that freeway at once!

But what actually happens when a machine receives a flood of datagrams too quickly for it to process? It stores them in a memory section called a *buffer*. Sounds great; it's just that this buffering action can solve the problem only if the datagrams are part of a small burst. If the datagram deluge continues, eventually exhausting the device's memory, its flood capacity will be exceeded and it will dump any and all additional datagrams it receives just like an inundated overflowing bucket!

Flow Control

Since floods and losing data can both be tragic, we have a fail-safe solution in place known as *flow control*. Its job is to ensure data integrity at the Transport layer by allowing applications to request reliable data transport between systems. Flow control prevents a sending host on one side of the connection from overflowing the buffers in the receiving host. Reliable data transport employs a connection-oriented communications session between systems, and the protocols involved ensure that the following will be achieved:

- The segments delivered are acknowledged back to the sender upon their reception.

- Any segments not acknowledged are retransmitted.

- Segments are sequenced back into their proper order upon arrival at their destination.

- A manageable data flow is maintained in order to avoid congestion, overloading, or worse, data loss.

The purpose of flow control is to provide a way for the receiving device to control the amount of data sent by the sender.

Because of the transport function, network flood control systems really work well. Instead of dumping and losing data, the Transport layer can issue a "not ready" indicator to the sender, or potential source of the flood. This mechanism works kind of like a stop-light, signaling the sending device to stop transmitting segment traffic to its overwhelmed peer. After the peer receiver processes the segments already in its memory reservoir—its buffer—it sends out a "ready" transport indicator. When the machine waiting to transmit the rest of its datagrams receives this "go" indicator, it resumes its transmission. The process is pictured in Figure 1.11.

FIGURE 1.11   Transmitting segments with flow control

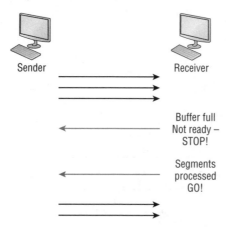

In a reliable, connection-oriented data transfer, datagrams are delivered to the receiving host hopefully in the same sequence they're transmitted. A failure will occur if any data segments are lost, duplicated, or damaged along the way—a problem solved by having the receiving host acknowledge that it has received each and every data segment.

A service is considered connection-oriented if it has the following characteristics:

- A virtual circuit, or "three-way handshake," is set up.
- It uses sequencing.
- It uses acknowledgments.
- It uses flow control.

The types of flow control are buffering, windowing, and congestion avoidance.

Windowing

Ideally, data throughput happens quickly and efficiently. And as you can imagine, it would be painfully slow if the transmitting machine had to actually wait for an acknowledgment after sending each and every segment! The quantity of data segments, measured in bytes, that the transmitting machine is allowed to send without receiving an acknowledgment is called a *window*.

Windows are used to control the amount of outstanding, unacknowledged data segments.

The size of the window controls how much information is transferred from one end to the other before an acknowledgement is required. While some protocols quantify information depending on the number of packets, TCP/IP measures it by counting the number of bytes.

As you can see in Figure 1.12, there are two window sizes—one set to 1 and one set to 3.

FIGURE 1.12   Windowing

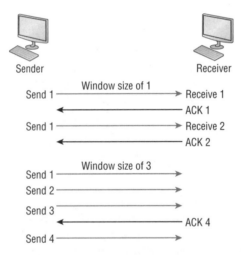

If you've configured a window size of 1, the sending machine will wait for an acknowledgment for each data segment it transmits before transmitting another one but will allow three to be transmitted before receiving an acknowledgement if the window size is set to 3.

In this simplified example, both the sending and receiving machines are workstations. Remember that in reality, the transmission isn't based on simple numbers but in the amount of bytes that can be sent!

If a receiving host fails to receive all the bytes that it should acknowledge, the host can improve the communication session by decreasing the window size.

Acknowledgments

Reliable data delivery ensures the integrity of a stream of data sent from one machine to the other through a fully functional data link. It guarantees that the data won't be duplicated or lost. This is achieved through something called *positive acknowledgment with retransmission*—a technique that requires a receiving machine to communicate with the transmitting source by sending an acknowledgment message back to the sender when it receives data. The sender documents each segment measured in bytes, then sends and waits for this acknowledgment before sending the next segment. Also important is that when it sends a segment, the transmitting machine starts a timer and will retransmit if it expires before it gets an acknowledgment back from the receiving end. Figure 1.13 shows the process I just described.

FIGURE 1.13   Transport layer reliable delivery

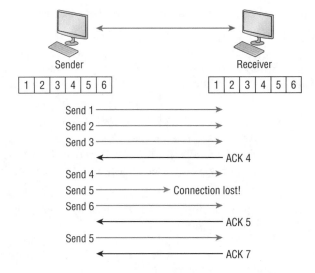

In the figure, the sending machine transmits segments 1, 2, and 3. The receiving node acknowledges that it has received them by requesting segment 4 (what it is expecting next). When it receives the acknowledgment, the sender then transmits segments 4, 5, and 6. If segment 5 doesn't make it to the destination, the receiving node acknowledges that event with a request for the segment to be re-sent. The sending machine will then resend the lost segment and wait for an acknowledgment, which it must receive in order to move on to the transmission of segment 7.

The Transport layer, working in tandem with the Session layer, also separates the data from different applications, an activity known as *session multiplexing*, and it happens when a client connects to a server with multiple browser sessions open. This is exactly what's taking place when you go someplace online like Amazon and click multiple links, opening them simultaneously to get information when comparison shopping. The client data from each browser session must be separate when the server application receives it, which is pretty slick technologically speaking, and it's the Transport layer to the rescue for that juggling act!

The Network Layer

The *Network layer*, or layer 3, manages device addressing, tracks the location of devices on the network, and determines the best way to move data. This means that it's up to the Network layer to transport traffic between devices that aren't locally attached. Routers, which are layer 3 devices, are specified at this layer and provide the routing services within an internetwork.

Here's how that works: first, when a packet is received on a router interface, the destination IP address is checked. If the packet isn't destined for that particular router, it will look up the destination network address in the routing table. Once the router chooses an exit interface, the packet will be sent to that interface to be framed and sent out on the local network. If the router can't find an entry for the packet's destination network in the routing table, the router drops the packet.

Data and route update packets are the two types of packets used at the Network layer:

Data Packets   These are used to transport user data through the internetwork. Protocols used to support data traffic are called routed protocols, and IP and IPv6 are key examples. I'll cover IP addressing in Chapter 3, "Introduction to TCP/IP," and Chapter 4, "Easy Subnetting," and I'll cover IPv6 in Chapter 14, "Internet Protocol Version 6 (IPv6)."

Route Update Packets   These packets are used to update neighboring routers about the networks connected to all routers within the internetwork. Protocols that send route update packets are called routing protocols; the most critical ones for CCNA are RIPv2, EIGRP, and OSPF. Route update packets are used to help build and maintain routing tables.

Figure 1.14 shows an example of a routing table. The routing table each router keeps and refers to includes the following information:

FIGURE 1.14   Routing table used in a router

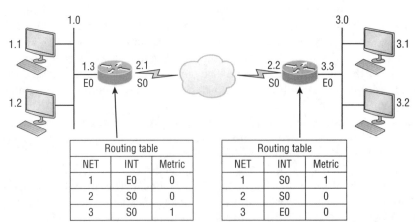

Network Addresses Protocol-specific network addresses. A router must maintain a routing table for individual routing protocols because each routed protocol keeps track of a network with a different addressing scheme. For example, the routing tables for IP and IPv6 are completely different, so the router keeps a table for each one. Think of it as a street sign in each of the different languages spoken by the American, Spanish, and French people living on a street; the street sign would read Cat/Gato/Chat.

Interface The exit interface a packet will take when destined for a specific network.

Metric The distance to the remote network. Different routing protocols use different ways of computing this distance. I'm going to cover routing protocols thoroughly in Chapter 9, "IP Routing." For now, know that some routing protocols like the Routing Information Protocol, or RIP, use hop count, which refers to the number of routers a packet passes through en route to a remote network. Others use bandwidth, delay of the line, or even tick count (1/18 of a second) to determine the best path for data to get to a given destination.

And as I mentioned earlier, routers break up broadcast domains, which means that by default, broadcasts aren't forwarded through a router. Do you remember why this is a good thing? Routers also break up collision domains, but you can also do that using layer 2 (Data Link layer) switches. Because each interface in a router represents a separate network, it must be assigned unique network identification numbers, and each host on the network connected to that router must use the same network number. Figure 1.15 shows how a router works in an internetwork.

FIGURE 1.15 A router in an internetwork. Each router LAN interface is a broadcast domain. Routers break up broadcast domains by default and provide WAN services.

Here are some router characteristics that you should never forget:

- Routers, by default, will not forward any broadcast or multicast packets.

- Routers use the logical address in a Network layer header to determine the next-hop router to forward the packet to.

- Routers can use access lists, created by an administrator, to control security based on the types of packets allowed to enter or exit an interface.

- Routers can provide layer 2 bridging functions if needed and can simultaneously route through the same interface.

- Layer 3 devices—in this case, routers—provide connections between *virtual LANs (VLANs)*.

- Routers can provide *quality of service (QoS)* for specific types of network traffic.

The Data Link Layer

The *Data Link layer* provides for the physical transmission of data and handles error notification, network topology, and flow control. This means that the Data Link layer will ensure that messages are delivered to the proper device on a LAN using hardware addresses and will translate messages from the Network layer into bits for the Physical layer to transmit.

The Data Link layer formats the messages, each called a *data frame*, and adds a customized header containing the hardware destination and source address. This added information forms a sort of capsule that surrounds the original message in much the same way that engines, navigational devices, and other tools were attached to the lunar modules of the Apollo project. These various pieces of equipment were useful only during certain stages of space flight and were stripped off the module and discarded when their designated stage was completed. The process of data traveling through networks is similar.

Figure 1.16 shows the Data Link layer with the Ethernet and IEEE specifications. When you check it out, notice that the IEEE 802.2 standard is used in conjunction with and adds functionality to the other IEEE standards. (You'll read more about the important IEEE 802 standards used with the Cisco objectives in Chapter 2, "Ethernet Networking and Data Encapsulation.")

FIGURE 1.16   Data Link layer

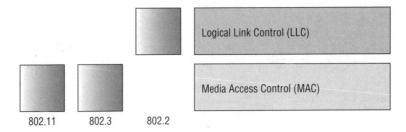

It's important for you to understand that routers, which work at the Network layer, don't care at all about where a particular host is located. They're only concerned about where networks are located and the best way to reach them—including remote ones. Routers are totally obsessive when it comes to networks, which in this case is a good thing! It's the Data Link layer that's responsible for the actual unique identification of each device that resides on a local network.

For a host to send packets to individual hosts on a local network as well as transmit packets between routers, the Data Link layer uses hardware addressing. Each time a packet is sent between routers, it's framed with control information at the Data Link layer, but that information is stripped off at the receiving router and only the original packet is left completely intact. This framing of the packet continues for each hop until the packet is finally delivered to the correct receiving host. It's really important to understand that the packet itself is never altered along the route; it's only encapsulated with the type of control information required for it to be properly passed on to the different media types.

The IEEE Ethernet Data Link layer has two sublayers:

Media Access Control (MAC)   Defines how packets are placed on the media. Contention for media access is "first come/first served" access where everyone shares the same bandwidth—hence the name. Physical addressing is defined here as well as logical topologies. What's a logical topology? It's the signal path through a physical topology. Line discipline, error notification (but not correction), the ordered delivery of frames, and optional flow control can also be used at this sublayer.

Logical Link Control (LLC)   Responsible for identifying Network layer protocols and then encapsulating them. An LLC header tells the Data Link layer what to do with a packet once a frame is received. It works like this: a host receives a frame and looks in the LLC header to find out where the packet is destined—for instance, the IP protocol at the Network layer. The LLC can also provide flow control and sequencing of control bits.

The switches and bridges I talked about near the beginning of the chapter both work at the Data Link layer and filter the network using hardware (MAC) addresses. I'll talk about these next.

As data is encoded with control information at each layer of the OSI model, the data is named with something called a protocol data unit (PDU). At the Transport layer, the PDU is called a segment, at the Network layer it's a packet, at the Data Link a frame, and at the Physical layer it's called bits. This method of naming the data at each layer is covered thoroughly in Chapter 2.

Switches and Bridges at the Data Link Layer

Layer 2 switching is considered hardware-based bridging because it uses specialized hardware called an *application-specific integrated circuit (ASIC)*. ASICs can run up to high gigabit speeds with very low latency rates.

Latency is the time measured from when a frame enters a port to when it exits a port.

Bridges and switches read each frame as it passes through the network. The layer 2 device then puts the source hardware address in a filter table and keeps track of which port the frame was received on. This information (logged in the bridge's or switch's filter table) is what helps the machine determine the location of the specific sending device. Figure 1.17 shows a switch in an internetwork and how John is sending packets to the Internet and Sally doesn't hear his frames because she is in a different collision domain. The destination frame goes directly to the default gateway router, and Sally doesn't see John's traffic, much to her relief.

FIGURE 1.17   A switch in an internetwork

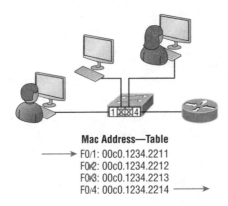

Mac Address—Table

F0/1: 00c0.1234.2211
F0/2: 00c0.1234.2212
F0/3: 00c0.1234.2213
F0/4: 00c0.1234.2214

The real estate business is all about location, location, location, and it's the same way for both layer 2 and layer 3 devices. Though both need to be able to negotiate the network, it's crucial to remember that they're concerned with very different parts of it. Primarily, layer 3 machines (such as routers) need to locate specific networks, whereas layer 2 machines (switches and bridges) need to eventually locate specific devices. So, networks are to routers as individual devices are to switches and bridges. And routing tables that "map" the internetwork are for routers as filter tables that "map" individual devices are for switches and bridges.

After a filter table is built on the layer 2 device, it will forward frames only to the segment where the destination hardware address is located. If the destination device is on the same segment as the frame, the layer 2 device will block the frame from going to any other segments. If the destination is on a different segment, the frame can be transmitted only to that segment. This is called *transparent bridging.*

When a switch interface receives a frame with a destination hardware address that isn't found in the device's filter table, it will forward the frame to all connected segments. If the unknown device that was sent the "mystery frame" replies to this forwarding action, the switch updates its filter table regarding that device's location. But in the event the destination address of the transmitting frame is a broadcast address, the switch will forward all broadcasts to every connected segment by default.

All devices that the broadcast is forwarded to are considered to be in the same broadcast domain. This can be a problem because layer 2 devices propagate layer 2 broadcast storms that can seriously choke performance, and the only way to stop a broadcast storm from propagating through an internetwork is with a layer 3 device—a router!

The biggest benefit of using switches instead of hubs in your internetwork is that each switch port is actually its own collision domain. Remember that a hub creates one large collision domain, which is not a good thing! But even armed with a switch, you still don't get to just break up broadcast domains by default because neither switches nor bridges will do that. They'll simply forward all broadcasts instead.

Another benefit of LAN switching over hub-centered implementations is that each device on every segment plugged into a switch can transmit simultaneously. Well, at least they can as long as there's only one host on each port and there isn't a hub plugged into a switch port! As you might have guessed, this is because hubs allow only one device per network segment to communicate at a time.

The Physical Layer

Finally arriving at the bottom, we find that the *Physical layer* does two things: it sends bits and receives bits. Bits come only in values of 1 or 0—a Morse code with numerical values. The Physical layer communicates directly with the various types of actual communication media. Different kinds of media represent these bit values in different ways. Some use audio tones, while others employ *state transitions*—changes in voltage from high to low and low to high. Specific protocols are needed for each type of media to describe the proper bit patterns to be used, how data is encoded into media signals, and the various qualities of the physical media's attachment interface.

The Physical layer specifies the electrical, mechanical, procedural, and functional requirements for activating, maintaining, and deactivating a physical link between end systems. This layer is also where you identify the interface between the *data terminal equipment (DTE)* and the *data communication equipment (DCE)*. (Some old phone-company employees still call DCE "data circuit-terminating equipment.") The DCE is usually located at the service provider, while the DTE is the attached device. The services available to the DTE are most often accessed via a modem or *channel service unit/data service unit (CSU/DSU)*.

The Physical layer's connectors and different physical topologies are defined by the OSI as standards, allowing disparate systems to communicate. The Cisco exam objectives are interested only in the IEEE Ethernet standards.

Hubs at the Physical Layer

A hub is really a multiple-port repeater. A repeater receives a digital signal, reamplifies or regenerates that signal, then forwards the signal out the other port without looking at any data. A hub does the same thing across all active ports: any digital signal received from a segment on a hub port is regenerated or reamplified and transmitted out all other ports on the hub. This means all devices plugged into a hub are in the same collision domain as well as in the same broadcast domain. Figure 1.18 shows a hub in a network and how when one host transmits, all other hosts must stop and listen.

FIGURE 1.18   A hub in a network

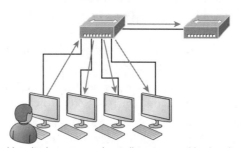

I love it when everyone has to listen to everything I say!

Hubs, like repeaters, don't examine any of the traffic as it enters or before it's transmitted out to the other parts of the physical media. And every device connected to the hub, or hubs, must listen if a device transmits. A physical star network, where the hub is a central device and cables extend in all directions out from it, is the type of topology a hub creates. Visually, the design really does resemble a star, whereas Ethernet networks run a logical bus topology, meaning that the signal has to run through the network from end to end.

Hubs and repeaters can be used to enlarge the area covered by a single LAN segment, but I really do not recommend going with this configuration! LAN switches are affordable for almost every situation and will make you much happier.

Topologies at the Physical layer

One last thing I want to discuss at the Physical layer is topologies, both physical and logical. Understand that every type of network has both a physical and a logical topology.

- The physical topology of a network refers to the physical layout of the devices, but mostly the cabling and cabling layout.

- The logical topology defines the logical path on which the signal will travel on the physical topology.

Figure 1.19 shows the four types of topologies.

FIGURE 1.19   Physical vs. Logical Topolgies

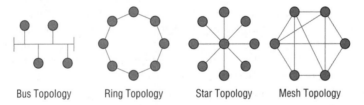

- Physical topology is the physical layout of the devices and cabling.
- The primary physical topology categories are bus, ring, star, and mesh.

Bus Topology   Ring Topology   Star Topology   Mesh Topology

Here are the topology types, although the most common, and pretty much the only network we use today is a physical star, logical bus technology, which is considered a hybrid topology (think Ethernet):

- Bus: In a bus topology, every workstation is connected to a single cable, meaning every host is directly connected to every other workstation in the network.

- Ring: In a ring topology, computers and other network devices are cabled together in a way that the last device is connected to the first to form a circle or ring.

- Star: The most common physical topology is a star topology, which is your Ethernet switching physical layout. A central cabling device (switch) connects the computers and other network devices together. This category includes star and extended star topologies. Physical connection is commonly made using twisted-pair wiring.

- Mesh: In a mesh topology, every network device is cabled together with connection to each other. Redundant links increase reliability and self-healing. The physical connection is commonly made using fiber or twisted-pair wiring.

- Hybrid: Ethernet uses a physical star layout (cables come from all directions), and the signal travels end-to-end, like a bus route.

Summary

Whew! I know this seemed like the chapter that wouldn't end, but it did—and you made it through! You're now armed with a ton of fundamental information; you're ready to build upon it and are well on your way to certification.

I started by discussing simple, basic networking and the differences between collision and broadcast domains.

I then discussed the OSI model—the seven-layer model used to help application developers design applications that can run on any type of system or network. Each layer has its special jobs and select responsibilities within the model to ensure that solid, effective communications do, in fact, occur. I provided you with complete details of each layer and discussed how Cisco views the specifications of the OSI model.

In addition, each layer in the OSI model specifies different types of devices, and I described the different devices used at each layer.

Remember that hubs are Physical layer devices and repeat the digital signal to all segments except the one from which it was received. Switches segment the network using hardware addresses and break up collision domains. Routers break up broadcast domains as well as collision domains and use logical addressing to send packets through an internetwork.

Exam Essentials

Identify the possible causes of LAN traffic congestion.   Too many hosts in a broadcast domain, broadcast storms, multicasting, and low bandwidth are all possible causes of LAN traffic congestion.

Describe the difference between a collision domain and a broadcast domain.   *Collision domain* is an Ethernet term used to describe a network collection of devices in which one particular device sends a packet on a network segment, forcing every other device on that same segment to pay attention to it. With a broadcast domain, a set of all devices on a network hears all broadcasts sent on all segments.

Differentiate a MAC address and an IP address and describe how and when each address type is used in a network.   A MAC address is a hexadecimal number identifying the physical connection of a host. MAC addresses are said to operate on layer 2 of the OSI model. IP addresses, which can be expressed in binary or decimal format, are logical identifiers that are said to be on layer 3 of the OSI model. Hosts on the same physical segment locate one another with MAC addresses, while IP addresses are used when they reside on different LAN segments or subnets.

Understand the difference between a hub, a bridge, a switch, and a router.   A hub creates one collision domain and one broadcast domain. A bridge breaks up collision domains but creates one large broadcast domain. They use hardware addresses to filter the network. Switches are really just multiple-port bridges with more intelligence; they break up collision domains but create one large broadcast domain by default. Bridges and switches use hardware addresses to filter the network. Routers break up broadcast domains (and collision domains) and use logical addressing to filter the network.

Identify the functions and advantages of routers.   Routers perform packet switching, filtering, and path selection, and they facilitate internetwork communication. One advantage of routers is that they reduce broadcast traffic.

Differentiate connection-oriented and connectionless network services and describe how each is handled during network communications.   Connection-oriented services use acknowledgments and flow control to create a reliable session. More overhead is used than in a connectionless network service. Connectionless services are used to send data with no acknowledgments or flow control. This is considered unreliable.

Define the OSI layers, understand the function of each, and describe how devices and networking protocols can be mapped to each layer.   You must remember the seven layers of the OSI model and what function each layer provides. The Application, Presentation, and Session layers are upper layers and are responsible for communicating from a user interface to an application. The Transport layer provides segmentation, sequencing, and virtual circuits. The Network layer provides logical network addressing and routing through an internetwork. The Data Link layer provides framing and placing of data on the network medium. The Physical layer is responsible for taking 1s and 0s and encoding them into a digital signal for transmission on the network segment.

Written Labs

In this section, you'll complete the following labs to make sure you've got the information and concepts contained within them fully dialed in:

   Lab 1.1: OSI Questions

   Lab 1.2: Defining the OSI Layers and Devices

   Lab 1.3: Identifying Collision and Broadcast Domains

   You can find the answers to these labs in Appendix A, "Answers to Written Labs."

Written Lab 1.1: OSI Questions

Answer the following questions about the OSI model:

1. Which layer chooses and determines the availability of communicating partners along with the resources necessary to make the connection, coordinates partnering applications, and forms a consensus on procedures for controlling data integrity and error recovery?

2. Which layer is responsible for converting data packets from the Data Link layer into electrical signals?

3. At which layer is routing implemented, enabling connections and path selection between two end systems?

4. Which layer defines how data is formatted, presented, encoded, and converted for use on the network?

5. Which layer is responsible for creating, managing, and terminating sessions between applications?

6. Which layer ensures the trustworthy transmission of data across a physical link and is primarily concerned with physical addressing, line discipline, network topology, error notification, ordered delivery of frames, and flow control?

7. Which layer is used for reliable communication between end nodes over the network and provides mechanisms for establishing, maintaining, and terminating virtual circuits; transport-fault detection and recovery; and controlling the flow of information?

8. Which layer provides logical addressing that routers will use for path determination?

9. Which layer specifies voltage, wire speed, and cable pinouts and moves bits between devices?

10. Which layer combines bits into bytes and bytes into frames, uses MAC addressing, and provides error detection?

11. Which layer is responsible for keeping the data from different applications separate on the network?

12. Which layer is represented by frames?

13. Which layer is represented by segments?

14. Which layer is represented by packets?

15. Which layer is represented by bits?

16. Rearrange the following in order of encapsulation:

    Packets

    Frames

    Bits

    Segments

17. Which layer segments and reassembles data into a data stream?

18. Which layer provides the physical transmission of the data and handles error notification, network topology, and flow control?

19. Which layer manages logical device addressing, tracks the location of devices on the internetwork, and determines the best way to move data?

20. What is the bit length and expression form of a MAC address?

Written Lab 1.2: Defining the OSI Layers and Devices

Fill in the blanks with the appropriate layer of the OSI or hub, switch, or router device.

Description	Device or OSI Layer
This device sends and receives information about the Network layer.	
This layer creates a virtual circuit before transmitting between two end stations.	
This device uses hardware addresses to filter a network.	
Ethernet is defined at these layers.	
This layer supports flow control, sequencing, and acknowledgments.	
This device can measure the distance to a remote network.	
Logical addressing is used at this layer.	
Hardware addresses are defined at this layer.	
This device creates one collision domain and one broadcast domain.	
This device creates many smaller collision domains, but the network is still one large broadcast domain.	
This device can never run full-duplex.	
This device breaks up collision domains and broadcast domains.	

Written Lab 1.3: Identifying Collision and Broadcast Domains

1. In the following exhibit, identify the number of collision domains and broadcast domains in each specified device. Each device is represented by a letter:

    A. Hub

    B. Bridge

    C. Switch

    D. Router

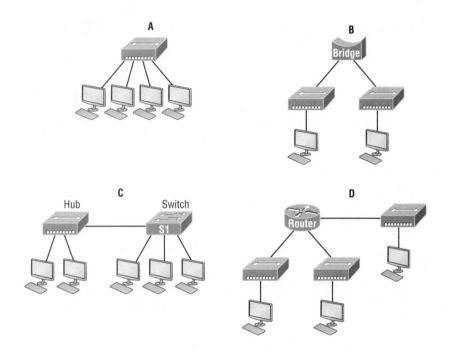

Review Questions

The following questions are designed to test your understanding of this chapter's material. For more information on how to get additional questions, please see www.lammle.com/ccna.

You can find the answers to these questions in Appendix B, "Answers to Review Questions."

1. Which of the following statements is/are true with regard to the device shown here? (Choose all that apply.)

   A. It includes one collision domain and one broadcast domain.

   B. It includes 10 collision domains and 10 broadcast domains.

   C. It includes 10 collision domains and one broadcast domain.

   D. It includes one collision domain and 10 broadcast domains.

2. With respect to the OSI model, which one of the following is the correct statement about PDUs?

   A. A segment contains IP addresses.

   B. A packet contains IP addresses.

   C. A segment contains MAC addresses.

   D. A packet contains MAC addresses.

3. You are the Cisco administrator for your company. A new branch office is opening and you are selecting the necessary hardware to support the network. There will be two groups of computers, each organized by department. The Sales group computers will be assigned IP addresses ranging from 192.168.1.2 to 192.168.1.50. The Accounting group will be assigned IP addresses ranging from 10.0.0.2 to 10.0.0.50. What type of device should you select to connect the two groups of computers so that data communication can occur?

   A. Hub

   B. Switch

   C. Router

   D. Bridge

4. The most effective way to mitigate congestion on a LAN would be to _____.

   A. Upgrade the network cards

   B. Change the cabling to CAT 6

C. Replace the hubs with switches

D. Upgrade the CPUs in the routers

5. In the following work area, draw a line from the OSI model layer to its PDU.

Layer	Description
Transport	Bits
Data Link	Segment
Physical	Packet
Network	Frame

6. What is a function of the WLAN Controller?

A. To monitor and control the incoming and outgoing network traffic

B. To automatically handle the configuration of wireless access points

C. To allow wireless devices to connect to a wired network

D. To connect networks and intelligently choose the best paths between networks

7. You need to provide network connectivity to 150 client computers that will reside in the same subnetwork, and each client computer must be allocated dedicated bandwidth. Which device should you use to accomplish the task?

A. Hub

B. Switch

C. Router

D. Bridge

8. In the following work area, draw a line from the OSI model layer definition on the left to its description on the right.

Layer	Description
Transport	Framing
Physical	End-to-end connection
Data Link	Routing
Network	Conversion to bits

9. What is the function of a firewall?

A. To automatically handle the configuration of wireless access points

B. To allow wireless devices to connect to a wired network

C. To monitor and control the incoming and outgoing network traffic

D. To connect networks and intelligently choose the best paths between networks

10. Which layer in the OSI reference model is responsible for determining the availability of the receiving program and checking to see whether enough resources exist for that communication?

    A. Transport

    B. Network

    C. Presentation

    D. Application

11. Which of the following correctly describe steps in the OSI data encapsulation process? (Choose two.)

    A. The Transport layer divides a data stream into segments and may add reliability and flow control information.

    B. The Data Link layer adds physical source and destination addresses and an FCS to the segment.

    C. Packets are created when the Network layer encapsulates a frame with source and destination host addresses and protocol-related control information.

    D. Packets are created when the Network layer adds layer 3 addresses and control information to a segment.

    E. The Presentation layer translates bits into voltages for transmission across the physical link.

12. Which of the following layers of the OSI model was later subdivided into two layers?

    A. Presentation

    B. Transport

    C. Data Link

    D. Physical

13. What is a function of an access point (AP)?

    A. To monitor and control the incoming and outgoing network traffic

    B. To automatically handle the configuration of wireless access point

    C. To allow wireless devices to connect to a wired network

    D. To connect networks and intelligently choose the best paths between networks

14. A _____ is an example of a device that operates only at the physical layer.

    A. Hub

    B. Switch

    C. Router

    D. Bridge

15. Which of the following is *not* a benefit of using a reference model?

    A. It divides the network communication process into smaller and simpler components.

    B. It encourages industry standardization.

   C. It enforces consistency across vendors.

   D. It allows various types of network hardware and software to communicate.

16. Which of the following statements is not true with regard to routers?

   A. They forward broadcasts by default.

   B. They can filter the network based on Network layer information.

   C. They perform path selection.

   D. They perform packet switching.

17. Switches break up _____ domains, and routers break up _____ domains.

   A. broadcast, broadcast

   B. collision, collision

   C. collision, broadcast

   D. broadcast, collision

18. How many collision domains are present in the following diagram?

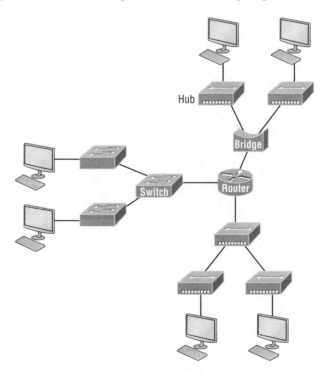

   A. 8

   B. 9

   C. 10

   D. 11

19. Which of the following layers of the OSI model is not involved in defining how the applications within the end stations will communicate with each other as well as with users?

   A. Transport

   B. Application

   C. Presentation

   D. Session

20. Which of the following is the *only* device that operates at all layers of the OSI model?

   A. Network host

   B. Switch

   C. Router

   D. Bridge

Chapter

2

Ethernet Networking and Data Encapsulation

THE FOLLOWING ICND1 EXAM TOPICS ARE COVERED IN THIS CHAPTER:

✓ **Network Fundamentals**

- 1.6 Select the appropriate cabling type based on implementation requirements

- 1.4 Compare and contrast collapsed core and three-tier architectures

✓ **LAN Switching Technologies**

- 2.2 Interpret Ethernet frame format

Before we begin exploring a set of key foundational topics like the TCP/IP DoD model, IP addressing, subnetting, and routing in the upcoming chapters, I really want you to grasp the big picture of LANs conceptually. The role Ethernet plays in today's networks as well as what Media Access Control (MAC) addresses are and how they are used are two more critical networking basics you'll want a solid understanding of as well.

We'll cover these important subjects and more in this chapter, beginning with Ethernet basics and the way MAC addresses are used on an Ethernet LAN, and then we'll focus in on the actual protocols used with Ethernet at the Data Link layer. To round out this discussion, you'll also learn about some very important Ethernet specifications.

You know by now that there are a whole bunch of different devices specified at the various layers of the OSI model and that it's essential to be really familiar with the many types of cables and connectors employed to hook them up to the network correctly. I'll review the types of cabling used with Cisco devices in this chapter, demonstrate how to connect to a router or switch, plus show you how to connect a router or switch via a console connection.

I'll also introduce you to a vital process of encoding data as it makes its way down the OSI stack, known as encapsulation.

I'm not nagging at all here—okay, maybe just a little, but promise that you'll actually work through the four written labs and 20 review questions I added to the end of this chapter just for you. You'll be so happy you did because they're written strategically to make sure all the important material covered in this chapter gets locked in, vault-tight into your memory. So don't skip them!

To find up-to-the-minute updates for this chapter, please see www.lammle.com/ccna or the book's web page via www.sybex.com/go/ccna.

Ethernet Networks in Review

Ethernet is a contention-based media access method that allows all hosts on a network to share the same link's bandwidth. Some reasons it's so popular are that Ethernet is really pretty simple to implement and it makes troubleshooting fairly straightforward as well. Ethernet is also readily scalable, meaning that it eases the process of integrating new technologies into an existing network infrastructure, like upgrading from Fast Ethernet to Gigabit Ethernet.

Ethernet uses both Data Link and Physical layer specifications, so you'll be presented with information relative to both layers, which you'll need to effectively implement, troubleshoot, and maintain an Ethernet network.

Collision Domain

In Chapter 1, "Internetworking," you learned that the Ethernet term *collision domain* refers to a network scenario wherein one device sends a frame out on a physical network segment forcing every other device on the same segment to pay attention to it. This is bad because if two devices on a single physical segment just happen to transmit simultaneously, it will cause a collision and require these devices to retransmit. Think of a collision event as a situation where each device's digital signals totally interfere with one another on the wire. Figure 2.1 shows an old, legacy network that's a single collision domain where only one host can transmit at a time.

FIGURE 2.1   Legacy collision domain design

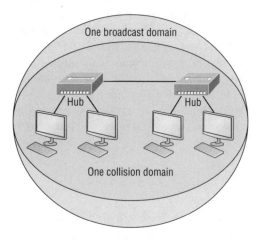

The hosts connected to each hub are in the same collision domain, so if one of them transmits, all the others must take the time to listen for and read the digital signal. It is easy to see how collisions can be a serious drag on network performance, so I'll show you how to strategically avoid them soon!

Okay—take another look at the network pictured in Figure 2.1. True, it has only one collision domain, but worse, it's also a single broadcast domain—what a mess! Let's check out an example, in Figure 2.2, of a typical network design still used today and see if it's any better.

FIGURE 2.2   A typical network you'd see today

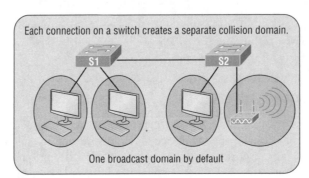

Because each port off a switch is a single collision domain, we gain more bandwidth for users, which is a great start. But switches don't break up broadcast domains by default, so this is still only one broadcast domain, which is not so good. This can work in a really small network, but to expand it at all, we would need to break up the network into smaller broadcast domains or our users won't get enough bandwidth! And you're probably wondering about that device in the lower-right corner, right? Well, that's a *wireless access point*, which is sometimes referred as an AP (which stands for access point). It's a wireless device that allows hosts to connect wirelessly using the IEEE 802.11 specification and I added it to the figure to demonstrate how these devices can be used to extend a collision domain. But still, understand that APs don't actually segment the network, they only extend them, meaning our LAN just got a lot bigger, with an unknown amount of hosts that are all still part of one measly broadcast domain! This clearly demonstrates why it's so important to understand exactly what a broadcast domain is, and now is a great time to talk about them in detail.

Broadcast Domain

Let me start by giving you the formal definition: *broadcast domain* refers to a group of devices on a specific network segment that hear all the broadcasts sent out on that specific network segment.

But even though a broadcast domain is usually a boundary delimited by physical media like switches and routers, the term can also refer to a logical division of a network segment, where all hosts can communicate via a Data Link layer, hardware address broadcast.

Figure 2.3 shows how a router would create a broadcast domain boundary.

Here you can see there are two router interfaces giving us two broadcast domains, and I count 10 switch segments, meaning we've got 10 collision domains.

The design depicted in Figure 2.3 is still in use today, and routers will be around for a long time, but in the latest, modern switched networks, it's important to create small broadcast domains. We achieve this by building virtual LANs (VLANs) within our switched networks, which I'll demonstrate shortly. Without employing VLANs in today's switched environments, there wouldn't be much bandwidth available to individual users. Switches break up collision domains with each port, which is awesome, but they're still only one broadcast domain by default! It's also one more reason why it's extremely important to design our networks very carefully.

FIGURE 2.3   A router creates broadcast domain boundaries.

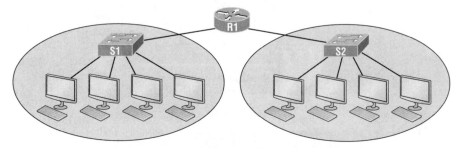

Two broadcast domains. How many collision domains do you see?

And key to carefully planning your network design is never to allow broadcast domains to grow too large and get out of control. Both collision and broadcast domains can easily be controlled with routers and VLANs, so there's just no excuse to allow user bandwidth to slow to a painful crawl when there are plenty of tools in your arsenal to prevent the suffering!

An important reason for this book's existence is to ensure that you really get the foundational basics of Cisco networks nailed down so you can effectively design, implement, configure, troubleshoot, and even dazzle colleagues and superiors with elegant designs that lavish your users with all the bandwidth their hearts could possibly desire.

To make it to the top of that mountain, you need more than just the basic story, so let's move on to explore the collision detection mechanism used in half-duplex Ethernet.

CSMA/CD

Ethernet networking uses a protocol called *Carrier Sense Multiple Access with Collision Detection (CSMA/CD)*, which helps devices share the bandwidth evenly while preventing two devices from transmitting simultaneously on the same network medium. CSMA/CD was actually created to overcome the problem of the collisions that occur when packets are transmitted from different nodes at the same time. And trust me—good collision management is crucial, because when a node transmits in a CSMA/CD network, all the other nodes on the network receive and examine that transmission. Only switches and routers can effectively prevent a transmission from propagating throughout the entire network!

So, how does the CSMA/CD protocol work? Let's start by taking a look at Figure 2.4.

FIGURE 2.4 CSMA/CD

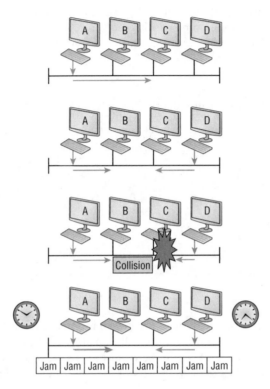

When a host wants to transmit over the network, it first checks for the presence of a digital signal on the wire. If all is clear and no other host is transmitting, the host will then proceed with its transmission.

But it doesn't stop there. The transmitting host constantly monitors the wire to make sure no other hosts begin transmitting. If the host detects another signal on the wire, it sends out an extended jam signal that causes all nodes on the segment to stop sending data—think busy signal.

The nodes respond to that jam signal by waiting a bit before attempting to transmit again. Backoff algorithms determine when the colliding stations can retransmit. If collisions keep occurring after 15 tries, the nodes attempting to transmit will then time out. Half-duplex can be pretty messy!

When a collision occurs on an Ethernet LAN, the following happens:

1. A jam signal informs all devices that a collision occurred.

2. The collision invokes a random backoff algorithm.

3. Each device on the Ethernet segment stops transmitting for a short time until its backoff timer expires.

4. All hosts have equal priority to transmit after the timers have expired.

The ugly effects of having a CSMA/CD network sustain heavy collisions are delay, low throughput, and congestion.

 Backoff on an Ethernet network is the retransmission delay that's enforced when a collision occurs. When that happens, a host will resume transmission only after the forced time delay has expired. Keep in mind that after the backoff has elapsed, all stations have equal priority to transmit data.

At this point, let's take a minute to talk about Ethernet in detail at both the Data Link layer (layer 2) and the Physical layer (layer 1).

Half- and Full-Duplex Ethernet

Half-duplex Ethernet is defined in the original IEEE 802.3 Ethernet specification, which differs a bit from how Cisco describes things. Cisco says Ethernet uses only one wire pair with a digital signal running in both directions on the wire. Even though the IEEE specifications discuss the half-duplex process somewhat differently, it's not actually a full-blown technical disagreement. Cisco is really just talking about a general sense of what's happening with Ethernet.

Half-duplex also uses the CSMA/CD protocol I just discussed to help prevent collisions and to permit retransmitting if one occurs. If a hub is attached to a switch, it must operate in half-duplex mode because the end stations must be able to detect collisions. Figure 2.5 shows a network with four hosts connected to a hub.

FIGURE 2.5 Half-duplex example

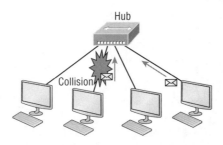

The problem here is that we can only run half-duplex, and if two hosts communicate at the same time there will be a collision. Also, half-duplex Ethernet is only about 30 to 40 percent efficient because a large 100Base-T network will usually only give you 30 to 40 Mbps, at most, due to overhead.

But full-duplex Ethernet uses two pairs of wires at the same time instead of a single wire pair like half-duplex. And full-duplex uses a point-to-point connection between the transmitter of the transmitting device and the receiver of the receiving device. This means that full-duplex data transfers happen a lot faster when compared to half-duplex transfers. Also, because the transmitted data is sent on a different set of wires than the received data, collisions won't happen. Figure 2.6 shows four hosts connected to a switch, plus a hub. Definitely try not to use hubs if you can help it!

FIGURE 2.6   Full-duplex example

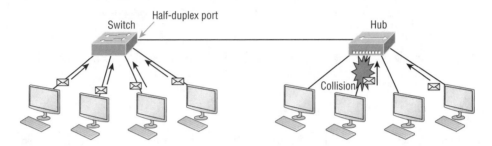

Theoretically all hosts connected to the switch in Figure 2.6 can communicate at the same time because they can run full-duplex. Just keep in mind that the switch port connecting to the hub as well as the hosts connecting to that hub must run at half-duplex.

The reason you don't need to worry about collisions is because now it's like a freeway with multiple lanes instead of the single-lane road provided by half-duplex. Full-duplex Ethernet is supposed to offer 100 percent efficiency in both directions—for example, you can get 20 Mbps with a 10 Mbps Ethernet running full-duplex, or 200 Mbps for Fast Ethernet. But this rate is known as an aggregate rate, which translates as "you're supposed to get" 100 percent efficiency. No guarantees, in networking as in life!

You can use full-duplex Ethernet in at least the following six situations:

- With a connection from a switch to a host
- With a connection from a switch to a switch
- With a connection from a host to a host
- With a connection from a switch to a router
- With a connection from a router to a router
- With a connection from a router to a host

Full-duplex Ethernet requires a point-to-point connection when only two nodes are present. You can run full-duplex with just about any device except a hub.

Now this may be a little confusing because this begs the question that if it's capable of all that speed, why wouldn't it actually deliver? Well, when a full-duplex Ethernet port is powered on, it first connects to the remote end and then negotiates with the other end of the Fast Ethernet link. This is called an *auto-detect mechanism*. This mechanism first decides on the exchange capability, which means it checks to see if it can run at 10, 100, or even 1000 Mbps. It then checks to see if it can run full-duplex, and if it can't, it will run half-duplex.

Remember that half-duplex Ethernet shares a collision domain and provides a lower effective throughput than full-duplex Ethernet, which typically has a private per-port collision domain plus a higher effective throughput.

Last, remember these important points:

- There are no collisions in full-duplex mode.

- A dedicated switch port is required for each full-duplex node.

- The host network card and the switch port must be capable of operating in full-duplex mode.

- The default behavior of 10Base-T and 100Base-T hosts is 10 Mbps half-duplex if the autodetect mechanism fails, so it is always good practice to set the speed and duplex of each port on a switch if you can.

Now let's take a look at how Ethernet works at the Data Link layer.

Ethernet at the Data Link Layer

Ethernet at the Data Link layer is responsible for Ethernet addressing, commonly referred to as MAC or hardware addressing. Ethernet is also responsible for framing packets received from the Network layer and preparing them for transmission on the local network through the Ethernet contention-based media access method.

Ethernet Addressing

Here's where we get into how Ethernet addressing works. It uses the *Media Access Control (MAC)* address burned into each and every Ethernet network interface card (NIC). The MAC, or hardware, address is a 48-bit (6-byte) address written in a hexadecimal format.

Figure 2.7 shows the 48-bit MAC addresses and how the bits are divided.

FIGURE 2.7   Ethernet addressing using MAC addresses

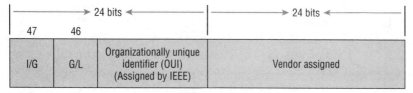

Example: 0000.0c12.3456

The *organizationally unique identifier (OUI)* is assigned by the IEEE to an organization. It's composed of 24 bits, or 3 bytes, and it in turn assigns a globally administered address also made up of 24 bits, or 3 bytes, that's supposedly unique to each and every adapter an organization manufactures. Surprisingly, there's no guarantee when it comes to that unique claim! Okay, now look closely at the figure. The high-order bit is the Individual/Group (I/G) bit. When it has a value of 0, we can assume that the address is the MAC address of a device and that it may well appear in the source portion of the MAC header. When it's a 1, we can assume that the address represents either a broadcast or multicast address in Ethernet.

The next bit is the Global/Local bit, sometimes called the G/L bit or U/L bit, where U means *universal*. When set to 0, this bit represents a globally administered address, as assigned by the IEEE, but when it's a 1, it represents a locally governed and administered address. The low-order 24 bits of an Ethernet address represent a locally administered or manufacturer-assigned code. This portion commonly starts with 24 0s for the first card made and continues in order until there are 24 1s for the last (16,777,216th) card made. You'll find that many manufacturers use these same six hex digits as the last six characters of their serial number on the same card.

Let's stop for a minute and go over some addressing schemes important in the Ethernet world.

Binary to Decimal and Hexadecimal Conversion

Before we get into working with the TCP/IP protocol and IP addressing, which we'll do in Chapter 3, "Introduction to TCP/IP," it's really important for you to truly grasp the differences between binary, decimal, and hexadecimal numbers and how to convert one format into the other.

We'll start with binary numbering, which is really pretty simple. The digits used are limited to either a 1 or a 0, and each digit is called a *bit*, which is short for *binary digit*. Typically, you group either 4 or 8 bits together, with these being referred to as a nibble and a byte, respectively.

The interesting thing about binary numbering is how the value is represented in a decimal format—the typical decimal format being the base-10 number scheme that we've all used since kindergarten. The binary numbers are placed in a value spot, starting at the right and moving left, with each spot having double the value of the previous spot.

Table 2.1 shows the decimal values of each bit location in a nibble and a byte. Remember, a nibble is 4 bits and a byte is 8 bits.

TABLE 2.1   Binary values

Nibble Values	Byte Values
8 4 2 1	128 64 32 16 8 4 2 1

What all this means is that if a one digit (1) is placed in a value spot, then the nibble or byte takes on that decimal value and adds it to any other value spots that have a 1. If a zero (0) is placed in a bit spot, you don't count that value.

Let me clarify this a little. If we have a 1 placed in each spot of our nibble, we would then add up 8 + 4 + 2 + 1 to give us a maximum value of 15. Another example for our nibble values would be 1001, meaning that the 8 bit and the 1 bit are turned on, which equals a decimal value of 9. If we have a nibble binary value of 0110, then our decimal value would be 6, because the 4 and 2 bits are turned on.

But the *byte* decimal values can add up to a number that's significantly higher than 15. This is how: If we counted every bit as a one (1), then the byte binary value would look like the following example because, remember, 8 bits equal a byte:

11111111

We would then count up every bit spot because each is turned on. It would look like this, which demonstrates the maximum value of a byte:

128 + 64 + 32 + 16 + 8 + 4 + 2 + 1 = 255

There are plenty of other decimal values that a binary number can equal. Let's work through a few examples:

10010110

Which bits are on? The 128, 16, 4, and 2 bits are on, so we'll just add them up: 128 + 16 + 4 + 2 = 150.

01101100

Which bits are on? The 64, 32, 8, and 4 bits are on, so we just need to add them up: 64 + 32 + 8 + 4 = 108.

11101000

Which bits are on? The 128, 64, 32, and 8 bits are on, so just add the values up: 128 + 64 + 32 + 8 = 232.

I highly recommend that you memorize Table 2.2 before braving the IP sections in Chapter 3, "Introduction to TCP/IP," and Chapter 4, "Easy Subnetting"!

TABLE 2.2   Binary to decimal memorization chart

Binary Value	Decimal Value
10000000	128
11000000	192
11100000	224
11110000	240

TABLE 2.2   Binary to decimal memorization chart *(continued)*

Binary Value	Decimal Value
11111000	248
11111100	252
11111110	254
11111111	255

Hexadecimal addressing is completely different than binary or decimal—it's converted by reading nibbles, not bytes. By using a nibble, we can convert these bits to hex pretty simply. First, understand that the hexadecimal addressing scheme uses only the characters 0 through 9. Because the numbers 10, 11, 12, and so on can't be used (because they are two-digit numbers), the letters *A*, *B*, *C*, *D*, *E*, and *F* are used instead to represent 10, 11, 12, 13, 14, and 15, respectively.

> *Hex* is short for *hexadecimal*, which is a numbering system that uses the first six letters of the alphabet, *A* through *F*, to extend beyond the available 10 characters in the decimal system. These values are not case sensitive.

Table 2.3 shows both the binary value and the decimal value for each hexadecimal digit.

TABLE 2.3   Hex to binary to decimal chart

Hexadecimal Value	Binary Value	Decimal Value
0	0000	0
1	0001	1
2	0010	2
3	0011	3
4	0100	4
5	0101	5
6	0110	6
7	0111	7

Hexadecimal Value	Binary Value	Decimal Value
8	1000	8
9	1001	9
A	1010	10
B	1011	11
C	1100	12
D	1101	13
E	1110	14
F	1111	15

Did you notice that the first 10 hexadecimal digits (0–9) are the same value as the decimal values? If not, look again because this handy fact makes those values super easy to convert!

Now suppose you have something like this: 0x6A. This is important because sometimes Cisco likes to put *0x* in front of characters so you know that they are a hex value. It doesn't have any other special meaning. So what are the binary and decimal values? All you have to remember is that each hex character is one nibble and that two hex characters joined together make a byte. To figure out the binary value, put the hex characters into two nibbles and then join them together into a byte. Six equals 0110, and A, which is 10 in hex, equals 1010, so the complete byte would be 01101010.

To convert from binary to hex, just take the byte and break it into nibbles. Let me clarify this.

Say you have the binary number 01010101. First, break it into nibbles—0101 and 0101—with the value of each nibble being 5 since the 1 and 4 bits are on. This makes the hex answer 0x55. And in decimal format, the binary number is 01010101, which converts to 64 + 16 + 4 + 1 = 85.

Here's another binary number:

11001100

Your answer would be 1100 = 12 and 1100 = 12, so therefore, it's converted to CC in hex. The decimal conversion answer would be 128 + 64 + 8 + 4 = 204.

One more example, then we need to get working on the Physical layer. Suppose you had the following binary number:

10110101

The hex answer would be 0xB5, since 1011 converts to B and 0101 converts to 5 in hex value. The decimal equivalent is 128 + 32 + 16 + 4 + 1 = 181.

Make sure you check out Written Lab 2.1 for more practice with binary/decimal/hex conversion!

Ethernet Frames

The Data Link layer is responsible for combining bits into bytes and bytes into frames. Frames are used at the Data Link layer to encapsulate packets handed down from the Network layer for transmission on a type of media access.

The function of Ethernet stations is to pass data frames between each other using a group of bits known as a MAC frame format. This provides error detection from a *cyclic redundancy check (CRC)*. But remember—this is error detection, not error correction. An example of a typical Ethernet frame used today is shown in Figure 2.8.

FIGURE 2.8   Typical Ethernet frame format

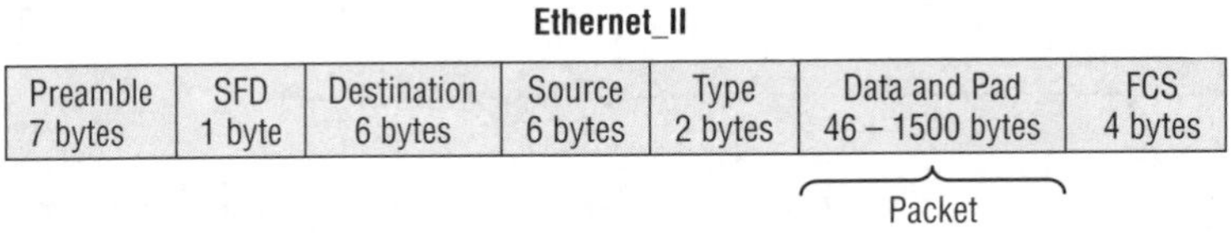

Ethernet_II

Preamble 7 bytes	SFD 1 byte	Destination 6 bytes	Source 6 bytes	Type 2 bytes	Data and Pad 46 – 1500 bytes	FCS 4 bytes

Packet

Encapsulating a frame within a different type of frame is called *tunneling*.

Following are the details of the various fields in the typical Ethernet frame type:

Preamble   An alternating 1,0 pattern provides a 5 MHz clock at the start of each packet, which allows the receiving devices to lock the incoming bit stream.

Start Frame Delimiter (SFD)/Synch   The preamble is seven octets and the SFD is one octet (synch). The SFD is 10101011, where the last pair of 1s allows the receiver to come into the alternating 1,0 pattern somewhere in the middle and still sync up to detect the beginning of the data.

Destination Address (DA)   This transmits a 48-bit value using the least significant bit (LSB) first. The DA is used by receiving stations to determine whether an incoming packet is addressed to a particular node. The destination address can be an individual address or a broadcast or multicast MAC address. Remember that a broadcast is all 1s—all *F*s in hex—and is sent to all devices. A multicast is sent only to a similar subset of nodes on a network.

Source Address (SA)   The SA is a 48-bit MAC address used to identify the transmitting device, and it uses the least significant bit first. Broadcast and multicast address formats are illegal within the SA field.

Length or Type   802.3 uses a Length field, but the Ethernet_II frame uses a Type field to identify the Network layer protocol. The old, original 802.3 cannot identify the upper-layer protocol and must be used with a proprietary LAN—IPX, for example.

Data   This is a packet sent down to the Data Link layer from the Network layer. The size can vary from 46 to 1,500 bytes.

Frame Check Sequence (FCS)   FCS is a field at the end of the frame that's used to store the cyclic redundancy check (CRC) answer. The CRC is a mathematical algorithm that's run when each frame is built based on the data in the frame. When a receiving host receives the frame and runs the CRC, the answer should be the same. If not, the frame is discarded, assuming errors have occurred.

Let's pause here for a minute and take a look at some frames caught on my trusty network analyzer. You can see that the frame below has only three fields: Destination, Source, and Type, which is shown as Protocol Type on this particular analyzer:

```
Destination:    00:60:f5:00:1f:27
Source:         00:60:f5:00:1f:2c
Protocol Type: 08-00 IP
```

This is an Ethernet_II frame. Notice that the Type field is IP, or 08-00, mostly just referred to as 0x800 in hexadecimal.

The next frame has the same fields, so it must be an Ethernet_II frame as well:

```
Destination:    ff:ff:ff:ff:ff:ff Ethernet Broadcast
Source:         02:07:01:22:de:a4
Protocol Type: 08-00 IP
```

Did you notice that this frame was a broadcast? You can tell because the destination hardware address is all 1s in binary, or all *F*s in hexadecimal.

Let's take a look at one more Ethernet_II frame. I'll talk about this next example again when we use IPv6 in Chapter 14, "Internet Protocol Version 6 (IPv6)," but you can see that the Ethernet frame is the same Ethernet_II frame used with the IPv4 routed protocol. The Type field has 0x86dd when the frame is carrying IPv6 data, and when we have IPv4 data, the frame uses 0x0800 in the protocol field:

```
Destination: IPv6-Neighbor-Discovery_00:01:00:03 (33:33:00:01:00:03)
Source: Aopen_3e:7f:dd (00:01:80:3e:7f:dd)
Type: IPv6 (0x86dd)
```

This is the beauty of the Ethernet_II frame. Because of the Type field, we can run any Network layer routed protocol and the frame will carry the data because it can identify the Network layer protocol!

Ethernet at the Physical Layer

Ethernet was first implemented by a group called DIX, which stands for Digital, Intel, and Xerox. They created and implemented the first Ethernet LAN specification, which the IEEE used to create the IEEE 802.3 committee. This was a 10 Mbps network that ran on coax and then eventually twisted-pair and fiber physical media.

The IEEE extended the 802.3 committee to three new committees known as 802.3u (Fast Ethernet), 802.3ab (Gigabit Ethernet on category 5), and then finally one more, 802.3ae (10 Gbps over fiber and coax). There are more standards evolving almost daily, such as the new 100 Gbps Ethernet (802.3ba)!

When designing your LAN, it's really important to understand the different types of Ethernet media available to you. Sure, it would be great to run Gigabit Ethernet to each desktop and 10 Gbps between switches, but you would need to figure out how to justify the cost of that network today! However, if you mix and match the different types of Ethernet media methods currently available, you can come up with a cost-effective network solution that works really great.

The *EIA/TIA* (Electronic Industries Alliance and the newer Telecommunications Industry Association) is the standards body that creates the Physical layer specifications for Ethernet. The EIA/TIA specifies that Ethernet use a *registered jack (RJ) connector* on *unshielded twisted-pair (UTP)* cabling (RJ45). But the industry is moving toward simply calling this an 8-pin modular connector.

Every Ethernet cable type that's specified by the EIA/TIA has inherent attenuation, which is defined as the loss of signal strength as it travels the length of a cable and is measured in decibels (dB). The cabling used in corporate and home markets is measured in categories. A higher-quality cable will have a higher-rated category and lower attenuation. For example, category 5 is better than category 3 because category 5 cables have more wire twists per foot and therefore less crosstalk. Crosstalk is the unwanted signal interference from adjacent pairs in the cable.

Here is a list of some of the most common IEEE Ethernet standards, starting with 10 Mbps Ethernet:

10Base-T (IEEE 802.3)   10 Mbps using category 3 unshielded twisted pair (UTP) wiring for runs up to 100 meters. Unlike with the 10Base-2 and 10Base-5 networks, each device must connect into a hub or switch, and you can have only one host per segment or wire. It uses an RJ45 connector (8-pin modular connector) with a physical star topology and a logical bus.

100Base-TX (IEEE 802.3u)   100Base-TX, most commonly known as Fast Ethernet, uses EIA/TIA category 5, 5E, or 6 UTP two-pair wiring. One user per segment; up to 100 meters long. It uses an RJ45 connector with a physical star topology and a logical bus.

100Base-FX (IEEE 802.3u)   Uses fiber cabling 62.5/125-micron multimode fiber. Point-to-point topology; up to 412 meters long. It uses ST and SC connectors, which are media-interface connectors.

1000Base-CX (IEEE 802.3z)   Copper twisted-pair, called twinax, is a balanced coaxial pair that can run only up to 25 meters and uses a special 9-pin connector known as the High Speed Serial Data Connector (HSSDC). This is used in Cisco's new Data Center technologies.

1000Base-T (IEEE 802.3ab)   Category 5, four-pair UTP wiring up to 100 meters long and up to 1 Gbps.

1000Base-SX (IEEE 802.3z)   The implementation of 1 Gigabit Ethernet running over multimode fiber-optic cable instead of copper twisted-pair cable, using short wavelength laser. Multimode fiber (MMF) using 62.5- and 50-micron core; uses an 850 nanometer (nm) laser and can go up to 220 meters with 62.5-micron, 550 meters with 50-micron.

1000Base-LX (IEEE 802.3z)   Single-mode fiber that uses a 9-micron core and 1300 nm laser and can go from 3 kilometers up to 10 kilometers.

1000Base-ZX (Cisco standard)   1000BaseZX, or 1000Base-ZX, is a Cisco specified standard for Gigabit Ethernet communication. 1000BaseZX operates on ordinary single-mode fiber-optic links with spans up to 43.5 miles (70 km).

10GBase-T (802.3.an)   10GBase-T is a standard proposed by the IEEE 802.3an committee to provide 10 Gbps connections over conventional UTP cables, (category 5e, 6, or 7 cables). 10GBase-T allows the conventional RJ45 used for Ethernet LANs and can support signal transmission at the full 100-meter distance specified for LAN wiring.

If you want to implement a network medium that is not susceptible to electromagnetic interference (EMI), fiber-optic cable provides a more secure, long-distance cable that is not susceptible to EMI at high speeds.

Armed with the basics covered so far in this chapter, you're equipped to go to the next level and put Ethernet to work using various Ethernet cabling.

 Real World Scenario

Interference or Host Distance Issue?

Quite a few years ago, I was consulting at a very large aerospace company in the Los Angeles area. In the very busy warehouse, they had hundreds of hosts providing many different services to the various departments working in that area.

However, a small group of hosts had been experiencing intermittent outages that no one could explain since most hosts in the same area had no problems whatsoever. So I decided to take a crack at this problem and see what I could find.

First, I traced the backbone connection from the main switch to multiple switches in the warehouse area. Assuming that the hosts with the issues were connected to the same switch, I traced each cable, and much to my surprise they were connected to various switches! Now my interest really peaked because the simplest issue had been eliminated right off the bat. It wasn't a simple switch problem!

I continued to trace each cable one by one, and this is what I found:

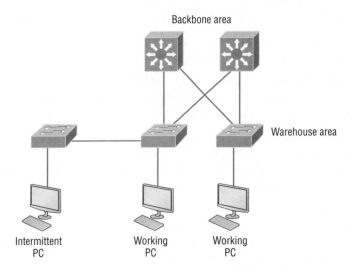

As I drew this network out, I noticed that they had many repeaters in place, which isn't a cause for immediate suspicion since bandwidth was not their biggest requirement here. So I looked deeper still. At this point, I decided to measure the distance of one of the intermittent hosts connecting to their hub/repeater.

This is what I measured. Can you see the problem?

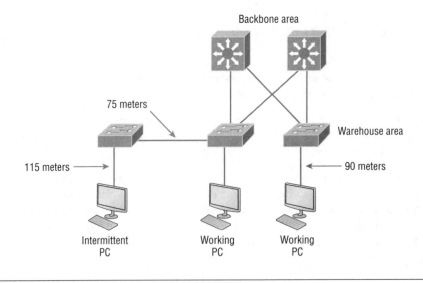

Having a hub or repeater in your network isn't a problem, unless you need better bandwidth (which they didn't in this case), but the distance was! It's not always easy to tell how far away a host is from its connection in an extremely large area, so these hosts ended up having a connection past the 100-meter Ethernet specification, which created a problem for the hosts not cabled correctly. Understand that this didn't stop the hosts from completely working, but the workers felt the hosts stopped working when they were at their most stressful point of the day. Sure, that makes sense, because whenever my host stops working, that becomes my most stressful part of the day!

Ethernet Cabling

A discussion about Ethernet cabling is an important one, especially if you are planning on taking the Cisco exams. You need to really understand the following three types of cables:

- Straight-through cable
- Crossover cable
- Rolled cable

We will look at each in the following sections, but first, let's take a look at the most common Ethernet cable used today, the category 5 Enhanced Unshielded Twisted Pair (UTP), shown in Figure 2.9.

FIGURE 2.9   Category 5 Enhanced UTP cable

The category 5 Enhanced UTP cable can handle speeds up to a gigabit with a distance of up to 100 meters. Typically we'd use this cable for 100 Mbps and category 6 for a gigabit, but the category 5 Enhanced is rated for gigabit speeds and category 6 is rated for 10 Gbps!

Straight-Through Cable

The *straight-through cable* is used to connect the following devices:

- Host to switch or hub
- Router to switch or hub

Four wires are used in straight-through cable to connect Ethernet devices. It's relatively simple to create this type, and Figure 2.10 shows the four wires used in a straight-through Ethernet cable.

FIGURE 2.10 Straight-through Ethernet cable

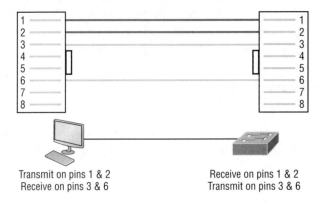

Transmit on pins 1 & 2
Receive on pins 3 & 6

Receive on pins 1 & 2
Transmit on pins 3 & 6

Notice that only pins 1, 2, 3, and 6 are used. Just connect 1 to 1, 2 to 2, 3 to 3, and 6 to 6 and you'll be up and networking in no time. However, remember that this would be a 10/100 Mbps Ethernet-only cable and wouldn't work with gigabit, voice, or other LAN or WAN technology.

Crossover Cable

The *crossover cable* can be used to connect the following devices:

▪ Switch to switch

▪ Hub to hub

▪ Host to host

▪ Hub to switch

▪ Router direct to host

▪ Router to router

The same four wires used in the straight-through cable are used in this cable—we just connect different pins together. Figure 2.11 shows how the four wires are used in a crossover Ethernet cable.

FIGURE 2.11   Crossover Ethernet cable

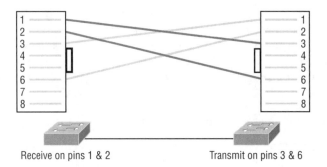

Receive on pins 1 & 2   Transmit on pins 3 & 6

Notice that instead of connecting 1 to 1, 2 to 2, and so on, here we connect pins 1 to 3 and 2 to 6 on each side of the cable. Figure 2.12 shows some typical uses of straight-through and crossover cables.

FIGURE 2.12   Typical uses for straight-through and cross-over Ethernet cables

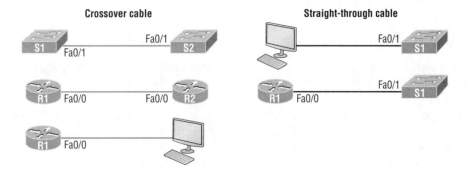

The crossover examples in Figure 2.12 are switch port to switch port, router Ethernet port to router Ethernet port, and router Ethernet port to PC Ethernet port. For the straight-through examples I used PC Ethernet to switch port and router Ethernet port to switch port.

It's very possible to connect a straight-through cable between two switches, and it will start working because of autodetect mechanisms called auto-mdix. But be advised that the CCNA objectives do not typically consider autodetect mechanisms valid between devices!

UTP Gigabit Wiring (1000Base-T)

In the previous examples of 10Base-T and 100Base-T UTP wiring, only two wire pairs were used, but that is not good enough for Gigabit UTP transmission.

1000Base-T UTP wiring (Figure 2.13) requires four wire pairs and uses more advanced electronics so that each and every pair in the cable can transmit simultaneously. Even so, gigabit wiring is almost identical to my earlier 10/100 example, except that we'll use the other two pairs in the cable.

FIGURE 2.13   UTP Gigabit crossover Ethernet cable

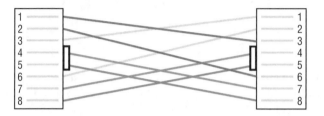

For a straight-through cable it's still 1 to 1, 2 to 2, and so on up to pin 8. And in creating the gigabit crossover cable, you'd still cross 1 to 3 and 2 to 6, but you would add 4 to 7 and 5 to 8—pretty straightforward!

Rolled Cable

Although *rolled cable* isn't used to connect any Ethernet connections together, you can use a rolled Ethernet cable to connect a host EIA-TIA 232 interface to a router console serial communication (COM) port.

If you have a Cisco router or switch, you would use this cable to connect your PC, Mac, or a device like an iPad to the Cisco hardware. Eight wires are used in this cable to connect serial devices, although not all eight are used to send information, just as in Ethernet networking. Figure 2.14 shows the eight wires used in a rolled cable.

FIGURE 2.14   Rolled Ethernet cable

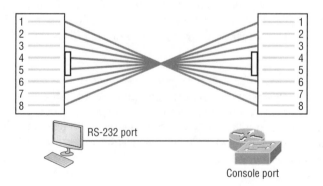

These are probably the easiest cables to make because you just cut the end off on one side of a straight-through cable, turn it over, and put it back on—with a new connector, of course!

Okay, once you have the correct cable connected from your PC to the Cisco router or switch console port, you can start your emulation program such as PuTTY or SecureCRT to create a console connection and configure the device. Set the configuration as shown in Figure 2.15.

FIGURE 2.15   Configuring your console emulation program

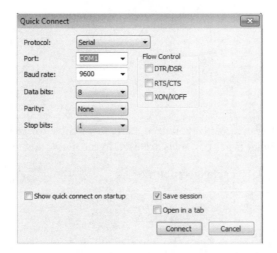

Notice that Baud Rate is set to 9600, Data Bits to 8, Parity to None, and no Flow Control options are set. At this point, you can click Connect and press the Enter key and you should be connected to your Cisco device console port.

Figure 2.16 shows a nice new 2960 switch with two console ports.

FIGURE 2.16   A Cisco 2960 console connections

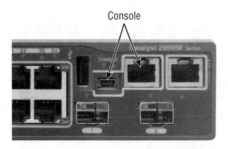

Console

Notice there are two console connections on this new switch—a typical original RJ45 connection and the newer mini type-B USB console. Remember that the new USB port supersedes the RJ45 port if you just happen to plug into both at the same time, and the USB port can have speeds up to 115,200 Kbps, which is awesome if you have to use Xmodem to update an IOS. I've even seen some cables that work on iPhones and iPads and allow them to connect to these mini USB ports!

Now that you've seen the various RJ45 unshielded twisted-pair (UTP) cables, what type of cable is used between the switches in Figure 2.17?

FIGURE 2.17   RJ45 UTP cable question #1

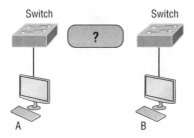

In order for host A to ping host B, you need a crossover cable to connect the two switches together. But what types of cables are used in the network shown in Figure 2.18?

FIGURE 2.18   RJ45 UTP cable question #2

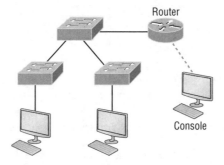

In Figure 2.18, there's a whole menu of cables in use. For the connection between the switches, we'd obviously use a crossover cable like we saw in Figure 2.13. The trouble is that you must understand that we have a console connection that uses a rolled cable. Plus, the connection from the router to the switch is a straight-through cable, as is true for the hosts to the switches. Keep in mind that if we had a serial connection, which we don't, we would use a V.35 to connect us to a WAN.

Fiber Optic

Fiber-optic cabling has been around for a long time and has some solid standards. The cable allows for very fast transmission of data, is made of glass (or even plastic!), is very thin, and works as a waveguide to transmit light between two ends of the fiber. Fiber optics has been used to go very long distances, as in intercontinental connections, but it is becoming more and more popular in Ethernet LAN networks due to the fast speeds avail-able and because, unlike UTP, it's immune to interference like cross-talk.

Some main components of this cable are the core and the cladding. The core will hold the light and the cladding confines the light in the core. The tighter the cladding, the smaller the core, and when the core is small, less light will be sent, but it can go faster and farther!

In Figure 2.19 you can see that there is a 9-micron core, which is very small and can be measured against a human hair, which is 50 microns.

FIGURE 2.19   Typical fiber cable

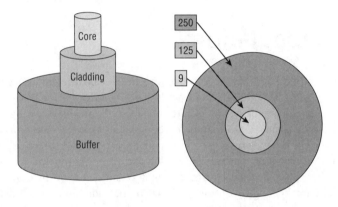

Dimensions are in um (10^{-6} meters). Not to scale.

The cladding is 125 microns, which is actually a fiber standard that allows manufacturers to make connectors for all fiber cables. The last piece of this cable is the buffer, which is there to protect the delicate glass.

There are two major types of fiber optics: single-mode and multimode. Figure 2.20 shows the differences between multimode and single-mode fibers.

FIGURE 2.20   Multimode and single-mode fibers

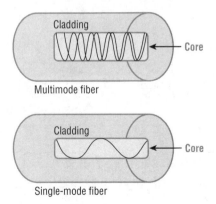

Single-mode is more expensive, has a tighter cladding, and can go much farther distances than multimode. The difference comes in the tightness of the cladding, which makes a smaller core, meaning that only one mode of light will propagate down the fiber. Multimode is looser and has a larger core so it allows multiple light particles to travel down the glass. These particles have to be put back together at the receiving end, so distance is less than that with single-mode fiber, which allows only very few light particles to travel down the fiber.

There are about 70 different connectors for fiber, and Cisco uses a few different types. Looking back at Figure 2.16, the two bottom ports are referred to as Small Form-Factor Pluggables, or SFPs.

Data Encapsulation

When a host transmits data across a network to another device, the data goes through a process called *encapsulation* and is wrapped with protocol information at each layer of the OSI model. Each layer communicates only with its peer layer on the receiving device.

To communicate and exchange information, each layer uses *protocol data units (PDUs)*. These hold the control information attached to the data at each layer of the model. They are usually attached to the header in front of the data field but can also be at the trailer, or end, of it.

Each PDU attaches to the data by encapsulating it at each layer of the OSI model, and each has a specific name depending on the information provided in each header. This PDU information is read only by the peer layer on the receiving device. After its read, it's stripped off and the data is then handed to the next layer up.

Figure 2.21 shows the PDUs and how they attach control information to each layer. This figure demonstrates how the upper-layer user data is converted for transmission on the network. The data stream is then handed down to the Transport layer, which sets up a virtual circuit to the receiving device by sending over a synch packet. Next, the data stream is broken up into smaller pieces, and a Transport layer header is created and attached to the header of the data field; now the piece of data is called a *segment* (a PDU). Each segment can be sequenced so the data stream can be put back together on the receiving side exactly as it was transmitted.

FIGURE 2.21 Data encapsulation

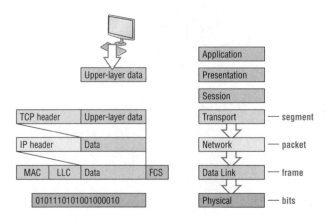

Each segment is then handed to the Network layer for network addressing and routing through the internetwork. Logical addressing (for example, IP and IPv6) is used to get each segment to the correct network. The Network layer protocol adds a control header to the segment handed down from the Transport layer, and what we have now is called a *packet* or *datagram*. Remember that the Transport and Network layers work together to rebuild a data stream on a receiving host, but it's not part of their work to place their PDUs on a local network segment—which is the only way to get the information to a router or host.

It's the Data Link layer that's responsible for taking packets from the Network layer and placing them on the network medium (cable or wireless). The Data Link layer encapsulates each packet in a *frame*, and the frame's header carries the hardware addresses of the source and destination hosts. If the destination device is on a remote network, then the frame is sent to a router to be routed through an internetwork. Once it gets to the destination network, a new frame is used to get the packet to the destination host.

To put this frame on the network, it must first be put into a digital signal. Since a frame is really a logical group of 1s and 0s, the physical layer is responsible for encoding these digits into a digital signal, which is read by devices on the same local network. The receiving devices will synchronize on the digital signal and extract (decode) the 1s and 0s from the digital signal. At this point, the devices reconstruct the frames, run a CRC, and then check their answer against the answer in the frame's FCS field. If it matches, the packet is pulled from the frame and what's left of the frame is discarded. This process is called *de-encapsulation*. The packet is handed to the Network layer, where the address is checked. If the address matches, the segment is pulled from the packet and what's left of the packet is discarded. The segment is processed at the Transport layer, which rebuilds the data stream and acknowledges to the transmitting station that it received each piece. It then happily hands the data stream to the upper-layer application.

At a transmitting device, the data encapsulation method works like this:

1. User information is converted to data for transmission on the network.

2. Data is converted to segments, and a reliable connection is set up between the transmitting and receiving hosts.

3. Segments are converted to packets or datagrams, and a logical address is placed in the header so each packet can be routed through an internetwork.

4. Packets or datagrams are converted to frames for transmission on the local network. Hardware (Ethernet) addresses are used to uniquely identify hosts on a local network segment.

5. Frames are converted to bits, and a digital encoding and clocking scheme is used.

To explain this in more detail using the layer addressing, I'll use Figure 2.22.

Remember that a data stream is handed down from the upper layer to the Transport layer. As technicians, we really don't care who the data stream comes from because that's really a programmer's problem. Our job is to rebuild the data stream reliably and hand it to the upper layers on the receiving device.

FIGURE 2.22   PDU and layer addressing

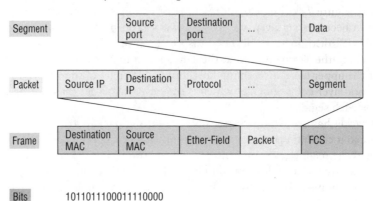

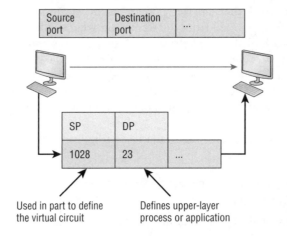

Before we go further in our discussion of Figure 2.22, let's discuss port numbers and make sure you understand them. The Transport layer uses port numbers to define both the virtual circuit and the upper-layer processes, as you can see from Figure 2.23.

FIGURE 2.23   Port numbers at the Transport layer

When using a connection-oriented protocol like TCP, the Transport layer takes the data stream, makes segments out of it, and establishes a reliable session by creating a virtual circuit. It then sequences (numbers) each segment and uses acknowledgments and flow control. If you're using TCP, the virtual circuit is defined by the source and destination port number plus the source and destination IP address and called a socket. Understand that the host just makes this up, starting at port number 1024 because 0 through 1023 are reserved for well-known port numbers. The destination port number defines the upper-layer process or application that the data stream is handed to when the data stream is reliably rebuilt on the receiving host.

Now that you understand port numbers and how they are used at the Transport layer, let's go back to Figure 2.22. Once the Transport layer header information is added to the piece of data, it becomes a segment that's handed down to the Network layer along with the destination IP address. As you know, the destination IP address was handed down from the upper layers to the Transport layer with the data stream and was identified via name resolution at the upper layers—probably with DNS.

The Network layer adds a header and adds the logical addressing such as IP addresses to the front of each segment. Once the header is added to the segment, the PDU is called a packet. The packet has a protocol field that describes where the segment came from (either UDP or TCP) so it can hand the segment to the correct protocol at the Transport layer when it reaches the receiving host.

The Network layer is responsible for finding the destination hardware address that dictates where the packet should be sent on the local network. It does this by using the Address Resolution Protocol (ARP)—something I'll talk about more in Chapter 3. IP at the Network layer looks at the destination IP address and compares that address to its own source IP address and subnet mask. If it turns out to be a local network request, the hardware address of the local host is requested via an ARP request. If the packet is destined for a host on a remote network, IP will look for the IP address of the default gateway (router) instead.

The packet, along with the destination hardware address of either the local host or default gateway, is then handed down to the Data Link layer. The Data Link layer will add a header to the front of the packet and the piece of data then becomes a frame. It's called a frame because both a header and a trailer are added to the packet, which makes it look like it's within bookends—a frame—as shown in Figure 2.22. The frame uses an Ether-Type field to describe which protocol the packet came from at the Network layer. Now a cyclic redundancy check is run on the frame, and the answer to the CRC is placed in the Frame Check Sequence field found in the trailer of the frame.

The frame is now ready to be handed down, one bit at a time, to the Physical layer, which will use bit-timing rules to encode the data in a digital signal. Every device on the network segment will receive the digital signal and synchronize with the clock and extract the 1s and 0s from the digital signal to build a frame. After the frame is rebuilt, a CRC is run to make sure the frame is in proper order. If everything turns out to be all good, the hosts will check the destination MAC and IP addresses to see if the frame is for them.

If all this is making your eyes cross and your brain freeze, don't freak. I'll be going over exactly how data is encapsulated and routed through an internetwork later, in Chapter 9, "IP Routing."

The Cisco Three-Layer Hierarchical Model

Most of us were exposed to hierarchy early in life. Anyone with older siblings learned what it was like to be at the bottom of the hierarchy. Regardless of where you first discovered the concept of hierarchy, most of us experience it in many aspects of our lives. It's *hierarchy* that helps us understand where things belong, how things fit together, and what functions go where. It brings order to otherwise complex models. If you want a pay raise, for instance, hierarchy dictates that you ask your boss, not your subordinate, because that's the person whose role it is to grant or deny your request. So basically, understanding hierarchy helps us discern where we should go to get what we need.

Hierarchy has many of the same benefits in network design that it does in other areas of life. When used properly, it makes networks more predictable and helps us define which areas should perform certain functions. Likewise, you can use tools such as access lists at certain levels in hierarchical networks and avoid them at others.

Let's face it: Large networks can be extremely complicated, with multiple protocols, detailed configurations, and diverse technologies. Hierarchy helps us summarize a complex collection of details into an understandable model, bringing order from the chaos. Then, as specific configurations are needed, the model dictates the appropriate manner in which to apply them.

The Cisco hierarchical model can help you design, implement, and maintain a scalable, reliable, cost-effective hierarchical internetwork. Cisco defines three layers of hierarchy, as shown in Figure 2.24, each with specific functions.

FIGURE 2.24   The Cisco hierarchical model

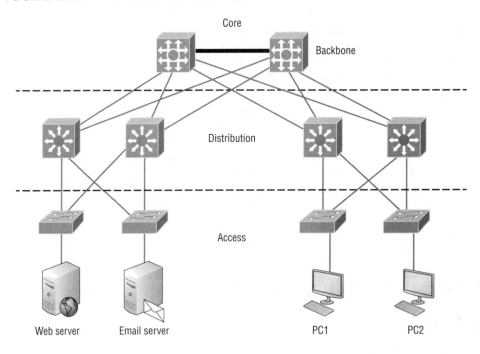

Each layer has specific responsibilities. Keep in mind that the three layers are logical and are not necessarily physical devices. Consider the OSI model, another logical hierarchy. Its seven layers describe functions but not necessarily protocols, right? Sometimes a protocol maps to more than one layer of the OSI model, and sometimes multiple protocols communicate within a single layer. In the same way, when we build physical implementations of hierarchical networks, we may have many devices in a single layer, or there may be a single device performing functions at two layers. Just remember that the definition of the layers is logical, not physical!

So let's take a closer look at each of the layers now.

The Core Layer

The *core layer* is literally the core of the network. At the top of the hierarchy, the core layer is responsible for transporting large amounts of traffic both reliably and quickly. The only purpose of the network's core layer is to switch traffic as fast as possible. The traffic transported across the core is common to a majority of users. But remember that user data is processed at the distribution layer, which forwards the requests to the core if needed.

If there's a failure in the core, *every single user* can be affected! This is why fault tolerance at this layer is so important. The core is likely to see large volumes of traffic, so speed and latency are driving concerns here. Given the function of the core, we can now consider some design specifics. Let's start with some things we don't want to do:

- Never do anything to slow down traffic. This includes making sure you don't use access lists, perform routing between virtual local area networks, or implement packet filtering.
- Don't support workgroup access here.
- Avoid expanding the core (e.g., adding routers when the internetwork grows). If performance becomes an issue in the core, give preference to upgrades over expansion.

Here's a list of things that we want to achieve as we design the core:

- Design the core for high reliability. Consider data-link technologies that facilitate both speed and redundancy, like Gigabit Ethernet with redundant links or even 10 Gigabit Ethernet.
- Design with speed in mind. The core should have very little latency.
- Select routing protocols with lower convergence times. Fast and redundant data-link connectivity is no help if your routing tables are shot!

The Distribution Layer

The *distribution layer* is sometimes referred to as the *workgroup layer* and is the communication point between the access layer and the core. The primary functions of the distribution layer are to provide routing, filtering, and WAN access and to determine how packets can access the core, if needed. The distribution layer must determine the fastest way that network service requests are handled—for example, how a file request is forwarded to a server. After the distribution layer determines the best path, it forwards the request to the core layer if necessary. The core layer then quickly transports the request to the correct service.

The distribution layer is where we want to implement policies for the network because we are allowed a lot of flexibility in defining network operation here. There are several things that should generally be handled at the distribution layer:

- Routing
- Implementing tools (such as access lists), packet filtering, and queuing
- Implementing security and network policies, including address translation and firewalls
- Redistributing between routing protocols, including static routing
- Routing between VLANs and other workgroup support functions
- Defining broadcast and multicast domains

Key things to avoid at the distribution layer are those that are limited to functions that exclusively belong to one of the other layers!

The Access Layer

The *access layer* controls user and workgroup access to internetwork resources. The access layer is sometimes referred to as the *desktop layer*. The network resources most users need will be available locally because the distribution layer handles any traffic for remote services.

The following are some of the functions to be included at the access layer:

- Continued (from distribution layer) use of access control and policies
- Creation of separate collision domains (microsegmentation/switches)
- Workgroup connectivity into the distribution layer
- Device connectivity
- Resiliency and security services
- Advanced technology capabilities (voice/video, etc.)

Technologies like Gigabit or Fast Ethernet switching are frequently seen in the access layer.

I can't stress this enough—just because there are three separate levels does not imply three separate devices! There could be fewer or there could be more. After all, this is a *layered* approach.

Summary

In this chapter, you learned the fundamentals of Ethernet networking, how hosts communicate on a network. You discovered how CSMA/CD works in an Ethernet half-duplex network.

I also talked about the differences between half- and full-duplex modes, and we discussed the collision detection mechanism called CSMA/CD.

I described the common Ethernet cable types used in today's networks in this chapter as well, and by the way, you'd be wise to study that section really well!

Important enough to not gloss over, this chapter provided an introduction to encapsulation. Encapsulation is the process of encoding data as it goes down the OSI stack.

Last, I covered the Cisco three-layer hierarchical model. I described in detail the three layers and how each is used to help design and implement a Cisco internetwork.

Exam Essentials

Describe the operation of Carrier Sense Multiple Access with Collision Detection (CSMA/CD).   CSMA/CD is a protocol that helps devices share the bandwidth evenly without having two devices transmit at the same time on the network medium. Although it does not eliminate collisions, it helps to greatly reduce them, which reduces retransmissions, resulting in a more efficient transmission of data for all devices.

Differentiate half-duplex and full-duplex communication and define the requirements to utilize each method.   Full-duplex Ethernet uses two pairs of wires at the same time instead of one wire pair like half-duplex. Full-duplex allows for sending and receiving at the same time, using different wires to eliminate collisions, while half-duplex can send or receive but not at the same time and still can suffer collisions. To use full-duplex, the devices at both ends of the cable must be capable of and configured to perform full-duplex.

Describe the sections of a MAC address and the information contained in each section.   The MAC, or hardware, address is a 48-bit (6-byte) address written in a hexadecimal format. The first 24 bits, or 3 bytes, are called the organizationally unique identifier (OUI), which is assigned by the IEEE to the manufacturer of the NIC. The balance of the number uniquely identifies the NIC.

Identify the binary and hexadecimal equivalent of a decimal number.   Any number expressed in one format can also be expressed in the other two. The ability to perform this conversion is critical to understanding IP addressing and subnetting. Be sure to go through the written labs covering binary to decimal to hexadecimal conversion.

Identify the fields in the Data Link portion of an Ethernet frame.   The fields in the Data Link portion of a frame include the preamble, Start Frame Delimiter, destination MAC address, source MAC address, Length or Type, Data, and Frame Check Sequence.

Identify the IEEE physical standards for Ethernet cabling.   These standards describe the capabilities and physical characteristics of various cable types and include but are not limited to 10Base-2, 10Base-5, and 10Base-T.

Differentiate types of Ethernet cabling and identify their proper application.   The three types of cables that can be created from an Ethernet cable are straight-through (to connect a PC's or router's Ethernet interface to a hub or switch), crossover (to connect hub to hub, hub to switch, switch to switch, or PC to PC), and rolled (for a console connection from a PC to a router or switch).

Describe the data encapsulation process and the role it plays in packet creation.   Data encapsulation is a process whereby information is added to the frame from each layer of the OSI model. This is also called packet creation. Each layer communicates only with its peer layer on the receiving device.

Understand how to connect a console cable from a PC to a router and switch.   Take a rolled cable and connect it from the COM port of the host to the console port of a router. Start your emulations program such as putty or SecureCRT and set the bits per second to 9600 and flow control to None.

Identify the layers in the Cisco three-layer model and describe the ideal function of each layer.   The three layers in the Cisco hierarchical model are the core (responsible for transporting large amounts of traffic both reliably and quickly), distribution (provides routing, filtering, and WAN access), and access (workgroup connectivity into the distribution layer).

Written Labs

In this section, you'll complete the following labs to make sure you've got the information and concepts contained within them fully dialed in:

   Lab 2.1: Binary/Decimal/Hexadecimal Conversion

   Lab 2.2: CSMA/CD Operations

   Lab 2.3: Cabling

   Lab 2.4: Encapsulation

   You can find the answers to these labs in Appendix A, "Answers to Written Labs."

Written Lab 2.1: Binary/Decimal/Hexadecimal Conversion

1.   Convert from decimal IP address to binary format.

   Complete the following table to express 192.168.10.15 in binary format.

128	64	32	16	8	4	2	1	Binary

Complete the following table to express 172.16.20.55 in binary format.

128	64	32	16	8	4	2	1	Binary

Complete the following table to express 10.11.12.99 in binary format.

128	64	32	16	8	4	2	1	Binary

2. Convert the following from binary format to decimal IP address.

   Complete the following table to express 11001100.00110011.10101010.01010101 in decimal IP address format.

128	64	32	16	8	4	2	1	Decimal

Complete the following table to express 11000110.11010011.00111001.11010001 in decimal IP address format.

128	64	32	16	8	4	2	1	Decimal

Complete the following table to express 10000100.11010010.10111000.10100110 in decimal IP address format.

128	64	32	16	8	4	2	1	Decimal

3. Convert the following from binary format to hexadecimal.

Complete the following table to express 11011000.00011011.00111101.01110110 in hexadecimal.

128	64	32	16	8	4	2	1	Hexadecimal

Complete the following table to express 11001010.11110101.10000011.11101011 in hexadecimal.

128	64	32	16	8	4	2	1	Hexadecimal

Complete the following table to express 10000100.11010010.01000011.10110011 in hexadecimal.

128	64	32	16	8	4	2	1	Hexadecimal

Written Lab 2.2: CSMA/CD Operations

Carrier Sense Multiple Access with Collision Detection (CSMA/CD) helps to minimize collisions in the network, thereby increasing data transmission efficiency. Place the following steps of its operation in the order in which they occur after a collision.

- All hosts have equal priority to transmit after the timers have expired.
- Each device on the Ethernet segment stops transmitting for a short time until the timers expire.
- The collision invokes a random backoff algorithm.
- A jam signal informs all devices that a collision occurred.

Written Lab 2.3: Cabling

For each of the following situations, determine whether a straight-through, crossover, or rolled cable would be used.

1. Host to host

2. Host to switch or hub

3. Router direct to host

4. Switch to switch

5. Router to switch or hub

6. Hub to hub

7. Hub to switch

8. Host to a router console serial communication (COM) port

Written Lab 2.4: Encapsulation

Place the following steps of the encapsulation process in the proper order.

- Packets or datagrams are converted to frames for transmission on the local network. Hardware (Ethernet) addresses are used to uniquely identify hosts on a local network segment.

- Segments are converted to packets or datagrams, and a logical address is placed in the header so each packet can be routed through an internetwork.

- User information is converted to data for transmission on the network.

- Frames are converted to bits, and a digital encoding and clocking scheme is used.

- Data is converted to segments, and a reliable connection is set up between the transmitting and receiving hosts.

Review Questions

 The following questions are designed to test your understanding of this chapter's material. For more information on how to get additional questions, please see www.lammle.com/ccna.

You can find the answers to these questions in Appendix B, "Answers to Review Questions."

1. In the accompanying graphic, what is the name for the section of the MAC address marked as unknown?

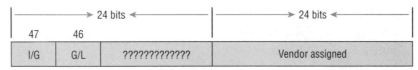

Example: 0000.0c12.3456

A. IOS

B. OSI

C. ISO

D. OUI

2. _____ on an Ethernet network is the retransmission delay that's enforced when a collision occurs.

A. Backoff

B. Carrier sense

C. Forward delay

D. Jamming

3. On which type of device could the situation shown in the diagram occur?

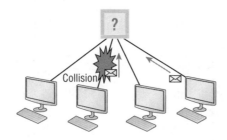

    A. Hub

    B. Switch

    C. Router

    D. Bridge

4. In the Ethernet II frame shown here, what is the function of the section labeled "FCS"?

Ethernet_II

Preamble 7 bytes	SFD 1 byte	Destination 6 bytes	Source 6 bytes	Type 2 bytes	Data and Pad 46 – 1500 bytes	FCS 4 bytes

    A. Allows the receiving devices to lock the incoming bit stream.

    B. Error detection

    C. Identifies the upper-layer protocol

    D. Identifies the transmitting device

5. A network interface port has collision detection and carrier sensing enabled on a shared twisted-pair network. From this statement, what is known about the network interface port?

    A. This is a 10 Mbps switch port.

    B. This is a 100 Mb/s switch port.

    C. This is an Ethernet port operating at half-duplex.

    D. This is an Ethernet port operating at full-duplex.

    E. This is a port on a network interface card in a PC.

6. For what two purposes does the Ethernet protocol use physical addresses? (Choose two.)

    A. To uniquely identify devices at layer 2

    B. To allow communication with devices on a different network

    C. To differentiate a layer 2 frame from a layer 3 packet

    D. To establish a priority system to determine which device gets to transmit first

    E. To allow communication between different devices on the same network

    F. To allow detection of a remote device when its physical address is unknown

7. Between which systems could you use a cable that uses the pinout pattern shown here?

    A. With a connection from a switch to a switch

    B. With a connection from a router to a router

    C. With a connection from a host to a host

    D. With a connection from a host to a switch

8. In an Ethernet network, under what two scenarios can devices transmit? (Choose two.)

    A. When they receive a special token

    B. When there is a carrier

    C. When they detect that no other devices are sending

    D. When the medium is idle

    E. When the server grants access

9. What type of cable uses the pinout shown here?

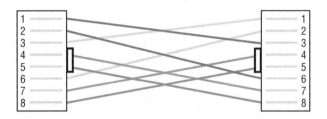

    A. Fiber optic

    B. Crossover Gigabit Ethernet cable

    C. Straight-through Fast Ethernet

    D. Coaxial

10. When configuring a terminal emulation program, which of the following is an incorrect setting?

    A. Bit rate: 9600

    B. Parity: None

    C. Flow control: None

    D. Data bits: 1

11. Which part of a MAC address indicates whether the address is a locally or globally administered address?

    A. FCS

    B. I/G bit

    C. OUI

    D. U/L bit

12. What cable type uses the pinout arrangement shown below?

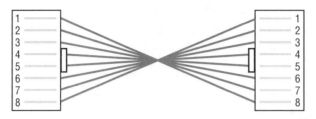

   A. Fiber optic

   B. Rolled

   C. Straight-through

   D. Crossover

13. Which of the following is *not* one of the actions taken in the operation of CSMA/CD when a collision occurs?

   A. A jam signal informs all devices that a collision occurred.

   B. The collision invokes a random backoff algorithm on the systems involved in the collision.

   C. Each device on the Ethernet segment stops transmitting for a short time until its back-off timer expires.

   D. All hosts have equal priority to transmit after the timers have expired.

14. Which of the following statements is *false* with regard to Ethernet?

   A. There are very few collisions in full-duplex mode.

   B. A dedicated switch port is required for each full-duplex node.

   C. The host network card and the switch port must be capable of operating in full-duplex mode to use full-duplex.

   D. The default behavior of 10Base-T and 100Base-T hosts is 10 Mbps half-duplex if the autodetect mechanism fails.

15. In the following diagram, identify the cable types required for connections A and B.

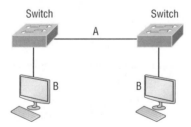

   A. A= crossover, B= crossover

   B. A= crossover, B= straight-through

   C. A= straight-through, B= straight-through

   D. A= straight-through, B= crossover

16. In the following image, match the cable type to the standard with which it goes.

1000Base-T	IEEE 802.3u
1000Base-SX	IEEE 802.3
10Base-T	IEEE 802.3ab
100Base-TX	IEEE 802.3z

17. The cable used to connect to the console port on a router or switch is called a _____ cable.

   A. Crossover

   B. Rollover

   C. Straight-through

   D. Full-duplex

18. Which of the following items does a socket comprise?

   A. IP address and MAC address

   B. IP address and port number

   C. Port number and MAC address

   D. MAC address and DLCI

19. Which of the following hexadecimal numbers converts to 28 in decimal?

   A. 1c

   B. 12

   C. 15

   D. ab

20. What cable type is shown in the following graphic?

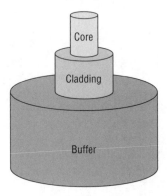

   A. Fiber optic

   B. Rollover

   C. Coaxial

   D. Full-duplex

Chapter

3

Introduction to TCP/IP

THE FOLLOWING ICND1 EXAM TOPICS ARE COVERED IN THIS CHAPTER:

✓ **Network Fundamentals**

- 1.1 Compare and contrast OSI and TCP/IP models

- 1.2 Compare and contrast TCP and UDP protocols

- 1.7 Apply troubleshooting methodologies to resolve problems

- 1.7.a Perform fault isolation and document

- 1.7.b Resolve or escalate

- 1.7.c Verify and monitor resolution

- 1.9 Compare and contrast IPv4 address types

  - 1.9.a Unicast

  - 1.9.b Broadcast

  - 1.9.c Multicast

- 1.10 Describe the need for private IPv4 addressing

The *Transmission Control Protocol/Internet Protocol (TCP/IP)* suite was designed and implemented by the Department of Defense (DoD) to ensure and preserve data integrity as well as maintain communications in the event of catastrophic war. So it follows that if designed and implemented correctly, a TCP/IP network can be a secure, dependable and resilient one. In this chapter, I'll cover the protocols of TCP/IP, and throughout this book, you'll learn how to create a solid TCP/IP network with Cisco routers and switches.

We'll begin by exploring the DoD's version of TCP/IP, then compare that version and its protocols with the OSI reference model that we discussed earlier.

Once you understand the protocols and processes used at the various levels of the DoD model, we'll take the next logical step by delving into the world of IP addressing and the different classes of IP addresses used in networks today.

 Subnetting is so vital, it will be covered in its own chapter, Chapter 4, "Easy Subnetting."

Because having a good grasp of the various IPv4 address types is critical to understanding IP addressing, subnetting, and variable length subnet masks (VLSMs), we'll explore these key topics in detail, ending this chapter by discussing the various types of IPv4 addresses that you'll need to have down for the exam.

I'm not going to cover Internet Protocol version 6 in this chapter because we'll get into that later, in Chapter 14, "Internet Protocol Version 6 (IPv6)." And just so you know, you'll simply see Internet Protocol version 4 written as just IP, rarely as IPv4.

 To find up-to-the-minute updates for this chapter, please see www.lammle .com/ccna or the book's web page via www.sybex.com/go/ccna.

Introducing TCP/IP

TCP/IP is at the very core of all things networking, so I really want to ensure that you have a comprehensive and functional command of it. I'll start by giving you the whole TCP/IP backstory, including its inception, and then move on to describe the important technical goals as defined by its original architects. And of course I'll include how TCP/IP compares to the theoretical OSI model.

A Brief History of TCP/IP

TCP first came on the scene way back in 1973, and in 1978, it was divided into two distinct protocols: TCP and IP. Later, in 1983, TCP/IP replaced the Network Control Protocol (NCP) and was authorized as the official means of data transport for anything connecting to ARPAnet, the Internet's ancestor. The DoD's Advanced Research Projects Agency (ARPA) created this ancient network way back in 1957 in a cold war reaction to the Soviet's launching of *Sputnik*. Also in 1983, ARPA was redubbed DARPA and divided into ARPAnet and MILNET until both were finally dissolved in 1990.

It may be counterintuitive, but most of the development work on TCP/IP happened at UC Berkeley in Northern California, where a group of scientists were simultaneously working on the Berkeley version of UNIX, which soon became known as the Berkeley Software Distribution (BSD) series of UNIX versions. Of course, because TCP/IP worked so well, it was packaged into subsequent releases of BSD Unix and offered to other universities and institutions if they bought the distribution tape. So basically, BSD Unix bundled with TCP/ IP began as shareware in the world of academia. As a result, it became the foundation for the tremendous success and unprecedented growth of today's Internet as well as smaller, private and corporate intranets.

As usual, what started as a small group of TCP/IP aficionados evolved, and as it did, the US government created a program to test any new published standards and make sure they passed certain criteria. This was to protect TCP/IP's integrity and to ensure that no developer changed anything too dramatically or added any proprietary features. It's this very quality—this open-systems approach to the TCP/IP family of protocols—that sealed its popularity because this quality guarantees a solid connection between myriad hardware and software platforms with no strings attached.

TCP/IP and the DoD Model

The DoD model is basically a condensed version of the OSI model that comprises four instead of seven layers:

- Process/Application layer
- Host-to-Host layer or Transport layer
- Internet layer
- Network Access layer or Link layer

Figure 3.1 offers a comparison of the DoD model and the OSI reference model. As you can see, the two are similar in concept, but each has a different number of layers with different names. Cisco may at times use different names for the same layer, such as both "Host-to-Host" and Transport" at the layer above the Internet layer, as well as "Network Access" and "Link" used to describe the bottom layer.

FIGURE 3.1   The DoD and OSI models

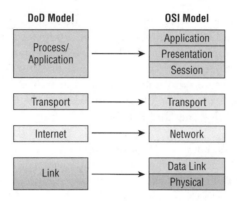

 When the different protocols in the IP stack are discussed, the layers of the OSI and DoD models are interchangeable. In other words, be prepared for the exam objectives to call the Host-to-Host layer the Transport layer!

A vast array of protocols join forces at the DoD model's *Process/Application layer.* These processes integrate the various activities and duties spanning the focus of the OSI's corresponding top three layers (Application, Presentation, and Session). We'll focus on a few of the most important applications found in the CCNA objectives. In short, the Process/Application layer defines protocols for node-to-node application communication and controls user-interface specifications.

The *Host-to-Host layer or Transport layer* parallels the functions of the OSI's Transport layer, defining protocols for setting up the level of transmission service for applications. It tackles issues like creating reliable end-to-end communication and ensuring the error-free delivery of data. It handles packet sequencing and maintains data integrity.

The *Internet layer* corresponds to the OSI's Network layer, designating the protocols relating to the logical transmission of packets over the entire network. It takes care of the addressing of hosts by giving them an IP (Internet Protocol) address and handles the routing of packets among multiple networks.

At the bottom of the DoD model, the *Network Access layer or Link layer* implements the data exchange between the host and the network. The equivalent of the Data Link and Physical layers of the OSI model, the Network Access layer oversees hardware addressing and defines protocols for the physical transmission of data. The reason TCP/IP became so popular is because there were no set physical layer specifications, so it could run on any existing or future physical network!

The DoD and OSI models are alike in design and concept and have similar functions in similar layers. Figure 3.2 shows the TCP/IP protocol suite and how its protocols relate to the DoD model layers.

FIGURE 3.2   The TCP/IP protocol suite

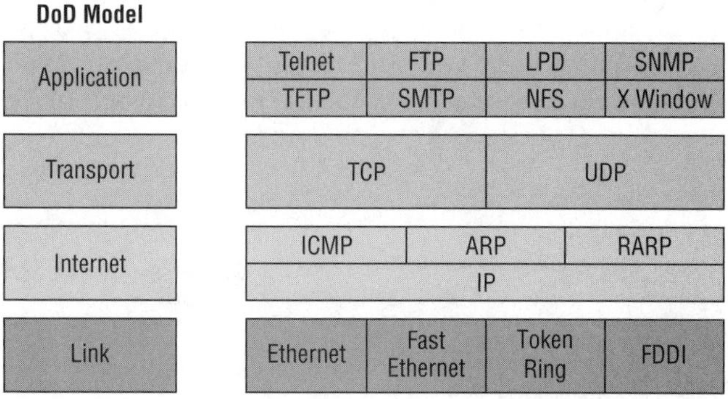

DoD Model

Application

Telnet	FTP	LPD	SNMP
TFTP	SMTP	NFS	X Window

Transport

TCP	UDP

Internet

ICMP	ARP	RARP
IP		

Link

Ethernet	Fast Ethernet	Token Ring	FDDI

In the following sections, we will look at the different protocols in more detail, beginning with those found at the Process/Application layer.

The Process/Application Layer Protocols

Coming up, I'll describe the different applications and services typically used in IP networks, and although there are many more protocols defined here, we'll focus in on the protocols most relevant to the CCNA objectives. Here's a list of the protocols and applications we'll cover in this section:

- Telnet
- SSH
- FTP
- TFTP
- SNMP
- HTTP
- HTTPS
- NTP
- DNS
- DHCP/BootP
- APIPA

Telnet

Telnet was one of the first Internet standards, developed in 1969, and is the chameleon of protocols—its specialty is terminal emulation. It allows a user on a remote client machine, called the Telnet client, to access the resources of another machine, the Telnet server, in order to access a command-line interface. Telnet achieves this by pulling a fast one on the Telnet server and making the client machine appear as though it were a terminal directly attached to the local network. This projection is actually a software image—a virtual terminal that can interact with the chosen remote host. A drawback is that there are no encryption techniques available within the Telnet protocol, so everything must be sent in clear text, including passwords! Figure 3.3 shows an example of a Telnet client trying to connect to a Telnet server.

FIGURE 3.3 Telnet

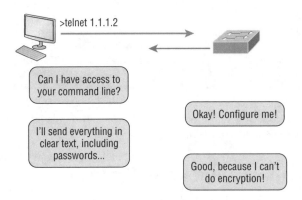

These emulated terminals are of the text-mode type and can execute defined procedures such as displaying menus that give users the opportunity to choose options and access the applications on the duped server. Users begin a Telnet session by running the Telnet client software and then logging into the Telnet server. Telnet uses an 8-bit, byte-oriented data connection over TCP, which makes it very thorough. It's still in use today because it is so simple and easy to use, with very low overhead, but again, with everything sent in clear text, it's not recommended in production.

Secure Shell (SSH)

Secure Shell (SSH) protocol sets up a secure session that's similar to Telnet over a standard TCP/IP connection and is employed for doing things like logging into systems, running programs on remote systems, and moving files from one system to another. And it does all of this while maintaining an encrypted connection. Figure 3.4 shows a SSH client trying to connect to a SSH server. The client must send the data encrypted!

You can think of it as the new-generation protocol that's now used in place of the antiquated and very unused rsh and rlogin—even Telnet.

File Transfer Protocol (FTP)

File Transfer Protocol (FTP) actually lets us transfer files, and it can accomplish this between any two machines using it. But FTP isn't just a protocol; it's also a program. Operating as a protocol, FTP is used by applications. As a program, it's employed by users to perform file tasks by hand. FTP also allows for access to both directories and files and can accomplish certain types of directory operations, such as relocating into different ones (Figure 3.5).

FIGURE 3.4   Secure Shell

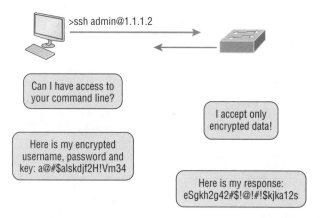

FIGURE 3.5   FTP

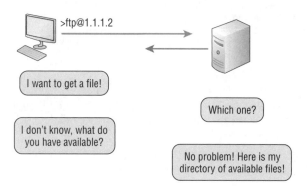

But accessing a host through FTP is only the first step. Users must then be subjected to an authentication login that's usually secured with passwords and usernames implemented by system administrators to restrict access. You can get around this somewhat by adopting the username *anonymous*, but you'll be limited in what you'll be able to access.

Even when employed by users manually as a program, FTP's functions are limited to listing and manipulating directories, typing file contents, and copying files between hosts. It can't execute remote files as programs.

Trivial File Transfer Protocol (TFTP)

Trivial File Transfer Protocol (TFTP) is the stripped-down, stock version of FTP, but it's the protocol of choice if you know exactly what you want and where to find it because it's fast and so easy to use!

But TFTP doesn't offer the abundance of functions that FTP does because it has no directory-browsing abilities, meaning that it can only send and receive files (Figure 3.6). Still, it's heavily used for managing file systems on Cisco devices, as I'll show you in Chapter 7, "Managing a Cisco Internetwork."

FIGURE 3.6   TFTP

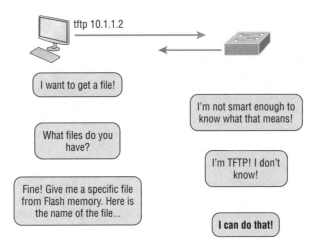

This compact little protocol also skimps in the data department, sending much smaller blocks of data than FTP. Also, there's no authentication as with FTP, so it's even more insecure, and few sites support it because of the inherent security risks.

🌐 **Real World Scenario**

When Should You Use FTP?

Let's say everyone at your San Francisco office needs a 50 GB file emailed to them right away. What do you do? Many email servers would reject that email due to size limits (a lot of ISPs don't allow files larger than 5 MB or 10 MB to be emailed), and even if there are no size limits on the server, it would still take a while to send this huge file. FTP to the rescue!

If you need to give someone a large file or you need to get a large file from someone, FTP is a nice choice. To use FTP, you would need to set up an FTP server on the Internet so that the files can be shared.

Besides resolving size issues, FTP is faster than email. In addition, because it uses TCP and is connection-oriented, if the session dies, FTP can sometimes start up where it left off. Try that with your email client!

Simple Network Management Protocol (SNMP)

Simple Network Management Protocol (SNMP) collects and manipulates valuable network information, as you can see in Figure 3.7. It gathers data by polling the devices on the network from a network management station (NMS) at fixed or random intervals, requiring them to disclose certain information, or even asking for certain information from the device. In addition, network devices can inform the NMS station about problems as they occur so the network administrator is alerted.

FIGURE 3.7   SNMP

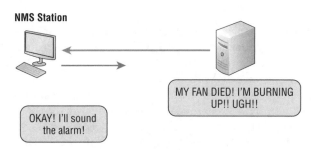

When all is well, SNMP receives something called a *baseline*—a report delimiting the operational traits of a healthy network. This protocol can also stand as a watchdog over the network, quickly notifying managers of any sudden turn of events. These network watchdogs are called *agents*, and when aberrations occur, agents send an alert called a *trap* to the management station.

SNMP Versions 1, 2, and 3

SNMP versions 1 and 2 are pretty much obsolete. This doesn't mean you won't see them in a network now and then, but you'll only come across v1 rarely, if ever. SNMPv2 provided improvements, especially in performance. But one of the best additions was called GETBULK, which allowed a host to retrieve a large amount of data at once. Even so, v2 never really caught on in the networking world and SNMPv3 is now the standard. Unlike v1, which used only UDP, v3 uses both TCP and UDP and added even more security, message integrity, authentication, and encryption.

Hypertext Transfer Protocol (HTTP)

All those snappy websites comprising a mélange of graphics, text, links, ads, and so on rely on the *Hypertext Transfer Protocol (HTTP)* to make it all possible (Figure 3.8). It's used to manage communications between web browsers and web servers and opens the right resource when you click a link, wherever that resource may actually reside.

FIGURE 3.8 HTTP

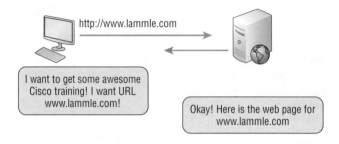

In order for a browser to display a web page, it must find the exact server that has the right web page, plus the exact details that identify the information requested. This information must be then be sent back to the browser. Nowadays, it's highly doubtful that a web server would have only one page to display!

Your browser can understand what you need when you enter a Uniform Resource Locator (URL), which we usually refer to as a web address, such as, for example, http://www.lammle.com/forum and http://www.lammle.com/blog.

So basically, each URL defines the protocol used to transfer data, the name of the server, and the particular web page on that server.

Hypertext Transfer Protocol Secure (HTTPS)

Hypertext Transfer Protocol Secure (HTTPS) is also known as Secure Hypertext Transfer Protocol. It uses Secure Sockets Layer (SSL). Sometimes you'll see it referred to as SHTTP or S-HTTP, which were slightly different protocols, but since Microsoft supported HTTPS, it became the de facto standard for securing web communication. But no matter—as indicated, it's a secure version of HTTP that arms you with a whole bunch of security tools for keeping transactions between a web browser and a server secure.

It's what your browser needs to fill out forms, sign in, authenticate, and encrypt an HTTP message when you do things online like make a reservation, access your bank, or buy something.

Network Time Protocol (NTP)

Kudos to Professor David Mills of the University of Delaware for coming up with this handy protocol that's used to synchronize the clocks on our computers to one standard time source (typically, an atomic clock). *Network Time Protocol (NTP)* works by synchronizing devices to ensure that all computers on a given network agree on the time (Figure 3.9).

This may sound pretty simple, but it's very important because so many of the transactions done today are time and date stamped. Think about databases—a server can get messed up pretty badly and even crash if it's out of sync with the machines connected to it by even mere seconds! You can't have a transaction entered by a machine at, say, 1:50 a.m. when the server records that transaction as having occurred at 1:45 a.m. So basically, NTP works to prevent a "back to the future *sans* DeLorean" scenario from bringing down the network—very important indeed!

FIGURE 3.9 NTP

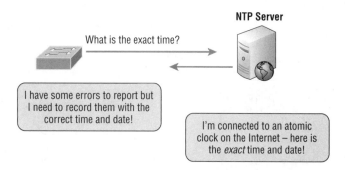

I'll tell you a lot more about NTP in Chapter 7, including how to configure this protocol in a Cisco environment.

Domain Name Service (DNS)

Domain Name Service (DNS) resolves hostnames—specifically, Internet names, such as www.lammle.com. But you don't have to actually use DNS. You just type in the IP address of any device you want to communicate with and find the IP address of a URL by using the Ping program. For example, >ping www.cisco.com will return the IP address resolved by DNS.

An IP address identifies hosts on a network and the Internet as well, but DNS was designed to make our lives easier. Think about this: What would happen if you wanted to move your web page to a different service provider? The IP address would change and no one would know what the new one is. DNS allows you to use a domain name to specify an IP address. You can change the IP address as often as you want and no one will know the difference.

To resolve a DNS address from a host, you'd typically type in the URL from your favorite browser, which would hand the data to the Application layer interface to be transmitted on the network. The application would look up the DNS address and send a UDP request to your DNS server to resolve the name (Figure 3.10).

If your first DNS server doesn't know the answer to the query, then the DNS server forwards a TCP request to its root DNS server. Once the query is resolved, the answer is transmitted back to the originating host, which means the host can now request the information from the correct web server.

DNS is used to resolve a *fully qualified domain name (FQDN)*—for example, www .lammle.com or todd.lammle.com. An FQDN is a hierarchy that can logically locate a system based on its domain identifier.

If you want to resolve the name *todd*, you either must type in the FQDN of todd .lammle.com or have a device such as a PC or router add the suffix for you. For example, on a Cisco router, you can use the command ip domain-name lammle.com to append each request with the lammle.com domain. If you don't do that, you'll have to type in the FQDN to get DNS to resolve the name.

FIGURE 3.10   DNS

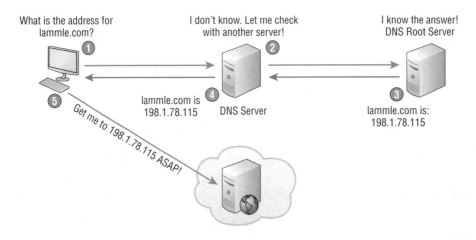

An important thing to remember about DNS is that if you can ping a device with an IP address but cannot use its FQDN, then you might have some type of DNS configuration failure.

Dynamic Host Configuration Protocol (DHCP)/Bootstrap Protocol (BootP)

Dynamic Host Configuration Protocol (DHCP) assigns IP addresses to hosts. It allows for easier administration and works well in small to very large network environments. Many types of hardware can be used as a DHCP server, including a Cisco router.

DHCP differs from BootP in that BootP assigns an IP address to a host but the host's hardware address must be entered manually in a BootP table. You can think of DHCP as a dynamic BootP. But remember that BootP is also used to send an operating system that a host can boot from. DHCP can't do that.

But there's still a lot of information a DHCP server can provide to a host when the host is requesting an IP address from the DHCP server. Here's a list of the most common types of information a DHCP server can provide:

- IP address
- Subnet mask
- Domain name
- Default gateway (routers)
- DNS server address
- WINS server address

A client that sends out a DHCP Discover message in order to receive an IP address sends out a broadcast at both layer 2 and layer 3.

- The layer 2 broadcast is all *F*s in hex, which looks like this: ff:ff:ff:ff:ff:ff.
- The layer 3 broadcast is 255.255.255.255, which means all networks and all hosts.

DHCP is connectionless, which means it uses User Datagram Protocol (UDP) at the Transport layer, also known as the Host-to-Host layer, which we'll talk about later.

Seeing is believing, so here's an example of output from my analyzer showing the layer 2 and layer 3 broadcasts:

```
Ethernet II, Src: 0.0.0.0 (00:0b:db:99:d3:5e),Dst: Broadcast(ff:ff:ff:ff:ff:ff)
Internet Protocol, Src: 0.0.0.0 (0.0.0.0),Dst: 255.255.255.255(255.255.255.255)
```

The Data Link and Network layers are both sending out "all hands" broadcasts saying, "Help—I don't know my IP address!"

DHCP will be discussed in more detail, including configuration on a Cisco router and switch, in Chapter 7, "Managing a Cisco Internetwork," and Chapter 9, "IP Routing."

Figure 3.11 shows the process of a client/server relationship using a DHCP connection.

FIGURE 3.11   DHCP client four-step process

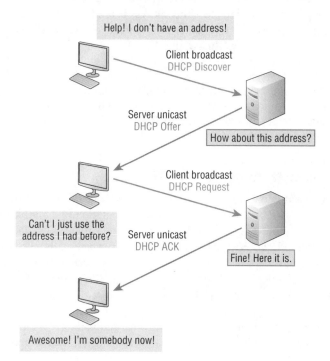

This is the four-step process a client takes to receive an IP address from a DHCP server:

1. The DHCP client broadcasts a DHCP Discover message looking for a DHCP server (Port 67).

2. The DHCP server that received the DHCP Discover message sends a layer 2 unicast DHCP Offer message back to the host.

3. The client then broadcasts to the server a DHCP Request message asking for the offered IP address and possibly other information.

4. The server finalizes the exchange with a unicast DHCP Acknowledgment message.

DHCP Conflicts

A DHCP address conflict occurs when two hosts use the same IP address. This sounds bad, and it is! We'll never even have to discuss this problem once we get to the chapter on IPv6!

During IP address assignment, a DHCP server checks for conflicts using the Ping program to test the availability of the address before it's assigned from the pool. If no host replies, then the DHCP server assumes that the IP address is not already allocated. This helps the server know that it's providing a good address, but what about the host? To provide extra protection against that terrible IP conflict issue, the host can broadcast for its own address!

A host uses something called a gratuitous ARP to help avoid a possible duplicate address. The DHCP client sends an ARP broadcast out on the local LAN or VLAN using its newly assigned address to solve conflicts before they occur.

So, if an IP address conflict is detected, the address is removed from the DHCP pool (scope), and it's really important to remember that the address will not be assigned to a host until the administrator resolves the conflict by hand!

Please see Chapter 9, "IP Routing," to check out a DHCP configuration on a Cisco router and also to find out what happens when a DHCP client is on one side of a router but the DHCP server is on the other side on a different network!

Automatic Private IP Addressing (APIPA)

Okay, so what happens if you have a few hosts connected together with a switch or hub and you don't have a DHCP server? You can add IP information by hand, known as *static IP addressing*, but later Windows operating systems provide a feature called Automatic Private IP Addressing (APIPA). With APIPA, clients can automatically self-configure an IP address and subnet mask—basic IP information that hosts use to communicate—when a DHCP server isn't available. The IP address range for APIPA is 169.254.0.1 through 169.254.255.254. The client also configures itself with a default Class B subnet mask of 255.255.0.0.

But when you're in your corporate network working and you have a DHCP server running, and your host shows that it's using this IP address range, it means that either your

DHCP client on the host is not working or the server is down or can't be reached due to some network issue. Believe me—I don't know anyone who's seen a host in this address range and has been happy about it!

Now, let's take a look at the Transport layer, or what the DoD calls the Host-to-Host layer.

The Host-to-Host or Transport Layer Protocols

The main purpose of the Host-to-Host layer is to shield the upper-layer applications from the complexities of the network. This layer says to the upper layer, "Just give me your data stream, with any instructions, and I'll begin the process of getting your information ready to send."

Coming up, I'll introduce you to the two protocols at this layer:

- Transmission Control Protocol (TCP)
- User Datagram Protocol (UDP)

In addition, we'll look at some of the key host-to-host protocol concepts, as well as the port numbers.

 Remember, this is still considered layer 4, and Cisco really likes the way layer 4 can use acknowledgments, sequencing, and flow control.

Transmission Control Protocol (TCP)

Transmission Control Protocol (TCP) takes large blocks of information from an application and breaks them into segments. It numbers and sequences each segment so that the destination's TCP stack can put the segments back into the order the application intended. After these segments are sent on the transmitting host, TCP waits for an acknowledgment of the receiving end's TCP virtual circuit session, retransmitting any segments that aren't acknowledged.

Before a transmitting host starts to send segments down the model, the sender's TCP stack contacts the destination's TCP stack to establish a connection. This creates a *virtual circuit*, and this type of communication is known as *connection-oriented*. During this initial handshake, the two TCP layers also agree on the amount of information that's going to be sent before the recipient's TCP sends back an acknowledgment. With everything agreed upon in advance, the path is paved for reliable communication to take place.

TCP is a full-duplex, connection-oriented, reliable, and accurate protocol, but establishing all these terms and conditions, in addition to error checking, is no small task. TCP is very complicated, and so not surprisingly, it's costly in terms of network overhead. And since today's networks are much more reliable than those of yore, this added reliability is often unnecessary. Most programmers use TCP because it removes a lot of programming work, but for real-time video and VoIP, *User Datagram Protocol (UDP)* is often better because using it results in less overhead.

TCP Segment Format

Since the upper layers just send a data stream to the protocols in the Transport layers, I'll use Figure 3.12 to demonstrate how TCP segments a data stream and prepares it for the Internet layer. When the Internet layer receives the data stream, it routes the segments as packets through an internetwork. The segments are handed to the receiving host's Host-to-Host layer protocol, which rebuilds the data stream for the upper-layer applications or protocols.

FIGURE 3.12   TCP segment format

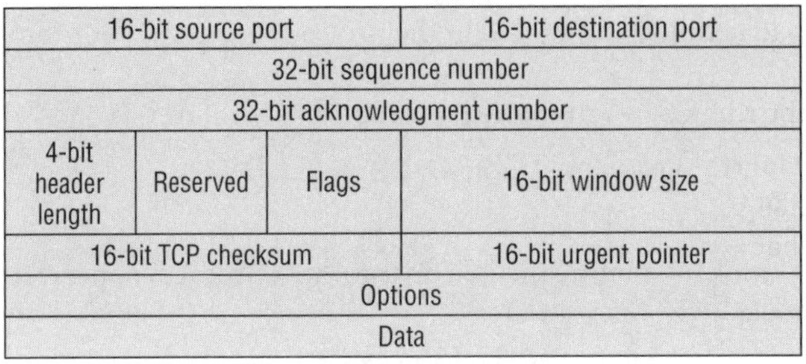

16-bit source port			16-bit destination port	
32-bit sequence number				
32-bit acknowledgment number				
4-bit header length	Reserved	Flags	16-bit window size	
16-bit TCP checksum			16-bit urgent pointer	
Options				
Data				

Figure 3.12 shows the TCP segment format and shows the different fields within the TCP header. This isn't important to memorize for the Cisco exam objectives, but you need to understand it well because it's really good foundational information.

The TCP header is 20 bytes long, or up to 24 bytes with options. You need to understand what each field in the TCP segment is in order to build a strong educational foundation:

Source port ⸳ This is the port number of the application on the host sending the data, which I'll talk about more thoroughly a little later in this chapter.

Destination port   This is the port number of the application requested on the destination host.

Sequence number   A number used by TCP that puts the data back in the correct order or retransmits missing or damaged data during a process called sequencing.

Acknowledgment number   The value is the TCP octet that is expected next.

Header length   The number of 32-bit words in the TCP header, which indicates where the data begins. The TCP header (even one including options) is an integral number of 32 bits in length.

Reserved   Always set to zero.

Code bits/flags   Controls functions used to set up and terminate a session.

Window   The window size the sender is willing to accept, in octets.

Checksum   The cyclic redundancy check (CRC), used because TCP doesn't trust the lower layers and checks everything. The CRC checks the header and data fields.

Urgent   A valid field only if the Urgent pointer in the code bits is set. If so, this value indicates the offset from the current sequence number, in octets, where the segment of non-urgent data begins.

Options   May be 0, meaning that no options have to be present, or a multiple of 32 bits. However, if any options are used that do not cause the option field to total a multiple of 32 bits, padding of 0s must be used to make sure the data begins on a 32-bit boundary. These boundaries are known as words.

Data   Handed down to the TCP protocol at the Transport layer, which includes the upper-layer headers.

Let's take a look at a TCP segment copied from a network analyzer:

```
TCP - Transport Control Protocol
  Source Port:        5973
  Destination Port: 23
  Sequence Number:  1456389907
  Ack Number:       1242056456
  Offset:           5
  Reserved:         %000000
  Code:             %011000
        Ack is valid
        Push Request
  Window:           61320
  Checksum:         0x61a6
  Urgent Pointer:   0
  No TCP Options
  TCP Data Area:
  vL.5.+.5.+.5.+.5  76 4c 19 35 11 2b 19 35 11 2b 19 35 11
    2b 19 35 +. 11 2b 19
 Frame Check Sequence: 0x0d00000f
```

Did you notice that everything I talked about earlier is in the segment? As you can see from the number of fields in the header, TCP creates a lot of overhead. Again, this is why application developers may opt for efficiency over reliability to save overhead and go with UDP instead. It's also defined at the Transport layer as an alternative to TCP.

User Datagram Protocol (UDP)

User Datagram Protocol (UDP) is basically the scaled-down economy model of TCP, which is why UDP is sometimes referred to as a thin protocol. Like a thin person on a park bench, a thin protocol doesn't take up a lot of room—or in this case, require much bandwidth on a network.

UDP doesn't offer all the bells and whistles of TCP either, but it does do a fabulous job of transporting information that doesn't require reliable delivery, using far less network resources. (UDP is covered thoroughly in Request for Comments 768.)

So clearly, there are times that it's wise for developers to opt for UDP rather than TCP, one of them being when reliability is already taken care of at the Process/Application layer. Network File System (NFS) handles its own reliability issues, making the use of TCP both impractical and redundant. But ultimately, it's up to the application developer to opt for using UDP or TCP, not the user who wants to transfer data faster!

UDP does *not* sequence the segments and does not care about the order in which the segments arrive at the destination. UDP just sends the segments off and forgets about them. It doesn't follow through, check up on them, or even allow for an acknowledgment of safe arrival—complete abandonment. Because of this, it's referred to as an unreliable protocol. This does not mean that UDP is ineffective, only that it doesn't deal with reliability issues at all.

Furthermore, UDP doesn't create a virtual circuit, nor does it contact the destination before delivering information to it. Because of this, it's also considered a *connectionless* protocol. Since UDP assumes that the application will use its own reliability method, it doesn't use any itself. This presents an application developer with a choice when running the Internet Protocol stack: TCP for reliability or UDP for faster transfers.

It's important to know how this process works because if the segments arrive out of order, which is commonplace in IP networks, they'll simply be passed up to the next layer in whatever order they were received. This can result in some seriously garbled data! On the other hand, TCP sequences the segments so they get put back together in exactly the right order, which is something UDP just can't do.

UDP Segment Format

Figure 3.13 clearly illustrates UDP's markedly lean overhead as compared to TCP's hungry requirements. Look at the figure carefully—can you see that UDP doesn't use windowing or provide for acknowledgments in the UDP header?

FIGURE 3.13   UDP segment

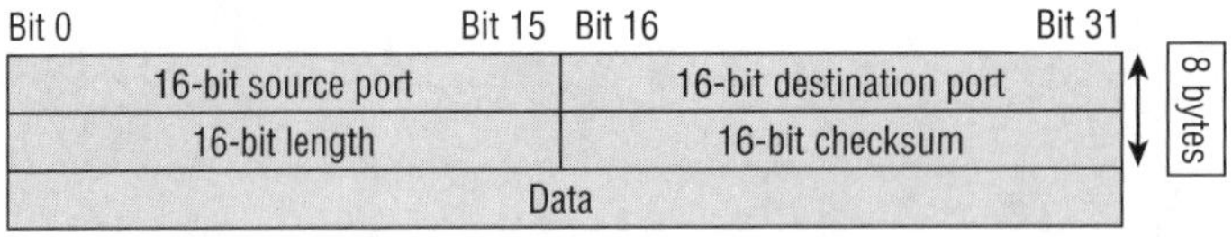

It's important for you to understand what each field in the UDP segment is:

Source port   Port number of the application on the host sending the data

Destination port   Port number of the application requested on the destination host

Length   Length of UDP header and UDP data

Checksum   Checksum of both the UDP header and UDP data fields

Data   Upper-layer data

UDP, like TCP, doesn't trust the lower layers and runs its own CRC. Remember that the Frame Check Sequence (FCS) is the field that houses the CRC, which is why you can see the FCS information.

The following shows a UDP segment caught on a network analyzer:

```
UDP - User Datagram Protocol
 Source Port:      1085
 Destination Port: 5136
 Length:           41
 Checksum:         0x7a3c
 UDP Data Area:
 ..Z......00 01 5a 96 00 01 00 00 00 00 00 11 0000 00
 ...C..2._C._C  2e 03 00 43 02 1e 32 0a 00 0a 00 80 43 00 80
Frame Check Sequence: 0x00000000
```

Notice that low overhead! Try to find the sequence number, ack number, and window size in the UDP segment. You can't because they just aren't there!

Key Concepts of Host-to-Host Protocols

Since you've now seen both a connection-oriented (TCP) and connectionless (UDP) protocol in action, it's a good time to summarize the two here. Table 3.1 highlights some of the key concepts about these two protocols for you to memorize.

TABLE 3.1 Key features of TCP and UDP

TCP	UDP
Sequenced	Unsequenced
Reliable	Unreliable
Connection-oriented	Connectionless
Virtual circuit	Low overhead
Acknowledgments	No acknowledgment
Windowing flow control	No windowing or flow control of any type

And if all this isn't quite clear yet, a telephone analogy will really help you understand how TCP works. Most of us know that before you speak to someone on a phone, you must first establish a connection with that other person no matter where they are. This is akin to establishing a virtual circuit with the TCP protocol. If you were giving someone important information during your conversation, you might say things like, "You know? or "Did you get that?" Saying things like this is a lot like a TCP acknowledgment—it's designed to get you verification. From time to time, especially on mobile phones, people ask, "Are you still there?" People end their conversations with a "Goodbye" of some kind, putting closure on the phone call, which you can think of as tearing down the virtual circuit that was created for your communication session. TCP performs these types of functions.

Conversely, using UDP is more like sending a postcard. To do that, you don't need to contact the other party first, you simply write your message, address the postcard, and send it off. This is analogous to UDP's connectionless orientation. Since the message on the postcard is probably not a matter of life or death, you don't need an acknowledgment of its receipt. Similarly, UDP does not involve acknowledgments.

Let's take a look at another figure, one that includes TCP, UDP, and the applications associated to each protocol: Figure 3.14 (discussed in the next section).

FIGURE 3.14   Port numbers for TCP and UDP

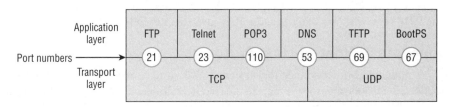

Port Numbers

TCP and UDP must use *port numbers* to communicate with the upper layers because these are what keep track of different conversations crossing the network simultaneously. Originating-source port numbers are dynamically assigned by the source host and will equal some number starting at 1024. Port number 1023 and below are defined in RFC 3232 (or just see www.iana.org), which discusses what we call well-known port numbers.

Virtual circuits that don't use an application with a well-known port number are assigned port numbers randomly from a specific range instead. These port numbers identify the source and destination application or process in the TCP segment.

> The Requests for Comments (RFCs) form a series of notes about the Internet (originally the ARPAnet) started in 1969. These notes discuss many aspects of computer communication, focusing on networking protocols, procedures, programs, and concepts, but they also include meeting notes, opinions, and sometimes even humor. You can find the RFCs by visiting www.iana.org.

Figure 3.14 illustrates how both TCP and UDP use port numbers. I'll cover the different port numbers that can be used next:

- Numbers below 1024 are considered well-known port numbers and are defined in RFC 3232.

- Numbers 1024 and above are used by the upper layers to set up sessions with other hosts and by TCP and UDP to use as source and destination addresses in the segment.

TCP Session: Source Port

Let's take a minute to check out analyzer output showing a TCP session I captured with my analyzer software session now:

```
TCP - Transport Control Protocol
  Source Port:       5973
  Destination Port: 23
  Sequence Number:  1456389907
  Ack Number:       1242056456
  Offset:            5
  Reserved:          %000000
  Code:              %011000
        Ack is valid
        Push Request
  Window:            61320
  Checksum:          0x61a6
  Urgent Pointer:    0
  No TCP Options
  TCP Data Area:
  vL.5.+.5.+.5.+.5   76 4c 19 35 11 2b 19 35 11 2b 19 35 11
   2b 19 35 +. 11 2b 19
Frame Check Sequence: 0x0d00000f
```

Notice that the source host makes up the source port, which in this case is 5973. The destination port is 23, which is used to tell the receiving host the purpose of the intended connection (Telnet).

By looking at this session, you can see that the source host makes up the source port by using numbers from 1024 to 65535. But why does the source make up a port number? To differentiate between sessions with different hosts because how would a server know where information is coming from if it didn't have a different number from a sending host? TCP and the upper layers don't use hardware and logical addresses to understand the sending host's address as the Data Link and Network layer protocols do. Instead, they use port numbers.

TCP Session: Destination Port

You'll sometimes look at an analyzer and see that only the source port is above 1024 and the destination port is a well-known port, as shown in the following trace:

```
TCP - Transport Control Protocol
  Source Port:       1144
  Destination Port: 80 World Wide Web HTTP
  Sequence Number:  9356570
  Ack Number:        0
```

```
Offset:         7
Reserved:       %000000
Code:           %000010
     Synch Sequence
Window:         8192
Checksum:       0x57E7
Urgent Pointer:  0
TCP Options:
 Option Type: 2 Maximum Segment Size
   Length:    4
   MSS:        536
 Option Type: 1 No Operation
 Option Type: 1 No Operation
 Option Type: 4
   Length:    2
   Opt Value:
 No More HTTP Data
Frame Check Sequence: 0x43697363
```

And sure enough, the source port is over 1024, but the destination port is 80, indicating an HTTP service. The server, or receiving host, will change the destination port if it needs to.

In the preceding trace, a "SYN" packet is sent to the destination device. This Synch (as shown in the output) sequence is what's used to inform the remote destination device that it wants to create a session.

TCP Session: Syn Packet Acknowledgment

The next trace shows an acknowledgment to the SYN packet:

```
TCP - Transport Control Protocol
 Source Port:      80 World Wide Web HTTP
 Destination Port: 1144
 Sequence Number:  2873580788
 Ack Number:       9356571
 Offset:           6
 Reserved:         %000000
 Code:             %010010
     Ack is valid
     Synch Sequence
 Window:           8576
 Checksum:         0x5F85
 Urgent Pointer:    0
```

```
TCP Options:
  Option Type: 2 Maximum Segment Size
     Length:    4
     MSS:       1460
  No More HTTP Data
Frame Check Sequence: 0x6E203132
```

Notice the *Ack is valid*, which means that the source port was accepted and the device agreed to create a virtual circuit with the originating host.

And here again, you can see that the response from the server shows that the source is 80 and the destination is the 1144 sent from the originating host—all's well!

Table 3.2 gives you a list of the typical applications used in the TCP/IP suite by showing their well-known port numbers and the Transport layer protocols used by each application or process. It's really key to memorize this table.

TABLE 3.2   Key protocols that use TCP and UDP

TCP	UDP
Telnet 23	SNMP 161
SMTP 25	TFTP 69
HTTP 80	DNS 53
FTP 20, 21	BooTPS/DHCP 67
DNS 53	
HTTPS 443	NTP 123
SSH 22	
POP3 110	
IMAP4 143	

Notice that DNS uses both TCP and UDP. Whether it opts for one or the other depends on what it's trying to do. Even though it's not the only application that can use both protocols, it's certainly one that you should make sure to remember in your studies.

 NOTE   What makes TCP reliable is sequencing, acknowledgments, and flow control (windowing). UDP does not have reliability.

Okay—I want to discuss one more item before we move down to the Internet layer—session multiplexing. Session multiplexing is used by both TCP and UDP and basically allows a single computer, with a single IP address, to have multiple sessions occurring simultaneously. Say you go to www.lammle.com and are browsing and then you click a link to another page. Doing this opens another session to your host. Now you go to www.lammle.com/forum from another window and that site opens a window as well. Now you have three sessions open using one IP address because the Session layer is sorting the separate requests based on the Transport layer port number. This is the job of the Session layer: to keep application layer data separate!

The Internet Layer Protocols

In the DoD model, there are two main reasons for the Internet layer's existence: routing and providing a single network interface to the upper layers.

None of the other upper- or lower-layer protocols have any functions relating to routing—that complex and important task belongs entirely to the Internet layer. The Internet layer's second duty is to provide a single network interface to the upper-layer protocols. Without this layer, application programmers would need to write "hooks" into every one of their applications for each different Network Access protocol. This would not only be a pain in the neck, but it would lead to different versions of each application—one for Ethernet, another one for wireless, and so on. To prevent this, IP provides one single network interface for the upper-layer protocols. With that mission accomplished, it's then the job of IP and the various Network Access protocols to get along and work together.

All network roads don't lead to Rome—they lead to IP. And all the other protocols at this layer, as well as all those at the upper layers, use it. Never forget that. All paths through the DoD model go through IP. Here's a list of the important protocols at the Internet layer that I'll cover individually in detail coming up:

- Internet Protocol (IP)
- Internet Control Message Protocol (ICMP)
- Address Resolution Protocol (ARP)

Internet Protocol (IP)

Internet Protocol (IP) essentially is the Internet layer. The other protocols found here merely exist to support it. IP holds the big picture and could be said to "see all," because it's aware of all the interconnected networks. It can do this because all the machines on the network have a software, or logical, address called an IP address, which we'll explore more thoroughly later in this chapter.

For now, understand that IP looks at each packet's address. Then, using a routing table, it decides where a packet is to be sent next, choosing the best path to send it upon. The protocols of the Network Access layer at the bottom of the DoD model don't possess IP's enlightened scope of the entire network; they deal only with physical links (local networks).

Identifying devices on networks requires answering these two questions: Which network is it on? And what is its ID on that network? The first answer is the *software address*, or *logical address*. You can think of this as the part of the address that specifies the correct street. The second answer is the hardware address, which goes a step further to specify the correct mailbox. All hosts on a network have a logical ID called an IP address. This is the software, or logical, address and contains valuable encoded information, greatly simplifying the complex task of routing. (IP is discussed in RFC 791.)

IP receives segments from the Host-to-Host layer and fragments them into datagrams (packets) if necessary. IP then reassembles datagrams back into segments on the receiving side. Each datagram is assigned the IP address of the sender and that of the recipient. Each router or switch (layer 3 device) that receives a datagram makes routing decisions based on the packet's destination IP address.

Figure 3.15 shows an IP header. This will give you a picture of what the IP protocol has to go through every time user data that is destined for a remote network is sent from the upper layers.

FIGURE 3.15 IP header

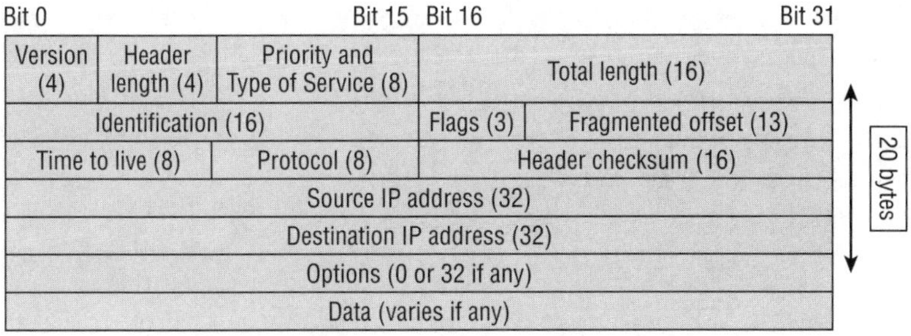

The following fields make up the IP header:

Version   IP version number.

Header length   Header length (HLEN) in 32-bit words.

Priority and Type of Service   Type of Service tells how the datagram should be handled. The first 3 bits are the priority bits, now called the differentiated services bits.

Total length   Length of the packet, including header and data.

Identification   Unique IP-packet value used to differentiate fragmented packets from different datagrams.

Flags   Specifies whether fragmentation should occur.

Fragment offset   Provides fragmentation and reassembly if the packet is too large to put in a frame. It also allows different maximum transmission units (MTUs) on the Internet.

Time To Live   The time to live (TTL) is set into a packet when it is originally generated. If it doesn't get to where it's supposed to go before the TTL expires, boom—it's gone. This stops IP packets from continuously circling the network looking for a home.

Protocol   Port of upper-layer protocol; for example, TCP is port 6 or UDP is port 17. Also supports Network layer protocols, like ARP and ICMP, and can be referred to as the Type field in some analyzers. We'll talk about this field more in a minute.

Header checksum   Cyclic redundancy check (CRC) on header only.

Source IP address   32-bit IP address of sending station.

Destination IP address   32-bit IP address of the station this packet is destined for.

Options   Used for network testing, debugging, security, and more.

Data   After the IP option field, will be the upper-layer data.

Here's a snapshot of an IP packet caught on a network analyzer. Notice that all the header information discussed previously appears here:

```
IP Header - Internet Protocol Datagram
 Version:              4
 Header Length:        5
 Precedence:           0
 Type of Service:      %000
 Unused:               %00
 Total Length:         187
 Identifier:           22486
 Fragmentation Flags:  %010 Do Not Fragment
 Fragment Offset:      0
 Time To Live:         60
 IP Type:              0x06 TCP
 Header Checksum:      0xd031
 Source IP Address:    10.7.1.30
 Dest. IP Address:     10.7.1.10
 No Internet Datagram Options
```

The Type field is typically a Protocol field, but this analyzer sees it as an IP Type field. This is important. If the header didn't carry the protocol information for the next layer, IP wouldn't know what to do with the data carried in the packet. The preceding example clearly tells IP to hand the segment to TCP.

Figure 3.16 demonstrates how the Network layer sees the protocols at the Transport layer when it needs to hand a packet up to the upper-layer protocols.

FIGURE 3.16   The Protocol field in an IP header

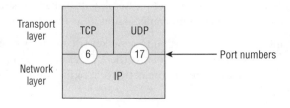

In this example, the Protocol field tells IP to send the data to either TCP port 6 or UDP port 17. But it will be UDP or TCP only if the data is part of a data stream headed for an upper-layer service or application. It could just as easily be destined for Internet Control Message Protocol (ICMP), Address Resolution Protocol (ARP), or some other type of Network layer protocol.

Table 3.3 is a list of some other popular protocols that can be specified in the Protocol field.

TABLE 3.3 Possible protocols found in the Protocol field of an IP header

Protocol	Protocol Number
ICMP	1
IP in IP (tunneling)	4
TCP	6
UDP	17
EIGRP	88
OSPF	89
IPv6	41
GRE	47
Layer 2 tunnel (L2TP)	115

 You can find a complete list of Protocol field numbers at www.iana.org/assignments/protocol-numbers.

Internet Control Message Protocol (ICMP)

Internet Control Message Protocol (ICMP) works at the Network layer and is used by IP for many different services. ICMP is basically a management protocol and messaging service provider for IP. Its messages are carried as IP datagrams. RFC 1256 is an annex to ICMP, which gives hosts extended capability in discovering routes to gateways.

ICMP packets have the following characteristics:

- They can provide hosts with information about network problems.
- They are encapsulated within IP datagrams.

The following are some common events and messages that ICMP relates to:

Destination unreachable If a router can't send an IP datagram any further, it uses ICMP to send a message back to the sender, advising it of the situation. For example, take a look at Figure 3.17, which shows that interface e0 of the Lab_B router is down.

FIGURE 3.17 ICMP error message is sent to the sending host from the remote router.

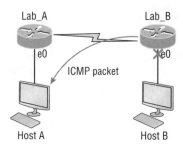

When Host A sends a packet destined for Host B, the Lab_B router will send an ICMP destination unreachable message back to the sending device, which is Host A in this example.

Buffer full/source quench If a router's memory buffer for receiving incoming datagrams is full, it will use ICMP to send out this message alert until the congestion abates.

Hops/time exceeded Each IP datagram is allotted a certain number of routers, called hops, to pass through. If it reaches its limit of hops before arriving at its destination, the last router to receive that datagram deletes it. The executioner router then uses ICMP to send an obituary message, informing the sending machine of the demise of its datagram.

Ping Packet Internet Groper (Ping) uses ICMP echo request and reply messages to check the physical and logical connectivity of machines on an internetwork.

Traceroute Using ICMP time-outs, Traceroute is used to discover the path a packet takes as it traverses an internetwork.

Traceroute is usually just called trace. Microsoft Windows uses tracert to allow you to verify address configurations in your internetwork.

The following data is from a network analyzer catching an ICMP echo request:

```
Flags:          0x00
 Status:         0x00
 Packet Length: 78
 Timestamp:     14:04:25.967000 12/20/03
Ethernet Header
 Destination: 00:a0:24:6e:0f:a8
```

```
Source:         00:80:c7:a8:f0:3d
Ether-Type:     08-00 IP
IP Header - Internet Protocol Datagram
Version:             4
Header Length:       5
Precedence:          0
Type of Service:     %000
Unused:              %00
Total Length:        60
Identifier:          56325
Fragmentation Flags: %000
Fragment Offset:     0
Time To Live:        32
IP Type:             0x01 ICMP
Header Checksum:     0x2df0
Source IP Address:   100.100.100.2
Dest. IP Address:    100.100.100.1
No Internet Datagram Options
ICMP - Internet Control Messages Protocol
ICMP Type:      8 Echo Request
Code:           0
Checksum:       0x395c
Identifier:     0x0300
Sequence Number: 4352
ICMP Data Area:
abcdefghijklmnop  61 62 63 64 65 66 67 68 69 6a 6b 6c 6d 6e 6f 70
qrstuvwabcdefghi  71 72 73 74 75 76 77 61 62 63 64 65 66 67 68 69
Frame Check Sequence: 0x00000000
```

Notice anything unusual? Did you catch the fact that even though ICMP works at the Internet (Network) layer, it still uses IP to do the Ping request? The Type field in the IP header is 0x01, which specifies that the data we're carrying is owned by the ICMP protocol. Remember, just as all roads lead to Rome, all segments or data *must* go through IP!

> The Ping program uses the alphabet in the data portion of the packet as a payload, typically around 100 bytes by default, unless, of course, you are pinging from a Windows device, which thinks the alphabet stops at the letter *W* (and doesn't include *X*, *Y*, or *Z*) and then starts at *A* again. Go figure!

If you remember reading about the Data Link layer and the different frame types in Chapter 2, "Ethernet Networking and Data Encapsulation," you should be able to look at the preceding trace and tell what type of Ethernet frame this is. The only fields are destination hardware address, source hardware address, and Ether-Type. The only frame that uses an Ether-Type field exclusively is an Ethernet_II frame.

We'll move on soon, but before we get into the ARP protocol, let's take another look at ICMP in action. Figure 3.18 shows an internetwork—it has a router, so it's an internetwork, right?

FIGURE 3.18   ICMP in action

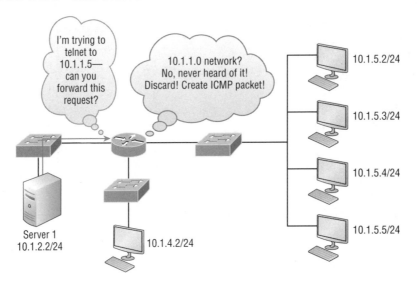

Server 1 (10.1.2.2) telnets to 10.1.1.5 from a DOS prompt. What do you think Server 1 will receive as a response? Server 1 will send the Telnet data to the default gateway, which is the router, and the router will drop the packet because there isn't a network 10.1.1.0 in the routing table. Because of this, Server 1 will receive an ICMP destination unreachable back from the router.

Address Resolution Protocol (ARP)

Address Resolution Protocol (ARP) finds the hardware address of a host from a known IP address. Here's how it works: When IP has a datagram to send, it must inform a Network Access protocol, such as Ethernet or wireless, of the destination's hardware address on the local network. Remember that it has already been informed by upper-layer protocols of the destination's IP address. If IP doesn't find the destination host's hardware address in the ARP cache, it uses ARP to find this information.

As IP's detective, ARP interrogates the local network by sending out a broadcast asking the machine with the specified IP address to reply with its hardware address. So basically, ARP translates the software (IP) address into a hardware address—for example, the destination machine's Ethernet adapter address—and from it, deduces its whereabouts on the LAN by broadcasting for this address. Figure 3.19 shows how an ARP broadcast looks to a local network.

FIGURE 3.19   Local ARP broadcast

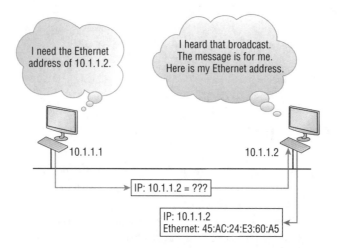

    ARP resolves IP addresses to Ethernet (MAC) addresses.

The following trace shows an ARP broadcast—notice that the destination hardware address is unknown and is all *F*s in hex (all 1s in binary)—and is a hardware address broadcast:

```
Flags:          0x00
Status:         0x00
Packet Length: 64
Timestamp:      09:17:29.574000 12/06/03
Ethernet Header
 Destination:   FF:FF:FF:FF:FF:FF Ethernet Broadcast
 Source:        00:A0:24:48:60:A5
 Protocol Type: 0x0806 IP ARP
ARP - Address Resolution Protocol
 Hardware:                 1 Ethernet (10Mb)
 Protocol:                 0x0800 IP
 Hardware Address Length: 6
 Protocol Address Length: 4
 Operation:                1 ARP Request
 Sender Hardware Address: 00:A0:24:48:60:A5
 Sender Internet Address: 172.16.10.3
```

```
Target Hardware Address: 00:00:00:00:00:00 (ignored)
Target Internet Address: 172.16.10.10
Extra bytes (Padding):
............... 0A 0A 0A 0A 0A 0A 0A 0A 0A 0A 0A 0A 0A
  0A 0A 0A 0A 0A
Frame Check Sequence: 0x00000000
```

IP Addressing

One of the most important topics in any discussion of TCP/IP is IP addressing. An *IP address* is a numeric identifier assigned to each machine on an IP network. It designates the specific location of a device on the network.

An IP address is a software address, not a hardware address—the latter is hard-coded on a network interface card (NIC) and used for finding hosts on a local network. IP addressing was designed to allow hosts on one network to communicate with a host on a different network regardless of the type of LANs the hosts are participating in.

Before we get into the more complicated aspects of IP addressing, you need to understand some of the basics. First I'm going to explain some of the fundamentals of IP addressing and its terminology. Then you'll learn about the hierarchical IP addressing scheme and private IP addresses.

IP Terminology

Throughout this chapter you're being introduced to several important terms that are vital to understanding the Internet Protocol. Here are a few to get you started:

Bit   A bit is one digit, either a 1 or a 0.

Byte   A byte is 7 or 8 bits, depending on whether parity is used. For the rest of this chapter, always assume a byte is 8 bits.

Octet   An octet, made up of 8 bits, is just an ordinary 8-bit binary number. In this chapter, the terms *byte* and *octet* are completely interchangeable.

Network address   This is the designation used in routing to send packets to a remote network—for example, 10.0.0.0, 172.16.0.0, and 192.168.10.0.

Broadcast address   The address used by applications and hosts to send information to all nodes on a network is called the broadcast address. Examples of layer 3 broadcasts include 255.255.255.255, which is any network, all nodes; 172.16.255.255, which is all subnets and hosts on network 172.16.0.0; and 10.255.255.255, which broadcasts to all subnets and hosts on network 10.0.0.0.

The Hierarchical IP Addressing Scheme

An IP address consists of 32 bits of information. These bits are divided into four sections, referred to as octets or bytes, with each containing 1 byte (8 bits). You can depict an IP address using one of three methods:

- Dotted-decimal, as in 172.16.30.56

- Binary, as in 10101100.00010000.00011110.00111000

- Hexadecimal, as in AC.10.1E.38

All these examples represent the same IP address. Pertaining to IP addressing, hexadecimal isn't used as often as dotted-decimal or binary, but you still might find an IP address stored in hexadecimal in some programs.

The 32-bit IP address is a structured or hierarchical address, as opposed to a flat or nonhierarchical address. Although either type of addressing scheme could have been used, *hierarchical addressing* was chosen for a good reason. The advantage of this scheme is that it can handle a large number of addresses, namely 4.3 billion (a 32-bit address space with two possible values for each position—either 0 or 1—gives you 2^{32}, or 4,294,967,296). The disadvantage of the flat addressing scheme, and the reason it's not used for IP addressing, relates to routing. If every address were unique, all routers on the Internet would need to store the address of each and every machine on the Internet. This would make efficient routing impossible, even if only a fraction of the possible addresses were used!

The solution to this problem is to use a two- or three-level hierarchical addressing scheme that is structured by network and host or by network, subnet, and host.

This two- or three-level scheme can also be compared to a telephone number. The first section, the area code, designates a very large area. The second section, the prefix, narrows the scope to a local calling area. The final segment, the customer number, zooms in on the specific connection. IP addresses use the same type of layered structure. Rather than all 32 bits being treated as a unique identifier, as in flat addressing, a part of the address is designated as the network address and the other part is designated as either the subnet and host or just the node address.

Next, we'll cover IP network addressing and the different classes of address we can use to address our networks.

Network Addressing

The *network address* (which can also be called the network number) uniquely identifies each network. Every machine on the same network shares that network address as part of its IP address. For example, in the IP address 172.16.30.56, 172.16 is the network address.

The *node address* is assigned to, and uniquely identifies, each machine on a network. This part of the address must be unique because it identifies a particular machine—an individual—as opposed to a network, which is a group. This number can also be referred to as a *host address*. In the sample IP address 172.16.30.56, the 30.56 specifies the node address.

The designers of the Internet decided to create classes of networks based on network size. For the small number of networks possessing a very large number of nodes, they created the rank *Class A network*. At the other extreme is the *Class C network*, which is reserved for the numerous networks with a small number of nodes. The class distinction for networks between very large and very small is predictably called the *Class B network*.

Subdividing an IP address into a network and node address is determined by the class designation of one's network. Figure 3.20 summarizes the three classes of networks used to address hosts—a subject I'll explain in much greater detail throughout this chapter.

FIGURE 3.20 Summary of the three classes of networks

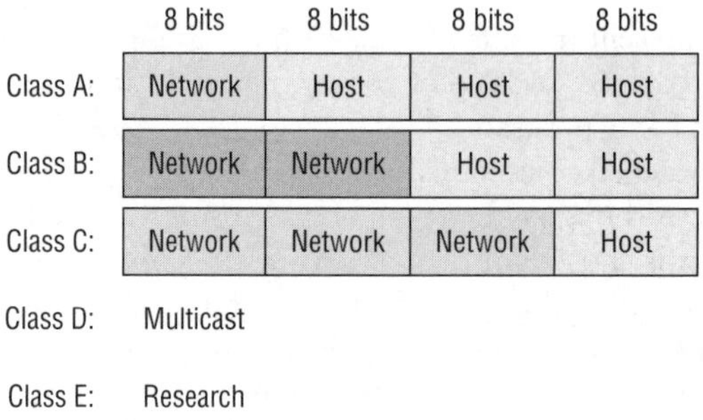

To ensure efficient routing, Internet designers defined a mandate for the leading-bits section of the address for each different network class. For example, since a router knows that a Class A network address always starts with a 0, the router might be able to speed a packet on its way after reading only the first bit of its address. This is where the address schemes define the difference between a Class A, a Class B, and a Class C address. Coming up, I'll discuss the differences between these three classes, followed by a discussion of the Class D and Class E addresses. Classes A, B, and C are the only ranges that are used to address hosts in our networks.

Network Address Range: Class A

The designers of the IP address scheme decided that the first bit of the first byte in a Class A network address must always be off, or 0. This means a Class A address must be between 0 and 127 in the first byte, inclusive.

Consider the following network address:

0xxxxxxx

If we turn the other 7 bits all off and then turn them all on, we'll find the Class A range of network addresses:

00000000 = 0
01111111 = 127

So, a Class A network is defined in the first octet between 0 and 127, and it can't be less or more. Understand that 0 and 127 are not valid in a Class A network because they're reserved addresses, which I'll explain soon.

Network Address Range: Class B

In a Class B network, the RFCs state that the first bit of the first byte must always be turned on but the second bit must always be turned off. If you turn the other 6 bits all off and then all on, you will find the range for a Class B network:

```
10000000 = 128
10111111 = 191
```

As you can see, a Class B network is defined when the first byte is configured from 128 to 191.

Network Address Range: Class C

For Class C networks, the RFCs define the first 2 bits of the first octet as always turned on, but the third bit can never be on. Following the same process as the previous classes, convert from binary to decimal to find the range. Here's the range for a Class C network:

```
11000000 = 192
11011111 = 223
```

So, if you see an IP address that starts at 192 and goes to 223, you'll know it is a Class C IP address.

Network Address Ranges: Classes D and E

The addresses between 224 to 255 are reserved for Class D and E networks. Class D (224–239) is used for multicast addresses and Class E (240–255) for scientific purposes, but I'm not going into these types of addresses because they are beyond the scope of knowledge you need to gain from this book.

Network Addresses: Special Purpose

Some IP addresses are reserved for special purposes, so network administrators can't ever assign these addresses to nodes. Table 3.4 lists the members of this exclusive little club and the reasons why they're included in it.

TABLE 3.4   Reserved IP addresses

Address	Function
Network address of all 0s	Interpreted to mean "this network or segment."
Network address of all 1s	Interpreted to mean "all networks."
Network 127.0.0.1	Reserved for loopback tests. Designates the local node and allows that node to send a test packet to itself without generating network traffic.

TABLE 3.4   Reserved IP addresses *(continued)*

Address	Function
Node address of all 0s	Interpreted to mean "network address" or any host on a specified network.
Node address of all 1s	Interpreted to mean "all nodes" on the specified network; for example, 128.2.255.255 means "all nodes" on network 128.2 (Class B address).
Entire IP address set to all 0s	Used by Cisco routers to designate the default route. Could also mean "any network."
Entire IP address set to all 1s (same as 255.255.255.255)	Broadcast to all nodes on the current network; sometimes called an "all 1s broadcast" or local broadcast.

Class A Addresses

In a Class A network address, the first byte is assigned to the network address and the three remaining bytes are used for the node addresses. The Class A format is as follows:

network.node.node.node

For example, in the IP address 49.22.102.70, the 49 is the network address and 22.102.70 is the node address. Every machine on this particular network would have the distinctive network address of 49.

Class A network addresses are 1 byte long, with the first bit of that byte reserved and the 7 remaining bits available for manipulation (addressing). As a result, the maximum number of Class A networks that can be created is 128. Why? Because each of the 7 bit positions can be either a 0 or a 1, thus 2^7, or 128.

To complicate matters further, the network address of all 0s (0000 0000) is reserved to designate the default route (see Table 3.4 in the previous section). Additionally, the address 127, which is reserved for diagnostics, can't be used either, which means that you can really only use the numbers 1 to 126 to designate Class A network addresses. This means the actual number of usable Class A network addresses is 128 minus 2, or 126.

The IP address 127.0.0.1 is used to test the IP stack on an individual node and cannot be used as a valid host address. However, the loopback address creates a shortcut method for TCP/IP applications and services that run on the same device to communicate with each other.

Each Class A address has 3 bytes (24-bit positions) for the node address of a machine. This means there are 2^{24}—or 16,777,216—unique combinations and, therefore, precisely that many possible unique node addresses for each Class A network. Because node addresses with the two patterns of all 0s and all 1s are reserved, the actual maximum usable number of nodes for a Class A network is 2^{24} minus 2, which equals 16,777,214. Either way, that's a huge number of hosts on a single network segment!

Class A Valid Host IDs

Here's an example of how to figure out the valid host IDs in a Class A network address:

- All host bits off is the network address: 10.0.0.0.
- All host bits on is the broadcast address: 10.255.255.255.

The valid hosts are the numbers in between the network address and the broadcast address: 10.0.0.1 through 10.255.255.254. Notice that 0s and 255s can be valid host IDs. All you need to remember when trying to find valid host addresses is that the host bits can't all be turned off or on at the same time.

Class B Addresses

In a Class B network address, the first 2 bytes are assigned to the network address and the remaining 2 bytes are used for node addresses. The format is as follows:

network.network.node.node

For example, in the IP address 172.16.30.56, the network address is 172.16 and the node address is 30.56.

With a network address being 2 bytes (8 bits each), you get 2^{16} unique combinations. But the Internet designers decided that all Class B network addresses should start with the binary digit 1, then 0. This leaves 14 bit positions to manipulate, therefore 16,384, or 2^{14} unique Class B network addresses.

A Class B address uses 2 bytes for node addresses. This is 2^{16} minus the two reserved patterns of all 0s and all 1s for a total of 65,534 possible node addresses for each Class B network.

Class B Valid Host IDs

Here's an example of how to find the valid hosts in a Class B network:

- All host bits turned off is the network address: 172.16.0.0.
- All host bits turned on is the broadcast address: 172.16.255.255.

The valid hosts would be the numbers in between the network address and the broadcast address: 172.16.0.1 through 172.16.255.254.

Class C Addresses

The first 3 bytes of a Class C network address are dedicated to the network portion of the address, with only 1 measly byte remaining for the node address. Here's the format:

network.network.network.node

Using the example IP address 192.168.100.102, the network address is 192.168.100 and the node address is 102.

In a Class C network address, the first three bit positions are always the binary 110. The calculation is as follows: 3 bytes, or 24 bits, minus 3 reserved positions leaves 21 positions. Hence, there are 2^{21}, or 2,097,152, possible Class C networks.

Each unique Class C network has 1 byte to use for node addresses. This leads to 2^8, or 256, minus the two reserved patterns of all 0s and all 1s, for a total of 254 node addresses for each Class C network.

Class C Valid Host IDs

Here's an example of how to find a valid host ID in a Class C network:

- All host bits turned off is the network ID: 192.168.100.0.
- All host bits turned on is the broadcast address: 192.168.100.255.

The valid hosts would be the numbers in between the network address and the broadcast address: 192.168.100.1 through 192.168.100.254.

Private IP Addresses (RFC 1918)

The people who created the IP addressing scheme also created private IP addresses. These addresses can be used on a private network, but they're not routable through the Internet. This is designed for the purpose of creating a measure of well-needed security, but it also conveniently saves valuable IP address space.

If every host on every network was required to have real routable IP addresses, we would have run out of IP addresses to hand out years ago. But by using private IP addresses, ISPs, corporations, and home users only need a relatively tiny group of bona fide IP addresses to connect their networks to the Internet. This is economical because they can use private IP addresses on their inside networks and get along just fine.

To accomplish this task, the ISP and the corporation—the end user, no matter who they are—need to use something called *Network Address Translation (NAT)*, which basically takes a private IP address and converts it for use on the Internet. NAT is covered in Chapter 13, "Network Address Translation (NAT)." Many people can use the same real IP address to transmit out onto the Internet. Doing things this way saves megatons of address space—good for us all!

The reserved private addresses are listed in Table 3.5.

TABLE 3.5 Reserved IP address space

Address Class	Reserved Address Space
Class A	10.0.0.0 through 10.255.255.255
Class B	172.16.0.0 through 172.31.255.255
Class C	192.168.0.0 through 192.168.255.255

You must know your private address space to become Cisco certified!

So, What Private IP Address Should I Use?

That's a really great question: Should you use Class A, Class B, or even Class C private addressing when setting up your network? Let's take Acme Corporation in SF as an example. This company is moving into a new building and needs a whole new network. It has 14 departments, with about 70 users in each. You could probably squeeze one or two Class C addresses to use, or maybe you could use a Class B, or even a Class A just for fun.

The rule of thumb in the consulting world is, when you're setting up a corporate network— regardless of how small it is—you should use a Class A network address because it gives you the most flexibility and growth options. For example, if you used the 10.0.0.0 network address with a /24 mask, then you'd have 65,536 networks, each with 254 hosts. Lots of room for growth with that network!

But if you're setting up a home network, you'd opt for a Class C address because it is the easiest for people to understand and configure. Using the default Class C mask gives you one network with 254 hosts—plenty for a home network.

With the Acme Corporation, a nice 10.1.x.0 with a /24 mask (the x is the subnet for each department) makes this easy to design, install, and troubleshoot.

IPv4 Address Types

Most people use the term *broadcast* as a generic term, and most of the time, we understand what they mean—but not always! For example, you might say, "The host broadcasted through a router to a DHCP server," but, well, it's pretty unlikely that this would ever really happen. What you probably mean—using the correct technical jargon—is, "The DHCP client broadcasted for an IP address and a router then forwarded this as a unicast packet to the DHCP server." Oh, and remember that with IPv4, broadcasts are pretty important, but with IPv6, there aren't any broadcasts sent at all—now there's something to look forward to reading about in Chapter 14!

Okay, I've referred to IP addresses throughout the preceding chapters and now all throughout this chapter, and even showed you some examples. But I really haven't gone into the different terms and uses associated with them yet, and it's about time I did. So here are the address types that I'd like to define for you:

Loopback (localhost)   Used to test the IP stack on the local computer. Can be any address from 127.0.0.1 through 127.255.255.254.

Layer 2 broadcasts   These are sent to all nodes on a LAN.

Broadcasts (layer 3)   These are sent to all nodes on the network.

Unicast   This is an address for a single interface, and these are used to send packets to a single destination host.

Multicast   These are packets sent from a single source and transmitted to many devices on different networks. Referred to as "one-to-many."

Layer 2 Broadcasts

First, understand that layer 2 broadcasts are also known as hardware broadcasts—they only go out on a LAN, but they don't go past the LAN boundary (router).

The typical hardware address is 6 bytes (48 bits) and looks something like 45:AC:24:E3:60:A5. The broadcast would be all 1s in binary, which would be all *F*s in hexadecimal, as in ff:ff:ff:ff:ff:ff and shown in Figure 3.21.

FIGURE 3.21   Local layer 2 broadcasts

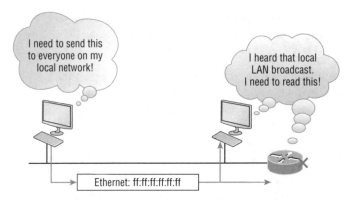

Every network interface card (NIC) will receive and read the frame, including the router, since this was a layer 2 broadcast, but the router would never, ever forward this!

Layer 3 Broadcasts

Then there are the plain old broadcast addresses at layer 3. Broadcast messages are meant to reach all hosts on a broadcast domain. These are the network broadcasts that have all host bits on.

Here's an example that you're already familiar with: The network address of 172.16.0.0 255.255.0.0 would have a broadcast address of 172.16.255.255—all host bits on. Broadcasts can also be "any network and all hosts," as indicated by 255.255.255.255, and shown in Figure 3.22.

FIGURE 3.22   Layer 3 broadcasts

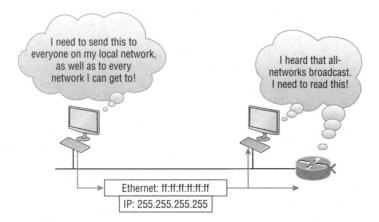

In Figure 3.22, all hosts on the LAN will get this broadcast on their NIC, including the router, but by default the router would never forward this packet.

Unicast Address

A unicast is defined as a single IP address that's assigned to a network interface card and is the destination IP address in a packet—in other words, it's used for directing packets to a specific host.

In Figure 3.23, both the MAC address and the destination IP address are for a single NIC on the network. All hosts on the broadcast domain would receive this frame and accept it. Only the destination NIC of 10.1.1.2 would accept the packet; the other NICs would discard the packet.

FIGURE 3.23   Unicast address

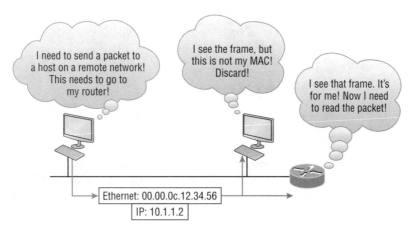

Multicast Address

Multicast is a different beast entirely. At first glance, it appears to be a hybrid of unicast and broadcast communication, but that isn't quite the case. Multicast does allow point-to-multipoint communication, which is similar to broadcasts, but it happens in a different manner. The crux of *multicast* is that it enables multiple recipients to receive messages without flooding the messages to all hosts on a broadcast domain. However, this is not the default behavior—it's what we *can* do with multicasting if it's configured correctly!

Multicast works by sending messages or data to IP *multicast group* addresses. Unlike with broadcasts, which aren't forwarded, routers then forward copies of the packet out to every interface that has hosts *subscribed* to that group address. This is where multicast differs from broadcast messages—with multicast communication, copies of packets, in theory, are sent only to subscribed hosts. For example, when I say in theory, I mean that the hosts will receive a multicast packet destined for 224.0.0.10. This is an EIGRP packet, and only a router running the EIGRP protocol will read these. All hosts on the broadcast LAN, and Ethernet is a broadcast multi-access LAN technology, will pick up the frame, read the destination address, then immediately discard the frame unless they're in the multicast group. This saves PC processing, not LAN bandwidth. Be warned though—multicasting can cause some serious LAN congestion if it's not implemented carefully! Figure 3.24 shows a Cisco router sending an EIGRP multicast packet on the local LAN and only the other Cisco router will accept and read this packet.

FIGURE 3.24 EIGRP multicast example

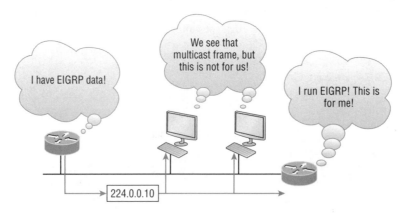

There are several different groups that users or applications can subscribe to. The range of multicast addresses starts with 224.0.0.0 and goes through 239.255.255.255. As you can see, this range of addresses falls within IP Class D address space based on classful IP assignment.

Summary

If you made it this far and understood everything the first time through, you should be extremely proud of yourself! We really covered a lot of ground in this chapter, but understand that the information in it is critical to being able to navigate well through the rest of this book.

If you didn't get a complete understanding the first time around, don't stress. It really wouldn't hurt you to read this chapter more than once. There is still a lot of ground to cover, so make sure you've got this material all nailed down. That way, you'll be ready for more, and just so you know, there's a lot more! What we're doing up to this point is building a solid foundation to build upon as you advance.

With that in mind, after you learned about the DoD model, the layers, and associated protocols, you learned about the oh-so-important topic of IP addressing. I discussed in detail the difference between each address class, how to find a network address and broadcast address, and what denotes a valid host address range. I can't stress enough how important it is for you to have this critical information unshakably understood before moving on to Chapter 4!

Since you've already come this far, there's no reason to stop now and waste all those brainwaves and new neural connections. So don't stop—go through the written labs and review questions at the end of this chapter and make sure you understand each answer's explanation. The best is yet to come!

Exam Essentials

Differentiate between the DoD and the OSI network models.   The DoD model is a condensed version of the OSI model, composed of four layers instead of seven, but is nonetheless like the OSI model in that it can be used to describe packet creation and devices and protocols can be mapped to its layers.

Identify Process/Application layer protocols.   Telnet is a terminal emulation program that allows you to log into a remote host and run programs. File Transfer Protocol (FTP) is a connection-oriented service that allows you to transfer files. Trivial FTP (TFTP) is a connectionless file transfer program. Simple Mail Transfer Protocol (SMTP) is a sendmail program.

Identify Host-to-Host layer protocols.   Transmission Control Protocol (TCP) is a connection-oriented protocol that provides reliable network service by using acknowledgments and flow control. User Datagram Protocol (UDP) is a connectionless protocol that provides low overhead and is considered unreliable.

Identify Internet layer protocols.   Internet Protocol (IP) is a connectionless protocol that provides network address and routing through an internetwork. Address Resolution Protocol (ARP) finds a hardware address from a known IP address. Reverse ARP (RARP) finds an IP address from a known hardware address. Internet Control Message Protocol (ICMP) provides diagnostics and destination unreachable messages.

Describe the functions of DNS and DHCP in the network.   Dynamic Host Configuration Protocol (DHCP) provides network configuration information (including IP addresses) to hosts, eliminating the need to perform the configurations manually. Domain Name Service (DNS) resolves hostnames—both Internet names such as www.lammle.com and device names such as Workstation 2—to IP addresses, eliminating the need to know the IP address of a device for connection purposes.

Identify what is contained in the TCP header of a connection-oriented transmission. The fields in the TCP header include the source port, destination port, sequence number, acknowledgment number, header length, a field reserved for future use, code bits, window size, checksum, urgent pointer, options field, and finally, the data field.

Identify what is contained in the UDP header of a connectionless transmission.   The fields in the UDP header include only the source port, destination port, length, checksum, and data. The smaller number of fields as compared to the TCP header comes at the expense of providing none of the more advanced functions of the TCP frame.

Identify what is contained in the IP header.   The fields of an IP header include version, header length, priority or type of service, total length, identification, flags, fragment offset, time to live, protocol, header checksum, source IP address, destination IP address, options, and finally, data.

Compare and contrast UDP and TCP characteristics and features.   TCP is connection-oriented, acknowledged, and sequenced and has flow and error control, while UDP is connectionless, unacknowledged, and not sequenced and provides no error or flow control.

Understand the role of port numbers.   Port numbers are used to identify the protocol or service that is to be used in the transmission.

Identify the role of ICMP.   Internet Control Message Protocol (ICMP) works at the Network layer and is used by IP for many different services. ICMP is a management protocol and messaging service provider for IP.

Define the Class A IP address range.   The IP range for a Class A network is 1–126. This provides 8 bits of network addressing and 24 bits of host addressing by default.

Define the Class B IP address range.   The IP range for a Class B network is 128–191. Class B addressing provides 16 bits of network addressing and 16 bits of host addressing by default.

Define the Class C IP address range.   The IP range for a Class C network is 192 through 223. Class C addressing provides 24 bits of network addressing and 8 bits of host addressing by default.

Identify the private IP ranges.   The Class A private address range is 10.0.0.0 through 10.255.255.255. The Class B private address range is 172.16.0.0 through 172.31.255.255. The Class C private address range is 192.168.0.0 through 192.168.255.255.

Understand the difference between a broadcast, unicast, and multicast address.   A broadcast is to all devices in a subnet, a unicast is to one device, and a multicast is to some but not all devices.

Written Labs

In this section, you'll complete the following labs to make sure you've got the information and concepts contained within them fully dialed in:

Lab 3.1: TCP/IP

Lab 3.2: Mapping Applications to the DoD Model

You can find the answers to these labs in Appendix A, "Answers to Written Labs."

Written Lab 3.1: TCP/IP

Answer the following questions about TCP/IP:

1. What is the Class C address range in decimal and in binary?
2. What layer of the DoD model is equivalent to the Transport layer of the OSI model?
3. What is the valid range of a Class A network address?
4. What is the 127.0.0.1 address used for?
5. How do you find the network address from a listed IP address?
6. How do you find the broadcast address from a listed IP address?
7. What is the Class A private IP address space?
8. What is the Class B private IP address space?
9. What is the Class C private IP address space?
10. What are all the available characters that you can use in hexadecimal addressing?

Written Lab 3.2: Mapping Applications to the DoD Model

The four layers of the DoD model are Process/Application, Host-to-Host, Internet, and Network Access. Identify the layer of the DoD model on which each of these protocols operates.

1. Internet Protocol (IP)
2. Telnet
3. FTP
4. SNMP
5. DNS
6. Address Resolution Protocol (ARP)
7. DHCP/BootP
8. Transmission Control Protocol (TCP)
9. X Window

10. User Datagram Protocol (UDP)

11. NFS

12. Internet Control Message Protocol (ICMP)

13. Reverse Address Resolution Protocol (RARP)

14. Proxy ARP

15. TFTP

16. SMTP

17. LPD

Review Questions

 The following questions are designed to test your understanding of this chapter's material. For more information on how to get additional questions, please see www.lammle.com/ccna.

You can find the answers to these questions in Appendix B, "Answers to Review Questions."

1. What must happen if a DHCP IP conflict occurs?

    A. Proxy ARP will fix the issue.

    B. The client uses a gratuitous ARP to fix the issue.

    C. The administrator must fix the conflict by hand at the DHCP server.

    D. The DHCP server will reassign new IP addresses to both computers.

2. Which of the following Application layer protocols sets up a secure session that's similar to Telnet?

    A. FTP

    B. SSH

    C. DNS

    D. DHCP

3. Which of the following mechanisms is used by the client to avoid a duplicate IP address during the DHCP process?

    A. Ping

    B. Traceroute

    C. Gratuitous ARP

    D. Pathping

4. What protocol is used to find the hardware address of a local device?

    A. RARP

    B. ARP

    C. IP

    D. ICMP

    E. BootP

5.   Which of the following are layers in the TCP/IP model? (Choose three.)

   A.   Application

   B.   Session

   C.   Transport

   D.   Internet

   E.   Data Link

   F.   Physical

6.   Which class of IP address provides a maximum of only 254 host addresses per network ID?

   A.   Class A

   B.   Class B

   C.   Class C

   D.   Class D

   E.   Class E

7.   Which of the following describe the DHCP Discover message? (Choose two.)

   A.   It uses ff:ff:ff:ff:ff:ff as a layer 2 broadcast.

   B.   It uses UDP as the Transport layer protocol.

   C.   It uses TCP as the Transport layer protocol.

   D.   It does not use a layer 2 destination address.

8.   Which layer 4 protocol is used for a Telnet connection?

   A.   IP

   B.   TCP

   C.   TCP/IP

   D.   UDP

   E.   ICMP

9.   Private IP addressing was specified in RFC _____ .

10. Which of the following services use TCP? (Choose three.)

   A.   DHCP

   B.   SMTP

   C.   SNMP

   D.   FTP

   E.   HTTP

   F.   TFTP

11. Which Class of IP addresses uses the pattern shown here?

Network	Network	Network	Host

A. Class A

B. Class B

C. Class C

D. Class D

12. Which of the following is an example of a multicast address?

A. 10.6.9.1

B. 192.168.10.6

C. 224.0.0.10

D. 172.16.9.5

13. The following illustration shows a data structure header. What protocol is this header from?

16-Bit Source Port		16-Bit Destination Port	
32-Bit Sequence Number			
32-Bit Acknowledgement Number			
4-Bit Header Length	Reserved	Flags	16-Bit Window Size
16-bit TCP Checksum		16-bit Urgent Pointer	
Options			
Data			

A. IP

B. ICMP

C. TCP

D. UDP

E. ARP

F. RARP

14. If you use either Telnet or FTP, what layer are you using to generate the data?

A. Application

B. Presentation

C. Session

D. Transport

15. The DoD model (also called the TCP/IP stack) has four layers. Which layer of the DoD model is equivalent to the Network layer of the OSI model?

  A. Application

  B. Host-to-Host

  C. Internet

  D. Network Access

16. Which two of the following are private IP addresses?

  A. 12.0.0.1

  B. 168.172.19.39

  C. 172.20.14.36

  D. 172.33.194.30

  E. 192.168.24.43

17. What layer in the TCP/IP stack is equivalent to the Transport layer of the OSI model?

  A. Application

  B. Host-to-Host

  C. Internet

  D. Network Access

18. Which statements are true regarding ICMP packets? (Choose two.)

  A. ICMP guarantees datagram delivery.

  B. ICMP can provide hosts with information about network problems.

  C. ICMP is encapsulated within IP datagrams.

  D. ICMP is encapsulated within UDP datagrams.

19. What is the address range of a Class B network address in binary?

  A. 01*xxxxxx*

  B. 0*xxxxxxx*

  C. 10*xxxxxx*

  D. 110*xxxxx*

20. Drag the steps in the DHCP process and place them in the correct order on the right.

  DHCPOffer   Drop Target A

  DHCPDiscover   Drop Target B

  DHCPAck   Drop Target C

  DHCPRequest   Drop Target D

Chapter

4

Easy Subnetting

THE FOLLOWING ICND1 EXAM TOPICS ARE COVERED IN THIS CHAPTER:

✓ **Network Fundamentals**

- 1.8 Configure, verify, and troubleshoot IPv4 addressing and subnetting

We'll pick up right where we left off in the last chapter and continue to explore the world of IP addressing. I'll open this chapter by telling you how to subnet an IP network—an indispensably crucial skill that's central to mastering networking in general! Forewarned is forearmed, so prepare yourself because being able to subnet quickly and accurately is pretty challenging and you'll need time to practice what you've learned to really nail it. So be patient and don't give up on this key aspect of networking until your skills are seriously sharp. I'm not kidding—this chapter is so important you should really just graft it into your brain!

So be ready because we're going to hit the ground running and thoroughly cover IP subnetting from the very start. And though I know this will sound weird to you, you'll be much better off if you just try to forget everything you've learned about subnetting before reading this chapter—especially if you've been to an official Cisco or Microsoft class! I think these forms of special torture often do more harm than good and sometimes even scare people away from networking completely. Those that survive and persevere usually at least question the sanity of continuing to study in this field. If this is you, relax, breathe, and know that you'll find that the way I tackle the issue of subnetting is relatively painless because I'm going to show you a whole new, much easier method to conquer this monster!

After working through this chapter, and I can't say this enough, after working through the extra study material at the end as well, you'll be able to tame the IP addressing/subnetting beast—just don't give up! I promise that you'll be really glad you didn't. It's one of those things that once you get it down, you'll wonder why you used to think it was so hard!

To find up-to-the minute updates for this chapter, please see www.lammle .com/ccna or the book's web page at www.sybex.com/go/ccna.

Subnetting Basics

In Chapter 3, "Introduction to TCP/IP," you learned how to define and find the valid host ranges used in a Class A, Class B, and Class C network address by turning the host bits all off and then all on. This is very good, but here's the catch: you were defining only one network, as shown in Figure 4.1.

FIGURE 4.1   One network

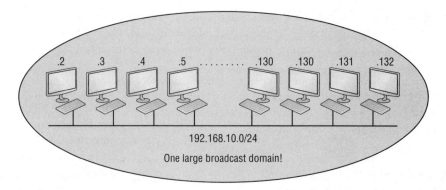

By now you know that having one large network is not a good thing because the first three chapters you just read were veritably peppered with me incessantly telling you that! But how would you fix the out-of-control problem that Figure 4.1 illustrates? Wouldn't it be nice to be able to break up that one, huge network address and create four manageable networks from it? You betcha it would, but to make that happen, you would need to apply the infamous trick of *subnetting* because it's the best way to break up a giant network into a bunch of smaller ones. Take a look at Figure 4.2 and see how this might look.

FIGURE 4.2   Multiple networks connected together

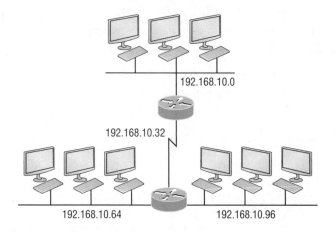

What are those 192.168.10.*x* addresses shown in the figure? Well that is what this chapter will explain—how to make one network into many networks!

Let's take off from where we left in Chapter 3 and start working in the host section (host bits) of a network address, where we can borrow bits to create subnets.

How to Create Subnets

Creating subnetworks is essentially the act of taking bits from the host portion of the address and reserving them to define the subnet address instead. Clearly this will result in fewer bits being available for defining your hosts, which is something you'll always want to keep in mind.

Later in this chapter, I'll guide you through the entire process of creating subnets starting with Class C addresses. As always in networking, before you actually implement anything, including subnetting, you must first determine your current requirements and make sure to plan for future conditions as well.

In this first section, we'll be discussing classful routing, which refers to the fact that all hosts (nodes) in the network are using the exact same subnet mask. Later, when we move on to cover variable length subnet masks (VLSMs), I'll tell you all about classless routing, which is an environment wherein each network segment *can* use a different subnet mask.

To create a subnet, we'll start by fulfilling these three steps:

1. Determine the number of required network IDs:
   - One for each LAN subnet
   - One for each wide area network connection
2. Determine the number of required host IDs per subnet:
   - One for each TCP/IP host
   - One for each router interface
3. Based on the previous requirements, create the following:
   - A unique subnet mask for your entire network
   - A unique subnet ID for each physical segment
   - A range of host IDs for each subnet

Subnet Masks

For the subnet address scheme to work, every machine on the network must know which part of the host address will be used as the subnet address. This condition is met by assigning a *subnet mask* to each machine. A subnet mask is a 32-bit value that allows the device that's receiving IP packets to distinguish the network ID portion of the IP address from the host ID portion of the IP address. This 32-bit subnet mask is composed of 1s and 0s, where the 1s represent the positions that refer to the network subnet addresses.

Not all networks need subnets, and if not, it really means that they're using the default subnet mask, which is basically the same as saying that a network doesn't have a subnet address. Table 4.1 shows the default subnet masks for Classes A, B, and C.

TABLE 4.1   Default subnet mask

Class	Format	Default Subnet Mask
A	*network.node.node.node*	255.0.0.0
B	*network.network.node.node*	255.255.0.0
C	*network.network.network.node*	255.255.255.0

Although you can use any mask in any way on an interface, typically it's not usually good to mess with the default masks. In other words, you don't want to make a Class B subnet mask read 255.0.0.0, and some hosts won't even let you type it in. But these days, most devices will. For a Class A network, you wouldn't change the first byte in a subnet mask because it should read 255.0.0.0 at a minimum. Similarly, you wouldn't assign 255.255.255.255 because this is all 1s, which is a broadcast address. A Class B address starts with 255.255.0.0, and a Class C starts with 255.255.255.0, and for the CCNA especially, there is no reason to change the defaults!

Understanding the Powers of 2

Powers of 2 are important to understand and memorize for use with IP subnetting. Reviewing powers of 2, remember that when you see a number noted with an exponent, it means you should multiply the number by itself as many times as the upper number specifies. For example, 2^3 is 2 x 2 x 2, which equals 8. Here's a list of powers of 2 to commit to memory:

$2^1 = 2$

$2^2 = 4$

$2^3 = 8$

$2^4 = 16$

$2^5 = 32$

$2^6 = 64$

$2^7 = 128$

$2^8 = 256$

$2^9 = 512$

$2^{10} = 1,024$

$2^{11} = 2,048$

$2^{12} = 4,096$

$2^{13} = 8,192$

$2^{14} = 16,384$

Memorizing these powers of 2 is a good idea, but it's not absolutely necessary. Just remember that since you're working with powers of 2, each successive power of 2 is double the previous one.

It works like this—all you have to do to remember the value of 2^9 is to first know that $2^8 = 256$. Why? Because when you double 2 to the eighth power (256), you get 2^9 (or 512). To determine the value of 2^{10}, simply start at $2^8 = 256$, and then double it twice.

You can go the other way as well. If you needed to know what 2^6 is, for example, you just cut 256 in half two times: once to reach 2^7 and then one more time to reach 2^6.

Classless Inter-Domain Routing (CIDR)

Another term you need to familiarize yourself with is *Classless Inter-Domain Routing (CIDR)*. It's basically the method that Internet service providers (ISPs) use to allocate a number of addresses to a company, a home—their customers. They provide addresses in a certain block size, something I'll talk about in greater detail soon.

When you receive a block of addresses from an ISP, what you get will look something like this: 192.168.10.32/28. This is telling you what your subnet mask is. The slash notation (/) means how many bits are turned on (1s). Obviously, the maximum could only be /32 because a byte is 8 bits and there are 4 bytes in an IP address: (4 × 8 = 32). But keep in mind that regardless of the class of address, the largest subnet mask available relevant to the Cisco exam objectives can only be a /30 because you've got to keep at least 2 bits for host bits.

Take, for example, a Class A default subnet mask, which is 255.0.0.0. This tells us that the first byte of the subnet mask is all ones (1s), or 11111111. When referring to a slash notation, you need to count all the 1 bits to figure out your mask. The 255.0.0.0 is considered a /8 because it has 8 bits that are 1s—that is, 8 bits that are turned on.

A Class B default mask would be 255.255.0.0, which is a /16 because 16 bits are ones (1s): 11111111.11111111.00000000.00000000.

Table 4.2 has a listing of every available subnet mask and its equivalent CIDR slash notation.

TABLE 4.2 CIDR values

Subnet Mask	CIDR Value
255.0.0.0	/8
255.128.0.0	/9

Subnet Mask	CIDR Value
255.192.0.0	/10
255.224.0.0	/11
255.240.0.0	/12
255.248.0.0	/13
255.252.0.0	/14
255.254.0.0	/15
255.255.0.0	/16
255.255.128.0	/17
255.255.192.0	/18
255.255.224.0	/19
255.255.240.0	/20
255.255.248.0	/21
255.255.252.0	/22
255.255.254.0	/23
255.255.255.0	/24
255.255.255.128	/25
255.255.255.192	/26
255.255.255.224	/27
255.255.255.240	/28
255.255.255.248	/29
255.255.255.252	/30

The /8 through /15 can only be used with Class A network addresses. /16 through /23 can be used by Class A and B network addresses. /24 through /30 can be used by Class A, B, and C network addresses. This is a big reason why most companies use Class A network addresses. Since they can use all subnet masks, they get the maximum flexibility in network design.

> No, you cannot configure a Cisco router using this slash format. But wouldn't that be nice? Nevertheless, it's *really* important for you to know subnet masks in the slash notation (CIDR).

IP Subnet-Zero

Even though `ip subnet-zero` is not a new command, Cisco courseware and Cisco exam objectives didn't used to cover it. Know that Cisco certainly covers it now! This command allows you to use the first and last subnet in your network design. For instance, the Class C mask of 255.255.255.192 provides subnets 64 and 128, another facet of subnetting that we'll discuss more thoroughly later in this chapter. But with the `ip subnet-zero` command, you now get to use subnets 0, 64, 128, and 192. It may not seem like a lot, but this provides two more subnets for every subnet mask we use.

Even though we don't discuss the command-line interface (CLI) until Chapter 6, "Cisco's Internetworking Operating System (IOS)," it's important for you to be at least a little familiar with this command at this point:

```
Router#sh running-config
Building configuration...
Current configuration : 827 bytes
!
hostname Pod1R1
!
ip subnet-zero
!
```

This router output shows that the command `ip subnet-zero` is enabled on the router. Cisco has turned this command on by default starting with Cisco IOS version 12.*x* and now we're running 15.*x* code.

When taking your Cisco exams, make sure you read very carefully to see if Cisco is asking you *not* to use `ip subnet-zero`. There are actually instances where this may happen.

Subnetting Class C Addresses

There are many different ways to subnet a network. The right way is the way that works best for you. In a Class C address, only 8 bits are available for defining the hosts. Remember that subnet bits start at the left and move to the right, without skipping bits. This means that the only Class C subnet masks can be the following:

```
Binary      Decimal   CIDR
-----------------------------------------------------------
00000000 = 255.255.255.0       /24
10000000 = 255.255.255.128     /25
11000000 = 255.255.255.192     /26
11100000 = 255.255.255.224     /27
11110000 = 255.255.255.240     /28
11111000 = 255.255.255.248     /29
11111100 = 255.255.255.252     /30
```

We can't use a /31 or /32 because, as I've said, we must have at least 2 host bits for assigning IP addresses to hosts. But this is only mostly true. Certainly we can never use a /32 because that would mean zero host bits available, yet Cisco has various forms of the IOS, as well as the new Cisco Nexus switches operating system, that support the /31 mask. The /31 is above the scope of the CCENT and CCNA objectives, so we won't be covering it in this book.

Coming up, I'm going to teach you that significantly less painful method of subnetting I promised you at the beginning of this chapter, which makes it ever so much easier to subnet larger numbers in a flash. Excited? Good! Because I'm not kidding when I tell you that you absolutely need to be able to subnet quickly and accurately to succeed in the networking real world and on the exam too!

Subnetting a Class C Address—The Fast Way!

When you've chosen a possible subnet mask for your network and need to determine the number of subnets, valid hosts, and the broadcast addresses of a subnet that mask will provide, all you need to do is answer five simple questions:

- How many subnets does the chosen subnet mask produce?
- How many valid hosts per subnet are available?
- What are the valid subnets?
- What's the broadcast address of each subnet?
- What are the valid hosts in each subnet?

This is where you'll be really glad you followed my advice and took the time to memorize your powers of 2. If you didn't, now would be a good time... Just refer back to the sidebar "Understanding the Powers of 2" earlier if you need to brush up. Here's how you arrive at the answers to those five big questions:

- *How many subnets?* 2^x = number of subnets. x is the number of masked bits, or the 1s. For example, in 11000000, the number of 1s gives us 2^2 subnets. So in this example, there are 4 subnets.

- *How many hosts per subnet?* $2^y - 2$ = number of hosts per subnet. y is the number of unmasked bits, or the 0s. For example, in 11000000, the number of 0s gives us $2^6 - 2$ hosts, or 62 hosts per subnet. You need to subtract 2 for the subnet address and the broadcast address, which are not valid hosts.

- *What are the valid subnets?* 256 – subnet mask = block size, or increment number. An example would be the 255.255.255.192 mask, where the interesting octet is the fourth octet (interesting because that is where our subnet numbers are). Just use this math: 256 – 192 = 64. The block size of a 192 mask is always 64. Start counting at zero in blocks of 64 until you reach the subnet mask value and these are your subnets in the fourth octet: 0, 64, 128, 192. Easy, huh?

- *What's the broadcast address for each subnet?* Now here's the really easy part. Since we counted our subnets in the last section as 0, 64, 128, and 192, the broadcast address is always the number right before the next subnet. For example, the 0 subnet has a broadcast address of 63 because the next subnet is 64. The 64 subnet has a broadcast address of 127 because the next subnet is 128, and so on. Remember, the broadcast address of the last subnet is always 255.

- *What are the valid hosts?* Valid hosts are the numbers between the subnets, omitting the all-0s and all-1s. For example, if 64 is the subnet number and 127 is the broadcast address, then 65–126 is the valid host range. Your valid range is *always* the group of numbers between the subnet address and the broadcast address.

If you're still confused, don't worry because it really isn't as hard as it seems to be at first—just hang in there! To help lift any mental fog, try a few of the practice examples next.

Subnetting Practice Examples: Class C Addresses

Here's your opportunity to practice subnetting Class C addresses using the method I just described. This is so cool. We're going to start with the first Class C subnet mask and work through every subnet that we can, using a Class C address. When we're done, I'll show you how easy this is with Class A and B networks too!

Practice Example #1C: 255.255.255.128 (/25)

Since 128 is 10000000 in binary, there is only 1 bit for subnetting and 7 bits for hosts. We're going to subnet the Class C network address 192.168.10.0.

192.168.10.0 = Network address

255.255.255.128 = Subnet mask

Now, let's answer our big five:

- *How many subnets?* Since 128 is 1 bit on (10000000), the answer would be $2^1 = 2$.

- *How many hosts per subnet?* We have 7 host bits off (**10000000**), so the equation would be $2^7 - 2 = 126$ hosts. Once you figure out the block size of a mask, the amount of hosts is always the block size minus 2. No need to do extra math if you don't need to!

- *What are the valid subnets?* 256 – 128 = 128. Remember, we'll start at zero and count in our block size, so our subnets are 0, 128. By just counting your subnets when counting in your block size, you really don't need to do steps 1 and 2. We can see we have two subnets, and in the step before this one, just remember that the amount of hosts is always the block size minus 2, and in this example, that gives us 2 subnets, each with 126 hosts.

- *What's the broadcast address for each subnet?* The number right before the value of the next subnet is all host bits turned on and equals the broadcast address. For the zero subnet, the next subnet is 128, so the broadcast of the 0 subnet is 127.

- *What are the valid hosts?* These are the numbers between the subnet and broadcast address. The easiest way to find the hosts is to write out the subnet address and the broadcast address, which makes valid hosts completely obvious. The following table shows the 0 and 128 subnets, the valid host ranges of each, and the broadcast address of both subnets:

Subnet	0	128
First host	1	129
Last host	126	254
Broadcast	127	255

Looking at a Class C /25, it's pretty clear that there are two subnets. But so what—why is this significant? Well actually, it's not because that's not the right question. What you really want to know is what you would do with this information!

I know this isn't exactly everyone's favorite pastime, but what we're about to do is really important, so bear with me; we're going to talk about subnetting—period. The key to understanding subnetting is to understand the very reason you need to do it, and I'm going to demonstrate this by going through the process of building a physical network.

Okay—because we added that router shown in Figure 4.3, in order for the hosts on our internetwork to communicate, they must now have a logical network addressing scheme. We could use IPv6, but IPv4 is still the most popular for now. It's also what we're studying at the moment, so that's what we're going with.

FIGURE 4.3   Implementing a Class C /25 logical network

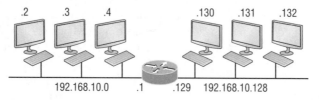

```
Router#show ip route
[output cut]
C 192.168.10.0 is directly connected to Ethernet 0
C 192.168.10.128 is directly connected to Ethernet 1
```

Looking at Figure 4.3, you can see that there are two physical networks, so we're going to implement a logical addressing scheme that allows for two logical networks. As always, it's a really good idea to look ahead and consider likely short- and long-term growth scenarios, but for this example in this book, a /25 gets it done.

Figure 4.3 shows us that both subnets have been assigned to a router interface, which creates our broadcast domains and assigns our subnets. Use the command show ip route to see the routing table on a router. Notice that instead of one large broadcast domain, there are now two smaller broadcast domains, providing for up to 126 hosts in each. The C in the router output translates to "directly connected network," and we can see we have two of those with two broadcast domains and that we created and implemented them. So congratulations—you did it! You have successfully subnetted a network and applied it to a network design. Nice! Let's do it again.

Practice Example #2C: 255.255.255.192 (/26)

This time, we're going to subnet the network address 192.168.10.0 using the subnet mask 255.255.255.192.

> 192.168.10.0 = Network address
>
> 255.255.255.192 = Subnet mask

Now, let's answer the big five:

- *How many subnets?* Since 192 is 2 bits on (**11**000000), the answer would be $2^2 = 4$ subnets.

- *How many hosts per subnet?* We have 6 host bits off (11**000000**), giving us $2^6 - 2 = 62$ hosts. The amount of hosts is always the block size minus 2.

- *What are the valid subnets?* 256 – 192 = 64. Remember to start at zero and count in our block size. This means our subnets are 0, 64, 128, and 192. We can see we have a block size of 64, so we have 4 subnets, each with 62 hosts.

- *What's the broadcast address for each subnet?* The number right before the value of the next subnet is all host bits turned on and equals the broadcast address. For the zero subnet, the next subnet is 64, so the broadcast address for the zero subnet is 63.

- *What are the valid hosts?* These are the numbers between the subnet and broadcast address. As I said, the easiest way to find the hosts is to write out the subnet address and the broadcast address, which clearly delimits our valid hosts. The following table shows the 0, 64, 128, and 192 subnets, the valid host ranges of each, and the broadcast address of each subnet:

The subnets (do this first)	0	64	128	192
Our first host (perform host addressing last)	1	65	129	193
Our last host	62	126	190	254
The broadcast address (do this second)	63	127	191	255

Again, before getting into the next example, you can see that we can now subnet a /26 as long as we can count in increments of 64. And what are you going to do with this fascinating information? Implement it! We'll use Figure 4.4 to practice a /26 network implementation.

FIGURE 4.4   Implementing a class C /26 (with three networks)

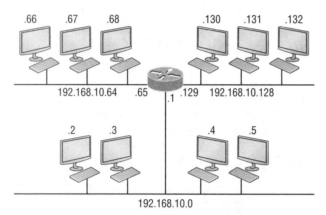

```
Router#show ip route
[output cut]
C 192.168.10.0 is directly connected to Ethernet 0
C 192.168.10.64 is directly connected to Ethernet 1
C 192.168.10.128 is directly connected to Ethernet 2
```

The /26 mask provides four subnetworks, and we need a subnet for each router interface. With this mask, in this example, we actually have room with a spare subnet to add to another router interface in the future. Always plan for growth if possible!

Practice Example #3C: 255.255.255.224 (/27)

This time, we'll subnet the network address 192.168.10.0 and subnet mask 255.255.255.224.

192.168.10.0 = Network address

255.255.255.224 = Subnet mask

- *How many subnets?* 224 is 11100000, so our equation would be $2^3 = 8$.

- *How many hosts?* $2^5 - 2 = 30$.

- *What are the valid subnets?* 256 − 224 = 32. We just start at zero and count to the subnet mask value in blocks (increments) of 32: 0, 32, 64, 96, 128, 160, 192, and 224.

- *What's the broadcast address for each subnet (always the number right before the next subnet)?*

- *What are the valid hosts (the numbers between the subnet number and the broadcast address)?*

To answer the last two questions, first just write out the subnets, then write out the broadcast addresses—the number right before the next subnet. Last, fill in the host addresses. The following table gives you all the subnets for the 255.255.255.224 Class C subnet mask:

The subnet address	0	32	64	96	128	160	192	224
The first valid host	1	33	65	97	129	161	193	225
The last valid host	30	62	94	126	158	190	222	254
The broadcast address	31	63	95	127	159	191	223	255

In practice example #3C, we're using a 255.255.255.224 (/27) network, which provides eight subnets as shown previously. We can take these subnets and implement them as shown in Figure 4.5 using any of the subnets available.

FIGURE 4.5   Implementing a Class C /27 logical network

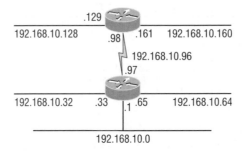

```
Router#show ip route
[output cut]
C 192.168.10.0 is directly connected to Ethernet 0
C 192.168.10.32 is directly connected to Ethernet 1
C 192.168.10.64 is directly connected to Ethernet 2
C 192.168.10.96 is directly connected to Serial 0
```

Notice that used six of the eight subnets available for my network design. The lightning bolt symbol in the figure represents a wide area network (WAN) such as a T1 or other serial connection through an ISP or telco. In other words, something you don't own, but it's still a subnet just like any LAN connection on a router. As usual, I used the first valid host in each subnet as the router's interface address. This is just a rule of thumb; you can use any address in the valid host range as long as you remember what address you configured so you can set the default gateways on your hosts to the router address.

Practice Example #4C: 255.255.255.240 (/28)

Let's practice another one:

192.168.10.0 = Network address

255.255.255.240 = Subnet mask

- *Subnets?* 240 is 11110000 in binary. $2^4 = 16$.

- *Hosts?* 4 host bits, or $2^4 - 2 = 14$.

- *Valid subnets?* 256 − 240 = 16. Start at 0: 0 + 16 = 16. 16 + 16 = 32. 32 + 16 = 48. 48 + 16 = 64. 64 + 16 = 80. 80 + 16 = 96. 96 + 16 = 112. 112 + 16 = 128. 128 + 16 = 144. 144 + 16 = 160. 160 + 16 = 176. 176 + 16 = 192. 192 + 16 = 208. 208 + 16 = 224. 224 + 16 = 240.

- *Broadcast address for each subnet?*

- *Valid hosts?*

To answer the last two questions, check out the following table. It gives you the subnets, valid hosts, and broadcast addresses for each subnet. First, find the address of each subnet using the block size (increment). Second, find the broadcast address of each subnet increment, which is always the number right before the next valid subnet, and then just fill in the host addresses. The following table shows the available subnets, hosts, and broadcast addresses provided from a Class C 255.255.255.240 mask.

Subnet	0	16	32	48	64	80	96	112	128	144	160	176	192	208	224	240
First host	1	17	33	49	65	81	97	113	129	145	161	177	193	209	225	241
Last host	14	30	46	62	78	94	110	126	142	158	174	190	206	222	238	254
Broadcast	15	31	47	63	79	95	111	127	143	159	175	191	207	223	239	255

Cisco has figured out that most people cannot count in 16s and therefore have a hard time finding valid subnets, hosts, and broadcast addresses with the Class C 255.255.255.240 mask. You'd be wise to study this mask.

Practice Example #5C: 255.255.255.248 (/29)

Let's keep practicing:

192.168.10.0 = Network address

255.255.255.248 = Subnet mask

- *Subnets?* 248 in binary = 11111000. $2^5 = 32$.

- *Hosts?* $2^3 - 2 = 6$.

- *Valid subnets?* 256 − 248 = 0, 8, 16, 24, 32, 40, 48, 56, 64, 72, 80, 88, 96, 104, 112, 120, 128, 136, 144, 152, 160, 168, 176, 184, 192, 200, 208, 216, 224, 232, 240, and 248.

- *Broadcast address for each subnet?*

- *Valid hosts?*

Take a look at the following table. It shows some of the subnets (first four and last four only), valid hosts, and broadcast addresses for the Class C 255.255.255.248 mask:

Subnet	0	8	16	24	...	224	232	240	248
First host	1	9	17	25	...	225	233	241	249
Last host	6	14	22	30	...	230	238	246	254
Broadcast	7	15	23	31	...	231	239	247	255

If you try to configure a router interface with the address 192.168.10.6 255.255.255.248 and receive the following error, It means that ip subnet-zero is not enabled:

```
Bad mask /29 for address 192.168.10.6
```

You must be able to subnet to see that the address used in this example is in the zero subnet!

Practice Example #6C: 255.255.255.252 (/30)

Okay—just one more:

    192.168.10.0 = Network address

    255.255.255.252 = Subnet mask

- *Subnets?* 64.
- *Hosts?* 2.
- *Valid subnets?* 0, 4, 8, 12, etc., all the way to 252.
- *Broadcast address for each subnet? (Always the number right before the next subnet.)*
- *Valid hosts?* (The numbers between the subnet number and the broadcast address.)

The following table shows you the subnet, valid host, and broadcast address of the first four and last four subnets in the 255.255.255.252 Class C subnet:

Subnet	0	4	8	12	...	240	244	248	252
First host	1	5	9	13	...	241	245	249	253
Last host	2	6	10	14	...	242	246	250	254
Broadcast	3	7	11	15	...	243	247	251	255

Real World Scenario

Should We Really Use This Mask That Provides Only Two Hosts?

You are the network administrator for Acme Corporation in San Francisco, with dozens of WAN links connecting to your corporate office. Right now your network is a classful network, which means that the same subnet mask is on each host and router interface. You've read about classless routing, where you can have different sized masks, but don't know what to use on your point-to-point WAN links. Is the 255.255.255.252 (/30) a helpful mask in this situation?

Yes, this is a very helpful mask in wide area networks and of course with any type of point-to-point link!

If you were to use the 255.255.255.0 mask in this situation, then each network would have 254 hosts. But you use only 2 addresses with a WAN or point-to-point link, which is a waste of 252 hosts per subnet! If you use the 255.255.255.252 mask, then each subnet has only 2 hosts, and you don't want to waste precious addresses. This is a really important subject, one that we'll address in a lot more detail in the section on VLSM network design in the next chapter!

Subnetting in Your Head: Class C Addresses

It really is possible to subnet in your head? Yes, and it's not all that hard either—take the following example:

192.168.10.50 = Node address

255.255.255.224 = Subnet mask

First, determine the subnet and broadcast address of the network in which the previous IP address resides. You can do this by answering question 3 of the big 5 questions: 256 – 224 = 32. 0, 32, 64, and so on. The address of 50 falls between the two subnets of 32 and 64 and must be part of the 192.168.10.32 subnet. The next subnet is 64, so the broadcast address of the 32 subnet is 63. Don't forget that the broadcast address of a subnet is always the number right before the next subnet. The valid host range equals the numbers between the subnet and broadcast address, or 33–62. This is too easy!

Let's try another one. We'll subnet another Class C address:

192.168.10.50 = Node address

255.255.255.240 = Subnet mask

What is the subnet and broadcast address of the network of which the previous IP address is a member? 256 – 240 = 16. Now just count by our increments of 16 until we pass the host address: 0, 16, 32, 48, 64. Bingo—the host address is between the 48 and 64 subnets. The subnet is 192.168.10.48, and the broadcast address is 63 because the next subnet is 64. The valid host range equals the numbers between the subnet number and the broadcast address, or 49–62.

Let's do a couple more to make sure you have this down.

You have a node address of 192.168.10.174 with a mask of 255.255.255.240. What is the valid host range?

The mask is 240, so we'd do a 256 – 240 = 16. This is our block size. Just keep adding 16 until we pass the host address of 174, starting at zero, of course: 0, 16, 32, 48, 64, 80, 96, 112, 128, 144, 160, 176. The host address of 174 is between 160 and 176, so the subnet is 160. The broadcast address is 175; the valid host range is 161–174. That was a tough one!

One more—just for fun. This one is the easiest of all Class C subnetting:

192.168.10.17 = Node address

255.255.255.252 = Subnet mask

What is the subnet and broadcast address of the subnet in which the previous IP address resides? 256 – 252 = 0 (always start at zero unless told otherwise). 0, 4, 8, 12, 16, 20, etc. You've got it! The host address is between the 16 and 20 subnets. The subnet is 192.168.10.16, and the broadcast address is 19. The valid host range is 17–18.

Now that you're all over Class C subnetting, let's move on to Class B subnetting. But before we do, let's go through a quick review.

What Do We Know?

Okay—here's where you can really apply what you've learned so far and begin committing it all to memory. This is a very cool section that I've been using in my classes for years. It will really help you nail down subnetting for good!

When you see a subnet mask or slash notation (CIDR), you should know the following:

/25   What do we know about a /25?

- 128 mask
- 1 bit on and 7 bits off (10000000)
- Block size of 128
- Subnets 0 and 128
- 2 subnets, each with 126 hosts

/26   What do we know about a /26?

- 192 mask
- 2 bits on and 6 bits off (11000000)

- Block size of 64
- Subnets 0, 64, 128, 192
- 4 subnets, each with 62 hosts

/27 What do we know about a /27?

- 224 mask
- 3 bits on and 5 bits off (11100000)
- Block size of 32
- Subnets 0, 32, 64, 96, 128, 160, 192, 224
- 8 subnets, each with 30 hosts

/28 What do we know about a /28?

- 240 mask
- 4 bits on and 4 bits off
- Block size of 16
- Subnets 0, 16, 32, 48, 64, 80, 96, 112, 128, 144, 160, 176, 192, 208, 224, 240
- 16 subnets, each with 14 hosts

/29 What do we know about a /29?

- 248 mask
- 5 bits on and 3 bits off
- Block size of 8
- Subnets 0, 8, 16, 24, 32, 40, 48, etc.
- 32 subnets, each with 6 hosts

/30 What do we know about a /30?

- 252 mask
- 6 bits on and 2 bits off
- Block size of 4
- Subnets 0, 4, 8, 12, 16, 20, 24, etc.
- 64 subnets, each with 2 hosts

Table 4.3 puts all of the previous information into one compact little table. You should practice writing this table out on scratch paper, and if you can do it, write it down before you start your exam!

TABLE 4.3   What do you know?

CIDR Notation	Mask	Bits	Block Size	Subnets	Hosts
/25	128	1 bit on and 7 bits off	128	0 and 128	2 subnets, each with 126 hosts
/26	192	2 bits on and 6 bits off	64	0, 64, 128, 192	4 subnets, each with 62 hosts
/27	224	3 bits on and 5 bits off	32	0, 32, 64, 96, 128, 160, 192, 224	8 subnets, each with 30 hosts
/28	240	4 bits on and 4 bits off	16	0, 16, 32, 48, 64, 80, 96, 112, 128, 144, 160, 176, 192, 208, 224, 240	16 subnets, each with 14 hosts
/29	248	5 bits on and 3 bits off	8	0, 8, 16, 24, 32, 40, 48, etc.	32 subnets, each with 6 hosts
/30	252	6 bits on and 2 bits off	4	0, 4, 8, 12, 16, 20, 24, etc.	64 subnets, each with 2 hosts

Regardless of whether you have a Class A, Class B, or Class C address, the /30 mask will provide you with only two hosts, ever. As suggested by Cisco, this mask is suited almost exclusively for use on point-to-point links.

If you can memorize this "What Do We Know?" section, you'll be much better off in your day-to-day job and in your studies. Try saying it out loud, which helps you memorize things—yes, your significant other and/or coworkers will think you've lost it, but they probably already do if you're in the networking field anyway. And if you're not yet in the networking field but are studying all this to break into it, get used to it!

It's also helpful to write these on some type of flashcards and have people test your skill. You'd be amazed at how fast you can get subnetting down if you memorize block sizes as well as this "What Do We Know?" section.

Subnetting Class B Addresses

Before we dive into this, let's look at all the possible Class B subnet masks first. Notice that we have a lot more possible subnet masks than we do with a Class C network address:

```
255.255.0.0     (/16)
255.255.128.0   (/17)      255.255.255.0    (/24)
255.255.192.0   (/18)      255.255.255.128  (/25)
```

```
255.255.224.0  (/19)      255.255.255.192  (/26)
255.255.240.0  (/20)      255.255.255.224  (/27)
255.255.248.0  (/21)      255.255.255.240  (/28)
255.255.252.0  (/22)      255.255.255.248  (/29)
255.255.254.0  (/23)      255.255.255.252  (/30)
```

We know the Class B network address has 16 bits available for host addressing. This means we can use up to 14 bits for subnetting because we need to leave at least 2 bits for host addressing. Using a /16 means you are not subnetting with Class B, but it *is* a mask you can use!

By the way, do you notice anything interesting about that list of subnet values—a pattern, maybe? Ah ha! That's exactly why I had you memorize the binary-to-decimal numbers earlier in Chapter 2, "Ethernet Networking and Data Encapsulation." Since subnet mask bits start on the left and move to the right and bits can't be skipped, the numbers are always the same regardless of the class of address. If you haven't already, memorize this pattern!

The process of subnetting a Class B network is pretty much the same as it is for a Class C, except that you have more host bits and you start in the third octet.

Use the same subnet numbers for the third octet with Class B that you used for the fourth octet with Class C, but add a zero to the network portion and a 255 to the broadcast section in the fourth octet. The following table shows you an example host range of two subnets used in a Class B 240 (/20) subnet mask:

Subnet address	16.0	32.0
Broadcast address	31.255	47.255

Just add the valid hosts between the numbers and you're set!

The preceding example is true only until you get up to /24. After that, it's numerically exactly like Class C.

Subnetting Practice Examples: Class B Addresses

The following sections will give you an opportunity to practice subnetting Class B addresses. Again, I have to mention that this is the same as subnetting with Class C, except we start in the third octet—with the exact same numbers!

Practice Example #1B: 255.255.128.0 (/17)

172.16.0.0 = Network address

255.255.128.0 = Subnet mask

- *Subnets?* 2^1 = 2 (same amount as Class C).
- *Hosts?* 2^{15} – 2 = 32,766 (7 bits in the third octet, and 8 in the fourth).
- *Valid subnets?* 256 – 128 = 128. 0, 128. Remember that subnetting is performed in the third octet, so the subnet numbers are really 0.0 and 128.0, as shown in the next table. These are the exact numbers we used with Class C; we use them in the third octet and add a 0 in the fourth octet for the network address.
- *Broadcast address for each subnet?*
- *Valid hosts?*

The following table shows the two subnets available, the valid host range, and the broadcast address of each:

Subnet	0.0	128.0
First host	0.1	128.1
Last host	127.254	255.254
Broadcast	127.255	255.255

Okay, notice that we just added the fourth octet's lowest and highest values and came up with the answers. And again, it's done exactly the same way as for a Class C subnet. We just used the same numbers in the third octet and added 0 and 255 in the fourth octet—pretty simple, huh? I really can't say this enough: it's just not that hard. The numbers never change; we just use them in different octets!

Question: Using the previous subnet mask, do you think 172.16.10.0 is a valid host address? What about 172.16.10.255? Can 0 and 255 in the fourth octet ever be a valid host address? The answer is absolutely, yes, those are valid hosts! Any number between the subnet number and the broadcast address is always a valid host.

Practice Example #2B: 255.255.192.0 (/18)

172.16.0.0 = Network address

255.255.192.0 = Subnet mask

- *Subnets?* 2^2 = 4.
- *Hosts?* 2^{14} – 2 = 16,382 (6 bits in the third octet, and 8 in the fourth).

- *Valid subnets?* 256 – 192 = 64. 0, 64, 128, 192. Remember that the subnetting is performed in the third octet, so the subnet numbers are really 0.0, 64.0, 128.0, and 192.0, as shown in the next table.
- *Broadcast address for each subnet?*
- *Valid hosts?*

The following table shows the four subnets available, the valid host range, and the broadcast address of each:

Subnet	0.0	64.0	128.0	192.0
First host	0.1	64.1	128.1	192.1
Last host	63.254	127.254	191.254	255.254
Broadcast	63.255	127.255	191.255	255.255

Again, it's pretty much the same as it is for a Class C subnet—we just added 0 and 255 in the fourth octet for each subnet in the third octet.

Practice Example #3B: 255.255.240.0 (/20)

172.16.0.0 = Network address

255.255.240.0 = Subnet mask

- *Subnets?* 2^4 = 16.
- *Hosts?* 2^{12} – 2 = 4094.
- *Valid subnets?* 256 – 240 = 0, 16, 32, 48, etc., up to 240. Notice that these are the same numbers as a Class C 240 mask—we just put them in the third octet and add a 0 and 255 in the fourth octet.
- *Broadcast address for each subnet?*
- *Valid hosts?*

The following table shows the first four subnets, valid hosts, and broadcast addresses in a Class B 255.255.240.0 mask:

Subnet	0.0	16.0	32.0	48.0
First host	0.1	16.1	32.1	48.1
Last host	15.254	31.254	47.254	63.254
Broadcast	15.255	31.255	47.255	63.255

Practice Example #4B: 255.255.248.0 (/21)

172.16.0.0 = Network address

255.255.248.0 = Subnet mask

- *Subnets?* 2^5 = 32.
- *Hosts?* 2^{11} – 2 = 2046.
- *Valid subnets?* 256 – 248 = 0, 8, 16, 24, 32, etc., up to 248.
- *Broadcast address for each subnet?*
- *Valid hosts?*

The following table shows the first five subnets, valid hosts, and broadcast addresses in a Class B 255.255.248.0 mask:

Subnet	0.0	8.0	16.0	24.0	32.0
First host	0.1	8.1	16.1	24.1	32.1
Last host	7.254	15.254	23.254	31.254	39.254
Broadcast	7.255	15.255	23.255	31.255	39.255

Practice Example #5B: 255.255.252.0 (/22)

172.16.0.0 = Network address

255.255.252.0 = Subnet mask

- *Subnets?* 2^6 = 64.
- *Hosts?* 2^{10} – 2 = 1022.
- *Valid subnets?* 256 – 252 = 0, 4, 8, 12, 16, etc., up to 252.
- *Broadcast address for each subnet?*
- *Valid hosts?*

The following table shows the first five subnets, valid hosts, and broadcast addresses in a Class B 255.255.252.0 mask:

Subnet	0.0	4.0	8.0	12.0	16.0
First host	0.1	4.1	8.1	12.1	16.1
Last host	3.254	7.254	11.254	15.254	19.254
Broadcast	3.255	7.255	11.255	15.255	19.255

Practice Example #6B: 255.255.254.0 (/23)

172.16.0.0 = Network address

255.255.254.0 = Subnet mask

- *Subnets?* $2^7 = 128$.
- *Hosts?* $2^9 - 2 = 510$.
- *Valid subnets?* $256 - 254 = 0, 2, 4, 6, 8$, etc., up to 254.
- *Broadcast address for each subnet?*
- *Valid hosts?*

The following table shows the first five subnets, valid hosts, and broadcast addresses in a Class B 255.255.254.0 mask:

Subnet	0.0	2.0	4.0	6.0	8.0
First host	0.1	2.1	4.1	6.1	8.1
Last host	1.254	3.254	5.254	7.254	9.254
Broadcast	1.255	3.255	5.255	7.255	9.255

Practice Example #7B: 255.255.255.0 (/24)

Contrary to popular belief, 255.255.255.0 used with a Class B network address is not called a Class B network with a Class C subnet mask. It's amazing how many people see this mask used in a Class B network and think it's a Class C subnet mask. This is a Class B subnet mask with 8 bits of subnetting—it's logically different from a Class C mask. Subnetting this address is fairly simple:

    172.16.0.0 = Network address

    255.255.255.0 = Subnet mask

- *Subnets?* $2^8 = 256$.
- *Hosts?* $2^8 - 2 = 254$.
- *Valid subnets?* $256 - 255 = 1. 0, 1, 2, 3$, etc., all the way to 255.
- *Broadcast address for each subnet?*
- *Valid hosts?*

The following table shows the first four and last two subnets, the valid hosts, and the broadcast addresses in a Class B 255.255.255.0 mask:

Subnet	0.0	1.0	2.0	3.0	...	254.0	255.0
First host	0.1	1.1	2.1	3.1	...	254.1	255.1
Last host	0.254	1.254	2.254	3.254	...	254.254	255.254
Broadcast	0.255	1.255	2.255	3.255	...	254.255	255.255

Practice Example #8B: 255.255.255.128 (/25)

This is actually one of the hardest subnet masks you can play with. And worse, it actually is a really good subnet to use in production because it creates over 500 subnets with 126 hosts for each subnet—a nice mixture. So, don't skip over it!

172.16.0.0 = Network address

255.255.255.128 = Subnet mask

- *Subnets?* 2^9 = 512.

- *Hosts?* $2^7 - 2$ = 126.

- *Valid subnets?* Now for the tricky part. 256 − 255 = 1. 0, 1, 2, 3, etc., for the third octet. But you can't forget the one subnet bit used in the fourth octet. Remember when I showed you how to figure one subnet bit with a Class C mask? You figure this the same way. You actually get two subnets for each third octet value, hence the 512 subnets. For example, if the third octet is showing subnet 3, the two subnets would actually be 3.0 and 3.128.

- *Broadcast address for each subnet?* The numbers right before the next subnet.

- *Valid hosts?* The numbers between the subnet numbers and the broadcast address.

The following graphic shows how you can create subnets, valid hosts, and broadcast addresses using the Class B 255.255.255.128 subnet mask. The first eight subnets are shown, followed by the last two subnets:

Subnet	0.0	0.128	1.0	1.128	2.0	2.128	3.0	3.128	...	255.0	255.128
First host	0.1	0.129	1.1	1.129	2.1	2.129	3.1	3.129	...	255.1	255.129
Last host	0.126	0.254	1.126	1.254	2.126	2.254	3.126	3.254	...	255.126	255.254
Broadcast	0.127	0.255	1.127	1.255	2.127	2.255	3.127	3.255	...	255.127	255.255

Practice Example #9B: 255.255.255.192 (/26)

Now, this is where Class B subnetting gets easy. Since the third octet has a 255 in the mask section, whatever number is listed in the third octet is a subnet number. And now that we have a subnet number in the fourth octet, we can subnet this octet just as we did with Class C subnetting. Let's try it out:

172.16.0.0 = Network address

255.255.255.192 = Subnet mask

- *Subnets?* 2^{10} = 1024.

- *Hosts?* $2^6 - 2$ = 62.

- *Valid subnets?* 256 – 192 = 64. The subnets are shown in the following table. Do these numbers look familiar?

- *Broadcast address for each subnet?*

- *Valid hosts?*

The following table shows the first eight subnet ranges, valid hosts, and broadcast addresses:

Subnet	0.0	0.64	0.128	0.192	1.0	1.64	1.128	1.192
First host	0.1	0.65	0.129	0.193	1.1	1.65	1.129	1.193
Last host	0.62	0.126	0.190	0.254	1.62	1.126	1.190	1.254
Broadcast	0.63	0.127	0.191	0.255	1.63	1.127	1.191	1.255

Notice that for each subnet value in the third octet, you get subnets 0, 64, 128, and 192 in the fourth octet.

Practice Example #10B: 255.255.255.224 (/27)

This one is done the same way as the preceding subnet mask, except that we just have more subnets and fewer hosts per subnet available.

172.16.0.0 = Network address

255.255.255.224 = Subnet mask

- *Subnets?* 2^{11} = 2048.

- *Hosts?* $2^5 - 2$ = 30.

- *Valid subnets?* 256 – 224 = 32. 0, 32, 64, 96, 128, 160, 192, 224.

- *Broadcast address for each subnet?*

- *Valid hosts?*

The following table shows the first eight subnets:

Subnet	0.0	0.32	0.64	0.96	0.128	0.160	0.192	0.224
First host	0.1	0.33	0.65	0.97	0.129	0.161	0.193	0.225
Last host	0.30	0.62	0.94	0.126	0.158	0.190	0.222	0.254
Broadcast	0.31	0.63	0.95	0.127	0.159	0.191	0.223	0.255

This next table shows the last eight subnets:

Subnet	255.0	255.32	255.64	255.96	255.128	255.160	255.192	255.224
First host	255.1	255.33	255.65	255.97	255.129	255.161	255.193	255.225
Last host	255.30	255.62	255.94	255.126	255.158	255.190	255.222	255.254
Broadcast	255.31	255.63	255.95	255.127	255.159	255.191	255.223	255.255

Subnetting in Your Head: Class B Addresses

Are you nuts? Subnet Class B addresses in our heads? It's actually easier than writing it out—I'm not kidding! Let me show you how:

Question: What is the subnet and broadcast address of the subnet in which 172.16.10.33 /27 resides?

Answer: The interesting octet is the fourth one. 256 – 224 = 32. 32 + 32 = 64. You've got it: 33 is between 32 and 64. But remember that the third octet is considered part of the subnet, so the answer would be the 10.32 subnet. The broadcast is 10.63, since 10.64 is the next subnet. That was a pretty easy one.

Question: What subnet and broadcast address is the IP address 172.16.66.10 255.255.192.0 (/18) a member of?

Answer: The interesting octet here is the third octet instead of the fourth one. 256 – 192 = 64. 0, 64, 128. The subnet is 172.16.64.0. The broadcast must be 172.16.127.255 since 128.0 is the next subnet.

Question: What subnet and broadcast address is the IP address 172.16.50.10 255.255.224.0 (/19) a member of?

Answer: 256 – 224 = 0, 32, 64 (remember, we always start counting at 0). The subnet is 172.16.32.0, and the broadcast must be 172.16.63.255 since 64.0 is the next subnet.

Question: What subnet and broadcast address is the IP address 172.16.46.255 255.255.240.0 (/20) a member of?

Answer: 256 – 240 = 16. The third octet is important here: 0, 16, 32, 48. This subnet address must be in the 172.16.32.0 subnet, and the broadcast must be 172.16.47.255 since 48.0 is the next subnet. So, yes, 172.16.46.255 is a valid host.

Question: What subnet and broadcast address is the IP address 172.16.45.14 255.255.255.252 (/30) a member of?

Answer: Where is our interesting octet? 256 – 252 = 0, 4, 8, 12, 16—the fourth. The subnet is 172.16.45.12, with a broadcast of 172.16.45.15 because the next subnet is 172.16.45.16.

Question: What is the subnet and broadcast address of the host 172.16.88.255/20?

Answer: What is a /20 written out in dotted decimal? If you can't answer this, you can't answer this question, can you? A /20 is 255.255.240.0, gives us a block size of 16 in the third octet, and since no subnet bits are on in the fourth octet, the answer is always 0 and 255 in the fourth octet: 0, 16, 32, 48, 64, 80, 96. Because 88 is between 80 and 96, the subnet is 80.0 and the broadcast address is 95.255.

Question: A router receives a packet on an interface with a destination address of 172.16.46.191/26. What will the router do with this packet?

Answer: Discard it. Do you know why? 172.16.46.191/26 is a 255.255.255.192 mask, which gives us a block size of 64. Our subnets are then 0, 64, 128 and 192. 191 is the broadcast address of the 128 subnet, and by default, a router will discard any broadcast packets.

Subnetting Class A Addresses

You don't go about Class A subnetting any differently than Classes B and C, but there are 24 bits to play with instead of the 16 in a Class B address and the 8 in a Class C address.

Let's start by listing all the Class A masks:

```
255.0.0.0      (/8)
255.128.0.0    (/9)      255.255.240.0    (/20)
255.192.0.0    (/10)     255.255.248.0    (/21)
255.224.0.0    (/11)     255.255.252.0    (/22)
255.240.0.0    (/12)     255.255.254.0    (/23)
255.248.0.0    (/13)     255.255.255.0    (/24)
255.252.0.0    (/14)     255.255.255.128  (/25)
255.254.0.0    (/15)     255.255.255.192  (/26)
255.255.0.0    (/16)     255.255.255.224  (/27)
255.255.128.0  (/17)     255.255.255.240  (/28)
255.255.192.0  (/18)     255.255.255.248  (/29)
255.255.224.0  (/19)     255.255.255.252  (/30)
```

That's it. You must leave at least 2 bits for defining hosts. I hope you can see the pattern by now. Remember, we're going to do this the same way as a Class B or C subnet. It's just that, again, we simply have more host bits and we just use the same subnet numbers we used with Class B and C, but we start using these numbers in the second octet. However, the reason Class A addresses are so popular to implement is because they give the most flexibility. You can subnet in the second, third or fourth octet. I'll show you this in the next examples.

Subnetting Practice Examples: Class A Addresses

When you look at an IP address and a subnet mask, you must be able to distinguish the bits used for subnets from the bits used for determining hosts. This is imperative. If you're still struggling with this concept, please reread the section "IP Addressing" in Chapter 3. It shows you how to determine the difference between the subnet and host bits and should help clear things up.

Practice Example #1A: 255.255.0.0 (/16)

Class A addresses use a default mask of 255.0.0.0, which leaves 22 bits for subnetting because you must leave 2 bits for host addressing. The 255.255.0.0 mask with a Class A address is using 8 subnet bits:

- *Subnets?* $2^8 = 256$.
- *Hosts?* $2^{16} - 2 = 65,534$.
- *Valid subnets?* What is the interesting octet? $256 - 255 = 1$. 0, 1, 2, 3, etc. (all in the second octet). The subnets would be 10.0.0.0, 10.1.0.0, 10.2.0.0, 10.3.0.0, etc., up to 10.255.0.0.
- *Broadcast address for each subnet?*
- *Valid hosts?*

The following table shows the first two and the last two subnets, the valid host range and the broadcast addresses for the private Class A 10.0.0.0 network:

Subnet	10.0.0.0	10.1.0.0	...	10.254.0.0	10.255.0.0
First host	10.0.0.1	10.1.0.1	...	10.254.0.1	10.255.0.1
Last host	10.0.255.254	10.1.255.254	...	10.254.255.254	10.255.255.254
Broadcast	10.0.255.255	10.1.255.255	...	10.254.255.255	10.255.255.255

Practice Example #2A: 255.255.240.0 (/20)

255.255.240.0 gives us 12 bits of subnetting and leaves us 12 bits for host addressing.

- *Subnets?* $2^{12} = 4096$.
- *Hosts?* $2^{12} - 2 = 4094$.
- *Valid subnets?* What is your interesting octet? $256 - 240 = 16$. The subnets in the second octet are a block size of 1 and the subnets in the third octet are 0, 16, 32, etc.
- *Broadcast address for each subnet?*
- *Valid hosts?*

The following table shows some examples of the host ranges—the first three subnets and the last subnet:

Subnet	10.0.0.0	10.0.16.0	10.0.32.0	...	10.255.240.0
First host	10.0.0.1	10.0.16.1	10.0.32.1	...	10.255.240.1
Last host	10.0.15.254	10.0.31.254	10.0.47.254	...	10.255.255.254
Broadcast	10.0.15.255	10.0.31.255	10.0.47.255	...	10.255.255.255

Practice Example #3A: 255.255.255.192 (/26)

Let's do one more example using the second, third, and fourth octets for subnetting:

- *Subnets?* 2^{18} = 262,144.
- *Hosts?* $2^6 - 2$ = 62.
- *Valid subnets?* In the second and third octet, the block size is 1, and in the fourth octet, the block size is 64.
- *Broadcast address for each subnet?*
- *Valid hosts?*

The following table shows the first four subnets and their valid hosts and broadcast addresses in the Class A 255.255.255.192 mask:

Subnet	10.0.0.0	10.0.0.64	10.0.0.128	10.0.0.192
First host	10.0.0.1	10.0.0.65	10.0.0.129	10.0.0.193
Last host	10.0.0.62	10.0.0.126	10.0.0.190	10.0.0.254
Broadcast	10.0.0.63	10.0.0.127	10.0.0.191	10.0.0.255

This table shows the last four subnets and their valid hosts and broadcast addresses:

Subnet	10.255.255.0	10.255.255.64	10.255.255.128	10.255.255.192
First host	10.255.255.1	10.255.255.65	10.255.255.129	10.255.255.193
Last host	10.255.255.62	10.255.255.126	10.255.255.190	10.255.255.254
Broadcast	10.255.255.63	10.255.255.127	10.255.255.191	10.255.255.255

Subnetting in Your Head: Class A Addresses

Again, I know this sounds hard, but as with Class C and Class B, the numbers are the same; we just start in the second octet. What makes this easy? You only need to worry about the octet that has the largest block size, which is typically called the interesting octet, and one that is something other than 0 or 255, such as, for example, 255.255.240.0 (/20) with a Class A network. The second octet has a block size of 1, so any number listed in that octet is a subnet. The third octet is a 240 mask, which means we have a block size of 16 in the third octet. If your host ID is 10.20.80.30, what is your subnet, broadcast address, and valid host range?

The subnet in the second octet is 20 with a block size of 1, but the third octet is in block sizes of 16, so we'll just count them out: 0, 16, 32, 48, 64, 80, 96... voilà! By the way, you can count by 16s by now, right? Good! This makes our subnet 10.20.80.0, with a broadcast address of 10.20.95.255 because the next subnet is 10.20.96.0. The valid host range is 10.20.80.1 through 10.20.95.254. And yes, no lie! You really can do this in your head if you just get your block sizes nailed!

Let's practice on one more, just for fun!

Host IP: 10.1.3.65/23

First, you can't answer this question if you don't know what a /23 is. It's 255.255.254.0. The interesting octet here is the third one: 256 – 254 = 2. Our subnets in the third octet are 0, 2, 4, 6, etc. The host in this question is in subnet 2.0, and the next subnet is 4.0, so that makes the broadcast address 3.255. And any address between 10.1.2.1 and 10.1.3.254 is considered a valid host.

Summary

Did you read Chapters 3 and 4 and understand everything on the first pass? If so, that is fantastic—congratulations! However, you probably really did get lost a couple of times. No worries because as I told you, that's what usually happens. Don't waste time feeling bad if you have to read each chapter more than once, or even 10 times, before you're truly good to go. If you do have to read the chapters more than once, you'll be seriously better off in the long run even if you were pretty comfortable the first time through!

This chapter provided you with an important understanding of IP subnetting—the painless way! And when you've got the key material presented in this chapter really nailed down, you should be able to subnet IP addresses in your head.

This chapter is extremely essential to your Cisco certification process, so if you just skimmed it, please go back, read it thoroughly, and don't forget to do all the written labs too!

Exam Essentials

Identify the advantages of subnetting.   Benefits of subnetting a physical network include reduced network traffic, optimized network performance, simplified management, and facilitated spanning of large geographical distances.

Describe the effect of the `ip subnet-zero` command.   This command allows you to use the first and last subnet in your network design.

Identify the steps to subnet a classful network.   Understand how IP addressing and subnetting work. First, determine your block size by using the 256-subnet mask math. Then count your subnets and determine the broadcast address of each subnet—it is always the number right before the next subnet. Your valid hosts are the numbers between the subnet address and the broadcast address.

Determine possible block sizes.   This is an important part of understanding IP addressing and subnetting. The valid block sizes are always 2, 4, 8, 16, 32, 64, 128, etc. You can determine your block size by using the 256-subnet mask math.

Describe the role of a subnet mask in IP addressing.   A subnet mask is a 32-bit value that allows the recipient of IP packets to distinguish the network ID portion of the IP address from the host ID portion of the IP address.

Understand and apply the $2^x - 2$ formula.   Use this formula to determine the proper subnet mask for a particular size network given the application of that subnet mask to a particular classful network.

Explain the impact of Classless Inter-Domain Routing (CIDR).   CIDR allows the creation of networks of a size other than those allowed with the classful subnetting by allowing more than the three classful subnet masks.

Written Labs

In this section, you'll complete the following labs to make sure you've got the information and concepts contained within them fully dialed in:

Lab 4.1: Written Subnet Practice #1

Lab 4.2: Written Subnet Practice #2

Lab 4.3: Written Subnet Practice #3

You can find the answers to these labs in Appendix A, "Answers to Written Labs."

Written Lab 4.1: Written Subnet Practice #1

Write the subnet, broadcast address, and a valid host range for question 1 through question 6. Then answer the remaining questions.

1. 192.168.100.25/30
2. 192.168.100.37/28
3. 192.168.100.66/27
4. 192.168.100.17/29
5. 192.168.100.99/26
6. 192.168.100.99/25
7. You have a Class B network and need 29 subnets. What is your mask?
8. What is the broadcast address of 192.168.192.10/29?
9. How many hosts are available with a Class C /29 mask?
10. What is the subnet for host ID 10.16.3.65/23?

Written Lab 4.2: Written Subnet Practice #2

Given a Class B network and the net bits identified (CIDR), complete the following table to identify the subnet mask and the number of host addresses possible for each mask.

Classful Address	Subnet Mask	Number of Hosts per Subnet ($2^x - 2$)
/16		
/17		
/18		
/19		
/20		
/21		
/22		
/23		
/24		
/25		
/26		
/27		
/28		
/29		
/30		

Written Lab 4.3: Written Subnet Practice #3

Complete the following based on the decimal IP address.

Decimal IP Address	Address Class	Number of Subnet and Host Bits	Number of Subnets (2^x)	Number of Hosts ($2^x - 2$)
10.25.66.154/23				
172.31.254.12/24				
192.168.20.123/28				
63.24.89.21/18				
128.1.1.254/20				
208.100.54.209/30				

Review Questions

The following questions are designed to test your understanding of this chapter's material. For more information on how to get additional questions, please see www.lammle.com/ccna.

You can find the answers to these questions in Appendix B, "Answers to Review Questions."

1. What is the maximum number of IP addresses that can be assigned to hosts on a local subnet that uses the 255.255.255.224 subnet mask?

    A. 14

    B. 15

    C. 16

    D. 30

    E. 31

    F. 62

2. You have a network that needs 29 subnets while maximizing the number of host addresses available on each subnet. How many bits must you borrow from the host field to provide the correct subnet mask?

    A. 2

    B. 3

    C. 4

    D. 5

    E. 6

    F. 7

3. What is the subnetwork address for a host with the IP address 200.10.5.68/28?

    A. 200.10.5.56

    B. 200.10.5.32

    C. 200.10.5.64

    D. 200.10.5.0

4. The network address of 172.16.0.0/19 provides how many subnets and hosts?

    A. 7 subnets, 30 hosts each

    B. 7 subnets, 2,046 hosts each

    C. 7 subnets, 8,190 hosts each

    D. 8 subnets, 30 hosts each

    E. 8 subnets, 2,046 hosts each

    F. 8 subnets, 8,190 hosts each

5. Which two statements describe the IP address 10.16.3.65/23? (Choose two.)

    A. The subnet address is 10.16.3.0 255.255.254.0.

    B. The lowest host address in the subnet is 10.16.2.1 255.255.254.0.

    C. The last valid host address in the subnet is 10.16.2.254 255.255.254.0.

    D. The broadcast address of the subnet is 10.16.3.255 255.255.254.0.

    E. The network is not subnetted.

6. If a host on a network has the address 172.16.45.14/30, what is the subnetwork this host belongs to?

    A. 172.16.45.0

    B. 172.16.45.4

    C. 172.16.45.8

    D. 172.16.45.12

    E. 172.16.45.16

7. Which mask should you use on point-to-point links in order to reduce the waste of IP addresses?

    A. /27

    B. /28

    C. /29

    D. /30

    E. /31

8. What is the subnetwork number of a host with an IP address of 172.16.66.0/21?

    A. 172.16.36.0

    B. 172.16.48.0

    C. 172.16.64.0

    D. 172.16.0.0

9. You have an interface on a router with the IP address of 192.168.192.10/29. Including the router interface, how many hosts can have IP addresses on the LAN attached to the router interface?

    A. 6

    B. 8

    C. 30

    D. 62

    E. 126

10. You need to configure a server that is on the subnet 192.168.19.24/29. The router has the first available host address. Which of the following should you assign to the server?

    A. 192.168.19.0 255.255.255.0

    B. 192.168.19.33 255.255.255.240

    C. 192.168.19.26 255.255.255.248

    D. 192.168.19.31 255.255.255.248

    E. 192.168.19.34 255.255.255.240

11. You have an interface on a router with the IP address of 192.168.192.10/29. What is the broadcast address the hosts will use on this LAN?

    A. 192.168.192.15

    B. 192.168.192.31

    C. 192.168.192.63

    D. 192.168.192.127

    E. 192.168.192.255

12. You need to subnet a network that has 5 subnets, each with at least 16 hosts. Which classful subnet mask would you use?

    A. 255.255.255.192

    B. 255.255.255.224

    C. 255.255.255.240

    D. 255.255.255.248

13. You configure a router interface with the IP address 192.168.10.62 255.255.255.192 and receive the following error:

    ```
    Bad mask /26 for address 192.168.10.62
    ```

    Why did you receive this error?

    A. You typed this mask on a WAN link and that is not allowed.

    B. This is not a valid host and subnet mask combination.

    C. `ip subnet-zero` is not enabled on the router.

    D. The router does not support IP.

14. If an Ethernet port on a router were assigned an IP address of 172.16.112.1/25, what would be the valid subnet address of this interface?

    A. 172.16.112.0

    B. 172.16.0.0

    C. 172.16.96.0

    D. 172.16.255.0

    E. 172.16.128.0

15. Using the following illustration, what would be the IP address of E0 if you were using the eighth subnet? The network ID is 192.168.10.0/28 and you need to use the last available IP address in the range. The zero subnet should not be considered valid for this question.

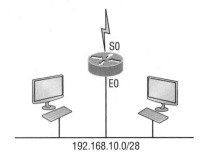

192.168.10.0/28

A. 192.168.10.142

B. 192.168.10.66

C. 192.168.100.254

D. 192.168.10.143

E. 192.168.10.126

16. Using the illustration from the previous question, what would be the IP address of S0 if you were using the first subnet? The network ID is 192.168.10.0/28 and you need to use the last available IP address in the range. Again, the zero subnet should not be considered valid for this question.

A. 192.168.10.24

B. 192.168.10.62

C. 192.168.10.30

D. 192.168.10.127

17. You have a network in your data center that needs 310 hosts. Which mask should you use so you waste the least amount of addresses?

A. 255.255.255.0

B. 255.255.254.0

C. 255.255.252.0

D. 255.255.248.0

18. You have a network with a host address of 172.16.17.0/22. From the following options, which is another valid host address in the same subnet?

A. 172.16.17.1 255.255.255.252

B. 172.16.0.1 255.255.240.0

C. 172.16.20.1 255.255.254.0

D. 172.16.16.1 255.255.255.240

E. 172.16.18.255 255.255.252.0

F. 172.16.0.1 255.255.255.0

19. Your router has the following IP address on Ethernet0: 172.16.2.1/23. Which of the following can be valid host IDs on the LAN interface attached to the router? (Choose two.)

A. 172.16.0.5

B. 172.16.1.100

C. 172.16.1.198

D. 172.16.2.255

E. 172.16.3.0

F. 172.16.3.255

20. Given an IP address 172.16.28.252 with a subnet mask of 255.255.240.0, what is the correct network address?

A. 172.16.16.0

B. 172.16.0.0

C. 172.16.24.0

D. 172.16.28.0

Chapter

5

VLSMs, Summarization, and Troubleshooting TCP/IP

THE FOLLOWING ICND1 EXAM TOPICS ARE COVERED IN THIS CHAPTER:

✓ **Network Fundamentals**

- 1.7 Apply troubleshooting methodologies to resolve problems

- 1.7.a Perform fault isolation and document

- 1.7.b Resolve or escalate

- 1.7.c Verify and monitor resolution

- 1.8 Configure, verify, and troubleshoot IPv4 addressing and subnetting

Now that IP addressing and subnetting have been thoroughly covered in the last two chapters, you're fully prepared and ready to learn all about variable length subnet masks (VLSMs). I'll also show you how to design and implement a network using VLSM in this chapter. After ensuring you've mastered VLSM design and implementation, I'll demonstrate how to summarize classful boundaries.

We'll wrap up the chapter by going over IP address troubleshooting, focusing on the steps Cisco recommends to follow when troubleshooting an IP network.

So get psyched because this chapter will give you powerful tools to hone your knowledge of IP addressing and networking and seriously refine the important skills you've gained so far. So stay with me—I guarantee that your hard work will pay off! Ready? Let's go!

To find up-to-the minute updates for this chapter, please see www.lammle.com/ccna or the book's web page at www.sybex.com/go/ccna.

Variable Length Subnet Masks (VLSMs)

Teaching you a simple way to create many networks from a large single network using subnet masks of different lengths in various kinds of network designs is what my primary focus will be in this chapter. Doing this is called VLSM networking, and it brings up another important subject I mentioned in Chapter 4, "Easy Subnetting," classful and classless networking.

Older routing protocols like Routing Information Protocol version 1 (RIPv1) do not have a field for subnet information, so the subnet information gets dropped. This means that if a router running RIP has a subnet mask of a certain value, it assumes that *all* interfaces within the classful address space have the same subnet mask. This is called classful routing, and RIP is considered a classful routing protocol. We'll cover RIP and the difference between classful and classless networks later on in Chapter 9, "IP Routing," but for now, just remember that if you try to mix and match subnet mask lengths in a network that's running an old routing protocol, such as RIP, it just won't work!

However, classless routing protocols do support the advertisement of subnet information, which means you can use VLSM with routing protocols such as RIPv2, Enhanced

Interior Gateway Protocol (EIGRP), and Open Shortest Path First (OSPF). The benefit of this type of network is that it saves a bunch of IP address space.

As the name suggests, VLSMs can use subnet masks with different lengths for different router interfaces. Check out Figure 5.1 to see an example of why classful network designs are inefficient.

FIGURE 5.1   Typical classful network

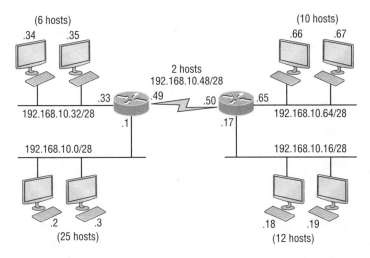

Looking at Figure 5.1, you can see that there are two routers, each with two LANs and connected together with a WAN serial link. In a typical classful network design that's running RIP, you could subnet a network like this:

192.168.10.0 = Network

255.255.255.240 (/28) = Mask

Our subnets would be—you know this part, right?— 0, 16, 32, 48, 64, 80, etc., which allows us to assign 16 subnets to our internetwork. But how many hosts would be available on each network? Well, as you know by now, each subnet provides only 14 hosts, so each LAN has only 14 valid hosts available (don't forget that the router interface needs an address too and is included in the amount of needed valid hosts). This means that one LAN doesn't even have enough addresses needed for all the hosts, and this network as it is shown would not work as addressed in the figure! Since the point-to-point WAN link also has 14 valid hosts, it would be great to be able to nick a few valid hosts from that WAN link to give to our LANs!

All hosts and router interfaces have the same subnet mask—again, known as classful routing—and if we want this network to be efficient, we would definitely need to add different masks to each router interface.

But that's not our only problem—the link between the two routers will never use more than two valid hosts! This wastes valuable IP address space, and it's the big reason you need to learn about VLSM network design.

VLSM Design

Let's take Figure 5.1 and use a classless design instead, which will become the new network shown in Figure 5.2. In the previous example, we wasted address space—one LAN didn't have enough addresses because every router interface and host used the same subnet mask. Not so good. A better solution would be to provide for only the needed number of hosts on each router interface, and we're going to use VLSMs to achieve that goal.

FIGURE 5.2   Classless network design

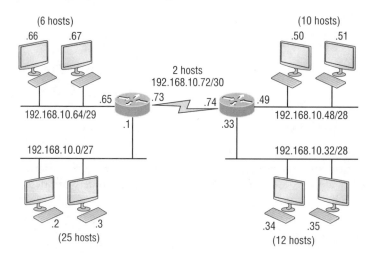

Now remember that we can use different size masks on each router interface. If we use a /30 on our WAN links and a /27, /28, and /29 on our LANs, we'll get 2 hosts per WAN interface and 30, 14, and 6 hosts per LAN interface—nice (remember to count your router interface as a host)! This makes a huge difference—not only can we get just the right amount of hosts on each LAN, we still have room to add more WANs and LANs using this same network!

To implement a VLSM design on your network, you need to have a routing protocol that sends subnet mask information with the route updates. The protocols that do that are RIPv2, EIGRP, and OSPF. Remember, RIPv1 will not work in classless networks, so it's considered a classful routing protocol.

Implementing VLSM Networks

To create VLSMs quickly and efficiently, you need to understand how block sizes and charts work together to create the VLSM masks. Table 5.1 shows you the block sizes used when creating VLSMs with Class C networks. For example, if you need 25 hosts, then you'll need a block size of 32. If you need 11 hosts, you'll use a block size of 16. Need 40 hosts? Then you'll need a block of 64. You cannot just make up block sizes—they've got to be the block sizes shown in Table 5.1. So memorize the block sizes in this table—it's easy. They're the same numbers we used with subnetting!

TABLE 5.1   Block sizes

Prefix	Mask	Hosts	Block Size
/25	128	126	128
/26	192	62	64
/27	224	30	32
/28	240	14	16
/29	248	6	8
/30	252	2	4

The next step is to create a VLSM table. Figure 5.3 shows you the table used in creating a VLSM network. The reason we use this table is so we don't accidentally overlap networks.

You'll find the sheet shown in Figure 5.3 very valuable because it lists every block size you can use for a network address. Notice that the block sizes start at 4 and advance all the way up to a block size of 128. If you have two networks with block sizes of 128, you can have only 2 networks. With a block size of 64, you can have only 4, and so on, all the way to 64 networks using a block size of 4. Of course, this is assuming you're using the ip subnet-zero command in your network design.

So now all you need to do is fill in the chart in the lower-left corner, then add the subnets to the worksheet and you're good to go!

Based on what you've learned so far about block sizes and the VLSM table, let's create a VLSM network using a Class C network address 192.168.10.0 for the network in Figure 5.4, then fill out the VLSM table, as shown in Figure 5.5.

In Figure 5.4, we have four WAN links and four LANs connected together, so we need to create a VLSM network that will save address space. Looks like we have two block sizes of 32, a block size of 16, and a block size of 8, and our WANs each have a block size of 4. Take a look and see how I filled out our VLSM chart in Figure 5.5.

FIGURE 5.3 The VLSM table

Subnet	Mask	Subnets	Hosts	Block
/25	128	2	126	128
/26	192	4	62	64
/27	224	8	30	32
/28	240	16	14	16
/29	248	32	6	8
/30	252	64	2	4

Network	Hosts	Block	Subnet	Mask
A				
B				
C				
D				
E				
F				
G				
H				
I				
J				
K				
L				

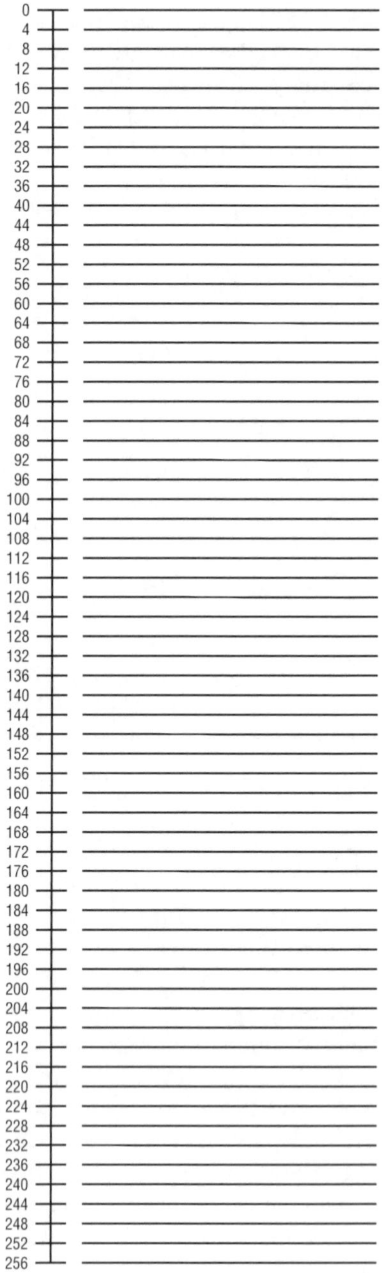

0
4
8
12
16
20
24
28
32
36
40
44
48
52
56
60
64
68
72
76
80
84
88
92
96
100
104
108
112
116
120
124
128
132
136
140
144
148
152
156
160
164
168
172
176
180
184
188
192
196
200
204
208
212
216
220
224
228
232
236
240
244
248
252
256

FIGURE 5.4 VLSM network example 1

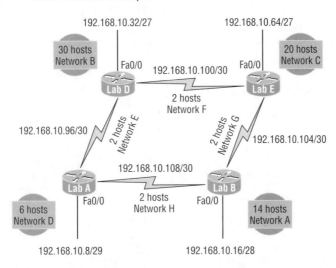

FIGURE 5.5 VLSM table example 1

Subnet	Mask	Subnets	Hosts	Block
/25	128	2	126	128
/26	192	4	62	64
/27	224	8	30	32
/28	240	16	14	16
/29	248	32	6	8
/30	252	64	2	4

Network	Hosts	Block	Subnet	Mask
A	14	16	/28	240
B	30	32	/27	224
C	20	32	/27	224
D	6	8	/29	248
E	2	4	/30	252
F	2	4	/30	252
G	2	4	/30	252
H	2	4	/30	252

```
0   ─┬─  ───────────────────────
4    ┼─  ───────────────────────
8    ┼─  ───────────────────────
12   ┼─  D — 192.168.10.8/29
16   ┼─  ───────────────────────
20   ┼─  ───────────────────────
24   ┼─  A — 192.168.10.16/28
28   ┼─  ───────────────────────
32   ┼─  ───────────────────────
36   ┼─  ───────────────────────
40   ┼─  ───────────────────────
44   ┼─  ───────────────────────
48   ┼─  B — 192.168.10.32/27
52   ┼─  ───────────────────────
56   ┼─  ───────────────────────
60   ┼─  ───────────────────────
64   ┼─  ───────────────────────
68   ┼─  ───────────────────────
72   ┼─  ───────────────────────
76   ┼─  ───────────────────────
80   ┼─  C — 192.168.10.64/27
84   ┼─  ───────────────────────
88   ┼─  ───────────────────────
92   ┼─  ───────────────────────
96   ┼─  E — 192.168.10.96/30
100  ┼─  F — 192.168.10.100/30
104  ┼─  G — 192.168.10.104/30
108  ┼─  H — 192.168.10.108/30
112  ┼─  ───────────────────────
116  ┼─  ───────────────────────
120  ┼─  ───────────────────────
124  ┼─  ───────────────────────
128  ┼─  ───────────────────────
132  ┼─  ───────────────────────
136  ┼─  ───────────────────────
140  ┼─  ───────────────────────
144  ┼─  ───────────────────────
148  ─┴─ ───────────────────────
         ---output cut---
```

There are two important things to note here. The first is that we still have plenty of room for growth with this VLSM network design. The second point is that we could never achieve this goal with one subnet mask using classful routing.

Let's do another one. Figure 5.6 shows a network with 11 networks, two block sizes of 64, one of 32, five of 16, and three of 4.

FIGURE 5.6   VLSM network example 2

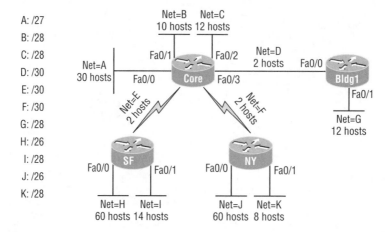

First, create your VLSM table and use your block size chart to fill in the table with the subnets you need. Figure 5.7 shows a possible solution.

Notice that I filled in this entire chart and only have room for one more block size of 4. You can only gain that amount of address space savings with a VLSM network!

Keep in mind that it doesn't matter where you start your block sizes as long as you always begin counting from zero. For example, if you had a block size of 16, you must start at 0 and incrementally progress from there—0, 16, 32, 48, and so on. You can't start with a block size of 16 or some value like 40, and you can't progress using anything but increments of 16.

Here's another example. If you had block sizes of 32, start at zero like this: 0, 32, 64, 96, etc. Again, you don't get to start wherever you want; you must always start counting from zero. In the example in Figure 5.7, I started at 64 and 128, with my two block sizes of 64. I didn't have much choice because my options are 0, 64, 128, and 192. However, I added the block size of 32, 16, 8, and 4 elsewhere, but they were always in the correct increments required of the specific block size. Remember that if you always start with the largest blocks first, then make your way to the smaller blocks sizes, you will automatically fall on an increment boundary. It also guarantees that you are using your address space in the most effective way.

Okay—you have three locations you need to address, and the IP network you have received is 192.168.55.0 to use as the addressing for the entire network. You'll use ip sub-net-zero and RIPv2 as the routing protocol because RIPv2 supports VLSM networks but

FIGURE 5.7 VLSM table example 2

Subnet	Mask	Subnets	Hosts	Block
/25	128	2	126	128
/26	192	4	62	64
/27	224	8	30	32
/28	240	16	14	16
/29	248	32	6	8
/30	252	64	2	4

Network	Hosts	Block	Subnet	Mask
A				
B				
C				
D				
E				
F				
G				
H				
I				
J				
K				

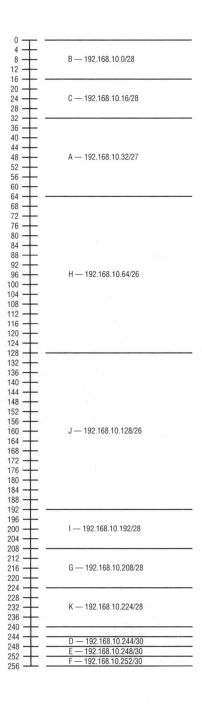

RIPv1 does not. Figure 5.8 shows the network diagram and the IP address of the RouterA S0/0 interface.

FIGURE 5.8   VLSM design example 1

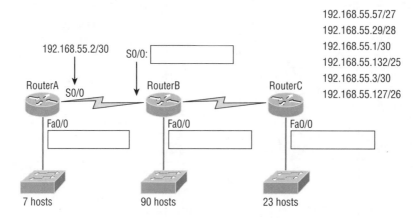

From the list of IP addresses on the right of the figure, which IP address do you think will be placed in each router's FastEthernet 0/0 interface and serial 0/0 of RouterB?

To answer this, look for clues in Figure 5.8. The first is that interface S0/0 on RouterA has IP address 192.168.55.2/30 assigned, which makes for an easy answer because A /30 is 255.255.255.252, which gives you a block size of 4. Your subnets are 0, 4, 8, etc. Since the known host has an IP address of 2, the only other valid host in the zero subnet is 1, so the third answer down is the right one for the S0/0 interface of RouterB.

The next clues are the listed number of hosts for each of the LANs. RouterA needs 7 hosts—a block size of 16 (/28). RouterB needs 90 hosts—a block size of 128 (/25). And RouterC needs 23 hosts—a block size of 32 (/27).

Figure 5.9 illustrates this solution.

FIGURE 5.9   Solution to VLSM design example 1

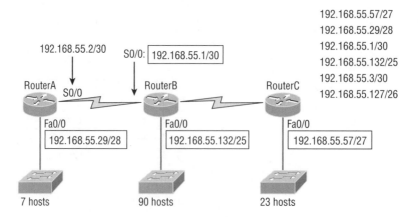

This is actually pretty simple because once you've figured out the block size needed for each LAN, all you need to get to the right solution is to identify proper clues and, of course, know your block sizes well!

One last example of VLSM design before we move on to summarization. Figure 5.10 shows three routers, all running RIPv2. Which Class C addressing scheme would you use to maintain the needs of this network while saving as much address space as possible?

FIGURE 5.10   VLSM design example 2

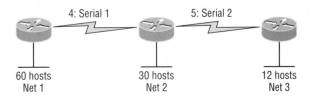

This is actually a pretty clean network design that's just waiting for you to fill out the chart. There are block sizes of 64, 32, and 16 and two block sizes of 4. Coming up with the right solution should be a slam dunk! Take a look at my answer in Figure 5.11.

FIGURE 5.11   Solution to VLSM design example 2

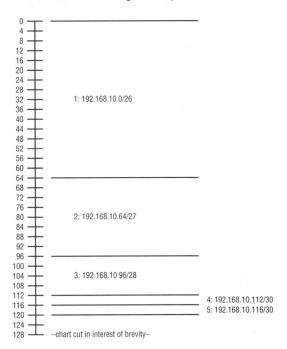

My solution began at subnet 0, and I used the block size of 64. Clearly, I didn't have to go with a block size of 64 because I could've chosen a block size of 4 instead. But I didn't because I usually like to start with the largest block size and move to the smallest. With that done, I added the block sizes of 32 and 16 as well as the two block sizes of 4. This solution is optimal because it still leaves lots of room to add subnets to this network!

Why Bother with VLSM Design?

You have just been hired by a new company and need to add on to their existing network. There are no restrictions to prevent you from starting over with a completely new IP address scheme. Should you use a VLSM classless network or opt for a classful network?

Let's say you happen to have plenty of address space because you're using the Class A 10.0.0.0 private network address, so you really can't imagine that you'd ever run out of IP addresses. So why would you want to bother with the VLSM design process in this environment?

Good question! Here's your answer...

By creating contiguous blocks of addresses to specific areas of your network, you can then easily summarize the network and keep route updates with a routing protocol to a minimum. Why would anyone want to advertise hundreds of networks between buildings when you can just send one summary route between buildings and achieve the same result? This approach will optimize the network's performance dramatically!

To make sure this is clear, let me take a second to explain summary routes. Summarization, also called supernetting, provides route updates in the most efficient way possible by advertising many routes in one advertisement instead of individually. This saves a ton of bandwidth and minimizes router processing. As always, you need to use blocks of addresses to configure your summary routes and watch your network's performance hum along efficiently! And remember, block sizes are used in all sorts of networks anyway.

Still, it's important to understand that summarization works only if you design your network properly. If you carelessly hand out IP subnets to any location on the network, you'll quickly notice that you no longer have any summary boundaries. And you won't get very far creating summary routes without those, so watch your step!

Summarization

Summarization, also called route aggregation, allows routing protocols to advertise many networks as one address. The purpose of this is to reduce the size of routing tables on routers to save memory, which also shortens the amount of time IP requires to parse the routing table when determining the best path to a remote network.

Figure 5.12 shows how a summary address would be used in an internetwork.

FIGURE 5.12   Summary address used in an internetwork

10.0.0.0/16
10.1.0.0/16
10.2.0.0/16
10.255.0.0/16   10.0.0.0/8

Summarization is pretty straightforward because all you really need to have down is a solid understanding of the block sizes we've been using for subnetting and VLSM design. For example, if you wanted to summarize the following networks into one network advertisement, you just have to find the block size first, which will make it easy to find your answer:

192.168.16.0 through network 192.168.31.0

Okay—so what's the block size? Well, there are exactly 16 Class C networks, which fit neatly into a block size of 16.

Now that we've determined the block size, we just need to find the network address and mask used to summarize these networks into one advertisement. The network address used to advertise the summary address is always the first network address in the block—in this example, 192.168.16.0. To figure out a summary mask, we just need to figure out which mask will get us a block size of 16. If you came up with 240, you got it right! 240 would be placed in the third octet, which is exactly the octet where we're summarizing, so the mask would be 255.255.240.0.

Here's another example:

Networks 172.16.32.0 through 172.16.50.0

This isn't as clean as the previous example because there are two possible answers. Here's why: Since you're starting at network 32, your options for block sizes are 4, 8, 16, 32, 64, etc., and block sizes of 16 and 32 could work as this summary address. Let's explore your two options:

- If you went with a block size of 16, then the network address would be 172.16.32.0 with a mask of 255.255.240.0 (240 provides a block of 16). The problem is that this only summarizes from 32 to 47, which means that networks 48 through 50 would be advertised as single networks. Even so, this could still be a good solution depending on your network design.

- If you decided to go with a block size of 32 instead, then your summary address would still be 172.16.32.0, but the mask would be 255.255.224.0 (224 provides a block of 32). The possible problem with this answer is that it will summarize networks 32 through 63 and we only have networks 32 to 50. No worries if you're planning on adding networks 51 to 63 later into the same network, but you could have serious problems in your internetwork if somehow networks 51 to 63 were to show up and be advertised from somewhere else in your network! So even though this option does allow for growth, it's a lot safer to go with option #1.

Let's take a look at another example: Your summary address is 192.168.144.0/20, so what's the range of host addresses that would be forwarded according to this summary? The /20 provides a summary address of 192.168.144.0 and mask of 255.255.240.0.

The third octet has a block size of 16, and starting at summary address 144, the next block of 16 is 160, so your network summary range is 144 to 159 in the third octet. This is why it comes in handy to be able to count in 16s!

A router with this summary address in the routing table will forward any packet having destination IP addresses of 192.168.144.1 through 192.168.159.254.

Only two more summarization examples, then we'll move on to troubleshooting.

In summarization example 4, Figure 5.13, the Ethernet networks connected to router R1 are being summarized to R2 as 192.168.144.0/20. Which range of IP addresses will R2 forward to R1 according to this summary?

FIGURE 5.13   Summarization example 4

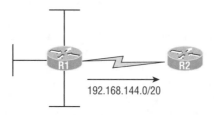

192.168.144.0/20

No worries—solving this is easier than it looks initially. The question actually has the summary address listed in it: 192.168.144.0/20. You already know that /20 is 255.255.240.0, which means you've got a block size of 16 in the third octet. Starting at 144, which is also right there in the question, makes the next block size of 16 equal 160. You can't go above 159 in the third octet, so the IP addresses that will be forwarded are 192.168.144.1 through 192.168.159.254.

Okay, last one. In Figure 5.14, there are five networks connected to router R1. What's the best summary address to R2?

FIGURE 5.14   Summarization example 5

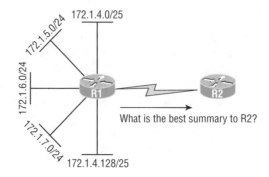

172.1.5.0/24
172.1.4.0/25
172.1.6.0/24
172.1.7.0/24
172.1.4.128/25
What is the best summary to R2?

I'll be honest with you—this is a much harder question than the one in Figure 5.13, so you're going to have to look carefully to see the answer. A good approach here would be to write down all the networks and see if you can find anything in common with all of them:

- 172.1.4.128/25
- 172.1.7.0/24
- 172.1.6.0/24
- 172.1.5.0/24
- 172.1.4.0/25

Do you see an octet that looks interesting to you? I do. It's the third octet. 4, 5, 6, 7, and yes, it's a block size of 4. So you can summarize 172.1.4.0 using a mask of 255.255.252.0, meaning you would use a block size of 4 in the third octet. The IP addresses forwarded with this summary would be 172.1.4.1 through 172.1.7.254.

To summarize the summarization section, if you've nailed down your block sizes, then finding and applying summary addresses and masks is a relatively straightforward task. But you're going to get bogged down pretty quickly if you don't know what a /20 is or if you can't count by 16s!

Troubleshooting IP Addressing

Because running into trouble now and then in networking is a given, being able to trouble-shoot IP addressing is clearly a vital skill. I'm not being negative here—just realistic. The positive side to this is that if you're the one equipped with the tools to diagnose and clear up the inevitable trouble, you get to be the hero when you save the day! Even better? You can usually fix an IP network regardless of whether you're on site or at home!

So this is where I'm going to show you the "Cisco way" of troubleshooting IP address-ing. Let's use Figure 5.15 as an example of your basic IP trouble—poor Sally can't log in to the Windows server. Do you deal with this by calling the Microsoft team to tell them their server is a pile of junk and causing all your problems? Though tempting, a better approach is to first double-check and verify your network instead.

FIGURE 5.15   Basic IP troubleshooting

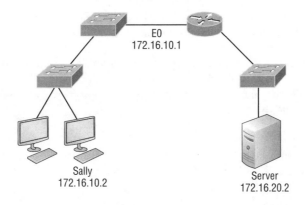

Okay, let's get started by going through the troubleshooting steps that Cisco recommends. They're pretty simple, but important nonetheless. Pretend you're at a customer host and they're complaining that they can't communicate to a server that just happens to be on a remote network. Here are the four troubleshooting steps Cisco recommends:

1. Open a Command window and ping 127.0.0.1. This is the diagnostic, or loopback, address, and if you get a successful ping, your IP stack is considered initialized. If it fails, then you have an IP stack failure and need to reinstall TCP/IP on the host.

```
C:\>ping 127.0.0.1
Pinging 127.0.0.1 with 32 bytes of data:
Reply from 127.0.0.1: bytes=32 time<1ms TTL=128
Reply from 127.0.0.1: bytes=32 time<1ms TTL=128
Reply from 127.0.0.1: bytes=32 time<1ms TTL=128
Reply from 127.0.0.1: bytes=32 time<1ms TTL=128
Ping statistics for 127.0.0.1:
    Packets: Sent &#x0003D; 4, Received = 4, Lost = 0 (0% loss),
Approximate round trip times in milli-seconds:
    Minimum = 0ms, Maximum = 0ms, Average = 0ms
```

2. From the Command window, ping the IP address of the local host (we'll assume correct configuration here, but always check the IP configuration too!). If that's successful, your network interface card (NIC) is functioning. If it fails, there is a problem with the NIC. Success here doesn't just mean that a cable is plugged into the NIC, only that the IP protocol stack on the host can communicate to the NIC via the LAN driver.

```
C:\>ping 172.16.10.2
Pinging 172.16.10.2 with 32 bytes of data:
Reply from 172.16.10.2: bytes=32 time<1ms TTL=128
Reply from 172.16.10.2: bytes=32 time<1ms TTL=128
Reply from 172.16.10.2: bytes=32 time<1ms TTL=128
Reply from 172.16.10.2: bytes=32 time<1ms TTL=128
Ping statistics for 172.16.10.2:
    Packets: Sent = 4, Received = 4, Lost = 0 (0% loss),
Approximate round trip times in milli-seconds:
    Minimum = 0ms, Maximum = 0ms, Average = 0ms
```

3. From the Command window, ping the default gateway (router). If the ping works, it means that the NIC is plugged into the network and can communicate on the local network. If it fails, you have a local physical network problem that could be anywhere from the NIC to the router.

```
C:\>ping 172.16.10.1
Pinging 172.16.10.1 with 32 bytes of data:
Reply from 172.16.10.1: bytes=32 time<1ms TTL=128
```

```
Reply from 172.16.10.1: bytes=32 time<1ms TTL=128
Reply from 172.16.10.1: bytes=32 time<1ms TTL=128
Reply from 172.16.10.1: bytes=32 time<1ms TTL=128
Ping statistics for 172.16.10.1:
    Packets: Sent = 4, Received = 4, Lost = 0 (0% loss),
Approximate round trip times in milli-seconds:
    Minimum = 0ms, Maximum = 0ms, Average = 0ms
```

4. If steps 1 through 3 were successful, try to ping the remote server. If that works, then you know that you have IP communication between the local host and the remote server. You also know that the remote physical network is working.

```
C:\>ping 172.16.20.2
Pinging 172.16.20.2 with 32 bytes of data:
Reply from 172.16.20.2: bytes=32 time<1ms TTL=128
Reply from 172.16.20.2: bytes=32 time<1ms TTL=128
Reply from 172.16.20.2: bytes=32 time<1ms TTL=128
Reply from 172.16.20.2: bytes=32 time<1ms TTL=128
Ping statistics for 172.16.20.2:
    Packets: Sent = 4, Received = 4, Lost = 0 (0% loss),
Approximate round trip times in milli-seconds:
    Minimum = 0ms, Maximum = 0ms, Average = 0ms
```

If the user still can't communicate with the server after steps 1 through 4 have been completed successfully, you probably have some type of name resolution problem and need to check your Domain Name System (DNS) settings. But if the ping to the remote server fails, then you know you have some type of remote physical network problem and need to go to the server and work through steps 1 through 3 until you find the snag.

Before we move on to determining IP address problems and how to fix them, I just want to mention some basic commands that you can use to help troubleshoot your network from both a PC and a Cisco router. Keep in mind that though these commands may do the same thing, they're implemented differently.

ping   Uses ICMP echo request and replies to test if a node IP stack is initialized and alive on the network.

traceroute   Displays the list of routers on a path to a network destination by using TTL time-outs and ICMP error messages. This command will not work from a command prompt.

tracert   Same function as traceroute, but it's a Microsoft Windows command and will not work on a Cisco router.

arp -a   Displays IP-to-MAC-address mappings on a Windows PC.

show ip arp   Same function as arp -a, but displays the ARP table on a Cisco router. Like the commands traceroute and tracert, arp -a and show ip arp are not interchangeable through DOS and Cisco.

`ipconfig /all`   Used only from a Windows command prompt; shows you the PC network configuration.

Once you've gone through all these steps and, if necessary, used the appropriate commands, what do you do when you find a problem? How do you go about fixing an IP address configuration error? Time to cover the next step—determining and fixing the issue at hand!

Determining IP Address Problems

It's common for a host, router, or other network device to be configured with the wrong IP address, subnet mask, or default gateway. Because this happens way too often, you must know how to find and fix IP address configuration errors.

A good way to start is to draw out the network and IP addressing scheme. If that's already been done, consider yourself lucky because though sensible, it's rarely done. Even if it is, it's usually outdated or inaccurate anyway. So either way, it's a good idea to bite the bullet and start from scratch.

> I'll show you how a great way to draw out your network using the Cisco Discovery Protocol (CDP) soon, in Chapter 7, "Managing a Cisco Internetwork."

Once you have your network accurately drawn out, including the IP addressing scheme, you need to verify each host's IP address, mask, and default gateway address to establish the problem. Of course, this is assuming that you don't have a physical layer problem, or if you did, that you've already fixed it.

Let's check out the example illustrated in Figure 5.16.

FIGURE 5.16   IP address problem 1

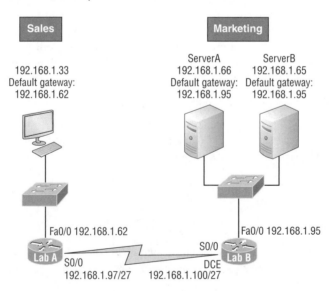

A user in the sales department calls and tells you that she can't get to ServerA in the marketing department. You ask her if she can get to ServerB in the marketing department, but she doesn't know because she doesn't have rights to log on to that server. What do you do?

First, guide your user through the four troubleshooting steps you learned in the preceding section. Okay—let's say steps 1 through 3 work but step 4 fails. By looking at the figure, can you determine the problem? Look for clues in the network drawing. First, the WAN link between the Lab A router and the Lab B router shows the mask as a /27. You should already know that this mask is 255.255.255.224 and determine that all networks are using this mask. The network address is 192.168.1.0. What are our valid subnets and hosts? 256 – 224 = 32, so this makes our subnets 0, 32, 64, 96, 128, etc. So, by looking at the figure, you can see that subnet 32 is being used by the sales department. The WAN link is using subnet 96, and the marketing department is using subnet 64.

Now you've got to establish what the valid host ranges are for each subnet. From what you learned at the beginning of this chapter, you should now be able to easily determine the subnet address, broadcast addresses, and valid host ranges. The valid hosts for the Sales LAN are 33 through 62, and the broadcast address is 63 because the next subnet is 64, right? For the Marketing LAN, the valid hosts are 65 through 94 (broadcast 95), and for the WAN link, 97 through 126 (broadcast 127). By closely examining the figure, you can determine that the default gateway on the Lab B router is incorrect. That address is the broadcast address for subnet 64, so there's no way it could be a valid host!

If you tried to configure that address on the Lab B router interface, you'd receive a bad mask error. Cisco routers don't let you type in subnet and broadcast addresses as valid hosts!

Did you get all that? Let's try another one to make sure. Figure 5.17 shows a network problem.

FIGURE 5.17   IP address problem 2

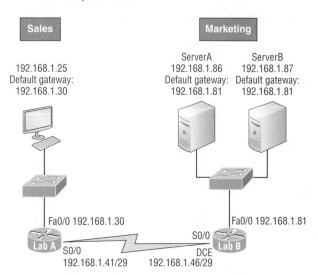

A user in the Sales LAN can't get to ServerB. You have the user run through the four basic troubleshooting steps and find that the host can communicate to the local network but not to the remote network. Find and define the IP addressing problem.

If you went through the same steps used to solve the last problem, you can see that first, the WAN link again provides the subnet mask to use— /29, or 255.255.255.248. Assuming classful addressing, you need to determine what the valid subnets, broadcast addresses, and valid host ranges are to solve this problem.

The 248 mask is a block size of 8 (256 – 248 = 8, as discussed in Chapter 4), so the subnets both start and increment in multiples of 8. By looking at the figure, you see that the Sales LAN is in the 24 subnet, the WAN is in the 40 subnet, and the Marketing LAN is in the 80 subnet. Can you see the problem yet? The valid host range for the Sales LAN is 25–30, and the configuration appears correct. The valid host range for the WAN link is 41–46, and this also appears correct. The valid host range for the 80 subnet is 81–86, with a broadcast address of 87 because the next subnet is 88. ServerB has been configured with the broadcast address of the subnet.

Okay, now that you can figure out misconfigured IP addresses on hosts, what do you do if a host doesn't have an IP address and you need to assign one? What you need to do is scrutinize the other hosts on the LAN and figure out the network, mask, and default gateway. Let's take a look at a couple of examples of how to find and apply valid IP addresses to hosts.

You need to assign a server and router IP addresses on a LAN. The subnet assigned on that segment is 192.168.20.24/29. The router needs to be assigned the first usable address and the server needs the last valid host ID. What is the IP address, mask, and default gateway assigned to the server?

To answer this, you must know that a /29 is a 255.255.255.248 mask, which provides a block size of 8. The subnet is known as 24, the next subnet in a block of 8 is 32, so the broadcast address of the 24 subnet is 31 and the valid host range is 25–30.

Server IP address: 192.168.20.30

Server mask: 255.255.255.248

Default gateway: 192.168.20.25 (router's IP address)

Take a look at Figure 5.18 and solve this problem.

FIGURE 5.18   Find the valid host #1

Router A

E0: 192.168.10.33/27

Look at the router's IP address on Ethernet0. What IP address, subnet mask, and valid host range could be assigned to the host?

The IP address of the router's Ethernet0 is 192.168.10.33/27. As you already know, a /27 is a 224 mask with a block size of 32. The router's interface is in the 32 subnet. The next subnet is 64, so that makes the broadcast address of the 32 subnet 63 and the valid host range 33–62.

> Host IP address: 192.168.10.34–62 (any address in the range except for 33, which is assigned to the router)
>
> Mask: 255.255.255.224
>
> Default gateway: 192.168.10.33

Figure 5.19 shows two routers with Ethernet configurations already assigned. What are the host addresses and subnet masks of HostA and HostB?

FIGURE 5.19   Find the valid host #2

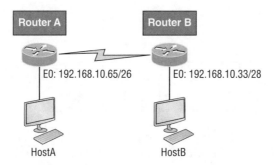

Router A has an IP address of 192.168.10.65/26 and Router B has an IP address of 192.168.10.33/28. What are the host configurations? Router A Ethernet0 is in the 192.168.10.64 subnet and Router B Ethernet0 is in the 192.168.10.32 network.

> Host A IP address: 192.168.10.66–126
>
> Host A mask: 255.255.255.192
>
> Host A default gateway: 192.168.10.65
>
> Host B IP address: 192.168.10.34–46
>
> Host B mask: 255.255.255.240
>
> Host B default gateway: 192.168.10.33

Just a couple more examples before you can put this chapter behind you—hang in there!

Figure 5.20 shows two routers. You need to configure the S0/0 interface on RouterA. The IP address assigned to the serial link is 172.16.17.0/22. What IP address can be assigned?

FIGURE 5.20   Find the valid host address #3

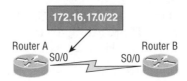

First, know that a /22 CIDR is 255.255.252.0, which makes a block size of 4 in the third octet. Since 17 is listed, the available range is 16.1 through 19.254, so in this example, the IP address S0/0 could be 172.16.18.255 since that's within the range.

Okay, last one! You need to find a classful network address that has one Class C network ID and you need to provide one usable subnet per city while allowing enough usable host addresses for each city specified in Figure 5.21. What is your mask?

FIGURE 5.21   Find the valid subnet mask

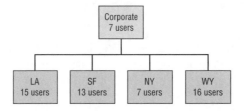

Actually, this is probably the easiest thing you've done all day! I count 5 subnets needed, and the Wyoming office needs 16 users—always look for the network that needs the most hosts! What block size is needed for the Wyoming office? Your answer is 32. You can't use a block size of 16 because you always have to subtract 2. What mask provides you with a block size of 32? 224 is your answer because this provides 8 subnets, each with 30 hosts.

You're done—the diva has sung and the chicken has safely crossed the road…whew! Time to take a break, but skip the shot and the beer if that's what you had in mind because you need to have your head straight to go through the written lab and review questions next!

Summary

Again, if you got to this point without getting lost along the way a few times, you're awesome, but if you did get lost, don't stress because most people do! Just be patient with yourself and go back over the material that tripped you up until it's all crystal clear. You'll get there!

This chapter provided you with keys to understanding the oh-so-very-important topic of variable length subnet masks. You should also know how to design and implement simple VLSM networks and be clear on summarization as well.

And make sure you understand and memorize Cisco's troubleshooting methods. You must remember the four steps that Cisco recommends to take when trying to narrow down exactly where a network and/or IP addressing problem is and then know how to proceed systematically to fix it. In addition, you should be able to find valid IP addresses and subnet masks by looking at a network diagram.

Exam Essentials

Describe the benefits of variable length subnet masks (VLSMs).   VLSMs enable the creation of subnets of specific sizes and allow the division of a classless network into smaller networks that do not need to be equal in size. This makes use of the address space more efficient because many times IP addresses are wasted with classful subnetting.

Understand the relationship between the subnet mask value and the resulting block size and the allowable IP addresses in each resulting subnet.   The relationship between the classful network being subdivided and the subnet mask used determines the number of possible hosts or the block size. It also determines where each subnet begins and ends and which IP addresses cannot be assigned to a host within each subnet.

Describe the process of summarization or route aggregation and its relationship to subnetting.   Summarization is the combining of subnets derived from a classful network for the purpose of advertising a single route to neighboring routers instead of multiple routes, reducing the size of routing tables and speeding the route process.

Calculate the summary mask that will advertise a single network representing all subnets.   The network address used to advertise the summary address is always the first network address in the block of subnets. The mask is the subnet mask value that yields the same block size.

Remember the four diagnostic steps.   The four simple steps that Cisco recommends for troubleshooting are ping the loopback address, ping the NIC, ping the default gateway, and ping the remote device.

Identify and mitigate an IP addressing problem.   Once you go through the four troubleshooting steps that Cisco recommends, you must be able to determine the IP addressing problem by drawing out the network and finding the valid and invalid hosts addressed in your network.

Understand the troubleshooting tools that you can use from your host and a Cisco router.   The ping 127.0.0.1 command tests your local IP stack, and tracert is a Windows command to track the path a packet takes through an internetwork to a destination. Cisco routers use the command traceroute, or just trace for short. Don't confuse the Windows and Cisco commands. Although they produce the same output, they don't work from the same prompts. The command ipconfig /all will display your PC network configuration from a DOS prompt, and arp -a (again from a DOS prompt) will display IP-to-MAC-address mapping on a Windows PC.

Written Lab 5

In this section, you'll complete the following lab to make sure you've got the information and concepts contained within them fully dialed in:

Lab 5.1: Summarization Practice

You can find the answers to this lab in Appendix A, "Answers to Written Labs."

Lab 5.1: Summarization Practice

For each of the following sets of networks, determine the summary address and the mask to be used that will summarize the subnets.

1. 192.168.1.0/24 through 192.168.12.0/24

2. 172.144.0.0 through 172.159.0.0

3. 192.168.32.0 through 192.168.63.0

4. 192.168.96.0 through 192.168.111.0

5. 66.66.0.0 through 66.66.15.0

6. 192.168.1.0 through 192.168.120.0

7. 172.16.1.0 through 172.16.7.0

8. 192.168.128.0 through 192.168.190.0

9. 53.60.96.0 through 53.60.127.0

10. 172.16.10.0 through 172.16.63.0

Review Questions

 The following questions are designed to test your understanding of this chapter's material. For more information on how to get additional questions, please see www.lammle.com/ccna.

You can find the answers to these questions in Appendix B, "Answers to Review Questions."

1. On a VLSM network, which mask should you use on point-to-point WAN links in order to reduce the waste of IP addresses?

    A. /27

    B. /28

    C. /29

    D. /30

    E. /31

2. In the network shown in the diagram, how many computers could be in Network B?

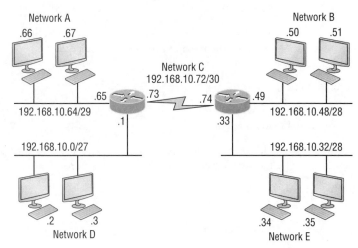

    A. 6

    B. 12

    C. 14

    D. 30

3. In the following diagram, in order to have IP addressing that's as efficient as possible, which network should use a /29 mask?

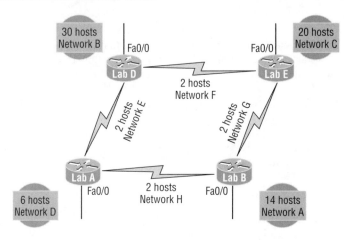

A. A

B. B

C. C

D. D

4. To use VLSM, what capability must the routing protocols in use possess?

A. Support for multicast

B. Multiprotocol support

C. Transmission of subnet mask information

D. Support for unequal load balancing

5. What summary address would cover all the networks shown and advertise a single, efficient route to Router B that won't advertise more networks than needed?

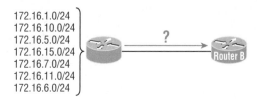

A. 172.16.0.0/24

B. 172.16.1.0/24

C. 172.16.0.0/24

D. 172.16.0.0/20

    E.   172.16.16.0/28

    F.   172.16.0.0/27

6.   In the following diagram, what is the most likely reason the station cannot ping outside of its network?

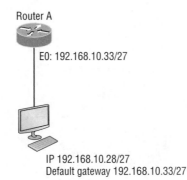

Router A

E0: 192.168.10.33/27

IP 192.168.10.28/27
Default gateway 192.168.10.33/27

    A.   The IP address is incorrect on interface E0 of the router.

    B.   The default gateway address is incorrect on the station.

    C.   The IP address on the station is incorrect.

    D.   The router is malfunctioning.

7.   If a host is configured with an incorrect default gateway and all the other computers and router are known to be configured correctly, which of the following statements is TRUE?

    A.   Host A cannot communicate with the router.

    B.   Host A can communicate with other hosts in the same subnet.

    C.   Host A can communicate with hosts in other subnets.

    D.   Host A can communicate with no other systems.

8.   Which of the following troubleshooting steps, if completed successfully, also confirms that the other steps will succeed as well?

    A.   Ping a remote computer.

    B.   Ping the loopback address.

    C.   Ping the NIC.

    D.   Ping the default gateway.

9.   When a ping to the local host IP address fails, what can you assume?

    A.   The IP address of the local host is incorrect.

    B.   The IP address of the remote host is incorrect.

    C.   The NIC is not functional.

    D.   The IP stack has failed to initialize.

10. When a ping to the local host IP address succeeds but a ping to the default gateway IP address fails, what can you rule out? (Choose all that apply.)

    A. The IP address of the local host is incorrect.

    B. The IP address of the gateway is incorrect.

    C. The NIC is not functional.

    D. The IP stack has failed to initialize.

11. Which of the networks in the diagram could use a /29 mask?

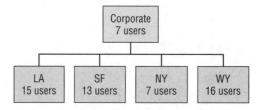

    A. Corporate

    B. LA

    C. SF

    D. NY

    E. None

12. What network service is the most likely problem if you can ping a computer by IP address but not by name?

    A. DNS

    B. DHCP

    C. ARP

    D. ICMP

13. When you issue the ping command, what protocol are you using?

    A. DNS

    B. DHCP

    C. ARP

    D. ICMP

14. Which of the following commands displays the networks traversed on a path to a network destination?

    A. ping

    B. traceroute

C. pingroute

D. pathroute

15. What command generated the output shown below?

```
Reply from 172.16.10.2: bytes=32 time<1ms TTL=128
Reply from 172.16.10.2: bytes=32 time<1ms TTL=128
Reply from 172.16.10.2: bytes=32 time<1ms TTL=128
Reply from 172.16.10.2: bytes=32 time<1ms TTL=128
```

A. traceroute

B. show ip route

C. ping

D. pathping

16. In the work area, match the command to its function on the right.

traceroute	=	Displays the list of routers on a path to a network destination
arp -	=	Displays IP-to_MAC
show ip arp	=	Cisco router ARP table
ipconfig /asll	=	PC Net config

17. Which of the following network addresses correctly summarizes the three networks shown below efficiently?

10.0.0.0/16

10.1.0.0/16

10.2.0.0/16

A. 10.0.0.0/15

B. 10.1.0.0/8

C. 10.0.0.0/14

D. 10.0.0.8/16

18. What command displays the ARP table on a Cisco router?

A. show ip arp

B. traceroute

C. arp -a

D. tracert

19. What switch must be added to the `ipconfig` command on a PC to verify DNS configuration?

    A. `/dns`

    B. `-dns`

    C. `/all`

    D. `showall`

20. Which of the following is the best summarization of the following networks: 192.168.128.0 through 192.168.159.0?

    A. 192.168.0.0/24

    B. 192.168.128.0/16

    C. 192.168.128.0/19

    D. 192.168.128.0/20

Chapter

6

Cisco's Internetworking Operating System (IOS)

THE FOLLOWING ICND1 EXAM TOPICS ARE COVERED IN THIS CHAPTER:

- ✓ **2.0 LAN Switching Technologies**

- ✓ **2.3 Troubleshoot interface and cable issues (collisions, errors, duplex, speed)**

- ✓ **5.0 Infrastructure Management**

- ✓ **5.3 Configure and verify initial device configuration**

- ✓ **5.4 Configure, verify, and troubleshoot basic device hardening**

- ✓ **5.4.a Local authentication**

- ✓ **5.4.b Secure password**

- ✓ **5.4.c Access to device**

    - ▪ 5.4.c. (i) Voice

    - ▪ 5.4.c. (ii) Video

- ✓ **5.4.c. (iii) Data**

- ✓ **5.4.d Source address Telnet/SSH**

- ✓ **5.4.e Login banner**

- ✓ **5.6 Use Cisco IOS tools to troubleshoot and resolve problems**

    - ▪ 5.6.a Ping and traceroute with extended option

    - ▪ 5.6.b Terminal monitor

    - ▪ 5.6.c Log events

It's time to introduce you to the Cisco Internetwork Operating System (IOS). The IOS is what runs Cisco routers as well as Cisco's switches, and it's also what we use to configure these devices.

So that's what you're going to learn about in this chapter. I'm going to show you how to configure a Cisco IOS device using the Cisco IOS command-line interface (CLI). Once proficient with this interface, you'll be able to configure hostnames, banners, passwords, and more as well as troubleshoot skillfully using the Cisco IOS.

We'll also begin the journey to mastering the basics of router and switch configurations plus command verifications in this chapter.

I'll start with a basic IOS switch to begin building the network we'll use throughout this book for configuration examples. Don't forget—I'll be using both switches and routers throughout this chapter, and we configure these devices pretty much the same way. Things diverge when we get to the interfaces where the differences between the two become key, so pay attention closely when we get to that point!

Just as it was with preceding chapters, the fundamentals presented in this chapter are important building blocks to have solidly in place before moving on to the more advanced material coming up in the next ones.

To find up-to-the minute updates for this chapter, please see www.lammle .com/ccna or the book's web page at www.sybex.com/go/ccna.

The IOS User Interface

The *Cisco Internetwork Operating System (IOS)* is the kernel of Cisco routers as well as all current Catalyst switches. In case you didn't know, a kernel is the elemental, indispensable part of an operating system that allocates resources and manages tasks like low-level hardware interfaces and security.

Coming up, I'll show you the Cisco IOS and how to configure a Cisco switch using the *command-line interface (CLI)*. By using the CLI, we can provide access to a Cisco device and provide voice, video, and data service. ... The configurations you'll see in this chapter are exactly the same as they are on a Cisco router.

Cisco IOS

The Cisco IOS is a proprietary kernel that provides routing, switching, internetworking, and telecommunications features. The first IOS was written by William Yeager in 1986 and enabled networked applications. It runs on most Cisco routers as well as a growing number of Cisco Catalyst switches, like the Catalyst 2960 and 3560 series switches used in this book. And it's an essential for the Cisco exam objectives!

Here's a short list of some important things that the Cisco router IOS software is responsible for:

- Carrying network protocols and functions
- Connecting high-speed traffic between devices
- Adding security to control access and stopping unauthorized network use
- Providing scalability for ease of network growth and redundancy
- Supplying network reliability for connecting to network resources

You can access the Cisco IOS through the console port of a router or switch, from a modem into the auxiliary (or aux) port on a router, or even through Telnet and Secure Shell (SSH). Access to the IOS command line is called an *EXEC session*.

Connecting to a Cisco IOS Device

We connect to a Cisco device to configure it, verify its configuration, and check statistics, and although there are different approaches to this, the first place you would usually connect to is the console port. The *console port* is usually an RJ45, 8-pin modular connection located at the back of the device, and there may or may not be a password set on it by default.

Look back into Chapter 2, "Ethernet Networking and Data Encapsulation," to review how to configure a PC and enable it to connect to a router console port.

You can also connect to a Cisco router through an *auxiliary port*, which is really the same thing as a console port, so it follows that you can use it as one. The main difference with an auxiliary port is that it also allows you to configure modem commands so that a modem can be connected to the router. This is a cool feature because it lets you dial up a remote router and attach to the auxiliary port if the router is down and you need to configure it remotely, *out-of-band*. One of the differences between Cisco routers and switches is that switches do not have an auxiliary port.

The third way to connect to a Cisco device is *in-band*, through the program *Telnet* or *Secure Shell (SSH)*. In-band means configuring the device via the network, the opposite of *out-of-band*. We covered Telnet and SSH in Chapter 3, "Introduction to TCP/IP," and in this chapter, I'll show you how to configure access to both of these protocols on a Cisco device.

Figure 6.1 shows an illustration of a Cisco 2960 switch. Really focus in on all the different kinds of interfaces and connections! On the right side is the 10/100/1000 uplink. You can use either the UTP port or the fiber port, but not both at the same time.

FIGURE 6.1   A Cisco 2960 switch

The 3560 switch I'll be using in this book looks a lot like the 2960, but it can perform layer 3 switching, unlike the 2960, which is limited to only layer 2 functions.

I also want to take a moment and tell you about the 2800 series router because that's the router series I'll be using in this book. This router is known as an Integrated Services Router (ISR) and Cisco has updated it to the 2900 series, but I still have plenty of 2800 series routers in my production networks. Figure 6.2 shows a new 1900 series router. The new ISR series of routers are nice; they are so named because many services, like security, are built into them. The ISR series router is a modular device, much faster and a lot sleeker than the older 2600 series routers, and it's elegantly designed to support a broad new range of interface options. The new ISR series router can offer multiple serial interfaces, which can be used for connecting a T1 using a serial V.35 WAN connection. And multiple Fast Ethernet or Gigabit Ethernet ports can be used on the router, depending on the model. This router also has one console via an RJ45 connector and another through the USB port. There is also an auxiliary connection to allow a console connection via a remote modem.

FIGURE 6.2   A new Cisco 1900 router

You need to keep in mind that for the most part, you get some serious bang for your buck with the 2800/2900—unless you start adding a bunch of interfaces to it. You've got to pony up for each one of those little beauties, so this can really start to add up and fast!

A couple of other series of routers that will set you back a lot less than the 2800 series are the 1800/1900s, so look into these routers if you want a less-expensive alternative to the 2800/2900 but still want to run the same IOS.

So even though I'm going to be using mostly 2800 series routers and 2960/3560 switches throughout this book to demonstrate examples of IOS configurations, I want to point out that the particular *router* model you use to practice for the Cisco exam isn't really important. The *switch* types are, though—you definitely need a couple 2960 switches as well as a 3560 switch if you want to measure up to the exam objectives!

You can find more information about all Cisco routers at www.cisco.com/en/US/products/hw/routers/index.html.

Bringing Up a Switch

When you first bring up a Cisco IOS device, it will run a power-on self-test—a POST. Upon passing that, the machine will look for and then load the Cisco IOS from flash memory if an IOS file is present, then expand it into RAM. As you probably know, flash memory is electronically erasable programmable read-only memory—an EEPROM. The next step is for the IOS to locate and load a valid configuration known as the startup-config that will be stored in *nonvolatile RAM (NVRAM)*.

Once the IOS is loaded and up and running, the startup-config will be copied from NVRAM into RAM and from then on referred to as the running-config.

But if a valid startup-config isn't found in NVRAM, your switch will enter setup mode, giving you a step-by-step dialog to help configure some basic parameters on it.

You can also enter setup mode at any time from the command line by typing the command **setup** from privileged mode, which I'll get to in a minute. Setup mode only covers some basic commands and generally isn't really all that helpful. Here's an example:

```
Would you like to enter the initial configuration dialog? [yes/no]: y

At any point you may enter a question mark '?' for help.
Use ctrl-c to abort configuration dialog at any prompt.
Default settings are in square brackets '[]'.


Basic management setup configures only enough connectivity
for management of the system, extended setup will ask you
to configure each interface on the system

Would you like to enter basic management setup? [yes/no]: y
Configuring global parameters:

  Enter host name [Switch]: Ctrl+C
Configuration aborted, no changes made.
```

 You can exit setup mode at any time by pressing Ctrl+C.

I highly recommend going through setup mode once, then never again because you should always use the CLI instead!

Command-Line Interface (CLI)

I sometimes refer to the CLI as "cash line interface" because the ability to create advanced configurations on Cisco routers and switches using the CLI will earn you some decent cash!

Entering the CLI

After the interface status messages appear and you press Enter, the Switch> prompt will pop up. This is called *user exec mode*, or user mode for short, and although it's mostly used to view statistics, it is also a stepping stone along the way to logging in to *privileged exec mode*, called privileged mode for short.

You can view and change the configuration of a Cisco router only while in privileged mode, and you enter it via the enable command like this:

```
Switch>enable
Switch#
```

The Switch# prompt signals you're in privileged mode where you can both view and change the switch configuration. You can go back from privileged mode into user mode by using the disable command:

```
Switch#disable
Switch>
```

You can type **logout** from either mode to exit the console:

```
Switch>logout
Switch con0 is now available
Press RETURN to get started.
```

Next, I'll show how to perform some basic administrative configurations.

Overview of Router Modes

To configure from a CLI, you can make global changes to the router by typing **configure terminal** or just **config t**. This will get you into global configuration mode where you can make changes to the running-config. Commands run from global configuration mode are predictably referred to as global commands, and they are typically set only once and affect the entire router.

Type **config** from the privileged-mode prompt and then press Enter to opt for the default of terminal like this:

```
Switch#config
Configuring from terminal, memory, or network [terminal]? [press enter]
Enter configuration commands, one per line.  End with CNTL/Z.
Switch(config)#
```

At this point, you make changes that affect the router as a whole (globally), hence the term *global configuration mode*. For instance, to change the running-config—the current configuration running in dynamic RAM (DRAM)—use the configure terminal command, as I just demonstrated.

CLI Prompts

Let's explore the different prompts you'll encounter when configuring a switch or router now, because knowing them well will really help you orient yourself and recognize exactly where you are at any given time while in configuration mode. I'm going to demonstrate some of the prompts used on a Cisco switch and cover the various terms used along the way. Make sure you're very familiar with them, and always check your prompts before making any changes to a router's configuration!

We're not going to venture into every last obscure command prompt you could potentially come across in the configuration mode world because that would get us deep into territory that's beyond the scope of this book. Instead, I'm going to focus on the prompts you absolutely must know to pass the exam plus the very handy and seriously vital ones you'll need and use the most in real-life networking—the cream of the crop.

> Don't freak! It's not important that you understand exactly what each of these command prompts accomplishes just yet because I'm going to completely fill you in on all of them really soon. For now, relax and focus on just becoming familiar with the different prompts available and all will be well!

Interfaces

To make changes to an interface, you use the interface command from global configuration mode:

```
Switch(config)#interface ?
  Async            Async interface
  BVI              Bridge-Group Virtual Interface
  CTunnel          CTunnel interface
  Dialer           Dialer interface
  FastEthernet     FastEthernet IEEE 802.3
  Filter           Filter interface
  Filtergroup      Filter Group interface
  GigabitEthernet  GigabitEthernet IEEE 802.3z
  Group-Async      Async Group interface
  Lex              Lex interface
  Loopback         Loopback interface
  Null             Null interface
  Port-channel     Ethernet Channel of interfaces
  Portgroup        Portgroup interface
  Pos-channel      POS Channel of interfaces
  Tunnel           Tunnel interface
```

```
Vif              PGM Multicast Host interface
Virtual-Template   Virtual Template interface
Virtual-TokenRing  Virtual TokenRing
Vlan             Catalyst Vlans
fcpa             Fiber Channel
range            interface range command
Switch(config)#interface fastEthernet 0/1
Switch(config-if)#)
```

Did you notice that the prompt changed to Switch(config-if)#? This tells you that you're in *interface configuration mode*. And wouldn't it be nice if the prompt also gave you an indication of what interface you were configuring? Well, at least for now we'll have to live without the prompt information, because it doesn't. But it should already be clear to you that you really need to pay attention when configuring an IOS device!

Line Commands

To configure user-mode passwords, use the line command. The prompt then becomes Switch(config-line)#:

```
Switch(config)#line ?
  <0-16>    First Line number
  console   Primary terminal line
  vty       Virtual terminal
Switch(config)#line console 0
Switch(config-line)#
```

The line console 0 command is a global command, and sometimes you'll also hear people refer to global commands as major commands. In this example, any command typed from the (config-line) prompt is known as a subcommand.

Access List Configurations

To configure a standard named access list, you'll need to get to the prompt Switch(config-std-nacl)#:

```
Switch#config t
Switch(config)#ip access-list standard Todd
Switch(config-std-nacl)#
```

What you see here is a typical basic standard ACL prompt. There are various ways to configure access lists, and the prompts are only slightly different from this particular example.

Routing Protocol Configurations

I need to point out that we don't use routing or router protocols on 2960 switches, but we can and will use them on my 3560 switches. Here is an example of configuring routing on a layer 3 switch:

```
Switch(config)#router rip
IP routing not enabled
Switch(config)#ip routing
Switch(config)#router rip
Switch(config-router)#
```

Did you notice that the prompt changed to Switch(config-router)#? To make sure you achieve the objectives specific to the Cisco exam and this book, I'll configure static routing, RIPv2, and RIPng. And don't worry—I'll explain all of these in detail soon, in Chapter 9, "IP Routing," and Chapter 14, "Internet Protocol Version 6 (IPv6)"!

Defining Router Terms

Table 6.1 defines some of the terms I've used so far.

TABLE 6.1   Router terms

Mode	Definition
User exec mode	Limited to basic monitoring commands
Privileged exec mode	Provides access to all other router commands
Global configuration mode	Commands that affect the entire system
Specific configuration modes	Commands that affect interfaces/processes only
Setup mode	Interactive configuration dialog

Editing and Help Features

The Cisco advanced editing features can also help you configure your router. If you type in a question mark (?) at any prompt, you'll be given a list of all the commands available from that prompt:

```
Switch#?
Exec commands:
  access-enable    Create a temporary Access-List entry
  access-template  Create a temporary Access-List entry
  archive          manage archive files
  cd               Change current directory
  clear            Reset functions
  clock            Manage the system clock
  cns              CNS agents
```

```
  configure        Enter configuration mode
  connect          Open a terminal connection
  copy             Copy from one file to another
  debug            Debugging functions (see also 'undebug')
  delete           Delete a file
  diagnostic       Diagnostic commands
  dir              List files on a filesystem
  disable          Turn off privileged commands
  disconnect       Disconnect an existing network connection
  dot1x            IEEE 802.1X Exec Commands
  enable           Turn on privileged commands
  eou              EAPoUDP
  erase            Erase a filesystem
  exit             Exit from the EXEC
 --More-- ?
Press RETURN for another line, SPACE for another page, anything else to quit
```

And if this is not enough information for you, you can press the spacebar to get another whole page of information, or you can press Enter to go one command at a time. You can also press Q, or any other key for that matter, to quit and return to the prompt. Notice that I typed a question mark (?) at the more prompt and it told me what my options were from that prompt.

Here's a shortcut: To find commands that start with a certain letter, use the letter and the question mark with no space between them, like this:

```
Switch#c?
cd       clear  clock  cns  configure
connect  copy
Switch#c
```

Okay, see that? By typing **c?**, I got a response listing all the commands that start with *c*. Also notice that the Switch#**c** prompt reappears after the list of commands is displayed. This can be really helpful when you happen to be working with long commands but you're short on patience and still need the next possible one. It would get old fast if you actually had to retype the entire command every time you used a question mark!

So with that, let's find the next command in a string by typing the first command and then a question mark:

```
Switch#clock ?
  set  Set the time and date

Switch#clock set ?
  hh:mm:ss  Current Time

Switch#clock set 2:34 ?
% Unrecognized command
```

```
Switch#clock set 2:34:01 ?
  <1-31>  Day of the month
  MONTH   Month of the year

Switch#clock set 2:34:01 21 july ?
  <1993-2035>  Year

Switch#clock set 2:34:01 21 august 2013
Switch#
00:19:45: %SYS-6-CLOCKUPDATE: System clock has been updated from 00:19:45
UTC Mon Mar 1 1993 to 02:34:01 UTC Wed Aug 21 2013, configured from console
by console.
```

I entered the **clock ?** command and got a list of the next possible parameters plus what they do. Make note of the fact that you can just keep typing a command, a space, and then a question mark until <cr> (carriage return) is your only option left.

And if you're typing commands and receive

```
Switch#clock set 11:15:11
% Incomplete command.
```

no worries—that's only telling you that the command string simply isn't complete quite yet. All you need to do is to press the up arrow key to redisplay the last command entered and then continue with the command by using your question mark.

But if you get the error

```
Switch(config)#access-list 100 permit host 1.1.1.1 host 2.2.2.2
                                              ^
% Invalid input detected at '^' marker.
```

all is not well because it means you actually have entered a command incorrectly. See that little caret—the ^? It's a very helpful tool that marks the exact point where you blew it and made a mess.

Here's another example of when you'll see that caret:

```
Switch#sh fastethernet 0/0
            ^
% Invalid input detected at '^' marker.
```

This command looks right, but be careful! The problem is that the full command is show interface fastethernet 0/0.

Now if you receive the error

```
Switch#sh cl
% Ambiguous command:  "sh cl"
```

you're being told that there are multiple commands that begin with the string you entered and it's not unique. Use the question mark to find the exact command you need:

```
Switch#sh cl?
class-map  clock  cluster
```

Case in point: There are three commands that start with show cl.
Table 6.2 lists the enhanced editing commands available on a Cisco router.

TABLE 6.2 Enhanced editing commands

Command	Meaning
Ctrl+A	Moves your cursor to the beginning of the line
Ctrl+E	Moves your cursor to the end of the line
Esc+B	Moves back one word
Ctrl+B	Moves back one character
Ctrl+F	Moves forward one character
Esc+F	Moves forward one word
Ctrl+D	Deletes a single character
Backspace	Deletes a single character
Ctrl+R	Redisplays a line
Ctrl+U	Erases a line
Ctrl+W	Erases a word
Ctrl+Z	Ends configuration mode and returns to EXEC
Tab	Finishes typing a command for you

Another really cool editing feature you need to know about is the automatic scrolling of long lines. In the following example, the command I typed reached the right margin and automatically moved 11 spaces to the left. How do I know this? Because the dollar sign [$] is telling me that the line has been scrolled to the left:

```
Switch#config t
Switch(config)#$ 100 permit ip host 192.168.10.1 192.168.10.0 0.0.0.255
```

You can review the router-command history with the commands shown in Table 6.3.

TABLE 6.3   IOS-command history

Command	Meaning
Ctrl+P or up arrow	Shows last command entered
Ctrl+N or down arrow	Shows previous commands entered
show history	Shows last 20 commands entered by default
show terminal	Shows terminal configurations and history buffer size
terminal history size	Changes buffer size (max 256)

The following example demonstrates the show history command as well as how to change the history's size. It also shows how to verify the history with the show terminal command. First, use the show history command, which will allow you to see the last 20 commands that were entered on the router (even though my particular router reveals only 10 commands because that's all I've entered since rebooting it). Check it out:

```
Switch#sh history
  sh fastethernet 0/0
  sh ru
  sh cl
  config t
  sh history
  sh flash
  sh running-config
  sh startup-config
  sh ver
  sh history
```

Okay—now, we'll use the show terminal command to verify the terminal history size:

```
Switch#sh terminal
Line 0, Location: "", Type: ""
Length: 24 lines, Width: 80 columns
Baud rate (TX/RX) is 9600/9600, no parity, 2 stopbits, 8 databits
Status: PSI Enabled, Ready, Active, Ctrl-c Enabled, Automore On
  0x40000
Capabilities: none
Modem state: Ready
```

```
[output cut]
Modem type is unknown.
Session limit is not set.
Time since activation: 00:17:22
Editing is enabled.
History is enabled, history size is 10.
DNS resolution in show commands is enabled
Full user help is disabled
Allowed input transports are none.
Allowed output transports are telnet.
Preferred transport is telnet.
No output characters are padded
No special data dispatching characters
```

When Should I Use the Cisco Editing Features?

You'll find yourself using a couple of editing features quite often and some not so much, if at all. Understand that Cisco didn't make these up; these are just old Unix commands! Even so, Ctrl+A is still a really helpful way to negate a command.

For example, if you were to put in a long command and then decide you didn't want to use that command in your configuration after all, or if it didn't work, then you could just press your up arrow key to show the last command entered, press Ctrl+A, type **no** and then a space, press Enter—and poof! The command is negated. This doesn't work on every command, but it works on a lot of them and saves some serious time!

Administrative Configurations

Even though the following sections aren't critical to making a router or switch *work* on a network, they're still really important. I'm going to guide you through configuring specific commands that are particularly helpful when administering your network.

You can configure the following administrative functions on a router and switch:

- Hostnames
- Banners
- Passwords
- Interface descriptions

Remember, none of these will make your routers or switches work better or faster, but trust me, your life will be a whole lot better if you just take the time to set these configurations on each of your network devices. This is because doing so makes trouble-shooting and maintaining your network a great deal easier—seriously! In this next section, I'll be demonstrating commands on a Cisco switch, but understand that these commands are used in the exact same way on a Cisco router.

Hostnames

We use the `hostname` command to set the identity of the router and switch. This is only locally significant, meaning it doesn't affect how the router or switch performs name lookups or how the device actually works on the internetwork. But the hostname is still important in routes because it's often used for authentication in many wide area networks (WANs). Here's an example:

```
Switch#config t
Switch(config)#hostname Todd
Todd(config)#hostname Chicago
Chicago(config)#hostname Todd
Todd(config)#
```

I know it's pretty tempting to configure the hostname after your own name, but it's usually a much better idea to name the device something that relates to its physical location. A name that maps to where the device lives will make finding it a whole lot easier, which among other things, confirms that you're actually configuring the correct device. Even though it seems like I'm completely ditching my own advice by naming mine *Todd*, I'm not, because this particular device really does live in "Todd's" office. Its name perfectly maps to where it is, so it won't be confused with those in the other networks I work with!

Banners

A very good reason for having a *banner* is to give any and all who dare attempt to telnet or sneak into your internetwork a little security notice. And they're very cool because you can create and customize them so that they'll greet anyone who shows up on the router with exactly the information you want them to have!

Here are the three types of banners you need to be sure you're familiar with:

- Exec process creation banner
- Login banner
- Message of the day banner

And you can see them all illustrated in the following code:

```
Todd(config)#banner ?
  LINE          c banner-text c, where 'c' is a delimiting character
  exec          Set EXEC process creation banner
```

```
incoming         Set incoming terminal line banner
login            Set login banner
motd             Set Message of the Day banner
prompt-timeout   Set Message for login authentication timeout
slip-ppp         Set Message for SLIP/PPP
```

Message of the day (MOTD) banners are the most widely used banners because they give a message to anyone connecting to the router via Telnet or an auxiliary port or even through a console port as seen here:

```
Todd(config)#banner motd ?
LINE c banner-text c, where 'c' is a delimiting character
Todd(config)#banner motd #
Enter TEXT message. End with the character '#'.
$ Acme.com network, then you must disconnect immediately.
#
```

Todd(config)#**^Z** (Press the control key + z keys to return to privileged mode)
Todd#**exit**
```
con0 is now available
Press RETURN to get started.
If you are not authorized to be in Acme.com network, then you
must disconnect immediately.
Todd#
```

This MOTD banner essentially tells anyone connecting to the device to get lost if they're not on the guest list. The part to focus upon here is the delimiting character, which is what informs the router the message is done. Clearly, you can use any character you want for it except for the delimiting character in the message itself. Once the message is complete, press Enter, then the delimiting character, and then press Enter again. Everything will still work if you don't follow this routine unless you have more than one banner. If that's the case, make sure you do follow it or your banners will all be combined into one message and put on a single line!

You can set a banner on one line like this:

```
Todd(config)#banner motd x Unauthorized access prohibited! x
```

Let's take a minute to go into more detail about the other two types of banners I mentioned:

Exec banner   You can configure a line-activation (exec) banner to be displayed when EXEC processes such as a line activation or an incoming connection to a VTY line have been created. Simply initiating a user exec session through a console port will activate the exec banner.

Login banner   You can configure a login banner for display on all connected terminals. It will show up after the MOTD banner but before the login prompts. This login banner can't be disabled on a per-line basis, so to globally disable it you've got to delete it with the no banner login command.

Here's what a login banner output looks like:

```
!
banner login ^C
-------------------------------------------------------------------------
Cisco Router and Security Device Manager (SDM) is installed on this device.
This feature requires the one-time use of the username "cisco"
with the password "cisco". The default username and password
have a privilege level of 15.
Please change these publicly known initial credentials using
SDM or the IOS CLI.
Here are the Cisco IOS commands.
username <myuser>  privilege 15 secret 0 <mypassword>
no username cisco
Replace <myuser> and <mypassword> with the username and
password you want to use.
For more information about SDM please follow the instructions
in the QUICK START GUIDE for your router or go to http://www.cisco.com/go/sdm
-------------------------------------------------------------------------
^C
!
```

The previous login banner should look pretty familiar to anyone who's ever logged into an ISR router because it's the banner Cisco has in the default configuration for its ISR routers.

Remember that the login banner is displayed before the login prompts and after the MOTD banner.

Setting Passwords

There are five passwords you'll need to secure your Cisco routers: console, auxiliary, telnet/SSH (VTY), enable password, and enable secret. The enable secret and enable password are the ones used to set the password for securing privileged mode. Once the enable commands are set, users will be prompted for a password. The other three are used to configure a password when user mode is accessed through the console port, through the auxiliary port, or via Telnet.

Let's take a look at each of these now.

Enable Passwords

You set the enable passwords from global configuration mode like this:

```
Todd(config)#enable ?
 last-resort Define enable action if no TACACS servers
            respond
```

```
password    Assign the privileged level password
secret      Assign the privileged level secret
use-tacacs  Use TACACS to check enable passwords
```

The following list describes the enable password parameters:

last-resort This allows you to still enter the device if you set up authentication through a TACACS server and it's not available. It won't be used if the TACACS server is working.

password This sets the enable password on older, pre-10.3 systems and isn't ever used if an enable secret is set.

secret The newer, encrypted password that overrides the enable password if it has been set.

use-tacacs This tells the router or switch to authenticate through a TACACS server. It comes in really handy when you have lots of routers because changing the password on a multitude of them can be insanely tedious. It's much easier to simply go through the TACACS server and change the password only once!

Here's an example that shows how to set the enable passwords:

```
Todd(config)#enable secret todd
Todd(config)#enable password todd
The enable password you have chosen is the same as your
  enable secret. This is not recommended. Re-enter the
  enable password.
```

If you try to set the enable secret and enable passwords the same, the device will give you a polite warning to change the second password. Make a note to yourself that if there aren't any old legacy routers involved, you don't even bother to use the enable password!

User-mode passwords are assigned via the line command like this:

```
Todd(config)#line ?
  <0-16>   First Line number
  console  Primary terminal line
  vty      Virtual terminal
```

And these two lines are especially important for the exam objectives:

console Sets a console user-mode password.

vty Sets a Telnet password on the device. If this password isn't set, then by default, Telnet can't be used.

To configure user-mode passwords, choose the line you want and configure it using the login command to make the switch prompt for authentication. Let's focus in on the configuration of individual lines now.

Console Password

We set the console password with the `line console 0` command, but look at what happened when I tried to type **line console ?** from the (config-line)# prompt—I received an error! Here's the example:

```
Todd(config-line)#line console ?
% Unrecognized command
Todd(config-line)#exit
Todd(config)#line console ?
  <0-0>  First Line number
Todd(config)#line console 0
Todd(config-line)#password console
Todd(config-line)#login
```

You can still type **line console 0** and that will be accepted, but the help screens just don't work from that prompt. Type **exit** to go back one level, and you'll find that your help screens now work. This is a "feature." Really.

Because there's only one console port, I can only choose line console 0. You can set all your line passwords to the same password, but doing this isn't exactly a brilliant security move!

And it's also important to remember to apply the `login` command or the console port won't prompt for authentication. The way Cisco has this process set up means you can't set the `login` command before a password is set on a line because if you set it but don't then set a password, that line won't be usable. You'll actually get prompted for a password that doesn't exist, so Cisco's method isn't just a hassle; it makes sense and is a feature after all!

> Definitely remember that although Cisco has this "password feature" on its routers starting with IOS 12.2 and above, it's not included in older IOSs.

Okay, there are a few other important commands you need to know regarding the console port.

For one, the `exec-timeout 0 0` command sets the time-out for the console EXEC session to zero, ensuring that it never times out. The default time-out is 10 minutes.

> If you're feeling mischievous, try this on people at work: Set the exec-timeout command to 0 1. This will make the console time out in 1 second, and to fix it, you have to continually press the down arrow key while changing the time-out time with your free hand!

`Logging synchronous` is such a cool command that it should be a default, but it's not. It's great because it's the antidote for those annoying console messages that disrupt the input you're trying to type. The messages will still pop up, but at least you get returned to your device prompt without your input being interrupted! This makes your input messages oh-so-much easier to read!

Here's an example of how to configure both commands:

```
Todd(config-line)#line con 0
Todd(config-line)#exec-timeout ?
  <0-35791>  Timeout in minutes
Todd(config-line)#exec-timeout 0 ?
  <0-2147483>  Timeout in seconds
  <cr>
Todd(config-line)#exec-timeout 0 0
Todd(config-line)#logging synchronous
```

> You can set the console to go from never timing out (0 0) to timing out in 35,791 minutes and 2,147,483 seconds. Remember that the default is 10 minutes.

Telnet Password

To set the user-mode password for Telnet access into the router or switch, use the line vty command. IOS switches typically have 16 lines, but routers running the Enterprise edition have considerably more. The best way to find out how many lines you have is to use that handy question mark like this:

```
Todd(config-line)#line vty 0 ?
% Unrecognized command
Todd(config-line)#exit
Todd(config)#line vty 0 ?
  <1-15>  Last Line number
  <cr>
Todd(config)#line vty 0 15
Todd(config-line)#password telnet
Todd(config-line)#login
```

This output clearly shows that you cannot get help from your (config-line)# prompt. You must go back to global config mode in order to use the question mark (?).

So what will happen if you try to telnet into a device that doesn't have a VTY password set? You'll receive an error saying the connection has been refused because the password isn't set. So, if you telnet into a switch and receive a message like this one that I got from Switch B

```
Todd#telnet SwitchB
Trying SwitchB (10.0.0.1)…Open

Password required, but none set
[Connection to SwitchB closed by foreign host]
Todd#
```

it means the switch doesn't have the VTY password set. But you can still get around this and tell the switch to allow Telnet connections without a password by using the no login command:

```
SwitchB(config-line)#line vty 0 15
SwitchB(config-line)#no login
```

 I definitely do not recommend using the no login command to allow Telnet connections without a password, unless you're in a testing or classroom environment. In a production network, always set your VTY password!

After your IOS devices are configured with an IP address, you can use the Telnet program to configure and check your routers instead of having to use a console cable. You can use the Telnet program by typing **telnet** from any command prompt (DOS or Cisco). I'll cover all things Telnet more thoroughly in Chapter 7, "Managing a Cisco Internetwork."

Auxiliary Password

To configure the auxiliary password on a router, go into global configuration mode and type **line aux ?**. And by the way, you won't find these ports on a switch. This output shows that you only get a choice of 0–0, which is because there's only one port:

```
Todd#config t
Todd(config)#line aux ?
  <0-0>  First Line number
Todd(config)#line aux 0
Todd(config-line)#login
% Login disabled on line 1, until 'password' is set
Todd(config-line)#password aux
Todd(config-line)#login
```

Setting Up Secure Shell (SSH)

I strongly recommend using Secure Shell (SSH) instead of Telnet because it creates a more secure session. The Telnet application uses an unencrypted data stream, but SSH uses encryption keys to send data so your username and password aren't sent in the clear, vulnerable to anyone lurking around!

Here are the steps for setting up SSH:

1. Set your hostname:

```
Router(config)#hostname Todd
```

2. Set the domain name—both the hostname and domain name are required for the encryption keys to be generated:

```
Todd(config)#ip domain-name Lammle.com
```

3. Set the username to allow SSH client access:

```
Todd(config)#username Todd password Lammle
```

4. Generate the encryption keys for securing the session:

```
Todd(config)#crypto key generate rsa
The name for the keys will be: Todd.Lammle.com
Choose the size of the key modulus in the range of 360 to
4096 for your General Purpose Keys. Choosing a key modulus
Greater than 512 may take a few minutes.

How many bits in the modulus [512]: 1024
% Generating 1024 bit RSA keys, keys will be non-exportable...
[OK] (elapsed time was 6 seconds)

Todd(config)#
1d14h: %SSH-5-ENABLED: SSH 1.99 has been enabled*June 24
19:25:30.035: %SSH-5-ENABLED: SSH 1.99 has been enabled
```

5. Enable SSH version 2 on the device—not mandatory, but strongly suggested:

```
Todd(config)#ip ssh version 2
```

6. Connect to the VTY lines of the switch or router:

```
Todd(config)#line vty 0 15
```

7. Tell the lines to use the local database for password:

```
Todd(config-line)#login local
```

8. Configure your access protocols:

```
Todd(config-line)#transport input ?
  all     All protocols
  none    No protocols
  ssh     TCP/IP SSH protocol
  telnet  TCP/IP Telnet protocol
```

Beware of this next line, and make sure you never use it in production because it's a horrendous security risk:

```
Todd(config-line)#transport input all
```

I recommend using the next line to secure your VTY lines with SSH:

```
Todd(config-line)#transport input ssh ?
  telnet  TCP/IP Telnet protocol
  <cr>
```

I actually do use Telnet once in a while when a situation arises that specifically calls for it. It just doesn't happen very often. But if you want to go with Telnet, here's how you do that:

```
Todd(config-line)#transport input ssh telnet
```

Know that if you don't use the keyword telnet at the end of the command string, then only SSH will work on the device. You can go with either, just so long as you understand that SSH is way more secure than Telnet.

Encrypting Your Passwords

Because only the enable secret password is encrypted by default, you'll need to manually configure the user-mode and enable passwords for encryption.

Notice that you can see all the passwords except the enable secret when performing a show running-config on a switch:

```
Todd#sh running-config
Building configuration...

Current configuration : 1020 bytes
!
! Last configuration change at 00:03:11 UTC Mon Mar 1 1993
!
version 15.0
no service pad
service timestamps debug datetime msec
service timestamps log datetime msec
no service password-encryption
!
hostname Todd
!
enable secret 4 ykw.3/tgsOuy9.6qmgG/EeYOYgBvfX4v.S8UNA9Rddg
enable password todd
!
[output cut]
!
line con 0
```

```
 password console
 login
line vty 0 4
 password telnet
 login
line vty 5 15
 password telnet
 login
!
end
```

To manually encrypt your passwords, use the service password-encryption command. Here's how:

```
Todd#config t
Todd(config)#service password-encryption
Todd(config)#exit
Todd#show run
Building configuration...
!
!
enable secret 4 ykw.3/tgsOuy9.6qmgG/EeYOYgBvfX4v.S8UNA9Rddg
enable password 7 1506040800
!
[output cut]
!
!
line con 0
 password 7 050809013243420C
 login
line vty 0 4
 password 7 06120A2D424B1D
 login
line vty 5 15
 password 7 06120A2D424B1D
 login
!
end
Todd#config t
Todd(config)#no service password-encryption
Todd(config)#^Z
Todd#
```

Nicely done—the passwords will now be encrypted. All you need to do is encrypt the passwords, perform a show run, then turn off the command if you want. This output clearly shows us that the enable password and the line passwords are all encrypted.

Before we move on to find out how to set descriptions on your interfaces, I want to stress some points about password encryption. As I said, if you set your passwords and then turn on the service password-encryption command, you have to perform a show running-config before you turn off the encryption service or your passwords won't be encrypted. You don't have to turn off the encryption service at all—you'd only do that if your switch is running low on processes. And if you turn on the service before you set your passwords, then you don't even have to view them to have them encrypted.

Descriptions

Setting descriptions on an interface is another administratively helpful thing, and like the hostname, it's also only locally significant. One case where the description command comes in really handy is when you want to keep track of circuit numbers on a switch or a router's serial WAN port.

Here's an example on my switch:

```
Todd#config t
Todd(config)#int fa0/1
Todd(config-if)#description Sales VLAN Trunk Link
Todd(config-if)#^Z
Todd#
```

And on a router serial WAN:

```
Router#config t
Router(config)#int s0/0/0
Router(config-if)#description WAN to Miami
Router(config-if)#^Z
```

You can view an interface's description with either the show running-config command or the show interface—even with the show interface description command:

```
Todd#sh run
Building configuration...

Current configuration : 855 bytes
!
interface FastEthernet0/1
 description Sales VLAN Trunk Link
!
 [output cut]
```

```
Todd#sh int f0/1
FastEthernet0/1 is up, line protocol is up (connected)
  Hardware is Fast Ethernet, address is ecc8.8202.8282 (bia ecc8.8202.8282)
  Description: Sales VLAN Trunk Link
  MTU 1500 bytes, BW 100000 Kbit/sec, DLY 100 usec,
[output cut]
```

```
Todd#sh int description
Interface                    Status       Protocol Description
Vl1                          up           up
Fa0/1                        up           up       Sales VLAN Trunk Link
Fa0/2                        up           up
```

Real World Scenario

***description*: A Helpful Command**

Bob, a senior network admin at Acme Corporation in San Francisco, has over 50 WAN links to branches throughout the United States and Canada. Whenever an interface goes down, Bob wastes lots of time trying to figure out the circuit number and the phone number of the provider of his ailing WAN link.

This kind of scenario shows just how helpful the interface description command can be. It would save Bob a lot of work because he could use it on his most important switch LAN links to find out exactly where every interface is connected. Bob's life would also be made a lot easier by adding circuit numbers to each and every WAN interface on his routers, along with the phone number of the responsible provider.

So if Bob had just taken time in advance to preventively add this information to his interfaces, he would have saved himself an ocean of stress and a ton of precious time when his WAN links inevitably go down!

Doing the *do* Command

In every previous example so far, we've had to run all show commands from privileged mode. But I've got great news—beginning with IOS version 12.3, Cisco has finally added a command to the IOS that allows you to view the configuration and statistics from within configuration mode!

In fact, with any IOS, you'd get the following error if you tried to view the configuration from global config:

```
Todd(config)#sh run
               ^
% Invalid input detected at '^' marker.
```

Compare that to the output I get from entering that same command on my router that's running the 15.0 IOS using the "do" syntax:

```
Todd(config)#do show run
Building configuration...

Current configuration : 759 bytes
!
version 15.0
no service pad
service timestamps debug datetime msec
service timestamps log datetime msec
no service password-encryption
!
hostname Todd
!
boot-start-marker
boot-end-marker
!
[output cut]
```

So now you can pretty much run any command from any configuration prompt—nice, huh? Looking back through all those examples for encrypting our passwords, you can see that the do command would definitely have gotten the party started sooner, making this innovation one to celebrate for sure!

Router and Switch Interfaces

Interface configuration is arguably the most important router configuration because without interfaces, a router is a pretty useless object. Furthermore, interface configurations must be totally precise to enable communication with other devices. Network layer addresses, media type, bandwidth, and other administrator commands are all used to configure an interface.

On a layer 2 switch, interface configurations typically involve a lot less work than router interface configuration. Check out the output from the powerful verification command show ip interface brief, which reveals all the interfaces on my 3560 switch:

```
Todd#sh ip interface brief
Interface          IP-Address      OK? Method Status          Protocol
Vlan1              192.168.255.8   YES DHCP   up                  up
FastEthernet0/1    unassigned      YES unset  up                  up
FastEthernet0/2    unassigned      YES unset  up                  up
```

```
FastEthernet0/3         unassigned      YES unset  down             down
FastEthernet0/4         unassigned      YES unset  down             down
FastEthernet0/5         unassigned      YES unset  up               up
FastEthernet0/6         unassigned      YES unset  up               up
FastEthernet0/7         unassigned      YES unset  down             down
FastEthernet0/8         unassigned      YES unset  down             down
GigabitEthernet0/1      unassigned      YES unset  down             down
```

The previous output shows the default routed port found on all Cisco switches (VLAN 1), plus nine switch FastEthernet interface ports, with one port being a Gigabit Ethernet port used for uplinks to other switches.

Different routers use different methods to choose the interfaces used on them. For instance, the following command shows one of my 2800 ISR Cisco routers with two FastEthernet interfaces along with two serial WAN interfaces:

```
Router>sh ip int brief
Interface       IP-Address      OK? Method Status              Protocol
FastEthernet0/0 192.168.255.11  YES DHCP   up                  up
FastEthernet0/1 unassigned      YES unset  administratively down down
Serial0/0/0     unassigned      YES unset  administratively down down
Serial0/1/0     unassigned      YES unset  administratively down down
Router>
```

Previously, we always used the interface type *number* sequence to configure an interface, but the newer routers come with an actual physical slot and include a port number on the module plugged into it. So on a modular router, the configuration would be interface type *slot/port*, as demonstrated here:

```
Todd#config t
Todd(config)#interface GigabitEthernet 0/1
Todd(config-if)#
```

You can see that we are now at the Gigabit Ethernet slot 0, port 1 prompt, and from here we can make configuration changes to the interface. Make note of the fact that you can't just type **int gigabitethernet 0**. No shortcuts on the slot/port—you've got to type the slot/port variables in the command: *type slot/port* or, for example, **int gigabitethernet 0/1** (or just **int g0/1**).

Once in interface configuration mode, we can configure various options. Keep in mind that speed and duplex are the two factors to be concerned with for the LAN:

```
Todd#config t
Todd(config)#interface GigabitEthernet 0/1
Todd(config-if)#speed 1000
Todd(config-if)#duplex full
```

So what's happened here? Well basically, this has shut off the auto-detect mechanism on the port, forcing it to only run gigabit speeds at full duplex. For the ISR series router, it's basically the same, but you get even more options! The LAN interfaces are the same, but the rest of the modules are different—they use three numbers instead of two. The three numbers used here can represent slot/subslot/port, but this depends on the card used in the ISR router. For the objectives, you just need to remember this: The first 0 is the router itself. You then choose the slot and then the port. Here's an example of a serial interface on my 2811:

```
Todd(config)#interface serial ?
  <0-2>  Serial interface number
Todd(config)#interface serial 0/0/?
  <0-1>  Serial interface number
Todd(config)#interface serial 0/0/0
Todd(config-if)#
```

This might look a little dicey to you, but I promise it's really not that hard! It helps to remember that you should always view the output of the show ip interface brief command or a show running-config output first so you know the exact interfaces you have to deal with. Here's one of my 2811's output that has even more serial interfaces installed:

```
Todd(config-if)#do show run
Building configuration...
[output cut]
!
interface FastEthernet0/0
 no ip address
 shutdown
 duplex auto
 speed auto
!
interface FastEthernet0/1
 no ip address
 shutdown
 duplex auto
 speed auto
!
interface Serial0/0/0
 no ip address
 shutdown
 no fair-queue
!
```

```
interface Serial0/0/1
 no ip address
 shutdown
!
interface Serial0/1/0
 no ip address
 shutdown
!
interface Serial0/2/0
 no ip address
 shutdown
 clock rate 2000000
!
 [output cut]
```

For the sake of brevity, I didn't include my complete running-config, but I've displayed all you really need. You can see the two built-in FastEthernet interfaces, the two serial interfaces in slot 0 (0/0/0 and 0/0/1), the serial interface in slot 1 (0/1/0), and the serial interface in slot 2 (0/2/0). And once you see the interfaces like this, it makes it a lot easier to understand how the modules are inserted into the router.

Just understand that if you type **interface e0** on an old 2500 series router, **interface fastethernet 0/0** on a modular router (such as the 2800 series router), or **interface serial 0/1/0** on an ISR router, all you're actually doing is choosing an interface to configure. Essentially, they're all configured the same way after that.

Let's delve deeper into our router interface discussion by exploring how to bring up the interface and set an IP address on it next.

Bringing Up an Interface

You can disable an interface with the interface command shutdown and enable it with the no shutdown command. Just to remind you, all switch ports are enabled by default and all router ports are disabled by default, so we're going to talk more about router ports than switch ports in the next few sections.

If an interface is shut down, it'll display as administratively down when you use the show interfaces command (sh int for short):

```
Router#sh int f0/0
FastEthernet0/1 is administratively down, line protocol is down
[output cut]
```

Another way to check an interface's status is via the show running-config command. You can bring up the router interface with the no shutdown command (no shut for short):

```
Router(config)#int f0/0
Router(config-if)#no shutdown
```

```
*August 21 13:45:08.455: %LINK-3-UPDOWN: Interface FastEthernet0/0,
    changed state to up
Router(config-if)#do show int f0/0
FastEthernet0/0 is up, line protocol is up
[output cut]
```

Configuring an IP Address on an Interface

Even though you don't have to use IP on your routers, it's usually what everyone uses. To configure IP addresses on an interface, use the ip address command from interface configuration mode and remember that you do not set an IP address on a layer 2 switch port!

```
Todd(config)#int f0/1
Todd(config-if)#ip address 172.16.10.2 255.255.255.0
```

Also, don't forget to enable the interface with the no shutdown command. Remember to look at the command show interface *int* output to see if the interface is administratively shut down or not. Show ip int brief and show running-config will also give you this information.

> The ip address *address mask* command starts the IP processing on the router interface. Again, you do not configure an IP address on a layer 2 switch interface!

Okay—now if you want to add a second subnet address to an interface, you have to use the secondary parameter. If you type another IP address and press Enter, it will replace the existing primary IP address and mask. This is definitely one of the Cisco IOS's coolest features!

So let's try it. To add a secondary IP address, just use the secondary parameter:

```
Todd(config-if)#ip address 172.16.20.2 255.255.255.0 ?
  secondary  Make this IP address a secondary address
  <cr>
Todd(config-if)#ip address 172.16.20.2 255.255.255.0 secondary
Todd(config-if)#do sh run
Building configuration...
[output cut]

interface FastEthernet0/1
 ip address 172.16.20.2 255.255.255.0 secondary
 ip address 172.16.10.2 255.255.255.0
 duplex auto
 speed auto
!
```

But I've got to stop here to tell you that I really wouldn't recommend having multiple IP addresses on an interface because it's really inefficient. I showed you how anyway just in case you someday find yourself dealing with an MIS manager who's in love with really bad network design and makes you administer it! And who knows? Maybe someone will ask you about it someday and you'll get to seem really smart because you know this.

Using the Pipe

No, not that pipe. I mean the output modifier. Although, I've got to say that some of the router configurations I've seen in my career make me wonder! Anyway, this pipe (|) allows us to wade through all the configurations or other long outputs and get straight to our goods fast. Here's an example:

```
Router#sh run | ?
  append   Append redirected output to URL (URLs supporting append
           operation only)
  begin    Begin with the line that matches
  exclude  Exclude lines that match
  include  Include lines that match
  redirect Redirect output to URL
  section  Filter a section of output
  tee      Copy output to URL

Router#sh run | begin interface
interface FastEthernet0/0
 description Sales VLAN
 ip address 10.10.10.1 255.255.255.248
 duplex auto
 speed auto
!
interface FastEthernet0/1
 ip address 172.16.20.2 255.255.255.0 secondary
 ip address 172.16.10.2 255.255.255.0
 duplex auto
 speed auto
!
interface Serial0/0/0
 description Wan to SF circuit number 6fdda 12345678
 no ip address
!
```

So basically, the pipe symbol—the output modifier—is what you need to help you get where you want to go light years faster than mucking around in a router's entire configuration. I use it a lot when scrutinizing a large routing table to find out whether a certain route is in the routing table. Here's an example:

```
Todd#sh ip route | include 192.168.3.32
R       192.168.3.32 [120/2] via 10.10.10.8, 00:00:25, FastEthernet0/0
Todd#
```

First, you need to know that this routing table had over 100 entries, so without my trusty pipe, I'd probably still be looking through that output! It's a powerfully efficient tool that saves you major time and effort by quickly finding a line in a configuration—or as the preceding example shows, a single route within a huge routing table.

Give yourself a little time to play around with the pipe command to get the hang of it and you'll be naturally high on your newfound ability to quickly parse through router output!

Serial Interface Commands

But wait! Before you just jump in and configure a serial interface, you need some key information, like knowing the interface will usually be attached to a CSU/DSU type of device that provides clocking for the line to the router. Check out Figure 6.3 for an example.

FIGURE 6.3 A typical WAN connection. Clocking is typically provided by a DCE network to routers. In nonproduction environments, a DCE network is not always present.

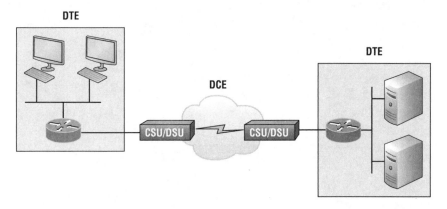

Here you can see that the serial interface is used to connect to a DCE network via a CSU/DSU that provides the clocking to the router interface. But if you have a back-to-back configuration, such as one that's used in a lab environment like the one in Figure 6.4, one end—the data communication equipment (DCE) end of the cable—must provide clocking!

FIGURE 6.4   Providing clocking on a nonproduction network

Set clock rate if needed

Todd# config t
Todd(config)# interface serial 0
Todd(config-if)#clock rate 1000000

DCE

DTE

DCE side determined by the cable.
Add clocking to DCE side only.

>**show controllers** *int* will show the cable connection type

By default, Cisco router serial interfaces are all data terminal equipment (DTE) interfaces, which means that you must configure an interface to provide clocking if you need it to act like a DCE device. Again, you would not provide clocking on a production WAN serial connection because you would have a CSU/DSU connected to your serial interface, as shown in Figure 6.3.

You configure a DCE serial interface with the clock rate command:

```
Router#config t
Enter configuration commands, one per line.  End with CNTL/Z.
Router(config)#int s0/0/0
Router(config-if)#clock rate ?
     Speed (bits per second)
  1200
  2400
  4800
  9600
  14400
  19200
  28800
  32000
  38400
  48000
  56000
  57600
  64000
  72000
  115200
  125000
  128000
```

```
148000
192000
250000
256000
384000
500000
512000
768000
800000
1000000
2000000
4000000
5300000
8000000
```

```
<300-8000000>    Choose clockrate from list above
Router(config-if)#clock rate 1000000
```

The clock rate command is set in bits per second. Besides looking at the cable end to check for a label of DCE or DTE, you can see if a router's serial interface has a DCE cable connected with the show controllers *int* command:

```
Router#sh controllers s0/0/0
Interface Serial0/0/0
Hardware is GT96K
DTE V.35idb at 0x4342FCB0, driver data structure at 0x434373D4
```

Here is an example of an output depicting a DCE connection:

```
Router#sh controllers s0/2/0
Interface Serial0/2/0
Hardware is GT96K
DCE V.35, clock rate 1000000
```

The next command you need to get acquainted with is the bandwidth command. Every Cisco router ships with a default serial link bandwidth of T1 (1.544 Mbps). But this has nothing to do with how data is transferred over a link. The bandwidth of a serial link is used by routing protocols such as EIGRP and OSPF to calculate the best cost path to a remote network. So if you're using RIP routing, the bandwidth setting of a serial link is irrelevant since RIP uses only hop count to determine this.

You may be rereading this part and thinking, "Huh? What? Routing protocols? Metrics?" But don't freak! I'm going over all of that soon in Chapter 9.

Here's an example of using the bandwidth command:

```
Router#config t
Router(config)#int s0/0/0
Router(config-if)#bandwidth ?
  <1-10000000>  Bandwidth in kilobits
  inherit       Specify that bandwidth is inherited
  receive       Specify receive-side bandwidth
Router(config-if)#bandwidth 1000
```

Did you notice that, unlike the clock rate command, the bandwidth command is configured in kilobits per second?

> After going through all these configuration examples regarding the clock rate command, understand that the new ISR routers automatically detect DCE connections and set clock rate to 2000000. But know that you still need to understand the clock rate command for the Cisco objectives, even though the new routers set it for you automatically!

Viewing, Saving, and Erasing Configurations

If you run through setup mode, you'll be asked if you want to use the configuration you just created. If you say yes, the configuration running in DRAM that's known as the running-config will be copied into NVRAM, and the file will be named startup-config. Hopefully, you'll be smart and always use the CLI, not setup mode!

You can manually save the file from DRAM, which is usually just called RAM, to NVRAM by using the copy running-config startup-config command. You can use the shortcut copy run start as well:

```
Todd#copy running-config startup-config
Destination filename [startup-config]? [press enter]
Building configuration...
[OK]
Todd#
Building configuration...
```

When you see a question with an answer in [], it means that if you just press Enter, you're choosing the default answer.

Also, when the command asks for the destination filename, the default answer is startup-config. The reason it asks is because you can copy the configuration to pretty much anywhere you want. Take a look at the output from my switch:

```
Todd#copy running-config ?
```

flash:	Copy to flash: file system
ftp:	Copy to ftp: file system
http:	Copy to http: file system
https:	Copy to https: file system
null:	Copy to null: file system
nvram:	Copy to nvram: file system
rcp:	Copy to rcp: file system
running-config	Update (merge with) current system configuration
scp:	Copy to scp: file system
startup-config	Copy to startup configuration
syslog:	Copy to syslog: file system
system:	Copy to system: file system
tftp:	Copy to tftp: file system
tmpsys:	Copy to tmpsys: file system
vb:	Copy to vb: file system

To reassure you, we'll get deeper into how and where to copy files in Chapter 7.

For now, you can view the files by typing **show running-config** or **show startup-config** from privileged mode. The sh run command, which is a shortcut for show running-config, tells us that we're viewing the current configuration:

```
Todd#sh run
Building configuration...

Current configuration : 855 bytes
!
! Last configuration change at 23:20:06 UTC Mon Mar 1 1993
!
version 15.0
[output cut]
```

The sh start command—one of the shortcuts for the show startup-config command—shows us the configuration that will be used the next time the router is reloaded. It also tells us how much NVRAM is being used to store the startup-config file. Here's an example:

```
Todd#sh start
Using 855 out of 524288 bytes
!
```

```
! Last configuration change at 23:20:06 UTC Mon Mar 1 1993
!
version 15.0
[output cut]
```

But beware—if you try and view the configuration and see

```
Todd#sh start
startup-config is not present
```

you have not saved your running-config to NVRAM, or you've deleted the backup configuration! Let me talk about just how you would do that now.

Deleting the Configuration and Reloading the Device

You can delete the startup-config file by using the erase startup-config command:

```
Todd#erase start
% Incomplete command.
```

First, notice that you can no longer use the shortcut commands for erasing the backup configuration. This started in IOS 12.4 with the ISR routers.

```
Todd#erase startup-config
Erasing the nvram filesystem will remove all configuration files! Continue?
[confirm]
[OK]
Erase of nvram: complete
Todd#
*Mar  5 01:59:45.206: %SYS-7-NV_BLOCK_INIT: Initialized the geometry of nvram
Todd#reload
Proceed with reload? [confirm]
```

Now if you reload or power the router down after using the erase startup-config command, you'll be offered setup mode because there's no configuration saved in NVRAM. You can press Ctrl+C to exit setup mode at any time, but the reload command can only be used from privileged mode.

At this point, you shouldn't use setup mode to configure your router. So just say **no** to setup mode, because it's there to help people who don't know how to use the command line interface (CLI), and this no longer applies to you. Be strong—you can do it!

Verifying Your Configuration

Obviously, show running-config would be the best way to verify your configuration and show startup-config would be the best way to verify the configuration that'll be used the next time the router is reloaded—right?

Well, once you take a look at the running-config, if all appears well, you can verify your configuration with utilities like Ping and Telnet. Ping is a program that uses ICMP echo requests and replies, which we covered in Chapter 3. For review, Ping sends a packet to a remote host, and if that host responds, you know that it's alive. But you don't know if it's alive and also *well*; just because you can ping a Microsoft server does not mean you can log in! Even so, Ping is an awesome starting point for troubleshooting an internetwork.

Did you know that you can ping with different protocols? You can, and you can test this by typing **ping ?** at either the router user-mode or privileged-mode prompt:

```
Todd#ping ?
  WORD  Ping destination address or hostname
  clns  CLNS echo
  ip    IP echo
  ipv6  IPv6 echo
  tag   Tag encapsulated IP echo
  <cr>
```

If you want to find a neighbor's Network layer address, either you go straight to the router or switch itself or you can type **show cdp entry * protocol** to get the Network layer addresses you need for pinging.

You can also use an extended ping to change the default variables, as shown here:

```
Todd#ping
Protocol [ip]:
Target IP address: 10.1.1.1
Repeat count [5]:
% A decimal number between 1 and 2147483647.
Repeat count [5]: 5000
Datagram size [100]:
% A decimal number between 36 and 18024.
Datagram size [100]: 1500
Timeout in seconds [2]:
Extended commands [n]: y
Source address or interface: FastEthernet 0/1
Source address or interface: Vlan 1
Type of service [0]:
Set DF bit in IP header? [no]:
Validate reply data? [no]:
Data pattern [0xABCD]:
Loose, Strict, Record, Timestamp, Verbose[none]:
Sweep range of sizes [n]:
Type escape sequence to abort.
Sending 5000, 1500-byte ICMP Echos to 10.1.1.1, timeout is 2 seconds:
Packet sent with a source address of 10.10.10.1
```

Notice that by using the question mark, I was able to determine that extended ping allows you to set the repeat count higher than the default of 5 and the datagram size larger.

This raises the MTU and allows for a more accurate testing of throughput. The source interface is one last important piece of information I'll pull out of the output. You can choose which interface the ping is sourced from, which is really helpful in certain diagnostic situations. Using my switch to display the extended ping capabilities, I had to use my only routed port, which is named VLAN 1, by default.

However, if you want to use a different diagnostic port, you can create a logical interface called a loopback interface as so:

```
Todd(config)#interface loopback ?
  <0-2147483647>  Loopback interface number

Todd(config)#interface loopback 0
*May 19 03:06:42.697: %LINEPROTO-5-UPDOWN: Line prot
 changed state to ups
Todd(config-if)#ip address 20.20.20.1 255.255.255.0
```

Now I can use this port for diagnostics, and even as my source port of my ping or traceroute, as so:

```
Todd#ping
Protocol [ip]:
Target IP address: 10.1.1.1
Repeat count [5]:
Datagram size [100]:
Timeout in seconds [2]:
Extended commands [n]: y
Source address or interface: 20.20.20.1
Type of service [0]:
Set DF bit in IP header? [no]:
Validate reply data? [no]:
Data pattern [0xABCD]:
Loose, Strict, Record, Timestamp, Verbose[none]:
Sweep range of sizes [n]:
Type escape sequence to abort.
Sending 5, 100-byte ICMP Echos to 10.1.1.1, timeout is 2 seconds:
Packet sent with a source address of 20.20.20.1
```

The logical interface are great for diagnostics and for using them in our home labs where we don't have any real interfaces to play with, but we'll also use them in our OSPF configurations in ICND2.

 Cisco Discovery Protocol (CDP) is covered in Chapter 7.

Traceroute uses ICMP with IP time to live (TTL) time-outs to track the path a given packet takes through an internetwork. This is in contrast to Ping, which just finds the host and responds. Traceroute can also be used with multiple protocols. Check out this output:

```
Todd#traceroute ?
  WORD       Trace route to destination address or hostname
  aaa        Define trace options for AAA events/actions/errors
  appletalk  AppleTalk Trace
  clns       ISO CLNS Trace
  ip         IP Trace
  ipv6       IPv6 Trace
  ipx        IPX Trace
  mac        Trace Layer2 path between 2 endpoints
  oldvines   Vines Trace (Cisco)
  vines      Vines Trace (Banyan)
  <cr>
```

And as with ping, we can perform an extended traceroute using additional parameters, typically used to change the source interface:

```
Todd#traceroute
Protocol [ip]:
Target IP address: 10.1.1.1
Source address: 172.16.10.1
Numeric display [n]:
Timeout in seconds [3]:
Probe count [3]:
Minimum Time to Live [1]: 255
Maximum Time to Live [30]:
Type escape sequence to abort.
Tracing the route to 10.1.1.1
```

Telnet, FTP, and HTTP are really the best tools because they use IP at the Network layer and TCP at the Transport layer to create a session with a remote host. If you can telnet, ftp, or http into a device, you know that your IP connectivity just has to be solid!

```
Todd#telnet ?
  WORD IP address or hostname of a remote system
  <cr>
Todd#telnet 10.1.1.1
```

When you telnet into a remote device, you won't see console messages by default. For example, you will not see debugging output. To allow console messages to be sent to your Telnet session, use the terminal monitor command, as shown on the SF router.

```
SF#terminal monitor
```

From the switch or router prompt, you just type a hostname or IP address and it will assume you want to telnet—you don't need to type the actual command, telnet.

Coming up, I'll show you how to verify the interface statistics.

Verifying with the *show interface* Command

Another way to verify your configuration is by typing show interface commands, the first of which is the show interface ? command. Doing this will reveal all the available interfaces to verify and configure.

> The show interfaces command, plural, displays the configurable parameters and statistics of all interfaces on a router.

This command comes in really handy when you're verifying and troubleshooting router and network issues.

The following output is from my freshly erased and rebooted 2811 router:

```
Router#sh int ?
  Async             Async interface
  BVI               Bridge-Group Virtual Interface
  CDMA-Ix           CDMA Ix interface
  CTunnel           CTunnel interface
  Dialer            Dialer interface
  FastEthernet      FastEthernet IEEE 802.3
  Loopback          Loopback interface
  MFR               Multilink Frame Relay bundle interface
  Multilink         Multilink-group interface
  Null              Null interface
  Port-channel      Ethernet Channel of interfaces
  Serial            Serial
  Tunnel            Tunnel interface
  Vif               PGM Multicast Host interface
  Virtual-PPP       Virtual PPP interface
  Virtual-Template  Virtual Template interface
  Virtual-TokenRing Virtual TokenRing
  accounting        Show interface accounting
  counters          Show interface counters
  crb               Show interface routing/bridging info
  dampening         Show interface dampening info
  description       Show interface description
  etherchannel      Show interface etherchannel information
  irb               Show interface routing/bridging info
  mac-accounting    Show interface MAC accounting info
```

```
mpls-exp          Show interface MPLS experimental accounting info
precedence        Show interface precedence accounting info
pruning           Show interface trunk VTP pruning information
rate-limit        Show interface rate-limit info
status            Show interface line status
summary           Show interface summary
switching         Show interface switching
switchport        Show interface switchport information
trunk             Show interface trunk information
|                 Output modifiers
<cr>
```

The only "real" physical interfaces are FastEthernet, Serial, and Async—the rest are all logical interfaces or commands you can use to verify with.

The next command is show interface fastethernet 0/0. It reveals the hardware address, logical address, and encapsulation method as well as statistics on collisions, as seen here:

```
Router#sh int f0/0
FastEthernet0/0 is up, line protocol is up
  Hardware is MV96340 Ethernet, address is 001a.2f55.c9e8 (bia 001a.2f55.c9e8)
  Internet address is 192.168.1.33/27
MTU 1500 bytes, BW 100000 Kbit, DLY 100 usec,
    reliability 255/255, txload 1/255, rxload 1/255
  Encapsulation ARPA, loopback not set
  Keepalive set (10 sec)
  Auto-duplex, Auto Speed, 100BaseTX/FX
  ARP type: ARPA, ARP Timeout 04:00:00
  Last input never, output 00:02:07, output hang never
  Last clearing of "show interface" counters never
  Input queue: 0/75/0/0 (size/max/drops/flushes); Total output drops: 0
  Queueing strategy: fifo
  Output queue: 0/40 (size/max)
  5 minute input rate 0 bits/sec, 0 packets/sec
  5 minute output rate 0 bits/sec, 0 packets/sec
     0 packets input, 0 bytes
     Received 0 broadcasts, 0 runts, 0 giants, 0 throttles
     0 input errors, 0 CRC, 0 frame, 0 overrun, 0 ignored
     0 watchdog
     0 input packets with dribble condition detected
     16 packets output, 960 bytes, 0 underruns
     0 output errors, 0 collisions, 0 interface resets
     0 babbles, 0 late collision, 0 deferred
```

```
     0 lost carrier, 0 no carrier
     0 output buffer failures, 0 output buffers swapped out
Router#
```

You probably guessed that we're going to go over the important statistics from this output, but first, just for fun, I've got to ask you, which subnet is FastEthernet 0/0 a member of and what's the broadcast address and valid host range?

I'm serious—you really have to be able to nail these things NASCAR-fast! Just in case you didn't, the address is 192.168.1.33/27. And I've gotta be honest—if you don't know what a /27 is at this point, you'll need a miracle to pass the exam! That or you need to actually read this book. (As a quick reminder, a /27 is 255.255.255.224.) The fourth octet is a block size of 32. The subnets are 0, 32, 64, etc.; the FastEthernet interface is in the 32 subnet; the broadcast address is 63; and the valid hosts are 33–62. All good now?

> If you struggled with any of this, please save yourself from certain doom and get yourself back into Chapter 4, "Easy Subnetting," now! Read and reread it until you've got it dialed in!

Okay—back to the output. The preceding interface is working and looks to be in good shape. The show interfaces command will show you if you're receiving errors on the interface, and it will also show you the maximum transmission unit (MTU). MTU is the maximum packet size allowed to transmit on that interface, bandwidth (BW) is for use with routing protocols, and 255/255 means that reliability is perfect! The load is 1/255, meaning no load.

Continuing through the output, can you figure out the bandwidth of the interface? Well, other than the easy giveaway of the interface being called a "FastEthernet" interface, we can see that the bandwidth is 100000 Kbit, which is 100,000,000. Kbit means to add three zeros, which is 100 Mbits per second, or FastEthernet. Gigabit would be 1000000 Kbits per second.

Be sure you don't miss the output errors and collisions, which show 0 in my output. If these numbers are increasing, then you have some sort of Physical or Data Link layer issue. Check your duplex! If you have one side as half-duplex and one at full-duplex, your interface will work, albeit really slow and those numbers will be increasing fast!

The most important statistic of the show interface command is the output of the line and Data Link protocol status. If the output reveals that FastEthernet 0/0 is up and the line protocol is up, then the interface is up and running:

```
Router#sh int fa0/0
FastEthernet0/0 is up, line protocol is up
```

The first parameter refers to the Physical layer, and it's up when it receives carrier detect. The second parameter refers to the Data Link layer, and it looks for keepalives from the connecting end. Keepalives are important because they're used between devices to make sure connectivity hasn't been dropped.

Here's an example of where your problem will often be found—on serial interfaces:

```
Router#sh int s0/0/0
Serial0/0 is up, line protocol is down
```

If you see that the line is up but the protocol is down, as displayed here, you're experiencing a clocking (keepalive) or framing problem—possibly an encapsulation mismatch. Check the keepalives on both ends to make sure they match. Make sure that the clock rate is set, if needed, and that the encapsulation type is equal on both ends. The preceding output tells us that there's a Data Link layer problem.

If you discover that both the line interface and the protocol are down, it's a cable or interface problem. The following output would indicate a Physical layer problem:

```
Router#sh int s0/0/0
Serial0/0 is down, line protocol is down
```

As you'll see next, if one end is administratively shut down, the remote end would present as down and down:

```
Router#sh int s0/0/0
Serial0/0 is administratively down, line protocol is down
```

To enable the interface, use the command no shutdown from interface configuration mode.

The next show interface serial 0/0/0 command demonstrates the serial line and the maximum transmission unit (MTU)—1,500 bytes by default. It also shows the default bandwidth (BW) on all Cisco serial links, which is 1.544 Kbps. This is used to determine the bandwidth of the line for routing protocols like EIGRP and OSPF. Another important configuration to notice is the keepalive, which is 10 seconds by default. Each router sends a keepalive message to its neighbor every 10 seconds, and if both routers aren't configured for the same keepalive time, it won't work! Check out this output:

```
Router#sh int s0/0/0
Serial0/0 is up, line protocol is up
 Hardware is HD64570
 MTU 1500 bytes, BW 1544 Kbit, DLY 20000 usec,
   reliability 255/255, txload 1/255, rxload 1/255
 Encapsulation HDLC, loopback not set, keepalive set
  (10 sec)
 Last input never, output never, output hang never
 Last clearing of "show interface" counters never
 Queueing strategy: fifo
 Output queue 0/40, 0 drops; input queue 0/75, 0 drops
 5 minute input rate 0 bits/sec, 0 packets/sec
 5 minute output rate 0 bits/sec, 0 packets/sec
  0 packets input, 0 bytes, 0 no buffer
```

```
Received 0 broadcasts, 0 runts, 0 giants, 0 throttles
0 input errors, 0 CRC, 0 frame, 0 overrun, 0 ignored,
0 abort
0 packets output, 0 bytes, 0 underruns
0 output errors, 0 collisions, 16 interface resets
0 output buffer failures, 0 output buffers swapped out
0 carrier transitions
DCD=down DSR=down DTR=down RTS=down CTS=down
```

You can clear the counters on the interface by typing the command **clear counters**:

```
Router#clear counters ?
  Async              Async interface
  BVI                Bridge-Group Virtual Interface
  CTunnel            CTunnel interface
  Dialer             Dialer interface
  FastEthernet       FastEthernet IEEE 802.3
  Group-Async        Async Group interface
  Line               Terminal line
  Loopback           Loopback interface
  MFR                Multilink Frame Relay bundle interface
  Multilink          Multilink-group interface
  Null               Null interface
  Serial             Serial
  Tunnel             Tunnel interface
  Vif                PGM Multicast Host interface
  Virtual-Template   Virtual Template interface
  Virtual-TokenRing  Virtual TokenRing
  <cr>
```

```
Router#clear counters s0/0/0
Clear "show interface" counters on this interface
  [confirm][enter]
Router#
00:17:35: %CLEAR-5-COUNTERS: Clear counter on interface
  Serial0/0/0 by console
Router#
```

Troubleshooting with the *show interfaces* Command

Let's take a look at the output of the show interfaces command one more time before I move on. There are some statistics in this output that are important for the Cisco objectives.

```
275496 packets input, 35226811 bytes, 0 no buffer
   Received 69748 broadcasts (58822 multicasts)
```

```
0 runts, 0 giants, 0 throttles
0 input errors, 0 CRC, 0 frame, 0 overrun, 0 ignored
0 watchdog, 58822 multicast, 0 pause input
0 input packets with dribble condition detected
2392529 packets output, 337933522 bytes, 0 underruns
0 output errors, 0 collisions, 1 interface resets
0 babbles, 0 late collision, 0 deferred
0 lost carrier, 0 no carrier, 0 PAUSE output
0 output buffer failures, 0 output buffers swapped out
```

Finding where to start when troubleshooting an interface can be the difficult part, but certainly we'll look for the number of input errors and CRCs right away. Typically we'd see those statistics increase with a duplex error, but it could be another Physical layer issue such as the cable might be receiving excessive interference or the network interface cards might have a failure. Typically you can tell if it is interference when the CRC and input errors output grow but the collision counters do not.

Let's take a look at some of the output:

No buffer   This isn't a number you want to see incrementing. This means you don't have any buffer room left for incoming packets. Any packets received once the buffers are full are discarded. You can see how many packets are dropped with the ignored output.

Ignored   If the packet buffers are full, packets will be dropped. You see this increment along with the no buffer output. Typically if the no buffer and ignored outputs are incrementing, you have some sort of broadcast storm on your LAN. This can be caused by a bad NIC or even a bad network design.

> I'll repeat this because it is so important for the exam objectives: Typically if the no buffer and ignored outputs are incrementing, you have some sort of broadcast storm on your LAN. This can be caused by a bad NIC or even a bad network design.

Runts   Frames that did not meet the minimum frame size requirement of 64 bytes. Typically caused by collisions.

Giants   Frames received that are larger than 1518 bytes

Input Errors   This is the total of many counters: runts, giants, no buffer, CRC, frame, overrun, and ignored counts.

CRC   At the end of each frame is a Frame Check Sequence (FCS) field that holds the answer to a cyclic redundancy check (CRC). If the receiving host's answer to the CRC does not match the sending host's answer, then a CRC error will occur.

Frame   This output increments when frames received are of an illegal format, or not complete, which is typically incremented when a collision occurs.

Packets Output   Total number of packets (frames) forwarded out to the interface.

Output Errors   Total number of packets (frames) that the switch port tried to transmit but for which some problem occurred.

Collisions   When transmitting a frame in half-duplex, the NIC listens on the receiving pair of the cable for another signal. If a signal is transmitted from another host, a collision has occurred. This output should not increment if you are running full-duplex.

Late Collisions   If all Ethernet specifications are followed during the cable install, all collisions should occur by the 64th byte of the frame. If a collision occurs after 64 bytes, the late collisions counter increments. This counter will increment on a duplex mismatched interface, or if cable length exceeds specifications.

> A duplex mismatch causes late collision errors at the end of the connection. To avoid this situation, manually set the duplex parameters of the switch to match the attached device.

A duplex mismatch is a situation in which the switch operates at full-duplex and the connected device operates at half-duplex, or vice versa. The result of a duplex mismatch is extremely slow performance, intermittent connectivity, and loss of connection. Other possible causes of data-link errors at full-duplex are bad cables, a faulty switch port, or NIC software or hardware issues. Use the show interface command to verify the duplex settings.

If the mismatch occurs between two Cisco devices with Cisco Discovery Protocol enabled, you will see Cisco Discovery Protocol error messages on the console or in the logging buffer of both devices.

```
%CDP-4-DUPLEX_MISMATCH: duplex mismatch discovered on FastEthernet0/2 (not
half duplex)
```

Cisco Discovery Protocol is useful for detecting errors and for gathering port and system statistics on nearby Cisco devices. CDP is covered in Chapter 7.

Verifying with the *show ip interface* Command

The show ip interface command will provide you with information regarding the layer 3 configurations of a router's interface, such as the IP address and subnet mask, MTU, and if an access list is set on the interface:

```
Router#sh ip interface
FastEthernet0/0 is up, line protocol is up
   Internet address is 1.1.1.1/24
   Broadcast address is 255.255.255.255
   Address determined by setup command
   MTU is 1500 bytes
```

```
Helper address is not set
Directed broadcast forwarding is disabled
Outgoing access list is not set
Inbound  access list is not set
Proxy ARP is enabled
Security level is default
Split horizon is enabled
[output cut]
```

The status of the interface, the IP address and mask, information on whether an access list is set on the interface, and basic IP information are all included in this output.

Using the *show ip interface brief* Command

The show ip interface brief command is probably one of the best commands that you can ever use on a Cisco router or switch. This command provides a quick overview of the devices interfaces, including the logical address and status:

```
Router#sh ip int brief
Interface         IP-Address    OK? Method Status   Protocol
FastEthernet0/0   unassigned    YES unset  up         up
FastEthernet0/1   unassigned    YES unset  up         up
Serial0/0/0       unassigned    YES unset  up         down
Serial0/0/1       unassigned    YES unset  administratively down down
Serial0/1/0       unassigned    YES unset  administratively down down
Serial0/2/0       unassigned    YES unset  administratively down down
```

Remember, administratively down means that you need to type no shutdown in order to enable the interface. Notice that Serial0/0/0 is up/down, which means that the Physical layer is good and carrier detect is sensed but no keepalives are being received from the remote end. In a nonproduction network, like the one I am working with, this tells us the clock rate hasn't been set.

Verifying with the *show protocols* Command

The show protocols command is also a really helpful command that you'd use in order to quickly see the status of layers 1 and 2 of each interface as well as the IP addresses used.

Here's a look at one of my production routers:

```
Router#sh protocols
Global values:
  Internet Protocol routing is enabled
Ethernet0/0 is administratively down, line protocol is down
Serial0/0 is up, line protocol is up
  Internet address is 100.30.31.5/24
```

```
Serial0/1 is administratively down, line protocol is down
Serial0/2 is up, line protocol is up
  Internet address is 100.50.31.2/24
Loopback0 is up, line protocol is up
  Internet address is 100.20.31.1/24
```

The show ip interface brief and show protocols commands provide the layer 1 and layer 2 statistics of an interface as well as the IP addresses. The next command, show controllers, only provides layer 1 information. Let's take a look.

Using the *show controllers* Command

The show controllers command displays information about the physical interface itself. It'll also give you the type of serial cable plugged into a serial port. Usually, this will only be a DTE cable that plugs into a type of data service unit (DSU).

```
Router#sh controllers serial 0/0
HD unit 0, idb = 0x1229E4, driver structure at 0x127E70
buffer size 1524 HD unit 0, V.35 DTE cable
```

```
Router#sh controllers serial 0/1
HD unit 1, idb = 0x12C174, driver structure at 0x131600
buffer size 1524 HD unit 1, V.35 DCE cable
```

Notice that serial 0/0 has a DTE cable, whereas the serial 0/1 connection has a DCE cable. Serial 0/1 would have to provide clocking with the clock rate command. Serial 0/0 would get its clocking from the DSU.

Let's look at this command again. In Figure 6.5, see the DTE/DCE cable between the two routers? Know that you will not see this in production networks!

FIGURE 6.5 Where do you configure clocking? Use the show controllers command on each router's serial interface to find out.

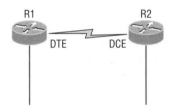

Router R1 has a DTE connection, which is typically the default for all Cisco routers. Routers R1 and R2 can't communicate. Check out the output of the show controllers s0/0 command here:

```
R1#sh controllers serial 0/0
HD unit 0, idb = 0x1229E4, driver structure at 0x127E70
buffer size 1524 HD unit 0, V.35 DCE cable
```

The show controllers s0/0 command reveals that the interface is a V.35 DCE cable. This means that R1 needs to provide clocking of the line to router R2. Basically, the interface has the wrong label on the cable on the R1 router's serial interface. But if you add clocking on the R1 router's serial interface, the network should come right up.

Let's check out another issue in Figure 6.6 that you can solve by using the show controllers command. Again, routers R1 and R2 can't communicate.

FIGURE 6.6   By looking at R1, the show controllers command reveals that R1 and R2 can't communicate.

Here's the output of R1's show controllers s0/0 command and show ip interface s0/0:

```
R1#sh controllers s0/0
HD unit 0, idb = 0x1229E4, driver structure at 0x127E70
buffer size 1524 HD unit 0,
DTE V.35 clocks stopped
cpb = 0xE2, eda = 0x4140, cda = 0x4000

R1#sh ip interface s0/0
Serial0/0 is up, line protocol is down
  Internet address is 192.168.10.2/24
  Broadcast address is 255.255.255.255
```

If you use the show controllers command and the show ip interface command, you'll see that router R1 isn't receiving the clocking of the line. This network is a nonproduction network, so no CSU/DSU is connected to provide clocking for it. This means the DCE end of the cable will be providing the clock rate—in this case, the R2 router. The show ip interface indicates that the interface is up but the protocol is down, which means that no keepalives are being received from the far end. In this example, the likely culprit is the result of bad cable, or simply the lack of clocking.

Summary

This was a fun chapter! I showed you a lot about the Cisco IOS, and I really hope you gained a lot of insight into the Cisco router world. I started off by explaining the Cisco Internetwork Operating System (IOS) and how you can use the IOS to run and configure Cisco routers. You learned how to bring a router up and what setup mode does. Oh, and by the way, since you can now basically configure Cisco routers, you should never use setup mode, right?

After I discussed how to connect to a router with a console and LAN connection, I covered the Cisco help features and how to use the CLI to find commands and command parameters. In addition, I discussed some basic show commands to help you verify your configurations.

Administrative functions on a router help you administer your network and verify that you are configuring the correct device. Setting router passwords is one of the most important configurations you can perform on your routers. I showed you the five passwords you must set, plus I introduced you to the hostname, interface description, and banners as tools to help you administer your router.

Well, that concludes your introduction to the Cisco IOS. And, as usual, it's super-important for you to have the basics that we went over in this chapter down rock-solid before you move on to the following chapters!

Exam Essentials

Describe the responsibilities of the IOS.   The Cisco router IOS software is responsible for network protocols and providing supporting functions, connecting high-speed traffic between devices, adding security to control access and prevent unauthorized network use, providing scalability for ease of network growth and redundancy, and supplying network reliability for connecting to network resources.

List the options available to connect to a Cisco device for management purposes.   The three options available are the console port, auxiliary port, and in-band communication, such as Telnet, SSH, and HTTP. Don't forget, a Telnet connection is not possible until an IP address has been configured and a Telnet password has been configured.

Understand the boot sequence of a router.   When you first bring up a Cisco router, it will run a power-on self-test (POST), and if that passes, it will look for and load the Cisco IOS from flash memory, if a file is present. The IOS then proceeds to load and looks for a valid configuration in NVRAM called the startup-config. If no file is present in NVRAM, the router will go into setup mode.

Describe the use of setup mode.   Setup mode is automatically started if a router boots and no startup-config is in NVRAM. You can also bring up setup mode by typing **setup** from privileged mode. Setup provides a minimum amount of configuration in an easy format for someone who does not understand how to configure a Cisco router from the command line.

Differentiate user, privileged, and global configuration modes, both visually and from a command capabilities perspective.   User mode, indicated by the **routername>** prompt, provides a command-line interface with very few available commands by default. User mode does not allow the configuration to be viewed or changed. Privileged mode, indicated by the **routername#** prompt, allows a user to both view and change the configuration of a router. You can enter privileged mode by typing the command **enable** and entering the enable password or enable secret password, if set. Global configuration mode, indicated by the **routername(config)#** prompt, allows configuration changes to be made that apply to the entire router (as opposed to a configuration change that might affect only one interface, for example).

Recognize additional prompts available in other modes and describe their use.   Additional modes are reached via the global configuration prompt, **routername(config)#**, and their prompts include interface, **router(config-if)#**, for making interface settings; line configuration mode, **router(config-line)#**, used to set passwords and make other settings to various connection methods; and routing protocol modes for various routing protocols; **router(config-router)#**, used to enable and configure routing protocols.

Access and utilize editing and help features.   Make use of typing a question mark at the end of commands for help in using the commands. Additionally, understand how to filter command help with the same question mark and letters. Use the command history to retrieve commands previously utilized without retyping. Understand the meaning of the caret when an incorrect command is rejected. Finally, identify useful hot key combinations.

Identify the information provided by the show version **command.**   The show version command will provide basic configuration for the system hardware as well as the software version, the names and sources of configuration files, the configuration register setting, and the boot images.

Set the hostname of a router.   The command sequence to set the hostname of a router is as follows:

```
enable
config t
hostname Todd
```

Differentiate the enable password and enable secret password.   Both of these passwords are used to gain access into privileged mode. However, the enable secret password is newer and is always encrypted by default. Also, if you set the enable password and then set the enable secret, only the enable secret will be used.

Describe the configuration and use of banners.   Banners provide information to users accessing the device and can be displayed at various login prompts. They are configured with the banner command and a keyword describing the specific type of banner.

Set the enable secret on a router.   To set the enable secret, you use the global config command enable secret. Do not use enable secret password *password* or you will set your password to *password password*. Here is an example:

```
enable
config t
enable secret todd
```

Set the console password on a router.   To set the console password, use the following sequence:

```
enable
config t
line console 0
password todd
login
```

Set the Telnet password on a router.   To set the Telnet password, the sequence is as follows:

```
enable
config t
line vty 0 4
password todd
login
```

Describe the advantages of using Secure Shell and list its requirements.   Secure Shell (SSH) uses encrypted keys to send data so that usernames and passwords are not sent in the clear. It requires that a hostname and domain name be configured and that encryption keys be generated.

Describe the process of preparing an interface for use.   To use an interface, you must configure it with an IP address and subnet mask in the same subnet of the hosts that will be connecting to the switch that is connected to that interface. It also must be enabled with the no shutdown command. A serial interface that is connected back to back with another router serial interface must also be configured with a clock rate on the DCE end of the serial cable.

Understand how to troubleshoot a serial link problem.   If you type **show interface serial 0/0** and see down, line protocol is down, this will be considered a Physical layer problem. If you see it as up, line protocol is down, then you have a Data Link layer problem.

Understand how to verify your router with the show interfaces command.   If you type **show interfaces**, you can view the statistics for the interfaces on the router, verify whether the interfaces are shut down, and see the IP address of each interface.

Describe how to view, edit, delete, and save a configuration.   The show running-config command is used to view the current configuration being used by the router. The show startup-config command displays the last configuration that was saved and is the one that will be used at next startup. The copy running-config startup-config command is used to save changes made to the running configuration in NVRAM. The erase startup-config command deletes the saved configuration and will result in the invocation of the setup menu when the router is rebooted because there will be no configuration present.

Written Lab 6: IOS Understanding

In this section, you'll complete the following lab to make sure you've got the information and concepts contained within them fully dialed in:

Lab 6.1: IOS Understanding

You can find the answers to this lab in Appendix A, "Answers to Written Labs."

Write out the command or commands for the following questions:

1. What command is used to set a serial interface to provide clocking to another router at 1000 Kb?

2. If you telnet into a switch and get the response `connection refused, password not set`, what commands would you execute on the destination device to stop receiving this message and not be prompted for a password?

3. If you type **show int fastethernet 0/1** and notice the port is administratively down, what commands would you execute to enable the interface?

4. If you wanted to delete the configuration stored in NVRAM, what command(s) would you type?

5. If you wanted to set the user-mode password to *todd* for the console port, what command(s) would you type?

6. If you wanted to set the enable secret password to *cisco*, what command(s) would you type?

7. If you wanted to determine if serial interface 0/2 on your router should provide clocking, what command would you use?

8. What command would you use to see the terminal history size?

9. You want to reinitialize the switch and totally replace the running-config with the current startup-config. What command will you use?

10. How would you set the name of a switch to *Sales*?

Hands-on Labs

In this section, you will perform commands on a Cisco switch (or you can use a router) that will help you understand what you learned in this chapter.

You'll need at least one Cisco device—two would be better, three would be outstanding. The hands-on labs in this section are included for use with real Cisco routers, but all of these labs work with the LammleSim IOS version (see www.lammle.com/ccna) or use the Cisco Packet Tracer router simulator. Last, for the Cisco exam it doesn't matter what model of switch or router you use with these labs, as long as you're running IOS 12.2 or newer. Yes, I know the objectives are 15 code, but that is not important for any of these labs.

It is assumed that the device you're going to use has no current configuration present. If necessary, erase any existing configuration with Hands-on Lab 6.1; otherwise, proceed to Hands-on Lab 6.2:

Lab 6.1: Erasing an Existing Configuration

Lab 6.2: Exploring User, Privileged, and Configuration Modes

Lab 6.3: Using the Help and Editing Features

Lab 6.4: Saving a Configuration

Lab 6.5: Setting Passwords

Lab 6.6: Setting the Hostname, Descriptions, IP Address, and Clock Rate

Hands-on Lab 6.1: Erasing an Existing Configuration

The following lab may require the knowledge of a username and password to enter privileged mode. If the router has a configuration with an unknown username and password for privileged mode, this procedure will not be possible. It is possible to erase a configuration without a privileged mode password, but the exact steps depend on the model and will not be covered until Chapter 7.

1. Start the switch up and when prompted, press Enter.

2. At the Switch> prompt, type **enable**.

3. If prompted, enter the username and press Enter. Then enter the correct password and press Enter.

4. At the privileged mode prompt, type **erase startup-config**.

5. At the privileged mode prompt, type **reload**, and when prompted to save the configuration, type **n** for no.

Hands-on Lab 6.2: Exploring User, Privileged, and Configuration Modes

In the following lab, you'll explore user, privileged, and configuration modes:

1. Plug the switch in, or turn the router on. If you just erased the configuration as in Hands-on Lab 6.1, when prompted to continue with the configuration dialog, enter **n** for no and press Enter. When prompted, press Enter to connect to your router. This will put you into user mode.

2. At the Switch> prompt, type a question mark (**?**).

3. Notice the -more- at the bottom of the screen.

4. Press the Enter key to view the commands line by line. Press the spacebar to view the commands a full screen at a time. You can type **q** at any time to quit.

5. Type **enable** or **en** and press Enter. This will put you into privileged mode where you can change and view the router configuration.

6. At the `Switch#` prompt, type a question mark (**?**). Notice how many options are available to you in privileged mode.

7. Type **q** to quit.

8. Type **config** and press Enter.

9. When prompted for a method, press Enter to configure your router using your terminal (which is the default).

10. At the `Switch(config)#` prompt, type a question mark (**?**), then **q** to quit, or press the spacebar to view the commands.

11. Type **interface f0/1** or **int f0/1** (or even **int gig0/1**) and press Enter. This will allow you to configure interface FastEthernet 0/1 or Gigabit 0/1.

12. At the `Switch(config-if)#` prompt, type a question mark (**?**).

13. If using a router, type **int s0/0**, **interface s0/0** or even **interface s0/0/0** and press Enter. This will allow you to configure interface serial 0/0. Notice that you can go from interface to interface easily.

14. Type **encapsulation ?**.

15. Type **exit**. Notice how this brings you back one level.

16. Press Ctrl+Z. Notice how this brings you out of configuration mode and places you back into privileged mode.

17. Type **disable**. This will put you into user mode.

18. Type **exit**, which will log you out of the router or switch.

Hands-on Lab 6.3: Using the Help and Editing Features

This lab will provide hands-on experience with Cisco's help and editing features.

1. Log into your device and go to privileged mode by typing **en** or **enable**.

2. Type a question mark (**?**).

3. Type **cl?** and then press Enter. Notice that you can see all the commands that start with *cl*.

4. Type **clock ?** and press Enter.

> **NOTE**   Notice the difference between steps 3 and 4. Step 3 has you type letters with no space and a question mark, which will give you all the commands that start with *cl*. Step 4 has you type a command, space, and question mark. By doing this, you will see the next available parameter.

5. Set the clock by typing **clock ?** and, following the help screens, setting the time and date. The following steps walk you through setting the date and time.

6. Type **clock ?**.

7. Type **clock set ?**.

8. Type **clock set 10:30:30 ?**.

9. Type **clock set 10:30:30 14 May ?**.

10. Type **clock set 10:30:30 14 May 2011**.

11. Press Enter.

12. Type **show clock** to see the time and date.

13. From privileged mode, type **show access-list 10**. Don't press Enter.

14. Press Ctrl+A. This takes you to the beginning of the line.

15. Press Ctrl+E. This should take you back to the end of the line.

16. Ctrl+A takes your cursor back to the beginning of the line, and then Ctrl+F moves your cursor forward one character.

17. Press Ctrl+B, which will move you back one character.

18. Press Enter, then press Ctrl+P. This will repeat the last command.

19. Press the up arrow key on your keyboard. This will also repeat the last command.

20. Type **sh history**. This shows you the last 10 commands entered.

21. Type **terminal history size ?**. This changes the history entry size. The ? is the number of allowed lines.

22. Type **show terminal** to gather terminal statistics and history size.

23. Type **terminal no editing**. This turns off advanced editing. Repeat steps 14 through 18 to see that the shortcut editing keys have no effect until you type **terminal editing**.

24. Type **terminal editing** and press Enter to re-enable advanced editing.

25. Type **sh run**, then press your Tab key. This will finish typing the command for you.

26. Type **sh start**, then press your Tab key. This will finish typing the command for you.

Hands-on Lab 6.4: Saving a Configuration

In this lab, you will get hands-on experience saving a configuration:

1. Log into your device and go into privileged mode by typing **en** or **enable**, then press Enter.

2. To see the configuration stored in NVRAM, type **sh start** and press Tab and Enter, or type **show startup-config** and press Enter. However, if no configuration has been saved, you will get an error message.

3. To save a configuration to NVRAM, which is known as startup-config, you can do one of the following:

   ▪ Type **copy run start** and press Enter.

   ▪ Type **copy running**, press Tab, type **start**, press Tab, and press Enter.

   ▪ Type **copy running-config startup-config** and press Enter.

4. Type **sh start**, press Tab, then press Enter.

5. Type **sh run**, press Tab, then press Enter.

6. Type **erase startup-config**, press Tab, then press Enter.

7. Type **sh start**, press Tab, then press Enter. The router will either tell you that NVRAM is not present or display some other type of message, depending on the IOS and hardware.

8. Type **reload**, then press Enter. Acknowledge the reload by pressing Enter. Wait for the device to reload.

9. Say no to entering setup mode, or just press Ctrl+C.

Hands-on Lab 6.5: Setting Passwords

This hands-on lab will have you set your passwords.

1. Log into the router and go into privileged mode by typing **en** or **enable**.

2. Type **config t** and press Enter.

3. Type **enable ?**.

4. Set your enable secret password by typing **enable secret *password*** (the third word should be your own personalized password) and pressing Enter. Do not add the parameter password after the parameter secret (this would make your password the word *password*). An example would be enable secret todd.

5. Now let's see what happens when you log all the way out of the router and then log in. Log out by pressing Ctrl+Z, and then type **exit** and press Enter. Go to privileged mode. Before you are allowed to enter privileged mode, you will be asked for a password. If you successfully enter the secret password, you can proceed.

6. Remove the secret password. Go to privileged mode, type **config t**, and press Enter. Type **no enable secret** and press Enter. Log out and then log back in again; now you should not be asked for a password.

7. One more password used to enter privileged mode is called the enable password. It is an older, less secure password and is not used if an enable secret password is set. Here is an example of how to set it:

```
config t
enable password todd1
```

8. Notice that the enable secret and enable passwords are different. They should never be set the same. Actually, you should never use the enable password, only enable secret.

9. Type **config t** to be at the right level to set your console and auxiliary passwords, then type **line ?**.

10. Notice that the parameters for the line commands are auxiliary, vty, and console. You will set all three if you're on a router; if you're on a switch, only the console and VTY lines are available.

11. To set the Telnet or VTY password, type **line vty 0 4** and then press Enter. The 0 4 is the range of the five available virtual lines used to connect with Telnet. If you have an enterprise IOS, the number of lines may vary. Use the question mark to determine the last line number available on your router.

12. The next command is used to set the authentication on or off. Type **login** and press Enter to prompt for a user-mode password when telnetting into the device. You will not be able to telnet into a Cisco device if the password is not set.

 You can use the no login command to disable the user-mode password prompt when using Telnet. Do not do this in production!

13. One more command you need to set for your VTY password is password. Type **password** *password* to set the password. (*password* is your password.)

14. Here is an example of how to set the VTY password:

```
config t
line vty 0 4
password todd
login
```

15. Set your auxiliary password by first typing **line auxiliary 0** or **line aux 0** (if you are using a router).

16. Type **login**.

17. Type **password** *password*.

18. Set your console password by first typing **line console 0** or **line con 0**.

19. Type **login**.

20. Type **password** *password*. Here is an example of the last two command sequences:

```
config t
line con 0
password todd1
login
line aux 0
password todd
login
```

21. You can add the Exec-timeout 0 0 command to the console 0 line. This will stop the console from timing out and logging you out. The command sequence will now look like this:

```
config t
line con 0
password todd2
```

```
login
exec-timeout 0 0
```

22. Set the console prompt to not overwrite the command you're typing with console messages by using the command `logging synchronous`.

```
config t
line con 0
logging synchronous
```

Hands-on Lab 6.6: Setting the Hostname, Descriptions, IP Address, and Clock Rate

This lab will have you set your administrative functions on each device.

1. Log into the switch or router and go into privileged mode by typing **en** or **enable**. If required, enter a username and password.

2. Set your hostname by using the `hostname` command. Notice that it is one word. Here is an example of setting your hostname on your router, but the switch uses the exact same command:

```
Router#config t
Router(config)#hostname RouterA
RouterA(config)#
```

Notice that the hostname of the router changed in the prompt as soon as you pressed Enter.

3. Set a banner that the network administrators will see by using the `banner` command, as shown in the following steps.

4. Type **config t**, then **banner ?**.

5. Notice that you can set at least four different banners. For this lab we are only interested in the login and message of the day (MOTD) banners.

6. Set your MOTD banner, which will be displayed when a console, auxiliary, or Telnet connection is made to the router, by typing this:

```
config t
banner motd #
This is an motd banner
#
```

7. The preceding example used a # sign as a delimiting character. This tells the router when the message is done. You cannot use the delimiting character in the message itself.

8. You can remove the MOTD banner by typing the following command:

```
config t
no banner motd
```

9. Set the login banner by typing this:

```
config t
banner login #
This is a login banner
#
```

10. The login banner will display immediately after the MOTD but before the user-mode password prompt. Remember that you set your user-mode passwords by setting the console, auxiliary, and VTY line passwords.

11. You can remove the login banner by typing this:

```
config t
no banner login
```

12. You can add an IP address to an interface with the `ip address` command if you are using a router. You need to get into interface configuration mode first; here is an example of how you do that:

```
config t
int f0/1
ip address 1.1.1.1 255.255.0.0
no shutdown
```

Notice that the IP address (1.1.1.1) and subnet mask (255.255.0.0) are configured on one line. The no shutdown (or no shut for short) command is used to enable the interface. All interfaces are shut down by default on a router. If you are on a layer 2 switch, you can set an IP address only on the VLAN 1 interface.

13. You can add identification to an interface by using the `description` command. This is useful for adding information about the connection. Here is an example:

```
config t
int f0/1
ip address 2.2.2.1 255.255.0.0
no shut
description LAN link to Finance
```

14. You can add the bandwidth of a serial link as well as the clock rate when simulating a DCE WAN link on a router. Here is an example:

```
config t
int s0/0
bandwidth 1000
clock rate 1000000
```

Review Questions

 The following questions are designed to test your understanding of this chapter's material. For more information on how to get additional questions, please see www.lammle.com/ccna.

You can find the answers to these questions in Appendix B, "Answers to Review Questions."

1. You type **show interfaces fa0/1** and get this output:

```
275496 packets input, 35226811 bytes, 0 no buffer
   Received 69748 broadcasts (58822 multicasts)
   0 runts, 0 giants, 0 throttles
   111395 input errors, 511987 CRC, 0 frame, 0 overrun, 0 ignored
   0 watchdog, 58822 multicast, 0 pause input
   0 input packets with dribble condition detected
   2392529 packets output, 337933522 bytes, 0 underruns
   0 output errors, 0 collisions, 1 interface resets
   0 babbles, 0 late collision, 0 deferred
   0 lost carrier, 0 no carrier, 0 PAUSE output
   0 output buffer failures, 0 output buffers swapped out
```

   What could the problem possibly be with this interface?

   A. Speed mismatch on directly connected interfaces

   B. Collisions causing CRC errors

   C. Frames received are too large

   D. Interference on the Ethernet cable

2. The output of the show running-config command comes from _____.

   A. NVRAM

   B. Flash

   C. RAM

   D. Firmware

3. Which two of the following commands are required when configuring SSH on your router? (Choose two.)

   A. enable secret *password*

   B. exec-timeout 0 0

   C. `ip domain-name` *name*

   D. `username` *name* `password` *password*

   E. `ip ssh version 2`

4. Which command will show you whether a DTE or a DCE cable is plugged into serial 0/0 on your router's WAN port?

   A. `sh int s0/0`

   B. `sh int serial0/0`

   C. `show controllers s0/0`

   D. `show serial0/0 controllers`

5. In the work area, drag the router term to its definition on the right.

Mode	Definition
user exec mode	Commands that affect the entire system
privileged exec mode	Commands that affect interfaces/processes only
Global configuration mode	Interactive configuration dialog
Specific configuration modes	Provides access to all other router commands
Setup mode	Limited to basic monitoring commands

6. Using the given output, what type of interface is shown?

```
[output cut]
Hardware is MV96340 Ethernet, address is 001a.2f55.c9e8 (bia 001a.2f55.c9e8)
Internet address is 192.168.1.33/27
MTU 1500 bytes, BW 100000 Kbit, DLY 100 usec,
    reliability 255/255, txload 1/255, rxload 1/255
```

   A. 10 Mb

   B. 100 Mb

   C. 1000 Mb

   D. 1000 MB

7. Which of the following commands will configure all the default VTY ports on a switch?

   A. `Switch#`**`line vty 0 4`**

   B. `Switch(config)#`**`line vty 0 4`**

   C. `Switch(config-if)#`**`line console 0`**

   D. `Switch(config)#`**`line vty all`**

8. Which of the following commands sets the privileged mode password to Cisco and encrypts the password?

   A. `enable secret password Cisco`

   B. `enable secret cisco`

   C. `enable secret Cisco`

   D. `enable password Cisco`

9. If you wanted administrators to see a message when logging into the switch, which command would you use?

   A. `message banner motd`

   B. `banner message motd`

   C. `banner motd`

   D. `message motd`

10. Which of the following prompts indicates that the switch is currently in privileged mode?

   A. `Switch(config)#`

   B. `Switch>`

   C. `Switch#`

   D. `Switch(config-if)`

11. What command do you type to save the configuration stored in RAM to NVRAM?

   A. `Switch(config)#`**`copy current to starting`**

   B. `Switch#`**`copy starting to running`**

   C. `Switch(config)#`**`copy running-config startup-config`**

   D. `Switch#`**`copy run start`**

12. You try to telnet into SF from router Corp and receive this message:

```
Corp#telnet SF
Trying SF (10.0.0.1)...Open

Password required, but none set
[Connection to SF closed by foreign host]
Corp#
```

Which of the following sequences will address this problem correctly?

   A. `Corp(config)#line console 0`
      `Corp(config-line)#password password`
      `Corp(config-line)#login`

   B. `SF config)#line console 0`
      `SF(config-line)#enable secret password`
      `SF(config-line)#login`

C. Corp(config)#line vty 0 4
Corp(config-line)#password *password*
Corp(config-line)#login

D. SF(config)#line vty 0 4
SF(config-line)#password *password*
SF(config-line)#login

13. Which command will delete the contents of NVRAM on a switch?

A. delete NVRAM

B. delete startup-config

C. erase flash

D. erase startup-config

E. erase start

14. What is the problem with an interface if you type **show interface g0/1** and receive the following message?

Gigabit 0/1 is administratively down, line protocol is down

A. The keepalives are different times.

B. The administrator has the interface shut down.

C. The administrator is pinging from the interface.

D. No cable is attached.

15. Which of the following commands displays the configurable parameters and statistics of all interfaces on a switch?

A. show running-config

B. show startup-config

C. show interfaces

D. show versions

16. If you delete the contents of NVRAM and reboot the switch, what mode will you be in?

A. Privileged mode

B. Global mode

C. Setup mode

D. NVRAM loaded mode

17. You type the following command into the switch and receive the following output:

Switch#**show fastethernet 0/1**
              ^
% Invalid input detected at '^' marker.

Why was this error message displayed?

A. You need to be in privileged mode.

B. You cannot have a space between `fastethernet` and `0/1`.

C. The switch does not have a FastEthernet 0/1 interface.

D. Part of the command is missing.

18. You type **Switch#sh r** and receive a `% ambiguous command` error. Why did you receive this message?

A. The command requires additional options or parameters.

B. There is more than one show command that starts with the letter *r*.

C. There is no show command that starts with *r*.

D. The command is being executed from the wrong mode.

19. Which of the following commands will display the current IP addressing and the layer 1 and 2 status of an interface? (Choose two.)

A. `show version`

B. `show interfaces`

C. `show controllers`

D. `show ip interface`

E. `show running-config`

20. At which layer of the OSI model would you assume the problem is if you type **show interface serial 1** and receive the following message?

`Serial1 is down, line protocol is down`

A. Physical layer

B. Data Link layer

C. Network layer

D. None; it is a router problem.

Chapter

7

Managing a Cisco Internetwork

THE FOLLOWING ICND1 EXAM TOPICS ARE COVERED IN THIS CHAPTER:

✓ **2.0 LAN Switching Technologies**

- 2.6 Configure and verify Layer 2 protocols
  - 2.6.a Cisco Discovery Protocol
  - 2.6.b LLDP

✓ **4.0 Infrastructure Services**

- 4.1 Describe DNS lookup operation
- 4.2 Troubleshoot client connectivity issues involving DNS
- 4.3 Configure and verify DHCP on a router (excluding static reservations)
  - 4.3.a Server
  - 4.3.b Relay
  - 4.3.c Client
  - 4.3.d TFTP, DNS, and gateway options
- 4.4 Troubleshoot client- and router-based DHCP connectivity issues
- 4.5 Configure and verify NTP operating in client/server mode

✓ **5.0 Infrastructure Management**

- 5.1 Configure and verify device-monitoring using syslog
- 5.2 Configure and verify device management
  - 5.2.a Backup and restore device configuration
  - 5.2.b Using Cisco Discovery Protocol and LLDP for device discovery
  - 5.2.d Logging
  - 5.2.e Timezone
  - 5.2.f Loopback

Here in Chapter 7, I'm going to show you how to manage Cisco routers and switches on an internetwork. You'll be learning about the main components of a router, as well as the router boot sequence. You'll also find out how to manage Cisco devices by using the copy command with a TFTP host and how to configure DHCP and NTP, plus you'll get a survey of the Cisco Discovery Protocol (CDP). I'll also show you how to resolve hostnames.

I'll wrap up the chapter by guiding you through some important Cisco IOS trouble-shooting techniques to ensure that you're well equipped with these key skills.

To find up-to-the minute updates for this chapter, please see www.lammle .com/ccna or the book's web page at www.sybex.com/go/ccna.

The Internal Components of a Cisco Router and Switch

Unless you happen to be really savvy about the inner and outer workings of all your car's systems and its machinery and how all of that technology works together, you'll take it to someone who *does* know how to keep it maintained, figure out what's wrong when it stops running, and get it up and running again. It's the same deal with Cisco networking devices—you need to know all about their major components, pieces, and parts as well as what they all do and why and how they all work together to make a network work. The more solid your knowledge, the more expert you are about these things and the better equipped you'll be to configure and troubleshoot a Cisco internetwork. Toward that goal, study Table 7.1 for an introductory description of a Cisco router's major components.

TABLE 7.1 Cisco router components

Component	Description
Bootstrap	Stored in the microcode of the ROM, the bootstrap is used to bring a router up during initialization. It boots the router up and then loads the IOS.
POST (power-on self-test)	Also stored in the microcode of the ROM, the POST is used to check the basic functionality of the router hardware and determines which interfaces are present.

Component	Description
ROM monitor	Again, stored in the microcode of the ROM, the ROM monitor is used for manufacturing, testing, and troubleshooting, as well as running a mini-IOS when the IOS in flash fails to load.
Mini-IOS	Called the RXBOOT or bootloader by Cisco, the mini-IOS is a small IOS in ROM that can be used to bring up an interface and load a Cisco IOS into flash memory. The mini-IOS can also perform a few other maintenance operations.
RAM (random access memory)	Used to hold packet buffers, ARP cache, routing tables, and also the software and data structures that allow the router to function. Running-config is stored in RAM, and most routers expand the IOS from flash into RAM upon boot.
ROM (read-only memory)	Used to start and maintain the router. Holds the POST and the bootstrap program as well as the mini-IOS.
Flash memory	Stores the Cisco IOS by default. Flash memory is not erased when the router is reloaded. It is EEPROM (electronically erasable programmable read-only memory) created by Intel.
NVRAM (nonvolatile RAM)	Used to hold the router and switch configuration. NVRAM is not erased when the router or switch is reloaded. Does not store an IOS. The configuration register is stored in NVRAM.
Configuration register	Used to control how the router boots up. This value can be found as the last line of the show version command output and by default is set to 0x2102, which tells the router to load the IOS from flash memory as well as to load the configuration from NVRAM.

The Router and Switch Boot Sequence

When a Cisco device boots up, it performs a series of steps, called the *boot sequence*, to test the hardware and load the necessary software. The boot sequence comprises the following steps, as shown in Figure 7.1:

1. The IOS device performs a POST, which tests the hardware to verify that all components of the device are present and operational. The post takes stock of the different interfaces on the switch or router, and it's stored in and runs from read-only memory (ROM).

2. The bootstrap in ROM then locates and loads the Cisco IOS software by executing programs responsible for finding where each IOS program is located. Once they are found, it then loads the proper files. By default, the IOS software is loaded from flash memory in all Cisco devices.

FIGURE 7.1   Router bootup process

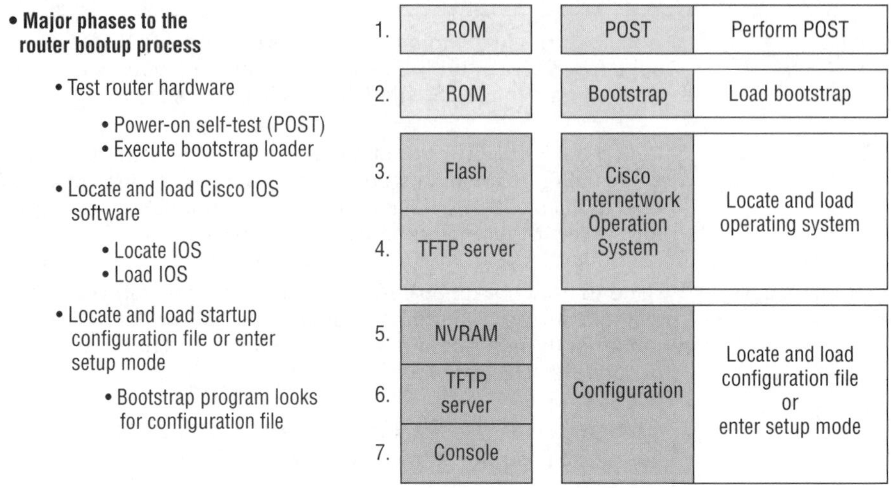

• **Major phases to the router bootup process**	1.	ROM	POST	Perform POST
• Test router hardware	2.	ROM	Bootstrap	Load bootstrap
• Power-on self-test (POST) • Execute bootstrap loader				
• Locate and load Cisco IOS software	3.	Flash	Cisco Internetwork Operation System	Locate and load operating system
• Locate IOS • Load IOS	4.	TFTP server		
• Locate and load startup configuration file or enter setup mode	5.	NVRAM	Configuration	Locate and load configuration file or enter setup mode
• Bootstrap program looks for configuration file	6.	TFTP server		
	7.	Console		

3. The IOS software then looks for a valid configuration file stored in NVRAM. This file is called startup-config and will be present only if an administrator has copied the running-config file into NVRAM.

4. If a startup-config file is found in NVRAM, the router or switch will copy it, place it in RAM, and name the file the running-config. The device will use this file to run, and the router/switch should now be operational. If a startup-config file is not in NVRAM, the router will broadcast out any interface that detects carrier detect (CD) for a TFTP host looking for a configuration, and when that fails (typically it will fail—most people won't even realize the router has attempted this process), it will start the setup mode configuration process.

The default order of an IOS loading from a Cisco device begins with flash, then TFTP server, and finally, ROM.

Backing Up and Restoring the Cisco Configuration

Any changes that you make to the configuration are stored in the running-config file. And if you don't enter a copy run start command after you make a change to running-config, that change will totally disappear if the device reboots or gets powered down. As always, backups are good, so you'll want to make another backup of the configuration information just in case the router or switch completely dies on you. Even if your machine is healthy and happy, it's good to have a backup for reference and documentation reasons!

Next, I'll cover how to copy the configuration of a router to a TFTP server as well as how to restore that configuration.

Backing Up the Cisco Configuration

To copy the configuration from an IOS device to a TFTP server, you can use either the copy running-config tftp or the copy startup-config tftp command. Either one will back up the router configuration that's currently running in DRAM or one that's stored in NVRAM.

Verifying the Current Configuration

To verify the configuration in DRAM, use the show running-config command (sh run for short) like this:

```
Router#show running-config
Building configuration...

Current configuration : 855 bytes
!
version 15.0
```

The current configuration information indicates that the router is running version 15.0 of the IOS.

Verifying the Stored Configuration

Next, you should check the configuration stored in NVRAM. To see this, use the show startup-config command (sh start for short) like this:

```
Router#sh start
Using 855 out of 524288 bytes
!
! Last configuration change at 04:49:14 UTC Fri Mar 5 1993
!
version 15.0
```

The first line shows you how much room your backup configuration is taking up. Here, we can see that NVRAM is about 524 KB and that only 855 bytes of it are being used. But memory is easier to reveal via the show version command when you're using an ISR router.

If you're not sure that the files are the same and the running-config file is what you want to go with, then use the copy running-config startup-config command. This will help you ensure that both files are in fact the same. I'll guide you through this in the next section.

Copying the Current Configuration to NVRAM

By copying running-config to NVRAM as a backup, as shown in the following output, you ensure that your running-config will always be reloaded if the router gets rebooted. Starting in the 12.0 IOS, you'll be prompted for the filename you want to use:

```
Router#copy running-config startup-config
Destination filename [startup-config]?[enter]
Building configuration...
[OK]
```

The reason the filename prompt appears is that there are now so many options you can use when using the copy command—check it out:

```
Router#copy running-config ?
  flash:          Copy to flash: file system
  ftp:            Copy to ftp: file system
  http:           Copy to http: file system
  https:          Copy to https: file system
  null:           Copy to null: file system
  nvram:          Copy to nvram: file system
  rcp:            Copy to rcp: file system
  running-config  Update (merge with) current system configuration
  scp:            Copy to scp: file system
  startup-config  Copy to startup configuration
  syslog:         Copy to syslog: file system
  system:         Copy to system: file system
  tftp:           Copy to tftp: file system
  tmpsys:         Copy to tmpsys: file system
```

Copying the Configuration to a TFTP Server

Once the file is copied to NVRAM, you can make a second backup to a TFTP server by using the copy running-config tftp command, or copy run tftp for short. I'm going to set the hostname to Todd before I run this command:

```
Todd#copy running-config tftp
Address or name of remote host []? 10.10.10.254
Destination filename [todd-confg]?
!!
776 bytes copied in 0.800 secs (970 bytes/sec)
```

If you have a hostname already configured, the command will automatically use the hostname plus the extension -confg as the name of the file.

Restoring the Cisco Configuration

What do you do if you've changed your running-config file and want to restore the configuration to the version in the startup-config file? The easiest way to get this done is to use the copy startup-config running-config command, or copy start run for short, but this will work only if you copied running-config into NVRAM before you made any changes! Of course, a reload of the device will work too!

If you did copy the configuration to a TFTP server as a second backup, you can restore the configuration using the copy tftp running-config command (copy tftp run for short), or the copy tftp startup-config command (copy tftp start for short), as shown in the following output. Just so you know, the old command we used to use for this is config net:

```
Todd#copy tftp running-config
Address or name of remote host []?10.10.10.254
Source filename []?todd-confg
Destination filename[running-config]?[enter]
Accessing tftp://10.10.10.254/todd-confg...
Loading todd-confg from 10.10.10.254 (via FastEthernet0/0):
!!
[OK - 776 bytes]
776 bytes copied in 9.212 secs (84 bytes/sec)
Todd#
*Mar  7 17:53:34.071: %SYS-5-CONFIG_I: Configured from
    tftp://10.10.10.254/todd-confg by console
```

Okay that the configuration file is an ASCII text file ... meaning that before you copy the configuration stored on a TFTP server back to a router, you can make changes to the file with any text editor.

Remember that when you copy or merge a configuration from a TFTP server to a freshly erased and rebooted router's RAM, the interfaces are shut down by default and you must manually enable each interface with the no shutdown command.

Erasing the Configuration

To delete the startup-config file on a Cisco router or switch, use the command erase startup-config, like this:

```
Todd#erase startup-config
Erasing the nvram filesystem will remove all configuration files!
    Continue? [confirm][enter]
```

```
[OK]
Erase of nvram: complete
*Mar  7 17:56:20.407: %SYS-7-NV_BLOCK_INIT: Initialized the geometry of nvram
Todd#reload
System configuration has been modified. Save? [yes/no]:n
Proceed with reload? [confirm][enter]
 *Mar  7 17:56:31.059: %SYS-5-RELOAD: Reload requested by console.
   Reload Reason: Reload Command.
```

This command deletes the contents of NVRAM on the switch and router. If you type **reload** while in privileged mode and say no to saving changes, the switch or router will reload and come up into setup mode.

Configuring DHCP

We went over DHCP in Chapter 3, "Introduction to TCP/IP," where I described how it works and what happens when there's a conflict. At this point, you're ready to learn how to configure DHCP on Cisco's IOS as well as how to configure a DHCP forwarder for when your hosts don't live on the same LAN as the DHCP server. Do you remember the four-step process hosts used to get an address from a server? If not, now would be a really great time to head back to Chapter 3 and thoroughly review that before moving on with this!

To configure a DHCP server for your hosts, you need the following information at minimum:

Network and mask for each LAN   Network ID, also called a scope. All addresses in a subnet can be leased to hosts by default.

Reserved/excluded addresses   Reserved addresses for printers, servers, routers, etc. These addresses will not be handed out to hosts. I usually reserve the first address of each subnet for the router, but you don't have to do this.

Default router   This is the router's address for each LAN.

DNS address   A list of DNS server addresses provided to hosts so they can resolve names.

Here are your configuration steps:

1. Exclude the addresses you want to reserve. The reason you do this step first is because as soon as you set a network ID, the DHCP service will start responding to client requests.

2. Create your pool for each LAN using a unique name.

3. Choose the network ID and subnet mask for the DHCP pool that the server will use to provide addresses to hosts.

4. Add the address used for the default gateway of the subnet.

5. Provide the DNS server address(es).

6. If you don't want to use the default lease time of 24 hours, you need to set the lease time in days, hours, and minutes.

I'll configure the switch in Figure 7.2 to be the DHCP server for the Sales wireless LAN.

FIGURE 7.2   DHCP configuration example on a switch

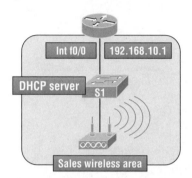

Understand that this configuration could just have easily been placed on the router in Figure 7.2. Here's how we'll configure DHCP using the 192.168.10.0/24 network ID:

```
Switch(config)#ip dhcp excluded-address 192.168.10.1 192.168.10.10
Switch(config)#ip dhcp pool Sales_Wireless
Switch(dhcp-config)#network 192.168.10.0 255.255.255.0
Switch(dhcp-config)#default-router 192.168.10.1
Switch(dhcp-config)#dns-server 4.4.4.4
Switch(dhcp-config)#lease 3 12 15
Switch(dhcp-config)#option 66 ascii tftp.lammle.com
```

First, you can see that I reserved 10 addresses in the range for the router, servers, and printers, etc. I then created the pool named Sales_Wireless, added the default gateway and DNS server, and set the lease to 3 days, 12 hours, and 15 minutes (which isn't really significant because I just set it that way for demonstration purposes). Lastly, I provided an example on you how you would set option 66, which is sending a TFTP server address to a DHCP client. Typically used for VoIP phones, or auto installs, and needs to be listed as a FQDN. Pretty straightforward, right? The switch will now respond to DHCP client requests. But what happens if we need to provide an IP address from a DHCP server to a host that's not in our broadcast domain, or if we want to receive a DHCP address for a client from a remote server?

DHCP Relay

If you need to provide addresses from a DHCP server to hosts that aren't on the same LAN as the DHCP server, you can configure your router interface to relay or forward the DHCP client requests, as shown in Figure 7.3. If we don't provide this service, our router would receive the DHCP client broadcast, promptly discard it, and the remote host would never receive an address—unless we added a DHCP server on every broadcast domain! Let's take a look at how we would typically configure DHCP service in today's networks.

FIGURE 7.3 Configuring a DHCP relay

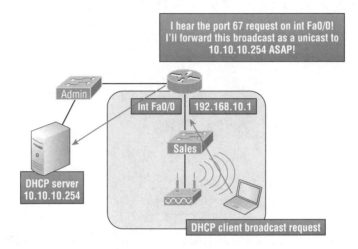

So we know that because the hosts off the router don't have access to a DHCP server, the router will simply drop their client request broadcast messages by default. To solve this problem, we can configure the Fa0/0 interface of the router to accept the DHCP client requests and forward them to the DHCP server like this:

```
Router#config t
Router(config)#interface fa0/0
Router(config-if)#ip helper-address 10.10.10.254
```

Now I know that was a pretty simple example, and there are definitely other ways to configure the relay, but rest assured that I've covered the objectives for you. Also, I want you to know that ip helper-address forwards more than just DHCP client requests, so be sure to research this command before you implement it! Now that I've demonstrated how to create the DHCP service, let's take a minute to verify DHCP before moving on to NTP.

Verifying DHCP on Cisco IOS

There are some really useful verification commands to use on a Cisco IOS device for monitoring and verifying a DHCP service. You'll get to see the output for these commands when I build the network in Chapter 9, "IP Routing," and add DHCP to the two remote LANs. I just want you to begin getting familiar with them, so here's a list of four very important ones and what they do:

show ip dhcp binding Lists state information about each IP address currently leased to a client.

show ip dhcp pool [poolname]   Lists the configured range of IP addresses, plus statistics for the number of currently leased addresses and the high watermark for leases from each pool.

show ip dhcp server statistics   Lists DHCP server statistics—a lot of them!

show ip dhcp conflict   If someone statically configures an IP address on a LAN and the DHCP server hands out that same address, you'll end up with a duplicate address. This isn't good, which is why this command is so helpful!

Again, no worries because we'll cover these vital commands thoroughly in Chapter 9.

Syslog

Reading system messages from a switch's or router's internal buffer is the most popular and efficient method of seeing what's going on with your network at a particular time. But the best way is to log messages to a *syslog* server, which stores messages from you and can even time-stamp and sequence them for you, and it's easy to set up and configure!

Syslog allows you to display, sort, and even search messages, all of which makes it a really great troubleshooting tool. The search feature is especially powerful because you can use keywords and even severity levels. Plus, the server can email admins based on the severity level of the message.

Network devices can be configured to generate a syslog message and forward it to various destinations. These four examples are popular ways to gather messages from Cisco devices:

- Logging buffer (on by default)
- Console line (on by default)
- Terminal lines (using the terminal monitor command)
- Syslog server

As you already know, all system messages and debug output generated by the IOS go out only the console port by default and are also logged in buffers in RAM. And you also know that Cisco routers aren't exactly shy about sending messages! To send a message to the VTY lines, use the terminal monitor command. We'll also add a small configuration needed for syslog, which I'll show you soon in the configuration section.

So by default, we'd see something like this on our console line:

```
*Oct 21 17:33:50.565:%LINK-5-CHANGED:Interface FastEthernet0/0, changed
state to administratively down
*Oct 21 17:33:51.565:%LINEPROTO-5-UPDOWN:Line protocol on Interface
FastEthernet0/0, changed state to down
```

And the Cisco router would send a general version of the message to the syslog server that would be formatted into something like this:

```
Seq no:timestamp: %facility-severity-MNEMONIC:description
```

The system message format can be broken down in this way:

seq no   This stamp logs messages with a sequence number, but not by default. If you want this output, you've got to configure it.

Timestamp   Data and time of the message or event, which again will show up only if configured.

Facility   The facility to which the message refers.

Severity   A single-digit code from 0 to 7 that indicates the severity of the message.

MNEMONIC   Text string that uniquely describes the message.

Description   Text string containing detailed information about the event being reported.

The severity levels, from the most severe level to the least severe, are explained in Table 7.2. Informational is the default and will result in all messages being sent to the buffers and console.

TABLE 7.2 Severity levels

Severity Level	Explanation
Emergency (severity 0)	System is unusable.
Alert (severity 1)	Immediate action is needed.
Critical (severity 2)	Critical condition.
Error (severity 3)	Error condition.
Warning (severity 4)	Warning condition.
Notification (severity 5)	Normal but significant condition.
Informational (severity 6)	Normal information message.
Debugging (severity 7)	Debugging message.

 If you are studying for your Cisco exam, you need to memorize Table 7.2 using this acronym: Every Awesome Cisco Engineer Will Need Icecream Daily.

Understand that only emergency-level messages will be displayed if you've configured severity level 0. But if, for example, you opt for level 4 instead, level 0 through 4 will be displayed, giving you emergency, alert, critical, error, and warning messages too. Level 7

is the highest-level security option and displays everything, but be warned that going with it could have a serious impact on the performance of your device. So always use debugging commands carefully, with an eye on the messages you really need to meet your specific business requirements!

Configuring and Verifying Syslog

As I said, Cisco devices send all log messages of the severity level you've chosen to the console. They'll also go to the buffer, and both happen by default. Because of this, it's good to know that you can disable and enable these features with the following commands:

```
Router(config)#logging ?
  Hostname or A.B.C.D  IP address of the logging host
  buffered             Set buffered logging parameters
  buginf               Enable buginf logging for debugging
  cns-events           Set CNS Event logging level
  console              Set console logging parameters
  count                Count every log message and timestamp last occurrence
  esm                  Set ESM filter restrictions
  exception            Limit size of exception flush output
  facility             Facility parameter for syslog messages
  filter               Specify logging filter
  history              Configure syslog history table
  host                 Set syslog server IP address and parameters
  monitor              Set terminal line (monitor) logging parameters
  on                   Enable logging to all enabled destinations
  origin-id            Add origin ID to syslog messages
  queue-limit          Set logger message queue size
  rate-limit           Set messages per second limit
  reload               Set reload logging level
  server-arp           Enable sending ARP requests for syslog servers when
                       first configured
  source-interface     Specify interface for source address in logging
                       transactions
  trap                 Set syslog server logging level
  userinfo             Enable logging of user info on privileged mode enabling

Router(config)#logging console
Router(config)#logging buffered
```

Wow—as you can see in this output, there are plenty of options you can use with the logging command! The preceding configuration enabled the console and buffer to receive all log messages of all severities, and don't forget that this is the default setting for all Cisco IOS devices. If you want to disable the defaults, use the following commands:

```
Router(config)#no logging console
Router(config)#no logging buffered
```

I like leaving the console and buffer commands on in order to receive the logging info, but that's up to you. You can see the buffers with the show logging command here:

```
Router#sh logging
Syslog logging: enabled (11 messages dropped, 1 messages rate-limited,
               0 flushes, 0 overruns, xml disabled, filtering disabled)
    Console logging: level debugging, 29 messages logged, xml disabled,
                     filtering disabled
    Monitor logging: level debugging, 0 messages logged, xml disabled,
                     filtering disabled
    Buffer logging: level debugging, 1 messages logged, xml disabled,
                    filtering disabled
    Logging Exception size (4096 bytes)
    Count and timestamp logging messages: disabled
No active filter modules.

    Trap logging: level informational, 33 message lines logged

Log Buffer (4096 bytes):
*Jun 21 23:09:37.822: %SYS-5-CONFIG_I: Configured from console by console
Router#
```

The default trap (message from device to NMS) level is debugging, but you can change this too. And now that you've seen the system message format on a Cisco device, I want to show you how you can also control the format of your messages via sequence numbers and time stamps, which aren't enabled by default. We'll begin with a basic, simple example of how to configure a device to send messages to a syslog server, demonstrated in Figure 7.4.

FIGURE 7.4 Messages sent to a syslog server

Syslog server

I want to look at the console messages
of the SF router from last night.

A syslog server saves copies of console messages and can time-stamp them for viewing at a later time. This is actually pretty easy to configure, and here's how doing that would look on the SF router:

```
SF(config)#logging 172.16.10.1
SF(config)#logging informational
```

This is awesome—now all the console messages will be stored in one location to be viewed at your convenience! I typically use the logging host *ip_address* command, but logging *IP_address* without the host keyword gets the same result.

We can limit the amount of messages sent to the syslog server, based on severity, with the following command:

```
SF(config)#logging trap ?
  <0-7>          Logging severity level
  alerts         Immediate action needed         (severity=1)
  critical       Critical conditions             (severity=2)
  debugging      Debugging messages              (severity=7)
  emergencies    System is unusable              (severity=0)
  errors         Error conditions                (severity=3)
  informational  Informational messages          (severity=6)
  notifications  Normal but significant conditions (severity=5)
  warnings       Warning conditions              (severity=4)
  <cr>
SF(config)#logging trap informational
```

Notice that we can use either the number or the actual severity level name—and they are in alphabetical order, not severity order, which makes it even harder to memorize the order! (Thanks, Cisco!) Since I went with severity level 6 (Informational), I'll receive messages for levels 0 through 6. These are referred to as local levels as well, such as, for example, local6—no difference.

Now let's configure the router to use sequence numbers:

```
SF(config)#no service timestamps
SF(config)#service sequence-numbers
SF(config)#^Z
000038: %SYS-5-CONFIG_I: Configured from console by console
```

When you exit configuration mode, the router will send a message like the one shown in the preceding code lines. Without the time stamps enabled, we'll no longer see a time and date, but we will see a sequence number.

So we now have the following:

- Sequence number: 000038
- Facility: %SYS

- Severity level: 5

- MNEMONIC: CONFIG_I

- Description: Configured from console by console

I want to stress that of all of these, the severity level is what you need to pay attention to the most for the Cisco exams as well as for a means to control the amount of messages sent to the syslog server.

Network Time Protocol (NTP)

Network Time Protocol provides pretty much what it describes: time to all your network devices. To be more precise, NTP synchronizes clocks of computer systems over packet-switched, variable-latency data networks.

Typically you'll have an NTP server that connects through the Internet to an atomic clock. This time can then be synchronized through the network to keep all routers, switches, servers, etc. receiving the same time information.

Correct network time within the network is important:

- Correct time allows the tracking of events in the network in the correct order.

- Clock synchronization is critical for the correct interpretation of events within the syslog data.

- Clock synchronization is critical for digital certificates.

Making sure all your devices have the correct time is especially helpful for your routers and switches for looking at logs regarding security issues or other maintenance issues. Routers and switches issue log messages when different events take place—for example, when an interface goes down and then back up. As you already know, all messages generated by the IOS go only to the console port by default. However, as shown in Figure 7.4, those console messages can be directed to a syslog server.

A syslog server saves copies of console messages and can time-stamp them so you can view them at a later time. This is actually rather easy to do. Here would be your configuration on the SF router:

```
SF(config)#service timestamps log datetime msec
```

Even though I had the messages time-stamped with the command `service timestamps log datetime msec`, this doesn't mean that we'll know the exact time if using default clock sources.

To make sure all devices are synchronized with the same time information, we'll configure our devices to receive the accurate time information from a centralized server, as shown here in the following command and in Figure 7.5:

```
SF(config)#ntp server 172.16.10.1 version 4
```

FIGURE 7.5   Synchronizing time information

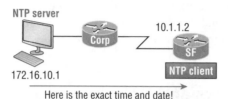

Here is the exact time and date!

Just use that one simple command on all your devices and each network device on your network will then have the same exact time and date information. You can then rest assured that your time stamps are accurate. You can also make your router or switch be an NTP server with the ntp master command.

To verify that our NTP client is receiving clocking information, we use the following commands:

```
SF#sh ntp ?
  associations  NTP associations
  status        NTP status  status      VTP domain status

SF#sh ntp status
Clock is unsynchronized, stratum 16, no reference clock
nominal freq is 119.2092 Hz, actual freq is 119.2092 Hz, precision is 2**18
reference time is 00000000.00000000 (00:00:00.000 UTC Mon Jan 1 1900)
clock offset is 0.0000 msec, root delay is 0.00 msec
S1#sh ntp associations

address     ref clock      st  when  poll reach  delay  offset     disp
~172.16.10.1  0.0.0.0            16    -    64    0     0.0      0.00  16000.
 * master (synced), # master (unsynced), + selected, - candidate, ~ configured
```

You can see in the example that the NTP client in SF is not synchronized with the server by using the show ntp status command. The stratum value is a number from 1 to 15, and a lower stratum value indicates a higher NTP priority; 16 means there is no clocking received.

There are many other configurations of an NTP client that are available, such as authentication of NTP so a router or switch isn't fooled into changing the time of an attack, for example.

Exploring Connected Devices Using CDP and LLDP

Cisco Discovery Protocol (CDP) is a proprietary Layer 2 protocol designed by Cisco to help administrators collect information about locally attached Cisco devices. Armed with CDP, you can gather hardware and protocol information about neighbor devices, which is crucial information to have when troubleshooting and documenting the network. Another dynamic discovery protocol is Link Layer Discovery Protocol (LLDP), but instead of being proprietary like CDP, it is vendor independent.

Let's start by exploring the CDP timer and CDP commands we'll need to verify our network.

Getting CDP Timers and Holdtime Information

The show cdp command (sh cdp for short) gives you information about two CDP global parameters that can be configured on Cisco devices:

- *CDP timer* delimits how often CDP packets are transmitted out all active interfaces.

- *CDP holdtime* delimits the amount of time that the device will hold packets received from neighbor devices.

Both Cisco routers and switches use the same parameters. Check out Figure 7.6 to see how CDP works within a switched network that I set up for my switching labs in this book.

FIGURE 7.6   Cisco Discovery Protocol

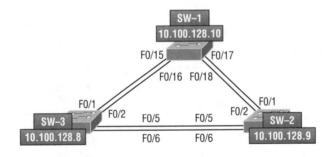

The output on my 3560 SW-3 looks like this:

```
SW-3#sh cdp
Global CDP information:
        Sending CDP packets every 60 seconds
        Sending a holdtime value of 180 seconds
        Sending CDPv2 advertisements is enabled
```

This output tells us that the default transmits every 60 seconds and will hold packets from a neighbor in the CDP table for 180 seconds. I can use the global commands cdp holdtime and cdp timer to configure the CDP holdtime and timer on a router if necessary like this:

```
SW-3(config)#cdp ?
  advertise-v2  CDP sends version-2 advertisements
  holdtime      Specify the holdtime (in sec) to be sent in packets
```

```
run          Enable CDP
timer        Specify the rate at which CDP packets are sent (in sec)
tlv          Enable exchange of specific tlv information
```

```
SW-3(config)#cdp holdtime ?
  <10-255> Length of time (in sec) that receiver must keep this packet
```

```
SW-3(config)#cdp timer ?
  <5-254>  Rate at which CDP packets are sent (in  sec)
```

You can turn off CDP completely with the no cdp run command from global configuration mode of a router and enable it with the cdp run command:

```
SW-3(config)#no cdp run
SW-3(config)#cdp run
```

To turn CDP off or on for an interface, use the no cdp enable and cdp enable commands.

Gathering Neighbor Information

The show cdp neighbor command (sh cdp nei for short) delivers information about directly connected devices. It's important to remember that CDP packets aren't passed through a Cisco switch and that you only see what's directly attached. So this means that if your router is connected to a switch, you won't see any of the Cisco devices connected beyond that switch!

The following output shows the show cdp neighbor command I used on my SW-3:

```
SW-3#sh cdp neighbors
Capability Codes: R - Router, T - Trans Bridge, B - Source Route Bridge
                  S - Switch, H - Host, I - IGMP, r - Repeater, P - Phone,
                  D - Remote, C - CVTA, M - Two-port Mac Relay Device ID
Local Intrfce    Holdtme    Capability  Platform  Port ID
SW-1   Fas 0/1    170          S I       WS-C3560- Fas 0/15
SW-1   Fas 0/2    170          S I       WS-C3560- Fas 0/16
SW-2   Fas 0/5    162          S I       WS-C3560- Fas 0/5
SW-2   Fas 0/6    162          S I       WS-C3560- Fas 0/6
```

Okay—we can see that I'm directly connected with a console cable to the SW-3 switch and also that SW-3 is directly connected to two other switches. However, do we really need the figure to draw out our network? We don't! CDP allows me to see who my directly connected neighbors are and gather information about them. From the SW-3 switch, we can see that there are two connections to SW-1 and two connections to SW-2. SW-3 connects to SW-1 with ports Fas 0/1 and Fas 0/2, and we have connections to SW-2 with local interfaces Fas 0/5 and Fas 0/6. Both the SW-1 and SW-2 switches are 3650 switches, and SW-1 is using ports Fas 0/15 and Fas 0/16 to connect to SW-3. SW-2 is using ports Fas 0/5 and Fas 0/6.

To sum this up, the device ID shows the configured hostname of the connected device, that the local interface is our interface, and the port ID is the remote devices' directly connected interface. Remember that all you get to view are directly connected devices!

Table 7.3 summarizes the information displayed by the show cdp neighbor command for each device.

TABLE 7.3 Output of the **show cdp neighbors** command

Field	Description
Device ID	The hostname of the device directly connected.
Local Interface	The port or interface on which you are receiving the CDP packet.
Holdtime	The remaining amount of time the router will hold the information before discarding it if no more CDP packets are received.
Capability	The capability of the neighbor—the router, switch, or repeater. The capability codes are listed at the top of the command output.
Platform	The type of Cisco device directly connected. In the previous output, the SW-3 shows it's directly connected to two 3560 switches.
Port ID	The neighbor device's port or interface on which the CDP packets are multicast.

It's imperative that you can look at the output of a show cdp neighbors command and decipher the information gained about the neighbor device's capability, whether it's a router or switch, the model number (platform), your port connecting to that device (local interface), and the port of the neighbor connecting to you (port ID).

Another command that will deliver the goods on neighbor information is the show cdp neighbors detail command (show cdp nei de for short). This command can be run on both routers and switches, and it displays detailed information about each device connected to the device you're running the command on. Check out the router output in Listing 7.1.

Listing 7.1: Showing CDP neighbors

```
SW-3#sh cdp neighbors detail
-------------------------
Device ID: SW-1
```

```
Entry address(es):
  IP address: 10.100.128.10
Platform: cisco WS-C3560-24TS,  Capabilities: Switch IGMP
Interface: FastEthernet0/1,  Port ID (outgoing port): FastEthernet0/15
Holdtime : 137 sec

Version :
Cisco IOS Software, C3560 Software (C3560-IPSERVICESK9-M), Version 12.2(55)SE7,
RELEASE SOFTWARE (fc1)
Technical Support: http://www.cisco.com/techsupport
Copyright (c) 1986-2013 by Cisco Systems, Inc.
Compiled Mon 28-Jan-13 10:10 by prod_rel_team

advertisement version: 2
Protocol Hello:  OUI=0x00000C, Protocol ID=0x0112; payload len=27, value=0000000
0FFFFFFFF010221FF000000000000001C575EC880Fc00f000
VTP Management Domain: 'NULL'
Native VLAN: 1
Duplex: full
Power Available TLV:

    Power request id: 0, Power management id: 1, Power available: 0, Power
management level: -1
Management address(es):
  IP address: 10.100.128.10
-------------------------

[ouput cut]

-------------------------
Device ID: SW-2
Entry address(es):
  IP address: 10.100.128.9
Platform: cisco WS-C3560-8PC,  Capabilities: Switch IGMP
Interface: FastEthernet0/5,  Port ID (outgoing port): FastEthernet0/5
Holdtime : 129 sec

Version :
Cisco IOS Software, C3560 Software (C3560-IPBASE-M), Version 12.2(35)SE5,
RELEASE SOFTWARE (fc1)
Copyright (c) 1986-2007 by Cisco Systems, Inc.
Compiled Thu 19-Jul-07 18:15 by nachen

advertisement version: 2
Protocol Hello:  OUI=0x00000C, Protocol ID=0x0112; payload len=27, value=0000000
0FFFFFFFF010221FF000000000000B41489D91880Fc00f000
VTP Management Domain: 'NULL'
```

```
Native VLAN: 1
Duplex: full
Power Available TLV:

    Power request id: 0, Power management id: 1, Power available: 0, Power
management level: -1
Management address(es):
  IP address: 10.100.128.9
[output cut]
```

So what's revealed here? First, we've been given the hostname and IP address of all directly connected devices. And in addition to the same information displayed by the show cdp neighbors command (see Table 7.3), the show cdp neighbors detail command tells us about the IOS version and IP address of the neighbor device—that's quite a bit!

The show cdp entry * command displays the same information as the show cdp neighbors detail command. There isn't any difference between these commands.

Real World Scenario

CDP Can Save Lives!

Karen has just been hired as a senior network consultant at a large hospital in Dallas, Texas, so she's expected to be able to take care of any problem that rears its ugly head. As if that weren't enough pressure, she also has to worry about the horrid possibility that people won't receive correct health care solutions—even the correct medications—if the network goes down. Talk about a potential life-or-death situation!

But Karen is confident and begins her job optimistically. Of course, it's not long before the network reveals that it has a few problems. Unfazed, she asks one of the junior administrators for a network map so she can troubleshoot the network. This person tells her that the old senior administrator, who she replaced, had them with him and now no one can find them. The sky begins to darken!

Doctors are calling every couple of minutes because they can't get the necessary information they need to take care of their patients. What should she do?

It's CDP to the rescue! And it's a gift that this hospital happens to be running Cisco routers and switches exclusively, because CDP is enabled by default on all Cisco devices. Karen is also in luck because the disgruntled former administrator didn't turn off CDP on any devices before he left!

So all Karen has to do now is to use the show cdp neighbor detail command to find all the information she needs about each device to help draw out the hospital network, bringing it back up to speed so the personnel who rely upon it can get on to the important business of saving lives!

The only snag for you nailing this in your own network is if you don't know the passwords of all those devices. Your only hope then is to somehow find out the access passwords or to perform password recovery on them.

So, use CDP—you never know when you may end up saving someone's life.

By the way, this is a true story!

Documenting a Network Topology Using CDP

With that moving real-life scenario in mind, I'm now going to show you how to document a sample network by using CDP. You'll learn to determine the appropriate router types, interface types, and IP addresses of various interfaces using only CDP commands and the show running-config command. And you can only console into the Lab_A router to document the network. You'll have to assign any remote routers the next IP address in each range. We'll use a different figure for this example—Figure 7.7— to help us to complete the necessary documentation.

FIGURE 7.7   Documenting a network topology using CDP

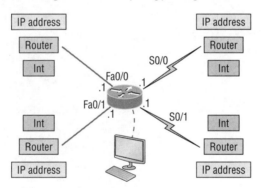

In this output, you can see that you have a router with four interfaces: two Fast Ethernet and two serial. First, determine the IP addresses of each interface by using the show running-config command like this:

```
Lab_A#sh running-config
Building configuration...

Current configuration : 960 bytes
!
version 12.2
service timestamps debug uptime
service timestamps log uptime
```

```
no service password-encryption
!
hostname Lab_A
!
ip subnet-zero
!
!
interface FastEthernet0/0
 ip address 192.168.21.1 255.255.255.0
 duplex auto
!
interface FastEthernet0/1
 ip address 192.168.18.1 255.255.255.0
 duplex auto
!
interface Serial0/0
ip address 192.168.23.1 255.255.255.0
!
interface Serial0/1
ip address 192.168.28.1 255.255.255.0
!
ip classless
!
line con 0
line aux 0
line vty 0 4
!
end
```

With this step completed, you can now write down the IP addresses of the Lab_A router's four interfaces. Next, you must determine the type of device on the other end of each of these interfaces. It's easy—just use the show cdp neighbors command:

```
Lab_A#sh cdp neighbors
Capability Codes: R - Router, T - Trans Bridge, B - Source Route Bridge
S - Switch, H - Host, I - IGMP, r - Repeater
Device ID    Local Intrfce    Holdtme    Capability Platform  Port ID
Lab_B        Fas 0/0          178        R          2501      E0
Lab_C        Fas 0/1          137        R          2621      Fa0/0
Lab_D        Ser 0/0          178        R          2514      S1
Lab_E        Ser 0/1          137        R          2620      S0/1
```

Wow—looks like we're connected to some old routers! But it's not our job to judge. Our mission is to draw out our network, so it's good that we've got some nice information to meet the challenge with now. By using both the show running-config and show cdp neighbors commands, we know about all the IP addresses of the Lab_A router, the types of routers connected to each of the Lab_A router's links, and all the interfaces of the remote routers.

Now that we're equipped with all the information gathered via show running-config and show cdp neighbors, we can accurately create the topology in Figure 7.8.

FIGURE 7.8   Network topology documented

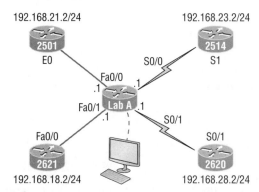

If we needed to, we could've also used the show cdp neighbors detail command to view the neighbor's IP addresses. But since we know the IP addresses of each link on the Lab_A router, we already know what the next available IP address is going to be.

Link Layer Discovery Protocol (LLDP)

Before moving on from CDP, I want to tell you about a nonproprietary discovery protocol that provides pretty much the same information as CDP but works in multi-vendor networks.

The IEEE created a new standardized discovery protocol called 802.1AB for Station and Media Access Control Connectivity Discovery. We'll just call it *Link Layer Discovery Protocol (LLDP)*.

LLDP defines basic discovery capabilities, but it was also enhanced to specifically address the voice application, and this version is called LLDP-MED (Media Endpoint Discovery). It's good to remember that LLDP and LLDP-MED are not compatible.

LLDP has the following configuration guidelines and limitations:

- LLDP must be enabled on the device before you can enable or disable it on any interface.

- LLDP is supported only on physical interfaces.

- LLDP can discover up to one device per port.

- LLDP can discover Linux servers.

You can turn off LLDP completely with the no lldp run command from global configuration mode of a device and enable it with the lldp run command, which enables it on all interfaces as well:

```
SW-3(config)#no lldp run
SW-3(config)#lldp run
```

To turn LLDP off or on for an interface, use the lldp transmit and lldp receive commands.

```
SW-3(config-if)#no lldp transmit
SW-3(config-if)#no lldp receive

SW-3(config-if)#lldp transmit
SW-3(config-if)#lldp receive
```

Using Telnet

As part of the TCP/IP protocol suite, *Telnet* is a virtual terminal protocol that allows you to make connections to remote devices, gather information, and run programs.

After your routers and switches are configured, you can use the Telnet program to reconfigure and/or check up on them without using a console cable. You run the Telnet program by typing **telnet** from any command prompt (Windows or Cisco), but you need to have VTY passwords set on the IOS devices for this to work.

Remember, you can't use CDP to gather information about routers and switches that aren't directly connected to your device. But you can use the Telnet application to connect to your neighbor devices and then run CDP on those remote devices to get information on them.

You can issue the telnet command from any router or switch prompt. In the following code, I'm trying to telnet from switch 1 to switch 3:

```
SW-1#telnet 10.100.128.8
Trying 10.100.128.8 ... Open

Password required, but none set

[Connection to 10.100.128.8 closed by foreign host]
```

Oops—clearly, I didn't set my passwords—how embarrassing! Remember that the VTY ports are default configured as login, meaning that we have to either set the VTY passwords or use the no login command. If you need to review the process of setting passwords, take a quick look back in Chapter 6, "Cisco's Internetworking Operating System (IOS)."

If you can't telnet into a device, it could be that the password on the remote device hasn't been set. It's also quite possible that an access control list is filtering the Telnet session.

On a Cisco device, you don't need to use the `telnet` command; you can just type in an IP address from a command prompt and the router will assume that you want to telnet to the device. Here's how that looks using just the IP address:

```
SW-1#10.100.128.8
Trying 10.100.128.8... Open

Password required, but none set

[Connection to 10.100.128.8 closed by foreign host]
SW-1#
```

Now would be a great time to set those VTY passwords on the SW-3 that I want to telnet into. Here's what I did on the switch named SW-3:

```
SW-3(config)#line vty 0 15
SW-3(config-line)#login
SW-3(config-line)#password telnet
SW-3(config-line)#login
SW-3(config-line)#^Z
```

Now let's try this again. This time, I'm connecting to SW-3 from the SW-1 console:

```
SW-1#10.100.128.8
Trying 10.100.128.8 ... Open

User Access Verification

Password:
SW-3>
```

Remember that the VTY password is the user-mode password, not the enable-mode password. Watch what happens when I try to go into privileged mode after telnetting into the switch:

```
SW-3>en
% No password set
SW-3>
```

It's totally slamming the door in my face, which happens to be a really nice security feature! After all, you don't want just anyone telnetting into your device and typing the enable command to get into privileged mode now, do you? You've got to set your enable-mode password or enable secret password to use Telnet to configure remote devices.

When you telnet into a remote device, you won't see console messages by default. For example, you will not see debugging output. To allow console messages to be sent to your Telnet session, use the `terminal monitor` command.

Using the next group of examples, I'll show you how to telnet into multiple devices simultaneously as well as how to use hostnames instead of IP addresses.

Telnetting into Multiple Devices Simultaneously

If you telnet to a router or switch, you can end the connection by typing **exit** at any time. But what if you want to keep your connection to a remote device going while still coming back to your original router console? To do that, you can press the Ctrl+Shift+6 key combination, release it, and then press X.

Here's an example of connecting to multiple devices from my SW-1 console:

```
SW-1#10.100.128.8
Trying 10.100.128.8... Open

User Access Verification

Password:
SW-3>Ctrl+Shift+6
SW-1#
```

Here you can see that I telnetted to SW-1 and then typed the password to enter user mode. Next, I pressed Ctrl+Shift+6, then X, but you won't see any of that because it doesn't show on the screen output. Notice that my command prompt now has me back at the SW-1 switch.

Now let's run through some verification commands.

Checking Telnet Connections

If you want to view the connections from your router or switch to a remote device, just use the show sessions command. In this case, I've telnetted into both the SW-3 and SW-2 switches from SW1:

```
SW-1#sh sessions
Conn Host            Address          Byte  Idle Conn Name
   1 10.100.128.9    10.100.128.9     0          10.100.128.9
*  2 10.100.128.8    10.100.128.8     0          10.100.128.8
SW-1#
```

See that asterisk (*) next to connection 2? It means that session 2 was the last session I connected to. You can return to your last session by pressing Enter twice. You can also return to any session by typing the number of the connection and then Enter.

Checking Telnet Users

You can reveal all active consoles and VTY ports in use on your router with the show users command:

```
SW-1#sh users
    Line       User       Host(s)           Idle        Location
*  0 con 0                10.100.128.9      00:00:01
                          10.100.128.8      00:01:06
```

In the command's output, con represents the local console, and we can see that the console session is connected to two remote IP addresses—in other words, two devices.

Closing Telnet Sessions

You can end Telnet sessions a few different ways. Typing exit or disconnect are probably the two quickest and easiest.

To end a session from a remote device, use the exit command:

```
SW-3>exit
[Connection to 10.100.128.8 closed by foreign host]
SW-1#
```

To end a session from a local device, use the disconnect command:

```
SW-1#sh session
Conn Host            Address          Byte  Idle Conn Name
  *2 10.100.128.9    10.100.128.9     0          10.100.128.9
SW-1#disconnect ?
  <2-2>  The number of an active network connection
  qdm    Disconnect QDM web-based clients
  ssh    Disconnect an active SSH connection
SW-1#disconnect 2
Closing connection to 10.100.128.9 [confirm][enter]
```

In this example, I used session number 2 because that was the connection I wanted to conclude. As demonstrated, you can use the show sessions command to see the connection number.

Resolving Hostnames

If you want to use a hostname instead of an IP address to connect to a remote device, the device that you're using to make the connection must be able to translate the hostname to an IP address.

There are two ways to resolve hostnames to IP addresses. The first is by building a host table on each router, and the second is to build a Domain Name System (DNS) server. The latter method is similar to creating a dynamic host table, assuming that you're dealing with dynamic DNS.

Building a Host Table

An important factor to remember is that although a host table provides name resolution, it does that only on the specific router that it was built upon. The command you use to build a host table on a router looks this:

```
ip host host_name [tcp_port_number] ip_address
```

The default is TCP port number 23, but you can create a session using Telnet with a different TCP port number if you want. You can also assign up to eight IP addresses to a hostname.

Here's how I configured a host table on the SW-1 switch with two entries to resolve the names for the SW-2 and SW-3:

```
SW-1#config t
SW-1(config)#ip host SW-2 ?
  <0-65535>   Default telnet port number
  A.B.C.D     Host IP address
  additional  Append addresses

SW-1(config)#ip host SW-2 10.100.128.9
SW-1(config)#ip host SW-3 10.100.128.8
```

Notice that I can just keep adding IP addresses to reference a unique host, one after another. To view our newly built host table, I'll just use the show hosts command:

```
SW-1(config)#do sho hosts
Default domain is not set
Name/address lookup uses domain service
Name servers are 255.255.255.255

Codes: u - unknown, e - expired, * - OK, ? - revalidate
       t - temporary, p - permanent
```

```
Host                    Port  Flags       Age Type  Address(es)
SW-3                    None  (perm, OK)   0   IP    10.100.128.8
SW-2                    None  (perm, OK)   0   IP    10.100.128.9
```

In this output, you can see the two hostnames plus their associated IP addresses. The perm in the Flags column means that the entry has been manually configured. If it read temp, it would be an entry that was resolved by DNS.

 The show hosts command provides information on temporary DNS entries and permanent name-to-address mappings created using the ip host command.

To verify that the host table resolves names, try typing the hostnames at a router prompt. Remember that if you don't specify the command, the router will assume you want to telnet.

In the following example, I'll use the hostnames to telnet into the remote devices and press Ctrl+Shift+6 and then X to return to the main console of the SW-1 router:

```
SW-1#sw-3
Trying SW-3 (10.100.128.8)... Open


User Access Verification


Password:
SW-3> Ctrl+Shift+6
SW-1#
```

It worked—I successfully used entries in the host table to create a session to the SW-3 device by using the name to telnet into it. And just so you know, names in the host table are not case sensitive.

Notice that the entries in the following show sessions output now display the hostnames and IP addresses instead of just the IP addresses:

```
SW-1#sh sessions
Conn Host            Address         Byte  Idle Conn Name
   1 SW-3            10.100.128.8     0     1   SW-3
*  2 SW-2            10.100.128.9     0     1   SW-2
SW-1#
```

If you want to remove a hostname from the table, all you need to do is use the no ip host command like this:

```
SW-1(config)#no ip host SW-3
```

The drawback to going with this host table method is that you must create a host table on each router in order to be able to resolve names. So clearly, if you have a whole bunch of routers and want to resolve names, using DNS is a much better option!

Using DNS to Resolve Names

If you have a lot of devices, you don't want to create a host table in each one of them unless you've also got a lot of time to waste. Since most of us don't, I highly recommend using a DNS server to resolve hostnames instead!

Anytime a Cisco device receives a command it doesn't understand, it will try to resolve it through DNS by default. Watch what happens when I type the special command todd at a Cisco router prompt:

```
SW-1#todd
Translating "todd"...domain server (255.255.255.255)
% Unknown command or computer name, or unable to find
  computer address
SW-1#
```

Because it doesn't know my name or the command I'm trying to type, it tries to resolve this through DNS. This is really annoying for two reasons: first, because it doesn't know my name <grin>, and second, because I need to hang out and wait for the name lookup to time out. You can get around this and prevent a time-consuming DNS lookup by using the no ip domain-lookup command on your router from global configuration mode.

So if you have a DNS server on your network, you'll need to add a few commands to make DNS name resolution work well for you:

- The first command is ip domain-lookup, which is turned on by default. It needs to be entered only if you previously turned it off with the no ip domain-lookup command. The command can be used without the hyphen as well with the syntax ip domain lookup.

- The second command is ip name-server. This sets the IP address of the DNS server. You can enter the IP addresses of up to six servers.

- The last command is ip domain-name. Although this command is optional, you really need to set it because it appends the domain name to the hostname you type in. Since DNS uses a fully qualified domain name (FQDN) system, you must have a second-level DNS name, in the form *domain.com*.

Here's an example of using these three commands:

```
SW-1#config t
SW-1(config)#ip domain-lookup
SW-1(config)#ip name-server ?
  A.B.C.D  Domain server IP address (maximum of 6)
SW-1(config)#ip name-server 4.4.4.4
```

```
SW-1(config)#ip domain-name lammle.com
SW-1(config)#^Z
```

After the DNS configurations have been set, you can test the DNS server by using a host-name to ping or telnet into a device like this:

```
SW-1#ping SW-3
Translating "SW-3"...domain server (4.4.4.4) [OK]
Type escape sequence to abort.
Sending 5, 100-byte ICMP Echos to 10.100.128.8, timeout is
  2 seconds:
!!!!!
Success rate is 100 percent (5/5), round-trip min/avg/max
  = 28/31/32 ms
```

Notice that the router uses the DNS server to resolve the name.

After a name is resolved using DNS, use the show hosts command to verify that the device cached this information in the host table. If I hadn't used the ip domain-name lammle.com command, I would have needed to type in ping sw-3.lammle.com, which is kind of a hassle.

 Real World Scenario

Should You Use a Host Table or a DNS Server?

Karen has finally finished mapping her network via CDP and the hospital's staff is now much happier. But Karen is still having a difficult time administering the network because she has to look at the network drawing to find an IP address every time she needs to tel-net to a remote router.

Karen was thinking about putting host tables on each router, but with literally hundreds of routers, this is a daunting task and not the best solution. What should she do?

Most networks have a DNS server now anyway, so adding a hundred or so hostnames into it would be much easier—certainly better than adding these hostnames to each and every router! She can just add the three commands on each router and voilà—she's resolving names!

Using a DNS server makes it easy to update any old entries too. Remember, for even one little change, her alternative would be to go to each and every router to manually update its table if she's using static host tables.

Keep in mind that this has nothing to do with name resolution on the network and noth-ing to do with what a host on the network is trying to accomplish. You only use this method when you're trying to resolve names from the router console.

Checking Network Connectivity and Troubleshooting

You can use the `ping` and `traceroute` commands to test connectivity to remote devices, and both of them can be used with many protocols, not just IP. But don't forget that the `show ip route` command is a great troubleshooting command for verifying your routing table and the `show interfaces` command will reveal the status of each interface to you.

I'm not going to get into the `show interfaces` commands here because we've already been over that in Chapter 6. But I am going to go over both the debug command and the `show processes` command, both of which come in very handy when you need to troubleshoot a router.

Using the *ping* Command

So far, you've seen lots of examples of pinging devices to test IP connectivity and name resolution using the DNS server. To see all the different protocols that you can use with the *Ping* program, type **ping ?**:

```
SW-1#ping ?
  WORD  Ping destination address or hostname
  clns  CLNS echo
  ip    IP echo
  ipv6  IPv6 echo
  tag   Tag encapsulated IP echo
  <cr>
```

The ping output displays the minimum, average, and maximum times it takes for a ping packet to find a specified system and return. Here's an example:

```
SW-1#ping SW-3
Translating "SW-3"...domain server (4.4.4.4) [OK]
Type escape sequence to abort.
Sending 5, 100-byte ICMP Echos to 10.100.128.8, timeout is
  2 seconds:
!!!!!
Success rate is 100 percent (5/5), round-trip min/avg/max
  = 28/31/32 ms
```

This output tells us that the DNS server was used to resolve the name, and the device was pinged in a minimum of 28 ms (milliseconds), an average of 31 ms, and up to 32 ms. This network has some latency!

The ping command can be used in user and privileged mode but not con-figuration mode!

Using the *traceroute* Command

Traceroute—the traceroute command, or trace for short—shows the path a packet takes to get to a remote device. It uses time to live (TTL), time-outs, and ICMP error messages to outline the path a packet takes through an internetwork to arrive at a remote host.

The trace command, which you can deploy from either user mode or privileged mode, allows you to figure out which router in the path to an unreachable network host should be examined more closely as the probable cause of your network's failure.

To see the protocols that you can use with the traceroute command, type **traceroute ?**:

```
SW-1#traceroute ?
  WORD      Trace route to destination address or hostname
  appletalk AppleTalk Trace
  clns      ISO CLNS Trace
  ip        IP Trace
  ipv6      IPv6 Trace
  ipx       IPX Trace
  mac       Trace Layer2 path between 2 endpoints
  oldvines  Vines Trace (Cisco)
  vines     Vines Trace (Banyan)
  <cr>
```

The traceroute command shows the hop or hops that a packet traverses on its way to a remote device.

Do not get confused! You can't use the tracert command; that's a Windows command. For a router, use the traceroute command!

Here's an example of using tracert on a Windows prompt—notice that the command is tracert, not traceroute:

```
C:\>tracert www.whitehouse.gov

Tracing route to a1289.g.akamai.net [69.8.201.107]
over a maximum of 30 hops:

  1    *        *        *       Request timed out.
  2    53 ms    61 ms    53 ms   hlrn-dsl-gw15-207.hlrn.qwest.net [207.225.112.207]
```

```
3    53 ms    55 ms    54 ms   hlrn-agw1.inet.qwest.net [71.217.188.113]
4    54 ms    53 ms    54 ms   hlr-core-01.inet.qwest.net [205.171.253.97]
5    54 ms    53 ms    54 ms   apa-cntr-01.inet.qwest.net [205.171.253.26]
6    54 ms    53 ms    53 ms   63.150.160.34
7    54 ms    54 ms    53 ms   www.whitehouse.gov [69.8.201.107]
```

Trace complete.

Okay, let's move on now and talk about how to troubleshoot your network using the debug command.

Debugging

Debug is a useful troubleshooting command that's available from the privileged exec mode of Cisco IOS. It's used to display information about various router operations and the related traffic generated or received by the router, plus any error messages.

Even though it's a helpful, informative tool, there are a few important facts that you need to know about it. Debug is regarded as a very high-overhead task because it can consume a huge amount of resources and the router is forced to process-switch the packets being debugged. So you don't just use debug as a monitoring tool—it's meant to be used for a short period of time and only as a troubleshooting tool. It's highly useful for discovering some truly significant facts about both working and faulty software and/or hardware components, but remember to limit its use as the beneficial troubleshooting tool it's designed to be.

Because debugging output takes priority over other network traffic, and because the debug all command generates more output than any other debug command, it can severely diminish the router's performance—even render it unusable! Because of this, it's nearly always best to use more specific debug commands.

As you can see from the following output, you can't enable debugging from user mode, only privileged mode:

```
SW-1>debug ?
% Unrecognized command
SW-1>en
SW-1#debug ?
  aaa                  AAA Authentication, Authorization and Accounting
  access-expression    Boolean access expression
  adjacency            adjacency
  aim                  Attachment Information Manager
  all                  Enable all debugging
  archive              debug archive commands
  arp                  IP ARP and HP Probe transactions
  authentication       Auth Manager debugging
  auto                 Debug Automation
```

```
beep                    BEEP debugging
bgp                     BGP information
bing                    Bing(d) debugging
call-admission          Call admission control
cca                     CCA activity
cdp                     CDP information
cef                     CEF address family independent operations
cfgdiff                 debug cfgdiff commands
cisp                    CISP debugging
clns                    CLNS information
cluster                 Cluster information
cmdhd                   Command Handler
cns                     CNS agents
condition               Condition
configuration           Debug Configuration behavior
[output cut]
```

If you've got the freedom to pretty much take out a router or switch and you really want to have some fun with debugging, use the debug all command:

```
Sw-1#debug all

This may severely impact network performance. Continue? (yes/[no]):yes
All possible debugging has been turned on
```

At this point my switch overloaded and crashed and I had to reboot it. Try this on your switch at work and see if you get the same results. Just kidding!

To disable debugging on a router, just use the command no in front of the debug command:

```
SW-1#no debug all
```

I typically just use the undebug all command since it is so easy when using the shortcut:

```
SW-1#un all
```

Remember that instead of using the debug all command, it's usually a much better idea to use specific commands—and only for short periods of time. Here's an example:

```
S1#debug ip icmp
ICMP packet debugging is on
S1#ping 192.168.10.17

Type escape sequence to abort.
Sending 5, 100-byte ICMP Echos to 192.168.10.17, timeout is 2 seconds:
!!!!!
```

```
Success rate is 100 percent (5/5), round-trip min/avg/max = 1/1/1 ms
S1#
1w4d: ICMP: echo reply sent, src 192.168.10.17, dst 192.168.10.17
1w4d: ICMP: echo reply rcvd, src 192.168.10.17, dst 192.168.10.17
1w4d: ICMP: echo reply sent, src 192.168.10.17, dst 192.168.10.17
1w4d: ICMP: echo reply rcvd, src 192.168.10.17, dst 192.168.10.17
1w4d: ICMP: echo reply sent, src 192.168.10.17, dst 192.168.10.17
1w4d: ICMP: echo reply rcvd, src 192.168.10.17, dst 192.168.10.17
1w4d: ICMP: echo reply sent, src 192.168.10.17, dst 192.168.10.17
1w4d: ICMP: echo reply rcvd, src 192.168.10.17, dst 192.168.10.17
1w4d: ICMP: echo reply sent, src 192.168.10.17, dst 192.168.10.17
1w4d: ICMP: echo reply rcvd, src 192.168.10.17, dst 192.168.10.17
SW-1#un all
```

I'm sure you can see that the debug command is one powerful command. And because of this, I'm also sure you realize that before you use any of the debugging commands, you should make sure you check the CPU utilization capacity of your router. This is important because in most cases, you don't want to negatively impact the device's ability to process the packets on your internetwork. You can determine a specific router's CPU utilization information by using the show processes command.

Remember, when you telnet into a remote device, you will not see console messages by default! For example, you will not see debugging output. To allow console messages to be sent to your Telnet session, use the terminal monitor command.

Using the *show processes* Command

As I've said, you've really got to be careful when using the debug command on your devices. If your router's CPU utilization is consistently at 50 percent or more, it's probably not a good idea to type in the debug all command unless you want to see what a router looks like when it crashes!

So what other approaches can you use? Well, the show processes (or show processes cpu) is a good tool for determining a given router's CPU utilization. Plus, it'll give you a list of active processes along with their corresponding process ID, priority, scheduler test (status), CPU time used, number of times invoked, and so on. Lots of great stuff! Plus, this command is super handy when you want to evaluate your router's performance and CPU utilization and are otherwise tempted to reach for the debug command!

Okay—what do you see in the following output? The first line shows the CPU utilization output for the last 5 seconds, 1 minute, and 5 minutes. The output provides 5%/0% in front of the CPU utilization for the last 5 seconds: The first number equals the total utilization, and the second one indicates the utilization due to interrupt routines. Take a look:

```
SW-1#sh processes
CPU utilization for five seconds: 5%/0%; one minute: 7%; five minutes: 8%
 PID QTy      PC Runtime(ms)  Invoked   uSecs    Stacks    TTY Process
   1 Cwe 29EBC58        0        22       0   5236/6000      0 Chunk Manager
   2 Csp 1B9CF10      241    206881       1   2516/3000      0 Load Meter
   3 Hwe 1F108D0        0         1       0   8768/9000      0 Connection Mgr
   4 Lst 29FA5C4 9437909    454026   20787   5540/6000      0 Check heaps
   5 Cwe 2A02468        0         2       0   5476/6000      0 Pool Manager
   6 Mst 1E98F04        0         2       0   5488/6000      0 Timers
   7 Hwe 13EB1B4     3686    101399      36   5740/6000      0 Net Input
   8 Mwe 13BCD84        0         1       0  23668/24000     0 Crash writer
   9 Mwe 1C591B4     4346     53691      80   4896/6000      0 ARP Input
  10 Lwe 1DA1504        0         1       0   5760/6000      0 CEF MIB API
  11 Lwe 1E76ACC        0         1       0   5764/6000      0 AAA_SERVER_DEADT
  12 Mwe 1E6F980        0         2       0   5476/6000      0 AAA high-capacit
  13 Mwe 1F56F24        0         1       0  11732/12000     0 Policy Manager [output cut]
```

So basically, the output from the show processes command reveals that our router is happily able to process debugging commands without being overloaded—nice!

Summary

In this chapter, you learned how Cisco routers are configured and how to manage those configurations.

We covered the internal components of a router, including ROM, RAM, NVRAM, and flash.

Next, you found out how to back up and restore the configuration of a Cisco router and switch.

You also learned how to use CDP and Telnet to gather information about remote devices. Finally, you discovered how to resolve hostnames and use the ping and trace commands to test network connectivity as well as how to use the debug and show processes commands—well done!

Exam Essentials

Define the Cisco router components.   Describe the functions of the bootstrap, POST, ROM monitor, mini-IOS, RAM, ROM, flash memory, NVRAM, and the configuration register.

Identify the steps in the router boot sequence.   The steps in the boot sequence are POST, loading the IOS, and copying the startup configuration from NVRAM to RAM.

Save the configuration of a router or switch.   There are a couple of ways to do this, but the most common method, as well as the most tested, is copy running-config startup-config.

Erase the configuration of a router or switch.   Type the privileged-mode command erase startup-config and reload the router.

Understand the various levels of syslog.   It's rather simple to configure syslog; however, there are a bunch of options you have to remember for the exam. To configure basic syslog with debugging as the default level, it's just this one command:

SF(config)#**logging 172.16.10.1**

   However, you must remember all eight options:

```
SF(config)#logging trap ?
  <0-7>          Logging severity level
  alerts         Immediate action needed          (severity=1)
  critical       Critical conditions              (severity=2)
  debugging      Debugging messages               (severity=7)
  emergencies    System is unusable               (severity=0)
  errors         Error conditions                 (severity=3)
  informational  Informational messages           (severity=6)
  notifications  Normal but significant conditions (severity=5)
  warnings       Warning conditions               (severity=4)
  <cr>
```

Understand how to configure NTP.   It's pretty simple to configure NTP, just like it was syslog, but we don't have to remember a bunch of options! It's just telling the syslog to mark the time and date and enabling NTP:

SF(config)#**service timestamps log datetime msec**
SF(config)#**ntp server 172.16.10.1 version 4**

Describe the value of CDP and LLDP.   Cisco Discovery Protocol can be used to help you document as well as troubleshoot your network; also, LLDP is a nonproprietary protocol that can provide the same information as CDP.

List the information provided by the output of the show cdp neighbors command.   The show cdp neighbors command provides the following information: device ID, local interface, holdtime, capability, platform, and port ID (remote interface).

Understand how to establish a Telnet session with multiple routers simultaneously.   If you telnet to a router or switch, you can end the connection by typing **exit** at any time.

However, if you want to keep your connection to a remote device but still come back to your original router console, you can press the Ctrl+Shift+6 key combination, release it, and then press X.

Identify current Telnet sessions.   The command show sessions will provide you with information about all the currently active sessions your router has with other routers.

Build a static host table on a router.   By using the global configuration command ip host *host_name ip_address*, you can build a static host table on your router. You can apply multiple IP addresses against the same host entry.

Verify the host table on a router.   You can verify the host table with the show hosts command.

Describe the function of the ping command.   Packet Internet Groper (ping) uses ICMP echo requests and ICMP echo replies to verify an active IP address on a network.

Ping a valid host ID from the correct prompt.   You can ping an IP address from a router's user mode or privileged mode but not from configuration mode, unless you use the do command. You must ping a valid address, such as 1.1.1.1.

Written Labs 7

In this section, you'll complete the following labs to make sure you've got the information and concepts contained within them fully dialed in:

Lab 7.1: IOS Management

Lab 7.2: Router Memory

You can find the answers to these labs in Appendix A, "Answers to Written Labs."

Written Lab 7.1: IOS Management

Write the answers to the following questions:

1. What is the command to copy the startup-config file to DRAM?

2. What command can you use to see the neighbor router's IP address from your router prompt?

3. What command can you use to see the hostname, local interface, platform, and remote port of a neighbor router?

4. What keystrokes can you use to telnet into multiple devices simultaneously?

5. What command will show you your active Telnet connections to neighbor and remote devices?

6. What command can you use to merge a backup configuration with the configuration in RAM?

7. What protocol can be used on a network to synchronize clock and date information?

8. What command is used by a router to forward a DHCP client request to a remote DHCP server?

9. What command enables your switch or router to receive clock and date information and synchronize with the NTP server?

10. Which NTP verification command will show the reference master for the client?

Written Lab 7.2: Router Memory

Identify the location in a router where each of the following files is stored by default.

1. Cisco IOS

2. Bootstrap

3. Startup configuration

4. POST routine

5. Running configuration

6. ARP cache

7. Mini-IOS

8. ROM Monitor

9. Routing tables

10. Packet buffers

Hands-on Labs

To complete the labs in this section, you need at least one router or switch (three would be best) and at least one PC running as a TFTP server. TFTP server software must be installed and running on the PC. For this lab, it is also assumed that your PC and the Cisco devices are connected together with a switch and that all interfaces (PC NIC and router interfaces) are in the same subnet. You can alternately connect the PC directly to the router or connect the routers directly to one another (use a crossover cable in that case). Remember that the labs listed here were created for use with real routers but can easily be used with the LammleSim IOS Version (see www.lammle.com/ccna) or you can use the Cisco Packet Tracer router simulator. Last, although it doesn't matter if you are using a switch or router in these labs, I'm just going to use my routers, but feel free to use your switch to go through these labs!

Here is a list of the labs in this chapter:

Lab 7.1: Backing Up the Router Configuration

Lab 7.2: Using the Cisco Discovery Protocol (CDP)

Lab 7.3: Using Telnet

Lab 7.4: Resolving Hostnames

Hands-on Lab 7.1: Backing Up the Router Configuration

In this lab, you'll back up the router configuration:

1. Log into your router and go into privileged mode by typing **en** or **enable**.

2. Ping the TFTP server to make sure you have IP connectivity.

3. From RouterB, type **copy run tftp**.

4. When prompted, type the IP address of the TFTP server (for example, 172.16.30.2) and press Enter.

5. By default, the router will prompt you for a filename. The hostname of the router is followed by the suffix -confg (yes, I spelled that correctly). You can use any name you want.

   ```
   Name of configuration file to write [RouterB-confg]?
   ```

   Press Enter to accept the default name.

   ```
   Write file RouterB-confg on host 172.16.30.2? [confirm]
   ```

   Press Enter to confirm.

Hands-on Lab 7.2: Using the Cisco Discovery Protocol (CDP)

CDP is an important objective for the Cisco exams. Please go through this lab and use CDP as much as possible during your studies.

1. Log into your router and go into privileged mode by typing **en** or **enable**.

2. From the router, type **sh cdp** and press Enter. You should see that CDP packets are being sent out to all active interfaces every 60 seconds and the holdtime is 180 seconds (these are the defaults).

3. To change the CDP update frequency to 90 seconds, type **cdp timer 90** in global configuration mode.

   ```
   Router#config t
   Enter configuration commands, one per line.  End with
     CNTL/Z.
   Router(config)#cdp timer ?
     <5-900>  Rate at which CDP packets are sent (in sec)
   Router(config)#cdp timer 90
   ```

4. Verify that your CDP timer frequency has changed by using the command **show cdp** in privileged mode.

```
Router#sh cdp
Global CDP information:
Sending CDP packets every 90 seconds
Sending a holdtime value of 180 seconds
```

5. Now use CDP to gather information about neighbor routers. You can get the list of available commands by typing **sh cdp ?**.

```
Router#sh cdp ?
  entry     Information for specific neighbor entry
  interface CDP interface status and configuration
  neighbors CDP neighbor entries
  traffic   CDP statistics
  <cr>
```

6. Type **sh cdp int** to see the interface information plus the default encapsulation used by the interface. It also shows the CDP timer information.

7. Type **sh cdp entry** * to see complete CDP information received from all devices.

8. Type **show cdp neighbors** to gather information about all connected neighbors. (You should know the specific information output by this command.)

9. Type **show cdp neighbors detail**. Notice that it produces the same output as show cdp entry *.

Hands-on Lab 7.3: Using Telnet

Secure Shell was covered in Chapter 6, and it is what you should use for remote access into a Cisco device. However, the Cisco objectives cover Telnet configuration, so let's do a lab on Telnet!

1. Log into your router and go into privileged mode by typing **en** or **enable**.

2. From RouterA, telnet into your remote router (RouterB) by typing **telnet** *ip_address* from the command prompt. Type **exit** to disconnect.

3. Now type in RouterB's IP address from RouterA's command prompt. Notice that the router automatically tries to telnet to the IP address you specified. You can use the telnet command or just type in the IP address.

4. From RouterB, press Ctrl+Shift+6 and then X to return to RouterA's command prompt. Now telnet into your third router, RouterC. Press Ctrl+Shift+6 and then X to return to RouterA.

5. From RouterA, type **show sessions**. Notice your two sessions. You can press the number displayed to the left of the session and press Enter twice to return to that session. The asterisk shows the default session. You can press Enter twice to return to that session.

6. Go to the session for your RouterB. Type **show users**. This shows the console connection and the remote connection. You can use the disconnect command to clear the session or just type **exit** from the prompt to close your session with RouterB.

7. Go to RouterC's console port by typing **show sessions** on the first router and using the connection number to return to RouterC. Type **show user** and notice the connection to your first router, RouterA.

8. Type **clear line line_number** to disconnect the Telnet session.

Hands-on Lab 7.4: Resolving Hostnames

It's best to use a DNS server for name resolution, but you can also create a local hosts table to resolve names. Let's take a look.

1. Log into your router and go into privileged mode by typing **en** or **enable**.

2. From RouterA, type **todd** and press Enter at the command prompt. Notice the error you receive and the delay. The router is trying to resolve the hostname to an IP address by looking for a DNS server. You can turn this feature off by using the no ip domain-lookup command from global configuration mode.

3. To build a host table, you use the ip host command. From RouterA, add a host table entry for RouterB and RouterC by entering the following commands:

```
ip host routerb ip_address
ip host routerc ip_address
```

Here is an example:

```
ip host routerb 172.16.20.2
ip host routerc 172.16.40.2
```

4. Test your host table by typing **ping routerb** from the privileged mode prompt (not the config prompt).

```
RouterA#ping routerb
Type escape sequence to abort.
Sending 5, 100-byte ICMP Echos to 172.16.20.2, timeout
  is 2 seconds:
!!!!!
Success rate is 100 percent (5/5), round-trip
  min/avg/max = 4/4/4 ms
```

5. Test your host table by typing **ping routerc**.

```
RouterA#ping routerc
Type escape sequence to abort.
Sending 5, 100-byte ICMP Echos to 172.16.40.2, timeout
```

```
   is 2 seconds:
!!!!!
Success rate is 100 percent (5/5), round-trip
  min/avg/max = 4/6/8 ms
```

6. Telnet to RouterB and keep your session to RouterB open to RouterA by pressing Ctrl+Shift+6, then X.

7. Telnet to RouterC by typing **routerc** at the command prompt.

8. Return to RouterA and keep the session to RouterC open by pressing Ctrl+Shift+6, then X.

9. View the host table by typing **show hosts** and pressing Enter.

```
Default domain is not set
Name/address lookup uses domain service
Name servers are 255.255.255.255
Host                 Flags      Age Type   Address(es)
routerb              (perm, OK)  0   IP     172.16.20.2
routerc              (perm, OK)  0   IP     172.16.40.2
```

Review Questions

The following questions are designed to test your understanding of this chapter's material. For more information on how to get additional questions, please see www.lammle.com/ccna.

You can find the answers to these questions in Appendix B, "Answers to Review Questions."

1. Which of the following is a standards-based protocol that provides dynamic network discovery?

   A. DHCP

   B. LLDP

   C. DDNS

   D. SSTP

   E. CDP

2. Which command can be used to determine a router's CPU utilization?

   A. `show version`

   B. `show controllers`

   C. `show processes cpu`

   D. `show memory`

3. You are troubleshooting a connectivity problem in your corporate network and want to isolate the problem. You suspect that a router on the route to an unreachable network is at fault. What IOS user exec command should you issue?

   A. `Router>ping`

   B. `Router>trace`

   C. `Router>show ip route`

   D. `Router>show interface`

   E. `Router>show cdp neighbors`

4. You copy a configuration from a network host to a router's RAM. The configuration looks correct, yet it is not working at all. What could the problem be?

   A. You copied the wrong configuration into RAM.

   B. You copied the configuration into flash memory instead.

   C. The copy did not override the `shutdown` command in running-config.

   D. The IOS became corrupted after the `copy` command was initiated.

5. In the following command, what does the IP address 10.10.10.254 refer to?

   ```
   Router#config t
   Router(config)#interface fa0/0
   Router(config-if)#ip helper-address 10.10.10.254
   ```

A. IP address of the ingress interface on the router

B. IP address of the egress interface on the router

C. IP address of the next hop on the path to the DHCP server

D. IP address of the DHCP server

6. The corporate office sends you a new router to connect, but upon connecting the console cable, you see that there is already a configuration on the router. What should be done before a new configuration is entered in the router?

A. RAM should be erased and the router restarted.

B. Flash should be erased and the router restarted.

C. NVRAM should be erased and the router restarted.

D. The new configuration should be entered and saved.

7. What command can you use to determine the IP address of a directly connected neighbor?

A. show cdp

B. show cdp neighbors

C. show cdp neighbors detail

D. show neighbor detail

8. According to the output, what interface does SW-2 use to connect to SW-3?

```
SW-3#sh cdp neighbors
Capability Codes: R - Router, T - Trans Bridge, B - Source Route BridgeS -
Switch, H - Host, I - IGMP, r - Repeater, P - Phone, D - Remote, C - CVTA,
M - Two-port Mac Relay Device ID
Local Intrfce    Holdtme    Capability  Platform  Port ID
SW-1   Fas 0/1      170         S I      WS-C3560- Fas 0/15
SW-1   Fas 0/2      170         S I      WS-C3560- Fas 0/16
SW-2   Fas 0/5      162         S I      WS-C3560- Fas 0/2
```

A. Fas 0/1

B. Fas 0/16

C. Fas 0/2

D. Fas 0/5

9. Which of the following commands enables syslog on a Cisco device with debugging as the level?

A. syslog 172.16.10.1

B. logging 172.16.10.1

C. remote console 172.16.10.1 syslog debugging

D. transmit console messages level 7 172.16.10.1

10. You save the configuration on a router with the `copy running-config startup-config` command and reboot the router. The router, however, comes up with a blank configuration. What can the problem be?

   A. You didn't boot the router with the correct command.

   B. NVRAM is corrupted.

   C. The configuration register setting is incorrect.

   D. The newly upgraded IOS is not compatible with the hardware of the router.

   E. The configuration you saved is not compatible with the hardware.

11. If you want to have more than one Telnet session open at the same time, what keystroke combination would you use?

   A. Tab+spacebar

   B. Ctrl+X, then 6

   C. Ctrl+Shift+X, then 6

   D. Ctrl+Shift+6, then X

12. You are unsuccessful in telnetting into a remote device from your switch, but you could telnet to the router earlier. However, you can still ping the remote device. What could the problem be? (Choose two.)

   A. IP addresses are incorrect.

   B. Access control list is filtering Telnet.

   C. There is a defective serial cable.

   D. The VTY password is missing.

13. What information is displayed by the `show hosts` command? (Choose two.)

   A. Temporary DNS entries

   B. The names of the routers created using the `hostname` command

   C. The IP addresses of workstations allowed to access the router

   D. Permanent name-to-address mappings created using the `ip host` command

   E. The length of time a host has been connected to the router via Telnet

14. Which three commands can be used to check LAN connectivity problems on an enterprise switch? (Choose three.)

   A. `show interfaces`

   B. `show ip route`

   C. `tracert`

   D. `ping`

   E. `dns lookups`

15. What is the default syslog facility level?

   A. local4

   B. local5

    C. local6

    D. local7

16. You telnet into a remote device and type debug ip icmp, but no output from the debug command is seen. What could the problem be?

    A. You must type the show ip icmp command first.

    B. IP addressing on the network is incorrect.

    C. You must use the terminal monitor command.

    D. Debug output is sent only to the console.

17. Which three statements about syslog utilization are true? (Choose three.)

    A. Utilizing syslog improves network performance.

    B. The syslog server automatically notifies the network administrator of network problems.

    C. A syslog server provides the storage space necessary to store log files without using router disk space.

    D. There are more syslog messages available within Cisco IOS than there are comparable SNMP trap messages.

    E. Enabling syslog on a router automatically enables NTP for accurate time stamping.

    F. A syslog server helps in aggregation of logs and alerts.

18. You need to gather the IP address of a remote switch that is located in Hawaii. What can you do to find the address?

    A. Fly to Hawaii, console into the switch, then relax and have a drink with an umbrella in it.

    B. Issue the show ip route command on the router connected to the switch.

    C. Issue the show cdp neighbor command on the router connected to the switch.

    D. Issue the show ip arp command on the router connected to the switch.

    E. Issue the show cdp neighbors detail command on the router connected to the switch.

19. You need to configure all your routers and switches so they synchronize their clocks from one time source. What command will you type for each device?

    A. clock synchronization *ip_address*

    B. ntp master ip_address

    C. sync ntp ip_address

    D. ntp server *ip_address* version *number*

20. A network administrator enters the following command on a router: logging trap 3. What are three message types that will be sent to the syslog server? (Choose three.)

    A. Informational

    B. Emergency

    C. Warning

    D. Critical

    E. Debug

    F. Error

Chapter

8

Managing Cisco Devices

THE FOLLOWING ICND1 EXAM TOPICS ARE COVERED IN THIS CHAPTER:

✓ **5.0 Infrastructure Management**

- 5.2 Configure and verify device management

  - 5.2.c Licensing

- 5.5 Perform device maintenance

  - 5.5.a Cisco IOS upgrades and recovery (SCP, FTP, TFTP, and MD5 verify)

  - 5.5.b Password recovery and configuration register

  - 5.5.c File system management

Here in Chapter 8, I'm going to show you how to manage Cisco routers on an internetwork. The Internetwork Operating System (IOS) and configuration files reside in different locations in a Cisco device, so it's really important to understand both where these files are located and how they work.

You'll be learning about the configuration register, including how to use the configuration register for password recovery.

Finally, I'll cover how to verify licenses on the ISRG2 routers as well as how to install a permanent license and configure evaluation features in the latest universal images.

To find up-to-the-minute updates for this chapter, please see www.lammle.com/ccna or the book's web page at www.sybex.com/go/ccna.

Managing the Configuration Register

All Cisco routers have a 16-bit software register that's written into NVRAM. By default, the *configuration register* is set to load the Cisco IOS from *flash memory* and to look for and load the startup-config file from NVRAM. In the following sections, I am going to discuss the configuration register settings and how to use these settings to provide password recovery on your routers.

Understanding the Configuration Register Bits

The 16 bits (2 bytes) of the configuration register are read from 15 to 0, from left to right. The default configuration setting on Cisco routers is 0x2102. This means that bits 13, 8, and 1 are on, as shown in Table 8.1. Notice that each set of 4 bits (called a nibble) is read in binary with a value of 8, 4, 2, 1.

TABLE 8.1 The configuration register bit numbers

Configuration Register		2				1				0			2	
Bit number	15	14	13	12	11	10	9	8	7	6	5	4	3	2	1	0
Binary	0	0	1	0	0	0	0	1	0	0	0	0	0	0	1	0

Add the prefix *0x* to the configuration register address. The *0x* means that the digits that follow are in hexadecimal.

Table 8.2 lists the software configuration bit meanings. Notice that bit 6 can be used to ignore the NVRAM contents. This bit is used for password recovery—something I'll go over with you soon in the section "Recovering Passwords," later in this chapter.

Remember that in hex, the scheme is 0–9 and A–F (A = 10, B = 11, C = 12, D = 13, E = 14, and F = 15). This means that a 210F setting for the configuration register is actually 210(15), or 1111 in binary.

TABLE 8.2 Software configuration meanings

Bit	Hex	Description
0–3	0x0000–0x000F	Boot field (see Table 8.3).
6	0x0040	Ignore NVRAM contents.
7	0x0080	OEM bit enabled.
8	0x101	Break disabled.
10	0x0400	IP broadcast with all zeros.
5, 11–12	0x0800–0x1000	Console line speed.
13	0x2000	Boot default ROM software if network boot fails.
14	0x4000	IP broadcasts do not have net numbers.
15	0x8000	Enable diagnostic messages and ignore NVRAM contents.

The boot field, which consists of bits 0–3 in the configuration register (the last 4 bits), controls the router boot sequence and locates the Cisco IOS. Table 8.3 describes the boot field bits.

TABLE 8.3   The boot field (configuration register bits 00–03)

Boot Field	Meaning	Use
00	ROM monitor mode	To boot to ROM monitor mode, set the configuration register to 2100. You must manually boot the router with the b command. The router will show the rommon> prompt.
01	Boot image from ROM	To boot the mini-IOS image stored in ROM, set the configuration register to 2101. The router will show the Router(boot)> prompt. The mini-IOS is not available in all routers and is also referred to as RXBOOT.
02–F	Specifies a default boot filename	Any value from 2102 through 210F tells the router to use the boot commands specified in NVRAM.

Checking the Current Configuration Register Value

You can see the current value of the configuration register by using the show version command (sh version or show ver for short), as demonstrated here:

```
Router>sh version
Cisco IOS Software, 2800 Software (C2800NM-ADVSECURITYK9-M),
Version 15.1(4)M6, RELEASE SOFTWARE (fc2)
[output cut]
Configuration register is 0x2102
```

The last information given from this command is the value of the configuration register. In this example, the value is 0x2102—the default setting. The configuration register setting of 0x2102 tells the router to look in NVRAM for the boot sequence.

Notice that the show version command also provides the IOS version, and in the preceding example, it shows the IOS version as 15.1(4)M6.

The show version command will display system hardware configuration information, system serial number, the software verision, and the names of the boot images on a router.

To change the configuration register, use the config-register command from global configuration mode:

```
Router(config)#config-register 0x2142
Router(config)#do sh ver
```

[output cut]
Configuration register is 0x2102 (will be 0x2142 at next reload)

It's important that you are careful when you set the configuration register!

 If you save your configuration and reload the router and it comes up in setup mode, the configuration register setting is probably incorrect.

Boot System Commands

Did you know that you can configure your router to boot another IOS if the flash is corrupted? Well, you can. You can boot all of your routers from a TFTP server, but it's old school, and people just don't do it anymore; it's just for backup in case of failure.

There are some boot commands you can play with that will help you manage the way your router boots the Cisco IOS—but please remember, we're talking about the router's IOS here, *not* the router's configuration!

```
Router>en
Router#config t
Enter configuration commands, one per line.  End with CNTL/Z.
Router(config)#boot ?
  bootstrap  Bootstrap image file
  config     Configuration file
  host       Router-specific config file
  network    Network-wide config file
  system     System image file
```

The boot command truly gives you a wealth of options, but first, I'll show you the typical settings that Cisco recommends. So let's get started—the boot system command will allow you to tell the router which system IOS file to boot from flash memory. Remember that the router, by default, boots the first system IOS file found in flash. You can change that with the following commands, as shown in the output:

```
Router(config)#boot system ?
  WORD   TFTP filename or URL
  flash  Boot from flash memory
  ftp    Boot from a server via ftp
  mop    Boot from a Decnet MOP server
  rcp    Boot from a server via rcp
  rom    Boot from rom
  tftp   Boot from a tftp server
Router(config)#boot system flash c2800nm-advsecurityk9-mz.151-4.M6.bin
```

Notice I could boot from FLASH, FTP, ROM, TFTP, or another useless options. The command I used configures the router to boot the IOS listed in it. This is a helpful command for when you load a new IOS into flash and want to test it, or even when you want to totally change which IOS is loading by default.

The next command is considered a fallback routine, but as I said, you can make it a permanent way to have your routers boot from a TFTP host. Personally, I wouldn't necessarily recommend doing this (single point of failure); I'm just showing you that it's possible:

```
Router(config)#boot system tftp ?
  WORD  System image filename
Router(config)#boot system tftp c2800nm-advsecurityk9-mz.151-4.M6.bin?
  Hostname or A.B.C.D  Address from which to download the file
  <cr>
Router(config)#boot system tftp c2800nm-advsecurityk9-mz.151-4.M6.bin 1.1.1.2
Router(config)#
```

As your last recommended fallback option—the one to go to if the IOS in flash doesn't load and the TFTP host does not produce the IOS—load the mini-IOS from ROM like this:

```
Router(config)#boot system rom
Router(config)#do show run | include boot system
boot system flash c2800nm-advsecurityk9-mz.151-4.M6.bin
boot system tftp c2800nm-advsecurityk9-mz.151-4.M6.bin 1.1.1.2
boot system rom
Router(config)#
```

If the preceding configuration is set, the router will try to boot from the TFTP server if flash fails, and if the TFTP boot fails, the mini-IOS will load after six unsuccessful attempts of trying to locate the TFTP server.

In the next section, I'll show you how to load the router into ROM monitor mode so you can perform password recovery.

Recovering Passwords

If you're locked out of a router because you forgot the password, you can change the configuration register to help you get back on your feet. As I said earlier, bit 6 in the configuration register is used to tell the router whether to use the contents of NVRAM to load a router configuration.

The default configuration register value is 0x2102, meaning that bit 6 is off. With the default setting, the router will look for and load a router configuration stored in NVRAM (startup-config). To recover a password, you need to turn on bit 6. Doing this will tell the router to ignore the NVRAM contents. The configuration register value to turn on bit 6 is 0x2142.

Here are the main steps to password recovery:

1. Boot the router and interrupt the boot sequence by performing a break, which will take the router into ROM monitor mode.

2. Change the configuration register to turn on bit 6 (with the value 0x2142).

3. Reload the router.

4. Say "no" to entering setup mode, then enter privileged mode.

5. Copy the startup-config file to running-config, and don't forget to verify that your interfaces are re-enabled.

6. Change the password.

7. Reset the configuration register to the default value.

8. Save the router configuration.

9. Reload the router (optional).

I'm going to cover these steps in more detail in the following sections. I'll also show you the commands to restore access to ISR series routers.

You can enter ROM monitor mode by pressing Ctrl+Break or Ctrl+Shift+6, then b, during router bootup. But if the IOS is corrupt or missing, if there's no network connectivity available to find a TFTP host, or if the mini-IOS from ROM doesn't load (meaning the default router fallback failed), the router will enter ROM monitor mode by default.

Interrupting the Router Boot Sequence

Your first step is to boot the router and perform a break. This is usually done by pressing the Ctrl+Break key combination when using HyperTerminal (personally, I use SecureCRT or PuTTY) while the router first reboots.

```
System Bootstrap, Version 15.1(4)M6, RELEASE SOFTWARE (fc2)
Copyright (c) 1999 by cisco Systems, Inc.
TAC:Home:SW:IOS:Specials for info
PC = 0xfff0a530, Vector = 0x500, SP = 0x680127b0
C2800 platform with 32768 Kbytes of main memory
PC = 0xfff0a530, Vector = 0x500, SP = 0x80004374
monitor: command "boot" aborted due to user interrupt
rommon 1 >
```

Notice the line monitor: command "boot" aborted due to user interrupt. At this point, you will be at the rommon 1> prompt, which is called the ROM monitor mode.

Changing the Configuration Register

As I explained earlier, you can change the configuration register from within the IOS by using the config-register command. To turn on bit 6, use the configuration register value 0x2142.

Remember that if you change the configuration register to 0x2142, the startup-config will be bypassed and the router will load into setup mode.

To change the bit value on a Cisco ISR series router, you just enter the following command at the `rommon 1>` prompt:

```
rommon 1 >confreg 0x2142
You must reset or power cycle for new config to take effect
rommon 2 >reset
```

Reloading the Router and Entering Privileged Mode

At this point, you need to reset the router like this:

- From the ISR series router, type **I** (for initialize) or **reset**.
- From an older series router, type **I**.

The router will reload and ask if you want to use setup mode (because no startup-config is used). Answer no to entering setup mode, press Enter to go into user mode, and then type **enable** to go into privileged mode.

Viewing and Changing the Configuration

Now you're past the point where you would need to enter the user-mode and privileged-mode passwords in a router. Copy the startup-config file to the running-config file:

```
copy startup-config running-config
```

Or use the shortcut:

```
copy start run
```

The configuration is now running in *random access memory (RAM)*, and you're in privileged mode, meaning that you can now view and change the configuration. But you can't view the enable secret setting for the password since it is encrypted. To change the password, do this:

```
config t
enable secret todd
```

Resetting the Configuration Register and Reloading the Router

After you're finished changing passwords, set the configuration register back to the default value with the `config-register` command:

```
config t
config-register 0x2102
```

It's important to remember to enable your interfaces after copying the configuration from NVRAM to RAM.

Finally, save the new configuration with a `copy running-config startup-config` and use `reload` to reload the router.

> If you save your configuration and reload the router and it comes up in setup mode, the configuration register setting is probably incorrect.

To sum this up, we now have Cisco's suggested IOS backup routine configured on our router: flash, TFTP host, ROM.

Backing Up and Restoring the Cisco IOS

Before you upgrade or restore a Cisco IOS, you really should copy the existing file to a *TFTP host* as a backup just in case the new image crashes and burns.

And you can use any TFTP host to accomplish this. By default, the flash memory in a router is used to store the Cisco IOS. In the following sections, I'll describe how to check the amount of flash memory, how to copy the Cisco IOS from flash memory to a TFTP host, and how to copy the IOS from a TFTP host to flash memory.

But before you back up an IOS image to a network server on your intranet, you've got to do these three things:

- Make sure you can access the network server.

- Ensure that the network server has adequate space for the code image.

- Verify the file naming and path requirements.

You can connect your laptop or workstation's Ethernet port directly to a router's Ethernet interface, as shown in Figure 8.1.

FIGURE 8.1   Copying an IOS from a router to a TFTP host

Copy the IOS to a TFTP host.
Router# copy flash tftp
- IP address of the TFTP server
- IOS filename

E0

Console

```
RouterX#copy flash tftp:
Source filename [] ?c2800nm-ipbase-mz.124-5a.bin
Address or name of remote host [] ? 10.1.1.1
Destination filename [c2800nm-ipbase-mz.124-5a.bin] [enter]
!!!!!!!!!!!!!!!!!!!!!!!!!!!!!!!!!!!!!!!!!!!!!!!!!!!!!!!!!!!!!!!!!!<output omitted>
12094416 bytes copied in 98.858 secs (122341 bytes/sec)
RouterX#
```

- TFTP server software must be running on the PC.
- The PC must be on the same subnet as the router's E0 interface.
- The `copy flash tftp` command must be supplied the IP address of the PC.

You need to verify the following before attempting to copy the image to or from the router:

- TFTP server software must be running on the laptop or workstation.
- The Ethernet connection between the router and the workstation must be made with a crossover cable.
- The workstation must be on the same subnet as the router's Ethernet interface.
- The copy flash tftp command must be supplied the IP address of the workstation if you are copying from the router flash.
- And if you're copying "into" flash, you need to verify that there's enough room in flash memory to accommodate the file to be copied.

Verifying Flash Memory

Before you attempt to upgrade the Cisco IOS on your router with a new IOS file, it's a good idea to verify that your flash memory has enough room to hold the new image. You verify the amount of flash memory and the file or files being stored in flash memory by using the show flash command (sh flash for short):

```
Router#sh flash
-#- --length-- -----date/time------ path
1    45392400 Apr 14 2013 05:31:44 +00:00 c2800nm-advsecurityk9-mz.151-4.M6.bin

18620416 bytes available (45395968 bytes used)
```

There are about 45 MB of flash used, but there are still about 18 MB available. If you want to copy a file into flash that is more than 18 MB in size, the router will ask you if you want to erase flash. Be careful here!

> The show flash command will display the amount of memory consumed by the current IOS image as well as tell you if there's enough room available to hold both current and new images. You should know that if there's not enough room for both the old and new image you want to load, the old image will be erased!

The amount of RAM and flash is actually easy to tally using the show version command on routers:

```
Router#show version
[output cut]
System returned to ROM by power-on
System image file is "flash:c2800nm-advsecurityk9-mz.151-4.M6.bin"
[output cut]
```

```
Cisco 2811 (revision 1.0) with 249856K/12288K bytes of memory.
Processor board ID FTX1049A1AB
2 FastEthernet interfaces
2 Serial(sync/async) interfaces
1 Virtual Private Network (VPN) Module
DRAM configuration is 64 bits wide with parity enabled.
239K bytes of non-volatile configuration memory.
62720K bytes of ATA CompactFlash (Read/Write)
```

The second highlighted line shows us that this router has about 256 MB of RAM, and you can see that the amount of flash shows up on the last line. By estimating up, we get the amount of flash to 64 MB.

Notice in the first highlighted line that the filename in this example is c2800nm-advsecurity k9-mz.151-4.M6.bin. The main difference in the output of the show flash and show version commands is that the show flash command displays all files in flash memory and the show version command shows the actual name of the file used to run the router and the location from which it was loaded, which is flash memory.

Backing Up the Cisco IOS

To back up the Cisco IOS to a TFTP server, you use the copy flash tftp command. It's a straightforward command that requires only the source filename and the IP address of the TFTP server.

The key to success in this backup routine is to make sure you've got good, solid connectivity to the TFTP server. Check this by pinging the TFTP device from the router console prompt like this:

```
Router#ping 1.1.1.2
Type escape sequence to abort.
Sending 5, 100-byte ICMP Echos to 1.1.1.2, timeout
  is 2 seconds:
!!!!!
Success rate is 100 percent (5/5), round-trip min/avg/max
  = 4/4/8 ms
```

After you ping the TFTP server to make sure that IP is working, you can use the copy flash tftp command to copy the IOS to the TFTP server as shown next:

```
Router#copy flash tftp
Source filename []?c2800nm-advsecurityk9-mz.151-4.M6.bin
Address or name of remote host []?1.1.1.2
Destination filename [c2800nm-advsecurityk9-mz.151-4.M6.bin]?[enter]
!!!!!!!!!!!!!!!!!!!!!!!!!!!!!!!!!!!!!!!!!!!!!!!!!!!!!!!!!!!!!!!!!!!!!!!!!!!!!!!!!!!
45395968 bytes copied in 123.724 secs (357532 bytes/sec)
Router#
```

Just copy the IOS filename from either the show flash or show version command and then paste it when prompted for the source filename.

In the preceding example, the contents of flash memory were copied successfully to the TFTP server. The address of the remote host is the IP address of the TFTP host, and the source filename is the file in flash memory.

WARNING Many newer Cisco routers have removable memory. You may see names for this memory such as flash0:, in which case the command in the preceding example would be copy flash0: tftp:. Alternately, you may see it as usbflash0:.

Restoring or Upgrading the Cisco Router IOS

What happens if you need to restore the Cisco IOS to flash memory to replace an original file that has been damaged or if you want to upgrade the IOS? You can download the file from a TFTP server to flash memory by using the copy tftp flash command. This command requires the IP address of the TFTP host and the name of the file you want to download.

However, since IOS's can be very large today, we may want to use something other than tftp, which is unreliable and can only transfer smaller files. Check this out:

```
Corp#copy ?
  /erase          Erase destination file system.
  /error          Allow to copy error file.
  /noverify       Don't verify image signature before reload.
  /verify         Verify image signature before reload.
  archive:        Copy from archive: file system
  cns:            Copy from cns: file system
  flash:          Copy from flash: file system
  ftp:            Copy from ftp: file system
  http:           Copy from http: file system
  https:          Copy from https: file system
  null:           Copy from null: file system
  nvram:          Copy from nvram: file system
  rcp:            Copy from rcp: file system
  running-config  Copy from current system configuration
  scp:            Copy from scp: file system
  startup-config  Copy from startup configuration
  system:         Copy from system: file system
  tar:            Copy from tar: file system
  tftp:           Copy from tftp: file system
  tmpsys:         Copy from tmpsys: file system
  xmodem:         Copy from xmodem: file system
  ymodem:         Copy from ymodem: file system
```

You can see from the output above that we have many options, and for the larger files we'll use ftp: or scp: to copy our IOS into or from routers and switches, and you can even perform an MD5 verification with the /verify at the end of a command.

Let's just use tftp for our examples in the chapter because it's easiest. But before you begin, make sure the file you want to place in flash memory is in the default TFTP directory on your host. When you issue the command, TFTP won't ask you where the file is, so if the file you want to use isn't in the default directory of the TFTP host, this just won't work.

```
Router#copy tftp flash
Address or name of remote host []?1.1.1.2
Source filename []?c2800nm-advsecurityk9-mz.151-4.M6.bin
Destination filename [c2800nm-advsecurityk9-mz.151-4.M6.bin]?[enter]
%Warning: There is a file already existing with this name
Do you want to over write? [confirm][enter]
Accessing tftp://1.1.1.2/ c2800nm-advsecurityk9-mz.151-4.M6.bin...
Loading c2800nm-advsecurityk9-mz.151-4.M6.bin from 1.1.1.2 (via
   FastEthernet0/0): !!!!!!!!!!!!!!!!!!!!!!!!!!!!!!!!!!!!!!!!!!!!!!!!!!!!!!!!!!!!!!!
[OK - 21710744 bytes]

45395968 bytes copied in 82.880 secs (261954 bytes/sec)
Router#
```

In the preceding example, I copied the same file into flash memory, so it asked me if I wanted to overwrite it. Remember that we are "playing" with files in flash memory. If I had just corrupted my file by overwriting it, I won't know for sure until I reboot the router. Be careful with this command! If the file is corrupted, you'll need to do an IOS-restore from ROM monitor mode.

If you are loading a new file and you don't have enough room in flash memory to store both the new and existing copies, the router will ask to erase the contents of flash memory before writing the new file into flash memory, and if you are able to copy the IOS without erasing the old version, then make sure you remember to use the boot system flash: *ios-file* command.

A Cisco router can become a TFTP server host for a router system image that's run in flash memory. The global configuration command is tftp-server flash: *ios-file*.

It's Monday Morning and You Just Upgraded Your IOS

You came in early to work to upgrade the IOS on your router. After the upgrade, you reload the router and the router now shows the rommon> prompt.

It seems that you're about to have a bad day! This is what I call an RGE: a resume-generating event! So, now what do you do? Just keep calm and chive on! Follow these steps to save your job:

```
rommon 1 > tftpdnld
```

```
Missing or illegal ip address for variable IP_ADDRESS
Illegal IP address.
```

```
usage: tftpdnld [-hr]
  Use this command for disaster recovery only to recover an image via TFTP.
  Monitor variables are used to set up parameters for the transfer.
  (Syntax: "VARIABLE_NAME=value" and use "set" to show current variables.)
  "ctrl-c" or "break" stops the transfer before flash erase begins.

  The following variables are REQUIRED to be set for tftpdnld:
          IP_ADDRESS: The IP address for this unit
      IP_SUBNET_MASK: The subnet mask for this unit
      DEFAULT_GATEWAY: The default gateway for this unit
          TFTP_SERVER: The IP address of the server to fetch from
            TFTP_FILE: The filename to fetch

  The following variables are OPTIONAL:
[unneeded output cut]
rommon 2 >set IP_Address:1.1.1.1
rommon 3 >set IP_SUBNET_MASK:255.0.0.0
rommon 4 >set DEFAULT_GATEWAY:1.1.1.2
rommon 5 >set TFTP_SERVER:1.1.1.2
rommon 6 >set TFTP_FILE: flash:c2800nm-advipservicesk9-mz.124-12.bin
rommon 7 >tftpdnld
```

From here you can see the variables you need to configure using the set command; be sure you use ALL_CAPS with these commands as well as underscore (_). From here, you need to set the IP address, mask, and default gateway of your router, then the IP address of the TFTP host, which in this example is a directly connected router that I made a TFTP server with this command:

```
Router(config)#tftp-server flash:c2800nm-advipservicesk9-mz.124-12.bin
```

And finally, you set the IOS filename of the file on your TFTP server. Whew! Job saved.

There is one other way you can restore the IOS on a router, but it takes a while. You can use what is called the Xmodem protocol to actually upload an IOS file into flash memory through the console port. You'd use the Xmodem through the console port procedure if you had no network connectivity to the router or switch.

Using the Cisco IOS File System (Cisco IFS)

Cisco has created a file system called Cisco IFS that allows you to work with files and directories just as you would from a Windows DOS prompt. The commands you use are dir, copy, more, delete, erase or format, cd and pwd, and mkdir and rmdir.

Working with IFS gives you the ability to view all files, even those on remote servers. And you definitely want to find out if an image on one of your remote servers is valid before you copy it, right? You also need to know how big it is—size matters here! It's also a really good idea to take a look at the remote server's configuration and make sure it's all good before loading that file on your router.

It's very cool that IFS makes the file system user interface universal—it's not platform specific anymore. You now get to use the same syntax for all your commands on all of your routers, no matter the platform!

Sound too good to be true? Well, it kind of is because you'll find out that support for all commands on each file system and platform just isn't there. But it's really no big deal since various file systems differ in the actions they perform; the commands that aren't relevant to a particular file system are the very ones that aren't supported on that file system. Be assured that any file system or platform will fully support all the commands you need to manage it.

Another cool IFS feature is that it cuts down on all those obligatory prompts for a lot of the commands. If you want to enter a command, all you have to do is type all the necessary info straight into the command line—no more jumping through hoops of prompts! So, if you want to copy a file to an FTP server, all you'd do is first indicate where the desired source file is on your router, pinpoint where the destination file is to be on the FTP server, determine the username and password you're going to use when you want to connect to that server, and type it all in on one line—sleek! And for those of you resistant to change, you can still have the router prompt you for all the information it needs and enjoy entering a more elegantly minimized version of the command than you did before.

But even in spite of all this, your router might still prompt you—even if you did everything right in your command line. It comes down to how you've got the file prompt command configured and which command you're trying to use. But no worries—if that happens, the default value will be entered right there in the command, and all you have to do is hit Enter to verify the correct values.

IFS also lets you explore various directories and inventory files in any directory you want. Plus, you can make subdirectories in flash memory or on a card, but you only get to do that if you're working on one of the more recent platforms.

And get this—the new file system interface uses URLs to determine the whereabouts of a file. So just as they pinpoint places on the Web, URLs now indicate where files are on your Cisco router, or even on a remote file server! You just type URLs right into your commands to identify where the file or directory is. It's really that easy—to copy a file from one place to another, you simply enter the copy *source-url destination-url* command—sweet! IFS URLs are a tad different than what you're used to though, and there's an array of formats to use that vary depending on where, exactly, the file is that you're after.

We're going to use Cisco IFS commands pretty much the same way that we used the copy command in the IOS section earlier:

- For backing up the IOS
- For upgrading the IOS
- For viewing text files

Okay—with all that down, let's take a look at the common IFS commands available to us for managing the IOS. I'll get into configuration files soon, but for now I'm going to get you started with going over the basics used to manage the new Cisco IOS.

dir   Same as with Windows, this command lets you view files in a directory. Type **dir**, hit Enter, and by default you get the contents of the flash:/ directory output.

copy   This is one popular command, often used to upgrade, restore, or back up an IOS. But as I said, when you use it, it's really important to focus on the details—what you're copying, where it's coming from, and where it's going to land.

more   Same as with Unix, this will take a text file and let you look at it on a card. You can use it to check out your configuration file or your backup configuration file. I'll go over it more when we get into actual configuration.

show file   This command will give you the skinny on a specified file or file system, but it's kind of obscure because people don't use it a lot.

delete   Three guesses—yep, it deletes stuff. But with some types of routers, not as well as you'd think. That's because even though it whacks the file, it doesn't always free up the space it was using. To actually get the space back, you have to use something called the squeeze command too.

erase/format   Use these with care—make sure that when you're copying files, you say no to the dialog that asks you if you want to erase the file system! The type of memory you're using determines if you can nix the flash drive or not.

cd/pwd   Same as with Unix and DOS, cd is the command you use to change directories. Use the pwd command to print (show) the working directory.

mkdir/rmdir   Use these commands on certain routers and switches to create and delete directories—the mkdir command for creation and the rmdir command for deletion. Use the cd and pwd commands to change into these directories.

The Cisco IFS uses the alternate term system:running-config as well as nvram:startup-config when copying the configurations on a router, although it is not mandatory that you use this naming convention.

Using the Cisco IFS to Upgrade an IOS

Let's take a look at some of these Cisco IFS commands on my ISR router (1841 series) with a hostname of R1.

We'll start with the pwd command to verify our default directory and then use the dir command to verify its contents (flash:/):

```
R1#pwd
flash:
R1#dir
Directory of flash:/
    1  -rw-    13937472  Dec 20 2006 19:58:18 +00:00  c1841-ipbase-
    mz.124-1c.bin
    2  -rw-        1821  Dec 20 2006 20:11:24 +00:00  sdmconfig-18xx.cfg
    3  -rw-     4734464  Dec 20 2006 20:12:00 +00:00  sdm.tar
    4  -rw-      833024  Dec 20 2006 20:12:24 +00:00  es.tar
    5  -rw-     1052160  Dec 20 2006 20:12:50 +00:00  common.tar
    6  -rw-        1038  Dec 20 2006 20:13:10 +00:00  home.shtml
    7  -rw-      102400  Dec 20 2006 20:13:30 +00:00  home.tar
    8  -rw-      491213  Dec 20 2006 20:13:56 +00:00  128MB.sdf
    9  -rw-     1684577  Dec 20 2006 20:14:34 +00:00  securedesktop-
    ios-3.1.1.27-k9.pkg
   10  -rw-      398305  Dec 20 2006 20:15:04 +00:00  sslclient-win-1.1.0.154.pkg

32071680 bytes total (8818688 bytes free)
```

What we can see here is that we have the basic IP IOS (c1841-ipbase-mz.124-1c.bin). Looks like we need to upgrade our 1841. You've just got to love how Cisco puts the IOS type in the filename now! First, let's check the size of the file that's in flash with the show file command (show flash would also work):

```
R1#show file info flash:c1841-ipbase-mz.124-1c.bin
flash:c1841-ipbase-mz.124-1c.bin:
  type is image (elf) []
  file size is 13937472 bytes, run size is 14103140 bytes
  Runnable image, entry point 0x8000F000, run from ram
```

With a file that size, the existing IOS will have to be erased before we can add our new IOS file (c1841-advipservicesk9-mz.124-12.bin), which is over 21 MB. We'll use the delete command, but remember, we can play with any file in flash memory and nothing serious will happen until we reboot—that is, if we made a mistake. So obviously, and as I pointed out earlier, we need to be very careful here!

```
R1#delete flash:c1841-ipbase-mz.124-1c.bin
Delete filename [c1841-ipbase-mz.124-1c.bin]?[enter]
Delete flash:c1841-ipbase-mz.124-1c.bin? [confirm][enter]
R1#sh flash
```

```
-#- --length-- -----date/time------ path
1          1821 Dec 20 2006 20:11:24 +00:00 sdmconfig-18xx.cfg
2       4734464 Dec 20 2006 20:12:00 +00:00 sdm.tar
3        833024 Dec 20 2006 20:12:24 +00:00 es.tar
4       1052160 Dec 20 2006 20:12:50 +00:00 common.tar
5          1038 Dec 20 2006 20:13:10 +00:00 home.shtml
6        102400 Dec 20 2006 20:13:30 +00:00 home.tar
7        491213 Dec 20 2006 20:13:56 +00:00 128MB.sdf
8       1684577 Dec 20 2006 20:14:34 +00:00 securedesktop-ios-3.1.1.27-k9.pkg
9        398305 Dec 20 2006 20:15:04 +00:00 sslclient-win-1.1.0.154.pkg
22757376 bytes available (9314304 bytes used)
R1#sh file info flash:c1841-ipbase-mz.124-1c.bin
%Error opening flash:c1841-ipbase-mz.124-1c.bin (File not found)
R1#
```

So with the preceding commands, we deleted the existing file and then verified the deletion by using both the show flash and show file commands. We'll add the new file with the copy command, but again, we need to make sure to be careful because this way isn't any safer than the first method I showed you earlier:

```
R1#copy tftp://1.1.1.2/c1841-advipservicesk9-mz.124-12.bin/ flash:/
    c1841-advipservicesk9-mz.124-12.bin
Source filename [/c1841-advipservicesk9-mz.124-12.bin/]?[enter]
Destination filename [c1841-advipservicesk9-mz.124-12.bin]?[enter]
Loading /c1841-advipservicesk9-mz.124-12.bin/ from 1.1.1.2 (via
    FastEthernet0/0): !!!!!!!!!!!!!!!!!!!!!!!!!!!!!!!!!!!!!!!!!!
[output cut]
!!!!!!!!!!!!!!!!!!!!!!!!!!!!!!!!!!!!!!!!!!!!!!!!!!!!!!!!
[OK - 22103052 bytes]
22103052 bytes copied in 72.008 secs (306953 bytes/sec)
R1#sh flash
-#- --length-- -----date/time------ path
1          1821 Dec 20 2006 20:11:24 +00:00 sdmconfig-18xx.cfg
2       4734464 Dec 20 2006 20:12:00 +00:00 sdm.tar
3        833024 Dec 20 2006 20:12:24 +00:00 es.tar
4       1052160 Dec 20 2006 20:12:50 +00:00 common.tar
5          1038 Dec 20 2006 20:13:10 +00:00 home.shtml
6        102400 Dec 20 2006 20:13:30 +00:00 home.tar
7        491213 Dec 20 2006 20:13:56 +00:00 128MB.sdf
8       1684577 Dec 20 2006 20:14:34 +00:00 securedesktop-ios-3.1.1.27-k9.pkg
9        398305 Dec 20 2006 20:15:04 +00:00 sslclient-win-1.1.0.154.pkg
```

```
10    22103052 Mar 10 2007 19:40:50 +00:00 c1841-advipservicesk9-mz.124-12.bin
651264 bytes available (31420416 bytes used)
R1#
```

We can also check the file information with the show file command:

```
R1#sh file information flash:c1841-advipservicesk9-mz.124-12.bin
flash:c1841-advipservicesk9-mz.124-12.bin:
  type is image (elf) []
  file size is 22103052 bytes, run size is 22268736 bytes
  Runnable image, entry point 0x8000F000, run from ram
```

Remember that the IOS is expanded into RAM when the router boots, so the new IOS will not run until you reload the router.

I really recommend experimenting with the Cisco IFS commands on a router just to get a good feel for them because, as I've said, they can definitely give you some grief if not executed properly!

 I mention "safer methods" a lot in this chapter. Clearly, I've caused myself some serious pain by not being careful enough when working in flash memory! I cannot stress this enough—pay attention when messing around with flash memory!

One of the brilliant features of the ISR routers is that they use the physical flash cards that are accessible from the front or back of any router. These typically have a name like usbflash0:, so to view the contents, you'd type **dir usbflash0:**, for example. You can pull these flash cards out, put them in an appropriate slot in your PC, and the card will show up as a drive. You can then add, change, and delete files. Just put the flash card back in your router and power up—instant upgrade. Nice!

Licensing

IOS licensing is now done quite differently than it was with previous versions of the IOS. Actually, there was no licensing before the new 15.0 IOS code, just your word and honor, and we can only guess based on how all products are downloaded on the Internet daily how well that has worked out for Cisco!

Starting with the IOS 15.0 code, things are much different—almost too different. I can imagine that Cisco will come back toward the middle on its licensing issues, so that the administration and management won't be as detailed as it is with the new 15.0 code license is now; but you can be the judge of that after reading this section.

A new ISR router is pre-installed with the software images and licenses that you ordered, so as long as you ordered and paid for everything you need, you're set! If not, you can just install another license, which can be a tad tedious at first—enough so that installing a license was made an objective on the Cisco exam! Of course, it can be done, but it definitely requires some effort. As is typical with Cisco, if you spend enough money on their products, they tend to make it easier on you and your administration, and the licensing for the newest IOS is no exception, as you'll soon see.

On a positive note, Cisco provides evaluation licenses for most software packages and features that are supported on the hardware you purchased, and it's always nice to be able to try it out before you buy. Once the temporary license expires after 60 days, you need to acquire a permanent license in order to continue to use the extended features that aren't available in your current version. This method of licensing allows you to enable a router to use different parts of the IOS. So, what happens after 60 days? Well, nothing—back to the honor system for now. This is now called *Right-To-Use (RTU) licensing*, and it probably won't always be available via your honor, but for now it is.

But that's not the best part of the new licensing features. Prior to the 15.0 code release, there were eight different software feature sets for each hardware router type. With the IOS 15.0 code, the packaging is now called a *universal image*, meaning all feature sets are available in one file with all features packed neatly inside. So instead of the pre-15.0 IOS file packages of one image per feature set, Cisco now just builds one universal image that includes all of them in the file. Even so, we still need a different universal image per router model or series, just not a different image for each feature set as we did with previous IOS versions.

To use the features in the IOS software, you must unlock them using the software activation process. Since all features available are inside the universal image already, you can just unlock the features you need as you need them, and of course pay for these features when you determine that they meet your business requirements. All routers come with something called the IP Base licensing, which is the prerequisite for installing all other features.

There are three different technology packages available for purchase that can be installed as additional feature packs on top of the prerequisite IP Base (default), which provides entry-level IOS functionality. These are as follows:

Data: MPLS, ATM, and multiprotocol support

Unified Communications: VoIP and IP telephony

Security: Cisco IOS Firewall, IPS, IPsec, 3DES, and VPN

For example, if you need MPLS and IPsec, you'll need the default IP Base, Data, and Security premium packages unlocked on your router.

To obtain the license, you'll need the unique device identifier (UDI), which has two components: the product ID (PID) and the serial number of the router. The show license UDI command provides this information in an output as shown:

```
Router#sh license udi
Device#   PID                 SN              UDI
-------------------------------------------------------------------
*0     CISCO2901/K9        FTX1641Y07J     CISCO2901/K9:FTX1641Y07J
```

After the time has expired for your 60-day evaluation period, you can either obtain the license file from the Cisco License Manager (CLM), which is an automated process, or use the manual process through the Cisco Product License Registration portal. Typically only larger companies will use the CLM because you'd need to install software on a server, which then keeps track of all your licenses for you. If you have just a few licenses that you use, you can opt for the manual web browser process found on the Cisco Product License Registration portal and then just add in a few CLI commands. After that, you just basically keep track of putting all the different license features together for each device you manage. Although this sounds like a lot of work, you don't need to perform these steps often. But clearly, going with the CLM makes a lot of sense if you have bunches of licenses to manage because it will put together all the little pieces of licensing for each router in one easy process.

When you purchase the software package with the features that you want to install, you need to permanently activate the software package using your UDI and the *product authorization key (PAK)* that you received with your purchase. This is essentially your receipt acknowledging that you purchased the license. You then need to connect the license with a particular router by combining the PAK and the UDI, which you do online at the Cisco Product License Registration portal (www.cisco.com/go/license). If you haven't already registered the license on a different router, and it is valid, Cisco will then email you your permanent license, or you can download it from your account.

But wait! You're still not done. You now need to activate the license on the router. Whew... maybe it's worthwhile to install the CLM on a server after all! Staying with the manual method, you need to make the new license file available to the router either via a USB port on the router or through a TFTP server. Once it's available to the router, you'll use the license install command from privileged mode.

Assuming that you copied the file into flash memory, the command would look like something like this:

```
Router#license install ?
  archive:  Install from archive: file system
  flash:    Install from flash: file system
  ftp:      Install from ftp: file system
  http:     Install from http: file system
  https:    Install from https: file system
  null:     Install from null: file system
  nvram:    Install from nvram: file system
  rcp:      Install from rcp: file system
  scp:      Install from scp: file system
  syslog:   Install from syslog: file system
  system:   Install from system: file system
  tftp:     Install from tftp: file system
  tmpsys:   Install from tmpsys: file system
  xmodem:   Install from xmodem: file system
  ymodem:   Install from ymodem: file system
Router#license install flash:FTX1628838P_201302111432454180.lic
```

```
Installing licenses from "flash::FTX1628838P_201302111432454180.lic"
Installing...Feature:datak9...Successful:Supported
1/1 licenses were successfully installed
0/1 licenses were existing licenses
0/1 licenses were failed to install
April 12 2:31:19.786: %LICENSE-6-INSTALL: Feature datak9 1.0 was
installed in this device. UDI=CISCO2901/K9:FTX1628838P; StoreIndex=1:Primary
License Storage

April 12 2:31:20.078: %IOS_LICENSE_IMAGE_APPLICATION-6-LICENSE_LEVEL: Module name
=c2800 Next reboot level = datak9 and License = datak9
```

You need to reboot to have the new license take effect. Now that you have your license installed and running, how do you use Right-To-Use licensing to check out new features on your router? Let's look into that now.

Right-To-Use Licenses (Evaluation Licenses)

Originally called evaluation licenses, Right-To-Use (RTU) licenses are what you need when you want to update your IOS to load a new feature but either don't want to wait to get the license or just want to test if this feature will truly meet your business requirements. This makes sense because if Cisco made it complicated to load and check out a feature, they could potentially miss out on a sale! Of course if the feature does work for you, they'll want you to buy a permanent license, but again, this is on the honor system at the time of this writing.

Cisco's license model allows you to install the feature you want without a PAK. The Right-To-Use license works for 60 days before you would need to install your permanent license. To enable the Right-To-Use license you would use the license boot module command. The following demonstrates starting the Right-To-Use license on my 2900 series router, enabling the security module named securityk9:

```
Router(config)#license boot module c2900 technology-package securityk9
PLEASE READ THE FOLLOWING TERMS CAREFULLY. INSTALLING THE LICENSE OR LICENSE KEY
PROVIDED FOR ANY CISCO PRODUCT FEATURE OR USING
SUCHPRODUCT FEATURE CONSTITUTES YOUR FULL ACCEPTANCE OF THE
FOLLOWING TERMS. YOU MUST NOT PROCEED FURTHER IF YOU ARE NOT WILLING
TO BE BOUND BY ALL THE TERMS SET FORTH HEREIN.
[output cut]
Activation of the software command line interface will be evidence of
your acceptance of this agreement.

ACCEPT? [yes/no]: yes
```

```
% use 'write' command to make license boot config take effect on next boot
Feb 12 01:35:45.060: %IOS_LICENSE_IMAGE_APPLICATION-6-LICENSE_LEVEL:
Module name =c2900 Next reboot level = securityk9 and License = securityk9

Feb 12 01:35:45.524: %LICENSE-6-EULA_ACCEPTED: EULA for feature
securityk9 1.0 has been accepted. UDI=CISCO2901/K9:FTX1628838P;
StoreIndex=0:Built-In License Storage
```

Once the router is reloaded, you can use the security feature set. And it is really nice that you don't need to reload the router again if you choose to install a permanent license for this feature. The show license command shows the licenses installed on the router:

```
Router#show license
Index 1 Feature: ipbasek9
     Period left: Life time
     License Type: Permanent
     License State: Active, In Use
     License Count: Non-Counted
     License Priority: Medium
Index 2 Feature: securityk9
     Period left: 8 weeks  2 days
     Period Used: 0  minute  0  second
     License Type: EvalRightToUse
     License State: Active, In Use
     License Count: Non-Counted
     License Priority: None
Index 3 Feature: uck9
     Period left: Life time
     License Type: Permanent
     License State: Active, In Use
     License Count: Non-Counted
     License Priority: Medium
Index 4 Feature: datak9
     Period left: Not Activated
     Period Used: 0  minute  0  second
     License Type: EvalRightToUse
     License State: Not in Use, EULA not accepted
     License Count: Non-Counted
     License Priority: None
Index 5 Feature: gatekeeper
 [output cut]
```

You can see in the preceding output that the ipbasek9 is permanent and the securityk9 has a license type of EvalRightToUse. The show license feature command provides the same information as show license, but it's summarized into one line as shown in the next output:

```
Router#sh license feature
```

Feature name	Enforcement	Evaluation	Subscription	Enabled	RightToUse
ipbasek9	no	no	no	yes	no
securityk9	yes	yes	no	no	yes
uck9	yes	yes	no	yes	yes
datak9	yes	yes	no	no	yes
gatekeeper	yes	yes	no	no	yes
SSL_VPN	yes	yes	no	no	yes
ios-ips-update	yes	yes	yes	no	yes
SNASw	yes	yes	no	no	yes
hseck9	yes	no	no	no	no
cme-srst	yes	yes	no	yes	yes
WAAS_Express	yes	yes	no	no	yes
UCVideo	yes	yes	no	no	yes

The show version command also shows the license information at the end of the command output:

```
Router#show version
[output cut]
License Info:

License UDI:

-------------------------------------------------
Device#   PID                   SN
-------------------------------------------------

*0       CISCO2901/K9          FTX1641Y07J


Technology Package License Information for Module:'c2900'


----------------------------------------------------------------
Technology   Technology-package        Technology-package
             Current      Type         Next reboot
----------------------------------------------------------------
ipbase       ipbasek9     Permanent    ipbasek9
security     None         None         None
```

```
uc            uck9          Permanent      uck9
data          None          None           None
```

```
Configuration register is 0x2102
```

The show version command shows if the license was activated. Don't forget, you'll need to reload the router to have the license features take effect if the license evaluation is not already active.

Backing Up and Uninstalling the License

It would be a shame to lose your license if it has been stored in flash and your flash files become corrupted. So always back up your IOS license!

If your license has been saved in a location other than flash, you can easily back it up to flash memory via the license save command:

```
Router#license save flash:Todd_License.lic
```

The previous command will save your current license to flash. You can restore your license with the license install command I demonstrated earlier.

There are two steps to uninstalling the license on a router. First, to uninstall the license you need to disable the technology package, using the no license boot module command with the keyword disable at the end of the command line:

```
Router#license boot module c2900 technology-package securityk9 disable
```

The second step is to clear the license. To achieve this from the router, use the license clear command and then remove the license with the no license boot module command:

```
Router#license clear securityk9
Router#config t
Router(config)#no license boot module c2900 technology-package securityk9
disable
Router(config)#exit
Router#reload
```

After you run through the preceding commands, the license will be removed from your router.

Here's a summary of the license commands I used in this chapter. These are important commands to have down and you really need to understand these to meet the Cisco objectives:

- show license determines the licenses that are active on your system. It also displays a group of lines for each feature in the currently running IOS image along with several status variables related to software activation and licensing, both licensed and unlicensed features.

- show license feature allows you to view the technology package licenses and feature licenses that are supported on your router along with several status variables related to software activation and licensing. This includes both licensed and unlicensed features.

- show license udi displays the unique device identifier (UDI) of the router, which comprises the product ID (PID) and serial number of the router.

- show version displays various pieces of information about the current IOS version, including the licensing details at the end of the command's output.

- license install *url* installs a license key file into a router.

- license boot module installs a Right-To-Use license feature on a router.

To help you organize a large amount of licenses, search on Cisco.com for the Cisco Smart Software Manager. This web page enables you to manage all your licenses from one centralized website. With Cisco Smart Software Manager, you organize and view your licenses in groups that are called *virtual accounts*, which are collections of licenses and product instances.

Summary

You now know how Cisco routers are configured and how to manage those configurations.

This chapter covered the internal components of a router, which included ROM, RAM, NVRAM, and flash.

In addition, I covered what happens when a router boots and which files are loaded at that time. The configuration register tells the router how to boot and where to find files. You learned how to change and verify the configuration register settings for password recovery purposes. I also showed you how to manage these files using the CLI and IFS.

Finally, the chapter covered licensing with the new 15.0 code, including how to install a permanent license and a Right-To-Use license to install features for 60 days. I also showed you the verification commands used to see what licenses are installed and to verify their status.

Exam Essentials

Define the Cisco router components. Describe the functions of the bootstrap, POST, ROM monitor, mini-IOS, RAM, ROM, flash memory, NVRAM, and the configuration register.

Identify the steps in the router boot sequence.   The steps in the boot sequence are POST, loading the IOS, and copying the startup configuration from NVRAM to RAM.

Understand configuration register commands and settings.   The 0x2102 setting is the default on all Cisco routers and tells the router to look in NVRAM for the boot sequence. 0x2101 tells the router to boot from ROM, and 0x2142 tells the router not to load the startup-config in NVRAM to provide password recovery.

Perform password recovery.   The steps in the password recovery process are interrupt the router boot sequence, change the configuration register, reload the router and enter privileged mode, copy the startup-config file to running-config and verify that your interfaces are re-enabled, change/set the password, save the new configuration, reset the configuration register, and reload the router.

Back up an IOS image.   By using the privileged-mode command copy flash tftp, you can back up a file from flash memory to a TFTP (network) server.

Restore or upgrade an IOS image.   By using the privileged-mode command copy tftp flash, you can restore or upgrade a file from a TFTP (network) server to flash memory.

Describe best practices to prepare to back up an IOS image to a network server.   Make sure that you can access the network server, ensure that the network server has adequate space for the code image, and verify the file naming and path requirement.

Understand and use Cisco IFS file system management commands.   The commands to use are dir, copy, more, delete, erase or format, cd and pwd, and mkdir and rmdir, as well as system:running-config and nvram:startup-config.

Remember how to install a permanent and Right-To-Use license.   To install a permanent license on a router, use the install license url command. To install an evaluation feature, use the license boot module command.

Remember the verification commands used for licensing in the new ISR G2 routers.   The show license command determines the licenses that are active on your system. The show license feature command allows you to view the technology package licenses and feature licenses that are supported on your router. The show license udi command displays the unique device identifier (UDI) of the router, which comprises the product ID (PID) and serial number of the router, and the show version command displays information about the current IOS version, including the licensing details at the end of the command's output.

Written Lab 8

You can find the answers to this labs in Appendix A, "Answers to Written Labs."

In this section, you'll complete the following lab to make sure you've got the information and concepts contained within them fully dialed in:

Lab 8.1: IOS Management

Written Lab 8.1: IOS Management

Write the answers to the following questions:

1. What is the command to copy a Cisco IOS to a TFTP server?

2. What do you set the configuration register setting to in order to boot the mini-IOS in ROM?

3. What is the configuration register setting to tell the router to look in NVRAM for the boot sequence?

4. What do you set the configuration register setting to in order to boot to ROM monitor mode?

5. What is used with a PAK to generate a license file?

6. What is the configuration register setting for password recovery?

7. Which command can change the location from which the system loads the IOS?

8. What is the first step of the router boot sequence?

9. What command can you use to upgrade a Cisco IOS?

10. Which command determines the licenses that are active on your system?

Hands-on Labs

To complete the labs in this section, you need at least one router (three would be best) and at least one PC running as a TFTP server. TFTP server software must be installed and running on the PC. For these labs, it is also assumed that your PC and the router(s) are connected together with a switch or hub and that all interfaces (PC NIC and router interfaces) are in the same subnet. You can alternately connect the PC directly to the router or connect the routers directly to one another (use a crossover cable in that case). Remember that the labs listed here were created for use with real routers but can easily be used with the LammleSim IOS version (found at www.lammle.com/ccna) or Cisco's Packet Tracer program.

Here is a list of the labs in this chapter:

Lab 8.1: Backing Up Your Router IOS

Lab 8.2: Upgrading or Restoring Your Router IOS

Hands-on Lab 8.1: Backing Up Your Router IOS

In this lab, we'll be backing up the IOS from flash to a TFTP host.

1. Log into your router and go into privileged mode by typing **en** or **enable**.

2. Make sure you can connect to the TFTP server that is on your network by pinging the IP address from the router console.

3. Type **show flash** to see the contents of flash memory.

4. Type **show version** at the router privileged-mode prompt to get the name of the IOS currently running on the router. If there is only one file in flash memory, the show flash and show version commands show the same file. Remember that the show version command shows you the file that is currently running and the show flash command shows you all of the files in flash memory.

5. Once you know you have good Ethernet connectivity to the TFTP server and you also know the IOS filename, back up your IOS by typing **copy flash tftp**. This command tells the router to copy a specified file from flash memory (this is where the IOS is stored by default) to a TFTP server.

6. Enter the IP address of the TFTP server and the source IOS filename. The file is now copied and stored in the TFTP server's default directory.

Hands-on Lab 8.2: Upgrading or Restoring Your Router IOS

In this lab, we'll be copying an IOS from a TFTP host to flash memory.

1. Log into your router and go into privileged mode by typing **en** or **enable**.

2. Make sure you can connect to the TFTP server by pinging the IP address of the server from the router console.

3. Once you know you have good Ethernet connectivity to the TFTP server, type the **copy tftp flash** command.

4. Confirm that the router will not function during the restore or upgrade by following the prompts provided on the router console. It is possible this prompt may not occur.

5. Enter the IP address of the TFTP server.

6. Enter the name of the IOS file you want to restore or upgrade.

7. Confirm that you understand that the contents of flash memory will be erased if there is not enough room in flash to store the new image.

8. Watch in amazement as your IOS is deleted out of flash memory and your new IOS is copied to flash memory.

If the file that was in flash memory is deleted but the new version wasn't copied to flash memory, the router will boot from ROM monitor mode. You'll need to figure out why the copy operation did not take place.

Review Questions

The following questions are designed to test your understanding of this chapter's material. For more information on how to get additional questions, please see www.lammle.com/ccna.

You can find the answers to these questions in Appendix B, "Answers to Review Questions."

1. What does the command `confreg 0x2142` provide?

    A. It is used to restart the router.

    B. It is used to bypass the configuration in NVRAM.

    C. It is used to enter ROM monitor mode.

    D. It is used to view the lost password.

2. Which command will copy the IOS to a backup host on your network?

    A. `transfer IOS to 172.16.10.1`

    B. `copy run start`

    C. `copy tftp flash`

    D. `copy start tftp`

    E. `copy flash tftp`

3. What command is used to permanently install a license on an ISR2 router?

    A. `install license`

    B. `license install`

    C. `boot system license`

    D. `boot license module`

4. You type the following into the router and reload. What will the router do?

    ```
    Router(config)#boot system flash c2800nm-advsecurityk9-mz.151-4.M6.bin
    Router(config)#config-register 0x2101
    Router(config)#do sh ver
    [output cut]
    Configuration register is 0x2102 (will be 0x2101 at next reload)
    ```

    A. The router will expand and run the c2800nm-advsecurityk9-mz.151-4.M6.bin IOS from flash memory.

    B. The router will go into setup mode.

    C. The router will load the mini-IOS from ROM.

    D. The router will enter ROM monitor mode.

5. A network administrator wants to upgrade the IOS of a router without removing the image currently installed. What command will display the amount of memory consumed by the current IOS image and indicate whether there is enough room available to hold both the current and new images?

   A. `show version`

   B. `show flash`

   C. `show memory`

   D. `show buffers`

   E. `show running-config`

6. The corporate office sends you a new router to connect, but upon connecting the console cable, you see that there is already a configuration on the router. What should be done before a new configuration is entered in the router?

   A. RAM should be erased and the router restarted.

   B. Flash should be erased and the router restarted.

   C. NVRAM should be erased and the router restarted.

   D. The new configuration should be entered and saved.

7. Which command loads a new version of the Cisco IOS into a router?

   A. `copy flash ftp`

   B. `copy nvram flash`

   C. `copy flash tftp`

   D. `copy tftp flash`

8. Which command will show you the IOS version running on your router?

   A. `sh IOS`

   B. `sh flash`

   C. `sh version`

   D. `sh protocols`

9. What should the configuration register value be after you successfully complete the password recovery procedure and return the router to normal operation?

   A. 0x2100

   B. 0x2101

   C. 0x2102

   D. 0x2142

10. You save the configuration on a router with the `copy running-config startup-config` command and reboot the router. The router, however, comes up with a blank configuration. What can the problem be?

   A. You didn't boot the router with the correct command.

   B. NVRAM is corrupted.

    C. The configuration register setting is incorrect.

    D. The newly upgraded IOS is not compatible with the hardware of the router.

    E. The configuration you saved is not compatible with the hardware.

11. Which command will install a Right-To-Use license so you can use an evaluation version of a feature?

    A. `install Right-To-Use license feature` *feature*

    B. `install temporary feature` *feature*

    C. `license install feature`

    D. `license boot module`

12. Which command determines the licenses that are active on your system along with several status variables?

    A. `show license`

    B. `show license feature`

    C. `show license udi`

    D. `show version`

13. Which command allows you to view the technology package licenses and feature licenses that are supported on your router along with several status variables?

    A. `show license`

    B. `show license feature`

    C. `show license udi`

    D. `show version`

14. Which command displays the unique device identifier that comprises the product ID and serial number of the router?

    A. `show license`

    B. `show license feature`

    C. `show license udi`

    D. `show version`

15. Which command displays various pieces of information about the current IOS version, including the licensing details at the end of the command's output?

    A. `show license`

    B. `show license feature`

    C. `show license udi`

    D. `show version`

16. Which command backs up your license to flash memory?

    A. `copy tftp flash`

    B. `save license flash`

    C. `license save flash`

    D. `copy license flash`

17. Which command displays the configuration register setting?

    A. `show ip route`

    B. `show boot version`

    C. `show version`

    D. `show flash`

18. What two steps are needed to remove a license from a router? (Choose two.)

    A. Use the `erase flash:license` command.

    B. Reload the system.

    C. Use the `license boot` command with the `disable` variable at the end of the command line.

    D. Clear the license with the `license clear` command.

19. You have your laptop directly connected into a router's Ethernet port. Which of the following are among the requirements for the `copy flash tftp` command to be successful? (Choose three.)

    A. TFTP server software must be running on the router.

    B. TFTP server software must be running on your laptop.

    C. The Ethernet cable connecting the laptop directly into the router's Ethernet port must be a straight-through cable.

    D. The laptop must be on the same subnet as the router's Ethernet interface.

    E. The `copy flash tftp` command must be supplied the IP address of the laptop.

    F. There must be enough room in the flash memory of the router to accommodate the file to be copied.

20. The configuration register setting of 0x2102 provides what function to a router?

    A. Tells the router to boot into ROM monitor mode

    B. Provides password recovery

    C. Tells the router to look in NVRAM for the boot sequence

    D. Boots the IOS from a TFTP server

    E. Boots an IOS image stored in ROM

Chapter

9

IP Routing

THE FOLLOWING ICND1 EXAM TOPICS ARE COVERED IN THIS CHAPTER:

✓ **3.0 Routing Technologies**

- 3.1 Describe the routing concepts
    - 3.1.a Packet handling along the path through a network
    - 3.1.b Forwarding decision based on route lookup
    - 3.1.c Frame rewrite
- 3.2 Interpret the components of routing table
    - 3.2.a Prefix
    - 3.2.b Network mask
    - 3.2.c Next hop
    - 3.2.d Routing protocol code
    - 3.2.e Administrative distance
    - 3.2.f Metric
    - 3.2.g Gateway of last resort
- 3.3 Describe how a routing table is populated by different routing information sources
    - 3.3.a Admin distance
- 3.5 Compare and contrast static routing and dynamic routing
- 3.6 Configure, verify, and troubleshoot IPv4 and IPv6 static routing
    - 3.6.a Default route
    - 3.6.b Network route
    - 3.6.c Host route
    - 3.6.d Floating static
- 3.7 Configure, verify, and troubleshoot RIPv2 for IPv4 (excluding authentication, filtering, manual summarization, redistribution)

It's time now to turn our focus toward the core topic of the ubiquitous IP routing process. It's integral to networking because it pertains to all routers and configurations that use it, which is easily the lion's share. IP routing is basically the process of moving packets from one network to another network using routers. And by routers, I mean Cisco routers, of course! However, the terms *router* and *layer 3 device* are interchangeable, and throughout this chapter when I use the term *router*, I am referring to any layer 3 device.

Before jumping into this chapter, I want to make sure you understand the difference between a *routing protocol* and a *routed protocol*. Routers use routing protocols to dynamically find all networks within the greater internetwork and to ensure that all routers have the same routing table. Routing protocols are also employed to determine the best path a packet should take through an internetwork to get to its destination most efficiently. RIP, RIPv2, EIGRP, and OSPF are great examples of the most common routing protocols.

Once all routers know about all networks, a routed protocol can be used to send user data (packets) through the established enterprise. Routed protocols are assigned to an interface and determine the method of packet delivery. Examples of routed protocols are IP and IPv6.

I'm pretty confident I don't have to underscore how crucial it is for you to have this chapter's material down to a near instinctive level. IP routing is innately what Cisco routers do, and they do it very well, so having a firm grasp of the fundamentals and basics of this topic is vital if you want to excel during the exam and in a real-world networking environment as well!

In this chapter, I'm going to show you how to configure and verify IP routing with Cisco routers and guide you through these five key subjects:

- Routing basics
- The IP routing process
- Static routing
- Default routing
- Dynamic routing

I want to start by nailing down the basics of how packets actually move through an internetwork, so let's get started!

To find up-to-the-minute updates for this chapter, please see www.lammle.com/ccna or the book's web page at www.sybex.com/go/ccna.

Routing Basics

Once you create an internetwork by connecting your WANs and LANs to a router, you'll need to configure logical network addresses, like IP addresses, to all hosts on that internetwork for them to communicate successfully throughout it.

The term *routing* refers to taking a packet from one device and sending it through the network to another device on a different network. Routers don't really care about hosts—they only care about networks and the best path to each one of them. The logical network address of the destination host is key to getting packets through a routed network. It's the hardware address of the host that's used to deliver the packet from a router and ensure it arrives at the correct destination host.

Routing is irrelevant if your network has no routers because their job is to route traffic to all the networks in your internetwork, but this is rarely the case! So here's an important list of the minimum factors a router must know to be able to effectively route packets:

- Destination address
- Neighbor routers from which it can learn about remote networks
- Possible routes to all remote networks
- The best route to each remote network
- How to maintain and verify routing information

The router learns about remote networks from neighboring routers or from an administrator. The router then builds a routing table, which is basically a map of the internetwork, and it describes how to find remote networks. If a network is directly connected, then the router already knows how to get to it.

But if a network isn't directly connected to the router, the router must use one of two ways to learn how to get to the remote network. The *static routing* method requires someone to hand-type all network locations into the routing table, which can be a pretty daunting task when used on all but the smallest of networks!

Conversely, when *dynamic routing* is used, a protocol on one router communicates with the same protocol running on neighboring routers. The routers then update each other about all the networks they know about and place this information into the routing table. If a change occurs in the network, the dynamic routing protocols automatically inform all routers about the event. If static routing is used, the administrator is responsible for updating all changes by hand onto all routers. Most people usually use a combination of dynamic and static routing to administer a large network.

Before we jump into the IP routing process, let's take a look at a very simple example that demonstrates how a router uses the routing table to route packets out of an interface. We'll be going into a more detailed study of the process soon, but I want to show you something called the "longest match rule" first. With it, IP will scan a routing table to find the longest match as compared to the destination address of a packet. Let's take a look at Figure 9.1 to get a picture of this process.

FIGURE 9.1 A simple routing example

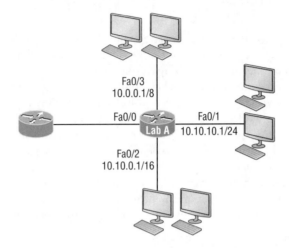

Figure 9.1 shows a simple network. Lab_A has four interfaces. Can you see which interface will be used to forward an IP datagram to a host with a destination IP address of 10.10.10.30?

By using the command show ip route on a router, we can see the routing table (map of the internetwork) that Lab_A has used to make its forwarding decisions:

```
Lab_A#sh ip route
Codes: L - local, C - connected, S - static,
[output cut]
        10.0.0.0/8 is variably subnetted, 6 subnets, 4 masks
C       10.0.0.0/8 is directly connected, FastEthernet0/3
L       10.0.0.1/32 is directly connected, FastEthernet0/3
C       10.10.0.0/16 is directly connected, FastEthernet0/2
L       10.10.0.1/32 is directly connected, FastEthernet0/2
C       10.10.10.0/24 is directly connected, FastEthernet0/1
L       10.10.10.1/32 is directly connected, FastEthernet0/1
S*      0.0.0.0/0 is directly connected, FastEthernet0/0
```

The C in the routing table output means that the networks listed are "directly connected," and until we add a routing protocol like RIPv2, OSPF, etc. to the routers in our internetwork, or enter static routes, only directly connected networks will show up in our routing table. But wait—what about that L in the routing table—that's new, isn't it? Yes it is, because in the new Cisco IOS 15 code, Cisco defines a different route, called a local host route. Each local route has a /32 prefix, defining a route just for the one address. So in this example, the router has relied upon these routes that list their own local IP addresses to more efficiently forward packets to the router itself.

So let's get back to the original question: By looking at the figure and the output of the routing table, can you determine what IP will do with a received packet that has a destination IP address of 10.10.10.30? The answer is that the router will packet-switch the packet to interface FastEthernet 0/1, which will frame the packet and then send it out on the network segment. This is referred to as frame rewrite. Based upon the longest match rule, IP would look for 10.10.10.30, and if that isn't found in the table, then IP would search for 10.10.10.0, then 10.10.0.0, and so on until a route is discovered.

Here's another example: Based on the output of the next routing table, which interface will a packet with a destination address of 10.10.10.14 be forwarded from?

```
Lab_A#sh ip route
[output cut]
Gateway of last resort is not set
C       10.10.10.16/28 is directly connected, FastEthernet0/0
L       10.10.10.17/32 is directly connected, FastEthernet0/0
C       10.10.10.8/29 is directly connected, FastEthernet0/1
L       10.10.10.9/32 is directly connected, FastEthernet0/1
C       10.10.10.4/30 is directly connected, FastEthernet0/2
L       10.10.10.5/32 is directly connected, FastEthernet0/2
C       10.10.10.0/30 is directly connected, Serial 0/0
L       10.10.10.1/32 is directly connected, Serial0/0
```

To figure this out, look closely at the output until you see that the network is subnetted and each interface has a different mask. And I have to tell you—you just can't answer this question if you can't subnet! 10.10.10.14 would be a host in the 10.10.10.8/29 subnet that's connected to the FastEthernet0/1 interface. Don't freak if you're struggling and don't get this! Instead, just go back and reread Chapter 4, "Easy Subnetting," until it becomes clear to you.

The IP Routing Process

The IP routing process is fairly simple and doesn't change, regardless of the size of your network. For a good example of this fact, I'll use Figure 9.2 to describe step-by-step what happens when Host A wants to communicate with Host B on a different network.

FIGURE 9.2 IP routing example using two hosts and one router

In Figure 9.2 a user on Host_A pinged Host_B's IP address. Routing doesn't get any simpler than this, but it still involves a lot of steps, so let's work through them now:

1. Internet Control Message Protocol (ICMP) creates an echo request payload, which is simply the alphabet in the data field.

2. ICMP hands that payload to Internet Protocol (IP), which then creates a packet. At a minimum, this packet contains an IP source address, an IP destination address, and a Protocol field with 01h. Don't forget that Cisco likes to use *0x* in front of hex characters, so this could also look like 0x01. This tells the receiving host to whom it should hand the payload when the destination is reached—in this example, ICMP.

3. Once the packet is created, IP determines whether the destination IP address is on the local network or a remote one.

4. Since IP has determined that this is a remote request, the packet must be sent to the default gateway so it can be routed to the remote network. The Registry in Windows is parsed to find the configured default gateway.

5. The default gateway of Host_A is configured to 172.16.10.1. For this packet to be sent to the default gateway, the hardware address of the router's interface Ethernet 0, which is configured with the IP address of 172.16.10.1, must be known. Why? So the packet can be handed down to the Data Link layer, framed, and sent to the router's interface that's connected to the 172.16.10.0 network. Because hosts communicate only via hardware addresses on the local LAN, it's important to recognize that for Host_A to communicate to Host_B, it has to send packets to the Media Access Control (MAC) address of the default gateway on the local network.

 MAC addresses are always local on the LAN and never go through and past a router.

6. Next, the Address Resolution Protocol (ARP) cache of the host is checked to see if the IP address of the default gateway has already been resolved to a hardware address.

   If it has, the packet is then free to be handed to the Data Link layer for framing. Remember that the hardware destination address is also handed down with that packet. To view the ARP cache on your host, use the following command:

```
C:\>arp -a
Interface: 172.16.10.2 --- 0x3
  Internet Address      Physical Address       Type
   172.16.10.1          00-15-05-06-31-b0      dynamic
```

   If the hardware address isn't already in the ARP cache of the host, an ARP broadcast will be sent out onto the local network to search for the 172.16.10.1 hardware address. The router then responds to the request and provides the hardware address of Ethernet 0, and the host caches this address.

7. Once the packet and destination hardware address are handed to the Data Link layer, the LAN driver is used to provide media access via the type of LAN being used, which

is Ethernet in this case. A frame is then generated, encapsulating the packet with control information. Within that frame are the hardware destination and source addresses plus, in this case, an Ether-Type field, which identifies the specific Network layer protocol that handed the packet to the Data Link layer. In this instance, it's IP. At the end of the frame is something called a Frame Check Sequence (FCS) field that houses the result of the cyclic redundancy check (CRC). The frame would look something like what I've detailed in Figure 9.3. It contains Host A's hardware (MAC) address and the destination hardware address of the default gateway. It does not include the remote host's MAC address—remember that!

FIGURE 9.3   Frame used from Host A to the Lab_A router when Host B is pinged

Destination MAC (router's E0 MAC address)	Source MAC (Host A MAC address)	Ether-Type field	Packet	FCS CRC

8. Once the frame is completed, it's handed down to the Physical layer to be put on the physical medium (in this example, twisted-pair wire) one bit at a time.

9. Every device in the collision domain receives these bits and builds the frame. They each run a CRC and check the answer in the FCS field. If the answers don't match, the frame is discarded.

    ▪ If the CRC matches, then the hardware destination address is checked to see if it matches (which, in this example, is the router's interface Ethernet 0).

    ▪ If it's a match, then the Ether-Type field is checked to find the protocol used at the Network layer.

10. The packet is pulled from the frame, and what is left of the frame is discarded. The packet is handed to the protocol listed in the Ether-Type field—it's given to IP.

11. IP receives the packet and checks the IP destination address. Since the packet's destination address doesn't match any of the addresses configured on the receiving router itself, the router will look up the destination IP network address in its routing table.

12. The routing table must have an entry for the network 172.16.20.0 or the packet will be discarded immediately and an ICMP message will be sent back to the originating device with a destination network unreachable message.

13. If the router does find an entry for the destination network in its table, the packet is switched to the exit interface—in this example, interface Ethernet 1. The following output displays the Lab_A router's routing table. The C means "directly connected." No routing protocols are needed in this network since all networks (all two of them) are directly connected.

```
Lab_A>sh ip route
C       172.16.10.0 is directly connected,    Ethernet0
L       172.16.10.1/32 is directly connected, Ethernet0
C       172.16.20.0 is directly connected,    Ethernet1
L       172.16.20.1/32 is directly connected, Ethernet1
```

14. The router packet-switches the packet to the Ethernet 1 buffer.

15. The Ethernet 1 buffer needs to know the hardware address of the destination host and first checks the ARP cache.
    - If the hardware address of Host_B has already been resolved and is in the router's ARP cache, then the packet and the hardware address will be handed down to the Data Link layer to be framed. Let's take a look at the ARP cache on the Lab_A router by using the show ip arp command:

    ```
    Lab_A#sh ip arp
    Protocol  Address       Age(min) Hardware Addr   Type   Interface
    Internet  172.16.20.1   -         00d0.58ad.05f4  ARPA   Ethernet1
    Internet  172.16.20.2   3         0030.9492.a5dd  ARPA   Ethernet1
    Internet  172.16.10.1   -         00d0.58ad.06aa  ARPA   Ethernet0
    Internet  172.16.10.2   12        0030.9492.a4ac  ARPA   Ethernet0
    ```

    The dash (-) signifies that this is the physical interface on the router. This output shows us that the router knows the 172.16.10.2 (Host_A) and 172.16.20.2 (Host_B) hardware addresses. Cisco routers will keep an entry in the ARP table for 4 hours.

    - Now if the hardware address hasn't already been resolved, the router will send an ARP request out E1 looking for the 172.16.20.2 hardware address. Host_B responds with its hardware address, and the packet and destination hardware addresses are then both sent to the Data Link layer for framing.

16. The Data Link layer creates a frame with the destination and source hardware addresses, Ether-Type field, and FCS field at the end. The frame is then handed to the Physical layer to be sent out on the physical medium one bit at a time.

17. Host_B receives the frame and immediately runs a CRC. If the result matches the information in the FCS field, the hardware destination address will then be checked next. If the host finds a match, the Ether-Type field is then checked to determine the protocol that the packet should be handed to at the Network layer—IP in this example.

18. At the Network layer, IP receives the packet and runs a CRC on the IP header. If that passes, IP then checks the destination address. Since a match has finally been made, the Protocol field is checked to find out to whom the payload should be given.

19. The payload is handed to ICMP, which understands that this is an echo request. ICMP responds to this by immediately discarding the packet and generating a new payload as an echo reply.

20. A packet is then created including the source and destination addresses, Protocol field, and payload. The destination device is now Host_A.

21. IP then checks to see whether the destination IP address is a device on the local LAN or on a remote network. Since the destination device is on a remote network, the packet needs to be sent to the default gateway.

22. The default gateway IP address is found in the Registry of the Windows device, and the ARP cache is checked to see if the hardware address has already been resolved from an IP address.

23. Once the hardware address of the default gateway is found, the packet and destination hardware addresses are handed down to the Data Link layer for framing.

24. The Data Link layer frames the packet of information and includes the following in the header:

- The destination and source hardware addresses
- The Ether-Type field with 0x0800 (IP) in it
- The FCS field with the CRC result in tow

25. The frame is now handed down to the Physical layer to be sent out over the network medium one bit at a time.

26. The router's Ethernet 1 interface receives the bits and builds a frame. The CRC is run, and the FCS field is checked to make sure the answers match.

27. Once the CRC is found to be okay, the hardware destination address is checked. Since the router's interface is a match, the packet is pulled from the frame and the Ether-Type field is checked to determine which protocol the packet should be delivered to at the Network layer.

28. The protocol is determined to be IP, so it gets the packet. IP runs a CRC check on the IP header first and then checks the destination IP address.

IP does not run a complete CRC as the Data Link layer does—it only checks the header for errors.

Since the IP destination address doesn't match any of the router's interfaces, the routing table is checked to see whether it has a route to 172.16.10.0. If it doesn't have a route over to the destination network, the packet will be discarded immediately. I want to take a minute to point out that this is exactly where the source of confusion begins for a lot of administrators because when a ping fails, most people think the packet never reached the destination host. But as we see here, that's not *always* the case. All it takes for this to happen is for even just one of the remote routers to lack a route back to the originating host's network and—*poof!*—the packet is dropped on the *return trip*, not on its way to the host!

Just a quick note to mention that when (and if) the packet is lost on the way back to the originating host, you will typically see a request timed-out message because it is an unknown error. If the error occurs because of a known issue, such as if a route is not in the routing table on the way to the destination device, you will see a destination unreachable message. This should help you determine if the problem occurred on the way to the destination or on the way back.

29. In this case, the router happens to know how to get to network 172.16.10.0—the exit interface is Ethernet 0—so the packet is switched to interface Ethernet 0.

30. The router then checks the ARP cache to determine whether the hardware address for 172.16.10.2 has already been resolved.

31. Since the hardware address to 172.16.10.2 is already cached from the originating trip to Host_B, the hardware address and packet are then handed to the Data Link layer.

32. The Data Link layer builds a frame with the destination hardware address and source hardware address and then puts IP in the Ether-Type field. A CRC is run on the frame and the result is placed in the FCS field.

33. The frame is then handed to the Physical layer to be sent out onto the local network one bit at a time.

34. The destination host receives the frame, runs a CRC, checks the destination hardware address, then looks into the Ether-Type field to find out to whom to hand the packet.

35. IP is the designated receiver, and after the packet is handed to IP at the Network layer, it checks the Protocol field for further direction. IP finds instructions to give the payload to ICMP, and ICMP determines the packet to be an ICMP echo reply.

36. ICMP acknowledges that it has received the reply by sending an exclamation point (!) to the user interface. ICMP then attempts to send four more echo requests to the destination host.

You've just experienced Todd's 36 easy steps to understanding IP routing. The key point here is that if you had a much larger network, the process would be the *same*. It's just that the larger the internetwork, the more hops the packet goes through before it finds the destination host.

It's super-important to remember that when Host_A sends a packet to Host_B, the destination hardware address used is the default gateway's Ethernet interface. Why? Because frames can't be placed on remote networks—only local networks. So packets destined for remote networks must go through the default gateway.

Let's take a look at Host_A's ARP cache now:

```
C:\ >arp -a
Interface: 172.16.10.2 --- 0x3
   Internet Address        Physical Address        Type
   172.16.10.1             00-15-05-06-31-b0       dynamic
   172.16.20.1             00-15-05-06-31-b0       dynamic
```

Did you notice that the hardware (MAC) address that Host_A uses to get to Host_B is the Lab_A E0 interface? Hardware addresses are *always* local, and they never pass through a router's interface. Understanding this process is as important as air to you, so carve this into your memory!

The Cisco Router Internal Process

One more thing before we get to testing your understanding of my 36 steps of IP routing. I think it's important to explain how a router forwards packets internally. For IP to look up a destination address in a routing table on a router, processing in the router must take place, and if there are tens of thousands of routes in that table, the amount of CPU time would be enormous. It results in a potentially overwhelming amount of overhead—think about a router at your ISP that has to calculate millions of packets per second and even subnet to find the correct exit interface! Even with the little network I'm using in this book, lots of processing would need to be done if there were actual hosts connected and sending data.

Cisco uses three types of packet-forwarding techniques.

Process switching   This is actually how many people see routers to this day, because it's true that routers actually did perform this type of bare-bones packet switching back in 1990 when Cisco released their very first router. But those days when traffic demands were unimaginably light are long gone—not in today's networks! This process is now extremely complex and involves looking up every destination in the routing table and finding the exit interface for every packet. This is pretty much how I just explained the process in my 36 steps. But even though what I wrote was absolutely true in concept, the internal process requires much more than packet-switching technology today because of the millions of packets per second that must now be processed. So Cisco came up with some other technologies to help with the "big process problem."

Fast switching   This solution was created to make the slow performance of process switching faster and more efficient. Fast switching uses a cache to store the most recently used destinations so that lookups are not required for every packet. By caching the exit interface of the destination device, as well as the layer 2 header, performance was dramatically improved, but as our networks evolved with the need for even more speed, Cisco created yet another technology!

Cisco Express Forwarding (CEF)   This is Cisco's newer creation, and it's the default packet-forwarding method used on all the latest Cisco routers. CEF makes many different cache tables to help improve performance and is change triggered, not packet triggered. Translated, this means that when the network topology changes, the cache changes along with it.

To see which packet switching method your router interface is using, use the command show ip interface.

Testing Your IP Routing Understanding

Since understanding IP routing is super-important, it's time for that little test I talked about earlier on how well you've got the IP routing process down so far. I'm going to do that by having you look at a couple of figures and answer some very basic IP routing questions based upon them.

Figure 9.4 shows a LAN connected to RouterA that's connected via a WAN link to RouterB. RouterB has a LAN connected with an HTTP server attached.

FIGURE 9.4   IP routing example 1

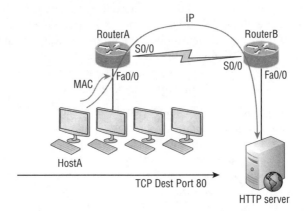

The critical information you want to obtain by looking at this figure is exactly how IP routing will occur in this example. Let's determine the characteristics of a frame as it leaves HostA. Okay—we'll cheat a bit. I'll give you the answer, but then you should go back over the figure and see if you can answer example 2 without looking at my three-step answer!

1. The destination address of a frame from HostA would be the MAC address of Router A's Fa0/0 interface.

2. The destination address of a packet would be the IP address of the HTTP server's network interface card (NIC).

3. The destination port number in the segment header would be 80.

That was a pretty simple, straightforward scenario. One thing to remember is that when multiple hosts are communicating to a server using HTTP, they must all use a different source port number. The source and destination IP addresses and port numbers are how the server keeps the data separated at the Transport layer.

Let's complicate matters by adding another device into the network and then see if you can find the answers. Figure 9.5 shows a network with only one router but two switches.

FIGURE 9.5   IP routing example 2

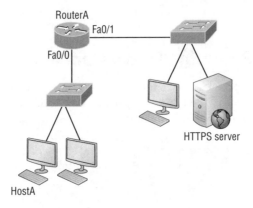

The key thing to understand about the IP routing process in this scenario is what happens when HostA sends data to the HTTPS server? Here's your answer:

1. The destination address of a frame from HostA would be the MAC address of RouterA's Fa0/0 interface.

2. The destination address of a packet is the IP address of the HTTPS server's network interface card (NIC).

3. The destination port number in the segment header will have a value of 443.

Did you notice that the switches weren't used as either a default gateway or any other destination? That's because switches have nothing to do with routing. I wonder how many of you chose the switch as the default gateway (destination) MAC address for HostA? If you did, don't feel bad—just take another look to see where you went wrong and why. It's very important to remember that the destination MAC address will always be the router's interface—if your packets are destined for outside the LAN, as they were in these last two examples!

Before moving on into some of the more advanced aspects of IP routing, let's look at another issue. Take a look at the output of this router's routing table:

```
Corp#sh ip route
[output cut]
R    192.168.215.0 [120/2] via 192.168.20.2, 00:00:23, Serial0/0
R    192.168.115.0 [120/1] via 192.168.20.2, 00:00:23, Serial0/0
R    192.168.30.0 [120/1] via 192.168.20.2, 00:00:23, Serial0/0
C    192.168.20.0 is directly connected, Serial0/0
L    192.168.20.1/32 is directly connected, Serial0/0
C    192.168.214.0 is directly connected, FastEthernet0/0
L    192.168.214.1/32 is directly connected, FastEthernet0/0
```

What do we see here? If I were to tell you that the corporate router received an IP packet with a source IP address of 192.168.214.20 and a destination address of 192.168.22.3, what do you think the Corp router will do with this packet?

If you said, "The packet came in on the FastEthernet 0/0 interface, but because the routing table doesn't show a route to network 192.168.22.0 (or a default route), the router will discard the packet and send an ICMP destination unreachable message back out to interface FastEthernet 0/0," you're a genius! The reason that's the correct answer is because that's the source LAN where the packet originated from.

Now, let's check out the next figure and talk about the frames and packets in detail. We're not really going over anything new here; I'm just making sure you totally, completely, thoroughly, fully understand basic IP routing! It is the crux of this book, and the topic the exam objectives are geared toward. It's all about IP routing, which means you need to be all over this stuff! We'll use Figure 9.6 for the next few scenarios.

FIGURE 9.6   Basic IP routing using MAC and IP addresses

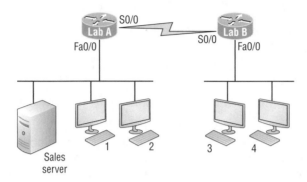

Referring to Figure 9.6, here's a list of all the answers to questions you need inscribed in your brain:

1. In order to begin communicating with the Sales server, Host 4 sends out an ARP request. How will the devices exhibited in the topology respond to this request?

2. Host 4 has received an ARP reply. Host 4 will now build a packet, then place this packet in the frame. What information will be placed in the header of the packet that leaves Host 4 if Host 4 is going to communicate to the Sales server?

3. The Lab_A router has received the packet and will send it out Fa0/0 onto the LAN toward the server. What will the frame have in the header as the source and destination addresses?

4. Host 4 is displaying two web documents from the Sales server in two browser windows at the same time. How did the data find its way to the correct browser windows?

The following should probably be written in a teensy font and put upside down in another part of the book so it would be really hard for you to cheat and peek, but since I'm not that mean and you really need to have this down, here are your answers in the same order that the scenarios were just presented:

1. In order to begin communicating with the server, Host 4 sends out an ARP request. How will the devices exhibited in the topology respond to this request? Since MAC addresses must stay on the local network, the Lab_B router will respond with the MAC address of the Fa0/0 interface and Host 4 will send all frames to the MAC address of the Lab_B Fa0/0 interface when sending packets to the Sales server.

2. Host 4 has received an ARP reply. Host 4 will now build a packet, then place this packet in the frame. What information will be placed in the header of the packet that leaves Host 4 if Host 4 is going to communicate to the Sales server? Since we're now talking about packets, not frames, the source address will be the IP address of Host 4 and the destination address will be the IP address of the Sales server.

3. Finally, the Lab_A router has received the packet and will send it out Fa0/0 onto the LAN toward the server. What will the frame have in the header as the source and

destination addresses? The source MAC address will be the Lab_A router's Fa0/0 interface, and the destination MAC address will be the Sales server's MAC address because all MAC addresses must be local on the LAN.

4. Host 4 is displaying two web documents from the Sales server in two different browser windows at the same time. How did the data find its way to the correct browser windows? TCP port numbers are used to direct the data to the correct application window.

Great! But we're not quite done yet. I've got a few more questions for you before you actually get to configure routing in a real network. Ready? Figure 9.7 shows a basic network, and Host 4 needs to get email. Which address will be placed in the destination address field of the frame when it leaves Host 4?

FIGURE 9.7   Testing basic routing knowledge

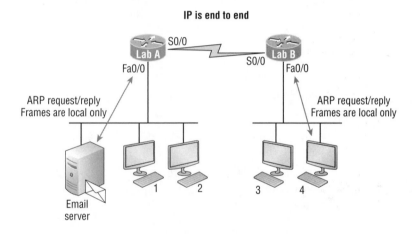

The answer is that Host 4 will use the destination MAC address of the Fa0/0 interface on the Lab_B router—you knew that, right? Look at Figure 9.7 again: What if Host 4 needs to communicate with Host 1—not the server, but with Host 1. Which OSI layer 3 source address will be found in the packet header when it reaches Host 1?

Hopefully you've got this: At layer 3, the source IP address will be Host 4 and the destination address in the packet will be the IP address of Host 1. Of course, the destination MAC address from Host 4 will always be the Fa0/0 address of the Lab_B router, right? And since we have more than one router, we'll need a routing protocol that communicates between both of them so that traffic can be forwarded in the right direction to reach the network that Host 1 is connected to.

Okay—one more scenario and you're on your way to being an IP routing machine! Again, using Figure 9.7, Host 4 is transferring a file to the email server connected to the Lab_A router. What would be the layer 2 destination address leaving Host 4? Yes, I've asked this question more than once. But not this one: What will be the source MAC address when the frame is received at the email server?

Hopefully, you answered that the layer 2 destination address leaving Host 4 is the MAC address of the Fa0/0 interface on the Lab_B router and that the source layer 2 address that the email server will receive is the Fa0/0 interface of the Lab_A router.

If you did, you're ready to discover how IP routing is handled in a larger network environment!

Configuring IP Routing

It's time to get serious and configure a real network. Figure 9.8 shows three routers: Corp, SF, and LA. Remember that, by default, these routers only know about networks that are directly connected to them. I'll continue to use this figure and network throughout the rest of the chapters in this book. As I progress through this book, I'll add more routers and switches as needed.

FIGURE 9.8   Configuring IP routing

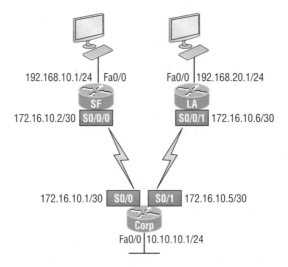

As you might guess, I've got quite a nice collection of routers for us to play with. But you don't need a closet full of devices to perform most, if not all, of the commands we'll use in this book. You can get by nicely with pretty much any router or even with a good router simulator.

Getting back to business, the Corp router has two serial interfaces, which will provide a WAN connection to the SF and LA router and two Fast Ethernet interfaces as well. The two remote routers have two serial interfaces and two Fast Ethernet interfaces.

The first step for this project is to correctly configure each router with an IP address on each interface. The following list shows the IP address scheme I'm going to use to configure the network. After we go over how the network is configured, I'll cover how to configure

IP routing. Pay attention to the subnet masks—they're important! The LANs all use a /24 mask, but the WANs are using a /30.

Corp

- Serial 0/0: 172.16.10.1/30
- Serial 0/1: 172.16.10.5/30
- Fa0/0: 10.10.10.1/24

SF

- S0/0/0: 172.16.10.2/30
- Fa0/0: 192.168.10.1/24

LA

- S0/0/0: 172.16.10.6/30
- Fa0/0: 192.168.20.1/24

The router configuration is really a pretty straightforward process since you just need to add IP addresses to your interfaces and then perform a no shutdown on those same interfaces. It gets a tad more complex later on, but for right now, let's configure the IP addresses in the network.

Corp Configuration

We need to configure three interfaces to configure the Corp router. And configuring the hostnames of each router will make identification much easier. While we're at it, let's set the interface descriptions, banner, and router passwords too because it's a really good idea to make a habit of configuring these commands on every router!

To get started, I performed an erase startup-config on the router and reloaded, so we'll start in setup mode. I chose no when prompted to enter setup mode, which will get us straight to the username prompt of the console. I'm going to configure all my routers this same way.

Here's how what I just did looks:

```
      --- System Configuration Dialog ---
Would you like to enter the initial configuration dialog? [yes/no]: n

Press RETURN to get started!
Router>en
Router#config t
Router(config)#hostname Corp
Corp(config)#enable secret GlobalNet
Corp(config)#no ip domain-lookup
Corp(config)#int f0/0
Corp(config-if)#desc Connection to LAN BackBone
```

```
Corp(config-if)#ip address 10.10.10.1 255.255.255.0
Corp(config-if)#no shut
Corp(config-if)#int s0/0
Corp(config-if)#desc WAN connection to SF
Corp(config-if)#ip address 172.16.10.1 255.255.255.252
Corp(config-if)#no shut
Corp(config-if)#int s0/1
Corp(config-if)#desc WAN connection to LA
Corp(config-if)#ip address 172.16.10.5 255.255.255.252
Corp(config-if)#no shut
Corp(config-if)#line con 0
Corp(config-line)#password console
Corp(config-line)#logging
Corp(config-line)#logging sync
Corp(config-line)#exit
Corp(config)#line vty 0 ?
  <1-181>  Last Line number
  <cr>
Corp(config)#line vty 0 181
Corp(config-line)#password telnet
Corp(config-line)#login
Corp(config-line)#exit
Corp(config)#banner motd # This is my Corp Router #
Corp(config)#^Z
Corp#copy run start
Destination filename [startup-config]?
Building configuration...
[OK]
Corp# [OK]
```

Let's talk about the configuration of the Corp router. First, I set the hostname and enable secret, but what is that no ip domain-lookup command? That command stops the router from trying to resolve hostnames, which is an annoying feature unless you've configured a host table or DNS. Next, I configured the three interfaces with descriptions and IP addresses and enabled them with the no shutdown command. The console and VTY passwords came next, but what is that logging sync command under the console line? The logging synchronous command stops console messages from writing over what you are typing in, meaning it's a sanity-saving command that you'll come to love! Last, I set my banner and then saved my configs.

If you're having a hard time understanding this configuration process, refer back to Chapter 6, "Cisco's Internetworking Operating System (IOS)."

To view the IP routing tables created on a Cisco router, use the command show ip route. Here's the command's output:

```
Corp#sh ip route
Codes: L - local, C - connected, S - static, R - RIP, M - mobile, B - BGP
   D - EIGRP, EX - EIGRP external, O - OSPF, IA - OSPF inter area
   N1 - OSPF NSSA external type 1, N2 - OSPF NSSA external type 2
   E1 - OSPF external type 1, E2 - OSPF external type 2
   i - IS-IS, su - IS-IS summary, L1 - IS-IS level-1, L2 - IS-IS level-2
   ia - IS-IS inter area, * - candidate default, U - per-user static route
   o - ODR, P - periodic downloaded static route, H - NHRP, l - LISP
   + - replicated route, % - next hop override
Gateway of last resort is not set


     10.0.0.0/24 is subnetted, 1 subnets
C       10.10.10.0 is directly connected, FastEthernet0/0
L       10.10.10.1/32 is directly connected, FastEthernet0/0
Corp#
```

It's important to remember that only configured, directly connected networks are going to show up in the routing table. So why is it that only the FastEthernet 0/0 interface shows up in the table? No worries—that's just because you won't see the serial interfaces come up until the other side of the links are operational. As soon as we configure our SF and LA routers, those interfaces should pop right up!

But did you notice the C on the left side of the output of the routing table? When you see that there, it means that the network is directly connected. The codes for each type of connection are listed at the top of the show ip route command, along with their descriptions.

For brevity, the codes at the top of the output will be cut in the rest of this chapter.

SF Configuration

Now we're ready to configure the next router—SF. To make that happen correctly, keep in mind that we have two interfaces to deal with: Serial 0/0/0 and FastEthernet 0/0. So let's make sure we don't forget to add the hostname, passwords, interface descriptions, and banners to the router configuration. As I did with the Corp router, I erased the configuration and reloaded since this router had already been configured before.

Here's the configuration I used:

```
R1#erase start
% Incomplete command.
```

```
R1#erase startup-config
Erasing the nvram filesystem will remove all configuration files!
  Continue? [confirm][enter]
[OK]
Erase of nvram: complete
R1#reload
Proceed with reload? [confirm][enter]
[output cut]
%Error opening tftp://255.255.255.255/network-confg (Timed out)
%Error opening tftp://255.255.255.255/cisconet.cfg (Timed out)


        --- System Configuration Dialog ---


Would you like to enter the initial configuration dialog? [yes/no]: n
```

Before we move on, let's talk about this output for a second. First, notice that beginning with IOS 12.4, ISR routers will no longer take the command erase start. The router has only one command after erase that starts with *s*, as shown here:

```
Router#erase s?
startup-config
```

I know, you'd think that the IOS would continue to accept the command, but nope—sorry! The second thing I want to point out is that the output tells us the router is looking for a TFTP host to see if it can download a configuration. When that fails, it goes straight into setup mode. This gives you a great picture of the Cisco router default boot sequence we talked about in Chapter 7, "Managing a Cisco Internetwork."

Let's get back to configuring our router:

```
Press RETURN to get started!
Router#config t
Router(config)#hostname SF
SF(config)#enable secret GlobalNet
SF(config)#no ip domain-lookup
SF(config)#int s0/0/0
SF(config-if)#desc WAN Connection to Corp
SF(config-if)#ip address 172.16.10.2 255.255.255.252
SF(config-if)#no shut
SF(config-if)#clock rate 1000000
SF(config-if)#int f0/0
SF(config-if)#desc SF LAN
SF(config-if)#ip address 192.168.10.1 255.255.255.0
SF(config-if)#no shut
```

```
SF(config-if)#line con 0
SF(config-line)#password console
SF(config-line)#login
SF(config-line)#logging sync
SF(config-line)#exit
SF(config)#line vty 0 ?
  <1-1180>  Last Line number
  <cr>
SF(config)#line vty 0 1180
SF(config-line)#password telnet
SF(config-line)#login
SF(config-line)#banner motd #This is the SF Branch router#
SF(config)#exit
SF#copy run start
Destination filename [startup-config]?
Building configuration...
 [OK]
```

Let's take a look at our configuration of the interfaces with the following two commands:

```
SF#sh run | begin int
interface FastEthernet0/0
 description SF LAN
 ip address 192.168.10.1 255.255.255.0
 duplex auto
 speed auto
!
interface FastEthernet0/1
 no ip address
 shutdown
 duplex auto
 speed auto
!
interface Serial0/0/0
 description WAN Connection to Corp
 ip address 172.16.10.2 255.255.255.252
 clock rate 1000000
!
SF#sh ip int brief
Interface            IP-Address      OK? Method Status          Protocol
FastEthernet0/0      192.168.10.1    YES manual up              up
```

```
FastEthernet0/1       unassigned      YES unset  administratively down down
Serial0/0/0           172.16.10.2     YES manual up                    up
Serial0/0/1           unassigned      YES unset  administratively down down
SF#
```

Now that both ends of the serial link are configured, the link comes up. Remember, the up/up status for the interfaces are Physical/Data Link layer status indicators that don't reflect the layer 3 status! I ask students in my classes, "If the link shows up/up, can you ping the directly connected network?" And they say, "Yes!" The correct answer is, "I don't know," because we can't see the layer 3 status with this command. We only see layers 1 and 2 and verify that the IP addresses don't have a typo. This is really important to understand!

The show ip route command for the SF router reveals the following:

```
SF#sh ip route
C    192.168.10.0/24 is directly connected, FastEthernet0/0
L    192.168.10.1/32 is directly connected, FastEthernet0/0
     172.16.0.0/30 is subnetted, 1 subnets
C       172.16.10.0 is directly connected, Serial0/0/0
L       172.16.10.2/32 is directly connected, Serial0/0/0
```

Notice that router SF knows how to get to networks 172.16.10.0/30 and 192.168.10.0/24; we can now ping to the Corp router from SF:

```
SF#ping 172.16.10.1

Type escape sequence to abort.
Sending 5, 100-byte ICMP Echos to 172.16.10.1, timeout is 2 seconds:
!!!!!
Success rate is 100 percent (5/5), round-trip min/avg/max = 1/3/4 ms
```

Now let's head back to the Corp router and check out the routing table:

```
Corp>sh ip route
     172.16.0.0/30 is subnetted, 1 subnets
C       172.16.10.0 is directly connected, Serial0/0
L       172.16.10.1/32 is directly connected, Serial0/0
     10.0.0.0/24 is subnetted, 1 subnets
C       10.10.10.0 is directly connected, FastEthernet0/0
L       10.10.10.1/32 is directly connected, FastEthernet0/0
```

On the SF router's serial interface 0/0/0 is a DCE connection, which means a clock rate needs to be set on the interface. Remember that you don't need to use the clock rate command in production. While true, it's still imperative that you know how/when you can use it and that you understand it really well when studying for your CCNA exam!

We can see our clocking with the show controllers command:

```
SF#sh controllers s0/0/0
Interface Serial0/0/0
Hardware is GT96K
DCE V.35, clock rate 1000000
```

```
Corp>sh controllers s0/0
Interface Serial0/0
Hardware is PowerQUICC MPC860
DTE V.35 TX and RX clocks detected.
```

Since the SF router has a DCE cable connection, I needed to add clock rate to this interface because DTE receives clock. Keep in mind that the new ISR routers will autodetect this and set the clock rate to 2000000. And you still need to make sure you're able to find an interface that is DCE and set clocking to meet the objectives.

Since the serial links are showing up, we can now see both networks in the Corp routing table. And once we configure LA, we'll see one more network in the routing table of the Corp router. The Corp router can't see the 192.168.10.0 network because we don't have any routing configured yet—routers see only directly connected networks by default.

LA Configuration

To configure LA, we're going to do pretty much the same thing we did with the other two routers. There are two interfaces to deal with, Serial 0/0/1 and FastEthernet 0/0, and again, we'll be sure to add the hostname, passwords, interface descriptions, and a banner to the router configuration:

```
Router(config)#hostname LA
LA(config)#enable secret GlobalNet
LA(config)#no ip domain-lookup
LA(config)#int s0/0/1
LA(config-if)#ip address 172.16.10.6 255.255.255.252
LA(config-if)#no shut
LA(config-if)#clock rate 1000000
LA(config-if)#description WAN To Corporate
LA(config-if)#int f0/0
LA(config-if)#ip address 192.168.20.1 255.255.255.0
LA(config-if)#no shut
LA(config-if)#description LA LAN
LA(config-if)#line con 0
LA(config-line)#password console
LA(config-line)#login
```

```
LA(config-line)#logging sync
LA(config-line)#exit
LA(config)#line vty 0 ?
  <1-1180>  Last Line number
  <cr>
LA(config)#line vty 0 1180
LA(config-line)#password telnet
LA(config-line)#login
LA(config-line)#exit
LA(config)#banner motd #This is my LA Router#
LA(config)#exit
LA#copy run start
Destination filename [startup-config]?
Building configuration...
[OK]
```

Nice—everything was pretty straightforward. The following output, which I gained via the show ip route command, displays the directly connected networks of 192.168.20.0 and 172.16.10.0:

```
LA#sh ip route
      172.16.0.0/30 is subnetted, 1 subnets
C        172.16.10.4 is directly connected, Serial0/0/1
L        172.16.10.6/32 is directly connected, Serial0/0/1
C     192.168.20.0/24 is directly connected, FastEthernet0/0
L     192.168.20.1/32 is directly connected, FastEthernet0/0
```

So now that we've configured all three routers with IP addresses and administrative functions, we can move on to deal with routing. But I want to do one more thing on the SF and LA routers—since this is a very small network, let's build a DHCP server on the Corp router for each LAN.

Configuring DHCP on Our Corp Router

While it's true that I could approach this task by going to each remote router and creating a pool, why bother with all that when I can easily create two pools on the Corp router and have the remote routers forward requests to the Corp router? Of course, you remember how to do this from Chapter 7!

Let's give it a shot:

```
Corp#config t
Corp(config)#ip dhcp excluded-address 192.168.10.1
Corp(config)#ip dhcp excluded-address 192.168.20.1
Corp(config)#ip dhcp pool SF_LAN
Corp(dhcp-config)#network 192.168.10.0 255.255.255.0
Corp(dhcp-config)#default-router 192.168.10.1
```

```
Corp(dhcp-config)#dns-server 4.4.4.4
Corp(dhcp-config)#exit
Corp(config)#ip dhcp pool LA_LAN
Corp(dhcp-config)#network 192.168.20.0 255.255.255.0
Corp(dhcp-config)#default-router 192.168.20.1
Corp(dhcp-config)#dns-server 4.4.4.4
Corp(dhcp-config)#exit
Corp(config)#exit
Corp#copy run start
Destination filename [startup-config]?
Building configuration...
```

Creating DHCP pools on a router is actually a simple process, and you would go about the configuration the same way on any router you wish to add a DHCP pool to. To designate a router as a DHCP server, you just create the pool name, add the network/subnet and the default gateway, and then exclude any addresses that you don't want handed out. You definitely want to make sure you've excluded the default gateway address, and you'd usually add a DNS server as well. I always add any exclusions first, and remember that you can conveniently exclude a range of addresses on a single line. Soon, I'll demonstrate those verification commands I promised I'd show you back in Chapter 7, but first, we need to figure out why the Corp router still can't get to the remote networks by default!

Now I'm pretty sure I configured DHCP correctly, but I just have this nagging feeling I forgot something important. What could that be? Well, the hosts are remote across a router, so what would I need to do that would allow them to get an address from a DHCP server? If you concluded that I've got to configure the SF and LA F0/0 interfaces to forward the DHCP client requests to the server, you got it!

Here's how we'd go about doing that:

```
LA#config t
LA(config)#int f0/0
LA(config-if)#ip helper-address 172.16.10.5

SF#config t
SF(config)#int f0/0
SF(config-if)#ip helper-address 172.16.10.1
```

I'm pretty sure I did this correctly, but we won't know until I have some type of routing configured and working. So let's get to that next!

Configuring IP Routing in Our Network

So is our network really good to go? After all, I've configured it with IP addressing, administrative functions, and even clocking that will automatically occur with the ISR routers. But how will our routers send packets to remote networks when they get their destination information by looking into their tables that only include directions about directly connected networks? And you know routers promptly discard packets they receive with addresses for networks that aren't listed in their routing table!

So we're not exactly ready to rock after all. But we will be soon because there are several ways to configure the routing tables to include all the networks in our little internetwork so that packets will be properly forwarded. As usual, one size fits all rarely fits at all, and what's best for one network isn't necessarily what's best for another. That's why understanding the different types of routing will be really helpful when choosing the best solution for your specific environment and business requirements.

These are the three routing methods I'm going to cover with you:

- Static routing
- Default routing
- Dynamic routing

We're going to start with the first way and implement static routing on our network, because if you can implement static routing *and* make it work, you've demonstrated that you definitely have a solid understanding of the internetwork. So let's get started.

Static Routing

Static routing is the process that ensues when you manually add routes in each router's routing table. Predictably, there are pros and cons to static routing, but that's true for all routing approaches.

Here are the pros:

- There is no overhead on the router CPU, which means you could probably make do with a cheaper router than you would need for dynamic routing.
- There is no bandwidth usage between routers, saving you money on WAN links as well as minimizing overhead on the router since you're not using a routing protocol.
- It adds security because you, the administrator, can be very exclusive and choose to allow routing access to certain networks only.

And here are the cons:

- Whoever the administrator is must have a vault-tight knowledge of the internetwork and how each router is connected in order to configure routes correctly. If you don't have a good, accurate map of your internetwork, things will get very messy quickly!
- If you add a network to the internetwork, you have to tediously add a route to it on all routers by hand, which only gets increasingly insane as the network grows.
- Due to the last point, it's just not feasible to use it in most large networks because maintaining it would be a full-time job in itself.

But that list of cons doesn't mean you get to skip learning all about it mainly because of that first disadvantage I listed—the fact that you must have such a solid understanding of a network to configure it properly and that your administrative knowledge has to practically verge on the supernatural! So let's dive in and develop those skills. Starting at the beginning, here's the command syntax you use to add a static route to a routing table from global config:

```
ip route [destination_network] [mask] [next-hop_address or
  exitinterface] [administrative_distance] [permanent]
```

This list describes each command in the string:

ip route The command used to create the static route.

destination_network The network you're placing in the routing table.

mask The subnet mask being used on the network.

next-hop_address This is the IP address of the next-hop router that will receive packets and forward them to the remote network, which must signify a router interface that's on a directly connected network. You must be able to successfully ping the router interface before you can add the route. Important note to self is that if you type in the wrong next-hop address or the interface to the correct router is down, the static route will show up in the router's configuration but not in the routing table.

exitinterface Used in place of the next-hop address if you want, and shows up as a directly connected route.

administrative_distance By default, static routes have an administrative distance of 1 or 0 if you use an exit interface instead of a next-hop address. You can change the default value by adding an administrative weight at the end of the command. I'll talk a lot more about this later in the chapter when we get to the section on dynamic routing.

permanent If the interface is shut down or the router can't communicate to the next-hop router, the route will automatically be discarded from the routing table by default. Choosing the permanent option keeps the entry in the routing table no matter what happens.

Before I guide you through configuring static routes, let's take a look at a sample static route to see what we can find out about it:

```
Router(config)#ip route 172.16.3.0 255.255.255.0 192.168.2.4
```

- The ip route command tells us simply that it's a static route.
- 172.16.3.0 is the remote network we want to send packets to.
- 255.255.255.0 is the mask of the remote network.
- 192.168.2.4 is the next hop, or router, that packets will be sent to.

But what if the static route looked like this instead?

```
Router(config)#ip route 172.16.3.0 255.255.255.0 192.168.2.4 150
```

That 150 at the end changes the default administrative distance (AD) of 1 to 150. As I said, I'll talk much more about AD when we get into dynamic routing, but for now, just remember that the AD is the trustworthiness of a route, where 0 is best and 255 is worst.

One more example, then we'll start configuring:

```
Router(config)#ip route 172.16.3.0 255.255.255.0 s0/0/0
```

Instead of using a next-hop address, we can use an exit interface that will make the route show up as a directly connected network. Functionally, the next hop and exit interface work exactly the same.

To help you understand how static routes work, I'll demonstrate the configuration on the internetwork shown previously in Figure 9.8. Here it is again in Figure 9.9 to save you the trouble of having to go back and forth to view the same figure.

FIGURE 9.9   Our internetwork

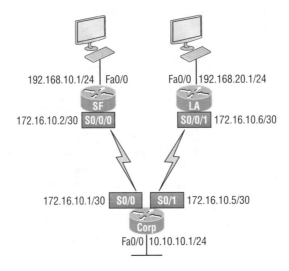

Corp

Each routing table automatically includes directly connected networks. To be able to route to all indirectly connected networks within the internetwork, the routing table must include information that describes where these other networks are located and how to get to them.

The Corp router is connected to three networks. For the Corp router to be able to route to all networks, the following networks have to be configured into its routing table:

- 192.168.10.0

- 192.168.20.0

The following router output shows the static routes on the Corp router and the routing table after the configuration. For the Corp router to find the remote networks, I had to place an entry into the routing table describing the remote network, the remote mask, and where to send the packets. I am going to add a 150 at the end of each line to raise the administrative distance. You'll see why soon when we get to dynamic routing. Many times this is also referred to as a floating static route because the static route has a higher administrative distance than any routing protocol and will only be used if the routes found with the routing protocols go down. Here's the output:

```
Corp#config t
Corp(config)#ip route 192.168.10.0 255.255.255.0 172.16.10.2 150
Corp(config)#ip route 192.168.20.0 255.255.255.0 s0/1 150
Corp(config)#do show run | begin ip route
ip route 192.168.10.0 255.255.255.0 172.16.10.2 150
ip route 192.168.20.0 255.255.255.0 Serial0/1 150
```

I needed to use different paths for networks 192.168.10.0 and 192.168.20.0, so I used a next-hop address for the SF router and an exit interface for the LA router. After the router has been configured, you can just type **show ip route** to see the static routes:

```
Corp(config)#do show ip route
S    192.168.10.0/24 [150/0] via 172.16.10.2
     172.16.0.0/30 is subnetted, 2 subnets
C       172.16.10.4 is directly connected, Serial0/1
L       172.16.10.5/32 is directly connected, Serial0/1
C       172.16.10.0 is directly connected, Serial0/0
L       172.16.10.1/32 is directly connected, Serial0/0
S    192.168.20.0/24 is directly connected, Serial0/1
     10.0.0.0/24 is subnetted, 1 subnets
C       10.10.10.0 is directly connected, FastEthernet0/0
L       10.10.10.1/32 is directly connected, FastEthernet0/0
```

The Corp router is configured to route and know all routes to all networks. But can you see a difference in the routing table for the routes to SF and LA? That's right! The next-hop configuration showed up as via, and the route configured with an exit interface configuration shows up as static but also as directly connected! This demonstrates how they are functionally the same but will display differently in the routing table.

Understand that if the routes don't appear in the routing table, it's because the router can't communicate with the next-hop address you've configured. But you can still use the permanent parameter to keep the route in the routing table even if the next-hop device can't be contacted.

The S in the first routing table entry means that the route is a static entry. The [150/0] stands for the administrative distance and metric to the remote network, respectively.

Okay—we're good. The Corp router now has all the information it needs to communicate with the other remote networks. Still, keep in mind that if the SF and LA routers aren't configured with all the same information, the packets will be discarded. We can fix this by configuring static routes.

Don't stress about the 150 at the end of the static route configuration at all, because I promise to get to it really soon in *this* chapter, not a later one! You really don't need to worry about it at this point.

SF

The SF router is directly connected to networks 172.16.10.0/30 and 192.168.10.0/24, which means I've got to configure the following static routes on the SF router:

- 10.10.10.0/24
- 192.168.20.0/24
- 172.16.10.4/30

The configuration for the SF router is revealed in the following output. Remember that we'll never create a static route to any network we're directly connected to as well as the fact that we must use the next hop of 172.16.10.1 since that's our only router connection. Let's check out the commands:

```
SF(config)#ip route 10.10.10.0 255.255.255.0 172.16.10.1 150
SF(config)#ip route 172.16.10.4 255.255.255.252 172.16.10.1 150
SF(config)#ip route 192.168.20.0 255.255.255.0 172.16.10.1 150
SF(config)#do show run | begin ip route
ip route 10.10.10.0 255.255.255.0 172.16.10.1 150
ip route 172.16.10.4 255.255.255.252 172.16.10.1 150
ip route 192.168.20.0 255.255.255.0 172.16.10.1 150
```

By looking at the routing table, you can see that the SF router now understands how to find each network:

```
SF(config)#do show ip route
C    192.168.10.0/24 is directly connected, FastEthernet0/0
L    192.168.10.1/32 is directly connected, FastEthernet0/0
     172.16.0.0/30 is subnetted, 3 subnets
S       172.16.10.4 [150/0] via 172.16.10.1
C       172.16.10.0 is directly connected, Serial0/0/0
L       172.16.10.2/32 is directly connected, Serial0/0
S    192.168.20.0/24 [150/0] via 172.16.10.1
     10.0.0.0/24 is subnetted, 1 subnets
S       10.10.10.0 [150/0] via 172.16.10.1
```

And we now can rest assured that the SF router has a complete routing table as well. As soon as the LA router has all the networks in its routing table, SF will be able to communicate with all remote networks!

LA

The LA router is directly connected to 192.168.20.0/24 and 172.16.10.4/30, so these are the routes that must be added:

- 10.10.10.0/24
- 172.16.10.0/30
- 192.168.10.0/24

And here's the LA router's configuration:

```
LA#config t
LA(config)#ip route 10.10.10.0 255.255.255.0 172.16.10.5 150
LA(config)#ip route 172.16.10.0 255.255.255.252 172.16.10.5 150
LA(config)#ip route 192.168.10.0 255.255.255.0 172.16.10.5 150
LA(config)#do show run | begin ip route
ip route 10.10.10.0 255.255.255.0 172.16.10.5 150
ip route 172.16.10.0 255.255.255.252 172.16.10.5 150
ip route 192.168.10.0 255.255.255.0 172.16.10.5 150
```

This output displays the routing table on the LA router:

```
LA(config)#do sho ip route
S    192.168.10.0/24 [150/0] via 172.16.10.5
     172.16.0.0/30 is subnetted, 3 subnets
C       172.16.10.4 is directly connected, Serial0/0/1
L       172.16.10.6/32 is directly connected, Serial0/0/1
S       172.16.10.0 [150/0] via 172.16.10.5
C    192.168.20.0/24 is directly connected, FastEthernet0/0
L    192.168.20.1/32 is directly connected, FastEthernet0/0
     10.0.0.0/24 is subnetted, 1 subnets
S       10.10.10.0 [150/0] via 172.16.10.5
```

LA now shows all five networks in the internetwork, so it too can now communicate with all routers and networks. But before we test our little network, as well as our DHCP server, let's cover one more topic.

Default Routing

The SF and LA routers that I've connected to the Corp router are considered stub routers. A *stub* indicates that the networks in this design have only one way out to reach all other networks, which means that instead of creating multiple static routes, we can just use a single default route. This default route is used by IP to forward any packet with a destination not found in the routing table, which is why it is also called a gateway of last resort. Here's the configuration I could have done on the LA router instead of typing in the static routes due to its stub status:

```
LA#config t
LA(config)#no ip route 10.10.10.0 255.255.255.0 172.16.10.5 150
LA(config)#no ip route 172.16.10.0 255.255.255.252 172.16.10.5 150
LA(config)#no ip route 192.168.10.0 255.255.255.0 172.16.10.5 150
LA(config)#ip route 0.0.0.0 0.0.0.0 172.16.10.5
LA(config)#do sho ip route
[output cut]
```

```
Gateway of last resort is 172.16.10.5 to network 0.0.0.0
172.16.0.0/30 is subnetted, 1 subnets
C        172.16.10.4 is directly connected, Serial0/0/1
L        172.16.10.6/32 is directly connected, Serial0/0/1
C     192.168.20.0/24 is directly connected, FastEthernet0/0
L     192.168.20.0/32 is directly connected, FastEthernet0/0
S*    0.0.0.0/0 [1/0] via 172.16.10.5
```

Okay—I've removed all the initial static routes I had configured, and adding a default route is a lot easier than typing a bunch of static routes! Can you see the default route listed last in the routing table? The S* shows that as a candidate for the default route. And I really want you to notice that the gateway of last resort is now set too. Everything the router receives with a destination not found in the routing table will be forwarded to 172.16.10.5. You need to be careful where you place default routes because you can easily create a network loop!

So we're there—we've configured all our routing tables! All the routers have the correct routing table, so all routers and hosts should be able to communicate without a hitch—for now. But if you add even one more network or another router to the internetwork, you'll have to update each and every router's routing tables by hand—ugh! Not really a problem at all if you've got a small network like we do, but it would be a time-consuming monster if you're dealing with a large internetwork!

Verifying Your Configuration

But we're not done yet—once all the routers' routing tables are configured, they must be verified. The best way to do this, besides using the show ip route command, is via Ping. I'll start by pinging from the Corp router to the SF router.

Here's the output I got:

```
Corp#ping 192.168.10.1
Type escape sequence to abort.
Sending 5, 100-byte ICMP Echos to 192.168.10.1, timeout is 2 seconds:
!!!!!
Success rate is 100 percent (5/5), round-trip min/avg/max = 4/4/4 ms
Corp#
```

Here you can see that I pinged from the Corp router to the remote interface of the SF router. Now let's ping the remote network on the LA router, and after that, we'll test our DHCP server and see if that is working too!

```
Corp#ping 192.168.20.1
Type escape sequence to abort.
Sending 5, 100-byte ICMP Echos to 192.168.20.1, timeout is 2 seconds:
!!!!!
Success rate is 100 percent (5/5), round-trip min/avg/max = 1/2/4 ms
Corp#
```

And why not test my configuration of the DHCP server on the Corp router while we're at it? I'm going to go to each host on the SF and LA routers and make them DHCP clients. By the way, I'm using an old router to represent "hosts," which just happens to work great for studying purposes. Here's how I did that:

```
SF_PC(config)#int e0
SF_PC(config-if)#ip address dhcp
SF_PC(config-if)#no shut
Interface Ethernet0 assigned DHCP address 192.168.10.8, mask 255.255.255.0
LA_PC(config)#int e0
LA_PC(config-if)#ip addr dhcp
LA_PC(config-if)#no shut
Interface Ethernet0 assigned DHCP address 192.168.20.4, mask 255.255.255.0
```

Nice! Don't you love it when things just work the first time? Sadly, this just isn't exactly a realistic expectation in the networking world, so we must be able to troubleshoot and verify our networks. Let's verify our DHCP server with a few of the commands you learned back in Chapter 7:

```
Corp#sh ip dhcp binding
Bindings from all pools not associated with VRF:
IP address          Client-ID/              Lease expiration          Type
                    Hardware address/
                    User name
192.168.10.8        0063.6973.636f.2d30.    Sept 16 2013 10:34 AM     Automatic
                    3035.302e.3062.6330.
                    2e30.3063.632d.4574.
                    30
192.168.20.4        0063.6973.636f.2d30.    Sept 16 2013 10:46 AM     Automatic
                    3030.322e.3137.3632.
                    2e64.3032.372d.4574.
                    30
```

We can see from earlier that our little DHCP server is working! Let's try another couple of commands:

```
Corp#sh ip dhcp pool SF_LAN
Pool SF_LAN :
 Utilization mark (high/low)    : 100 / 0
 Subnet size (first/next)       : 0 / 0
 Total addresses                : 254
 Leased addresses               : 3
 Pending event                  : none
 1 subnet is currently in the pool :
```

```
Current index        IP address range                      Leased addresses
192.168.10.9         192.168.10.1      - 192.168.10.254     3
```

Corp#sh ip dhcp conflict
```
IP address       Detection method   Detection time         VRF
```

The last command would tell us if we had two hosts with the same IP address, so it's good news because there are no conflicts reported! Two detection methods are used to confirm this:

- A ping from the DHCP server to make sure no other host responds before handing out an address

- A gratuitous ARP from a host that receives a DHCP address from the server

The DHCP client will send an ARP request with its new IP address looking to see if anyone responds, and if so, it will report the conflict to the server.

Okay, since we can communicate from end to end and to each host without a problem while receiving DHCP addresses from our server, I'd say our static and default route configurations have been a success—cheers!

Dynamic Routing

Dynamic routing is when protocols are used to find networks and update routing tables on routers. This is whole lot easier than using static or default routing, but it will cost you in terms of router CPU processing and bandwidth on network links. A routing protocol defines the set of rules used by a router when it communicates routing information between neighboring routers.

The routing protocol I'm going to talk about in this chapter is Routing Information Protocol (RIP) versions 1 and 2.

Two types of routing protocols are used in internetworks: *interior gateway protocols (IGPs)* and *exterior gateway protocols (EGPs)*. IGPs are used to exchange routing information with routers in the same *autonomous system (AS)*. An AS is either a single network or a collection of networks under a common administrative domain, which basically means that all routers sharing the same routing-table information are in the same AS. EGPs are used to communicate between ASs. An example of an EGP is Border Gateway Protocol (BGP), which we're not going to bother with because it's beyond the scope of this book.

Since routing protocols are so essential to dynamic routing, I'm going to give you the basic information you need to know about them next. Later on in this chapter, we'll focus on configuration.

Routing Protocol Basics

There are some important things you should know about routing protocols before we get deeper into RIP routing. Being familiar with administrative distances and the three different kinds of routing protocols, for example. Let's take a look.

Administrative Distances

The *administrative distance (AD)* is used to rate the trustworthiness of routing information received on a router from a neighbor router. An administrative distance is an integer from 0 to 255, where 0 is the most trusted and 255 means no traffic will be passed via this route.

If a router receives two updates listing the same remote network, the first thing the router checks is the AD. If one of the advertised routes has a lower AD than the other, then the route with the lowest AD will be chosen and placed in the routing table.

If both advertised routes to the same network have the same AD, then routing protocol metrics like *hop count* and/or the bandwidth of the lines will be used to find the best path to the remote network. The advertised route with the lowest metric will be placed in the routing table, but if both advertised routes have the same AD as well as the same metrics, then the routing protocol will load-balance to the remote network, meaning the protocol will send data down each link.

Table 9.1 shows the default administrative distances that a Cisco router uses to decide which route to take to a remote network.

TABLE 9.1   Default administrative distances

Route Source	Default AD
Connected interface	0
Static route	1
External BGP	20
EIGRP	90
OSPF	110
RIP	120
External EIGRP	170
Internal BGP	200
Unknown	255 (This route will never be used.)

If a network is directly connected, the router will always use the interface connected to the network. If you configure a static route, the router will then believe that route over any other ones it learns about. You can change the administrative distance of static routes, but by default, they have an AD of 1. In our previous static route configuration, the AD of each route is set at 150. This AD allows us to configure routing protocols without having to remove the static routes because it's nice to have them there for backup in case the routing protocol experiences some kind of failure.

If you have a static route, an RIP-advertised route, and an EIGRP-advertised route listing the same network, which route will the router go with? That's right—by default, the router will always use the static route unless you change its AD—which we did!

Routing Protocols

There are three classes of routing protocols:

Distance vector   The distance-vector protocols in use today find the best path to a remote network by judging distance. In RIP routing, each instance where a packet goes through a router is called a hop, and the route with the least number of hops to the network will be chosen as the best one. The vector indicates the direction to the remote network. RIP is a distance-vector routing protocol and periodically sends out the entire routing table to directly connected neighbors.

Link state   In link-state protocols, also called shortest-path-first (SPF) protocols, the routers each create three separate tables. One of these tables keeps track of directly attached neighbors, one determines the topology of the entire internetwork, and one is used as the routing table. Link-state routers know more about the internetwork than any distance-vector routing protocol ever could. OSPF is an IP routing protocol that's completely link-state. Link-state routing tables are not exchanged periodically. Instead, triggered updates containing only specific link-state information are sent. Periodic keepalives that are small and efficient, in the form of hello messages, are exchanged between directly connected neighbors to establish and maintain neighbor relationships.

Advanced distance vector   Advanced distance-vector protocols use aspects of both distance-vector and link-state protocols, and EIGRP is a great example. EIGRP may act like a link-state routing protocol because it uses a Hello protocol to discover neighbors and form neighbor relationships and because only partial updates are sent when a change occurs. However, EIGRP is still based on the key distance-vector routing protocol principle that information about the rest of the network is learned from directly connected neighbors.

There's no set of rules to follow that dictate exactly how to broadly configure routing protocols for every situation. It's a task that really must be undertaken on a case-by-case basis, with an eye on specific requirements of each one. If you understand how the different routing protocols work, you can make good, solid decisions that will solidly meet the individual needs of any business!

Routing Information Protocol (RIP)

Routing Information Protocol (RIP) is a true distance-vector routing protocol. RIP sends the complete routing table out of all active interfaces every 30 seconds. It relies on hop count to determine the best way to a remote network, but it has a maximum allowable hop count of 15 by default, so a destination of 16 would be considered unreachable. RIP works okay in very small networks, but it's super inefficient on large networks with slow WAN links or on networks with a large number of routers installed and completely useless on networks that have links with variable bandwidths!

RIP version 1 uses only *classful routing*, which means that all devices in the network must use the same subnet mask. This is because RIP version 1 doesn't send updates with subnet mask information in tow. RIP version 2 provides something called *prefix routing* and does send subnet mask information with its route updates. This is called *classless routing*.

So, with that let's configure our current network with RIPv2, before we move onto the next chapter.

Configuring RIP Routing

To configure RIP routing, just turn on the protocol with the `router rip` command and tell the RIP routing protocol the networks to advertise. Remember that with static routing, we always configured remote networks and never typed a route to our directly connected networks? Well, dynamic routing is carried out the complete opposite way. You would never type a *remote* network under your routing protocol—only enter your directly connected networks! Let's configure our three-router internetwork, revisited in Figure 9.9, with RIP routing.

Corp

RIP has an administrative distance of 120. Static routes have an administrative distance of 1 by default, and since we currently have static routes configured, the routing tables won't be populated with RIP information by default. We're still good though because I added the 150 to the end of each static route!

You can add the RIP routing protocol by using the `router rip` command and the `network` command. The `network` command tells the routing protocol which classful network to advertise. By doing this, you're activating the RIP routing process on the interfaces whose addressing falls within the specified classful networks configured with the `network` command under the RIP routing process.

Look at the Corp router configuration to see how easy this is. Oh wait—first, I want to verify my directly connected networks so I know what to configure RIP with:

```
Corp#sh ip int brief
Interface       IP-Address    OK? Method Status                 Protocol
FastEthernet0/0 10.10.10.1    YES manual up                     up
Serial0/0       172.16.10.1   YES manual up                     up
FastEthernet0/1 unassigned    YES unset  administratively down  down
Serial0/1       172.16.10.5   YES manual up                     up
Corp#config t
Corp(config)#router rip
Corp(config-router)#network 10.0.0.0
Corp(config-router)#network 172.16.0.0
Corp(config-router)#version 2
Corp(config-router)#no auto-summary
```

That's it—really! Typically just two or three commands and you're done, which sure makes your job a lot easier than dealing with static routes, doesn't it? Be sure to keep in mind the extra router CPU process and bandwidth that you're consuming.

Anyway, so what exactly did I do here? I enabled the RIP routing protocol, added my directly connected networks, made sure I was only running RIPv2, which is a classless routing protocol, and then I disabled auto-summary. We typically don't want our routing protocols summarizing for us because it's better to do that manually and both RIP and EIGRP (before 15.x code) auto-summarize by default. So a general rule of thumb is to disable auto-summary, which allows them to advertise subnets.

Notice I didn't type in subnets, only the classful network address, which is betrayed by the fact that all subnet bits and host bits are off! That's because with dynamic routing, it's not my job and it's up to the routing protocol to find the subnets and populate the routing tables. And since we have no router buddies running RIP, we won't see any RIP routes in the routing table yet.

Remember that RIP uses the classful address when configuring the network address. To clarify this, refer to the example in our network with an address of 172.16.0.0/24 using subnets 172.16.10.0 and 172.16.20.0. You would only type in the classful network address of 172.16.0.0 and let RIP find the subnets and place them in the routing table. This doesn't mean you are running a classful routing protocol; this is just the way that both RIP and EIGRP are configured.

SF

Let's configure our SF router now, which is connected to two networks. We need to configure both directly connected classful networks, not subnets:

```
SF#sh ip int brief
Interface        IP-Address     OK? Method Status                  Protocol
FastEthernet0/0  192.168.10.1   YES manual up                      up
FastEthernet0/1  unassigned     YES unset  administratively down down
Serial0/0/0      172.16.10.2    YES manual up                      up
Serial0/0/1      unassigned     YES unset  administratively down down
SF#config
SF(config)#router rip
SF(config-router)#network 192.168.10.0
SF(config-router)#network 172.16.0.0
SF(config-router)#version 2
SF(config-router)#no auto-summary
SF(config-router)#do show ip route
C    192.168.10.0/24 is directly connected, FastEthernet0/0
L    192.168.10.1/32 is directly connected, FastEthernet0/0
```

```
       172.16.0.0/30 is subnetted, 3 subnets
R        172.16.10.4 [120/1] via 172.16.10.1, 00:00:08, Serial0/0/0
C        172.16.10.0 is directly connected, Serial0/0/0
L        172.16.10.2/32 is directly connected, Serial0/0
S      192.168.20.0/24 [150/0] via 172.16.10.1
       10.0.0.0/24 is subnetted, 1 subnets
R        10.10.10.0 [120/1] via 172.16.10.1, 00:00:08, Serial0/0/0
```

That was pretty straightforward. Let's talk about this routing table. Since we have one RIP buddy out there with whom we are exchanging routing tables, we can see the RIP networks coming from the Corp router. All the other routes still show up as static and local. RIP also found both connections through the Corp router to networks 10.10.10.0 and 172.16.10.4. But we're not done yet!

LA

Let's configure our LA router with RIP, only I'm going to remove the default route first, even though I don't have to. You'll see why soon:

```
LA#config t
LA(config)#no ip route 0.0.0.0 0.0.0.0
LA(config)#router rip
LA(config-router)#network 192.168.20.0
LA(config-router)#network 172.16.0.0
LA(config-router)#no auto
LA(config-router)#vers 2
LA(config-router)#do show ip route
R    192.168.10.0/24 [120/2] via 172.16.10.5, 00:00:10, Serial0/0/1
     172.16.0.0/30 is subnetted, 3 subnets
C        172.16.10.4 is directly connected, Serial0/0/1
L        172.16.10.6/32 is directly connected, Serial0/0/1
R        172.16.10.0 [120/1] via 172.16.10.5, 00:00:10, Serial0/0/1
C    192.168.20.0/24 is directly connected, FastEthernet0/0
L    192.168.20.1/32 is directly connected, FastEthernet0/0
     10.0.0.0/24 is subnetted, 1 subnets
R        10.10.10.0 [120/1] via 172.16.10.5, 00:00:10, Serial0/0/1
```

The routing table is sprouting new R's as we add RIP buddies! We can still see that all routes are in the routing table.

This output shows us basically the same routing table and the same entries that it had when we were using static routes—except for those R's. An R indicates that the networks were added dynamically using the RIP routing protocol. The [120/1] is the administrative distance of the route (120) along with the metric, which for RIP is the number of hops to that remote network (1). From the Corp router, all networks are one hop away.

So, while yes, it's true that RIP has worked in our little internetwork, it's just not a great solution for most enterprises. Its maximum hop count of only 15 is a highly limiting factor. And it performs full routing-table updates every 30 seconds, which would bring a larger internetwork to a painful crawl in no time!

There's still one more thing I want to show you about RIP routing tables and the parameters used to advertise remote networks. Using a different router on a different network as an example for a second, look into the following output. Can you spot where the following routing table shows [120/15] in the 10.1.3.0 network metric? This means that the administrative distance is 120, the default for RIP, but the hop count is 15. Remember that each time a router sends out an update to a neighbor router, the hop count goes up by one incrementally for each route! Here's that output now:

```
Router#sh ip route
     10.0.0.0/24 is subnetted, 12 subnets
C       10.1.11.0 is directly connected, FastEthernet0/1
L       10.1.11.1/32 is directly connected, FastEthernet0/1
C       10.1.10.0 is directly connected, FastEthernet0/0
L       10.1.10.1/32 is directly connected, FastEthernet/0/0
R       10.1.9.0 [120/2] via 10.1.5.1, 00:00:15, Serial0/0/1
R       10.1.8.0 [120/2] via 10.1.5.1, 00:00:15, Serial0/0/1
R       10.1.12.0 [120/1] via 10.1.11.2, 00:00:00, FastEthernet0/1
R       10.1.3.0 [120/15] via 10.1.5.1, 00:00:15, Serial0/0/1
R       10.1.2.0 [120/1] via 10.1.5.1, 00:00:15, Serial0/0/1
R       10.1.1.0 [120/1] via 10.1.5.1, 00:00:15, Serial0/0/1
R       10.1.7.0 [120/2] via 10.1.5.1, 00:00:15, Serial0/0/1
R       10.1.6.0 [120/2] via 10.1.5.1, 00:00:15, Serial0/0/1
C       10.1.5.0 is directly connected, Serial0/0/1
L       10.1.5.1/32 is directly connected, Serial0/0/1
R       10.1.4.0 [120/1] via 10.1.5.1, 00:00:15, Serial0/0/1
```

So this [120/15] is really bad. We're basically doomed because the next router that receives the table from this router will just discard the route to network 10.1.3.0 since the hop count would rise to 16, which is invalid!

 NOTE If a router receives a routing update that contains a higher-cost path to a network that's already in its routing table, the update will be ignored.

Holding Down RIP Propagations

You probably don't want your RIP network advertised everywhere on your LAN and WAN. There's enough stress in networking already and not a whole lot to be gained by advertising your RIP network to the Internet!

There are a few different ways to stop unwanted RIP updates from propagating across your LANs and WANs, and the easiest one is through the `passive-interface` command. This command prevents RIP update broadcasts from being sent out of a specified interface but still allows that same interface to receive RIP updates.

Here's an example of how to configure a `passive-interface` on the Corp router's Fa0/1 interface, which we will pretend is connected to a LAN that we don't want RIP on (and the interface isn't shown in the figure):

```
Corp#config t
Corp(config)#router rip
Corp(config-router)#passive-interface FastEthernet 0/1
```

This command will stop RIP updates from being propagated out of FastEthernet interface 0/1, but it can still receive RIP updates.

 Real World Scenario

Should We Really Use RIP in an Internetwork?

You have been hired as a consultant to install a couple of Cisco routers into a growing network. They have a couple of old Unix routers that they want to keep in the network. These routers do not support any routing protocol except RIP. I guess this means you just have to run RIP on the entire network. If you were balding before, your head now shines like chrome.

No need for hairs abandoning ship though—you can run RIP on a router connecting that old network, but you certainly don't need to run RIP throughout the whole internetwork!

You can do what is called *redistribution*, which is basically translating from one type of routing protocol to another. This means that you can support those old routers using RIP but use something much better like Enhanced IGRP on the rest of your network.

This will prevent RIP routes from being sent all over the internetwork gobbling up all that precious bandwidth!

Advertising a Default Route Using RIP

Now I'm going to guide you through how to advertise a way out of your autonomous system to other routers, and you'll see this is completed the same way with OSPF. Imagine that our Corp router's Fa0/0 interface is connected to some type of Metro-Ethernet as a connection to the Internet. This is a pretty common configuration today that uses a LAN interface to connect to the ISP instead of a serial interface.

If we do add an Internet connection to Corp, all routers in our AS (SF and LA) must know where to send packets destined for networks on the Internet or they'll just drop the packets when they get a remote request. One solution to this little hitch would be to place a default route on every router and funnel the information to Corp, which in turn would have a default route to the ISP. Most people do this type of configuration in small- to medium-size networks because it actually works pretty well!

But since I'm running RIPv2 on all routers, I'll just add a default route on the Corp router to our ISP, as I would normally. I'll then add another command to advertise my network to the other routers in the AS as the default route to show them where to send packets destined for the Internet.

Here's my new Corp configuration:

```
Corp(config)#ip route 0.0.0.0 0.0.0.0 fa0/0
Corp(config)#router rip
Corp(config-router)#default-information originate
```

Now, let's take a look at the last entry found in the Corp routing table:

```
S*   0.0.0.0/0 is directly connected, FastEthernet0/0
```

Let's see if the LA router can see this same entry:

```
LA#sh ip route
Gateway of last resort is 172.16.10.5 to network 0.0.0.0

R    192.168.10.0/24 [120/2] via 172.16.10.5, 00:00:04, Serial0/0/1
     172.16.0.0/30 is subnetted, 2 subnets
C       172.16.10.4 is directly connected, Serial0/0/1
L       172.16.10.5/32 is directly connected, Serial0/0/1
R       172.16.10.0 [120/1] via 172.16.10.5, 00:00:04, Serial0/0/1
C    192.168.20.0/24 is directly connected, FastEthernet0/0
L    192.168.20.1/32 is directly connected, FastEthernet0/0
     10.0.0.0/24 is subnetted, 1 subnets
R       10.10.10.0 [120/1] via 172.16.10.5, 00:00:04, Serial0/0/1
R    192.168.218.0/24 [120/3] via 172.16.10.5, 00:00:04, Serial0/0/1
R    192.168.118.0/24 [120/2] via 172.16.10.5, 00:00:05, Serial0/0/1
R*   0.0.0.0/0 [120/1] via 172.16.10.5, 00:00:05, Serial0/0/1
```

Can you see that last entry? It screams that it's an RIP injected route, but it's also a default route, so our `default-information originate` command is working! Last, notice that the gateway of last resort is now set as well.

If all of what you've learned is clear and understood, congratulations—you're ready to move on to the next chapter right after you go through the written and hands-on labs, and while you're at it, don't forget the review questions!

Summary

This chapter covered IP routing in detail. Again, it's extremely important to fully understand the basics we covered in this chapter because everything that's done on a Cisco router will typically have some kind of IP routing configured and running.

You learned how IP routing uses frames to transport packets between routers and to the destination host. From there, we configured static routing on our routers and discussed the administrative distance used by IP to determine the best route to a destination network. You found out that if you have a stub network, you can configure default routing, which sets the gateway of last resort on a router.

We then discussed dynamic routing, specifically RIPv2 and how it works on an internetwork, which is not very well!

Exam Essentials

Describe the basic IP routing process.   You need to remember that the frame changes at each hop but that the packet is never changed or manipulated in any way until it reaches the destination device (the TTL field in the IP header is decremented for each hop, but that's it!).

List the information required by a router to successfully route packets.   To be able to route packets, a router must know, at a minimum, the destination address, the location of neighboring routers through which it can reach remote networks, possible routes to all remote networks, the best route to each remote network, and how to maintain and verify routing information.

Describe how MAC addresses are used during the routing process.   A MAC (hardware) address will only be used on a local LAN. It will never pass a router's interface. A frame uses MAC (hardware) addresses to send a packet on a LAN. The frame will take the packet to either a host on the LAN or a router's interface (if the packet is destined for a remote network). As packets move from one router to another, the MAC addresses used will change, but normally the original source and destination IP addresses within the packet will not.

View and interpret the routing table of a router.   Use the show ip route command to view the routing table. Each route will be listed along with the source of the routing information. A C to the left of the route will indicate directly connected routes, and other letters next to the route can also indicate a particular routing protocol that provided the information, such as, for example, R for RIP.

Differentiate the three types of routing.   The three types of routing are static (in which routes are manually configured at the CLI), dynamic (in which the routers share routing information via a routing protocol), and default routing (in which a special route is configured for all traffic without a more specific destination network found in the table).

Compare and contrast static and dynamic routing.   Static routing creates no routing update traffic and creates less overhead on the router and network links, but it must be configured manually and does not have the ability to react to link outages. Dynamic routing creates routing update traffic and uses more overhead on the router and network links.

Configure static routes at the CLI.   The command syntax to add a route is `ip route [destination_network] [mask] [next-hop_address or exitinterface] [administrative_distance] [permanent]`.

Create a default route.   To add a default route, use the command syntax `ip route 0.0.0.0 0.0.0.0 ip-address` or `exit interface type and number`.

Understand administrative distance and its role in the selection of the best route. Administrative distance (AD) is used to rate the trustworthiness of routing information received on a router from a neighbor router. Administrative distance is an integer from 0 to 255, where 0 is the most trusted and 255 means no traffic will be passed via this route. All routing protocols are assigned a default AD, but it can be changed at the CLI.

Differentiate distance-vector, link-state, and hybrid routing protocols.   Distance-vector routing protocols make routing decisions based on hop count (think RIP), while link-state routing protocols are able to consider multiple factors such as bandwidth available and building a topology table. Hybrid routing protocols exhibit characteristics of both types.

Configure RIPv2 routing.   To configure RIP routing, first you must be in global configuration mode and then you type the command `router rip`. Then you add all directly connected networks, making sure to use the classful address and the `version 2` command and to disable auto-summarization with the `no auto-summary` command.

Written Lab 9

In this section, you'll complete the following lab to make sure you've got the information and concepts contained within them fully dialed in:

Lab 9.1: IP Routing

You can find the answers to this lab in Appendix A, "Answers to Written Labs." Write the answers to the following questions:

1. At the appropriate command prompt, create a static route to network 172.16.10.0/24 with a next-hop gateway of 172.16.20.1 and an administrative distance of 150.

2. When a PC sends a packet to another PC in a remote network, what destination addresses will be in the frame that it sends to its default gateway?

3. At the appropriate command prompt, create a default route to 172.16.40.1.

4. On which type of network is a default route most beneficial?

5. At the appropriate command prompt, display the routing table on your router.

6. When creating a static or default route, you don't have to use the next-hop IP address; you can use the _____.

7. True/False: To reach a remote host, you must know the MAC address of the remote host.

8. True/False: To reach a remote host, you must know the IP address of the remote host.

9. At the appropriate command prompt(s), prevent a router from propagating RIP information out serial 1.

10. True/False: RIPv2 is considered classless.

Hands-on Labs

In the following hands-on labs, you will configure a network with three routers. These exercises assume all the same setup requirements as the labs found in earlier chapters. You can use real routers, the LammleSim IOS version found at www.lammle.com/ccna, or the Cisco Packet Tracer program to run these labs.

This chapter includes the following labs:

Lab 9.1: Creating Static Routes

Lab 9.2: Configuring RIP Routing

The internetwork shown in the following graphic will be used to configure all routers.

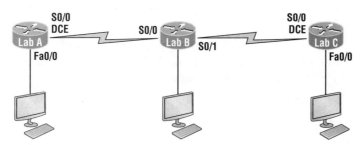

Table 9.2 shows our IP addresses for each router (each interface uses a /24 mask).

TABLE 9.2   Our IP addresses

Router	Interface	IP Address
Lab_A	Fa0/0	172.16.10.1
Lab_A	S0/0	172.16.20.1
Lab_B	S0/0	172.16.20.2
Lab_B	S0/1	172.16.30.1
Lab_C	S0/0	172.16.30.2
Lab_C	Fa0/0	172.16.40.1

These labs were written without using the LAN interface on the Lab_B router. You can choose to add that LAN into the labs if necessary. Also, if you have enough LAN interfaces, then you don't need to add the serial interfaces into this lab. Using all LAN interfaces is fine.

Hands-on Lab 9.1: Creating Static Routes

In this lab, you will create a static route in all three routers so that the routers see all networks. Verify with the Ping program when complete.

1. The Lab_A router is connected to two networks, 172.16.10.0 and 172.16.20.0. You need to add routes to networks 172.16.30.0 and 172.16.40.0. Use the following commands to add the static routes:

```
Lab_A#config t
Lab_A(config)#ip route 172.16.30.0 255.255.255.0
   172.16.20.2
Lab_A(config)#ip route 172.16.40.0 255.255.255.0
   172.16.20.2
```

2. Save the current configuration for the Lab_A router by going to privileged mode, typing **copy run start**, and pressing Enter.

3. On the Lab_B router, you have direct connections to networks 172.16.20.0 and 172.16.30.0. You need to add routes to networks 172.16.10.0 and 172.16.40.0. Use the following commands to add the static routes:

```
Lab_B#config t
Lab_B(config)#ip route 172.16.10.0 255.255.255.0
   172.16.20.1
Lab_B(config)#ip route 172.16.40.0 255.255.255.0
   172.16.30.2
```

4. Save the current configuration for router Lab_B by going to the enabled mode, typing **copy run start**, and pressing Enter.

5. On router Lab_C, create a static route to networks 172.16.10.0 and 172.16.20.0, which are not directly connected. Create static routes so that router Lab_C can see all networks, using the commands shown here:

```
Lab_C#config t
Lab_C(config)#ip route 172.16.10.0 255.255.255.0
   172.16.30.1
Lab_C(config)#ip route 172.16.20.0 255.255.255.0
   172.16.30.1
```

6. Save the current configuration for router Lab_C by going to the enable mode, typing **copy run start**, and pressing Enter.

7. Check your routing tables to make sure all four networks show up by executing the **show ip route** command.

8. Now ping from each router to your hosts and from each router to each router. If it is set up correctly, it will work.

Hands-on Lab 9.2: Configuring RIP Routing

In this lab, we will use the dynamic routing protocol RIP instead of static routing.

1. Remove any static routes or default routes configured on your routers by using the no ip route command. For example, here is how you would remove the static routes on the Lab_A router:

```
Lab_A#config t
Lab_A(config)#no ip route 172.16.30.0 255.255.255.0
  172.16.20.2
Lab_A(config)#no ip route 172.16.40.0 255.255.255.0
  172.16.20.2
```

Do the same thing for routers Lab_B and Lab_C. Verify that only your directly connected networks are in the routing tables.

2. After your static and default routes are clear, go into configuration mode on router Lab_A by typing **config t**.

3. Tell your router to use RIP routing by typing **router rip** and pressing Enter, as shown here:

```
config t
router rip
```

4. Add the network number for the networks you want to advertise. Since router Lab_A has two interfaces that are in two different networks, you must enter a network statement using the network ID of the network in which each interface resides. Alternately, you could use a summarization of these networks and use a single statement, minimizing the size of the routing table. Since the two networks are 172.16.10.0/24 and 172.16.20.0/24, the network summarization 172.16.0.0 would include both subnets. Do this by typing **network 172.16.0.0** and pressing Enter.

5. Press Ctrl+Z to get out of configuration mode.

6. The interfaces on Lab_B and Lab_C are in the 172.16.20.0/24 and 172.16.30.0/24 networks; therefore, the same summarized network statement will work there as well. Type the same commands, as shown here:

```
Config t
Router rip
network 172.16.0.0
```

7. Verify that RIP is running at each router by typing the following commands at each router:

   `show ip protocols`

   (Should indicate to you that RIP is present on the router.)

   `show ip route`

   (Should have routes present with an R to the left of them.)

   `show running-config or show run`

   (Should indicate that RIP is present and the networks are being advertised.)

8. Save your configurations by typing **`copy run start`** or **`copy running-config startup-config`** and pressing Enter at each router.

9. Verify the network by pinging all remote networks and hosts.

Review Questions

 The following questions are designed to test your understanding of this chapter's material. For more information on how to get additional questions, please see www.lammle.com/ccna.

You can find the answers to these questions in Appendix B, "Answers to Review Questions."

1. What command was used to generate the following output?

    ```
    Codes: L - local, C - connected, S - static,
    [output cut]
            10.0.0.0/8 is variably subnetted, 6 subnets, 4 masks
    C       10.0.0.0/8 is directly connected, FastEthernet0/3
    L       10.0.0.1/32 is directly connected, FastEthernet0/3
    C       10.10.0.0/16 is directly connected, FastEthernet0/2
    L       10.10.0.1/32 is directly connected, FastEthernet0/2
    C       10.10.10.0/24 is directly connected, FastEthernet0/1
    L       10.10.10.1/32 is directly connected, FastEthernet0/1
    S*      0.0.0.0/0 is directly connected, FastEthernet0/0
    ```

2. You are viewing the routing table and you see an entry 10.1.1.1/32. What legend code would you expect to see next to this route?

    A. C

    B. L

    C. S

    D. D

3. Which of the following statements are true regarding the command ip route 172.16.4.0 255.255.255.0 192.168.4.2? (Choose two.)

    A. The command is used to establish a static route.

    B. The default administrative distance is used.

    C. The command is used to configure the default route.

    D. The subnet mask for the source address is 255.255.255.0.

    E. The command is used to establish a stub network.

4. What destination addresses will be used by HostA to send data to the HTTPS server as shown in the following network? (Choose two.)

    A. The IP address of the switch

    B. The MAC address of the remote switch

    C. The IP address of the HTTPS server

D. The MAC address of the HTTPS server

E. The IP address of RouterA's Fa0/0 interface

F. The MAC address of RouterA's Fa0/0 interface

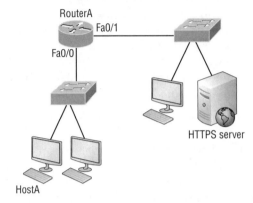

5. Using the output shown, what protocol was used to learn the MAC address for 172.16.10.1?

```
Interface: 172.16.10.2 --- 0x3
  Internet Address      Physical Address      Type
  172.16.10.1           00-15-05-06-31-b0     dynamic
```

A. ICMP

B. ARP

C. TCP

D. UDP

6. Which of the following is called an advanced distance-vector routing protocol?

A. OSPF

B. EIGRP

C. BGP

D. RIP

7. When a packet is routed across a network, the _____ in the packet changes at every hop while the _____ does not.

A. MAC address, IP address

B. IP address, MAC address

C. Port number, IP address

D. IP address, port number

8. Which statements are true regarding classless routing protocols? (Choose two.)

    A. The use of discontiguous networks is not allowed.

    B. The use of variable length subnet masks is permitted.

    C. RIPv1 is a classless routing protocol.

    D. IGRP supports classless routing within the same autonomous system.

    E. RIPv2 supports classless routing.

9. Which two of the following are true regarding the distance-vector and link-state routing protocols? (Choose two.)

    A. Link state sends its complete routing table out of all active interfaces at periodic time intervals.

    B. Distance vector sends its complete routing table out of all active interfaces at periodic time intervals.

    C. Link state sends updates containing the state of its own links to all routers in the internetwork.

    D. Distance vector sends updates containing the state of its own links to all routers in the internetwork.

10. When a router looks up the destination in the routing table for every single packet, it is called _____ .

    A. dynamic switching

    B. fast switching

    C. process switching

    D. Cisco Express Forwarding

11. What type(s) of route is the following? (Choose all that apply.)

```
S*   0.0.0.0/0 [1/0] via 172.16.10.5
```

    A. Default

    B. Subnetted

    C. Static

    D. Local

12. A network administrator views the output from the show ip route command. A network that is advertised by both RIP and EIGRP appears in the routing table flagged as an EIGRP route. Why is the RIP route to this network not used in the routing table?

    A. EIGRP has a faster update timer.

    B. EIGRP has a lower administrative distance.

    C. RIP has a higher metric value for that route.

    D. The EIGRP route has fewer hops.

    E. The RIP path has a routing loop.

13. Which of the following is *not* an advantage of static routing?

    A. Less overhead on the router CPU

    B. No bandwidth usage between routers

    C. Adds security

    D. Recovers automatically from lost routes

14. What metric does RIPv2 use to find the best path to a remote network?

    A. Hop count

    B. MTU

    C. Cumulative interface delay

    D. Load

    E. Path bandwidth value

15. The Corporate router receives an IP packet with a source IP address of 192.168.214.20 and a destination address of 192.168.22.3. Looking at the output from the Corp router, what will the router do with this packet?

```
Corp#sh ip route
[output cut]
R    192.168.215.0 [120/2] via 192.168.20.2, 00:00:23, Serial0/0
R    192.168.115.0 [120/1] via 192.168.20.2, 00:00:23, Serial0/0
R    192.168.30.0 [120/1] via 192.168.20.2, 00:00:23, Serial0/0
C    192.168.20.0 is directly connected, Serial0/0
C    192.168.214.0 is directly connected, FastEthernet0/0
```

    A. The packet will be discarded.

    B. The packet will be routed out of the S0/0 interface.

    C. The router will broadcast looking for the destination.

    D. The packet will be routed out of the Fa0/0 interface.

16. If your routing table has a static, an RIP, and an EIGRP route to the same network, which route will be used to route packets by default?

    A. Any available route

    B. RIP route

    C. Static route

    D. EIGRP route

    E. They will all load-balance.

17. Which of the following is an EGP?

    A. RIPv2

    B. EIGRP

    C. BGP

    D. RIP

18. Which of the following is an advantage of static routing?

   A. Less overhead on the router CPU

   B. No bandwidth usage between routers

   C. Adds security

   D. Recovers automatically from lost routes

19. What command produced the following output?

```
Interface          IP-Address      OK? Method Status                  Protocol
FastEthernet0/0    192.168.10.1    YES manual up                      up
FastEthernet0/1    unassigned      YES unset  administratively down   down
Serial0/0/0        172.16.10.2     YES manual up                      up
Serial0/0/1        unassigned      YES unset  administratively down   down
```

   A. `show ip route`

   B. `show interfaces`

   C. `show ip interface brief`

   D. `show ip arp`

20. What does the 150 at the end of the following command mean?

```
Router(config)#ip route 172.16.3.0 255.255.255.0 192.168.2.4 150
```

   A. Metric

   B. Administrative distance

   C. Hop count

   D. Cost

Chapter

10

Layer 2 Switching

THE FOLLOWING ICND1 EXAM TOPICS ARE COVERED IN THIS CHAPTER:

✓ **2.0 LAN Switching Technologies**

- 2.1 Describe and verify switching concepts

  - 2.1.a MAC learning and aging

  - 2.1.b Frame switching

  - 2.1.c Frame flooding

  - 2.1.d MAC address table

- 2.7 Configure, verify, and troubleshoot port security

  - 2.7.a Static

  - 2.7.b Dynamic

  - 2.7.c Sticky

  - 2.7.d Max MAC addresses

  - 2.7.e Violation actions

  - 2.7.f Err-disable recovery

When people at Cisco discuss switching in regards to the Cisco exam objectives, they're talking about layer 2 switching unless they say otherwise. Layer 2 switching is the process of using the hardware address of devices on a LAN to segment a network. Since you've got the basic idea of how that works nailed down by now, we're going to dive deeper into the particulars of layer 2 switching to ensure that your concept of how it works is solid and complete.

You already know that we rely on switching to break up large collision domains into smaller ones and that a collision domain is a network segment with two or more devices sharing the same bandwidth. A hub network is a typical example of this type of technology. But since each port on a switch is actually its own collision domain, we were able to create a much better Ethernet LAN network by simply replacing our hubs with switches!

Switches truly have changed the way networks are designed and implemented. If a pure switched design is properly implemented, it absolutely will result in a clean, cost-effective, and resilient internetwork. In this chapter, we'll survey and compare how networks were designed before and after switching technologies were introduced.

I'll be using three switches to begin our configuration of a switched network, and we'll actually continue with their configurations in Chapter 11, "VLANs and Inter-VLAN Routing."

To find up-to-the-minute updates for this chapter, please see www.lammle.com/ccna or the book's web page at www.sybex.com/go/ccna.

Switching Services

Unlike old bridges, which used software to create and manage a Content Addressable Memory (CAM) filter table, our new, fast switches use application-specific integrated circuits (ASICs) to build and maintain their MAC filter tables. But it's still okay to think of a layer 2 switch as a multiport bridge because their basic reason for being is the same: to break up collision domains.

Layer 2 switches and bridges are faster than routers because they don't take up time looking at the Network layer header information. Instead, they look at the frame's hardware addresses before deciding to either forward, flood, or drop the frame.

Unlike hubs, switches create private, dedicated collision domains and provide independent bandwidth exclusive on each port.

Here's a list of four important advantages we gain when using layer 2 switching:

- Hardware-based bridging (ASICs)
- Wire speed
- Low latency
- Low cost

A big reason layer 2 switching is so efficient is that no modification to the data packet takes place. The device only reads the frame encapsulating the packet, which makes the switching process considerably faster and less error-prone than routing processes are.

And if you use layer 2 switching for both workgroup connectivity and network segmentation (breaking up collision domains), you can create more network segments than you can with traditional routed networks. Plus, layer 2 switching increases bandwidth for each user because, again, each connection, or interface into the switch, is its own, self-contained collision domain.

Three Switch Functions at Layer 2

There are three distinct functions of layer 2 switching that are vital for you to remember: *address learning*, *forward/filter decisions*, and *loop avoidance*.

Address learning   Layer 2 switches remember the source hardware address of each frame received on an interface and enter this information into a MAC database called a forward/filter table.

Forward/filter decisions   When a frame is received on an interface, the switch looks at the destination hardware address, then chooses the appropriate exit interface for it in the MAC database. This way, the frame is only forwarded out of the correct destination port.

Loop avoidance   If multiple connections between switches are created for redundancy purposes, network loops can occur. Spanning Tree Protocol (STP) is used to prevent network loops while still permitting redundancy.

Next, I'm going to talk about address learning and forward/filtering decisions. Loop avoidance is beyond the scope of the objectives being covered in this chapter.

Address Learning

When a switch is first powered on, the MAC forward/filter table (CAM) is empty, as shown in Figure 10.1.

FIGURE 10.1   Empty forward/filter table on a switch

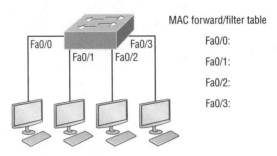

    When a device transmits and an interface receives a frame, the switch places the frame's source address in the MAC forward/filter table, allowing it to refer to the precise interface the sending device is located on. The switch then has no choice but to flood the network with this frame out of every port except the source port because it has no idea where the destination device is actually located.

    If a device answers this flooded frame and sends a frame back, then the switch will take the source address from that frame and place that MAC address in its database as well, associating this address with the interface that received the frame. Because the switch now has both of the relevant MAC addresses in its filtering table, the two devices can now make a point-to-point connection. The switch doesn't need to flood the frame as it did the first time because now the frames can and will only be forwarded between these two devices. This is exactly why layer 2 switches are so superior to hubs. In a hub network, all frames are forwarded out all ports every time—no matter what. Figure 10.2 shows the processes involved in building a MAC database.

FIGURE 10.2   How switches learn hosts' locations

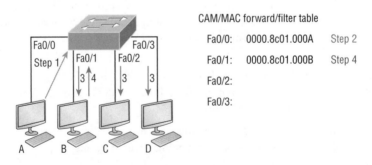

    In this figure, you can see four hosts attached to a switch. When the switch is powered on, it has nothing in its MAC address forward/filter table, just as in Figure 10.1. But when the hosts start communicating, the switch places the source hardware address of each frame into the table along with the port that the frame's source address corresponds to.

Let me give you an example of how a forward/filter table is populated using Figure 10.2:

1. Host A sends a frame to Host B. Host A's MAC address is 0000.8c01.000A; Host B's MAC address is 0000.8c01.000B.

2. The switch receives the frame on the Fa0/0 interface and places the source address in the MAC address table.

3. Since the destination address isn't in the MAC database, the frame is forwarded out all interfaces except the source port.

4. Host B receives the frame and responds to Host A. The switch receives this frame on interface Fa0/1 and places the source hardware address in the MAC database.

5. Host A and Host B can now make a point-to-point connection and only these specific devices will receive the frames. Hosts C and D won't see the frames, nor will their MAC addresses be found in the database because they haven't sent a frame to the switch yet.

If Host A and Host B don't communicate to the switch again within a certain time period, the switch will flush their entries from the database to keep it as current as possible.

Forward/Filter Decisions

When a frame arrives at a switch interface, the destination hardware address is compared to the forward/filter MAC database. If the destination hardware address is known and listed in the database, the frame is only sent out of the appropriate exit interface. The switch won't transmit the frame out any interface except for the destination interface, which preserves bandwidth on the other network segments. This process is called *frame filtering*.

But if the destination hardware address isn't listed in the MAC database, then the frame will be flooded out all active interfaces except the interface it was received on. If a device answers the flooded frame, the MAC database is then updated with the device's location— its correct interface.

If a host or server sends a broadcast on the LAN, by default, the switch will flood the frame out all active ports except the source port. Remember, the switch creates smaller collision domains, but it's always still one large broadcast domain by default.

In Figure 10.3, Host A sends a data frame to Host D. What do you think the switch will do when it receives the frame from Host A?

FIGURE 10.3   Forward/filter table

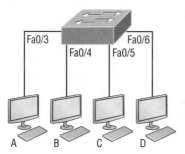

Switch# show mac address-table

VLAN	Mac Address	Ports
1	0005.dccb.d74b	Fa0/4
1	000a.f467.9e80	Fa0/5
1	000a.f467.9e8b	Fa0/6

Let's examine Figure 10.4 to find the answer.

FIGURE 10.4   Forward/filter table answer

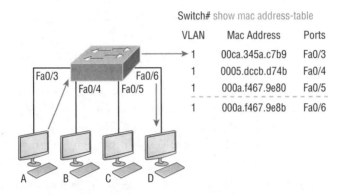

Switch# show mac address-table

VLAN	Mac Address	Ports
1	00ca.345a.c7b9	Fa0/3
1	0005.dccb.d74b	Fa0/4
1	000a.f467.9e80	Fa0/5
1	000a.f467.9e8b	Fa0/6

Since Host A's MAC address is not in the forward/filter table, the switch will add the source address and port to the MAC address table, then forward the frame to Host D. It's really important to remember that the source MAC is always checked first to make sure it's in the CAM table. After that, if Host D's MAC address wasn't found in the forward/filter table, the switch would've flooded the frame out all ports except for port Fa0/3 because that's the specific port the frame was received on.

Now let's take a look at the output that results from using a show mac address-table command:

```
Switch#sh mac address-table
Vlan    Mac Address      Type       Ports
----    -----------      --------   -----
   1    0005.dccb.d74b   DYNAMIC    Fa0/1
   1    000a.f467.9e80   DYNAMIC    Fa0/3
   1    000a.f467.9e8b   DYNAMIC    Fa0/4
   1    000a.f467.9e8c   DYNAMIC    Fa0/3
   1    0010.7b7f.c2b0   DYNAMIC    Fa0/3
   1    0030.80dc.460b   DYNAMIC    Fa0/3
   1    0030.9492.a5dd   DYNAMIC    Fa0/1
   1    00d0.58ad.05f4   DYNAMIC    Fa0/1
```

But let's say the preceding switch received a frame with the following MAC addresses:

Source MAC: **0005.dccb.d74b**

Destination MAC: **000a.f467.9e8c**

How will the switch handle this frame? The right answer is that the destination MAC address will be found in the MAC address table and the frame will only be forwarded out Fa0/3. Never forget that if the destination MAC address isn't found in the forward/filter table, the frame will be forwarded out all of the switch's ports except for the one on which it was originally received in an attempt to locate the destination device. Now that you can see the MAC address table and how switches add host addresses to the forward filter table, how do think we can secure it from unauthorized users?

Port Security

It's usually not a good thing to have your switches available for anyone to just plug into and play around with. I mean, we worry about wireless security, so why wouldn't we demand switch security just as much, if not more?

But just how do we actually prevent someone from simply plugging a host into one of our switch ports—or worse, adding a hub, switch, or access point into the Ethernet jack in their office? By default, MAC addresses will just dynamically appear in your MAC forward/filter database and you can stop them in their tracks by using port security!

Figure 10.5 shows two hosts connected to the single switch port Fa0/3 via either a hub or access point (AP).

FIGURE 10.5   "Port security" on a switch port restricts port access by MAC address.

Port Fa0/3 is configured to observe and allow only certain MAC addresses to associate with the specific port, so in this example, Host A is denied access, but Host B is allowed to associate with the port.

By using port security, you can limit the number of MAC addresses that can be assigned dynamically to a port, set static MAC addresses, and—here's my favorite part—set penalties for users who abuse your policy! Personally, I like to have the port shut down when the security policy is violated. Making abusers bring me a memo from their boss explaining why they violated the security policy brings with it a certain poetic justice, which is nice. And I'll also require something like that before I'll enable their port again. Things like this really seem to help people remember to behave!

This is all good, but you still need to balance your particular security needs with the time that implementing and managing them will realistically require. If you have tons of time on your hands, then go ahead and seriously lock your network down vault-tight! If you're busy like the rest of us, I'm here to reassure you that there are ways to secure things nicely without being totally overwhelmed with a massive amount of administrative overhead. First, and painlessly, always remember to shut down unused ports or assign them to an unused VLAN. All ports are enabled by default, so you need to make sure there's no access to unused switch ports!

Here are your options for configuring port security:

```
Switch#config t
Switch(config)#int f0/1
Switch(config-if)#switchport mode access
Switch(config-if)#switchport port-security
Switch(config-if)#switchport port-security ?
    aging           Port-security aging commands
    mac-address     Secure mac address
    maximum         Max secure addresses
    violation       Security violation mode
    <cr>
```

Most Cisco switches ship with their ports in desirable mode, which means that those ports will desire to trunk when sensing that another switch has just been connected. So first, we need to change the port out from desirable mode and make it an access port instead. If we don't do that, we won't be able to configure port security on it at all! Once that's out of the way, we can move on using our port-security commands, never forgetting that we must enable port security on the interface with the basic command switchport port-security. Notice that I did this after I made the port an access port!

The preceding output clearly illustrates that the switchport port-security command can be used with four options. You can use the switchport port-security mac-address *mac-address* command to assign individual MAC addresses to each switch port, but be warned because if you go with that option, you had better have boatloads of time on your hands!

You can configure the device to take one of the following actions when a security violation occurs by using the switchport port-security command:

- Protect: The protect violation mode drops packets with unknown source addresses until you remove enough secure MAC addresses to drop below the maximum value.

- Restrict: The restrict violation mode also drops packets with unknown source addresses until you remove enough secure MAC addresses to drop below the maximum value. However, it also generates a log message, causes the security violation counter to increment, and sends an SNMP trap.

- Shutdown: Shutdown is the default violation mode. The shutdown violation mode puts the interface into an error-disabled state immediately. The entire port is shut down. Also, in this mode, the system generates a log message, sends an SNMP trap, and increments the violation counter. To make the interface usable, you must perform a shut/no shut on the interface.

If you want to set up a switch port to allow only one host per port and make sure the port will shut down if this rule is violated, use the following commands like this:

```
Switch(config-if)#switchport port-security maximum 1
Switch(config-if)#switchport port-security violation shutdown
```

These commands really are probably the most popular because they prevent random users from connecting to a specific switch or access point that's in their office. The port security default that's immediately set on a port when it's enabled is `maximum 1` and `violation shutdown`. This sounds okay, but the drawback to this is that it only allows a single MAC address to be used on the port, so if anyone, including you, tries to add another host on that segment, the switch port will immediately enter error-disabled state and the port will turn amber. And when that happens, you have to manually go into the switch and re-enable the port by cycling it with a `shutdown` and then a `no shutdown` command.

Probably one of my favorite commands is the `sticky` command, and not just because it's got a cool name. It also makes very cool things happen! You can find this command under the `mac-address` command:

```
Switch(config-if)#switchport port-security mac-address sticky
Switch(config-if)#switchport port-security maximum 2
Switch(config-if)#switchport port-security violation shutdown
```

Basically, with the `sticky` command you can provide static MAC address security without having to type in absolutely everyone's MAC address on the network. I like things that save me time like that!

In the preceding example, the first two MAC addresses coming into the port "stick" to it as static addresses and will be placed in the running-config, but when a third address tried to connect, the port would shut down immediately.

I'll be going over port security CCENT objectives again in the configuration examples later in this chapter. They're important!

Let me show you one more example. Figure 10.6 displays a host in a company lobby that needs to be secured against the Ethernet cable used by anyone other than a single authorized individual.

FIGURE 10.6   Protecting a PC in a lobby

What can you do to ensure that only the MAC address of the lobby PC is allowed by switch port Fa0/1?

The solution is pretty straightforward because in this case, the defaults for port security will work well. All I have left to do is add a static MAC entry:

```
Switch(config-if)#switchport port-security
Switch(config-if)#switchport port-security violation restrict
Switch(config-if)#switchport port-security mac-address aa.bb.cc.dd.ee.ff
```

To protect the lobby PC, we would set the maximum allowed MAC addresses to 1 and the violation to restrict so the port didn't get shut down every time someone tried to use the Ethernet cable (which would be constantly). By using violation restrict, the unauthorized frames would just be dropped. But did you notice that I enabled port-security and then set a static MAC address? Remember that as soon as you enable port-security on a port, it defaults to violation shutdown and a maximum of 1. So all I needed to do was change the violation mode and add the static MAC address and our business requirement is solidly met!

 Real World Scenario

Lobby PC Always Being Disconnected Becomes a Security Risk

At a large Fortune 50 company in San Jose, California, there was a PC in the lobby that held the company directory. With no security guard present in the lobby, the Ethernet cable connecting the PC was free game to all vendors, contractors, and visitors waiting in the lobby.

Port security to the rescue! When port security was enabled on the port with the switchport port-security command, the switch port connecting to the PC was automatically secured with the defaults of allowing only one MAC address to associate to the port and violation shutdown. However, the port was always going into err-shutdown mode whenever anyone tried to use the Ethernet port. When the violation mode was changed to restrict and a static MAC address was set for the port with the switchport port-security mac-address command, only the Lobby PC was able to connect and communicate on the network! Problem solved!

Loop Avoidance

Redundant links between switches are important to have in place because they help prevent nasty network failures in the event that one link stops working.

But while it's true that redundant links can be extremely helpful, they can also cause more problems than they solve! This is because frames can be flooded down all redundant links simultaneously, creating network loops as well as other evils. Here's a list of some of the ugliest problems that can occur:

- If no loop avoidance schemes are put in place, the switches will flood broadcasts endlessly throughout the internetwork. This is sometimes referred to as a *broadcast storm*. Most of the time, they're referred to in very unprintable ways! Figure 10.7 illustrates how a broadcast can be propagated throughout the network. Observe how a frame is continually being flooded through the internetwork's physical network media.

FIGURE 10.7   Broadcast storm

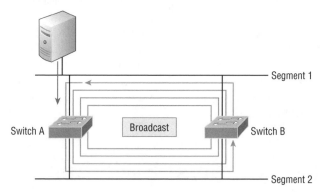

- A device can receive multiple copies of the same frame because that frame can arrive from different segments at the same time. Figure 10.8 demonstrates how a whole bunch of frames can arrive from multiple segments simultaneously. The server in the figure sends a unicast frame to Router C. Because it's a unicast frame, Switch A forwards the frame and Switch B provides the same service—it forwards the unicast. This is bad because it means that Router C receives that unicast frame twice, causing additional overhead on the network.

FIGURE 10.8   Multiple frame copies

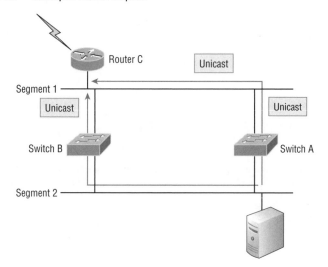

- You may have thought of this one: The MAC address filter table could be totally confused about the source device's location because the switch can receive the frame from more than one link. Worse, the bewildered switch could get so caught up in constantly updating the MAC filter table with source hardware address locations that it will fail to forward a frame! This is called thrashing the MAC table.

- One of the most vile events is when multiple loops propagate throughout a network. Loops can occur within other loops, and if a broadcast storm were to occur simultaneously, the network wouldn't be able to perform frame switching—period!

All of these problems spell disaster or close, and they're all evil situations that must be avoided or fixed somehow. That's where the Spanning Tree Protocol comes into play. It was actually developed to solve each and every one of the problems I just told you about!

Now that I explained the issues that can occur when you have redundant links, or when you have links that are improperly implemented, I'm sure you understand how vital it is to prevent them. However, the best solutions are beyond the scope of this chapter and among the territory covered in the more advanced Cisco exam objectives. For now, let's focus on configuring some switching!

Configuring Catalyst Switches

Cisco Catalyst switches come in many flavors; some run 10 Mbps, while others can speed all the way up to 10 Gbps or higher switched ports with a combination of twisted-pair and fiber. These newer switches, like the 3850, also have more intelligence, so they can give you data fast—mixed media services, too!

With that in mind, it's time to show you how to start up and configure a Cisco Catalyst switch using the command-line interface (CLI). After you get the basic commands down in this chapter, I'll show you how to configure virtual LANs (VLANs) plus Inter-Switch Link (ISL) and 802.1q trunking in the next one.

Here's a list of the basic tasks we'll be covering next:

- Administrative functions
- Configuring the IP address and subnet mask
- Setting the IP default gateway
- Setting port security
- Testing and verifying the network

 You can learn all about the Cisco family of Catalyst switches at www.cisco .com/en/US/products/hw/switches/index.html.

Catalyst Switch Configuration

But before we actually get into configuring one of the Catalyst switches, I've got to fill you in regarding the boot process of these switches, just as I did with the routers in Chapter 7, "Managing a Cisco Internetwork." Figure 10.9 shows a typical Cisco Catalyst switch, and I need to tell you about the different interfaces and features of this device.

FIGURE 10.9   A Cisco Catalyst switch

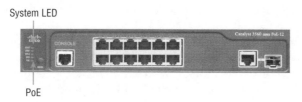

The first thing I want to point out is that the console port for the Catalyst switches are typically located on the back of the switch. Yet, on a smaller switch like the 3560 shown in the figure, the console is right in the front to make it easier to use. (The eight-port 2960 looks exactly the same.) If the POST completes successfully, the system LED turns green, but if the POST fails, it will turn amber. And seeing that amber glow is an ominous thing—typically fatal. So you may just want to keep a spare switch around—especially in case it's a production switch that's croaked! The bottom button is used to show you which lights are providing Power over Ethernet (PoE). You can see this by pressing the Mode button. The PoE is a very nice feature of these switches. It allows me to power my access point and phone by just connecting them into the switch with an Ethernet cable—sweet.

Just as we did with the routers we configured in Chapter 9, "IP Routing," we'll use a diagram and switch setup in this chapter as well as in Chapter 11. Figure 10.10 shows the switched network we'll be working on.

FIGURE 10.10   Our switched network

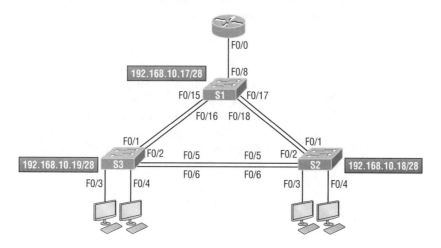

I'm going to use three 3560 switches, which I also used for demonstration in Chapter 6, "Cisco's Internetworking Operating System (IOS)," and Chapter 7. You can use any layer 2 switches for this chapter to follow the configuration, but when we get to Chapter 11, you'll need at least one router as well as a layer 3 switch, like my 3560.

Now if we connect our switches to each other, as shown in Figure 10.10, remember that first we'll need a crossover cable between the switches. My 3560 switches autodetect the connection type, so I was able to use straight-through cables. But not all switches autodetect the cable type. Different switches have different needs and abilities, so just keep this in mind when connecting your various switches together. Make a note that in the Cisco exam objectives, switches never autodetect!

When you first connect the switch ports to each other, the link lights are amber and then turn green, indicating normal operation. What you're actually watching is spanning-tree converging, and this process takes around 50 seconds with no extensions enabled. But if you connect into a switch port and the switch port LED is alternating green and amber, it means the port is experiencing errors. If this happens, check the host NIC or the cabling, possibly even the duplex settings on the port to make sure they match the host setting.

Do We Need to Put an IP Address on a Switch?

Absolutely not! Switches have all ports enabled and ready to rock. Take the switch out of the box, plug it in, and the switch starts learning MAC addresses in the CAM. So why would I need an IP address since switches are providing layer 2 services? Because you still need it for in-band management purposes! Telnet, SSH, SNMP, etc. all need an IP address in order to communicate with the switch through the network (in-band). Remember, since all ports are enabled by default, you need to shut down unused ports or assign them to an unused VLAN for security reasons.

So where do we put this management IP address the switch needs for management purposes? On what is predictably called the management VLAN interface—a routed interface on every Cisco switch and called interface VLAN 1. This management interface can be changed, and Cisco recommends that you do change this to a different management interface for security purposes. No worries—I'll demonstrate how to do this in Chapter 11.

Let's configure our switches now so you can watch how I configure the management interfaces on each switch.

S1

We're going to begin our configuration by connecting into each switch and setting the administrative functions. We'll also assign an IP address to each switch, but as I said, doing that isn't really necessary to make our network function. The only reason we're going to do that is so we can manage/administer it remotely, via Telnet for example. Let's use a simple IP scheme like 192.168.10.16/28. This mask should be familiar to you! Check out the following output:

```
Switch>en
Switch#config t
```

```
Switch(config)#hostname S1
S1(config)#enable secret todd
S1(config)#int f0/15
S1(config-if)#description 1st connection to S3
S1(config-if)#int f0/16
S1(config-if)#description 2nd connection to S3
S1(config-if)#int f0/17
S1(config-if)#description 1st connection to S2
S1(config-if)#int f0/18
S1(config-if)#description 2nd connection to S2
S1(config-if)#int f0/8
S1(config-if)#desc Connection to IVR
S1(config-if)#line con 0
S1(config-line)#password console
S1(config-line)#login
S1(config-line)#line vty 0 15
S1(config-line)#password telnet
S1(config-line)#login
S1(config-line)#int vlan 1
S1(config-if)#ip address 192.168.10.17 255.255.255.240
S1(config-if)#no shut
S1(config-if)#exit
S1(config)#banner motd #this is my S1 switch#
S1(config)#exit
S1#copy run start
Destination filename [startup-config]? [enter]
Building configuration...
[OK]
S1#
```

The first thing to notice about this is that there's no IP address configured on the switch's physical interfaces. Since all ports on a switch are enabled by default, there's not really a whole lot to configure! The IP address is configured under a logical interface, called a management domain or VLAN. You can use the default VLAN 1 to manage a switched network just as we're doing here, or you can opt to use a different VLAN for management.

The rest of the configuration is basically the same as the process you go through for router configuration. So remember... no IP addresses on physical switch interfaces, no routing protocols, and so on. We're performing layer 2 switching at this point, not routing! Also, make a note to self that there is no AUX port on Cisco switches.

S2

Here is the S2 configuration:

```
Switch#config t
Switch(config)#hostname S2
S2(config)#enable secret todd
S2(config)#int f0/1
S2(config-if)#desc 1st connection to S1
S2(config-if)#int f0/2
S2(config-if)#desc 2nd connection to s2
S2(config-if)#int f0/5
S2(config-if)#desc 1st connection to S3
S2(config-if)#int f0/6
S2(config-if)#desc 2nd connection to s3
S2(config-if)#line con 0
S2(config-line)#password console
S2(config-line)#login
S2(config-line)#line vty 0 15
S2(config-line)#password telnet
S2(config-line)#login
S2(config-line)#int vlan 1
S2(config-if)#ip address 192.168.10.18 255.255.255.240
S2(config)#exit
S2#copy run start
Destination filename [startup-config]?[enter]
Building configuration...
[OK]
S2#
```

We should now be able to ping from S2 to S1. Let's try it:

```
S2#ping 192.168.10.17

Type escape sequence to abort.
Sending 5, 100-byte ICMP Echos to 192.168.10.17, timeout is 2 seconds:
.!!!!
Success rate is 80 percent (4/5), round-trip min/avg/max = 1/1/1 ms
S2#
```

Okay—now why did I get only four pings to work instead of five? The first period [.] is a time-out, but the exclamation point [!] is a success.

It's a good question, and here's your answer: the first ping didn't work because of the time that ARP takes to resolve the IP address to its corresponding hardware MAC address.

S3

Check out the S3 switch configuration:

```
Switch>en
Switch#config t
SW-3(config)#hostname S3
S3(config)#enable secret todd
S3(config)#int f0/1
S3(config-if)#desc 1st connection to S1
S3(config-if)#int f0/2
S3(config-if)#desc 2nd connection to S1
S3(config-if)#int f0/5
S3(config-if)#desc 1st connection to S2
S3(config-if)#int f0/6
S3(config-if)#desc 2nd connection to S2
S3(config-if)#line con 0
S3(config-line)#password console
S3(config-line)#login
S3(config-line)#line vty 0 15
S3(config-line)#password telnet
S3(config-line)#login
S3(config-line)#int vlan 1
S3(config-if)#ip address 192.168.10.19 255.255.255.240
S3(config-if)#no shut
S3(config-if)#banner motd #This is the S3 switch#
S3(config)#exit
S3#copy run start
Destination filename [startup-config]?[enter]
Building configuration...
[OK]
S3#
```

Now let's ping to S1 and S2 from the S3 switch and see what happens:

```
S3#ping 192.168.10.17
Type escape sequence to abort.
Sending 5, 100-byte ICMP Echos to 192.168.10.17, timeout is 2 seconds:
.!!!!
Success rate is 80 percent (4/5), round-trip min/avg/max = 1/3/9 ms
```

```
S3#ping 192.168.10.18
Type escape sequence to abort.
Sending 5, 100-byte ICMP Echos to 192.168.10.18, timeout is 2 seconds:
.!!!!
Success rate is 80 percent (4/5), round-trip min/avg/max = 1/3/9 ms
S3#sh ip arp
Protocol  Address          Age (min)   Hardware Addr   Type   Interface
Internet  192.168.10.17           0    001c.575e.c8c0  ARPA   Vlan1
Internet  192.168.10.18           0    b414.89d9.18c0  ARPA   Vlan1
Internet  192.168.10.19           -    ecc8.8202.82c0  ARPA   Vlan1
S3#
```

In the output of the show ip arp command, the dash (-) in the minutes column means that it is the physical interface of the device.

Now, before we move on to verifying the switch configurations, there's one more command you need to know about, even though we don't really need it in our current network because we don't have a router involved. It's the ip default-gateway command. If you want to manage your switches from outside your LAN, you must set a default gateway on the switches just as you would with a host, and you do this from global config. Here's an example where we introduce our router with an IP address using the last IP address in our subnet range:

```
S3#config t
S3(config)#ip default-gateway 192.168.10.30
```

Now that we have all three switches basically configured, let's have some fun with them!

Port Security

A secured switch port can associate anywhere from 1 to 8,192 MAC addresses, but the 3560s I am using can support only 6,144, which seems like way more than enough to me. You can choose to allow the switch to learn these values dynamically, or you can set static addresses for each port using the switchport port-security mac-address *mac-address* command.

So let's set port security on our S3 switch now. Ports Fa0/3 and Fa0/4 will have only one device connected in our lab. By using port security, we're assured that no other device can connect once our hosts in ports Fa0/3 and in Fa0/4 are connected. Here's how to easily do that with just a couple commands:

```
S3#config t
S3(config)#int range f0/3-4
S3(config-if-range)#switchport mode access
S3(config-if-range)#switchport port-security
S3(config-if-range)#do show port-security int f0/3
```

```
Port Security               : Enabled
Port Status                 : Secure-down
Violation Mode              : Shutdown
Aging Time                  : 0 mins
Aging Type                  : Absolute
SecureStatic Address Aging  : Disabled
Maximum MAC Addresses       : 1
Total MAC Addresses         : 0
Configured MAC Addresses    : 0
Sticky MAC Addresses        : 0
Last Source Address:Vlan    : 0000.0000.0000:0
Security Violation Count    : 0
```

The first command sets the mode of the ports to "access" ports. These ports must be access or trunk ports to enable port security. By using the command switchport port-security on the interface, I've enabled port security with a maximum MAC address of 1 and violation of shutdown. These are the defaults, and you can see them in the highlighted output of the show port-security int f0/3 command in the preceding code.

Port security is enabled, as displayed on the first line, but the second line shows Secure-down because I haven't connected my hosts into the ports yet. Once I do, the status will show Secure-up and would become Secure-shutdown if a violation occurs.

I've just got to point out this all-so-important fact one more time: It's very important to remember that you can set parameters for port security but it won't work until you enable port security at the interface level. Notice the output for port F0/6:

```
S3#config t
S3(config)#int range f0/6
S3(config-if-range)#switchport mode access
S3(config-if-range)#switchport port-security violation restrict
S3(config-if-range)#do show port-security int f0/6
Port Security               : Disabled
Port Status                 : Secure-up
Violation Mode              : restrict
[output cut]
```

Port Fa0/6 has been configured with a violation of restrict, but the first line shows that port security has not been enabled on the port yet. Remember, you must use this command at interface level to enable port security on a port:

```
S3(config-if-range)#switchport port-security
```

There are two other modes you can use instead of just shutting down the port. The restrict and protect modes mean that another host can connect up to the maximum MAC addresses allowed, but after the maximum has been met, all frames will just be dropped and the port won't be shut down. Additionally, both the restrict and shutdown violation modes alert you via SNMP that a violation has occurred on a port. You can then call the abuser and tell them they're so busted—you can see them, you know what they did, and they're in serious trouble!

If you've configured ports with the `violation shutdown` command, then the ports will look like this when a violation occurs:

```
S3#sh port-security int f0/3
Port Security              : Enabled
Port Status                : Secure-shutdown
Violation Mode             : Shutdown
Aging Time                 : 0 mins
Aging Type                 : Absolute
SecureStatic Address Aging : Disabled
Maximum MAC Addresses      : 1
Total MAC Addresses        : 2
Configured MAC Addresses   : 0
Sticky MAC Addresses       : 0
Last Source Address:Vlan   : 0013:0ca69:00bb3:00ba8:1
Security Violation Count   : 1
```

Here you can see that the port is in `Secure-shutdown` mode and the light for the port would be amber. To enable the port again, you'd need to do the following:

```
S3(config-if)#shutdown
S3(config-if)#no shutdown
```

Let's verify our switch configurations before we move onto VLANs in the next chapter. Beware that even though some switches will show `err-disabled` instead of `Secure-shutdown` as my switch shows, there is no difference between the two.

Verifying Cisco Catalyst Switches

The first thing I like to do with any router or switch is to run through the configurations with a `show running-config` command. Why? Because doing this gives me a really great overview of each device. But it is time consuming, and showing you all the configs would take up way too many pages in this book. Besides, we can instead run other commands that will still stock us up with really good information.

For example, to verify the IP address set on a switch, we can use the `show interface` command. Here's the output:

```
S3#sh int vlan 1
Vlan1 is up, line protocol is up
  Hardware is EtherSVI, address is ecc8.8202.82c0 (bia ecc8.8202.82c0)
```

```
Internet address is 192.168.10.19/28
MTU 1500 bytes, BW 1000000 Kbit/sec, DLY 10 usec,
    reliability 255/255, txload 1/255, rxload 1/255
Encapsulation ARPA, loopback not set
[output cut]
```

The previous output shows the interface is in up/up status. Remember to always check this interface, either with this command or the show ip interface brief command. Lots of people tend to forget that this interface is shutdown by default.

 Never forget that IP addresses aren't needed on a switch for it to operate. The only reason we would set an IP address, mask, and default gateway is for management purposes.

show mac address-table

I'm sure you remember being shown this command earlier in the chapter. Using it displays the forward filter table, also called a content addressable memory (CAM) table. Here's the output from the S1 switch:

```
S3#sh mac address-table
          Mac Address Table
-------------------------------------------
Vlan    Mac Address       Type        Ports
----    -----------       --------    -----
 All    0100.0ccc.cccc    STATIC      CPU
[output cut]
  1     000e.83b2.e34b    DYNAMIC     Fa0/1
  1     0011.1191.556f    DYNAMIC     Fa0/1
  1     0011.3206.25cb    DYNAMIC     Fa0/1
  1     001a.2f55.c9e8    DYNAMIC     Fa0/1
  1     001a.4d55.2f7e    DYNAMIC     Fa0/1
  1     001c.575e.c891    DYNAMIC     Fa0/1
  1     b414.89d9.1886    DYNAMIC     Fa0/5
  1     b414.89d9.1887    DYNAMIC     Fa0/6
```

The switches use things called base MAC addresses, which are assigned to the CPU. The first one listed is the base mac address of the switch. From the preceding output, you can see that we have six MAC addresses dynamically assigned to Fa0/1, meaning that port Fa0/1 is connected to another switch. Ports Fa0/5 and Fa0/6 only have one MAC address assigned, and all ports are assigned to VLAN 1.

Let's take a look at the S2 switch CAM and see what we can find out.

```
S2#sh mac address-table
         Mac Address Table
-------------------------------------------
Vlan    Mac Address      Type      Ports
----    -----------      --------  -----
 All    0100.0ccc.cccc   STATIC    CPU
[output cut
  1     000e.83b2.e34b   DYNAMIC   Fa0/5
  1     0011.1191.556f   DYNAMIC   Fa0/5
  1     0011.3206.25cb   DYNAMIC   Fa0/5
  1     001a.4d55.2f7e   DYNAMIC   Fa0/5
  1     581f.aaff.86b8   DYNAMIC   Fa0/5
  1     ecc8.8202.8286   DYNAMIC   Fa0/5
  1     ecc8.8202.82c0   DYNAMIC   Fa0/5
Total Mac Addresses for this criterion: 27
S2#
```

This output tells us that we have seven MAC addresses assigned to Fa0/5, which is our connection to S3. But where's port 6? Since port 6 is a redundant link to S3, STP placed Fa0/6 into blocking mode.

Assigning Static MAC Addresses

You can set a static MAC address in the MAC address table, but like setting static MAC port security without the sticky command, it's a ton of work. Just in case you want to do it, here's how it's done:

```
S3(config)#mac address-table ?
  aging-time    Set MAC address table entry maximum age
  learning      Enable MAC table learning feature
  move          Move keyword
  notification  Enable/Disable MAC Notification on the switch
  static        static keyword

S3(config)#mac address-table static aaaa.bbbb.cccc vlan 1 int fa0/7
S3(config)#do show mac address-table
         Mac Address Table
-------------------------------------------
Vlan    Mac Address      Type      Ports
----    -----------      --------  -----
 All    0100.0ccc.cccc   STATIC    CPU
[output cut]
  1     000e.83b2.e34b   DYNAMIC   Fa0/1
  1     0011.1191.556f   DYNAMIC   Fa0/1
```

```
1     0011.3206.25cb    DYNAMIC    Fa0/1
1     001a.4d55.2f7e    DYNAMIC    Fa0/1
1     001b.d40a.0538    DYNAMIC    Fa0/1
1     001c.575e.c891    DYNAMIC    Fa0/1
1     aaaa.bbbb.0ccc    STATIC     Fa0/7
[output cut]
Total Mac Addresses for this criterion: 59
```

As shown on the left side of the output, you can see that a static MAC address has now been assigned permanently to interface Fa0/7 and that it's also been assigned to VLAN 1 only.

Now admit it—this chapter had a lot of great information, and you really did learn a lot and, well, maybe even had a little fun along the way too! You've now configured and verified all switches and set port security. That means you're now ready to learn all about virtual LANs! I'm going to save all our switch configurations so we'll be able to start right from here in Chapter 11.

Summary

In this chapter, I talked about the differences between switches and bridges and how they both work at layer 2. They create MAC address forward/filter tables in order to make decisions on whether to forward or flood a frame.

Although everything in this chapter is important, I wrote two port-security sections—one to provide a foundation and one with a configuration example. You must know both these sections in detail.

I also covered some problems that can occur if you have multiple links between bridges (switches).

Finally, I covered detailed configuration of Cisco's Catalyst switches, including verifying the configuration.

Exam Essentials

Remember the three switch functions.   Address learning, forward/filter decisions, and loop avoidance are the functions of a switch.

Remember the command `show mac address-table`.   The command show mac address-table will show you the forward/filter table used on the LAN switch.

Understand the reason for port security.   Port security restricts access to a switch based on MAC addresses.

Know the command to enable port security.   To enable port security on a port, you must first make sure the port is an access port with `switchport mode access` and then use the `switchport port-security` command at the interface level. You can set the port security parameters before or after enabling port security.

Know the commands to verify port security.   To verify port security, use the `show port-security`, `show port-security interface` *interface*, and `show running-config` commands.

Written Lab 10

In this section, you'll complete the following lab to make sure you've got the information and concepts contained within them fully dialed in:

Lab 10.1: Layer 2 Switching

You can find the answers to this lab in Appendix A, "Answers to Written Labs."

Write the answers to the following questions:

1. What command will show you the forward/filter table?

2. If a destination MAC address is not in the forward/filter table, what will the switch do with the frame?

3. What are the three switch functions at layer 2?

4. If a frame is received on a switch port and the source MAC address is not in the forward/filter table, what will the switch do?

5. What are the default modes for a switch port configured with port security?

6. Which two violation modes send out an SNMP trap?

7. Which violation mode drops packets with unknown source addresses until you remove enough secure MAC addresses to drop below the maximum but also generates a log message, causes the security violation counter to increment, and sends an SNMP trap but does not disable the port?

8. What does the `sticky` keyword in the `port-security` command provide?

9. What two commands can you use to verify that port security has been configured on a port FastEthernet 0/12 on a switch?

10. True/False: The layer 2 switch must have an IP address set and the PCs connecting to the switch must use that address as their default gateway.

Hands-on Labs

In this section, you will use the following switched network to configure your switching labs. You can use any Cisco switches to do this lab, as well as LammleSim IOS version simulator found at `www.lammle.com/ccna`. They do not need to be multilayer switches, just layer 2 switches.

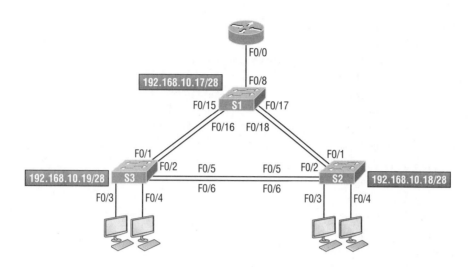

The first lab (Lab 10.1) requires you to configure three switches, and then you will verify them in Lab 10.2.

The labs in this chapter are as follows:

Hands-on Lab 10.1: Configuring Layer 2 Switches

Hands-on Lab 10.2: Verifying Layer 2 Switches

Hands-on Lab 10.3: Configuring Port Security

Lab 10.1: Configuring Layer 2 Switches

In this lab, you will configure the three switches in the graphic:

1. Connect to the S1 switch and configure the following, not in any particular order:

    - Hostname

    - Banner

    - Interface description

    - Passwords

    - IP address, subnet mask, default gateway

```
Switch>en
Switch#config t
Switch(config)#hostname S1
S1(config)#enable secret todd
S1(config)#int f0/15
S1(config-if)#description 1st connection to S3
S1(config-if)#int f0/16
```

```
S1(config-if)#description 2nd connection to S3
S1(config-if)#int f0/17
S1(config-if)#description 1st connection to S2
S1(config-if)#int f0/18
S1(config-if)#description 2nd connection to S2
S1(config-if)#int f0/8
S1(config-if)#desc Connection to IVR
S1(config-if)#line con 0
S1(config-line)#password console
S1(config-line)#login
S1(config-line)#line vty 0 15
S1(config-line)#password telnet
S1(config-line)#login
S1(config-line)#int vlan 1
S1(config-if)#ip address 192.168.10.17 255.255.255.240
S1(config-if)#no shut
S1(config-if)#exit
S1(config)#banner motd #this is my S1 switch#
S1(config)#exit
S1#copy run start
Destination filename [startup-config]? [enter]
Building configuration...
```

2. Connect to the S2 switch and configure all the settings you used in step 1. Do not forget to use a different IP address on the switch.

3. Connect to the S3 switch and configure all the settings you used in steps 1 and 2. Do not forget to use a different IP address on the switch.

Lab 10.2: Verifying Layer 2 Switches

Once you configure a device, you must be able to verify it.

1. Connect to each switch and verify the management interface.

    ```
    S1#sh interface vlan 1
    ```

2. Connect to each switch and verify the CAM.

    ```
    S1#sh mac address-table
    ```

3. Verify your configurations with the following commands:

    ```
    S1#sh running-config
    S1#sh ip int brief
    ```

Lab 10.3: Configuring Port Security

Port security is a big Cisco objective. Do not skip this lab!

1. Connect to your S3 switch.

2. Configure port Fa0/3 with port security.

    ```
    S3#config t
    S(config)#int fa0/3
    S3(config-if#Switchport mode access
    S3(config-if#switchport port-security
    ```

3. Check your default setting for port security.

    ```
    S3#show port-security int f0/3
    ```

4. Change the settings to have a maximum of two MAC addresses that can associate to
    interface Fa0/3.

    ```
    S3#config t
    S(config)#int fa0/3
    S3(config-if#switchport port-security maximum 2
    ```

5. Change the violation mode to restrict.

    ```
    S3#config t
    S(config)#int fa0/3
    S3(config-if#switchport port-security violation restrict
    ```

6. Verify your configuration with the following commands:

    ```
    S3#show port-security
    S3#show port-security int fa0/3
    S3#show running-config
    ```

Review Questions

The following questions are designed to test your understanding of this chapter's material. For more information on how to get additional questions, please see www.lammle.com/ccna.

You can find the answers to these questions in Appendix B, "Answers to Review Questions."

1. Which of the following statements is *not* true with regard to layer 2 switching?

   A. Layer 2 switches and bridges are faster than routers because they don't take up time looking at the Data Link layer header information.

   B. Layer 2 switches and bridges look at the frame's hardware addresses before deciding to either forward, flood, or drop the frame.

   C. Switches create private, dedicated collision domains and provide independent bandwidth on each port.

   D. Switches use application-specific integrated circuits (ASICs) to build and maintain their MAC filter tables.

2. List the two commands that generated the last entry in the MAC address table shown.

   ```
   Mac Address Table
   -------------------------------------------

   Vlan    Mac Address      Type       Ports
   ----    -----------      --------   -----
    All    0100.0ccc.cccc   STATIC     CPU
   [output cut]
      1     000e.83b2.e34b   DYNAMIC    Fa0/1
      1     0011.1191.556f   DYNAMIC    Fa0/1
      1     0011.3206.25cb   DYNAMIC    Fa0/1
      1     001a.4d55.2f7e   DYNAMIC    Fa0/1
      1     001b.d40a.0538   DYNAMIC    Fa0/1
      1     001c.575e.c891   DYNAMIC    Fa0/1
      1     aaaa.bbbb.0ccc   STATIC     Fa0/7
   ```

3. In the diagram shown, what will the switch do if a frame with a destination MAC address of 000a.f467.63b1 is received on Fa0/4? (Choose all that apply.)

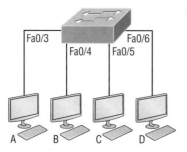

Switch# show mac address-table

VLAN	Mac Address	Ports
1	0005.dccb.d74b	Fa0/4
1	000a.f467.9e80	Fa0/5
1	000a.f467.9e8b	Fa0/6

A. Drop the frame.

B. Send the frame out of Fa0/3.

C. Send the frame out of Fa0/4.

D. Send the frame out of Fa0/5.

E. Send the frame out of Fa0/6.

4. Write the command that generated the following output.

```
        Mac Address Table
-------------------------------------------
Vlan    Mac Address     Type      Ports
----    -----------     --------  -----
All     0100.0ccc.cccc  STATIC    CPU
[output cut]
   1    000e.83b2.e34b  DYNAMIC   Fa0/1
   1    0011.1191.556f  DYNAMIC   Fa0/1
   1    0011.3206.25cb  DYNAMIC   Fa0/1
   1    001a.2f55.c9e8  DYNAMIC   Fa0/1
   1    001a.4d55.2f7e  DYNAMIC   Fa0/1
   1    001c.575e.c891  DYNAMIC   Fa0/1
   1    b414.89d9.1886  DYNAMIC   Fa0/5
   1    b414.89d9.1887  DYNAMIC   Fa0/6
```

5. In the work area in the following graphic, draw the functions of a switch from the list on the left to the right.

Address learning	Target 1
Packet forwarding	Target 2
Layer 3 security	Target 3
Forward/filter decisions	
Loop avoidance	

6. What statement(s) is/are true about the output shown here? (Choose all that apply.)

```
S3#sh port-security int f0/3
Port Security              : Enabled
Port Status                : Secure-shutdown
Violation Mode             : Shutdown
Aging Time                 : 0 mins
Aging Type                 : Absolute
SecureStatic Address Aging : Disabled
Maximum MAC Addresses      : 1
Total MAC Addresses        : 2
Configured MAC Addresses   : 0
Sticky MAC Addresses       : 0
Last Source Address:Vlan   : 0013:0ca69:00bb3:00ba8:1
Security Violation Count   : 1
```

A. The port light for F0/3 will be amber in color.

B. The F0/3 port is forwarding frames.

C. This problem will resolve itself in a few minutes.

D. This port requires the shutdown command to function.

7. Write the command that would limit the number of MAC addresses allowed on a port to 2. Write only the command and not the prompt.

8. Which of the following commands in this configuration is a prerequisite for the other commands to function?

```
S3#config t
S(config)#int fa0/3
S3(config-if#switchport port-security
S3(config-if#switchport port-security maximum 3
S3(config-if#switchport port-security violation restrict
S3(config-if#Switchport mode-security aging time 10
```

A. switchport mode-security aging time 10

B. switchport port-security

C. switchport port-security maximum 3

D. switchport port-security violation restrict

9. Which if the following is *not* an issue addressed by STP?

A. Broadcast storms

B. Gateway redundancy

C. A device receiving multiple copies of the same frame

D. Constant updating of the MAC filter table

10. What issue that arises when redundancy exists between switches is shown in the figure?

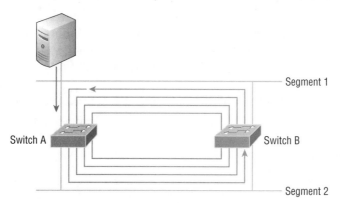

A. Broadcast storm

B. Routing loop

C. Port violation

D. Loss of gateway

11. Which two of the following switch port violation modes will alert you via SNMP that a violation has occurred on a port?

A. `restrict`

B. `protect`

C. `shutdown`

D. `err-disable`

12. _____ is the loop avoidance mechanism used by switches.

13. Write the command that must be present on any switch that you need to manage from a different subnet.

14. On which default interface have you configured an IP address for a switch?

A. `int fa0/0`

B. `int vty 0 15`

C. `int vlan 1`

D. `int s/0/0`

15. Which Cisco IOS command is used to verify the port security configuration of a switch port?

A. `show interfaces port-security`

B. `show port-security interface`

C. show ip interface

D. show interfaces switchport

16. Write the command that will save a dynamically learned MAC address in the running-configuration of a Cisco switch?

17. Which of the following methods will ensure that only one specific host can connect to port F0/3 on a switch? (Choose two. Each correct answer is a separate solution.)

A. Configure port security on F0/3 to accept traffic other than that of the MAC address of the host.

B. Configure the MAC address of the host as a static entry associated with port F0/3.

C. Configure an inbound access control list on port F0/3 limiting traffic to the IP address of the host.

D. Configure port security on F0/3 to accept traffic only from the MAC address of the host.

18. What will be the effect of executing the following command on port F0/1?

switch(config-if)# switchport port-security mac-address 00C0.35F0.8301

A. The command configures an inbound access control list on port F0/1, limiting traffic to the IP address of the host.

B. The command expressly prohibits the MAC address of 00c0.35F0.8301 as an allowed host on the switch port.

C. The command encrypts all traffic on the port from the MAC address of 00c0.35F0.8301.

D. The command statically defines the MAC address of 00c0.35F0.8301 as an allowed host on the switch port.

19. The conference room has a switch port available for use by the presenter during classes, and each presenter uses the same PC attached to the port. You would like to prevent other PCs from using that port. You have completely removed the former configuration in order to start anew. Which of the following steps is *not* required to prevent any other PCs from using that port?

A. Enable port security.

B. Assign the MAC address of the PC to the port.

C. Make the port an access port.

D. Make the port a trunk port.

20. Write the command required to disable the port if a security violation occurs. Write only the command and not the prompt.

Chapter

11

VLANs and Inter-VLAN Routing

THE FOLLOWING ICND1 EXAM TOPICS ARE COVERED IN THIS CHAPTER:

✓ **2.0 LAN Switching Technologies**

- 2.4 Configure, verify, and troubleshoot VLANs (normal range) spanning multiple switches

  - 2.4.a Access ports (data and voice)

  - 2.4.b Default VLAN

- 2.5 Configure, verify, and troubleshoot interswitch connectivity

  - 2.5.a Trunk ports

  - 2.5.b 802.1Q

  - 2.5.c Native VLAN

✓ **3.0 Routing Technologies**

- 3.4 Configure, verify, and troubleshoot inter-VLAN routing

  - 3.4.a Router on a stick

I know I keep telling you this, but so you never forget it, here I go, one last time: By default, switches break up collision domains and routers break up broadcast domains. Okay, I feel better! Now we can move on.

In contrast to the networks of yesterday that were based on collapsed backbones, today's network design is characterized by a flatter architecture—thanks to switches. So now what? How do we break up broadcast domains in a pure switched internetwork? By creating virtual local area networks (VLANs). A VLAN is a logical grouping of network users and resources connected to administratively defined ports on a switch. When you create VLANs, you're given the ability to create smaller broadcast domains within a layer 2 switched internetwork by assigning different ports on the switch to service different subnetworks. A VLAN is treated like its own subnet or broadcast domain, meaning that frames broadcast onto the network are only switched between the ports logically grouped within the same VLAN.

So, does this mean we no longer need routers? Maybe yes; maybe no. It really depends on what your particular networking needs and goals are. By default, hosts in a specific VLAN can't communicate with hosts that are members of another VLAN, so if you want inter-VLAN communication, the answer is that you still need a router or Inter-VLAN Routing (IVR).

In this chapter, you're going to comprehensively learn exactly what a VLAN is and how VLAN memberships are used in a switched network. You'll also become well-versed in what a trunk link is and how to configure and verify them.

I'll finish this chapter by demonstrating how you can make inter-VLAN communication happen by introducing a router into a switched network. Of course, we'll configure our familiar switched network layout we used in the last chapter for creating VLANs and for implementing trunking and Inter-VLAN routing on a layer 3 switch by creating switched virtual interfaces (SVIs).

To find up-to-the-minute updates for this chapter, please see www.lammle .com/ccna or the book's web page at www.sybex.com/go/ccna.

VLAN Basics

Figure 11.1 illustrates the flat network architecture that used to be so typical for layer 2 switched networks. With this configuration, every broadcast packet transmitted is seen by every device on the network regardless of whether the device needs to receive that data or not.

FIGURE 11.1   Flat network structure

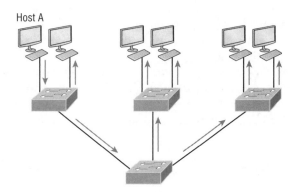

By default, routers allow broadcasts to occur only within the originating network, while switches forward broadcasts to all segments. Oh, and by the way, the reason it's called a *flat network* is because it's one *broadcast domain*, not because the actual design is physically flat. In Figure 11.1 we see Host A sending out a broadcast and all ports on all switches forwarding it—all except the port that originally received it.

Now check out Figure 11.2. It pictures a switched network and shows Host A sending a frame with Host D as its destination. Clearly, the important factor here is that the frame is only forwarded out the port where Host D is located.

FIGURE 11.2   The benefit of a switched network

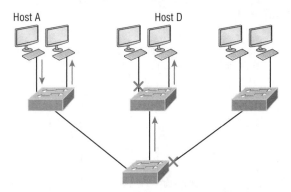

This is a huge improvement over the old hub networks, unless having one *collision domain* by default is what you really want for some reason!

Okay—you already know that the biggest benefit gained by having a layer 2 switched network is that it creates individual collision domain segments for each device plugged into each port on the switch. This scenario frees us from the old Ethernet density constraints and makes us able to build larger networks. But too often, each new advance comes with new issues. For instance, the more users and devices that populate and use a network, the more broadcasts and packets each switch must handle.

And there's another big issue—security! This one is real trouble because within the typical layer 2 switched internetwork, all users can see all devices by default. And you can't stop devices from broadcasting, plus you can't stop users from trying to respond to broadcasts. This means your security options are dismally limited to placing passwords on your servers and other devices.

But wait—there's hope if you create a *virtual LAN (VLAN)*! You can solve many of the problems associated with layer 2 switching with VLANs, as you'll soon see.

VLANs work like this: Figure 11.3 shows all hosts in this very small company connected to one switch, meaning all hosts will receive all frames, which is the default behavior of all switches.

FIGURE 11.3 One switch, one LAN: Before VLANs, there were no separations between hosts.

If we want to separate the host's data, we could either buy another switch or create virtual LANs, as shown in Figure 11.4.

FIGURE 11.4 One switch, two virtual LANs (*logical* separation between hosts): Still physically one switch, but this switch acts as many separate devices.

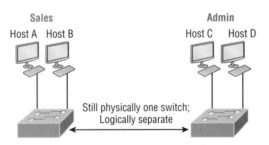

In Figure 11.4, I configured the switch to be two separate LANs, two subnets, two broadcast domains, two VLANs—they all mean the same thing—without buying another switch. We can do this 1,000 times on most Cisco switches, which saves thousands of dollars and more!

Notice that even though the separation is virtual and the hosts are all still connected to the same switch, the LANs can't send data to each other by default. This is because they are still separate networks, but no worries—we'll get into inter-VLAN communication later in this chapter.

Here's a short list of ways VLANs simplify network management:

- Network adds, moves, and changes are achieved with ease by just configuring a port into the appropriate VLAN.

- A group of users that need an unusually high level of security can be put into its own VLAN so that users outside of that VLAN can't communicate with the group's users.

- As a logical grouping of users by function, VLANs can be considered independent from their physical or geographic locations.

- VLANs greatly enhance network security if implemented correctly.

- VLANs increase the number of broadcast domains while decreasing their size.

Coming up, we'll thoroughly explore the world of switching, and you learn exactly how and why switches provide us with much better network services than hubs can in our networks today.

Broadcast Control

Broadcasts occur in every protocol, but how often they occur depends upon three things:

- The type of protocol

- The application(s) running on the internetwork

- How these services are used

Some older applications have been rewritten to reduce their bandwidth consumption, but there's a new generation of applications that are so bandwidth greedy they'll consume any and all they can find. These gluttons are the legion of multimedia applications that use both broadcasts and multicasts extensively. As if they weren't enough trouble, factors like faulty equipment, inadequate segmentation, and poorly designed firewalls can seriously compound the problems already caused by these broadcast-intensive applications. All of this has added a major new dimension to network design and presents a bunch of new challenges for an administrator. Positively making sure your network is properly segmented so you can quickly isolate a single segment's problems to prevent them from propagating throughout your entire internetwork is now imperative. And the most effective way to do that is through strategic switching and routing!

Since switches have become more affordable, most everyone has replaced their flat hub networks with pure switched network and VLAN environments. All devices within a VLAN are members of the same broadcast domain and receive all broadcasts relevant to it. By default, these broadcasts are filtered from all ports on a switch that aren't members of the same VLAN. This is great because you get all the benefits you would with a switched design without getting hit with all the problems you'd have if all your users were in the same broadcast domain—sweet!

Security

But there's always a catch, right? Time to get back to those security issues. A flat internetwork's security used to be tackled by connecting hubs and switches together with routers. So it was basically the router's job to maintain security. This arrangement was pretty ineffective for several reasons. First, anyone connecting to the physical network could access the network resources located on that particular physical LAN. Second, all anyone had to do to observe any and all traffic traversing that network was to simply plug a network analyzer into the hub. And similar to that last, scary, fact, users could easily join a workgroup by just plugging their workstations into the existing hub. That's about as secure as a barrel of honey in a bear enclosure!

But that's exactly what makes VLANs so cool. If you build them and create multiple broadcast groups, you can still have total control over each port and user! So the days when anyone could just plug their workstations into any switch port and gain access to network resources are history because now you get to control each port and any resources it can access.

And that's not even all—VLANs can be created in harmony with a specific user's need for the network resources. Plus, switches can be configured to inform a network management station about unauthorized access to those vital network resources. And if you need inter-VLAN communication, you can implement restrictions on a router to make sure this all happens securely. You can also place restrictions on hardware addresses, protocols, and applications. *Now* we're talking security—our honey barrel is now sealed tightly, made of solid titanium and wrapped in razor wire!

Flexibility and Scalability

If you've been paying attention so far, you know that layer 2 switches only read frames for filtering because they don't look at the Network layer protocol. You also know that by default, switches forward broadcasts to all ports. But if you create and implement VLANs, you're essentially creating smaller broadcast domains at layer 2.

As a result, broadcasts sent out from a node in one VLAN won't be forwarded to ports configured to belong to a different VLAN. But if we assign switch ports or users to VLAN groups on a switch or on a group of connected switches, we gain the flexibility to exclusively add only the users we want to let into that broadcast domain regardless of their physical location. This setup can also work to block broadcast storms caused by a faulty network interface card (NIC) as well as prevent an intermediate device from propagating broadcast storms throughout the entire internetwork. Those evils can still happen on the VLAN where the problem originated, but the disease will be fully contained in that one ailing VLAN!

Another advantage is that when a VLAN gets too big, you can simply create more VLANs to keep the broadcasts from consuming too much bandwidth. The fewer users in a VLAN, the fewer users affected by broadcasts. This is all good, but you seriously need to keep network services in mind and understand how the users connect to these services when creating a VLAN. A good strategy is to try to keep all services, except for the email and Internet access that everyone needs, local to all users whenever possible.

Identifying VLANs

Switch ports are layer 2–only interfaces that are associated with a physical port that can belong to only one VLAN if it's an access port or all VLANs if it's a trunk port.

Switches are definitely pretty busy devices. As myriad frames are switched throughout the network, switches have to be able to keep track of all of them, plus understand what to do with them depending on their associated hardware addresses. And remember—frames are handled differently according to the type of link they're traversing.

There are two different types of ports in a switched environment. Let's take a look at the first type in Figure 11.5.

FIGURE 11.5   Access ports

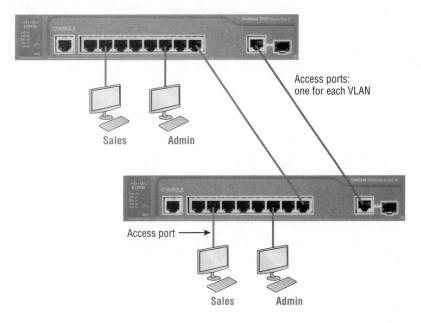

Notice there are access ports for each host and an access port between switches—one for each VLAN.

Access ports   An *access port* belongs to and carries the traffic of only one VLAN. Traffic is both received and sent in native formats with no VLAN information (tagging) whatsoever. Anything arriving on an access port is simply assumed to belong to the VLAN assigned to the port. Because an access port doesn't look at the source address, tagged traffic—a frame with added VLAN information—can be correctly forwarded and received only on trunk ports.

With an access link, this can be referred to as the *configured VLAN* of the port. Any device attached to an *access link* is unaware of a VLAN membership—the device just assumes it's part of some broadcast domain. But it doesn't have the big picture, so it doesn't understand the physical network topology at all.

Another good bit of information to know is that switches remove any VLAN information from the frame before it's forwarded out to an access-link device. Remember that access-link devices can't communicate with devices outside their VLAN unless the packet is routed. Also, you can only create a switch port to be either an access port or a trunk port—not both. So you've got to choose one or the other and know that if you make it an access port, that port can be assigned to one VLAN only. In Figure 11.5, only the hosts in the Sales VLAN can talk to other hosts in the same VLAN. This is the same with the Admin VLAN, and they can both communicate to hosts on the other switch because of an access link for each VLAN configured between switches.

> **Voice access ports**   Not to confuse you, but all that I just said about the fact that an access port can be assigned to only one VLAN is really only sort of true. Nowadays, most switches will allow you to add a second VLAN to an access port on a switch port for your voice traffic, called the voice VLAN. The voice VLAN used to be called the auxiliary VLAN, which allowed it to be overlaid on top of the data VLAN, enabling both types of traffic to travel through the same port. Even though this is technically considered to be a different type of link, it's still just an access port that can be configured for both data and voice VLANs. This allows you to connect both a phone and a PC device to one switch port but still have each device in a separate VLAN.

Trunk ports   Believe it or not, the term *trunk port* was inspired by the telephone system trunks, which carry multiple telephone conversations at a time. So it follows that trunk ports can similarly carry multiple VLANs at a time as well.

A *trunk link* is a 100, 1,000, or 10,000 Mbps point-to-point link between two switches, between a switch and router, or even between a switch and server, and it carries the traffic of multiple VLANs—from 1 to 4,094 VLANs at a time. But the amount is really only up to 1,001 unless you're going with something called extended VLANs.

Instead of an access link for each VLAN between switches, we'll create a trunk link, demonstrated in Figure 11.6.

FIGURE 11.6 VLANs can span across multiple switches by using trunk links, which carry traffic for multiple VLANs.

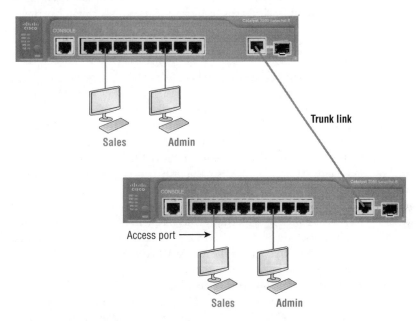

Trunking can be a real advantage because with it, you get to make a single port part of a whole bunch of different VLANs at the same time. This is a great feature because you can actually set ports up to have a server in two separate broadcast domains simultaneously so your users won't have to cross a layer 3 device (router) to log in and access it. Another benefit to trunking comes into play when you're connecting switches. Trunk links can carry the frames of various VLANs across them, but by default, if the links between your switches aren't trunked, only information from the configured access VLAN will be switched across that link.

It's also good to know that all VLANs send information on a trunked link unless you clear each VLAN by hand, and no worries, I'll show you how to clear individual VLANs from a trunk in a bit.

Okay—it's finally time to tell you about frame tagging and the VLAN identification methods used in it across our trunk links.

Frame Tagging

As you now know, you can set up your VLANs to span more than one connected switch. You can see that going on in Figure 11.6, which depicts hosts from two VLANs spread across two switches. This flexible, power-packed capability is probably the main advantage to implementing VLANs, and we can do this with up to a thousand VLANs and thousands upon thousands of hosts!

All this can get kind of complicated—even for a switch—so there needs to be a way for each one to keep track of all the users and frames as they travel the switch fabric and VLANs. When I say, "switch fabric," I'm just referring to a group of switches that share the same VLAN information. And this just happens to be where *frame tagging* enters the scene. This frame identification method uniquely assigns a user-defined VLAN ID to each frame.

Here's how it works: Once within the switch fabric, each switch that the frame reaches must first identify the VLAN ID from the frame tag. It then finds out what to do with the frame by looking at the information in what's known as the filter table. If the frame reaches a switch that has another trunked link, the frame will be forwarded out of the trunk-link port.

Once the frame reaches an exit that's determined by the forward/filter table to be an access link matching the frame's VLAN ID, the switch will remove the VLAN identifier. This is so the destination device can receive the frames without being required to understand their VLAN identification information.

Another great thing about trunk ports is that they'll support tagged and untagged traffic simultaneously if you're using 802.1q trunking, which we will talk about next. The trunk port is assigned a default port VLAN ID (PVID) for a VLAN upon which all untagged traffic will travel. This VLAN is also called the native VLAN and is always VLAN 1 by default, but it can be changed to any VLAN number.

Similarly, any untagged or tagged traffic with a NULL (unassigned) VLAN ID is assumed to belong to the VLAN with the port default PVID. Again, this would be VLAN 1 by default. A packet with a VLAN ID equal to the outgoing port native VLAN is sent untagged and can communicate to only hosts or devices in that same VLAN. All other VLAN traffic has to be sent with a VLAN tag to communicate within a particular VLAN that corresponds with that tag.

VLAN Identification Methods

VLAN identification is what switches use to keep track of all those frames as they're traversing a switch fabric. It's how switches identify which frames belong to which VLANs, and there's more than one trunking method.

Inter-Switch Link (ISL)

Inter-Switch Link (ISL) is a way of explicitly tagging VLAN information onto an Ethernet frame. This tagging information allows VLANs to be multiplexed over a trunk link through an external encapsulation method. This allows the switch to identify the VLAN membership of a frame received over the trunked link.

By running ISL, you can interconnect multiple switches and still maintain VLAN information as traffic travels between switches on trunk links. ISL functions at layer 2 by encapsulating a data frame with a new header and by performing a new cyclic redundancy check (CRC).

Of note is that ISL is proprietary to Cisco switches and is pretty versatile as well. ISL can be used on a switch port, router interfaces, and server interface cards to trunk a server.

Although some Cisco switches still support ISL frame tagging, Cisco is moving toward using only 802.1q.

IEEE 802.1q

Created by the IEEE as a standard method of frame tagging, IEEE 802.1q actually inserts a field into the frame to identify the VLAN. If you're trunking between a Cisco switched link and a different brand of switch, you've got to use 802.1q for the trunk to work.

Unlike ISL, which encapsulates the frame with control information, 802.1q inserts an 802.1q field along with tag control information, as shown in Figure 11.7.

FIGURE 11.7   IEEE 802.1q encapsulation with and without the 802.1q tag

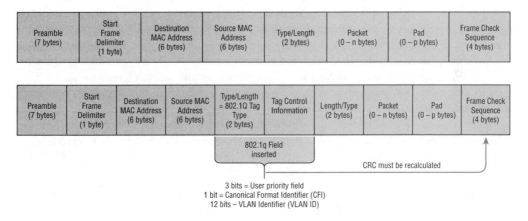

For the Cisco exam objectives, it's only the 12-bit VLAN ID that matters. This field identifies the VLAN and can be 2 to the 12th, minus 2 for the 0 and 4,095 reserved VLANs, which means an 802.1q tagged frame can carry information for 4,094 VLANs.

It works like this: You first designate each port that's going to be a trunk with 802.1q encapsulation. The other ports must be assigned a specific VLAN ID in order for them to communicate. VLAN 1 is the default native VLAN, and when using 802.1q, all traffic for a native VLAN is untagged. The ports that populate the same trunk create a group with this native VLAN and each port gets tagged with an identification number reflecting that. Again the default is VLAN 1. The native VLAN allows the trunks to accept information that was received without any VLAN identification or frame tag.

Most 2960 model switches only support the IEEE 802.1q trunking protocol, but the 3560 will support both the ISL and IEEE methods, which you'll see later in this chapter.

The basic purpose of ISL and 802.1q frame-tagging methods is to provide inter-switch VLAN communication. Remember that any ISL or 802.1q frame tagging is removed if a frame is forwarded out an access link—tagging is used internally and across trunk links only!

Routing between VLANs

Hosts in a VLAN live in their own broadcast domain and can communicate freely. VLANs create network partitioning and traffic separation at layer 2 of the OSI, and as I said when I told you why we still need routers, if you want hosts or any other IP-addressable device to communicate between VLANs, you must have a layer 3 device to provide routing.

For this, you can use a router that has an interface for each VLAN or a router that supports ISL or 802.1q routing. The least expensive router that supports ISL or 802.1q routing is the 2600 series router. You'd have to buy that from a used-equipment reseller because they are end-of-life, or EOL. I'd recommend at least a 2800 as a bare minimum, but even that only supports 802.1q; Cisco is really moving away from ISL, so you probably should only be using 802.1q anyway. Some 2800s may support both ISL and 802.1q; I've just never seen it supported.

Anyway, as shown in Figure 11.8, if you had two or three VLANs, you could get by with a router equipped with two or three FastEthernet connections. And 10Base-T is okay for home study purposes, and I mean only for your studies, but for anything else I'd highly recommend Gigabit interfaces for real power under the hood!

What we see in Figure 11.8 is that each router interface is plugged into an access link. This means that each of the routers' interface IP addresses would then become the default gateway address for each host in each respective VLAN.

FIGURE 11.8   Router connecting three VLANs together for inter-VLAN communication, one router interface for each VLAN

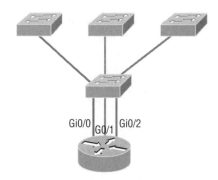

If you have more VLANs available than router interfaces, you can configure trunking on one FastEthernet interface or buy a layer 3 switch, like the old and now cheap 3560 or a higher-end switch like a 3850. You could even opt for a 6800 if you've got money to burn!

Instead of using a router interface for each VLAN, you can use one FastEthernet interface and run ISL or 802.1q trunking. Figure 11.9 shows how a FastEthernet interface on a router will look when configured with ISL or 802.1q trunking. This allows all VLANs to communicate through one interface. Cisco calls this a router on a stick (ROAS).

FIGURE 11.9   Router on a stick: single router interface connecting all three VLANs together for inter-VLAN communication

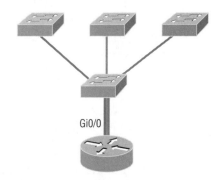

Gi0/0

I really want to point out that this creates a potential bottleneck, as well as a single point of failure, so your host/VLAN count is limited. To how many? Well, that depends on your traffic level. To really make things right, you'd be better off using a higher-end switch and routing on the backplane. But if you just happen to have a router sitting around, configuring this method is free, right?

Figure 11.10 shows how we would create a router on a stick using a router's physical interface by creating logical interfaces—one for each VLAN.

FIGURE 11.10   A router creates logical interfaces.

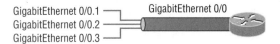

GigabitEthernet 0/0.1 —
GigabitEthernet 0/0.2 —   GigabitEthernet 0/0
GigabitEthernet 0/0.3 —

Here we see one physical interface divided into multiple subinterfaces, with one subnet assigned per VLAN, each subinterface being the default gateway address for each VLAN/subnet. An encapsulation identifier must be assigned to each subinterface to define the VLAN ID of that subinterface. In the next section where I'll configure VLANs and inter-VLAN routing, I'll configure our switched network with a router on a stick and demonstrate this configuration for you.

But wait, there's still one more way to go about routing! Instead of using an external router interface for each VLAN, or an external router on a stick, we can configure logical interfaces on the backplane of the layer 3 switch; this is called inter-VLAN routing (IVR), and it's configured with a switched virtual interface (SVI). Figure 11.11 shows how hosts see these virtual interfaces.

FIGURE 11.11   With IVR, routing runs on the backplane of the switch, and it appears to the hosts that a router is present.

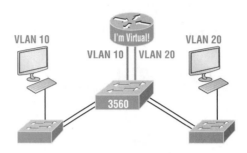

In Figure 11.11, it appears there's a router present, but there is no physical router present as there was when we used router on a stick. The IVR process takes little effort and is easy to implement, which makes it very cool! Plus, it's a lot more efficient for inter-VLAN routing than an external router is. To implement IVR on a multilayer switch, we just need to create logical interfaces in the switch configuration for each VLAN. We'll configure this method in a minute, but first let's take our existing switched network from Chapter 10, "Layer 2 Switching," and add some VLANs, then configure VLAN memberships and trunk links between our switches.

Configuring VLANs

Now this may come as a surprise to you, but configuring VLANs is actually pretty easy. It's just that figuring out which users you want in each VLAN is not, and doing that can eat up a lot of your time! But once you've decided on the number of VLANs you want to create and established which users you want belonging to each one, it's time to bring your first VLAN into the world.

To configure VLANs on a Cisco Catalyst switch, use the global config `vlan` command. In the following example, I'm going to demonstrate how to configure VLANs on the S1 switch by creating three VLANs for three different departments—again, remember that VLAN 1 is the native and management VLAN by default:

```
S1(config)#vlan ?
  WORD        ISL VLAN IDs 1-4094
  access-map  Create vlan access-map or enter vlan access-map command mode
  dot1q       dot1q parameters
  filter      Apply a VLAN Map
  group       Create a vlan group
  internal    internal VLAN
```

```
S1(config)#vlan 2
S1(config-vlan)#name Sales
S1(config-vlan)#vlan 3
S1(config-vlan)#name Marketing
S1(config-vlan)#vlan 4
S1(config-vlan)#name Accounting
S1(config-vlan)#vlan 5
S1(config-vlan)#name Voice
S1(config-vlan)#^Z
S1#
```

In this output, you can see that you can create VLANs from 1 to 4094. But this is only mostly true. As I said, VLANs can really only be created up to 1001, and you can't use, change, rename, or delete VLANs 1 or 1002 through 1005 because they're reserved. The VLAN numbers above 1005 are called extended VLANs and won't be saved in the database unless your switch is set to what is called VLAN Trunking Protocol (VTP) transparent mode. You won't see these VLAN numbers used too often in production. Here's an example of me attempting to set my S1 switch to VLAN 4000 when my switch is set to VTP server mode (the default VTP mode):

```
S1#config t
S1(config)#vlan 4000
S1(config-vlan)#^Z
% Failed to create VLANs 4000
Extended VLAN(s) not allowed in current VTP mode.
%Failed to commit extended VLAN(s) changes.
```

After you create the VLANs that you want, you can use the show vlan command to check them out. But notice that, by default, all ports on the switch are in VLAN 1. To change the VLAN associated with a port, you need to go to each interface and specifically tell it which VLAN to be a part of.

Remember that a created VLAN is unused until it is assigned to a switch port or ports and that all ports are always assigned in VLAN 1 unless set otherwise.

Once the VLANs are created, verify your configuration with the show vlan command (sh vlan for short):

```
S1#sh vlan
VLAN Name                            Status    Ports
---- -------------------------- --------- -------------------------------
1    default                     active    Fa0/1, Fa0/2, Fa0/3, Fa0/4
                                           Fa0/5, Fa0/6, Fa0/7, Fa0/8
                                           Fa0/9, Fa0/10, Fa0/11, Fa0/12
```

```
                                    Fa0/13, Fa0/14, Fa0/19, Fa0/20
                                    Fa0/21, Fa0/22, Fa0/23, Gi0/1
                                    Gi0/2
2     Sales                         active
3     Marketing                     active
4     Accounting                    active
5     Voice                         active
[output cut]
```

This may seem repetitive, but it's important, and I want you to remember it: You can't change, delete, or rename VLAN 1 because it's the default VLAN and you just can't change that—period. It's also the native VLAN of all switches by default, and Cisco recommends that you use it as your management VLAN. If you're worried about security issues, then change it! Basically, any ports that aren't specifically assigned to a different VLAN will be sent down to the native VLAN—VLAN 1.

In the preceding S1 output, you can see that ports Fa0/1 through Fa0/14, Fa0/19 through 23, and Gi0/1 and Gi0/2 uplinks are all in VLAN 1. But where are ports 15 through 18? First, understand that the command show vlan only displays access ports, so now that you know what you're looking at with the show vlan command, where do you think ports Fa15–18 are? That's right! They are trunked ports. Cisco switches run a proprietary protocol called *Dynamic Trunk Protocol (DTP)*, and if there is a compatible switch connected, they will start trunking automatically, which is precisely where my four ports are. You have to use the show interfaces trunk command to see your trunked ports like this:

```
S1# show interfaces trunk
Port      Mode          Encapsulation  Status     Native vlan
Fa0/15    desirable     n-isl          trunking   1
Fa0/16    desirable     n-isl          trunking   1
Fa0/17    desirable     n-isl          trunking   1
Fa0/18    desirable     n-isl          trunking   1

Port      Vlans allowed on trunk
Fa0/15    1-4094
Fa0/16    1-4094
Fa0/17    1-4094
Fa0/18    1-4094

[output cut]
```

This output reveals that the VLANs from 1 to 4094 are allowed across the trunk by default. Another helpful command, which is also part of the Cisco exam objectives, is the show interfaces *interface* switchport command:

```
S1#sh interfaces fastEthernet 0/15 switchport
Name: Fa0/15
Switchport: Enabled
```

```
Administrative Mode: dynamic desirable
Operational Mode: trunk
Administrative Trunking Encapsulation: negotiate
Operational Trunking Encapsulation: isl
Negotiation of Trunking: On
Access Mode VLAN: 1 (default)
Trunking Native Mode VLAN: 1 (default)
Administrative Native VLAN tagging: enabled
Voice VLAN: none
[output cut]
```

The highlighted output shows us the administrative mode of dynamic desirable, that the port is a trunk port, and that DTP was used to negotiate the frame-tagging method of ISL. It also predictably shows that the native VLAN is the default of 1.

Now that we can see the VLANs created, we can assign switch ports to specific ones. Each port can be part of only one VLAN, with the exception of voice access ports. Using trunking, you can make a port available to traffic from all VLANs. I'll cover that next.

Assigning Switch Ports to VLANs

You configure a port to belong to a VLAN by assigning a membership mode that specifies the kind of traffic the port carries plus the number of VLANs it can belong to. You can also configure each port on a switch to be in a specific VLAN (access port) by using the interface switchport command. You can even configure multiple ports at the same time with the interface range command.

In the next example, I'll configure interface Fa0/3 to VLAN 3. This is the connection from the S3 switch to the host device:

```
S3#config t
S3(config)#int fa0/3
S3(config-if)#switchport ?
  access         Set access mode characteristics of the interface
  autostate      Include or exclude this port from vlan link up calculation
  backup         Set backup for the interface
  block          Disable forwarding of unknown uni/multi cast addresses
  host           Set port host
  mode           Set trunking mode of the interface
  nonegotiate    Device will not engage in negotiation protocol on this
                 interface
  port-security  Security related command
  priority       Set appliance 802.1p priority
  private-vlan   Set the private VLAN configuration
```

```
protected      Configure an interface to be a protected port
trunk          Set trunking characteristics of the interface
voice          Voice appliance attributes voice
```

Well now, what do we have here? There's some new stuff showing up in our output now. We can see various commands—some that I've already covered, but no worries because I'm going to cover the access, mode, nonegotiate, and trunk commands very soon. Let's start with setting an access port on S1, which is probably the most widely used type of port you'll find on production switches that have VLANs configured:

```
S3(config-if)#switchport mode ?
    access       Set trunking mode to ACCESS unconditionally
  dot1q-tunnel  set trunking mode to TUNNEL unconditionally
  dynamic        Set trunking mode to dynamically negotiate access or trunk mode
  private-vlan  Set private-vlan mode
  trunk          Set trunking mode to TRUNK unconditionally

S3(config-if)#switchport mode access
S3(config-if)#switchport access vlan 3
S3(config-if)#switchport voice vlan 5
```

By starting with the switchport mode access command, you're telling the switch that this is a nontrunking layer 2 port. You can then assign a VLAN to the port with the switchport access command, as well as configure the same port to be a member of a different type of VLAN, called the voice VLAN. This allows you to connect a laptop into a phone, and the phone into a single switch port. Remember, you can choose many ports to configure simultaneously with the interface range command.

Let's take a look at our VLANs now:

```
S3#show vlan
VLAN Name                     Status    Ports
---- ----------------------- --------- -------------------------------
1    default                 active    Fa0/4, Fa0/5, Fa0/6, Fa0/7
                                       Fa0/8, Fa0/9, Fa0/10, Fa0/11,
                                       Fa0/12, Fa0/13, Fa0/14, Fa0/19,
                                       Fa0/20, Fa0/21, Fa0/22, Fa0/23,
                                       Gi0/1 ,Gi0/2
2    Sales                   active
3    Marketing               active    Fa0/3
5    Voice                   active    Fa0/3
```

Notice that port Fa0/3 is now a member of VLAN 3 and VLAN 5—two different types of VLANs. But, can you tell me where ports 1 and 2 are? And why aren't they showing up in the output of show vlan? That's right, because they are trunk ports!

We can also see this with the show interfaces *interface* switchport command:

```
S3#sh int fa0/3 switchport
Name: Fa0/3
```

```
Switchport: Enabled
Administrative Mode: static access
Operational Mode: static access
Administrative Trunking Encapsulation: negotiate
Negotiation of Trunking: Off
Access Mode VLAN: 3 (Marketing)
Trunking Native Mode VLAN: 1 (default)
Administrative Native VLAN tagging: enabled
Voice VLAN: 5 (Voice)
```

The highlighted output shows that Fa0/3 is an access port and a member of VLAN 3 (Marketing), as well as a member of the Voice VLAN 5.

That's it. Well, sort of. If you plugged devices into each VLAN port, they can only talk to other devices in the same VLAN. But as soon as you learn a bit more about trunking, we're going to enable inter-VLAN communication!

Configuring Trunk Ports

The 2960 switch only runs the IEEE 802.1q encapsulation method. To configure trunking on a FastEthernet port, use the interface command switchport mode trunk. It's a tad different on the 3560 switch.

The following switch output shows the trunk configuration on interfaces Fa0/15–18 as set to trunk:

```
S1(config)#int range f0/15-18
S1(config-if-range)#switchport trunk encapsulation dot1q
S1(config-if-range)#switchport mode trunk
```

If you have a switch that only runs the 802.1q encapsulation method, then you wouldn't use the encapsulation command as I did in the preceding output. Let's check out our trunk ports now:

```
S1(config-if-range)#do sh int f0/15 swi
Name: Fa0/15
Switchport: Enabled
Administrative Mode: trunk
Operational Mode: trunk
Administrative Trunking Encapsulation: dot1q
Operational Trunking Encapsulation: dot1q
Negotiation of Trunking: On
Access Mode VLAN: 1 (default)
Trunking Native Mode VLAN: 1 (default)
Administrative Native VLAN tagging: enabled
Voice VLAN: none
```

Notice that port Fa0/15 is a trunk and running 802.1q. Let's take another look:

```
S1(config-if-range)#do sh int trunk
Port        Mode            Encapsulation   Status        Native vlan
Fa0/15      on              802.1q          trunking      1
Fa0/16      on              802.1q          trunking      1
Fa0/17      on              802.1q          trunking      1
Fa0/18      on              802.1q          trunking      1
Port        Vlans allowed on trunk
Fa0/15      1-4094
Fa0/16      1-4094
Fa0/17      1-4094
Fa0/18      1-4094
```

Take note of the fact that ports 15–18 are now in the trunk mode of on and the encapsulation is now 802.1q instead of the negotiated ISL. Here's a description of the different options available when configuring a switch interface:

switchport mode access   I discussed this in the previous section, but this puts the interface (access port) into permanent nontrunking mode and negotiates to convert the link into a nontrunk link. The interface becomes a nontrunk interface regardless of whether the neighboring interface is a trunk interface. The port would be a dedicated layer 2 access port.

switchport mode dynamic auto   This mode makes the interface able to convert the link to a trunk link. The interface becomes a trunk interface if the neighboring interface is set to trunk or desirable mode. The default is dynamic auto on a lot of Cisco switches, but that default trunk method is changing to dynamic desirable on most new models.

switchport mode dynamic desirable   This one makes the interface actively attempt to convert the link to a trunk link. The interface becomes a trunk interface if the neighboring interface is set to trunk, desirable, or auto mode. I used to see this mode as the default on some switches, but not any longer. This is now the default switch port mode for all Ethernet interfaces on all new Cisco switches.

switchport mode trunk   Puts the interface into permanent trunking mode and negotiates to convert the neighboring link into a trunk link. The interface becomes a trunk interface even if the neighboring interface isn't a trunk interface.

switchport nonegotiate   Prevents the interface from generating DTP frames. You can use this command only when the interface switchport mode is access or trunk. You must manually configure the neighboring interface as a trunk interface to establish a trunk link.

Dynamic Trunking Protocol (DTP) is used for negotiating trunking on a link between two devices as well as negotiating the encapsulation type of either 802.1q or ISL. I use the nonegotiate command when I want dedicated trunk ports; no questions asked.

To disable trunking on an interface, use the `switchport mode access` command, which sets the port back to a dedicated layer 2 access switch port.

Defining the Allowed VLANs on a Trunk

As I've mentioned, trunk ports send and receive information from all VLANs by default, and if a frame is untagged, it's sent to the management VLAN. Understand that this applies to the extended range VLANs too.

But we can remove VLANs from the allowed list to prevent traffic from certain VLANs from traversing a trunked link. I'll show you how you'd do that, but first let me again demonstrate that all VLANs are allowed across the trunk link by default:

```
S1#sh int trunk
[output cut]
Port        Vlans allowed on trunk
Fa0/15      1-4094
Fa0/16      1-4094
Fa0/17      1-4094
Fa0/18      1-4094
S1(config)#int f0/15
S1(config-if)#switchport trunk allowed vlan 4,6,12,15
S1(config-if)#do show int trunk
[output cut]
Port        Vlans allowed on trunk
Fa0/15      4,6,12,15
Fa0/16      1-4094
Fa0/17      1-4094
Fa0/18      1-4094
```

The preceding command affected the trunk link configured on S1 port F0/15, causing it to permit all traffic sent and received for VLANs 4, 6, 12, and 15. You can try to remove VLAN 1 on a trunk link, but it will still send and receive management like CDP, DTP, and VTP, so what's the point?

To remove a range of VLANs, just use the hyphen:

```
S1(config-if)#switchport trunk allowed vlan remove 4-8
```

If by chance someone has removed some VLANs from a trunk link and you want to set the trunk back to default, just use this command:

```
S1(config-if)#switchport trunk allowed vlan all
```

Next, I want to show you how to configure a native VLAN for a trunk before we start routing between VLANs.

Changing or Modifying the Trunk Native VLAN

You can change the trunk port native VLAN from VLAN 1, which many people do for security reasons. To change the native VLAN, use the following command:

```
S1(config)#int f0/15
S1(config-if)#switchport trunk native vlan ?
  <1-4094>  VLAN ID of the native VLAN when this port is in trunking mode

S1(config-if)#switchport trunk native vlan 4
1w6d: %CDP-4-NATIVE_VLAN_MISMATCH: Native VLAN mismatch discovered on
FastEthernet0/15 (4), with S3 FastEthernet0/1 (1).
```

So we've changed our native VLAN on our trunk link to 4, and by using the show running-config command, I can see the configuration under the trunk link:

```
S1#sh run int f0/15
Building configuration...

Current configuration : 202 bytes
!
interface FastEthernet0/15
 description 1st connection to S3
 switchport trunk encapsulation dot1q
 switchport trunk native vlan 4
 switchport trunk allowed vlan 4,6,12,15
 switchport mode trunk
end

S1#!
```

Oops—wait a minute! You didn't think it would be this easy and would just start working, did you? Of course not! Here's the rub: If all switches don't have the same native VLAN configured on the given trunk links, then we'll start to receive this error, which happened immediately after I entered the command:

```
1w6d: %CDP-4-NATIVE_VLAN_MISMATCH: Native VLAN mismatch discovered
on FastEthernet0/15 (4), with S3 FastEthernet0/1 (1).
```

Actually, this is a good, noncryptic error, so either we can go to the other end of our trunk link(s) and change the native VLAN or we set the native VLAN back to the default to fix it. Here's how we'd do that:

```
S1(config-if)#no switchport trunk native vlan
1w6d: %SPANTREE-2-UNBLOCK_CONSIST_PORT: Unblocking FastEthernet0/15
on VLAN0004. Port consistency restored.
```

Now our trunk link is using the default VLAN 1 as the native VLAN. Just remember that all switches on a given trunk must use the same native VLAN or you'll have some serious management problems. These issues won't affect user data, just management traffic between switches. Now, let's mix it up by connecting a router into our switched network and configure inter-VLAN communication.

Configuring Inter-VLAN Routing

By default, only hosts that are members of the same VLAN can communicate. To change this and allow inter-VLAN communication, you need a router or a layer 3 switch. I'm going to start with the router approach.

To support ISL or 802.1q routing on a FastEthernet interface, the router's interface is divided into logical interfaces—one for each VLAN—as was shown in Figure 11.10. These are called *subinterfaces*. From a FastEthernet or Gigabit interface, you can set the interface to trunk with the encapsulation command:

```
ISR#config t
ISR(config)#int f0/0.1
ISR(config-subif)#encapsulation ?
  dot1Q  IEEE 802.1Q Virtual LAN
ISR(config-subif)#encapsulation dot1Q ?
  <1-4094>  IEEE 802.1Q VLAN ID
```

Notice that my 2811 router (named ISR) only supports 802.1q. We'd need an older-model router to run the ISL encapsulation, but why bother?

The subinterface number is only locally significant, so it doesn't matter which subinterface numbers are configured on the router. Most of the time, I'll configure a subinterface with the same number as the VLAN I want to route. It's easy to remember that way since the subinterface number is used only for administrative purposes.

It's really important that you understand that each VLAN is actually a separate subnet. True, I know—they don't *have* to be. But it really is a good idea to configure your VLANs as separate subnets, so just do that. Before we move on, I want to define *upstream routing*. This is a term used to define the router on a stick. This router will provide inter-VLAN routing, but it can also be used to forward traffic upstream from the switched network to other parts of the corporate network or Internet.

Now, I need to make sure you're fully prepared to configure inter-VLAN routing as well as determine the IP addresses of hosts connected in a switched VLAN environment. And as always, it's also a good idea to be able to fix any problems that may arise. To set you up for success, let me give you few examples.

First, start by looking at Figure 11.12 and read the router and switch configuration within it. By this point in the book, you should be able to determine the IP address, masks, and default gateways of each of the hosts in the VLANs.

FIGURE 11.12   Configuring inter-VLAN example 1

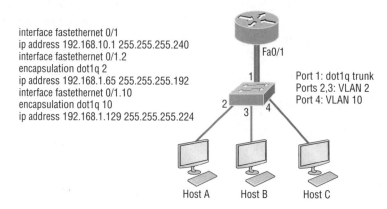

```
interface fastethernet 0/1
ip address 192.168.10.1 255.255.255.240
interface fastethernet 0/1.2
encapsulation dot1q 2
ip address 192.168.1.65 255.255.255.192
interface fastethernet 0/1.10
encapsulation dot1q 10
ip address 192.168.1.129 255.255.255.224
```

Fa0/1

Port 1: dot1q trunk
Ports 2,3: VLAN 2
Port 4: VLAN 10

Host A   Host B   Host C

The next step is to figure out which subnets are being used. By looking at the router configuration in the figure, you can see that we're using 192.168.10.0/28 for VLAN1, 192.168.1.64/26 with VLAN 2, and 192.168.1.128/27 for VLAN 10.

By looking at the switch configuration, you can see that ports 2 and 3 are in VLAN 2 and port 4 is in VLAN 10. This means that Host A and Host B are in VLAN 2 and Host C is in VLAN 10.

But wait—what's that IP address doing there under the physical interface? Can we even do that? Sure we can! If we place an IP address under the physical interface, the result is that frames sent from the IP address would be untagged. So what VLAN would those frames be a member of? By default, they would belong to VLAN 1, our management VLAN. This means the address 192.168.10.1/28 is my native VLAN IP address for this switch.

Here's what the hosts' IP addresses should be:

Host A: 192.168.1.66, 255.255.255.192, default gateway 192.168.1.65

Host B: 192.168.1.67, 255.255.255.192, default gateway 192.168.1.65

Host C: 192.168.1.130, 255.255.255.224, default gateway 192.168.1.129

The hosts could be any address in the range—I just chose the first available IP address after the default gateway address. That wasn't so hard, was it?

Now, again using Figure 11.12, let's go through the commands necessary to configure switch port 1 so it will establish a link with the router and provide inter-VLAN communication using the IEEE version for encapsulation. Keep in mind that the commands can vary slightly depending on what type of switch you're dealing with.

For a 2960 switch, use the following:

```
2960#config t
2960(config)#interface fa0/1
2960(config-if)#switchport mode trunk
```

That's it! As you already know, the 2960 switch can only run the 802.1q encapsulation, so there's no need to specify it. You can't anyway. For a 3560, it's basically the same, but because it can run ISL and 802.1q, you have to specify the trunking encapsulation protocol you're going to use.

> Remember that when you create a trunked link, all VLANs are allowed to pass data by default.

Let's take a look at Figure 11.13 and see what we can determine. This figure shows three VLANs, with two hosts in each of them. The router in Figure 11.13 is connected to the Fa0/1 switch port, and VLAN 4 is configured on port F0/6.

When looking at this diagram, keep in mind that these three factors are what Cisco expects you to know:

- The router is connected to the switch using subinterfaces.
- The switch port connecting to the router is a trunk port.
- The switch ports connecting to the clients and the hub are access ports, not trunk ports.

FIGURE 11.13 Inter-VLAN example 2

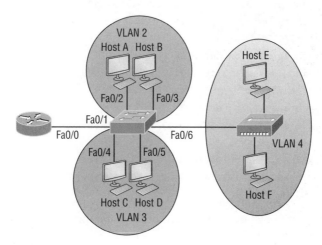

The configuration of the switch would look something like this:

```
2960#config t
2960(config)#int f0/1
2960(config-if)#switchport mode trunk
```

```
2960(config-if)#int f0/2
2960(config-if)#switchport access vlan 2
2960(config-if)#int f0/3
2960(config-if)#switchport access vlan 2
2960(config-if)#int f0/4
2960(config-if)#switchport access vlan 3
2960(config-if)#int f0/5
2960(config-if)#switchport access vlan 3
2960(config-if)#int f0/6
2960(config-if)#switchport access vlan 4
```

Before we configure the router, we need to design our logical network:

VLAN 1: 192.168.10.0/28

VLAN 2: 192.168.10.16/28

VLAN 3: 192.168.10.32/28

VLAN 4: 192.168.10.48/28

The configuration of the router would then look like this:

```
ISR#config t
ISR(config)#int fa0/0
ISR(config-if)#ip address 192.168.10.1 255.255.255.240
ISR(config-if)#no shutdown
ISR(config-if)#int f0/0.2
ISR(config-subif)#encapsulation dot1q 2
ISR(config-subif)#ip address 192.168.10.17 255.255.255.240
ISR(config-subif)#int f0/0.3
ISR(config-subif)#encapsulation dot1q 3
ISR(config-subif)#ip address 192.168.10.33 255.255.255.240
ISR(config-subif)#int f0/0.4
ISR(config-subif)#encapsulation dot1q 4
ISR(config-subif)#ip address 192.168.10.49 255.255.255.240
```

Notice I didn't tag VLAN 1. Even though I could have created a subinterface and tagged VLAN 1, it's not necessary with 802.1q because untagged frames are members of the native VLAN.

The hosts in each VLAN would be assigned an address from their subnet range, and the default gateway would be the IP address assigned to the router's subinterface in that VLAN.

Now, let's take a look at another figure and see if you can determine the switch and router configurations without looking at the answer—no cheating! Figure 11.14 shows a router connected to a 2960 switch with two VLANs. One host in each VLAN is assigned an IP address. What would your router and switch configurations be based on these IP addresses?

FIGURE 11.14   Inter-VLAN example 3

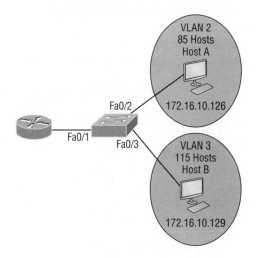

Since the hosts don't list a subnet mask, you have to look for the number of hosts used in each VLAN to figure out the block size. VLAN 2 has 85 hosts and VLAN 3 has 115 hosts. Each of these will fit in a block size of 128, which is a /25 mask, or 255.255.255.128.

You should know by now that the subnets are 0 and 128; the 0 subnet (VLAN 2) has a host range of 1–126, and the 128 subnet (VLAN 3) has a range of 129–254. You can almost be fooled since Host A has an IP address of 126, which makes it *almost* seem that Host A and B are in the same subnet. But they're not, and you're way too smart by now to be fooled by this one!

Here is the switch configuration:

```
2960#config t
2960(config)#int f0/1
2960(config-if)#switchport mode trunk
2960(config-if)#int f0/2
2960(config-if)#switchport access vlan 2
2960(config-if)#int f0/3
2960(config-if)#switchport access vlan 3
```

Here is the router configuration:

```
ISR#config t
ISR(config)#int f0/0
```

```
ISR(config-if)#ip address 192.168.10.1 255.255.255.0
ISR(config-if)#no shutdown
ISR(config-if)#int f0/0.2
ISR(config-subif)#encapsulation dot1q 2
ISR(config-subif)#ip address 172.16.10.1 255.255.255.128
ISR(config-subif)#int f0/0.3
ISR(config-subif)#encapsulation dot1q 3
ISR(config-subif)#ip address 172.16.10.254 255.255.255.128
```

I used the first address in the host range for VLAN 2 and the last address in the range for VLAN 3, but any address in the range would work. You would just have to configure the host's default gateway to whatever you make the router's address. Also, I used a different subnet for my physical interface, which is my management VLAN router's address.

Now, before we go on to the next example, I need to make sure you know how to set the IP address on the switch. Since VLAN 1 is typically the administrative VLAN, we'll use an IP address from out of that pool of addresses. Here's how to set the IP address of the switch (not nagging, but you really should already know this!):

```
2960#config t
2960(config)#int vlan 1
2960(config-if)#ip address 192.168.10.2 255.255.255.0
2960(config-if)#no shutdown
2960(config-if)#exit
2960(config)#ip default-gateway 192.168.10.1
```

Yes, you have to execute a no shutdown on the VLAN interface and set the ip default-gateway address to the router.

One more example, and then we'll move on to IVR using a multilayer switch—another important subject that you definitely don't want to miss! In Figure 11.15 there are two VLANs, plus the management VLAN 1. By looking at the router configuration, what's the IP address, subnet mask, and default gateway of Host A? Use the last IP address in the range for Host A's address.

If you really look carefully at the router configuration (the hostname in this configuration is just Router), there's a simple and quick answer. All subnets are using a /28, which is a 255.255.255.240 mask. This is a block size of 16. The router's address for VLAN 2 is in subnet 128. The next subnet is 144, so the broadcast address of VLAN 2 is 143 and the valid host range is 129–142. So the host address would be this:

IP address: 192.168.10.142

Mask: 255.255.255.240

Default gateway: 192.168.10.129

FIGURE 11.15 Inter-VLAN example 4

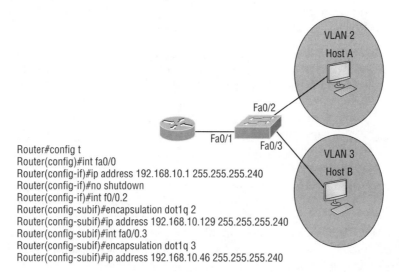

```
Router#config t
Router(config)#int fa0/0
Router(config-if)#ip address 192.168.10.1 255.255.255.240
Router(config-if)#no shutdown
Router(config-if)#int f0/0.2
Router(config-subif)#encapsulation dot1q 2
Router(config-subif)#ip address 192.168.10.129 255.255.255.240
Router(config-subif)#int fa0/0.3
Router(config-subif)#encapsulation dot1q 3
Router(config-subif)#ip address 192.168.10.46 255.255.255.240
```

This section was probably the hardest part of this entire book, and I honestly created the simplest configuration you can possibly get away with using to help you through it!

I'll use Figure 11.16 to demonstrate configuring inter-VLAN routing (IVR) with a multilayer switch, which is often referred to as a switched virtual interface (SVI). I'm going to use the same network that I used to discuss a multilayer switch back in Figure 11.11, and I'll use this IP address scheme: 192.168.*x*.0/24, where *x* represents the VLAN subnet. In my example this will be the same as the VLAN number.

FIGURE 11.16 Inter-VLAN routing with a multilayer switch

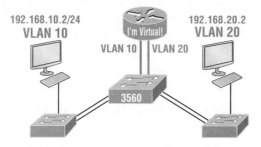

The hosts are already configured with the IP address, subnet mask, and default gateway address using the first address in the range. Now I just need to configure the routing on the switch, which is pretty simple actually:

```
S1(config)#ip routing
S1(config)#int vlan 10
```

```
S1(config-if)#ip address 192.168.10.1 255.255.255.0
S1(config-if)#int vlan 20
S1(config-if)#ip address 192.168.20.1 255.255.255.0
```

And that's it! Enable IP routing and create one logical interface for each VLAN using the interface vlan number command and voilà! You've now accomplished making inter-VLAN routing work on the backplane of the switch!

Summary

In this chapter, I introduced you to the world of virtual LANs and described how Cisco switches can use them. We talked about how VLANs break up broadcast domains in a switched internetwork—a very important, necessary thing because layer 2 switches only break up collision domains, and by default, all switches make up one large broadcast domain. I also described access links to you, and we went over how trunked VLANs work across a FastEthernet or faster link.

Trunking is a crucial technology to understand really well when you're dealing with a network populated by multiple switches that are running several VLANs.

You were also presented with some key troubleshooting and configuration examples for access and trunk ports, configuring trunking options, and a huge section on IVR.

Exam Essentials

Understand the term *frame tagging*.   *Frame tagging* refers to VLAN identification; this is what switches use to keep track of all those frames as they're traversing a switch fabric. It's how switches identify which frames belong to which VLANs.

Understand the 802.1q VLAN identification method.   This is a nonproprietary IEEE method of frame tagging. If you're trunking between a Cisco switched link and a different brand of switch, you have to use 802.1q for the trunk to work.

Remember how to set a trunk port on a 2960 switch.   To set a port to trunking on a 2960, use the switchport mode trunk command.

Remember to check a switch port's VLAN assignment when plugging in a new host.   If you plug a new host into a switch, then you must verify the VLAN membership of that port. If the membership is different than what is needed for that host, the host will not be able to reach the needed network services, such as a workgroup server or printer.

Remember how to create a Cisco router on a stick to provide inter-VLAN communication.   You can use a Cisco FastEthernet or Gigabit Ethernet interface to provide inter-VLAN routing. The switch port connected to the router must be a trunk port; then you must create virtual interfaces (subinterfaces) on the router port for each VLAN connecting to it. The hosts in each VLAN will use this subinterface address as their default gateway address.

Remember how to provide inter-VLAN routing with a layer 3 switch.   You can use a layer 3 (multilayer) switch to provide IVR just as with a router on a stick, but using a layer 3 switch is more efficient and faster. First you start the routing process with the command `ip routing`, then create a virtual interface for each VLAN using the command `interface vlan vlan`, and then apply the IP address for that VLAN under that logical interface.

Written Lab 11

In this section, you'll complete the following lab to make sure you've got the information and concepts contained within them fully dialed in:

Lab 11.1: VLANs

You can find the answers to this lab in Appendix A, "Answers to Written Labs."
Write the answers to the following questions:

1.   True/False: To provide IVR with a layer 3 switch, you place an IP address on each interface of the switch.

2.   What protocol will stop loops in a layer 2 switched network?

3.   VLANs break up _____ domains in a layer 2 switched network.

4.   Which VLAN numbers are reserved by default?

5.   If you have a switch that provides both ISL and 802.1q frame tagging, what command under the trunk interface will make the trunk use 802.1q?

6.   What does trunking provide?

7.   How many VLANs can you create on an IOS switch by default?

8.   True/False: The 802.1q encapsulation is removed from the frame if the frame is forwarded out an access link.

9.   What type of link on a switch is a member of only one VLAN?

10. You want to change from the default of VLAN 1 to VLAN 4 for untagged traffic. What command will you use?

Hands-on Labs

In these labs, you will use three switches and a router. To perform the last lab, you'll need a layer 3 switch.

Lab 11.1: Configuring and Verifying VLANs

Lab 11.2: Configuring and Verifying Trunk Links

Lab 11.3: Configuring Router on a Stick Routing

Lab 11.4: Configuring IVR with a Layer 3 Switch

In these labs, I'll use the following layout:

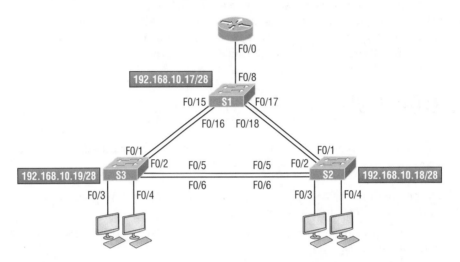

Hands-on Lab 11.1: Configuring and Verifying VLANs

This lab will have you configure VLANs from global configuration mode and then verify the VLANs.

1. Configure two VLANs on each switch, VLAN 10 and VLAN 20.

   ```
   S1(config)#vlan 10
   S1(config-vlan)#vlan 20

   S2(config)#vlan 10
   S2(config-vlan)#vlan 20

   S3(config)#vlan 10
   S3(config-vlan)#vlan 20
   ```

2. Use the show vlan and show vlan brief commands to verify your VLANs. Notice that all interfaces are in VLAN 1 by default.

   ```
   S1#sh vlan
   S1#sh vlan brief
   ```

Hands-on Lab 11.2: Configuring and Verifying Trunk Links

This lab will have you configure trunk links and then verify them.

1. Connect to each switch and configure trunking on all switch links. If you are using a switch that supports both 802.1q and ISL frame tagging, then use the encapsulation command; if not, then skip that command.

```
S1#config t
S1(config)#interface fa0/15
S1(config-if)#switchport trunk encapsulation ?
  dot1q  Interface uses only 802.1q trunking encapsulation when trunking
  isl    Interface uses only ISL trunking encapsulation when trunking
  negotiate   Device will negotiate trunking encapsulation with peer on
interface
```

Again, if you typed the previous and received an error, then your switch does not support both encapsulation methods:

```
S1 (config-if)#switchport trunk encapsulation dot1q
S1 (config-if)#switchport mode trunk
S1 (config-if)#interface fa0/16
S1 (config-if)#switchport trunk encapsulation dot1q
S1 (config-if)#switchport mode trunk
S1 (config-if)#interface fa0/17
S1 (config-if)#switchport trunk encapsulation dot1q
S1 (config-if)#switchport mode trunk
S1 (config-f)#interface fa0/18
S1 (config-if)#switchport trunk encapsulation dot1q
S1 (config-if)#switchport mode trunk
```

2. Configure the trunk links on your other switches.

3. On each switch, verify your trunk ports with the `show interface trunk` command:

```
S1#show interface trunk
```

4. Verify the switchport configuration with the following:

```
S1#show interface interface switchport
```

The second *interface* in the command is a variable, such as Fa0/15.

Hands-on Lab 11.3: Configuring Router on a Stick Routing

In this lab, you'll use the router connected to port F0/8 of switch S1 to configure ROAS.

1. Configure the F0/0 of the router with two subinterfaces to provide inter-VLAN routing using 802.1q encapsulation. Use 172.16.10.0/24 for your management VLAN, 10.10.10.0/24 for VLAN 10, and 20.20.20.0/24 for VLAN 20.

```
Router#config t
Router (config)#int f0/0
Router (config-if)#ip address 172.16.10.1 255.255.255.0
Router (config-if)#interface f0/0.10
Router (config-subif)#encapsulation dot1q 10
Router (config-subif)#ip address 10.10.10.1 255.255.255.0
Router (config-subif)#interface f0/0.20
Router (config-subif)#encapsulation dot1q 20
Router (config-subif)#ip address 20.20.20.1 255.255.255.0
```

2. Verify the configuration with the show running-config command.

3. Configure trunking on interface F0/8 of the S1 switch connecting to your router.

4. Verify that your VLANs are still configured on your switches with the sh vlan command.

5. Configure your hosts to be in VLAN 10 and VLAN 20 with the switchport access vlan x command.

6. Ping from your PC to the router's subinterface configured for your VLAN.

7. Ping from your PC to your PC in the other VLAN. You are now routing through the router!

Hands-on Lab 11.4: Configuring IVR with a Layer 3 Switch

In this lab, you will disable the router and use the S1 switch to provide inter-VLAN routing by creating SVI's.

1. Connect to the S1 switch and make interface F0/8 an access port, which will make the router stop providing inter-VLAN routing.

2. Enable IP routing on the S1 switch.

```
S1(config)#ip routing
```

3. Create two new interfaces on the S1 switch to provide IVR.

```
S1(config)#interface vlan 10
S1(config-if)#ip address 10.10.10.1 255.255.255.0
S1(config-if)#interface vlan 20
S1(config-if)#ip address 20.20.20.1 255.255.255.0
```

4. Clear the ARP cache on the switch and hosts.

```
S1#clear arp
```

5. Ping from your PC to the router's subinterface configured for your VLAN.

6. Ping from your PC to your PC in the other VLAN. You are now routing through the S1 switch!

Review Questions

The following questions are designed to test your understanding of this chapter's material. For more information on how to get additional questions, please see www.lammle.com/ccna.

You can find the answers to these questions in Appendix B, "Answers to Review Questions."

1. Which of the following statements is true with regard to VLANs?

    A. VLANs greatly reduce network security.

    B. VLANs increase the number of collision domains while decreasing their size.

    C. VLANs decrease the number of broadcast domains while decreasing their size.

    D. Network adds, moves, and changes are achieved with ease by just configuring a port into the appropriate VLAN.

2. Write the command that must be present for this layer 3 switch to provide inter-VLAN routing between the two VLANs created with these commands:

    ```
    S1(config)#int vlan 10
    S1(config-if)#ip address 192.168.10.1 255.255.255.0
    S1(config-if)#int vlan 20
    S1(config-if)#ip address 192.168.20.1 255.255.255.0
    ```

3. In the following diagram, how must the port on each end of the line be configured to carry traffic between the four hosts?

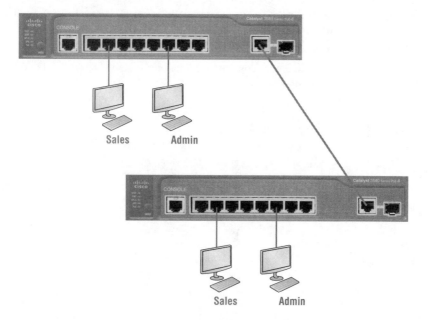

    A. Access port

    B. 10 GB

    C. Trunk

    D. Spanning

4. What is the only type of *second* VLAN of which an access port can be a member?

    A. Secondary

    B. Voice

    C. Primary

    D. Trunk

5. In the following configuration, what command is missing in the creation of the VLAN interface?

```
2960#config t
2960(config)#int vlan 1
2960(config-if)#ip address 192.168.10.2 255.255.255.0
2960(config-if)#exit
2960(config)#ip default-gateway 192.168.10.1
```

    A. `no shutdown` under int vlan 1

    B. `encapsulation dot1q 1` under int vlan 1

    C. `switchport access vlan 1`

    D. `passive-interface`

6. Which of the following statements is true with regard to ISL and 802.1q?

    A. 802.1q encapsulates the frame with control information; ISL inserts an ISL field along with tag control information.

    B. 802.1q is Cisco proprietary.

    C. ISL encapsulates the frame with control information; 802.1q inserts an 802.1q field along with tag control information.

    D. ISL is a standard.

7. What concept is depicted in the diagram?

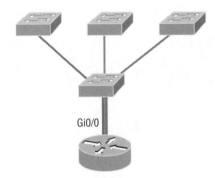

A. Multiprotocol routing

B. Passive interface

C. Gateway redundancy

D. Router on a stick

8. Write the command that places an interface into VLAN 2. Write only the command and not the prompt.

9. Write the command that generated the following output:

```
VLAN Name                      Status    Ports
---- ------------------------- --------- ------------------------
1    default                   active    Fa0/1, Fa0/2, Fa0/3, Fa0/4
                                         Fa0/5, Fa0/6, Fa0/7, Fa0/8
                                         Fa0/9, Fa0/10, Fa0/11, Fa0/12
                                         Fa0/13, Fa0/14, Fa0/19, Fa0/20
                                         Fa0/21, Fa0/22, Fa0/23, Gi0/1
                                         Gi0/2
2    Sales                     active
3    Marketing                 active
4    Accounting                active
[output cut]
```

10. In the configuration and diagram shown, what command is missing to enable inter-VLAN routing between VLAN 2 and VLAN 3?

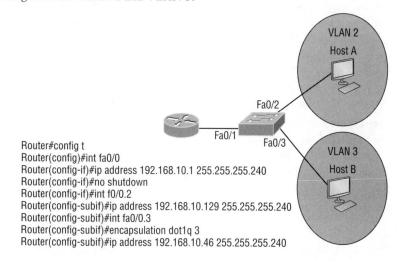

```
Router#config t
Router(config)#int fa0/0
Router(config-if)#ip address 192.168.10.1 255.255.255.240
Router(config-if)#no shutdown
Router(config-if)#int f0/0.2
Router(config-subif)#ip address 192.168.10.129 255.255.255.240
Router(config-subif)#int fa0/0.3
Router(config-subif)#encapsulation dot1q 3
Router(config-subif)#ip address 192.168.10.46 255.255.255.240
```

A. encapsulation dot1q 3 under int f0/0.2

B. encapsulation dot1q 2 under int f0/0.2

C. no shutdown under int f0/0.2

D. no shutdown under int f0/0.3

11. Based on the configuration shown here, what statement is true?

```
S1(config)#ip routing
S1(config)#int vlan 10
S1(config-if)#ip address 192.168.10.1 255.255.255.0
S1(config-if)#int vlan 20
S1(config-if)#ip address 192.168.20.1 255.255.255.0
```

A. This is a multilayer switch.

B. The two VLANs are in the same subnet.

C. Encapsulation must be configured.

D. VLAN 10 is the management VLAN.

12. What is true of the output shown here?

```
S1#sh vlan
```

VLAN	Name	Status	Ports
1	default	active	Fa0/1, Fa0/2, Fa0/3, Fa0/4
			Fa0/5, Fa0/6, Fa0/7, Fa0/8
			Fa0/9, Fa0/10, Fa0/11, Fa0/12
			Fa0/13, Fa0/14, Fa0/19, Fa0/20,
			Fa0/22, Fa0/23, Gi0/1, Gi0/2
2	Sales	active	
3	Marketing	active	Fa0/21
4	Accounting	active	

[output cut]

A. Interface F0/15 is a trunk port.

B. Interface F0/17 is an access port.

C. Interface F0/21 is a trunk port.

D. VLAN 1 was populated manually.

13. 802.1q untagged frames are members of the _____ VLAN.

A. Auxiliary

B. Voice

C. Native

D. Private

14. Write the command that generated the following output. Write only the command and not the prompt:

```
Name: Fa0/15
Switchport: Enabled
Administrative Mode: dynamic desirable
Operational Mode: trunk
Administrative Trunking Encapsulation: negotiate
Operational Trunking Encapsulation: isl
Negotiation of Trunking: On
Access Mode VLAN: 1 (default)
Trunking Native Mode VLAN: 1 (default)
Administrative Native VLAN tagging: enabled
Voice VLAN: none
[output cut]
```

15. In the switch output of question 12, how many broadcast domains are shown?

   A. 1

   B. 2

   C. 4

   D. 1001

16. In the diagram, what should be the default gateway address of Host B?

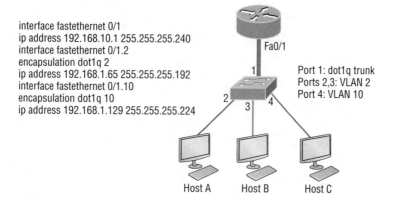

```
interface fastethernet 0/1
ip address 192.168.10.1 255.255.255.240
interface fastethernet 0/1.2
encapsulation dot1q 2
ip address 192.168.1.65 255.255.255.192
interface fastethernet 0/1.10
encapsulation dot1q 10
ip address 192.168.1.129 255.255.255.224
```

Fa0/1

Port 1: dot1q trunk
Ports 2,3: VLAN 2
Port 4: VLAN 10

Host A   Host B   Host C

   A. 192.168.10.1

   B. 192.168.1.65

   C. 192.168.1.129

   D. 192.168.1.2

17. What is the purpose of frame tagging in virtual LAN (VLAN) configurations?

A. Inter-VLAN routing

B. Encryption of network packets

C. Frame identification over trunk links

D. Frame identification over access links

18. Write the command to create VLAN 2 on a layer 2 switch. Write only the command and not the prompt.

19. Which statement is true regarding 802.1q frame tagging?

A. 802.1q adds a 26-byte trailer and 4-byte header.

B. 802.1q uses a native VLAN.

C. The original Ethernet frame is not modified.

D. 802.1q only works with Cisco switches.

20. Write the command that prevents an interface from generating DTP frames. Write only the command and not the prompt.

Chapter

12

Security

THE FOLLOWING ICND1 EXAM TOPICS ARE COVERED IN THIS CHAPTER:

✓ **4.0 Infrastructure Services**

- 4.6 Configure, verify, and troubleshoot IPv4 standard numbered and named access list for routed interfaces

If you're a sys admin, it's my guess that shielding sensitive, critical data, as well as your network's resources, from every possible evil exploit is a top priority of yours, right? Good to know you're on the right page because Cisco has some really effective security solutions to equip you with the tools you'll need to make this happen in a very real way!

The first power tool I'm going to hand you is known as the access control list (ACL). Being able to execute an ACL proficiently is an integral part of Cisco's security solution, so I'm going to begin by showing you how to create and implement simple ACLs. From there, I'll move to demonstrating more advanced ACLs and describe how to implement them strategically to provide serious armor for an internetwork in today's challenging, high-risk environment.

In Appendix C, "Disabling and Configuring Network Services," I'll show you how to mitigate most security-oriented network threats. Make sure you don't skip this appendix because it is chock full of great security information, and the information it contains is part of the Cisco exam objectives as well!

The proper use and configuration of access lists is a vital part of router configuration because access lists are such versatile networking accessories. Contributing mightily to the efficiency and operation of your network, access lists give network managers a huge amount of control over traffic flow throughout the enterprise. With access lists, we can gather basic statistics on packet flow and security policies can be implemented. These dynamic tools also enable us to protect sensitive devices from the dangers of unauthorized access.

In this chapter, we'll cover ACLs for TCP/IP as well as explore effective ways available to us for testing and monitoring how well applied access lists are functioning. We'll begin now by discussing key security measures deployed using hardware devices and VLANs and then I'll introduce you to ACLs.

To find up-to-the-minute updates for this chapter, please see www.lammle.com/ccna or the book's web page at www.sybex.com/go/ccna.

Perimeter, Firewall, and Internal Routers

You see this a lot—typically, in medium to large enterprise networks—the various strategies for security are based on some mix of internal and perimeter routers plus firewall devices. Internal routers provide additional security by screening traffic to various parts of the protected corporate network, and they achieve this using access lists. You can see where each of these types of devices would be found in Figure 12.1.

FIGURE 12.1   A typical secured network

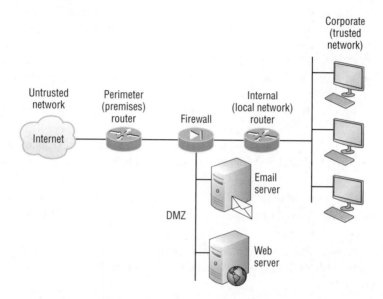

I'll use the terms *trusted network* and *untrusted network* throughout this chapter, so it's important that you can see where they're found in a typical secured network. The demilitarized zone (DMZ) can be global (real) Internet addresses or private addresses, depending on how you configure your firewall, but this is typically where you'll find the HTTP, DNS, email, and other Internet-type corporate servers.

As you now know, instead of using routers, we can create VLANs with switches on the inside trusted network. Multilayer switches containing their own security features can sometimes replace internal (LAN) routers to provide higher performance in VLAN architectures.

Let's look at some ways of protecting the internetwork using access lists.

Introduction to Access Lists

An *access list* is essentially a list of conditions that categorize packets, and they really come in handy when you need to exercise control over network traffic. An ACL would be your tool of choice for decision making in these situations.

One of the most common and easiest-to-understand uses of access lists is to filter unwanted packets when implementing security policies. For example, you can set them up to make very specific decisions about regulating traffic patterns so that they'll allow only certain hosts to access web resources on the Internet while restricting others. With the right combination of access lists, network managers arm themselves with the power to enforce nearly any security policy they can invent.

Creating access lists is really a lot like programming a series of if-then statements—if a given condition is met, then a given action is taken. If the specific condition isn't met, nothing happens and the next statement is evaluated. Access-list statements are basically packet filters that packets are compared against, categorized by, and acted upon accordingly. Once the lists are built, they can be applied to either inbound or outbound traffic on any interface. Applying an access list causes the router to analyze every packet crossing that interface in the specified direction and take the appropriate action.

There are three important rules that a packet follows when it's being compared with an access list:

- The packet is always compared with each line of the access list in sequential order—it will always start with the first line of the access list, move on to line 2, then line 3, and so on.

- The packet is compared with lines of the access list only until a match is made. Once it matches the condition on a line of the access list, the packet is acted upon and no further comparisons take place.

- There is an implicit "deny" at the end of each access list—this means that if a packet doesn't match the condition on any of the lines in the access list, the packet will be discarded.

Each of these rules has some powerful implications when filtering IP packets with access lists, so keep in mind that creating effective access lists definitely takes some practice.

There are two main types of access lists:

Standard access lists   These ACLs use only the source IP address in an IP packet as the condition test. All decisions are made based on the source IP address. This means that standard access lists basically permit or deny an entire suite of protocols. They don't distinguish between any of the many types of IP traffic such as Web, Telnet, UDP, and so on.

Extended access lists   Extended access lists can evaluate many of the other fields in the layer 3 and layer 4 headers of an IP packet. They can evaluate source and destination IP addresses, the Protocol field in the Network layer header, and the port number at the Transport layer header. This gives extended access lists the ability to make much more granular decisions when controlling traffic.

Named access lists   Hey, wait a minute—I said there were only two types of access lists but listed three! Well, technically there really are only two since *named access lists* are either standard or extended and not actually a distinct type. I'm just distinguishing them because they're created and referred to differently than standard and extended access lists are, but they're still functionally the same.

   We'll cover these types of access lists in more depth later in the chapter.

Once you create an access list, it's not really going to do anything until you apply it. Yes, they're there on the router, but they're inactive until you tell that router what to do with them. To use an access list as a packet filter, you need to apply it to an interface on the router where you want the traffic filtered. And you've got to specify which direction of traffic you want the access list applied to. There's a good reason for this—you may want different controls in place for traffic leaving your enterprise destined for the Internet than you'd want for traffic coming into your enterprise from the Internet. So, by specifying the direction of traffic, you can and must use different access lists for inbound and outbound traffic on a single interface:

Inbound access lists   When an access list is applied to inbound packets on an interface, those packets are processed through the access list before being routed to the outbound interface. Any packets that are denied won't be routed because they're discarded before the routing process is invoked.

Outbound access lists   When an access list is applied to outbound packets on an interface, packets are routed to the outbound interface and then processed through the access list before being queued.

There are some general access-list guidelines that you should keep in mind when creating and implementing access lists on a router:

- You can assign only one access list per interface per protocol per direction. This means that when applying IP access lists, you can have only one inbound access list and one outbound access list per interface.

When you consider the implications of the implicit deny at the end of any access list, it makes sense that you can't have multiple access lists applied on the same interface in the same direction for the same protocol. That's because any packets that don't match some condition in the first access list would be denied and there wouldn't be any packets left over to compare against a second access list!

- Organize your access lists so that the more specific tests are at the top.
- Anytime a new entry is added to the access list, it will be placed at the bottom of the list, which is why I highly recommend using a text editor for access lists.
- You can't remove one line from an access list. If you try to do this, you will remove the entire list. This is why it's best to copy the access list to a text editor before trying to edit the list. The only exception is when you're using named access lists.

You can edit, add, or delete a single line from a named access list. I'll show you how shortly.

- Unless your access list ends with a `permit any` command, all packets will be discarded if they do not meet any of the list's tests. This means every list should have at least one `permit` statement or it will deny all traffic.

- Create access lists and then apply them to an interface. Any access list applied to an interface without access-list test statements present will not filter traffic.

- Access lists are designed to filter traffic going through the router. They will not filter traffic that has originated from the router.

- Place IP standard access lists as close to the destination as possible. This is the reason we don't really want to use standard access lists in our networks. You can't put a standard access list close to the source host or network because you can only filter based on source address and all destinations would be affected as a result.

- Place IP extended access lists as close to the source as possible. Since extended access lists can filter on very specific addresses and protocols, you don't want your traffic to traverse the entire network just to be denied. By placing this list as close to the source address as possible, you can filter traffic before it uses up precious bandwidth.

Before I move on to demonstrate how to configure basic and extended ACLs, let's talk about how they can be used to mitigate the security threats I mentioned earlier.

Mitigating Security Issues with ACLs

The most common attack is a denial of service (DoS) attack. Although ACLs can help with a DoS, you really need an intrusion detection system (IDS) and intrusion prevention system (IPS) to help prevent these common attacks. Cisco sells the Adaptive Security Appliance (ASA), which has IDS/IPS modules, but lots of other companies sell IDS/IPS products too.

Here's a list of the many security threats you can mitigate with ACLs:

- IP address spoofing, inbound

- IP address spoofing, outbound

- Denial of service (DoS) TCP SYN attacks, blocking external attacks

- DoS TCP SYN attacks, using TCP Intercept

- DoS smurf attacks

- Denying/filtering ICMP messages, inbound

- Denying/filtering ICMP messages, outbound

- Denying/filtering Traceroute

This is not an "introduction to security" book, so you may have to research some of the preceding terms if you don't understand them.

It's generally a bad idea to allow into a private network any external IP packets that contain the source address of any internal hosts or networks—just don't do it!

Here's a list of rules to live by when configuring ACLs from the Internet to your production network to mitigate security problems:

- Deny any source addresses from your internal networks.

- Deny any local host addresses (127.0.0.0/8).

- Deny any reserved private addresses (RFC 1918).

- Deny any addresses in the IP multicast address range (224.0.0.0/4).

None of these source addresses should be ever be allowed to enter your internetwork. Now finally, let's get our hands dirty and configure some basic and advanced access lists!

Standard Access Lists

Standard IP access lists filter network traffic by examining the source IP address in a packet. You create a *standard IP access list* by using the access-list numbers 1–99 or numbers in the expanded range of 1300–1999 because the type of ACL is generally differentiated using a number. Based on the number used when the access list is created, the router knows which type of syntax to expect as the list is entered. By using numbers 1–99 or 1300–1999, you're telling the router that you want to create a standard IP access list, so the router will expect syntax specifying only the source IP address in the test lines.

The following output displays a good example of the many access-list number ranges that you can use to filter traffic on your network. The IOS version delimits the protocols you can specify access for:

```
Corp(config)#access-list ?
```

```
  <1-99>             IP standard access list
  <100-199>          IP extended access list
  <1000-1099>        IPX SAP access list
  <1100-1199>        Extended 48-bit MAC address access list
  <1200-1299>        IPX summary address access list
  <1300-1999>        IP standard access list (expanded range)
  <200-299>          Protocol type-code access list
  <2000-2699>        IP extended access list (expanded range)
  <2700-2799>        MPLS access list
  <300-399>          DECnet access list
  <700-799>          48-bit MAC address access list
  <800-899>          IPX standard access list
  <900-999>          IPX extended access list
  dynamic-extended   Extend the dynamic ACL absolute timer
  rate-limit         Simple rate-limit specific access list
```

Wow—there certainly are lot of old protocols listed in that output! IPX and DECnet would no longer be used in any of today's networks. Let's take a look at the syntax used when creating a standard IP access list:

```
Corp(config)#access-list 10 ?
  deny    Specify packets to reject
```

```
permit  Specify packets to forward
remark  Access list entry comment
```

As I said, by using the access-list numbers 1–99 or 1300–1999, you're telling the router that you want to create a standard IP access list, which means you can only filter on source IP address.

Once you've chosen the access-list number, you need to decide whether you're creating a permit or deny statement. I'm going to create a deny statement now:

```
Corp(config)#access-list 10 deny ?
  Hostname or A.B.C.D  Address to match
  any                  Any source host
  host                 A single host address
```

The next step is more detailed because there are three options available in it:

1. The first option is the any parameter, which is used to permit or deny any source host or network.

2. The second choice is to use an IP address to specify either a single host or a range of them.

3. The last option is to use the host command to specify a specific host only.

The any command is pretty obvious—any source address matches the statement, so every packet compared against this line will match. The host command is relatively simple too, as you can see here:

```
Corp(config)#access-list 10 deny host ?
  Hostname or A.B.C.D  Host address
Corp(config)#access-list 10 deny host 172.16.30.2
```

This tells the list to deny any packets from host 172.16.30.2. The default parameter is host. In other words, if you type **access-list 10 deny 172.16.30.2**, the router assumes you mean host 172.16.30.2 and that's exactly how it will show in your running-config.

But there's another way to specify either a particular host or a range of hosts, and it's known as wildcard masking. In fact, to specify any range of hosts, you must use wildcard masking in the access list.

So exactly what is wildcard masking? Coming up, I'm going to show you using a standard access list example. I'll also guide you through how to control access to a virtual terminal.

Wildcard Masking

Wildcards are used with access lists to specify an individual host, a network, or a specific range of a network or networks. The block sizes you learned about earlier used to specify a range of addresses are key to understanding wildcards.

Let me pause here for a quick review of block sizes before we go any further. I'm sure you remember that the different block sizes available are 64, 32, 16, 8, and 4. When you need to specify a range of addresses, you choose the next-largest block size for your needs. So if you need to specify 34 networks, you need a block size of 64. If you want to specify 18 hosts, you need a block size of 32. If you specify only 2 networks, then go with a block size of 4.

Wildcards are used with the host or network address to tell the router a range of available addresses to filter. To specify a host, the address would look like this:

```
172.16.30.5 0.0.0.0
```

The four zeros represent each octet of the address. Whenever a zero is present, it indicates that the octet in the address must match the corresponding reference octet exactly. To specify that an octet can be any value, use the value 255. Here's an example of how a /24 subnet is specified with a wildcard mask:

```
172.16.30.0 0.0.0.255
```

This tells the router to match up the first three octets exactly, but the fourth octet can be any value.

Okay—that was the easy part. But what if you want to specify only a small range of subnets? This is where block sizes come in. You have to specify the range of values in a block size, so you can't choose to specify 20 networks. You can only specify the exact amount that the block size value allows. This means that the range would have to be either 16 or 32, but not 20.

Let's say that you want to block access to the part of the network that ranges from 172.16.8.0 through 172.16.15.0. To do that, you would go with a block size of 8, your network number would be 172.16.8.0, and the wildcard would be 0.0.7.255. The 7.255 equals the value the router will use to determine the block size. So together, the network number and the wildcard tell the router to begin at 172.16.8.0 and go up a block size of eight addresses to network 172.16.15.0.

This really is easier than it looks! I could certainly go through the binary math for you, but no one needs that kind of pain because all you have to do is remember that the wildcard is always one number less than the block size. So, in our example, the wildcard would be 7 since our block size is 8. If you used a block size of 16, the wildcard would be 15. Easy, right?

Just to make you've got this, we'll go through some examples that will definitely help you nail it down. The following example tells the router to match the first three octets exactly but that the fourth octet can be anything:

```
Corp(config)#access-list 10 deny 172.16.10.0 0.0.0.255
```

The next example tells the router to match the first two octets and that the last two octets can be any value:

```
Corp(config)#access-list 10 deny 172.16.0.0 0.0.255.255
```

Now, try to figure out this next line:

```
Corp(config)#access-list 10 deny 172.16.16.0 0.0.3.255
```

This configuration tells the router to start at network 172.16.16.0 and use a block size of 4. The range would then be 172.16.16.0 through 172.16.19.255, and by the way, the Cisco objectives seem to really like this one!

Let's keep practicing. What about this next one?

```
Corp(config)#access-list 10 deny 172.16.16.0 0.0.7.255
```

This example reveals an access list starting at 172.16.16.0 going up a block size of 8 to 172.16.23.255.

Let's keep at it... What do you think the range of this one is?

```
Corp(config)#access-list 10 deny 172.16.32.0 0.0.15.255
```

This one begins at network 172.16.32.0 and goes up a block size of 16 to 172.16.47.255. You're almost done practicing! After a couple more, we'll configure some real ACLs.

```
Corp(config)#access-list 10 deny 172.16.64.0 0.0.63.255
```

This example starts at network 172.16.64.0 and goes up a block size of 64 to 172.16.127.255.

What about this last example?

```
Corp(config)#access-list 10 deny 192.168.160.0 0.0.31.255
```

This one shows us that it begins at network 192.168.160.0 and goes up a block size of 32 to 192.168.191.255.

Here are two more things to keep in mind when working with block sizes and wildcards:

- Each block size must start at 0 or a multiple of the block size. For example, you can't say that you want a block size of 8 and then start at 12. You must use 0–7, 8–15, 16–23, etc. For a block size of 32, the ranges are 0–31, 32–63, 64–95, etc.

- The command any is the same thing as writing out the wildcard 0.0.0.0 255.255.255.255.

 Wildcard masking is a crucial skill to master when creating IP access lists, and it's used identically when creating standard and extended IP access lists.

Standard Access List Example

In this section, you'll learn how to use a standard access list to stop specific users from gaining access to the Finance department LAN.

In Figure 12.2, a router has three LAN connections and one WAN connection to the Internet. Users on the Sales LAN should not have access to the Finance LAN, but they should be able to access the Internet and the marketing department files. The Marketing LAN needs to access the Finance LAN for application services.

FIGURE 12.2   IP access list example with three LANs and a WAN connection

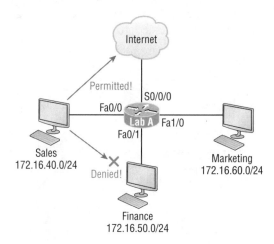

We can see that the following standard IP access list is configured on the router:

```
Lab_A#config t
Lab_A(config)#access-list 10 deny 172.16.40.0 0.0.0.255
Lab_A(config)#access-list 10 permit any
```

It's very important to remember that the any command is the same thing as saying the following using wildcard masking:

```
Lab_A(config)#access-list 10 permit 0.0.0.0 255.255.255.255
```

Since the wildcard mask says that none of the octets are to be evaluated, every address matches the test condition, so this is functionally doing the same as using the any keyword.

At this point, the access list is configured to deny source addresses from the Sales LAN to the Finance LAN and to allow everyone else. But remember, no action will be taken until the access list is applied on an interface in a specific direction!

But where should this access list be placed? If you place it as an incoming access list on Fa0/0, you might as well shut down the FastEthernet interface because all of the Sales LAN devices will be denied access to all networks attached to the router. The best place to apply this access list is on the Fa0/1 interface as an outbound list:

```
Lab_A(config)#int fa0/1
Lab_A(config-if)#ip access-group 10 out
```

Doing this completely stops traffic from 172.16.40.0 from getting out FastEthernet0/1. It has no effect on the hosts from the Sales LAN accessing the Marketing LAN and the Internet because traffic to those destinations doesn't go through interface Fa0/1. Any packet trying to exit out Fa0/1 will have to go through the access list first. If there were an inbound list placed on F0/0, then any packet trying to enter interface F0/0 would have to go through the access list before being routed to an exit interface.

Now, let's take a look at another standard access list example. Figure 12.3 shows an internetwork of two routers with four LANs.

FIGURE 12.3   IP standard access list example 2

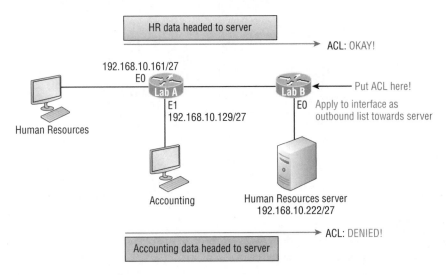

Now we're going to stop the Accounting users from accessing the Human Resources server attached to the Lab_B router but allow all other users access to that LAN using a standard ACL. What kind of standard access list would we need to create and where would we place it to achieve our goals?

The real answer is that we should use an extended access list and place it closest to the source! But this question specifies using a standard access list, and as a rule, standard ACLs are placed closest to the destination. In this example, Ethernet 0 is the outbound interface on the Lab_B router and here's the access list that should be placed on it:

```
Lab_B#config t
Lab_B(config)#access-list 10 deny 192.168.10.128 0.0.0.31
Lab_B(config)#access-list 10 permit any
Lab_B(config)#interface Ethernet 0
Lab_B(config-if)#ip access-group 10 out
```

Keep in mind that to be able to answer this question correctly, you really need to understand subnetting, wildcard masks, and how to configure and implement ACLs. The accounting subnet is the 192.168.10.128/27, which is a 255.255.255.224, with a block size of 32 in the fourth octet.

With all this in mind and before we move on to restricting Telnet access on a router, let's take a look at one more standard access list example. This one is going to require some thought. In Figure 12.4, you have a router with four LAN connections and one WAN connection to the Internet.

FIGURE 12.4   IP standard access list example 3

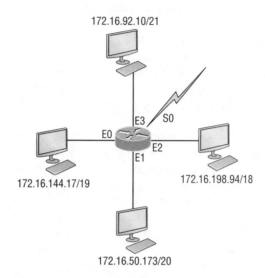

Okay—you need to write an access list that will stop access from each of the four LANs shown in the diagram to the Internet. Each of the LANs reveals a single host's IP address, which you need to use to determine the subnet and wildcards of each LAN to configure the access list.

Here is an example of what your answer should look like, beginning with the network on E0 and working through to E3:

```
Router(config)#access-list 1 deny 172.16.128.0 0.0.31.255
Router(config)#access-list 1 deny 172.16.48.0 0.0.15.255
Router(config)#access-list 1 deny 172.16.192.0 0.0.63.255
Router(config)#access-list 1 deny 172.16.88.0 0.0.7.255
Router(config)#access-list 1 permit any
Router(config)#interface serial 0
Router(config-if)#ip access-group 1 out
```

Sure, you could have done this with one line:

```
Router(config)#access-list 1 deny 172.16.0.0 0.0.255.255
```

But what fun is that?

And remember the reasons for creating this list. If you actually applied this ACL on the router, you'd effectively shut down access to the Internet, so why even have an Internet connection? I included this exercise so you can practice how to use block sizes with access lists, which is vital for succeeding when you take the Cisco exam!

Controlling VTY (Telnet/SSH) Access

Trying to stop users from telnetting or trying to SSH to a router is really challenging because any active interface on a router is fair game for VTY/SSH access. Creating an extended IP ACL that limits access to every IP address on the router may sound like a solution, but if you did that, you'd have to apply it inbound on every interface, which really wouldn't scale well if you happen to have dozens, even hundreds, of interfaces, now would it? And think of all the latency dragging down your network as a result of each and every router checking every packet just in case the packet was trying to access your VTY lines—horrible!

Don't give up—there's always a solution! And in this case, a much better one, which employs a standard IP access list to control access to the VTY lines themselves.

Why does this work so well? Because when you apply an access list to the VTY lines, you don't need to specify the protocol since access to the VTY already implies terminal access via the Telnet or SSH protocols. You also don't need to specify a destination address because it really doesn't matter which interface address the user used as a target for the Telnet session. All you really need control of is where the user is coming from, which is betrayed by their source IP address.

You need to do these two things to make this happen:

1. Create a standard IP access list that permits only the host or hosts you want to be able to telnet into the routers.

2. Apply the access list to the VTY line with the access-class in command.

Here, I'm allowing only host 172.16.10.3 to telnet into a router:

```
Lab_A(config)#access-list 50 permit host 172.16.10.3
Lab_A(config)#line vty 0 4
Lab_A(config-line)#access-class 50 in
```

Because of the implied deny any at the end of the list, the ACL stops any host from telnetting into the router except the host 172.16.10.3, regardless of the individual IP address on the router being used as a target. It's a good idea to include an admin subnet address as the source instead of a single host, but the reason I demonstrated this was to show you how to create security on your VTY lines without adding latency to your router.

Real World Scenario

Should You Secure Your VTY Lines on a Router?

You're monitoring your network and notice that someone has telnetted into your core router by using the show users command. You use the disconnect command and they're disconnected from the router, but you notice that they're right back in there a few minutes later. You consider putting an ACL on the router interfaces, but you don't want to add latency on each interface since your router is already pushing a lot of packets. At this point, you think about putting an access list on the VTY lines themselves, but not having done this before, you're not sure if this is a safe alternative to putting an ACL on each interface. Would placing an ACL on the VTY lines be a good idea for this network?

Yes—absolutely! And the access-class command covered in this chapter is the way to do it. Why? Because it doesn't use an access list that just sits on an interface looking at every packet, resulting in unnecessary overhead and latency.

When you put the access-class in command on the VTY lines, only packets trying to telnet into the router will be checked and compared, providing easy-to-configure yet solid security for your router!

 Just a reminder—Cisco recommends using Secure Shell (SSH) instead of Telnet on the VTY lines of a router, as we covered in Chapter 6, "Cisco's Internetworking Operating System (IOS)," so review that chapter if you need a refresher on SSH and how to configure it on your routers and switches.

Extended Access Lists

Let's go back to the standard IP access list example where you had to block all access from the Sales LAN to the finance department and add a new requirement. You now must allow Sales to gain access to a certain server on the Finance LAN but not to other network services for security reasons. What's the solution? Applying a standard IP access list won't allow users to get to one network service but not another because a standard ACL won't allow you to make decisions based on both source and destination addresses. It makes decisions based only on source address, so we need another way to achieve our new goal—but what is it?

Using an *extended access list* will save the day because extended ACLs allow us to specify source and destination addresses as well as the protocol and port number that identify the upper-layer protocol or application. An extended ACL is just what we need to affectively allow users access to a physical LAN while denying them access to specific hosts—even specific services on those hosts!

Yes, I am well aware there are no ICND1 objectives for extended access lists, but you need to understand Extended ACL's for when you get to ICND2 troubleshooting, so I added foundation here.

We're going to take a look at the commands we have in our arsenal, but first, you need to know that you must use the extended access-list range from 100 to 199. The 2000–2699 range is also available for extended IP access lists.

After choosing a number in the extended range, you need to decide what type of list entry to make. For this example, I'm going with a deny list entry:

```
Corp(config)#access-list 110 ?
  deny      Specify packets to reject
  dynamic   Specify a DYNAMIC list of PERMITs or DENYs
  permit    Specify packets to forward
  remark    Access list entry comment
```

And once you've settled on the type of ACL, you then need to select a protocol field entry:

```
Corp(config)#access-list 110 deny ?
  <0-255>   An IP protocol number
  ahp       Authentication Header Protocol
  eigrp     Cisco's EIGRP routing protocol
  esp       Encapsulation Security Payload
  gre       Cisco's GRE tunneling
  icmp      Internet Control Message Protocol
  igmp      Internet Gateway Message Protocol
  ip        Any Internet Protocol
  ipinip    IP in IP tunneling
  nos       KA9Q NOS compatible IP over IP tunneling
  ospf      OSPF routing protocol
  pcp       Payload Compression Protocol
  pim       Protocol Independent Multicast
  tcp       Transmission Control Protocol
  udp       User Datagram Protocol
```

If you want to filter by Application layer protocol, you have to choose the appropriate layer 4 transport protocol after the permit or deny statement. For example, to filter Telnet or FTP, choose TCP since both Telnet and FTP use TCP at the Transport layer. Selecting IP wouldn't allow you to specify a particular application protocol later and only filter based on source and destination addresses.

So now, let's filter an Application layer protocol that uses TCP by selecting TCP as the protocol and indicating the specific destination TCP port at the end of the line. Next, we'll be prompted for the source IP address of the host or network and we'll choose the any command to allow any source address:

```
Corp(config)#access-list 110 deny tcp ?
  A.B.C.D  Source address
  any      Any source host
  host     A single source host
```

After we've selected the source address, we can then choose the specific destination address:

```
Corp(config)#access-list 110 deny tcp any ?
  A.B.C.D  Destination address
  any      Any destination host
  eq       Match only packets on a given port number
  gt       Match only packets with a greater port number
  host     A single destination host
  lt       Match only packets with a lower port number
  neq      Match only packets not on a given port number
  range    Match only packets in the range of port numbers
```

In this output, you can see that any source IP address that has a destination IP address of 172.16.30.2 has been denied:

```
Corp(config)#access-list 110 deny tcp any host 172.16.30.2 ?
  ack          Match on the ACK bit
  dscp         Match packets with given dscp value
  eq           Match only packets on a given port number
  established  Match established connections
  fin          Match on the FIN bit
  fragments    Check non-initial fragments
  gt           Match only packets with a greater port number
  log          Log matches against this entry
  log-input    Log matches against this entry, including input interface
  lt           Match only packets with a lower port number
  neq          Match only packets not on a given port number
  precedence   Match packets with given precedence value
  psh          Match on the PSH bit
  range        Match only packets in the range of port numbers
  rst          Match on the RST bit
  syn          Match on the SYN bit
```

```
time-range    Specify a time-range
tos           Match packets with given TOS value
urg           Match on the URG bit
<cr>
```

And once we have the destination host addresses in place, we just need to specify the type of service to deny using the equal to command, entered as eq. The following help screen reveals the options available now. You can choose a port number or use the application name:

```
Corp(config)#access-list 110 deny tcp any host 172.16.30.2 eq ?
  <0-65535>   Port number
  bgp         Border Gateway Protocol (179)
  chargen     Character generator (19)
  cmd         Remote commands (rcmd, 514)
  daytime     Daytime (13)
  discard     Discard (9)
  domain      Domain Name Service (53)
  drip        Dynamic Routing Information Protocol (3949)
  echo        Echo (7)
  exec        Exec (rsh, 512)
  finger      Finger (79)
  ftp         File Transfer Protocol (21)
  ftp-data    FTP data connections (20)
  gopher      Gopher (70)
  hostname    NIC hostname server (101)
  ident       Ident Protocol (113)
  irc         Internet Relay Chat (194)
  klogin      Kerberos login (543)
  kshell      Kerberos shell (544)
  login       Login (rlogin, 513)
  lpd         Printer service (515)
  nntp        Network News Transport Protocol (119)
  pim-auto-rp PIM Auto-RP (496)
  pop2        Post Office Protocol v2 (109)
  pop3        Post Office Protocol v3 (110)
  smtp        Simple Mail Transport Protocol (25)
  sunrpc      Sun Remote Procedure Call (111)
  syslog      Syslog (514)
  tacacs      TAC Access Control System (49)
  talk        Talk (517)
  telnet      Telnet (23)
```

```
time           Time (37)
uucp           Unix-to-Unix Copy Program (540)
whois          Nicname (43)
www            World Wide Web (HTTP, 80)
```

Now let's block Telnet (port 23) to host 172.16.30.2 only. If the users want to use FTP, fine—that's allowed. The log command is used to log messages every time the access list entry is hit. This can be an extremely cool way to monitor inappropriate access attempts, but be careful because in a large network, this command can overload your console's screen with messages!

Here's our result:

```
Corp(config)#access-list 110 deny tcp any host 172.16.30.2 eq 23 log
```

This line says to deny any source host trying to telnet to destination host 172.16.30.2. Keep in mind that the next line is an implicit deny by default. If you apply this access list to an interface, you might as well just shut the interface down because by default, there's an implicit deny all at the end of every access list. So we've got to follow up the access list with the following command:

```
Corp(config)#access-list 110 permit ip any any
```

The IP in this line is important because it will permit the IP stack. If TCP was used instead of IP in this line, then UDP, etc. would all be denied. Remember, the 0.0.0.0 255.255.255.255 is the same command as any, so the command could also look like this:

```
Corp(config)#access-list 110 permit ip 0.0.0.0 255.255.255.255
0.0.0.0 255.255.255.255
```

But if you did this, when you looked at the running-config, the commands would be replaced with the any any. I like efficiency so I'll just use the any command because it requires less typing.

As always, once our access list is created, we must apply it to an interface with the same command used for the IP standard list:

```
Corp(config-if)#ip access-group 110 in
```

Or this:

```
Corp(config-if)#ip access-group 110 out
```

Next, we'll check out some examples of how to use an extended access list.

Extended Access List Example 1

For our first scenario, we'll use Figure 12.5. What do we need to do to deny access to a host at 172.16.50.5 on the finance department LAN for both Telnet and FTP services? All other services on this and all other hosts are acceptable for the sales and marketing departments to access.

FIGURE 12.5   Extended ACL example 1

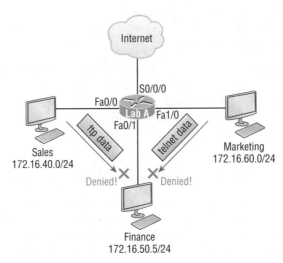

Here's the ACL we must create:

```
Lab_A#config t
Lab_A(config)#access-list 110 deny tcp any host 172.16.50.5 eq 21
Lab_A(config)#access-list 110 deny tcp any host 172.16.50.5 eq 23
Lab_A(config)#access-list 110 permit ip any any
```

The access-list 110 tells the router we're creating an extended IP ACL. The tcp is the protocol field in the Network layer header. If the list doesn't say tcp here, you cannot filter by TCP port numbers 21 and 23 as shown in the example. Remember that these values indicate FTP and Telnet, which both use TCP for connection-oriented services. The any command is the source, which means any source IP address, and the host is the destination IP address. This ACL says that all IP traffic will be permitted from any host except FTP and Telnet to host 172.16.50.5 from any source.

    Remember that instead of the host 172.16.50.5 command when we created the extended access list, we could have entered 172.16.50.5 0.0.0.0. There would be no difference in the result other than the router would change the command to host 172.16.50.5 in the running-config.

After the list is created, it must be applied to the FastEthernet 0/1 interface outbound because we want to block all traffic from getting to host 172.16.50.5 and performing FTP and Telnet. If this list was created to block access only from the Sales LAN to host 172.16.50.5, then we'd have put this list closer to the source, or on FastEthernet 0/0. In that situation, we'd apply the list to inbound traffic. This highlights the fact that you really need to analyze each situation carefully before creating and applying ACLs!

Now let's go ahead and apply the list to interface Fa0/1 to block all outside FTP and Telnet access to the host 172.16.50.5:

```
Lab_A(config)#int fa0/1
Lab_A(config-if)#ip access-group 110 out
```

Extended Access List Example 2

We're going to use Figure 12.4 again, which has four LANs and a serial connection. We need to prevent Telnet access to the networks attached to the E1 and E2 interfaces.

The configuration on the router would look something like this, although the answer can vary:

```
Router(config)#access-list 110 deny tcp any 172.16.48.0 0.0.15.255
eq 23
Router(config)#access-list 110 deny tcp any 172.16.192.0 0.0.63.255
eq 23
Router(config)#access-list 110 permit ip any any
Router(config)#interface Ethernet 1
Router(config-if)#ip access-group 110 out
Router(config-if)#interface Ethernet 2
Router(config-if)#ip access-group 110 out
```

Here are the key factors to understand from this list:

- First, you need to verify that the number range is correct for the type of access list you are creating. In this example, it's extended, so the range must be 100–199.

- Second, you must verify that the protocol field matches the upper-layer process or application, which in this case, is TCP port 23 (Telnet).

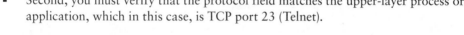

> The protocol parameter must be TCP since Telnet uses TCP. If it were TFTP instead, then the protocol parameter would have to be UDP because TFTP uses UDP at the Transport layer.

- Third, verify that the destination port number matches the application you're filtering for. In this case, port 23 matches Telnet, which is correct, but know that you can also type **telnet** at the end of the line instead of 23.

- Finally, the test statement permit ip any any is important to have there at the end of the list because it means to enable all packets other than Telnet packets destined for the LANs connected to Ethernet 1 and Ethernet 2.

Extended Access List Example 3

I want to guide you through one more extended ACL example before we move on to named ACLs. Figure 12.6 displays the network we're going to use for this last scenario.

FIGURE 12.6   Extended ACL example 3

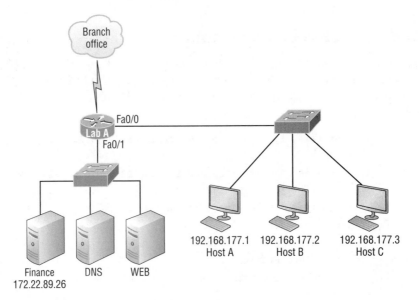

In this example, we're going to allow HTTP access to the Finance server from source Host B only. All other traffic will be permitted. We need to be able to configure this in only three test statements, and then we'll need to add the interface configuration.

Let's take what we've learned and knock this one out:

```
Lab_A#config t
Lab_A(config)#access-list 110 permit tcp host 192.168.177.2 host 172.22.89.26 eq 80
Lab_A(config)#access-list 110 deny tcp any host 172.22.89.26 eq 80
Lab_A(config)#access-list 110 permit ip any any
```

This is really pretty simple! First we need to permit Host B HTTP access to the Finance server. But since all other traffic must be allowed, we must detail who cannot HTTP to the Finance server, so the second test statement is there to deny anyone else from using HTTP on the Finance server. Finally, now that Host B can HTTP to the Finance server and everyone else can't, we'll permit all other traffic with our third test statement.

Not so bad—this just takes a little thought! But wait—we're not done yet because we still need to apply this to an interface. Since extended access lists are typically applied closest to the source, we should simply place this inbound on F0/0, right? Well, this is one time we're not going to follow the rules. Our challenge required us to allow only HTTP traffic to the Finance server from Host B. If we apply the ACL inbound on Fa0/0, then the branch office would be able to access the Finance server and perform HTTP. So in this example, we need to place the ACL closest to the destination:

```
Lab_A(config)#interface fastethernet 0/1
Lab_A(config-if)#ip access-group 110 out
```

Perfect! Now let's get into how to create ACLs using names.

Named ACLs

As I said earlier, *named* access lists are just another way to create standard and extended access lists. In medium to large enterprises, managing ACLs can become a real hassle over time! A handy way to make things easier is to copy the access list to a text editor, edit the list, then paste the new list back into the router, which works pretty well if it weren't for the "pack rat" mentality. It's really common to think things like, "What if I find a problem with the new list and need to back out of the change?" This and other factors cause people to hoard unapplied ACLs, and over time, they can seriously build up on a router, leading to more questions, like, "What were these ACLs for? Are they important? Do I need them?" All good questions, and named access lists are the answer to this problem!

And of course, this kind of thing can also apply to access lists that are up and running. Let's say you come into an existing network and are looking at access lists on a router. Suppose you find an access list 177, which happens to be an extended access list that's a whopping 93 lines long. This leads to more of the same bunch of questions and can even lead to needless existential despair! Instead, wouldn't it be a whole lot easier to identify an access with a name like "FinanceLAN" rather than one mysteriously dubbed "177"?

To our collective relief, named access lists allow us to use names for creating and applying either standard or extended access lists. There's really nothing new or different about these ACLs aside from being readily identifiable in a way that makes sense to humans, but there are some subtle changes to the syntax. So let's re-create the standard access list we created earlier for our test network in Figure 12.2 using a named access list:

```
Lab_A#config t
Lab_A(config)# ip access-list ?
  extended    Extended Access List
  log-update  Control access list log updates
  logging     Control access list logging
  resequence  Resequence Access List
  standard    Standard Access List
```

Notice that I started by typing **ip access-list**, not **access-list**. Doing this allows me to enter a named access list. Next, I'll need to specify it as a standard access list:

```
Lab_A(config)#ip access-list standard ?
  <1-99>       Standard IP access-list number
```

```
  <1300-1999>  Standard IP access-list number (expanded range)
  WORD         Access-list name
```

Lab_A(config)#**ip access-list standard BlockSales**
Lab_A(config-std-nacl)#

I've specified a standard access list, then added the name, BlockSales. I definitely could've used a number for a standard access list, but instead, I chose to use a nice, clear, descriptive name. And notice that after entering the name, I hit Enter and the router prompt changed. This confirms that I'm now in named access list configuration mode and that I'm entering the named access list:

```
Lab_A(config-std-nacl)#?
Standard Access List configuration commands:
  default  Set a command to its defaults
  deny     Specify packets to reject
  exit     Exit from access-list configuration mode
  no       Negate a command or set its defaults
  permit   Specify packets to forward
```

Lab_A(config-std-nacl)#**deny 172.16.40.0 0.0.0.255**
Lab_A(config-std-nacl)#**permit any**
Lab_A(config-std-nacl)#**exit**
Lab_A(config)#**^Z**
Lab_A#

So I've entered the access list and then exited configuration mode. Next, I'll take a look at the running configuration to verify that the access list is indeed in the router:

Lab_A#**sh running-config | begin ip access**
```
ip access-list standard BlockSales
 deny   172.16.40.0 0.0.0.255
 permit any
!
```

And there it is: the BlockSales access list has truly been created and is in the running-config of the router. Next, I'll need to apply the access list to the correct interface:

Lab_A#**config t**
Lab_A(config)#**int fa0/1**
Lab_A(config-if)#**ip access-group BlockSales out**

Clear skies! At this point, we've re-created the work done earlier using a named access list. But let's take our IP extended example, shown in Figure 12.6, and redo that list using a named ACL instead as well.

Same business requirements: Allow HTTP access to the Finance server from source Host B only. All other traffic is permitted.

```
Lab_A#config t
Lab_A(config)#ip access-list extended 110
Lab_A(config-ext-nacl)#permit tcp host 192.168.177.2 host 172.22.89.26 eq 80
Lab_A(config-ext-nacl)#deny tcp any host 172.22.89.26 eq 80
Lab_A(config-ext-nacl)#permit ip any any
Lab_A(config-ext-nacl)#int fa0/1
Lab_A(config-if)#ip access-group 110 out
```

Okay—true—I named the extended list with a number, but sometimes it's okay to do that! I'm guessing that named ACLs don't seem all that exciting or different to you, do they? Maybe not in this configuration, except that I don't need to start every line with `access-list 110`, which is nice. But where named ACLs really shine is that they allow us to insert, delete, or edit a single line. That isn't just nice, it's wonderful! Numbered ACLs just can't compare with that, and I'll demonstrate this in a minute.

Remarks

The `remark` keyword is really important because it arms you with the ability to include comments—remarks—regarding the entries you've made in both your IP standard and extended ACLs. Remarks are very cool because they efficiently increase your ability to examine and understand your ACLs to superhero level! Without them, you'd be caught in a quagmire of potentially meaningless numbers without anything to help you recall what all those numbers mean.

Even though you have the option of placing your remarks either before or after a `permit` or deny statement, I totally recommend that you choose to position them consistently so you don't get confused about which remark is relevant to a specific `permit` or deny statement.

To get this going for both standard and extended ACLs, just use the `access-list` *access-list number* `remark` *remark* global configuration command like this:

```
R2#config t
R2(config)#access-list 110 remark Permit Bob from Sales Only To Finance
R2(config)#access-list 110 permit ip host 172.16.40.1 172.16.50.0 0.0.0.255
R2(config)#access-list 110 deny ip 172.16.40.0 0.0.0.255 172.16.50.0 0.0.0.255
R2(config)#ip access-list extended No_Telnet
R2(config-ext-nacl)#remark Deny all of Sales from Telnetting to Marketing
R2(config-ext-nacl)#deny tcp 172.16.40.0 0.0.0.255 172.16.60.0 0.0.0.255 eq 23
R2(config-ext-nacl)#permit ip any any
R2(config-ext-nacl)#do show run
[output cut]
!
```

```
ip access-list extended No_Telnet
 remark Stop all of Sales from Telnetting to Marketing
 deny    tcp 172.16.40.0 0.0.0.255 172.16.60.0 0.0.0.255 eq telnet
 permit ip any any
!
access-list 110 remark Permit Bob from Sales Only To Finance
access-list 110 permit ip host 172.16.40.1 172.16.50.0 0.0.0.255
access-list 110 deny   ip 172.16.40.0 0.0.0.255 172.16.50.0 0.0.0.255
access-list 110 permit ip any any
!
```

Sweet—I was able to add a remark to both an extended list and a named access list. Keep in mind that you cannot see these remarks in the output of the show access-list command, which we'll cover next, because they only show up in the running-config.

Speaking of ACLs, I still need to show you how to monitor and verify them. This is an important topic, so pay attention!

Monitoring Access Lists

It's always good to be able to verify a router's configuration. Table 12.1 lists the commands that we can use to achieve that.

TABLE 12.1 Commands used to verify access-list configuration

Command	Effect
show access-list	Displays all access lists and their parameters configured on the router. Also shows statistics about how many times the line either permitted or denied a packet. This command does not show you which interface the list is applied on.
show access-list 110	Reveals only the parameters for access list 110. Again, this command will not reveal the specific interface the list is set on.
show ip access-list	Shows only the IP access lists configured on the router.
show ip interface	Displays which interfaces have access lists set on them.
show running-config	Shows the access lists and the specific interfaces that have ACLs applied on them.

We've already used the show running-config command to verify that a named access list was in the router, so now let's take a look at the output from some of the other commands.

The show access-list command will list all ACLs on the router, whether they're applied to an interface or not:

```
Lab_A#show access-list
Standard IP access list 10
    10 deny    172.16.40.0, wildcard bits 0.0.0.255
    20 permit any
Standard IP access list BlockSales
    10 deny    172.16.40.0, wildcard bits 0.0.0.255
    20 permit any
Extended IP access list 110
    10 deny tcp any host 172.16.30.5 eq ftp
    20 deny tcp any host 172.16.30.5 eq telnet
    30 permit ip any any
    40 permit tcp host 192.168.177.2 host 172.22.89.26 eq www
    50 deny tcp any host 172.22.89.26 eq www
Lab_A#
```

First, notice that access list 10 as well as both of our named access lists appear on this list—remember, my extended named ACL was named 110! Second, notice that even though I entered actual numbers for TCP ports in access list 110, the show command gives us the protocol names rather than TCP ports for serious clarity.

But wait! The best part is those numbers on the left side: 10, 20, 30, etc. Those are called sequence numbers, and they allow us to edit our named ACL. Here's an example where I added a line into the named extended ACL 110:

```
Lab_A (config)#ip access-list extended 110
Lab_A (config-ext-nacl)#21 deny udp any host 172.16.30.5 eq 69
Lab_A#show access-list
[output cut]
Extended IP access list 110
    10 deny tcp any host 172.16.30.5 eq ftp
    20 deny tcp any host 172.16.30.5 eq telnet
    21 deny udp any host 172.16.30.5 eq tftp
    30 permit ip any any
    40 permit tcp host 192.168.177.2 host 172.22.89.26 eq www
    50 deny tcp any host 172.22.89.26 eq www
```

You can see that I added line 21. I could have deleted a line or edited an existing line as well—very nice!

Here's the output of the show ip interface command:

```
Lab_A#show ip interface fa0/1
FastEthernet0/1 is up, line protocol is up
  Internet address is 172.16.30.1/24
  Broadcast address is 255.255.255.255
  Address determined by non-volatile memory
  MTU is 1500 bytes
  Helper address is not set
  Directed broadcast forwarding is disabled
  Outgoing access list is 110
  Inbound access list is not set
  Proxy ARP is enabled
  Security level is default
  Split horizon is enabled
[output cut]
```

Be sure to notice the bold line indicating that the outgoing list on this interface is 110, yet the inbound access list isn't set. What happened to BlockSales? I had configured that outbound on Fa0/1! That's true, I did, but I configured my extended named ACL 110 and applied it to Fa0/1 as well. You can't have two lists on the same interface, in the same direction, so what happened here is that my last configuration overwrote the BlockSales configuration.

And as I've already mentioned, you can use the show running-config command to see any and all access lists.

Summary

In this chapter you learned how to configure standard access lists to properly filter IP traffic. You discovered what a standard access list is and how to apply it to a Cisco router to add security to your network. You also learned how to configure extended access lists to further filter IP traffic. We also covered the key differences between standard and extended access lists as well as how to apply them to Cisco routers.

Moving on, you found out how to configure named access lists and apply them to interfaces on the router and learned that named access lists offer the huge advantage of being easily identifiable and, therefore, a whole lot easier to manage than mysterious access lists that are simply referred to by obscure numbers.

Appendix C, "Disabling and Configuring Network Services," which takes off from this chapter, has a fun section in it: turning off default services. I've always found performing this administration task fun, and the auto secure command can help us configure basic, much-needed security on our routers.

The chapter wrapped up by showing you how to monitor and verify selected access-list configurations on a router.

Exam Essentials

Remember the standard and extended IP access-list number ranges.   The number ranges you can use to configure a standard IP access list are 1–99 and 1300–1999. The number ranges for an extended IP access list are 100–199 and 2000–2699.

Understand the term implicit deny.   At the end of every access list is an *implicit deny*. What this means is that if a packet does not match any of the lines in the access list, it will be discarded. Also, if you have nothing but deny statements in your list, the list will not permit any packets.

Understand the standard IP access-list configuration command.   To configure a standard IP access list, use the access-list numbers 1–99 or 1300–1999 in global configuration mode. Choose permit or deny, then choose the source IP address you want to filter on using one of the three techniques covered in this chapter.

Understand the extended IP access-list configuration command.   To configure an extended IP access list, use the access-list numbers 100–199 or 2000–2699 in global configuration mode. Choose permit or deny, the Network layer protocol field, the source IP address you want to filter on, the destination address you want to filter on, and finally, the Transport layer port number if TCP or UDP has been specified as the protocol.

Remember the command to verify an access list on a router interface.   To see whether an access list is set on an interface and in which direction it is filtering, use the show ip interface command. This command will not show you the contents of the access list, merely which access lists are applied on the interface.

Remember the command to verify the access-list configuration.   To see the configured access lists on your router, use the show access-list command. This command will not show you which interfaces have an access list set.

Written Lab 12

In this section, you'll complete the following lab to make sure you've got the information and concepts contained within them fully dialed in:

Lab 12.1: Security

The answers to this lab can be found in Appendix A, "Answers to Written Labs."

In this section, write the answers to the following questions:

1.   What command would you use to configure a standard IP access list to prevent all machines on network 172.16.0.0/16 from accessing your Ethernet network?

2.   What command would you use to apply the access list you created in question 1 to an Ethernet interface outbound?

3. What command(s) would you use to create an access list that denies host 192.168.15.5 access to an Ethernet network?

4. Which command verifies that you've entered the access list correctly?

5. What two tools can help notify and prevent DoS attacks?

6. What command(s) would you use to create an extended access list that stops host 172.16.10.1 from telnetting to host 172.16.30.5?

7. What command would you use to set an access list on a VTY line?

8. Write the same standard IP access list you wrote in question 1 but this time as a named access list.

9. Write the command to apply the named access list you created in question 8 to an Ethernet interface outbound.

10. Which command verifies the placement and direction of an access list?

Hands-on Labs

In this section, you will complete two labs. To complete these labs, you will need at least three routers. You can easily perform these labs with the Cisco Packet Tracer program. If you are studying to take your Cisco exam, you really need to do these labs!

Lab 12.1: Standard IP Access Lists

Lab 12.2: Extended IP Access Lists

All of the labs will use the following diagram for configuring the routers.

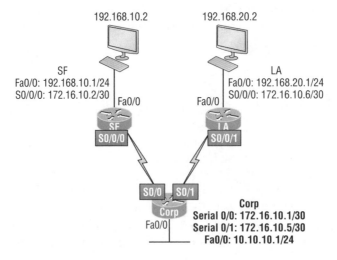

Hands-on Lab 12.1: Standard IP Access Lists

In this lab, you will allow only packets from a single host on the SF LAN to enter the LA LAN.

1. Go to LA router and enter global configuration mode by typing **config t**.

2. From global configuration mode, type **access-list ?** to get a list of all the different access lists available.

3. Choose an access-list number that will allow you to create an IP standard access list. This is a number between 1 and 99 or 1300 and 1399.

4. Choose to permit host 192.168.10.2, which is the host address:

    ```
    LA(config)#access-list 10 permit 192.168.20.2 ?
      A.B.C.D  Wildcard bits
      <cr>
    ```

    To specify only host 192.168.20.2, use the wildcards 0.0.0.0:

    ```
    LA(config)#access-list 10 permit 192.168.20.2
      0.0.0.0
    ```

5. Now that the access list is created, you must apply it to an interface to make it work:

    ```
    LA(config)#int f0/0
    Lab_A(config-if)#ip access-group 10 out
    ```

6. Verify your access list with the following commands:

    ```
    LA#sh access-list
    Standard IP access list 10
        permit 192.168.20.2
    LA#sh run
    [output cut]
    interface FastEthernet0/0
     ip address 192.168.20.1 255.255.255.0
     ip access-group 10 out
    ```

7. Test your access list by pinging from 192.168.10.2 to 192.168.20.2.

8. If you have another host on the LA LAN, ping that address, which should fail if your ACL is working.

Hands-on Lab 12.2: Extended IP Access Lists

In this lab, you will use an extended IP access list to stop host 192.168.10.2 from creating a Telnet session to router LA (172.16.10.6). However, the host still should be able to ping the LA router. IP extended lists should be placed close to the source, so add the extended list on router SF. Pay attention to the log command used in step 6. It is a Cisco objective!

1. Remove any access lists on SF and add an extended list to SF.

2. Choose a number to create an extended IP list. The IP extended lists use 100–199 or 2000–2699.

3. Use a deny statement. (You'll add a permit statement in step 7 to allow other traffic to still work.)

```
SF(config)#access-list 110 deny ?
  <0-255>  An IP protocol number
  ahp      Authentication Header Protocol
  eigrp    Cisco's EIGRP routing protocol
  esp      Encapsulation Security Payload
  gre      Cisco's GRE tunneling
  icmp     Internet Control Message Protocol
  igmp     Internet Gateway Message Protocol
  igrp     Cisco's IGRP routing protocol
  ip       Any Internet Protocol
  ipinip   IP in IP tunneling
  nos      KA9Q NOS compatible IP over IP tunneling
  ospf     OSPF routing protocol
  pcp      Payload Compression Protocol
  tcp      Transmission Control Protocol
  udp      User Datagram Protocol
```

4. Since you are going to deny Telnet, you must choose TCP as a Transport layer protocol:

```
SF(config)#access-list 110 deny tcp ?
  A.B.C.D  Source address
  any      Any source host
  host     A single source host
```

5. Add the source IP address you want to filter on, then add the destination host IP address. Use the host command instead of wildcard bits.

```
SF(config)#access-list 110 deny tcp host
  192.168.10.2 host 172.16.10.6 ?
  ack             Match on the ACK bit
```

eq	Match only packets on a given port number
established	Match established connections
fin	Match on the FIN bit
fragments	Check fragments
gt	Match only packets with a greater port number
log	Log matches against this entry
log-input	Log matches against this entry, including input interface
lt	Match only packets with a lower port number
neq	Match only packets not on a given port number
precedence	Match packets with given precedence value
psh	Match on the PSH bit
range	Match only packets in the range of port numbers
rst	Match on the RST bit
syn	Match on the SYN bit
tos	Match packets with given TOS value
urg	Match on the URG bit
<cr>	

6. At this point, you can add the eq telnet command to filter host 192.168.10.2 from telnetting to 172.16.10.6. The log command can also be used at the end of the command so that whenever the access-list line is hit, a log will be generated on the console.

```
SF(config)#access-list 110 deny tcp host
   192.168.10.2 host 172.16.10.6 eq telnet log
```

7. It is important to add this line next to create a permit statement. (Remember that 0.0.0.0 255.255.255.255 is the same as the any command.)

```
SF(config)#access-list 110 permit ip any 0.0.0.0
   255.255.255.255
```

You must create a permit statement; if you just add a deny statement, nothing will be permitted at all. Please see the sections earlier in this chapter for more detailed information on the deny any command implied at the end of every ACL.

8. Apply the access list to the FastEthernet0/0 on SF to stop the Telnet traffic as soon as it hits the first router interface.

```
SF(config)#int f0/0
SF(config-if)#ip access-group 110 in
SF(config-if)#^Z
```

9. Try telnetting from host 192.168.10.2 to LA using the destination IP address of 172.16.10.6. This should fail, but the ping command should work.

10. On the console of SF, because of the log command, the output should appear as follows:

```
01:11:48: %SEC-6-IPACCESSLOGP: list 110 denied tcp
   192.168.10.2(1030) -> 172.16.10.6(23), 1 packet
01:13:04: %SEC-6-IPACCESSLOGP: list 110 denied tcp
   192.168.10.2(1030) -> 172.16.10.6(23), 3 packets
```

Review Questions

 The following questions are designed to test your understanding of this chapter's material. For more information on how to get additional questions, please see www.lammle.com/ccna.

You can find the answers to these questions in Appendix B, "Answers to Review Questions."

1. Which of the following statements is false when a packet is being compared to an access list?

    A. It's always compared with each line of the access list in sequential order.

    B. Once the packet matches the condition on a line of the access list, the packet is acted upon and no further comparisons take place.

    C. There is an implicit "deny" at the end of each access list.

    D. Until all lines have been analyzed, the comparison is not over.

2. You need to create an access list that will prevent hosts in the network range of 192.168.160.0 to 192.168.191.0. Which of the following lists will you use?

    A. `access-list 10 deny 192.168.160.0 255.255.224.0`

    B. `access-list 10 deny 192.168.160.0 0.0.191.255`

    C. `access-list 10 deny 192.168.160.0 0.0.31.255`

    D. `access-list 10 deny 192.168.0.0 0.0.31.255`

3. You have created a named access list called BlockSales. Which of the following is a valid command for applying this to packets trying to enter interface Fa0/0 of your router?

    A. `(config)#ip access-group 110 in`

    B. `(config-if)#ip access-group 110 in`

    C. `(config-if)#ip access-group Blocksales in`

    D. `(config-if)#BlockSales ip access-list in`

4. Which access list statement will permit all HTTP sessions to network 192.168.144.0/24 containing web servers?

    A. `access-list 110 permit tcp 192.168.144.0 0.0.0.255 any eq 80`

    B. `access-list 110 permit tcp any 192.168.144.0 0.0.0.255 eq 80`

    C. `access-list 110 permit tcp 192.168.144.0 0.0.0.255 192.168.144.0 0.0.0.255 any eq 80`

    D. `access-list 110 permit udp any 192.168.144.0 eq 80`

5. Which of the following access lists will allow only HTTP traffic into network 196.15.7.0?

    A. `access-list 100 permit tcp any 196.15.7.0 0.0.0.255 eq www`

    B. `access-list 10 deny tcp any 196.15.7.0 eq www`

    C. `access-list 100 permit 196.15.7.0 0.0.0.255 eq www`

D. `access-list 110 permit ip any 196.15.7.0 0.0.0.255`

E. `access-list 110 permit www 196.15.7.0 0.0.0.255`

6. What router command allows you to determine whether an IP access list is enabled on a particular interface?

   A. `show ip port`

   B. `show access-lists`

   C. `show ip interface`

   D. `show access-lists interface`

7. In the work area, connect the show command to its function on the right.

show access-list	Shows only the parameters for the access list 110. This command does not show you the interface the list is set on.
show access-list 110	Shows only the IP access lists configured on the router.
show ip access-list	Shows which interfaces have access lists set.
show ip interface	Displays all access lists and their parameters configured on the router. This command does not show you which interface the list is set on.

8. If you wanted to deny all Telnet connections to only network 192.168.10.0, which command could you use?

   A. `access-list 100 deny tcp 192.168.10.0 255.255.255.0 eq telnet`

   B. `access-list 100 deny tcp 192.168.10.0 0.255.255.255 eq telnet`

   C. `access-list 100 deny tcp any 192.168.10.0 0.0.0.255 eq 23`

   D. `access-list 100 deny 192.168.10.0 0.0.0.255 any eq 23`

9. If you wanted to deny FTP access from network 200.200.10.0 to network 200.199.11.0 but allow everything else, which of the following command strings is valid?

   A. `access-list 110 deny 200.200.10.0 to network 200.199.11.0 eq ftp`

      `access-list 111 permit ip any 0.0.0.0 255.255.255.255`

   B. `access-list 1 deny ftp 200.200.10.0 200.199.11.0 any any`

   C. `access-list 100 deny tcp 200.200.10.0 0.0.0.255 200.199.11.0 0.0.0.255 eq ftp`

   D. `access-list 198 deny tcp 200.200.10.0 0.0.0.255 200.199.11.0 0.0.0.255 eq ftp`

      `access-list 198 permit ip any 0.0.0.0 255.255.255.255`

10. You want to create an extended access list that denies the subnet of the following host: 172.16.50.172/20. Which of the following would you start your list with?

   A. `access-list 110 deny ip 172.16.48.0 255.255.240.0 any`

   B. `access-list 110 udp deny 172.16.0.0 0.0.255.255 ip any`

C. `access-list 110 deny tcp 172.16.64.0 0.0.31.255 any eq 80`

D. `access-list 110 deny ip 172.16.48.0 0.0.15.255 any`

11. Which of the following is the wildcard (inverse) version of a /27 mask?

A. 0.0.0.7

B. 0.0.0.31

C. 0.0.0.27

D. 0.0.31.255

12. You want to create an extended access list that denies the subnet of the following host: 172.16.198.94/19. Which of the following would you start your list with?

A. `access-list 110 deny ip 172.16.192.0 0.0.31.255 any`

B. `access-list 110 deny ip 172.16.0.0 0.0.255.255 any`

C. `access-list 10 deny ip 172.16.172.0 0.0.31.255 any`

D. `access-list 110 deny ip 172.16.188.0 0.0.15.255 any`

13. The following access list has been applied to an interface on a router:

`access-list 101 deny tcp 199.111.16.32 0.0.0.31 host 199.168.5.60`

Which of the following IP addresses will be blocked because of this single rule in the list? (Choose all that apply.)

A. 199.111.16.67

B. 199.111.16.38

C. 199.111.16.65

D. 199.11.16.54

14. Which of the following commands connects access list 110 inbound to interface Ethernet0?

A. `Router(config)#ip access-group 110 in`

B. `Router(config)#ip access-list 110 in`

C. `Router(config-if)#ip access-group 110 in`

D. `Router(config-if)#ip access-list 110 in`

15. What is the effect of this single-line access list?

`access-list 110 deny ip 172.16.10.0 0.0.0.255 host 1.1.1.1`

A. Denies only the computer at 172.16.10

B. Denies all traffic

C. Denies the subnet 172.16.10.0/26

D. Denies the subnet 172.16.10.0/25

16. You configure the following access list. What will the result of this access list be?

`access-list 110 deny tcp 10.1.1.128 0.0.0.63 any eq smtp`
`access-list 110 deny tcp any any eq 23`

```
int ethernet 0
ip access-group 110 out
```

   A. Email and Telnet will be allowed out E0.

   B. Email and Telnet will be allowed in E0.

   C. Everything but email and Telnet will be allowed out E0.

   D. No IP traffic will be allowed out E0.

17. Which of the following series of commands will restrict Telnet access to the router?

   A. Lab_A(config)#**access-list 10 permit 172.16.1.1**

      Lab_A(config)#**line con 0**

      Lab_A(config-line)#**ip access-group 10 in**

   B. Lab_A(config)#**access-list 10 permit 172.16.1.1**

      Lab_A(config)#**line vty 0 4**

      Lab_A(config-line)#**access-class 10 out**

   C. Lab_A(config)#**access-list 10 permit 172.16.1.1**

      Lab_A(config)#**line vty 0 4**

      Lab_A(config-line)#**access-class 10 in**

   D. Lab_A(config)#**access-list 10 permit 172.16.1.1**

      Lab_A(config)#**line vty 0 4**

      Lab_A(config-line)#**ip access-group 10 in**

18. Which of the following is true regarding access lists applied to an interface?

   A. You can place as many access lists as you want on any interface until you run out of memory.

   B. You can apply only one access list on any interface.

   C. One access list may be configured, per direction, for each layer 3 protocol configured on an interface.

   D. You can apply two access lists to any interface.

19. What is the most common attack on a network today?

   A. Lock picking

   B. Naggle

   C. DoS

   D. auto secure

20. You need to stop DoS attacks in real time and have a log of anyone who has tried to attack your network. What should you do your network?

   A. Add more routers.

   B. Use the auto secure command.

   C. Implement IDS/IPS.

   D. Configure Naggle.

Chapter
13

Network Address Translation (NAT)

THE FOLLOWING ICND1 EXAM TOPICS ARE COVERED IN THIS CHAPTER:

✓ **4.0 Infrastructure Services**

- 4.7 Configure, verify, and troubleshoot inside source NAT

  - 4.7.a Static

  - 4.7.b Pool

  - 4.7.c PAT

In this chapter, we're going to dig into Network Address Translation (NAT), Dynamic NAT, and Port Address Translation (PAT), also known as NAT Overload. Of course, I'll demonstrate all the NAT commands. I also provided some fantastic hands-on labs for you to configure at the end of this chapter, so be sure not to miss those!

It's important to understand the Cisco objectives for this chapter. They are very straightforward: you have hosts on your inside Corporate network using RFC 1918 addresses and you need to allow those hosts access to the Internet by configuring NAT translations. With that objective in mind, that will be my direction with this chapter.

Because we'll be using ACLs in our NAT configurations, it's important that you're really comfortable with the skills you learned in the previous chapter before proceeding with this one.

To find up-to-the-minute updates for this chapter, please see www.lammle.com/ccna or the book's web page at www.sybex.com/go/ccna.

When Do We Use NAT?

Network Address Translation (NAT) is similar to Classless Inter-Domain Routing (CIDR) in that the original intention for NAT was to slow the depletion of available IP address space by allowing multiple private IP addresses to be represented by a much smaller number of public IP addresses.

Since then, it's been discovered that NAT is also a useful tool for network migrations and mergers, server load sharing, and creating "virtual servers." So in this chapter, I'm going to describe the basics of NAT functionality and the terminology common to NAT.

Because NAT really decreases the overwhelming amount of public IP addresses required in a networking environment, it comes in really handy when two companies that have duplicate internal addressing schemes merge. NAT is also a great tool to use when an organization changes its Internet service provider (ISP) but the networking manager needs to avoid the hassle of changing the internal address scheme.

Here's a list of situations when NAT can be especially helpful:

- When you need to connect to the Internet and your hosts don't have globally unique IP addresses

- When you've changed to a new ISP that requires you to renumber your network
- When you need to merge two intranets with duplicate addresses

You typically use NAT on a border router. For example, in Figure 13.1, NAT is used on the Corporate router connected to the Internet.

FIGURE 13.1 Where to configure NAT

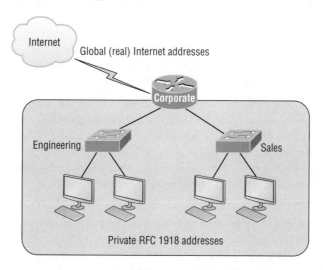

Now you may be thinking, "NAT's totally cool and I just gotta have it!" But don't get too excited yet because there are some serious snags related to using NAT that you need to understand first. Don't get me wrong—it can truly be a lifesaver sometimes, but NAT has a bit of a dark side you need to know about too. For the pros and cons linked to using NAT, check out Table 13.1.

TABLE 13.1 Advantages and disadvantages of implementing NAT

Advantages	Disadvantages
Conserves legally registered addresses.	Translation results in switching path delays.
Remedies address overlap events.	Causes loss of end-to-end IP traceability
Increases flexibility when connecting to the Internet.	Certain applications will not function with NAT enabled
Eliminates address renumbering as a network evolves.	Complicates tunneling protocols such as IPsec because NAT modifies the values in the header

The most obvious advantage associated with NAT is that it allows you to conserve your legally registered address scheme. But a version of it known as PAT is also why we've only just recently run out of IPv4 addresses. Without NAT/PAT, we'd have run out of IPv4 addresses more than a decade ago!

Types of Network Address Translation

In this section, I'm going to go over the three types of NATs with you:

Static NAT (one-to-one)   This type of NAT is designed to allow one-to-one mapping between local and global addresses. Keep in mind that the static version requires you to have one real Internet IP address for every host on your network.

Dynamic NAT (many-to-many)   This version gives you the ability to map an unregistered IP address to a registered IP address from out of a pool of registered IP addresses. You don't have to statically configure your router to map each inside address to an individual outside address as you would using static NAT, but you do have to have enough real, bona fide IP addresses for everyone who's going to be sending packets to and receiving them from the Internet at the same time.

Overloading (one-to-many)   This is the most popular type of NAT configuration. Understand that overloading really is a form of dynamic NAT that maps multiple unregistered IP addresses to a single registered IP address (many-to-one) by using different source ports. Now, why is this so special? Well, because it's also known as *Port Address Translation (PAT)*, which is also commonly referred to as NAT Overload. Using PAT allows you to permit thousands of users to connect to the Internet using only one real global IP address—pretty slick, right? Seriously, NAT Overload is the real reason we haven't run out of valid IP addresses on the Internet. Really—I'm not joking!

 I'll show you how to configure all three types of NAT throughout this chapter and at the end of this chapter with the hands-on labs.

NAT Names

The names we use to describe the addresses used with NAT are fairly straightforward. Addresses used after NAT translations are called *global addresses*. These are usually the public addresses used on the Internet, which you don't need if you aren't going on the Internet.

Local addresses are the ones we use before NAT translation. This means that the inside local address is actually the private address of the sending host that's attempting to get to the Internet. The outside local address would typically be the router interface connected to your ISP and is also usually a public address used as the packet begins its journey.

After translation, the inside local address is then called the *inside global address* and the outside global address then becomes the address of the destination host. Check out Table 13.2, which lists all this terminology and offers a clear picture of the various names used with NAT. Keep in mind that these terms and their definitions can vary somewhat based on implementation. The table shows how they're used according to the Cisco exam objectives.

TABLE 13.2   NAT terms

Names	Meaning
Inside local	Source host inside address before translation—typically an RFC 1918 address.
Outside local	Address of an outside host as it appears to the inside network. This is usually the address of the router interface connected to ISP—the actual Internet address.
Inside global	Source host address used after translation to get onto the Internet. This is also the actual Internet address.
Outside global	Address of outside destination host and, again, the real Internet address.

How NAT Works

Okay, it's time to look at how this whole NAT thing works. I'm going to start by using Figure 13.2 to describe basic NAT translation.

FIGURE 13.2   Basic NAT translation

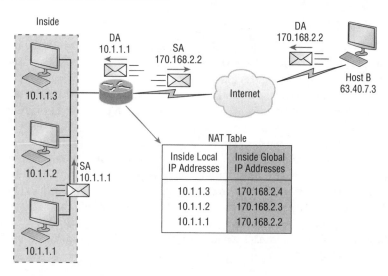

In this figure, we can see host 10.1.1.1 sending an Internet-bound packet to the border router configured with NAT. The router identifies the source IP address as an inside local IP address destined for an outside network, translates the source IP address in the packet, and documents the translation in the NAT table.

The packet is sent to the outside interface with the new translated source address. The external host returns the packet to the destination host and the NAT router translates the inside global IP address back to the inside local IP address using the NAT table. This is as simple as it gets!

Let's take a look at a more complex configuration using overloading, also referred to as PAT. I'll use Figure 13.3 to demonstrate how PAT works by having an inside host HTTP to a server on the Internet.

FIGURE 13.3 NAT overloading example (PAT)

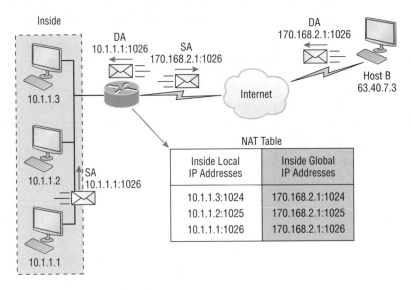

With PAT, all inside hosts get translated to one single IP address, hence the term *overloading*. Again, the reason we've just run out of available global IP addresses on the Internet is because of overloading (PAT).

Take a look at the NAT table in Figure 13.3 again. In addition to the inside local IP address and inside global IP address, we now have port numbers. These port numbers help the router identify which host should receive the return traffic. The router uses the source port number from each host to differentiate the traffic from each of them. Understand that the packet has a destination port number of 80 when it leaves the router, and the HTTP server sends back the data with a destination port number of 1026, in this example. This allows the NAT translation router to differentiate between hosts in the NAT table and then translate the destination IP address back to the inside local address.

Port numbers are used at the Transport layer to identify the local host in this example. If we had to use real global IP addresses to identify the source hosts, that's called *static NAT* and we would run out of addresses. PAT allows us to use the Transport layer to identify the hosts, which in turn allows us to theoretically use up to about 65,000 hosts with only one real IP address!

Static NAT Configuration

Let's take a look at a simple example of a basic static NAT configuration:

```
ip nat inside source static 10.1.1.1 170.46.2.2
!
interface Ethernet0
 ip address 10.1.1.10 255.255.255.0
 ip nat inside
!
interface Serial0
 ip address 170.46.2.1 255.255.255.0
 ip nat outside
!
```

In the preceding router output, the ip nat inside source command identifies which IP addresses will be translated. In this configuration example, the ip nat inside source command configures a static translation between the inside local IP address 10.1.1.1 and the outside global IP address 170.46.2.2.

Scrolling farther down in the configuration, we find an ip nat command under each interface. The ip nat inside command identifies that interface as the inside interface. The ip nat outside command identifies that interface as the outside interface. When you look back at the ip nat inside source command, you can see that the command is referencing the inside interface as the source or starting point of the translation. You could also use the command like this: ip nat outside source. This option indicates the interface that you designated as the outside interface should become the source or starting point for the translation.

Dynamic NAT Configuration

Basically, dynamic NAT really means we have a pool of addresses that we'll use to provide real IP addresses to a group of users on the inside. Because we don't use port numbers, we must have real IP addresses for every user who's trying to get outside the local network simultaneously.

Here is a sample output of a dynamic NAT configuration:

```
ip nat pool todd 170.168.2.3 170.168.2.254
    netmask 255.255.255.0
ip nat inside source list 1 pool todd
```

```
!
interface Ethernet0
 ip address 10.1.1.10 255.255.255.0
 ip nat inside
!
interface Serial0
 ip address 170.168.2.1 255.255.255.0
 ip nat outside
!
access-list 1 permit 10.1.1.0 0.0.0.255
!
```

The `ip nat inside source list 1 pool todd` command tells the router to translate IP addresses that match `access-list 1` to an address found in the IP NAT pool named todd. Here the ACL isn't there to filter traffic for security reasons by permitting or denying traffic. In this case, it's there to select or designate what we often call interesting traffic. When interesting traffic has been matched with the access list, it's pulled into the NAT process to be translated. This is actually a common use for access lists, which aren't always just stuck with the dull job of just blocking traffic at an interface!

The command `ip nat pool todd 170.168.2.3 170.168.2.254 netmask 255.255.255.0` creates a pool of addresses that will be distributed to the specific hosts that require global addresses. When troubleshooting NAT for the Cisco objectives, always check this pool to confirm that there are enough addresses in it to provide translation for all the inside hosts. Last, check to make sure the pool names match exactly on both lines, remembering that they are case sensitive; if they don't, the pool won't work!

PAT (Overloading) Configuration

This last example shows how to configure inside global address overloading. This is the typical form of NAT that we would use today. It's actually now rare to use static or dynamic NAT unless it is for something like statically mapping a server, for example.

Here is a sample output of a PAT configuration:

```
ip nat pool globalnet 170.168.2.1 170.168.2.1 netmask 255.255.255.0
ip nat inside source list 1 pool globalnet overload
!
interface Ethernet0/0
 ip address 10.1.1.10 255.255.255.0
 ip nat inside
!
interface Serial0/0
 ip address 170.168.2.1 255.255.255.0
 ip nat outside
!
access-list 1 permit 10.1.1.0 0.0.0.255
```

The nice thing about PAT is that these are only a few differences between this configuration and the previous dynamic NAT configuration:

- Our pool of addresses has shrunk to only one IP address.

- We included the `overload` keyword at the end of our `ip nat inside source` command.

A really key factor to see in the example is that the one IP address that's in the pool for us to use is the IP address of the outside interface. This is perfect if you are configuring NAT Overload for yourself at home or for a small office that only has one IP address from your ISP. You could, however, use an additional address such as 170.168.2.2 if you had that address available to you as well, and doing that could prove very helpful in a very large implementation where you've got such an abundance of simultaneously active internal users that you need to have more than one overloaded IP address on the outside!

Simple Verification of NAT

As always, once you've chosen and configured the type of NAT you're going to run, which is typically PAT, you must be able to verify your configuration.

To see basic IP address translation information, use the following command:

`Router#`**`show ip nat translations`**

When looking at the IP NAT translations, you may see many translations from the same host to the corresponding host at the destination. Understand that this is typical when there are many connections to the same server.

You can also verify your NAT configuration via the `debug ip nat` command. This output will show the sending address, the translation, and the destination address on each debug line:

`Router#`**`debug ip nat`**

But wait—how do you clear your NAT entries from the translation table? Just use the `clear ip nat translation` command, and if you want to clear all entries from the NAT table, just use an asterisk (*) at the end of the command.

Testing and Troubleshooting NAT

Cisco's NAT gives you some serious power—and it does so without much effort, because the configurations are really pretty simple. But we all know nothing's perfect, so in case something goes wrong, you can figure out some of the more common culprits by running through this list of potential causes:

- Check the dynamic pools. Are they composed of the right scope of addresses?

- Check to see if any dynamic pools overlap.

- Check to see if the addresses used for static mapping and those in the dynamic pools overlap.

- Ensure that your access lists specify the correct addresses for translation.

- Make sure there aren't any addresses left out that need to be there, and ensure that none are included that shouldn't be.

- Check to make sure you've got both the inside and outside interfaces delimited properly.

A key thing to keep in mind is that one of the most common problems with a new NAT configuration often isn't specific to NAT at all—it usually involves a routing blooper. So, because you're changing a source or destination address in a packet, make sure your router still knows what to do with the new address after the translation!

The first command you should typically use is the show ip nat translations command:

```
Router#show ip nat trans
Pro   Inside global   Inside local   Outside local   Outside global
---   192.2.2.1       10.1.1.1       ---             ---
---   192.2.2.2       10.1.1.2       ---             ---
```

After checking out this output, can you tell me if the configuration on the router is static or dynamic NAT? The answer is yes, either static or dynamic NAT is configured because there's a one-to-one translation from the inside local to the inside global. Basically, by looking at the output, you can't tell if it's static or dynamic per se, but you absolutely can tell that you're not using PAT because there are no port numbers.

Let's take a look at another output:

```
Router#sh ip nat trans
Pro Inside global       Inside local      Outside local     Outside global
tcp 170.168.2.1:11003   10.1.1.1:11003    172.40.2.2:23     172.40.2.2:23
tcp 170.168.2.1:1067    10.1.1.1:1067     172.40.2.3:23     172.40.2.3:23
```

Okay, you can easily see that the previous output is using NAT Overload (PAT). The protocol in this output is TCP, and the inside global address is the same for both entries.

Supposedly the sky's the limit regarding the number of mappings the NAT table can hold. But this is reality, so things like memory and CPU, or even the boundaries set in place by the scope of available addresses or ports, can cause limitations on the actual number of entries. Consider that each NAT mapping devours about 160 bytes of memory. And sometimes the amount of entries must be limited for the sake of performance or because of policy restrictions, but this doesn't happen very often. In situations like these, just go to the ip nat translation max-entries command for help.

Another handy command for troubleshooting is show ip nat statistics. Deploying this gives you a summary of the NAT configuration, and it will count the number of active translation types too. Also counted are hits to an existing mapping as well any misses, with the latter causing an attempt to create a mapping. This command will also reveal expired translations. If you want to check into dynamic pools, their types, the total available addresses, how many addresses have been allocated and how many have failed, plus the number of translations that have occurred, just use the pool keyword after statistics.

Here is an example of the basic NAT debugging command:

```
Router#debug ip nat
NAT: s=10.1.1.1->192.168.2.1, d=172.16.2.2 [0]
NAT: s=172.16.2.2, d=192.168.2.1->10.1.1.1 [0]
NAT: s=10.1.1.1->192.168.2.1, d=172.16.2.2 [1]
NAT: s=10.1.1.1->192.168.2.1, d=172.16.2.2 [2]
NAT: s=10.1.1.1->192.168.2.1, d=172.16.2.2 [3]
NAT*: s=172.16.2.2, d=192.168.2.1->10.1.1.1 [1]
```

Notice the last line in the output and how the NAT at the beginning of the line has an asterisk (*). This means the packet was translated and fast-switched to the destination. What's fast-switched? Well in brief, fast-switching has gone by several aliases such as cache-based switching and this nicely descriptive name, "route once switch many." The fast-switching process is used on Cisco routers to create a cache of layer 3 routing information to be accessed at layer 2 so packets can be forwarded quickly through a router without the routing table having to be parsed for every packet. As packets are packet switched (looked up in the routing table), this information is stored in the cache for later use if needed for faster routing processing.

Let's get back to verifying NAT. Did you know you can manually clear dynamic NAT entries from the NAT table? You can, and doing this can come in seriously handy if you need to get rid of a specific rotten entry without sitting around waiting for the timeout to expire! A manual clear is also really useful when you want to clear the whole NAT table to reconfigure a pool of addresses.

You also need to know that the Cisco IOS software just won't allow you to change or delete an address pool if any of that pool's addresses are mapped in the NAT table. The clear ip nat translations command clears entries—you can indicate a single entry via the global and local address and through TCP and UDP translations, including ports, or you can just type in an asterisk (*) to wipe out the entire table. But know that if you do that, only dynamic entries will be cleared because this command won't remove static entries.

Oh, and there's more—any outside device's packet destination address that happens to be responding to any inside device is known as the inside global (IG) address. This means that the initial mapping has to be held in the NAT table so that all packets arriving from a specific connection get translated consistently. Holding entries in the NAT table also cuts down on repeated translation operations happening each time the same inside machine sends packets to the same outside destinations on a regular basis.

Let me clarify: When an entry is placed into the NAT table the first time, a timer begins ticking and its duration is known as the translation timeout. Each time a packet for a given entry translates through the router, the timer gets reset. If the timer expires, the entry will be unceremoniously removed from the NAT table and the dynamically assigned address will then be returned to the pool. Cisco's default translation timeout is 86,400 seconds (24 hours), but you can change that with the ip nat translation timeout command.

Before we move on to the configuration section and actually use the commands I just talked about, let's go through a couple of NAT examples and see if you can figure out the best configuration to go with. To start, look at Figure 13.4 and ask yourself two things: Where would you implement NAT in this design? What type of NAT would you configure?

FIGURE 13.4 NAT example

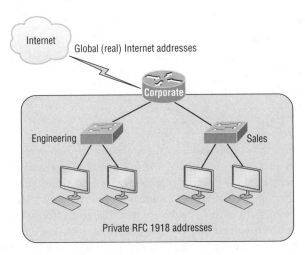

In Figure 13.4, the NAT configuration would be placed on the corporate router, just as I demonstrated with Figure 13.1, and the configuration would be dynamic NAT with overload (PAT). In this next NAT example, what type of NAT is being used?

```
ip nat pool todd-nat 170.168.10.10 170.168.10.20 netmask 255.255.255.0
ip nat inside source list 1 pool todd-nat
```

The preceding command uses dynamic NAT without PAT. The pool in the command gives the answer away as dynamic, plus there's more than one address in the pool and there is no overload command at the end of our ip nat inside source command. This means we are not using PAT!

In the next NAT example, refer to Figure 13.5 and see if you can come up with the configuration needed.

FIGURE 13.5 Another NAT example

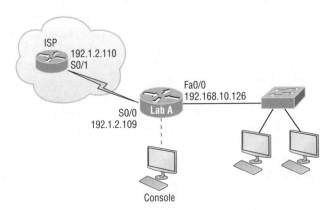

Figure 13.5 shows a border router that needs to be configured with NAT and allow the use of six public IP addresses to the inside locals, 192.1.2.109 through 192.1.2.114. However, on the inside network, you have 62 hosts that use the private addresses of 192.168.10.65 through 192.168.10.126. What would your NAT configuration be on the border router?

Actually, two different answers would both work here, but the following would be my first choice based on the exam objectives:

```
ip nat pool Todd 192.1.2.109 192.1.2.109 netmask 255.255.255.248
access-list 1 permit 192.168.10.64 0.0.0.63
ip nat inside source list 1 pool Todd overload
```

The command ip nat pool Todd 192.1.2.109 192.1.2.109 netmask 255.255.255.248 sets the pool name as Todd and creates a dynamic pool of only one address using NAT address 192.1.2.109. Instead of the netmask command, you can use the prefix-length 29 statement. Just in case you're wondering, you cannot do this on router interfaces as well!

The second answer would get you the exact same result of having only 192.1.2.109 as your inside global, but you can type this in and it will also work: ip nat pool Todd 192.1.2.109 192.1.2.114 netmask 255.255.255.248. But this option really is a waste because the second through sixth addresses would only be used if there was a conflict with a TCP port number. You would use something like what I've shown in this example if you literally had about ten thousand hosts with one Internet connection! You would need it to help with the TCP-Reset issue when two hosts are trying to use the same source port number and get a negative acknowledgment (NAK). But in our example, we've only got up to 62 hosts connecting to the Internet at the same time, so having more than one inside global gets us nothing!

If you're fuzzy on the second line where the access list is set in the NAT configuration, do a quick review of Chapter 12, "Security." But this isn't difficult to grasp because it's easy to see in this access-list line that it's just the *network number* and *wildcard* used with that command. I always say, "Every question is a subnet question," and this one is no exception. The inside locals in this example were 192.168.10.65–126, which is a block of 64, or a 255.255.255.192 mask. As I've said in pretty much every chapter, you really need to be able to subnet quickly!

The command ip nat inside source list 1 pool Todd overload sets the dynamic pool to use PAT by using the overload command.

And be sure to add the ip nat inside and ip nat outside statements on the appropriate interfaces.

If you're planning on testing for any Cisco exam, configure the hands-on labs at the end of this chapter until you're really comfortable with doing that!

One more example, and then you are off to the written lab, hands-on labs, and review questions.

The network in Figure 13.6 is already configured with IP addresses as shown in the figure, and there is only one configured host. However, you need to add 25 more hosts to the LAN. Now, all 26 hosts must be able to get to the Internet at the same time.

FIGURE 13.6   Last NAT example

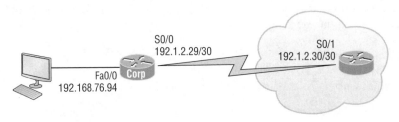

By looking at the configured network, use only the following inside addresses to configure NAT on the Corp router to allow all hosts to reach the Internet:

- Inside globals: 198.18.41.129 through 198.18.41.134
- Inside locals: 192.168.76.65 through 192.168.76.94

This one is a bit more challenging because all we have to help us figure out the configuration is the inside globals and the inside locals. But even meagerly armed with these crumbs of information, plus the IP addresses of the router interfaces shown in the figure, we can still configure this correctly.

To do that, we must first determine what our block sizes are so we can get our subnet mask for our NAT pool. This will also equip us to configure the wildcard for the access list.

You should easily be able to see that the block size of the inside globals is 8 and the block size of the inside locals is 32. Know that it's critical not to stumble on this foundational information!

So we can configure NAT now that we have our block sizes:

```
ip nat pool Corp 198.18.41.129 198.18.41.134 netmask 255.255.255.248
ip nat inside source list 1 pool Corp overload
access-list 1 permit 192.168.76.64 0.0.0.31
```

Since we had a block of only 8 for our pool, we had to use the `overload` command to make sure all 26 hosts can get to the Internet at the same time.

There is one other simple way to configure NAT, and I use this command at my home office to connect to my ISP. One command line and it's done! Here it is:

```
ip nat inside source list 1 int s0/0/0 overload
```

I can't say enough how much I love efficiency, and being able to achieve something cool using one measly line always makes me happy! My one little powerfully elegant line essentially says, "Use my outside local as my inside global and overload it." Nice! Of course, I still had to create ACL 1 and add the inside and outside interface commands to the configuration, but this is a really nice, fast way to configure NAT if you don't have a pool of addresses to use.

Summary

Now this really was a fun chapter. Come on—admit it! You learned a lot about Network Address Translation (NAT) and how it's configured as static and dynamic as well as with Port Address Translation (PAT), also called NAT Overload.

I also described how each flavor of NAT is used in a network as well as how each type is configured.

We finished up by going through some verification and troubleshooting commands. Now don't forget to practice all the wonderfully helpful labs until you've got them nailed down tight!

Exam Essentials

Understand the term *NAT*.   This may come as news to you, because I didn't—okay, failed to—mention it earlier, but NAT has a few nicknames. In the industry, it's referred to as network masquerading, IP-masquerading, and (for those who are besieged with OCD and compelled to spell everything out) Network Address Translation. Whatever you want to dub it, basically, they all refer to the process of rewriting the source/destination addresses of IP packets when they go through a router or firewall. Just focus on the process that's occurring and your understanding of it (i.e., the important part) and you're on it for sure!

Remember the three methods of NAT.   The three methods are static, dynamic, and overloading; the latter is also called PAT.

Understand static NAT.   This type of NAT is designed to allow one-to-one mapping between local and global addresses.

Understand dynamic NAT.   This version gives you the ability to map a range of unregistered IP addresses to a registered IP address from out of a pool of registered IP addresses.

Understand overloading.   Overloading really is a form of dynamic NAT that maps multiple unregistered IP addresses to a single registered IP address (many-to-one) by using different ports. It's also known as *PAT*.

Written Lab 13

In this section, you'll complete the following lab to make sure you've got the information and concepts contained within it fully dialed in:

   Lab 13.1: NAT

   You can find the answers to this lab in Appendix A, "Answers to Written Labs."

In this section, write the answers to the following questions:

1. What type of address translation can use only one address to allow thousands of hosts to be translated globally?

2. What command can you use to show the NAT translations as they occur on your router?

3. What command will show you the translation table?

4. What command will clear all your NAT entries from the translation table?

5. An inside local is before or after translation?

6. An inside global is before or after translation?

7. Which command can be used for troubleshooting and displays a summary of the NAT configuration as well as counts of active translation types and hits to an existing mapping?

8. What commands must be used on your router interfaces before NAT will translate addresses?

9. In the following output, what type of NAT is being used?

    ```
    ip nat pool todd-nat 170.168.10.10 170.168.10.20 netmask 255.255.255.0
    ```

10. Instead of the netmask command, you can use the ＿＿＿＿＿＿ statement.

Hands-on Labs

I am going to use some basic routers for these labs, but really, almost any Cisco router will work. Also, you can use the LammleSim IOS version to run through all the labs in this (and every) chapter in this book.

Here is a list of the labs in this chapter:

Lab 13.1: Preparing for NAT

Lab 13.2: Configuring Dynamic NAT

Lab 13.3: Configuring PAT

I am going to use the network shown in the following diagram for our hands-on labs. I highly recommend you connect up some routers and run through these labs. You will configure NAT on router Lab_A to translate the private IP address of 192.168.10.0 to a public address of 171.16.10.0.

Table 13.3 shows the commands we will use and the purpose of each command.

TABLE 13.3 Command summary for NAT/PAT hands-on labs

Command	Purpose
ip nat inside source list *acl* pool *name*	Translates IPs that match the ACL to the pool
ip nat inside source static *inside_addr outside_addr*	Statically maps an inside local address to an outside global address
ip nat pool *name*	Creates an address pool
ip nat inside	Sets an interface to be an inside interface
ip nat outside	Sets an interface to be an outside interface
show ip nat translations	Shows current NAT translations

Lab 13.1: Preparing for NAT

In this lab, you'll set up your routers with IP addresses and RIP routing.

1. Configure the routers with the IP addresses listed in the following table:

Router	Interface	IP Address
ISP	S0	171.16.10.1/24
Lab_A	S0/2	171.16.10.2/24
Lab_A	S0/0	192.168.20.1/24
Lab_B	S0	192.168.20.2/24
Lab_B	E0	192.168.30.1/24
Lab_C	E0	192.168.30.2/24

After you configure IP addresses on the routers, you should be able to ping from router to router, but since we do not have a routing protocol running until the next step, you can verify only from one router to another but not through the network until RIP is set up. You can use any routing protocol you wish; I am just using RIP for simplicity's sake to get this up and running.

2. On Lab_A, configure RIP routing, set a passive interface, and configure the default network.

```
Lab_A#config t
Lab_A(config)#router rip
```

```
Lab_A(config-router)#network 192.168.20.0
Lab_A(config-router)#network 171.16.0.0
Lab_A(config-router)#passive-interface s0/2
Lab_A(config-router)#exit
Lab_A(config)#ip default-network 171.16.10.1
```

The passive-interface command stops RIP updates from being sent to the ISP and
the ip default-network command advertises a default network to the other routers so
they know how to get to the Internet.

3. On Lab_B, configure RIP routing:

```
Lab_B#config t
Lab_B(config)#router rip
Lab_B(config-router)#network 192.168.30.0
Lab_B(config-router)#network 192.168.20.0
```

4. On Lab_C, configure RIP routing:

```
Lab_C#config t
Lab_C(config)#router rip
Lab_C(config-router)#network 192.168.30.0
```

5. On the ISP router, configure a default route to the corporate network:

```
ISP#config t
ISP(config)#ip route 0.0.0.0 0.0.0.0 s0
```

6. Configure the ISP router so you can telnet into the router without being prompted for a
password:

```
ISP#config t
ISP(config)#line vty 0 4
ISP(config-line)#no login
```

7. Verify that you can ping from the ISP router to the Lab_C router and from the Lab_C
router to the ISP router. If you cannot, troubleshoot your network.

Lab 13.2: Configuring Dynamic NAT

In this lab, you'll configure dynamic NAT on the Lab_A router.

1. Create a pool of addresses called GlobalNet on the Lab_A router. The pool should
contain a range of addresses of 171.16.10.50 through 171.16.10.55.

```
Lab_A(config)#ip nat pool GlobalNet 171.16.10.50 171.16.10.55
net 255.255.255.0
```

2. Create access list 1. This list permits traffic from the 192.168.20.0 and 192.168.30.0 network to be translated.

```
Lab_A(config)#access-list 1 permit 192.168.20.0 0.0.0.255
Lab_A(config)#access-list 1 permit 192.168.30.0 0.0.0.255
```

3. Map the access list to the pool that was created.

```
Lab_A(config)#ip nat inside source list 1 pool GlobalNet
```

4. Configure serial 0/0 as an inside NAT interface.

```
Lab_A(config)#int s0/0
Lab_A(config-if)#ip nat inside
```

5. Configure serial 0/2 as an outside NAT interface.

```
Lab_A(config-if)#int s0/2
Lab_A(config-if)#ip nat outside
```

6. Move the console connection to the Lab_C router. Log in to the Lab_C router. Telnet from the Lab_C router to the ISP router.

```
Lab_C#telnet 171.16.10.1
```

7. Move the console connection to the Lab_B router. Log in to the Lab_B router. Telnet from the Lab_B router to the ISP router.

```
Lab_B#telnet 171.16.10.1
```

8. Execute the command **show users** from the ISP router. (This shows who is accessing the VTY lines.)

```
ISP#show users
```

a. What does it show as your source IP address?_____

b. What is your real source IP address?_____

The show users output should look something like this:

```
ISP>sh users
     Line        User      Host(s)           Idle        Location
    0 con 0                idle              00:03:32
    2 vty 0                idle              00:01:33 171.16.10.50
*   3 vty 1                idle              00:00:09 171.16.10.51
   Interface  User     Mode              Idle Peer Address
ISP>
```

> Notice that there is a one-to-one translation. This means you must have a real IP address for every host that wants to get to the Internet, which is not typically possible.

9. Leave the session open on the ISP router and connect to Lab_A. (Use **Ctrl+Shift+6**, let go, and then press **X**.)

10. Log in to your Lab_A router and view your current translations by entering the show ip nat translations command. You should see something like this:

```
Lab_A#sh ip nat translations
Pro Inside global     Inside local     Outside local     Outside global
--- 171.16.10.50      192.168.30.2     ---               ---
--- 171.16.10.51      192.168.20.2     ---               ---
Lab_A#
```

11. If you turn on debug ip nat on the Lab_A router and then ping through the router, you will see the actual NAT process take place, which will look something like this:

```
00:32:47: NAT*: s=192.168.30.2->171.16.10.50, d=171.16.10.1 [5]
00:32:47: NAT*: s=171.16.10.1, d=171.16.10.50->192.168.30.2
```

Lab 13.3: Configuring PAT

In this lab, you'll configure PAT on the Lab_A router. We will use PAT because we don't want a one-to-one translation, which uses just one IP address for every user on the network.

1. On the Lab_A router, delete the translation table and remove the dynamic NAT pool.

```
Lab_A#clear ip nat translations *
Lab_A#config t
Lab_A(config)#no ip nat pool GlobalNet 171.16.10.50
171.16.10.55 netmask 255.255.255.0
Lab_A(config)#no ip nat inside source list 1 pool GlobalNet
```

2. On the Lab_A router, create a NAT pool with one address called Lammle. The pool should contain a single address, 171.16.10.100. Enter the following command:

```
Lab_A#config t
Lab_A(config)#ip nat pool Lammle 171.16.10.100 171.16.10.100
net 255.255.255.0
```

3. Create access list 2. It should permit networks 192.168.20.0 and 192.168.30.0 to be translated.

```
Lab_A(config)#access-list 2 permit 192.168.20.0 0.0.0.255
Lab_A(config)#access-list 2 permit 192.168.30.0 0.0.0.255
```

4. Map access list 2 to the new pool, allowing PAT to occur by using the overload command.

```
Lab_A(config)#ip nat inside source list 2 pool Lammle overload
```

5. Log in to the Lab_C router and telnet to the ISP router; also, log in to the Lab_B router and telnet to the ISP router.

6. From the ISP router, use the show users command. The output should look like this:

```
ISP>sh users
    Line        User      Host(s)            Idle         Location
*   0 con 0               idle               00:00:00
    2 vty 0               idle               00:00:39 171.16.10.100
    4 vty 2               idle               00:00:37 171.16.10.100


    Interface  User      Mode               Idle Peer Address

ISP>
```

7. From the Lab_A router, use the show ip nat translations command.

```
Lab_A#sh ip nat translations
Pro Inside global  Inside local  Outside local Outside global
tcp 171.16.10.100:11001 192.168.20.2:11001 171.16.10.1:23
171.16.10.1:23
tcp 171.16.10.100:11002 192.168.30.2:11002 171.16.10.1:23
171.16.10.1:23
```

8. Also make sure the debug ip nat command is on for the Lab_A router. If you ping from the Lab_C router to the ISP router, the output will look like this:

```
01:12:36: NAT: s=192.168.30.2->171.16.10.100, d=171.16.10.1 [35]
01:12:36: NAT*: s=171.16.10.1, d=171.16.10.100->192.168.30.2 [35]
01:12:36: NAT*: s=192.168.30.2->171.16.10.100, d=171.16.10.1 [36]
01:12:36: NAT*: s=171.16.10.1, d=171.16.10.100->192.168.30.2 [36]
01:12:36: NAT*: s=192.168.30.2->171.16.10.100, d=171.16.10.1 [37]
01:12:36: NAT*: s=171.16.10.1, d=171.16.10.100->192.168.30.2 [37]
01:12:36: NAT*: s=192.168.30.2->171.16.10.100, d=171.16.10.1 [38]
01:12:36: NAT*: s=171.16.10.1, d=171.16.10.100->192.168.30.2 [38]
01:12:37: NAT*: s=192.168.30.2->171.16.10.100, d=171.16.10.1 [39]
01:12:37: NAT*: s=171.16.10.1, d=171.16.10.100->192.168.30.2 [39]
```

Review Questions

 The following questions are designed to test your understanding of this chapter's material. For more information on how to get additional questions, please see www.lammle.com/ccna.

You can find the answers to these questions in Appendix B, "Answers to Review Questions."

1. Which of the following are disadvantages of using NAT? (Choose three.)

    A. Translation introduces switching path delays.

    B. NAT conserves legally registered addresses.

    C. NAT causes loss of end-to-end IP traceability.

    D. NAT increases flexibility when connecting to the Internet.

    E. Certain applications will not function with NAT enabled.

    F. NAT reduces address overlap occurrence.

2. Which of the following are advantages of using NAT? (Choose three.)

    A. Translation introduces switching path delays.

    B. NAT conserves legally registered addresses.

    C. NAT causes loss of end-to-end IP traceability.

    D. NAT increases flexibility when connecting to the Internet.

    E. Certain applications will not function with NAT enabled.

    F. NAT remedies address overlap occurrence.

3. Which command will allow you to see real-time translations on your router?

    A. `show ip nat translations`

    B. `show ip nat statistics`

    C. `debug ip nat`

    D. `clear ip nat translations *`

4. Which command will show you all the translations active on your router?

    A. `show ip nat translations`

    B. `show ip nat statistics`

    C. `debug ip nat`

    D. `clear ip nat translations *`

5. Which command will clear all the translations active on your router?

    A. `show ip nat translations`

    B. `show ip nat statistics`

    C. `debug ip nat`

    D. `clear ip nat translations *`

6. Which command will show you the summary of the NAT configuration?

    A. `show ip nat translations`

    B. `show ip nat statistics`

    C. `debug ip nat`

    D. `clear ip nat translations *`

7. Which command will create a dynamic pool named Todd that will provide you with 30 global addresses?

    A. `ip nat pool Todd 171.16.10.65 171.16.10.94 net 255.255.255.240`

    B. `ip nat pool Todd 171.16.10.65 171.16.10.94 net 255.255.255.224`

    C. `ip nat pool todd 171.16.10.65 171.16.10.94 net 255.255.255.224`

    D. `ip nat pool Todd 171.16.10.1 171.16.10.254 net 255.255.255.0`

8. Which of the following are methods of NAT? (Choose three.)

    A. Static

    B. IP NAT pool

    C. Dynamic

    D. NAT double-translation

    E. Overload

9. When creating a pool of global addresses, which of the following can be used instead of the netmask command?

    A. / (slash notation)

    B. `prefix-length`

    C. `no mask`

    D. `block-size`

10. Which of the following would be a good starting point for troubleshooting if your router is not translating?

    A. Reboot.

    B. Call Cisco.

    C. Check your interfaces for the correct configuration.

    D. Run the `debug all` command.

11. Which of the following would be good reasons to run NAT? (Choose three.)

    A. You need to connect to the Internet and your hosts don't have globally unique IP addresses.

    B. You change to a new ISP that requires you to renumber your network.

    C. You don't want any hosts connecting to the Internet.

    D. You require two intranets with duplicate addresses to merge.

12. Which of the following is considered to be the inside host's address after translation?

    A. Inside local

    B. Outside local

    C. Inside global

    D. Outside global

13. Which of the following is considered to be the inside host's address before translation?

    A. Inside local

    B. Outside local

    C. Inside global

    D. Outside global

14. By looking at the following output, determine which of the following commands would allow dynamic translations?

    ```
    Router#show ip nat trans
    Pro   Inside global   Inside local   Outside local Outside global
    ---   1.1.128.1       10.1.1.1       ---           ---
    ---   1.1.130.178     10.1.1.2       ---           ---
    ---   1.1.129.174     10.1.1.10      ---           ---
    ---   1.1.130.101     10.1.1.89      ---           ---
    ---   1.1.134.169     10.1.1.100     ---           ---
    ---   1.1.135.174     10.1.1.200     ---           ---
    ```

    A. `ip nat inside source pool todd 1.1.128.1 1.1.135.254 prefix-length 19`

    B. `ip nat pool todd 1.1.128.1 1.1.135.254 prefix-length 19`

    C. `ip nat pool todd 1.1.128.1 1.1.135.254 prefix-length 18`

    D. `ip nat pool todd 1.1.128.1 1.1.135.254 prefix-length 21`

15. Your inside locals are not being translated to the inside global addresses. Which of the following commands will show you if your inside globals are allowed to use the NAT pool?

    ```
    ip nat pool Corp 198.18.41.129 198.18.41.134 netmask 255.255.255.248
    ip nat inside source list 100 int s0/0 Corp overload
    ```

    A. `debug ip nat`

    B. `show access-list`

    C. `show ip nat translation`

    D. `show ip nat statistics`

16. Which command would you place on the interface of a private network?

  A. ip nat inside

  B. ip nat outside

  C. ip outside global

  D. ip inside local

17. Which command would you place on an interface connected to the Internet?

  A. ip nat inside

  B. ip nat outside

  C. ip outside global

  D. ip inside local

18. Port Address Translation is also called what?

  A. NAT Fast

  B. NAT Static

  C. NAT Overload

  D. Overloading Static

19. What does the asterisk (*) represent in the following output?

```
NAT*: s=172.16.2.2, d=192.168.2.1->10.1.1.1 [1]
```

  A. The packet was destined for a local interface on the router.

  B. The packet was translated and fast-switched to the destination.

  C. The packet attempted to be translated but failed.

  D. The packet was translated but there was no response from the remote host.

20. Which of the following needs to be added to the configuration to enable PAT?

```
ip nat pool Corp 198.18.41.129 198.18.41.134 netmask 255.255.255.248
access-list 1 permit 192.168.76.64 0.0.0.31
```

  A. ip nat pool inside overload

  B. ip nat inside source list 1 pool Corp overload

  C. ip nat pool outside overload

  D. ip nat pool Corp 198.41.129 net 255.255.255.0 overload

Chapter

14

Internet Protocol Version 6 (IPv6)

THE FOLLOWING ICND1 EXAM TOPICS ARE COVERED IN THIS CHAPTER:

✓ **1.11 Identify the appropriate IPv6 addressing scheme to satisfy addressing requirements in a LAN/WAN environment**

✓ **1.12 Configure, verify, and troubleshoot IPv6 addressing**

✓ **1.13 Configure and verify IPv6 Stateless Address Auto Configuration**

✓ **1.14 Compare and contrast IPv6 address types**

- 1.14.a Global unicast

- 1.14.b Unique local

- 1.14.c Link local

- 1.14.d Multicast

- 1.14.e Modified EUI 64

- 1.14.f Autoconfiguration

- 1.14.g Anycast

✓ **3.6 Configure, verify, and troubleshoot IPv4 and IPv6 static routing**

- 3.6.a Default route

We've covered a lot of ground in this book, and though the journey has been tough at times, it's been well worth it! But our networking expedition isn't quite over yet because we still have the vastly important frontier of IPv6 to explore. There's still some expansive territory to cover with this sweeping new subject, so gear up and get ready to discover all you need to know about IPv6. Understanding IPv6 is vital now, so you'll be much better equipped and prepared to meet today's real-world networking challenges as well as to ace the exam. This final chapter is packed and brimming with all the IPv6 information you'll need to complete your Cisco exam trek successfully, so get psyched—we're in the home stretch!

I probably don't need to say this, but I will anyway because I really want to go the distance and do everything I can to ensure that you arrive and achieve . . . You absolutely must have a solid hold on IPv4 by now, but if you're still not confident with it, or feel you could use a refresher, just page back to the chapters on TCP/IP and subnetting. And if you're not crystal clear on the address problems inherent to IPv4, you really need to review Chapter 13, "Network Address Translation (NAT)", before we decamp for this chapter's IPv6 summit push!

People refer to IPv6 as "the next-generation Internet protocol," and it was originally created as the solution to IPv4's inevitable and impending address-exhaustion crisis. Though you've probably heard a thing or two about IPv6 already, it has been improved even further in the quest to bring us the flexibility, efficiency, capability, and optimized functionality that can effectively meet our world's seemingly insatiable thirst for ever-evolving technologies and increasing access. The capacity of its predecessor, IPv4, pales wan and ghostly in comparison, which is why IPv4 is destined to fade into history completely, making way for IPv6 and the future.

The IPv6 header and address structure has been completely overhauled, and many of the features that were basically just afterthoughts and addenda in IPv4 are now included as full-blown standards in IPv6. It's power-packed, well equipped with robust and elegant features, poised and prepared to manage the mind-blowing demands of the Internet to come!

After an introduction like that, I understand if you're a little apprehensive, but I promise—really—to make this chapter and its VIP topic pretty painless for you. In fact, you might even find yourself actually enjoying it—I definitely did! Because IPv6 is so complex, while still being so elegant, innovative, and powerful, it fascinates me like some weird combination of a sleek, new Aston Martin and a riveting futuristic novel. Hopefully you'll experience this chapter as an awesome ride and enjoy reading it as much as I did writing it!

To find up-to-the-minute updates for this chapter, please see www.lammle .com/ccna or the book's web page at www.sybex.com/go/ccna.

Why Do We Need IPv6?

Well, the short answer is because we need to communicate and our current system isn't really cutting it anymore. It's kind of like the Pony Express trying to compete with airmail! Consider how much time and effort we've been investing for years while we scratch our heads to resourcefully come up with slick new ways to conserve bandwidth and IP addresses. Sure, variable length subnet masks (VLSMs) are wonderful and cool, but they're really just another invention to help us cope while we desperately struggle to overcome the worsening address drought.

I'm not exaggerating, at all, about how dire things are getting, because it's simply reality. The number of people and devices that connect to networks increases dramatically each and every day, which is not a bad thing. We're just finding new and exciting ways to communicate to more people, more often, which is good thing. And it's not likely to go away or even decrease in the littlest bit, because communicating and making connections are, in fact, basic human needs—they're in our very nature. But with our numbers increasing along with the rising tide of people joining the communications party increasing as well, the forecast for our current system isn't exactly clear skies and smooth sailing. IPv4, upon which our ability to do all this connecting and communicating is presently dependent, is quickly running out of addresses for us to use.

IPv4 has only about 4.3 billion addresses available—in theory—and we know that we don't even get to use most of those! Sure, the use of Classless Inter-Domain Routing (CIDR) and Network Address Translation (NAT) has helped to extend the inevitable dearth of addresses, but we will still run out of them, and it's going to happen within a few years. China is barely online, and we know there's a huge population of people and corporations there that surely want to be. There are myriad reports that give us all kinds of numbers, but all you really need to think about to realize that I'm not just being an alarmist is this: there are about 7 billion people in the world today, and it's estimated that only just over 10 percent of that population is currently connected to the Internet—wow!

That statistic is basically screaming at us the ugly truth that based on IPv4's capacity, every person can't even have a computer, let alone all the other IP devices we use with them! I have more than one computer, and it's pretty likely that you do too, and I'm not even including phones, laptops, game consoles, fax machines, routers, switches, and a mother lode of other devices we use every day into the mix! So I think I've made it pretty clear that we've got to do something before we run out of addresses and lose the ability to connect with each other as we know it. And that "something" just happens to be implementing IPv6.

The Benefits and Uses of IPv6

So what's so fabulous about IPv6? Is it really the answer to our coming dilemma? Is it really worth it to upgrade from IPv4? All good questions—you may even think of a few more. Of course, there's going to be that group of people with the time-tested "resistance to change syndrome," but don't listen to them. If we had done that years ago, we'd still be waiting weeks, even months for our mail to arrive via horseback. Instead, just know that the answer is a resounding *yes*, it is really the answer, and it is worth the upgrade! Not only does IPv6 give us lots of addresses (3.4×10^{38} = definitely enough), there are tons of other features built into this version that make it well worth the cost, time, and effort required to migrate to it.

Today's networks, as well as the Internet, have a ton of unforeseen requirements that simply weren't even considerations when IPv4 was created. We've tried to compensate with a collection of add-ons that can actually make implementing them more difficult than they would be if they were required by a standard. By default, IPv6 has improved upon and included many of those features as standard and mandatory. One of these sweet new standards is IPsec—a feature that provides end-to-end security.

But it's the efficiency features that are really going to rock the house! For starters, the headers in an IPv6 packet have half the fields, and they are aligned to 64 bits, which gives us some seriously souped-up processing speed. Compared to IPv4, lookups happen at light speed! Most of the information that used to be bound into the IPv4 header was taken out, and now you can choose to put it, or parts of it, back into the header in the form of optional extension headers that follow the basic header fields.

And of course there's that whole new universe of addresses—the 3.4×10^{38} I just mentioned—but where did we get them? Did some genie just suddenly arrive and make them magically appear? That huge proliferation of addresses had to come from somewhere! Well it just so happens that IPv6 gives us a substantially larger address space, meaning the address itself is a whole lot bigger—four times bigger as a matter of fact! An IPv6 address is actually 128 bits in length, and no worries—I'm going to break down the address piece by piece and show you exactly what it looks like coming up in the section "IPv6 Addressing and Expressions." For now, let me just say that all that additional room permits more levels of hierarchy inside the address space and a more flexible addressing architecture. It also makes routing much more efficient and scalable because the addresses can be aggregated a lot more effectively. And IPv6 also allows multiple addresses for hosts and networks. This is especially important for enterprises veritably drooling for enhanced access and availability. Plus, the new version of IP now includes an expanded use of multicast communication—one device sending to many hosts or to a select group—that joins in to seriously boost efficiency on networks because communications will be more specific.

IPv4 uses broadcasts quite prolifically, causing a bunch of problems, the worst of which is of course the dreaded broadcast storm. This is that uncontrolled deluge of forwarded broadcast traffic that can bring an entire network to its knees and devour every last bit of bandwidth! Another nasty thing about broadcast traffic is that it interrupts each and every device on the network. When a broadcast is sent out, every machine has to stop what it's doing and respond to the traffic whether the broadcast is relevant to it or not.

But smile assuredly, everyone. There's no such thing as a broadcast in IPv6 because it uses multicast traffic instead. And there are two other types of communications as well: unicast, which is the same as it is in IPv4, and a new type called *anycast*. Anycast communication allows the same address to be placed on more than one device so that when traffic is sent to the device service addressed in this way, it's routed to the nearest host that shares the same address. And this is just the beginning—we'll get into the various types of communication later in the section called "Address Types."

IPv6 Addressing and Expressions

Just as understanding how IP addresses are structured and used is critical with IPv4 addressing, it's also vital when it comes to IPv6. You've already read about the fact that at 128 bits, an IPv6 address is much larger than an IPv4 address. Because of this, as well as the new ways the addresses can be used, you've probably guessed that IPv6 will be more complicated to manage. But no worries! As I said, I'll break down the basics and show you what the address looks like and how you can write it as well as many of its common uses. It's going to be a little weird at first, but before you know it, you'll have it nailed!

So let's take a look at Figure 14.1, which has a sample IPv6 address broken down into sections.

FIGURE 14.1   IPv6 address example

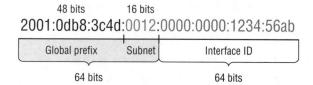

As you can clearly see, the address is definitely much larger. But what else is different? Well, first, notice that it has eight groups of numbers instead of four and also that those groups are separated by colons instead of periods. And hey, wait a second . . . there are letters in that address! Yep, the address is expressed in hexadecimal just like a MAC address is, so you could say this address has eight 16-bit hexadecimal colon-delimited blocks. That's already quite a mouthful, and you probably haven't even tried to say the address out loud yet!

There are four hexadecimal characters (16 bits) in each IPv6 field (with eight fields total), separated by colons.

Shortened Expression

The good news is there are a few tricks to help rescue us when writing these monster addresses. For one thing, you can actually leave out parts of the address to abbreviate it, but to get away with doing that you have to follow a couple of rules. First, you can drop any leading zeros in each of the individual blocks. After you do that, the sample address from earlier would then look like this:

```
2001:db8:3c4d:12:0:0:1234:56ab
```

That's a definite improvement—at least we don't have to write all of those extra zeros! But what about whole blocks that don't have anything in them except zeros? Well, we can kind of lose those too—at least some of them. Again referring to our sample address, we can remove the two consecutive blocks of zeros by replacing them with a doubled colon, like this:

```
2001:db8:3c4d:12::1234:56ab
```

Cool—we replaced the blocks of all zeros with a doubled colon. The rule you have to follow to get away with this is that you can replace only one contiguous block of such zeros in an address. So if my address has four blocks of zeros and each of them were separated, I just don't get to replace them all because I can replace only one contiguous block with a doubled colon. Check out this example:

```
2001:0000:0000:0012:0000:0000:1234:56ab
```

And just know that you *can't* do this:

```
2001::12::1234:56ab
```

Instead, the best you can do is this:

```
2001::12:0:0:1234:56ab
```

The reason the preceding example is our best shot is that if we remove two sets of zeros, the device looking at the address will have no way of knowing where the zeros go back in. Basically, the router would look at the incorrect address and say, "Well, do I place two blocks into the first set of doubled colons and two into the second set, or do I place three blocks into the first set and one block into the second set?" And on and on it would go because the information the router needs just isn't there.

Address Types

We're all familiar with IPv4's unicast, broadcast, and multicast addresses that basically define who or at least how many other devices we're talking to. But as I mentioned, IPv6 modifies that trio and introduces the anycast. Broadcasts, as we know them, have been eliminated in IPv6 because of their cumbersome inefficiency and basic tendency to drive us insane!

So let's find out what each of these types of IPv6 addressing and communication methods do for us:

Unicast Packets addressed to a unicast address are delivered to a single interface. For load balancing, multiple interfaces across several devices can use the same address, but we'll call that an anycast address. There are a few different types of unicast addresses, but we don't need to get further into that here.

Global unicast addresses (2000::/3)   These are your typical publicly routable addresses and they're the same as in IPv4. Global addresses start at 2000::/3. Figure 14.2 shows how a unicast address breaks down. The ISP can provide you with a minimum /48 network ID, which in turn provides you 16-bits to create a unique 64-bit router interface address. The last 64-bits are the unique host ID.

FIGURE 14.2   IPv6 global unicast addresses

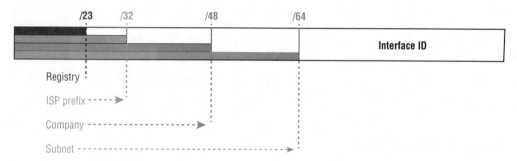

Link-local addresses (FE80::/10)   These are like the Automatic Private IP Address (APIPA) addresses that Microsoft uses to automatically provide addresses in IPv4 in that they're not meant to be routed. In IPv6 they start with FE80::/10, as shown in Figure 14.3. Think of these addresses as handy tools that give you the ability to throw a temporary LAN together for meetings or create a small LAN that's not going to be routed but still needs to share and access files and services locally.

FIGURE 14.3   IPv6 link local FE80::/10: The first 10 bits define the address type.

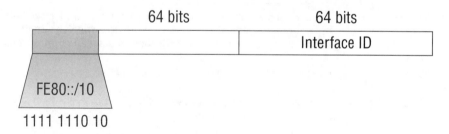

Unique local addresses (FC00::/7)   These addresses are also intended for nonrouting purposes over the Internet, but they are nearly globally unique, so it's unlikely you'll ever have one of them overlap. Unique local addresses were designed to replace site-local addresses, so they basically do almost exactly what IPv4 private addresses do: allow communication throughout a site while being routable to multiple local networks. Site-local addresses were deprecated as of September 2004.

Multicast (FF00::/8)   Again, as in IPv4, packets addressed to a multicast address are delivered to all interfaces tuned into the multicast address. Sometimes people call them "one-to-many" addresses. It's really easy to spot a multicast address in IPv6 because they always start with *FF*. We'll get deeper into multicast operation coming up, in "How IPv6 Works in an Internetwork."

Anycast   Like multicast addresses, an anycast address identifies multiple interfaces on multiple devices. But there's a big difference: the anycast packet is delivered to only one device—actually, to the closest one it finds defined in terms of routing distance. And again, this address is special because you can apply a single address to more than one host. These are referred to as "one-to-nearest" addresses. Anycast addresses are typically only configured on routers, never hosts, and a source address could never be an anycast address. Of note is that the IETF did reserve the top 128 addresses for each /64 for use with anycast addresses.

You're probably wondering if there are any special, reserved addresses in IPv6 because you know they're there in IPv4. Well there are—plenty of them! Let's go over those now.

Special Addresses

I'm going to list some of the addresses and address ranges (in Table 14.1) that you should definitely make sure to remember because you'll eventually use them. They're all special or reserved for a specific use, but unlike IPv4, IPv6 gives us a galaxy of addresses, so reserving a few here and there doesn't hurt at all!

TABLE 14.1   Special IPv6 addresses

Address	Meaning
0:0:0:0:0:0:0:0	Equals ::. This is the equivalent of IPv4's 0.0.0.0 and is typically the source address of a host before the host receives an IP address when you're using DHCP-driven stateful configuration.
0:0:0:0:0:0:0:1	Equals ::1. The equivalent of 127.0.0.1 in IPv4.
0:0:0:0:0:0:192.168.100.1	This is how an IPv4 address would be written in a mixed IPv6/IPv4 network environment.
2000::/3	The global unicast address range.
FC00::/7	The unique local unicast range.
FE80::/10	The link-local unicast range.
FF00::/8	The multicast range.

Address	Meaning
3FFF:FFFF::/32	Reserved for examples and documentation.
2001:0DB8::/32	Also reserved for examples and documentation.
2002::/16	Used with 6-to-4 tunneling, which is an IPv4-to-IPv6 transition system. The structure allows IPv6 packets to be transmitted over an IPv4 network without the need to configure explicit tunnels.

When you run IPv4 and IPv6 on a router, you have what is called "dual-stack."

Let me show you how IPv6 actually works in an internetwork. We all know how IPv4 works, so let's see what's new!

How IPv6 Works in an Internetwork

It's time to explore the finer points of IPv6. A great place to start is by showing you how to address a host and what gives it the ability to find other hosts and resources on a network.

I'll also demonstrate a device's ability to automatically address itself—something called stateless autoconfiguration—plus another type of autoconfiguration known as stateful. Keep in mind that stateful autoconfiguration uses a DHCP server in a very similar way to how it's used in an IPv4 configuration. I'll also show you how Internet Control Message Protocol (ICMP) and multicasting works for us in an IPv6 network environment.

Manual Address Assignment

In order to enable IPv6 on a router, you have to use the `ipv6 unicast-routing` global configuration command:

```
Corp(config)#ipv6 unicast-routing
```

By default, IPv6 traffic forwarding is disabled, so using this command enables it. Also, as you've probably guessed, IPv6 isn't enabled by default on any interfaces either, so we have to go to each interface individually and enable it.

There are a few different ways to do this, but a really easy way is to just add an address to the interface. You use the interface configuration command `ipv6 address <ipv6prefix>/<prefix-length>` [eui-64]to get this done.

Here's an example:

```
Corp(config-if)#ipv6 address 2001:db8:3c4d:1:0260:d6FF.FE73:1987/64
```

You can specify the entire 128-bit global IPv6 address as I just demonstrated with the preceding command, or you can use the EUI-64 option. Remember, the EUI-64 (extended unique identifier) format allows the device to use its MAC address and pad it to make the interface ID. Check it out:

```
Corp(config-if)#ipv6 address 2001:db8:3c4d:1::/64 eui-64
```

As an alternative to typing in an IPv6 address on a router, you can enable the interface instead to permit the application of an automatic link-local address.

To configure a router so that it uses only link-local addresses, use the ipv6 enable interface configuration command:

```
Corp(config-if)#ipv6 enable
```

Remember, if you have only a link-local address, you will be able to communicate only on that local subnet.

Stateless Autoconfiguration (eui-64)

Autoconfiguration is an especially useful solution because it allows devices on a network to address themselves with a link-local unicast address as well as with a global unicast address. This process happens through first learning the prefix information from the router and then appending the device's own interface address as the interface ID. But where does it get that interface ID? Well, you know every device on an Ethernet network has a physical MAC address, which is exactly what's used for the interface ID. But since the interface ID in an IPv6 address is 64 bits in length and a MAC address is only 48 bits, where do the extra 16 bits come from? The MAC address is padded in the middle with the extra bits—it's padded with FFFE.

For example, let's say I have a device with a MAC address that looks like this: 0060:d673:1987. After it's been padded, it would look like this: 0260:d6FF:FE73:1987. Figure 14.4 illustrates what an EUI-64 address looks like.

FIGURE 14.4 EUI-64 interface ID assignment

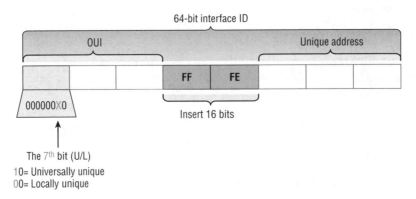

So where did that 2 in the beginning of the address come from? Another good question. You see that part of the process of padding, called modified EUI-64 format, changes a bit to specify if the address is locally unique or globally unique. And the bit that gets changed is the 7th bit in the address.

The reason for modifying the U/L bit is that, when using manually assigned addresses on an interface, it means you can simply assign the address 2001:db8:1:9::1/64 instead of the much longer 2001:db8:1:9:0200::1/64. Also, if you are going to manually assign a link-local address, you can assign the short address fe80::1 instead of the long fe80::0200:0:0:1 or fe80:0:0:0:0200::1. So, even though at first glance it seems the IETF made this harder for you to simply understand IPv6 addressing by flipping the 7th bit, in reality this made addressing much simpler. Also, since most people don't typically override the burned-in address, the U/L bit is a 0, which means that you'll see this inverted to a 1 most of the time. But because you're studying the Cisco exam objectives, you'll need to look at inverting it both ways.

Here are a few examples:

- MAC address 0090:2716:fd0f

- IPv6 EUI-64 address: 2001:0db8:0:1:0290:27ff:fe16:fd0f

That one was easy! Too easy for the Cisco exam, so let's do another:

- MAC address aa12:bcbc:1234

- IPv6 EUI-64 address: 2001:0db8:0:1:a812:bcff:febc:1234

10101010 represents the first 8 bits of the MAC address (aa), which when inverting the 7th bit becomes 10101000. The answer becomes A8. I can't tell you how important this is for you to understand, so bear with me and work through a couple more!

- MAC address 0c0c:dede:1234

- IPv6 EUI-64 address: 2001:0db8:0:1:0e0c:deff:fede:1234

0c is 00001100 in the first 8 bits of the MAC address, which then becomes 00001110 when flipping the 7th bit. The answer is then 0e. Let's practice one more:

- MAC address 0b34:ba12:1234

- IPv6 EUI-64 address: 2001:0db8:0:1:0934:baff:fe12:1234

0b in binary is 00001011, the first 8 bits of the MAC address, which then becomes 00001001. The answer is 09.

Pay extra-special attention to this EUI-64 address assignment and be able to convert the 7th bit based on the EUI-64 rules! Written Lab 14.2 will help you practice this.

To perform autoconfiguration, a host goes through a basic two-step process:

1. First, the host needs the prefix information, similar to the network portion of an IPv4 address, to configure its interface, so it sends a router solicitation (RS) request for it. This RS is then sent out as a multicast to all routers (FF02::2). The actual information

being sent is a type of ICMP message, and like everything in networking, this ICMP message has a number that identifies it. The RS message is ICMP type 133.

2. The router answers back with the required prefix information via a router advertisement (RA). An RA message also happens to be a multicast packet that's sent to the all-nodes multicast address (FF02::1) and is ICMP type 134. RA messages are sent on a periodic basis, but the host sends the RS for an immediate response so it doesn't have to wait until the next scheduled RA to get what it needs.

These two steps are shown in Figure 14.5.

FIGURE 14.5 Two steps to IPv6 autoconfiguration

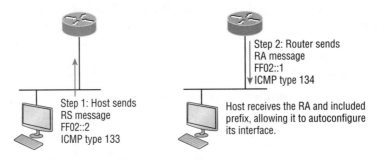

By the way, this type of autoconfiguration is also known as stateless autoconfiguration because it doesn't contact or connect to and receive any further information from the other device. We'll get to stateful configuration when we talk about DHCPv6 next.

But before we do that, first take a look at Figure 14.6. In this figure, the Branch router needs to be configured, but I just don't feel like typing in an IPv6 address on the interface connecting to the Corp router. I also don't feel like typing in any routing commands, but I need more than a link-local address on that interface, so I'm going to have to do something! So basically, I want to have the Branch router work with IPv6 on the internetwork with the least amount of effort from me. Let's see if I can get away with that.

FIGURE 14.6 IPv6 autoconfiguration example

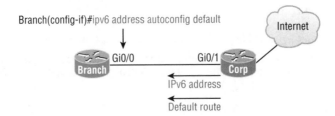

Ah ha—there is an easy way! I love IPv6 because it allows me to be relatively lazy when dealing with some parts of my network, yet it still works really well. By using the command `ipv6 address autoconfig`, the interface will listen for RAs and then, via the EUI-64 format, it will assign itself a global address—sweet!

This is all really great, but you're hopefully wondering what that `default` is doing there at the end of the command. If so, good catch! It happens to be a wonderful, optional part of the command that smoothly delivers a default route received from the Corp router, which will be automatically injected into my routing table and set as the default route—so easy!

DHCPv6 (Stateful)

DHCPv6 works pretty much the same way DHCP does in v4, with the obvious difference that it supports IPv6's new addressing scheme. And it might come as a surprise, but there are a couple of other options that DHCP still provides for us that autoconfiguration doesn't. And no, I'm not kidding— in autoconfiguration, there's absolutely no mention of DNS servers, domain names, or many of the other options that DHCP has always generously provided for us via IPv4. This is a big reason that the odds favor DHCP's continued use into the future in IPv6 at least partially—maybe even most of the time!

Upon booting up in IPv4, a client sends out a DHCP Discover message looking for a server to give it the information it needs. But remember, in IPv6, the RS and RA process happens first, so if there's a DHCPv6 server on the network, the RA that comes back to the client will tell it if DHCP is available for use. If a router isn't found, the client will respond by sending out a DHCP Solicit message, which is actually a multicast message addressed with a destination of ff02::1:2 that calls out, "All DHCP agents, both servers and relays."

It's good to know that there's some support for DHCPv6 in the Cisco IOS even though it's limited. This rather miserly support is reserved for stateless DHCP servers and tells us it doesn't offer any address management of the pool or the options available for configuring that address pool other than the DNS, domain name, default gateway, and SIP servers.

This means that you're definitely going to need another server around to supply and dispense all the additional, required information—maybe to even manage the address assignment, if needed!

Remember for the objectives that both stateless and stateful autoconfiguration can dynamically assign IPv6 addresses.

IPv6 Header

An IPv4 header is 20 bytes long, so since an IPv6 address is four times the size of IPv4 at 128 bits, its header must then be 80 bytes long, right? That makes sense and is totally intuitive, but it's also completely wrong! When IPv6 designers devised the header, they created fewer, streamlined fields that would also result in a faster routed protocol at the same time. Let's take a look at the streamlined IPv6 header using Figure 14.7.

FIGURE 14.7 IPv6 header

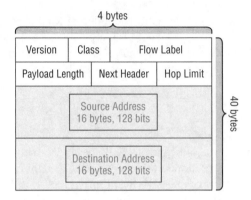

The basic IPv6 header contains eight fields, making it only twice as large as an IP header at 40 bytes. Let's zoom in on these fields:

Version This 4-bit field contains the number 6, instead of the number 4 as in IPv4.

Traffic Class This 8-bit field is like the Type of Service (ToS) field in IPv4.

Flow Label This new field, which is 24 bits long, is used to mark packets and traffic flows. A flow is a sequence of packets from a single source to a single destination host, an anycast or multicast address. The field enables efficient IPv6 flow classification.

Payload Length IPv4 had a total length field delimiting the length of the packet. IPv6's payload length describes the length of the payload only.

Next Header Since there are optional extension headers with IPv6, this field defines the next header to be read. This is in contrast to IPv4, which demands static headers with each packet.

Hop Limit This field specifies the maximum number of hops that an IPv6 packet can traverse.

 For objectives remember that the Hop Limit field is equivalent to the TTL field in IPv4's header, and the Extension header (after the destination address and not shown in the figure) is used instead of the IPv4 Fragmentation field.

Source Address This field of 16 bytes, or 128 bits, identifies the source of the packet.

Destination Address This field of 16 bytes, or 128 bits, identifies the destination of the packet.

There are also some optional extension headers following these eight fields, which carry other Network layer information. These header lengths are not a fixed number—they're of variable size.

So what's different in the IPv6 header from the IPv4 header? Let's look at that:

- The Internet Header Length field was removed because it is no longer required. Unlike the variable-length IPv4 header, the IPv6 header is fixed at 40 bytes.

- Fragmentation is processed differently in IPv6 and does not need the Flags field in the basic IPv4 header. In IPv6, routers no longer process fragmentation; the host is responsible for fragmentation.

- The Header Checksum field at the IP layer was removed because most Data Link layer technologies already perform checksum and error control, which forces formerly optional upper-layer checksums (UDP, for example) to become mandatory.

For the objectives, remember that unlike IPv4 headers, IPv6 headers have a fixed length, use an extension header instead of the IPv4 Fragmentation field, and eliminate the IPv4 checksum field.

It's time to move on to talk about another IPv4 familiar face and find out how a certain very important, built-in protocol has evolved in IPv6.

ICMPv6

IPv4 used the ICMP workhorse for lots of tasks, including error messages like destination unreachable and troubleshooting functions like Ping and Traceroute. ICMPv6 still does those things for us, but unlike its predecessor, the v6 flavor isn't implemented as a separate layer 3 protocol. Instead, it's an integrated part of IPv6 and is carried after the basic IPv6 header information as an extension header. And ICMPv6 gives us another really cool feature—by default, it prevents IPv6 from doing any fragmentation through an ICMPv6 process called path MTU discovery. Figure 14.8 shows how ICMPv6 has evolved to become part of the IPv6 packet itself.

FIGURE 14.8   ICMPv6

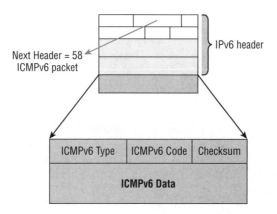

The ICMPv6 packet is identified by the value 58 in the Next Header field, located inside the ICMPv6 packet. The Type field identifies the particular kind of ICMP message that's being carried, and the Code field further details the specifics of the message. The Data field contains the ICMPv6 payload.

Table 14.2 shows the ICMP Type codes.

TABLE 14.2 ICMPv6 types

ICMPv6 Type	Description
1	Destination Unreachable
128	Echo Request
129	Echo Reply
133	Router Solicitation
134	Router Advertisement
135	Neighbor Solicitation
136	Neighbor Advertisement

And this is how it works: The source node of a connection sends a packet that's equal to the MTU size of its local link's MTU. As this packet traverses the path toward its destination, any link that has an MTU smaller than the size of the current packet will force the intermediate router to send a "packet too big" message back to the source machine. This message tells the source node the maximum size the restrictive link will allow and asks the source to send a new, scaled-down packet that can pass through. This process will continue until the destination is finally reached, with the source node now sporting the new path's MTU. So now, when the rest of the data packets are transmitted, they'll be protected from fragmentation.

ICMPv6 is used for router solicitation and advertisement, for neighbor solicitation and advertisement (i.e., finding the MAC data addresses for IPv6 neighbors), and for redirecting the host to the best router (default gateway).

Neighbor Discovery (NDP)

ICMPv6 also takes over the task of finding the address of other devices on the local link. The Address Resolution Protocol is used to perform this function for IPv4, but that's been renamed neighbor discovery (ND) in ICMPv6. This process is now achieved via a multicast address called the solicited-node address because all hosts join this multicast group upon connecting to the network.

Neighbor discovery enables these functions:

- Determining the MAC address of neighbors
- Router solicitation (RS) FF02::2 type code 133
- Router advertisements (RA) FF02::1 type code 134
- Neighbor solicitation (NS) Type code 135
- Neighbor advertisement (NA) Type code 136
- Duplicate address detection (DAD)

The part of the IPv6 address designated by the 24 bits farthest to the right is added to the end of the multicast address FF02:0:0:0:0:1:FF/104 prefix and is referred to as the *solicited-node address*. When this address is queried, the corresponding host will send back its layer 2 address.

Devices can find and keep track of other neighbor devices on the network in pretty much the same way. When I talked about RA and RS messages earlier and told you that they use multicast traffic to request and send address information, that too is actually a function of ICMPv6—specifically, neighbor discovery.

In IPv4, the protocol IGMP was used to allow a host device to tell its local router that it was joining a multicast group and would like to receive the traffic for that group. This IGMP function has been replaced by ICMPv6, and the process has been renamed multicast listener discovery.

With IPv4, our hosts could have only one default gateway configured, and if that router went down we had to either fix the router, change the default gateway, or run some type of virtual default gateway with other protocols created as a solution for this inadequacy in IPv4. Figure 14.9 shows how IPv6 devices find their default gateways using neighbor discovery.

FIGURE 14.9   Router solicitation (RS) and router advertisement (RA)

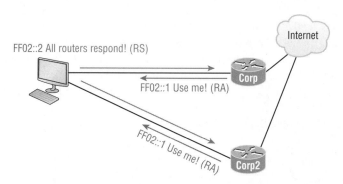

IPv6 hosts send a router solicitation (RS) onto their data link asking for all routers to respond, and they use the multicast address FF02::2 to achieve this. Routers on the same link respond with a unicast to the requesting host, or with a router advertisement (RA) using FF02::1.

But that's not all! Hosts also can send solicitations and advertisements between themselves using a neighbor solicitation (NS) and neighbor advertisement (NA), as shown in Figure 14.10. Remember that RA and RS gather or provide information about routers, and NS and NA gather information about hosts. Remember that a "neighbor" is a host on the same data link or VLAN.

FIGURE 14.10   Neighbor solicitation (NS) and neighbor advertisement (NA)

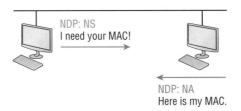

Solicited-Node and Multicast Mapping over Ethernet

If an IPv6 address is known, then the associated IPv6 solicited-node multicast address is known, and if an IPv6 multicast address is known, then the associated Ethernet MAC address is known.

For example, the IPv6 address 2001:DB8:2002:F:2C0:10FF:FE18:FC0F will have a known solicited-node address of FF02::1:FF18:FC0F.

Now we'll form the multicast Ethernet addresses by adding the last 32 bits of the IPv6 multicast address to 33:33.

For example, if the IPv6 solicited-node multicast address is FF02::1:FF18:FC0F, the associated Ethernet MAC address is 33:33:FF:18:FC:0F and is a virtual address.

Duplicate Address Detection (DAD)

So what do you think are the odds that two hosts will assign themselves the same random IPv6 address? Personally, I think you could probably win the lotto every day for a year and still not come close to the odds against two hosts on the same data link duplicating an IPv6 address! Still, to make sure this doesn't ever happen, duplicate address detection (DAD) was created, which isn't an actual protocol, but a function of the NS/NA messages. Figure 14.11 shows how a host sends an NDP NS when it receives or creates an IPv6 address.

FIGURE 14.11   Duplicate address detection (DAD)

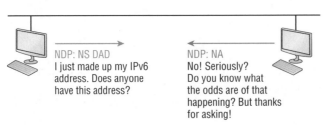

When hosts make up or receive an IPv6 address, they send three DADs out via NDP NS asking if anyone has this same address. The odds are unlikely that this will ever happen, but they ask anyway.

 Remember for the objectives that ICMPv6 uses type 134 for router advertisement messages, and the advertised prefix must be 64 bits in length.

IPv6 Routing Protocols

All of the routing protocols we've already discussed have been tweaked and upgraded for use in IPv6 networks, so it figures that many of the functions and configurations that you've already learned will be used in almost the same way as they are now. Knowing that broadcasts have been eliminated in IPv6, it's safe to conclude that any protocols relying entirely on broadcast traffic will go the way of the dodo. But unlike with the dodo, it'll be really nice to say goodbye to these bandwidth-hogging, performance-annihilating little gremlins!

The routing protocols we'll still use in IPv6 have been renovated and given new names. Even though this chapter's focus is on the Cisco exam objectives, which cover only static and default routing, I want to discuss a few of the more important ones too.

First on the list is the IPv6 RIPng (next generation). Those of you who've been in IT for a while know that RIP has worked pretty well for us on smaller networks. This happens to be the very reason it didn't get whacked and will still be around in IPv6. And we still have EIGRPv6 because EIGRP already had protocol-dependent modules and all we had to do was add a new one to it to fit in nicely with the IPv6 protocol. Rounding out our group of protocol survivors is OSPFv3—that's not a typo, it really is v3! OSPF for IPv4 was actually v2, so when it got its upgrade to IPv6, it became OSPFv3. Lastly, for the new objectives, we'll list MP-BGP4 as a multiprotocol BGP-4 protocol for IPv6. Please understand for the objectives at this point in the book, we only need to understand static and default routing.

Static Routing with IPv6

Okay, now don't let the heading of this section scare you into looking on Monster.com for some job that has nothing to do with networking! I know that static routing has always run a chill up our collective spines because it's cumbersome, difficult, and really easy to screw up. And I won't lie to you—it's certainly not any easier with IPv6's longer addresses, but you can do it!

We know that to make static routing work, whether in IP or IPv6, you need these three tools:

- An accurate, up-to-date network map of your entire internetwork
- Next-hop address and exit interface for each neighbor connection
- All the remote subnet IDs

Of course, we don't need to have any of these for dynamic routing, which is why we mostly use dynamic routing. It's just so awesome to have the routing protocol do all that work for us by finding all the remote subnets and automatically placing them into the routing table!

Figure 14.12 shows a really good example of how to use static routing with IPv6. It really doesn't have to be that hard, but just as with IPv4, you absolutely need an accurate network map to make static routing work!

FIGURE 14.12   IPv6 static and default routing

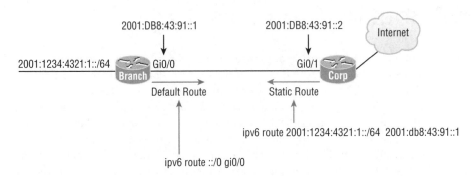

So here's what I did: First, I created a static route on the Corp router to the remote network 2001:1234:4321:1::/64 using the next hop address. I could've just as easily used the Corp router's exit interface. Next, I just set up a default route for the Branch router with ::/0 and the Branch exit interface of Gi0/0—not so bad!

Configuring IPv6 on Our Internetwork

We're going to continue working on the same internetwork we've been configuring throughout this book, as shown in Figure 14.13. Let's add IPv6 to the Corp, SF, and LA routers by using a simple subnet scheme of 11, 12, 13, 14, and 15. After that, we'll add the OSPFv3 routing protocol. Notice in Figure 14.13 how the subnet numbers are the same on each end of the WAN links. Keep in mind that we'll finish this chapter by running through some verification commands.

As usual, I'll start with the Corp router:

```
Corp#config t
Corp(config)#ipv6 unicast-routing
Corp(config)#int f0/0
Corp(config-if)#ipv6 address 2001:db8:3c4d:11::/64 eui-64
Corp(config-if)#int s0/0
Corp(config-if)#ipv6 address 2001:db8:3c4d:12::/64 eui-64
```

```
Corp(config-if)#int s0/1
Corp(config-if)#ipv6 address 2001:db8:3c4d:13::/64 eui-64
Corp(config-if)#^Z
Corp#copy run start
Destination filename [startup-config]?[enter]
Building configuration...
[OK]
```

FIGURE 14.13   Our internetwork

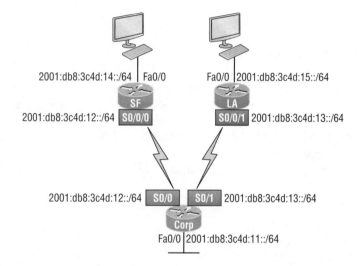

Pretty simple! In the previous configuration, I only changed the subnet address for each interface slightly. Let's take a look at the routing table now:

```
Corp(config-if)#do sho ipv6 route
C   2001:DB8:3C4D:11::/64 [0/0]
     via ::, FastEthernet0/0
L   2001:DB8:3C4D:11:20D:BDFF:FE3B:D80/128 [0/0]
     via ::, FastEthernet0/0
C   2001:DB8:3C4D:12::/64 [0/0]
     via ::, Serial0/0
L   2001:DB8:3C4D:12:20D:BDFF:FE3B:D80/128 [0/0]
     via ::, Serial0/0
C   2001:DB8:3C4D:13::/64 [0/0]
     via ::, Serial0/1
L   2001:DB8:3C4D:13:20D:BDFF:FE3B:D80/128 [0/0]
     via ::, Serial0/1
```

```
L   FE80::/10 [0/0]
      via ::, Null0
L   FF00::/8 [0/0]
      via ::, Null0
Corp(config-if)#
```

Alright, but what's up with those two addresses for each interface? One shows C for connected, one shows L. The connected address indicates the IPv6 address I configured on each interface and the L is the link-local that's been automatically assigned. Notice in the link-local address that the FF:FE is inserted into the address to create the EUI-64 address.

Let's configure the SF router now:

```
SF#config t
SF(config)#ipv6 unicast-routing
SF(config)#int s0/0/0
SF(config-if)#ipv6 address 2001:db8:3c4d:12::/64
% 2001:DB8:3C4D:12::/64 should not be configured on Serial0/0/0, a subnet router
anycast
SF(config-if)#ipv6 address 2001:db8:3c4d:12::/64 eui-64
SF(config-if)#int fa0/0
SF(config-if)#ipv6 address 2001:db8:3c4d:14::/64 eui-64
SF(config-if)#^Z
SF#show ipv6 route
C   2001:DB8:3C4D:12::/64 [0/0]
      via ::, Serial0/0/0
L   2001:DB8:3C4D:12::/128 [0/0]
      via ::, Serial0/0/0
L   2001:DB8:3C4D:12:21A:2FFF:FEE7:4398/128 [0/0]
      via ::, Serial0/0/0
C   2001:DB8:3C4D:14::/64 [0/0]
      via ::, FastEthernet0/0
L   2001:DB8:3C4D:14:21A:2FFF:FEE7:4398/128 [0/0]
      via ::, FastEthernet0/0
L   FE80::/10 [0/0]
      via ::, Null0
L   FF00::/8 [0/0]
      via ::, Null0
```

Did you notice that I used the exact IPv6 subnet addresses on each side of the serial link? Good . . . but wait—what's with that anycast error I received when trying to configure the interfaces on the SF router? I didn't meant to create that error; it happened because I forgot to add the eui-64 at the end of the address. Still, what's behind that error? An anycast address is a host address of all 0s, meaning the last 64 bits are all off, but by typing in /64 without the eui-64, I was telling the interface that the unique identifier would be nothing but zeros, and that's not allowed!

Let's configure the LA router now, and then add OSPFv3:

```
SF#config t
SF(config)#ipv6 unicast-routing
SF(config)#int s0/0/1
SF(config-if)#ipv6 address 2001:db8:3c4d:13::/64 eui-64
SF(config-if)#int f0/0
SF(config-if)#ipv6 address 2001:db8:3c4d:15::/64 eui-64
SF(config-if)#do show ipv6 route
C   2001:DB8:3C4D:13::/64 [0/0]
     via ::, Serial0/0/1
L   2001:DB8:3C4D:13:21A:6CFF:FEA1:1F48/128 [0/0]
     via ::, Serial0/0/1
C   2001:DB8:3C4D:15::/64 [0/0]
     via ::, FastEthernet0/0
L   2001:DB8:3C4D:15:21A:6CFF:FEA1:1F48/128 [0/0]
     via ::, FastEthernet0/0
L   FE80::/10 [0/0]
     via ::, Null0
L   FF00::/8 [0/0]
     via ::, Null0
```

This looks good, but I want you to notice that I used the exact same IPv6 subnet addresses on each side of the links from the Corp router to the SF router as well as from the Corp to the LA router.

Configuring Routing on Our Internetwork

I'll start at the Corp router and add simple static routes. Check it out:

```
Corp(config)#ipv6 route 2001:db8:3c4d:14::/64  2001:DB8:3C4D:12:21A:2FFF:
FEE7:4398 150
Corp(config)#ipv6 route 2001:DB8:3C4D:15::/64 s0/1 150
Corp(config)#do sho ipv6 route static
[output cut]
S   2001:DB8:3C4D:14::/64 [150/0]
     via 2001:DB8:3C4D:12:21A:2FFF:FEE7:4398
```

Okay—I agree that first static route line was pretty long because I used the next-hop address, but notice that I used the exit interface on the second entry. But it still wasn't really all that hard to create the longer static route entry. I just went to the SF router, used the command show ipv6 int brief, and then copied and pasted the interface address used for the next hop. You'll get used to IPv6 addresses (You'll get used to doing a lot of copy/paste moves!).

Now since I put an AD of 150 on the static routes, once I configure a routing protocol such as OSPF, they'll be replaced with an OSPF injected route. Let's go to the SF and LA routers and put a single entry in each router to get to remote subnet 11.

```
SF(config)#ipv6 route 2001:db8:3c4d:11::/64 s0/0/0 150
```

That's it! I'm going to head over to LA and put a default route on that router now:

```
LA(config)#ipv6 route ::/0 s0/0/1
```

Let's take a peek at the Corp router's routing table and see if our static routes are in there.

```
Corp#sh ipv6 route static
[output cut]
S   2001:DB8:3C4D:14::/64 [150/0]
     via 2001:DB8:3C4D:12:21A:2FFF:FEE7:4398
S   2001:DB8:3C4D:15::/64 [150/0]
     via ::, Serial0/1
```

Voilà! I can see both of my static routes in the routing table, so IPv6 can now route to those networks. But we're not done because we still need to test our network! First I'm going to go to the SF router and get the IPv6 address of the Fa0/0 interface:

```
SF#sh ipv6 int brief
FastEthernet0/0            [up/up]
   FE80::21A:2FFF:FEE7:4398
   2001:DB8:3C4D:14:21A:2FFF:FEE7:4398
FastEthernet0/1            [administratively down/down]
Serial0/0/0                [up/up]
   FE80::21A:2FFF:FEE7:4398
   2001:DB8:3C4D:12:21A:2FFF:FEE7:4398
```

Next, I'm going to go back to the Corporate router and ping that remote interface by copying and pasting in the address. No sense doing all that typing when copy/paste works great!

```
Corp#ping ipv6 2001:DB8:3C4D:14:21A:2FFF:FEE7:4398
Type escape sequence to abort.
Sending 5, 100-byte ICMP Echos to 2001:DB8:3C4D:14:21A:2FFF:FEE7:4398, timeout
is 2 seconds:
!!!!!
```

```
Success rate is 100 percent (5/5), round-trip min/avg/max = 0/0/0 ms
Corp#
```

We can see that static route worked, so next, I'll go get the IPv6 address of the LA router and ping that remote interface as well:

```
LA#sh ipv6 int brief
FastEthernet0/0          [up/up]
    FE80::21A:6CFF:FEA1:1F48
    2001:DB8:3C4D:15:21A:6CFF:FEA1:1F48
Serial0/0/1              [up/up]
    FE80::21A:6CFF:FEA1:1F48
    2001:DB8:3C4D:13:21A:6CFF:FEA1:1F48
```

It's time to head over to Corp and ping LA:

```
Corp#ping ipv6 2001:DB8:3C4D:15:21A:6CFF:FEA1:1F48
Type escape sequence to abort.
Sending 5, 100-byte ICMP Echos to 2001:DB8:3C4D:15:21A:6CFF:FEA1:1F48, timeout
is 2 seconds:
!!!!!
Success rate is 100 percent (5/5), round-trip min/avg/max = 4/4/4 ms
Corp#
```

Now let's use one of my favorite commands:

```
Corp#sh ipv6 int brief
FastEthernet0/0          [up/up]
    FE80::20D:BDFF:FE3B:D80
    2001:DB8:3C4D:11:20D:BDFF:FE3B:D80
Serial0/0                [up/up]
    FE80::20D:BDFF:FE3B:D80
    2001:DB8:3C4D:12:20D:BDFF:FE3B:D80
FastEthernet0/1          [administratively down/down]
    unassigned
Serial0/1                [up/up]
    FE80::20D:BDFF:FE3B:D80
    2001:DB8:3C4D:13:20D:BDFF:FE3B:D80
Loopback0                [up/up]
    unassigned
Corp#
```

What a nice output! All our interfaces are up/up, and we can see the link-local and assigned global address.

Static routing really isn't so bad with IPv6! I'm not saying I'd like to do this in a ginormous network—no way—I wouldn't want to opt for doing that with IPv4 either! But you can see that it can be done. Also, notice how easy it was to ping an IPv6 address. Copy/paste really is your friend!

Before we finish the chapter, let's add another router to our network and connect it to the Corp Fa0/0 LAN. For our new router I really don't feel like doing any work, so I'll just type this:

```
Boulder#config t
Boulder(config)#int f0/0
Boulder(config-if)#ipv6 address autoconfig default
```

Nice and easy! This configures stateless autoconfiguration on the interface, and the `default` keyword will advertise itself as the default route for the local link!

I hope you found this chapter as rewarding as I did. The best thing you can do to learn IPv6 is to get some routers and just go at it. Don't give up because it's seriously worth your time!

Summary

This last chapter introduced you to some very key IPv6 structural elements as well as how to make IPv6 work within a Cisco internetwork. You now know that even when covering and configuring IPv6 basics, there's still a great deal to understand—and we just scratched the surface! But you're still well equipped with all you need to meet the Cisco exam objectives.

You learned the vital reasons why we need IPv6 and the benefits associated with it. I covered IPv6 addressing and the importance of using the shortened expressions. As I covered addressing with IPv6, I also showed you the different address types, plus the special addresses reserved in IPv6.

IPv6 will mostly be deployed automatically, meaning hosts will employ autoconfiguration. I demonstrated how IPv6 utilizes autoconfiguration and how it comes into play when configuring a Cisco router. You also learned that in IPv6, we can and still should use a DHCP server to the router to provide options to hosts just as we've been doing for years with IPv4—not necessarily IPv6 addresses, but other mission-critical options like providing a DNS server address.

From there, I discussed the evolution of some more integral and familiar protocols like ICMP and OSPF. They've been upgraded to work in the IPv6 environment, but these networking workhorses are still vital and relevant to operations, and I detailed how ICMP works with IPv6, followed by how to configure OSPFv3. I wrapped up this pivotal chapter by demonstrating key methods to use when verifying that all is running correctly in your IPv6 network. So take some time and work through all the essential study material, especially the written labs, to ensure that you meet your networking goals!

Exam Essentials

Understand why we need IPv6.   Without IPv6, the world would be depleted of IP addresses.

Understand link-local.   Link-local is like an IPv4 private IP address, but it can't be routed at all, not even in your organization.

Understand unique local.   This, like link-local, is like a private IP address in IPv4 and cannot be routed to the Internet. However, the difference between link-local and unique local is that unique local can be routed within your organization or company.

Remember IPv6 addressing.   IPv6 addressing is not like IPv4 addressing. IPv6 addressing has much more address space, is 128 bits long, and represented in hexadecimal, unlike IPv4, which is only 32 bits long and represented in decimal.

Understand and be able to read a EUI-64 address with the 7th bit inverted.   Hosts can use autoconfiguration to obtain an IPv6 address, and one of the ways it can do that is through what is called EUI-64. This takes the unique MAC address of a host and inserts FF:FE in the middle of the address to change a 48-bit MAC address to a 64-bit interface ID. In addition to inserting the 16 bits into the interface ID, the 7th bit of the 1st byte is inverted, typically from a 0 to a 1. Practice this with Written Lab 14.2.

Written Labs 14

In this section, you'll complete the following labs to make sure you've got the information and concepts contained within them fully dialed in:

   Lab 14.1: IPv6

   Lab 14.2: Converting EUI addresses

   You can find the answers to these labs in Appendix A, "Answers to Written Labs."

Written Lab 14.1

In this section, write the answers to the following IPv6 questions:

1.   Which two ICMPv6 types are used for testing IPv6 reachability?

2.   What is the corresponding Ethernet address for FF02:0000:0000:0000:0000:0001:FF 17:FC0F?

3.   Which type of address is not meant to be routed?

4.   What type of address is this: FE80::/10?

5.   Which type of address is meant to be delivered to multiple interfaces?

6. Which type of address identifies multiple interfaces, but packets are delivered only to the first address it finds?

7. Which routing protocol uses multicast address FF02::5?

8. IPv4 had a loopback address of 127.0.0.1. What is the IPv6 loopback address?

9. What does a link-local address always start with?

10. Which IPv6 address is the all-router multicast group?

Written Lab 14.2

In this section, you will practice inverting the 7th bit of a EUI-64 address. Use the prefix 2001:db8:1:1/64 for each address.

1. Convert the following MAC address into a EUI-64 address: 0b0c:abcd:1234.

2. Convert the following MAC address into a EUI-64 address: 060c:32f1:a4d2.

3. Convert the following MAC address into a EUI-64 address: 10bc:abcd:1234.

4. Convert the following MAC address into a EUI-64 address: 0d01:3a2f:1234.

5. Convert the following MAC address into a EUI-64 address: 0a0c.abac.caba.

Hands-on Labs

You'll need at least three routers to complete these labs; five would be better, but if you are using the LammleSim IOS version, then these lab layouts are preconfigured for you. This section will have you configure the following labs:

Lab 14.1: Manual and Stateful Autoconfiguration

Lab 14.2: Static and Default Routing

Here is our network:

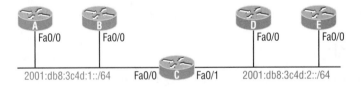

Hands-on Lab 14.1: Manual and Stateful Autoconfiguration

In this lab, you will configure the C router with manual IPv6 addresses on the Fa0/0 and Fa0/1 interfaces and then configure the other routers to automatically assign themselves an IPv6 address.

1. Log in to the C router and configure IPv6 addresses on each interface based on the subnets (1 and 2) shown in the graphic.

```
C(config)#ipv6 unicast-routing
C(config)#int fa0/0
C(config-if)#ipv6 address 2001:db8:3c4d:1::1/64
C(config-if)#int fa0/1
C(config-if)#ipv6 address 2001:db8:3c4d:2::1/64
```

2. Verify the interfaces with the show ipv6 route connected and sho ipv6 int brief commands.

```
C(config-if)#do show ipv6 route connected
[output cut]
C    2001:DB8:3C4D:1::/64 [0/0]
     via ::, FastEthernet0/0
C    2001:DB8:3C4D:2::/64 [0/0]
     via ::, FastEthernet0/0
C(config-if)#sh ipv6 int brief
FastEthernet0/0             [up/up]
    FE80::20D:BDFF:FE3B:D80
    2001:DB8:3C4D:1::1
FastEthernet0/1             [up/up]
    FE80::20D:BDFF:FE3B:D81
    2001:DB8:3C4D:2::1
Loopback0                   [up/up]
    Unassigned
```

3. Go to your other routers and configure the Fa0/0 on each router to autoconfigure an IPv6 address.

```
A(config)#ipv6 unicast-routing
A(config)#int f0/0
A(config-if)#ipv6 address autoconfig
A(config-if)#no shut


B(config)#ipv6 unicast-routing
B(config)#int fa0/0
B(config-if)#ipv6 address autoconfig
B(config-if)#no shut


D(config)#ipv6 unicast-routing
D(config)#int fa0/0
D(config-if)#ipv6 address autoconfig
D(config-if)#no shut
```

```
E(config)#ipv6 unicast-routing
E(config)#int fa0/0
E(config-if)#ipv6 address autoconfig
E(config-if)#no shut
```

4. Verify that your routers received an IPv6 address.

```
A#sh ipv6 int brief
FastEthernet0/0              [up/up]
    FE80::20D:BDFF:FE3B:C20
    2001:DB8:3C4D:1:20D:BDFF:FE3B:C20
```

Continue to verify your addresses on all your other routers.

Hands-on Lab 14.2: Static and Default Routing

Router C is directly connected to both subnets, so no routing of any type needs to be configured. However, all the other routers are connected to only one subnet, so at least one route needs to be configured on each router.

1. On the A router, configure a static route to the 2001:db8:3c4d:2::/64 subnet.

    `A(config)#ipv6 route 2001:db8:3c4d:2::/64 fa0/0`

2. On the B router, configure a default route.

    `B(config)#ipv6 route ::/0 fa0/0`

3. On the D router, create a static route to the remote subnet.

    `D(config)#ipv6 route 2001:db8:3c4d:1::/64 fa0/0`

4. On the E router, create a static route to the remote subnet.

    `E(config)#ipv6 route 2001:db8:3c4d:1::/64 fa0/0`

5. Verify your configurations with a show running-config and show ipv6 route.

6. Ping from router D to router A. First, you need to get router A's IPv6 address with a show ipv6 int brief command. Here is an example:

```
A#sh ipv6 int brief
FastEthernet0/0              [up/up]
    FE80::20D:BDFF:FE3B:C20
    2001:DB8:3C4D:1:20D:BDFF:FE3B:C20
```

7. Now go to router D and ping the IPv6 address from router A:

```
D#ping ipv6 2001:DB8:3C4D:1:20D:BDFF:FE3B:C20
Type escape sequence to abort.
Sending 5, 100-byte ICMP Echos to 2001:DB8:3C4D:1:20D:BDFF:FE3B:C20, timeout
is 2 seconds:
!!!!!
Success rate is 100 percent (5/5), round-trip min/avg/max = 0/2/4 ms
```

Review Questions

The following questions are designed to test your understanding of this chapter's material. For more information on how to get additional questions, please see www.lammle.com/ccna.

The answers to these questions can be found in Appendix B, "Answers to Chapter Review Questions."

1. How is an EUI-64 format interface ID created from a 48-bit MAC address?

    A. By appending 0xFF to the MAC address

    B. By prefixing the MAC address with 0xFFEE

    C. By prefixing the MAC address with 0xFF and appending 0xFF to it

    D. By inserting 0xFFFE between the upper 3 bytes and the lower 3 bytes of the MAC address

    E. By prefixing the MAC address with 0xF and inserting 0xF after each of its first three bytes

2. Which option is a valid IPv6 address?

    A. 2001:0000:130F::099a::12a

    B. 2002:7654:A1AD:61:81AF:CCC1

    C. FEC0:ABCD:WXYZ:0067::2A4

    D. 2004:1:25A4:886F::1

3. Which three statements about IPv6 prefixes are true? (Choose three.)

    A. FF00:/8 is used for IPv6 multicast.

    B. FE80::/10 is used for link-local unicast.

    C. FC00::/7 is used in private networks.

    D. 2001::1/127 is used for loopback addresses.

    E. FE80::/8 is used for link-local unicast.

    F. FEC0::/10 is used for IPv6 broadcast.

4. What are three approaches that are used when migrating from an IPv4 addressing scheme to an IPv6 scheme? (Choose three.)

    A. Enable dual-stack routing.

    B. Configure IPv6 directly.

    C. Configure IPv4 tunnels between IPv6 islands.

    D. Use proxying and translation to translate IPv6 packets into IPv4 packets.

    E. Statically map IPv4 addresses to IPv6 addresses.

    F. Use DHCPv6 to map IPv4 addresses to IPv6 addresses.

5. Which two statements about IPv6 router advertisement messages are true? (Choose two.)

   A. They use ICMPv6 type 134.

   B. The advertised prefix length must be 64 bits.

   C. The advertised prefix length must be 48 bits.

   D. They are sourced from the configured IPv6 interface address.

   E. Their destination is always the link-local address of the neighboring node.

6. Which of the following is true when describing an IPv6 anycast address?

   A. One-to-many communication model

   B. One-to-nearest communication model

   C. Any-to-many communication model

   D. A unique IPv6 address for each device in the group

   E. The same address for multiple devices in the group

   F. Delivery of packets to the group interface that is closest to the sending device

7. You want to ping the loopback address of your IPv6 local host. What will you type?

   A. `ping 127.0.0.1`

   B. `ping 0.0.0.0`

   C. `ping ::1`

   D. `trace 0.0.::1`

8. What are three features of the IPv6 protocol? (Choose three.)

   A. Optional IPsec

   B. Autoconfiguration

   C. No broadcasts

   D. Complicated header

   E. Plug-and-play

   F. Checksums

9. Which two statements describe characteristics of IPv6 unicast addressing? (Choose two.)

   A. Global addresses start with 2000::/3.

   B. Link-local addresses start with FE00:/12.

   C. Link-local addresses start with FF00::/10.

   D. There is only one loopback address and it is ::1.

   E. If a global address is assigned to an interface, then that is the only allowable address for the interface.

10. A host sends a router solicitation (RS) on the data link. What destination address is sent with this request?

   A. FF02::A

   B. FF02::9

    C. FF02::2

    D. FF02::1

    E. FF02::5

11. What are two valid reasons for adopting IPv6 over IPv4? (Choose two.)

    A. No broadcast

    B. Change of source address in the IPv6 header

    C. Change of destination address in the IPv6 header

    D. No password required for Telnet access

    E. Autoconfiguration

    F. NAT

12. A host sends a type of NDP message providing the MAC address that was requested. Which type of NDP was sent?

    A. NA

    B. RS

    C. RA

    D. NS

13. Which is known as "one-to-nearest" addressing in IPv6?

    A. Global unicast

    B. Anycast

    C. Multicast

    D. Unspecified address

14. Which of the following statements about IPv6 addresses are true? (Choose two.)

    A. Leading zeros are required.

    B. Two colons (::) are used to represent successive hexadecimal fields of zeros.

    C. Two colons (::) are used to separate fields.

    D. A single interface will have multiple IPv6 addresses of different types.

15. Which three ways are an IPv6 header simpler than an IPv4 header? (Choose three.)

    A. Unlike IPv4 headers, IPv6 headers have a fixed length.

    B. IPv6 uses an extension header instead of the IPv4 Fragmentation field.

    C. IPv6 headers eliminate the IPv4 Checksum field.

    D. IPv6 headers use the Fragment Offset field in place of the IPv4 Fragmentation field.

    E. IPv6 headers use a smaller Option field size than IPv4 headers.

    F. IPv6 headers use a 4-bit TTL field, and IPv4 headers use an 8-bit TTL field.

16. Which of the following descriptions about IPv6 is correct?

    A. Addresses are not hierarchical and are assigned at random.

    B. Broadcasts have been eliminated and replaced with multicasts.

    C. There are 2.7 billion addresses.

    D. An interface can only be configured with one IPv6 address.

17. How many bits are in an IPv6 address field?

    A. 24

    B. 4

    C. 3

    D. 16

    E. 32

    F. 128

18. Which of the following correctly describe characteristics of IPv6 unicast addressing? (Choose two.)

    A. Global addresses start with 2000::/3.

    B. Link-local addresses start with FF00::/10.

    C. Link-local addresses start with FE00:/12.

    D. There is only one loopback address and it is ::1.

19. Which of the following statements are true of IPv6 address representation? (Choose two.)

    A. The first 64 bits represent the dynamically created interface ID.

    B. A single interface may be assigned multiple IPv6 addresses of any type.

    C. Every IPv6 interface contains at least one loopback address.

    D. Leading zeroes in an IPv6 16-bit hexadecimal field are mandatory.

20. Which command enables IPv6 forwarding on a Cisco router?

    A. `ipv6 local`

    B. `ipv6 host`

    C. `ipv6 unicast-routing`

    D. `ipv6 neighbor`

ICND2

PART II

Chapter

15

Enhanced Switched Technologies

THE FOLLOWING ICND2 EXAM TOPICS ARE COVERED IN THIS CHAPTER:

✓ **1.0 LAN Switching Technologies**

- 1.1 Configure, verify, and troubleshoot VLANs (normal/extended range) spanning multiple switches

  - 1.1.a Access ports (data and voice)

  - 1.1.b Default VLAN

- 1.2 Configure, verify, and troubleshoot interswitch connectivity

  - 1.2.a Add and remove VLANs on a trunk

  - 1.2.b DTP and VTP (v1&v2)

  - 1.3 Configure, verify, and troubleshoot STP protocols

  - 1.3.a STP mode (PVST+ and RPVST+)

  - 1.3.b STP root bridge selection

- 1.4 Configure, verify, and troubleshoot STP-related optional features

  - 1.4.a PortFast

  - 1.4.b BPDU guard

- 1.5 Configure, verify, and troubleshoot (Layer 2/Layer 3) EtherChannel

  - 1.5.a Static

  - 1.5.b PAGP

  - 1.5.c LACP

- 1.7 Describe common access layer threat mitigation techniques

  - 1.7.c Nondefault native VLAN

✓ **2.0 Routing Technologies**

- 2.1 Configure, verify, and troubleshoot Inter-VLAN routing

  - 2.1.a Router on a stick

  - 2.1.b SVI

Long ago, a company called Digital Equipment Corporation (DEC) created the original version of *Spanning Tree Protocol (STP)*. The IEEE later created its own version of STP called 802.1d. Cisco has moved toward another industry standard in its newer switches called 802.1w. We'll explore both the old and new versions of STP in this chapter, but first, I'll define some important STP basics.

Routing protocols like RIP, EIGRP, and OSPF have processes for preventing loops from occurring at the Network layer, but if you have redundant physical links between your switches, these protocols won't do a thing to stop loops from occurring at the Data Link layer. That's exactly why STP was developed—to put an end to loop issues in a layer 2 switched network. It's also why we'll be thoroughly exploring the key features of this vital protocol as well as how it works within a switched network in this chapter.

After covering STP in detail, we'll move on to explore EtherChannel.

To find up-to-the-minute updates for this chapter, please see www.lammle.com/ccna or the book's web page at www.sybex.com/go/ccna.

VLAN Review

As you may remember from ICND1, configuring VLANs is actually pretty easy. It's just that figuring out which users you want in each VLAN is not, and doing that can eat up a lot of your time! But once you've decided on the number of VLANs you want to create and established which users you want to belong to each one, it's time to bring your first VLAN into the world.

To configure VLANs on a Cisco Catalyst switch, use the global config vlan command. In the following example, I'm going to demonstrate how to configure VLANs on the S1 switch by creating three VLANs for three different departments—again, remember that VLAN 1 is the native and management VLAN by default:

```
S1(config)#vlan ?
  WORD        ISL VLAN IDs 1-4094
  access-map  Create vlan access-map or enter vlan access-map command mode
  dot1q       dot1q parameters
  filter      Apply a VLAN Map
```

```
 group        Create a vlan group
 internal     internal VLAN
S1(config)#vlan 2
S1(config-vlan)#name Sales
S1(config-vlan)#vlan 3
S1(config-vlan)#name Marketing
S1(config-vlan)#vlan 4
S1(config-vlan)#name Accounting
S1(config-vlan)#^Z
S1#
```

In this output, you can see that you can create VLANs from 1 to 4094. But this is only mostly true. As I said, VLANs can really only be created up to 1001, and you can't use, change, rename, or delete VLANs 1 or 1002 through 1005 because they're reserved. The VLAN with numbers above 1005 are called extended VLANs and won't be saved in the database unless your switch is set to what is called VLAN Trunking Protocol (VTP) transparent mode. You won't see these VLAN numbers used too often in production. Here's an example of me attempting to set my S1 switch to VLAN 4000 when my switch is set to VTP server mode (the default VTP mode, which we'll talk about shortly):

```
S1#config t
S1(config)#vlan 4000
S1(config-vlan)#^Z
% Failed to create VLANs 4000
Extended VLAN(s) not allowed in current VTP mode.
%Failed to commit extended VLAN(s) changes.
```

After you create the VLANs that you want, you can use the show vlan command to check them out. But notice that, by default, all ports on the switch are in VLAN 1. To change the VLAN associated with a port, you need to go to each interface and specifically tell it which VLAN to be a part of.

Remember that a created VLAN is unused until it is assigned to a switch port or ports and that all ports are always assigned in VLAN 1 unless set otherwise.

Once the VLANs are created, verify your configuration with the show vlan command (sh vlan for short):

```
S1#sh vlan
```

VLAN	Name	Status	Ports
1	default	active	Fa0/1, Fa0/2, Fa0/3, Fa0/4
			Fa0/5, Fa0/6, Fa0/7, Fa0/8

```
                                         Fa0/9, Fa0/10, Fa0/11, Fa0/12
                                         Fa0/13, Fa0/14, Fa0/19, Fa0/20
                                         Fa0/21, Fa0/22, Fa0/23, Gi0/1
                                         Gi0/2
2    Sales                      active
3    Marketing                  active
4    Accounting                 active
[output cut]
```

If you want to see which ports are assigned to a particular VLAN (for example, VLAN 200), you can obviously use the show vlan command as shown above, or you can use the show vlan id 200 command to get ports assigned only to VLAN 200.

This may seem repetitive, but it's important, and I want you to remember it: You can't change, delete, or rename VLAN 1 because it's the default VLAN and you just can't change that—period. It's also the native VLAN of all switches by default, and Cisco recommends that you use it as your management VLAN. If you're worried about security issues, then change the native VLAN! Basically, any ports that aren't specifically assigned to a different VLAN will be sent down to the native VLAN—VLAN 1.

In the preceding S1 output, you can see that ports Fa0/1 through Fa0/14, Fa0/19 through 23, and the Gi0/1 and Gi02 uplinks are all in VLAN 1. But where are ports 15 through 18? First, understand that the command show vlan only displays access ports, so now that you know what you're looking at with the show vlan command, where do you think ports Fa15–18 are? That's right! They are trunked ports. Cisco switches run a proprietary protocol called *Dynamic Trunk Protocol (DTP)*, and if there is a compatible switch connected, they will start trunking automatically, which is precisely where my four ports are. You have to use the show interfaces trunk command to see your trunked ports like this:

```
S1# show interfaces trunk
Port       Mode            Encapsulation  Status        Native vlan
Fa0/15     desirable       n-isl          trunking      1
Fa0/16     desirable       n-isl          trunking      1
Fa0/17     desirable       n-isl          trunking      1
Fa0/18     desirable       n-isl          trunking      1

Port       Vlans allowed on trunk
Fa0/15     1-4094
Fa0/16     1-4094
Fa0/17     1-4094
Fa0/18     1-4094

[output cut]
```

This output reveals that the VLANs from 1 to 4094 are allowed across the trunk by default. Another helpful command, which is also part of the Cisco exam objectives, is the show interfaces *interface* switchport command:

```
S1#sh interfaces fastEthernet 0/15 switchport
Name: Fa0/15
Switchport: Enabled
Administrative Mode: dynamic desirable
Operational Mode: trunk
Administrative Trunking Encapsulation: negotiate
Operational Trunking Encapsulation: isl
Negotiation of Trunking: On
Access Mode VLAN: 1 (default)
Trunking Native Mode VLAN: 1 (default)
Administrative Native VLAN tagging: enabled
Voice VLAN: none
[output cut]
```

The highlighted output shows us the administrative mode of dynamic desirable, that the port is a trunk port, and that DTP was used to negotiate the frame-tagging method of ISL. It also predictably shows that the native VLAN is the default of 1.

Now that we can see the VLANs created, we can assign switch ports to specific ones. Each port can be part of only one VLAN, with the exception of voice access ports. Using trunking, you can make a port available to traffic from all VLANs. I'll cover that next.

Assigning Switch Ports to VLANs

You configure a port to belong to a VLAN by assigning a membership mode that specifies the kind of traffic the port carries plus the number of VLANs it can belong to. You can also configure each port on a switch to be in a specific VLAN (access port) by using the interface switchport command. You can even configure multiple ports at the same time with the interface range command.

In the next example, I'll configure interface Fa0/3 to VLAN 3. This is the connection from the S3 switch to the host device:

```
S3#config t
S3(config)#int fa0/3
S3(config-if)#switchport ?
  access     Set access mode characteristics of the interface
  autostate  Include or exclude this port from vlan link up calculation
  backup     Set backup for the interface
  block      Disable forwarding of unknown uni/multi cast addresses
  host       Set port host
```

```
mode          Set trunking mode of the interface
nonegotiate   Device will not engage in negotiation protocol on this
              interface
port-security Security related command
priority      Set appliance 802.1p priority
private-vlan  Set the private VLAN configuration
protected     Configure an interface to be a protected port
trunk         Set trunking characteristics of the interface
voice         Voice appliance attributes  voice
```

Well now, what do we have here? There's some new stuff showing up in our output now. We can see various commands—some that I've already covered, but no worries because I'm going to cover the access, mode, nonegotiate, and trunk commands very soon. Let's start with setting an access port on S1, which is probably the most widely used type of port you'll find on production switches that have VLANs configured:

```
S3(config-if)#switchport mode ?
    access       Set trunking mode to ACCESS unconditionally
  dot1q-tunnel   set trunking mode to TUNNEL unconditionally
    dynamic      Set trunking mode to dynamically negotiate access or trunk mode
  private-vlan   Set private-vlan mode
    trunk        Set trunking mode to TRUNK unconditionally


S3(config-if)#switchport mode access
S3(config-if)#switchport access vlan 3
```

By starting with the switchport mode access command, you're telling the switch that this is a nontrunking layer 2 port. You can then assign a VLAN to the port with the switchport access command. Remember, you can choose many ports to configure simultaneously with the interface range command.

Let's take a look at our VLANs now:

```
S3#show vlan
VLAN Name                       Status    Ports
---- ------------------------   --------- ------------------------------
1    default                    active    Fa0/4, Fa0/5, Fa0/6, Fa0/7
                                          Fa0/8, Fa0/9, Fa0/10, Fa0/11,
                                          Fa0/12, Fa0/13, Fa0/14, Fa0/19,
                                          Fa0/20, Fa0/21, Fa0/22, Fa0/23,
                                          Gi0/1,Gi0/2

2    Sales                      active
3    Marketing                  active    Fa0/3
```

Notice that port Fa0/3 is now a member of VLAN 3. But, can you tell me where ports 1 and 2 are? And why aren't they showing up in the output of show vlan? That's right, because they are trunk ports!

We can also see this with the show interfaces interface switchport command:

```
S3#sh int fa0/3 switchport
Name: Fa0/3
Switchport: Enabled
Administrative Mode: static access
Operational Mode: static access
Administrative Trunking Encapsulation: negotiate
Negotiation of Trunking: Off
Access Mode VLAN: 3 (Marketing)
```

The highlighted output shows that Fa0/3 is an access port and a member of VLAN 3 (Marketing).

Before we move onto trunking and VTP, let's add a voice VLAN on our switch. When an IP phone is connected to a switch port, this port should have a voice VLAN associated with it. By creating a separate VLAN for voice traffic, which of course you would do, what happens when you have a PC or laptop that connects via Ethernet into an IP phone? The phone connects to the Ethernet port and into one port on the switch. You're now sending both voice and data to the single switch port.

All you need to do is add another VLAN to the same switch port like so to fix this issue and separate the data at the switch port into two VLANs:

```
S1(config)#vlan 10
S1(config-vlan)#name Voice
S1(config-vlan)#int g0/1
S1(config-if)#switchport voice vlan 10
```

That's it. Well, sort of. If you plugged devices into each VLAN port, they can only talk to other devices in the same VLAN. But as soon as you learn a bit more about trunking, we're going to enable inter-VLAN communication!

Configuring Trunk Ports

The 2960 switch only runs the IEEE 802.1q encapsulation method. To configure trunking on a FastEthernet port, use the interface command switchport mode trunk. It's a tad different on the 3560 switch.

The following switch output shows the trunk configuration on interfaces Fa0/15–18 as set to trunk:

```
S1(config)#int range f0/15-18
S1(config-if-range)#switchport trunk encapsulation dot1q
S1(config-if-range)#switchport mode trunk
```

If you have a switch that only runs the 802.1q encapsulation method, then you wouldn't use the encapsulation command as I did in the preceding output. Let's check out our trunk ports now:

```
S1(config-if-range)#do sh int f0/15 switchport
Name: Fa0/15
Switchport: Enabled
Administrative Mode: trunk
Operational Mode: trunk
Administrative Trunking Encapsulation: dot1q
Operational Trunking Encapsulation: dot1q
Negotiation of Trunking: On
Access Mode VLAN: 1 (default)
Trunking Native Mode VLAN: 1 (default)
Administrative Native VLAN tagging: enabled
Voice VLAN: none
```

Notice that port Fa0/15 is a trunk and running 802.1q. Let's take another look:

```
S1(config-if-range)#do sh int trunk
Port        Mode             Encapsulation  Status      Native vlan
Fa0/15      on               802.1q         trunking    1
Fa0/16      on               802.1q         trunking    1
Fa0/17      on               802.1q         trunking    1
Fa0/18      on               802.1q         trunking    1
Port        Vlans allowed on trunk
Fa0/15      1-4094
Fa0/16      1-4094
Fa0/17      1-4094
Fa0/18      1-4094
```

Take note of the fact that ports 15–18 are now in the trunk mode of on and the encapsulation is now 802.1q instead of the negotiated ISL. Here's a description of the different options available when configuring a switch interface:

switchport mode access I discussed this in the previous section, but this puts the interface (access port) into permanent nontrunking mode and negotiates to convert the link into a nontrunk link. The interface becomes a nontrunk interface regardless of whether the neighboring interface is a trunk interface. The port would be a dedicated layer 2 access port.

switchport mode dynamic auto This mode makes the interface able to convert the link to a trunk link. The interface becomes a trunk interface if the neighboring interface is set to trunk or desirable mode. The default is dynamic auto on a lot of Cisco switches, but that default trunk method is changing to dynamic desirable on most new models.

switchport mode dynamic desirable This one makes the interface actively attempt to convert the link to a trunk link. The interface becomes a trunk interface if the neighboring interface is set to trunk, desirable, or auto mode. This is now the default switch port mode for all Ethernet interfaces on all new Cisco switches.

switchport mode trunk   Puts the interface into permanent trunking mode and negotiates to convert the neighboring link into a trunk link. The interface becomes a trunk interface even if the neighboring interface isn't a trunk interface.

switchport nonegotiate   Prevents the interface from generating DTP frames. You can use this command only when the interface switchport mode is access or trunk. You must manually configure the neighboring interface as a trunk interface to establish a trunk link.

> Dynamic Trunking Protocol (DTP) is used for negotiating trunking on a link between two devices as well as negotiating the encapsulation type of either 802.1q or ISL. I use the nonegotiate command when I want dedicated trunk ports; no questions asked.

To disable trunking on an interface, use the switchport mode access command, which sets the port back to a dedicated layer 2 access switch port.

Defining the Allowed VLANs on a Trunk

As I've mentioned, trunk ports send and receive information from all VLANs by default, and if a frame is untagged, it's sent to the management VLAN. Understand that this applies to the extended range VLANs too.

But we can remove VLANs from the allowed list to prevent traffic from certain VLANs from traversing a trunked link. I'll show you how you'd do that, but first let me again demonstrate that all VLANs are allowed across the trunk link by default:

```
S1#sh int trunk
[output cut]
Port        Vlans allowed on trunk
Fa0/15      1-4094
Fa0/16      1-4094
Fa0/17      1-4094
Fa0/18      1-4094
S1(config)#int f0/15
S1(config-if)#switchport trunk allowed vlan 4,6,12,15
S1(config-if)#do show int trunk
[output cut]
Port        Vlans allowed on trunk
Fa0/15      4,6,12,15
Fa0/16      1-4094
Fa0/17      1-4094
Fa0/18      1-4094
```

The preceding command affected the trunk link configured on S1 port Fa0/15, causing it to permit all traffic sent and received for VLANs 4, 6, 12, and 15. You can try to remove VLAN 1 on a trunk link, but it will still send and receive management data like CDP, DTP, and VTP, so what's the point?

To remove a range of VLANs, just use the hyphen:

```
S1(config-if)#switchport trunk allowed vlan remove 4-8
```

If by chance someone has removed some VLANs from a trunk link and you want to set the trunk back to default, just use this command:

```
S1(config-if)#switchport trunk allowed vlan all
```

Next, I want to show you how to configure a native VLAN for a trunk before we start routing between VLANs.

Changing or Modifying the Trunk Native VLAN

You can change the trunk port native VLAN from VLAN 1, which many people do for security reasons. To change the native VLAN, use the following command:

```
S1(config)#int f0/15
S1(config-if)#switchport trunk native vlan ?
  <1-4094>  VLAN ID of the native VLAN when this port is in trunking mode

S1(config-if)#switchport trunk native vlan 4
1w6d: %CDP-4-NATIVE_VLAN_MISMATCH: Native VLAN mismatch discovered on
FastEthernet0/15 (4), with S3 FastEthernet0/1 (1).
```

So we've changed our native VLAN on our trunk link to 4, and by using the show running-config command, I can see the configuration under the trunk link:

```
S1#sh run int f0/15
Building configuration...

Current configuration : 202 bytes
!
interface FastEthernet0/15
 description 1st connection to S3
 switchport trunk encapsulation dot1q
 switchport trunk native vlan 4
 switchport trunk allowed vlan 4,6,12,15
 switchport mode trunk
end

S1#!
```

Oops—wait a minute! You didn't think it would be this easy and would just start working, did you? Of course not! Here's the rub: If all switches don't have the same native VLAN configured on the given trunk links, then we'll start to receive this error, which happened immediately after I entered the command:

```
1w6d: %CDP-4-NATIVE_VLAN_MISMATCH: Native VLAN mismatch discovered
on FastEthernet0/15 (4), with S3 FastEthernet0/1 (1).
```

Actually, this is a good, noncryptic error, so either we can go to the other end of our trunk link(s) and change the native VLAN or we set the native VLAN back to the default to fix it. Here's how we'd do that:

```
S1(config-if)#no switchport trunk native vlan
1w6d: %SPANTREE-2-UNBLOCK_CONSIST_PORT: Unblocking FastEthernet0/15
on VLAN0004. Port consistency restored.
```

Now our trunk link is using the default VLAN 1 as the native VLAN. Just remember that all switches on a given trunk must use the same native VLAN or you'll have some serious management problems. These issues won't affect user data, just management traffic between switches. Now, let's mix it up by connecting a router into our switched network and configure inter-VLAN communication.

VLAN Trunking Protocol (VTP)

Cisco created this one too. The basic goals of *VLAN Trunking Protocol (VTP)* are to manage all configured VLANs across a switched internetwork and to maintain consistency throughout that network. VTP allows you to add, delete, and rename VLANs—information that is then propagated to all other switches in the VTP domain.

Here's a list of some of the cool features VTP has to offer:

- Consistent VLAN configuration across all switches in the network
- VLAN trunking over mixed networks, such as Ethernet to ATM LANE or even FDDI
- Accurate tracking and monitoring of VLANs
- Dynamic reporting of added VLANs to all switches in the VTP domain
- Adding VLANs using Plug and Play

Very nice, but before you can get VTP to manage your VLANs across the network, you have to create a VTP server (really, you don't need to even do that since all switches default to VTP server mode, but just make sure you have a server). All servers that need to share VLAN information must use the same domain name, and a switch can be in only one domain at a time. So basically, this means that a switch can share VTP domain information with other switches only if they're configured into the same VTP domain. You can use a VTP domain if you have more than one switch connected in a network, but if you've got all your switches in only one VLAN, you just don't need to use VTP. Do keep in mind that VTP information is sent between switches only via a trunk port.

Switches advertise VTP management domain information as well as a configuration revision number and all known VLANs with any specific parameters. But there's also something called *VTP transparent mode*. In it, you can configure switches to forward VTP information through trunk ports but not to accept information updates or update their VLAN databases.

If you've got sneaky users adding switches to your VTP domain behind your back, you can include passwords, but don't forget—every switch must be set up with the same password. And as you can imagine, this little snag can be a real hassle administratively!

Switches detect any added VLANs within a VTP advertisement and then prepare to send information on their trunk ports with the newly defined VLAN in tow. Updates are sent out as revision numbers that consist of summary advertisements. Anytime a switch sees a higher revision number, it knows the information it's getting is more current, so it will overwrite the existing VLAN database with the latest information.

You should know these four requirements for VTP to communicate VLAN information between switches:

- The VTP version must be set the same
- The VTP management domain name of both switches must be set the same.
- One of the switches has to be configured as a VTP server.
- Set a VTP password if used.

No router is necessary and is not a requirement. Now that you've got that down, we're going to delve deeper into the world of VTP with VTP modes and VTP pruning.

VTP Modes of Operation

Figure 15.1 shows you how a VTP server will update the connected VTP client's VLAN database when a change occurs in the VLAN database on the server.

FIGURE 15.1   VTP modes

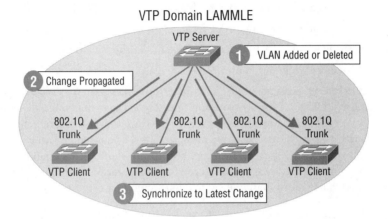

Server   This is the default mode for all Catalyst switches. You need at least one server in your VTP domain to propagate VLAN information throughout that domain. Also important: The switch must be in server mode to be able to create, add, and delete VLANs in a VTP domain. VLAN information has to be changed in server mode, and any change made to VLANs on a switch in server mode will be advertised to the entire VTP domain. In VTP server mode, VLAN configurations are saved in NVRAM on the switch.

Client   In client mode, switches receive information from VTP servers, but they also receive and forward updates, so in this way, they behave like VTP servers. The difference is that they can't create, change, or delete VLANs. Plus, none of the ports on a client switch can be added to a new VLAN before the VTP server notifies the client switch of the new VLAN and the VLAN exists in the client's VLAN database. Also good to know is that VLAN information sent from a VTP server isn't stored in NVRAM, which is important because it means that if the switch is reset or reloaded, the VLAN information will be deleted. Here's a hint: If you want a switch to become a server, first make it a client so it receives all the correct VLAN information, then change it to a server—so much easier!

So basically, a switch in VTP client mode will forward VTP summary advertisements and process them. This switch will learn about but won't save the VTP configuration in the running configuration, and it won't save it in NVRAM. Switches that are in VTP client mode will only learn about and pass along VTP information—that's it!

 **Real World Scenario**

So, When Do I Need to Consider Using VTP?

Here's a scenario for you. Bob, a senior network administrator at Acme Corporation in San Francisco, has about 25 switches all connected together, and he wants to configure VLANs to break up broadcast domains. When do you think he should start to consider using VTP?

If you answered that he should have used VTP the moment he had more than one switch and multiple VLANs, you're right. If you have only one switch, then VTP is irrelevant. It also isn't a player if you're not configuring VLANs in your network. But if you do have multiple switches that use multiple VLANs, you'd better configure your VTP server and clients, and you better do it right!

When you first bring up your switched network, verify that your main switch is a VTP server and that all the other ones are VTP clients. When you create VLANs on the main VTP server, all switches will receive the VLAN database.

If you have an existing switched network and you want to add a new switch, make sure to configure it as a VTP client before you install it. If you don't, it's possible—okay, highly probable—that your new little beauty will send out a new VTP database to all your other switches, effectively wiping out all your existing VLANs like a nuclear blast. No one needs that!

Transparent Switches in transparent mode don't participate in the VTP domain or share its VLAN database, but they'll still forward VTP advertisements through any configured trunk links. They can create, modify, and delete VLANs because they keep their own database—one they keep secret from the other switches. Despite being kept in NVRAM, the VLAN database in transparent mode is actually only locally significant. The whole purpose of transparent mode is to allow remote switches to receive the VLAN database from a VTP Server configured switch through a switch that is not participating in the same VLAN assignments.

VTP only learns about normal-range VLANs, with VLAN IDs 1 to 1005; VLANs with IDs greater than 1005 are called extended-range VLANs and they're not stored in the VLAN database. The switch must be in VTP transparent mode when you create VLAN IDs from 1006 to 4094, so it would be pretty rare that you'd ever use these VLANs. One other thing: VLAN IDs 1 and 1002 to 1005 are automatically created on all switches and can't be removed.

VTP Pruning

VTP gives you a way to preserve bandwidth by configuring it to reduce the amount of broadcasts, multicasts, and unicast packets. This is called *pruning*. Switches enabled for VTP pruning send broadcasts only to trunk links that actually must have the information.

Here's what this means: If Switch A doesn't have any ports configured for VLAN 5 and a broadcast is sent throughout VLAN 5, that broadcast wouldn't traverse the trunk link to Switch A. By default, VTP pruning is disabled on all switches. Seems to me this would be a good default parameter. When you enable pruning on a VTP server, you enable it for the entire domain. By default, VLANs 2 through 1001 are pruning eligible, but VLAN 1 can never be pruned because it's an administrative VLAN. VTP pruning is supported with both VTP version 1 and version 2.

By using the show interface trunk command, we can see that all VLANs are allowed across a trunked link by default:

```
S1#sh int trunk

Port        Mode         Encapsulation  Status        Native vlan
Fa0/1       auto         802.1q         trunking      1
Fa0/2       auto         802.1q         trunking      1

Port        Vlans allowed on trunk
Fa0/1       1-4094
Fa0/2       1-4094

Port        Vlans allowed and active in management domain
Fa0/1       1
Fa0/2       1

Port        Vlans in spanning tree forwarding state and not pruned
```

```
Fa0/1     1
Fa0/2     none
S1#
```

Looking at the preceding output, you can see that VTP pruning is disabled by default. I'm going to go ahead and enable pruning. It only takes one command and it is enabled on your entire switched network for the listed VLANs. Let's see what happens:

```
S1#config t
S1(config)#int f0/1
S1(config-if)#switchport trunk ?
  allowed  Set allowed VLAN characteristics when interface is
  in trunking mode
  native   Set trunking native characteristics when interface
  is in trunking mode
  pruning  Set pruning VLAN characteristics when interface is
  in trunking mode
S1(config-if)#switchport trunk pruning ?
  vlan  Set VLANs enabled for pruning when interface is in
  trunking mode
S1(config-if)#switchport trunk pruning vlan 3-4
```

The valid VLANs that can be pruned are 2 to 1001. Extended-range VLANs (VLAN IDs 1006 to 4094) can't be pruned, and these pruning-ineligible VLANs can receive a flood of traffic.

Configuring VTP

All Cisco switches are configured to be VTP servers by default. To configure VTP, first you have to configure the domain name you want to use. And of course, once you configure the VTP information on a switch, you need to verify it.

When you create the VTP domain, you have a few options, including setting the VTP version, domain name, password, operating mode, and pruning capabilities of the switch. Use the vtp global configuration mode command to set all this information. In the following example, I'll set the S1 switch to vtp server, the VTP domain to Lammle, and the VTP password to todd:

```
S1#config t
S1#(config)#vtp mode server
Device mode already VTP SERVER.
S1(config)#vtp domain Lammle
Changing VTP domain name from null to Lammle
S1(config)#vtp password todd
```

```
Setting device VLAN database password to todd
S1(config)#do show vtp password
VTP Password: todd
S1(config)#do show vtp status
VTP Version                      : 2
Configuration Revision           : 0
Maximum VLANs supported locally  : 255
Number of existing VLANs         : 8
VTP Operating Mode               : Server
VTP Domain Name                  : Lammle
VTP Pruning Mode                 : Disabled
VTP V2 Mode                      : Disabled
VTP Traps Generation             : Disabled
MD5 digest                       : 0x15 0x54 0x88 0xF2 0x50 0xD9 0x03 0x07
Configuration last modified by 192.168.24.6 at 3-14-93 15:47:32
Local updater ID is 192.168.24.6 on interface Vl1 (lowest numbered VLAN
interface found)
```

Please make sure you remember that all switches are set to VTP server mode by default, and if you want to change and distribute any VLAN information on a switch, you absolutely must be in VTP server mode. After you configure the VTP information, you can verify it with the show vtp status command as shown in the preceding output.

The preceding switch output shows the VTP Version, Configuration Revision, Maximum VLANs supported locally, Number of existing VLANs, VTP Operating Mode, VTP domain, the VTP domain, and the VTP password listed as an MD5 Digest. You can use show vtp password in privileged mode to see the password.

Troubleshooting VTP

You connect your switches with crossover cables, the lights go green on both ends, and you're up and running! Yeah—in a perfect world, right? Don't you wish it was that easy? Well, actually, it pretty much is—without VLANs, of course. But if you're using VLANs—and you definitely should be—then you need to use VTP if you have multiple VLANs configured in your switched network.

But here there be monsters: If VTP is not configured correctly, it (surprise!) will not work, so you absolutely must be capable of troubleshooting VTP. Let's take a look at a couple of configurations and solve the problems. Study the output from the two following switches:

```
SwitchA#sh vtp status
VTP Version                      : 2
Configuration Revision           : 0
Maximum VLANs supported locally  : 64
```

```
Number of existing VLANs      : 7
VTP Operating Mode            : Server
VTP Domain Name               : Lammle
VTP Pruning Mode              : Disabled
VTP V2 Mode                   : Disabled
VTP Traps Generation          : Disabled


SwitchB#sh vtp status
VTP Version                   : 2
Configuration Revision        : 1
Maximum VLANs supported locally : 64
Number of existing VLANs      : 7
VTP Operating Mode            : Server
VTP Domain Name               : GlobalNet
VTP Pruning Mode              : Disabled
VTP V2 Mode                   : Disabled
VTP Traps Generation          : Disabled
```

So what's happening with these two switches? Why won't they share VLAN information? At first glance, it seems that both servers are in VTP server mode, but that's not the problem. Servers in VTP server mode will share VLAN information using VTP. The problem is that they're in two different VTP *domains*. SwitchA is in VTP domain Lammle and SwitchB is in VTP domain GlobalNet. They will never share VTP information because the VTP domain names are configured differently.

Now that you know how to look for common VTP domain configuration errors in your switches, let's take a look at another switch configuration:

```
SwitchC#sh vtp status
VTP Version                   : 2
Configuration Revision        : 1
Maximum VLANs supported locally : 64
Number of existing VLANs      : 7
VTP Operating Mode            : Client
VTP Domain Name               : Todd
VTP Pruning Mode              : Disabled
VTP V2 Mode                   : Disabled
VTP Traps Generation          : Disabled
```

Here's what will happen when you have the preceding VTP configuration:

```
SwitchC(config)#vlan 50
VTP VLAN configuration not allowed when device is in CLIENT mode.
```

There you are just trying to create a new VLAN on SwitchC and what do you get for your trouble? A loathsome error! Why can't you create a VLAN on SwitchC? Well, the VTP domain name isn't the important thing in this example. What is critical here is the VTP *mode*. The VTP mode is client, and a VTP client cannot create, delete, or change VLANs, remember? VTP clients only keep the VTP database in RAM, and that's not saved to NVRAM. So, in order to create a VLAN on this switch, you've got to make the switch a VTP server first.

So to fix this problem, here's what you need to do:

```
SwitchC(config)#vtp mode server
Setting device to VTP SERVER mode
SwitchC(config)#vlan 50
SwitchC(config-vlan)#
```

Wait, we're not done. Now take a look at the output from these two switches and determine why SwitchB is not receiving VLAN information from SwitchA:

```
SwitchA#sh vtp status
VTP Version                    : 2
Configuration Revision         : 4
Maximum VLANs supported locally : 64
Number of existing VLANs       : 7
VTP Operating Mode             : Server
VTP Domain Name                : GlobalNet
VTP Pruning Mode               : Disabled
VTP V2 Mode                    : Disabled
VTP Traps Generation           : Disabled


SwitchB#sh vtp status
VTP Version                    : 2
Configuration Revision         : 14
Maximum VLANs supported locally : 64
Number of existing VLANs       : 7
VTP Operating Mode             : Server
VTP Domain Name                : GlobalNet
VTP Pruning Mode               : Disabled
VTP V2 Mode                    : Disabled
VTP Traps Generation           : Disabled
```

You may be tempted to say it's because they're both VTP servers, but that is not the problem. All your switches can be servers and they can still share VLAN information. As a matter of fact, Cisco actually suggests that all switches stay VTP servers and that you just make sure the switch you want to advertise VTP VLAN information has the highest revision number. If all switches are VTP servers, then all of the switches will save the VLAN database. But SwitchB isn't receiving VLAN information from SwitchA because SwitchB has a higher revision number than SwitchA. It's very important that you can recognize this problem.

There are a couple ways to go about resolving this issue. The first thing you could do is to change the VTP domain name on SwitchB to another name, then set it back to GlobalNet, which will reset the revision number to zero (0) on SwitchB. The second approach would be to create or delete VLANs on SwitchA until the revision number passes the revision number on SwitchB. I didn't say the second way was better; I just said it's another way to fix it!

Let's look at one more. Why is SwitchB not receiving VLAN information from SwitchA?

```
SwitchA#sh vtp status
VTP Version                   : 1
Configuration Revision        : 4
Maximum VLANs supported locally : 64
Number of existing VLANs      : 7
VTP Operating Mode            : Server
VTP Domain Name               : GlobalNet
VTP Pruning Mode              : Disabled
VTP V2 Mode                   : Disabled
VTP Traps Generation          : Disabled

SwitchB#sh vtp status
VTP Version                   : 2
Configuration Revision        : 3
Maximum VLANs supported locally : 64
Number of existing VLANs      : 5
VTP Operating Mode            : Server
VTP Domain Name               :
VTP Pruning Mode              : Disabled
VTP V2 Mode                   : Disabled
VTP Traps Generation          : Disabled
```

I know your first instinct is to notice that SwitchB doesn't have a domain name set and consider that the issue. That's not the problem! When a switch comes up, a VTP server with a domain name set will send VTP advertisements, and a new switch out of the box will configure itself using the advertisement with the received domain name and also download the VLAN database.

The problem with the above switches is that they are set to different VTP versions—but that still isn't the full problem.

By default, VTP operates in version 1. You can configure VTP version 2 if you want support for these features, which are not supported in version 1:

- Token Ring support—Hmmm...doesn't seem like much of a reason to go to version 2 today. Let's look at some other reasons.

- Unrecognized Type-Length-Value (TLV) support—A VTP server or client propagates configuration changes to its other trunks, even for TLVs it is not able to parse. The unrecognized TLV is saved in NVRAM when the switch is operating in VTP server mode.

- Version-Dependent Transparent Mode—In VTP version 1, a VTP transparent switch inspects VTP messages for the domain name and version and forwards a message only if the version and domain name match. Because VTP version 2 supports only one domain, it forwards VTP messages in transparent mode without inspecting the version and domain name.

- Consistency Checks—In VTP version 2, VLAN consistency checks (such as checking the consistency of VLAN names and values) are performed only when you enter new information through the CLI or SNMP. Consistency checks are not performed when new information is obtained from a VTP message or when information is read from NVRAM. If the MD5 digest on a received VTP message is correct, its information is accepted.

Wait! Nothing is that easy. Just set SwitchA to version 2 and we're up and running? Nope! The interesting thing about VTP version 2 is that if you set one switch in your network (VTP domain) to version 2, all switches would set their version to 2 automatically—very cool! So then what is the problem? SwitchA doesn't support VTP version 2, which is the actual answer to this question. Crazy! I think you can see that VTP will drive you to drink if you're not careful!

Okay, get a coffee, expresso or Mountain Dew and hold onto your hats—it's spanning tree time!

Spanning Tree Protocol (STP)

Spanning Tree Protocol (STP) achieves its primary objective of preventing network loops on layer 2 network bridges or switches by monitoring the network to track all links and shut down the redundant ones. STP uses the spanning-tree algorithm (STA) to first create a topology database and then search out and disable redundant links. With STP running, frames will be forwarded on only premium, STP-chosen links.

The Spanning Tree Protocol is a great protocol to use in networks like the one shown in Figure 15.2.

FIGURE 15.2   A switched network with switching loops

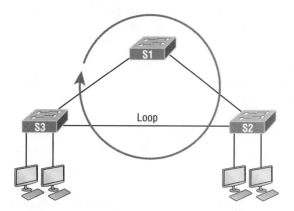

This is a switched network with a redundant topology that includes switching loops. Without some type of layer 2 mechanism in place to prevent a network loop, this network is vulnerable to nasty issues like broadcast storms, multiple frame copies, and MAC table thrashing! Figure 15.3 shows how this network would work with STP working on the switches.

FIGURE 15.3   A switched network with STP

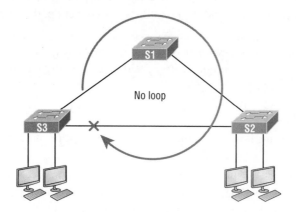

There a few types of spanning-tree protocols, but I'll start with the IEEE version 802.1d, which happens to be the default on all Cisco IOS switches.

Spanning-Tree Terms

Now, before I get into describing the details of how STP works within a network, it would be good for you to have these basic ideas and terms down first:

Root bridge   The *root bridge* is the bridge with the lowest and, therefore, the best bridge ID. The switches within the STP network elect a root bridge, which becomes the focal point in the network. All other decisions in the network, like which ports on the non-root bridges should be blocked or put in forwarding mode, are made from the perspective of the root bridge, and once it has been elected, all other bridges must create a single path to it. The port with the best path to the root bridge is called the root port.

Non-root bridges   These are all bridges that aren't the root bridge. Non-root bridges exchange BPDUs with all the other bridges and update the STP topology database on all switches. This prevents loops and helps defend against link failures.

BPDU   All switches exchange information to use for the subsequent configuration of the network. Each switch compares the parameters in the *Bridge Protocol Data Unit (BPDU)* that it sends to a neighbor with the parameters in the BPDU that it receives from other neighbors. Inside the BPDU is the bridge ID.

Bridge ID   The bridge ID is how STP keeps track of all the switches in the network. It's determined by a combination of the bridge priority, which is 32,768 by default on all Cisco switches, and the base MAC address. The bridge with the lowest bridge ID becomes the root bridge in the network. Once the root bridge is established, every other switch must make a single path to it. Most networks benefit by forcing a specific bridge or switch to be on the root bridge by setting its bridge priority lower than the default value.

Port cost   Port cost determines the best path when multiple links are used between two switches. The cost of a link is determined by the bandwidth of a link, and this path cost is the deciding factor used by every bridge to find the most efficient path to the root bridge.

Path cost   A switch may encounter one or more switches on its path to the root bridge, and there may be more than one possible path. All unique paths are analyzed individually, and a path cost is calculated for each unique path by adding the individual port costs encountered on the way to the root bridge.

Bridge Port Roles

STP uses roles to determine how a port on a switch will act within the spanning-tree algorithm.

Root port   The root port is the link with the lowest path cost to the root bridge. If more than one link connects to the root bridge, then a port cost is found by checking the bandwidth of each link. The lowest-cost port becomes the root port. When multiple links connect to the same device, the port connected to the lowest port number on the upstream switch will be the one that's used. The root bridge can never have a root port designation, while every other switch in a network must have one and only one root port.

Designated port   A *designated port* is one that's been determined to have the best (lowest) cost to get to on a given network segment, compared to other ports on that segment. A designated port will be marked as a forwarding port, and you can have only one forwarding port per network segment.

Non-designated port   A *non-designated port* is one with a higher cost than the designated port. These are basically the ones left over after the root ports and designated ports have been determined. Non-designated ports are put in blocking or discarding mode—they are not forwarding ports!

Forwarding port   A forwarding port forwards frames and will be either a root port or a designated port.

Blocked port   A blocked port won't forward frames in order to prevent loops. A blocked port will still always listen to BPDU frames from neighbor switches, but it will drop any and all other frames received and will never transmit a frame.

Alternate port   This corresponds to the blocking state of 802.1d and is a term used with the newer 802.1w (Rapid Spanning Tree Protocol). An alternative port is located on a switch connected to a LAN segment with two or more switches connected, and one of the other switches holds the designated port.

Backup port   This corresponds to the blocking state of 802.1d and is a term now used with the newer 802.1w. A backup port is connected to a LAN segment where another port on that switch is acting as the designated port.

Spanning-Tree Port States

Okay, so you plug your host into a switch port and the light turns amber and your host doesn't get a DHCP address from the server. You wait and wait and finally the light goes green after almost a full minute—that's an eternity in today's networks! This is the STA transitioning through the different port states verifying that you didn't just create a loop with the device you just plugged in. STP would rather time out your new host than allow a loop into the network because that would effectively bring your network to its knees. Let's talk about the transition states; then later in this chapter we'll talk about how to speed this process up.

The ports on a bridge or switch running IEEE 802.1d STP can transition through five different states:

Disabled (technically, not a transition state)   A port in the administratively disabled state doesn't participate in frame forwarding or STP. A port in the disabled state is virtually nonoperational.

Blocking   As I mentioned, a blocked port won't forward frames; it just listens to BPDUs. The purpose of the blocking state is to prevent the use of looped paths. All ports are in blocking state by default when the switch is powered up.

Listening   This port listens to BPDUs to make sure no loops occur on the network before passing data frames. A port in listening state prepares to forward data frames without populating the MAC address table.

Learning   The switch port listens to BPDUs and learns all the paths in the switched network. A port in learning state populates the MAC address table but still doesn't forward data frames. Forward delay refers to the time it takes to transition a port from listening to learning mode, or from learning to forwarding mode, which is set to 15 seconds by default and can be seen in the `show spanning-tree` output.

Forwarding This port sends and receives all data frames on the bridged port. If the port is still a designated or root port at the end of the learning state, it will enter the forwarding state.

 Switches populate the MAC address table in learning and forwarding modes only.

Switch ports are most often in either the blocking or forwarding state. A forwarding port is typically the one that's been determined to have the lowest (best) cost to the root bridge. But when and if the network experiences a topology change due to a failed link or because someone has added in a new switch, you'll see the ports on a switch transitioning through listening and learning states.

As I said earlier, blocking ports is a strategy for preventing network loops. Once a switch determines the best path to the root bridge for its root port and any designated ports, all other redundant ports will be in blocking mode. Blocked ports can still receive BPDUs—they just don't send out any frames.

If a switch determines that a blocked port should become the designated or root port because of a topology change, it will go into listening mode and check all BPDUs it receives to make sure it won't create a loop once the port moves into forwarding mode.

Convergence

Convergence occurs when all ports on bridges and switches have transitioned to either forwarding or blocking modes. No data will be forwarded until convergence is complete. Yes—you read that right: When STP is converging, all host data stops transmitting through the switches! So if you want to remain on speaking terms with your network's users, or remain employed for any length of time, you must make sure that your switched network is physically designed really well so that STP can converge quickly!

Convergence is vital because it ensures that all devices have a coherent database. And making sure this happens efficiently will definitely require your time and attention. The original STP (802.1d) takes 50 seconds to go from blocking to forwarding mode by default and I don't recommend changing the default STP timers. You can adjust those timers for a large network, but the better solution is simply to opt out of using 802.1d at all! We'll get to the various STP versions in a minute.

Link Costs

Now that you know about the different port roles and states, you need to really understand all about path cost before we put this all together. Port cost is based on the speed of the link, and Table 15.1 breaks down the need-to-know path costs for you. Port cost is the cost of a single link, whereas path cost is the sum of the various port costs to the root bridge.

TABLE 15.1   IEEE STP link costs

Speed	Cost
10 Mb/s	100
100 Mb/s	19
1000 Mb/s	4
10,000 Mb/s	2

These costs will be used in the STP calculations to choose a single root port on each bridge. You absolutely need to memorize this table, but no worries—I'll guide you through lots of examples in this chapter to help you do that quite easily! Now it's time to take everything we've learned so far and put it all together.

Spanning-Tree Operations

Let's start neatly summarizing what you've learned so far using the simple three-switch network connected together as shown in Figure 15.4.

FIGURE 15.4   STP operations

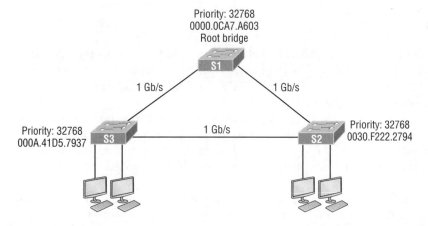

Basically, STP's job is to find all the links in the network and shut down any redundant ones, thereby preventing network loops from occurring. It achieves this by first electing a root bridge that will have all ports forwarding and will also act as a point of reference for all other devices within the STP domain. In Figure 15.4, S1 has been elected the root bridge based on bridge ID. Since the priorities are all equal to 32,768, we'll compare MAC addresses and find that the MAC address of S1 is lower than that of S2 and S3, meaning that S1 has a better bridge ID.

Once all switches agree on the root bridge, they must then determine their one and only root port—the single path to the root bridge. It's really important to remember that a bridge can go through many other bridges to get to the root, so it's not always the shortest path that will be chosen. That role will be given to the port that happens to offer the fastest, highest bandwidth. Figure 15.5 shows the root ports for both non-root bridges (the *RP* signifies a root port and the *F* signifies a designated forwarding port).

FIGURE 15.5   STP operations

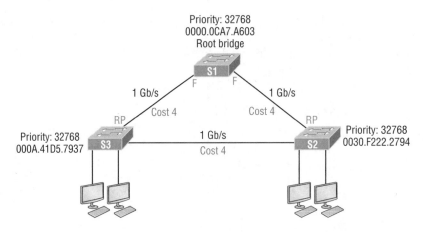

Looking at the cost of each link, it's clear why S2 and S3 are using their directly connected links, because a gigabit link has a cost of 4. For example, if S3 chose the path through S2 as its root port, we'd have to add up each port cost along the way to the root, which would be 4 + 4 for a total cost of 8.

Every port on the root bridge is a designated, or forwarding, port for a segment, and after the dust settles on all other non-root bridges, any port connection between switches that isn't either a root port or a designated port will predictably become a non-designated port. These will again be put into the blocking state to prevent switching loops.

Okay—at this point, we have our root bridge with all ports in forwarding state and we've found our root ports for each non-root bridge. Now the only thing left to do is to choose the one forwarding port on the segment between S2 and S3. Both bridges can't be forwarding on a segment because that's exactly how we would end up with loops. So, based on the bridge ID, the port with the best and lowest would become the only bridge forwarding on that segment, with the one having the highest, worst bridge ID put into blocking mode. Figure 15.6 shows the network after STP has converged.

FIGURE 15.6 STP operations

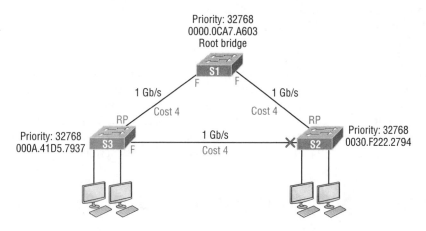

Since S3 had a lower bridge ID (better), S2's port went into blocking mode. Let's discuss the root bridge election process more completely now.

Selecting the Root Bridge

The bridge ID is used to elect the root bridge in the STP domain and to determine the root port for each of the remaining devices when there's more than one potential root port available because they have equal-cost paths. This key bridge ID is 8 bytes long and includes both the priority and the MAC address of the device, as illustrated in Figure 15.7. Remember—the default priority on all devices running the IEEE STP version is 32,768.

FIGURE 15.7 STP operations

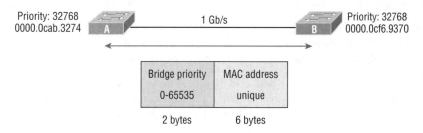

So, to determine the root bridge, you combine the priority of each bridge with its MAC address. If two switches or bridges happen to have the same priority value, the MAC address becomes the tiebreaker for figuring out which one has the lowest and, therefore, best ID. This means that because the two switches in Figure 15.7 are both using the default priority of 32,768, the MAC address will be the determining factor instead. And because Switch A's MAC address is 0000.0cab.3274 and Switch B's MAC address is 0000.0cf6.9370, Switch

A wins and will become the root bridge. A really easy way to figure out the lowest MAC address is to just start reading from the left toward the right until you find a lesser value. For Switch A, I only needed to get to 0000.0ca before stopping. Switch A wins since switch B is 0000.0cf. Never forget that the lower value is always the better one when it comes to electing a root bridge!

I want to point out that prior to the election of the root bridge, BPDUs are sent every 2 seconds out all active ports on a bridge/switch by default, and they're received and processed by all bridges. The root bridge is elected based on this information. You can change the bridge's ID by lowering its priority so that it will become a root bridge automatically. Being able to do that is important in a large switched network because it ensures that the best paths will actually be the ones chosen. Efficiency is always awesome in networking!

Types of Spanning-tree Protocols

There are several varieties of spanning-tree protocols in use today:

IEEE 802.1d   The original standard for bridging and STP, which is really slow but requires very little bridge resources. It's also referred to as Common Spanning Tree (CST).

PVST+ (Cisco default version)   Per-VLAN Spanning Tree+ (PVST+) is the Cisco proprietary enhancement for STP that provides a separate 802.1d spanning-tree instance for each VLAN. Know that this is just as slow as the CST protocol, but with it, we get to have multiple root bridges. This creates more efficiency of the links in the network, but it does use more bridge resources than CST does.

IEEE 802.1w   Also called Rapid Spanning Tree Protocol (RSTP), this iteration enhanced the BPDU exchange and paved the way for much faster network convergence, but it still only allows for one root bridge per network like CST. The bridge resources used with RSTP are higher than CST's but less than PVST+.

802.1s (MSTP)   IEEE standard that started out as Cisco propriety MISTP. Maps multiple VLANs into the same spanning-tree instance to save processing on the switch. It's basically a spanning-tree protocol that rides on top of another spanning-tree protocol.

Rapid PVST+   Cisco's version of RSTP that also uses PVST+ and provides a separate instance of 802.1w per VLAN. It gives us really fast convergence times and optimal traffic flow but predictably requires the most CPU and memory of all.

Common Spanning Tree

If you're running Common Spanning Tree (CST) in your switched network with redundant links, there will be an election to choose what STP considers to be the best root bridge for your network. That switch will also become the root for all VLANs in your network and all bridges in your network will create a single path to it. You can manually override this selection and pick whichever bridge you want if it makes sense for your particular network.

Figure 15.8 shows how a typical root bridge would look on your switched network when running CST.

FIGURE 15.8   Common STP example

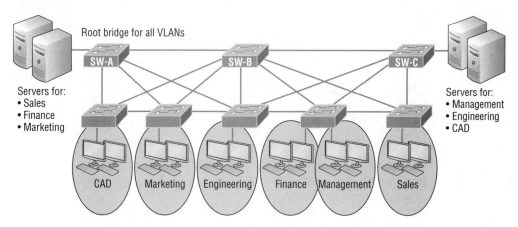

Notice that switch A is the root bridge for all VLANs even though it's really not the best path for some VLANs because all switches must make a single path to it! This is where Per-VLAN Spanning Tree+ (PVST+) comes into play. Because it allows for a separate instance of STP for each VLAN, it frees up the individual selection of the most optimal path.

Per-VLAN Spanning Tree+

PVST+ is a Cisco proprietary extension to 801.2d STP that provides a separate 802.1 spanning-tree instance for each VLAN configured on your switches. All of the Cisco proprietary extensions were created to improve convergence times, which is 50 seconds by default. Cisco IOS switches run 802.1d PVST+ by default, which means you'll have optimal path selection, but the convergence time will still be slow.

Creating a per-VLAN STP instance for each VLAN is worth the increased CPU and memory requirements, because it allows for per-VLAN root bridges. This feature allows the STP tree to be optimized for the traffic of each VLAN by allowing you to configure the root bridge in the center of each of them. Figure 15.9 shows how PVST+ would look in an optimized switched network with multiple redundant links.

This root bridge placement clearly enables faster convergence as well as optimal path determination. This version's convergence is really similar to 802.1 CST's, which has one instance of STP no matter how many VLANs you have configured on your network. The difference is that with PVST+, convergence happens on a per-VLAN basis, with each VLAN running its own instance of STP. Figure 15.9 shows us that we now have a nice, efficient root bridge selection for each VLAN.

FIGURE 15.9 PVST+ provides efficient root bridge selection.

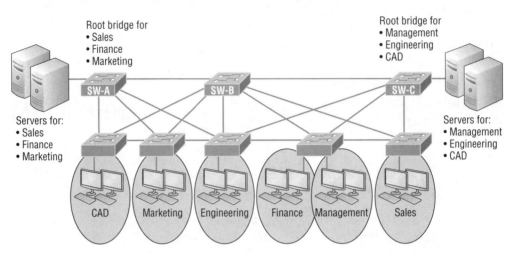

To allow for the PVST+ to operate, there's a field inserted into the BPDU to accommodate the extended system ID so that PVST+ can have a root bridge configured on a per-STP instance, shown in Figure 15.10. The bridge ID actually becomes smaller—only 4 bits—which means that we would configure the bridge priority in blocks of 4,096 rather than in increments of 1 as we did with CST. The extended system ID (VLAN ID) is a 12-bit field, and we can even see what this field is carrying via show spanning-tree command output, which I'll show you soon.

FIGURE 15.10 PVST+ unique bridge ID

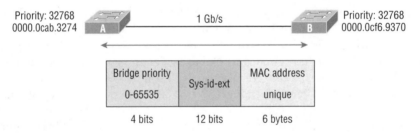

But still, isn't there a way we can do better than a 50-second convergence time? That's a really long time in today's world!

Rapid Spanning Tree Protocol 802.1w

Wouldn't it be wonderful to have a solid STP configuration running on your switched network, regardless of switch type, and still have all the features we just discussed built in and enabled on every one of your switches too? Rapid Spanning Tree Protocol (RSTP) serves up exactly this amazing capacity right to our networking table!

Cisco created proprietary extensions to "fix" all the sinkholes and liabilities the IEEE 802.1d standard threw at us, with the main drawback to them being they require extra configuration because they're Cisco proprietary. But RSTP, the new 802.1w standard, brings us most of the patches needed in one concise solution. Again, efficiency is golden!

RSTP, or IEEE 802.1w, is essentially an evolution of STP that allows for much faster convergence. But even though it does address all the convergence issues, it still only permits a single STP instance, so it doesn't help to take the edge off suboptimal traffic flow issues. And as I mentioned, to support that faster convergence, the CPU usage and memory demands are slightly higher than CST's. The good news is that Cisco IOS can run the Rapid PVST+ protocol—a Cisco enhancement of RSTP that provides a separate 802.1w spanning-tree instance for each VLAN configured within the network. But all that power needs fuel, and although this version addresses both convergence and traffic flow issues, it also demands the most CPU and memory of all solutions. And it's also good news that Cisco's newest switches don't have a problem with this protocol running on them.

 Keep in mind that Cisco documentation may say STP 802.1d and RSTP 802.1w, but it is referring to the PVST+ enhancement of each version.

Understand that RSTP wasn't meant to be something completely new and different. The protocol is more of an evolution than an innovation of the 802.1d standard, which offers faster convergence whenever a topology change occurs. Backward compatibility was a must when 802.1w was created.

So, RSTP helps with convergence issues that were the bane of traditional STP. Rapid PVST+ is based on the 802.1w standard in the same way that PVST+ is based on 802.1d. The operation of Rapid PVST+ is simply a separate instance of 802.1w for each VLAN. Here's a list to clarify how this all breaks down:

- RSTP speeds the recalculation of the spanning tree when the layer 2 network topology changes.

- It's an IEEE standard that redefines STP port roles, states, and BPDUs.

- RSTP is extremely proactive and very quick, so it doesn't need the 802.1d delay timers.

- RSTP (802.1w) supersedes 802.1d while remaining backward compatible.

- Much of the 802.1d terminology and most parameters remain unchanged.

- 802.1w is capable of reverting to 802.1d to interoperate with traditional switches on a per-port basis.

And to clear up confusion, there are also five terminology adjustments between 802.1d's five port states and 802.1w's, compared here, respectively:

802.1d State		802.1w State
Disabled	=	Discarding
Blocking	=	Discarding
Listening	=	Discarding
Learning	=	Learning
Forwarding	=	Forwarding

Make note of the fact that RSTP basically just goes from discarding to learning to forwarding, whereas 802.1d requires five states to transition.

The task of determining the root bridge, root ports, and designated ports hasn't changed from 802.1d to RSTP, and understanding the cost of each link is still key to making these decisions well. Let's take a look at an example of how to determine ports using the revised IEEE cost specifications in Figure 15.11.

FIGURE 15.11 RSTP example 1

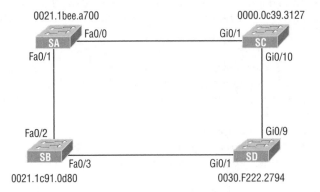

Can you figure out which is the root bridge? How about which port is the root and which ones are designated? Well, because SC has the lowest MAC address, it becomes the root bridge, and since all ports on a root bridge are forwarding designated ports, well, that's easy, right? Ports Gi0/1 and Gi0/10 become designated forwarding ports on SC.

But which one would be the root port for SA? To figure that out, we must first find the port cost for the direct link between SA and SC. Even though the root bridge (SC) has a Gigabit Ethernet port, it's running at 100 Mbps because SA's port is a 100-Mbps port, giving it a cost of 19. If the paths between SA and SC were both Gigabit Ethernet, their costs would only be 4, but because they're running 100 Mbps links instead, the cost jumps to a whopping 19!

Can you find SD's root port? A quick glance at the link between SC and SD tells us that's a Gigabit Ethernet link with a cost of 4, so the root port for SD would be its Gi0/9 port.

The cost of the link between SB and SD is also 19 because it's also a Fast Ethernet link, bringing the full cost from SB to SD to the root (SC) to a total cost of 19 + 4 = 23. If SB were to go through SA to get to SC, then the cost would be 19 + 19, or 38, so the root port of SB becomes the Fa0/3 port.

The root port for SA would be the Fa0/0 port since that's a direct link with a cost of 19. Going through SB to SD would be 19 + 19 + 4 = 42, so we'll use that as a backup link for SA to get to the root just in case we need to.

Now all we need is a forwarding port on the link between SA and SB. Because SA has the lowest bridge ID, Fa0/1 on SA wins that role. Also, the Gi0/1 port on SD would become a designated forwarding port. This is because the SB Fa0/3 port is a designed root port and you must have a forwarding port on a network segment! This leaves us with the Fa0/2 port on SB. Since it isn't a root port or designated forwarding port, it will be placed into blocking mode, which will prevent looks in our network.

Let's take a look at this example network when it has converged in Figure 15.12.

FIGURE 15.12   RSTP example 1 answer

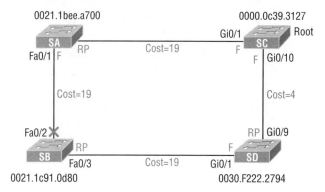

If this isn't clear and still seems confusing, just remember to always tackle this process following these three steps:

1. Find your root bridge by looking at bridge IDs.

2. Determine your root ports by finding the lowest path cost to the root bridge.

3. Find your designated ports by looking at bridge IDs.

As usual, the best way to nail this down is to practice, so let's explore another scenario, shown in Figure 15.13.

FIGURE 15.13   RSTP example 2

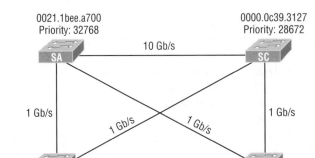

So which bridge is our root bridge? Checking priorities first tells us that SC is the root bridge, which means all ports on SC are designated forwarding ports. Now we need to find our root ports.

We can quickly see that SA has a 10-gigabit port to SC, so that would be a port cost of 2, and it would be our root port. SD has a direct Gigabit Ethernet port to SC, so that would be the root port for SD with a port cost of 4. SB's best path would also be the direct Gigabit Ethernet port to SC with a port cost of 4.

Now that we've determined our root bridge and found the three root ports we need, we've got to find our designated ports next. Whatever is left over simply goes into the discarding role. Let's take a look at Figure 15.14 and see what we have.

FIGURE 15.14   RSTP example 2, answer 1

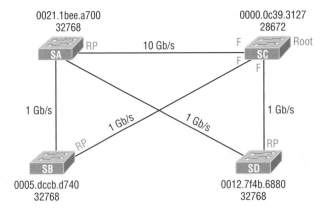

All right, it looks like there are two links to choose between to find one designated port per segment. Let's start with the link between SA and SD. Which one has the best bridge

ID? They're both running the same default priority, so by looking at the MAC address, we can see that SD has the better bridge ID (lower), so the SA port toward SD will go into a discarding role, or will it? The SD port will go into discarding mode, because the link from SA to the root has the lowest accumulated path costs to the root bridge, and that is used before the bridge ID in this circumstance. It makes sense to let the bridge with the fastest path to the root bridge be a designated forwarding port. Let's talk about this a little more in depth.

As you know, once your root bridge and root ports have been chosen, you're left with finding your designated ports. Anything left over goes into a discarding role. But how are the designated ports chosen? Is it just bridge ID? Here are the rules:

1. To choose the switch that will forward on the segment, we select the switch with the lowest accumulated path cost to the root bridge. We want the fast path to the root bridge.

2. If there is a tie on the accumulated path cost from both switches to the root bridge, then we'll use bridge ID, which was what we used in our previous example (but not with this latest RSTP example; not with a 10-Gigabit Ethernet link to the root bridge available!).

3. Port priorities can be set manually if we want a specific port chosen. The default priority is 32, but we can lower that if needed.

4. If there are two links between switches, and the bridge ID and priority are tied, the port with the lowest number will be chosen—for example, Fa0/1 would be chosen over Fa0/2.

Let's take a look at our answer now, but before we do, can you find the forwarding port between SA and SB? Take a look at Figure 15.15 for the answer.

FIGURE 15.15   RSTP example 2, answer 2

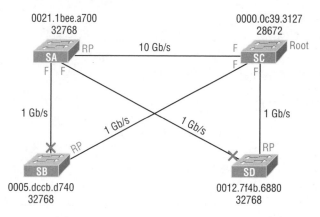

Again, to get the right answer to this question we're going to let the switch on the network segment with the lowest accumulated path cost to the root bridge forward on that segment. This is definitely SA, meaning the SB port goes into discarding role—not so hard at all!

802.1s (MSTP)

Multiple Spanning Tree Protocol (MSTP), also known as IEEE 802.ls, gives us the same fast convergence as RSTP but reduces the number of required STP instances by allowing us to map multiple VLANs with the same traffic flow requirements into the same spanning-tree instance. It essentially allows us to create VLAN sets and basically is a spanning-tree protocol that runs on top of another spanning-tree protocol.

So clearly, you would opt to use MSTP over RSTP when you've got a configuration involving lots of VLANs, resulting in CPU and memory requirements that would be too high otherwise. But there's no free lunch—though MSTP reduces the demands of Rapid PVST+, you've got to configure it correctly because MSTP does nothing by itself!

Modifying and Verifying the Bridge ID

To verify spanning tree on a Cisco switch, just use the command show spanning-tree. From its output, we can determine our root bridge, priorities, root ports, and designated and blocking/discarding ports.

Let's use the same simple three-switch network we used earlier as the base to play around with the configuration of STP. Figure 15.16 shows the network we'll work with in this section.

FIGURE 15.16   Our simple three-switch network

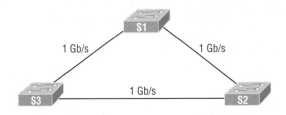

Let's start by taking a look at the output from S1:

```
S1#sh spanning-tree vlan 1
VLAN0001
  Spanning tree enabled protocol ieee
  Root ID    Priority    32769
             Address     0001.42A7.A603
             This bridge is the root
             Hello Time  2 sec  Max Age 20 sec  Forward Delay 15 sec

  Bridge ID  Priority    32769  (priority 32768 sys-id-ext 1)
             Address     0001.42A7.A603 him
```

```
            Hello Time  2 sec  Max Age 20 sec  Forward Delay 15 sec
            Aging Time  20


Interface         Role Sts Cost      Prio.Nbr Type
---------------- ---- --- --------- -------- -------------------------------
Gi1/1             Desg FWD 4         128.25   P2p
Gi1/2             Desg FWD 4         128.26   P2p
```

First, we can see that we're running the IEEE 802.1d STP version by default, and don't forget that this is really 802.1d PVST+! Looking at the output, we can see that S1 is the root bridge for VLAN 1. When you use this command, the top information is about the root bridge, and the Bridge ID output refers to the bridge you're looking at. In this example, they are one and the same. Notice the sys-id-ext 1 (for VLAN 1). This is the 12-bit PVST+ field that is placed into the BPDU so it can carry multiple-VLAN information. You add the priority and sys-id-ext to come up with the true priority for the VLAN. We can also see from the output that both Gigabit Ethernet interfaces are designated forwarding ports. You will not see a blocked/discarding port on a root bridge. Now let's take a look at S3's output:

```
S3#sh spanning-tree
VLAN0001
  Spanning tree enabled protocol ieee
  Root ID    Priority    32769
             Address     0001.42A7.A603
             Cost        4
             Port        26(GigabitEthernet1/2)
             Hello Time  2 sec  Max Age 20 sec  Forward Delay 15 sec

  Bridge ID  Priority    32769   (priority 32768 sys-id-ext 1)
             Address     000A.41D5.7937
             Hello Time  2 sec  Max Age 20 sec  Forward Delay 15 sec
             Aging Time  20


Interface         Role Sts Cost      Prio.Nbr Type
---------------- ---- --- --------- -------- -------------------------------
Gi1/1             Desg FWD 4         128.25   P2p
Gi1/2             Root FWD 4         128.26   P2p
```

Looking at the Root ID, it's easy to see that S3 isn't the root bridge, but the output tells us it's a cost of 4 to get to the root bridge and also that it's located out port 26 of the switch (Gi1/2). This tells us that the root bridge is one Gigabit Ethernet link away, which we already know is S1, but we can confirm this with the show cdp neighbors command:

```
Switch#sh cdp nei
Capability Codes: R - Router, T - Trans Bridge, B - Source Route Bridge
                  S - Switch, H - Host, I - IGMP, r - Repeater, P - Phone
Device ID   Local Intrfce   Holdtme   Capability   Platform   Port ID
S3          Gig 1/1         135          S          2960       Gig 1/1
S1          Gig 1/2         135          S          2960       Gig 1/1
```

That's how simple it is to find your root bridge if you don't have the nice figure as we do. Use the show spanning-tree command, find your root port, and then use the show cdp neighbors command. Let's see what S2's output has to tell us now:

```
S2#sh spanning-tree
VLAN0001
  Spanning tree enabled protocol ieee
  Root ID    Priority    32769
             Address     0001.42A7.A603
             Cost        4
             Port        26(GigabitEthernet1/2)
             Hello Time  2 sec  Max Age 20 sec  Forward Delay 15 sec

  Bridge ID  Priority    32769  (priority 32768 sys-id-ext 1)
             Address     0030.F222.2794
             Hello Time  2 sec  Max Age 20 sec  Forward Delay 15 sec
             Aging Time  20

Interface         Role Sts Cost      Prio.Nbr Type
---------------- ---- --- --------- -------- --------------------------------
Gi1/1             Altn BLK 4         128.25   P2p
Gi1/2             Root FWD 4         128.26   P2p
```

We're certainly not looking at a root bridge since we're seeing a blocked port, which is S2's connection to S3!

Let's have some fun by making S2 the root bridge for VLAN 2 and for VLAN 3. Here's how easy that is to do:

```
S2#sh spanning-tree vlan 2
VLAN0002
  Spanning tree enabled protocol ieee
  Root ID    Priority    32770
             Address     0001.42A7.A603
```

```
          Cost        4
          Port        26(GigabitEthernet1/2)
          Hello Time  2 sec  Max Age 20 sec  Forward Delay 15 sec

Bridge ID  Priority    32770  (priority 32768 sys-id-ext 2)
          Address     0030.F222.2794
          Hello Time  2 sec  Max Age 20 sec  Forward Delay 15 sec
          Aging Time  20

Interface         Role Sts Cost      Prio.Nbr Type
----------------  ---- --- --------- -------- --------------------------------
Gi1/1             Altn BLK 4         128.25   P2p
Gi1/2             Root FWD 4         128.26   P2p
```

We can see that the root bridge cost is 4, meaning that the root bridge is one gigabit link away. One more key factor I want to talk about before making S2 the root bridge for VLANs 2 and 3 is the sys-id-ext, which shows up as 2 in this output because this output is for VLAN 2. This sys-id-ext is added to the bridge priority, which in this case is 32768 + 2, which makes the priority 32770. Now that you understand what that output is telling us, let's make S2 the root bridge:

```
S2(config)#spanning-tree vlan 2 ?
  priority  Set the bridge priority for the spanning tree
  root      Configure switch as root
  <cr>
S2(config)#spanning-tree vlan 2 priority ?
  <0-61440>  bridge priority in increments of 4096
S2(config)#spanning-tree vlan 2 priority 16384
```

You can set the priority to any value from 0 through 61440 in increments of 4096. Setting it to zero (0) means that the switch will always be a root as long as it has a lower MAC address than another switch that also has its bridge ID set to 0. If you want to set a switch to be the root bridge for every VLAN in your network, then you have to change the priority for each VLAN, with 0 being the lowest priority you can use. But trust me—it's never a good idea to set all switches to a priority of 0!

Furthermore, you don't actually need to change priorities because there is yet another way to configure the root bridge. Take a look:

```
S2(config)#spanning-tree vlan 3 root ?
  primary    Configure this switch as primary root for this spanning tree
  secondary  Configure switch as secondary root
S2(config)#spanning-tree vlan 3 root primary
S3(config)#spanning-tree vlan 3 root secondary
```

Notice that you can set a bridge to either primary or secondary—very cool! If both the primary and secondary switches go down, then the next highest priority will take over as root.

Let's check to see if S2 is actually the root bridge for VLANs 2 and 3 now:

```
S2#sh spanning-tree vlan 2
VLAN0002
  Spanning tree enabled protocol ieee
  Root ID    Priority    16386
             Address     0030.F222.2794
             This bridge is the root
             Hello Time  2 sec  Max Age 20 sec  Forward Delay 15 sec

  Bridge ID  Priority    16386  (priority 16384 sys-id-ext 2)
             Address     0030.F222.2794
             Hello Time  2 sec  Max Age 20 sec  Forward Delay 15 sec
             Aging Time  20

Interface         Role Sts Cost     Prio.Nbr Type
----------------  ---- --- -------- -------- -------------------------------
Gi1/1             Desg FWD 4        128.25   P2p
Gi1/2             Desg FWD 4        128.26   P2p
```

Nice—S2 is the root bridge for VLAN 2, with a priority of 16386 (16384 + 2). Let's take a look to see the root bridge for VLAN 3. I'll use a different command for that this time. Check it out:

```
S2#sh spanning-tree summary
Switch is in pvst mode
Root bridge for: VLAN0002 VLAN0003
Extended system ID          is enabled
Portfast Default            is disabled
PortFast BPDU Guard Default is disabled
Portfast BPDU Filter Default is disabled
Loopguard Default           is disabled
EtherChannel misconfig guard is disabled
UplinkFast                  is disabled
BackboneFast                is disabled
Configured Pathcost method used is short

Name                    Blocking Listening Learning Forwarding STP Active
--------------------- -------- --------- -------- ---------- ----------
VLAN0001                     1         0        0          1          2
```

VLAN0002	0	0	0	2	2
VLAN0003	0	0	0	2	2
----------------------	--------	---------	--------	----------	----------
3 vlans	1	0	0	5	6

The preceding output tells us that S2 is the root for the two VLANs, but we can see we have a blocked port for VLAN 1 on S2, so it's not the root bridge for VLAN 1. This is because there's another bridge with a better bridge ID for VLAN 1 than S2's.

One last burning question: How do you enable RSTP on a Cisco switch? Well, doing that is actually the easiest part of this chapter! Take a look:

```
S2(config)#spanning-tree mode rapid-pvst
```

Is that really all there is to it? Yes, because it's a global command, not per VLAN. Let's verify we're running RSTP now:

```
S2#sh spanning-tree
VLAN0001
  Spanning tree enabled protocol rstp
  Root ID    Priority    32769
             Address     0001.42A7.A603
             Cost        4
             Port        26(GigabitEthernet1/2)
             Hello Time  2 sec  Max Age 20 sec  Forward Delay 15 sec
[output cut
S2#sh spanning-tree summary
Switch is in rapid-pvst mode
Root bridge for: VLAN0002 VLAN0003
```

Looks like we're set! We're running RSTP, S1 is our root bridge for VLAN 1, and S2 is the root bridge for VLANs 2 and 3. I know this doesn't seem hard, and it really isn't, but you still need to practice what we've covered so far in this chapter to really get your skills solid!

Spanning-Tree Failure Consequences

Clearly, there will be consequences when a routing protocol fails on a single router, but mainly, you'll just lose connectivity to the networks directly connected to that router, and it usually does not affect the rest of your network. This definitely makes it easier to troubleshoot and fix the issue!

There are two failure types with STP. One of them causes the same type of issue I mentioned with a routing protocol; when certain ports have been placed in a blocking state they should be forwarding on a network segment instead. This situation makes the network segment unusable, but the rest of the network will still be working. But what happens when blocked ports are placed into forwarding state when they should be blocking? Let's work through this second failure issue now, using the same layout we used in the last section. Let's start with Figure 15.17 and then find out what happens when STP fails. Squeamish readers be warned—this isn't pretty!

Looking at Figure 15.17, what do you think will happen if SD transitions its blocked port to the forwarding state?

FIGURE 15.17 STP stopping loops

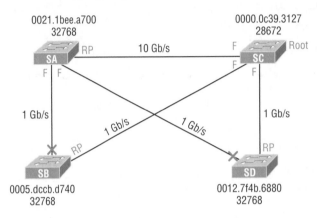

Clearly, the consequences to the entire network will be pretty devastating! Frames that already had a destination address recorded in the MAC address table of the switches are forwarded to the port they're associated with; however, any broadcast, multicast, and unicasts not in the CAM are now in an endless loop. Figure 15.18 shows us the carnage— when you see all the lights on each port blinking super-fast amber/green, this means serious errors are occurring, and lots of them!

FIGURE 15.18 STP failure

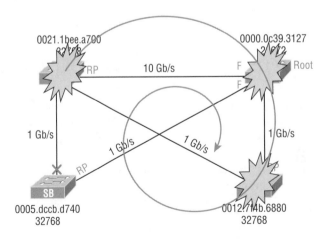

As frames begin building up on the network, the bandwidth starts getting saturated. The CPU percentage goes way up on the switches until they'll just give up and stop working completely, and all this within a few seconds!

Here is a list of the problems that will occur in a failed STP network that you must be aware of and you must be able to find in your production network—and of course, you must know them to meet the exam objectives:

- The load on all links begins increasing and more and more frames enter the loop. Remember, this loop affects all the other links in the network because these frames are always flooded out all ports. This scenario is a little less dire if the loop occurs within a single VLAN. In that case, the snag will be isolated to ports only in that VLAN membership, plus all trunk links that carry information for that VLAN.

- If you have more than one loop, traffic will increase on the switches because all the circling frames actually get duplicated. Switches basically receive a frame, make a copy of it, and send it out all ports. And they do this over and over and over again with the same frame, as well as for any new ones!

- The MAC address table is now completely unstable. It no longer knows where any source MAC address hosts are actually located because the same source address comes in via multiple ports on the switch.

- With the overwhelmingly high load on the links and the CPUs, now possibly at 100% or close to that, the devices become unresponsive, making it impossible to troubleshoot— it's a terrible thing!

At this point your only option is to systematically remove every redundant link between switches until you can find the source of the problem. And don't freak because, eventually, your ravaged network will calm down and come back to life after STP converges. Your fried switches will regain consciousness, but the network will need some serious therapy, so you're not out of the woods yet!

Now is when you start troubleshooting to find out what caused the disaster in the first place. A good strategy is to place the redundant links back into your network one at a time and wait to see when a problem begins to occur. You could have a failing switch port, or even a dead switch. Once you've replaced all your redundant links, you need to carefully monitor the network and have a back-out plan to quickly isolate the problem if it reoccurs. You don't want to go through this again!

You're probably wondering how to prevent these STP problems from ever darkening your doorstep in the first place. Well, just hang on, because after the next section, I'll tell you all about EtherChannel, which can stop ports from being placed in the blocked/discarding state on redundant links to save the day! But before we add more links to our switches and then bundle them, let's talk about PortFast.

PortFast and BPDU Guard

If you have a server or other devices connected into your switch that you're totally sure won't create a switching loop if STP is disabled, you can use a Cisco proprietary extension to the 802.1d standard called PortFast on these ports. With this tool, the port won't spend the usual 50 seconds to come up into forwarding mode while STP is converging, which is what makes it so cool.

Since ports will transition from blocking to forwarding state immediately, PortFast can prevent our hosts from being potentially unable to receive a DHCP address due to STP's slow convergence. If the host's DHCP request times out, or if every time you plug a host in you're just tired of looking at the switch port being amber for almost a minute before it transitions to forwarding state and turns green, PortFast can really help you out!

Figure 15.19 illustrates a network with three switches, each with a trunk to each of the others and a host and server off the S1 switch.

FIGURE 15.19   PortFast

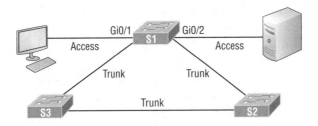

We can use PortFast on the ports on S1 to help them transition to the STP forwarding state immediately upon connecting to the switch.

Here are the commands, first from global config mode—they're pretty simple:

```
S1(config)#spanning-tree portfast ?
  bpdufilter  Enable portfast bdpu filter on this switch
  bpduguard   Enable portfast bpdu guard on this switch
  default     Enable portfast by default on all access ports
```

If you were to type spanning-tree portfast default, you would enable all nontrunking ports with PortFast. From interface mode, you can be more specific, which is the better way to go:

```
S1(config-if)#spanning-tree portfast ?
  disable  Disable portfast for this interface
  trunk    Enable portfast on the interface even in trunk mode
  <cr>
```

From interface mode you can actually configure PortFast on a trunk port, but you would do that only if the port connects to a server or router, not to another switch, so we won't use that here. So let's take a look at the message I get when I turn on PortFast on interface Gi0/1:

```
S1#config t
S1#config)#int range gi0/1 - 2
```

```
S1(config-if)#spanning-tree portfast
%Warning: portfast should only be enabled on ports connected to a single
  host. Connecting hubs, concentrators, switches, bridges, etc... to this
  interface  when portfast is enabled, can cause temporary bridging loops.
  Use with CAUTION

%Portfast has been configured on GigabitEthernet0/1 but will only
  have effect when the interface is in a non-trunking mode.
```

PortFast is enabled on port Gi0/1 and Gi0/2, but notice that you get a pretty long message that's essentially telling you to be careful. This is because when using PortFast, you definitely don't want to create a network loop by plugging another switch or hub into a port that's also configured with PortFast! Why? Because if you let this happen, even though the network may still sort of work, data will pass super slowly, and worse, it could take you a really long time to find the source of the problem, making you very unpopular. So proceed with caution!

At this juncture, you would be happy to know that there are some safeguard commands to have handy when using PortFast just in case someone causes a loop in a port that's configured with PortFast enabled. Let's talk about a really key safeguard command now.

BPDU Guard

If you turn on PortFast for a switch port, it's a really good idea to turn on BPDU Guard as well. In fact, it's such a great idea, I personally feel that it should be enabled by default whenever a port is configured with PortFast!

This is because if a switch port that has PortFast enabled receives a BPDU on that port, it will place the port into error disabled (shutdown) state, effectively preventing anyone from accidentally connecting another switch or hub port into a switch port configured with PortFast. Basically, you're preventing (guarding) your network from being severely crippled or even brought down. So let's configure our S1 interface, which is already configured with PortFast, with BPDU Guard now—it's easy!

Here's how to set it globally:

```
S1(config)# spanning-tree portfast bpduguard default
```

And specifically on an interface:

```
S1(config-if)#spanning-tree bpduguard enable
```

It's important to know that you would only configure this command on your access layer switches—switches where users are directly connected.

Real World Scenario

Hedging My Bets Created Bad Switch Ports during the Super Bowl

A junior admin called me frantically telling me all switch ports had just gone bad on the core switch, which was located at the data center where I was lead consultant for a data center upgrade. Now these things happen, but keep in mind that I just happened to be at a Super Bowl party having a great time watching my favorite team play in the "Big One" when I received this call! So I took a deep breath to refocus. I needed to find out some key information to determine just how bad the situation really was, and my client was in as big of a hurry as I was to get to a solution!

First I asked the junior admin exactly what he did. Of course, he said, "Nothing, I swear!" I figured that's what he'd say, so I pressed him for more info and finally asked for stats on the switch. The admin told me that all the ports on the 10/100/1000 line card went amber at the same time—finally some information I could use! I confirmed that, as suspected, these ports trunked to uplink distribution switches. Wow—this was not good!

At this point, though, I found it hard to believe that all 24 ports would suddenly go bad, but it's possible, so I asked if he had a spare card to try. He told me that he had already put in the new card but the same thing was still happening. Well, it's not the card, or the ports, but maybe something happened with the other switches. I knew there were a lot of switches involved, so someone must have screwed something up to make this catastrophe happen! Or, maybe the fiber distribution closet went down somehow? If so, how? Was there a fire in the closet or something? Some serious internal shenanigans would be the only answer if that were the cause!

So remaining ever patient (because, to quote Dr. House, "Patients lie"), I again had to ask the admin exactly what he did, and sure enough, he finally admitted that he tried to plug his personal laptop into the core switch so he could watch the Super Bowl, and he quickly added, "...but that's it, I didn't do anything else!" I'll skip over the fact that this guy was about to have the ugliest Monday ever, but something still didn't make sense, and here's why.

Knowing that the ports on that card would all connect to distribution switches, I configured the ports with PortFast so they wouldn't have to transition through the STP process. And because I wanted to make sure no one plugged a switch into any of those ports, I enabled BPDU Guard on the entire line card.

But a host would not bring down those ports, so I asked him if he had plugged in the laptop directly or used something in between. He admitted that he had indeed used another switch because, turns out, there were lots of people from the office who wanted to plug into the core switch and watch the game too. Was he kidding me? The security policy wouldn't allow connecting from their offices, so wouldn't you think they'd consider the core even more off-limits? Some people!

But wait... This doesn't explain all ports turning amber, because only the one he plugged into should be doing that. It took me a second, but I figured out what he did and finally got him to confess. When he plugged the switch in, the port turned amber so he thought it went bad. So what do think he did? Well, if at first you don't succeed, try, try again, and that's just what he did—he actually kept trying ports—all 24 of them to be exact! Now that's what I call determined!

Sad to say, I got back to the party in time just to watch my team lose in the last few minutes! A dark day, indeed!

EtherChannel

Know that almost all Ethernet networks today will typically have multiple links between switches because this kind of design provides redundancy and resiliency. On a physical design that includes multiple links between switches, STP will do its job and put a port or ports into blocking mode. In addition to that, routing protocols like OSPF and EIGRP could see all these redundant links as individual ones, depending on the configuration, which can mean an increase in routing overhead.

We can gain the benefits from multiple links between switches by using port channeling. EtherChannel is a port channel technology that was originally developed by Cisco as a switch-to-switch technique for grouping several Fast Ethernet or Gigabit Ethernet ports into one logical channel.

Also important to note is that once your port channel (EtherChannel) is up and working, layer 2 STP and layer 3 routing protocols will treat those bundled links as a single one, which would stop STP from performing blocking. An additional nice result is that because the routing protocols now only see this as a single link, a single adjacency across the link can be formed—elegant!

Figure 15.20 shows how a network would look if we had four connections between switches, before and after configuring port channels.

FIGURE 15.20   Before and after port channels

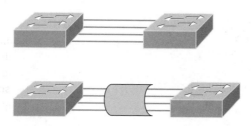

Now as usual, there's the Cisco version and the IEEE version of port channel negotiation protocols to choose from—take your pick. Cisco's version is called Port Aggregation Protocol (PAgP), and the IEEE 802.3ad standard is called Link Aggregation Control Protocol (LACP). Both versions work equally well, but the way you configure each is slightly different. Keep in mind that both PAgP and LACP are negotiation protocols and that EtherChannel can actually be statically configured without PAgP or LACP. Still, it's better to use one of these protocols to help with compatibility issues as well as to manage link additions and failures between two switches.

Cisco EtherChannel allows us to bundle up to eight ports active between switches. The links must have the same speed, duplex setting, and VLAN configuration—in other words, you can't mix interface types and configurations into the same bundle.

There are a few differences in configuring PAgP and LACP, but first, let's go over some terms so you don't get confused:

Port channeling   Refers to combining two to eight Fast Ethernet or two Gigabit Ethernet ports together between two switches into one aggregated logical link to achieve more bandwidth and resiliency.

EtherChannel   Cisco's proprietary term for port channeling.

PAgP   This is a Cisco proprietary port channel negotiation protocol that aids in the automatic creation for EtherChannel links. All links in the bundle must match the same parameters (speed, duplex, VLAN info), and when PAgP identifies matched links, it groups the links into an EtherChannel. This is then added to STP as a single bridge port. At this point, PAgP's job is to send packets every 30 seconds to manage the link for consistency, any link additions, and failures.

LACP (802.3ad)   This has the exact same purpose as PAgP, but it's nonproprietary so it can work between multi-vendor networks.

`channel-group`   This is a command on Ethernet interfaces used to add the specified interface to a single EtherChannel. The number following this command is the port channel ID.

`interface port-channel`   Here's a command that creates the bundled interface. Ports can be added to this interface with the `channel-group` command. Keep in mind that the interface number must match the group number.

Now let's see if you can make some sense out of all these terms by actually configuring something!

Configuring and Verifying Port Channels

Let's use Figure 15.21 for our simple example of how to configure port channels.

FIGURE 15.21   EtherChannel example

You can enable your channel-group for each channel by setting the channel mode for each interface to either active or passive if using LACP. When a port is configured in passive mode, it will respond to the LACP packets it receives, but it won't initiate an LACP negotiation. When a port is configured for active mode, the port initiates negotiations with other ports by sending LACP packets.

Let me show you a simple example of configuring port channels and then verifying them. First I'll go to global configuration mode and create a port channel interface, and then I'll add this port channel to the physical interfaces.

Remember, all parameters and configurations of the ports must be the same, so I'll start by trunking the interfaces before I configure EtherChannel, like this:

```
S1(config)#int range g0/1 - 2
S1(config-if-range)#switchport trunk encapsulation dot1q
S1(config-if-range)#switchport mode trunk
```

All ports in your bundles must be configured the same, so I'll configure both sides with the same trunking configuration. Now I can assign these ports to a bundle:

```
S1(config-if-range)#channel-group 1 mode ?
  active     Enable LACP unconditionally
  auto       Enable PAgP only if a PAgP device is detected
  desirable  Enable PAgP unconditionally
  on         Enable Etherchannel only
  passive    Enable LACP only if a LACP device is detected
S1(config-if-range)#channel-group 1 mode active
S1(config-if-range)#exit
```

To configure the IEEE nonproprietary LACP, I'll use the active or passive command; if I wanted to use Cisco's PAgP, I'd use the auto or desirable command. You can't mix and match these on either end of the bundle, and really, it doesn't matter which one you use in a pure Cisco environment, as long as you configure them the same on both ends (setting the mode to on would be statically configuring your EtherChannel bundle).

At this point in the configuration, I'd have to set the mode to active on the S2 interfaces if I wanted the bundle to come up with LACP because, again, all parameters must be the same on both ends of the link. Let's configure our port channel interface, which was created when we used the channel-group command:

```
S1(config)#int port-channel 1
S1(config-if)#switchport trunk encapsulation dot1q
S1(config-if)#switchport mode trunk
S1(config-if)#switchport trunk allowed vlan 1,2,3
```

Notice that I set the same trunking method under the port channel interface as I did the physical interfaces, as well as VLAN information too. Nicely, all command performed under the port-channel are inherited at the interface level, so you can just easily configure the port-channel with all parameters.

Time to configure the interfaces, channel groups, and port channel interface on the S2 switch:

```
S2(config)#int range g0/13 - 14
S2(config-if-range)#switchport trunk encapsulation dot1q
S2(config-if-range)#switchport mode trunk
S2(config-if-range)#channel-group 1 mode active
S2(config-if-range)#exit
S2(config)#int port-channel 1
S2(config-if)#switchport trunk encapsulation dot1q
S2(config-if)#switchport mode trunk
S2(config-if)#switchport trunk allowed vlan 1,2,3
```

On each switch, I configured the ports I wanted to bundle with the same configuration, then created the port channel. After that, I added the ports into the port channel with the channel-group command.

Remember, for LACP we'll use either active/active on each side of the bundle or active/passive, but you can't use passive/passive. Same goes for PAgP; you can use desirable/desirable or auto/desirable but not auto/auto.

Let's verify our EtherChannel with a few commands. We'll start with the show etherchannel port-channel command to see information about a specific port channel interface:

```
S2#sh etherchannel port-channel
              Channel-group listing:
              ----------------------


Group: 1
----------
              Port-channels in the group:
              --------------------------


Port-channel: Po1    (Primary Aggregator)
------------

Age of the Port-channel   = 00d:00h:46m:49s
Logical slot/port   = 2/1       Number of ports = 2
GC                  = 0x00000000      HotStandBy port = null
Port state          = Port-channel
Protocol            =    LACP
Port Security       = Disabled
```

```
Ports in the Port-channel:

Index  Load   Port   EC state          No of bits
------+------+------+-----------------+-----------
  0    00     Gig0/2  Active              0
  0    00     Gig0/1  Active              0
Time since last port bundled:    00d:00h:46m:47s    Gig0/1
S2#
```

Notice that we have one group and that we're running the IEEE LACP version of port channeling. We're in Active mode, and that Port-channel: Po1 interface has two physical interfaces. The heading Load is not the load over the interfaces, it's a hexadecimal value that decides which interface will be chosen to specify the flow of traffic.

The show etherchannel summary command displays one line of information per port channel:

```
S2#sh etherchannel summary
Flags:  D - down        P - in port-channel
        I - stand-alone s - suspended
        H - Hot-standby (LACP only)
        R - Layer3      S - Layer2
        U - in use      f - failed to allocate aggregator
        u - unsuitable for bundling
        w - waiting to be aggregated
        d - default port

Number of channel-groups in use: 1
Number of aggregators:          1

Group  Port-channel  Protocol    Ports
------+-------------+-----------+------------------------------------------------

1      Po1(SU)        LACP    Gig0/1(P) Gig0/2(P)
```

This command shows that we have one group, that we're running LACP, and Gig0/1 and Gig0/2 or (P), which means these ports are in port-channel mode. This command isn't really all that helpful unless you have multiple channel groups, but it does tell us our group is working well!

Layer 3 EtherChannel

One last item to discuss before we finish this chapter and that is layer 3 EtherChannel. You'd use layer 3 EtherChannel when connecting a switch to multiple ports on a router, for example. It's important to understand that you wouldn't put IP addresses under the physical interfaces of the router, instead you'd actually add the IP address of the bundle under the logical port-channel interface.

Here is an example on how to create the logical port channel 1 and assign 20.2.2.2 as its IP address:

```
Router#config t
Router(config)#int port-channel 1
Router(config-if)#ip address 20.2.2.2 255.255.255.0
```

Now we need to add the physical ports into port channel 1:

```
Router(config-if)#int range g0/0-1
Router(config-if-range)#channel-group 1
GigabitEthernet0/0 added as member-1 to port-channel1
GigabitEthernet0/1 added as member-2 to port-channel1
```

Now let's take a look at the running-config. Notice there are no IP addresses under the physical interface of the router:

```
!
interface Port-channel1
 ip address 20.2.2.2 255.255.255.0
 load-interval 30
!
 interface GigabitEthernet0/0
 no ip address
 load-interval 30
 duplex auto
 speed auto
 channel-group 1
!
 interface GigabitEthernet0/1
 no ip address
 load-interval 30
 duplex auto
 speed auto
 channel-group 1
```

Summary

This chapter was all about switching technologies, with a particular focus on the Spanning Tree Protocol (STP) and its evolution to newer versions like RSTP and then Cisco's PVST+.

You learned about the problems that can occur if you have multiple links between bridges (switches) and the solutions attained with STP.

I also talked about and demonstrated issues that can occur if you have multiple links between bridges (switches), plus how to solve these problems by using the Spanning Tree Protocol (STP).

I covered a detailed configuration of Cisco's Catalyst switches, including verifying the configuration, setting the Cisco STP extensions, and changing the root bridge by setting a bridge priority.

Finally, we discussed, configured, and verified the EtherChannel technology that helps us bundle multiple links between switches.

Exam Essentials

Understand the main purpose of the Spanning Tree Protocol in a switched LAN.   The main purpose of STP is to prevent switching loops in a network with redundant switched paths.

Remember the states of STP.   The purpose of the blocking state is to prevent the use of looped paths. A port in listening state prepares to forward data frames without populating the MAC address table. A port in learning state populates the MAC address table but doesn't forward data frames. A port in forwarding state sends and receives all data frames on the bridged port. Also, a port in the disabled state is virtually nonoperational.

Remember the command `show spanning-tree`.   You must be familiar with the command `show spanning-tree` and how to determine the root bridge of each VLAN. Also, you can use the `show spanning-tree summary` command to help you get a quick glimpse of your STP network and root bridges.

Understand what PortFast and BPDU Guard provide.   PortFast allows a port to transition to the forwarding state immediately upon a connection. Because you don't want other switches connecting to this port, BPDU Guard will shut down a PortFast port if it receives a BPDU.

Understand what EtherChannel is and how to configure it.   EtherChannel allows you to bundle links to get more bandwidth, instead of allowing STP to shut down redundant ports. You can configure Cisco's PAgP or the IEEE version, LACP, by creating a port channel interface and assigning the port channel group number to the interfaces you are bundling.

Written Lab 15

You can find the answers to this lab in Appendix A, "Answers to Written Labs."
   Write the answers to the following questions:

1.   Which of the following is Cisco proprietary: LACP or PAgP?

2.   What command will show you the STP root bridge for a VLAN?

3. What standard is RSTP PVST+ based on?

4. Which protocol is used in a layer 2 network to maintain a loop-free network?

5. Which proprietary Cisco STP extension would put a switch port into error disabled mode if a BPDU is received on this port?

6. You want to configure a switch port to not transition through the STP port states but to go immediately to forwarding mode. What command will you use on a per-port basis?

7. What command will you use to see information about a specific port channel interface?

8. What command can you use to set a switch so that it will be the root bridge for VLAN 3 over any other switch?

9. You need to find the VLANs for which your switch is the root bridge. What two commands can you use?

10. What are the two modes you can set with LACP?

Hands-on Labs

In this section, you will configure and verify STP, as well as configure PortFast and BPDU Guard, and finally, bundle links together with EtherChannel.

Note that the labs in this chapter were written to be used with real equipment using 2960 switches. However, you can use the free LammleSim IOS version simulator or Cisco's Packet Tracer to run through these labs.

The labs in this chapter are as follows:

Lab 15.1: Verifying STP and Finding Your Root Bridge

Lab 15.2: Configuring and Verifying Your Root Bridge

Lab 15.3: Configuring PortFast and BPDU Guard

Lab 15.4: Configuring and Verifying EtherChannel

We'll use the following illustration for all four labs:

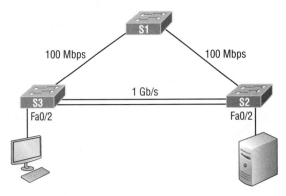

Hands-on Lab 15.1: Verifying STP and Finding Your Root Bridge

This lab will assume that you have added VLANs 2 and 3 to each of your switches and all of your links are trunked.

1. From one of your switches, use the show spanning-tree vlan 2 command. Verify the output.

```
S3#sh spanning-tree vlan 2
VLAN0002
  Spanning tree enabled protocol ieee
  Root ID    Priority    32770
             Address     0001.C9A5.8748
             Cost        19
             Port        1(FastEthernet0/1)
             Hello Time  2 sec  Max Age 20 sec  Forward Delay 15 sec

  Bridge ID  Priority    32770   (priority 32768 sys-id-ext 2)
             Address     0004.9A04.ED97
             Hello Time  2 sec  Max Age 20 sec  Forward Delay 15 sec
             Aging Time  20

Interface         Role Sts Cost      Prio.Nbr Type
---------------- ---- --- --------- -------- --------------------------------
Fa0/1             Root FWD 19        128.1    P2p
Fa0/2             Desg FWD 19        128.2    P2p
Gi1/1             Altn BLK 4         128.25   P2p
Gi1/2             Altn BLK 4         128.26   P2p
```

Notice that S3 is not the root bridge, so to find your root bridge, just follow the root port and see what bridge is connected to that port. Port Fa0/1 is the root port with a cost of 19, which means the switch that is off the Fa0/1 port is the root port connecting to the root bridge because it is a cost of 19, meaning one Fast Ethernet link away.

2. Find the bridge that is off of Fa0/1, which will be our root.

```
S3#sh cdp neighbors
Capability Codes: R - Router, T - Trans Bridge, B - Source Route Bridge
                  S - Switch, H - Host, I - IGMP, r - Repeater, P - Phone
Device ID    Local Intrfce   Holdtme   Capability   Platform   Port ID
S1           Fas 0/1         158          S          2960       Fas 0/1
S2           Gig 1/1         151          S          2960       Gig 1/1
```

S2	Gig 1/2	151	S	2960	Gig 1/2	

```
S3#
```

Notice that S1 is connected to the local interface Fa0/1, so let's go to S1 and verify our root bridge.

3. Verify the root bridge for each of the three VLANs. From S1, use the show spanning-tree summary command.

```
S1#sh spanning-tree summary
Switch is in pvst mode
Root bridge for: default VLAN0002 VLAN0003
Extended system ID         is enabled
Portfast Default           is disabled
PortFast BPDU Guard Default is disabled
Portfast BPDU Filter Default is disabled
Loopguard Default          is disabled
EtherChannel misconfig guard is disabled
UplinkFast                 is disabled
BackboneFast               is disabled
Configured Pathcost method used is short
```

Name	Blocking	Listening	Learning	Forwarding	STP Active
VLAN0001	0	0	0	2	2
VLAN0002	0	0	0	2	2
VLAN0003	0	0	0	2	2
3 vlans	0	0	0	6	6

```
S1#
```

Notice that S1 is the root bridge for all three VLANs.

4. Make note of all your root bridges, for all three VLANs, if you have more than one root bridge.

Hands-on Lab 15.2: Configuring and Verifying Your Root Bridge

This lab will assume you have performed Lab 1 and now know who your root bridge is for each VLAN.

1. Go to one of your non-root bridges and verify the bridge ID with the show spanning-tree vlan command.

```
S3#sh spanning-tree vlan 1
VLAN0001
  Spanning tree enabled protocol ieee
  Root ID    Priority    32769
             Address     0001.C9A5.8748
             Cost        19
             Port        1(FastEthernet0/1)
             Hello Time  2 sec  Max Age 20 sec  Forward Delay 15 sec

  Bridge ID  Priority    32769   (priority 32768 sys-id-ext 1)
             Address     0004.9A04.ED97
             Hello Time  2 sec  Max Age 20 sec  Forward Delay 15 sec
             Aging Time  20


Interface        Role Sts Cost      Prio.Nbr Type
---------------- ---- --- --------- -------- --------------------------------
Fa0/1            Root FWD 19        128.1    P2p
Fa0/2            Desg FWD 19        128.2    P2p
Gi1/1            Altn BLK 4         128.25   P2p
Gi1/2            Altn BLK 4         128.26   P2p
```

Notice that this bridge is not the root bridge for VLAN 1 and the root port is Fa0/1 with a cost of 19, which means the root bridge is directly connected one Fast Ethernet link away.

2. Make one of your non-root bridges the root bridge for VLAN 1. Use priority 16,384, which is lower than the 32,768 of the current root.

```
S3(config)#spanning-tree vlan 1 priority ?
  <0-61440>  bridge priority in increments of 4096
S3(config)#spanning-tree vlan 1 priority 16384
```

3. Verify the root bridge for VLAN 1.

```
S3#sh spanning-tree vlan 1
VLAN0001
  Spanning tree enabled protocol ieee
  Root ID    Priority    16385
             Address     0004.9A04.ED97
             This bridge is the root
             Hello Time  2 sec  Max Age 20 sec  Forward Delay 15 sec
```

```
Bridge ID  Priority    16385  (priority 16384 sys-id-ext 1)
           Address     0004.9A04.ED97
           Hello Time  2 sec  Max Age 20 sec  Forward Delay 15 sec
           Aging Time  20

Interface         Role Sts Cost      Prio.Nbr Type
----------------  ---- --- --------- -------- --------------------------------
Fa0/1             Desg FWD 19        128.1    P2p
Fa0/2             Desg FWD 19        128.2    P2p
Gi1/1             Desg FWD 4         128.25   P2p
Gi1/2             Desg FWD 4         128.26   P2p
```

Notice that this bridge is indeed the root and all ports are in Desg FWD mode.

Hands-on Lab 15.3: Configuring PortFast and BPDU Guard

This lab will have you configure ports on switches S3 and S2 to allow the PC and server to automatically go into forward mode when they connect into the port.

1. Connect to your switch that has a host connected and enable PortFast for the interface.

   ```
   S3#config t
   S3(config)#int fa0/2
   S3(config-if)#spanning-tree portfast
   %Warning: portfast should only be enabled on ports connected to a single
   host. Connecting hubs, concentrators, switches, bridges, etc... to this
   interface  when portfast is enabled, can cause temporary bridging loops.
   Use with CAUTION

   %Portfast has been configured on FastEthernet0/2 but will only
   have effect when the interface is in a non-trunking mode.
   ```

2. Verify that the switch port will be shut down if another switch Ethernet cable plugs into this port.

   ```
   S3(config-if)#spanning-tree bpduguard enable
   ```

3. Verify your configuration with the show running-config command.

   ```
   !
   interface FastEthernet0/2
    switchport mode trunk
    spanning-tree portfast
    spanning-tree bpduguard enable
   !
   ```

Hands-on Lab 15.4: Configuring and Verifying EtherChannel

This lab will have you configure the Cisco EtherChannel PAgP version on the switches used in this lab. Because I have preconfigured the switches, I have set up the trunks on all inter-switch ports. We'll use the Gigabit Ethernet ports between switches S3 and S2.

1. Configure the S3 switch with EtherChannel by creating a port channel interface.

    ```
    S3#config t
    S3(config)#inter port-channel 1
    ```

2. Configure the ports to be in the bundle with the channel-group command.

    ```
    S3(config-if)#int range g1/1 - 2
    S3(config-if-range)#channel-group 1 mode ?
      active     Enable LACP unconditionally
      auto       Enable PAgP only if a PAgP device is detected
      desirable  Enable PAgP unconditionally
      on         Enable Etherchannel only
      passive    Enable LACP only if a LACP device is detected
    S3(config-if-range)#channel-group 1 mode desirable
    ```

    I chose the PAgP desirable mode for the S3 switch.

3. Configure the S2 switch with EtherChannel, using the same parameters as S3.

    ```
    S2#config t
    S2(config)#interface port-channel 1
    S2(config-if)#int rang g1/1 - 2
    S2(config-if-range)#channel-group 1 mode desirable
    %LINK-5-CHANGED: Interface Port-channel 1, changed state to up

    %LINEPROTO-5-UPDOWN: Line protocol on Interface Port-channel 1, changed state
    to up
    ```

    Pretty simple, really. Just a couple of commands.

4. Verify with the show etherchannel port-channel command.

    ```
    S3#sh etherchannel port-channel
                    Channel-group listing:
                    ----------------------


    Group: 1
    ----------
                    Port-channels in the group:
                    --------------------------
    ```

```
Port-channel: Po1
------------


Age of the Port-channel   = 00d:00h:06m:43s
Logical slot/port   = 2/1       Number of ports = 2
GC                  = 0x00000000      HotStandBy port = null
Port state          = Port-channel
Protocol            =   PAGP
Port Security       = Disabled


Ports in the Port-channel:

Index   Load   Port    EC state          No of bits
------+------+------+------------------+-----------
  0     00     Gig1/1  Desirable-Sl        0
  0     00     Gig1/2  Desirable-Sl        0
Time since last port bundled:     00d:00h:01m:30s    Gig1/2
```

5. Verify with the show etherchannel summary command.

```
S3#sh etherchannel summary
Flags:  D - down        P - in port-channel
        I - stand-alone s - suspended
        H - Hot-standby (LACP only)
        R - Layer3      S - Layer2
        U - in use      f - failed to allocate aggregator
        u - unsuitable for bundling
        w - waiting to be aggregated
        d - default port


Number of channel-groups in use: 1
Number of aggregators:          1


Group  Port-channel  Protocol    Ports
------+-------------+-----------+----------------------------------

1      Po1(SU)          PAgP   Gig1/1(P) Gig1/2(P)
S3#
```

Review Questions

The following questions are designed to test your understanding of this chapter's material. For more information on how to get additional questions, please see www.lammle.com/ccna.

You can find the answers to these questions in Appendix B, "Answers to Review Questions."

1. You receive the following output from a switch:

```
S2#sh spanning-tree
VLAN0001
  Spanning tree enabled protocol rstp
  Root ID    Priority    32769
             Address     0001.42A7.A603
             Cost        4
             Port        26(GigabitEthernet1/2)
             Hello Time  2 sec  Max Age 20 sec  Forward Delay 15 sec
[output cut]
```

Which are true regarding this switch? (Choose two.)

   A. The switch is a root bridge.

   B. The switch is a non-root bridge.

   C. The root bridge is four switches away.

   D. The switch is running 802.1w.

   E. The switch is running STP PVST+.

2. You have configured your switches with the `spanning-tree vlan x root primary` and `spanning-tree vlan x root secondary` commands. Which of the following tertiary switch will take over if both switches fail?

   A. A switch with priority 4096

   B. A switch with priority 8192

   C. A switch with priority 12288

   D. A switch with priority 20480

3. Which of the following would you use to find the VLANs for which your switch is the root bridge? (Choose two.)

   A. `show spanning-tree`

   B. `show root all`

   C. `show spanning-tree port root VLAN`

   D. `show spanning-tree summary`

4. You want to run the new 802.1w on your switches. Which of the following would enable this protocol?

   A. `Switch(config)#spanning-tree mode rapid-pvst`

   B. `Switch#spanning-tree mode rapid-pvst`

   C. `Switch(config)#spanning-tree mode 802.1w`

   D. `Switch#spanning-tree mode 802.1w`

5. Which of the following is a layer 2 protocol used to maintain a loop-free network?

   A. VTP

   B. STP

   C. RIP

   D. CDP

6. Which statement describes a spanning-tree network that has converged?

   A. All switch and bridge ports are in the forwarding state.

   B. All switch and bridge ports are assigned as either root or designated ports.

   C. All switch and bridge ports are in either the forwarding or blocking state.

   D. All switch and bridge ports are either blocking or looping.

7. Which of the following modes enable LACP EtherChannel? (Choose two.)

   A. On

   B. Prevent

   C. Passive

   D. Auto

   E. Active

   F. Desirable

8. Which of the following are true regarding RSTP? (Choose three.)

   A. RSTP speeds the recalculation of the spanning tree when the layer 2 network topology changes.

   B. RSTP is an IEEE standard that redefines STP port roles, states, and BPDUs.

   C. RSTP is extremely proactive and very quick, and therefore it absolutely needs the 802.1 delay timers.

   D. RSTP (802.1w) supersedes 802.1d while remaining proprietary.

   E. All of the 802.1d terminology and most parameters have been changed.

   F. 802.1w is capable of reverting to 802.1d to interoperate with traditional switches on a per-port basis.

9. What does BPDU Guard perform?

   A. Makes sure the port is receiving BPDUs from the correct upstream switch.

   B. Makes sure the port is not receiving BPDUs from the upstream switch, only the root.

C. If a BPDU is received on a BPDU Guard port, PortFast is used to shut down the port.

D. Shuts down a port if a BPDU is seen on that port.

10. How many bits is the `sys-id-ext` field in a BPDU?

A. 4

B. 8

C. 12

D. 16

11. There are four connections between two switches running RSTP PVST+ and you want to figure out how to achieve higher bandwidth without sacrificing the resiliency that RSTP provides. What can you configure between these two switches to achieve higher bandwidth than the default configuration is already providing?

A. Set PortFast and BPDU Guard, which provides faster convergence.

B. Configure unequal cost load balancing with RSTP PVST+.

C. Place all four links into the same EtherChannel bundle.

D. Configure PPP and use multilink.

12. In which circumstance are multiple copies of the same unicast frame likely to be transmitted in a switched LAN?

A. During high-traffic periods

B. After broken links are reestablished

C. When upper-layer protocols require high reliability

D. In an improperly implemented redundant topology

13. You want to configure LACP. Which do you need to make sure are configured exactly the same on all switch interfaces you are using? (Choose three.)

A. Virtual MAC address

B. Port speeds

C. Duplex

D. PortFast enabled

E. VLAN information

14. Which of the following modes enable PAgP EtherChannel? (Choose two.)

A. On

B. Prevent

C. Passive

D. Auto

E. Active

F. Desirable

15. For this question, refer to the following illustration. SB's RP to the root bridge has failed.

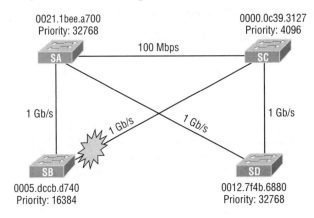

What is the new cost for SB to make a single path to the root bridge?

  A. 4

  B. 8

  C. 23

  D. 12

16. Which of the following would put switch interfaces into EtherChannel port number 1, using LACP? (Choose two.)

  A. `Switch(config)#interface port-channel 1`

  B. `Switch(config)#channel-group 1 mode active`

  C. `Switch#interface port-channel 1`

  D. `Switch(config-if)#channel-group 1 mode active`

17. Which two commands would guarantee your switch to be the root bridge for VLAN 30? (Choose two.)

  A. `spanning-tree vlan 30 priority 0`

  B. `spanning-tree vlan 30 priority 16384`

  C. `spanning-tree vlan 30 root guarantee`

  D. `spanning-tree vlan 30 root primary`

18. Why does Cisco use its proprietary extension of PVST+ with STP and RSTP?

  A. Root bridge placement enables faster convergence as well as optimal path determination.

  B. Non-root bridge placement clearly enables faster convergence as well as optimal path determination.

   C. PVST+ allows for faster discarding of non-IP frames.

   D. PVST+ is actually an IEEE standard called 802.1w.

19. Which are states in 802.1d? (Choose all that apply.)

   A. Blocking

   B. Discarding

   C. Listening

   D. Learning

   E. Forwarding

   F. Alternate

20. Which of the following are roles in STP? (Choose all that apply.)

   A. Blocking

   B. Discarding

   C. Root

   D. Non-designated

   E. Forwarding

   F. Designated

Chapter

16

Network Device Management and Security

THE FOLLOWING ICND2 EXAM TOPICS ARE COVERED IN THIS CHAPTER:

✓ **1.7 Describe common access layer threat mitigation techniques**

- 1.7.a 802.1x
- 1.7.b DHCP snooping

✓ **4.0 Infrastructure Services**

✓ **4.1 Configure, verify, and troubleshoot basic HSRP**

- 4.1.a Priority
- 4.1.b Preemption
- 4.1.c Version

✓ **5.0 Infrastructure Maintenance**

✓ **5.1 Configure and verify device-monitoring protocols**

- 5.1.a SNMPv2
- 5.1.b SNMPv3

✓ **5.4 Describe device management using AAA with TACACS+ and RADIUS**

We're going to start this chapter by discussing how to mitigate threats at the access layer using various security techniques.

Keeping our discussion on security, we're then going to turn our attention to external authentication with authentication, authorization, and accounting (AAA) of our network devices using RADIUS and TACACS+.

Next, we're going to look at Simple Network Management Protocol (SNMP) and the type of alerts sent to the network management station (NMS).

Last, I'm going to show you how to integrate redundancy and load-balancing features into your network elegantly with the routers that you likely have already. Acquiring some overpriced load-balancing device just isn't always necessary because knowing how to properly configure and use Hot Standby Router Protocol (HSRP) can often meet your needs instead.

To find up-to-the-minute updates for this chapter, please see www.lammle .com/ccna or the book's web page at www.sybex.com/go/ccna.

Mitigating Threats at the Access Layer

The Cisco hierarchical model can help you design, implement, and maintain a scalable, reliable, cost-effective hierarchical internetwork.

The access layer controls user and workgroup access to internetwork resources and is also sometimes referred to as the desktop layer. The network resources most users need at this layer will be available locally because the distribution layer handles any traffic for remote services.

The following are some of the functions to be included at the access layer:

- Continued (from the distribution layer) use of access control and policies
- Creation of separate collision domains (microsegmentation/switches)
- Workgroup connectivity into the distribution layer
- Device connectivity
- Resiliency and security services
- Advanced technology capabilities (voice/video, PoE, port-security, etc.)
- Interfaces like Gigabit or FastEthernet switching frequently seen in the access layer

Since the access layer is both the point at which user devices connect to the network and the connection point between the network and client device, protecting it plays an important role in protecting other users, applications, and the network itself from attacks.

Here are some of the ways to protect the access layer (also shown in Figure 16.1):

FIGURE 16.1   Mitigating threats at the access layer

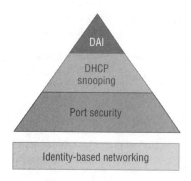

Port security   You're already very familiar with port security (or you should be!), but restricting a port to a specific set of MAC addresses is the most common way to defend the access layer.

DHCP snooping   DHCP snooping is a layer 2 security feature that validates DHCP messages by acting like a firewall between untrusted hosts and trusted DHCP servers.

In order to stop rogue DHCP servers in the network, switch interfaces are configured as trusted or untrusted, where trusted interfaces allow all types of DHCP messages and untrusted interfaces allow only requests. Trusted interfaces are interfaces that connect to a DHCP server or are an uplink toward the DHCP server, as shown in Figure 16.2.

FIGURE 16.2   DHCP snooping and DAI

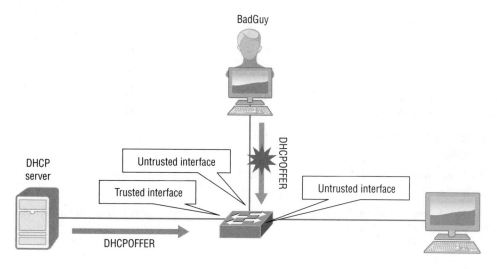

With DHCP snooping enabled, a switch also builds a DHCP snooping binding database, where each entry includes the MAC and IP address of the host as well as the DHCP lease time, binding type, VLAN, and interface. Dynamic ARP inspection also uses this DHCP snooping binding database.

Dynamic ARP inspection (DAI)   DAI, used with DHCP snooping, tracks IP-to-MAC bindings from DHCP transactions to protect against ARP poisoning (which is an attacker trying to have your traffic be sent to him instead of to your valid destination). DHCP snooping is required in order to build the MAC-to-IP bindings for DAI validation.

Identity-based networking   Identity-based networking is a concept that ties together several authentication, access control, and user policy components in order to provide users with the network services you want them to have.

In the past, for a user to connect to the Finance services, for example, a user had to be plugged into the Finance LAN or VLAN. However, with user mobility as one of the core requirements of modern networks, this is no longer practical, nor does it provide sufficient security.

Identity-based networking allows you to verify users when they connect to a switch port by authenticating them and placing them in the right VLAN based on their identity. Should any users fail to pass the authentication process, their access can be rejected, or they might be simply put in a guest VLAN. Figure 16.3 shows this process.

FIGURE 16.3   Identity-based networking

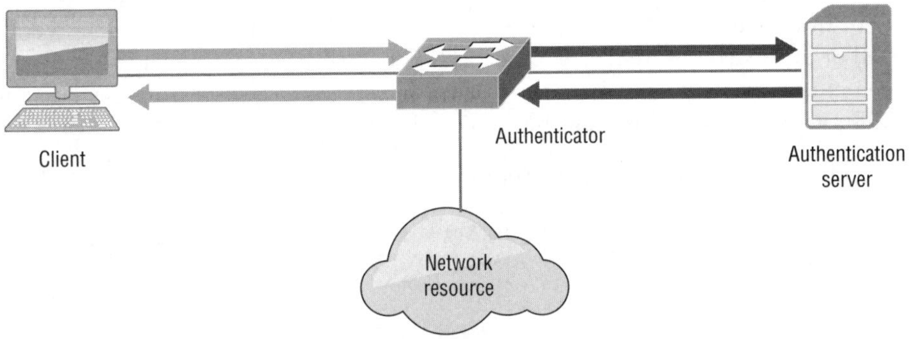

The IEEE 802.1x standard allows you to implement identity-based networking on wired and wireless hosts by using client/server access control. There are three roles:

Client   Also referred to as a supplicant, this software runs on a client that is 802.1x compliant.

Authenticator   Typically a switch, this controls physical access to the network and is a proxy between the client and the authentication server.

Authentication server (RADIUS)   This is a server that authenticates each client before making available any services.

External Authentication Options

Of course we only want authorized IT folks to have administrative access to our network devices such as routers and switches, and in a small to medium-sized network, just using local authentication is sufficient.

However, if you have hundreds of devices, managing administrative connectivity would be nearly impossible since you'd have to configure local authentication on each device by hand, and if you changed just one password, it can take hours to update your network.

Since maintaining the local database for each network device for the size of the network is usually not feasible, you can use an external AAA server that will manage all user and administrative access needs for an entire network.

The two most popular options for external AAA are RADIUS and TACACS+, both covered next.

RADIUS

Remote Authentication Dial-In User Service, or RADIUS, was developed by the Internet Engineering Task Force—the IETF—and is basically a security system that works to guard the network against unauthorized access. RADIUS, which uses only UDP, is an open standard implemented by most major vendors, and it's one of the most popular types of security servers around because it combines authentication and authorization services into a single process. So after users are authenticated, they are then authorized for network services.

RADIUS implements a client/server architecture, where the typical client is a router, switch, or AP and the typical server is a Windows or Unix device that's running RADIUS software.

The authentication process has three distinct stages:

1. The user is prompted for a username and password.

2. The username and encrypted password are sent over the network to the RADIUS server.

3. The RADIUS server replies with one of the following:

Response	Meaning
Accept	The user has been successfully authenticated.
Reject	The username and password are not valid.
Challenge	The RADIUS server requests additional information.
Change Password	The user should select a new password.

It's important to remember that RADIUS encrypts only the password in the access-request packet from the client to the server. The remainder of the packet is unencrypted.

Configuring RADIUS

To configure a RADIUS server for console and VTY access, first you need to enable AAA services in order to configure all the AAA commands. Configure the aaa new-model command in the global configuration mode.

```
Router(config)# aaa new-model
```

The aaa new-model command immediately applies local authentication to all lines and interfaces (except line con 0). So, to avoid being locked out of the router or switch, you should define a local username and password before starting the AAA configuration.

Now, configure a local user:

```
Router(config)#username Todd password Lammle
```

Creating this user is super important because you can then use this same locally created user if the external authentication server fails! If you don't create this and you can't get to the server, you're going to end up doing a password recovery.

Next, configure a RADIUS server using any name and the RADIUS key that is configured on the server.

```
Router(config)#radius server SecureLogin
Router(config-radius-server)#address ipv4 10.10.10.254
Router(config-radius-server)#key MyRadiusPassword
```

Now, add your newly created RADIUS server to an AAA group of any name.

```
Router(config)#aaa group server radius MyRadiusGroup
Router(config-sg-radius)#server name SecureLogin
```

Last, configure this newly created group to be used for AAA login authentication. If the RADIUS server fails, the fallback to local authentication should be set.

```
Router(config)# aaa authentication login default group MyRadiusGroup local
```

TACACS+

Terminal Access Controller Access Control System (TACACS+) is also a security server that's Cisco proprietary and uses TCP. It's really similar in many ways to RADIUS; however, it does all that RADIUS does and more, including multiprotocol support.

TACACS+ was developed by Cisco Systems, so it's specifically designed to interact with Cisco's AAA services. If you're using TACACS+, you have the entire menu of AAA features available to you—and it handles each security aspect separately, unlike RADIUS:

- Authentication includes messaging support in addition to login and password functions.
- Authorization enables explicit control over user capabilities.
- Accounting supplies detailed information about user activities.

Configuring TACACS+

This is pretty much identical to the RADIUS configuration.

To configure a TACACS+ server for console and VTY access, first you need to enable AAA services in order to configure all the AAA commands. Configure the aaa new-model command in the global configuration mode (if it isn't already enabled).

```
Router(config)# aaa new-model
```

Now, configure a local user if you haven't already.

```
Router(config)#username Todd password Lammle
```

Next, configure a TACACS+ server using any name and the key that is configured on the server.

```
Router(config)#radius server SecureLoginTACACS+
Router(config-radius-server)#address ipv4 10.10.10.254
Router(config-radius-server)#key MyTACACS+Password
```

Now, add your newly created TACACS+ server to a AAA group of any name.

```
Router(config)#aaa group server radius MyTACACS+Group
Router(config-sg-radius)#server name SecureLoginTACACS+
```

Last configure this newly created group to be used for AAA login authentication. If the TACACS+ server fails, the fallback to local authentication should be set.

```
Router(config)# aaa authentication login default group MyTACACS+Group local
```

SNMP

Although *Simple Network Management Protocol (SNMP)* certainly isn't the oldest protocol ever, it's still pretty old, considering it was created way back in 1988 (RFC 1065)!

SNMP is an Application layer protocol that provides a message format for agents on a variety of devices to communicate with network management stations (NMSs)—for example, Cisco Prime or HP Openview. These agents send messages to the NMS station, which then either reads or writes information in the database that's stored on the NMS and called a management information base (MIB).

The NMS periodically queries or polls the SNMP agent on a device to gather and analyze statistics via GET messages. End devices running SNMP agents would send an SNMP trap to the NMS if a problem occurs. This is demonstrated in Figure 16.4.

FIGURE 16.4   SNMP GET and TRAP messages

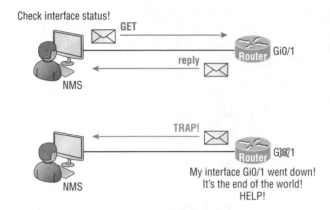

Admins can also use SNMP to provide some configurations to agents as well, called SET messages. In addition to polling to obtain statistics, SNMP can be used for analyzing information and compiling the results in a report or even a graph. Thresholds can be used to trigger a notification process when exceeded. Graphing tools are used to monitor the CPU statistics of Cisco devices like a core router. The CPU should be monitored continuously and the NMS can graph the statistics. Notification will be sent when any threshold you've set has been exceeded.

SNMP has three versions, with version 1 being rarely, if ever, implemented today. Here's a summary of these three versions:

SNMPv1   Supports plaintext authentication with community strings and uses only UDP.

SNMPv2c   Supports plaintext authentication with community strings with no encryption but provides GET BULK, which is a way to gather many types of information at once and minimize the number of GET requests. It offers a more detailed error message reporting method called INFORM, but it's not more secure than v1. It uses UDP even though it can be configured to use TCP.

SNMPv3   Supports strong authentication with MD5 or SHA, providing confidentiality (encryption) and data integrity of messages via DES or DES-256 encryption between agents and managers. GET BULK is a supported feature of SNMPv3, and this version also uses TCP.

Management Information Base (MIB)

With so many kinds of devices and so much data that can be accessed, there needed to be a standard way to organize this plethora of data, so MIB to the rescue! A *management information base (MIB)* is a collection of information that's organized hierarchically and can be accessed by protocols like SNMP. RFCs define some common public variables, but most organizations define their own private branches along with basic SNMP standards. Organizational IDs (OIDs) are laid out as a tree with different levels assigned by different organizations, with top-level MIB OIDs belonging to various standards organizations.

Vendors assign private branches in their own products. Let's take a look at Cisco's OIDs, which are described in words or numbers to locate a particular variable in the tree, as shown in Figure 16.5.

FIGURE 16.5   Cisco's MIB OIDs

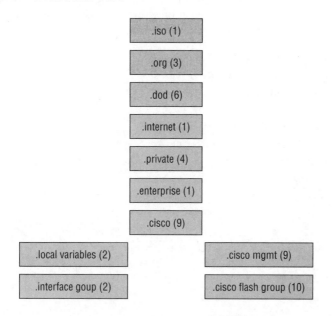

Luckily, you don't need to memorize the OIDs in Figure 16.5 for the Cisco exams!

To obtain information from the MIB on the SNMP agent, you can use several different operations:

- GET: This operation is used to get information from the MIB to an SNMP agent.

- SET: This operation is used to get information to the MIB from an SNMP manager.

- WALK: This operation is used to list information from successive MIB objects within a specified MIB.

- TRAP: This operation is used by the SNMP agent to send a triggered piece of information to the SNMP manager.

- INFORM: This operation is the same as a trap, but it adds an acknowledgment that a trap does not provide.

Configuring SNMP

Configuring SNMP is a pretty straightforward process for which you only need a few commands. These five steps are all you need to run through to configure a Cisco device for SNMP access:

1.   Configure where the traps are to be sent.

2.   Enable SNMP read-write access to the router.

3. Configure SNMP contact information.

4. Configure SNMP location.

5. Configure an ACL to restrict SNMP access to the NMS hosts.

The only required configuration is the IP address of the NMS station and the community string (which acts as a password or authentication string) because the other three are optional. Here's an example of a typical SNMP router configuration:

```
Router(config)#snmp-server host 1.2.3.4
Router(config)#snmp-server community ?
  WORD  SNMP community string

Router(config)#snmp-server community Todd ?
  <1-99>      Std IP accesslist allowing access with this community string
  <1300-1999> Expanded IP accesslist allowing access with this community
              string
  WORD        Access-list name
  ipv6        Specify IPv6 Named Access-List
  ro          Read-only access with this community string
  rw          Read-write access with this community string
  view        Restrict this community to a named MIB view
  <cr>

Router(config)#snmp-server community Todd rw
Router(config)#snmp-server location Boulder
Router(config)#snmp-server contact Todd Lammle
Router(config)#ip access-list standard Protect_NMS_Station
Router(config-std-nacl)#permit host 192.168.10.254
```

Entering the snmp-server command enables SNMPv1 on the Cisco device.

You can enter the ACL directly in the SNMP configuration to provide security, using either a number or a name. Here is an example:

```
Router(config)#snmp-server community Todd Protect_NMS_Station rw
```

Notice that even though there's a boatload of configuration options under SNMP, you only really need to work with a few of them to configure a basic SNMP trap setup on a router. First, I set the IP address of the NMS station where the router will send the traps; then I chose the community name of Todd with RW access (read-write), which means the NMS will be able to retrieve and modify MIB objects from the router. Location and contact information comes in really handy for troubleshooting the configuration. Make sure you understand that the ACL protects the NMS from access, not the devices with the agents!

Let's define the SNMP read and write options.

Read-only   Gives authorized management stations read access to all objects in the MIB except the community strings and doesn't allow write access

Read-write   Gives authorized management stations read and write access to all objects in the MIB but doesn't allow access to the community strings

Next we'll explore a Cisco proprietary method of configuring redundant default gateways for hosts.

Client Redundancy Issues

If you're wondering how you can possibly configure a client to send data off its local link when its default gateway router has gone down, you've targeted a key issue because the answer is that, usually, you can't! Most host operating systems just don't allow you to change data routing. Sure, if a host's default gateway router goes down, the rest of the network will still converge, but it won't share that information with the hosts. Take a look at Figure 16.6 to see what I am talking about. There are actually two routers available to forward data for the local subnet, but the hosts know about only one of them. They learn about this router when you provide them with the default gateway either statically or through DHCP.

FIGURE 16.6   Default gateway

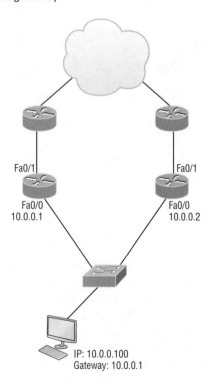

This begs the question: Is there another way to use the second active router? The answer is a bit complicated, but bear with me. There is a feature that's enabled by default on Cisco routers called Proxy Address Resolution Protocol (Proxy ARP). Proxy ARP enables hosts, which have no knowledge of routing options, to obtain the MAC address of a gateway router that can forward packets for them.

You can see how this happens in Figure 16.7. If a Proxy ARP–enabled router receives an ARP request for an IP address that it knows isn't on the same subnet as the requesting host, it will respond with an ARP reply packet to the host. The router will give its own local MAC address—the MAC address of its interface on the host's subnet—as the destination MAC address for the IP address that the host is seeking to be resolved. After receiving the destination MAC address, the host will then send all the packets to the router, not knowing that what it sees as the destination host is really a router. The router will then forward the packets toward the intended host.

FIGURE 16.7   Proxy ARP

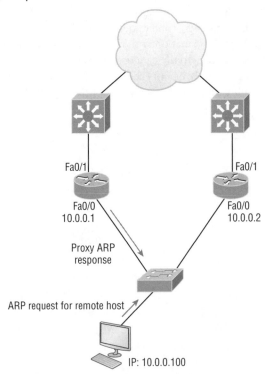

So with Proxy ARP, the host device sends traffic as if the destination device were located on its own network segment. If the router that responded to the ARP request fails, the source host continues to send packets for that destination to the same MAC address. But because they're being sent to a failed router, the packets will be sent to the other router on the network that is also responding to ARP requests for remote hosts.

After the time-out period on the host, the proxy ARP MAC address ages out of the ARP cache. The host can then make a new ARP request for the destination and get the address of another proxy ARP router. Still, keep in mind that the host cannot send packets off of its subnet during the failover time. This isn't exactly a perfect situation, so there has to be a better way, right? Well, there is, and that's precisely where redundancy protocols come to the rescue!

Introducing First Hop Redundancy Protocols (FHRPs)

First hop redundancy protocols (FHRPs) work by giving you a way to configure more than one physical router to appear as if they were only a single logical one. This makes client configuration and communication easier because you can simply configure a single default gateway and the host machine can use its standard protocols to communicate. *First hop* is a reference to the default router being the first router, or first router hop, through which a packet must pass.

So how does a redundancy protocol accomplish this? The protocols I'm going to describe to you do this basically by presenting a virtual router to all of the clients. The virtual router has its own IP and MAC addresses. The virtual IP address is the address that's configured on each of the host machines as the default gateway. The virtual MAC address is the address that will be returned when an ARP request is sent by a host. The hosts don't know or care which physical router is actually forwarding the traffic, as you can see in Figure 16.8.

FIGURE 16.8   FHRPs use a virtual router with a virtual IP address and virtual MAC address.

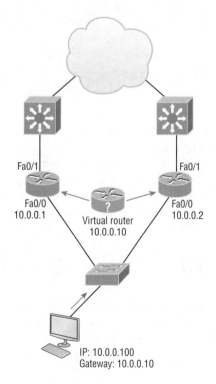

It's the responsibility of the redundancy protocol to decide which physical router will actively forward traffic and which one will be placed on standby in case the active router fails. Even if the active router fails, the transition to the standby router will be transparent to the hosts because the virtual router, which is identified by the virtual IP and MAC addresses, is now used by the standby router. The hosts never change default gateway information, so traffic keeps flowing.

Fault-tolerant solutions provide continued operation in the event of a device failure, and load-balancing solutions distribute the workload over multiple devices.

There are three important redundancy protocols, but only HSRP is covered on the CCNA objectives now:

Hot Standby Router Protocol (HSRP)   HSRP is by far Cisco's favorite protocol ever! Don't buy just one router; buy up to eight routers to provide the same service, and keep seven as backup in case of failure! HSRP is a Cisco proprietary protocol that provides a redundant gateway for hosts on a local subnet, but this isn't a load-balanced solution. HSRP allows you to configure two or more routers into a standby group that shares an IP address and MAC address and provides a default gateway. When the IP and MAC addresses are independent from the routers' physical addresses (on a virtual interface, not tied to a specific interface), HSRP can swap control of an address if the current forwarding and active router fails. But there is actually a way you can sort of achieve load balancing with HSRP—by using multiple VLANs and designating a specific router active for one VLAN, then an alternate router as active for the other VLAN via trunking. This still isn't a true load-balancing solution and it's not nearly as solid as what you can achieve with GLBP!

Virtual Router Redundancy Protocol (VRRP)   Also provides a redundant—but again, not load-balanced—gateway for hosts on a local subnet. It's an open standard protocol that functions almost identically to HSRP.

Gateway Load Balancing Protocol (GLBP)   For the life of me I can't figure out how GLBP isn't a CCNA objective anymore! GLBP doesn't just stop at providing us with a redundant gateway; it's a true load-balancing solution for routers. GLBP allows a maximum of four routers in each forwarding group. By default, the active router directs the traffic from hosts to each successive router in the group using a round-robin algorithm. The hosts are directed to send their traffic toward a specific router by being given the MAC address of the next router in line to be used.

Hot Standby Router Protocol (HSRP)

Again, HSRP is a Cisco proprietary protocol that can be run on most, but not all, of Cisco's router and multilayer switch models. It defines a standby group, and each standby group that you define includes the following routers:

- Active router
- Standby router
- Virtual router
- Any other routers that maybe attached to the subnet

The problem with HSRP is that with it, only one router is active and two or more routers just sit there in standby mode and won't be used unless a failure occurs—not very cost effective or efficient! Figure 16.9 shows how only one router is used at a time in an HSRP group.

The standby group will always have at least two routers participating in it. The primary players in the group are the one active router and one standby router that communicate to each other using multicast Hello messages. The Hello messages provide all of the required communication for the routers. The Hellos contain the information required to accomplish the election that determines the active and standby router positions. They also hold the key to the failover process. If the standby router stops receiving Hello packets from the active router, it then takes over the active router role, as shown in Figure 16.9 and Figure 16.10.

FIGURE 16.9   HSRP active and standby routers

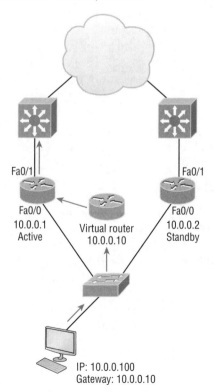

FIGURE 16.10   Example of HSRP active and standby routers swapping interfaces

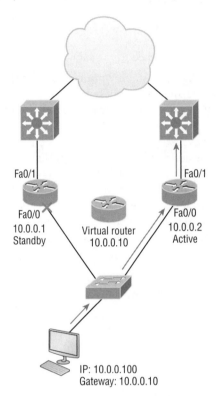

As soon as the active router stops responding to Hellos, the standby router automatically becomes the active router and starts responding to host requests.

Virtual MAC Address

A virtual router in an HSRP group has a virtual IP address and a virtual MAC address. So where does that virtual MAC come from? The virtual IP address isn't that hard to figure out; it just has to be a unique IP address on the same subnet as the hosts defined in the configuration. But MAC addresses are a little different, right? Or are they? The answer is yes—sort of. With HSRP, you create a totally new, made-up MAC address in addition to the IP address.

The HSRP MAC address has only one variable piece in it. The first 24 bits still identify the vendor who manufactured the device (the organizationally unique identifier, or OUI).

The next 16 bits in the address tell us that the MAC address is a well-known HSRP MAC address. Finally, the last 8 bits of the address are the hexadecimal representation of the HSRP group number.

Let me clarify all this with an example of what an HSRP MAC address would look like:

```
0000.0c07.ac0a
```

- The first 24 bits (0000.0c) are the vendor ID of the address; in the case of HSRP being a Cisco protocol, the ID is assigned to Cisco.

- The next 16 bits (07.ac) are the well-known HSRP ID. This part of the address was assigned by Cisco in the protocol, so it's always easy to recognize that this address is for use with HSRP.

- The last 8 bits (0a) are the only variable bits and represent the HSRP group number that you assign. In this case, the group number is 10 and converted to hexadecimal when placed in the MAC address, where it becomes the 0a that you see.

You can see this displayed with every MAC address added to the ARP cache of every router in the HSRP group. There will be the translation from the IP address to the MAC address, as well as the interface on which it's located.

HSRP Timers

Before we get deeper into the roles that each of the routers can have in an HSRP group, I want to define the HSRP timers for HSRP to function because they ensure communication between the routers, and if something goes wrong, they allow the standby router to take over. The HSRP timers include *hello*, *hold*, *active*, and *standby*.

Hello timer   The hello timer is the defined interval during which each of the routers send out Hello messages. Their default interval is 3 seconds and they identify the state that each router is in. This is important because the particular state determines the specific role of each router and, as a result, the actions each will take within the group. Figure 16.11 shows the Hello messages being sent and the router using the hello timer to keep the network flowing in case of a failure.

This timer can be changed, and people used to avoid doing so because it was thought that lowering the hello value would place an unnecessary load on the routers. That isn't true with most of the routers today; in fact, you can configure the timers in milliseconds, meaning the failover time can be in milliseconds! Still, keep in mind that increasing the value will make the standby router wait longer before taking over for the active router when it fails or can't communicate.

FIGURE 16.11   HSRP Hellos

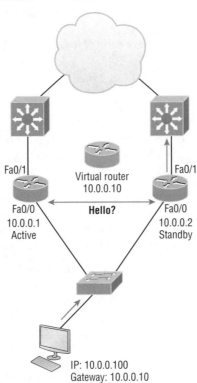

Hold timer   The hold timer specifies the interval the standby router uses to determine whether the active router is offline or out of communication. By default, the hold timer is 10 seconds, roughly three times the default for the hello timer. If one timer is changed for some reason, I recommend using this multiplier to adjust the other timers too. By setting the hold timer at three times the hello timer, you ensure that the standby router doesn't take over the active role every time there's a short break in communication.

Active timer   The active timer monitors the state of the active router. The timer resets each time a router in the standby group receives a Hello packet from the active router. This timer expires based on the hold time value that's set in the corresponding field of the HSRP Hello message.

Standby timer   The standby timer is used to monitor the state of the standby router. The timer resets anytime a router in the standby group receives a Hello packet from the standby router and expires based on the hold time value that's set in the respective Hello packet.

🌐 Real World Scenario

Large Enterprise Network Outages with FHRPs

Years ago when HSRP was all the rage, and before VRRP and GLBP, enterprises used hundreds of HSRP groups. With the hello timer set to 3 seconds and a hold time of 10 seconds, these timers worked just fine and we had great redundancy with our core routers.

However, as we've seen in the last few years and certainly will see in the future, 10 seconds is now a lifetime! Some of my customers have been complaining with the failover time and loss of connectivity to their virtual server farm.

So lately I've been changing the timers to well below the defaults. Cisco had changed the timers so you could use sub-second times for failover. Because these are multicast packets, the overhead that is seen on a current high-speed network is almost nothing.

The hello timer is typically set to 200 msec and the hold time is 700 msec. The command is as follows:

```
(config-if)#Standby 1 timers msec 200 msec 700
```

This almost ensures that not even a single packet is lost when there is an outage.

Group Roles

Each of the routers in the standby group has a specific function and role to fulfill. The three main roles are as virtual router, active router, and standby router. Additional routers can also be included in the group.

Virtual router   As its name implies, the virtual router is not a physical entity. It really just defines the role that's held by one of the physical routers. The physical router that communicates as the virtual router is the current active router. The virtual router is nothing more than a separate IP address and MAC address to which packets are sent.

Active router   The active router is the physical router that receives data sent to the virtual router address and routes it onward to its various destinations. As I mentioned, this router accepts all the data sent to the MAC address of the virtual router in addition to the data that's been sent to its own physical MAC address. The active router processes the data that's being forwarded and will also answer any ARP requests destined for the virtual router's IP address.

Standby router   The standby router is the backup to the active router. Its job is to monitor the status of the HSRP group and quickly take over packet-forwarding responsibilities if the active router fails or loses communication. Both the active and standby routers transmit Hello messages to inform all other routers in the group of their role and status.

Other routers   An HSRP group can include additional routers, which are members of the group but don't take the primary roles of either active or standby states. These routers monitor the Hello messages sent by the active and standby routers to ensure that an active and standby router exists for the HSRP group that they belong to. They will forward data that's specifically addressed to their own IP addresses, but they will never forward data addressed to the virtual router unless elected to the active or standby state. These routers send "speak" messages based on the hello timer interval that informs other routers of their position in an election.

Interface Tracking

By now, you probably understand why having a virtual router on a LAN is a great idea. You also know why it's a very good thing that the active router can change dynamically, giving us much needed redundancy on our inside network. But what about the links to the upstream network or the Internet connection off of those HSRP-enabled routers? And how will the inside hosts know if an outside interface goes down or if they are sending packets to an active router that can't route to a remote network? Key questions and HSRP do provide a solution for them; it's called interface tracking.

Figure 16.12 shows how HSRP-enabled routers can keep track of the interface status of the outside interfaces and how they can switch the inside active router as needed to keep the inside hosts from losing connectivity upstream.

FIGURE 16.12   Interface tracking setup

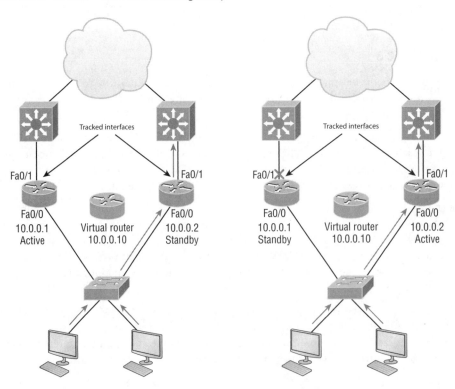

If the outside link of the active router goes down, the standby router will take over and become the active router. There is a default priority of 100 on routers configured with an HSRP interface, and if you raise this priority (we'll do this in a minute), it means your router has a higher priority to become the active router. The reason I am bringing this up now is because when a tracked interface goes down, it decrements the priority of this router.

Configuring and Verifying HSRP

Configuring and verifying the different FHRPs can be pretty simple, especially regarding the Cisco objectives, but as with most technologies, you can quickly get into advanced configurations and territory with the different FHRPs if you're not careful, so I'll show you exactly what you need to know.

The Cisco objectives don't cover much about the configuration of FHRPs, but verification and troubleshooting is important, so I'll use a simple configuration on two routers here. Figure 16.13 shows the network I'll use to demonstrate HSRP.

FIGURE 16.13   HSRP configuration and verification

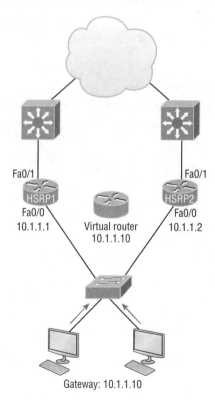

Gateway: 10.1.1.10

This is a simple configuration for which you really need only one command: standby *group* ip *virtual_ip*. After using this single mandatory command, I'll name the group and set the interface on router HSRP1 so it wins the election and becomes the active router by default.

```
HSRP1#config t
HSRP1(config)#int fa0/0
HSRP1(config-if)#standby ?
  <0-255>         group number
  authentication  Authentication
  delay           HSRP initialisation delay
  ip              Enable HSRP and set the virtual IP address
  mac-address     Virtual MAC address
  name            Redundancy name string
  preempt         Overthrow lower priority Active routers
  priority        Priority level
  redirect        Configure sending of ICMP Redirect messages with an HSRP
                  virtual IP address as the gateway IP address
  timers          Hello and hold timers
  track           Priority tracking
  use-bia         HSRP uses interface's burned in address
  version         HSRP version

HSRP1(config-if)#standby 1 ip 10.1.1.10
HSRP1(config-if)#standby 1 name HSRP_Test
HSRP1(config-if)#standby 1 priority ?
  <0-255>  Priority value

HSRP1(config-if)#standby 1 priority 110
000047: %HSRP-5-STATECHANGE: FastEthernet0/0 Grp 1 state Speak -> Standby
000048: %HSRP-5-STATECHANGE: FastEthernet0/0 Grp 1 state Standby -> Active110
```

There are quite a few commands available to use in an advanced setting with the standby command, but we'll stick with the simple commands that follow the Cisco objectives. First, I numbered the group (1), which must be the same on all routers sharing HSRP duties; then I added the virtual IP address shared by all routers in the HSRP group. Optionally, I named the group and then set the priority of HSRP1 to 110, and I left HSRP2 to a default of 100. The router with the highest priority will win the election to become the active router. Let's configure the HSRP2 router now:

```
HSRP2#config t
HSRP2(config)#int fa0/0
HSRP2(config-if)#standby 1 ip 10.1.1.10
HSRP2(config-if)#standby 1 name HSRP_Test
```

```
*Jun 23 21:40:10.699:%HSRP-5-STATECHANGE:FastEthernet0/0 Grp 1 state
Speak -> Standby
```

I really only needed the first command—naming it was for administrative purposes only. Notice that the link came up and HSRP2 became the standby router because it had the lower priority of 100 (the default). Make a note that this priority comes into play only if both routers were to come up at the same time. This means that HSRP2 would be the active router, regardless of the priority, if it comes up first.

Let's take a look at the configurations with the show standby and show standby brief commands:

```
HSRP1(config-if)#do show standby
FastEthernet0/0 - Group 1
  State is Active
    2 state changes, last state change 00:03:40
  Virtual IP address is 10.1.1.10
  Active virtual MAC address is 0000.0c07.ac01
    Local virtual MAC address is 0000.0c07.ac01 (v1 default)
  Hello time 3 sec, hold time 10 sec
    Next hello sent in 1.076 secs
  Preemption disabled
  Active router is local
  Standby router is 10.1.1.2, priority 100 (expires in 7.448 sec)
  Priority 110 (configured 110)
  IP redundancy name is "HSRP_Test" (cfgd)

HSRP1(config-if)#do show standby brief
                     P indicates configured to preempt.
                     |
Interface  Grp Prio P State   Active        Standby        Virtual IP
Fa0/0      1   110    Active  local         10.1.1.2       10.1.1.10
```

Notice the group number in each output—it's a key troubleshooting spot! Each router must be configured in the same group or they won't work. Also, you can see the virtual MAC and configured virtual IP address, as well as the hello time of 3 seconds. The standby and virtual IP addresses are also displayed.

HSRP2's output tells us that it's in standby mode:

```
HSRP2(config-if)#do show standby brief
                     P indicates configured to preempt.
                     |
Interface  Grp Prio P State    Active       Standby        Virtual IP
Fa0/0      1   100    Standby  10.1.1.1     local          10.1.1.10
HRSP2(config-if)#
```

Notice so far that you have seen HSRP states of active and standby, but watch what happens when I disable Fa0/0:

```
HSRP1#config t
HSRP1(config)#interface Fa0/0
HSRP1(config-if)#shutdown
*Nov 20 10:06:52.369: %HSRP-5-STATECHANGE: Ethernet0/0 Grp 1 state Active ->
Init
```

The HSRP went into Init state, meaning it's trying to initialize with a peer. The possible interface states for HSRP are shown in Table 16.1.

TABLE 16.1 HSRP states

State	Definition
Initial (INIT)	This is the state at the start. This state indicates that HSRP does not run. This state is entered through a configuration change or when an interface first becomes available.
Learn	The router has not determined the virtual IP address and has not yet seen an authenticated Hello message from the active router. In this state, the router still waits to hear from the active router.
Listen	The router knows the virtual IP address, but the router is neither the active router nor the standby router. It listens for Hello messages from those routers.
Speak	The router sends periodic Hello messages and actively participates in the election of the active and/or standby router. A router cannot enter speak state unless the router has the virtual IP address.
Standby	The router is a candidate to become the next active router and sends periodic Hello messages. With the exclusion of transient conditions, there is, at most, one router in the group in standby state.
Active	The router currently forwards packets that are sent to the group virtual MAC address. The router sends periodic Hello messages. With the exclusion of transient conditions, there must be, at most, one router in active state in the group.

There is one other command that I want to cover. If you're studying and want to understand HSRP, you should learn to use this debug command and have your active and standby routers move. You'll really get to see what is going on.

```
HSRP2#debug standby
*Sep 15 00:07:32.344:HSRP:Fa0/0 Interface UP
*Sep 15 00:07:32.344:HSRP:Fa0/0 Initialize swsb, Intf state Up
*Sep 15 00:07:32.344:HSRP:Fa0/0 Starting minimum intf delay (1 secs)
*Sep 15 00:07:32.344:HSRP:Fa0/0 Grp 1 Set virtual MAC 0000.0c07.ac01
type: v1 default
*Sep 15 00:07:32.344:HSRP:Fa0/0 MAC hash entry 0000.0c07.ac01, Added
Fa0/0 Grp 1 to list
*Sep 15 00:07:32.348:HSRP:Fa0/0 Added 10.1.1.10 to hash table
*Sep 15 00:07:32.348:HSRP:Fa0/0 Grp 1 Has mac changed? cur 0000.0c07.ac01
new 0000.0c07.ac01
*Sep 15 00:07:32.348:HSRP:Fa0/0 Grp 1 Disabled -> Init
*Sep 15 00:07:32.348:HSRP:Fa0/0 Grp 1 Redundancy "hsrp-Fa0/0-1" state
Disabled -> Init
*Sep 15 00:07:32.348:HSRP:Fa0/0 IP Redundancy "hsrp-Fa0/0-1" added
*Sep 15 00:07:32.348:HSRP:Fa0/0 IP Redundancy "hsrp-Fa0/0-1" update,
Disabled -> Init
*Sep 15 00:07:33.352:HSRP:Fa0/0 Intf min delay expired
*Sep 15 00:07:39.936:HSRP:Fa0/0 Grp 1 MAC addr update Delete from SMF
0000.0c07.ac01
*Sep 15 00:07:39.936:HSRP:Fa0/0 Grp 1 MAC addr update Delete from SMF
0000.0c07.ac01
*Sep 15 00:07:39.940:HSRP:Fa0/0 ARP reload
```

HSRP Load Balancing

As you know, HSRP doesn't really perform true load balancing, but it can be configured to use more than one router at a time for use with different VLANs. This is different from the true load balancing that's possible with GLBP, which I'll demonstrate in a minute, but HSRP still performs a load-balancing act of sorts. Figure 16.14 shows how load balancing would look with HSRP.

How can you get two HSRP routers active at the same time? Well for the same subnet with this simple configuration, you can't, but if you trunk the links to each router, they'll run and be configured with a "router on a stick" (ROAS) configuration. This means that each router can be the default gateway for different VLANs, but you still can have only one active router per VLAN. Typically, in a more advanced setting you won't use HSRP for load balancing; you'll use GLBP, but you can do load-sharing with HSRP, and that is the topic of an objective, so we'll remember that, right? It comes in handy because it prevents situations where a single point of failure causes traffic interruptions. This HSRP feature improves network resilience by allowing for load-balancing and redundancy capabilities between subnets and VLANs.

FIGURE 16.14   HSRP load balancing per VLAN

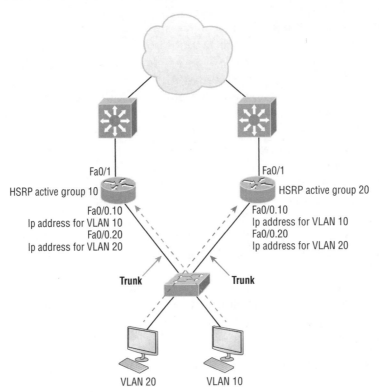

HSRP Troubleshooting

Besides HSRP verification, the troubleshooting of HSRP is the Cisco objective hotspot, so let's go through this.

Most of your HSRP misconfiguration issues can be solved by checking the output of the show standby command. In the output, you can see the active IP and the MAC address, the timers, the active router, and more, as shown earlier in the verification section.

There are several possible misconfigurations of HSRP, but these are what you need to pay attention to for your CCNA:

Different HSRP virtual IP addresses configured on the peers   Console messages will notify you about this, of course, but if you configure it this way and the active router fails, the standby router takes over with a virtual IP address, which is different than the one used previously, and different than the one configured as the default-gateway address for end devices, so your hosts stop working, which defeats the purpose of a FHRP.

Different HSRP groups configured on the peers   This misconfiguration leads to both peers becoming active, and you'll start receiving duplicate IP address warnings. It seems like this would be easy to troubleshoot, but the next issue has the same warnings.

Different HSRP versions configured on the peers or ports blocked   HSRP comes in two versions, 1 and 2. If there is a version mismatch, both routers will become active and you'll again have duplicate IP address warnings.

In version 1, HSRP messages are sent to the multicast IP address 224.0.0.2 and UDP port 1985. HSRP version 2 uses the multicast IP address 224.0.0.102 and UDP port 1985. These IP addresses and ports need to be permitted in the inbound access lists. If the packets are blocked, the peers will not see each other and there will be no HSRP redundancy.

Summary

I started this chapter by discussing how to mitigate security threats at the access layer and then also discussed external authentication for our network devices for ease of management.

SNMP is an Application layer protocol that provides a message format for agents on a variety of devices to communicate to network management stations (NMSs). I discussed the basic information you need to use syslog and SNMP, that is, configuration and verification.

Last, I showed you how to integrate redundancy and load-balancing features into your network elegantly with the routers that you likely have already. HSRP is Cisco proprietary; acquiring some overpriced load-balancing device just isn't always necessary because knowing how to properly configure and use Hot Standby Router Protocol (HSRP) can often meet your needs instead.

Exam Essentials

Understand how to mitigate threats at the access layer.   You can mitigate threats at the access layer by using port security, DHCP snooping, dynamic ARP inspection, and identity-based networking.

Understand TACACS+ and RADIUS.   TACACS+ is Cisco proprietary, uses TCP, and can separate services. RADIUS is an open standard, uses UDP, and cannot separate services.

Remember the differences between SNMPv2 and SNMPv3.   SNMPv2 uses UDP but can use TCP; however, v2 still sends data to the NMS station in clear text, exactly like SNMPv1, plus SNMPv2 implemented GETBULK and INFORM messages. SNMPv3 uses TCP and authenticates users, plus it can use ACLs in the SNMP strings to protect the NMS station from unauthorized use.

Understand FHRPs, especially HSRP. The FHRPs are HSRP, VRRP, and GLBP, with HSRP and GLBP being Cisco proprietary.

Remember the HSRP virtual address. The HSRP MAC address has only one variable piece in it. The first 24 bits still identify the vendor who manufactured the device (the organizationally unique identifier, or OUI). The next 16 bits in the address tell us that the MAC address is a well-known HSRP MAC address. Finally, the last 8 bits of the address are the hexadecimal representation of the HSRP group number.

Let me clarify all this with an example of what an HSRP MAC address would look like:

```
0000.0c07.ac0a
```

Written Lab 16

You can find the answers to this lab in Appendix A, "Answers to Written Labs."

1. Which operation used by SNMP is the same as a trap but adds an acknowledgment that a trap does not provide?

2. Which operation is used by SNMP to get information from the MIB to an SNMP agent?

3. Which operation used by the SNMP agent to send a triggered piece of information to the SNMP manager?

4. Which operation is used to get information to the MIB from an SNMP manager?

5. This operation is used to list information from successive MIB objects within a specified MIB.

6. You have different HSRP virtual IP addresses configured on peers. What is the result?

7. You configure HSRP on peers with different group numbers. What is the result?

8. You configure your HSRP peers with different versions (v1 and v2). What is the result?

9. What is the multicast and port number used for both HSRP versions 1 and 2?

10. The two most popular options for external AAA are what, and which one of them is Cisco proprietary?

Review Questions

The following questions are designed to test your understanding of this chapter's material. For more information on how to get additional questions, please see www.lammle.com/ccna.

You can find the answers to these questions in Appendix B, "Answers to Review Questions."

1. How can you efficiently restrict the read-only function of a requesting SNMP management station based on the IP address?

   A. Place an ACL on the logical control plane.

   B. Place an ACL on the line when configuring the RO community string.

   C. Place an ACL on the VTY line.

   D. Place an ACL on all router interfaces.

2. What is the default priority setting on an HSRP router?

   A. 25

   B. 50

   C. 100

   D. 125

3. Which of the following commands will enable AAA on a router?

   A. `aaa enable`

   B. `enable aaa`

   C. `new-model aaa`

   D. `aaa new-model`

4. Which of the following will mitigate access layer threats? (Choose two.)

   A. Port security

   B. Access lists

   C. Dynamic ARP inspection

   D. AAA

5. Which of the following is not true about DHCP snooping?

   A. DHCP snooping validates DHCP messages received from untrusted sources and filters out invalid messages.

   B. DHCP snooping builds and maintains the DHCP snooping binding database, which contains information about untrusted hosts with leased IP addresses.

   C. DHCP snooping rate-limits DHCP traffic from trusted and untrusted sources.

   D. DHCP snooping is a layer 2 security feature that acts like a firewall between hosts.

6. Which of the following are true about TACACS+? (Choose two.)

A. TACACS+ is a Cisco proprietary security mechanism.

B. TACACS+ uses UDP.

C. TACACS+ combines authentication and authorization services as a single process—after users are authenticated, they are also authorized.

D. TACACS+ offers multiprotocol support.

7. Which of the following is not true about RADIUS?

A. RADIUS is an open standard protocol.

B. RADIUS separates AAA services.

C. RADIUS uses UDP.

D. RADIUS encrypts only the password in the access-request packet from the client to the server. The remainder of the packet is unencrypted.

8. A switch is configured with the `snmp-server community Cisco RO` command running SNMPv2c. An NMS is trying to communicate to this router via SNMP, so what can be performed by the NMS? (Choose two.)

A. The NMS can only graph obtained results.

B. The NMS can graph obtained results and change the hostname of the router.

C. The NMS can only change the hostname of the router.

D. The NMS can use GETBULK and return many results.

9. What is true regarding any type of FHRP?

A. The FHRP supplies hosts with routing information.

B. The FHRP is a routing protocol.

C. The FHRP provides default gateway redundancy.

D. The FHRP is only standards-based.

10. Which of the following are HSRP states? (Choose two.)

A. INIT

B. Active

C. Established

D. Idle

11. Which command configures an interface to enable HSRP with the virtual router IP address 10.1.1.10?

A. `standby 1 ip 10.1.1.10`

B. `ip hsrp 1 standby 10.1.1.10`

C. `hsrp 1 ip 10.1.1.10`

D. `standby 1 hsrp ip 10.1.1.10`

12. Which command displays the status of all HSRP groups on a Cisco router or layer 3 switch?

  A. `show ip hsrp`

  B. `show hsrp`

  C. `show standby hsrp`

  D. `show standby`

  E. `show hsrp groups`

13. Two routers are part of a HSRP standby group and there is no priority configured on the routers for the HSRP group. Which of the statements below is correct?

  A. Both routers will be in the active state.

  B. Both routers will be in the standby state.

  C. Both routers will be in the listen state.

  D. One router will be active, the other standby.

14. Which of the following statement is true about the HSRP version 1 Hello packet?

  A. HSRP Hello packets are sent to multicast address 224.0.0.5.

  B. HSRP RP Hello packets are sent to multicast address 224.0.0.2 with TCP port 1985.

  C. HSRP Hello packets are sent to multicast address 224.0.0.2 with UDP port 1985.

  D. HSRP Hello packets are sent to multicast address 224.0.0.10 with UDP port 1986.

15. Routers HSRP1 and HSRP2 are in HSRP group 1. HSRP1 is the active router with a priority of 120 and HSRP2 has the default priority. When HSRP1 reboots, HSRP2 will become the active router. Once HSRP1 comes back up, which of the following statements will be true? (Choose two.)

  A. HSRP1 will become the active router.

  B. HSRP2 will stay the active router.

  C. HSRP1 will become the active router if it is also configured to preempt.

  D. Both routers will go into speak state.

16. What is the multicast address and port number used for HSRP version 2?

  A. 224.0.0.2, UDP port 1985

  B. 224.0.0.2, TCP port 1985

  C. 224.0.0.102, UDP port 1985

  D. 224.0.0.102, TCP port 1985

17. Which is true regarding SNMP? (Choose two.)

  A. SNMPv2c offers more security than SNMPv1.

  B. SNMPv3 uses TCP and introduced the GETBULK operation.

  C. SNMPv2c introduced the INFORM operation.

  D. SNMPv3 provides the best security of the three versions.

18. You want to configure RADIUS so your network devices have external authentication, but you also need to make sure you can fall back to local authentication. Which command will you use?

    A. `aaa authentication login local group MyRadiusGroup`

    B. `aaa authentication login group MyRadiusGroup fallback local`

    C. `aaa authentication login default group MyRadiusGroup external local`

    D. `aaa authentication login default group MyRadiusGroup local`

19. Which is true about DAI?

    A. It must use TCP, BootP, and DHCP snooping in order to work.

    B. DHCP snooping is required in order to build the MAC-to-IP bindings for DAI validation.

    C. DAI is required in order to build the MAC-to-IP bindings, which protect against man-in-the-middle attacks.

    D. DAI tracks ICMP-to-MAC bindings from DHCP.

20. The IEEE 802.1x standard allows you to implement identity-based networking on wired and wireless hosts by using client/server access control. There are three roles. Which of the following are these three roles?

    A. Client

    B. Forwarder

    C. Security access control

    D. Authenticator

    E. Authentication server

Chapter

17

Enhanced IGRP

THE FOLLOWING ICND2 EXAM TOPICS ARE COVERED IN THIS CHAPTER:

✓ **2.0 Routing Technologies**

- ▪ 2.2 Compare and contrast distance vector and link-state routing protocols

- ▪ 2.3 Compare and contrast interior and exterior routing protocols

- ▪ 2.6 Configure, verify, and troubleshoot EIGRP for IPv4 (excluding authentication, filtering, manual summarization, redistribution, stub)

- ▪ 2.7 Configure, verify, and troubleshoot EIGRP for IPv6 (excluding authentication, filtering, manual summarization, redistribution, stub

Enhanced Interior Gateway Routing Protocol (EIGRP) is a Cisco protocol that runs on Cisco routers and on some Cisco switches. In this chapter, I'll cover the many features and functions of EIGRP, with an added focus on the unique way that it discovers, selects, and advertises routes.

EIGRP has a number of features that make it especially useful within large, complex networks. A real standout among these is its support of VLSM, which is crucial to its ultra-efficient scalability. EIGRP even includes benefits gained through other common protocols like OSPF and RIPv2, such as the ability to create route summaries at any location you choose.

I'll also cover key EIGRP configuration details and give you examples of each, as well as demonstrate the various commands required to verify that EIGRP is working properly. Finally, I'll wrap up the chapter by showing you how to configure and verify EIGRPv6. I promise that after you get through it, you'll agree that EIGRPv6 is truly the easiest part of this chapter!

To find up-to-the-minute updates for this chapter, please see www.lammle.com/ccna or the book's web page at www.sybex.com/go/ccna.

EIGRP Features and Operations

EIGRP is a classless, distance-vector protocol that uses the concept of an autonomous system to describe a set of contiguous routers that run the same routing protocol and share routing information; it also includes the subnet mask in its route updates. This is a very big deal because by advertising subnet information, this robust protocol enables us to use VLSM and permits summarization to be included within the design of EIGRP networks.

EIGRP is sometimes referred to as a *hybrid routing protocol* or an *advanced distance-vector protocol* because it has characteristics of both distance-vector and some link-state protocols. For example, EIGRP doesn't send link-state packets like OSPF does. Instead, it sends traditional distance-vector updates that include information about networks plus the cost of reaching them from the perspective of the advertising router.

EIGRP has link-state characteristics as well—it synchronizes network topology information between neighbors at startup and then sends specific updates only when topology changes occur (bounded updates). This particular feature is a huge advancement over RIP and is a big reason that EIGRP works so well in very large networks.

EIGRP has a default hop count of 100, with a maximum of 255, but don't let this confuse you because EIGRP doesn't rely on hop count as a metric like RIP does. In

EIGRP-speak, hop count refers to how many routers an EIGRP route update packet can go through before it will be discarded, which limits the size of the autonomous system (AS). So don't forget that this isn't how metrics are calculated with EIGRP!

There are a bunch of powerful features that make EIGRP a real standout from other protocols. Here's a list of some of the major ones:

- Support for IP and IPv6 (and some other useless routed protocols) via protocol-dependent modules

- Considered classless (same as RIPv2 and OSPF)

- Support for VLSM/CIDR

- Support for summaries and discontiguous networks

- Efficient neighbor discovery

- Communication via Reliable Transport Protocol (RTP)

- Best path selection via Diffusing Update Algorithm (DUAL)

- Reduced bandwidth usage with bounded updates

- No broadcasts

Cisco refers to EIGRP as a distance-vector routing protocol but also as an advanced distance-vector or even a hybrid routing protocol.

Neighbor Discovery

Before EIGRP routers can exchange routes with each other, they must become neighbors, and there are three conditions that must be met before this can happen, as shown in Figure 17.1.

FIGURE 17.1 EIGRP neighbor discovery

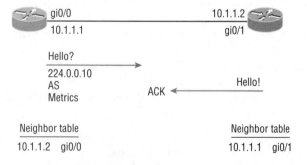

And these three things will be exchanged with directly connected neighbors:

- Hello or ACK received

- AS numbers match

- Identical metrics (K values)

Link-state protocols often use Hello messages to establish who their neighbors are because they usually don't send out periodic route updates but still need a way to help neighbors know when a new peer has arrived or an old one has gone down. And because Hellos are also used to maintain neighbor relationships, it follows that EIGRP routers must also continuously receive Hellos from their neighbors.

But EIGRP routers that belong to different ASs don't automatically share routing information and, therefore, don't become neighbors. This factor is really helpful operating in larger networks because it reduces the amount of route information propagated through a specific AS. But it also means that manual redistribution can sometimes be required between different ASs as a result. Because metrics play a big role in choosing between the five possible factors to be evaluated when choosing the best possible route, it's important that all EIGRP neighbors agree on how a specific route is chosen. This is vital because the calculations on one router depend upon the calculations of its neighbors.

Hellos between EIGRP routers are set to 5 seconds by default. Another timer that's related to the *hello timer* is the *hold timer*. The hold timer determines the amount of time a router is willing to wait to get a Hello from a neighbor before declaring it dead. Once a neighbor is declared dead, it's removed from the neighbor table and all routes that depended upon it are recalculated. Interestingly, the hold timer configuration doesn't determine how long a router waits before it declares neighbors dead; it establishes how long the router will tell others to wait before they can declare it dead. This means that the hold timers on neighboring routers don't need to match because they only tell the others how long to wait.

The only time EIGRP advertises its entire information is when it discovers a new neighbor and forms a relationship or adjacency with it by exchanging Hello packets. When this happens, both neighbors then advertise their complete information to one another. After each has learned its neighbor's routes, only changes to the routing table will be propagated.

During each EIGRP session running on a router, a neighbor table is created in which the router stores information about all routers known to be directly connected neighbors. Each neighboring router's IP address, hold time interval, *smooth round-trip timer (SRTT)*, and queue information are all kept in this table. It's an important reference used to establish that topology changes have occurred that neighboring routers need to know about.

To sum this all up, remember that EIGRP routers receive their neighbors' updates and store them in a local topology table that contains all known routes from all known neighbors and serves as the raw material from which the best routes are selected.

Let's define some terms before we move on:

Reported/advertised distance (RD/AD)   This is the metric of a remote network, as reported by a neighbor. It's also the routing table metric of the neighbor and is the same as the second number in parentheses as displayed in the topology table. The first number is the administrative distance, and I'll discuss more about these values in a minute. In Figure 17.2, routers SF and NY are both advertising the path to network 10.0.0.0 to the Corp router, but the cost through SF to network 10.0.0.0 is less than NY.

FIGURE 17.2 Advertised distance

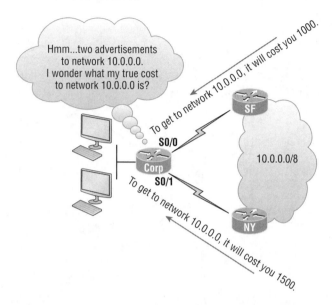

We're not done yet because the Corp router still needs to calculate its cost to each neighbor.

Feasible distance (FD) This is the best metric among all paths to a remote network, including the metric to the neighbor that's advertising the remote network. The route with the lowest FD is the route that you'll find in the routing table because it's considered the best path. The metric of a feasible distance is calculated using the metric reported by the neighbor that's referred to as the reported or advertised distance plus the metric to the neighbor reporting the route. In Figure 17.3, the Corp router will have the path through router SF to network 10.0.0.0 in the routing table since it's the lowest feasible distance. It's the lowest true cost from end to end.

Take a look at an EIGRP route that's been injected into a routing table and find the FD listed in the entry.

```
D    10.0.0.0/8 [90/2195456] via 172.16.10.2, 00:27:06,Serial0/0
```

First, the D means Dual, and it's an EIGRP injected route and the route used by EIGRP to forward traffic to the 10.0.0.0 network via its neighbor, 172.16.10.2. But that's not what I want to focus on right now. See the [90/2195456] entry in the line? The first number (90) is the administrative distance (AD), which is not to be confused with advertised distance (AD), which is why a lot of people call it the reported distance! The second number, is the feasible distance (FD), or the entire cost for this router to get to network 10.0.0.0. To sum this up, the neighbor router sends a reported, or advertised, distance (RD/AD) for network 10.0.0.0, and EIGRP calculates the cost to get to that neighbor and then adds those two numbers together to get the FD, or total cost.

FIGURE 17.3   Feasible distance

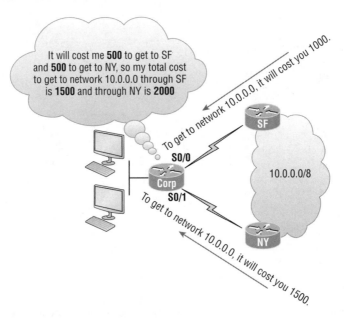

Neighbor table   Each router keeps state information about adjacent neighbors. When a newly discovered neighbor is found, its address and interface are recorded and the information is held in the neighbor table, stored in RAM. Sequence numbers are used to match acknowledgments with update packets. The last sequence number received from the neighbor is recorded so that out-of-order packets can be detected. We'll get into this more, later in the chapter, when we look at the neighbor table and find out how it's useful for troubleshooting links between neighbor routers.

Topology table   The topology table is populated by the neighbor table and the Diffusing Update Algorithm (DUAL) calculates the best loop-free path to each remote network. It contains all destinations advertised by neighboring routers, holding each destination address and a list of neighbors that have advertised the destination. For each neighbor, the advertised metric (distance), which comes only from the neighbor's routing table, is recorded, as well as the FD. The best path to each remote network is copied and placed in the routing table and then IP will use this route to forward traffic to the remote network. The path copied to the routing table is called a successor router—think "successful" to help you remember. The path with a good, but less desirable, cost will be entered in the topology table as a backup link and called the feasible successor. Let's talk more about these terms now.

The neighbor and topology tables are stored in RAM and maintained through the use of Hello and update packets. While the routing table is also stored in RAM, the information stored in the routing table is gathered only from the topology table.

Feasible successor (FS)   So a feasible successor is basically an entry in the topology table that represents a path that's inferior to the successor route(s). An FS is defined as a path whose advertised distance is less than the feasible distance of the current successor and considered a backup route. EIGRP will keep up to 32 feasible successors in the topology table in 15.0 code but only up to 16 in previous IOS versions, which is still a lot! Only the path with the best metric—the successor—is copied and placed in the routing table. The show ip eigrp topology command will display all the EIGRP feasible successor routes known to the router.

> A feasible successor is a backup route and is stored in the topology table. A successor route is stored in the topology table and is copied and placed in the routing table.

Successor   A successor route—again, think "successful"—is the best route to a remote network. A successor route is the lowest cost to a destination and stored in the topology table along with everything else. However, this particular best route is copied and placed in the routing table so IP can use it to get to the remote network. The successor route is backed up by a feasible successor route, which is also stored in the topology table, if there's one available. The routing table contains only successor routes; the topology table contains successor and feasible successor routes.

Figure 17.4 illustrates that the SF and NY routers each have subnets of the 10.0.0.0 network and the Corp router has two paths to get to this network.

FIGURE 17.4   The tables used by EIGRP

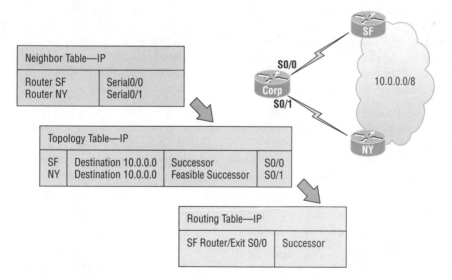

As shown in Figure 17.4, there are two paths to network 10.0.0.0 that can be used by the Corp router. EIGRP picks the best path and places it in the routing table, but if both links have equal-cost paths, EIGRP would load-balance between them—up to four links, by default. By using the successor, and having feasible successors in the topology table as backup links, the network can converge instantly and updates to any neighbor make up the only traffic sent from EIGRP—very clean!

Reliable Transport Protocol (RTP)

EIGRP depends on a proprietary protocol, called *Reliable Transport Protocol (RTP)*, to manage the communication of messages between EIGRP-speaking routers. As the name suggests, reliability is a key concern of this protocol, so Cisco designed this mechanism, which leverages multicasts and unicasts, to ensure that updates are delivered quickly and that data reception is tracked accurately.

But how does this really work? Well, when EIGRP sends multicast traffic, it uses the Class D address 224.0.0.10, and each EIGRP router knows who its neighbors are. For each multicast it sends out, a list is built and maintained that includes all the neighbors who have replied. If a router doesn't get a reply from a neighbor via the multicast, EIGRP will then try using unicasts to resend the same data. If there's no reply from a neighbor after 16 unicast attempts, that neighbor will then be declared dead. This process is often referred to as *reliable multicast.*

Routers keep track of the information they send by assigning a sequence number to each packet that enables them to identify old, redundant information and data that's out of sequence. You'll get to actually see this information in the neighbor table coming up when we get into configuring EIGRP.

Remember, EIGRP is all about topology changes and updates, making it the quiet, performance-optimizing protocol it is. Its ability to synchronize routing databases at startup time, while maintaining the consistency of databases over time, is achieved quietly by communicating only necessary changes. The downside here is that you can end up with a corrupted routing database if any packets have been permanently lost or if packets have been mishandled out of order!

Here's a description of the five different types of packets used by EIGRP:

Update   An *Update packet* contains route information. When these are sent in response to metric or topology changes, they use reliable multicasts. In the event that only one router needs an update, like when a new neighbor is discovered, it's sent via unicasts. Keep in mind that the unicast method still requires an acknowledgment, so updates are always reliable regardless of their underlying delivery mechanism.

Query   A *Query packet* is a request for specific routes and always uses the reliable multicast method. Routers send queries when they realize they've lost the path to a particular network and are searching for alternatives.

Reply   A *Reply packet* is sent in response to a query via the unicast method. Replies either include a specific route to the queried destination or declare that there's no known route.

Hello   A *Hello packet* is used to discover EIGRP neighbors and is sent via unreliable multicast, meaning it doesn't require an acknowledgment.

ACK   An *ACK packet* is sent in response to an update and is always unicast. ACKs are never sent reliably because this would require another ACK sent for acknowledgment, which would just create a ton of useless traffic!

It's helpful to think of all these different packet types like envelopes. They're really just types of containers that EIGRP routers use to communicate with their neighbors. What's really interesting is the actual content envelopes these communications and the procedures that guide their conversations, and that's what we'll be exploring next!

Diffusing Update Algorithm (DUAL)

I mentioned that EIGRP uses *Diffusing Update Algorithm (DUAL)* for selecting and maintaining the best path to each remote network. DUAL allows EIGRP to carry out these vital tasks:

- Figure out a backup route if there's one available.
- Support variable length subnet masks (VLSMs).
- Perform dynamic route recoveries.
- Query neighbors for unknown alternate routes.
- Send out queries for an alternate route.

Quite an impressive list, but what really makes DUAL so great is that it enables EIGRP to converge amazingly fast! The key to the speed is twofold: First, EIGRP routers maintain a copy of all of their neighbors' routes to refer to for calculating their own cost to each remote network. So if the best path goes down, all it often takes to find another one is a quick scan of the topology table looking for a feasible successor. Second, if that quick table survey doesn't work out, EIGRP routers immediately ask their neighbors for help finding the best path. It's exactly this, ahem, DUAL strategy of reliance upon, and the leveraging of, other routers' information that accounts for the algorithm's "diffusing" character. Unlike other routing protocols where the change is propagated through the entire network, EIGRP bounded updates are propagated only as far as needed.

Three critical conditions must be met for DUAL to work properly:

- Neighbors are discovered or noted as dead within a finite time.
- All transmitted messages are received correctly.
- All changes and messages are processed in the order in which they're detected.

As you already know, the Hello protocol ensures the rapid detection of new or dead neighbors, and RTP provides a reliable method of conveying and sequencing messages. Based upon this solid foundation, DUAL can then select and maintain information about the best paths. Let's check further into the process of route discovery and maintenance next.

Route Discovery and Maintenance

The hybrid nature of EIGRP is fully revealed in its approach to route discovery and maintenance. Like many link-state protocols, EIGRP supports the concept of neighbors that are formally discovered via a Hello process and whose state is monitored thereafter. And like many distance-vector protocols, EIGRP uses the routing-by-rumor approach, which implies that many routers within an AS never actually hear about a route update firsthand. Instead, these devices rely on "network gossip" to hear about neighbors and their respective status via another router that may have also gotten the info from yet another router and so on.

Given all of the information that EIGRP routers have to collect, it follows that they must have a place to store it, and they do this in the tables I referred to earlier in this chapter. As you know, EIGRP doesn't depend on just one table—it actually uses three of them to store important information about its environment:

Neighbor table   Contains information about the specific routers with whom neighbor relationships have been formed. It also displays information about the Hello transmit interval and queue counts for unaccounted Hello acknowledgment.

Topology table   Stores the route advertisements received from each neighbor. All routes in the AS are stored in the topology table, both successors and feasible successors.

Route table   Stores the routes that are currently in use to make local routing decisions. Anything in the routing table is considered a successor route.

We'll explore more of EIGRP's features in greater detail soon, beginning with a look at the metrics associated with particular routes. After that, I'll cover the decision-making process that's used to select the best routes, and then we'll review the procedures followed when routes change.

Configuring EIGRP

I know what you're thinking! "We're going to jump in to configuring EIGRP already when I've heard how complex it is?" No worries here—what I'm about to show is basic, and I know you won't have a problem with it at all! We're going to start with the easy part of EIGRP, and by configuring it on our little internetwork, you'll learn a lot more this way than you would if I just continued explaining more at this point. After we've completed the initial configuration, we'll fine-tune it and have fun experimenting with it throughout this chapter!

Okay, there are two modes for entering EIGRP commands: router configuration mode and interface configuration mode. In router configuration mode, we'll enable the protocol, determine which networks will run EIGRP, and set global factors. When in interface configuration mode, we'll customize summaries and bandwidth.

To initiate an EIGRP session on a router, I'll use the `router eigrp` command followed by our network's AS number. After that, we'll enter the specific numbers of the networks that we want to connect to the router using the `network` command followed by the network number. This is pretty straightforward stuff—if you can configure RIP, then you can configure EIGRP!

Just so you know, we'll use the same network I used in the previous CCENT routing chapters, but I'm going to connect more networks so we can look deeper into EIGRP. With that, I'm going to enable EIGRP for autonomous system 20 on our Corp router connected to four networks.

Figure 17.5 shows the network we'll be configuring throughout this chapter and the next chapter. Here's the Corp configuration:

FIGURE 17.5   Configuring our little internetwork with EIGRP

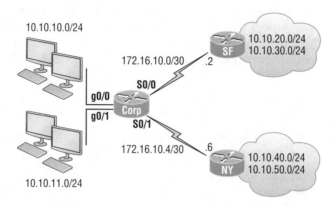

```
Corp#config t
Corp(config)#router eigrp 20
Corp(config-router)#network 172.16.0.0
Corp(config-router)#network 10.0.0.0
```

Remember, just as we would when configuring RIP, we need to use the classful network address, which is all subnet and host bits turned off. This is another thing that makes EIGRP so great: it has the complexity of a link-state protocol running in the background and the same easy configuration process used for RIP!

 Understand that the AS number is irrelevant—that is, as long as all routers use the same number! You can use any number from 1 to 65,535.

But wait, the EIGRP configuration can't be that easy, can it? A few simple EIGRP commands and my network just works? Well, it can be and usually is, but not always. Remember the wildcards you learned about in your access list configurations in your preparation for the Cisco exam? Let's say, for example, that we wanted to advertise all the directly connected networks with EIGRP off the Corp router. By using the command network 10.0.0.0, we can effectively advertise to all subnets within that classful network; however, take a look at this configuration now:

```
Corp#config t
Corp(config)#router eigrp 20
Corp(config-router)#network 10.10.11.0 0.0.0.255
Corp(config-router)#network 172.16.10.0 0.0.0.3
Corp(config-router)#network 172.16.10.4 0.0.0.3
```

This configuration should look pretty familiar to you because by now you should have a solid understanding of how wildcards are configured. This configuration will advertise the network connected to g0/1 on the Corp router as well as the two WAN links. Still, all we accomplished with this configuration was to stop the g0/0 interface from being placed into the EIGRP process, and unless you have tens of thousands of networks worldwide, then there is really no need to use wildcards because they don't provide any other administrative purpose other than what I've already described.

Now let's take a look at the simple configuration needed for the SF and NY routers in our internetwork:

```
SF(config)#router eigrp 20
SF(config-router)#network 172.16.0.0
SF(config-router)#network 10.0.0.0
000060:&#x00025;DUAL-5-NBRCHANGE:IP-EIGRP(0) 20:Neighbor 172.16.10.1
(Serial0/0/0) is up:
new adjacency


NY(config)#router eigrp 20
NY(config-router)#network 172.16.0.0
NY(config-router)#network 10.0.0.0
*Jun 26 02:41:36:%DUAL-5-NBRCHANGE:IP-EIGRP(0) 20:Neighbor 172.16.10.5
(Serial0/0/1) is up: new adjacency
```

Nice and easy—or is it? We can see that the SF and NY router created an adjacency to the Corp router, but are they actually sharing routing information? To find out, let's take a look at the number that I pointed out as the autonomous system (AS) number in the configuration.

EIGRP uses ASs to identify the group of routers that will share route information. Only routers that have the same AS share routes. The range of values we can use to create an AS with EIGRP is 1–65535:

```
Corp(config)#router eigrp ?
  <1-65535>  Autonomous System
  WORD       EIGRP Virtual-Instance Name
Corp(config)#router eigrp 20
```

Notice that I could have used any number from 1 to 65,535, but I chose to use 20 because it just felt good at the time. As long as all routers use the same number, they'll create an adjacency. Okay, now the AS makes sense, but it looks like I can type a word in the place of the AS number, and I can! Let's take a look at the configuration:

```
Corp(config)#router eigrp Todd
Corp(config-router)#address-family ipv4 autonomous-system 20
Corp(config-router-af)#network 10.0.0.0
Corp(config-router-af)#network 172.16.0.0
```

What I just showed you is not part of the Cisco exam objectives, but it's also not really necessary for any IPv4 routing configuration in your network. The previous configuration examples I've gone through so far in this chapter covers the objectives and work just fine, but I included this last configuration example because it's now an option in IOS 15.0 code.

VLSM Support and Summarization

Being one of the more sophisticated classless routing protocols, EIGRP supports using variable length subnet masks. This is good because it allows us to conserve address space by using subnet masks that map to specific host requirements in a much better way. Being able to use 30-bit subnet masks for the point-to-point networks that I configured in our internetwork is a great example. Plus, because the subnet mask is propagated with every route update, EIGRP also supports the use of discontiguous subnets, giving us greater administrative flexibility when designing a network IP address scheme. Another versatile feature is that EIGRP allows us to use and place route summaries at strategically optimal locations throughout the EIGRP network to reduce the size of the routing table.

Keep in mind that EIGRP automatically summarizes networks at their classful boundaries and supports the manual creation of summaries at any and all EIGRP routers. This is usually a good thing, but by checking out the routing table in the Corp router, you can see the possible complications that auto-summarization can cause:

```
Corp#sh ip route
[output cut]
     172.16.0.0/16 is variably subnetted, 3 subnets, 2 masks
C        172.16.10.4/30 is directly connected, Serial0/1
C        172.16.10.0/30 is directly connected, Serial0/0
D        172.16.0.0/16 is a summary, 00:01:37, Null0
     10.0.0.0/8 is variably subnetted, 3 subnets, 2 masks
C        10.10.10.0/24 is directly connected, GigabitEthernet0/0
D        10.0.0.0/8 is a summary, 00:01:19, Null0
C        10.10.11.0/24 is directly connected, GigabitEthernet0/1
```

Now this just doesn't look so good—both 172.16.0.0 and 10.0.0.0/8 are being advertised as summary routes injected by EIGRP, but we have multiple subnets in the 10.0.0.0/8 classful network address, so how would the Corp router know how to route to a specific network like 10.10.20.0? The answer is, it wouldn't. Let's see why in Figure 17.6.

The networks we're using make up what is considered a discontinuous network because we have the 10.0.0.0/8 network subnetted across a different class of address, the 172.16.0.0 network, with 10.0.0.0/8 subnets on both sides of the WAN links.

You can see that the SF and NY routers will both create an automatic summary of 10.0.0.0/8 and then inject it into their routing tables. This is a common problem, and an important one that Cisco really wants you to understand (by including it in the objectives)! With this type of topology, disabling automatic summarization is definitely the better option. Actually, it's the only option if we want this network to work.

FIGURE 17.6 Discontiguous networks

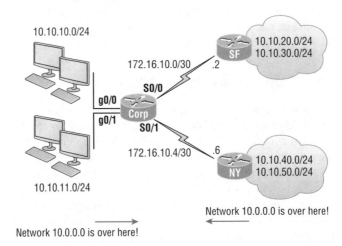

Let's take a look at the routing tables on the NY and SF routers to find out what they're seeing:

```
SF>sh ip route
[output cut]
     172.16.0.0/16 is variably subnetted, 3 subnets, 3 masks
C       172.16.10.0/30 is directly connected, Serial0/0/0
D       172.16.10.0/24 [90/2681856] via 172.16.10.1, 00:54:58, Serial0/0/0
D       172.16.0.0/16 is a summary, 00:55:12, Null0
     10.0.0.0/8 is variably subnetted, 3 subnets, 2 masks
D       10.0.0.0/8 is a summary, 00:54:58, Null0
C       10.10.20.0/24 is directly connected, FastEthernet0/0
C       10.10.30.0/24 is directly connected, Loopback0
SF>
```

```
NY>sh ip route
[output cut]
     172.16.0.0/16 is variably subnetted, 2 subnets, 2 masks
C       172.16.10.4/30 is directly connected, Serial0/0/1
D       172.16.0.0/16 is a summary, 00:55:56, Null0
     10.0.0.0/8 is variably subnetted, 3 subnets, 2 masks
D       10.0.0.0/8 is a summary, 00:55:26, Null0
C       10.10.40.0/24 is directly connected, FastEthernet0/0
C       10.10.50.0/24 is directly connected, Loopback0
NY>ping 10.10.10.1
Type escape sequence to abort.
```

```
Sending 5, 100-byte ICMP Echos to 10.10.10.1, timeout is 2 seconds:
.....
Success rate is 0 percent (0/5)
NY>
```

The confirmed answer is that our network isn't working because we're discontiguous and our classful boundaries are auto-summarizing. We can see that EIGRP is injecting summary routes into both the SF and NY routing tables.

We need to advertise our subnets in order to make this work, and here's how we make that happen, starting with the Corp router:

```
Corp#config t
Corp(config)#router eigrp 20
Corp(config-router)#no auto-summary
Corp(config-router)#
*Feb 25 18:29:30%DUAL-5-NBRCHANGE:IP-EIGRP(0) 20:Neighbor 172.16.10.6
(Serial0/1)
 is resync: summary configured
*Feb 25 18:29:30%DUAL-5-NBRCHANGE:IP-EIGRP(0) 20:Neighbor 172.16.10.2
(Serial0/0)
 is resync: summary configured
Corp(config-router)#
```

Okay—our network still isn't working because the other routers are still sending a summary. So let's configure the SF and NY routers to advertise subnets:

```
SF#config t
SF(config)#router eigrp 20
SF(config-router)#no auto-summary
SF(config-router)#
000090:%DUAL-5-NBRCHANGE:IP-EIGRP(0) 20:Neighbor 172.16.10.1 (Serial0/0/0) is
resync: summary configured
```

```
NY#config t
NY(config)#router eigrp 20
NY(config-router)#no auto-summary
NY(config-router)#
*Jun 26 21:31:08%DUAL-5-NBRCHANGE:IP-EIGRP(0) 20:Neighbor 172.16.10.5
(Serial0/0/1)
is resync: summary configured
```

Let's take a look at the Corp router's output now:

```
Corp(config-router)#do show ip route
[output cut]
```

```
        172.16.0.0/30 is subnetted, 2 subnets
C       172.16.10.4 is directly connected, Serial0/1
C       172.16.10.0 is directly connected, Serial0/0
        10.0.0.0/24 is subnetted, 6 subnets
C       10.10.10.0 is directly connected, GigabitEthernet0/0
C       10.10.11.0 is directly connected, GigabitEthernet0/1
D       10.10.20.0 [90/3200000] via 172.16.10.2, 00:00:27, Serial0/0
D       10.10.30.0 [90/3200000] via 172.16.10.2, 00:00:27, Serial0/0
D       10.10.40.0 [90/2297856] via 172.16.10.6, 00:00:29, Serial0/1
D       10.10.50.0 [90/2297856] via 172.16.10.6, 00:00:30, Serial0/1
Corp# ping 10.10.20.1

Type escape sequence to abort.
Sending 5, 100-byte ICMP Echos to 10.10.20.1, timeout is 2 seconds:
!!!!!
Success rate is 100 percent (5/5), round-trip min/avg/max = 1/2/4 ms
```

Wow, what a difference compared to the previous routing table output! We can see all the subnets now. It would be hard to justify using auto-summarization today. If you want to summarize, it should definitely be done manually. Always typing in no auto-summary under RIPv2 and EIGRP is common practice today.

> The new 15.x code auto-summarization feature is disabled by default, as it should be. But don't think that discontiguous networks and disabling auto-summary are no longer topics in the Cisco exam objectives, because they most certainly are! When troubleshooting EIGRP on the exam, verify the code version, and if it is 15.x code, then you can assume that auto-summary is not a problem.

Controlling EIGRP Traffic

But what if you need to stop EIGRP from working on a specific interface? Maybe it's a connection to your ISP, or where we didn't want to have the g0/0 interface be part of the EIGRP process as in our earlier example. All you need to do is to flag the interface as passive, and to do this from an EIGRP session, just use this command:

```
passive-interface interface-type interface-number
```

This works because the interface-type portion defines the type of interface and the interface-number portion defines the number of the interface. The following command makes interface serial 0/0 into a passive interface:

```
Corp(config)#router eigrp 20
Corp(config-router)#passive-interface g0/0
```

What we've accomplished here is to prevent this interface from sending or reading received Hello packets so that it will no longer form adjacencies or send or receive route information. But this still won't stop EIGRP from advertising the subnet of this interface out all other interfaces without using wildcards. This really illustrates the reason you must understand why and when to use wildcards as well as what the passive-interface command does. This knowledge really helps you to make an informed decision on which command you need to use to meet your specific business requirements!

> The impact of the passive-interface command depends upon the routing protocol under which the command is issued. For example, on an interface running RIP, the passive-interface command will prohibit sending route updates but will permit receiving them. An RIP router with a passive interface will still learn about the networks advertised by other routers. This is different from EIGRP, where an interface configured with the passive-interface command will neither send nor read received Hellos.

Typically, EIGRP neighbors use multicast to exchange routing updates. You can change this by specifically telling the router about a particular neighbor, which will ensure that unicast packets will only be used for the routing updates with that specific neighbor. To take advantage of this feature, apply the neighbor command and execute it under the EIGRP process.

I'm going to configure the Corp router with information about routers SF and NY:

```
Corp(config)#router eigrp 20
Corp(config-router)#neighbor 172.16.10.2
Corp(config-router)#neighbor 172.16.10.6
```

Understand that you don't need to use the preceding commands to create neighbor relationships, but they're available if you need them.

EIGRP Metrics

Unlike many other protocols that use a single element to compare routes and select the best possible path, EIGRP uses a combination of these four factors:

- *Bandwidth*
- *Delay*
- *Load*
- *Reliability*

It's worth noting that there's a fifth element, *maximum transmission unit (MTU)*, which has never been used in EIGRP metrics calculations though it's still a required parameter in some EIGRP-related commands—especially those involving redistribution. The value of the MTU element represents the smallest MTU value encountered along the path to the destination network.

Also good to know is that there's a mathematical formula that combines the four main elements to create a single value representing just how good a given route actually is. The higher the metric associated with it, the less desirable the route. Here's that formula:

$$metric = [K_1 \times Bandwidth + (K_2 \times Bandwidth)/(256 - Load) + K_3 \times Delay] \times [K_5/(Reliability + K_4)]$$

The formula's components break down like this:

- By default, $K_1 = 1$, $K_2 = 0$, $K_3 = 1$, $K_4 = 0$, $K_5 = 0$.
- *Delay* equals the sum of all the delays of the links along the path.
  - *Delay* = [Delay in 10s of microseconds] × 256.
- *Bandwidth* is the lowest bandwidth of the links along the path.
  - *Bandwidth* = [10000000 / (bandwidth in Kbps)] × 256.
- By default, *metric* = lowest bandwidth along path + sum of all delays along path.

If necessary, you can adjust the constant K values on a per-interface basis, but I would recommend that you only do this under the direction of the Cisco Technical Assistance Center (TAC). Metrics are tuned to change the manner in which routes are calculated. The K values can be seen with a show ip protocols output:

```
Corp#sh ip protocols
*** IP Routing is NSF aware ***

Routing Protocol is "eigrp 1"
  Outgoing update filter list for all interfaces is not set
  Incoming update filter list for all interfaces is not set
  Default networks flagged in outgoing updates
  Default networks accepted from incoming updates
  EIGRP-IPv4 Protocol for AS(1)
    Metric weight K1=1, K2=0, K3=1, K4=0, K5=0
```

Notice that that the K1 and K3 values are enabled by default—for example, K1 = 1. Table 17.1 shows the relationship between each constant and the metric it affects.

Each constant is used to assign a weight to a specific variable, meaning that when the metric is calculated, the algorithm will assign a greater importance to the specified metric. This is very cool because it means that by assigning a weight, you get to specify the factor that's most important to you. For example, if bandwidth is your priority, you would assign K1 to weight it accordingly, but if delay is totally unacceptable, then K3 would be assigned a greater weight. A word of caution though: Always remember that any changes to the default values could result in instability and convergence problems, particularly if delay or reliability values are constantly changing! But if you're looking for something to do on a rainy Saturday, it's an interesting experiment to pass some time and gain some nice networking insight!

TABLE 17.1   Metric association of K values

Constant	Metric
K1	Bandwidth (B_e)
K2	Load (utilization on path)
K3	Delay (D_c)
K4	Reliability (r)
K5	MTU

Maximum Paths and Hop Count

By default, EIGRP can provide equal-cost load balancing across up to 4 links. RIP and OSPF do this too. But you can have EIGRP actually load-balance across up to 32 links with 15.0 code (equal or unequal) by using the following command:

```
Corp(config)#router eigrp 10
Corp(config-router)#maximum-paths ?
  <1-32>  Number of paths
```

As I mentioned, pre–15.0 code routers allowed up to 16 paths to remote networks, which is still a lot!

EIGRP has a default maximum hop count of 100 for route update packets, but it can be set up to 255. Chances are you wouldn't want to ever change this, but if you did, here is how you would do it:

```
Corp(config)#router eigrp 10
Corp(config-router)#metric maximum-hops ?
  <1-255>  Hop count
```

As you can see from this router output, EIGRP can be set to a maximum of 255 hops. Even though it doesn't use hop count in the path metric calculation, it still uses the maximum hop count to limit the scope of the AS.

Route Selection

Now that you've got a good idea how EIGRP works and also how easy it actually is to configure, it's probably clear that determining the best path simply comes down to seeing which one gets awarded the lowest metric. But it's not the winning path that really sets EIGRP apart from other protocols. You know that EIGRP stores route information from its neighbors in its topology table and that as long as a given neighbor remains alive, it will rarely throw out anything it has learned from that neighbor. This makes EIGRP able to flag the best routes in its topology table for positioning in its local routing table, enabling it to flag the next-best routes as alternatives if the best route goes down.

In Figure 17.7, you can see that I added another Fast Ethernet link between the SF and NY routers. This will give us a great opportunity to play with the topology and routing tables!

FIGURE 17.7   EIGRP route selection process

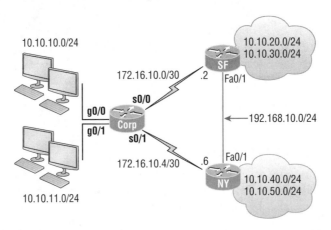

First, let's take another look at the routing table on the Corp router before I bring up the new interfaces:

```
172.16.0.0/30 is subnetted, 2 subnets
C       172.16.10.4 is directly connected, Serial0/1
C       172.16.10.0 is directly connected, Serial0/0
     10.0.0.0/24 is subnetted, 6 subnets
C       10.10.10.0 is directly connected, GigabitEthernet0/0
C       10.10.11.0 is directly connected, GigabitEthernet0/1
D       10.10.20.0 [90/3200000] via 172.16.10.2, 00:00:27, Serial0/0
D       10.10.30.0 [90/3200000] via 172.16.10.2, 00:00:27, Serial0/0
D       10.10.40.0 [90/2297856] via 172.16.10.6, 00:00:29, Serial0/1
D       10.10.50.0 [90/2297856] via 172.16.10.6, 00:00:30, Serial0/1
```

We can see the three directly connected interfaces as well as the other four networks injected into the routing table by EIGRP. Now I'll add the network 192.168.10.0/24 between the SF and NY routers, then enable the interfaces.

And let's check out the routing table of the Corp router now that I've configured that link:

```
D    192.168.10.0/24 [90/2172416] via 172.16.10.6, 00:04:27, Serial0/1
     172.16.0.0/30 is subnetted, 2 subnets
C       172.16.10.4 is directly connected, Serial0/1
C       172.16.10.0 is directly connected, Serial0/0
     10.0.0.0/24 is subnetted, 6 subnets
```

```
C       10.10.10.0 is directly connected, GigabitEthernet0/0
C       10.10.11.0 is directly connected, GigabitEthernet0/1
D       10.10.20.0 [90/3200000] via 172.16.10.2, 00:00:27, Serial0/0
D       10.10.30.0 [90/3200000] via 172.16.10.2, 00:00:27, Serial0/0
D       10.10.40.0 [90/2297856] via 172.16.10.6, 00:00:29, Serial0/1
D       10.10.50.0 [90/2297856] via 172.16.10.6, 00:00:30, Serial0/1
```

Okay—that's weird. The only thing different I see is one path to the 192.168.10.0/24 network listed first. Glad it is there, which means that we can route to that network. Notice that we can reach the network from the Serial0/1 interface, but what happened to my link to the SF router—shouldn't we have an advertisement from that router and be load-balancing? Let's take a look the topology table to find out what's going on:

```
Corp#sh ip eigrp topology
IP-EIGRP Topology Table for AS(20)/ID(10.10.11.1)

Codes: P - Passive, A - Active, U - Update, Q - Query, R - Reply,
       r - reply Status, s - sia Status

P 10.10.10.0/24, 1 successors, FD is 128256
        via Connected, GigbitEthernet0/0
P 10.10.11.0/24, 1 successors, FD is 128256
        via Connected, GigbitEthernet0/1
P 10.10.20.0/24, 1 successors, FD is 2300416
        via 172.16.10.6 (2300416/156160), Serial0/1
        via 172.16.10.2 (3200000/128256), Serial0/0
P 10.10.30.0/24, 1 successors, FD is 2300416
        via 172.16.10.6 (2300416/156160), Serial0/1
        via 172.16.10.2 (3200000/128256), Serial0/0
P 10.10.40.0/24, 1 successors, FD is 2297856
        via 172.16.10.6 (2297856/128256), Serial0/1
        via 172.16.10.2 (3202560/156160), Serial0/0
P 10.10.50.0/24, 1 successors, FD is 2297856
        via 172.16.10.6 (2297856/128256), Serial0/1
        via 172.16.10.2 (3202560/156160), Serial0/0
P 192.168.10.0/24, 1 successors, FD is 2172416
        via 172.16.10.6 (2172416/28160), Serial0/1
        via 172.16.10.2 (3074560/28160), Serial0/0
P 172.16.10.4/30, 1 successors, FD is 2169856
        via Connected, Serial0/1
P 172.16.10.0/30, 1 successors, FD is 3072000
        via Connected, Serial0/0
```

Okay, we can see there are two paths to the 192.168.10.0/24 network, but it's using the next hop of 172.16.10.6 (NY) because the feasible distance (FD) is less! The advertised distance from both routers is 28160, but the cost to get to each router via the WAN links is not the same. This means the FD is not the same, meaning we're not load-balancing by default.

Both WAN links are a T1, so this should have load-balanced by default, but EIGRP has determined that it costs more to go through SF than through NY. Since EIGRP uses bandwidth and delay of the line to determine the best path, we can use the show interfaces command to verify our stats like this:

```
Corp#sh int s0/0
Serial0/0 is up, line protocol is up
  Hardware is PowerQUICC Serial
  Description: <<Connection to CR1>>
  Internet address is 172.16.10.1/30
  MTU 1500 bytes, BW 1000 Kbit, DLY 20000 usec,
    reliability 255/255, txload 1/255, rxload 1/255
  Encapsulation HDLC, loopback not set Keepalive set (10 sec)


Corp#sh int s0/1
Serial0/1 is up, line protocol is up
  Hardware is PowerQUICC Serial
  Internet address is 172.16.10.5/30
  MTU 1500 bytes, BW 1544 Kbit, DLY 20000 usec,
    reliability 255/255, txload 1/255, rxload 1/255
  Encapsulation HDLC, loopback not set Keepalive set (10 sec)
```

I highlighted the statistics that EIGRP uses to determine the metrics to a next-hop router: MTU, bandwidth, delay, reliability, and load, with bandwidth and delay enabled by default. We can see that the bandwidth on the Serial0/0 interface is set to 1000 Kbit, which is not the default bandwidth. Serial0/1 is set to the default bandwidth of 1544 Kbit.

Let's set the bandwidth back to the default on the s0/0 interface and we should start load-balancing to the 192.168.10.0 network. I'll just use the no bandwidth command, which will set it back to its default of 1544 Mbps:

```
Corp#config t
Corp(config)#int s0/0
Corp(config-if)#no bandwidth
Corp(config-if)#^Z
```

Now let's take a look at the topology table and see if we're equal.

```
Corp#sh ip eigrp topo | section 192.168.10.0
P 192.168.10.0/24, 2 successors, FD is 2172416
        via 172.16.10.2 (2172416/28160), Serial0/0
        via 172.16.10.6 (2172416/28160), Serial0/1
```

Since the topology tables can get really huge in most networks, the show ip eigrp topology | section *network* command comes in handy because it allows us to see information about the network we want to look into in a couple of lines.

Let's use the show ip route *network* command and check out what is going on there:

```
Corp#sh ip route 192.168.10.0
Routing entry for 192.168.10.0/24
  Known via "eigrp 20", distance 90, metric 2172416, type internal
  Redistributing via eigrp 20
  Last update from 172.16.10.2 on Serial0/0, 00:05:18 ago
  Routing Descriptor Blocks:
  * 172.16.10.6, from 172.16.10.6, 00:05:18 ago, via Serial0/1
      Route metric is 2172416, traffic share count is 1
      Total delay is 20100 microseconds, minimum bandwidth is 1544 Kbit
      Reliability 255/255, minimum MTU 1500 bytes
      Loading 1/255, Hops 1
    172.16.10.2, from 172.16.10.2, 00:05:18 ago, via Serial0/0
      Route metric is 2172416, traffic share count is 1
      Total delay is 20100 microseconds, minimum bandwidth is 1544 Kbit
      Reliability 255/255, minimum MTU 1500 bytes
      Loading 1/255, Hops 1
```

Lots of detail about our routes to the 192.168.10.0 network! The Corp route has two equal-cost links to the 192.168.10.0 network. And to reveal load balancing even better, we'll just use the plain, ever useful show ip route command:

```
Corp#sh ip route
[output cut]
D    192.168.10.0/24 [90/2172416] via 172.16.10.6, 00:05:35, Serial0/1
                     [90/2172416] via 172.16.10.2, 00:05:35, Serial0/0
```

Now we can see that there are two successor routes to the 192.168.10.0 network. Pretty sweet! But in the routing table, there's one path to 192.168.20.0 and 192.168.30.0, with the link between the SF and NY routers being feasible successors. And it's the same with the 192.168.40.0 and 192.168.50.0 networks. Let's take a look at the topology table to examine this more closely:

```
Corp#sh ip eigrp topology
IP-EIGRP Topology Table for AS(20)/ID(10.10.11.1)

Codes: P - Passive, A - Active, U - Update, Q - Query, R - Reply,
       r - reply Status, s - sia Status

P 10.10.10.0/24, 1 successors, FD is 128256
        via Connected, GigabitEthernet0/0
```

```
P 10.10.11.0/24, 1 successors, FD is 128256
        via Connected, GigabitEthernet0/1
P 10.10.20.0/24, 1 successors, FD is 2297856
        via 172.16.10.2 (2297856/128256), Serial0/0
        via 172.16.10.6 (2300416/156160), Serial0/1
P 10.10.30.0/24, 1 successors, FD is 2297856
        via 172.16.10.2 (2297856/128256), Serial0/0
        via 172.16.10.6 (2300416/156160), Serial0/1
P 10.10.40.0/24, 1 successors, FD is 2297856
        via 172.16.10.6 (2297856/128256), Serial0/1
        via 172.16.10.2 (2300416/156160), Serial0/0
P 10.10.50.0/24, 1 successors, FD is 2297856
        via 172.16.10.6 (2297856/128256), Serial0/1
        via 172.16.10.2 (2300416/156160), Serial0/0
P 192.168.10.0/24, 2 successors, FD is 2172416
        via 172.16.10.2 (2172416/28160), Serial0/0
        via 172.16.10.6 (2172416/28160), Serial0/1
P 172.16.10.4/30, 1 successors, FD is 2169856
        via Connected, Serial0/1
P 172.16.10.0/30, 1 successors, FD is 2169856
        via Connected, Serial0/0
```

It is nice that we can see that we have a successor and a feasible successor to each network, so we know that EIGRP is doing its job. Let's take a close look at the links to 10.10.20.0 now and dissect what it's telling us:

```
P 10.10.20.0/24, 1 successors, FD is 2297856
        via 172.16.10.2 (2297856/128256), Serial0/0
        via 172.16.10.6 (2300416/156160), Serial0/1
```

Okay—first, we can see that it's passive (P), which means that it has found all the usable paths to the network 10.10.20.0 and is happy! If we see active (A), that means that EIGRP is not happy at all and is querying its neighbors for a new path to that network. The (2297856/128256) is the FD/AD, meaning that the SF router is advertising the 10.10.20.0 network as a cost of 128256, which is the AD. The Corp router adds the bandwidth and delay of the line to get to the SF router and then adds that number to the AD (128256) to come up with a total cost (FD) of 2297856 to get to network 10.10.20.0.

 WARNING   To become a CCNA R/S, you must understand how to read a topology table!

Unequal-Cost Load Balancing

As with all routing protocols running on Cisco routers, EIGRP automatically supports load balancing over four equal-cost routes and can be configured to support up to 32 equal-cost paths with IOS 15.0 code. As you know, previous IOS versions supported up to 16. I've mentioned this a few times in this chapter already, but I want to show you how to configure unequal-cost load balancing with EIGRP. First let's take a look at the Corp router by typing in the show ip protocols command:

```
Corp#sh ip protocols
Routing Protocol is "eigrp 20"
  Outgoing update filter list for all interfaces is not set
  Incoming update filter list for all interfaces is not set
  Default networks flagged in outgoing updates
  Default networks accepted from incoming updates
  EIGRP metric weight K1=1, K2=0, K3=1, K4=0, K5=0
  EIGRP maximum hopcount 100
  EIGRP maximum metric variance 1
  Redistributing: eigrp 20
  EIGRP NSF-aware route hold timer is 240s
  Automatic network summarization is not in effect
  Maximum path: 4
  Routing for Networks:
    10.0.0.0
    172.16.0.0
  Routing Information Sources:
    Gateway         Distance      Last Update
    (this router)         90      19:15:10
    172.16.10.6          90      00:25:38
    172.16.10.2          90      00:25:38
  Distance: internal 90 external 170
```

The variance 1 means equal-path load balancing with the maximum paths set to 4 by default. Unlike most other protocols, EIGRP also supports unequal-cost load balancing through the use of the variance parameter.

To clarify, let's say the parameter has been set to a variance of 2. This would effectively load-balance traffic across the best route plus any route with a feasible distance of up to twice as large. But still keep in mind that load balancing occurs in proportion with and relative to the cost of the route, meaning that more traffic would travel across the best route than the suboptimal one.

Let's configure the variance on the Corp router and see if we can load-balance across our feasible successors now:

```
Corp# config t
Corp(config)#router eigrp 20
Corp(config-router)#variance 2
Corp(config-router)#
*Feb 26 22:24:24:IP-EIGRP(Default-IP-Routing-Table:20):route installed for
10.10.20.0
*Feb 26 22:24:24:IP-EIGRP(Default-IP-Routing-Table:20):route installed for
10.10.20.0
*Feb 26 22:24:24:IP-EIGRP(Default-IP-Routing-Table:20):route installed for
10.10.30.0
*Feb 26 22:24:24:IP-EIGRP(Default-IP-Routing-Table:20):route installed for
10.10.30.0
*Feb 26 22:24:24:IP-EIGRP(Default-IP-Routing-Table:20):route installed for
10.10.40.0
*Feb 26 22:24:24:IP-EIGRP(Default-IP-Routing-Table:20):route installed for
10.10.40.0
*Feb 26 22:24:24:IP-EIGRP(Default-IP-Routing-Table:20):route installed for
10.10.50.0
*Feb 26 22:24:24:IP-EIGRP(Default-IP-Routing-Table:20):route installed for
10.10.50.0
*Feb 26 22:24:24:IP-EIGRP(Default-IP-Routing-Table:20):route installed for
192.168.10.0
*Feb 26 22:24:24:IP-EIGRP(Default-IP-Routing-Table:20):route installed for
192.168.10.0
Corp(config-router)#do show ip route
[output cut]
D    192.168.10.0/24 [90/2172416] via 172.16.10.6, 00:00:18, Serial0/1
                     [90/2172416] via 172.16.10.2, 00:00:18, Serial0/0
     172.16.0.0/30 is subnetted, 2 subnets
C       172.16.10.4 is directly connected, Serial0/1
C       172.16.10.0 is directly connected, Serial0/0
     10.0.0.0/24 is subnetted, 6 subnets
C       10.10.10.0 is directly connected, GigabitEthernet0/0
C       10.10.11.0 is directly connected, GigabitEthernet0/1
D       10.10.20.0 [90/2300416] via 172.16.10.6, 00:00:18, Serial0/1
                   [90/2297856] via 172.16.10.2, 00:00:19, Serial0/0
D       10.10.30.0 [90/2300416] via 172.16.10.6, 00:00:19, Serial0/1
                   [90/2297856] via 172.16.10.2, 00:00:19, Serial0/0
D       10.10.40.0 [90/2297856] via 172.16.10.6, 00:00:19, Serial0/1
                   [90/2300416] via 172.16.10.2, 00:00:19, Serial0/0
```

```
D       10.10.50.0 [90/2297856] via 172.16.10.6, 00:00:20, Serial0/1
                   [90/2300416] via 172.16.10.2, 00:00:20, Serial0/0
Corp(config-router)#
```

Nice—it worked! Now we have two paths to each remote network in the routing table, even though the feasible distances to each route aren't equal. Don't forget that unequal load balancing is not enabled by default and that you can perform load balancing through paths that have up to 128 times worse metrics than the successor route!

Split Horizon

Split horizon is enabled on interfaces by default, which means that if a route update is received on an interface from a neighbor router, this interface will not advertise those networks back out to the neighbor router who sent them. Let's take a look at an interface and then go through an example:

```
Corp#sh ip int s0/0
Serial0/0 is up, line protocol is up
  Internet address is 172.16.10.1/24
  Broadcast address is 255.255.255.255
  Address determined by setup command
  MTU is 1500 bytes
  Helper address is not set
  Directed broadcast forwarding is disabled
  Multicast reserved groups joined: 224.0.0.10
  Outgoing access list is not set
  Inbound  access list is not set
  Proxy ARP is enabled
  Local Proxy ARP is disabled
  Security level is default
  Split horizon is enabled
[output cut]
```

Okay—we can see that split horizon is enabled by default. But what does this really mean? Most of the time it's more helpful than harmful, but let's check out our internetwork in Figure 17.8 so I can really explain what split horizon is doing.

Notice that the SF and NY routers are each advertising their routes to the Corp router. Now, let's see what the Corp router sends back to each router in Figure 17.9.

Can you see that the Corp router is not advertising back out the advertised networks that it received on each interface? This is saving the SF and NY routers from receiving the incorrect route information that they could possibly get to their own network through the Corp router, which we know is wrong.

FIGURE 17.8 Split horizon in action, part 1

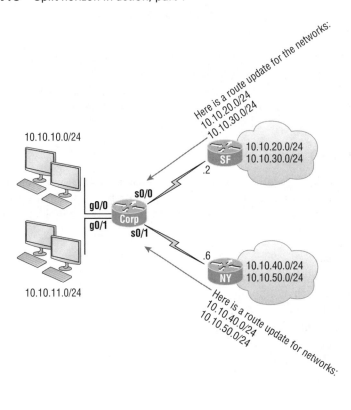

FIGURE 17.9 Split horizon in action, part 2

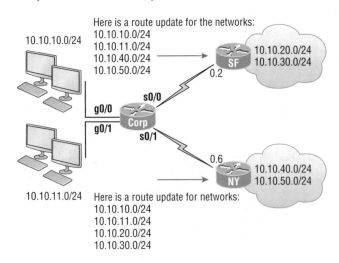

So how can this cause a problem? After all, it seems reasonable not to send misinformation back to an originating router, right? You'll see this create a problem on point-to-multipoint links, such as Frame Relay, when multiple remote routers connect to a single interface at the Corp location. We can use logical interfaces, called subinterfaces, which I'll tell you all about in Chapter 21, "Wide Area Networks," to solve the split horizon issue on a point-to-multipoint interface.

Verifying and Troubleshooting EIGRP

Even though EIGRP usually runs smoothly and is relatively low maintenance, there are several commands you need to memorize for using on a router that can be super helpful when troubleshooting EIGRP! I've already shown you a few of them, but I'm going to demonstrate all the tools you'll need to verify and troubleshoot EIGRP now. Table 17.2 contains all of the commands you need to know for verifying that EIGRP is functioning well and offers a brief description of what each command does.

TABLE 17.2   EIGRP troubleshooting commands

Command	Description/Function
show ip eigrp neighbors	Shows all EIGRP neighbors, their IP addresses, and the retransmit interval and queue counts for the adjacent routers
show ip eigrp interfaces	Lists the interfaces on which the router has actually enabled EIGRP
show ip route eigrp	Shows EIGRP entries in the routing table
show ip eigrp topology	Shows entries in the EIGRP topology table
show ip eigrp traffic	Shows the packet count for EIGRP packets sent and received
show ip protocols	Shows information about the active protocol sessions

When troubleshooting an EIGRP problem, it's always a good idea to start by getting an accurate map of the network, and the best way to do that is by using the show ip eigrp neighbors command to find out who your directly connected neighbors are. This command shows all adjacent routers that share route information within a given AS. If neighbors are missing, check the configuration, AS number, and link status on both routers to verify that the protocol has been configured correctly.

Let's execute the command on the Corp router:

Corp#**sh ip eigrp neighbors**

IP-EIGRP neighbors for process 20

H	Address	Interface	Hold (sec)	Uptime	SRTT (ms)	RTO	Q Cnt	Seq Num
1	172.16.10.2	Se0/0	11	03:54:25	1	200	0	127
0	172.16.10.6	Se0/1	11	04:14:47	1	200	0	2010

Here's a breakdown of the important information we can see in the preceding output:

- H indicates the order in which the neighbor was discovered.
- Hold time in seconds is how long this router will wait for a Hello packet to arrive from a specific neighbor.
- The Uptime value indicates how long the neighbor relationship has been established.
- The SRTT field is the smooth round-trip timer and represents how long it takes to complete a round-trip from this router to its neighbor and back. This value delimits how long to wait after a multicast for a reply from this neighbor. As mentioned earlier, the router will attempt to establish communication via unicasts if it doesn't receive a reply.
- The time between multicast attempts is specified by the Retransmission Time Out (RTO) field, which is based upon the SRTT values.
- The Q value tells us if there are any outstanding messages in the queue. We can make a mental note that there's a problem if we see consistently large values here!
- Finally, the Seq field shows the sequence number of the last update from that neighbor, which is used to maintain synchronization and avoid duplicate messages or their out-of-sequence processing.

The neighbors command is a great command, but we can get local status of our router by also using the show ip eigrp interface command like this:

Corp#**sh ip eigrp interfaces**

IP-EIGRP interfaces for process 20

Interface	Peers	Xmit Queue Un/Reliable	Mean SRTT	Pacing Time Un/Reliable	Multicast Flow Timer	Pending Routes
Gi0/0	0	0/0	0	0/1	0	0
Se0/1	1	0/0	1	0/15	50	0
Se0/0	1	0/0	1	0/15	50	0
Gi0/1	0	0/0	0	0/1	0	0

Corp#**sh ip eigrp interface detail s0/0**

IP-EIGRP interfaces for process 20

Interface	Peers	Xmit Queue Un/Reliable	Mean SRTT	Pacing Time Un/Reliable	Multicast Flow Timer	Pending Routes
Se0/0	1	0/0	1	0/15	50	0

```
  Hello interval is 5 sec
  Next xmit serial <none>
  Un/reliable mcasts: 0/0  Un/reliable ucasts: 21/26
  Mcast exceptions: 0  CR packets: 0  ACKs suppressed: 9
  Retransmissions sent: 0  Out-of-sequence rcvd: 0
  Authentication mode is not set
```

The first command, show ip eigrp interfaces, lists all interfaces for which EIGRP is enabled as well as those the router is currently sending Hello messages to in an attempt to find new EIGRP neighbors. The show ip eigrp interface detail *interface* command lists more details per interface, including the local router's own Hello interval. Understand that you can use these commands to verify that all your interfaces are within the AS process used by EIGRP, but also note that the passive interfaces won't show up in these outputs. So be sure to also check to see if an interface has been configured as passive if is not present in the outputs.

Okay, if all neighbors are present, then verify the routes learned. By executing the show ip route eigrp command, you're given a quick picture of the routes in the routing table. If a certain route doesn't appear in the routing table, you need to verify its source. If the source is functioning properly, then check the topology table.

The routing table according to Corp looks like this:

```
D     192.168.10.0/24 [90/2172416] via 172.16.10.6, 02:29:09, Serial0/1
                      [90/2172416] via 172.16.10.2, 02:29:09, Serial0/0
      172.16.0.0/30 is subnetted, 2 subnets
C        172.16.10.4 is directly connected, Serial0/1
C        172.16.10.0 is directly connected, Serial0/0
      10.0.0.0/24 is subnetted, 6 subnets
C        10.10.10.0 is directly connected, Loopback0
C        10.10.11.0 is directly connected, Loopback1
D        10.10.20.0 [90/2300416] via 172.16.10.6, 02:29:09, Serial0/1
                    [90/2297856] via 172.16.10.2, 02:29:10, Serial0/0
D        10.10.30.0 [90/2300416] via 172.16.10.6, 02:29:10, Serial0/1
                    [90/2297856] via 172.16.10.2, 02:29:10, Serial0/0
D        10.10.40.0 [90/2297856] via 172.16.10.6, 02:29:10, Serial0/1
                    [90/2300416] via 172.16.10.2, 02:29:10, Serial0/0
D        10.10.50.0 [90/2297856] via 172.16.10.6, 02:29:11, Serial0/1
                    [90/2300416] via 172.16.10.2, 02:29:11, Serial0/0
```

You can see here that most EIGRP routes are referenced with a D and that their administrative distance is 90. Remember that the [90/2300416] represents AD/FD, and in the preceding output, EIGRP is performing equal- and unequal-cost load balancing between two links to our remote networks.

We can see this by looking closer at two different networks. Pay special attention to the FD of each output:

```
Corp#sh ip route | section 192.168.10.0
D    192.168.10.0/24 [90/2172416] via 172.16.10.6, 01:15:44, Serial0/1
                     [90/2172416] via 172.16.10.2, 01:15:44, Serial0/0
```

The preceding output shows equal-cost load balancing, and here's our unequal-cost load balancing in action:

```
Corp#sh ip route | section 10.10.50.0
D    10.10.50.0 [90/2297856] via 172.16.10.6, 01:16:16, Serial0/1
                [90/2300416] via 172.16.10.2, 01:16:16, Serial0/0
```

We can get the topology table displayed for us via the show ip eigrp topology command. If the route is in the topology table but not in the routing table, it's a pretty safe assumption that there's a problem between the topology database and the routing table. After all, there must be a good reason the topology database isn't adding the route into the routing table, right? We discussed this issue in detail earlier in the chapter, and it's oh so important!

Corp's topology table looks like this:

```
P 10.10.10.0/24, 1 successors, FD is 128256
        via Connected, GigabitEthernet0/0
P 10.10.11.0/24, 1 successors, FD is 128256
        via Connected, GigabitEthernet0/1
P 10.10.20.0/24, 1 successors, FD is 2297856
        via 172.16.10.2 (2297856/128256), Serial0/0
        via 172.16.10.6 (2300416/156160), Serial0/1
P 10.10.30.0/24, 1 successors, FD is 2297856
        via 172.16.10.2 (2297856/128256), Serial0/0
        via 172.16.10.6 (2300416/156160), Serial0/1
P 10.10.40.0/24, 1 successors, FD is 2297856
        via 172.16.10.6 (2297856/128256), Serial0/1
        via 172.16.10.2 (2300416/156160), Serial0/0
P 10.10.50.0/24, 1 successors, FD is 2297856
        via 172.16.10.6 (2297856/128256), Serial0/1
        via 172.16.10.2 (2300416/156160), Serial0/0
P 192.168.10.0/24, 2 successors, FD is 2172416
        via 172.16.10.2 (2172416/28160), Serial0/0
        via 172.16.10.6 (2172416/28160), Serial0/1
P 172.16.10.4/30, 1 successors, FD is 2169856
        via Connected, Serial0/1
P 172.16.10.0/30, 1 successors, FD is 2169856
        via Connected, Serial0/0
```

Notice that every route in this output is preceded by a P, which shows that these routes are in a *passive state*. This is good because routes in the active state indicate that the router has lost its path to this network and is searching for a replacement. Each entry also reveals the feasible distance, or FD, to each remote network as well as the next-hop neighbor through which packets will travel to this destination. Each entry also has two numbers in brackets, with the first indicating the feasible distance and the second, the advertised distance to a remote network.

Again, here's our equal- and unequal-cost load-balancing output shown in the topology table:

```
Corp#sh ip eigrp top | section 192.168.10.0
P 192.168.10.0/24, 2 successors, FD is 2172416
        via 172.16.10.2 (2172416/28160), Serial0/0
        via 172.16.10.6 (2172416/28160), Serial0/1
```

The preceding output shows equal-cost load balancing, and here is our unequal-cost load balancing in action:

```
Corp#sh ip eigrp top | section 10.10.50.0
P 10.10.50.0/24, 1 successors, FD is 2297856
        via 172.16.10.6 (2297856/128256), Serial0/1
        via 172.16.10.2 (2300416/156160), Serial0/0
```

The command show ip eigrp traffic enables us to see if updates are being sent. If the counters for EIGRP input and output packets don't increase, it means that no EIGRP information is being sent between peers. The following output indicates that the Corp router is experiencing normal traffic:

```
Corp#show ip eigrp traffic
IP-EIGRP Traffic Statistics for process 200
  Hellos sent/received: 2208/2310
  Updates sent/received: 184/183
  Queries sent/received: 17/4
  Replies sent/received: 4/18
  Acks sent/received: 62/65
  Input queue high water mark 2, 0 drops
```

All of the packet types I talked about in the section on RTP are represented in the output of this command. And we can't forget the always useful troubleshooting command show ip protocols. Here's the output the Corp router gives us after using it:

```
Routing Protocol is "eigrp 20"
  Outgoing update filter list for all interfaces is not set
  Incoming update filter list for all interfaces is not set
  Default networks flagged in outgoing updates
  Default networks accepted from incoming updates
```

```
EIGRP metric weight K1=1, K2=0, K3=1, K4=0, K5=0
EIGRP maximum hopcount 100
EIGRP maximum metric variance 2
Redistributing: eigrp 20
EIGRP NSF-aware route hold timer is 240s
Automatic network summarization is not in effect
Maximum path: 4
Routing for Networks:
  10.0.0.0
  172.16.0.0
Routing Information Sources:
  Gateway         Distance      Last Update
  (this router)         90      04:23:51
  172.16.10.6           90      02:30:48
  172.16.10.2           90      02:30:48
Distance: internal 90 external 170
```

In this output, we can see that EIGRP is enabled for autonomous system 20 and that the K values are set to their defaults. The variance is 2, so both equal- and unequal-cost load balancing is happening here. Automatic summarization has been turned off. We can also see that EIGRP is advertising two classful networks and that it sees two neighbors.

The show ip eigrp events command displays a log of every EIGRP event: when routes are injected and removed from the routing table and when EIGRP adjacencies are reset or fail. This information is so helpful in determining if there are routing instabilities in the network! Be advised that this command can result in quite a flood of information even for really simple configurations like ours. To demonstrate, here's the output the Corp router divulged after I used it:

```
Corp#show ip eigrp events
Event information for AS 20:
1    22:24:24.258 Metric set: 172.16.10.0/30 2169856
2    22:24:24.258 FC sat rdbmet/succmet: 2169856 0
3    22:24:24.258 FC sat nh/ndbmet: 0.0.0.0 2169856
4    22:24:24.258 Find FS: 172.16.10.0/30 2169856
5    22:24:24.258 Metric set: 172.16.10.4/30 2169856
6    22:24:24.258 FC sat rdbmet/succmet: 2169856 0
7    22:24:24.258 FC sat nh/ndbmet: 0.0.0.0 2169856
8    22:24:24.258 Find FS: 172.16.10.4/30 2169856
9    22:24:24.258 Metric set: 192.168.10.0/24 2172416
10   22:24:24.258 Route install: 192.168.10.0/24 172.16.10.2
11   22:24:24.258 Route install: 192.168.10.0/24 172.16.10.6
12   22:24:24.254 FC sat rdbmet/succmet: 2172416 28160
13   22:24:24.254 FC sat nh/ndbmet: 172.16.10.6 2172416
```

```
14    22:24:24.254 Find FS: 192.168.10.0/24 2172416
15    22:24:24.254 Metric set: 10.10.50.0/24 2297856
16    22:24:24.254 Route install: 10.10.50.0/24 172.16.10.6
17    22:24:24.254 FC sat rdbmet/succmet: 2297856 128256
18    22:24:24.254 FC sat nh/ndbmet: 172.16.10.6 2297856
19    22:24:24.254 Find FS: 10.10.50.0/24 2297856
20    22:24:24.254 Metric set: 10.10.40.0/24 2297856
21    22:24:24.254 Route install: 10.10.40.0/24 172.16.10.6
22    22:24:24.250 FC sat rdbmet/succmet: 2297856 128256
 --More--
```

Troubleshooting Example with EIGRP

Throughout this chapter I've covered many of the problems that commonly occur with EIGRP and how to verify and troubleshoot these issues. Make sure you clearly understand what I have shown you so far in this chapter so you're prepared to answer any question the Cisco exam could possibly throw at you!

Just to make sure you're solidly armed with all the skills you need to ace the exam as well as successfully administer a network, I'm going to provide even more examples about verifying EIGRP. We'll be dealing with mostly the same commands and problems we've already covered, but this is so important, and the best way to get this all nailed down is to practice troubleshooting an EIGRP network as much as possible!

With that, after you've configured EIGRP, you would first test connectivity to the remote network by using the Ping program. If that fails, you need to check whether the directly connected router is in the neighbor table.

Here are some key things to look for if neighbors haven't formed an adjacency:

- Interfaces between the devices are down.
- The two routers have mismatching EIGRP autonomous system numbers.
- Proper interfaces are not enabled for the EIGRP process.
- An interface is configured as passive.
- The K values are mismatched.
- EIGRP authentication is misconfigured.

Also, if the adjacency is up but you're not receiving remote network updates, there may be a routing problem, likely caused by these issues:

- The proper networks aren't being advertised under the EIGRP process.
- An access list is blocking the advertisements from remote networks.
- Automatic summary is causing confusion in your discontiguous network.

Let's use Figure 17.10 as our example network and run through some troubleshooting scenarios. I've preconfigured the routers with IP addresses, and without having to try too hard, I also snuck in a few snags for us to find and fix. Let's see what we're facing.

FIGURE 17.10   Troubleshooting scenario

A good place to start is by checking to see if we have an adjacency with show ip eigrp neighbors and show ip eigrp interfaces. It's also smart to see what information the show ip eigrp topology command reveals:

```
Corp#sh ip eigrp neighbors
IP-EIGRP neighbors for process 20
Corp#
```

```
Corp#sh ip eigrp interfaces
IP-EIGRP interfaces for process 20
```

		Xmit Queue	Mean	Pacing Time	Multicast	Pending
Interface	Peers	Un/Reliable	SRTT	Un/Reliable	Flow Timer	Routes
Se0/1	0	0/0	0	0/15	50	0
Fa0/0	0	0/0	0	0/1	0	0
Se0/0	0	0/0	0	0/15	50	0

```
Corp#sh ip eigrp top
IP-EIGRP Topology Table for AS(20)/ID(10.10.11.1)

Codes: P - Passive, A - Active, U - Update, Q - Query, R - Reply,
       r - reply Status, s - sia Status


P 10.1.1.0/24, 1 successors, FD is 28160
        via Connected, FastEthernet0/0
```

Alright—we can see by looking at the neighbor and the interface as well as the topology table command that our LAN is up on the Corp router but the serial link isn't working between routers because we don't have an adjacency. From the show ip eigrp interfaces command, we can establish that EIGRP is running on all interfaces, so that means our network statements under the EIGRP process are probably correct, but we'll verify that later.

Let's move on by checking into our Physical and Data Link status with the show ip int brief command because maybe there's a physical problem between routers:

```
Corp#sh ip int brief
Interface              IP-Address     OK? Method Status        Protocol
```

```
FastEthernet0/0          10.1.1.1       YES manual up                          up
Serial0/0                192.168.1.1    YES manual up                          up
FastEthernet0/1          unassigned     YES manual administratively down down
Serial0/1                172.16.10.5    YES manual administratively down down
Corp#
Corp#sh protocols s0/0
Serial0/0 is up, line protocol is up
  Internet address is 192.168.1.1/30
```

Well, since the Serial0/0 interface shows the correct IP address and the status is up/up, it means we have a good Data Link connection between routers, so it's not a physical link issue between the routers, which is good! Notice I also used the show protocols command, which gave me the subnet mask for the link. Remember, the information obtained via the two commands gives us only layer 1 and layer 2 status and doesn't mean we can ping across the link. In other words, we might have a layer 3 issue, so let's check the Branch router with the same commands:

```
Branch#sh ip int brief
Interface                IP-Address     OK? Method Status              Protocol
FastEthernet0/0          10.2.2.2       YES manual up                          up
FastEthernet0/1          unassigned     YES manual administratively down down
Serial0/0/0              192.168.1.2    YES manual up                          up
Serial0/0/1              unassigned     YES unset  administratively down down
Branch#sh proto s0/0/0
Serial0/0/0 is up, line protocol is up
  Internet address is 192.168.1.2/30
```

Okay, well, we can see that our IP address and mask are correct, and that the link shows up/up, so we're looking pretty good! Let's try to ping from the Corp router to the Branch router now:

```
Corp#ping 192.168.1.2

Type escape sequence to abort.
Sending 5, 100-byte ICMP Echos to 192.168.1.2, timeout is 2 seconds:
!!!!!
Success rate is 100 percent (5/5), round-trip min/avg/max = 1/3/4 ms
```

Now because that was successful, we've ruled out layer 1, 2, or 3 issues between routers at this point! Since everything seems to be working between the routers, except

EIGRP, checking our EIGRP configurations is our next move. Let's start with the show ip protocols command:

```
Corp#sh ip protocols
Routing Protocol is "eigrp 20"
  Outgoing update filter list for all interfaces is not set
  Incoming update filter list for all interfaces is not set
  Default networks flagged in outgoing updates
  Default networks accepted from incoming updates
  EIGRP metric weight K1=1, K2=0, K3=1, K4=0, K5=0
  EIGRP maximum hopcount 100
  EIGRP maximum metric variance 2
  Redistributing: eigrp 20
  EIGRP NSF-aware route hold timer is 240s
  Automatic network summarization is in effect
  Maximum path: 4
  Routing for Networks:
    10.0.0.0
    172.16.0.0
    192.168.1.0
Passive Interface(s):
    FastEthernet0/1
  Routing Information Sources:
    Gateway         Distance      Last Update
    (this router)         90      20:51:48
    192.168.1.2          90      00:22:58
    172.16.10.6          90      01:58:46
    172.16.10.2          90      01:59:52
  Distance: internal 90 external 170
```

This output shows us we're using AS 20, that we don't have an access-list filter list set on the routing tables, and that our K values are set to default. We can see that we're routing for the 10.0.0.0, 172.16.0.0, and 192.168.1.0 networks and that we have a passive interface on interface FastEthernet0/1. We don't have an interface configured for the 172.16.0.0 network, which means that this entry is an extra network statement under EIGRP. But that won't hurt anything, so this is not causing our issue. Last, the passive interface is not causing a problem with this network either, because we're not using interface Fa0/1. Still, keep in mind that when troubleshooting, it's always good to see if there are any interfaces set to passive.

Let's see what the show interfaces command will tell us:

```
Corp#sh interfaces s0/0
Serial0/0 is up, line protocol is up
  Hardware is PowerQUICC Serial
  Description: <<Connection to Branch>>
```

```
Internet address is 192.168.1.1/30
MTU 1500 bytes, BW 1544 Kbit, DLY 20000 usec,
   reliability 255/255, txload 1/255, rxload 1/255
Encapsulation HDLC, loopback not set
[output cut]
```

Looks like our statistics are set to defaults, so nothing really pops as a problem here. But remember when I covered the steps to check if there is no adjacency back at the beginning of this section? In case you forgot, here's a list of things to investigate:

- The interface between the devices are down.
- The two routers have mismatching EIGRP autonomous system numbers.
- The proper interfaces aren't enabled for the EIGRP process.
- An interface is configured as passive.
- K values are mismatched.
- EIGRP authentication is misconfigured.

Okay, our interfaces are not down, our AS number matches, layer 3 is working between routers, all the interfaces show up under the EIGRP process, and none of our needed interfaces are passive, so now we'll have to look even deeper into the EIGRP configuration to uncover the problem.

Since the Corp router has the basic default configurations, we need to check the Branch router's EIGRP configuration:

```
Branch#sh ip protocols
Routing Protocol is "eigrp 20"
  Outgoing update filter list for all interfaces is 10
  Incoming update filter list for all interfaces is not set
  Default networks flagged in outgoing updates
  Default networks accepted from incoming updates
  EIGRP metric weight K1=1, K2=0, K3=0, K4=0, K5=0
  EIGRP maximum hopcount 100
  EIGRP maximum metric variance 1
  Redistributing: eigrp 20
  EIGRP NSF-aware route hold timer is 240s
  Automatic network summarization is not in effect
  Maximum path: 4
  Routing for Networks:
    10.0.0.0
    192.168.1.0
  Routing Information Sources:
    Gateway         Distance      Last Update
    192.168.1.1           90      00:27:09
  Distance: internal 90 external 170
```

This router has the correct AS—always check this first—and we're routing for the correct networks. But I see two possible snags here, do you? First, the outgoing ACL filter list is set, but the metrics are not set to default. Remember, just because an ACL is set doesn't mean it's automatically giving you grief. Second, the K values must match, and we know these values are not matching the Corp router!

Let's take a look at the Branch interface statistics to see what else might be wrong:

```
Branch>sh int s0/0/0
Serial0/0/0 is up, line protocol is up
  Hardware is GT96K Serial
  Internet address is 192.168.1.2/30
  MTU 1500 bytes, BW 512 Kbit, DLY 30000 usec,
    reliability 255/255, txload 1/255, rxload 1/255
  Encapsulation HDLC, loopback not set
[output cut]
```

Aha! The bandwidth and delay are not set to their defaults and don't match the directly connected Corp router. Let's start by changing those back to the default and see if that fixes our problem:

```
Branch#config t
Branch(config)#int s0/0/0
Branch(config-if)#no bandwidth
Branch(config-if)#no delay
```

And let's check out our stats now to see if we're back to defaults:

```
Branch#sh int s0/0/0
Serial0/0/0 is up, line protocol is up
  Hardware is GT96K Serial
  Internet address is 192.168.1.2/30
  MTU 1500 bytes, BW 1544 Kbit, DLY 20000 usec,
    reliability 255/255, txload 1/255, rxload 1/255
  Encapsulation HDLC, loopback not set
[output cut]
```

The bandwidth and delay are now at the defaults, so let's check our adjacencies next:

```
Corp#sh ip eigrp neighbors
IP-EIGRP neighbors for process 20
```

Okay, so it wasn't the bandwidth and delay settings because our adjacency didn't come up, so let's set our K values back to default like this:

```
Branch#config t
Branch(config)#router eigrp 20
```

```
Branch(config-router)#metric weights 0 1 0 1 0 0
Branch(config-router)#do sho ip proto
Routing Protocol is "eigrp 20"
  Outgoing update filter list for all interfaces is 10
  Incoming update filter list for all interfaces is not set
  Default networks flagged in outgoing updates
  Default networks accepted from incoming updates
  EIGRP metric weight K1=1, K2=0, K3=1, K4=0, K5=0
[output cut]
```

I know this probably seems a little complicated at first, but it's something you shouldn't have to do much, if ever. Remember, there are five K values, so why 6 numbers? The first number listed is type of service (ToS), so always just set that to 0, which means you must type in six numbers as shown in my configuration example. After we chose the default of 0 first, the default K values are then 1 0 1 0 0, which is bandwidth and delay enabled. Let's check our adjacency now:

```
Corp#sh ip eigrp neighbors
IP-EIGRP neighbors for process 20
H   Address               Interface      Hold Uptime   SRTT   RTO  Q   Seq
                                         (sec)         (ms)        Cnt Num
0   192.168.1.2           Se0/0            14 00:02:09    7   200  0   18
```

Bam! There we go! Looks like mismatched K values were our problem. Now let's just check to make sure we can ping from end to end and we're done:

```
Corp#ping 10.2.2.2

Type escape sequence to abort.
Sending 5, 100-byte ICMP Echos to 10.2.2.2, timeout is 2 seconds:
.....
Success rate is 0 percent (0/5)
Corp#
```

Rats! It looks like even though we have our adjacency, we still can't reach our remote network. Next step? Let's see what the routing table shows us:

```
Corp#sh ip route
[output cut]

     10.0.0.0/8 is variably subnetted, 2 subnets, 2 masks
C       10.1.1.0/24 is directly connected, FastEthernet0/0
D       10.0.0.0/8 is a summary, 00:18:55, Null0
     192.168.1.0/24 is variably subnetted, 2 subnets, 2 masks
C       192.168.1.0/30 is directly connected, Serial0/0
D       192.168.1.0/24 is a summary, 00:18:55, Null0
```

The problem is screamingly clear now because I went through this in detail throughout this chapter. But just in case you still can't find it, let's look at the show ip protocols command output:

```
Routing Protocol is "eigrp 20"
  Outgoing update filter list for all interfaces is not set
  Incoming update filter list for all interfaces is not set
  Default networks flagged in outgoing updates
  Default networks accepted from incoming updates
  EIGRP metric weight K1=1, K2=0, K3=1, K4=0, K5=0
  EIGRP maximum hopcount 100
  EIGRP maximum metric variance 2
  Redistributing: eigrp 20
  EIGRP NSF-aware route hold timer is 240s
  Automatic network summarization is in effect
  Automatic address summarization:
    192.168.1.0/24 for FastEthernet0/0
      Summarizing with metric 2169856
    10.0.0.0/8 for Serial0/0
      Summarizing with metric 28160
  [output cut]
```

By looking at the Figure 17.10, you should have noticed right away that we had a discontiguous network. This means that unless they are running 15.0 IOS code, the routers will auto-summarize, so we need to disable auto-summary:

```
Branch(config)#router eigrp 20
Branch(config-router)#no auto-summary
008412:%DUAL-5-NBRCHANGE:IP-EIGRP(0) 20:Neighbor 192.168.1.1 (Serial0/0/0) is
resync:
peer graceful-restart


Corp(config)#router eigrp 20
Corp(config-router)#no auto-summary
Corp(config-router)#
*Feb 27 19:52:54:%DUAL-5-NBRCHANGE: IP-EIGRP(0) 20:Neighbor 192.168.1.2
(Serial0/0)
 is resync: summary configured
*Feb 27 19:52:54.177:IP-EIGRP(Default-IP-Routing-Table:20):10.1.1.0/24 - do
advertise
 out Serial0/0
*Feb 27 19:52:54:IP-EIGRP(Default-IP-Routing-Table:20):Int 10.1.1.0/24 metric
2816
```

```
0 - 25600 2560
*Feb 27 19:52:54:IP-EIGRP(Default-IP-Routing-Table:20):192.168.1.0/30 - do
advertise out Serial0/0
*Feb 27 19:52:54:IP-EIGRP(Default-IP-Routing-Table:20):192.168.1.0/24 - do
advertise out Serial0/0
*Feb 27 19:52:54:IP-EIGRP(Default-IP-Routing-Table:20):Int 192.168.1.0/24 metric
4294967295 - 0 4294967295
*Feb 27 19:52:54:IP-EIGRP(Default-IP-Routing-Table:20):10.0.0.0/8 - do advertise
 out Serial0/0
Corp(config-router)#
*Feb 27 19:52:54:IP-EIGRP(Default-IP-Routing-Table:20):Int 10.0.0.0/8 metric
4294967295 - 0 4294967295
*Feb 27 19:52:54:IP-EIGRP(Default-IP-Routing-Table:20):Processing incoming REPLY
packet
*Feb 27 19:52:54:IP-EIGRP(Default-IP-Routing-Table:20):Int 192.168.1.0/24 M
4294967295 - 1657856 4294967295 SM 4294967295 - 1657856 4294967295
*Feb 27 19:52:54:IP-EIGRP(Default-IP-Routing-Table:20):Int 10.0.0.0/8 M
4294967295 - 25600 4294967295 SM 4294967295 - 25600 4294967295
*Feb 27 19:52:54:IP-EIGRP(Default-IP-Routing-Table:20):Processing incoming
UPDATE packet
```

Finally the Corp looks happy, so it looks like we're good to go! Let's just check our routing table to be sure:

```
Corp#sh ip route
[output cut]
     10.0.0.0/24 is subnetted, 1 subnets
C       10.1.1.0 is directly connected, FastEthernet0/0
     192.168.1.0/30 is subnetted, 1 subnets
C       192.168.1.0 is directly connected, Serial0/0
```

What the heck? How can this be! We saw all those updates on the Corp console, right? Let's check the configuration of EIGRP by looking at the active configuration on the Branch router:

```
Branch#sh run
[output cut]
!
router eigrp 20
 network 10.0.0.0
 network 192.168.1.0
 distribute-list 10 out
 no auto-summary
!
```

We can see that the access list is set outbound on the routing table of the Branch router. This may be preventing us from receiving the updates from remote networks! Let's see what the ACL 10 list is doing:

```
Branch#sh access-lists
Standard IP access list 10
    10 deny    any (40 matches)
    20 permit any
```

Now who in the world would stick an access list like this on a router? This ACL says to deny every packet, which makes the second line of the ACL irrelevant since every single packet will match the first line! This has got to be the source of our troubles, so let's remove that list and see if the Corp router starts working:

```
Branch#config t
Branch(config)#router eigrp 20
Branch(config-router)#no distribute-list 10 out
```

Okay, with that ugly thing gone, let's check to see if we're receiving our remote networks now:

```
Corp#sh ip route
[output cut]
     10.0.0.0/24 is subnetted, 2 subnets
D       10.2.2.0 [90/2172416] via 192.168.1.2, 00:00:24, Serial0/0
C       10.1.1.0 is directly connected, FastEthernet0/0
     192.168.1.0/30 is subnetted, 1 subnets
C       192.168.1.0 is directly connected, Serial0/0
Corp#
Corp#ping 10.2.2.2

Type escape sequence to abort.
Sending 5, 100-byte ICMP Echos to 10.2.2.2, timeout is 2 seconds:
!!!!!
Success rate is 100 percent (5/5), round-trip min/avg/max = 1/3/4 ms
Corp#
```

Clear skies! We're up and running. We had mismatched K values, discontiguous networking, and a nasty ACL on our routing table. For the CCNA R/S objectives, always check for an ACL on the actual interface as well, not just in the routing table. It could be set on the interface or routing table, either one, or both! And never forget to check for passive interfaces when troubleshooting a routing protocol issue!

All of these commands are seriously powerful tools in the hands of a savvy professional faced with the task of troubleshooting myriad network issues. I could go on and on about the profusion of information these commands can generate and how well they can equip us to solve virtually every networking ill, but that would be way outside the scope of this book. Even so, I have no doubt that the foundation I've given you here will prove practical and valuable for certification purposes as well as for working in the real networking world.

Simple Troubleshooting EIGRP for the CCNA

Let's do one more troubleshooting scenario. You have two routers not forming an adjacency. What would you do first? Well, we went through a lot in this chapter, but let me make it super easy for you when you're troubleshooting on the CCNA exam.

All you need to do is perform a show running-config on each router. That's it! I can then fix anything regarding EIGRP. Remember that dynamic routing is all about the router you are looking at—it's not important to be looking at another router's configuration to get EIGRP correct on the router you're configuring as long as you know your AS number.

Let's look at each router's configuration and determine what the problem is—no network figure needed here because this is all about the router you're looking at.

Here is the first router's configuration:

```
R1#sh run
Building configuration...

Current configuration : 737 bytes
!
version 15.1
!
interface Loopback0
 ip address 10.1.1.1 255.255.255.255
int FastEthernet0/0
 ip address 192.168.16.1 255.255.255.0
int Serial1/1
 ip address 192.168.13.1 255.255.255.0
 bandwidth 1000
int Serial1/3
 ip address 192.168.12.1 255.255.255.0
!
router eigrp 1
 network 192.168.12.0
 network 192.168.13.0
 network 192.168.16.0
```

Here is the neighbor router's configuration:

```
R2#sh run
Building configuration...
```

```
Current configuration : 737 bytes
!
version 15.1
!
interface Loopback0
 ip address 10.2.2.2 255.255.255.255
interface Loopback1
 ip address 10.5.5.5 255.255.255.255
interface Loopback2
 ip address 10.5.5.55 255.255.255.255
int FastEthernet0/0
 ip address 192.168.123.2 255.255.255.0
int Serial2/1
 ip address 192.168.12.2 255.255.255.0
!
router eigrp 2
 network 10.2.2.2 0.0.0.0
 network 192.168.12.0
 network 192.168.123.0
```

Can you see the problems? Pretty simple. First, notice that we're running 15.1 code so we don't need to worry about discontiguous networks or need to configure the no auto-summary command. One thing down!

Now, let's look at each interface and either remember or write down the network numbers under each interface, including the loopback interfaces. Once we do that we can then make sure our EIGRP configuration is correct.

Here is the new configuration for R1:

```
R1#config t
R1(config)#router eigrp 1
R1(config-router)#network 10.1.1.1 0.0.0.0
```

That's it! I just added the missing network statement from the loopback0 interface under the EIGRP process; all the other networks were already under the EIGRP process. We're golden on R1. Let's fix R2 now:

```
R2#config t
R2(config)#no router eigrp 2
R2(config)#router eigrp 1
R2(config-router)#network 10.2.2.2 0.0.0
R2(config-router)#network 10.5.5.5 0.0.0.0
R2(config-router)#network 10.5.5.55 0.0.0.0
R2(config-router)#network 192.168.123.0
R2(config-router)#network 192.168.12.0
```

Notice I started by deleting the wrong AS number—they have to match! I then created another EIGRP process using AS 1 and then added all the networks found under every interface, including the loopback interfaces.

It's that easy! Just perform a Show running-config on each router, add any missing networks found under each interface to the EIGRP process, make sure the AS numbers match, and you're set!

Now it's time to relax a bit as we move into the easiest part of this chapter, seriously—not joking! You still need to pay attention though.

EIGRPv6

As I was just saying, welcome to the easiest part of the chapter! Of course, I only mostly mean that, and here's why: I talked about IPv6 in the earlier ICND1 chapters, and in order to continue on with this section of the chapter, you need to have that vital, foundational part of IPv6 down solidly before you dare to dwell here! If you do, you're pretty much set and this will all be pretty simple for you.

EIGRPv6 works much the same way as its IPv4 predecessor does—most of the features that EIGRP provided before EIGRPv6 will still be available.

EIGRPv6 is still an advanced distance-vector protocol that has some link-state features. The neighbor discovery process using Hellos still happens, and it still provides reliable communication with Reliable Transport Protocol that gives us loop-free fast convergence using the Diffusing Update Algorithm (DUAL).

Hello packets and updates are sent using multicast transmission, and as with RIPng, EIGRPv6's multicast address stayed almost the same. In IPv4 it was 224.0.0.10; in IPv6, it's FF02::A (A = 10 in hexadecimal notation).

But clearly, there are key differences between the two versions. Most notably the use of the pesky network command is gone, so it's hard to make a mistake with EIGRPv6. Also, the network and interface to be advertised must be enabled from interface configuration mode with one simple command.

But you still have to use the router configuration mode to enable the routing protocol in EIGRPv6 because the routing process must be literally enabled like an interface with the no shutdown command—interesting! However, the 15.0 code does enable this by default, so this command actually may or may not be needed.

Here's an example of enabling EIGRPv6 on the Corp router:

```
Corp(config)#ipv6 unicast-routing
Corp(config)#ipv6 router eigrp 10
```

The 10 in this case is still the AS number. The prompt changes to (config-rtr), and from here, just initiate a no shutdown if needed:

```
Corp(config-rtr)#no shutdown
```

Other options also can be configured in this mode, like redistribution and router ID (RID). So now, let's go to the interface and enable IPv6:

```
Corp(config-if)#ipv6 eigrp 10
```

The 10 in the interface command again references the AS number that was enabled in the configuration mode.

Figure 17.11 shows the layout we've been using throughout this chapter, only with IPv6 addresses now assigned to interfaces. I used the EUI-64 option on each interface so each router assigned itself an IPv6 address after I typed in the 64-bit network/subnet address.

FIGURE 17.11   Configuring EIGRPv6 on our internetwork

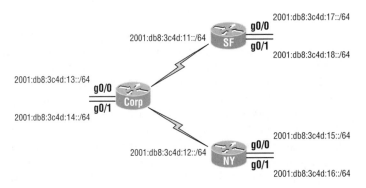

We'll start with the Corp router. Really, all we need to know in order to enable EIGRPv6 are which interfaces we're using and want to advertise our networks.

```
Corp#config t
Corp(config)#ipv6 router eigrp 10
Corp(config-rtr)#no shut
Corp(config-rtr)#router-id 1.1.1.1
Corp(config-rtr)#int s0/0/0
Corp(config-if)#ipv6 eigrp 10
Corp(config-if)#int s0/0/1
Corp(config-if)#ipv6 eigrp 10
Corp(config-if)#int g0/0
Corp(config-if)#ipv6 eigrp 10
Corp(config-if)#int g0/1
Corp(config-if)#ipv6 eigrp 10
```

I had erased and reloaded the routers before I started this EIGRPv6 section of the chapter. What this means is that there were no 32-bit addresses on the router in order to create the RID for EIGRP, so I had to set it under the IPv6 router global command, which is the same command used with EIGRP and EIGRPv6. Unlike with OSPF, the RID isn't that important, and it can actually be the same address on every router. You just can't get away with doing this with OSPF! The configuration for EIGRPv6 was pretty straightforward because unless you type the AS number wrong, it's pretty hard to screw this up!

Okay, let's configure the SF and NY routers now, and then we'll verify our networks:

```
SF#config t
SF(config)#ipv6 router eigrp 10
SF(config-rtr)#no shut
SF(config-rtr)#router-id 2.2.2.2
SF(config-rtr)#int s0/0/0
SF(config-if)#ipv6 eigrp 10
SF(config-if)#int g0/0
SF(config-if)#ipv6 eigrp 10
SF(config-if)#int g0/1
SF(config-if)#ipv6 eigrp 10


NY#config t
NY(config)#ipv6 router eigrp 10
NY(config-rtr)#no shut
NY(config-rtr)#router-id 3.3.3.3
NY(config-rtr)#int s0/0/0
NY(config-if)#ipv6 eigrp 10
NY(config-if)#int g0/0
NY(config-if)#ipv6 eigrp 10
NY(config-if)#int g0/1
```

Since we configured EIGRPv6 on a per-interface basis, no worries about having to use the passive-interface command. This is because if we don't enable the routing protocol on an interface, it's just not part of the EIGRPv6 process. We can see which interfaces are part of the EIGRPv6 process with the show ipv6 eigrp interfaces command like this:

```
Corp#sh ipv6 eigrp interfaces
IPv6-EIGRP interfaces for process 10
                      Xmit Queue   Mean   Pacing Time   Multicast     Pending
Interface      Peers  Un/Reliable  SRTT   Un/Reliable   Flow Timer    Routes
Se0/0/0          1       0/0       1236      0/10           0            0
Se0/0/1          1       0/0       1236      0/10           0            0
Gig0/1           0       0/0       1236      0/10           0            0
Gig0/0           0       0/0       1236      0/10           0            0
Corp#
```

Looks great so far—all the interfaces we want in our AS are listed, so we're looking good for our Corp's local configuration. Now it's time to check if our adjacencies came up with the show ipv6 eigrp neighbors command:

```
Corp#sh ipv6 eigrp neighbors
IPv6-EIGRP neighbors for process 10
H   Address                 Interface     Hold    Uptime     SRTT    RTO   Q   Seq
                                          (sec)              (ms)          Cnt Num
0   Link-local address:     Se0/0/0        10     00:01:40    40     1000  0   11
    FE80::201:C9FF:FED0:3301
1   Link-local address:     Se0/0/1        14     00:01:24    40     1000  0   11
    FE80::209:7CFF:FE51:B401
```

It's great that we can see neighbors listed off of each serial interface, but do you notice something missing from the preceding output? That's right, the actual IPv6 network/subnet addresses of the links aren't listed in the neighbor table! Only the link-local addresses are used for forming EIGRP neighbor adjacencies. With IPv6, neighbor interfaces and next-hop addresses are always link-local.

We can verify our configuration with the show ip protocols command:

```
Corp#sh ipv6 protocols
IPv6 Routing Protocol is "connected"
IPv6 Routing Protocol is "static
IPv6 Routing Protocol is "eigrp 10 "
  EIGRP metric weight K1=1, K2=0, K3=1, K4=0, K5=0
  EIGRP maximum hopcount 100
  EIGRP maximum metric variance 1
  Interfaces:
    Serial0/0/0
    Serial0/0/1
    GigabitEthernet0/0
    GigabitEthernet0/1
Redistributing: eigrp 10
  Maximum path: 16
  Distance: internal 90 external 170
```

You can verify the AS number from this output, but be sure to verify your K values, variance, and interfaces too. Remember that the AS number and interfaces are the first factors to check when troubleshooting.

The topology table lists all feasible routes in the network, so this output can be rather long, but let's see what this shows us:

```
Corp#sh ipv6 eigrp topology
IPv6-EIGRP Topology Table for AS 10/ID(1.1.1.1)

Codes: P - Passive, A - Active, U - Update, Q - Query, R - Reply,
       r - Reply status
```

```
P 2001:DB8:C34D:11::/64, 1 successors, FD is 2169856
        via Connected, Serial0/0/0
P 2001:DB8:C34D:12::/64, 1 successors, FD is 2169856
        via Connected, Serial0/0/1
P 2001:DB8:C34D:14::/64, 1 successors, FD is 2816
        via Connected, GigabitEthernet0/1
P 2001:DB8:C34D:13::/64, 1 successors, FD is 2816
        via Connected, GigabitEthernet0/0
P 2001:DB8:C34D:17::/64, 1 successors, FD is 2170112
        via FE80::201:C9FF:FED0:3301 (2170112/2816), Serial0/0/0
P 2001:DB8:C34D:18::/64, 1 successors, FD is 2170112
        via FE80::201:C9FF:FED0:3301 (2170112/2816), Serial0/0/0
P 2001:DB8:C34D:15::/64, 1 successors, FD is 2170112
        via FE80::209:7CFF:FE51:B401 (2170112/2816), Serial0/0/1
P 2001:DB8:C34D:16::/64, 1 successors, FD is 2170112
        via FE80::209:7CFF:FE51:B401 (2170112/2816), Serial0/0/1
```

Since we only have eight networks in our internetwork, we can see all eight networks in the topology table, which clearly is as it should be. I've highlighted a couple of things I want to discuss, and the first is that you need to be able to read and understand a topology table. This includes understanding which routes are directly connected and which are being advertised via neighbors. The via Connected shows us our directly connected networks. The second item I want to show you is (2170112/2816), which is the FD/AD, and by the way, it's no different than if you're working with IPv4.

So let's wrap up this chapter by taking a look at a routing table:

```
Corp#sh ipv6 route eigrp
IPv6 Routing Table - 13 entries
Codes: C - Connected, L - Local, S - Static, R - RIP, B - BGP
       U - Per-user Static route, M - MIPv6
       I1 - ISIS L1, I2 - ISIS L2, IA - ISIS interarea, IS - ISIS summary
       O - OSPF intra, OI - OSPF inter, OE1 - OSPF ext 1, OE2 - OSPF ext 2
       ON1 - OSPF NSSA ext 1, ON2 - OSPF NSSA ext 2
       D - EIGRP, EX - EIGRP external
C   2001:DB8:C34D:11::/64 [0/0]
    via ::, Serial0/0/0
L   2001:DB8:C34D:11:230:A3FF:FE36:B101/128 [0/0]
    via ::, Serial0/0/0
C   2001:DB8:C34D:12::/64 [0/0]
    via ::, Serial0/0/1
L   2001:DB8:C34D:12:230:A3FF:FE36:B102/128 [0/0]
    via ::, Serial0/0/1
```

```
C    2001:DB8:C34D:13::/64 [0/0]
       via ::, GigabitEthernet0/0
L    2001:DB8:C34D:13:2E0:F7FF:FEDA:7501/128 [0/0]
       via ::, GigabitEthernet0/0
C    2001:DB8:C34D:14::/64 [0/0]
       via ::, GigabitEthernet0/1
L    2001:DB8:C34D:14:2E0:F7FF:FEDA:7502/128 [0/0]
       via ::, GigabitEthernet0/1
D    2001:DB8:C34D:15::/64 [90/2170112]
       via FE80::209:7CFF:FE51:B401, Serial0/0/1
D    2001:DB8:C34D:16::/64 [90/2170112]
       via FE80::209:7CFF:FE51:B401, Serial0/0/1
D    2001:DB8:C34D:17::/64 [90/2170112]
       via FE80::201:C9FF:FED0:3301, Serial0/0/0
D    2001:DB8:C34D:18::/64 [90/2170112]
       via FE80::201:C9FF:FED0:3301, Serial0/0/0
L    FF00::/8 [0/0]
       via ::, Null0
```

I highlighted the EIGRPv6 injected routes that were injected into the routing table. It's important to notice that in order for IPv6 to get to a remote network, the router uses the next-hop link-local address. Do you see that in the table? For example, via FE80::209:7CFF:FE51:B401, Serial0/0/1 is the link-local address of the NY router.

See? I told you it was easy!

Summary

It's true that this chapter has been pretty extensive, so let's briefly recap what we covered in it. EIGRP, the main focus of the chapter, is a hybrid of link-state routing and typically referred to as an advanced distance-vector protocol. It allows for unequal-cost load balancing, controlled routing updates, and formal neighbor adjacencies called relationships to be formed.

EIGRP uses the capabilities of the Reliable Transport Protocol (RTP) to communicate between neighbors and utilizes the Diffusing Update Algorithm (DUAL) to compute the best path to each remote network.

We also covered the configuration of EIGRP and explored a number of troubleshooting commands plus key ways and means to help solve some common networking issues.

Moving on, EIGRP facilitates unequal-cost load balancing, controlled routing updates, and formal neighbor adjacencies.

I also went over the configuration of EIGRP and explored a number of troubleshooting commands as well as taking you through a highly informative scenario that will not only help you to ace the exam, it will help you confront and overcome many troubleshooting issues common to today's internetworks!

Finally, I went over the easiest topic at the end of this long chapter: EIGRPv6. Easy to understand, configure, and verify!

Exam Essentials

Know EIGRP features.   EIGRP is a classless, advanced distance-vector protocol that supports IP and now IPv6. EIGRP uses a unique algorithm, called DUAL, to maintain route information and uses RTP to communicate with other EIGRP routers reliably.

Know how to configure EIGRP.   Be able to configure basic EIGRP. This is configured the same as RIP with classful addresses.

Know how to verify EIGRP operation.   Know all of the EIGRP show commands and be familiar with their output and the interpretation of the main components of their output.

Be able to read an EIGRP topology table.   Understand which are successors, which are feasible successors, and which routes will become successors if the main successor fails.

You must be able to troubleshoot EIGRP.   Go through the EIGRP troubleshooting scenario and make sure you understand to look for the AS number, ACLs, passive interfaces, variance, and other factors.

Be able to read an EIGRP neighbor table.   Understand the output of the show ip eigrp neighbor command.

Understand how to configure EIGRPv6.   To configure EIGRPv6, first create the autonomous system from global configuration mode and perform a no shutdown. Then enable EIGRPv6 on each interface individually.

Written Lab 17

You can find the answers to this lab in Appendix A, "Answers to Written Labs."

1.   What is the command to enable EIGRPv6 from global configuration mode?

2.   What is the EIGRPv6 multicast address?

3.   True/False: Each router within an EIGRP domain must use different AS numbers.

4.   If you have two routers with various K values assigned, what will this do to the link?

5.   What type of EIGRP interface will neither send nor receive Hello packets?

6.   Which type of EIGRP route entry describes a feasible successor?

Hands-on Labs

In this section, you will use the following network and add EIGRP and EIGRPv6 routing.

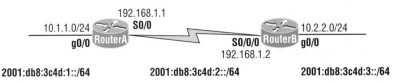

The first lab requires you to configure two routers for EIGRP and then view the configuration. In the last lab, you will be asked to enable EIGRPv6 routing on the same network. Note that the labs in this chapter were written to be used with real equipment—real cheap equipment, that is. I wrote these labs with the cheapest, oldest routers I had lying around so you can see that you don't need expensive gear to get through some of the hardest labs in this book. However, you can use the free LammleSim IOS version simulator or Cisco's Packet Tracer to run through these labs.

The labs in this chapter are as follows:

Lab 17.1: Configuring and Verifying EIGRP

Lab 17.2: Configuring and Verifying EIGRPv6

Hands-on Lab 17.1: Configuring and Verifying EIGRP

This lab will assume you have configured the IP addresses on the interfaces as shown in the preceding diagram.

1. Implement EIGRP on RouterA.

    ```
    RouterA#conf t
    Enter configuration commands, one per line.
      End with CNTL/Z.
    RouterA(config)#router eigrp 100
    RouterA(config-router)#network 192.168.1.0
    RouterA(config-router)#network 10.0.0.0
    RouterA(config-router)#^Z
    RouterA#
    ```

2. Implement EIGRP on RouterB.

    ```
    RouterB#conf t
    Enter configuration commands, one per line.
      End with CNTL/Z.
    RouterB(config)#router eigrp 100
    ```

```
RouterB(config-router)#network 192.168.1.0
RouterA(config-router)#network 10.0.0.0
RouterB(config-router)#exit
RouterB#
```

3. Display the topology table for RouterA.
   ```
   RouterA#show ip eigrp topology
   ```

4. Display the routing table for RouterA.
   ```
   RouterA #show ip route
   ```

5. Display the neighbor table for RouterA.
   ```
   RouterA show ip eigrp neighbor
   ```

6. Type the command on each router to fix the routing problem. You did see a problem, didn't you? Yes, the network is discontiguous.
   ```
   RouterA#config t
   RouterA(config)#router eigrp 100
   RouterA(config-router)#no auto-summary

   RouterB#config t
   RouterA(config)#router eigrp 100
   RouterA(config-router)#no auto-summary
   ```

7. Verify your routes with the show ip route command.

Hands-on Lab 17.2: Configuring and Verifying EIGRPv6

This lab will assume you configured the IPv6 address as shown in the diagram preceding Lab 5.1.

1. Implement EIGRPv6 on RouterA with AS 100.
   ```
   RouterA#config t
   RouterA (config)#ipv6 router eigrp 100
   RouterA (config-rtr)#no shut
   RouterA (config-rtr)#router-id 2.2.2.2
   RouterA (config-rtr)#int s0/0
   RouterA (config-if)#ipv6 eigrp 100
   RouterA (config-if)#int g0/0
   RouterA (config-if)#ipv6 eigrp 100
   ```

2. Implement EIGRP on RouterB.
   ```
   RouterA#config t
   RouterB(config)#ipv6 router eigrp 100
   ```

```
RouterB(config-rtr)#no shut
RouterB(config-rtr)#router-id 2.2.2.2
RouterB(config-rtr)#int s0/0
RouterB(config-if)#ipv6 eigrp 100
RouterB(config-if)#int g0/0
RouterB(config-if)#ipv6 eigrp 100
```

3. Display the topology table RouterA.

```
RouterA#show ipv6 eigrp topology
```

4. Display the routing table for RouterA.

```
RouterA #show ipv6 route
```

5. Display the neighbor table for RouterA.

```
RouterA show ipv6 eigrp neighbor
```

Review Questions

 The following questions are designed to test your understanding of this chapter's material. For more information on how to get additional questions, please see www.lammle.com/ccna.

You can find the answers to these questions in Appendix B, "Answers to Review Questions."

1. There are three possible routes for a router to reach a destination network. The first route is from OSPF with a metric of 782. The second route is from RIPv2 with a metric of 4. The third is from EIGRP with a composite metric of 20514560. Which route will be installed by the router in its routing table?

   A. RIPv2

   B. EIGRP

   C. OSPF

   D. All three

2. Which EIGRP information is held in RAM and maintained through the use of Hello and update packets? (Choose two.)

   A. Neighbor table

   B. STP table

   C. Topology table

   D. DUAL table

3. What will be the reported distance to a downstream neighbor router for the 10.10.30.0 network, with the neighbor adding the cost to find the true FD?

   ```
   P 10.10.30.0/24, 1 successors, FD is 2297856
           via 172.16.10.2 (2297856/128256), Serial0/0
   ```

   A. Four hops

   B. 2297856

   C. 128256

   D. EIGRP doesn't use reported distances.

4. Where are EIGRP successor routes stored?

   A. In the routing table only

   B. In the neighbor table only

   C. In the topology table only

   D. In the routing table and the neighbor table

    E. In the routing table and the topology table

    F. In the topology table and the neighbor table

5. Which command will display all the EIGRP feasible successor routes known to a router?

    A. `show ip routes *`

    B. `show ip eigrp summary`

    C. `show ip eigrp topology`

    D. `show ip eigrp adjacencies`

    E. `show ip eigrp neighbors detail`

6. Which of the following commands are used when routing with EIGRP or EIGRPv6? (Choose three.)

    A. `network 10.0.0.0`

    B. `eigrp router-id`

    C. `variance`

    D. `router eigrp`

    E. `maximum-paths`

7. Serial0/0 goes down. How will EIGRP send packets to the 10.1.1.0 network?

`Corp#`**`show ip eigrp topology`**

`[output cut]`

`P 10.1.1.0/24, 2 successors, FD is 2681842`

`        via 10.1.2.2 (2681842/2169856), Serial0/0`

`        via 10.1.3.1 (2973467/2579243), Serial0/2`

`        via 10.1.3.3 (2681842/2169856), Serial0/1`

    A. EIGRP will put the 10.1.1.0 network into active mode.

    B. EIGRP will drop all packets destined for 10.1.1.0.

    C. EIGRP will just keep sending packets out s0/1.

    D. EIGRP will use s0/2 as the successor and keep routing to 10.1.1.0.

8. What command do you use to enable EIGRPv6 on an interface?

    A. `router eigrp as`

    B. `ip router eigrp as`

    C. `router eigrpv6 as`

    D. `ipv6 eigrp as`

9. What command was typed in to have these two paths to network 10.10.50.0 in the routing table?

```
D        10.10.50.0 [90/2297856] via 172.16.10.6, 00:00:20, Serial0/1
                    [90/6893568] via 172.16.10.2, 00:00:20, Serial0/0
```

- **A.** maximum-paths 2
- **B.** variance 2
- **C.** variance 3
- **D.** maximum-hops 2

10. A route to network 10.10.10.0 goes down. How does EIGRP respond in the local routing table? (Choose two.)

- **A.** It sends a poison reverse with a maximum hop of 16.
- **B.** If there is a feasible successor, that is copied and placed into the routing table.
- **C.** If a feasible successor is not found, a query will be sent to all neighbors asking for a path to network 10.10.10.0.
- **D.** EIGRP will broadcast out all interfaces that the link to network 10.10.10.0 is down and that it is looking for a feasible successor.

11. You need the IP address of the devices with which the router has established an adjacency. Also, the retransmit interval and the queue counts for the adjacent routers need to be checked. What command will display the required information?

- **A.** show ip eigrp adjacency
- **B.** show ip eigrp topology
- **C.** show ip eigrp interfaces
- **D.** show ip eigrp neighbors

12. For some reason, you cannot establish an adjacency relationship on a common Ethernet link between two routers. Looking at the output shown here, what are the causes of the problem? (Choose two.)

```
RouterA##show ip protocols
Routing Protocol is "eigrp 20"
  Outgoing update filter list for all interfaces is not set
  Incoming update filter list for all interfaces is not set
  Default networks flagged in outgoing updates
  Default networks accepted from incoming updates
  EIGRP metric weight K1=1, K2=0, K3=1, K4=0, K5=0

RouterB##show ip protocols
Routing Protocol is "eigrp 220"
  Outgoing update filter list for all interfaces is not set
  Incoming update filter list for all interfaces is not set
  Default networks flagged in outgoing updates
  Default networks accepted from incoming updates
  EIGRP metric weight K1=1, K2=1, K3=1, K4=0, K5=0
```

A. EIGRP is running on RouterA and OSPF is running on RouterB.

B. There is an ACL set on the routing protocol.

C. The AS numbers don't match.

D. There is no default network accepted from incoming updates.

E. The K values don't match.

F. There is a passive interface set.

13. Which are true regarding EIGRP successor routes? (Choose two.)

A. A successor route is used by EIGRP to forward traffic to a destination.

B. Successor routes are saved in the topology table to be used if the primary route fails.

C. Successor routes are flagged as "active" in the routing table.

D. A successor route may be backed up by a feasible successor route.

E. Successor routes are stored in the neighbor table following the discovery process.

14. The remote RouterB router has a directly connected network of 10.255.255.64/27. Which two of the following EIGRP network statements could you use so this directly connected network will be advertised under the EIGRP process? (Choose two.)

A. network 10.255.255.64

B. network 10.255.255.64 0.0.0.31

C. network 10.255.255.64 0.0.0.0

D. network 10.255.255.64 0.0.0.15

15. RouterA and RouterB are connected via their Serial 0/0 interfaces, but they have not formed an adjacency. Based on the following output, what could be the problem?

```
RouterA#sh ip protocols
Routing Protocol is "eigrp 220"
  Outgoing update filter list for all interfaces is not set
  Incoming update filter list for all interfaces is not set
  Default networks flagged in outgoing updates
  Default networks accepted from incoming updates
  EIGRP metric weight K1=1, K2=0, K3=1, K4=0, K5=0
  EIGRP maximum hopcount 100
  EIGRP maximum metric variance 2
  Redistributing: eigrp 220
  EIGRP NSF-aware route hold timer is 240s
  Automatic network summarization is in effect
  Maximum path: 4
  Routing for Networks:
    10.0.0.0
    172.16.0.0
    192.168.1.0
  Routing Information Sources:
    Gateway         Distance      Last Update
    (this router)         90      20:51:48
    192.168.1.2           90      00:22:58
    172.16.10.6           90      01:58:46
    172.16.10.2           90      01:59:52
  Distance: internal 90 external 170
```

```
RouterB#sh ip protocols
Routing Protocol is "eigrp 220"
  Outgoing update filter list for all interfaces is not set
  Incoming update filter list for all interfaces is not set
  Default networks flagged in outgoing updates
  Default networks accepted from incoming updates
  EIGRP metric weight K1=1, K2=0, K3=1, K4=0, K5=0
  EIGRP maximum hopcount 100
  EIGRP maximum metric variance 2
  Redistributing: eigrp 220
  EIGRP NSF-aware route hold timer is 240s
  Automatic network summarization is in effect
  Maximum path: 4
  Routing for Networks:
    10.0.0.0
    172.16.0.0
    192.168.1.0
Passive Interface(s):
    Serial0/0
  Routing Information Sources:
    Gateway         Distance      Last Update
    (this router)        90       20:51:48
    192.168.1.2          90       00:22:58
    172.16.10.6          90       01:58:46
    172.16.10.2          90       01:59:52
  Distance: internal 90 external 170
```

A. The metric K values don't match.

B. The AS numbers don't match.

C. There is a passive interface on RouterB.

D. There is an ACL set on RouterA.

16. How many paths will EIGRPv6 load-balance by default?

    A. 16

    B. 32

    C. 4

    D. None

17. What would your configurations be on RouterB based on the illustration? (Choose two.)

    A. (config)#router eigrp 10

    B. (config)#ipv6 router eigrp 10

    C. (config)#ipv6 router 2001:db8:3c4d:15::/64

    D. (config-if)#ip eigrp 10

    E. (config-if)#ipv6 eigrp 10

    F. (config-if)#ipv6 router eigrp 10

18. RouterA has a feasible successor not shown in the following output. Based on what you can learn from the output, which one of the following will be the successor for 2001:db8:c34d:18::/64 if the current successor fails?

```
via FE80::201:C9FF:FED0:3301 (29110112/33316), Serial0/0/0
via FE80::209:7CFF:FE51:B401 (4470112/42216), Serial0/0/1
via FE80::209:7CFF:FE51:B401 (2170112/2816), Serial0/0/2
```

  A. Serial0/0/0

  B. Serial0/0/1

  C. Serial0/0/2

  D. There is no feasible successor.

19. You have router output as shown in the following illustrations with routers running IOS 12.4. However, the two networks are not sharing routing table route entries. What is the problem?

```
RouterA#sh ip protocols
Routing Protocol is "eigrp 930"
  Outgoing update filter list for all interfaces is not set
  Incoming update filter list for all interfaces is not set
  Default networks flagged in outgoing updates
  Default networks accepted from incoming updates
  EIGRP metric weight K1=1, K2=0, K3=1, K4=0, K5=0
  EIGRP maximum hopcount 100
  EIGRP maximum metric variance 2
  Redistributing: eigrp 930
  EIGRP NSF-aware route hold timer is 240s
  Automatic network summarization is in effect
  Automatic address summarization:
    192.168.1.0/24 for FastEthernet0/0
      Summarizing with metric 2169856
    10.0.0.0/8 for Serial0/0
      Summarizing with metric 28160
  [output cut]

RouterB#sh ip protocols
Routing Protocol is "eigrp 930"
  Outgoing update filter list for all interfaces is not set
  Incoming update filter list for all interfaces is not set
  Default networks flagged in outgoing updates
  Default networks accepted from incoming updates
  EIGRP metric weight K1=1, K2=0, K3=1, K4=0, K5=0
  EIGRP maximum hopcount 100
  EIGRP maximum metric variance 3
  Redistributing: eigrp 930
  EIGRP NSF-aware route hold timer is 240s
  Automatic network summarization is in effect
  Maximum path: 4
  Routing for Networks:
    10.0.0.0
    192.168.1.0
  Passive Interface(s):
    Serial0/0
  Routing Information Sources:
    Gateway         Distance      Last Update
    (this router)        90       20:51:48
    192.168.1.2          90       00:22:58
    172.16.10.6          90       01:58:46
    172.16.10.2          90       01:59:52
  Distance: internal 90 external 170
```

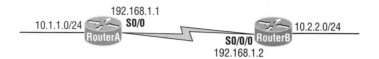

A. The variances don't match between routers.

B. The metrics are not valid between neighbors.

C. There is a discontiguous network.

D. There is a passive interface on RouterB.

E. An ACL is set on the router.

20. Which should you look for when troubleshooting an adjacency? (Choose four.)

A. Verify the AS numbers.

B. Verify that you have the proper interfaces enabled for EIGRP.

C. Make sure there are no mismatched K values.

D. Check your passive interface settings.

E. Make sure your remote routers are not connected to the Internet.

F. If authentication is configured, make sure all routers use different passwords.

Chapter
18

Open Shortest Path First (OSPF)

THE FOLLOWING ICND1 EXAM TOPICS ARE COVERED IN THIS CHAPTER:

- ✓ 2.0 Routing Technologies

- ✓ 2.2 Compare and contrast distance vector and link-state routing protocols

- ✓ 2.3 Compare and contrast interior and exterior routing protocols

- ✓ 2.4 Configure, verify, and troubleshoot single area and multiarea OSPFv2 for IPv4 (excluding authentication, filtering, manual summarization, redistribution, stub, virtual-link, and LSAs)

- ✓ 2.5 Configure, verify, and troubleshoot single area and multiarea OSPFv3 for IPv6 (excluding authentication, filtering, manual summarization, redistribution, stub, virtual-link, and LSAs)

Open Shortest Path First (OSPF) is by far the most popular and important routing protocol in use today—so important, I'm devoting this entire chapter to it! Sticking with the same approach we've adhered to throughout this book, we'll begin with the basics by completely familiarizing you with key OSPF terminology. Once we've covered that thoroughly, I'll guide you through OSPF's internal operation and then move on to tell you all about OSPF's many advantages over RIP.

This chapter is going to be more than chock full of vitally important information and it's also going to be really exciting because together, we'll explore some seriously critical factors and issues innate to implementing OSPF! I'll walk you through exactly how to implement single-area OSPF in a variety of networking environments and then demonstrate some great techniques you'll need to verify that everything is configured correctly and running smoothly.

To find up-to-the-minute updates for this chapter, please see www.lammle .com/ccna or the book's web page at www.sybex.com/go/ccna.

Open Shortest Path First (OSPF) Basics

Open Shortest Path First is an open standard routing protocol that's been implemented by a wide variety of network vendors, including Cisco. And it's that open standard characteristic that's the key to OSPF's flexibility and popularity.

Most people opt for OSPF, which works by using the Dijkstra algorithm to initially construct a shortest path tree and follows that by populating the routing table with the resulting best paths. EIGRP's convergence time may be blindingly fast, but OSPF isn't that far behind, and its quick convergence is another reason it's a favorite. Another two great advantages OSPF offers are that it supports multiple, equal-cost routes to the same destination and, like EIGRP, it also supports both IP and IPv6 routed protocols.

Here's a list that summarizes some of OSPF's best features:

- Allows for the creation of areas and autonomous systems
- Minimizes routing update traffic
- Is highly flexible, versatile, and scalable
- Supports VLSM/CIDR

- Offers an unlimited hop count
- Is open standard and supports multi-vendor deployment

Because OSPF is the first link-state routing protocol that most people run into, it's a good idea to size it up against more traditional distance-vector protocols like RIPv2 and RIPv1. Table 18.1 presents a nice comparison of all three of these common protocols.

TABLE 18.1   OSPF and RIP comparison

Characteristic	OSPF	RIPv2	RIPv1
Type of protocol	Link state	Distance vector	Distance vector
Classless support	Yes	Yes	No
VLSM support	Yes	Yes	No
Auto-summarization	No	Yes	Yes
Manual summarization	Yes	Yes	No
Noncontiguous support	Yes	Yes	No
Route propagation	Multicast on change	Periodic multicast	Periodic broadcast
Path metric	Bandwidth	Hops	Hops
Hop count limit	None	15	15
Convergence	Fast	Slow	Slow
Peer authentication	Yes	Yes	No
Hierarchical network requirement	Yes (using areas)	No (flat only)	No (flat only)
Updates	Event triggered	Periodic	Periodic
Route computation	Dijkstra	Bellman-Ford	Bellman-Ford

I want you know that OSPF has many features beyond the few I've listed in Table 18.1, and all of them combine to produce a fast, scalable, robust protocol that's also flexible enough to be actively deployed in a vast array of production networks!

One of OSPF's most useful traits is that its design is intended to be hierarchical in use, meaning that it allows us to subdivide the larger internetwork into smaller internetworks called areas. It's a really powerful feature that I recommend using, and I promise to show you how to do that later in the chapter.

Here are three of the biggest reasons to implement OSPF in a way that makes full use of its intentional, hierarchical design:

▪ To decrease routing overhead

▪ To speed up convergence

▪ To confine network instability to single areas of the network

Because free lunches are invariably hard to come by, all this wonderful functionality predictably comes at a price and doesn't exactly make configuring OSPF any easier. But no worries—we'll crush it!

Let's start by checking out Figure 18.1, which shows a very typical, yet simple OSPF design. I really want to point out the fact that some routers connect to the backbone—called area 0—the backbone area. OSPF absolutely must have an area 0, and all other areas should connect to it except for those connected via virtual links, which are beyond the scope of this book. A router that connects other areas to the backbone area within an AS is called an *area border router (ABR)*, and even these must have at least one of their interfaces connected to area 0.

FIGURE 18.1   OSPF design example. An OSPF hierarchical design minimizes routing table entries and keeps the impact of any topology changes contained within a specific area.

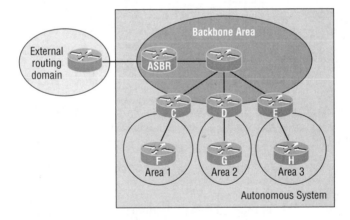

OSPF runs great inside an autonomous system, but it can also connect multiple autonomous systems together. The router that connects these ASs is called an *autonomous system boundary router (ASBR)*. Ideally, your aim is to create other areas of networks to help keep route updates to a minimum, especially in larger networks. Doing this also keeps problems from propagating throughout the network, effectively isolating them to a single area.

But let's pause here to cover some key OSPF terms that are really essential for you to nail down before we move on any further.

OSPF Terminology

Imagine being given a map and compass with no prior concept of east, west, north or south—not even what rivers, mountains, lakes, or deserts are. I'm guessing that without any ability to orient yourself in a basic way, your cool, new tools wouldn't help you get anywhere but completely lost, right? This is exactly why we're going to begin exploring OSPF by getting you solidly acquainted with a fairly long list of terms before setting out from base camp into the great unknown! Here are those vital terms to commit to memory now:

Link   A *link* is a network or router interface assigned to any given network. When an interface is added to the OSPF process, it's considered to be a link. This link, or interface, will have up or down state information associated with it as well as one or more IP addresses.

Router ID   The *router ID (RID)* is an IP address used to identify the router. Cisco chooses the router ID by using the highest IP address of all configured loopback interfaces. If no loopback interfaces are configured with addresses, OSPF will choose the highest IP address out of all active physical interfaces. To OSPF, this is basically the "name" of each router.

Neighbor   *Neighbors* are two or more routers that have an interface on a common network, such as two routers connected on a point-to-point serial link. OSPF neighbors must have a number of common configuration options to be able to successfully establish a neighbor relationship, and all of these options must be configured exactly the same way:

- Area ID
- Stub area flag
- Authentication password (if using one)
- Hello and Dead intervals

Adjacency   An *adjacency* is a relationship between two OSPF routers that permits the direct exchange of route updates. Unlike EIGRP, which directly shares routes with all of its neighbors, OSPF is really picky about sharing routing information and will directly share routes only with neighbors that have also established adjacencies. And not all neighbors will become adjacent—this depends upon both the type of network and the configuration of the routers. In multi-access networks, routers form adjacencies with designated and backup designated routers. In point-to-point and point-to-multipoint networks, routers form adjacencies with the router on the opposite side of the connection.

Designated router   A *designated router (DR)* is elected whenever OSPF routers are connected to the same broadcast network to minimize the number of adjacencies formed and to publicize received routing information to and from the remaining routers on the broadcast network or link. Elections are won based upon a router's priority level, with the one having the highest priority becoming the winner. If there's a tie, the router ID will be used to break it. All routers on the shared network will establish adjacencies with the DR and the BDR, which ensures that all routers' topology tables are synchronized.

Backup designated router   A *backup designated router (BDR)* is a hot standby for the DR on broadcast, or multi-access, links. The BDR receives all routing updates from OSPF adjacent routers but does not disperse LSA updates.

Hello protocol   The OSPF Hello protocol provides dynamic neighbor discovery and maintains neighbor relationships. Hello packets and Link State Advertisements (LSAs) build and maintain the topological database. Hello packets are addressed to multicast address 224.0.0.5.

Neighborship database   The *neighborship database* is a list of all OSPF routers for which Hello packets have been seen. A variety of details, including the router ID and state, are maintained on each router in the neighborship database.

Topological database   The *topological database* contains information from all of the Link State Advertisement packets that have been received for an area. The router uses the information from the topology database as input into the Dijkstra algorithm that computes the shortest path to every network.

LSA packets are used to update and maintain the topological database.

Link State Advertisement   A *Link State Advertisement (LSA)* is an OSPF data packet containing link-state and routing information that's shared among OSPF routers. An OSPF router will exchange LSA packets only with routers to which it has established adjacencies.

OSPF areas   An *OSPF area* is a grouping of contiguous networks and routers. All routers in the same area share a common area ID. Because a router can be a member of more than one area at a time, the area ID is associated with specific interfaces on the router. This would allow some interfaces to belong to area 1 while the remaining interfaces can belong to area 0. All of the routers within the same area have the same topology table. When configuring OSPF with multiple areas, you've got to remember that there must be an area 0 and that this is typically considered the backbone area. Areas also play a role in establishing a hierarchical network organization—something that really enhances the scalability of OSPF!

Broadcast (multi-access)   *Broadcast (multi-access) networks* such as Ethernet allow multiple devices to connect to or access the same network, enabling a *broadcast* ability in which a single packet is delivered to all nodes on the network. In OSPF, a DR and BDR must be elected for each broadcast multi-access network.

Nonbroadcast multi-access   *Nonbroadcast multi-access (NBMA)* networks are networks such as Frame Relay, X.25, and Asynchronous Transfer Mode (ATM). These types of networks allow for multi-access without broadcast ability like Ethernet. NBMA networks require special OSPF configuration to function properly.

Point-to-point   *Point-to-point* refers to a type of network topology made up of a direct connection between two routers that provides a single communication path. The point-to-point connection can be physical—for example, a serial cable that directly connects two routers—or logical, where two routers thousands of miles apart are connected by a circuit in a Frame Relay network. Either way, point-to-point configurations eliminate the need for DRs or BDRs.

Point-to-multipoint   *Point-to-multipoint* refers to a type of network topology made up of a series of connections between a single interface on one router and multiple destination routers. All interfaces on all routers share the point-to-multipoint connection and belong to the same network. Point-to-multipoint networks can be further classified according to whether they support broadcasts or not. This is important because it defines the kind of OSPF configurations you can deploy.

All of these terms play a critical role when you're trying to understand how OSPF actually works, so again, make sure you're familiar with each of them. Having these terms down will enable you to confidently place them in their proper context as we progress on our journey through the rest of this chapter!

OSPF Operation

Fully equipped with your newly acquired knowledge of the terms and technologies we just covered, it's now time to delve into how OSPF discovers, propagates, and ultimately chooses routes. Once you know how OSPF achieves these tasks, you'll understand how OSPF operates internally really well.

OSPF operation is basically divided into these three categories:

- Neighbor and adjacency initialization
- LSA flooding
- SPF tree calculation

The beginning neighbor/adjacency formation stage is a very big part of OSPF operation. When OSPF is initialized on a router, the router allocates memory for it, as well as for the maintenance of both neighbor and topology tables. Once the router determines which interfaces have been configured for OSPF, it will then check to see if they're active and begin sending Hello packets as shown in Figure 18.2.

FIGURE 18.2   The Hello protocol

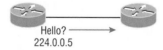

The Hello protocol is used to discover neighbors, establish adjacencies, and maintain relationships with other OSPF routers. Hello packets are periodically sent out of each enabled OSPF interface and in environments that support multicast.

The address used for this is 224.0.0.5, and the frequency with which Hello packets are sent out depends upon the network type and topology. Broadcast and point-to-point networks send Hellos every 10 seconds, whereas non-broadcast and point-to-multipoint networks send them every 30 seconds.

LSA Flooding

LSA flooding is the method OSPF uses to share routing information. Via Link State Updates (LSU's) packets, LSA information containing link-state data is shared with all OSPF routers within an area. The network topology is created from the LSA updates, and flooding is used so that all OSPF routers have the same topology map to make SPF calculations with.

Efficient flooding is achieved through the use of a reserved multicast address: 224.0.0.5 (AllSPFRouters). LSA updates, which indicate that something in the topology has changed, are handled a bit differently. The network type determines the multicast address used for sending updates. Table 18.2 contains the multicast addresses associated with LSA flooding. Point-to-multipoint networks use the adjacent router's unicast IP address.

TABLE 18.2 LSA update multicast addresses

Network Type	Multicast Address	Description
Point-to-point	224.0.0.5	AllSPFRouters
Broadcast	224.0.0.6	AllDRouters
Point-to-multipoint	NA	NA

Once the LSA updates have been flooded throughout the network, each recipient must acknowledge that the flooded update has been received. It's also important for recipients to validate the LSA update.

SPF Tree Calculation

Within an area, each router calculates the best/shortest path to every network in that same area. This calculation is based upon the information collected in the topology database and an algorithm called shortest path first (SPF). Picture each router in an area constructing a tree—much like a family tree—where the router is the root and all other networks are arranged along the branches and leaves. This is the shortest-path tree used by the router to insert OSPF routes into the routing table.

It's important to understand that this tree contains only networks that exist in the same area as the router itself does. If a router has interfaces in multiple areas, then separate trees will be constructed for each area. One of the key criteria considered during the route selection process of the SPF algorithm is the metric or cost of each potential path to a network. But this SPF calculation doesn't apply to routes from other areas.

OSPF Metrics

OSPF uses a metric referred to as *cost*. A cost is associated with every outgoing interface included in an SPF tree. The cost of the entire path is the sum of the costs of the outgoing interfaces along the path. Because cost is an arbitrary value as defined in RFC 2338, Cisco had to implement its own method of calculating the cost for each OSPF-enabled interface. Cisco uses a simple equation of $10^8/bandwidth$, where *bandwidth* is the configured bandwidth for the interface. Using this rule, a 100 Mbps Fast Ethernet interface would have a default OSPF cost of 1 and a 1,000 Mbps Ethernet interface would have a cost of 1.

Important to note is that this value can be overridden with the `ip ospf cost` command. The cost is manipulated by changing the value to a number within the range of 1 to 65,535. Because the cost is assigned to each link, the value must be changed on the specific interface you want to change the cost on.

Cisco bases link cost on bandwidth. Other vendors may use other metrics to calculate a given link's cost. When connecting links between routers from different vendors, you'll probably have to adjust the cost to match another vendor's router because both routers must assign the same cost to the link for OSPF to work properly.

Configuring OSPF

Configuring basic OSPF isn't as simple as configuring RIP and EIGRP, and it can get really complex once the many options that are allowed within OSPF are factored in. But that's okay because you really only need to focus on basic, single-area OSPF configuration at this point. Coming up, I'll show you how to configure single-area OSPF.

The two factors that are foundational to OSPF configuration are enabling OSPF and configuring OSPF areas.

Enabling OSPF

The easiest and also least scalable way to configure OSPF is to just use a single area. Doing this requires a minimum of two commands.

The first command used to activate the OSPF routing process is as follows:

```
Router(config)#router ospf ?
<1-65535> Process ID
```

A value in the range from 1 to 65,535 identifies the OSPF process ID. It's a unique number on this router that groups a series of OSPF configuration commands under a specific running process. Different OSPF routers don't have to use the same process ID to communicate. It's a purely local value that doesn't mean a lot, but you still need to remember that it cannot start at 0; it has to start at a minimum of 1.

You can have more than one OSPF process running simultaneously on the same router if you want, but this isn't the same as running multi-area OSPF. The second process will maintain an entirely separate copy of its topology table and manage its communications independently of the first one and you use it when you want OSPF to connect multiple ASs together. Also, because the Cisco exam objectives only cover single-area OSPF with each router running a single OSPF process, that's what we'll focus on in this book.

The OSPF process ID is needed to identify a unique instance of an OSPF database and is locally significant.

Configuring OSPF Areas

After identifying the OSPF process, you need to identify the interfaces that you want to activate OSPF communications on as well as the area in which each resides. This will also configure the networks you're going to advertise to others.

Here's an example of a basic OSPF configuration for you, showing our second minimum command needed, the network command:

```
Router#config t
Router(config)#router ospf 1
Router(config-router)#network 10.0.0.0 0.255.255.255 area ?
  <0-4294967295>  OSPF area ID as a decimal value
  A.B.C.D         OSPF area ID in IP address format
Router(config-router)#network 10.0.0.0 0.255.255.255 area 0
```

The areas can be any number from 0 to 4.2 billion. Don't get these numbers confused with the process ID, which ranges from 1 to 65,535.

Remember, the OSPF process ID number is irrelevant. It can be the same on every router on the network, or it can be different—doesn't matter. It's locally significant and just enables the OSPF routing on the router.

The arguments of the network command are the network number (10.0.0.0) and the wildcard mask (0.255.255.255). The combination of these two numbers identifies the interfaces that OSPF will operate on and will also be included in its OSPF LSA advertisements. Based on my sample configuration, OSPF will use this command to find any interface on the router configured in the 10.0.0.0 network and will place any interface it finds into area 0.

Notice that you can create about 4.2 billion areas! In reality, a router wouldn't let you create that many, but you can certainly name them using the numbers up to 4.2 billion. You can also label an area using an IP address format.

Let me stop here a minute to give you a quick explanation of wildcards: A 0 octet in the wildcard mask indicates that the corresponding octet in the network must match exactly. On the other hand, a 255 indicates that you don't care what the corresponding octet is in the network number. A network and wildcard mask combination of 1.1.1.1 0.0.0.0 would match an interface configured exactly with 1.1.1.1 only, and nothing else. This is really useful if you want to activate OSPF on a specific interface in a very clear and simple way. If you insist on matching a range of networks, the network and wildcard mask combination of 1.1.0.0 0.0.255.255 would match any interface in the range of 1.1.0.0 to 1.1.255.255. Because of this, it's simpler and safer to stick to using wildcard masks of 0.0.0.0 and identify each OSPF interface individually. Once configured, they'll function exactly the same—one way really isn't better than the other.

The final argument is the area number. It indicates the area to which the interfaces identified in the network and wildcard mask portion belong. Remember that OSPF routers will become neighbors only if their interfaces share a network that's configured to belong to the same area number. The format of the area number is either a decimal value from the range 0 to 4,294,967,295 or a value represented in standard dotted-decimal notation. For example, area 0.0.0.0 is a legitimate area and is identical to area 0.

Wildcard Example

Before getting down to configuring our network, let's take a quick peek at a more complex OSPF network configuration to find out what our OSPF network statements would be if we were using subnets and wildcards.

In this scenario, you have a router with these four subnets connected to four different interfaces:

- 192.168.10.64/28
- 192.168.10.80/28
- 192.168.10.96/28
- 192.168.10.8/30

All interfaces need to be in area 0, so it seems to me the easiest configuration would look like this:

```
Test#config t
Test(config)#router ospf 1
Test(config-router)#network 192.168.10.0 0.0.0.255 area 0
```

I'll admit that the preceding example is actually pretty simple, but easy isn't always best—especially when dealing with OSPF! So even though this is an easy-button way to configure OSPF, it doesn't make good use of its capabilities and what fun is that? Worse yet, the objectives aren't very likely to present something this simple for you! So let's create a separate network statement for each interface using the subnet numbers and wildcards. Doing that would look something like this:

```
Test#config t
Test(config)#router ospf 1
Test(config-router)#network 192.168.10.64 0.0.0.15 area 0
Test(config-router)#network 192.168.10.80 0.0.0.15 area 0
Test(config-router)#network 192.168.10.96 0.0.0.15 area 0
Test(config-router)#network 192.168.10.8 0.0.0.3 area 0
```

Wow, now that's a different looking config! Truthfully, OSPF would work exactly the same way as it would with the easy configuration I showed you first—but unlike the easy configuration, this one covers the objectives!

And although this looks a bit complicated, trust me, it really isn't. All you need for clarity is to fully understand your block sizes! Just remember that when configuring wildcards, they're always one less than the block size. A /28 is a block size of 16, so we would add our network statement using the subnet number and then add a wildcard of 15 in the interesting octet. For the /30, which is a block size of 4, we would go with a wildcard of 3. Once you practice this a few times, it gets really easy. And do practice because we'll deal with them again when we get to access lists later on!

Let's use Figure 18.3 as an example and configure that network with OSPF using wild-cards to make sure you have a solid grip on this. The figure shows a three-router network with the IP addresses of each interface.

FIGURE 18.3   Sample OSPF wildcard configuration

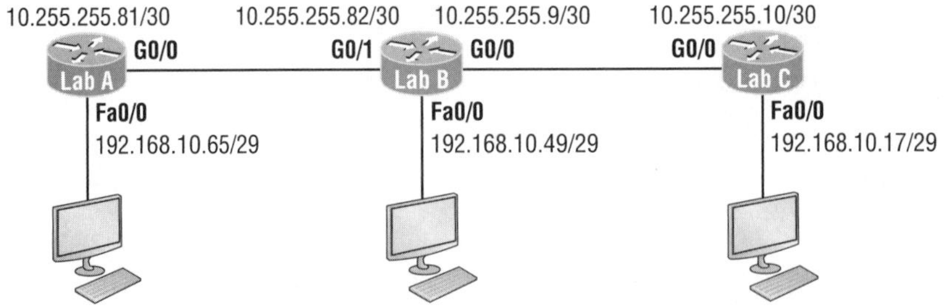

The very first thing you need to be able to do is to look at each interface and determine the subnet that the addresses are in. Hold on, I know what you're thinking: "Why don't I just use the exact IP addresses of the interface with the 0.0.0.0 wildcard?" Well, you can, but we're paying attention to Cisco exam objectives here, not just what's easiest, remember?

The IP addresses for each interface are shown in the figure. The Lab_A router has two directly connected subnets: 192.168.10.64/29 and 10.255.255.80/30. Here's the OSPF configuration using wildcards:

```
Lab_A#config t
Lab_A(config)#router ospf 1
Lab_A(config-router)#network 192.168.10.64 0.0.0.7 area 0
Lab_A(config-router)#network 10.255.255.80 0.0.0.3 area 0
```

The Lab_A router is using a /29, or 255.255.255.248, mask on the Fa0/0 interface. This is a block size of 8, which is a wildcard of 7. The G0/0 interface is a mask of 255.255.255.252— block size of 4, with a wildcard of 3. Notice that I typed in the network number, not the interface number. You can't configure OSPF this way if you can't look at the IP address and slash notation and then figure out the subnet, mask, and wildcard, can you? So don't take your exam until you can do this.

Here are other two configurations to help you practice:

```
Lab_B#config t
Lab_B(config)#router ospf 1
Lab_B(config-router)#network 192.168.10.48 0.0.0.7 area 0
Lab_B(config-router)#network 10.255.255.80 0.0.0.3 area 0
Lab_B(config-router)#network 10.255.255.8 0.0.0.3 area 0

Lab_C#config t
Lab_C(config)#router ospf 1
Lab_C(config-router)#network 192.168.10.16 0.0.0.7 area 0
Lab_C(config-router)#network 10.255.255.8 0.0.0.3 area 0
```

As I mentioned with the Lab_A configuration, you've got to be able to determine the subnet, mask, and wildcard just by looking at the IP address and mask of an interface. If you can't do that, you won't be able to configure OSPF using wildcards as I just demonstrated. So go over this until you're really comfortable with it!

Configuring Our Network with OSPF

Now we get to have some fun! Let's configure our internetwork with OSPF using just area 0. OSPF has an administrative distance of 110, but let's remove RIP while we're at it because I don't want you to get in the habit of having RIP running on your network.

There's a bunch of different ways to configure OSPF, and as I said, the simplest and easiest is to use the wildcard mask 0.0.0.0. But I want to demonstrate that we can configure each router differently with OSPF and still come up with the exact same result. This is one reason why OSPF is more fun and challenging than other routing protocols—it gives us all a lot more ways to screw things up, which automatically provides a troubleshooting opportunity! We'll use our network as shown in Figure 18.4 to configure OSPF, and by the way, notice I added a new router!

FIGURE 18.4   Our new network layout

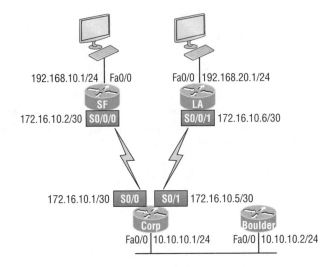

Corp

Here's the Corp router's configuration:

```
Corp#sh ip int brief
Interface       IP-Address    OK? Method Status                 Protocol
FastEthernet0/0 10.10.10.1    YES manual up                     up
Serial0/0       172.16.10.1   YES manual up                     up
FastEthernet0/1 unassigned    YES unset  administratively down  down
Serial0/1       172.16.10.5   YES manual up                     up
Corp#config t
Corp(config)#no router rip
Corp(config)#router ospf 132
Corp(config-router)#network 10.10.10.1 0.0.0.0 area 0
Corp(config-router)#network 172.16.10.1 0.0.0.0 area 0
Corp(config-router)#network 172.16.10.5 0.0.0.0 area 0
```

Alright—it looks like we have a few things to talk about here. First, I removed RIP and then added OSPF. Why did I use OSPF 132? It really doesn't matter—the number is irrelevant. I guess it just felt good to use 132. But notice that I started with the show ip int brief command, just like when I was configuring RIP. I did this because it's always important to verify exactly what you are directly connected to. Doing this really helps prevent typos!

The network commands are pretty straightforward. I typed in the IP address of each interface and used the wildcard mask of 0.0.0.0, which means that the IP address must precisely match each octet. This is actually one of those times where easier is better, so just do this:

```
Corp(config)#router ospf 132
Corp(config-router)#network 172.16.10.0 0.0.0.255 area 0
```

Nice—there's only one line instead of two for the 172.16.10.0 network! I really want you to understand that OSPF will work the same here no matter which way you configure the network statement. Now, let's move on to SF. To simplify things, we're going to use our same sample configuration.

SF

The SF router has two directly connected networks. I'll use the IP addresses on each interface to configure this router.

```
SF#sh ip int brief
Interface      IP-Address      OK? Method Status                Protocol
FastEthernet0/0 192.168.10.1    YES manual up                    up
FastEthernet0/1 unassigned      YES unset  administratively down down
Serial0/0/0    172.16.10.2     YES manual up                    up
Serial0/0/1    unassigned      YES unset  administratively down down
SF#config t
SF(config)#no router rip
SF(config)#router ospf 300
SF(config-router)#network 192.168.10.1 0.0.0.0 area 0
SF(config-router)#network 172.16.10.2 0.0.0.0 area 0
*Apr 30 00:25:43.810: %OSPF-5-ADJCHG: Process 300, Nbr 172.16.10.5 on
Serial0/0/0 from LOADING to FULL, Loading Done
```

Here, all I did was to first disable RIP, turn on OSPF routing process 300, and then I added my two directly connected networks. Now let's move on to LA!

LA

We're going to give some attention to the LA router that's directly connected to two networks:

```
LA#sh ip int brief
Interface      IP-Address      OK? Method Status                Protocol
FastEthernet0/0 192.168.20.1    YES manual up                    up
```

```
FastEthernet0/1 unassigned    YES unset  administratively down down
Serial0/0/0     unassigned    YES unset  administratively down down
Serial0/0/1     172.16.10.6   YES manual up                     up
LA#config t
LA(config)#router ospf 100
LA(config-router)#network 192.168.20.0 0.0.0.255 area 0
LA(config-router)#network 172.16.0.0 0.0.255.255 area 0
*Apr 30 00:56:37.090: %OSPF-5-ADJCHG: Process 100, Nbr 172.16.10.5 on
Serial0/0/1 from LOADING to FULL, Loading Done
```

Remember that when you're configuring dynamic routing, using the show ip int brief command first will make it all so much easier!

And don't forget, I can use any process ID I want, as long as it's a value from 1 to 65,535, because it doesn't matter if all routers use the same process ID. Also, notice that I used different wildcards in this example. Doing this works really well too.

Okay, I want you to think about something for a second before we move onto more advanced OSPF topics: What if the Fa0/1 interface of the LA router was connected to a link that we didn't need OSPF running on, as shown in Figure 18.5?

FIGURE 18.5   Adding a non-OSPF network to the LA router

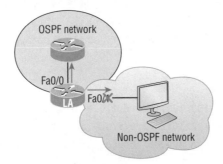

You've seen this before because I demonstrated this already back in the RIP section. We can use the same command that we did under that routing process here as well! Take a look:

```
LA(config)#router ospf 100
LA(config-router)#passive-interface fastEthernet 0/1
```

Even though this is pretty simple, you've really got to be careful before you configure this command on your router! I added this command as an example on interface Fa0/1, which happens to be an interface we're not using in this network because I want OSPF to work on my other router's interfaces.

Now it's time to configure our Corp router to advertise a default route to the SF and LA routers because doing so will make our lives a lot easier. Instead of having to configure all our routers with a default route, we'll only configure one router and then advertise that this router is the one that holds the default route—elegant!

In Figure 18.4, keep in mind that, for now, the corporate router is connected to the Internet off of Fa0/0. We'll create a default route toward this imaginary Internet and then tell the other routers that this is the route they'll use to get to the Internet. Here is the configuration:

```
Corp#config t
Corp(config)#ip route 0.0.0.0 0.0.0.0 Fa0/0
Corp(config)#router ospf 1
Corp(config-router)#default-information originate
```

Now, let's check and see if our other routers have received this default route from the Corp router:

```
SF#show ip route
[output cut]
E1 - OSPF external type 1, E2 - OSPF external type 2
[output cut]
O*E2 0.0.0.0/0 [110/1] via 172.16.10.1, 00:01:54, Serial0/0/0
SF#
```

Sure enough—the last line in the SF router shows that it received the advertisement from the Corp router regarding the fact that the corporate router is the one holding the default route out of the AS.

But hold on a second! I need to configure our new router into my lab to create the example network we'll use from here on. Here's the configuration of the new router that I connected to the same network that the Corp router is connected to via the Fa0/0 interface:

```
Router#config t
Router(config)#hostname Boulder
Boulder(config)#int f0/0
Boulder(config-if)#ip address 10.10.10.2 255.255.255.0
Boulder(config-if)#no shut
*Apr  6 18:01:38.007: %LINEPROTO-5-UPDOWN: Line protocol on Interface
FastEthernet0/0, changed state to up
Boulder(config-if)#router ospf 2
Boulder(config-router)#network 10.0.0.0 0.255.255.255 area 0
*Apr  6 18:03:27.267: %OSPF-5-ADJCHG: Process 2, Nbr 223.255.255.254 on
FastEthernet0/0 from LOADING to FULL, Loading Done
```

This is all good, but I need to make sure that you don't follow my example to a tee because here, I just quickly brought a router up without setting my passwords first. I can get away with this only because I am in a nonproduction network, so don't do this in the real world where security is key!

Anyway, now that I have my new router nicely connected with a basic configuration, we're going to move on to cover loopback interfaces, how to set the router ID (RID) used with OSPF, and finally, how to verify OSPF.

OSPF and Loopback Interfaces

It's really vital to configure loopback interfaces when using OSPF. In fact, Cisco suggests using them whenever you configure OSPF on a router for stability purposes.

Loopback interfaces are logical interfaces, which means they're virtual, software-only interfaces, not actual, physical router interfaces. A big reason we use loopback interfaces with OSPF configurations is because they ensure that an interface is always active and available for OSPF processes.

Loopback interfaces also come in very handy for diagnostic purposes as well as for OSPF configuration. Understand that if you don't configure a loopback interface on a router, the highest active IP address on a router will become that router's RID during bootup! Figure 18.6 illustrates how routers know each other by their router ID.

FIGURE 18.6   OSPF router ID (RID)

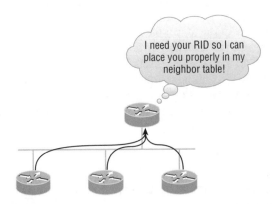

The RID is not only used to advertise routes, it's also used to elect the designated router (DR) and the backup designated router (BDR). These designated routers create adjacencies when a new router comes up and exchanges LSAs to build topological databases.

> By default, OSPF uses the highest IP address on any active interface at the moment OSPF starts up to determine the RID of the router. But this behavior can be overridden via a logical interface. Remember—the highest IP address of any logical interface will always become a router's RID!

Now it's time to show you how to configure these logical loopback interfaces and how to verify them, as well as verify RIDs.

Configuring Loopback Interfaces

Configuring loopback interfaces rocks mostly because it's the easiest part of OSPF configuration, and we all need a break about now—right? So hang on—we're in the home stretch!

First, let's see what the RID is on the Corp router with the show ip ospf command:

```
Corp#sh ip ospf
 Routing Process "ospf 1" with ID 172.16.10.5
[output cut]
```

Okay, we can see that the RID is 172.16.10.5—the Serial0/1 interface of the router. So let's configure a loopback interface using a completely different IP addressing scheme:

```
Corp(config)#int loopback 0
*Mar 22 01:23:14.206: %LINEPROTO-5-UPDOWN: Line protocol on Interface
    Loopback0, changed state to up
Corp(config-if)#ip address 172.31.1.1 255.255.255.255
```

The IP scheme really doesn't matter here, but each one being in a separate subnet does! By using the /32 mask, we can use any IP address we want as long as the addresses are never the same on any two routers.

Let's configure the other routers now:

```
SF#config t
SF(config)#int loopback 0
*Mar 22 01:25:11.206: %LINEPROTO-5-UPDOWN: Line protocol on Interface
    Loopback0, changed state to up
SF(config-if)#ip address 172.31.1.2 255.255.255.255
```

Here's the configuration of the loopback interface on LA:

```
LA#config t
LA(config)#int loopback 0
*Mar 22 02:21:59.686: %LINEPROTO-5-UPDOWN: Line protocol on Interface
    Loopback0, changed state to up
LA(config-if)#ip address 172.31.1.3 255.255.255.255
```

I'm pretty sure you're wondering what the IP address mask of 255.255.255.255 (/32) means and why we don't just use 255.255.255.0 instead. While it's true that either mask works, the /32 mask is called a host mask and works fine for loopback interfaces. It also allows us to save subnets. Notice how I was able to use 172.31.1.1, .2, .3, and .4? If I didn't use the /32, I'd have to use a separate subnet for each and every router—not good!

One important question to answer before we move on is did we actually change the RIDs of our router by setting the loopback interfaces? Let's find out by taking a look at the Corp's RID:

```
Corp#sh ip ospf
 Routing Process "ospf 1" with ID 172.16.10.5
```

What happened here? You would think that because we set logical interfaces, the IP addresses under them would automatically become the RID of the router, right? Well, sort of, but only if you do one of two things: either reboot the router or delete OSPF and re-create the database on your router. Neither is all that great an option, so try to remember to create your logical interfaces before you start OSPF routing. That way, the loopback interface would always become your RID straight away!

With all this in mind, I'm going with rebooting the Corp router because it's the easier of the two options I have right now.

Now let's look and see what our RID is:

```
Corp#sh ip ospf
 Routing Process "ospf 1" with ID 172.31.1.1
```

That did the trick! The Corp router now has a new RID, so I guess I'll just go ahead and reboot all my routers to get their RIDs reset to our logical addresses. But should I really do that?

Maybe not because there is *one* other way. What do you think about adding a new RID for the router right under the router ospf *process-id* command instead? Sounds good, so I'd say let's give that a shot! Here's an example of doing that on the Corp router:

```
Corp#config t
Corp(config)#router ospf 1
Corp(config-router)#router-id 223.255.255.254
Reload or use "clear ip ospf process" command, for this to take effect
Corp(config-router)#do clear ip ospf process
Reset ALL OSPF processes? [no]: yes
*Jan 16 14:20:36.906: %OSPF-5-ADJCHG: Process 1, Nbr 192.168.20.1
on Serial0/1 from FULL to DOWN, Neighbor Down: Interface down
or detached
*Jan 16 14:20:36.906: %OSPF-5-ADJCHG: Process 1, Nbr 192.168.10.1
on Serial0/0 from FULL to DOWN, Neighbor Down: Interface down
or detached
*Jan 16 14:20:36.982: %OSPF-5-ADJCHG: Process 1, Nbr 192.168.20.1
on Serial0/1 from LOADING to FULL, Loading Done
*Jan 16 14:20:36.982: %OSPF-5-ADJCHG: Process 1, Nbr 192.168.10.1
on Serial0/0 from LOADING to FULL, Loading Done
Corp(config-router)#do sh ip ospf
 Routing Process "ospf 1" with ID 223.255.255.254
```

Now look at that—it worked! We changed the RID without reloading the router! But wait—remember, we set a logical loopback interface earlier. Does that mean the loopback interface will win over the `router-id` command? Well, we can see our answer...
A loopback interface will *not* override the `router-id` command, and we don't have to reboot the router to make it take effect as the RID!

So this process follows this hierarchy:

1. Highest active interface by default.

2. Highest logical interface overrides a physical interface.

3. The `router-id` overrides the interface and loopback interface.

The only thing left now is to decide whether you want to advertise the loopback interfaces under OSPF. There are pros and cons to using an address that won't be advertised versus using an address that will be. Using an unadvertised address saves on real IP address space, but the address won't appear in the OSPF table, which means you can't ping it.

So basically, what you're faced with here is a choice that equals a trade-off between the ease of debugging the network and conservation of address space—what to do? A really tight strategy is to use a private IP address scheme as I did. Do this and all will be well!

Now that we've configured all the routers with OSPF, what's next? Miller time? Nope—not yet. It's that verification thing again. We still have to make sure that OSPF is really working, and that's exactly what we're going to do next.

Verifying OSPF Configuration

There are several ways to verify proper OSPF configuration and operation, so next, I'm going to demonstrate the various OSPF show commands you need to know in order to achieve this. We're going to start by taking a quick look at the routing table of the Corp router.

First, let's issue a `show ip route` command on the Corp router:

```
O    192.168.10.0/24 [110/65] via 172.16.10.2, 1d17h, Serial0/0
        172.131.0.0/32 is subnetted, 1 subnets
     172.131.0.0/32 is subnetted, 1 subnets
C        172.131.1.1 is directly connected, Loopback0
     172.16.0.0/30 is subnetted, 4 subnets
C       172.16.10.4 is directly connected, Serial0/1
L       172.16.10.5/32 is directly connected, Serial0/1
C       172.16.10.0 is directly connected, Serial0/0
L       172.16.10.1/32 is directly connected, Serial0/0
O    192.168.20.0/24 [110/65] via 172.16.10.6, 1d17h, Serial0/1
        10.0.0.0/24 is subnetted, 2 subnets
C       10.10.10.0 is directly connected, FastEthernet0/0
L       10.10.10.1/32 is directly connected, FastEthernet0/0
```

The Corp router shows only two dynamic routes for the internetwork, with the O representing OSPF internal routes. The Cs are clearly our directly connected networks, and our two remote networks are showing up too—nice! Notice the 110/65, which is our administrative distance/metric.

Now that's a really sweet-looking OSPF routing table! It's important to make it easier to troubleshoot and fix an OSPF network, which is why I always use the show ip int brief command when configuring my routing protocols. It's very easy to make little mistakes with OSPF, so keep your eyes on the details!

It's time to show you all the OSPF verification commands that you need in your toolbox for now.

The *show ip ospf* Command

The show ip ospf command is what you'll need to display OSPF information for one or all OSPF processes running on the router. Information contained therein includes the router ID, area information, SPF statistics, and LSA timer information. Let's check out the output from the Corp router:

```
Corp#sh ip ospf
 Routing Process "ospf 1" with ID 223.255.255.254
 Start time: 00:08:41.724, Time elapsed: 2d16h
 Supports only single TOS(TOS0) routes
 Supports opaque LSA
 Supports Link-local Signaling (LLS)
 Supports area transit capability
 Router is not originating router-LSAs with maximum metric
 Initial SPF schedule delay 5000 msecs
 Minimum hold time between two consecutive SPFs 10000 msecs
 Maximum wait time between two consecutive SPFs 10000 msecs
 Incremental-SPF disabled
 Minimum LSA interval 5 secs
 Minimum LSA arrival 1000 msecs
 LSA group pacing timer 240 secs
 Interface flood pacing timer 33 msecs
 Retransmission pacing timer 66 msecs
 Number of external LSA 0. Checksum Sum 0x000000
 Number of opaque AS LSA 0. Checksum Sum 0x000000
 Number of DCbitless external and opaque AS LSA 0
 Number of DoNotAge external and opaque AS LSA 0
 Number of areas in this router is 1. 1 normal 0 stub 0 nssa
 Number of areas transit capable is 0
 External flood list length 0
 IETF NSF helper support enabled
```

```
Cisco NSF helper support enabled
   Area BACKBONE(0)
       Number of interfaces in this area is 3
       Area has no authentication
       SPF algorithm last executed 00:11:08.760 ago
       SPF algorithm executed 5 times
       Area ranges are
       Number of LSA 6. Checksum Sum 0x03B054
       Number of opaque link LSA 0. Checksum Sum 0x000000
       Number of DCbitless LSA 0
       Number of indication LSA 0
       Number of DoNotAge LSA 0
       Flood list length 0
```

Notice the router ID (RID) of 223.255.255.254, which is the highest IP address configured on the router. Hopefully, you also noticed that I set the RID of the corporate router to the highest IP address available with IPv4.

The *show ip ospf database* Command

Using the show ip ospf database command will give you information about the number of routers in the internetwork (AS) plus the neighboring router's ID—the topology database I mentioned earlier. Unlike the show ip eigrp topology command, this command reveals the OSPF routers, but not each and every link in the AS like EIGRP does.

The output is broken down by area. Here's a sample output, again from Corp:

```
Corp#sh ip ospf database

                OSPF Router with ID (223.255.255.254) (Process ID 1)
Router Link States (Area 0)

Link ID          ADV Router       Age     Seq#        Checksum Link count
10.10.10.2       10.10.10.2       966     0x80000001 0x007162 1
172.31.1.4       172.31.1.4       885     0x80000002 0x00D27E 1
192.168.10.1     192.168.10.1     886     0x8000007A 0x00BC95 3
192.168.20.1     192.168.20.1     1133    0x8000007A 0x00E348 3
223.255.255.254 223.255.255.254 925      0x8000004D 0x000B90 5


                Net Link States (Area 0)

Link ID          ADV Router       Age     Seq#        Checksum
10.10.10.1       223.255.255.254 884      0x80000002 0x008CFE
```

You can see all the routers and the RID of each router—the highest IP address on each of them. For example, the link ID and ADV router of my new Boulder router shows up twice: once with the directly connected IP address (10.10.10.2) and as the RID that I set under the OSPF process (172.31.1.4).

The router output shows the link ID—remember that an interface is also a link—and the RID of the router on that link under the ADV router, or advertising router.

The *show ip ospf interface* Command

The show ip ospf interface command reveals all interface-related OSPF information. Data is displayed about OSPF information for all OSPF-enabled interfaces or for specified interfaces. I'll highlight some of the more important factors for you. Check it out:

```
Corp#sh ip ospf int f0/0
FastEthernet0/0 is up, line protocol is up
  Internet Address 10.10.10.1/24, Area 0
  Process ID 1, Router ID 223.255.255.254, Network Type BROADCAST, Cost: 1
  Transmit Delay is 1 sec, State DR, Priority 1
  Designated Router (ID) 223.255.255.254, Interface address 10.10.10.1
  Backup Designated router (ID) 172.31.1.4, Interface address 10.10.10.2
  Timer intervals configured, Hello 10, Dead 40, Wait 40, Retransmit 5
    oob-resync timeout 40
    Hello due in 00:00:08
  Supports Link-local Signaling (LLS)
  Cisco NSF helper support enabled
  IETF NSF helper support enabled
  Index 3/3, flood queue length 0
  Next 0x0(0)/0x0(0)
  Last flood scan length is 1, maximum is 1
  Last flood scan time is 0 msec, maximum is 0 msec
  Neighbor Count is 1, Adjacent neighbor count is 1
    Adjacent with neighbor 172.31.1.  Suppress hello for 0 neighbor(s)
```

So this command has given us the following information:

- Interface IP address
- Area assignment
- Process ID
- Router ID
- Network type
- Cost
- Priority

- DR/BDR election information (if applicable)
- Hello and Dead timer intervals
- Adjacent neighbor information

The reason I used the `show ip ospf interface f0/0` command is because I knew that there would be a designated router elected on the FastEthernet broadcast multi-access network between our Corp and Boulder routers. The information that I highlighted is all very important, so make sure you've noted it! A good question to ask you here is what are the Hello and Dead timers set to by default?

What if you type in the `show ip ospf interface` command and receive this response:

```
Corp#sh ip ospf int f0/0
%OSPF: OSPF not enabled on FastEthernet0/0
```

This error occurs when OSPF is enabled on the router, but not the interface. When this happens, you need to check your network statements because it means that the interface you're trying to verify is not in your OSPF process!

The *show ip ospf neighbor* Command

The `show ip ospf neighbor` command is super-useful because it summarizes the pertinent OSPF information regarding neighbors and the adjacency state. If a DR or BDR exists, that information will also be displayed. Here's a sample:

```
Corp#sh ip ospf neighbor

Neighbor ID     Pri   State      Dead Time   Address       Interface
172.31.1.4       1    FULL/BDR   00:00:34    10.10.10.2    FastEthernet0/0
192.168.20.1     0    FULL/  -   00:00:31    172.16.10.6   Serial0/1
192.168.10.1     0    FULL/  -   00:00:32    172.16.10.2   Serial0/0
```

 Real World Scenario

An Admin Connects Two Disparate Routers Together with OSPF and the Link between them Never Comes Up

Quite a few years ago, an admin called me in a panic because he couldn't get OSPF working between two routers, one of which was an older router that they needed to use while they were waiting for their new router to be shipped to them.

OSPF can be used in a multi-vendor network, so he was confused as to why this wasn't working. He turned on RIP and it worked, so he was super confused with why OSPF was

> not creating adjacencies. I had him use the `show ip ospf interface` command to look at the link between the two routers and sure enough, the hello and dead timers didn't match. I had him configure the mismatched parameters so they would match, but it still wouldn't create an adjacency. Looking more closely at the `show ip ospf interface` command, I noticed the cost did not match! Cisco calculated the bandwidth differently than the other vendor. Once I had him configure both as the same value, the link came up! Always remember, just because OSPF can be used in a multi-vendor network does not mean it will work out of the box!

This is a critical command to understand because it's extremely useful in production networks. Let's take a look at the Boulder router output:

```
Boulder>sh ip ospf neighbor

Neighbor ID      Pri   State    Dead Time   Address       Interface
223.255.255.254   1    FULL/DR  00:00:31    10.10.10.1    FastEthernet0/0
```

Here we can see that since there's an Ethernet link (broadcast multi-access) on the link between the Boulder and the Corp router, there's going to be an election to determine who will be the designated router (DR) and who will be the backup designated router (BDR). We can see that the Corp became the designated router, and it won because it had the highest IP address on the network—the highest RID.

Now the reason that the Corp connections to SF and LA don't have a DR or BDR listed in the output is that by default, elections don't happen on point-to-point links and they show FULL/ - . But we can still determine that the Corp router is fully adjacent to all three routers from its output.

The *show ip protocols* Command

The `show ip protocols` command is also highly useful, whether you're running OSPF, EIGRP, RIP, BGP, IS-IS, or any other routing protocol that can be configured on your router. It provides an excellent overview of the actual operation of all currently running protocols!

Check out the output from the Corp router:

```
Corp#sh ip protocols
Routing Protocol is "ospf 1"
  Outgoing update filter list for all interfaces is not set
  Incoming update filter list for all interfaces is not set
  Router ID 223.255.255.254
```

```
Number of areas in this router is 1. 1 normal 0 stub 0 nssa
Maximum path: 4
Routing for Networks:
   10.10.10.1 0.0.0.0 area 0
   172.16.10.1 0.0.0.0 area 0
   172.16.10.5 0.0.0.0 area 0
 Reference bandwidth unit is 100 mbps
 Routing Information Sources:
    Gateway         Distance      Last Update
    192.168.10.1         110      00:21:53
    192.168.20.1         110      00:21:53
 Distance: (default is 110) Distance: (default is 110)
```

From looking at this output, you can determine the OSPF process ID, OSPF router ID, type of OSPF area, networks and areas configured for OSPF, and the OSPF router IDs of neighbors—that's a lot. It's super-efficient!

Summary

This chapter gave you a great deal of information about OSPF. It's really difficult to include everything about OSPF because so much of it falls outside the scope of this chapter and book, but I've given you a few tips here and there, so you're good to go—as long as you make sure you've got what I presented to you dialed in, that is!

I talked about a lot of OSPF topics, including terminology, operations, and configuration as well as verification and monitoring.

Each of these topics encompasses quite a bit of information—the terminology section just scratched the surface of OSPF. But you've got the goods you really need for your studies. Finally, I gave you a tight survey of commands highly useful for observing the operation of OSPF so you can verify that things are moving along as they should. So eat it all up, and you're set!

Exam Essentials

Compare OSPF and RIPv1.   OSPF is a link-state protocol that supports VLSM and classless routing; RIPv1 is a distance-vector protocol that does not support VLSM and supports only classful routing.

Know how OSPF routers become neighbors and/or adjacent.   OSPF routers become neighbors when each router sees the other's Hello packets and the timers match between routers.

Be able to configure single-area OSPF.   A minimal single-area configuration involves only two commands: router ospf *process-id* and network *x.x.x.x y.y.y.y area Z.*

Be able to verify the operation of OSPF.   There are many show commands that provide useful details on OSPF, and it is useful to be completely familiar with the output of each: show ip ospf, show ip ospf database, show ip ospf interface, show ip ospf neighbor, and show ip protocols.

Written Lab 18

You can find the answers to this lab in Appendix A, "Answers to Written Labs."

1. Write the command that will enable the OSPF process 101 on a router.

2. Write the command that will display details of all OSPF routing processes enabled on a router.

3. Write the command that will display interface-specific OSPF information.

4. Write the command that will display all OSPF neighbors.

5. Write the command that will display all different OSPF route types that are currently known by the router.

6. Which parameter or parameters are used to calculate OSPF cost in Cisco routers?

7. Two routers are not forming an adjacency. What are all the reasons that OSPF will not form this adjacency with the neighbor router?

8. Which command is used to display the collection of OSPF link states?

9. What is the default administrative distance of OSPF?

10. What is the default to which hello and dead timers are set?

Hands-on Labs

In this section, you will use the following network and add OSPF routing.

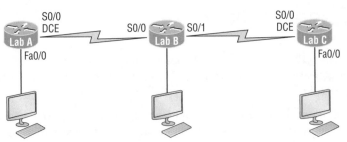

The first lab (Lab 18.1) requires you to configure three routers for OSPF and then view the configuration. Note that the labs in this chapter were written to be used with real equipment—but they can be used with any router simulator. You can replace the WAN links with Ethernet links if you want to.

The labs in this chapter are as follows:

Lab 18.1: Enabling the OSPF Process

Lab 18.2: Configuring OSPF Interfaces

Lab 18.3: Verifying OSPF Operation

Table 18.3 shows our IP addresses for each router (each interface uses a /24 mask).

TABLE 18.3   Our IP addresses

Router	Interface	IP address
Lab_A	Fa0/0	172.16.10.1
Lab_A	S0/0	172.16.20.1
Lab_B	S0/0	172.16.20.2
Lab_B	S0/1	172.16.30.1
Lab_C	S0/0	172.16.30.2
Lab_C	Fa0/0	172.16.40.1

Hands-on Lab 18.1: Enabling the OSPF Process

This is the first mandatory step in OSPF configuration.

1. Enable OSPF process 100 on Lab_A:

```
Lab_A#conf t
Enter configuration commands, one per line.
  End with CNTL/Z.
Lab_A (config)#router ospf 100
Lab_A (config-router)#^Z
```

2. Enable OSPF process 101 on Lab_B:

```
Lab_B#conf t
Enter configuration commands, one per line.
  End with CNTL/Z.
```

```
Lab_B (config)#router ospf 101
Lab_B (config-router)#^Z
```

3. Enable OSPF process 102 on Lab_C:

```
Lab_C#conf t
Enter configuration commands, one per line.
  End with CNTL/Z.
Lab_C (config)#router ospf 102
Lab_C (config-router)#^Z
```

Hands-on Lab 18.2: Configuring OSPF Interfaces

The second mandatory step in OSPF is adding your network statements.

1. Configure the LAN and the network between Lab_A and Lab_B. Assign it to area 0.

```
Lab_A#conf t
Enter configuration commands, one per line.
  End with CNTL/Z.
Lab_A (config)#router ospf 100
Lab_A (config-router)#network 172.16.10.1 0.0.0.0 area 0
Lab_A (config-router)#network 172.16.20.1 0.0.0.0 area 0
Lab_A (config-router)#^Z
Lab_A #
```

2. Configure the networks on the Lab_B router. Assign them to area 0.

```
Lab_B#conf t
Enter configuration commands, one per line.
  End with CNTL/Z.
Lab_B(config)#router ospf 101
Lab_B(config-router)#network 172.16.20.2 0.0.0.0 area 0
Lab_B(config-router)#network 172.16.30.1 0.0.0.0 area 0
Lab_B(config-router)#^Z
Lab_B #
```

3. Configure the networks on the Lab_C router. Assign them to area 0.

```
Lab_C#conf t
Enter configuration commands, one per line.
  End with CNTL/Z.
Lab_C(config)#router ospf 102
Lab_C(config-router)#network 172.16.30.2 0.0.0.0 area 0
```

```
Lab_C(config-router)#network 172.16.40.1 0.0.0.0 area 0
Lab_C(config-router)#^Z
Lab_C#
```

Hands-on Lab 18.3: Verifying OSPF Operation

You need to be able to verify what you configure.

1. Execute a show ip ospf neighbors command from the Lab_A router and view the results.

   ```
   Lab_A#sho ip ospf neighbors
   ```

2. Execute a show ip route command to verify that all other routers are learning all routes.

   ```
   Lab_A#sho ip route
   ```

3. Execute a show ip protocols command to verify OSPF information.

   ```
   Lab_A#sho ip protocols
   ```

4. Execute a show ip OSPF command to verify your RID.

   ```
   Lab_A#sho ip ospf
   ```

5. Execute a show ip ospf interface f0/0 command to verify your timers.

   ```
   Lab_A#sho ip ospf int f0/0
   ```

Review Questions

NOTE   The following questions are designed to test your understanding of this chapter's material. For more information on how to get additional questions, please see www.lammle.com/ccna.

You can find the answers to these questions in Appendix B, "Answers to Review Questions."

1. There are three possible routes for a router to reach a destination network. The first route is from OSPF with a metric of 782. The second route is from RIPv2 with a metric of 4. The third is from EIGRP with a composite metric of 20514560. Which route will be installed by the router in its routing table?

   A. RIPv2

   B. EIGRP

   C. OSPF

   D. All three

2. In the accompanying diagram, which of the routers must be ABRs? (Choose all that apply.)

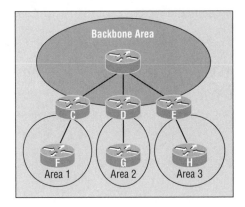

   A. C

   B. D

   C. E

   D. F

   E. G

   F. H

3. Which of the following describe the process identifier that is used to run OSPF on a router? (Choose two.)

   A. It is locally significant.

   B. It is globally significant.

   C. It is needed to identify a unique instance of an OSPF database.

   D. It is an optional parameter required only if multiple OSPF processes are running on the router.

   E. All routes in the same OSPF area must have the same process ID if they are to exchange routing information.

4. All of the following must match for two OSPF routers to become neighbors except which?

   A. Area ID

   B. Router ID

   C. Stub area flag

   D. Authentication password if using one

5. In the diagram, by default what will be the router ID of Lab_B?

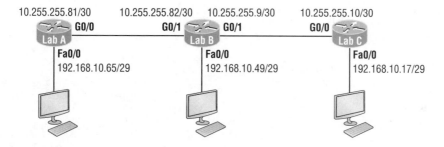

   A. 10.255.255.82

   B. 10.255.255.9

   C. 192.168.10.49

   D. 10.255.255.81

6. You get a call from a network administrator who tells you that he typed the following into his router:

```
Router(config)#router ospf 1
Router(config-router)#network 10.0.0.0 255.0.0.0 area 0
```

   He tells you he still can't see any routes in the routing table. What configuration error did the administrator make?

   A. The wildcard mask is incorrect.

   B. The OSPF area is wrong.

    C. The OSPF process ID is incorrect.

    D. The AS configuration is wrong.

7. Which of the following statements is true with regard to the output shown?

```
Corp#sh ip ospf neighbor
Neighbor ID      Pri   State       Dead Time   Address      Interface
172.31.1.4        1    FULL/BDR    00:00:34    10.10.10.2   FastEthernet0/0
192.168.20.1      0    FULL/  -    00:00:31    172.16.10.6  Serial0/1
192.168.10.1      0    FULL/  -    00:00:32    172.16.10.2  Serial0/0
```

    A. There is no DR on the link to 192.168.20.1.

    B. The Corp router is the BDR on the link to 172.31.1.4.

    C. The Corp router is the DR on the link to 192.168.20.1.

    D. The link to 192.168.10.1 is Active.

8. What is the administrative distance of OSPF?

    A. 90

    B. 100

    C. 120

    D. 110

9. In OSPF, Hellos are sent to what IP address?

    A. 224.0.0.5

    B. 224.0.0.9

    C. 224.0.0.10

    D. 224.0.0.1

10. What command generated the following output?

```
172.31.1.4        1    FULL/BDR    00:00:34    10.10.10.2   FastEthernet0/0
192.168.20.1      0    FULL/  -    00:00:31    172.16.10.6  Serial0/1
192.168.10.1      0    FULL/  -    00:00:32    172.16.10.2  Serial0/0
```

    A. show ip ospf neighbor

    B. show ip ospf database

    C. show ip route

    D. show ip ospf interface

11. Updates addressed to 224.0.0.6 are destined for which type of OSPF router?

    A. DR

    B. ASBR

    C. ABR

    D. All OSPF routers

12. For some reason, you cannot establish an adjacency relationship on a common Ethernet link between two routers. Looking at this output, what is the cause of the problem?

```
RouterA#
Ethernet0/0 is up, line protocol is up
  Internet Address 172.16.1.2/16, Area 0
  Process ID 2, Router ID 172.126.1.2, Network Type BROADCAST, Cost: 10
  Transmit Delay is 1 sec, State DR, Priority 1
  Designated Router (ID) 172.16.1.2, interface address 172.16.1.1
  No backup designated router on this network
  Timer intervals configured, Hello 5, Dead 20, Wait 20, Retransmit 5

RouterB#
Ethernet0/0 is up, line protocol is up
  Internet Address 172.16.1.1/16, Area 0
  Process ID 2, Router ID 172.126.1.1, Network Type BROADCAST, Cost: 10
  Transmit Delay is 1 sec, State DR, Priority 1
  Designated Router (ID) 172.16.1.1, interface address 172.16.1.2
  No backup designated router on this network
  Timer intervals configured, Hello 10, Dead 40, Wait 40, Retransmit 5
```

    A. The OSPF area is not configured properly.

    B. The priority on RouterA should be set higher.

    C. The cost on RouterA should be set higher.

    D. The Hello and Dead timers are not configured properly.

    E. A backup designated router needs to be added to the network.

    F. The OSPF process ID numbers must match.

13. In the work area, match each OSPF term (by line) to its definition.

Designated router	Contains only the best routes
Topological database	Elected on broadcast networks
Hello protocol	Contains all routes learned
Routing table	Provides dynamic neighbor discovery

14. Type the command that will disable OSPF on the Fa0/1 interface under the routing process. Write only the command and not the prompt.

15. Which two of the following commands will place network 10.2.3.0/24 into area 0? (Choose two.)

   A. `router eigrp 10`

   B. `router ospf 10`

   C. `router rip`

   D. `network 10.0.0.0`

   E. `network 10.2.3.0 255.255.255.0 area 0`

   F. `network 10.2.3.0 0.0.0.255 area0`

   G. `network 10.2.3.0 0.0.0.255 area 0`

16. Given the following output, which statement or statements can be determined to be true? (Choose all that apply.)

```
RouterA2# show ip ospf neighbor

Neighbor ID Pri State Dead Time Address Interface
192.168.23.2 1 FULL/BDR 00:00:29 10.24.4.2 FastEthernet1/0
192.168.45.2 2 FULL/BDR 00:00:24 10.1.0.5 FastEthernet0/0
192.168.85.1 1 FULL/- 00:00:33 10.6.4.10 Serial0/1
192.168.90.3 1 FULL/DR 00:00:32 10.5.5.2 FastEthernet0/1
192.168.67.3 1 FULL/DR 00:00:20 10.4.9.20 FastEthernet0/2
192.168.90.1 1 FULL/BDR 00:00:23 10.5.5.4 FastEthernet0/1
<<output omitted>>
```

   A. The DR for the network connected to Fa0/0 has an interface priority higher than 2.

   B. This router (A2) is the BDR for subnet 10.1.0.0.

   C. The DR for the network connected to Fa0/1 has a router ID of 10.5.5.2.

   D. The DR for the serial subnet is 192.168.85.1.

17. What are three reasons for creating OSPF in a hierarchical design? (Choose three.)

   A. To decrease routing overhead

   B. To speed up convergence

   C. To confine network instability to single areas of the network

   D. To make configuring OSPF easier

18. Type the command that produced the following output. Write only the command and not the prompt.

```
FastEthernet0/0 is up, line protocol is up
  Internet Address 10.10.10.1/24, Area 0
  Process ID 1, Router ID 223.255.255.254, Network Type BROADCAST, Cost:
1 Transmit Delay is 1 sec, State DR, Priority 1
  Designated Router (ID) 223.255.255.254, Interface address 10.10.10.1
```

```
Backup Designated router (ID) 172.31.1.4, Interface address 10.10.10.2
Timer intervals configured, Hello 10, Dead 40, Wait 40, Retransmit 5
    oob-resync timeout 40
    Hello due in 00:00:08
  Supports Link-local Signaling (LLS)
  Cisco NSF helper support enabled
  IETF NSF helper support enabled
  Index 3/3, flood queue length 0
  Next 0x0(0)/0x0(0)
  Last flood scan length is 1, maximum is 1
  Last flood scan time is 0 msec, maximum is 0 msec
  Neighbor Count is 1, Adjacent neighbor count is 1
    Adjacent with neighbor 172.31.1.  Suppress hello for 0 neighbor(s)
```

19. A(n) _____ is an OSPF data packet containing link-state and routing information that is shared among OSPF routers.

   A. LSA

   B. TSA

   C. Hello

   D. SPF

20. If routers in a single area are configured with the same priority value, what value does a router use for the OSPF router ID in the absence of a loopback interface?

   A. The lowest IP address of any physical interface

   B. The highest IP address of any physical interface

   C. The lowest IP address of any logical interface

   D. The highest IP address of any logical interface

Chapter

19

Multi-Area OSPF

THE FOLLOWING ICND2 EXAM TOPICS ARE COVERED IN THIS CHAPTER:

✓ 2.0   Routing Technologies

✓ 2.2   Compare and contrast distance vector and link-state routing protocols

✓ 2.3   Compare and contrast interior and exterior routing protocols

✓ 2.4   Configure, verify, and troubleshoot single area and multiarea OSPFv2 for IPv4 (excluding authentication, filtering, manual summarization, redistribution, stub, virtual-link, and LSAs)

✓ 2.5   Configure, verify, and troubleshoot single area and multiarea OSPFv3 for IPv6 (excluding authentication, filtering, manual summarization, redistribution, stub, virtual-link, and LSAs)

We'll begin this chapter by focusing on the scalability constraints of an Open Shortest Path First (OSPF) network with a single area and move on from there to explore the concept of multi-area OSPF as a solution to these scalability limitations.

I'll also identify and introduce you to the various categories of routers used in multi-area configurations, including backbone routers, internal routers, area border routers (ABRs), and autonomous system boundary routers (ASBRs).

The functions of different OSPF Link-State Advertisements (LSAs) are absolutely crucial for you to understand for success in taking the Cisco exam, so I'll go into detail about the types of LSAs used by OSPF as well as the Hello protocol and different neighbor states when an adjacency is taking place.

And because troubleshooting is always a vital skill to have, I'll guide you through the process with a collection of show commands that can be effectively used to monitor and troubleshoot a multi-area OSPF implementation. Finally, I'll end the chapter with the easiest part: configuring and verifying OSPFv3.

To find up-to-the-minute updates for this chapter, please see www.lammle.com/ccna or the book's web page at www.sybex.com/go/ccna.

OSPF Scalability

At this point, and before you read this chapter, be sure that you have the foundation of single-area OSPF down pat. I'm sure you remember OSPF's significant advantage over distance-vector protocols like RIP, due to OSPF's ability to represent an entire network within its link-state database, which dramatically reduces the time required for convergence!

But what does a router actually go through to give us this great performance? Each router recalculates its database every time there's a topology change. If you have numerous routers in an area, they'll clearly have lots of links. Every time a link goes up or down, an LSA Type 1 packet is advertised, forcing all of the routers in the same area to recalculate their shortest path first (SPF) tree. Predictably, this kind of heavy lifting requires a ton of CPU overhead. On top of that, each router must hold the entire link-state database that represents the topology of the entire network, which results in considerable memory overhead. As if all that weren't enough, each router also holds a complete copy of the routing table, adding more to the already heavy overhead burden on memory. And keep in mind that the number of entries in the routing table can be much greater than the number of networks in the routing table because there are typically multiple routes to the same remote networks!

Considering these OSPF factors, it's easy to imagine that in a really large network, single-area OSPF presents some serious scalability challenges, as shown in Figure 19.1. We'll move on in a bit to compare the single-area OSPF network in that illustration to our multi-area networks.

FIGURE 19.1   OSPF single-area network: All routers flood the network with link-state information to all other routers within the same area.

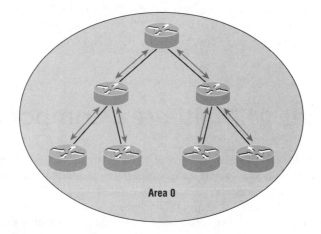

Single-area OSPF design places all routers into a single OSPF area, which results in many LSAs being processed on every router.

Fortunately, OSPF allows us to take a large OSPF topology and break it down into multiple, more manageable areas, as illustrated in Figure 19.2.

FIGURE 19.2   OSPF multi-area network: All routers flood the network only within their area.

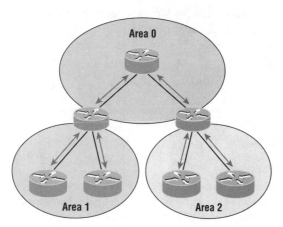

Just take a minute to think about the advantages of this hierarchical approach. First, routers that are internal to a defined area don't need to worry about having a link-state database for the entire network because they need one for only their own areas. This factor seriously reduces memory overhead! Second, routers that are internal to a defined area now have to recalculate their link-state database only when there's a topology change within their given area. Topology changes in one area won't cause global OSPF recalculations, further reducing processor overhead. Finally, because routes can be summarized at area boundaries, the routing tables on each router just don't need to be nearly as huge as they would be in a single-area environment!

But of course there's a catch: As you start subdividing your OSPF topology into multiple areas, the configuration gets more complex, so we'll explore some strategic ways to finesse the configuration plus look at some cool tricks for effectively troubleshooting multi-area OSPF networks.

Categories of Multi-area Components

In the following sections, I'm going to cover the various roles that routers play in a multi-area OSPF network. You'll find routers serving as backbone routers, internal routers, area border routers, and autonomous system boundary routers. I'll also introduce you to the different types of advertisements used in an OSPF network.

Link-State Advertisements (LSAs) describe a router and the networks that are connected to it by sending the LSAs to neighbor routers. Routers exchange LSAs and learn the complete topology of the network until all routers have the exact same topology database. After the topology database is built, OSPF uses the Dijkstra algorithm to find the best path to each remote network and places only the best routes into the routing table.

Adjacency Requirements

Once neighbors have been identified, adjacencies must be established so that routing (LSA) information can be exchanged. There are two steps required to change a neighboring OSPF router into an adjacent OSPF router:

1. Two-way communication (achieved via the Hello protocol)
2. Database synchronization, which consists of three packet types being exchanged between routers:

    ▪ Database Description (DD) packets

    ▪ Link-State Request (LSR) packets

    ▪ Link-State Update (LSU) packets

Once database synchronization is complete, the two routers are considered adjacent. This is how adjacency is achieved, but you need to know when an adjacency will occur.

It's important to remember that neighbors will not form an adjacency if the following do not match:

- Area ID
- Subnet
- Hello and dead timers
- Authentication (if configured)

When adjacencies form depends on the network type. If the link is point-to-point, the two neighbors will become adjacent if the Hello packet information for both routers is configured properly. On broadcast multi-access networks, adjacencies are formed only between the OSPF routers on the network and the DR and BDR.

OSPF Router Roles

Routers within a multi-area OSPF network fall into different categories. Check out Figure 19.3 to see the various roles that routers can play.

FIGURE 19.3   Router roles: Routers within an area are called internal routers.

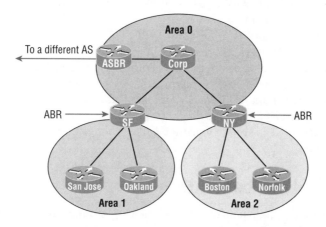

Notice that there are four routers that are part of area 0: the Corp router, SF and NY, and the autonomous system border router (ASBR). When configuring multi-area OSPF, one area must be called area 0, referred to as the *backbone area*. All other areas must connect to area 0. The four routers are referred to as the backbone routers, which are any routers that exist either partially or completely in OSPF area 0.

Another key distinction about the SF and NY routers connecting to other areas is that they have interfaces in more than one area. This makes them *area border routers (ABRs)* because in addition to having an interface in area 0, SF has an interface in area 1 and NY has an interface in area 2.

An ABR is a router that belongs to more than one OSPF area. It maintains information from all directly connected areas in its topology table but doesn't share the topological details from one area with the other. But it will forward routing information from one area to the other. The key concept here is that an ABR separates the LSA flooding zone, is a primary point for area address summarization, and typically has the source default route, all while maintaining the link-state database (LSDB) for each area it's connected to.

> Remember that a router can play more than one role. In Figure 19.3, SF and NY are both backbone routers and area border routers.

Let's turn our focus to the San Jose and Oakland routers. You can see that all interfaces on both of these routers reside only in area 1. Because all of San Jose's and Oakland's interfaces are internal to a single area, they're called internal routers. An *internal router* is any router with all of its interfaces included as members of the same area. This also applies to the Boston and Norfolk routers and their relationship to area 2. The Corp router is internal to area 0.

Finally, the ASBR is unique among all routers in our example because of its connection to an external *autonomous system (AS)*. When an OSPF network is connected to an EIGRP network, a *Border Gateway Protocol (BGP)* network, or a network running any other external routing process, it's referred to as an AS.

An *autonomous system boundary router (ASBR)* is an OSPF router with at least one interface connected to an external network or different AS. A network is considered external if a route received is from a routing protocol other than OSPF. An ASBR is responsible for injecting route information learned via the external network into OSPF.

I want to point out that an ASBR doesn't automatically exchange routing information between its OSPF routing process and the external routing process that it's connected to. These routes are exchanged through a method called *route redistribution*, which is beyond the scope of this book.

Link-State Advertisements

You know that a router's link-state database is made up of *Link-State Advertisements (LSAs)*. But just as there are several OSPF router categories to remember, there are also various types of LSAs to keep in mind—five of them, to be exact. These LSA classifications may not seem important at first, but you'll see why they are when we cover how the various types of OSPF areas operate. Let's start by exploring the different types of LSAs that Cisco uses:

Type 1 LSA   Referred to as a *router link advertisement (RLA)*, or just router LSA, a *Type 1 LSA* is sent by every router to other routers in its area. This advertisement contains the status of a router's link in the area to which it is connected. If a router is connected to multiple areas, then it will send separate Type 1 LSAs for each of the areas it's connected to. Type 1 LSAs contain the router ID (RID), interfaces, IP information, and current interface state. For example, in the network in Figure 19.4, router SF will send an LSA Type 1 advertisement for its interface into area 0 and a separate LSA Type 1 advertisement for its interfaces into area 1 describing the state of its links. The same will happen with the other routers in Figure 19.4.

FIGURE 19.4   Type 1 Link-State Advertisements

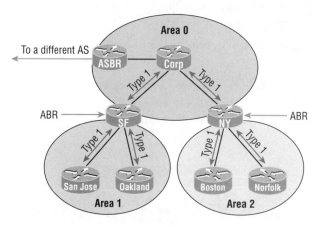

Type 1: Here is the status of my links!

Type 2 LSA   Referred to as a *network link advertisement (NLA)*, a *Type 2 LSA* is generated by designated routers (DRs). Remember that a designated router is elected to represent other routers in its network, and it establishes adjacencies with them. The DR uses a Type 2 LSA to send out information about the state of other routers that are part of the same network. Note that the Type 2 LSA is flooded to all routers that are in the same area as the one containing the specific network but not to any outside of that area. These updates contain the DR and BDR IP information.

Type 3 LSA   Referred to as a *summary link advertisement (SLA)*, a *Type 3 LSA* is generated by area border routers. These ABRs send Type 3 LSAs toward the area external to the one where they were generated. The Type 3 LSA advertises networks, and these LSAs advertise *inter-area routes* to the backbone area (area 0). Advertisements contain the IP information and RID of the ABR that is advertising an LSA Type 3.

The word *summary* often invokes images of a summarized network address that hides the details of many small subnets within the advertisement of a single large one. But in OSPF, summary link advertisements don't necessarily contain network summaries. Unless the administrator manually creates a summary, the full list of individual networks available within an area will be advertised by the SLAs.

Type 4 LSA *Type 4 LSAs* are generated by area border routers. These ABRs send a Type 4 LSA toward the area external to the one in which they were generated. These are also summary LSAs like Type 3, but Type 4 are specifically used to inform the rest of the OSPF areas how to get to the ASBR.

Type 5 LSA Referred to as *AS external link advertisements*, a *Type 5 LSA* is sent by autonomous system boundary routers to advertise routes that are external to the OSPF autonomous system and are flooded everywhere. A Type 5 LSA is generated for each individual external network advertised by the ASBR.

Figure 19.5 shows how each LSA type would be used in a multi-area OSPF network.

FIGURE 19.5 Basic LSA types

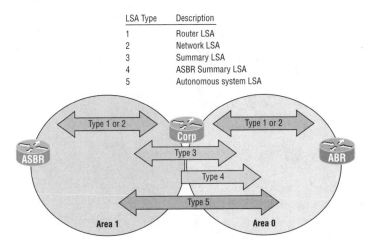

It's important to understand the different LSA types and how they work. Looking at Figure 19.5, you can see that Type 1 and 2 are flooded between routers in their same area. Type 3 LSAs from the Corp router (which is an ABR and maintains the LSDB for each area it is connected to) will summarize information learned from area 1 into area 0 and vice versa. The ASBR will flood Type 5 LSAs into area 1, and the Corp router will then flood Type 4 LSAs into area 0, telling all routers how to get to the ASBR, basically becoming a proxy ASBR.

OSPF Hello Protocol

The Hello protocol provides a lot of information to neighbors. The following is communicated between neighbors, by default, every 10 seconds:

Router ID (RID) This is the highest active IP address on the router. The highest loopback IP addresses are used first. If no loopback interfaces are configured, OSPF will choose from physical interfaces instead.

Hello/Dead interval   The period between Hello packets is the Hello time, which is 10 seconds by default. The dead time is the length of time allotted for a Hello packet to be received before a neighbor is considered down—four times the Hello interval, unless otherwise configured.

Neighbors   The information includes a list of the router IDs for all the originating router's neighbors, neighbors being defined as routers that are attached to a common IP subnet and use identical subnet masks.

Area ID   This represents the area that the originating router interface belongs to.

Router priority   The priority is an 8-bit value used to aid in the election of the DR and BDR. This isn't set on point-to-point links!

DR IP address   This is the router ID of the current DR.

BDR IP address   This is the router ID of the current BDR.

Authentication data   This is the authentication type and corresponding information (if configured).

The mandatory information within the Hello update that must match exactly are the hello and dead timer values intervals, area ID, OSPF area type, subnet, and authentication data if used. If any of those don't match perfectly, no adjacency will occur!

Neighbor States

Before we move on to configuration, verification, and troubleshooting OSPF, it's important for you to grasp how OSPF routers traverse different states when adjacencies are being established.

When OSPF routers are initialized, they first start exchanging information using the Hello protocol via the multicast address 224.0.0.5. After the neighbor relationship is established between routers, the routers synchronize their link-state database (LSDB) by reliably exchanging LSAs. They actually exchange quite a bit of vital information when they start up.

The relationship that one router has with another consists of eight possible states. All OSPF routers begin in the DOWN state, and if all is well, they'll progress to either the 2WAY or FULL state with their neighbors. Figure 19.6 shows this neighbor state progression.

FIGURE 19.6   OSPF neighbor states, part 1

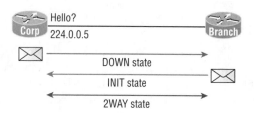

The process starts by sending out Hello packets. Every listening router will then add the originating router to the neighbor database. The responding routers will reply with all of their Hello information so that the originating router can add them to its own neighbor table. At this point, we will have reached the 2WAY state—only certain routers will advance beyond this to establish adjacencies.

Here's a definition of the eight possible relationship states:

DOWN   In the *DOWN state*, no Hello packets have been received on the interface. Bear in mind that this does not imply that the interface itself is physically down.

ATTEMPT   In the *ATTEMPT state*, neighbors must be configured manually. It applies only to nonbroadcast multi-access (NBMA) network connections.

INIT   In the *INIT state*, Hello packets have been received from another router. Still, the absence of the router ID for the receiving router in the Neighbor field indicates that bidirectional communication hasn't been established yet.

2WAY   In the *2WAY state*, Hello packets that include their own router ID in the Neighbor field have been received. Bidirectional communication has been established. In broadcast multi-access networks, an election can occur after this point.

After the DR and BDR have been selected, the routers will enter into the EXSTART state and the routers are ready to discover the link-state information about the internetwork and create their LSDB. This process is illustrated in Figure 19.7.

FIGURE 19.7   OSPF router neighbor states, part 2

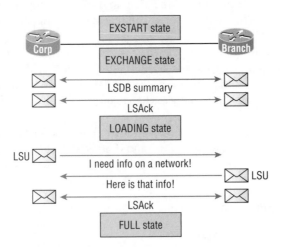

EXSTART   In the *EXSTART state*, the DR and BDR establish adjacencies with each router in the network. A master-slave relationship is created between each router and its adjacent DR and DBR. The router with the highest RID becomes the master, and the master-slave election dictates which router will start the exchange. Once routers exchange DBD packets, the routers will move into the EXCHANGE state.

One reason two neighbor routers won't get past the EXSTART state is that they have different MTUs.

EXCHANGE   In the *EXCHANGE state*, routing information is exchanged using Database Description (DBD or DD) packets, and Link-State Request (LSR) and Link-State Update packets may also be sent. When routers start sending LSRs, they're considered to be in the LOADING state.

LOADING   In the *LOADING state*, Link-State Request (LSR) packets are sent to neighbors to request any Link-State Advertisements (LSAs) that may have been missed or corrupted while the routers were in the EXCHANGE state. Neighbors respond with Link-State Update (LSU) packets, which are in turn acknowledged with Link-State Acknowledgement (LSAck) packets. When all LSRs have been satisfied for a given router, the adjacent routers are considered synchronized and enter the FULL state.

FULL   In the *FULL state*, all LSA information is synchronized among neighbors and adjacency has been established. OSPF routing can begin only after the FULL state has been reached!

It's important to understand that routers should be in the 2WAY and FULL states and the others are considered transitory. Routers shouldn't remain in any other state for extended period of times. Let's configure OSPF now to see what we've covered so far in action.

Basic Multi-area Configuration

Basic multi-area configuration isn't all that hard. Understanding your design, layout, and types of LSAs and DRs and configuring the elections, troubleshooting, and fully comprehending what's happening in the background are really the most complicated aspects of OSPF.

As I was saying, configuring OSPF is pretty simple, and you'll see toward the end of this chapter that configuring OSPFv3 is even easier! After I show you the basic OSPF multi-area configuration in this section, we'll work on the verification of OSPF and then go through a detailed troubleshooting scenario just as we did with EIGRP. Let's get the ball rolling with the multi-area configuration shown in Figure 19.8.

We'll use the same routers we've been working with throughout all the chapters, but we're going to create three areas. The routers are still configured with the IPv6 addresses from my last EIGRPv6 section in Chapter 3, and I've also verified that the IPv4 addresses are on the interfaces and working as well since then, so we're all set to rock the configs for this chapter! Here's the Corp configuration:

```
Corp#config t
Corp(config)#router ospf 1
Corp(config-router)#router-id 1.1.1.1
```

Reload or use "clear ip ospf process" command, for this to
take effect

```
Corp(config-router)#network 10.10.0.0 0.0.255.255 area 0
Corp(config-router)#network 172.16.10.0 0.0.0.3 area 1
Corp(config-router)#network 172.16.10.4 0.0.0.3 area 2
```

FIGURE 19.8   Our internetwork

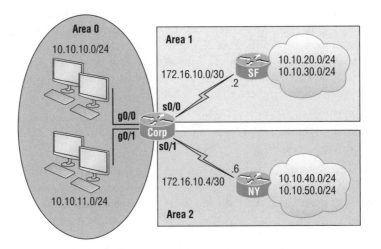

Pretty straightforward, but let's talk about it anyway. First I started the OSPF process
with the router ospf *process-id* command, using any number from 1–65,535 because
they're only locally significant, so they don't need to match my neighbor routers. I set the
RID of the router only to remind you that this can be configured under the router process,
but with our small network it wouldn't really be necessary to mess with RIDs if this was
an actual production network. The one thing that you need to keep in mind here is that
in OSPF, the RID must be different on each router. With EIGRP, they can all be the same
because they are not as important in that process. Still, as I showed you in the EIGRPv6
section, we still need them!

Anyway, at this point in the configurations I needed to choose my network statements
for the OSPF process to use, which allowed me to place my four interfaces on the Corp
router into three different areas. In the first network statement, 10.10.0.0 0.0.255.255, I
placed the g0/0 and g0/1 interfaces into area 0. The second and third statements needed to
be more exact since there are /30 networks. 172.16.10.0 0.0.0.3 tells OSPF process 1 to go
find an active interface that's configured with 172.16.10.1 or .2 and to place that interface
into area 1. The last line tells the OSPF process to go find any active interface configured

with 172.16.10.5 or .6 and place that interface into area 2. The wildcard of 0.0.0.3 means the first three octets can match any value, but the last octet is a block size of 4.

The only thing different about these configurations from those in the single-area OSPF is the different areas at the end of the command—that's it!

Here is the configuration for the SF and NY routers:

```
SF(config)#router ospf 1
SF(config-router)#network 10.10.0.0 0.0.255.255 area 1
SF(config-router)#network 172.16.0.0 0.0.255.255 area 1

NY(config)#router ospf 1
NY(config-router)#network 0.0.0.0 255.255.255.255 area 2
00:01:07: %OSPF-5-ADJCHG: Process 1, Nbr 1.1.1.1 on Serial0/0/0 from LOADING
to FULL,
Loading Done
```

I configured each one slightly different from the Corp router, but since they didn't have an interface in more than area 1, I had more leeway in configuring them. For the NY router I just configured a network statement (0.0.0.0 255.255.255.255) that says "go find any active interface and place it into area 2!" I'm not recommending that you configure your routers in such a broad manner; I just wanted to show you your options.

Before we move onto verifying our network, let me show you another way that the CCNA objectives configure OSPF. For the Corp router, we had three network statements, which covered the four interfaces used. We could have configured the OSPF process like this on the Corp router (or all routers); it doesn't matter which way you choose:

```
Corp(config)#router ospf 1
Corp(config-router)#router-id 1.1.1.1
Corp(config-router)#int g0/0
Corp(config-if)#ip ospf 1 area 0
Corp(config-if)#int g0/1
Corp(config-if)#ip ospf 1 area 0
Corp(config-if)#int s0/0
Corp(config-if)#ip ospf 1 area 1
Corp(config-if)#int s0/1
Corp(config-if)#ip ospf 1 area 2
```

First I chose my process ID, then set my RID (this absolutely must be different on every router in your internetwork!), then I just went to each interface and told it what area it was in. Easy! No network commands to screw up! Nice. Again, you can configure it with the network statement or the interface statement, it doesn't matter, but you need to really remember this for the CCNA objectives!

Now that our three routers are configured, let's verify our internetwork.

Verifying and Troubleshooting Multi-area OSPF Networks

Cisco's IOS has several show and debug commands that can help you monitor and troubleshoot OSPF networks. A sampling of these commands, which can be used to gain information about various OSPF characteristics, is included in Table 19.1.

TABLE 19.1   OSPF verification commands

Command	Provides the following
show ip ospf neighbor	Verifies your OSPF-enabled interfaces
show ip ospf interface	Displays OSPF-related information on an OSPF-enabled interface
show ip protocols	Verifies the OSPF process ID and that OSPF is enabled on the router
show ip route	Verifies the routing table, and displays any OSPF injected routes
show ip ospf database	Lists a summary of the LSAs in the database, with one line of output per LSA, organized by type

Let's go through some verification commands—the same commands we used to verify our single-area OSPF network—then we'll move onto the OSPF troubleshooting scenario section.

Okay, once you've checked the link between your neighbors and can use the Ping program, the best command when verifying a routing protocol is to always check the status of your neighbor's connection first. The show ip ospf neighbor command is super useful because it summarizes the pertinent OSPF information regarding neighbors and their adjacency state. If a DR or BDR exists, that information will also be displayed. Here's a sample:

```
Corp#sh ip ospf neighbor
Neighbor ID     Pri   State          Dead Time   Address       Interface
172.16.10.2       0   FULL/  -       00:00:34    172.16.10.2   Serial0/0/0
172.16.10.6       0   FULL/  -       00:00:31    172.16.10.6   Serial0/0/1


SF#sh ip ospf neighbor
Neighbor ID     Pri   State          Dead Time   Address       Interface
1.1.1.1           0   FULL/  -       00:00:39    172.16.10.1   Serial0/0/0
```

```
NY#sh ip ospf neighbor
Neighbor ID    Pri   State        Dead Time    Address       Interface
1.1.1.1          0   FULL/  -     00:00:34     172.16.10.5   Serial0/0/0
```

The reason that the Corp connections to SF and LA don't have a DR or BDR listed in the output is that by default, elections don't happen on point-to-point links and they show FULL/-. But we can see that the Corp router is fully adjacent to all three routers from its output.

The output of this command shows the neighbor ID, which is the RID of the router. Notice in the output of the Corp router that the RIDs for the SF and NY routers were chosen based on highest IP address of any active interface when I started the OSPF process on those routers. Both the SF and NY routers see the Corp router RID as 1.1.1.1 because I set that manually under the router ospf process command.

Next we see the Pri field, which is the priority field that's set to 1 by default. Don't forget that on point-to-point links, elections don't happen, so the interfaces are all set to 0 in this example because none of these routers will have elections on these interfaces with each other over this serial WAN network. The state field shows Full/-, which means all routers are synchronized with their LSDB, and the /- means there is no election on this type of interface. The dead timer is counting down, and if the router does not hear from this neighbor before this expires, the link will be considered down. The Address field is the actual address of the neighbor's interface connecting to the router.

The *show ip ospf* Command

We use the show ip ospf command to display OSPF information for one or all OSPF processes running on the router. Information contained therein includes the router ID, area information, SPF statistics, and LSA timer information. Let's check out the output from the Corp router:

```
Corp#sh ip ospf
 Routing Process "ospf 1" with ID 1.1.1.1
 Supports only single TOS(TOS0) routes
 Supports opaque LSA
 It is an area border router
 SPF schedule delay 5 secs, Hold time between two SPFs 10 secs
 Minimum LSA interval 5 secs. Minimum LSA arrival 1 secs
 Number of external LSA 0. Checksum Sum 0x000000
 Number of opaque AS LSA 0. Checksum Sum 0x000000
 Number of DCbitless external and opaque AS LSA 0
 Number of DoNotAge external and opaque AS LSA 0
 Number of areas in this router is 3. 3 normal 0 stub 0 nssa
 External flood list length 0
```

```
Area BACKBONE(0)
    Number of interfaces in this area is 2
    Area has no authentication
    SPF algorithm executed 19 times
    Area ranges are
    Number of LSA 7. Checksum Sum 0x0384d5
    Number of opaque link LSA 0. Checksum Sum 0x000000
    Number of DCbitless LSA 0
    Number of indication LSA 0
    Number of DoNotAge LSA 0
    Flood list length 0
Area 1
    Number of interfaces in this area is 1
    Area has no authentication
    SPF algorithm executed 43 times
    Area ranges are
    Number of LSA 7. Checksum Sum 0x0435f8
    Number of opaque link LSA 0. Checksum Sum 0x000000
    Number of DCbitless LSA 0
    Number of indication LSA 0
    Number of DoNotAge LSA 0
    Flood list length 0
Area 2
    Number of interfaces in this area is 1
    Area has no authentication
    SPF algorithm executed 38 times
    Area ranges are
    Number of LSA 7. Checksum Sum 0x0319ed
    Number of opaque link LSA 0. Checksum Sum 0x000000
    Number of DCbitless LSA 0
    Number of indication LSA 0
    Number of DoNotAge LSA 0
    Flood list length 0
```

You'll notice that most of the preceding information wasn't displayed with this command output in single-area OSPF. We have more displayed here because it's providing information about each area we've configured on this router.

The *show ip ospf interface* Command

The show ip ospf interface command displays all interface-related OSPF information. Data is displayed for all OSPF-enabled interfaces or for specified interfaces. I'll highlight some important portions I want you to pay special attention to.

```
Corp#sh ip ospf interface gi0/0
GigabitEthernet0/0 is up, line protocol is up
  Internet address is 10.10.10.1/24, Area 0
  Process ID 1, Router ID 1.1.1.1, Network Type BROADCAST, Cost: 1
  Transmit Delay is 1 sec, State DR, Priority 1
  Designated Router (ID) 1.1.1.1, Interface address 10.10.10.1
  No backup designated router on this network
  Timer intervals configured, Hello 10, Dead 40, Wait 40, Retransmit 5
    Hello due in 00:00:05
  Index 1/1, flood queue length 0
  Next 0x0(0)/0x0(0)
  Last flood scan length is 1, maximum is 1
  Last flood scan time is 0 msec, maximum is 0 msec
  Neighbor Count is 0, Adjacent neighbor count is 0
  Suppress hello for 0 neighbor(s)
```

Let's take a look at a serial interface so we can compare it to the Gigabit Ethernet interface just shown. The Ethernet network is a broadcast multi-access network by default, and the serial interface is a point-to-point nonbroadcast multi-access network, so they will act differently with OSPF:

```
Corp#sh ip ospf interface s0/0/0
Serial0/0/0 is up, line protocol is up
  Internet address is 172.16.10.1/30, Area 1
  Process ID 1, Router ID 1.1.1.1, Network Type POINT-TO-POINT, Cost: 64
  Transmit Delay is 1 sec, State POINT-TO-POINT, Priority 0
  No designated router on this network
  No backup designated router on this network
  Timer intervals configured, Hello 10, Dead 40, Wait 40, Retransmit 5
    Hello due in 00:00:02
  Index 3/3, flood queue length 0
  Next 0x0(0)/0x0(0)
  Last flood scan length is 1, maximum is 1
  Last flood scan time is 0 msec, maximum is 0 msec
  Neighbor Count is 1 , Adjacent neighbor count is 1
    Adjacent with neighbor 172.16.10.2
  Suppress hello for 0 neighbor(s)
```

The following information is displayed via this command:

- Interface IP address
- Area assignment
- Process ID
- Router ID

- Network type
- Cost
- Priority
- DR/BDR election information (if applicable)
- Hello and dead timer intervals
- Adjacent neighbor information

I used the `show ip ospf interface gi0/0` command first because I knew that there would be a designated router elected on the Ethernet broadcast multi-access network on the Corp router, even though it has no one to run against, which means the Corp router automatically wins. The information that I bolded is all very important! What are the hello and dead timers set to by default? Even though I haven't talked much about the cost output on an interface, it can also be very important. Two OSPF routers still could create an adjacency if the costs don't match, but it could lead to certain links not being utilized. We'll discuss this more at the end of the verification section.

 Real World Scenario

Neighbor Routers Don't Form an Adjacency

I'd like to talk more about the adjacency issue and how the `show ip ospf interface` command can help you solve problems, especially in multi-vendor networks.

Years ago I was consulting with the folks at a large PC/laptop manufacturer and was helping them build out their large internetwork. They were using OSPF because their company was a worldwide company and used many types of routers from all manufacturers.

I received a call from a remote branch informing me that they installed a new router but it was not seeing the Cisco router off their Ethernet interface. Of course it was an emergency because this new router was holding some important WAN links to a new remote location that needed to be up yesterday!

After calming down the person on the phone, I simply had the admin use the `show ip ospf interface fa0/0` command and verify the hello and dead timers and the area configured for that interface and then had him verify that the IP addresses were correct between routers and that there was no passive interface set.

Then I had him verify that same information on the neighbor, and sure enough the neighbor's hello and dead timers didn't match. Quick and easy fix on the interface of the Cisco router with the `ip ospf dead 30` command, and they were up!

Always remember that OSPF can work with multi-vendor routers, but no one ever said it works out of the box between various vendors!

The *show ip protocols* Command

The show ip protocols command is also useful, whether you're running OSPF, EIGRP, RIP, BGP, IS-IS, or any other routing protocol that can be configured on your router. It provides an excellent overview of the actual operation of all currently running protocols.

Check the output from the Corp router:

```
Corp#sh ip protocols
Routing Protocol is "ospf 1"
  Outgoing update filter list for all interfaces is not set
  Incoming update filter list for all interfaces is not set
  Router ID 1.1.1.1
  Number of areas in this router is 3. 3 normal 0 stub 0 nssa
  Maximum path: 4
  Routing for Networks:
    10.10.0.0 0.0.255.255 area 0
    172.16.10.0 0.0.0.3 area 1
    172.16.10.4 0.0.0.3 area 2
  Routing Information Sources:
    Gateway         Distance      Last Update
    1.1.1.1             110       00:17:42
    172.16.10.2         110       00:17:42
    172.16.10.6         110       00:17:42
  Distance: (default is 110)
```

Here we can determine the OSPF process ID, OSPF router ID, type of OSPF area, networks, and the three areas configured for OSPF as well as the OSPF router IDs of neighbors—that's a lot. Read efficient!

The *show ip route* Command

Now would be a great time to issue a show ip route command on the Corp router. The Corp router shows only four dynamic routes for our internetwork, with the O representing OSPF internal routes. The Cs clearly represent our directly connected networks, but our four remote networks are also showing up—nice! Notice the 110/65, which is the administrative distance/metric:

```
Corp#sh ip route
[output cut]
      10.0.0.0/8 is variably subnetted, 8 subnets, 2 masks
C        10.10.10.0/24 is directly connected, GigabitEthernet0/0
L        10.10.10.1/32 is directly connected, GigabitEthernet0/0
C        10.10.11.0/24 is directly connected, GigabitEthernet0/1
```

```
L      10.10.11.1/32 is directly connected, GigabitEthernet0/1
O      10.10.20.0/24 [110/65] via 172.16.10.2, 02:18:27, Serial0/0/0
O      10.10.30.0/24 [110/65] via 172.16.10.2, 02:18:27, Serial0/0/0
O      10.10.40.0/24 [110/65] via 172.16.10.6, 03:37:24, Serial0/0/1
O      10.10.50.0/24 [110/65] via 172.16.10.6, 03:37:24, Serial0/0/1
    172.16.0.0/16 is variably subnetted, 4 subnets, 2 masks
C      172.16.10.0/30 is directly connected, Serial0/0/0
L      172.16.10.1/32 is directly connected, Serial0/0/0
C      172.16.10.4/30 is directly connected, Serial0/0/1
L      172.16.10.5/32 is directly connected, Serial0/0/1
```

In addition, you can use the show ip route ospf command to get only OSPF-injected routes in your routing table. I can't stress enough how useful this is when dealing with large networks!

```
Corp#sh ip route ospf
    10.0.0.0/8 is variably subnetted, 8 subnets, 2 masks
O      10.10.20.0 [110/65] via 172.16.10.2, 02:18:33, Serial0/0/0
O      10.10.30.0 [110/65] via 172.16.10.2, 02:18:33, Serial0/0/0
O      10.10.40.0 [110/65] via 172.16.10.6, 03:37:30, Serial0/0/1
O      10.10.50.0 [110/65] via 172.16.10.6, 03:37:30, Serial0/0/1
```

Now that's a really nice-looking OSPF routing table! Troubleshooting and fixing an OSPF network is as vital a skill to have as it is in any other networking environment, which is why I always use the show ip int brief command when configuring my routing protocols. It's very easy to make little mistakes with OSPF, so pay very close attention to the details—especially when troubleshooting!

The *show ip ospf database* Command

Using the show ip ospf database command will give you information about the number of routers in the internetwork (AS), plus the neighboring router's ID. This is the topology database I referred to earlier.

The output is broken down by area. Here's a sample, again from Corp:

```
Corp#sh ip ospf database
            OSPF Router with ID (1.1.1.1) (Process ID 1)

            Router Link States (Area 0)

Link ID        ADV Router        Age        Seq#        Checksum Link count
1.1.1.1        1.1.1.1           196        0x8000001a 0x006d76 2
```

```
                   Summary Net Link States (Area 0)
Link ID            ADV Router       Age        Seq#        Checksum
172.16.10.0        1.1.1.1          182        0x80000095 0x00be04
172.16.10.4        1.1.1.1          177        0x80000096 0x009429
10.10.40.0         1.1.1.1          1166       0x80000091 0x00222b
10.10.50.0         1.1.1.1          1166       0x80000092 0x00b190
10.10.20.0         1.1.1.1          1114       0x80000093 0x00fa64
10.10.30.0         1.1.1.1          1114       0x80000094 0x008ac9
```

Router Link States (Area 1)

```
Link ID            ADV Router       Age        Seq#        Checksum Link count
1.1.1.1            1.1.1.1          1118       0x8000002a 0x00a59a 2
172.16.10.2        172.16.10.2      1119       0x80000031 0x00af47 4
```

```
                   Summary Net Link States (Area 1)
Link ID            ADV Router       Age        Seq#        Checksum
10.10.10.0         1.1.1.1          178        0x80000076 0x0021a5
10.10.11.0         1.1.1.1          178        0x80000077 0x0014b0
172.16.10.4        1.1.1.1          173        0x80000078 0x00d00b
10.10.40.0         1.1.1.1          1164       0x80000074 0x005c0e
10.10.50.0         1.1.1.1          1164       0x80000075 0x00eb73
```

Router Link States (Area 2)

```
Link ID            ADV Router       Age        Seq#        Checksum Link count
1.1.1.1            1.1.1.1          1119       0x8000002b 0x005cd6 2
172.16.10.6        172.16.10.6      1119       0x8000002d 0x0020a3 4
```

```
                   Summary Net Link States (Area 2)
Link ID            ADV Router       Age        Seq#        Checksum
10.10.10.0         1.1.1.1          179        0x8000007a 0x0019a9
10.10.11.0         1.1.1.1          179        0x8000007b 0x000cb4
172.16.10.0        1.1.1.1          179        0x8000007c 0x00f0ea
10.10.20.0         1.1.1.1          1104       0x80000078 0x003149
10.10.30.0         1.1.1.1          1104       0x80000079 0x00c0ae
Corp#
```

Considering we only have eight networks configured in our internetwork, there's a huge amount of information in this database! You can see all the routers and the RID of each—the highest IP address related to individual routers. And each output under each area represents LSA Type 1, indicating the area they're connected to.

The router output also shows the link ID. Remember that an interface is also a link, as is the RID of the router on that link under the ADV router—the advertising router.

So far, this has been a great chapter, brimming with detailed OSPF information, a whole lot more than what was needed to meet past Cisco objectives, for sure! Next, we'll use the same sample network that I built in Chapter 3 on EIGRP and run through a troubleshooting scenario using multi-area OSPF.

Troubleshooting OSPF Scenario

When you notice problems with your OSPF network, it's wise to first test your layer 3 connectivity with Ping and the traceroute command to see if your issue is a local one. If all looks good locally, then follow these Cisco-provided guidelines:

1. Verify your adjacency with your neighbor routers using the show ip ospf neighbors command. If you are not seeing your neighbor adjacencies, then you need to verify that the interfaces are operational and enabled for OSPF. If all is well with the interfaces, verify the hello and dead timers next, and establish that the interfaces are in the same area and that you don't have a passive interface configured.

2. Once you've determined that your adjacencies to all neighbors are working, use the show ip route to verify your layer 3 routes to all remote networks. If you see no OSPF routes in the routing table, you need to verify that you don't have another routing protocol running with a lower administrative distance. You can use show ip protocols to see all routing protocols running on your router. If no other protocols are running, then verify your network statements under the OSPF process. In a multi-area network, make sure all non–backbone area routers are directly connected to area 0 through an ABR or they won't be able to send and receive updates.

3. If you can see all the remote networks in the routing table, move on to verify the path for each network and that each path for each specific network is correct. If not, you need to verify the cost on your interfaces with the show ip ospf interface command. You may need to adjust the cost on an interface either higher or lower, depending on which path you want OSPF to use for sending packets to a remote network. Remember— the path with the lowest cost is the preferred path!

Okay, with our marching orders for troubleshooting OSPF in hand, let's take a look at Figure 19.9, which we'll use to verify our network now.

FIGURE 19.9   Our internetwork

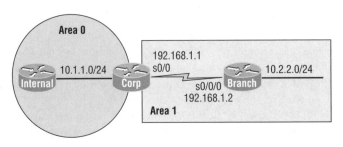

Here's the OSPF configuration on the three routers:

```
Corp(config-if)#router ospf 1
Corp(config-router)#network 10.1.1.0 0.0.0.255 area 0
Corp(config-router)#network 192.168.1.0 0.0.0.3 area 1

Internal(config)#router ospf 3
Internal(config-router)#network 10.1.1.2 0.0.0.0 area 0

Branch(config-if)#router ospf 2
Branch(config-router)#network 192.168.1.2 0.0.0.0 area 1
Branch(config-router)#network 10.2.2.1 0.0.0.0 area 1
```

Let's check out our network now, beginning by checking the layer 1 and layer 2 status between routers:

```
Corp#sh ip int brief
Interface          IP-Address      OK? Method Status        Protocol
FastEthernet0/0    10.1.1.1        YES manual up            up
Serial0/0          192.168.1.1     YES manual up            up
```

The IP addresses look correct and the layer 1 and 2 status is up/up, so next we'll use the Ping program to check connectivity like this:

```
Corp#ping 192.168.1.2
Type escape sequence to abort.
Sending 5, 100-byte ICMP Echos to 192.168.1.2, timeout is 2 seconds:
!!!!!
Success rate is 100 percent (5/5), round-trip min/avg/max = 1/2/4 ms
Corp#ping 10.1.1.2
Type escape sequence to abort.
Sending 5, 100-byte ICMP Echos to 10.1.1.2, timeout is 2 seconds:
!!!!!
Success rate is 100 percent (5/5), round-trip min/avg/max = 1/2/4 ms
```

Nice—I can ping both directly connected neighbors, so this means layers 1, 2, and 3 are working between neighbor routers. This is a great start, but it still doesn't mean OSPF is actually working yet. If any of the preceding commands had failed, I first would've verified layers 1 and 2 to make sure my data link was working between neighbors and then moved on to verify my layer 3 IP configuration.

Since our data link appears to be working between each neighbor, our next move is to check the OSPF configuration and status of the routing protocol. I'll start with the interfaces:

```
Corp#sh ip ospf interface s0/0
Serial0/0 is up, line protocol is up
```

```
Internet Address 192.168.1.1/30, Area 1
Process ID 1, Router ID 192.168.1.1, Network Type POINT_TO_POINT, Cost: 100
Transmit Delay is 1 sec, State POINT_TO_POINT
Timer intervals configured, Hello 10, Dead 40, Wait 40, Retransmit 5
  oob-resync timeout 40
  Hello due in 00:00:03
Supports Link-local Signaling (LLS)
Cisco NSF helper support enabled
IETF NSF helper support enabled
Index 1/2, flood queue length 0
Next 0x0(0)/0x0(0)
Last flood scan length is 1, maximum is 1
Last flood scan time is 0 msec, maximum is 0 msec
Neighbor Count is 1, Adjacent neighbor count is 1
  Adjacent with neighbor 192.168.1.2
Suppress hello for 0 neighbor(s)
```

I've highlighted the important statistics that you should always check first on an OSPF interface. You need to verify that the interface is configured in the same area as the neighbor and that the hello and dead timers match. A cost mismatch won't stop an adjacency from forming, but it could cause ugly routing issues. We'll explore that more in a minute.

For now let's take a look at the LAN interface that's connecting to the Internal router:

```
Corp#sh ip ospf int f0/0
FastEthernet0/0 is up, line protocol is up
  Internet Address 10.1.1.1/24, Area 0
  Process ID 1, Router ID 192.168.1.1, Network Type BROADCAST, Cost: 1
  Transmit Delay is 1 sec, State DR, Priority 1
  Designated Router (ID) 192.168.1.1, Interface address 10.1.1.1
  Backup Designated router (ID) 10.1.1.2, Interface address 10.1.1.2
  Timer intervals configured, Hello 10, Dead 40, Wait 40, Retransmit 5
    oob-resync timeout 40
    Hello due in 00:00:00
  Supports Link-local Signaling (LLS)
  Cisco NSF helper support enabled
  IETF NSF helper support enabled
  Index 1/1, flood queue length 0
  Next 0x0(0)/0x0(0)
  Last flood scan length is 1, maximum is 1
  Last flood scan time is 0 msec, maximum is 0 msec
  Neighbor Count is 1, Adjacent neighbor count is 1
    Adjacent with neighbor 10.1.1.2  (Backup Designated Router)
  Suppress hello for 0 neighbor(s)
```

We'll focus on the same key factors on a LAN interface that we did on our serial interface: the area ID and hello and dead timers. Notice that the cost is 1. According to Cisco's method of calculating cost, anything 100 Mbps or higher will always be a cost of 1 and serial links with the default bandwidth are always 64. This can cause problems in a large network with lots of high-bandwidth links. One thing to take special note of is that there's a designated and backup designated router on a broadcast multi-access network. DRs and BDRs won't cause a routing problem between neighbors, but it's still a consideration when designing and configuring in a really large internetwork environment. But we won't be focusing on that for our purposes here. It's just something to keep in mind.

Staying with the troubleshooting step of checking our interfaces, look at the error I received when I tried to verify OSPF on the fa0/1 interface of the Corp router (which we're not using):

```
Corp#sh ip ospf int fa0/1
%OSPF: OSPF not enabled on FastEthernet0/1
```

I got this error because the network statements under the OSPF process are not enabled for the network on the fa0/1 interface. If you receive this error, immediately check your network statements!

Next, let's check out the networks we're routing for with the show ip protocols command:

```
Corp#sh ip protocols
Routing Protocol is "ospf 1"
  Outgoing update filter list for all interfaces is not set
  Incoming update filter list for all interfaces is not set
  Router ID 192.168.1.1
  It is an area border router
  Number of areas in this router is 2. 2 normal 0 stub 0 nssa
  Maximum path: 4
  Routing for Networks:
    10.1.1.0 0.0.0.255 area 0
    192.168.1.0 0.0.0.3 area 1
  Reference bandwidth unit is 100 mbps
  Routing Information Sources:
    Gateway         Distance      Last Update
    192.168.1.2          110      00:28:40
  Distance: (default is 110)
```

From this output we can check our process ID as well as reveal if we have an ACL set on our routing protocol, just as we found when troubleshooting EIGRP in Chapter 3. But this time, we'll first examine the network statements and the area they're configured for—most important, the specific areas that each interface is configured for. This is key, because if your neighbor's interface isn't in the same area, you won't be able to form an adjacency!

This command's output provides a great view of what exactly we typed in for the network statements under the OSPF process. Also, notice that the default reference bandwidth is set to 100 Mbps. I'll talk about this factor at the end of this section.

I want to point out that the neighbor IP address and administrative distance is listed. OSPF uses 110 by default, so remember that if EIGRP were running here, we wouldn't see OSPF routes in the routing table because EIGRP has an AD of 90!

Next, we'll look at our neighbor table on the Corp router to find out if OSPF has formed an adjacency with the Branch router:

```
Corp#sh ip ospf neighbor
Neighbor ID    Pri   State       Dead Time   Address      Interface
10.1.1.2        1    FULL/BDR    00:00:39    10.1.1.2     FastEthernet0/0
```

Okay, we've finally zeroed in on our problem—the Corp router can see the Internal router in area 0 but not the Branch router in area 1! What now?

First, let's review what we know so far about the Corp and Branch router. The data link is good, and we can use Ping successfully between the routers. This shouts out that we have a routing protocol issue, so we'll look further into the details of the OSPF configuration on each router. Let's run a show ip protocols on the Branch router:

```
Branch#sh ip protocols
Routing Protocol is "eigrp 20"
  Outgoing update filter list for all interfaces is not set
  Incoming update filter list for all interfaces is not set
  Default networks flagged in outgoing updates
  Default networks accepted from incoming updates
  EIGRP metric weight K1=1, K2=0, K3=1, K4=0, K5=0
  EIGRP maximum hopcount 100
  EIGRP maximum metric variance 1
  Redistributing: eigrp 20
  EIGRP NSF-aware route hold timer is 240s
  Automatic network summarization is not in effect
  Maximum path: 4
  Routing for Networks:
    10.0.0.0
    192.168.1.0
  Routing Information Sources:
    Gateway          Distance      Last Update
    (this router)          90      3d22h
    192.168.1.1            90      00:00:07
  Distance: internal 90 external 170
```

```
Routing Protocol is "ospf 2"
  Outgoing update filter list for all interfaces is not set
  Incoming update filter list for all interfaces is not set
  Router ID 192.168.1.2
  Number of areas in this router is 1. 1 normal 0 stub 0 nssa
  Maximum path: 4
  Routing for Networks:
    10.2.2.1 0.0.0.0 area 1
    192.168.1.2 0.0.0.0 area 1
  Reference bandwidth unit is 100 mbps
  Passive Interface(s):
    Serial0/0/0
  Routing Information Sources:
    Gateway         Distance      Last Update
    192.168.1.1          110      03:29:07
  Distance: (default is 110)
```

Do you see two routing protocols running on the Branch router? Both EIGRP and OSPF are running, but that's not necessarily our problem. The Corp router would need to be running EIGRP, and if so, we would have only EIGRP routes in our routing table because EIGRPs have the lower AD of 90 versus OSPF's AD of 110.

Let's check the routing table of the Branch router and see if the Corp router is also running EIGRP. This will be easy to determine if we discover EIGRP-injected routes in the table:

```
Branch#sh ip route
[output cut]
     10.0.0.0/24 is subnetted, 2 subnets
C       10.2.2.0 is directly connected, FastEthernet0/0
D       10.1.1.0 [90/2172416] via 192.168.1.1, 00:02:35, Serial0/0/0
     192.168.1.0/30 is subnetted, 1 subnets
C       192.168.1.0 is directly connected, Serial0/0/0
```

Okay—so yes, the Corp router is clearly running EIGRP. This is a leftover configuration from Chapter 3. All I need to do to fix this issue is disable EIGRP on the Branch router. After that, we should see OSPF in the routing table:

```
Branch#config t
Branch(config)#no router eigrp 20
Branch(config)#do sh ip route
[output cut]
     10.0.0.0/24 is subnetted, 1 subnets
```

```
C        10.2.2.0 is directly connected, FastEthernet0/0
     192.168.1.0/30 is subnetted, 1 subnets
C        192.168.1.0 is directly connected, Serial0/0/0
```

That's not so good—I disabled the EIGRP protocol on the Branch router, but we still didn't receive OSPF updates! Let investigate further using the show ip protocols command on the Branch router:

```
Branch#sh ip protocols
Routing Protocol is "ospf 2"
  Outgoing update filter list for all interfaces is not set
  Incoming update filter list for all interfaces is not set
  Router ID 192.168.1.2
  Number of areas in this router is 1. 1 normal 0 stub 0 nssa
  Maximum path: 4
  Routing for Networks:
    10.2.2.1 0.0.0.0 area 1
    192.168.1.2 0.0.0.0 area 1
 Reference bandwidth unit is 100 mbps
  Passive Interface(s):
    Serial0/0/0
  Routing Information Sources:
    Gateway         Distance      Last Update
    192.168.1.1          110      03:34:19
  Distance: (default is 110)
```

Do you see the problem? There's no ACL, the networks are configured correctly, but see the passive interface for Serial0/0/0? That will definitely prevent an adjacency from happening between the Corp and Branch routers! Let's fix that:

```
Branach#show run
[output cut]
!
router ospf 2
 log-adjacency-changes
 passive-interface Serial0/0/0
 network 10.2.2.1 0.0.0.0 area 1
 network 192.168.1.2 0.0.0.0 area 1
!
[output cut]
Branch#config t
Branch(config)#router ospf 2
Branch(config-router)#no passive-interface serial 0/0/0
```

Let's see what our neighbor table and routing table look like now:

```
Branch#sh ip ospf neighbor
Neighbor ID    Pri  State          Dead Time   Address        Interface
192.168.1.1      0  FULL/ -        00:00:32    192.168.1.1    Serial0/0/0

Branch#sh ip route
     10.0.0.0/24 is subnetted, 2 subnets
C       10.2.2.0 is directly connected, FastEthernet0/0
O IA    10.1.1.0 [110/65] via 192.168.1.1, 00:01:21, Serial0/0/0
     192.168.1.0/30 is subnetted, 1 subnets
C       192.168.1.0 is directly connected, Serial0/0/0
```

Awesome—our little internetwork is finally happy! That was actually pretty fun and really not all that hard once you know what to look for.

But there's one more thing we need to cover before moving onto OSPFv3—load balancing with OSPF. To explore that, we'll use Figure 19.10, wherein I added another link between the Corp and Branch routers.

FIGURE 19.10   Our internetwork with dual links

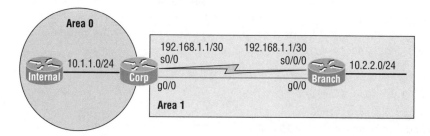

First, it's clear that having a Gigabit Ethernet interface between our two routers is way better than any serial link we could possibly have, which means we want the routers to use the LAN link. We can either disconnect the serial link or use it as a backup link.

Let's start by looking at the routing table and seeing what OSPF found:

```
Corp#sh ip route ospf
     10.0.0.0/8 is variably subnetted, 3 subnets, 2 masks
O       10.2.2.0 [110/2] via 192.168.1.6, 00:00:13, GigabitEthernet0/1
```

Look at that! OSPF wisely went with the Gigabit Ethernet link because it has the lowest cost. Although it's possible you'll have to mess with the links to help OSPF choose the best paths, it's likely best to just leave it alone at this point.

But that wouldn't be very much fun, now would it? Instead, let's configure OSPF to fool it into thinking the links are equal so it will use both of them by setting the cost on the interfaces to the same value:

```
Corp#config t
Corp(config)#int g0/1
```

```
Corp(config-if)#ip ospf cost 10
Corp(config-if)#int s0/0/0
Corp(config-if)#ip ospf cost 10
```

Obviously you need to deploy this configuration on both sides of the link, and I've already configured the Branch router as well. Now that both sides are configured with the same cost, let's check out our routing table now:

```
Corp#sh ip route ospf
     10.0.0.0/8 is variably subnetted, 3 subnets, 2 masks
O       10.2.2.0 [110/11] via 192.168.1.2, 00:01:23, Serial0/0/0
                 [110/11] via 192.168.1.6, 00:01:23, GigabitEthernet0/1
```

I'm not saying you should configure a serial link and Gigabit Ethernet link as equal costs as I just demonstrated, but there are times when you need to adjust the cost for OSPF. If you don't have multiple links to any remote networks, you really don't need to worry about this, but with regard to the objectives, you absolutely must understand the cost, how it works, and how to set it so OSPF can choose a preferred path. And there's still one more thing about cost I want to cover with you.

It's possible to change the reference bandwidth of the router, but you need to make sure all the routers within the OSPF AS have the same reference bandwidth. The default reference bandwidth is 10^8, which is 100,000,000, or the equivalent of the bandwidth of Fast Ethernet, which is 100 Mbps, as demonstrated via show ip ospf and the show ip protocols command:

```
Routing for Networks:
    10.2.2.1 0.0.0.0 area 1
    192.168.1.2 0.0.0.0 area 1
Reference bandwidth unit is 100 mbps
```

This will basically make any interface running 100 Mbps or higher have a cost of 1. The default is 100, and if you change it to 1,000, it will increase the cost by a factor of 10. Again, if you do want to change this, you must make sure to configure the change on all routers in your AS! Here is how you would do that:

```
Corp(route)#router ospf 1
Corp(config-router)#auto-cost reference-bandwidth ?
  <1-4294967>  The reference bandwidth in terms of Mbits per second
```

Simple Troubleshooting OSPF for the CCNA

Let's do a troubleshooting scenario. You have two routers not forming an adjacency. What would you do first? Well, we went through a lot in this chapter, but let me make it super easy for you when troubleshooting on the CCNA exam.

All you need to do is perform a *show running-config* on each router. That's it! You can then fix anything regarding OSPF because all the problems will be shown there if you know what to look for. Unlike with EIGRP, where you don't need to see a neighbor router's configuration to verify the protocol, with OSPF we need to compare directly connected interfaces to make sure they match up.

Let's look at each router's configuration and determine what the problems are.

Here is the first router's configuration:

```
R1#sh run
Building configuration...
!
interface Loopback0
 ip address 10.1.1.1 255.255.255.255
 ip ospf 3 area 0
!
int FastEthernet0/0
 Description **Connected to R2 F0/0**
 ip address 192.168.16.1 255.255.255.0
 ip ospf 3 area 0
 ip ospf hello-interval 25
!
router ospf 3
 router-id 192.168.3.3
```

Here is the neighbor router's configuration:

```
R2#sh run
Building configuration...
!
interface Loopback0
 ip address 10.1.1.2 255.255.255.255
 ip ospf 6 area 0
!
 Description **Connected to R1 F0/0**
 int FastEthernet0/0
 ip address 192.168.17.2 255.255.255.0
 ip ospf 6 area 1
!
router ospf 6
 router-id 192.168.3.3
```

Can you see the problems? Pretty simple. Just use the show running-config on each router and compare directly connected interfaces.

The loopbacks on each router are fine. I don't see a problem with their configuration, and they don't connect to each other, so whatever configuration they would have wouldn't matter.

However on the FastEthernet 0/0 interface of each router, where the description tells us that R1 and R2 are directly connected with interface f0/0, we can see a few problems. First, R1 is not using the default hellointerval of 10 seconds as R2 is, so that will never work. On R1 under the f0/0 interface, configure the no ip ospf hello-interval 25 command.

Let's dig deeper. Both routers have a different process ID, but that's not a problem. However, the areas are configured differently on each interface, and the IP addresses are not in the same subnet.

Last, they are both using the same RID under their process ID—this will never work!

Now, finally, let's get to the easy section of the chapter!

OSPFv3

The new version of OSPF continues the trend of routing protocols having a lot in common with their IPv4 versions. The foundation of OSPF remains the same—it's still a link-state routing protocol that divides an entire internetwork or autonomous system into areas, establishing a hierarchy.

In OSPF version 2, the router ID (RID) is determined by the highest IP addresses assigned to the router. And as you now know, the RID can be assigned. In version 3, nothing has really changed because you can still assign the RID, area ID, and link-state ID, which remain 32-bit values.

Adjacencies and next-hop attributes now use link-local addresses, but OSPFv3 still uses multi-cast traffic to send its updates and acknowledgements. It uses the addresses FF02::5 for OSPF routers and FF02::6 for OSPF-designated routers. These new addresses are the replacements for 224.0.0.5 and 224.0.0.6, respectively.

Other, less flexible IPv4 protocols don't give us the ability that OSPFv2 does to assign specific networks and interfaces into the OSPF process, but this is still configured under the router configuration process. And with OSPFv3, just as with the EIGRPv6 routing protocols we've talked about, the interfaces and therefore the networks attached to them are configured directly on the interface in interface configuration mode.

The configuration of OSPFv3 is going to look like this: First, optionally start by assigning the RID, but if you have IPv4 addresses assigned to your interface, you can let OSPF pick the RID just as we did with OSPFv2:

```
Router(config)#ipv6 router ospf 10
Router(config-rtr)#router-id 1.1.1.1
```

You get to perform some other configurations from router configuration mode, like summarization and redistribution, but again, we don't even need to configure OSPFv3 from this prompt if we configure it from the interface!

A simple interface configuration looks like this:

```
Router(config-if)#ipv6 ospf 10 area 0.0.0.0
```

So, if we just go to each interface and assign a process ID and area—poof, we're done! See? Easy! As the configuration shows, I configured the area as 0.0.0.0, which is the same thing as just typing area 0. We'll use Figure 19.11, which is the same network and IPv6-addressing we used in the EIGRPv6 section in Chapter 3.

FIGURE 19.11 Configuring OSPFv3

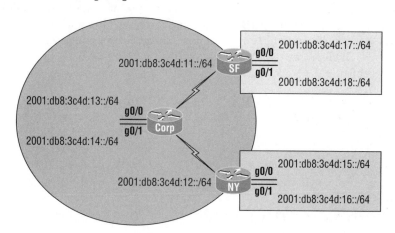

Okay, so all we have to do to enable OSPF on the internetwork is go to each interface that we want to run it on. Here's the Corp configuration:

```
Corp#config t
Corp(config)#int g0/0
Corp(config-if)#ipv6 ospf 1 area 0
Corp(config-if)#int g0/1
Corp(config-if)#ipv6 ospf 1 area 0
Corp(config-if)#int s0/0/0
Corp(config-if)#ipv6 ospf 1 area 0
Corp(config-if)#int s0/0/1
Corp(config-if)#ipv6 ospf 1 area 0
```

That wasn't so bad—much easier than it was with IPv4! To configure OSPFv3, you just need to establish the specific interfaces you'll be using! Let's configure the other two routers now:

```
SF#config t
SF(config)#int g0/0
```

```
SF(config-if)#ipv6 ospf 1 area 1
SF(config-if)#int g0/1
SF(config-if)#ipv6 ospf 1 area 1
SF(config-if)#int s0/0/0
SF(config-if)#ipv6 ospf 1 area 0
01:03:55: %OSPFv3-5-ADJCHG: Process 1, Nbr 192.168.1.5 on Serial0/0/0 from
LOADING to
FULL, Loading Done
```

Sweet—the SF has become adjacent to the Corp router! One interesting output line I want to point out is that the IPv4 RID is being used in the OSPFv3 adjacent change. I didn't set the RIDs manually because I knew I had interfaces with IPv4 addresses already on them, which the OSPF process would use for a RID.

Now let's configure the NY router:

```
NY(config)#int g0/0
NY(config-if)#ipv6 ospf 1 area 2
%OSPFv3-4-NORTRID:OSPFv3 process 1 could not pick a router-id,please configure
manually
NY(config-if)#ipv6 router ospf 1
NY(config-rtr)#router-id 1.1.1.1
NY(config-if)#int g0/0
NY(config-if)#ipv6 ospf 1 area 2
NY(config-if)#int g0/1
NY(config-if)#ipv6 ospf 1 area 2
NY(config-if)#int s0/0/0
NY(config-if)#ipv6 ospf 1 area 0
00:09:00: %OSPFv3-5-ADJCHG: Process 1, Nbr 192.168.1.5 on Serial0/0/0 from
LOADING to
FULL, Loading Done
```

Our adjacency popped up—this is great. But did you notice that I had to set the RID? That's because there wasn't an IPv4 32-bit address already on an interface for the router to use as the RID, so it was mandatory to set the RID manually!

Without even verifying our network, it appears it's up and running. Even so, it's always important to verify!

Verifying OSPFv3

I'll start as usual with the show ipv6 route ospf command:

```
Corp#sh ipv6 route ospf
OI  2001:DB8:3C4D:15::/64 [110/65]
     via FE80::201:C9FF:FED2:5E01, Serial0/0/1
```

```
OI  2001:DB8:3C4D:16::/64 [110/65]
      via FE80::201:C9FF:FED2:5E01, Serial0/0/1
O   2001:DB8:C34D:11::/64 [110/128]
      via FE80::2E0:F7FF:FE13:5E01, Serial0/0/0
OI  2001:DB8:C34D:17::/64 [110/65]
      via FE80::2E0:F7FF:FE13:5E01, Serial0/0/0
OI  2001:DB8:C34D:18::/64 [110/65]
      via FE80::2E0:F7FF:FE13:5E01, Serial0/0/0
```

Perfect. I see all six subnets. Notice the O and OI? The O is intra-area and the OI is inter-area, meaning it's a route from a different area. You can't simply distinguish the area by looking at the routing table though. Plus, don't forget that the routers communicate with their neighbor via link-local addresses: via FE80::2E0:F7FF:FE13:5E01, Serial0/0/0, for example.

Let's take a look at the show ipv6 protocols command:

```
Corp#sh ipv6 protocols
IPv6 Routing Protocol is "connected"
IPv6 Routing Protocol is "static
IPv6 Routing Protocol is "ospf 1"
  Interfaces (Area 0)
    GigabitEthernet0/0
    GigabitEthernet0/1
    Serial0/0/0
    Serial0/0/1
```

This just tells us which interfaces are part of OSPF process 1, area 0. To configure OSPFv3, you absolutely have to know which interfaces are in use. Show ip int brief can really help you if you're having a problem finding your active interfaces.

Let's take a look at the Gigabit Ethernet OSPFv3 active interface on the Corp router:

```
Corp#sh ipv6 ospf int g0/0
GigabitEthernet0/0 is up, line protocol is up
  Link Local Address FE80::2E0:F7FF:FE0A:3301 , Interface ID 1
  Area 0, Process ID 1, Instance ID 0, Router ID 192.168.1.5
  Network Type BROADCAST, Cost: 1
  Transmit Delay is 1 sec, State DR, Priority 1
  Designated Router (ID) 192.168.1.5, local address FE80::2E0:F7FF:FE0A:3301
  No backup designated router on this network
  Timer intervals configured, Hello 10, Dead 40, Wait 40, Retransmit 5
    Hello due in 00:00:09
  Index 1/1, flood queue length 0
```

```
Next 0x0(0)/0x0(0)
Last flood scan length is 1, maximum is 1
Last flood scan time is 0 msec, maximum is 0 msec
Neighbor Count is 0, Adjacent neighbor count is 0
Suppress hello for 0 neighbor(s)
```

This is basically the same information we saw earlier in the verification and trouble-shooting section. Let's take a look at the neighbor table on the Corp router via show ipv6 ospf neighbor:

```
Corp#sh ipv6 ospf neighbor
Neighbor ID    Pri   State        Dead Time   Interface ID   Interface
2.2.2.2          0   FULL/  -     00:00:36    4              Serial0/0/1
192.168.1.6      0   FULL/  -     00:00:39    4              Serial0/0/0
```

Okay, we can see our two neighbors, and there's also a slight difference in this version's command from OSPFv2. We still see the RID on the left and that we're also fully adjacent with both our neighbors—the dash is there because there are no elections on serial point-to-point links. But we don't see the neighbor's IPv6 address listed as we did with OSPFv2's IPv4 addresses, which were listed in the interface ID field.

There's one other command I want to finish with—the show ipv6 ospf command:

```
Corp#sh ipv6 ospf
 Routing Process "ospfv3 1" with ID 192.168.1.5
 SPF schedule delay 5 secs, Hold time between two SPFs 10 secs
 Minimum LSA interval 5 secs. Minimum LSA arrival 1 secs
 LSA group pacing timer 240 secs
 Interface flood pacing timer 33 msecs
 Retransmission pacing timer 66 msecs
 Number of external LSA 0. Checksum Sum 0x000000
 Number of areas in this router is 1. 1 normal 0 stub 0 nssa
 Reference bandwidth unit is 100 mbps
    Area BACKBONE(0)
        Number of interfaces in this area is 4
        SPF algorithm executed 10 times
        Number of LSA 10. Checksum Sum 0x05aebb
        Number of DCbitless LSA 0
        Number of indication LSA 0
        Number of DoNotAge LSA 0
        Flood list length 0
```

This shows the process ID and RID, our reference bandwidth for this interface, and how many interfaces we have in each area, which in our example is only area 0.

Holy output! Now that's what I call a fun chapter. The best thing you can do to get a solid grasp of OSPF and OSPv3 multi-area networks is to gather up some routers and spend some quality time with them, practicing everything we've covered!

Summary

In this chapter, you learned about the scalability constraints of a single-area OSPF network, and you were introduced to the concept of multi-area OSPF as a solution to these scalability limitations.

You're now able to identify the different categories of routers used in multi-area configurations, including the backbone router, internal router, area border router, and autonomous system boundary router.

I detailed the function of different OSPF Link-State Advertisements (LSAs) and you discovered how these LSAs can be minimized through the effective implementation of specific OSPF area types. I discussed the Hello protocols and the different neighbor states experienced when an adjacency is taking place.

Verification and troubleshooting are very large parts of the objectives, and I covered everything you need to know in order to verify and troubleshoot OSPFv2 and meet those requirements.

Finally, we ended the chapter with the easiest part: configuring and verifying OSPFv3.

Exam Essentials

Know the scalability issues multi-area OSPF addresses.   The primary problems in single-area OSPF networks are the large size of the topology and routing tables as well as the excessive computation of the SPF algorithm due to the large number of link-state updates that occur in this single area.

Know the different types of OSPF routers.   Backbone routers have at least one interface in area 0. Area border routers (ABRs) belong to two or more OSPF areas simultaneously. Internal routers have all of their interfaces within the same area. Autonomous system boundary routers (ASBRs) have at least one interface connected to an external network.

Know the different types of LSA packets.   There are seven different types of LSA packets that Cisco uses, but here are the ones you need to remember: Type 1 LSAs (router link advertisements), Type 2 LSAs (network link advertisements), Type 3 and 4 LSAs (summary LSAs), and Type 5 LSAs (AS external link advertisements). Know how each functions.

Be able to monitor multi-area OSPF.   There are a number of commands that provide information useful in a multi-area OSPF environment: show ip route ospf, show ip ospf neighbor, show ip ospf, and show ip ospf database. It's important to understand what each provides.

Be able to troubleshoot OSPF networks. It's important that you can work your way through the troubleshooting scenario that I presented in this chapter. Be able to look for neighbor adjacencies, and if they are not there, look for ACLs set on the routing protocol, passive interfaces, and wrong network statements.

Understand how to configure OSPFv3. OSPFv3 uses the same basic mechanisms that OSPFv2 uses, but OSPFv3 is more easily configured by placing the configuring OSPFv3 on a per-interface basis with `ipv6 ospf` *process-ID* area *area*.

Written Lab 19

You can find the answers to this lab in Appendix A, "Answers to Written Labs."

1. What type of LSAs are sent by an ASBR?

2. What state would a router adjacency be in after the INIT state has finished?

3. What LSA types are sent by ABR toward the area external to the one in which they were generated?

4. When would you see an adjacency show this: FULL/-?

5. True/False: OSPFv3 is configured per area, per interface.

6. Which OSPF state uses DBD packets and LSRs?

7. Which LSA type is referred to as a router link advertisement (RLA)?

8. What is the command to configure OSPFv3 on an interface with process ID 1 into area 0?

9. What must match exactly between two routers to form an adjacency when using OSPFv3?

10. How can you see all the routing protocols configured and running on your router from user mode?

Hands-on Labs

In this section, you will use the following network and add OSPF and OSPFv3 routing.

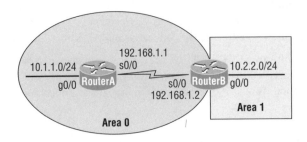

The first lab requires you to configure two routers with OSPF and then verify the configuration. In the second, you will be asked to enable OSPFv3 routing on the same network. Note that the labs in this chapter were written to be used with real equipment—real cheap equipment, that is. As with the chapter on EIGRP, I wrote these labs with the cheapest, oldest routers I had lying around so you can see that you don't need expensive gear to get through some of the hardest labs in this book. However, you can use the free LammleSim IOS version simulator or Cisco's Packet Tracer to run through these labs.

The labs in this chapter are as follows:

Lab 19.1: Configuring and Verifying Multi-Area OSPF

Lab 19.2: Configuring and Verifying OSPFv3

Hands-on Lab 19.1: Configuring and Verifying OSPF Multi-Area

In this lab, you'll configure and verify multi-area OSPF:

1. Implement OSPFv2 on RouterA based on the information in the diagram.

```
RouterA#conf t
RouterA(config)#router ospf 10
RouterA(config-router)#network 10.0.0.0 0.255.255.255 area 0
RouterA(config-router)#network 192.168.1.0 0.0.0.255 area 0
```

2. Implement OSPF on RouterB based on the diagram.

```
RouterB#conf t
RouterB(config)#router ospf 1
RouterB(config-router)#network 192.168.1.2 0.0.0.0 area 0
RouterB(config-router)#network 10.2.2.0 0.0.0.255 area 1
```

3. Display all the LSAs received on RouterA.

```
RouterA#sh ip ospf database

          OSPF Router with ID (192.168.1.1) (Process ID 10)

              Router Link States (Area 0)

Link ID        ADV Router      Age       Seq#        Checksum Link count
10.1.1.2       10.1.1.2        380       0x80000035 0x0012AB 1
192.168.1.1    192.168.1.1     13        0x8000000A 0x00729F 3
192.168.1.2    192.168.1.2     10        0x80000002 0x0090F9 2

              Net Link States (Area 0)

Link ID        ADV Router      Age       Seq#        Checksum
10.1.1.2       10.1.1.2        381       0x80000001 0x003371
```

```
             Summary Net Link States (Area 0)

Link ID          ADV Router        Age        Seq#         Checksum
10.2.2.0         192.168.1.2       8          0x80000001 0x00C3FD
```

4. Display the routing table for RouterA.

```
RouterA#sh ip route
Codes: C - connected, S - static, R - RIP, M - mobile, B - BGP
       D - EIGRP, EX - EIGRP external, O - OSPF, IA - OSPF inter area
       N1 - OSPF NSSA external type 1, N2 - OSPF NSSA external type 2
       E1 - OSPF external type 1, E2 - OSPF external type 2
       i - IS-IS, su - IS-IS summary, L1 - IS-IS level-1, L2 - IS-IS level-2
       ia -IS-IS inter area,* - candidate default,U - per-user static route
       o - ODR, P - periodic downloaded static route

Gateway of last resort is not set

     10.0.0.0/24 is subnetted, 2 subnets
O IA    10.2.2.0 [110/101] via 192.168.1.2, 00:00:29, Serial0/0
C       10.1.1.0 is directly connected, FastEthernet0/0
     192.168.1.0/30 is subnetted, 1 subnets
C       192.168.1.0 is directly connected, Serial0/0
```

5. Display the neighbor table for RouterA.

```
RouterA#sh ip ospf neighbor

Neighbor ID     Pri   State        Dead Time   Address         Interface
192.168.1.2       0   FULL/  -     00:00:35    192.168.1.2     Serial0/0
10.1.1.2          1   FULL/DR      00:00:34    10.1.1.2        FastEthernet0/0
```

6. Use the show ip ospf command on RouterB to see that it is an ABR.

```
RouterB#sh ip ospf
 Routing Process "ospf 1" with ID 192.168.1.2
 Start time: 1w4d, Time elapsed: 00:07:04.100
 Supports only single TOS(TOS0) routes
 Supports opaque LSA
 Supports Link-local Signaling (LLS)
 Supports area transit capability
 It is an area border router
 Router is not originating router-LSAs with maximum metric
```

Initial SPF schedule delay 5000 msecs
Minimum hold time between two consecutive SPFs 10000 msecs
Maximum wait time between two consecutive SPFs 10000 msecs
Incremental-SPF disabled
Minimum LSA interval 5 secs
Minimum LSA arrival 1000 msecs
LSA group pacing timer 240 secs
Interface flood pacing timer 33 msecs
Retransmission pacing timer 66 msecs
Number of external LSA 0. Checksum Sum 0x000000
Number of opaque AS LSA 0. Checksum Sum 0x000000
Number of DCbitless external and opaque AS LSA 0
Number of DoNotAge external and opaque AS LSA 0
Number of areas in this router is 2. 2 normal 0 stub 0 nssa
Number of areas transit capable is 0
External flood list length 0
    Area BACKBONE(0)
        Number of interfaces in this area is 1
        Area has no authentication
        SPF algorithm last executed 00:06:44.492 ago
        SPF algorithm executed 3 times
        Area ranges are
        Number of LSA 5. Checksum Sum 0x020DB1
        Number of opaque link LSA 0. Checksum Sum 0x000000
        Number of DCbitless LSA 0
        Number of indication LSA 0
        Number of DoNotAge LSA 0
        Flood list length 0
    Area 1
        Number of interfaces in this area is 1
        Area has no authentication
        SPF algorithm last executed 00:06:45.640 ago
        SPF algorithm executed 2 times
        Area ranges are
        Number of LSA 3. Checksum Sum 0x00F204
        Number of opaque link LSA 0. Checksum Sum 0x000000
        Number of DCbitless LSA 0
        Number of indication LSA 0
        Number of DoNotAge LSA 0
        Flood list length 0

Hands-on Lab 19.2: Configuring and Verifying OSPFv3

In this lab, you will configure and verify OSPFv3:

1. Implement OSPFv3 on RouterA. Since the routers have IPv4 addresses, we don't need to set the RID of the router.

```
RouterA#config t
RouterA(config)#int g0/0
RouterA(config-if)#ipv6 ospf 1 area 0
RouterA(config-if)#int s0/0
RouterA(config-if)#ipv6 ospf 1 area 0
```

That's all there is to it! Nice.

2. Implement OSPFv3 on RouterB.

```
RouterB#config t
RouterB(config)#int s0/0/0
RouterB(config-if)#ipv6 ospf 1 area 0
RouterB(config-if)#int f0/0
RouterB(config-if)#ipv6 ospf 1 area 1
```

Again, that's all there is to it!

3. Display the routing table for RouterA.

```
RouterA#sh ipv6 route ospf
IPv6 Routing Table - 11 entries
Codes: C - Connected, L - Local, S - Static, R - RIP, B - BGP
       U - Per-user Static route
       I1 - ISIS L1, I2 - ISIS L2, IA - ISIS interarea, IS - ISIS summary
       O - OSPF intra, OI - OSPF inter, OE1 - OSPF ext 1, OE2 - OSPF ext 2
       ON1 - OSPF NSSA ext 1, ON2 - OSPF NSSA ext 2
       D - EIGRP, EX - EIGRP external
OI  2001:DB8:3C4D:15::/64 [110/65]
     via FE80::21A:2FFF:FEE7:4398, Serial0/0
```

Notice that the one route OSPFv3 found is an inter-area route, meaning the network is in another area.

4. Display the neighbor table for RouterA.

```
RouterA#sh ipv6 ospf neighbor

Neighbor ID     Pri   State        Dead Time   Interface ID   Interface
192.168.1.2      1    FULL/  -     00:00:32    6              Serial0/0
```

5. Display the show `ipv6 ospf` command on RouterB.

```
RouterB#sh ipv6 ospf
 Routing Process "ospfv3 1" with ID 192.168.1.2
 It is an area border router
 SPF schedule delay 5 secs, Hold time between two SPFs 10 secs
 Minimum LSA interval 5 secs. Minimum LSA arrival 1 secs
 LSA group pacing timer 240 secs
 Interface flood pacing timer 33 msecs
 Retransmission pacing timer 66 msecs
 Number of external LSA 0. Checksum Sum 0x000000
 Number of areas in this router is 2. 2 normal 0 stub 0 nssa
 Reference bandwidth unit is 100 mbps
    Area BACKBONE(0)
        Number of interfaces in this area is 1
        SPF algorithm executed 3 times
        Number of LSA 7. Checksum Sum 0x041C1B
        Number of DCbitless LSA 0
        Number of indication LSA 0
        Number of DoNotAge LSA 0
        Flood list length 0
    Area 1
        Number of interfaces in this area is 1
        SPF algorithm executed 2 times
        Number of LSA 5. Checksum Sum 0x02C608
        Number of DCbitless LSA 0
        Number of indication LSA 0
        Number of DoNotAge LSA 0
        Flood list length 0
```

Review Questions

The following questions are designed to test your understanding of this chapter's material. For more information on how to get additional questions, please see www.lammle.com/ccna.

You can find the answers to these questions in Appendix B, "Answers to Review Questions."

1. Which of the following are scalability issues with single-area OSPF networks? (Choose all that apply.)

   A. Size of the routing table

   B. Size of the OSPF database

   C. Maximum hop-count limitation

   D. Recalculation of the OSPF database

2. Which of the following describes a router that connects to an external routing process (e.g., EIGRP)?

   A. ABR

   B. ASBR

   C. Type 2 LSA

   D. Stub router

3. Which of the following must match in order for an adjacency to occur between routers? (Choose three.)

   A. Process ID

   B. Hello and dead timers

   C. Link cost

   D. Area

   E. IP address/subnet mask

4. In which OSPF state do two routers forming an adjacency appear as in the show ip ospf neighbor output after adding neighbors into the table and exchanging hello information?

   A. ATTEMPT

   B. INIT

   C. 2WAY

   D. EXSTART

   E. FULL

5. You need to set up a preferred link that OSPF will use to route information to a remote network. Which command will allow you to set the interface link as preferred over another?

   A. ip ospf preferred 10

   B. ip ospf priority 10

   C. `ospf bandwidth 10`

   D. `ip ospf cost 10`

6. When would a router's neighbor table show the FULL/DR state?

   A. After the first Hello packets are received by a neighbor

   B. When all information is synchronized among adjacent neighbors

   C. When the router's neighbor table is too full of information and is discarding neighbor information

   D. After the EXSTART state

7. Which is/are true regarding OSPFv3? (Choose all that apply.)

   A. You must add network statements under the OSPF process.

   B. There are no network statements in OSPFv3 configurations.

   C. OSPFv3 uses a 128-bit RID.

   D. If you have IPv4 configured on the router, it is not mandatory that you configure the RID.

   E. If you don't have IPv4 configured on the router, it is mandatory that you configure the RID.

   F. OSPFv3 doesn't use LSAs like OSPFv2 does.

8. When a router undergoes the exchange protocol within OSPF, in what order does it pass through each state?

   A. EXSTART state > LOADING state > EXCHANGE state > FULL state

   B. EXSTART state > EXCHANGE state > LOADING state > FULL state

   C. EXSTART state > FULL state > LOADING state > EXCHANGE state

   D. LOADING state > EXCHANGE state > FULL state > EXSTART state

9. Which type of LSA is generated by DRs and referred to as a network link advertisement (NLA)?

   A. Type 1

   B. Type 2

   C. Type 3

   D. Type 4

   E. Type 5

10. Which type of LSA is generated by ABRs and is referred to as a summary link advertisement (SLA)?

   A. Type 1

   B. Type 2

   C. Type 3

   D. Type 4

   E. Type 5

11. Which command will show all the LSAs known by a router?

   A. `show ip ospf`

   B. `show ip ospf neighbor`

    C. `show ip ospf interface`

    D. `show ip ospf database`

12. Using the following illustration, what is the cost from R1's routing table to reach the network with Server 1? Each Gigabit Ethernet link has a cost of 4, and each serial link has a cost of 15.

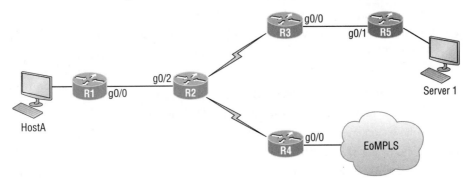

    A. 100

    B. 23

    C. 64

    D. 19

    E. 27

13. Using the following illustration, which of the following are true? (Choose all that apply.)

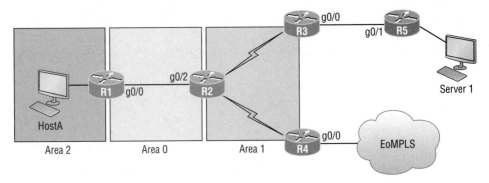

    A. R1 is an internal router.

    B. R3 would see the networks connected to the R1 router as an inter-area route.

    C. R2 is an ASBR.

    D. R3 and R4 would receive information from R2 about the backbone area, and the same LSA information would be in both LSDBs.

    E. R4 is an ABR.

14. Which of the following could cause two routers to not form an adjacency? (Choose all that apply.)

   A. They are configured in different areas.

   B. Each router sees the directly connected link as different costs.

   C. Two different process IDs are configured.

   D. ACL is configured on the routing protocol.

   E. There is an IP address/mask mismatch.

   F. Passive interface is configured.

   G. They both have been configured with the same RID.

15. Which of the following IOS commands shows the state of an adjacency with directly connected routers?

   A. debug ospf events

   B. show ip ospf border-routers

   C. show ip ospf neighbor

   D. show ip ospf database

16. What command will show you the DR and DBR address of the area you are connected to directly with an interface?

   A. show interface s0/0/0

   B. show interface fa0/0

   C. show ip ospf interface s0/0/0

   D. show ip ospf interface fa0/0

17. Which of the following could be causing a problem with the Corp router not forming an adjacency with its neighbor router? (Choose all that apply.)

```
Corp#sh ip protocols
Routing Protocol is "ospf 1"
  Outgoing update filter list for all interfaces is not set
  Incoming update filter list for all interfaces is 10
  Router ID 1.1.1.1
  Number of areas in this router is 3. 3 normal 0 stub 0 nssa
  Maximum path: 4
  Routing for Networks:
    10.10.0.0 0.0.255.255 area 0
    172.16.10.0 0.0.0.3 area 1
    172.16.10.4 0.0.0.3 area 2
  Reference bandwidth unit is 100 mbps
  Passive Interface(s):
    Serial0/0/0
  Routing Information Sources:
    Gateway         Distance      Last Update
    1.1.1.1              110       00:17:42
    172.16.10.2          110       00:17:42
    172.16.10.6          110       00:17:42
  Distance: (default is 110)
```

    A. The routers are configured with the wrong network statements.

    B. They have different maximum paths configured.

    C. There is a passive interface configured.

    D. There is an ACL set stopping Hellos.

    E. The costs of the links between the routers are configured differently.

    F. They are in different areas.

18. Which of the following is/are true? (Choose all that apply.)

    A. The reference bandwidth for OSPF and OSPFv3 is 1.

    B. The reference bandwidth for OSPF and OSPFv3 is 100.

    C. You change the reference bandwidth from global config with the command `auto-cost reference bandwidth` *number*.

    D. You change the reference bandwidth under the OSPF router process with the command `auto-cost reference bandwidth` *number*.

    E. Only one router needs to set the reference bandwidth if it is changed from its default.

    F. All routers in a single area must set the reference bandwidth if it is changed from its default.

    G. All routers in the AS must set the reference bandwidth if it is changed from its default.

19. Which two statements about the OSPF router ID are true? (Choose two.)

    A. It identifies the source of a Type 1 LSA.

    B. It should be the same on all routers in an OSPF routing instance.

    C. By default, the lowest IP address on the router becomes the OSPF router ID.

    D. The router automatically chooses the IP address of a loopback as the OSPF router ID.

    E. It is created using the MAC address of the loopback interface.

20. What are two benefits of using a single OSPF area network design? (Choose two.)

    A. It is less CPU intensive for routers in the single area.

    B. It reduces the types of LSAs that are generated.

    C. It removes the need for virtual links.

    D. It increases LSA response times.

    E. It reduces the number of required OSPF neighbor adjacencies.

Chapter

20

Troubleshooting IP, IPv6, and VLANs

THE FOLLOWING ICND2 EXAM TOPICS ARE COVERED IN THIS CHAPTER:

✓ **1.7 Describe common access layer threat mitigation techniques**

- 1.7.c Nondefault native VLAN

✓ **4.0 Infrastructure Services**

✓ **4.4 Configure, verify, and troubleshoot IPv4 and IPv6 access list for traffic filtering**

- 4.4.a Standard

- 4.4.b Extended

- 4.4.c Named

✓ **5.0 Infrastructure Maintenance**

✓ **5.2 Troubleshoot network connectivity issues using ICMP echo-based IP SLA**

✓ **5.3 Use local SPAN to troubleshoot and resolve problems**

In this chapter, especially at first, it's going to seem like we're going over lot of the same ground and concepts already covered in other chapters. The reason for this is that troubleshooting is such a major focus of the Cisco ICND1 and ICND2 objectives that I've got to make sure I've guided you through this vital topic in depth. If not, then I just haven't done all I can to really set you up for success! So to make that happen, we're going to thoroughly examine troubleshooting with IP, IPv6, and *virtual LANs (VLANs)* now. And I can't stress the point enough that you absolutely must have a solid, fundamental understanding of IP and IPv6 routing as well as a complete understanding of VLANs and trunking nailed down tight if you're going to win at this!

To help you do that, I'll be using different scenarios to walk you through the Cisco troubleshooting steps to correctly solve the problems you're likely to be faced with. Although it's hard to tell exactly what the ICND1 and ICND2 exams will throw at you, you can read and completely understand the objectives so that no matter what, you'll be prepared, equipped, and up to the challenge. The way to do this is by building upon a really strong foundation, including being skilled at troubleshooting. This chapter is precisely designed, and exactly what you need, to seriously help solidify your troubleshooting foundation.

The previous chapters on EIGRP and OSPF each had their own troubleshooting section. Troubleshooting WAN protocols will be thoroughly covered in Chapter 21. In this chapter we'll concentrate solely on IP, IPv6, and VLAN troubleshooting.

 To find up-to-the-minute updates for this chapter, please see www.lammle .com/ccna or the book's web page at www.sybex.com/go/ccna.

Troubleshooting IP Network Connectivity

Let's start out by taking a moment for a short and sweet review of IP routing. Always remember that when a host wants to transmit a packet, IP looks at the destination address and determines if it's a local or remote request. If it's determined to be a local request, IP just broadcasts a frame out on the local network looking for the local host using an ARP request. If it's a remote request, the host sends an ARP request to the default gateway to discover the MAC address of the router.

Once the hosts have the default gateway address, they'll send each packet that needs to be transmitted to the Data Link layer for framing, and newly framed packets are then sent out on the local collision domain. The router will receive the frame and remove the packet from the frame, and IP will then parse the routing table looking for the exit interface on the router. If the destination is found in the routing table, it will packet-switch the packet to the exit interface. At this point, the packet will be framed with new source and destination MAC addresses.

Okay, with that short review in mind, what would you say to someone who called you saying they weren't able to get to a server on a remote network? What's the first thing you would have this user do (besides reboot Windows) or that you would do yourself to test network connectivity? If you came up with using the Ping program, that's a great place to start. The Ping program is a great tool for finding out if a host is alive on the network with a simple ICMP echo request and echo reply. But being able to ping the host as well as the server doesn't guarantee that all is well in the network! Keep in mind that there's more to the Ping program than just being used as a quick and simple testing protocol.

To be prepared for the exam objectives, it's a great idea to get used to connecting to various routers and pinging from them. Of course, pinging from a router is not as good as pinging from the host reporting the problem, but that doesn't mean we can't isolate some problems from the routers themselves.

Let's use Figure 20.1 as a basis to run through some troubleshooting scenarios.

FIGURE 20.1   Troubleshooting scenario

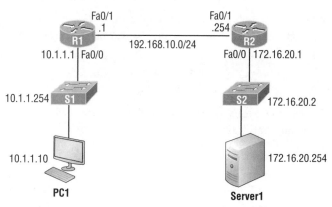

In this first scenario, a manager calls you and says that he cannot log in to Server1 from PC1. Your job is to find out why and fix it. The Cisco objectives are clear on the troubleshooting steps you need to take when a problem has been reported, and here they are:

1. Check the cables to find out if there's a faulty cable or interface in the mix and verify the interface's statistics.

2. Make sure that devices are determining the correct path from the source to the destination. Manipulate the routing information if needed.

3. Verify that the default gateway is correct.

4. Verify that name resolution settings are correct.

5. Verify that there are no *access control lists (ACLs)* blocking traffic.

In order to effectively troubleshoot this problem, we'll narrow down the possibilities by process of elimination. We'll start with PC1 and verify that it's configured correctly and also that IP is working correctly.

There are four steps for checking the PC1 configuration:

1. Test that the local IP stack is working by pinging the loopback address.

2. Test that the local IP stack is talking to the Data Link layer (LAN driver) by pinging the local IP address.

3. Test that the host is working on the LAN by pinging the default gateway.

4. Test that the host can get to remote networks by pinging remote Server1.

Let's check out the PC1 configuration by using the ipconfig command, or ifconfig on a Mac:

```
C:\Users\Todd Lammle>ipconfig

Windows IP Configuration

Ethernet adapter Local Area Connection:

    Connection-specific DNS Suffix   . : localdomain
    Link-local IPv6 Address . . . . . : fe80::64e3:76a2:541f:ebcb%11
    IPv4 Address. . . . . . . . . . . : 10.1.1.10
    Subnet Mask . . . . . . . . . . . : 255.255.255.0
    Default Gateway . . . . . . . . . : 10.1.1.1
```

We can also check the route table on the host with the route print command to see if it truly does know the default gateway:

```
C:\Users\Todd Lammle>route print
[output cut]
IPv4 Route Table
===========================================================================
Active Routes:
Network Destination        Netmask          Gateway       Interface  Metric
          0.0.0.0          0.0.0.0       10.1.1.10       10.1.1.1   10
[output cut]
```

Between the output of the ipconfig command and the route print command, we can be assured that the hosts are aware of the correct default gateway.

For the Cisco objectives, it's extremely important to be able to check and verify the default gateway on a host and also that this address matches the router's interface!

So, let's verify that the local IP stack is initialized by pinging the loopback address now:

```
C:\Users\Todd Lammle>ping 127.0.0.1

Pinging 127.0.0.1 with 32 bytes of data:
Reply from 127.0.0.1: bytes=32 time<1ms TTL=128
Reply from 127.0.0.1: bytes=32 time<1ms TTL=128
Reply from 127.0.0.1: bytes=32 time<1ms TTL=128
Reply from 127.0.0.1: bytes=32 time<1ms TTL=128

Ping statistics for 127.0.0.1:
    Packets: Sent = 4, Received = 4, Lost = 0 (0% loss),
Approximate round trip times in milli-seconds:
    Minimum = 0ms, Maximum = 0ms, Average = 0ms
```

This first output confirms the IP address and configured default gateway of the host, and then I verified the fact that the local IP stack is working. Our next move is to verify that the IP stack is talking to the LAN driver by pinging the local IP address.

```
C:\Users\Todd Lammle>ping 10.1.1.10

Pinging 10.1.1.10 with 32 bytes of data:
Reply from 10.1.1.10: bytes=32 time<1ms TTL=128
Reply from 10.1.1.10: bytes=32 time<1ms TTL=128
Reply from 10.1.1.10: bytes=32 time<1ms TTL=128
Reply from 10.1.1.10: bytes=32 time<1ms TTL=128

Ping statistics for 10.1.1.10:
    Packets: Sent = 4, Received = 4, Lost = 0 (0% loss),
Approximate round trip times in milli-seconds:
    Minimum = 0ms, Maximum = 0ms, Average = 0ms
```

And now that we know the local stack is solid and the IP stack is communicating to the LAN driver, it's time to check our local LAN connectivity by pinging the default gateway:

```
C:\Users\Todd Lammle>ping 10.1.1.1

Pinging 10.1.1.1 with 32 bytes of data:
Reply from 10.1.1.1: bytes=32 time<1ms TTL=128
Reply from 10.1.1.1: bytes=32 time<1ms TTL=128
Reply from 10.1.1.1: bytes=32 time<1ms TTL=128
Reply from 10.1.1.1: bytes=32 time<1ms TTL=128
```

```
Ping statistics for 10.1.1.1:
    Packets: Sent = 4, Received = 4, Lost = 0 (0% loss),
Approximate round trip times in milli-seconds:
    Minimum = 0ms, Maximum = 0ms, Average = 0ms
```

Looking good! I'd say our host is in good shape. Let's try to ping the remote server next to see if our host is actually getting off the local LAN to communicate remotely:

```
C:\Users\Todd Lammle>ping 172.16.20.254

Pinging 172.16.20.254 with 32 bytes of data:
Request timed out.
Request timed out.
Request timed out.
Request timed out.

Ping statistics for 172.16.20.254:
    Packets: Sent = 4, Received = 0, Lost = 4 (100% loss),
```

Well, looks like we've confirmed local connectivity but not remote connectivity, so we're going to have to dig deeper to isolate our problem. But first, and just as important, it's key to make note of what we can rule out at this point:

1. The PC is configured with the correct IP address and the local IP stack is working.

2. The default gateway is configured correctly and the PC's default gateway configuration matches the router interface IP address.

3. The local switch is working because we can ping through the switch to the router.

4. We don't have a local LAN issue, meaning our Physical layer is good because we can ping the router. If we couldn't ping the router, we would need to verify our physical cables and interfaces.

Let's see if we can narrow the problem down further using the traceroute command:

```
C:\Users\Todd Lammle>tracert 172.16.20.254

Tracing route to 172.16.20.254 over a maximum of 30 hops

  1     1 ms      1 ms     <1 ms   10.1.1.1
  2     *         *         *       Request timed out.
  3     *         *         *       Request timed out.
```

Well, we didn't get beyond our default gateway, so let's go over to R2 and see if we can talk locally to the server:

```
R2#ping 172.16.20.254

Pinging 172.16.20.254 with 32 bytes of data:
Reply from 172.16.20.254: bytes=32 time<1ms TTL=128
```

```
Reply from 172.16.20.254: bytes=32 time<1ms TTL=128
Reply from 172.16.20.254: bytes=32 time<1ms TTL=128
Reply from 172.16.20.254: bytes=32 time<1ms TTL=128

Ping statistics for 172.16.20.254:
    Packets: Sent = 4, Received = 0, Lost = 4 (100% loss),
```

Okay, we just eliminated a local LAN problem by connecting to Server1 from the R2 router, so we're good there. Let's summarize what we know so far:

1. PC1 is configured correctly.

2. The switch located on the 10.1.1.0 LAN is working.

3. PC1's default gateway is configured correctly.

4. R2 can communicate to Server1, so we don't have a remote LAN issue.

But something is still clearly wrong, so what should we check now? Now would be a great time to verify the Server1 IP configuration and make sure the default gateway is configured correctly. Let's take a look:

```
C:\Users\Server1>ipconfig

Windows IP Configuration

Ethernet adapter Local Area Connection:

    Connection-specific DNS Suffix  . : localdomain
    Link-local IPv6 Address . . . . . : fe80::7723:76a2:e73c:2acb%11
    IPv4 Address. . . . . . . . . . . : 172.16.20.254
    Subnet Mask . . . . . . . . . . . : 255.255.255.0
    Default Gateway . . . . . . . . . : 172.16.20.1
```

Okay—the Server1 configuration looks good and the R2 router can ping the server, so it seems that the server's local LAN is solid, the local switch is working, and there are no cable or interface issues. But let's zoom in on interface Fa0/0 on R2 and talk about what to expect if there were errors on this interface:

```
R2#sh int fa0/0
FastEthernet0/0 is up, line protocol is up
[output cut]
  Full-duplex, 100Mb/s, 100BaseTX/FX
  ARP type: ARPA, ARP Timeout 04:00:00
  Last input 00:00:05, output 00:00:01, output hang never
  Last clearing of "show interface" counters never
  Input queue: 0/75/0/0 (size/max/drops/flushes); Total output drops: 0
  Queueing strategy: fifo
  Output queue: 0/40 (size/max)
  5 minute input rate 0 bits/sec, 0 packets/sec
```

```
5 minute output rate 0 bits/sec, 0 packets/sec
   1325 packets input, 157823 bytes
   Received 1157 broadcasts (0 IP multicasts)
   0 runts, 0 giants, 0 throttles
   0 input errors, 0 CRC, 0 frame, 0 overrun, 0 ignored
   0 watchdog
   0 input packets with dribble condition detected
   2294 packets output, 244630 bytes, 0 underruns
   0 output errors, 0 collisions, 3 interface resets
   347 unknown protocol drops
   0 babbles, 0 late collision, 0 deferred
   4 lost carrier, 0 no carrier
   0 output buffer failures, 0 output buffers swapped out
```

You've got to be able to analyze interface statistics to find problems there if they exist, so let's pick out the important factors relevant to meeting that challenge effectively now.

Speed and duplex settings   Good to know that the most common cause of interface errors is a mismatched duplex mode between two ends of an Ethernet link. This is why it's so important to make sure that the switch and its hosts (PCs, router interfaces, etc.) have the same speed setting. If not, they just won't connect. And if they have mismatched duplex settings, you'll receive a legion of errors, which cause nasty performance issues, intermittent connectivity—even total loss of communication!

Using autonegotiation for speed and duplex is a very common practice, and it's enabled by default. But if this fails for some reason, you'll have to set the configuration manually like this:

```
Switch(config)#int gi0/1
Switch(config-if)#speed ?
   10    Force 10 Mbps operation
   100   Force 100 Mbps operation
   1000  Force 1000 Mbps operation
   auto  Enable AUTO speed configuration
Switch(config-if)#speed 1000
Switch(config-if)#duplex ?
   auto  Enable AUTO duplex configuration
   full  Force full duplex operation
   half  Force half-duplex operation
Switch(config-if)#duplex  full
```

If you have a duplex mismatch, a telling sign is that the late collision counter will increment.

Input queue drops If the input queue drops counter increments, this signifies that more traffic is being delivered to the router that it can process. If this is consistently high, try to determine exactly when these counters are increasing and how the events relate to CPU usage. You'll see the ignored and throttle counters increment as well.

Output queue drops This counter indicates that packets were dropped due to interface congestion, leading to queuing delays. When this occurs, applications like VoIP will experience performance issues. If you observe this constantly incrementing, consider QoS.

Input errors Input errors often indicate high errors such as CRCs. This can point to cabling problems, hardware issues, or duplex mismatches.

Output errors This is the total number of frames that the port tried to transmit when an issue such as a collision occurred.

We're going to move on in our troubleshooting process of elimination by analyzing the routers' actual configurations. Here's R1's routing table:

```
R1>sh ip route
[output cut]
Gateway of last resort is 192.168.10.254 to network 0.0.0.0

S*    0.0.0.0/0 [1/0] via 192.168.10.254
      10.0.0.0/8 is variably subnetted, 2 subnets, 2 masks
C        10.1.1.0/24 is directly connected, FastEthernet0/0
L        10.1.1.1/32 is directly connected, FastEthernet0/0
      192.168.10.0/24 is variably subnetted, 2 subnets, 2 masks
C        192.168.10.0/24 is directly connected, FastEthernet0/1
L        192.168.10.1/32 is directly connected, FastEthernet0/1
```

This actually looks pretty good! Both of our directly connected networks are in the table and we can confirm that we have a default route going to the R2 router. So now let's verify the connectivity to R2 from R1:

```
R1>sh ip int brief
Interface          IP-Address     OK? Method Status                 Protocol
FastEthernet0/0    10.1.1.1       YES manual up                     up
FastEthernet0/1    192.168.10.1   YES manual up                     up
Serial0/0/0        unassigned     YES unset  administratively down  down
Serial0/1/0        unassigned     YES unset  administratively down  down
R1>ping 192.168.10.254
Type escape sequence to abort.
Sending 5, 100-byte ICMP Echos to 192.168.10.254, timeout is 2 seconds:
!!!!!
Success rate is 100 percent (5/5), round-trip min/avg/max = 1/2/4 ms
```

This looks great too! Our interfaces are correctly configured with the right IP address and the Physical and Data Link layers are up. By the way, I also tested layer 3 connectivity by pinging the R2 Fa0/1 interface.

Since everything looks good so far, our next step is to check into the status of R2's interfaces:

```
R2>sh ip int brief
Interface              IP-Address       OK? Method Status           Protocol
FastEthernet0/0        172.16.20.1      YES manual up                  up
FastEthernet0/1        192.168.10.254   YES manual up                  up
R2>ping 192.168.10.1
Type escape sequence to abort.
Sending 5, 100-byte ICMP Echos to 192.168.10.1, timeout is 2 seconds:
!!!!!
Success rate is 100 percent (5/5), round-trip min/avg/max = 1/2/4 ms
```

Well, everything still checks out at this point. The IP addresses are correct and the Physical and Data Link layers are up. I also tested the layer 3 connectivity with a ping to R1, so we're all good so far. We'll examine the routing table next:

```
R2>sh ip route
[output cut]
Gateway of last resort is not set

     10.0.0.0/24 is subnetted, 1 subnets
S        10.1.1.0 is directly connected, FastEthernet0/0
     172.16.0.0/16 is variably subnetted, 2 subnets, 2 masks
C        172.16.20.0/24 is directly connected, FastEthernet0/0
L        172.16.20.1/32 is directly connected, FastEthernet0/0
     192.168.10.0/24 is variably subnetted, 2 subnets, 2 masks
C        192.168.10.0/24 is directly connected, FastEthernet0/1
L        192.168.10.254/32 is directly connected, FastEthernet0/1
```

Okay—we can see that all our local interfaces are in the table, as well as a static route to the 10.1.1.0 network. But do you see the problem? Look closely at the static route. The route was entered with an exit interface of Fa0/0, and the path to the 10.1.1.0 network is out Fa0/1! Aha! We've found our problem! Let's fix R2:

```
R2#config t
R2(config)#no ip route 10.1.1.0 255.255.255.0 fa0/0
R2(config)#ip route 10.1.1.0 255.255.255.0 192.168.10.1
```

That should do it. Let's verify from PC1:

```
C:\Users\Todd Lammle>ping 172.16.20.254
```

```
Pinging 172.16.20.254 with 32 bytes of data:
Reply from 172.16.20.254: bytes=32 time<1ms TTL=128
Reply from 172.16.20.254: bytes=32 time<1ms TTL=128
Reply from 172.16.20.254: bytes=32 time<1ms TTL=128
Reply from 172.16.20.254: bytes=32 time<1ms TTL=128

Ping statistics for 172.16.20.254
    Packets: Sent = 4, Received = 4, Lost = 0 (0% loss),
Approximate round trip times in milli-seconds:
    Minimum = 0ms, Maximum = 0ms, Average = 0ms
```

Our snag appears to be solved, but just to make sure, we really need to verify with a higher-level protocol like Telnet:

```
C:\Users\Todd Lammle>telnet 172.16.20.254
Connecting To 172.16.20.254...Could not open connection to the host, on
port 23: Connect failed
```

Okay, that's not good! We can ping to Server1, but we can't telnet to it. In the past, I've verified that telnetting to this server worked, but it's still possible that we have a failure on the server side. To find out, let's verify our network first, starting at R1:

```
R1>ping 172.16.20.254
Type escape sequence to abort.
Sending 5, 100-byte ICMP Echos to 172.16.20.254, timeout is 2 seconds:
!!!!!
Success rate is 100 percent (5/5), round-trip min/avg/max = 1/1/4 ms
R1>telnet 172.16.20.254
Trying 172.16.20.254 ...
% Destination unreachable; gateway or host down
```

This is some pretty ominous output! Let's try from R2 and see what happens:

```
R2#telnet 172.16.20.254
Trying 172.16.20.254 ... Open

User Access Verification

Password:
```

Oh my—I can ping the server from a remote network, but I can't telnet to it; however, the local router R2 can! These factors eliminate the server being a problem since I can telnet to the server when I'm on the local LAN.

And we know we don't have a routing problem because we fixed that already. So what's next? Let's check to see if there's an ACL on R2:

```
R2>sh access-lists
```

```
Extended IP access list 110
    10 permit icmp any any (25 matches)
```

Seriously? What a loopy access list to have on a router! This ridiculous list permits ICMP, but that's it. It denies everything except ICMP due to the implicit deny ip any any at the end of every ACL. But before we uncork the champagne, we need to see if this foolish list has been applied to our interfaces on R2 to confirm that this is really our problem:

```
R2>sh ip int fa0/0
FastEthernet0/0 is up, line protocol is up
  Internet address is 172.16.20.1/24
  Broadcast address is 255.255.255.255
  Address determined by setup command
  MTU is 1500 bytes
  Helper address is not set
  Directed broadcast forwarding is disabled
  Outgoing access list is 110
  Inbound  access list is not set
```

There it is—that's our problem all right! In case you're wondering why R2 could telnet to Server1, it's because an ACL filters only packets trying to go through the router—not packets generated at the router. Let's get to work and fix this:

```
R2#config t
R2(config)#no access-list 110
```

I just verified that I can telnet from PC1 to Server1, but let's try telnetting from R1 again:

```
R1#telnet 172.16.20.254
Trying 172.16.20.254 ... Open

User Access Verification

Password:
```

Nice—looks like we're set, but what about using the name?

```
R1#telnet Server1
Translating "Server1"...domain server (255.255.255.255)

% Bad IP address or host name
```

Well, we're not all set just yet. Let's fix R1 so that it can provide name resolution:

```
R1(config)#ip host Server1 172.16.20.254
```

```
R1#telnet Server1
Trying Server1 (172.16.20.254)... Open

User Access Verification

Password:
```

Great—things are looking good from the router, but if the customer can't telnet to the remote host using the name, we've got to check the DNS server to confirm connectivity and for the correct entry to the server. Another option would be to configure the local host table manually on PC1.

The last thing to do is to check the server to see if it's responding to HTTP requests via the telnet command, believe it or not! Here's an example:

```
R1#telnet 172.16.20.254 80
Trying 172.16.20.254, 80 ... Open
```

Yes—finally! Server1 is responding to requests on port 80, so we're in the clear.

Using IP SLA for Troubleshooting

I want to mention one more thing that can help you troubleshoot your IP network, and this is using IP service-level agreements (SLAs), which will allow us to use IP SLA ICMP echo to test far-end devices instead of pinging manually.

There are several reasons to use the IP SLA measurements:

- Edge-to-edge network availability monitoring
  - For example, packet loss statistics
- Network performance monitoring and network performance visibility
  - For example, network latency and response time
- Troubleshooting basic network operation
  - For example, end-to-end network connectivity

Step 1: Enable an IP SLA operation that enters the IP SLA configuration mode. Chose any number from 1 to 2.1 billion as an operation number.

```
R1(config)#ip sla 1
```

Step 2: Configure the IP SLA ICMP echo test and destination.

```
R1(config-ip-sla)#icmp?
icmp-echo  icmp-jitter

R1(config-ip-sla)#icmp-echo ?
  Hostname or X:X:X:X::X
  Hostname or A.B.C.D  Destination IPv6/IP address or hostname

R1(config-ip-sla)#icmp-echo 172.16.20.254
```

Step 3: Set the test frequency.

```
R1(config-ip-sla-echo)#frequency ?
  <1-604800>  Frequency in seconds (default 60)

R1(config-ip-sla-echo)#frequency 10
```

Step 4: Schedule your IP SLA test.

```
R1(config-ip-sla-echo)#exit
R1(config)#ip sla schedule ?
  <1-2147483647>  Entry number

R1(config)#ip sla schedule 1 life ?
  <0-2147483647>  Life seconds (default 3600)
  forever         continue running forever

R1(config)#ip sla schedule 1 life forever start-time ?
  after      Start after a certain amount of time from now
  hh:mm      Start time (hh:mm)
  hh:mm:ss   Start time (hh:mm:ss)
  now        Start now
  pending    Start pending

R1(config)#ip sla schedule 1 life forever start-time now
```

Step 5: Verify the IP SLA operation. Use the following commands:

```
Show ip sla configuration
Show ip sla statistics
```

R1 should have an ICMP Echo test configured to the remote server address, and the test should run every 10 seconds and be scheduled to run forever.

```
R1#show ip sla configuration
IP SLAs Infrastructure Engine-II
Entry number: 1
Owner:
Tag:
Type of operation to perform: icmp-echo
Target address/Source address: 172.16.20.254/0.0.0.0
Type Of Service parameter: 0x0
Request size (ARR data portion): 28
Operation timeout (milliseconds): 5000
Verify data: No
```

```
Vrf Name:
Schedule:
    Operation frequency (seconds): 10   (not considered if randomly scheduled)
    Next Scheduled Start Time: Start Time already passed
    Group Scheduled : FALSE
    Randomly Scheduled : FALSE
    Life (seconds): Forever
    Entry Ageout (seconds): never
    Recurring (Starting Everyday): FALSE
    Status of entry (SNMP RowStatus): Active
[output cut]
```

```
R1#sh ip sla statistics
IPSLAs Latest Operation Statistics

IPSLA operation id: 1
Type of operation: icmp-echo
        Latest RTT: 1 milliseconds
Latest operation start time: *15:27:51.365 UTC Mon Jun 6 2016
Latest operation return code: OK
Number of successes: 38
Number of failures: 0
Operation time to live: Forever
```

The IP SLA 1 test on R1 has been successfully performed 38 times and the test never failed.

Using SPAN for Troubleshooting

A traffic sniffer can be a valuable tool for monitoring and troubleshooting your network. However, since the inception of switches into our networks more than 20 years ago, troubleshooting has become more difficult because we can't just plug an analyzer into a switch port and be able to read all the network traffic. Before we had switches, we used hubs, and when a hub received a digital signal on one port, the hub sent that digital signal out on all ports except the port it was received on. This allows a traffic sniffer that is connected to a hub port to receive all traffic in the network.

Modern local networks are essentially switched networks. After a switch boots, it starts to build up a layer 2 forwarding table based on the source MAC addresses of the different packets that the switch receives. After the switch builds this forwarding table, it forwards traffic that is destined for a MAC address directly to the exit port. By default, this prevents a traffic sniffer that is connected to another port from receiving the unicast traffic. The SPAN feature was therefore introduced on switches to help solve this problem (see Figure 20.2).

FIGURE 20.2   Using SPAN for troubleshooting

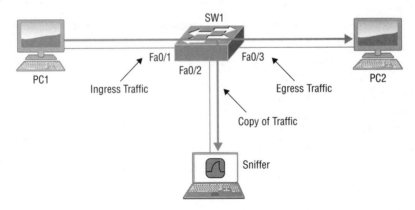

The SPAN feature allows you to analyze network traffic passing through the port and send a copy of the traffic to another port on the switch that has been connected to a network analyzer or other monitoring device. SPAN copies the traffic that the device receives and/or sends on source ports to a destination port for analysis.

For example, if you would like to analyze the traffic flowing from PC1 to PC2, shown in Figure 20.2, you need to specify a source port where you want to capture the data. You can either configure the interface Fa0/1 to capture the ingress traffic or configure the interface Fa0/3 to capture the egress traffic—your choice! Next, specify the destination port interface where the sniffer is connected and will capture the data, in this example Fa0/2. The traffic flowing from PC1 to PC2 will then be copied to that interface, and you will be able to analyze it with a traffic sniffer.

Step 1: Associate a SPAN session number with the source port of what you want to monitor.

```
S1(config)#monitor session 1 source interface f0/1
```

Step 2: Associate a SPAN session number of the sniffer with the destination interface.

```
S1(config)#monitor session 1 dest interface f0/2
```

Step 3: Verify that the SPAN session has been configured correctly.

```
S1(config)#do sh monitor
Session 1
---------
Type                 : Local Session
Source Ports         :
    Both             : Fa0/1
Destination Ports    : Fa0/2
    Encapsulation    : Native
          Ingress    : Disabled
```

Now connect up your network analyzer into port F0/2 and enjoy!

Configuring and Verifying Extended Access Lists

Even though I went through some very basic troubleshooting with ACLs earlier in this chapter, let's dig a little deeper to make sure we really understand extended named ACLs before hitting IPv6.

First off, you should be familiar with ACLs from your ICND1 studies; if not, head back and read that chapter, including the standard and extended ACLs section. I'm going to focus solely on extended named ACLs, since that is what the ICND2 objectives are all about.

As you know, standard access lists focus only on IP or IPv6 source addresses. Extended ACLs, however, filter based on the source *and* destination layer 3 addresses at a minimum, but in addition can filter using the protocol field in the IP header (Next Header field in IPv6), as well as the source and destination port numbers at layer 4, all shown in Figure 20.3

FIGURE 20.3   Extended ACLs

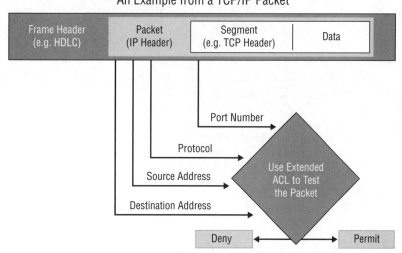

Using the network layout in Figure 20.1, let's create an extended named ACL that blocks Telnet to the 172.16.20.254 server from 10.1.1.10. It's an extended list, so we'll place it closest to the source address as possible.

Step 1: Test that you can telnet to the remote host.

```
R1#telnet 172.16.20.254
Trying 172.16.20.254 ... Open
Server1>
```

Okay, great!

Step 2: Create an ACL on R1 that stops telnetting to the remote host of 172.16.20.254. Using a named ACL, start with the protocol (IP or IPv6), choose either a standard or extended list, and then name it. The name is absolutely case sensitive when applying to an interface.

```
R1(config)#ip access-list extended Block_Telnet
R1(config-ext-nacl)#
```

Step 3: Once you have created the named list, add your test parameters.

```
R1(config-ext-nacl)#deny tcp host 10.1.1.1 host 172.16.20.254 eq 23
R1(config-ext-nacl)#permit ip any any
```

Step 4: Verify your access list.

```
R1(config-ext-nacl)#do sh access-list
Extended IP access list Block_Telnet
    10 deny tcp host 10.1.1.1 host 172.16.20.254 eq telnet
    20 permit ip any any
```

Notice the numbers 10 and 20 on the left side for each test statement. These are called sequence numbers. We can use these number to then edit a single line, delete it, or even add a new line in between two sequence numbers. Named ACLs can be edited; numbered ACLs cannot.

Step 5: Configure your ACL on your router interface.

Since we're adding this to the R1 router in Figure 20.3, we'll add it inbound to interface FastEthernet 0/0, stopping traffic closest to the source.

```
R1(config)#int fa0/0
R1(config-if)#ip access-group Block_Telnet in
```

Step 6: Test your access list.

```
R1#telnet 172.16.20.254
Trying 172.16.20.254 ... Open
Server1>
```

Hmm...okay, that didn't work because I'm still able to telnet to the remote host. Let's take a look at our list, verify our interface, and then fix the problem.

```
R1#sh access-list
Extended IP access list Block_Telnet
    10 deny tcp host 10.1.1.1 host 172.16.20.254 eq telnet
    20 permit ip any any
```

By verifying the IP addresses in the deny statement in line sequence 10, you can see that my source address is 10.1.1.1 and instead should have been 10.1.1.10.

Step 7: Fix and/or edit your access list. Delete the bad line and reconfigure the ACL to the correct IP.

```
R1(config)#ip access-list extended Block_Telnet
R1(config-ext-nacl)#no 10
R1(config-ext-nacl)#10 deny tcp host 10.1.1.10 host 172.16.20.254 eq 80
```

Verify that your list is working.

```
R1#telnet 172.16.20.254
Trying 172.16.20.254 ...
% Destination unreachable; gateway or host down
```

Step 8: Display the ACL again and observe the updated hit counters with each line, and also verify that the interface is set with the ACL.

```
R1#sh access-list
Extended IP access list Block_Telnet
    10 deny tcp host 10.1.1.10 host 172.16.20.254 eq telnet (58 matches)
    20 permit ip any any (86 matches)
```

```
R1#sh ip int f0/0
FastEthernet0/0 is up, line protocol is up
  Internet address is 10.10.10.1/24
  Broadcast address is 255.255.255.255
  Address determined by non-volatile memory
  MTU is 1500 bytes
  Helper address is not set
  Directed broadcast forwarding is disabled
  Multicast reserved groups joined: 224.0.0.10
  Outgoing access list is not set
  Inbound  access list is Block_Telnet
  Proxy ARP is enabled
[output cut]
```

The interface was up and working, so verifying at this point was a little overkill, but you must be able to look at an interface and troubleshoot issues, such as ACLs set on an interface. So be sure to remember the show ip interface command.

Now, let's mix things up a little by adding IPv6 to our network and work through the same troubleshooting steps.

Troubleshooting IPv6 Network Connectivity

I'm going to be straight with you: there isn't a lot that's going to be much different between this section and the process you just went through with the IPv4 troubleshooting steps. Except regarding the addressing of course! So other than that key factor, we'll take the same approach, using Figure 20.4, specifically because I really want to highlight the differences associated with IPv6. So the problem scenario I'm going to use will also stay the same: PC1 cannot communicate to Server1.

FIGURE 20.4   IPv6 troubleshooting scenario

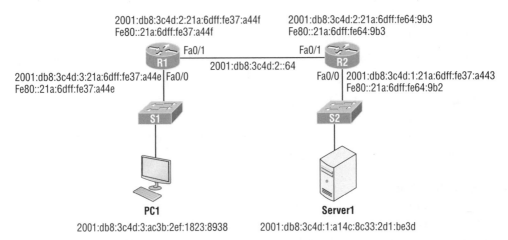

I want to point out that this is not an "introduction to IPv6" chapter, so I'm assuming you've got some IPv6 fundamentals down.

Notice that I documented both the *link-local* and *global addresses* assigned to each router interface in Figure 20.4. We need both in order to troubleshoot, so right away, you can see that things get a bit more complicated because of the longer addresses and the fact that there are multiple addresses per interface involved!

But *before* we start troubleshooting the IPv6 network in Figure 20.4, I want to refresh your memory on the ICMPv6 protocol, which is an important protocol in our troubleshooting arsenal.

ICMPv6

IPv4 used the ICMP workhorse for lots of tasks, including error messages like destination unreachable and troubleshooting functions like Ping and Traceroute. ICMPv6 still does those things for us, but unlike its predecessor, the v6 flavor isn't implemented as a separate layer 3 protocol. Instead, it's an integrated part of IPv6 and is carried after the basic IPv6 header information as an extension header.

ICMPv6 is used for router solicitation and advertisement, for neighbor solicitation and advertisement (i.e., finding the MAC addresses for IPv6 neighbors), and for redirecting the host to the best router (default gateway).

Neighbor Discovery (NDP)

ICMPv6 also takes over the task of finding the address of other devices on the local link. The Address Resolution Protocol is used to perform this function for IPv4, but that's been renamed Neighbor Discovery (ND or NDP) in ICMPv6. This process is now achieved via a multicast address called the solicited node address because all hosts join this multicast group upon connecting to the network.

Neighbor discovery enables these functions:

- Determining the MAC address of neighbors
- Router solicitation (RS) FF02::2
- Router advertisements (RA) FF02::1
- Neighbor solicitation (NS)
- Neighbor advertisement (NA)
- Duplicate address detection (DAD)

The part of the IPv6 address designated by the 24 bits farthest to the right is added to the end of the multicast address FF02:0:0:0:0:1:FF/104. When this address is queried, the corresponding host will send back its layer 2 address. Devices can find and keep track of other neighbor devices on the network in pretty much the same way. When I talked about RA and RS messages earlier in the CCENT chapters, and told you that they use multicast traffic to request and send address information, that too is actually a function of ICMPv6—specifically, neighbor discovery.

In IPv4, the protocol IGMP was used to allow a host device to tell its local router that it was joining a multicast group and would like to receive the traffic for that group. This IGMP function has been replaced by ICMPv6, and the process has been renamed multicast listener discovery.

With IPv4, our hosts could have only one default gateway configured, and if that router went down we had to fix the router, change the default gateway, or run some type of virtual default gateway with other protocols created as a solution for this inadequacy in IPv4. Figure 20.5 shows how IPv6 devices find their default gateways using neighbor discovery.

FIGURE 20.5   Router solicitation (RS) and router advertisement (RA)

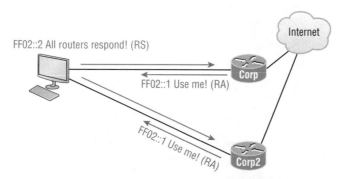

IPv6 hosts send a router solicitation (RS) onto their data link asking for all routers to respond, and they use the multicast address FF02::2 to achieve this. Routers on the same link respond with a unicast to the requesting host, or with a router advertisement (RA) using FF02::1.

But that's not all! Hosts also can send solicitations and advertisements between themselves using a neighbor solicitation (NS) and neighbor advertisement (NA), as shown in Figure 20.6.

FIGURE 20.6   Neighbor solicitation (NS) and neighbor advertisement (NA)

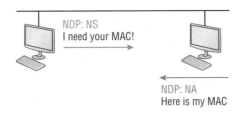

Remember that RA and RS gather or provide information about routers and NS and NA gather information about hosts. Also, remember that a "neighbor" is a host on the same data link or VLAN.

With that foundation review in mind, here are the troubleshooting steps we'll progress through in our investigation:

1. Check the cables because there might be a faulty cable or interface. Verify interface statistics.

2. Make sure that devices are determining the correct path from the source to the destination. Manipulate the routing information if needed.

3. Verify that the default gateway is correct.

4. Verify that name resolution settings are correct, and especially for IPv6, make sure the DNS server is reachable via IPv4 and IPv6.

5. Verify that there are no ACLs that are blocking traffic.

In order to troubleshoot this problem, we'll use the same process of elimination, beginning with PC1. We must verify that it's configured correctly and that IP is working properly. Let's start by pinging the loopback address to verify the IPv6 stack:

```
C:\Users\Todd Lammle>ping ::1

Pinging ::1 with 32 bytes of data:
Reply from ::1: time<1ms
Reply from ::1: time<1ms
Reply from ::1: time<1ms
Reply from ::1: time<1ms
```

Well, the IPv6 stack checks out, so let's ping the Fa0/0 of R1, which PC1 is directly connected to on the same LAN, starting with the link-local address:

```
C:\Users\Todd Lammle>ping fe80::21a:6dff:fe37:a44e
```

```
Pinging fe80:21a:6dff:fe37:a44e with 32 bytes of data:
Reply from fe80::21a:6dff:fe37:a44e: time<1ms
Reply from fe80::21a:6dff:fe37:a44e: time<1ms
Reply from fe80::21a:6dff:fe37:a44e: time<1ms
Reply from fe80::21a:6dff:fe37:a44e: time<1ms
```

Next, we'll ping the global address on Fa0/0:

```
C:\Users\Todd Lammle>ping 2001:db8:3c4d:3:21a:6dff:fe37:a44e
```

```
Pinging 2001:db8:3c4d:3:21a:6dff:fe37:a44e with 32 bytes of data:
Reply from 2001:db8:3c4d:3:21a:6dff:fe37:a44e: time<1ms
Reply from 2001:db8:3c4d:3:21a:6dff:fe37:a44e: time<1ms
Reply from 2001:db8:3c4d:3:21a:6dff:fe37:a44e: time<1ms
Reply from 2001:db8:3c4d:3:21a:6dff:fe37:a44e: time<1ms
```

Okay—looks like PC1 is configured and working on the local LAN to the R1 router, so we've confirmed the Physical, Data Link, and Network layers between the PC1 and the R1 router Fa0/0 interface.

Our next move is to check the local connection on Server1 to the R2 router to verify that LAN. First we'll ping the link-local address of the router from Server1:

```
C:\Users\Server1>ping fe80::21a:6dff:fe64:9b2
```

```
Pinging fe80::21a:6dff:fe64:9b2  with 32 bytes of data:
Reply from fe80::21a:6dff:fe64:9b2: time<1ms
Reply from fe80::21a:6dff:fe64:9b2: time<1ms
Reply from fe80::21a:6dff:fe64:9b2: time<1ms
Reply from fe80::21a:6dff:fe64:9b2: time<1ms
```

And next, we'll ping the global address of Fa0/0 on R2:

```
C:\Users\Server1>ping 2001:db8:3c4d:1:21a:6dff:fe37:a443
```

```
Pinging 2001:db8:3c4d:1:21a:6dff:fe37:a443 with 32 bytes of data:
Reply from 2001:db8:3c4d:1:21a:6dff:fe37:a443: time<1ms
Reply from 2001:db8:3c4d:1:21a:6dff:fe37:a443: time<1ms
Reply from 2001:db8:3c4d:1:21a:6dff:fe37:a443: time<1ms
Reply from 2001:db8:3c4d:1:21a:6dff:fe37:a443: time<1ms
```

Let's quickly summarize what we know at this point:

1. By using the ipconfig /all command on PC1 and Server1, I was able to document their global and link-local IPv6 addresses.

2. We know the IPv6 link-local addresses of each router interface.

3. We know the IPv6 global address of each router interface.

4. We can ping from PC1 to router R1's Fa0/0 interface.

5. We can ping from Server1 to router R2's Fa0/0 interface.

6. We can eliminate a local problem on both LANs.

From here, we'll go to PC1 and see if we can route to Server1:

```
C:\Users\Todd Lammle>tracert 2001:db8:3c4d:1:a14c:8c33:2d1:be3d

Tracing route to 2001:db8:3c4d:1:a14c:8c33:2d1:be3d over a maximum of 30 hops

  1    Destination host unreachable.
```

Okay, now that's not good. Looks like we might have a routing problem. And on this little network, we're doing static IPv6 routing, so getting to the bottom of things will definitely take a little effort! But before we start looking into our potential routing issue, let's check the link between R1 and R2. We'll ping R2 from R1 to test the directly connected link.

The first thing you need to do before attempting to ping between routers is verify your addresses—yes, verify them again! Let's check out both routers, then try pinging from R1 to R2:

```
R1#sh ipv6 int brief
FastEthernet0/0           [up/up]
    FE80::21A:6DFF:FE37:A44E
    2001:DB8:3C4D:3:21A:6DFF:FE37:A44E
FastEthernet0/1           [up/up]
    FE80::21A:6DFF:FE37:A44F
    2001:DB8:3C4D:2:21A:6DFF:FE37:A44F

R2#sh ipv6 int brief
FastEthernet0/0           [up/up]
    FE80::21A:6DFF:FE64:9B2
    2001:DB8:3C4D:1:21A:6DFF:FE37:A443
FastEthernet0/1           [up/up]
    FE80::21A:6DFF:FE64:9B3
    2001:DB8:3C4D:2:21A:6DFF:FE64:9B3

R1#ping 2001:DB8:3C4D:2:21A:6DFF:FE64:9B3
Type escape sequence to abort.
Sending 5, 100-byte ICMP Echos to ping 2001:DB8:3C4D:2:21A:6DFF:FE64:9B3,
timeout
is 2 seconds:
!!!!!
Success rate is 100 percent (5/5), round-trip min/avg/max = 0/2/8 ms
```

In the preceding output, you can see that I now have the IPv6 addresses for both the R1 and R2 directly connected interfaces. The output also shows that I used the Ping program to verify layer 3 connectivity. Just as with IPv4, we need to resolve the logical (IPv6) address to a MAC address in order to communicate on the local LAN. But unlike IPv4, IPv6 doesn't use ARP—it uses ICMPv6 neighbor solicitations instead—so after the successful ping, we can now see the neighbor resolution table on R1:

```
R1#sh ipv6 neighbors
IPv6 Address                      Age Link-layer Addr State Interface
FE80::21A:6DFF:FE64:9B3             0 001a.6c46.9b09  DELAY Fa0/1
2001:DB8:3C4D:2:21A:6DFF:FE64:9B3   0 001a.6c46.9b09  REACH Fa0/1
```

Let's take a minute to talk about the possible states that a resolved address shows us:

INCMP (incomplete)   Address resolution is being performed on the entry. A neighbor solicitation message has been sent, but the neighbor message has not yet been received.

REACH (reachable)   Positive confirmation has been received confirming that the path to the neighbor is functioning correctly. REACH is good!

STALE   The state is STALE when the interface has not communicated within the neighbor reachable time frame. The next time the neighbor communicates, the state will change back to REACH.

DELAY   Occurs after the STALE state, when no reachability confirmation has been received within what's known as the DELAY_FIRST_PROBE_TIME. This means that the path was functioning but it hasn't had communication within the neighbor reachable time frame.

PROBE   When in PROBE state, the configured interface is resending a neighbor solicitation and waiting for a reachability confirmation from a neighbor.

We can verify our default gateway with IPv6 with the ipconfig command like this:

```
C:\Users\Todd Lammle>ipconfig
   Connection-specific DNS Suffix  . : localdomain
   IPv6 Address. . . . . . . . . . . : 2001:db8:3c4d:3:ac3b:2ef:1823:8938
   Temporary IPv6 Address. . . . . . : 2001:db8:3c4d:3:2f33:44dd:211:1c3d
   Link-local IPv6 Address . . . . . : fe80::ac3b:2ef:1823:8938%11
   IPv4 Address. . . . . . . . . . . : 10.1.1.10
   Subnet Mask . . . . . . . . . . . : 255.255.255.0
   Default Gateway . . . . . . . . . : Fe80::21a:6dff:fe37:a44e%11
      10.1.1.1
```

It's important to understand that the default gateway will be the link-local address of the router, and in this case, we can see that the address the host learned is truly the link-local address of the Fa0/0 interface of R1. The %11 is just used to identify an interface and isn't used as part of the IPv6 address.

Temporary IPv6 Addresses

The temporary IPv6 address, listed under the unicast IPv6 address as 2001:db8:3c4d:3:2f33: 44dd:211:1c3d, was created by Windows to provide privacy from the EUI-64 format. This creates a global address for your host without using your MAC address by generating a random number for the interface and hashing it; the result is then appended to the /64 prefix from the router. You can disable this feature with the following commands:

```
netsh interface ipv6 set global randomizeidentifiers=disabled
netsh interface ipv6 set privacy state-disabled
```

In addition to the `ipconfig` command, we can use the command `netsh interface ipv6 show neighbor` to verify our default gateway address:

```
C:\Users\Todd Lammle>netsh interface ipv6 show neighbor
[output cut]

Interface 11: Local Area Connection

Internet Address                           Physical Address   Type
-------------------------------------      -----------------  -----------
2001:db8:3c4d:3:21a:6dff:fe37:a44e         00-1a-6d-37-a4-4e  (Router)
Fe80::21a:6dff:fe37:a44e                   00-1a-6d-37-a4-4e  (Router)
ff02::1                                    33-33-00-00-00-01  Permanent
ff02::2                                    33-33-00-00-00-02  Permanent
ff02::c                                    33-33-00-00-00-0c  Permanent
ff02::16                                   33-33-00-00-00-16  Permanent
ff02::fb                                   33-33-00-00-00-fb  Permanent
ff02::1:2                                  33-33-00-01-00-02  Permanent
ff02::1:3                                  33-33-00-01-00-03  Permanent
ff02::1:ff1f:ebcb                          33-33-ff-1f-eb-cb  Permanent
```

 I've checked the default gateway addresses on Server1 and they are correct. They should be, because this is provided directly from the router with an ICMPv6 RA (router advertisement) message. The output for that verification is not shown.

Let's establish the information we have right now:

1. Our PC1 and Server1 configurations are working and have been verified.

2. The LANs are working and verified, so there is no Physical layer issue.

3.   The default gateways are correct.

4.   The link between the R1 and R2 routers is working and verified.

So all this tells us is that it's now time to check our routing tables! We'll start with the R1 router:

```
R1#sh ipv6 route
C    2001:DB8:3C4D:2::/64 [0/0]
       via FastEthernet0/1, directly connected
L    2001:DB8:3C4D:2:21A:6DFF:FE37:A44F/128 [0/0]
       via FastEthernet0/1, receive
C    2001:DB8:3C4D:3::/64 [0/0]
       via FastEthernet0/0, directly connected
L    2001:DB8:3C4D:3:21A:6DFF:FE37:A44E/128 [0/0]
       via FastEthernet0/0, receive
L    FF00::/8 [0/0]
       via Null0, receive
```

All we can see in the output is the two directly connected interfaces configured on the router, and that won't help us send IPv6 packets to the 2001:db8:3c4d:1::/64 subnet off of Fa0/0 on R2. So let's find out what R2 can tell us:

```
R2#sh ipv6 route
C    2001:DB8:3C4D:1::/64 [0/0]
       via FastEthernet0/0, directly connected
L    2001:DB8:3C4D:1:21A:6DFF:FE37:A443/128 [0/0]
       via FastEthernet0/0, receive
C    2001:DB8:3C4D:2::/64 [0/0]
       via FastEthernet0/1, directly connected
L    2001:DB8:3C4D:2:21A:6DFF:FE64:9B3/128 [0/0]
       via FastEthernet0/1, receive
S    2001:DB8:3C4D:3::/64 [1/0]
       via 2001:DB8:3C4D:2:21B:D4FF:FE0A:539
L    FF00::/8 [0/0]
       via Null0, receive
```

Now we're talking—that tells us a lot more than R1's table did! We have both of our directly connected configured LANs, Fa0/0 and Fa0/1, right there in the routing table, as well as a static route to 2001:DB8:3C4D:3::/64, which is the remote LAN Fa0/0 off of R1, which is good. Now let's fix the route problem on R1 by adding a route that gives us access to the Server1 network.

```
R1(config)#ipv6 route ::/0 fastethernet 0/1 FE80::21A:6DFF:FE64:9B3
```

I want to point out that I didn't need to make the default route as difficult as I did. I entered both the exit interface and next-hop link-local address when just the exit interface or next-hop global addresses would be mandatory, but not the link-local. So it could have simply just been this:

```
R1(config)#ipv6 route ::/0 fa0/1
```

Next, we'll verify that we can now ping from PC1 to Server1:

```
C:\Users\Todd Lammle>ping 2001:db8:3c4d:1:a14c:8c33:2d1:be3d

Pinging 2001:db8:3c4d:1:a14c:8c33:2d1:be3d with 32 bytes of data:
Reply from 2001:db8:3c4d:1:a14c:8c33:2d1:be3d: time<1ms
Reply from 2001:db8:3c4d:1:a14c:8c33:2d1:be3d: time<1ms
Reply from 2001:db8:3c4d:1:a14c:8c33:2d1:be3d: time<1ms
Reply from 2001:db8:3c4d:1:a14c:8c33:2d1:be3d: time<1ms
```

Sweet—we're looking golden with this particular scenario! But know that it is still possible to have name resolution issues. If that were the case, you would just need to check your DNS server or local host table.

Moving on in the same way we did in the IPv4 troubleshooting section, it's a good time to check into your ACLs, especially if you're still having a problem after troubleshooting all your local LANs and all other potential routing issues.

Troubleshooting IPv6 Extended Access Lists

Let's create an extended IPv6 ACL on R2, pretty much just like we did in the IPv4 troubleshooting section.

First, understand that you can only create named extended IPv6 ACLs, so you don't need to specify standard or extended in your named list, and although you won't see any sequence numbers, you can still somewhat edit a named IPv6 ACL, meaning you can delete a single line but there is no way to insert a line other than at the end of the ACL.

In addition, every IPv4 access list has an implicit deny ip any any at the bottom; however, IPv6 access lists actually have *three* implied statements at the bottom:

- permit icmp any any nd-na
- permit icmp any any nd-ns
- deny ipv6 any any

The two permit statements are required for neighbor discovery, which is an important protocol in IPv6, because it's the replacement for ARP.

Using the network layout and IPv6 addresses in Figure 20.4, let's create an IPv6 extended named ACL that blocks Telnet to Server1 (with an IPv6 address of 2001:db8:3c4d:1:a14c:8c33:2d1:be3d) from PC1 (with a destination IPv6 address of 2001:db8:3c4d:3:2ef:1823:8938). Since it's an IPv6 extended named ACL (always), we'll place it closest to the source address if possible.

Step 1: Test that you can telnet to the remote host.

```
R1#telnet 2001:db8:3c4d:1:a14c:8c33:2d1:be3d
Trying 2001:db8:3c4d:1:a14c:8c33:2d1:be3d... Open

Server1>
```

Okay, great—but that was way too much effort! Let's create an entry into the hosts table of R1 so we don't have to type an IPv6 address when trying to access that host.

```
R1(config)#ipv6 host Server1 2001:db8:3c4d:1:a14c:8c33:2d1:be3d
R1(config)#do sh host
[output cut]

Host Port Flags Age Type Address(es)
Server1 None (perm, OK) 0 IPV6 2001:DB8:3C4D:1:A14C:8C33:2D1:BE3D
```

Now we can just type this from now on (the name is case sensitive).

```
R1#telnet Server1
Trying 2001:DB8:3C4D:1:A14C:8C33:2D1:BE3D... Open

Server1>
```

Or better yet, just the name (Telnet is the default).

```
R1#Server1
Trying 2001:DB8:3C4D:1:A14C:8C33:2D1:BE3D... Open

Server1>exit
```

Also, ping using the name.

```
R1#ping Server1
Type escape sequence to abort.
Sending 5, 100-byte ICMP Echos to 2001:DB8:3C4D:1:A14C:8C33:2D1:BE3D, timeout is
2 seconds:
!!!!!
Success rate is 100 percent (5/5), round-trip min/avg/max = 0/0/1 ms
```

Step 2: Create an ACL on R2 that stops Telnet to the remote host Server1 (2001:db8 :3c4d:1:a14c:8c33:2d1:be3d). The name is absolutely case sensitive when applying to an interface.

```
R2(config)#ipv6 access-list Block_Telnet
R2(config-ipv6-acl)#
```

Step 3: Once you have created the named list, add your test parameters.

```
R2(config-ipv6-acl)#deny tcp host 2001:DB8:3C4D:2:21A:6DFF:FE37:A44F host
2001:DB8:3C4D:1:A14C:8C33:2D1:BE3D eq telnet
R2(config-ipv6-acl)#permit ipv6 any any
```

Step 4: Configure your ACL on your router interface.

Since we're adding this to the R2 router in Figure 20.4, we'll add it to interface FastEthernet 0/1, stopping traffic closest to the source, and use the command ipv6 traffic-filter.

```
R2(config)#int fa0/1
R2(config-if)#ipv6 traffic-filter Block_Telnet out
```

Step 5: Test your access list by telnetting from Server1 on the R1 router.

```
R1#Server1
Trying 2001:DB8:3C4D:1:A14C:8C33:2D1:BE3D ...Open


Server1>
```

Hmm… and I tried really hard not to make a typo! Let's take a look.

```
R2#sh access-lists
IPv6 access list Block_Telnet
     deny tcp host 2001:DB8:3C4D:2:21A:6DFF:FE37:A44F host
2001:DB8:3C4D:1:A14C:8C33:2D1:BE3D eq telnet (96 match(es))
     permit ipv6 any any (181 match(es))
```

By verifying the IPv6 addresses with the interfaces of the routers, this list looks correct. It's important to verify your addresses with a show ipv6 interface brief command. Let's take a look.

```
R1#sh ipv6 int brief
FastEthernet0/0 [up/up]
     FE80::2E0:B0FF:FED2:B701
     2001:DB8:3C4D:3:21A:6DFF:FE37:A44E
FastEthernet0/1 [up/up]
     FE80::2E0:B0FF:FED2:B702
     2001:DB8:3C4D:2:21A:6DFF:FE37:A44F
```

Since R1 Fa0/1 is my source address, we can see that this address is correct in my ACL. Let's take a look at the destination device.

```
Server1#sh ipv6 int br
FastEthernet0/0 [up/up]
     FE80::260:70FF:FED8:DD01
     2001:DB8:3C4D:1:A14C:8C33:2D1:BE3D
```

Yup, this one is correct too! My IPv6 ACL is correct, so now we need to check our interface.

Step 6: Fix and/or edit your access list and/or interfaces.

```
R2#show running-config
[output cut]
!
interface FastEthernet0/0
     no ip address
     duplex auto
     speed auto
     ipv6 address 2001:DB8:3C4D:1:21A:6DFF:FE37:A443/64
     ipv6 rip 1 enable
!
interface FastEthernet0/1
     no ip address
     ipv6 traffic-filter Block_Telnet out
     duplex auto
     speed auto
     ipv6 address 2001:DB8:3C4D:2:21A:6DFF:FE64:9B3/64
     ipv6 rip 1 enable
!
```

Unlike IPv4, where we can use the show ip interface command to see if an ACL is set, we can only use the show running-config command to verify if an IPv6 ACL is set on an interface. In the above output, we can see that I certainly did set the ACL to the interface Fa0/1, but I configured it to out instead of in on the interface. Let's fix that.

```
R2#config t
R2(config)#int fa0/1
R2(config-if)#no ipv6 traffic-filter Block_Telnet out
R2(config-if)#ipv6 traffic-filter Block_Telnet in
```

Step 7: Retest your ACL.

```
R1#Server1

Trying 2001:DB8:3C4D:1:A14C:8C33:2D1:BE3D ...% Connection timed out; remote host
not responding
R1#
```

Looks good! Although I don't recommend using this method to block Telnet to a router, it was a great way to test our IPv6 ACLs.

Troubleshooting VLAN Connectivity

You know by now that VLANs are used to break up broadcast domains in a layer 2 switched network. You've also learned that we assign ports on a switch into a VLAN broadcast domain by using the switchport access vlan command.

The access port carries traffic for a single VLAN that the port is a member of. If members of one VLAN want to communicate to members in the same VLAN that are located on a different switch, then a port between the two switches needs to be either configured to be a member of this single VLAN or configured as a trunk link, which passes information on all VLANs by default.

We're going to use Figure 20.7 to reference as we go through the procedures for troubleshooting VLAN and trunking.

FIGURE 20.7   VLAN connectivity

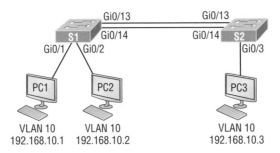

I'm going to begin with VLAN troubleshooting and then move on to trunk troubleshooting.

VLAN Troubleshooting

A couple of key times to troubleshoot VLANs are when and if you lose connectivity between hosts and when you're configuring new hosts into a VLAN but they're not working.

Here are the steps we'll follow to troubleshoot VLANs:

1. Verify the VLAN database on all your switches.
2. Verify your *Content Addressable Memory (CAM)* table.
3. Verify that your port VLAN assignments are configured correctly.

And here's a list of the commands we'll be using in the following sections:

```
Show vlan
Show mac address-table
Show interfaces interface switchport
switchport access vlan vlan
```

VLAN Troubleshooting Scenario

A manager calls and says they can't communicate to the new sales team member that just connected to the network. How would you proceed to solve this issue? Well, because the sales hosts are in VLAN 10, we'll begin with step 1 and verify that our databases on both switches are correct.

First, I'll use the show vlan or show vlan brief command to check if the expected VLAN is actually in the database. Here's a look at the VLAN database on S1:

S1#**sh vlan**

VLAN	Name	Status	Ports
1	default	active	Gi0/3, Gi0/4, Gi0/5, Gi0/6
			Gi0/7, Gi0/8, Gi0/9, Gi0/10
			Gi0/11, Gi0/12, Gi0/13, Gi0/14
			Gi0/15, Gi0/16, Gi0/17, Gi0/18
			Gi0/19, Gi0/20, Gi0/21, Gi0/22
			Gi0/23, Gi0/24, Gi0/25, Gi0/26
			Gi0/27, Gi0/28
10	**Sales**	**active**	**Gi0/1, Gi0/2**
20	Accounting	active	
26	Automation10	active	
27	VLAN0027	active	
30	Engineering	active	
170	VLAN0170	active	
501	Private501	active	
502	Private500	active	

[output cut]

This output shows that VLAN 10 is in the local database and that Gi0/1 and Gi0/2 are associated to VLAN 10.

So next, we'll go to step 2 and verify the CAM with the show mac address-table command:

S1#**sh mac address-table**

```
      Mac Address Table
-------------------------------------------
```

Vlan	Mac Address	Type	Ports
All	0100.0ccc.cccc	STATIC	CPU
[output cut]			
1	000d.2830.2f00	DYNAMIC	Gi0/24
1	0021.1c91.0d8d	DYNAMIC	Gi0/13
1	0021.1c91.0d8e	DYNAMIC	Gi0/14
1	b414.89d9.1882	DYNAMIC	Gi0/17
1	b414.89d9.1883	DYNAMIC	Gi0/18
1	ecc8.8202.8282	DYNAMIC	Gi0/15

```
   1    ecc8.8202.8283    DYNAMIC     Gi0/16
  10    001a.2f55.c9e8    DYNAMIC     Gi0/1
  10    001b.d40a.0538    DYNAMIC     Gi0/2
```
Total Mac Addresses for this criterion: 29

Okay—know that your switch will show quite a few MAC addresses assigned to the CPU at the top of the output; those MAC addresses are used by the switch to manage the ports. The very first MAC address listed is the base MAC address of the switch and used by STP in the bridge ID. In the preceding output, we can see that there are two MAC addresses associated with VLAN 10 and that it was dynamically learned. We can also establish that this MAC address is associated to Gi0/1. S1 looks really good!

Let's take a look at S2 now. First, let's confirm that port PC3 is connected and check its configuration. I'll use the show interfaces *interface* switchport command to do that:

S2#**sh interfaces gi0/3 switchport**
Name: Gi0/3
Switchport: Enabled
Administrative Mode: dynamic desirable
Operational Mode: static access
Administrative Trunking Encapsulation: negotiate
Operational Trunking Encapsulation: native
Negotiation of Trunking: On
Access Mode VLAN: 10 (Inactive)
Trunking Native Mode VLAN: 1 (default)
[output cut]

Okay—we can see that the port is enabled and that it's set to dynamic desirable. This means that if it connects to another Cisco switch, it will desire to trunk on that link. But keep in mind that we're using it as an access port, which is confirmed by the operational mode of static access. At the end of the output, the text shows Access Mode VLAN: 10 (Inactive). This is not a good thing! Let's examine S2's CAM and see what we find out:

S2#**sh mac address-table**
```
          Mac Address Table
-------------------------------------------

Vlan    Mac Address      Type      Ports
----    -----------      --------  -----
All     0100.0ccc.cccc   STATIC    CPU
[output cut]
  1     001b.d40a.0538   DYNAMIC   Gi0/13
  1     0021.1bee.a70d   DYNAMIC   Gi0/13
  1     b414.89d9.1884   DYNAMIC   Gi0/17
```

```
   1     b414.89d9.1885    DYNAMIC     Gi0/18
   1     ecc8.8202.8285    DYNAMIC     Gi0/16
Total Mac Addresses for this criterion: 26
```

Referring back to Figure 20.7, we can see that the host is connected to Gi0/3. The problem here is that we don't see a MAC address dynamically associated to Gi0/3 in the MAC address table. So what do we know so far that can help us? Well first, we can see that Gi0/3 is configured into VLAN 10, but that VLAN is inactive. Second, the host off of Gi0/3 doesn't appear in the CAM table. Now would be a good time to take a look at the VLAN database like this:

```
S2#sh vlan brief

VLAN Name                             Status    Ports
---- -------------------------------- --------- -------------------------------
1    default                          active    Gi0/1, Gi0/2, Gi0/4, Gi0/5
                                                Gi0/6, Gi0/7, Gi0/8, Gi0/9
                                                Gi0/10, Gi0/11, Gi0/12, Gi0/13
                                                Gi0/14, Gi0/15, Gi0/16, Gi0/17
                                                Gi0/18, Gi0/19, Gi0/20, Gi0/21
                                                Gi0/22, Gi0/23, Gi0/24, Gi0/25
                                                Gi0/26, Gi0/27, Gi0/28
26   Automation10                     active
27   VLAN0027                         active
30   Engineering                      active
170  VLAN0170                         active
[output cut]
```

Look at that: there is no VLAN 10 in the database! Clearly the problem, but also an easy one to fix by simply creating the VLAN in the database:

```
S2#config t
S2(config)#vlan 10
S2(config-vlan)#name Sales
```

That's all there is to it. Now let's check the CAM again:

```
S2#sh mac address-table
          Mac Address Table
-------------------------------------------

Vlan    Mac Address     Type      Ports
----    -----------     --------  -----
 All    0100.0ccc.cccc  STATIC    CPU
[output cut]
```

```
  1     0021.1bee.a70d    DYNAMIC     Gi0/13
 10     001a.6c46.9b09    DYNAMIC     Gi0/3
Total Mac Addresses for this criterion: 22
```

We're good to go—the MAC address off of Gi0/3 shows in the MAC address table configured into VLAN 10.

That was pretty straightforward, but if the port had been assigned to the wrong VLAN, I would have used the switch access vlan command to correct the VLAN membership. Here's an example of how to do that:

```
S2#config t
S2(config)#int gi0/3
S2(config-if)#switchport access vlan 10
S2(config-if)#do sh vlan
```

```
VLAN Name                            Status    Ports
---- -------------------------------- --------- -------------------------------
1    default                          active    Gi0/1, Gi0/2, Gi0/4, Gi0/5
                                                Gi0/6, Gi0/7, Gi0/8, Gi0/9
                                                Gi0/10, Gi0/11, Gi0/12, Gi0/13
                                                Gi0/14, Gi0/15, Gi0/16, Gi0/17
                                                Gi0/18, Gi0/19, Gi0/20, Gi0/21
                                                Gi0/22, Gi0/23, Gi0/24, Gi0/25
                                                Gi0/26, Gi0/27, Gi0/28
10   Sales                            active    Gi0/3
```

Okay, great—we can see that our port Gi0/3 is in the VLAN 10 membership. Now let's try to ping from PC1 to PC3:

```
PC1#ping 192.168.10.3
Type escape sequence to abort.
Sending 5, 100-byte ICMP Echos to 192.168.10.3, timeout is 2 seconds:
.....
Success rate is 0 percent (0/5)
```

No luck, so let's see if PC1 can ping PC2:

```
PC1#ping 192.168.10.2
Type escape sequence to abort.
Sending 5, 100-byte ICMP Echos to 192.168.10.2, timeout is 2 seconds:
!!!!!
Success rate is 100 percent (5/5), round-trip min/avg/max = 1/2/4 ms
PC1#
```

That worked! I can ping a host that's a member of the same VLAN connected to the same switch, but I can't ping to a host on another switch that's a member of the same VLAN, which is VLAN 10. To get to the bottom of this, let's quickly summarize what we've learned so far:

1. We know that the VLAN database is now correct on each switch.

2. The MAC address table shows the ARP entries for each host as well as a connection to each switch.

3. We've verified that our VLAN memberships are now correct on all the ports we're using.

But since we still can't ping to a host on another switch, we need to start checking out the connections between our switches.

Trunk Troubleshooting

You'll need to troubleshoot trunk links when you lose connectivity between hosts that are in the same VLAN but are located on different switches. Cisco refers to this as "VLAN leaking." Seems to me we are leaking VLAN 10 between switches somehow.

These are the steps we'll take to troubleshoot VLANs:

1. Verify that the interface configuration is set to the correct trunk parameters.

2. Verify that the ports are configured correctly.

3. Verify the native VLAN on each switch.

And here are the commands we'll use to perform trunk troubleshooting:

```
Show interfaces trunk
Show vlan
Show interfaces interface trunk
Show interfaces interface switchport
Show dtp interface interface
switchport mode
switchport mode dynamic
switchport trunk native vlan vlan
```

Okay, let's get started by checking ports Gi0/13 and Gi0/14 on each switch because these are what the figure is showing as forming the connection between our switches. We'll start with the show interfaces trunk command:

```
S1>sh interfaces trunk
```

```
S2>sh interfaces trunk
```

Not a scrap of output—that's definitely a bad sign! Let's take another look at the show vlan output on S1 and see what we can find out:

```
S1>sh vlan brief
```

```
VLAN Name                            Status    Ports
---- -------------------------------- --------- -------------------------------
1    default                          active    Gi0/3, Gi0/4, Gi0/5, Gi0/6
                                                Gi0/7, Gi0/8, Gi0/9, Gi0/10
                                                Gi0/11, Gi0/12, Gi0/13, Gi0/14
                                                Gi0/15, Gi0/16, Gi0/17, Gi0/18
                                                Gi0/19, Gi0/20, Gi0/21, Gi0/22
                                                Gi0/23, Gi0/24, Gi0/25, Gi0/26
                                                Gi0/27, Gi0/28
10   Sales                            active    Gi0/1, Gi0/2
20   Accounting                       active
[output cut]
```

Nothing new from when we checked it a few minutes ago, but look there under VLAN 1—we can see interfaces Gi0/13 and Gi0/14. This means that our ports between switches are members of VLAN 1 and will pass only VLAN 1 frames!

Typically I'll tell my students that if you type the show vlan command, you're really typing the nonexistent "show access ports" command since this output shows interfaces in access mode but doesn't show the trunk interfaces. This means that our ports between switches are access ports instead of trunk ports, so they'll pass information about only VLAN 1.

Let's go back over to the S2 switch to verify and see which port interfaces Gi0/13 and Gi0/14 are members of:

S2>sh vlan brief

```
VLAN Name                            Status    Ports
---- -------------------------------- --------- ------------------------------
1    default                          active    Gi0/1, Gi0/2, Gi0/4, Gi0/5
                                                Gi0/6, Gi0/7, Gi0/8, Gi0/9
                                                Gi0/10, Gi0/11, Gi0/12, Gi0/13
                                                Gi0/14, Gi0/15, Gi0/16, Gi0/17
                                                Gi0/18, Gi0/19, Gi0/20, Gi0/21
                                                Gi0/22, Gi0/23, Gi0/24, Gi0/25
                                                Gi0/26, Gi0/27, Gi0/28
10   Sales                            active    Gi0/3
```

Again, as with S1, the links between switches are showing in the output of the show vlan command, which means that they are not trunk ports. We can use the show interfaces *interface* switchport command to verify this as well:

S1#sho interfaces gi0/13 switchport
```
Name: Gi0/13
```

```
Switchport: Enabled
Administrative Mode: dynamic auto
Operational Mode: static access
Administrative Trunking Encapsulation: negotiate
Operational Trunking Encapsulation: native
Negotiation of Trunking: On
Access Mode VLAN: 1 (default)
Trunking Native Mode VLAN: 1 (default)
```

This output tells us that interface Gi0/13 is in dynamic auto mode. But its operational mode is static access, meaning it's not a trunk port. We can look closer at its trunking capabilities with the show interfaces *interface* trunk command:

S1#**sh interfaces gi0/1 trunk**

```
Port          Mode         Encapsulation  Status        Native vlan
Gi0/1         auto         negotiate      not-trunking  1
[output cut]
```

Sure enough—the port is not trunking, but we already knew that. Now we know it again. Notice that we can see that the native VLAN is set to VLAN 1, which is the default native VLAN. This means that VLAN 1 is the default VLAN for untagged traffic.

Now, before we check the native VLAN on S2 to verify that there isn't a mismatch, I want to point out a key fact about trunking and how we would get these ports between switches to do that.

Many Cisco switches support the Cisco proprietary *Dynamic Trunking Protocol (DTP)*, which is used to manage automatic trunk negotiation between switches. Cisco recommends that you don't allow this and to configure your switch ports manually instead. I agree with them!

Okay, with that in mind, let's check out our switch port Gi0/13 on S1 and view its DTP status. I'll use the show dtp interface *interface* command to view the DTP statistics:

S1#**sh dtp interface gi0/13**
```
DTP information for GigabitEthernet0/13:
  TOS/TAS/TNS:                          ACCESS/AUTO/ACCESS
  TOT/TAT/TNT:                          NATIVE/NEGOTIATE/NATIVE
  Neighbor address 1:                   00211C910D8D
  Neighbor address 2:                   000000000000
  Hello timer expiration (sec/state):   12/RUNNING
  Access timer expiration (sec/state):  never/STOPPED
```

Did you notice that our port GI0/13 from S1 to S2 is an access port configured to auto-negotiate using DTP? That's interesting, and I want to delve a bit deeper into the different port configurations and how they affect trunking capabilities to clarify why.

Access   Trunking is not allowed on a port set to access mode.

Auto   Will trunk to neighbor switch only if the remote port is set to on or to desirable mode. This creates the trunk based on the DTP request from the neighboring switch.

Desirable   This will trunk with all port modes except access. Ports set to dynamic desirable will communicate via DTP that the interface is attempting to become a trunk if the neighboring switch interface is able to become a trunk.

Nonegotiate   No DTP frames are generated from the interface. Can only be used if the neighbor interface is manually set as trunk or access.

Trunk (on)   Trunks with all switch port modes except access. Automatically enables trunking regardless of the state of the neighboring switch and regardless of any DTP requests.

Let's check out the different options available on the S1 switch with the switchport mode dynamic command:

```
S1(config-if)#switchport mode ?
  access       Set trunking mode to ACCESS unconditionally
  dot1q-tunnel set trunking mode to TUNNEL unconditionally
  dynamic      Set trunking mode to dynamically negotiate access or trunk mode
  private-vlan Set private-vlan mode
  trunk        Set trunking mode to TRUNK unconditionally

S1(config-if)#switchport mode dynamic ?
  auto     Set trunking mode dynamic negotiation parameter to AUTO
  desirable Set trunking mode dynamic negotiation parameter to DESIRABLE
```

From interface mode, use the switch mode trunk command to turn trunking on. You can also use the switch mode dynamic command to set the port to auto or desirable trunking modes. To turn off DTP and any type of negotiation, use the switchport nonegotiate command.

Let's take a look at S2 and see if we can figure out why our two switches didn't create a trunk:

```
S2#sh int gi0/13 switchport
Name: Gi0/13
Switchport: Enabled
Administrative Mode: dynamic auto
Operational Mode: static access
Administrative Trunking Encapsulation: negotiate
Operational Trunking Encapsulation: native
Negotiation of Trunking: On
```

Okay—we can see that the port is in dynamic auto and that it's operating as an access port. Let's look into this further:

```
S2#sh dtp interface gi0/13
DTP information for GigabitEthernet0/3:
  DTP information for GigabitEthernet0/13:
  TOS/TAS/TNS:                        ACCESS/AUTO/ACCESS
  TOT/TAT/TNT:                        NATIVE/NEGOTIATE/NATIVE
  Neighbor address 1:                 000000000000
  Neighbor address 2:                 000000000000
  Hello timer expiration (sec/state): 17/RUNNING
  Access timer expiration (sec/state): never/STOPPED
```

Do you see the problem? Don't be fooled—it's not that they're running in access mode; it's because two ports in dynamic auto will not form a trunk! This is a really common problem to look for since most Cisco switches ship in dynamic auto. The other issue you need to be aware of, as well as check for, is the frame-tagging method. Some switches run 802.1q, some run both 802.1q and *Inter-Switch Link (ISL) routing*, so be sure the tagging method is compatible between all of your switches!

It's time to fix our problem on the trunk ports between S1 and S2. All we need to do is to just fix one side of each link since dynamic auto will trunk with a port set to desirable or on:

```
S2(config)#int gi0/13
S2(config-if)#switchport mode dynamic desirable
23:11:37:%LINEPROTO-5-UPDOWN:Line protocol on Interface GigabitEthernet0/13,
changed state to down
23:11:37:%LINEPROTO-5-UPDOWN:Line protocol on Interface Vlan1, changed state to
down
23:11:40:%LINEPROTO-5-UPDOWN:Line protocol on Interface GigabitEthernet0/13,
changed state to up
23:12:10:%LINEPROTO-5-UPDOWN:Line protocol on Interface Vlan1, changed state to
up
S2(config-if)#do show int trunk

Port       Mode        Encapsulation  Status     Native vlan
Gi0/13     desirable   n-isl          trunking   1
[output cut]
```

Nice—it worked! With one side in Auto and the other now in Desirable, DTPs will be exchanged and they will trunk. Notice in the preceding output that the mode of S2's Gi0/13 link is desirable and that the switches actually negotiated ISL as a trunk encapsulation— go figure! But don't forget to notice the native VLAN. We'll work on the frame-tagging method and native VLAN in a minute, but first, let's configure our other link:

```
S2(config-if)#int gi0/14
S2(config-if)#switchport mode dynamic desirable
23:12:%LINEPROTO-5-UPDOWN:Line protocol on Interface GigabitEthernet0/14,
changed state to down
```

```
23:12:%LINEPROTO-5-UPDOWN:Line protocol on Interface GigabitEthernet0/14,
changed state to up
S2(config-if)#do show int trunk

Port       Mode          Encapsulation  Status        Native vlan
Gi0/13     desirable     n-isl          trunking      1
Gi0/14     desirable     n-isl          trunking      1

Port       Vlans allowed on trunk
Gi0/13     1-4094
Gi0/14     1-4094
[output cut]
```

Great, we now have two trunked links between switches. But I've got to say, I really don't like the ISL method of frame tagging since it can't send untagged frames across the link. So let's change our native VLAN from the default of 1 to 392. The number 392 just randomly sounded good at the moment. Here's what I entered on S1:

```
S1(config-if)#switchport trunk native vlan 392
S1(config-if)#
23:17:40: Port is not 802.1Q trunk, no action
```

See what I mean? I tried to change the native VLAN and ISL basically responded with, "What's a native VLAN?" Very annoying, so I'm going to take care of that now!

```
S1(config-if)#int range gi0/13 - 14
S1(config-if-range)#switchport trunk encapsulation ?
  dot1q      Interface uses only 802.1q trunking encapsulation when trunking
  isl        Interface uses only ISL trunking encapsulation when trunking
  negotiate  Device will negotiate trunking encapsulation with peer on
             interface

S1(config-if-range)#switchport trunk encapsulation dot1q
23:23:%LINEPROTO-5-UPDOWN:Line protocol on Interface GigabitEthernet0/13,
changed state to down
23:23:%LINEPROTO-5-UPDOWN: Line protocol on Interface GigabitEthernet0/14,
changed state to down
23:23:%CDP-4-NATIVE_VLAN_MISMATCH: Native VLAN mismatch discovered on
GigabitEthernet0/13 (392), with S2 GigabitEthernet0/13 (1).
23:23:%LINEPROTO-5-UPDOWN: Line protocol on Interface GigabitEthernet0/14,
changed state to up
23:23:%LINEPROTO-5-UPDOWN: Line protocol on Interface GigabitEthernet0/13,
changed state to up
23:23:%CDP-4-NATIVE_VLAN_MISMATCH: Native VLAN mismatch discovered on
GigabitEthernet0/13 (392), with S2 GigabitEthernet0/13 (1).
```

Okay, that's more like it! As soon as I changed the encapsulation type on S1, DTP frames changed the frame-tagging method between S2 to 802.1q. Since I had already changed the native VLAN on port Gi0/13 on S1, the switch lets us know, via CDP, that we now have a native VLAN mismatch. Let's proceed to deal with this by verifying our interfaces with the show interface trunk command:

```
S1#sh int trunk
Port       Mode       Encapsulation  Status     Native vlan
Gi0/13     auto       802.1q         trunking   392
Gi0/14     auto       802.1q         trunking   1

S2#sh int trunk
Port       Mode       Encapsulation  Status     Native vlan
Gi0/13     desirable  n-802.1q       trunking   1
Gi0/14     desirable  n-802.1q       trunking   1
```

Now notice that both links are running 802.1q and that S1 is in auto mode and S2 is in desirable mode. And we can see a native VLAN mismatch on port Gi0/13. We can also see the mismatched native VLAN with the show interfaces *interface* switchport command by looking at both sides of the link like this:

```
S2#sh interfaces gi0/13 switchport
Name: Gi0/13
Switchport: Enabled
Administrative Mode: dynamic desirable
Operational Mode: trunk
Administrative Trunking Encapsulation: negotiate
Operational Trunking Encapsulation: dot1q
Negotiation of Trunking: On
Access Mode VLAN: 1 (default)
Trunking Native Mode VLAN: 1 (default)

S1#sh int gi0/13 switchport
Name: Gi0/13
Switchport: Enabled
Administrative Mode: dynamic auto
Operational Mode: trunk
Administrative Trunking Encapsulation: dot1q
Operational Trunking Encapsulation: dot1q
Negotiation of Trunking: On
Access Mode VLAN: 1 (default)
Trunking Native Mode VLAN: 392 (Inactive)
```

So this has got to be bad, right? I mean really—are we sending any frames down that link or not? Let's see if we solved our little problem of not being able to ping to hosts from S1 to S2 and find out:

```
PC1#ping 192.168.10.3
Type escape sequence to abort.
Sending 5, 100-byte ICMP Echos to 192.168.10.3, timeout is 2 seconds:
!!!!!
Success rate is 100 percent (5/5), round-trip min/avg/max = 1/1/4 ms
```

Yes, it works! Not so bad after all. We've solved our problem, or at least most of it. Having a native VLAN mismatch only means you can't send untagged frames down the link, which are essentially management frames like CDP, for example. So although it's not the end of the world, it will prevent us from being able to remotely manage the switch, or even sending any other types of traffic down just that one VLAN.

So am I saying you can just leave this issue the way it is? Well, you could, but you won't. No, you'll fix it because if you don't, CDP will send you a message every minute telling you that there's a mismatch, which will drive you mad! So, this is how we'll stop that from happening:

```
S2(config)#int gi0/13
S2(config-if)#switchport trunk native vlan 392
S2(config-if)#^Z
S2#sh int trunk
```

Port	Mode	Encapsulation	Status	Native vlan
Gi0/13	desirable	n-802.1q	trunking	392
Gi0/14	desirable	n-802.1q	trunking	1
[output cut]				

All better! Both sides of the same link between switches are now using native VLAN 392 on Gigabit Ethernet 0/13. I want you to know that it's fine to have different native VLANs for each link if that's what works best for you. Each network is different and you have to make choices between options that will end up meeting your particular business requirements the most optimal way.

Summary

This chapter covered troubleshooting techniques from basic to advanced. Although most chapters in this book cover troubleshooting, this chapter focused purely on IPv4, IPv6, and VLAN/trunk troubleshooting.

You learned how to troubleshoot step-by-step from a host to a remote device. Starting with IPv4, you learned the steps to test the host and the local connectivity and then how to troubleshoot remote connectivity.

We then moved on to IPv6 and proceeded to troubleshoot using the same techniques that you learned with IPv4. It's important that you can use the verification commands that I used in each step of this chapter.

Last, I covered VLAN and trunk troubleshooting and how to go step-by-step through a switched network using verification commands and narrowing down the problem.

Exam Essentials

Remember the Cisco steps in troubleshooting an IPv4 and IPv6 network.

1. Check the cables to find out if there's a faulty cable or interface in the mix and verify the interface's statistics.
2. Make sure that devices are determining the correct path from the source to the destination. Manipulate the routing information if needed.
3. Verify that the default gateway is correct.
4. Verify that name resolution settings are correct.
5. Verify that there are no ACLs blocking traffic.

Remember the commands to verify and troubleshoot IPv4 and IPv6.   You need to remember and practice the commands used in this chapter, especially ping and traceroute (tracert on Windows). But we also used the Windows commands ipconfig and route print and Cisco's commands show ip int brief, show interface, and show route.

Remember how to verify an ARP cache with IPv6.   The command show ipv6 neighbors shows the IP-to-MAC-address resolution table on a Cisco router.

Remember to look at the statistics on a router and switch interface to determine problems.   You've got to be able to analyze interface statistics to find problems if they exist, and this includes speed and duplex settings, input queue drops, output queue drops, and input and output errors.

Understand what a native VLAN is and how to change it.   A native VLAN works with only 802.1q trunks and allows untagged traffic to traverse the trunk link. This is VLAN 1 by default on all Cisco switches, but it can be changed for security reasons with the switchport native vlan *vlan* command.

Written Lab 20

You can find the answers to this lab in Appendix A, "Answers to Written Labs."

Write the answers to the following questions:

1. If your IPv6 ARP cache shows an entry of INCMP, what does this mean?

2. You want traffic from VLAN 66 to traverse a trunked link untagged. Which command will you use?

3. What are the five modes you can set a switch port to?

4. You are having a network problem and have checked the cables to find out if there's a faulty cable or interface in the mix and also verified the interface's statistics, made sure that devices are determining the correct path from the source to the destination, and verified that you don't need to manipulate the routing. What are your next trouble-shooting steps?

5. You need to find out if the local IPv6 stack is working on a host. What command will you use?

Hands-on Labs for Troubleshooting

Please check www.lammle.com/ccna for the latest information and downloads available for studying when using my books. Preconfigured hands-on troubleshooting labs are available for download, with the answers to the troubleshooting problems found on my forum.

Review Questions

 The following questions are designed to test your understanding of this chapter's material. For more information on how to get additional questions, please www.lammle.com/ccna.

You can find the answers to these questions in Appendix B, "Answers to Review Questions."

1. You need to verify the IPv6 ARP cache on a router and see that the state of an entry is REACH. What does REACH mean?

    A. The router is reaching out to get the address.

    B. The entry is incomplete.

    C. The entry has reached the end of life and will be discarded from the table.

    D. A positive confirmation has been received by the neighbor and the path to it is functioning correctly.

2. What is the most common cause of interface errors?

    A. Speed mismatch

    B. Duplex mismatch

    C. Buffer overflows

    D. Collisions between a dedicated switch port and an NIC

3. Which command will verify the DTP status on a switch interface?

    A. `sh dtp status`

    B. `sh dtp status interface` *interface*

    C. `sh interface` *interface* `dtp`

    D. `sh dtp interface` *interface*

4. What mode will not allow DTP frames generated from a switch port?

    A. Nonegotiate

    B. Trunk

    C. Access

    D. Auto

5. The following output was generated by which command?

```
IPv6 Address                          Age Link-layer Addr State Interface
FE80::21A:6DFF:FE64:9B3                 0 001a.6c46.9b09  DELAY Fa0/1
2001:DB8:3C4D:2:21A:6DFF:FE64:9B3       0 001a.6c46.9b09  REACH Fa0/1
```

    A. show ip arp

    B. show ipv6 arp

    C. show ip neighbors

    D. show ipv6 neighbors

6. Which of the following states tells you that an interface has not communicated within the neighbor-reachable time frame?

    A. REACH

    B. STALE

    C. TIMEOUT

    D. CLEARED

7. You receive a call from a user who says that they cannot log in to a remote server, which only runs IPv6. Based on the output, what could the problem be?

```
C:\Users\Todd Lammle>ipconfig
    Connection-specific DNS Suffix  . : localdomain
    IPv6 Address. . . . . . . . . . . : 2001:db8:3c4d:3:ac3b:2ef:1823:8938
    Temporary IPv6 Address. . . . . . : 2001:db8:3c4d:3:2f33:44dd:211:1c3d
    Link-local IPv6 Address . . . . . : fe80::ac3b:2ef:1823:8938%11
    IPv4 Address. . . . . . . . . . . : 10.1.1.10
    Subnet Mask . . . . . . . . . . . : 255.255.255.0
    Default Gateway . . . . . . . . . : 10.1.1.1
```

    A. The global address is in the wrong subnet.

    B. The IPv6 default gateway has not been configured or received from the router.

    C. The link-local address has not been resolved, so the host cannot communicate to the router.

    D. There are two IPv6 global addresses configured. One must be removed from the configuration.

8. Your host cannot reach remote networks. Based on the output, what is the problem?

```
C:\Users\Server1>ipconfig

Windows IP Configuration

Ethernet adapter Local Area Connection:

    Connection-specific DNS Suffix  . : localdomain
    Link-local IPv6 Address . . . . . : fe80::7723:76a2:e73c:2acb%11
    IPv4 Address. . . . . . . . . . . : 172.16.20.254
    Subnet Mask . . . . . . . . . . . : 255.255.255.0
    Default Gateway . . . . . . . . . : 172.16.2.1
```

    A. The link-local IPv6 address is wrong.

    B. The IPv6 global address is missing.

   C. There is no DNS server configuration.

   D. The IPv4 default gateway address is misconfigured.

9. Which two commands will show you if you have a native VLAN mismatch?

   A. `show interface native vlan`

   B. `show interface trunk`

   C. `show interface interface switchport`

   D. `show switchport interface`

10. You connect two new Cisco 3560 switches together and expect them to use DTP and create a trunk. However, when you check statistics, you find that they are access ports and didn't negotiate. Why didn't DTP work on these Cisco switches?

   A. The ports on each side of the link are set to auto trunking.

   B. The ports on each side of the link are set to on.

   C. The ports on each side of the link are set to dynamic.

   D. The ports on each side of the link are set to desirable.

Chapter

21

Wide Area Networks

THE FOLLOWING ICND2 EXAM TOPICS ARE COVERED IN THIS CHAPTER:

✓ **3.0   WAN Technologies**

✓ **3.1   Configure and verify PPP and MLPPP on WAN interfaces using local authentication**

✓ **3.2   Configure, verify, and troubleshoot PPPoE client-side interfaces using local authentication**

✓ **3.3   Configure, verify, and troubleshoot GRE tunnel connectivity**

✓ **3.4   Describe WAN topology options**

   ▪ 3.4.a Point-to-point

   ▪ 3.4.b Hub and spoke

   ▪ 3.4.c Full mesh

   ▪ 3.4.d Single vs dual-homed

✓ **3.5   Describe WAN access connectivity options**

   ▪ 3.5.a MPLS

   ▪ 3.5.b MetroEthernet

   ▪ 3.5.c Broadband PPPoE

   ▪ 3.5.d Internet VPN (DMVPN, site-to-site VPN, client VPN)

✓ **3.6   Configure and verify single-homed branch connectivity using eBGP IPv4 (limited to peering and route advertisement using Network command only)**

The Cisco IOS supports a ton of different wide area network (WAN) protocols that help you extend your local LANs to other LANs at remote sites. And I don't think I have to tell you how essential information exchange between disparate sites is these days—it's absolutely vital! But even so, it wouldn't exactly be cost effective or efficient to install your own cable and connect all of your company's remote locations yourself, would it? A much better way to get this done is to just lease the existing installations that service providers already have in place.

This is exactly why I'm going to devote most of this chapter to covering the various types of connections, technologies, and devices used in today's WANs.

We'll also delve into how to implement and configure High-Level Data-Link Control (HDLC), and Point-to-Point Protocol (PPP). I'll describe Point-to-Point Protocol over Ethernet (PPPoE), cable, digital subscriber line (DSL), MultiProtocol Label Switching (MPLS), and Metro Ethernet plus last mile and long-range WAN technologies. I'll also introduce you to WAN security concepts, tunneling, virtual private networks (VPNs) and how to create a tunnel using GRE (Generic Routing Encapsulation). Finally, I'll close the chapter with a discussion on Border Gateway Protocol (BGP) and how to configure External BGP.

To find up-to-the-minute updates for this chapter, please see www.lammle .com/ccna or the book's web page at www.sybex.com/go/ccna.

Introduction to Wide Area Networks

Let's begin exploring WAN basics by asking, what's the difference between a *wide area network (WAN)* and a local area network (LAN)? Clearly there's the distance factor, but modern wireless LANs can cover some serious turf, so there's more to it than that. What about bandwidth? Here again, some really big pipes can be had for a price in many places, so that's not it either. What's the answer we're looking for?

A major distinction between a WAN and a LAN is that while you generally own a LAN infrastructure, you usually lease a WAN infrastructure from a service provider. And to be honest, modern technologies even blur this characteristic somewhat, but it still fits neatly into the context of Cisco's exam objectives!

I've already talked about the data link that you usually own back when we covered Ethernet, so now I'm going to focus on the type you usually don't own—the kind you typically lease from a service provider.

There are several reasons why WANs are necessary in corporate environments today.

LAN technologies provide amazing speeds (10/40/100 Gbps is now common) and at a great bang for your buck! But these type of solutions can only work well in relatively small geographic areas. You still need WANs in a communications environment because some business needs require connections to remote sites for many reasons, including the following:

- People in the regional or branch offices of an organization need to be able to communicate and share data.

- Organizations often want to share information with other organizations across large distances.

- Employees who travel on company business frequently need to access information that resides on their corporate networks.

Here are three major characteristics of WANs:

- WANs generally connect devices that are separated by a broader geographic area than a LAN can serve.

- WANs use the services of carriers such as telcos, cable companies, satellite systems, and network providers.

- WANs use serial connections of various types to provide access to bandwidth over large geographic areas.

The first key to understanding WAN technologies is to be familiar with the different WAN topologies, terms, and connection types commonly used by service providers to join your LAN networks together. We'll begin covering these topics now.

WAN Topology Options

A physical topology describes the physical layout of the network, in contrast to logical topologies, which describe the path a signal takes through the physical topology. There are three basic topologies for a WAN design.

Star or hub-and-spoke topology   This topology features a single hub (central router) that provides access from remote networks to a core router. Figure 21.1 illustrates a hub-and-spoke topology:

FIGURE 21.1   Hub-and-spoke

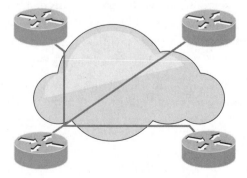

All communication among the networks travels through the core router. The advantages of a star physical topology are less cost and easier administration, but the disadvantages can be significant:

▪ The central router (hub) represents a single point of failure.

▪ The central router limits the overall performance for access to centralized resources. It is a single pipe that manages all traffic intended either for the centralized resources or for the other regional routers.

Fully meshed topology   In this topology, each routing node on the edge of a given packet-switching network has a direct path to every other node on the cloud. Figure 21.2 shows a fully meshed topology.

FIGURE 21.2   Fully meshed topology

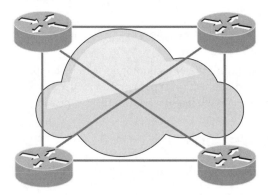

This configuration clearly provides a high level of redundancy, but the costs are the highest. So a fully meshed topology really isn't viable in large packet-switched networks. Here are some issues you'll contend with using a fully meshed topology:

▪ Many virtual circuits are required—one for every connection between routers, which brings up the cost.

▪ Configuration is more complex for routers without multicast support in non-broadcast environments.

Partially meshed topology   This type of topology reduces the number of routers within a network that have direct connections to all other routers in the topology. Figure 21.3 depicts a partially meshed topology.

FIGURE 21.3   Partially meshed topology

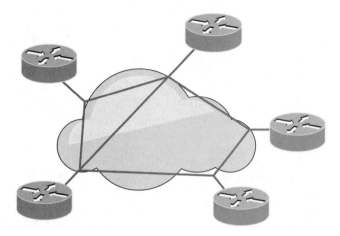

Unlike in the full mesh network, all routers are not connected to all other routers, but it still provides more redundancy than a typical hub-and-spoke design will. This is actually considered the most balanced design because it provides more virtual circuits, plus redundancy and performance.

Defining WAN Terms

Before you run out and order a WAN service type from a provider, you really need to understand the following terms that service providers typically use. Take a look at these in Figure 21.4:

FIGURE 21.4   WAN terms

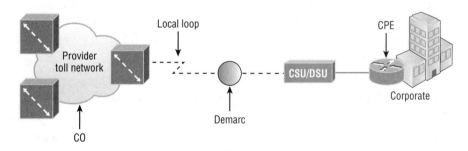

Customer premises equipment (CPE)   *Customer premises equipment (CPE)* is equipment that's typically owned by the subscriber and located on the subscriber's premises.

CSU/DSU   A channel service unit/data service unit (CSU/DSU) is a device that is used to connect data terminal equipment (DTE) to a digital circuit, such as a T1/T3 line. A device is considered DTE if it is either a source or destination for digital data—for example, PCs, servers, and routers. In Figure 21.4, the router is considered DTE because it is passing data to the CSU/DSU, which will forward the data to the service provider. Although the CSU/DSU connects to the service provider infrastructure using a telephone or coaxial cable, such as a T1 or E1 line, it connects to the router with a serial cable. The most important aspect to remember for the CCNA objectives is that the CSU/DSU provides clocking of the line to the router. You really need to understand this completely, which is why I'll cover it in depth later in the cabling the serial WAN interface configuration section!

Demarcation point   The *demarcation point* (demarc for short) is the precise spot where the service provider's responsibility ends and the CPE begins. It's generally a device in a telecommunications closet owned and installed by the telecommunications company (telco). It's your responsibility to cable (extended demarc) from this box to the CPE, which is usually a connection to a CSU/DSU, although more recently we see the provider giving us an Ethernet connection. Nice!

Local loop   The *local loop* connects the demarc to the closest switching office, referred to as the central office.

Central office (CO)   This point connects the customer's network to the provider's switching network. Make a mental note that a *central office (CO)* is sometimes also referred to as a *point of presence (POP)*.

Toll network   The *toll network* is a trunk line inside a WAN provider's network. This network is a collection of switches and facilities owned by the Internet service provider (ISP).

Optical fiber converters   Even though I'm not employing this device in Figure 21.4, optical fiber converters are used where a fiber-optic link terminates to convert optical signals into electrical signals and vice versa. You can also implement the converter as a router or switch module.

Definitely familiarize yourself with these terms, what they represent, and where they're located, as shown in Figure 21.4, because they're key to understanding WAN technologies.

WAN Connection Bandwidth

Next, I want you to know these basic but very important bandwidth terms used when referring to WAN connections:

Digital Signal 0 (DS0)   This is the basic digital signaling rate of 64 Kbps, equivalent to one channel. Europe uses the E0 and Japan uses the J0 to reference the same channel speed. Typical to T-carrier transmission, this is the generic term used by several multiplexed digital carrier systems and is also the smallest-capacity digital circuit. One DS0 = One voice/data line.

T1   Also referred to as a DS1, a T1 comprises 24 DS0 circuits bundled together for a total bandwidth of 1.544 Mbps.

E1   This is the European equivalent of a T1 and comprises 30 DS0 circuits bundled together for a bandwidth of 2.048 Mbps.

T3   Referred to as a DS3, a T3 comprises 28 DS1s bundled together, or 672 DS0s, for a bandwidth of 44.736 Mbps.

OC-3   Optical Carrier (OC) 3 uses fiber and is made up of three DS3s bundled together. It's made up of 2,016 DS0s and avails a total bandwidth of 155.52 Mbps.

OC-12   Optical Carrier 12 is made up of four OC-3s bundled together and contains 8,064 DS0s for a total bandwidth of 622.08 Mbps.

OC-48   Optical Carrier 48 is made up of four OC-12s bundled together and contains 32,256 DS0s for a total bandwidth of 2488.32 Mbps.

OC-192   Optical Carrier 192 is four OC-48s and contains 129,024 DS0s for a total bandwidth of 9953.28 Mbps.

WAN Connection Types

You're probably aware that a WAN can use a number of different connection types available on the market today. Figure 21.5 shows the different WAN connection types that can be used to connect your LANs (made up of data terminal equipment, or DTE) together over the data communication equipment (DCE) network.

FIGURE 21.5   WAN connection types

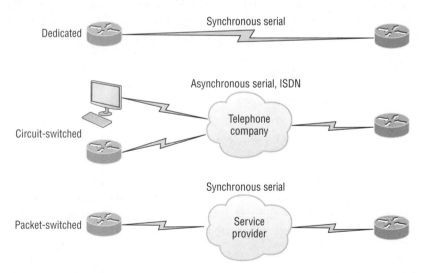

Let me explain the different WAN connection types in detail now:

Dedicated (leased lines)   These are usually referred to as a *point-to-point* or dedicated connections. A *leased line* is a pre-established WAN communications path that goes from the CPE through the DCE switch, then over to the CPE of the remote site. The CPE enables DTE networks to communicate at any time with no cumbersome setup procedures to muddle through before transmitting data. When you've got plenty of cash, this is definitely the way to go because it uses synchronous serial lines up to 45 Mbps. HDLC and PPP encapsulations are frequently used on leased lines, and I'll go over these with you soon.

Circuit switching   When you hear the term *circuit switching*, think phone call. The big advantage is cost; most plain old telephone service (POTS) and ISDN dial-up connections are not flat rate, which is their advantage over dedicated lines because you pay only for what you use, and you pay only when the call is established. No data can transfer before an end-to-end connection is established. Circuit switching uses dial-up modems or ISDN and is used for low-bandwidth data transfers. Okay, I know what you're thinking, "Modems? Did he say modems? Aren't those found only in museums now?" After all, with all the wireless technologies available, who would use a modem these days? Well, some people do have ISDN; it's still viable and there are a few who still use a modem now and then. And circuit switching can be used in some of the newer WAN technologies as well.

Packet switching   This is a WAN switching method that allows you to share bandwidth with other companies to save money, just like a super old party line, where homes shared the same phone number and line to save money. *Packet switching* can be thought of as a network that's designed to look like a leased line yet it charges you less, like circuit switching does. As usual, you get what you pay for, and there's definitely a serious downside to this technology. If you need to transfer data constantly, well, just forget about this option and get a leased line instead! Packet switching will only really work for you if your data transfers are bursty, not continuous; think of a highway, where you can only go as fast as the traffic—packet switching is the same thing. Frame Relay and X.25 are packet-switching technologies with speeds that can range from 56 Kbps up to T3 (45 Mbps).

MultiProtocol Label Switching (MPLS) uses a combination of both circuit switching and packet switching.

WAN Support

Cisco supports many layer 2 WAN encapsulations on its serial interfaces, including HDLC, PPP, and Frame Relay, which map to the Cisco exam objectives. You can view them via the encapsulation ? command from any serial interface, but understand that the output you'll get can vary based upon the specific IOS version you're running:

```
Corp#config t
Corp(config)#int s0/0/0
Corp(config-if)#encapsulation ?
  atm-dxi       ATM-DXI encapsulation
  frame-relay   Frame Relay networks
```

```
hdlc          Serial HDLC synchronous
lapb          LAPB (X.25 Level 2)
ppp           Point-to-Point protocol
smds          Switched Megabit Data Service (SMDS)
x25           X.25
```

I also want to point out that if I had other types of interfaces on my router, I would have a different set of encapsulation options. And never forget that you can't configure an Ethernet encapsulation on a serial interface or vice versa!

Next, I'm going to define the most prominently known WAN protocols used in the latest Cisco exam objectives: Frame Relay, ISDN, HDLC, PPP, PPPoE, cable, DSL, MPLS, ATM, Cellular 3G/4G, VSAT, and Metro Ethernet. Just so you know, the only WAN protocols you'll usually find configured on a serial interface are HDLC, PPP, and Frame Relay, but who said you're stuck with using only serial interfaces for wide area connections? Actually, we're beginning to see fewer and fewer serial connections because they're not as scalable or cost effective as a Fast Ethernet connection to your ISP.

Frame Relay   A packet-switched technology that made its debut in the early 1990s, *Frame Relay* is a high-performance Data Link and Physical layer specification. It's pretty much a successor to X.25, except that much of the technology in X.25 that was used to compensate for physical errors like noisy lines has been eliminated. An upside to Frame Relay is that it can be more cost effective than point-to-point links, plus it typically runs at speeds of 64 Kbps up to 45 Mbps (T3). Another Frame Relay benefit is that it provides features for dynamic bandwidth allocation and congestion control.

ISDN   *Integrated Services Digital Network (ISDN)* is a set of digital services that transmit voice and data over existing phone lines. ISDN offers a cost-effective solution for remote users who need a higher-speed connection than analog POTS dial-up links can give them, and it's also a good choice to use as a backup link for other types of links, such as Frame Relay or T1 connections.

HDLC   *High-Level Data-Link Control (HDLC)* was derived from Synchronous Data Link Control (SDLC), which was created by IBM as a Data Link connection protocol. HDLC works at the Data Link layer and creates very little overhead compared to Link Access Procedure, Balanced (LAPB).

Generic HDLC wasn't intended to encapsulate multiple Network layer protocols across the same link—the HDLC header doesn't contain any identification about the type of protocol being carried inside the HDLC encapsulation. Because of this, each vendor that uses HDLC has its own way of identifying the Network layer protocol, meaning each vendor's HDLC is proprietary with regard to its specific equipment.

PPP   *Point-to-Point Protocol (PPP)* is a pretty famous, industry-standard protocol. Because all multiprotocol versions of HDLC are proprietary, PPP can be used to create point-to-point links between different vendors' equipment. It uses a Network Control Protocol field in the Data Link header to identify the Network layer protocol being carried and allows authentication and multilink connections to be run over asynchronous and synchronous links.

PPPoE   *Point-to-Point Protocol over Ethernet* encapsulates PPP frames in Ethernet frames and is usually used in conjunction with xDSL services. It gives you a lot of the familiar PPP features like authentication, encryption, and compression, but there's a downside—it has a lower maximum transmission unit (MTU) than standard Ethernet does. If your firewall isn't solidly configured, this little factor can really give you some grief!

Still somewhat popular in the United States, PPPoE's main feature is that it adds a direct connection to Ethernet interfaces while also providing DSL support. It's often used by many hosts on a shared Ethernet interface for opening PPP sessions to various destinations via at least one bridging modem.

Cable   In a modern *hybrid fiber-coaxial (HFC)* network, typically 500 to 2,000 active data subscribers are connected to a certain cable network segment, all sharing the upstream and downstream bandwidth. HFC is a telecommunications industry term for a network that incorporates both optical fiber and coaxial cables to create a broadband network. The actual bandwidth for Internet service over a cable TV (CATV) line can be up to about 27 Mbps on the download path to the subscriber, with about 2.5 Mbps of bandwidth on the upload path. Typically users get an access speed from 256 Kbps to 6 Mbps. This data rate varies greatly throughout the United States and can be much, much higher today.

DSL   Digital subscriber line is a technology used by traditional telephone companies to deliver advanced services such as high-speed data and sometimes video over twisted-pair copper telephone wires. It typically has lower data-carrying capacity than HFC networks, and data speeds can be limited in range by line lengths and quality. Digital subscriber line is not a complete end-to-end solution but rather a Physical layer transmission technology like dial-up, cable, or wireless. DSL connections are deployed in the last mile of a local telephone network—the local loop. The connection is set up between a pair of DSL modems on either end of a copper wire located between the customer premises equipment (CPE) and the Digital Subscriber Line Access Multiplexer (DSLAM). A DSLAM is the device that is located at the provider's central office (CO) and concentrates connections from multiple DSL subscribers.

MPLS   *MultiProtocol Label Switching (MPLS)* is a data-carrying mechanism that emulates some properties of a circuit-switched network over a packet-switched network. MPLS is a switching mechanism that imposes labels (numbers) to packets and then uses them to forward the packets. The labels are assigned on the edge of the MPLS network, and forwarding inside the MPLS network is carried out solely based on the labels. The labels usually correspond to a path to layer 3 destination addresses, which is on par with IP destination-based routing. MPLS was designed to support the forwarding of protocols other than TCP/IP. Because of this, label switching within the network is achieved the same way irrespective of the layer 3 protocol. In larger networks, the result of MPLS labeling is that only the edge routers perform a routing lookup. All the core routers forward packets based on the labels, which makes forwarding the packets through the service provider network faster. This is a big reason most companies have replaced their Frame Relay networks with MPLS service today. Last, you can use Ethernet with MPLS to connect a WAN, and this is called Ethernet over MPLS, or EoMPLS.

ATM   Asynchronous Transfer Mode (ATM) was created for time-sensitive traffic, providing simultaneous transmission of voice, video, and data. ATM uses cells that are a fixed 53 bytes long instead of packets. It also can use isochronous clocking (external clocking) to help the data move faster. Typically, if you're running Frame Relay today, you will be running Frame Relay over ATM.

Cellular 3G/4G   Having a wireless hot spot in your pocket is pretty normal these days. If you have a pretty current cellular phone, then you can probably can gain access through your phone to the Internet. You can even get a 3G/4G card for an ISR router that's useful for a small remote office that's in the coverage area.

VSAT   Very Small Aperture Terminal (VSAT) can be used if you have many locations geographically spread out in a large area. VSAT uses a two-way satellite ground station with dishes available through many companies like Dish Network or Hughes and connects to satellites in geosynchronous orbit. A good example of where VSATs are a useful, cost-effective solution would be companies that use satellite communications to VSATs, like gasoline stations that have hundreds or thousands of locations spread out over the entire country. How could you connect them otherwise? Using leased lines would be cost prohibitive and dial-ups would be way too slow and hard to manage. Instead, the signal from the satellite connects to many remote locations at once, which is much more cost effective and efficient! It's a lot faster than a modem (about 10x faster), but the upload speeds only come in at about 10 percent of their download speeds.

Metro Ethernet   Metropolitan-area Ethernet is a metropolitan area network (MAN) that's based on Ethernet standards and can connect a customer to a larger network and the Internet. If available, businesses can use Metro Ethernet to connect their own offices together, which is another very cost-effective connection option. MPLS-based Metro Ethernet networks use MPLS in the ISP by providing an Ethernet or fiber cable to the customer as a connection. From the customer, it leaves the Ethernet cable, jumps onto MPLS, and then Ethernet again on the remote side. This is a smart and thrifty solution that's very popular if you can get it in your area.

Cisco Intelligent WAN (IWAN)

Bottom line, WANs are expensive, and if they're not deployed correctly, they can be a very costly mistake! Here's a short list of how most companies are currently deployingWANs:

- Using MPLS links for the branch and remote locations to headquarters.
- Leveraging low-cost, high-bandwidth Internet links as backup for the MPLS links.

Still, even these solutions are no longer good enough. The pressure on today's WANs has increased dramatically to make them handle more and more, as shown in Figure 21.6:

- Steadily increasing cloud traffic like Google Docs, Office365, etc.

- Unprecedented proliferation of mobile devices.

- A legion of high-bandwidth applications like Video—lots of video!

FIGURE 21.6   Branch WAN challenges

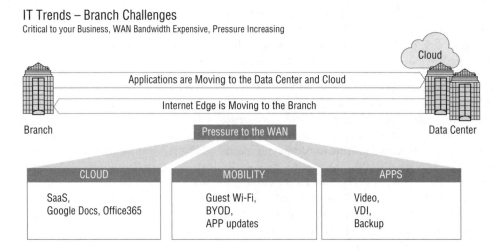

Here are two new winning strategies that many businesses in today's fast paced market utilize:

- Using a low-cost Internet link set in an active/active mode rather than just sitting there idly most of the time in active/standby mode.

- Leveraging the Internet link for remote employees accessing public clouds or the Internet as well as for guest users' access.

These new strategies offer cost reductions for your company plus increased WAN capacity. They result in improved performance and scalability from the end user point of view and pave the way for implementing cloud, mobility, and BYOD effectively.

So what does the Cisco Intelligent WAN (IWAN) have to do with all this? The Cisco IWAN enables application service-level agreements (SLAs), endpoint type, and network conditions so that Cisco IWAN traffic is dynamically routed to deliver the best-quality experience. The savings over traditional WANs not only allows companies to pay for the infrastructure upgrades, they can also free up resources for new business innovation.

IT organizations can now provide more bandwidth to their branch office connections by using less-expensive WAN transport options, all without affecting performance, security, or reliability, as pictured in Figure 21.7:

FIGURE 21.7   Intelligent WAN

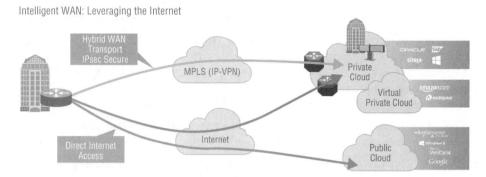

- Saves customers money – 6 month ROI
- Improves application response times
- Enables cloud, mobility, and BYOD in the branch

Cisco's IWAN solution is based upon four technology pillars demonstrated in Figure 21.8:

FIGURE 21.8   IWAN four technology pillars

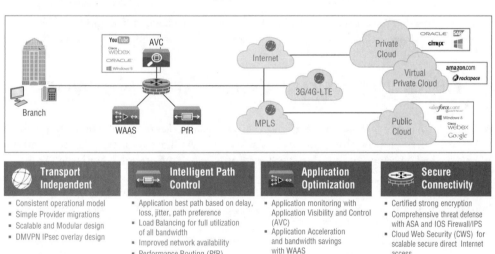

Transport Independent Connectivity   IWAN should provide consistent connectivity over the entire access network while also providing simplicity, scalability, and modularity. It also allows for a simple, efficient migration strategy. Keep in mind that you don't typically use a design based on DMVPN to achieve this.

Intelligent Path Control   This solution is intended to help utilize full WAN links without over-subscribing lines. Through Intelligent Path Control (Path Selection), routing decisions are made dynamically by looking at application type, policies, and path status. This allows new cloud traffic and guest services as well as video services to easily load-balance across multiple links!

Application Optimization   This solution provides an application-aware network for optimized performance, providing full visibility and control at the Application layer (layer 7). It uses technologies like AVC and NBAR2, NetFlow, QoS, and more to reach optimization goals.

High Secure Connectivity   US government FIPS 140-2 certified IPsec solutions provide security, privacy, and dynamic site-to-site IP Security (IPsec) tunnels with DMVPN. Threat defense with zone-based firewalls permit access to the Internet using the Cloud Web Security (CWS) Connector.

IWAN also gives us more useful technologies, like the following:

Intelligent Virtualization   Cisco's IWAN offers a virtual WAN overlay over any transport type, which doesn't compromise application performance, availability, or security.

Automation   This Cisco IWAN technology provides network services by provisioning security and application policies.

Cloud Integration   An innovation that permits private cloud integration through APIC and public cloud application optimization with security.

Service Virtualization   Cisco's IWAN delivers virtual services on specialized router platforms as well as virtual routers and services on x86 server platforms.

Self-Learning Networks   Using policies, this technology leverages network analytics to proactively optimize the infrastructure.

We're going to pause a second and head back in time to cover some good old serial connections, which still actually happen to be a valid form of connecting via a WAN.

Cabling the Serial Wide Area Network

As you can imagine, there are a few things that you need to know before connecting your WAN to ensure that everything goes well. For starters, you have to understand the kind of WAN Physical layer implementation that Cisco provides and be familiar with the various types of WAN serial connectors involved.

The good news is that Cisco serial connections support almost any type of WAN service. Your typical WAN connection is a dedicated leased line using HDLC or PPP, with speeds that can kick it up to 45 Mbps (T3).

HDLC, PPP, and Frame Relay can use the same Physical layer specifications. I'll go over the various types of connections and then move on to tell you all about the WAN protocols specified in the ICND2 and CCNA R/S objectives.

Serial Transmission

WAN serial connectors use *serial transmission*, something that takes place 1 bit at a time over a single channel.

Older Cisco routers have used a proprietary 60-pin serial connector that you have to get from Cisco or a provider of Cisco equipment. Cisco also has a new, smaller proprietary serial connection that's about one-tenth the size of the 60-pin basic serial cable called the *smart-serial.* You have to verify that you have the right type of interface in your router before using this cable connector.

The type of connector you have on the other end of the cable depends on your service provider and its particular end-device requirements. There are several different types of ends you'll run into:

- EIA/TIA-232—Allowed speed up to 64 Kbps on 24-pin connector

- EIA/TIA-449

- V.35—Standard used to connect to a CSU/DSU, with speeds up to 2.048 Mbps using a 34-pin rectangular connector

- EIA-530

Make sure you're clear on these things: Serial links are described in frequency, or cycles per second (hertz). The amount of data that can be carried within these frequencies is called *bandwidth*. Bandwidth is the amount of data in bits per second that the serial channel can carry.

Data Terminal Equipment and Data Communication Equipment

By default, router interfaces are typically *data terminal equipment (DTE)*, and they connect into *data communication equipment (DCE)* like a *channel service unit/data service unit (CSU/DSU)* using a V.35 connector. CSU/DSU then plugs into a demarcation location (demarc) and is the service provider's last responsibility. Most of the time, the demarc is a jack that has an RJ45 (8-pin modular) female connector located in a telecommunications closet.

Actually, you may already have heard of demarcs. If you've ever had the glorious experience of reporting a problem to your service provider, they'll usually tell you everything tests out fine up to the demarc, so the problem must be the CPE, or customer premises equipment. In other words, it's your problem, not theirs!

Figure 21.9 shows a typical DTE-DCE-DTE connection and the devices used in the network.

FIGURE 21.9   DTE-DCE-DTE WAN connection: Clocking is typically provided by the DCE network to routers. In nonproduction environments, a DCE network is not always present.

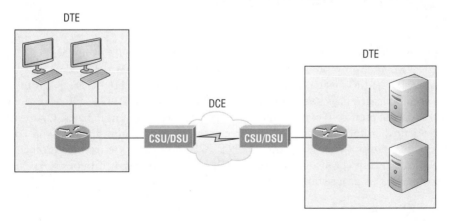

The idea behind a WAN is to be able to connect two DTE networks through a DCE network. The DCE network includes the CSU/DSU, through the provider's wiring and switches, all the way to the CSU/DSU at the other end. The network's DCE device (CSU/DSU) provides clocking to the DTE-connected interface (the router's serial interface).

As mentioned, the DCE network provides clocking to the router; this is the CSU/DSU. If you have a nonproduction network and you're using a WAN crossover type of cable and do not have a CSU/DSU, then you need to provide clocking on the DCE end of the cable by using the clock rate command. To find out which interface needs the clock rate command, use the show controllers *int* command:

```
Corp#sh controllers s0/0/0
Interface Serial0/0/0
Hardware is PowerQUICC MPC860
DCE V.35, clock rate 2000000
```

The preceding output shows a DCE interface that has the clock rate set to 2000000, which is the default for ISR routers. This next output shows a DTE connector, so you don't need enter the clock rate command on this interface:

```
SF#sh controllers s0/0/0
Interface Serial0/0/0
Hardware is PowerQUICC MPC860
DTE V.35 TX and RX clocks detected
```

Terms such as *EIA/TIA-232, V.35, X.21*, and *HSSI (High-Speed Serial Interface)* describe the Physical layer between the DTE (router) and DCE device (CSU/DSU).

High-Level Data-Link Control (HDLC) Protocol

The High-Level Data-Link Control (HDLC) protocol is a popular ISO-standard, bit-oriented, Data Link layer protocol. It specifies an encapsulation method for data on synchronous serial data links using frame characters and checksums. HDLC is a point-to-point protocol used on leased lines. No authentication is provided by HDLC.

In byte-oriented protocols, control information is encoded using entire bytes. On the other hand, bit-oriented protocols use single bits to represent the control information. Some common bit-oriented protocols are SDLC and HDLC; TCP and IP are byte-oriented protocols.

HDLC is the default encapsulation used by Cisco routers over synchronous serial links. And Cisco's HDLC is proprietary, meaning it won't communicate with any other vendor's

HDLC implementation. But don't give Cisco grief for it—*everyone's* HDLC implementation is proprietary. Figure 21.10 shows the Cisco HDLC format.

FIGURE 21.10   Cisco's HDLC frame format: Each vendor's HDLC has a proprietary data field to support multiprotocol environments.

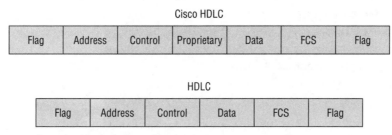

The reason every vendor has a proprietary HDLC encapsulation method is that each vendor has a different way for the HDLC protocol to encapsulate multiple Network layer protocols. If the vendors didn't have a way for HDLC to communicate the different layer 3 protocols, then HDLC would be able to operate in only a single layer 3 protocol environment. This proprietary header is placed in the data field of the HDLC encapsulation.

It's pretty simple to configure a serial interface if you're just going to connect two Cisco routers across a T1, for example. Figure 21.11 shows a point-to-point connection between two cities.

FIGURE 21.11   Configuring Cisco's HDLC proprietary WAN encapsulation

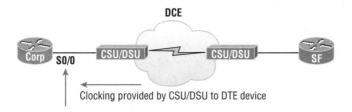

We can easily configure the routers with a basic IP address and then enable the interface. Assuming the link to the ISP is up, the routers will start communicating using the default HDLC encapsulation. Let's take a look at the Corp router configuration so you can see just how easy this can be:

```
Corp(config)#int s0/0
Corp(config-if)#ip address 172.16.10.1 255.255.255.252
Corp(config-if)#no shut


Corp#sh int s0/0
```

```
Serial0/0 is up, line protocol is up
  Hardware is PowerQUICC Serial
  Internet address is 172.16.10.1/30
  MTU 1500 bytes, BW 1544 Kbit, DLY 20000 usec,
    reliability 255/255, txload 1/255, rxload 1/255
  Encapsulation HDLC, loopback not set
  Keepalive set (10 sec)
```

```
Corp#sh run | begin interface Serial0/0
interface Serial0/0
 ip address 172.16.10.1 255.255.255.252
```

Note that all I did was add an IP address before I then enabled the interface—pretty simple! Now, as long as the SF router is running the default serial encapsulation, this link will come up. Notice in the preceding output that the show interface command does show the encapsulation type of HDLC, but the output of show running-config does not. This is important—remember that if you don't see an encapsulation type listed under a serial interface in the active configuration file, you know it's running the default encapsulation of HDLC.

So let's say you have only one Cisco router and you need to connect to a non-Cisco router because your other Cisco router is on order or something. What would you do? You couldn't use the default HDLC serial encapsulation because it wouldn't work. Instead, you would need to go with an option like PPP, an ISO-standard way of identifying the upper-layer protocols. Now is a great time to get into more detail about PPP as well as how to connect to routers using the PPP encapsulation. You can check out RFC 1661 for more information on the origins and standards of PPP.

Point-to-Point Protocol (PPP)

Point-to-Point Protocol (PPP) is a Data Link layer protocol that can be used over either asynchronous serial (dial-up) or synchronous serial media. It relies on Link Control Protocol (LCP) to build and maintain data-link connections. Network Control Protocol (NCP) enables multiple Network layer protocols (routed protocols) to be used on a point-to-point connection.

Because HDLC is the default serial encapsulation on Cisco serial links and it works great, why in the world would you choose to use PPP? Well, the basic purpose of PPP is to transport layer 3 packets across a Data Link layer point-to-point link, and it's nonproprietary. So unless you have all Cisco routers, you need PPP on your serial interfaces because the HDLC encapsulation is Cisco proprietary, remember? Plus, since PPP can encapsulate several layer 3 routed protocols and provide authentication, dynamic addressing, and callback, PPP could actually be the best encapsulation solution for you over HDLC anyway.

Figure 21.12 shows the PPP protocol stack compared to the OSI reference model.

FIGURE 21.12   Point-to-Point Protocol stack

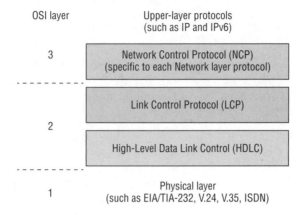

PPP contains four main components:

EIA/TIA-232-C, V.24, V.35, and ISDN   A Physical layer international standard for serial communication.

HDLC   A method for encapsulating datagrams over serial links.

LCP   A method of establishing, configuring, maintaining, and terminating the point-to-point connection. It also provides features such as authentication. I'll give you a complete list of these features in the next section.

NCP   NCP is a method of establishing and configuring different Network layer protocols for transport across the PPP link. NCP is designed to allow the simultaneous use of multiple Network layer protocols. Two examples of protocols here are Internet Protocol Control Protocol (IPCP) and Cisco Discovery Protocol Control Protocol (CDPCP).

Burn it into your mind that the PPP protocol stack is specified at the Physical and Data Link layers only. NCP is used to allow communication of multiple Network layer protocols by identifying and encapsulating the protocols across a PPP data link.

Remember that if you have a Cisco router and a non-Cisco router connected with a serial connection, you must configure PPP or another encapsulation method like Frame Relay because the HDLC default just won't work!

Next, we'll cover the options for LCP and PPP session establishment.

Link Control Protocol (LCP) Configuration Options

Link Control Protocol (LCP) offers different PPP encapsulation options, including the following:

Authentication   This option tells the calling side of the link to send information that can identify the user. The two methods for this task are PAP and CHAP.

Compression   This is used to increase the throughput of PPP connections by compressing the data or payload prior to transmission. PPP decompresses the data frame on the receiving end.

Error detection   PPP uses Quality and Magic Number options to ensure a reliable, loop-free data link.

Multilink PPP (MLP)   Starting with IOS version 11.1, multilink is supported on PPP links with Cisco routers. This option makes several separate physical paths appear to be one logical path at layer 3. For example, two T1s running multilink PPP would show up as a single 3 Mbps path to a layer 3 routing protocol.

PPP callback   On a dial-up connection, PPP can be configured to call back after successful authentication. *PPP callback* can be a very good thing because it allows us to keep track of usage based upon access charges for accounting records and a bunch of other reasons. With callback enabled, a calling router (client) will contact a remote router (server) and authenticate. Predictably, both routers have to be configured for the callback feature for this to work. Once authentication is completed, the remote router will terminate the connection and then reinitiate a connection to the calling router from the remote router.

PPP Session Establishment

When PPP connections are started, the links go through three phases of session establishment, as shown in Figure 21.13:

FIGURE 21.13   PPP session establishment

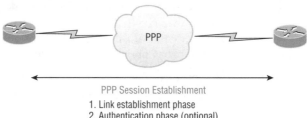

PPP Session Establishment
1. Link establishment phase
2. Authentication phase (optional)
3. Network layer protocol phase

Link-establishment phase   LCP packets are sent by each PPP device to configure and test the link. These packets contain a field called Configuration Option that allows each device to see the size of the data, the compression, and authentication. If no Configuration Option field is present, then the default configurations will be used.

Authentication phase   If required, either CHAP or PAP can be used to authenticate a link. Authentication takes place before Network layer protocol information is read, and it's also possible that link-quality determination will occur simultaneously.

Network layer protocol phase   PPP uses the *Network Control Protocol (NCP)* to allow multiple Network layer protocols to be encapsulated and sent over a PPP data link. Each Network layer protocol (e.g., IP, IPv6, which are routed protocols) establishes a service with NCP.

PPP Authentication Methods

There are two methods of authentication that can be used with PPP links:

Password Authentication Protocol (PAP)   The *Password Authentication Protocol (PAP)* is the less secure of the two methods. Passwords are sent in clear text and PAP is performed only upon the initial link establishment. When the PPP link is first established, the remote node sends the username and password back to the originating target router until authentication is acknowledged. Not exactly Fort Knox!

Challenge Handshake Authentication Protocol (CHAP)   The *Challenge Handshake Authentication Protocol (CHAP)* is used at the initial startup of a link and at periodic checkups on the link to ensure that the router is still communicating with the same host.

After PPP finishes its initial link-establishment phase, the local router sends a challenge request to the remote device. The remote device sends a value calculated using a one-way hash function called MD5. The local router checks this hash value to make sure it matches. If the values don't match, the link is immediately terminated.

CHAP authenticates at the beginning of the session and periodically throughout the session.

Configuring PPP on Cisco Routers

Configuring PPP encapsulation on an interface is really pretty straightforward. To configure it from the CLI, use these simple router commands:

```
Router#config t
Router(config)#int s0
Router(config-if)#encapsulation ppp
Router(config-if)#^Z
```

Of course, PPP encapsulation has to be enabled on both interfaces connected to a serial line in order to work, and there are several additional configuration options available to you via the ppp ? command.

Configuring PPP Authentication

After you configure your serial interface to support PPP encapsulation, you can then configure authentication using PPP between routers. But first, you must set the hostname of the router if it hasn't been set already. After that, you set the username and password for the remote router that will be connecting to your router, like this:

```
Router#config t
Router(config)#hostname RouterA
RouterA(config)#username RouterB password cisco
```

When using the `username` command, remember that the username is the hostname of the remote router that's connecting to your router. And it's case sensitive too. Also, the password on both routers must be the same. It's a plain-text password that you can see with a `show run` command, and you can encrypt the password by using the command `service password-encryption`. You must have a username and password configured for each remote system you plan to connect to. The remote routers must also be similarly configured with usernames and passwords.

Now, after you've set the hostname, usernames, and passwords, choose either CHAP or PAP as the authentication method:

```
RouterA#config t
RouterA(config)#int s0
RouterA(config-if)#ppp authentication chap pap
RouterA(config-if)#^Z
```

If both methods are configured on the same line as I've demonstrated here, then only the first method will be used during link negotiation. The second acts as a backup just in case the first method fails.

There is yet another command you can use if you're using PAP authentication for some reason. The `ppp pap sent-username <username> password <password>` command enables outbound PAP authentication. The local router uses the username and password that the `ppp pap sent-username` command specifies to authenticate itself to a remote device. The other router must have this same username/password configured as well.

Verifying and Troubleshooting Serial Links

Now that PPP encapsulation is enabled, you need to verify that it's up and running. First, let's take a look at a figure of a sample nonproduction network serial link. Figure 21.14 shows two routers connected with a point-to-point serial connection, with the DCE side on the Pod1R1 router.

FIGURE 21.14   PPP authentication example

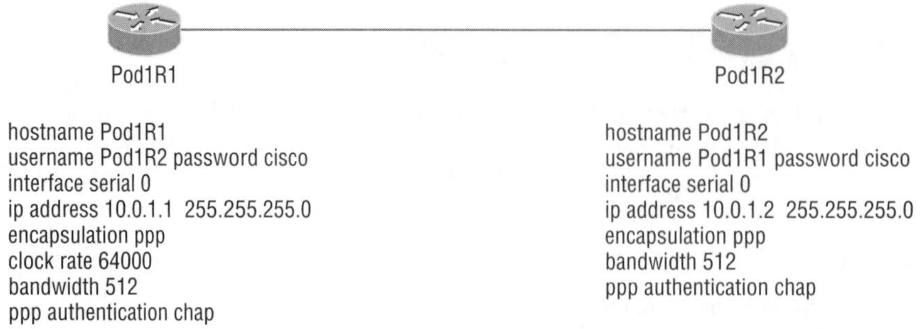

Pod1R1

Pod1R2

hostname Pod1R1
username Pod1R2 password cisco
interface serial 0
ip address 10.0.1.1 255.255.255.0
encapsulation ppp
clock rate 64000
bandwidth 512
ppp authentication chap

hostname Pod1R2
username Pod1R1 password cisco
interface serial 0
ip address 10.0.1.2 255.255.255.0
encapsulation ppp
bandwidth 512
ppp authentication chap

You can start verifying the configuration with the show interface command like this:

```
Pod1R1#sh int s0/0
Serial0/0 is up, line protocol is up
  Hardware is PowerQUICC Serial
  Internet address is 10.0.1.1/24
  MTU 1500 bytes, BW 1544 Kbit, DLY 20000 usec,
     reliability 239/255, txload 1/255, rxload 1/255
  Encapsulation PPP
  loopback not set
  Keepalive set (10 sec)
  LCP Open
  Open: IPCP, CDPCP
[output cut]
```

The first line of output is important because it tells us that Serial 0/0 is up/up. Notice that the interface encapsulation is PPP and that LCP is open. This means that it has negotiated the session establishment and all is well. The last line tells us that NCP is listening for the protocols IP and CDP, shown with the NCP headers IPCP and CDPCP.

But what would you see if everything isn't so perfect? I'm going to type in the configuration shown in Figure 21.15 to find out.

FIGURE 21.15   Failed PPP authentication

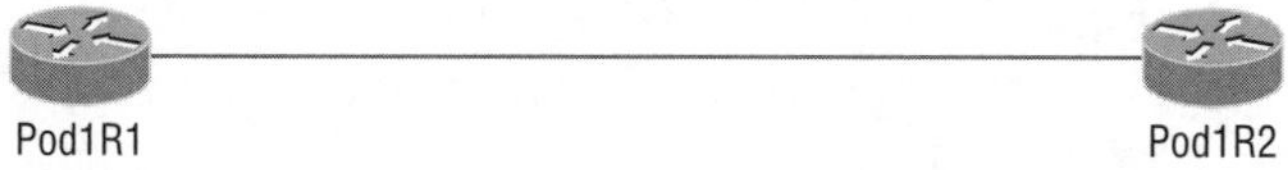

Pod1R1   Pod1R2

```
hostname Pod1R1                    hostname Pod1R2
username Pod1R2 password Cisco     username Pod1R1 password cisco
interface serial 0                 interface serial 0
ip address 10.0.1.1 255.255.255.0  ip address 10.0.1.2 255.255.255.0
clock rate 64000                   bandwidth 512
bandwidth 512                      encapsulation ppp
encapsulation ppp                  ppp authentication chap
ppp authentication chap
```

What's wrong here? Take a look at the usernames and passwords. Do you see the problem now? That's right, the C is capitalized on the Pod1R2 username command found in the configuration of router Pod1R1. This is wrong because the usernames and passwords are case sensitive. Now let's take a look at the show interface command and see what happens:

```
Pod1R1#sh int s0/0
Serial0/0 is up, line protocol is down
  Hardware is PowerQUICC Serial
```

```
Internet address is 10.0.1.1/24
MTU 1500 bytes, BW 1544 Kbit, DLY 20000 usec,
    reliability 243/255, txload 1/255, rxload 1/255
Encapsulation PPP, loopback not set
Keepalive set (10 sec)
LCP Closed
Closed: IPCP, CDPCP
```

First, notice that the first line of output shows us that Serial0/0 is up and line protocol is down. This is because there are no keepalives coming from the remote router. The next thing I want you to notice is that the LCP and NCP are closed because the authentication failed.

Debugging PPP Authentication

To display the CHAP authentication process as it occurs between two routers in the network, just use the command debug ppp authentication.

If your PPP encapsulation and authentication are set up correctly on both routers and your usernames and passwords are all good, then the debug ppp authentication command will display an output that looks like the following output, which is called the three-way handshake:

```
d16h: Se0/0 PPP: Using default call direction
1d16h: Se0/0 PPP: Treating connection as a dedicated line
1d16h: Se0/0 CHAP: O CHALLENGE id 219 len 27 from "Pod1R1"
1d16h: Se0/0 CHAP: I CHALLENGE id 208 len 27 from "Pod1R2"
1d16h: Se0/0 CHAP: O RESPONSE id 208 len 27 from "Pod1R1"
1d16h: Se0/0 CHAP: I RESPONSE id 219 len 27 from "Pod1R2"
1d16h: Se0/0 CHAP: O SUCCESS id 219 len 4
1d16h: Se0/0 CHAP: I SUCCESS id 208 len 4
```

But if you have the password wrong as they were previously in the PPP authentication failure example back in Figure 21.15, the output would look something like this:

```
1d16h: Se0/0 PPP: Using default call direction
1d16h: Se0/0 PPP: Treating connection as a dedicated line
1d16h: %SYS-5-CONFIG_I: Configured from console by console
1d16h: Se0/0 CHAP: O CHALLENGE id 220 len 27 from "Pod1R1"
1d16h: Se0/0 CHAP: I CHALLENGE id 209 len 27 from "Pod1R2"
1d16h: Se0/0 CHAP: O RESPONSE id 209 len 27 from "Pod1R1"
1d16h: Se0/0 CHAP: I RESPONSE id 220 len 27 from "Pod1R2"
1d16h: Se0/0 CHAP: O FAILURE id 220 len 25 msg is "MD/DES compare failed"
```

PPP with CHAP authentication is a three-way authentication, and if the username and passwords aren't configured exactly the way they should be, then the authentication will fail and the link will go down.

Mismatched WAN Encapsulations

If you have a point-to-point link but the encapsulations aren't the same, the link will never come up. Figure 21.16 shows one link with PPP and one with HDLC.

FIGURE 21.16   Mismatched WAN encapsulations

Pod1R1   Pod1R2

hostname Pod1R1	hostname Pod1R2
username Pod1R2 password cisco	username Pod1R1 password cisco
interface serial 0	interface serial 0
ip address 10.0.1.1 255.255.255.0	ip address 10.0.1.2 255.255.255.0
clock rate 64000	bandwidth 512
bandwidth 512	encapsulation hdlc
encapsulation ppp	

Look at router Pod1R1 in this output:

```
Pod1R1#sh int s0/0
Serial0/0 is up, line protocol is down
  Hardware is PowerQUICC Serial
  Internet address is 10.0.1.1/24
  MTU 1500 bytes, BW 1544 Kbit, DLY 20000 usec,
     reliability 254/255, txload 1/255, rxload 1/255
  Encapsulation PPP, loopback not set
  Keepalive set (10 sec)
  LCP REQsent
Closed: IPCP, CDPCP
```

The serial interface is up/down and LCP is sending requests but will never receive any responses because router Pod1R2 is using the HDLC encapsulation. To fix this problem, you would have to go to router Pod1R2 and configure the PPP encapsulation on the serial interface. One more thing: Even though the usernames are configured incorrectly, it doesn't matter because the command ppp authentication chap isn't used under the serial interface configuration. This means that the username command isn't relevant in this example.

You can set a Cisco serial interface back to the default of HDLC with the no encapsulation command like this:

```
Router(config)#int s0/0
Router(config-if)#no encapsulation
*Feb 7 16:00:18.678:%LINEPROTO-5-UPDOWN: Line protocol on Interface Serial0/0,
changed state to up
```

Notice the link came up because it now matches the encapsulation on the other end of the link!

> Always remember that you just can't have PPP on one side and HDLC on the other—they don't get along!

Mismatched IP Addresses

A tricky problem to spot is if you have HDLC or PPP configured on your serial interface but your IP addresses are wrong. Things seem to be just fine because the interfaces will show that they are up. Take a look at Figure 21.17 and see if you can see what I mean—the two routers are connected with different subnets—router Pod1R1 with 10.0.1.1/24 and router Pod1R2 with 10.2.1.2/24.

FIGURE 21.17 Mismatched IP addresses

Pod1R1   Pod1R2

```
hostname Pod1R1                    hostname Pod1R2
username Pod1R2 password cisco     username Pod1R1 password cisco
interface serial 0                 interface serial 0
ip address 10.0.1.1 255.255.255.0  ip address 10.2.1.2 255.255.255.0
clock rate 64000                   bandwidth 512
bandwidth 512                      encapsulation ppp
encapsulation ppp                  ppp authentication chap
ppp authentication chap
```

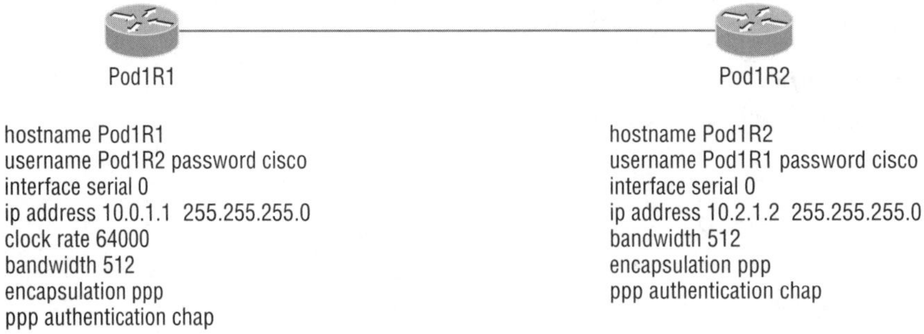

This will never work. Let's take a look at the output:

```
Pod1R1#sh int s0/0
Serial0/0 is up, line protocol is up
  Hardware is PowerQUICC Serial
  Internet address is 10.0.1.1/24
  MTU 1500 bytes, BW 1544 Kbit, DLY 20000 usec,
     reliability 255/255, txload 1/255, rxload 1/255
  Encapsulation PPP, loopback not set
  Keepalive set (10 sec)
  LCP Open
  Open: IPCP, CDPCP
```

See that? The IP addresses between the routers are wrong but the link appears to be working just fine. This is because PPP, like HDLC and Frame Relay, is a layer 2 WAN encapsulation, so it doesn't care about layer three addressing at all. So yes, the link is up, but you can't use IP across this link since it's misconfigured, or can you? Well, yes and no. If you try to ping, you'll see that this actually works! This is a feature of PPP, but not HDLC or Frame Relay. But just because you can ping to an IP address that's not in the same subnet doesn't mean your network traffic and routing protocols will work. So be careful with this issue, especially when troubleshooting PPP links!

Take a look at the routing table of Pod1R1 and see if you can find the mismatched IP address problem:

```
[output cut]
  10.0.0.0/8 is variably subnetted, 2 subnets, 2 masks
C       10.2.1.2/32 is directly connected, Serial0/0
C       10.0.1.0/24 is directly connected, Serial0/0
```

Interesting! We can see our serial interface S0/0 address of 10.0.1.0/24, but what is that other address on interface S0/0—10.2.1.2/32? That's our remote router's interface IP address! PPP determines and places the neighbor's IP address in the routing table as a connected interface, which then allows you to ping it even though it's actually configured on a separate IP subnet.

For the Cisco objectives, you need to be able to troubleshoot PPP from the routing table as I just described.

To find and fix this problem, you can also use the show running-config, show interfaces, or show ip interfaces brief command on each router, or you can use the show cdp neighbors detail command:

```
Pod1R1#sh cdp neighbors detail
-------------------------
Device ID: Pod1R2
Entry address(es):
  IP address: 10.2.1.2
```

Since the layer 1 Physical and layer 2 Data Link is up/up, you can view and verify the directly connected neighbor's IP address and then solve your problem.

Multilink PPP (MLP)

There are many load-balancing mechanisms available, but this one is free for use on serial WAN links! It provides multivendor support and is specified in RFC 1990, which details the fragmentation and packet sequencing specifications.

You can use MLP to connect your home network to an Internet service provider using two traditional modems or to connect a company via two leased lines.

The MLP feature provides a load-balancing functionality over multiple WAN links while allowing for multivendor interoperability. It offers support for packet fragmentation, proper sequencing, and load calculation on both inbound and outbound traffic.

MLP allows packets to be fragmented and then sent simultaneously over multiple point-to-point links to the same remote address. It can work over synchronous and asynchronous serial types.

MLP combines multiple physical links into a logical link called an MLP bundle, which is essentially a single, virtual interface that connects to the remote router. None of the links inside the bundle have any knowledge about the traffic on the other links.

The MLP over serial interfaces feature provides us with the following benefits:

Load balancing   MLP provides bandwidth on demand, utilizing load balancing on up to 10 links and can even calculate the load on traffic between specific sites. You don't actually need to make all links the same bandwidth, but doing so is recommended. Another key MLP advantage is that it splits packets and fragments across all links, which reduces latency across the WAN.

Increased redundancy   This one is pretty straightforward... If a link fails, the others will still transmit and receive.

Link fragmentation and interleaving   The fragmentation mechanism in MLP works by fragmenting large packets, then sending the packet fragments over the multiple point-to-point links. Smaller real-time packets are not fragmented. So interleaving basically means real-time packets can be sent in between sending the fragmented, non-real-time packets, which helps reduce delay on the lines. So let's configure MLP now to get a good feel for how it actually works now.

Configuring MLP

We're going to use Figure 21.18 to demonstrate how to configure MLP between two routers.

FIGURE 21.18   MLP between Corp and SF routers

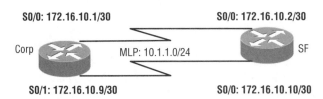

But first, I want you to study the configuration of the two serial interfaces on the Corp router that we're going to use for making our bundle:

```
Corp# show interfaces Serial0/0
Serial0/0 is up, line protocol is up
  Hardware is M4T
  Internet address is 172.16.10.1/30
  MTU 1500 bytes, BW 1544 Kbit/sec, DLY 20000 usec,
      reliability 255/255, txload 1/255, rxload 1/255
  Encapsulation PPP, LCP Open
```

```
  Open: IPCP, CDPCP, crc 16, loopback not set

Corp# show interfaces Serial1/1
Serial1/1 is up, line protocol is up
  Hardware is M4T
  Internet address is 172.16.10.9/30
  MTU 1500 bytes, BW 1544 Kbit/sec, DLY 20000 usec,
     reliability 255/255, txload 1/255, rxload 1/255
  Encapsulation PPP, LCP Open
  Open: IPCP, CDPCP, crc 16, loopback not set
```

Did you notice that each serial connection is on a different subnet (they have to be) and that the encapsulation is PPP?

When you configure MLP, you must first remove your IP addresses off your physical interface. Then, you configure a multilink bundle by creating a multilink interface on both sides of the link. After that, you assign an IP address to this multilink interface, which effectively restricts a physical link so that it can only join the designated multilink group interface.

So first I'm going to remove the IP addresses from the physical interfaces that I'm going to include in my PPP bundle.

```
Corp# config t
Corp(config)# int Serial0/0
Corp(config-if)# no ip address
Corp(config-if)# int Serial1/1
Corp(config-if)# no ip address
Corp(config-if)# end
Corp#


SF# config t
SF(config)# int Serial0/0
SF(config-if)# no ip address
SF(config-if)# int Serial0/1
SF(config-if)# no ip address
SF(config-if)# end
SF#
```

Now we create the multilink interface on each side of the link and the MLP commands to enable the bundle.

```
Corp#config t
Corp(config)# interface Multilink1
Corp(config-if)# ip address 10.1.1.1 255.255.255.0
Corp(config-if)# ppp multilink
```

```
Corp(config-if)# ppp multilink group 1
Corp(config-if)# end

SF#config t
SF(config)# interface Multilink1
SF(config-if)# ip address 10.1.1.2 255.255.255.0
SF(config-if)# ppp multilink
SF(config-if)# ppp multilink group 1
SF(config-if)# exit
```

We can see that a link joins an MLP bundle only if it negotiates to use the bundle when a connection is established and the identification information that has been exchanged matches the info for an existing bundle.

When you configure the ppp multilink group command on a link, that link won't be allowed to join any bundle other than the indicated group interface.

Verifying MLP

To verify that your bundle is up and running, just use the show ppp multilink and show interfaces multilink1 commands:

```
Corp# show ppp multilink

Multilink1
   Bundle name: Corp
   Remote Endpoint Discriminator: [1] SF
   Local Endpoint Discriminator: [1] Corp
   Bundle up for 02:12:05, total bandwidth 4188, load 1/255
   Receive buffer limit 24000 bytes, frag timeout 1000 ms
     0/0 fragments/bytes in reassembly list
     0 lost fragments, 53 reordered
     0/0 discarded fragments/bytes, 0 lost received
     0x56E received sequence, 0x572 sent sequence
   Member links: 2 active, 0 inactive (max 255, min not set)
     Se0/1, since 01:32:05
     Se1/2, since 01:31:31
No inactive multilink interfaces
```

We can see that the physical interfaces, Se0/1 and Se1/1, are members of the logical interface bundle Multilink 1. So now we'll verify the status of the interface Multilink1 on the Corp router:

```
Corp# show int Multilink1
Multilink1 is up, line protocol is up
   Hardware is multilink group interface
```

```
  Internet address is 10.1.1.1/24
  MTU 1500 bytes, BW 1544 Kbit/sec, DLY 20000 usec,
     reliability 255/255, txload 1/255, rxload 1/255
Encapsulation PPP, LCP Open, multilink Open
Open: IPCP, CDPCP, loopback not set
 Keepalive set (10 sec)
[output cut]
```

Let's move on to configure a PPPoE client on a Cisco router.

PPP Client (PPPoE)

Used with ADSL services, PPPoE (Point-to-Point Protocol over Ethernet) encapsulates PPP frames in Ethernet frames and uses common PPP features like authentication, encryption, and compression. But as I said earlier, it can be trouble. This is especially true if you've got a badly configured firewall!

Basically, PPPoE is a tunneling protocol that layers IP and other protocols running over PPP with the attributes of a PPP link. This is done so protocols can then be used to contact other Ethernet devices and initiate a point-to-point connection to transport IP packets.

Figure 21.19 displays typical usage of PPPoE over ADSL. As you can see, a PPP session is connected from the PC of the end user to the router. Subsequently, the subscriber PC IP address is assigned by the router via IPCP.

FIGURE 21.19   PPPoE with ADSL

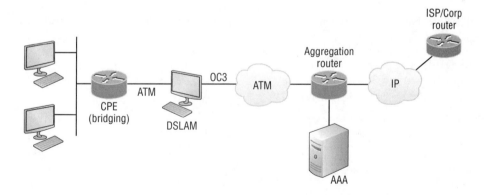

Your ISP will typically provide you with a DSL line and this will act as a bridge if your line doesn't provide enhanced features. This means only one host will connect using PPPoE. By using a Cisco router, you can run the PPPoE client IOS feature which will connect multiple PCs on the Ethernet segment that is connected to the router.

Configuring a PPPoE Client

The PPPoE client configuration is simple and straightforward. First, you need to create a dialer interface and then tie it to a physical interface.

Here are the easy steps:

1. Create a dialer interface using the `interface dialer` *number* command.

2. Instruct the client to use an IP address provided by the PPPoE server with the `ip address negotiated` command.

3. Set the encapsulation type to PPP.

4. Configure the dialer pool and number.

5. Under the physical interface, use the `pppoe-client dial-pool number` *number* command.

On your PPPoE client router, enter the following commands:

```
R1# conf t
R1(config)# int dialer1
R1(config-if)# ip address negotiated
R1(config-if)# encapsulation ppp
R1(config-if)# dialer pool 1
R1(config-if)# interface f0/1
R1(config-if)# no ip address
R1(config-if)# pppoe-client dial-pool-number 1
*May 1 1:09:07.540: %DIALER-6-BIND: Interface Vi2 bound to profile Di1
*May 1 1:09:07.541: %LINK-3-UPDOWN: Interface Virtual-Access2, changed state to
up
```

That's it! Now let's verify the interface with the `show ip interface brief` and the `show pppoe session` commands:

```
R1# show ip int brief
Interface            IP-Address     OK? Method Status          Protocol
FastEthernet0/1      unassigned     YES manual up              up
<output cut>
Dialer1              10.10.10.3     YES IPCP   up              up
Loopback0            192.168.1.1    YES NVRAM  up              up
Loopback1            172.16.1.1     YES NVRAM  up              up
Virtual-Access1      unassigned     YES unset  up              up
Virtual-Access2      unassigned     YES unset  up              up

R1#show pppoe session
    1 client session
```

```
Uniq ID  PPPoE  RemMAC          Port              VT  VA        State
         SID    LocMAC                                VA-st     Type
   N/A     4    aacb.cc00.1419  FEt0/1            Di1 Vi2        UP
                aacb.cc00.1f01                        UP
```

Our connection using a PPPoE client is up and running. Now let's take a look at VPNs.

Virtual Private Networks

I'd be pretty willing to bet you've heard the term *VPN* more than once before. Maybe you even know what one is, but just in case, a *virtual private network (VPN)* allows the creation of private networks across the Internet, enabling privacy and tunneling of IP and non-TCP/IP protocols. VPNs are used daily to give remote users and disjointed networks connectivity over a public medium like the Internet instead of using more expensive permanent means.

No worries—VPNs aren't really that hard to understand. A VPN fits somewhere between a LAN and WAN, with the WAN often simulating a LAN link because your computer, on one LAN, connects to a different, remote LAN and uses its resources remotely. The key drawback to using VPNs is a big one—security! So the definition of connecting a LAN (or VLAN) to a WAN may sound the same as using a VPN, but a VPN is actually much more.

Here's the difference: A typical WAN connects two or more remote LANs together using a router and someone else's network, like, say, your Internet service provider's. Your local host and router see these networks as remote networks and not as local networks or local resources. This would be a WAN in its most general definition. A VPN actually makes your local host part of the remote network by using the WAN link that connects you to the remote LAN. The VPN will make your host appear as though it's actually local on the remote network. This means that we now have access to the remote LAN's resources, and that access is also very secure!

This may sound a lot like a VLAN definition, and really, the concept is the same: "Take my host and make it appear local to the remote resources." Just remember this key distinction: For networks that are physically local, using VLANs is a good solution, but for physically remote networks that span a WAN, opt for using VPNs instead.

For a simple VPN example, let's use my home office in Boulder, Colorado. Here, I have my personal host, but I want it to appear as if it's on a LAN in my corporate office in Dallas, Texas, so I can get to my remote servers. VPN is the solution I would opt for to achieve my goal.

Figure 21.20 shows this example of my host using a VPN connection from Boulder to Dallas, which allows me to access the remote network services and servers as if my host were right there on the same VLAN as my servers.

FIGURE 21.20 Example of using a VPN

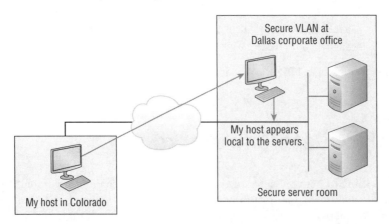

Why is this so important? If you answered, "Because my servers in Dallas are secure, and only the hosts on the same VLAN are allowed to connect to them and use the resources of these servers," you nailed it! A VPN allows me to connect to these resources by locally attaching to the VLAN through a VPN across the WAN. The other option is to open up my network and servers to everyone on the Internet or another WAN service, in which case my security goes "poof." So clearly, it's imperative I have a VPN!

Benefits of VPNs

There are many benefits to using VPNs on your corporate and even home network. The benefits covered in the CCNA R/S objectives are as follows:

Security VPNs can provide very good security by using advanced encryption and authentication protocols, which will help protect your network from unauthorized access. IPsec and SSL fall into this category. Secure Sockets Layer (SSL) is an encryption technology used with web browsers, which has native SSL encryption, and is known as Web VPN. You can also use the Cisco AnyConnect SSL VPN client installed on your PC to provide an SSL VPN solution, as well as the Clientless Cisco SSL VPN.

Cost savings By connecting the corporate remote offices to their closest Internet provider, and then creating a VPN tunnel with encryption and authentication, I gain a huge savings over opting for traditional leased point-to-point lines. This also permits higher bandwidth links and security, all for far less money than traditional connections.

Scalability VPNs scale very well to quickly bring up new offices or have mobile users connect securely while traveling or when connecting from home.

Compatibility with broadband technology For remote and traveling users and remote offices, any Internet access can provide a connection to the corporate VPN. This allows users to take advantage of the high-speed Internet access of DSL or cable modems.

Enterprise- and Provider-Managed VPNs

VPNs are categorized based upon the role they play in a business—for example, enterprise-managed VPNs and provider-managed VPNs.

You'd use an enterprise-managed VPNs if your company manages its own VPNs, which happens to be a very popular way of providing this service. To get a picture of this, check out Figure 21.21.

FIGURE 21.21   Enterprise-managed VPNs

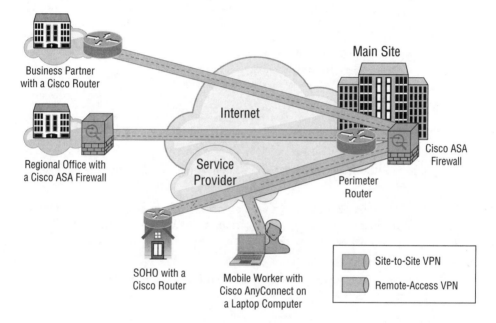

There are three different categories of enterprise-managed VPNs:

Remote-access VPNs allow remote users such as telecommuters to securely access the corporate network wherever and whenever they need to.

Site-to-site VPNs, or intranet VPNs, allow a company to connect its remote sites to the corporate backbone securely over a public medium like the Internet instead of requiring more expensive WAN connections like Frame Relay.

Extranet VPNs allow an organization's suppliers, partners, and customers to be connected to the corporate network in a limited way for business-to-business (B2B) communications.

Provider-managed VPNs are pictured in Figure 21.22.

FIGURE 21.22   Provider-managed VPNs

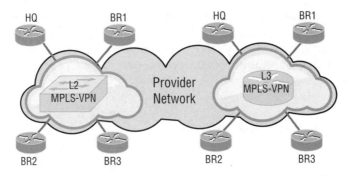

Layer 2 MPLS VPN (VPLS and VPWS):
- Customer routers exchange routes directly.
- Some applications need Layer 2 connectivity to work.

Layer 3 MPLS VPN:
- Customer routers exchange routes with SP routers.
- It provides Layer 3 service across the backbone.

And you need to be familiar with the two different categories of provider-managed VPNs:

Layer 2 MPLS VPN   Layer 2 VPNs are a type of virtual private network (VPN) that use MPLS labels to transport data. The communication occurs between routers known as provider edge routers (PEs) because they sit on the edge of the provider's network, next to the customer's network.

Internet providers who have an existing layer 2 network can opt to use these VPNs instead of the other common layer 3 MPLS VPNs.

There are two typical technologies of layer 2 MPLS VPNs:

Virtual private wire service (VPWS)   VPWS is the simplest form for enabling Ethernet services over MPLS. It is also known as ETHoMPLS (Ethernet over MPLS), or VLL (Virtual Leased Line). VPWS has the characteristics of a fixed relationship between an attachment-virtual circuit and an emulated virtual circuit. VPWS-based services are point-to-point, such as, for example, Frame-Relay/ATM/Ethernet services over IP/MPLS.

Virtual private LAN switching service (VPLS)   This is an end-to-end service and is virtual because multiple instances of this service share the same Ethernet broadcast domain virtually. However, each connection is independent and isolated from the others in the network. A dynamic, "learned" relationship exists between an attachment-virtual circuit and emulated virtual circuits, which is determined by the customer's MAC address.

In this type of network, the customer manages its own routing protocols. One advantage that a layer 2 VPN has over its layer 3 counterpart is that some applications just won't work if nodes are not in the same layer 2 network.

Layer 3 MPLS VPN   Layer 3 MPLS VPN provides a layer 3 service across the backbone. A different IP subnet connects each site. Since you would typically deploy a routing protocol over this VPN, you must communicate with the service provider to participate in the exchange of routes. Neighbor adjacency is established between your router, called CE, and the provider router that's called PE. The service provider network has many core routers called P routers and it's the P routers' job to provide connectivity between the PE routers.

If you really want to totally outsource your layer 3 VPN, then this service is for you. Your service provider will maintain and manage routing for all your sites. From your perspective as a customer who's outsourced your VPNs, this will appear to you that your service provider network is one big virtual switch.

Now you're interested in VPNs, huh? And since VPNs are inexpensive and secure, I'm guessing you just can't wait to find out how to create VPNs now! There's more than one way to bring a VPN into being. The first approach uses IPsec to create authentication and encryption services between endpoints on an IP network. The second way is via tunneling protocols, which allow you to establish a tunnel between endpoints on a network. And understand that the tunnel itself is a means for data or protocols to be encapsulated inside another protocol—pretty clean!

I'm going to go over IPsec in a minute, but first I really want to describe four of the most common tunneling protocols in use today:

Layer 2 Forwarding (L2F) is a Cisco-proprietary tunneling protocol, and it was Cisco's first tunneling protocol created for virtual private dial-up networks (VPDNs). A VPDN allows a device to use a dial-up connection to create a secure connection to a corporate network. L2F was later replaced by L2TP, which is backward compatible with L2F.

Point-to-Point Tunneling Protocol (PPTP) was created by Microsoft and others to allow the secure transfer of data from remote networks to the corporate network.

Layer 2 Tunneling Protocol (L2TP) was created by Cisco and Microsoft to replace L2F and PPTP. L2TP merged the capabilities of both L2F and PPTP into one tunneling protocol.

Generic Routing Encapsulation (GRE) is another Cisco-proprietary tunneling protocol. It forms virtual point-to-point links, allowing for a variety of protocols to be encapsulated in IP tunnels. I'll cover GRE in more detail, including how to configure it, at the end of this chapter.

Now that you're clear on both exactly what a VPN is and the various types of VPNs available, it's time to dive into IPsec.

Introduction to Cisco IOS IPsec

Simply put, IPsec is an industry-wide standard framework of protocols and algorithms that allows for secure data transmission over an IP-based network and functions at the layer 3 Network layer of the OSI model.

Did you notice I said IP-based network? That's really important because by itself, IPsec can't be used to encrypt non-IP traffic. This means that if you run into a situation where you have to encrypt non-IP traffic, you'll need to create a Generic Routing Encapsulation (GRE) tunnel for it (which I explain later) and then use IPsec to encrypt that tunnel!

IPsec Transforms

An *IPsec transform* specifies a single security protocol with its corresponding security algorithm; without these transforms, IPsec wouldn't be able to give us its glory. It's important to be familiar with these technologies, so let me take a second to define the security protocols and briefly introduce the supporting encryption and hashing algorithms that IPsec relies upon.

Security Protocols

The two primary security protocols used by IPsec are *Authentication Header (AH)* and *Encapsulating Security Payload (ESP)*.

Authentication Header (AH)

The AH protocol provides authentication for the data and the IP header of a packet using a one-way hash for packet authentication. It works like this: The sender generates a one-way hash; then the receiver generates the same one-way hash. If the packet has changed in any way, it won't be authenticated and will be dropped since the hash values won't match. So basically, IPsec relies upon AH to guarantee authenticity. AH checks the entire packet, but it doesn't offer any encryption services.

This is unlike ESP, which only provides an integrity check on the data of a packet.

Encapsulating Security Payload (ESP)

It won't tell you when or how the NASDAQ's gonna bounce up and down like a superball, but ESP will provide confidentiality, data origin authentication, connectionless integrity, anti-replay service, and limited traffic-flow confidentiality by defeating traffic flow analysis—which is almost as good! Anyway, there are five components of ESP:

Confidentiality (encryption) This allows the sending device to encrypt the packets before transmitting in order to prevent eavesdropping. Confidentiality is provided through the use of symmetric encryption algorithms like DES or 3DES. Confidentiality can be selected separately from all other services, but the confidentiality selected must be the same on both endpoints of your VPN.

Data integrity Data integrity allows the receiver to verify that the data received was not altered in any way along the way. IPsec uses checksums as a simple check of the data.

Authentication Authentication ensures that the connection is made with the correct partner. The receiver can authenticate the source of the packet by guaranteeing and certifying the source of the information.

Anti-replay service Anti-replay election is based upon the receiver, meaning the service is effective only if the receiver checks the sequence number. In case you were wondering, a replay attack is when a hacker nicks a copy of an authenticated packet and later transmits it to the intended destination. When the duplicate, authenticated IP packet gets to the destination, it can disrupt services and generally wreak havoc. The *Sequence Number* field is designed to foil this type of attack.

Traffic flow   For traffic flow confidentiality to work, you have to have at least tunnel mode selected. It's most effective if it's implemented at a security gateway where tons of traffic amasses because it's precisely the kind of environment that can mask the true source-destination patterns to bad guys who are trying to breach your network's security.

Encryption

VPNs create a private network over a public network infrastructure, but to maintain confidentiality and security, we really need to use IPsec with our VPNs. IPsec uses various types of protocols to perform encryption. The types of encryption algorithms used today are as follows:

Symmetric encryption   This encryption requires a shared secret to encrypt and decrypt. Each computer encrypts the data before sending info across the network, with this same key being used to both encrypt and decrypt the data. Examples of symmetric key encryption are Data Encryption Standard (DES), Triple DES (3DES), and Advanced Encryption Standard (AES).

Asymmetric encryption   Devices that use asymmetric encryption use different keys for encryption than they do for decryption. These keys are called private and public keys.

Private keys encrypt a hash from the message to create a digital signature, which is then verified via decryption using the public key. Public keys encrypt a symmetric key for secure distribution to the receiving host, which then decrypts that symmetric key using its exclusively held private key. It's not possible to encrypt and decrypt using the same key. This is a variant of public key encryption that uses a combination of both a public and private keys. An example of an asymmetric encryption is Rivest, Shamir, and Adleman (RSA).

As you can see from the amount of information I've thrown at you so far, establishing a VPN connection between two sites takes study, time, and practice. And I am just scratching the surface here! I know it can be difficult at times, and it can take quite a bit of patience. Cisco does have some GUI interfaces to help with this process, and they can be very helpful for configuring VPNs with IPsec. Though highly useful and very interesting, they are just beyond the scope of this book, so I'm not going to delve further into this topic here.

GRE Tunnels

Generic Routing Encapsulation (GRE) is a tunneling protocol that can encapsulate many protocols inside IP tunnels. Some examples would be routing protocols such as EIGRP and OSPF and the routed protocol IPv6. Figure 21.23 shows the different pieces of a GRE header.

FIGURE 21.23   Generic Routing Encapsulation (GRE) tunnel structure

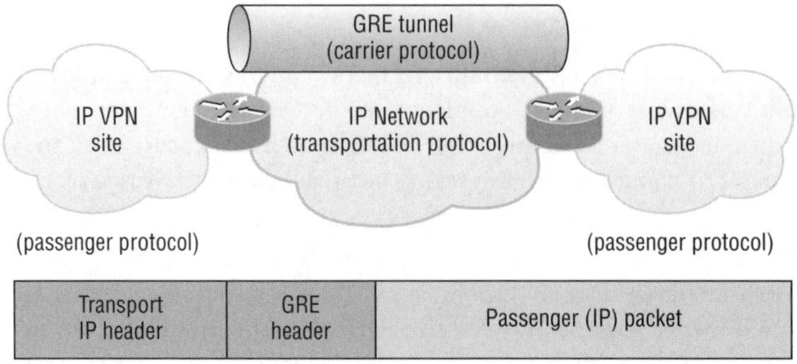

A GRE tunnel interface supports a header for each of the following:

- A passenger protocol or encapsulated protocols like IP or IPv6, which is the protocol being encapsulated by GRE

- GRE encapsulation protocol

- A transport delivery protocol, typically IP

GRE tunnels have the following characteristics:

- GRE uses a protocol-type field in the GRE header so any layer 3 protocol can be used through the tunnel.

- GRE is stateless and has no flow control.

- GRE offers no security.

- GRE creates additional overhead for tunneled packets—at least 24 bytes.

GRE over IPsec

As I just mentioned, GRE by itself provides no security—no form of payload confidentiality or encryption. If the packets are sniffed over the public networks, their contents are in plain-text, and although IPsec provides a secure method for tunneling data across an IP network, it has limitations.

IPsec does not support IP broadcast or IP multicast, preventing the use of protocols that need them, like routing protocols. IPsec also does not support the use of the multiprotocol traffic. GRE is a protocol that can be used to "carry" other passenger protocols like IP broadcast or IP multicast, as well as non-IP protocols. So using GRE tunnels with IPsec allows you to run a routing protocol, IP multicast, as well as multiprotocol traffic across your network.

With a generic hub-and-spoke topology (corp to branch, for example), you can implement static tunnels, typically GRE over IPsec, between the corporate office and branch offices. When you want to add a new spoke to the network, all you need to do is configure it on the hub router. The traffic between spokes has to traverse the hub, where it must exit one tunnel and enter another. Static tunnels can be an appropriate solution for small networks, but this solution actually becomes an unacceptable problem as the number of spokes grows larger and larger!

Cisco DMVPN (Cisco Proprietary)

The Cisco Dynamic Multipoint Virtual Private Network (DMVPN) feature enables you to easily scale large and small IPsec VPNs. The Cisco DMVPN is Cisco's answer to allow a corporate office to connect to branch offices with low cost, easy configuration, and flexibility. DMVPN has one central router, such as a corporate router, which is referred to as the hub, and the branches are called spokes. So the corporate to branch connection is referred to as the hub-and-spoke interconnection. Also supported is the spoke-to-spoke design used for branch-to-branch interconnections. If you're thinking this design sounds eerily similar to your old Frame Relay network, you're right! The DMPVN features enables you to configure a single GRE tunnel interface and a single IPsec profile on the hub router to manage all spoke routers, which keeps the size of the configuration on the hub router basically the same even if you add more spoke routers to the network. DMVPN also allows spoke router to dynamically create VPN tunnels between them as network data travels from one spoke to another.

Cisco IPsec VTI (Cisco Proprietary)

The IPsec Virtual Tunnel Interface (VTI) mode of an IPsec configuration can greatly simplify a VPN configuration when protection is needed for remote access. And it's a simpler option to GRE or L2TP for encapsulation and crypto maps used with IPsec. Like GRE, it sends routing protocol and multicast traffic, but you don't need the GRE protocol and all the overhead that brings. A nice simple configuration and routing adjacency directly over the VTI offers many benefits. Understand that all traffic is encrypted and that it supports only one protocol—either IPv4 or IPv6, just like standard IPsec.

Now let's take a look at how to configure a GRE tunnel. It's actually pretty simple.

Configuring GRE Tunnels

Before you attempt to configure a GRE tunnel, you need to create an implementation plan. Here's a checklist for what you need to configure and implement a GRE:

1. Use IP addressing.
2. Create the logical tunnel interfaces.
3. Specify that you're using GRE tunnel mode under the tunnel interface (this is optional since this is the default tunnel mode).
4. Specify the tunnel source and destination IP addresses.
5. Configure an IP address for the tunnel interface.

Let's take a look at how to bring up a simple GRE tunnel. Figure 21.24 shows the network with two routers.

FIGURE 21.24   Example of GRE configuration

First, we need to make the logical tunnel with the `interface tunnel` *number* command. We can use any number up to 2.14 billion.

```
Corp(config)#int s0/0/0
Corp(config-if)#ip address 63.1.1.1 255.255.255.252
Corp(config)#int tunnel ?
  <0-2147483647>  Tunnel interface number
Corp(config)#int tunnel 0
*Jan 5 16:58:22.719:%LINEPROTO-5-UPDOWN: Line protocol on Interface Tunnel0,
changed state to down
```

Once we have configured our interface and created the logical tunnel, we need to configure the mode and then the transport protocol.

```
Corp(config-if)#tunnel mode ?
  aurp     AURP TunnelTalk AppleTalk encapsulation
  cayman   Cayman TunnelTalk AppleTalk encapsulation
  dvmrp    DVMRP multicast tunnel
  eon      EON compatible CLNS tunnel
  gre      generic route encapsulation protocol
  ipip     IP over IP encapsulation
  ipsec    IPSec tunnel encapsulation
  iptalk   Apple IPTalk encapsulation
  ipv6     Generic packet tunneling in IPv6
  ipv6ip   IPv6 over IP encapsulation
  nos      IP over IP encapsulation (KA9Q/NOS compatible)
  rbscp    RBSCP in IP tunnel
Corp(config-if)#tunnel mode gre ?
  ip          over IP
  ipv6        over IPv6
  multipoint  over IP (multipoint)

Corp(config-if)#tunnel mode gre ip
```

Now that we've created the tunnel interface, the type, and the transport protocol, we must configure our IP addresses for use inside of the tunnel. Of course, you need to use your actual physical interface IP for the tunnel to send traffic across the Internet, but you also need to configure the tunnel source and tunnel destination addresses.

```
Corp(config-if)#ip address 192.168.10.1 255.255.255.0
Corp(config-if)#tunnel source 63.1.1.1
Corp(config-if)#tunnel destination 63.1.1.2

Corp#sho run interface tunnel 0
Building configuration...

Current configuration : 117 bytes
!
interface Tunnel0
 ip address 192.168.10.1 255.255.255.0
 tunnel source 63.1.1.1
 tunnel destination 63.1.1.2
end
```

Now let's configure the other end of the serial link and watch the tunnel pop up!

```
SF(config)#int s0/0/0
SF(config-if)#ip address 63.1.1.2 255.255.255.252
SF(config-if)#int t0
SF(config-if)#ip address 192.168.10.2 255.255.255.0
SF(config-if)#tunnel source 63.1.1.2
SF(config-if)#tun destination 63.1.1.1
*May 19 22:46:37.099: %LINEPROTO-5-UPDOWN: Line protocol on Interface Tunnel0,
changed state to up
```

Oops—did I forget to set my tunnel mode and transport to GRE and IP on the SF router? No, I didn't need to because it's the default tunnel mode on Cisco IOS. Nice! So, first I set the physical interface IP address (which used a global address even though I didn't have to), then I created the tunnel interface and set the IP address of the tunnel interface. It's really important that you remember to configure the tunnel interface with the actual source and destination IP addresses to use or the tunnel won't come up. In my example, the 63.1.1.2 was the source and 63.1.1.1 was the destination.

Verifying GRP Tunnels

As usual I'll start with my favorite troubleshooting command, show ip interface brief.

```
Corp#sh ip int brief
Interface       IP-Address   OK? Method Status        Protocol
FastEthernet0/0 10.10.10.5   YES manual up            up
```

```
Serial0/0          63.1.1.1       YES manual up                          up
FastEthernet0/1    unassigned     YES unset  administratively down down
Serial0/1          unassigned     YES unset  administratively down down
Tunnel0            192.168.10.1   YES manual up                          up
```

In this output, you can see that the tunnel interface is now showing as an interface on my router. You can see the IP address of the tunnel interface, and the Physical and Data Link status show as up/up. So far so good. Let's take a look at the interface with the show interfaces tunnel 0 command.

```
Corp#sh int tun 0
Tunnel0 is up, line protocol is up
  Hardware is Tunnel
  Internet address is 192.168.10.1/24
  MTU 1514 bytes, BW 9 Kbit, DLY 500000 usec,
     reliability 255/255, txload 1/255, rxload 1/255
  Encapsulation TUNNEL, loopback not set
  Keepalive not set
  Tunnel source 63.1.1.1, destination 63.1.1.2
  Tunnel protocol/transport GRE/IP
    Key disabled, sequencing disabled
    Checksumming of packets disabled
  Tunnel TTL 255
  Fast tunneling enabled
  Tunnel transmit bandwidth 8000 (kbps)
  Tunnel receive bandwidth 8000 (kbps)
```

The show interfaces command shows the configuration settings and the interface status as well as the IP address, tunnel source, and destination address. The output also shows the tunnel protocol, which is GRE/IP. Last, let's take a look at the routing table with the show ip route command.

```
Corp#sh ip route
[output cut]
     192.168.10.0/24 is subnetted, 2 subnets
C       192.168.10.0/24 is directly connected, Tunnel0
L       192.168.10.1/32 is directly connected, Tunnel0
     63.0.0.0/30 is subnetted, 2 subnets
C       63.1.1.0 is directly connected, Serial0/0
L       63.1.1.1/32 is directly connected, Serial0/0
```

The tunnel0 interface shows up as a directly connected interface, and although it's a logical interface, the router treats it as a physical interface, just like serial 0/0 in the routing table.

```
Corp#ping 192.168.10.2

Type escape sequence to abort.
Sending 5, 100-byte ICMP Echos to 192.168.10.2, timeout is 2 seconds:
!!!!!
Success rate is 100 percent (5/5)
```

Did you notice that I just pinged 192.168.10.2 across the Internet? I hope so! Anyway, there's one last thing I want to cover before we move on to EBGP, and that's troubleshooting an output, which is showing a tunnel routing error. If you configure your GRE tunnel and receive this GRE flapping message

```
          Line protocol on Interface Tunnel0, changed state to up
07:11:55: %TUN-5-RECURDOWN:
          Tunnel0 temporarily disabled due to recursive routing
07:11:59: %LINEPROTO-5-UPDOWN:
          Line protocol on Interface Tunnel0, changed state to down
07:12:59: %LINEPROTO-5-UPDOWN:
```

it means that you've misconfigured your tunnel, which will cause your router to try and route to the tunnel destination address using the tunnel interface itself!

Single-Homed EBGP

The *Border Gateway Protocol (BGP)* is perhaps one of the most well-known routing protocols in the world of networking. This is understandable because BGP is the routing protocol that powers the Internet and makes possible what we take for granted: connecting to remote systems on the other side of the country or planet. Because of its pervasive use, it's likely that each of us will have to deal with it at some point in our careers. So it's appropriate that we spend some time learning about BGP.

BGP version 4 has a long and storied history. Although the most recent definition was published in 1995 as RFC 1771 by Rekhter and Li, BGP's roots can be traced back to RFCs 827 and 904, which specified a protocol called the exterior gateway protocol (EGP). These earlier specifications date from 1982 and 1984, respectively—ages ago! Although BGP obsoletes EGP, it uses many of the techniques first defined by EGP and draws upon the many lessons learned from its use.

Way back in 1982, many organizations were connected to the ARPAnet, the noncommercial predecessor of the Internet. When a new network was added to ARPAnet, it would typically be added in a relatively unstructured way and would begin participating in a common routing protocol, the Gateway to Gateway Protocol (GGP). As you might expect, this solution did not scale well. GGP suffered from excessive overhead in managing large routing tables and from the difficulty of troubleshooting in an environment in which there was no central administrative control.

To address these deficiencies, EGP was developed, and with it the concept of *autonomous systems (ASs)*. RFC 827 was very clear in laying out the problems with GGP and in pointing out that a new type of routing protocol was required, an *exterior gateway protocol (EGP)*. The purpose of this new protocol was to facilitate the flow of traffic among a series of autonomous systems by exchanging information about routes contained in each system. The complexities of this network of networks, the Internet, would be hidden from the end user who simply views the Internet as a single address space through which they travel, unaware of the exact path they take.

The BGP that we know today flows directly from this work on EGP and builds upon it. So that you can get a better understanding of BGP, I will provide an overview of its features next.

Protocol Comparison and Overview

Because BGP is the first exterior gateway protocol we've encountered, I'll briefly compare it to a more familiar interior gateway protocol, like OSPF, so that we can put its features into context. After that comes a brief overview of BGP so that you can quickly become aware of its main capabilities.

Just to clarify things, with this comparison, I'm not implying that OSPF could be a substitute for BGP. In fact, there are a number of reasons that BGP is far better suited as an exterior gateway protocol than OSPF. For example, the requirement that all OSPF areas be connected to area 0 simply doesn't allow OSPF to scale to the size required by the Internet. Thousands of areas would have to connect to area 0, overwhelming it with route updates. In addition, OSPF uses a metric based on bandwidth, but in the context of the Internet, routing decisions are also based on political and business issues. OSPF does not have any mechanism to modify path selection based upon factors such as interconnection agreements between Internet service providers.

Although BGP can be thought of as just another routing protocol, the differences between it and protocols like OSPF are significant enough to catapult it into an entirely different category. Table 21.1 contains a comparison of BGP and OSPF.

TABLE 21.1   Comparison of BGP and OSPF

Characteristic	BGP	OSPF
Routing algorithm	Distance vector	Link state
Classless support	Yes	Yes
VLSM support	Yes	Yes
Summarization	Any BGP router	ASBR/ABR

Characteristic	BGP	OSPF
Metric	Various	Bandwidth
Hierarchy	No	Yes
Building blocks	Autonomous systems	Areas
Base protocol	TCP port 179	Protocol value 89
Traffic type	Unicast	Multicast
Neighbors	Specifically configured	Discovered/configured
Route exchange	Only with neighbors	Only with adjacent neighbors
Initial update	Synchronize database	Synchronize database
Update frequency	Incremental	Incremental with 60-minute timer
Hello timer	60 seconds	10 or 30 seconds
Hold timer	180 seconds	40 or 120 seconds
Internal route exchange	Internal BGP sessions	LSA Types 1 and 2
External route exchange	External BGP sessions	LSA Types 3, 4, and 5
Route updates	Contain network, attributes, AS path	Contain network, metric (Types 3 and 4 LSAs)
Network statement	Advertises network	Activates OSPF on interface
Special features	Route reflectors	Stub, totally stubby, NSSA areas

It's easy to get lost in the specific details of BGP, so at the risk of a small amount of repetition later on, the following is a high-level overview of the BGP protocol and its main characteristics as listed in Table 21.1.

BGP is a distance-vector protocol, which means that it advertises all or a portion of its route table to its neighbors. The advertised routes include the network being advertised, a list of attributes that influence the selection of the best path, the next-hop address through which the network can be reached, and a list of autonomous systems (ASs) through which the route update has passed. BGP routers use the list of autonomous systems to ensure a loop-free path by enforcing the rule that no AS path list is allowed to contain the same AS number twice.

BGP supports classless networks, the use of variable length subnet masks (VLSMs), and summarization. These characteristics allow BGP to work with networks that are not organized on purely classful boundaries and to create summaries of networks to reduce the size of the routing tables.

- BGP uses a rich variety of metrics called *attributes* to influence the selection of the best path to remote networks in the event that there are multiple advertised paths. Network administrators far removed from the initial origin of the advertised networks can manipulate these attributes. Paths can be chosen simply because a neighbor AS is preferred for political or economic reasons, thus overriding more traditional measures such as the distance to the advertised route.

- BGP supports a nonhierarchical network structure and allows a complex combination of interconnections among neighbors. There is no counterpart in BGP to the OSPF concept of area 0, which is the single area through which interarea traffic passes. Traffic between different BGP autonomous systems may follow a variety of different paths.

- BGP uses the concept of autonomous systems to define the boundaries of networks and treats communications among neighbors differently depending on whether the neighbors belong to the same autonomous system or not. An autonomous system is a collection of routers that are under a common administrative control and that present a common route policy to the outside world. It is not necessary that all of the routers run the same routing protocol, just that they all be controlled and coordinated by the same administrative authority.

- An AS uses BGP to advertise routes that are in its network and need to be visible outside of the network; it also uses BGP to learn about the reachability of routes by listening to advertisement announcements from other autonomous systems. Each AS can have a specific policy regarding the routes it wishes to advertise externally. These policies can be different for every point in which the AS attaches to the outside world.

- Inside autonomous networks, *interior gateway protocols (IGPs)* are used to discover the connectivity among a set of IP subnets. IGPs are well-known protocols such as the Routing Information Protocol (RIP), Interior Gateway Routing Protocol (IGRP), Open Shortest Path First (OSPF), and Enhanced Interior Gateway Routing Protocol (EIGRP).

BGP relies upon TCP for connection-oriented, acknowledged communications using port 179. BGP routers are specifically configured as neighbors of one another and use unicast packets to exchange route information, keepalives, and a variety of other messages. BGP routers go through a variety of stages as they establish communications with their configured neighbors, verify consistent parameter configuration, and begin the initial synchronization of their route information. After the initial synchronization is complete, BGP neighbors exchange updates on a triggered basis and monitor their connection state via periodic keepalives.

BGP neighbors either live in the same AS, in which case they are referred to as *internal BGP (iBGP) neighbors,* or live in different ASs, in which case they are referred to as *external BGP (eBGP) neighbors*. Internal BGP neighbors do not need to share a common network and can be separated by many other routers that don't need to run BGP. However, every iBGP router must be configured as a neighbor to every other iBGP router in the same area. External BGP neighbors are normally required to share a common network and are directly accessible to each other. There is no requirement that every eBGP router be a neighbor to every other eBGP router.

BGP can advertise networks that are learned dynamically, statically, or through redistribution. The network command, which is used in most other protocols to cause the router's interface(s) to begin listening for and sending route updates, is used in BGP routers to advertise specific networks. There are a number of rules, like the synchronization rule, that govern BGP's interaction with interior gateway protocols and the routes that are advertised as a result of this interaction.

Finally, BGP can implement a variety of mechanisms to improve scalability. Summarization is certainly one of these mechanisms, as is the use of route reflectors. Route reflectors provide a means to eliminate the requirement for a full mesh of neighbor relationships among iBGP neighbors, thus permitting larger BGP environments with less traffic.

Configuring and Verifying EBGP

If you're configuring BGP between a customer network and an ISP, this process is called external BGP (EBGP). If you're configuring BGP peers between two routers in the same AS, it's not considered EBGP.

You must have the basic information to configure EBGP:

- AS numbers (your own, and all remote AS numbers, which must be different)
- All the neighbors (peers) that are involved in BGP, and IP addressing that is used among the BGP neighbors
- Networks that need to be advertised into BGP

For an example of configuring EBGP, here's Figure 21.25.

FIGURE 21.25   Example of EBGP lay layout

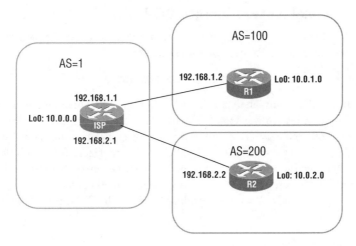

There are three main steps to configure basic BGP:

1. Define the BGP process.
2. Establish one or more neighbor relationships.
3. Advertise the local networks into BGP.

Define the BGP Process

To start the BGP process on a router, use the router bgp *AS* command. Each process must be assigned a local AS number. There can only be one BGP process in a router, which means that each router can only be in one AS at any given time.

Here is an example:

```
ISP#config t
ISP(config)#router bgp ?
<1-65535> Autonomous system number
ISP(config)#router bgp 1
```

Notice the AS number can be from 1 to 65,535.

Establish One or More Neighbor Relationships

Since BGP does not automatically discover neighbors like other routing protocols do, you have to explicitly configure them using the neighbor *peer-ip-address* remote-as *peer-as-number* command. Here is an example of configuring the ISP router in Figure 21.25:

```
ISP(config-router)#neighbor 192.168.1.2 remote-as 100
ISP(config-router)#neighbor 192.168.2.2 remote-as 200
```

Be sure to understand that the above command is the neighbor's IP address and neighbor's AS number.

Advertise the Local Networks Into BGP

To specify your local networks and advertise them into BGP, you use the network command with the mask keyword and then the subnet mask:

```
ISP(config-router)#network 10.0.0.0 mask 255.255.255.0
```

These network numbers must match what is found on the local router's forwarding table exactly, which can be seen with the show ip route or show ip int brief command. For other routing protocols, the network command has a different meaning. For OSPF and EIGRP, for example, the network command indicates the interfaces for which the routing protocol will send and receive route updates. In BGP, the network command indicates which routes should be injected into the BGP table on the local router.

Figure 21.25 displays the BGP routing configuration for the R1 and R2 routers:

```
R1#config t
R1(config)#router bgp 100
```

```
R1(config-router)#neighbor 192.168.1.1 remote-as 1
R1(config-router)#network 10.0.1.0 mask 255.255.255.0

R2#config t
R2(config)#router bgp 200
R2(config-router)#neighbor 192.168.2.1 remote-as 1
R2(config-router)#network 10.0.2.0 mask 255.255.255.0
```

That's it! Pretty simple. Now let's verify our configuration.

Verifying EBGP

We'll use the following commands to verify our little EBGP network.

- show ip bgp summary
- show ip bgp
- show ip bgp neighbors

The *show ip bgp summary* Command

The show ip bgp summary command gives you an overview of the BGP status. Each configured neighbor is listed in the output of the command. The output will display the IP address and AS number of the neighbor, along with the status of the session. You can use this information to verify that BGP sessions are up and established, or to verify the IP address and AS number of the configured BGP neighbor.

```
ISP#sh ip bgp summary
BGP router identifier 10.0.0.1, local AS number 1
BGP table version is 4, main routing table version 6
3 network entries using 396 bytes of memory
3 path entries using 156 bytes of memory
2/2 BGP path/bestpath attribute entries using 368 bytes of memory
3 BGP AS-PATH entries using 72 bytes of memory
0 BGP route-map cache entries using 0 bytes of memory
0 BGP filter-list cache entries using 0 bytes of memory
Bitfield cache entries: current 1 (at peak 1) using 32 bytes of memory
BGP using 1024 total bytes of memory
BGP activity 3/0 prefixes, 3/0 paths, scan interval 60 secs

Neighbor        V    AS MsgRcvd MsgSent   TblVer  InQ OutQ Up/Down State/PfxRcd
192.168.1.2     4   100      56      55        4    0    0 00:53:33         4
192.168.2.2     4   200      47      46        4    0    0 00:44:53         4
```

The first section of the show ip bgp summary command output describes the BGP table and its content:

- The router ID of the router and local AS number.

- The BGP table version is the version number of the local BGP table. This number is increased every time the table is changed.

The second section of the show ip bgp summary command output is a table in which the current neighbor statuses are shown. Here's information about what you see displayed in the output of this command:

- IP address of the neighbor.

- BGP version number that is used by the router when communicating with the neighbor (v4).

- AS number of the remote neighbor.

- Number of messages and updates that have been received from the neighbor since the session was established.

- Number of messages and updates that have been sent to the neighbor since the session was established.

- Version number of the local BGP table that has been included in the most recent update to the neighbor.

- Number of messages that are waiting to be processed in the incoming queue from this neighbor.

- Number of messages that are waiting in the outgoing queue for transmission to the neighbor.

- How long the neighbor has been in the current state and the name of the current state. Interestingly, notice there is no state listed, which is actually what you want because that means the peers are established.

- Number of received prefixes from the neighbor.

- ISP1 has two established sessions with the following neighbors:

  - 192.168.1.2, which is the IP address of R1 router and is in AS 100

  - 192.168.2.2, which is the IP address of R2 router and is in AS 200

- From each of the neighbors, ISP1 has received one prefix (one network).

Now, for the CCNA objectives, remember that if you see this type of output at the end of the show ip bgp summary command, that the BGP session is not established between peers:

```
Neighbor        V    AS MsgRcvd MsgSent    TblVer   InQ OutQ Up/Down State/PfxRcd
192.168.1.2     4    64       0       0         0     0    0 never    Active
```

Notice the state of Active. Remember, seeing no state output is good! Active means we're actively trying to establish with the peer.

The *show ip bgp* Command

With the show ip bgp command, the entire BGP table is displayed. A list of information about each route is displayed, so this is a nice command to get quick information on your BGP routes.

```
ISP#sh ip bgp
BGP table version is 4, local router ID is 10.0.0.1
Status codes: s suppressed, d damped, h history, * valid, > best, i - internal,
r RIB-failure, S Stale
Origin codes: i - IGP, e - EGP, ? - incomplete

Network Next Hop Metric LocPrf Weight Path
*> 10.0.0.0/24 0.0.0.0 0 0 32768 i
*> 10.0.1.0/24 192.168.1.2 0 0 0 100 i
*> 10.0.2.0/24 192.168.2.2 0 0 0 200 i
```

The output is sorted in network number order, and if the BGP table contains more than one route to the same network, the backup routes are displayed on separate lines. We don't have multiple routes, so none are shown.

The BGP path selection process selects one of the available routes to each of the networks as the best. This route is pointed out by the > character in the left column.

ISP1 has the following networks in the BGP table:

- 10.0.0.0/24, which is locally originated via the network command in BGP on the ISP router

- 10.0.1.0/24, which has been advertised from 192.168.1.2 (R1) neighbor

- 10.0.2.0/24, which has been advertised from 192.168.2.2 (R2) neighbor

Since the command displays all routing information, note that network 10.0.0.0/24, with the next-hop attribute set to 0.0.0.0, is also displayed. The next-hop attribute is set to 0.0.0.0 when you view the BGP table on the router that originates the route in BGP. The 10.0.0.0/24 network is the network that I locally configured on ISP1 into BGP.

The *show ip bgp neighbors* Command

The show ip bgp neighbors command provides more information about BGP connections to neighbors than the show ip bgp command does. This command can be used to get information about the TCP sessions and the BGP parameters of the session, as well as the showing the TCP timers and counters, and it's a long output! I'll just give you the top part of the command here:

```
ISP#sh ip bgp neighbors
BGP neighbor is 192.168.1.2, remote AS 100, external link
BGP version 4, remote router ID 10.0.1.1
BGP state = Established, up for 00:10:55
Last read 00:10:55, last write 00:10:55, hold time is 180, keepalive interval is
60 seconds
```

```
Neighbor capabilities:
Route refresh: advertised and received(new)
Address family IPv4 Unicast: advertised and received
Message statistics:
InQ depth is 0
OutQ depth is 0
```
[*output cut*]

Notice (and remember!) you can use the show ip bgp neighbors command to see the hold time on two BGP peers, and in the above example from the ISP to R1, the holdtime is 180 seconds.

Summary

In this chapter, you learned the difference between the following WAN services: cable, DSL, HDLC, PPP, and PPPoE. You also learned that you can use a VPN once any of those services are up and running as well as create and verify a tunnel interface.

It's so important for you to understand High-Level Data-Link Control (HDLC) and how to verify with the show interface command that HDLC is enabled! You've been provided with some really important HDLC information as well as information on how the Point-to-Point Protocol (PPP) is used if you need more features than HDLC offers or if you're using two different brands of routers. You now know that this is because various versions of HDLC are proprietary and won't work between two different vendors' routers.

When we went through the section on PPP, I discussed the various LCP options as well as the two types of authentication that can be used: PAP and CHAP.

We then discussed virtual private networks, IPsec, and encryption, and I explained GRE and how to configure the tunnel and then verify it.

We finished up the chapter with a discussion on BGP.

Exam Essentials

Remember the default serial encapsulation on Cisco routers.   Cisco routers use a proprietary High-Level Data-Link Control (HDLC) encapsulation on all their serial links by default.

Remember the PPP Data Link layer protocols.   The three Data Link layer protocols are Network Control Protocol (NCP), which defines the Network layer protocols; Link Control Protocol (LCP), a method of establishing, configuring, maintaining, and terminating the point-to-point connection; and High-Level Data-Link Control (HDLC), the MAC layer protocol that encapsulates the packets.

Be able to troubleshoot a PPP link.   Understand that a PPP link between two routers will show up and a ping would even work between the router if the layer 3 addresses are wrong.

Remember the various types of serial WAN connections.   The serial WAN connections that are most widely used are HDLC, PPP, and Frame Relay.

Understand the term *virtual private network*.   You need to understand why and how to use a VPN between two sites and the purpose that IPsec serves with VPNs.

Understand how to configure and verify a GRE tunnel.   To configure GRE, first configure the logical tunnel with the `interface tunnel` *number* command. Configure the mode and transport, if needed, with the `tunnel mode` *mode protocol* command, then configure the IP addresses on the tunnel interfaces, the tunnel source and tunnel destination addresses, and your physical interfaces with global addresses. Verify with the `show interface tunnel` command as well as the Ping protocol.

Written Lab 21

You can find the answers to this lab in Appendix A, "Answers to Written Labs."
   Write the answers to the following WAN questions:

1.   True/False: The IWAN allows transport-independent connectivity.

2.   True/False: BGP runs between two peers in the same autonomous system (AS). It is referred to as External BGP (EBGP).

3.   TCP port 179 is used for which protocol?

4.   Which command can you use to know the hold time on the two BGP peers?

5.   Which command will not tell you if the GRE tunnel is in up/up state?

6.   True/False: A GRE tunnel is considered secure.

7.   What protocol would you use if you were running xDSL and needed authentication?

8.   What are the three protocols specified in PPP?

9.   List two technologies that are examples of layer 2 MPLS VPN technologies.

10.   List two VPNs that are examples of VPNs managed by service providers.

Hands-on Labs

In this section, you will configure Cisco routers in three different WAN labs using the figure supplied in each lab. (These labs are included for use with real Cisco routers but work perfectly with the LammleSim IOS version simulator and with Cisco's Packet Tracer program.)

   Lab 21.1: Configuring PPP Encapsulation and Authentication

   Lab 21.2: Configuring and Monitoring HDLC

   Lab 21.3: Configuring a GRE Tunnel

Hands-on Lab 21.1: Configuring PPP Encapsulation and Authentication

By default, Cisco routers use High-Level Data-Link Control (HDLC) as a point-to-point encapsulation method on serial links. If you are connecting to non-Cisco equipment, then you can use the PPP encapsulation method to communicate.

Labs 21.1 and 21.2 will have you configure the network in the following diagram.

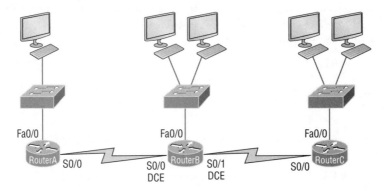

1. Type **sh int s0/0** on RouterA and RouterB to see the encapsulation method.
2. Make sure each router has the hostname assigned.

   ```
   RouterA#config t
   RouterA(config)#hostname RouterA

   RouterB#config t
   RouterB(config)#hostname RouterB
   ```

3. To change the default HDLC encapsulation method to PPP on both routers, use the encapsulation command at interface configuration. Both ends of the link must run the same encapsulation method.

   ```
   RouterA#Config t
   RouterA(config)#int s0
   RouterA(config-if)#encap ppp
   ```

4. Now go to RouterB and set serial 0/0 to PPP encapsulation.

   ```
   RouterB#config t
   RouterB(config)#int s0
   RouterB(config-if)#encap ppp
   ```

5. Verify the configuration by typing **sh int s0/0** on both routers.

6. Notice the IPCP and CDPCP (assuming the interface is up). This is the information used to transmit the upper-layer (Network layer) information across the HDLC at the MAC sublayer.

7. Define a username and password on each router. Notice that the username is the name of the remote router. Also, the password must be the same.

```
RouterA#config t
RouterA(config)#username RouterB password todd

RouterB#config t
RouterB(config)#username RouterA password todd
```

8. Enable CHAP or PAP authentication on each interface.

```
RouterA(config)#int s0
RouterA(config-if)#ppp authentication chap

RouterB(config)#int s0
RouterB(config-if)#ppp authentication chap
```

9. Verify the PPP configuration on each router by using these commands.

```
RouterB(config-if)#shut
RouterB(config-if)#debug ppp authentication
RouterB(config-if)#no shut
```

Hands-on Lab 21.2: Configuring and Monitoring HDLC

There really is no configuration required for HDLC (as it is the default configuration on Cisco serial interfaces), but if you completed Lab 21.1, then the PPP encapsulation would be set on both routers. This is why I put the PPP lab first. This lab allows you to actually configure HDLC encapsulation on a router.

 For this second lab, you will use the same configuration you used for Lab 21.1.

1. Set the encapsulation for each serial interface by using the encapsulation hdlc command.

```
RouterA#config t
RouterA(config)#int s0
RouterA(config-if)#encapsulation hdlc
```

```
RouterB#config t
RouterB(config)#int s0
RouterB(config-if)#encapsulation hdlc
```

2. Verify the HDLC encapsulation by using the show interface s0 command on each router.

Hands-on Lab 21.3: Configuring a GRE Tunnel

In this lab you will configure two point-to-point routers with a simple IP GRE tunnel. You can use a real router, LammleSim IOS version, or Packet Tracer to do this lab.

1. First, configure the logical tunnel with the interface tunnel *number* command.

```
Corp(config)#int s0/0/0
Corp(config-if)#ip address 63.1.1.2 255.255.255.252
Corp(config)#int tunnel ?
  <0-2147483647>  Tunnel interface number
Corp(config)#int tunnel 0
*Jan  5 16:58:22.719: %LINEPROTO-5-UPDOWN: Line protocol
on Interface Tunnel0, changed state to down
```

2. Once you have configured your interface and created the logical tunnel, you need to configure the mode and then the transport protocol.

```
Corp(config-if)#tunnel mode ?
  aurp    AURP TunnelTalk AppleTalk encapsulation
  cayman  Cayman TunnelTalk AppleTalk encapsulation
  dvmrp   DVMRP multicast tunnel
  eon     EON compatible CLNS tunnel
  gre     generic route encapsulation protocol
  ipip    IP over IP encapsulation
  ipsec   IPSec tunnel encapsulation
  iptalk  Apple IPTalk encapsulation
  ipv6    Generic packet tunneling in IPv6
  ipv6ip  IPv6 over IP encapsulation
  nos     IP over IP encapsulation (KA9Q/NOS compatible)
  rbscp   RBSCP in IP tunnel
Corp(config-if)#tunnel mode gre ?
  ip          over IP
  ipv6        over IPv6
  multipoint  over IP (multipoint)

Corp(config-if)#tunnel mode gre ip
```

3. Now that you have created the tunnel interface, the type, and the transport protocol, you need to configure your IP addresses. Of course, you need to use your actual interface IP for the tunnel, but you also need to configure the tunnel source and tunnel destination addresses.

```
Corp(config-if)#int t0
Corp(config-if)#ip address 192.168.10.1 255.255.255.0
Corp(config-if)#tunnel source 63.1.1.1
Corp(config-if)#tunnel destination 63.1.1.2

Corp#sho run interface tunnel 0
Building configuration...

Current configuration : 117 bytes
!
interface Tunnel0
 ip address 192.168.10.1 255.255.255.0
 tunnel source 63.1.1.1
 tunnel destination 63.1.1.2
end
```

4. Now configure the other end of the serial link and watch the tunnel pop up!

```
SF(config)#int s0/0/0
SF(config-if)#ip address 63.1.1.2 255.255.255.252
SF(config-if)#int t0
SF(config-if)#ip address 192.168.10.2 255.255.255.0
SF(config-if)#tunnel source 63.1.1.2
SF(config-if)#tun destination 63.1.1.1
*May 19 22:46:37.099: %LINEPROTO-5-UPDOWN: Line protocol on Interface
Tunnel0, changed state to up
```

Remember, you don't need to configure your tunnel mode and transport protocol because GRE and IP are the defaults. It's really important that you remember to configure the tunnel interface with the actual source and destination IP addresses to use or the tunnel won't come up. In my example, 63.1.1.2 was the source and 63.1.1.1 was the destination.

5. Verify with the following commands:

```
Corp#sh ip int brief
```

You should see that the tunnel interface is now showing as an interface on your router. The IP address of the tunnel interface and the physical and data link status shows as up/up.

```
Corp#sh int tun 0
```

The show interfaces command shows the configuration settings and the interface status as well as the IP address and tunnel source and destination address.

Corp#**sh ip route**

The tunnel0 interface shows up as a directly connected interface, and although it's a logical interface, the router treats it as a physical interface just like serial0/0 in the routing table.

Review Questions

The following questions are designed to test your understanding of this chapter's material. For more information on how to get additional questions, please see www.lammle.com/ccna.

You can find the answers to these questions in Appendix B, "Answers to Review Questions."

1. Which command will display the CHAP authentication process as it occurs between two routers in the network?

   A. show chap authentication

   B. show interface serial 0

   C. debug ppp authentication

   D. debug chap authentication

2. Which of the following are true regarding the following command? (Choose two.)

   R1(config-router)# **neighbor 10.10.200.1 remote-as 6200**

   A. The local router R1 uses AS 6200.

   B. The remote router uses AS 6200.

   C. The local interface of R1 is 10.10.200.1.

   D. The neighbor IP address is 10.10.200.1.

   E. The neighbor's loopback interface is 10.10.200.1.

3. BGP uses which Transport layer protocol and port number?

   A. UDP/123

   B. TCP/123

   C. UDP/179

   D. TCP/179

   E. UDP/169

   F. TCP/169

4. Which command can you use to know the hold time on the two BGP peers?

   A. show ip bgp

   B. show ip bgp summary

   C. show ip bgp all

   D. show ip bgp neighbor

5. What does a next hop of 0.0.0.0 mean in the show ip bgp command output?

```
Network          Next Hop          Metric LocPrf Weight Path
*> 10.1.1.0/24    0.0.0.0                  0          32768 ?
*> 10.13.13.0/24  0.0.0.0                  0          32768 ?
```

    A. The router does not know the next hop.

    B. The network is locally originated via the network command in BGP.

    C. It is not a valid network.

    D. The next hop is not reachable.

6. Which two of the following are GRE characteristics? (Choose two.)

    A. GRE encapsulation uses a protocol-type field in the GRE header to support the encapsulation of any OSI layer 3 protocol.

    B. GRE itself is stateful. It includes flow-control mechanisms, by default.

    C. GRE includes strong security mechanisms to protect its payload.

    D. The GRE header, together with the tunneling IP header, creates at least 24 bytes of additional overhead for tunneled packets.

7. A GRE tunnel is flapping with the following error message:

```
07:11:49: %LINEPROTO-5-UPDOWN:
          Line protocol on Interface Tunnel0, changed state to up
07:11:55: %TUN-5-RECURDOWN:
          Tunnel0 temporarily disabled due to recursive routing
07:11:59: %LINEPROTO-5-UPDOWN:
          Line protocol on Interface Tunnel0, changed state to down
07:12:59: %LINEPROTO-5-UPDOWN:
```

What could be the reason for the tunnel flapping?

    A. IP routing has not been enabled on tunnel interface.

    B. There's an MTU issue on the tunnel interface.

    C. The router is trying to route to the tunnel destination address using the tunnel interface itself.

    D. An access list is blocking traffic on the tunnel interface.

8. Which of the following commands will not tell you if the GRE tunnel 0 is in up/up state?

    A. show ip interface brief

    B. show interface tunnel 0

    C. show ip interface tunnel 0

    D. show run interface tunnel 0

9. Which of the following PPP authentication protocols authenticates a device on the other end of a link with an encrypted password?

    A. MD5

    B. PAP

    C. CHAP

    D. DES

10. Which of the following encapsulates PPP frames in Ethernet frames and uses common PPP features like authentication, encryption, and compression?

    A. PPP

    B. PPPoA

    C. PPPoE

    D. Token Ring

11. Shown is the output of a `show interfaces` command on an interface that is configured to use PPP. A ping of the IP address on the other end of the link fails. Which two of the following could be the reason for the problem? (Choose two.)

    ```
    R1# show interfaces serial 0/0/1
    Serial0/0/0 is up, line protocol is down
      Hardware is GT96K Serial
    Internet address is 10.0.1.1/30
    ```

    A. The CSU/DSU connected to the other router is not powered on.

    B. The IP address on the router at the other end of the link is not in subnet 192.168.2.0/24.

    C. CHAP authentication failed.

    D. The router on the other end of the link has been configured to use HDLC.

12. You have configured a serial interface with GRE IP commands on a corporate router with a point-to-point link to a remote office. What command will show you the IP addresses and tunnel source and destination addresses of the interfaces?

    A. `show int serial 0/0`

    B. `show ip int brief`

    C. `show interface tunnel 0`

    D. `show tunnel ip status`

    E. `debug ip interface tunnel`

13. Which of the following is true regarding WAN technologies? (Choose three.)

    A. You must use PPP on a link connecting two routers using a point-to-point lease line.

    B. You can use a T1 to connect a customer site to the ISP.

    C. You can use a T1 to connect a Frame Relay connection to the ISP.

D. You can use Ethernet as a WAN service by using EoMPLS.

E. When using an Ethernet WAN, you must configure the DLCI.

14. You want to allow remote users to send protected packets to the corporate site, but you don't want to install software on the remote client machines. What is the best solution that you could implement?

A. GRE tunnel

B. Web VPN

C. VPN Anywhere

D. IPsec

15. Why won't the serial link between the Corp router and the Remote router come up?

```
Corp#sh int s0/0
Serial0/0 is up, line protocol is down
  Hardware is PowerQUICC Serial
  Internet address is 10.0.1.1/24
  MTU 1500 bytes, BW 1544 Kbit, DLY 20000 usec,
     reliability 254/255, txload 1/255, rxload 1/255
  Encapsulation PPP, loopback not set
Remote#sh int s0/0
Serial0/0 is up, line protocol is down
  Hardware is PowerQUICC Serial
  Internet address is 10.0.1.2/24
  MTU 1500 bytes, BW 1544 Kbit, DLY 20000 usec,
     reliability 254/255, txload 1/255, rxload 1/255
  Encapsulation HDLC, loopback not set
```

A. The serial cable is faulty.

B. The IP addresses are not in the same subnet.

C. The subnet masks are not correct.

D. The keepalive settings are not correct.

E. The layer 2 frame types are not compatible.

16. Which of the following are benefits of using a VPN in your internetwork? (Choose three.)

A. Security

B. Private high-bandwidth links

C. Cost savings

D. Incompatibility with broadband technologies

E. Scalability

17. Which two technologies are examples of layer 2 MPLS VPN technologies? (Choose two.)

    A. VPLS

    B. DMVPM

    C. GETVPN

    D. VPWS

18. Which of the following is an industry-wide standard suite of protocols and algorithms that allows for secure data transmission over an IP-based network that functions at the layer 3 (Network layer) of the OSI model?

    A. HDLC

    B. Cable

    C. VPN

    D. IPsec

    E. xDSL

19. Which of the following describes the creation of private networks across the Internet, enabling privacy and tunneling of non-TCP/IP protocols?

    A. HDLC

    B. Cable

    C. VPN

    D. IPsec

    E. xDSL

20. Which two VPNs are examples of service provider–managed VPNs? (Choose two.)

    A. Remote-access VPN

    B. Layer 2 MPLS VPN

    C. Layer 3 MPLS VPN

    D. DMVPN

Chapter

22

Evolution of Intelligent Networks

THE FOLLOWING ICND2 EXAM TOPICS ARE COVERED IN THIS CHAPTER:

✓ **1.6 Describe the benefits of switch stacking and chassis aggregation**

✓ **4.2 Describe the effects of cloud resources on enterprise network architecture**

-   4.2.a Traffic path to internal and external cloud services

-   4.2.b Virtual services

-   4.2.c Basic virtual network infrastructure

✓ **4.3 Describe basic QoS concepts**

-   4.3.a Marking

-   4.3.b Device trust

-   4.3.c Prioritization

-   4.3.c.

-   (i) Voice 4.3.c.

-   (ii) Video 4.3.c.

-   (iii) Data

-   4.3.d Shaping

-   4.3.e Policing

-   4.3.f Congestion management

✓ **4.5 Verify ACLs using the APIC-EM Path Trace ACL analysis tool**

✓ **5.5 Describe network programmability in enterprise network architecture**

-   5.5.a Function of a controller

-   5.5.b Separation of control plane and data plane

-   5.5.c Northbound and southbound APIs

This all-new chapter is totally focused on the CCNA objectives for intelligent networks. I'll start by covering switch stacking using StackWise and then move on to discuss the important realm of cloud computing and its effect on the enterprise network.

I'm going to stick really close to the objectives on the more difficult subjects to help you tune in specifically to the content that's important for the CCNA, including the following: Software Defined Networking (SDN), application programming interfaces (APIs), Cisco's Application Policy Infrastructure Controller Enterprise Module (APIC-EM), Intelligent WAN, and finally, quality of service (QoS). While it's good to understand the cloud and SDN because they're certainly objectives for the CCNA, just know that they aren't as critical for the objectives as the QoS section found in this chapter.

In this chapter, I really only have the space to introduce the concepts of network programmability and SDN because the topic is simply too large in scope. Plus, this chapter is already super challenging because it's a foundational chapter containing no configurations. Just remember that I'm going to spotlight the objectives in this chapter to make this chapter and its vital content as potent but painless as possible! We'll check off every exam objective by the time we're through.

To find up-to-the-minute updates for this chapter, please see www.lammle .com/ccna or the book's web page at www.sybex.com/go/ccna.

Switch Stacking

It's hard to believe that Cisco is using switch stacking to start their "Evolution of Intelligent Networks" objectives because switch stacking has been around since the word *cloud* meant 420 in my home town of Boulder, but I digress.

A typical access closet contains access switches placed next to each other in the same rack and uses high-speed redundant links with copper, or more typically fiber, to the distribution layer switches.

Here are three big drawbacks to a typical switch topology:

- Management overhead is high.
- STP will block half of the uplinks.
- There is no direct communication between switches.

Cisco StackWise technology connects switches that are mounted in the same rack together so they basically become one larger switch. By doing this, you can incrementally add more access ports for each closet while avoiding the cost of upgrading to a bigger switch. So you're adding ports as you grow your company instead of front loading the investment into a pricier, larger switch all at once. And since these stacks are managed as a single unit, it reduces the management in your network.

All switches in a stack share configuration and routing information, so you can easily add or remove switches at any time without disrupting your network or affecting its performance.

Figure 22.1 shows a typical access layer StackWise unit.

FIGURE 22.1   Switch stacking

To create a StackWise unit, you combine individual switches into a single, logical unit using special stack interconnect cables as shown in Figure 22.1. This creates a bidirectional, closed-loop path in the stack.

Here are some other features of StackWise:

- Any changes to the network topology or routing information are updated continuously through the stack interconnect.

- A master switch manages the stack as a single unit. The master switch is elected from one of the stack member switches.

- You can join up to nine separate switches in a stack.

- Each stack of switches has only a single IP address, and the stack is managed as a single object. You'll use this single IP address for managing the stack, including fault detection, VLAN database updates, security, and QoS controls. Each stack has only one configuration file, which is distributed to each switch in the StackWise.

- Using Cisco StackWise will produce some management overhead, but at the same time, multiple switches in a stack can create an EtherChannel connection, eliminating the need for STP.

These are the benefits to using StackWise technology, specifically mapped to the CCNA objectives to memorize:

- StackWise provides a method to join multiple physical switches into a single logical switching unit.

- Switches are united by special interconnect cables.

- The master switch is elected.
- The stack is managed as a single object and has a single management IP address.
- Management overhead is reduced.
- STP is no longer needed if you use EtherChannel.
- Up to nine switches can be in a StackWise unit.

One more very cool thing…When you add a new switch to the stack, the master switch automatically configures the unit with the currently running IOS image as well as the configuration of the stack. So you don't have to do anything to bring up the switch before its ready to operate…nice!

Cloud Computing and Its Effect on the Enterprise Network

Cloud computing is by far one of the hottest topics in today's IT world. Basically, cloud computing can provide virtualized processing, storage, and computing resources to users remotely, making the resources transparently available regardless of the user connection. To put it simply, some people just refer to the cloud as "someone else's hard drive." This is true, of course, but the cloud is much more than just storage.

The history of the consolidation and virtualization of our servers tells us that this has become the de facto way of implementing servers because of basic resource efficiency. Two physical servers will use twice the amount of electricity as one server, but through virtualization, one physical server can host two virtual machines, hence the main thrust toward virtualization. With it, network components can simply be shared more efficiently.

Users connecting to a cloud provider's network, whether it be for storage or applications, really don't care about the underlying infrastructure because as computing becomes a service rather than a product, it's then considered an on-demand resource, described in Figure 22.2.

FIGURE 22.2   Cloud computing is on-demand.

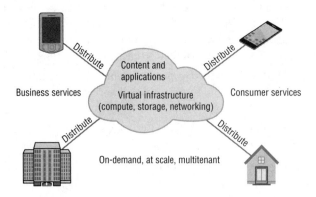

Centralization/consolidation of resources, automation of services, virtualization, and standardization are just a few of the big benefits cloud services offer. Let's take a look in Figure 22.3.

FIGURE 22.3 Advantages of cloud computing

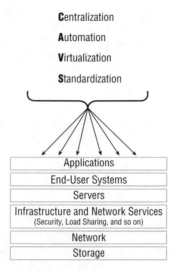

Cloud computing has several advantages over the traditional use of computer resources. Following are advantages to the provider and to the cloud user.

Here are the advantages to a cloud service builder or provider:

- Cost reduction, standardization, and automation
- High utilization through virtualized, shared resources
- Easier administration
- Fall-in-place operations model

Here are the advantages to cloud users:

- On-demand, self-service resource provisioning
- Fast deployment cycles
- Cost effective
- Centralized appearance of resources
- Highly available, horizontally scaled application architectures
- No local backups

Having centralized resources is critical for today's workforce. For example, if you have your documents stored locally on your laptop and your laptop gets stolen, you're pretty much screwed unless you're doing constant local backups. That is so 2005!

After I lost my laptop and all the files for the book I was writing at the time, I swore (yes, I did that too) to never have my files stored locally again. I started using only Google

Drive, OneDrive, and Dropbox for all my files, and they became my best backup friends. If I lose my laptop now, I just need to log in from any computer from anywhere to my service provider's logical drives and presto, I have all my files again. This is clearly a simple example of using cloud computing, specifically SaaS (which is discussed next), and it's wonderful!

So cloud computing provides for the sharing of resources, lower cost operations passed to the cloud consumer, computing scaling, and the ability to dynamically add new servers without going through the procurement and deployment process.

Service Models

Cloud providers can offer you different available resources based on your needs and budget. You can choose just a vitalized network platform or go all in with the network, OS, and application resources.

Figure 22.4 shows the three service models available depending on the type of service you choose to get from a cloud.

FIGURE 22.4   Cloud computing service

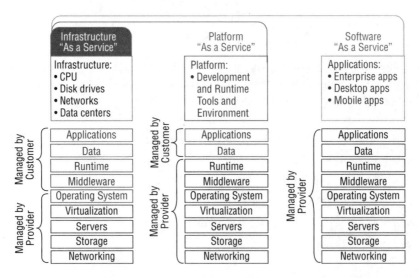

You can see that IaaS allows the customer to manage most of the network, whereas SaaS doesn't allow any management by the customer, and PaaS is somewhere in the middle of the two. Clearly, choices can be cost driven, so the most important thing is that the customer pays only for the services or infrastructure they use.

Let's take a look at each service:

Infrastructure as a Service (IaaS): Provides only the network.   Delivers computer infrastructure—a platform virtualization environment—where the customer has the most control and management capability.

Platform as a Service (PaaS): Provides the operating system and the network. Delivers a computing platform and solution stack, allowing customers to develop, run, and manage applications without the complexity of building and maintaining the infrastructure typically associated with developing and launching an application. An example is Windows Azure.

Software as a Service (SaaS): Provides the required software, operating system, and network. SaaS is common application software such as databases, web servers, and email software that's hosted by the SaaS vendor. The customer accesses this software over the Internet. Instead of having users install software on their computers or servers, the SaaS vendor owns the software and runs it on computers in its data center. Microsoft Office 365 and many Amazon Web Services (AWS) offerings are perfect examples of SaaS.

So depending on your business requirements and budget, cloud service providers market a very broad offering of cloud computing products from highly specialized offerings to a large selection of services.

What's nice here is that you're is offered a fixed price for each service that you use, which allows you to easily budget wisely for the future. It's true—at first, you'll have to spend a little cash on staff training, but with automation you can do more with less staff because administration will be easier and less complex. All of this works to free up the company resources to work on new business requirements and be more agile and innovative in the long run.

Overview of Network Programmability in Enterprise Network

Right now in our current, traditional networks, our router and switch ports are the only devices that are not virtualized. So this is what we're really trying to do here—virtualize our physical ports.

First, understand that our current routers and switches run an operating system, such as Cisco IOS, that provides network functionality. This has worked well for us for 25 years or so, but it is way too cumbersome now to configure, implement, and troubleshoot these autonomous devices in today's large, complicated networks. Before you even get started, you have to understand the business requirements and then push that out to all the devices. This can take weeks or even months since each device is configured, maintained, and monitored separately.

Before we can talk about the new way to network our ports, you need to understand how our current networks forward data, which happens via these two planes:

Data plane This plane, also referred to as the forwarding plane, is physically responsible for forwarding frames of packets from its ingress to egress interfaces using protocols managed in the control plane. Here, data is received, the destination interface is looked up, and the forwarding of frames and packets happens, so the data plane relies completely on the control plane to provide solid information.

Control plane   This plane is responsible for managing and controlling any forwarding table that the data plane uses. For example, routing protocols such as OSPF, EIGRP, RIP, and BGP as well as IPv4 ARP, IPv6 NDP, switch MAC address learning, and STP are all managed by the control plane.

Now that you understand that there are two planes used to forward traffic in our current or legacy network, let's take a look at the future of networking.

Application Programming Interfaces (APIs)

If you have worked on any enterprise Wi-Fi installations in the last decade, you would have designed your physical network and then configured a type of network controller that managed all the wireless APs in the network. It's hard to imagine that anyone would install a wireless network today without some type of controller in an enterprise network, where the access points (APs) receive their directions from the controller on how to manage the wireless frames and the APs have no operating system or brains to make many decisions on their own.

The same is now true for our physical router and switch ports, and it's precisely this centralized management of network frames and packets that Software Defined Networking (SDN) provides to us.

SDN removes the control plane intelligence from the network devices by having a central controller manage the network instead of having a full operating system (Cisco IOS, for example) on the devices. In turn, the controller manages the network by separating the control and data (forwarding) planes, which automates configuration and the remediation of all devices.

So instead of the network devices each having individual control planes, we now have a centralized control plane, which consolidates all network operations in the SDN controller. APIs allow for applications to control and configure the network without human intervention. The APIs are another type of configuration interface just like the CLI, SNMP, or GUI interfaces, which facilitate machine-to-machine operations.

The SDN architecture slightly differs from the architecture of traditional networks by adding a third layer, the application plane, as described here and shown in Figure 22.5:

Data (or forwarding) plane   Contains network elements, meaning any physical or virtual device that deals with data traffic.

Control plane   Usually a software solution, the SDN controllers reside here to provide centralized control of the router and switches that populate the data plane, removing the control plane from individual devices.

Application plane   This new layer contains the applications that communicate their network requirements toward the controller using APIs.

FIGURE 22.5 The SDN architecture

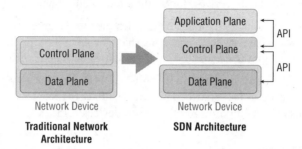

SDN is pretty cool because your applications tell the network what to do based on business needs instead of you having to do it. Then the controller uses the APIs to pass instructions on to your routers, switches, or other network gear. So instead of taking weeks or months to push out a business requirement, the solution now only takes minutes.

There are two sets of APIs that SDN uses and they are very different. As you already know, the SDN controller uses APIs to communicate with both the application and data plane. Communication with the data plane is defined with southbound interfaces, while services are offered to the application plane using the northbound interface. Let's take a deeper look at this oh-so-vital CCNA objective.

Southbound APIs

Logical southbound interface (SBI) APIs (or device-to-control-plane interfaces) are used for communication between the controllers and network devices. They allow the two devices to communicate so that the controller can program the data plane forwarding tables of your routers and switches. SBIs are pictured in Figure 22.6.

FIGURE 22.6 Southbound interfaces

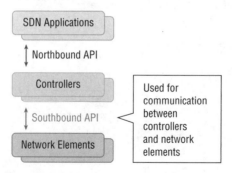

Since all the network drawings had the network gear below the controller, the APIs that talked to the devices became known as southbound, meaning, "out the southbound interface of the controller." And don't forget that with SDN, the term *interface* is no longer referring to a physical interface!

Unlike northbound APIs, southbound APIs have many standards, and you absolutely must know them well for the objectives. Let's talk about them now:

OpenFlow   Describes an industry-standard API, which the ONF (opennetworking.org) defines. It configures white label switches, meaning that they are nonproprietary, and as a result defines the flow path through the network. All the configuration is done through NETCONF.

NETCONF   Although not all devices support NETCONF yet, what this provides is a network management protocol standardized by the IETF. Using RPC, you can install, manipulate, and delete the configuration of network devices using XML.

 NETCONF is a protocol that allows you to modify the configuration of a networking device, but if you want to modify the device's forwarding table, then the OpenFlow protocol is the way to go.

onePK   A Cisco proprietary SBI that allows you to inspect or modify the network element configuration without hardware upgrades. This makes life easier for developers by providing software development kits for Java, C, and Python.

OpFlex   The name of the southbound API in the Cisco ACI world is OpFlex, an open-standard, distributed control system. Understand that OpenFlow first sends detailed and complex instructions to the control plane of the network elements in order to implement a new application policy—something called an imperative SDN model. On the other hand, OpFlex uses a declarative SDN model because the controller, which Cisco calls the APIC, sends a more abstract, "summary policy" to the network elements. The summary policy makes the controller believe that the network elements will implement the required changes using their own control planes, since the devices will use a partially centralized control plane.

Northbound APIs

To communicate from the SDN controller and the applications running over the network, you'll use northbound interfaces (NBIs), pictured in Figure 22.7.

FIGURE 22.7   Northbound interfaces

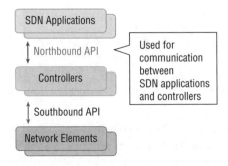

By setting up a framework that allows the application to demand the network setup with the configuration that it needs, the NBIs allow your applications to manage and control the network. This is priceless for saving time because you no longer need to adjust and tweak your network to get a service or application running correctly.

The NBI applications include a wide variety of automated network services, from network virtualization and dynamic virtual network provisioning to more granular firewall monitoring, user identity management, and access policy control. This allows for cloud orchestration applications that tie together, for server provisioning, storage, and networking that enables a complete rollout of new cloud services in minutes instead of weeks!

Sadly, at this writing there is no single northbound interface that you can use for communication between the controller and all applications. So instead, you use various and sundry northbound APIs, with each one working only with a specific set of applications.

Most of the time, applications used by NBIs will be on the same system as the APIC controller, so the APIs don't need to send messages over the network since both programs run on the same system. However, if they don't reside on the same system, REST (Representational State Transfer) comes into play; it uses HTTP messages to transfer data over the API for applications that sit on different hosts.

Cisco APIC-EM

Cisco Application Policy Infrastructure Controller Enterprise Module (APIC-EM) is a Cisco SDN controller, which uses the previously mentioned open APIs for policy-based management and security through a single controller, abstracting the network and making network services simpler. APIC-EM provides centralized automation of policy-based application profiles, and the APIC-EM northbound interface is the only API that you'll need to control your network programmatically. Through this programmability, automated network control helps IT to respond quickly to new business opportunities. The APIC-EM also includes support for greenfield (new installations) and brownfield (current or old installations) deployments, which allows you to implement programmability and automation with the infrastructure that you already have.

APIC-EM is pretty cool, easy to use (that's up for debate), and automates the tasks that network engineers have been doing for well over 20 years. At first glance this seems like it will replace our current jobs, and in some circumstances, people resistant to change will certainly be replaced. But you don't have to be one of them if you start planning now. Figure 22.8 demonstrates exactly where the APCI-EM controller sits in the SDN stack.

FIGURE 22.8   Where APIC-EM fits in the SDN stack

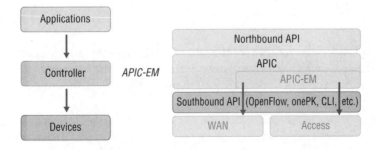

Cisco APIC-EM's northbound interface is only an API, but southbound interfaces are implemented with something called a service abstraction layer (SAL), which talks to the network elements via SNMP and CLI. Using the SNMP and the CLI allows APIC-EM to work with legacy Cisco products, and soon APIC-EM will be able to use NETCONF too.

The network devices can be either physical or virtual, including Nexus data center switches, ASA firewalls, ASR routers, or even third-party load balancers. The managed devices must be specific to ACI; in other words, a special NX-OS or ASR IOS version is required to add the southbound APIs required to communicate with the APIC controller.

The APIC-EM API is REST based, which as you know allows you to discover and control your network using HTTP by using the GET, POST, PUT, and DELETE options along with JSON (JavaScript Object Notation) and XML (eXtensible Markup Language) syntax.

Here are some important features of Cisco APIC-EM that are covered in the CCNA objectives, and shown in Figure 22.9:

FIGURE 22.9   APIC-Enterprise Module

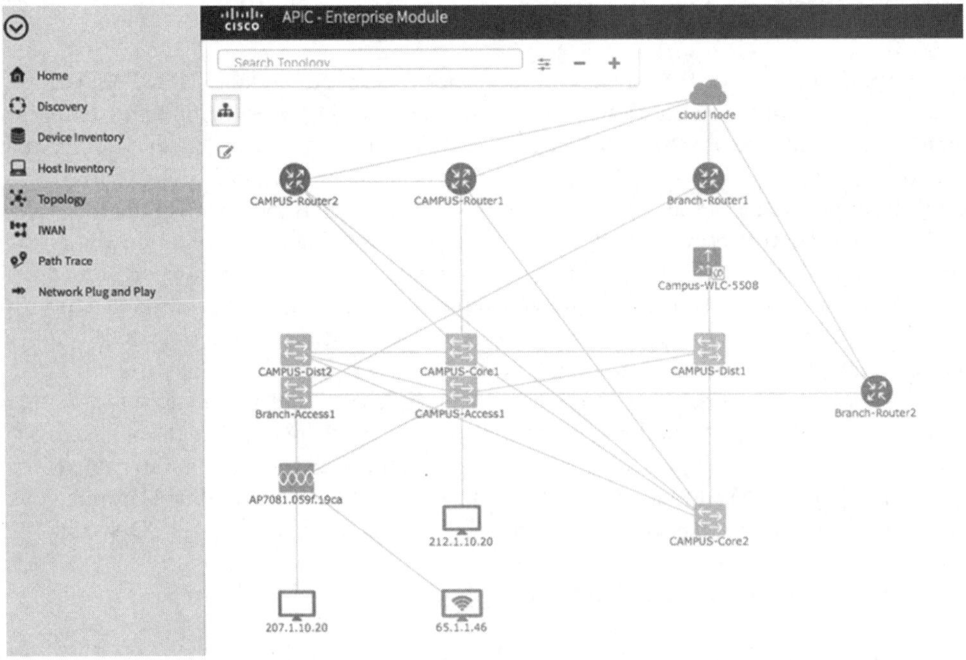

On the left of the screen you can see the Discover button. This provides the network information database, which scans the network and provides the inventory, including all network devices; the network devices are also shown in the Device Inventory.

There's also a network topology visualization, which reveals the physical topology discovered, as shown in the layout on Figure 22.9. This auto-discovers and maps network devices to a physical topology with detailed device-level data, including the discovered hosts. And take note of that IWAN button. It provides the provisioning of IWAN network profiles with simple business policies. Plus there is a Path Trace button, which I will talk about next.

But wait… Before I move on to the Path Trace functionality of APIC-EM, let me go over a few more promising features with you. In the APIC-EM is the Zero-Touch Deployment feature, which finds a new device via the controller scanner and automatically configures it. You can track user identities and endpoints by exchanging the information with the Cisco Identity Service Engine (Cisco ISE) via the Identity Manager. You can also quickly set and enforce QoS priority policies with the QoS deployment and change management feature and accelerate ACL management by querying and analyzing ACLs on each network device. This means you can quickly identify ACL misconfiguration using the ACL analysis! And last but not least, using the Policy Manager, the controller translates a business policy into a network-device-level policy. The Policy Manager can enforce the policy for a specific user at various times of the day, across wired and wireless networks.

Now let's take a look at the very vital path tracing feature of APIC-EM.

Using APIC-EM for Path Tracing

An important objective in this intelligent networks chapter is the path tracing ability in the APIC-EM. Matter of fact, I've mostly been using the APIC-EM for just this feature in order to help me troubleshoot my virtual networks, and it does it very well. And it looks cool too!

Pushing toward staying tight to the CCNA objectives here, you really want to know that you can use the path trace service of APIC-EM for ACL analysis. Doing this allows you to examine the path that a specific type of packet travels as it makes its way across the network from a source to a destination node, and it can use IP and TCP/UDP ports when diagnosing an application issue. If there is an ACL on an interface that blocks a certain application, you'll see this in a GUI output. I cannot tell you how extremely helpful this is in the day-to-day administration of your networks!

The result of a path trace will be a GUI representation of the path that a packet takes across all the devices and links between the source and destination, and you can choose to provide the output of a reverse path as well. Although I could easily do this same work manually, it would certainly be a whole lot more time consuming if I did! APIC-EM's Path Trace app actually does the work for you with just a few clicks at the user interface.

Once you fill in the fields for the source, destination, and optionally, the application, the path trace is initiated. You'll then see the path between hosts, plus the list of each device along the path, illustrated in Figure 22.10.

FIGURE 22.10 APIC-Enterprise Module path trace sample

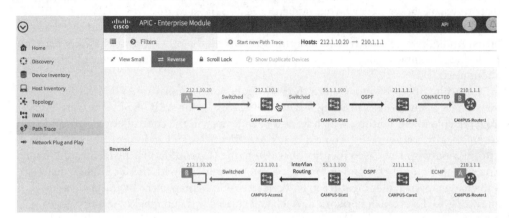

Okay, here you can see the complete path taken from host A to host B. I chose to view the reverse path as well. In this particular case, we weren't being blocked by an ACL, but if a packet actually was being blocked for a certain application, we'd see the exact interface where the application was blocked and why. Here is more detail on how my trace occurred.

First, the APIC-EM Discovery finds the network topology. At this point I can now choose the source and destination address of a packet and, alternately, port numbers and the application that can be used. The MAC address table, IP routing tables, and so on are used by the APIC-EM to find the path of the packet through the network. Finally, the GUI will show you the path, complete with device and interface information.

Last point: The APIC-EM is free, and most of the applications off the NBI are built in and included, but there are some solution applications that need a license. So if you have a VM with at least 64 gigs of RAM, you're set!

Cisco Intelligent WAN

This topic was covered in the chapter "Wide Area Networks," but it's important to at least touch on it here since it's included in the "Evolution of Intelligent Networks" CCNA objectives. We'll also take a peek at the APIC-EM for IWAN in this section. What Cisco's IWAN solution provides is a way to take advantage of cheaper bandwidth at remote locations, without compromising application performance, availability, or even security and in an easy-to-configure manner—nice!

Clearly, this allows us to use low-cost or inexpensive Internet connections, which have become more reliable and cost effective compared to the dedicated WAN links we used to use, and it means that we can now take advantage of this low-cost technology with Cisco's new Cisco Intelligent WAN (Cisco IWAN). Add in the failover and redundancy features that IWAN provides and you'll definitely see the reason large enterprises are deploying

Cisco's IWAN. The downside? Well, nothing to you and me, because we always use Cisco's gear from end to end in all our networks, right?

IWAN can provide great long-distance connections for your organization by dynamically routing based on the application service-level agreement (SLA) while paying attention to network conditions. And it can do this over any type of network!

Figure 22.11 pictures the IWAN Aggregation Site tab on the IWAN screen.

A feature of the APCI-EM is the IWAN discovery and configuration.

FIGURE 22.11   APIC-Enterprise Module IWAN

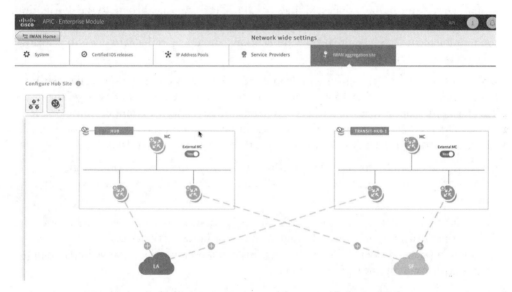

There are four components of Cisco's IWAN:

Transport-independent connectivity   Cisco IWAN provides a type of advanced VPN connection across all available routes to remote locations, providing one network with a single routing domain. This allows you to easily multihome the network across different types of connections, including MPLS, broadband, and cellular.

Intelligent path control   By using Cisco Performance Routing (Cisco PfR), Cisco IWAN improves delivery and WAN efficiency of applications.

Application optimization   Via Cisco's Application Visibility and Control (Cisco AVC), as well as Cisco's Wide Area Application Services (Cisco WAAS), you can now optimize application performance over WAN links.

Highly secure connectivity   Using VPNs, firewalls, network segmentation, and security features, Cisco IWAN helps ensure that these solutions actually provide the security you need over the public Internet.

Quality of Service

Quality of service (QoS) refers to the way the resources are controlled so that the quality of services is maintained. It's basically the ability to provide a different priority to one or more types of traffic over other levels for different applications, data flows, or users so that they can be guaranteed a certain performance level. QoS is used to manage contention for network resources for better end-user experience.

QoS methods focus on problems that can affect data as it traverses network cable:

Delay   Data can run into congested lines or take a less-than-ideal route to the destination, and delays like these can make some applications, such as VoIP, fail. This is the best reason to implement QoS when real-time applications are in use in the network—to prioritize delay-sensitive traffic.

Dropped Packets   Some routers will drop packets if they receive a packet while their buffers are full. If the receiving application is waiting for the packets but doesn't get them, it will usually request that the packets be retransmitted—another common cause of a service(s) delay. With QoS, when there is contention on a link, less important traffic is delayed or dropped in favor of delay-sensitive business-important traffic.

Error   Packets can be corrupted in transit and arrive at the destination in an unacceptable format, again requiring retransmission and resulting in delays such as video and voice.

Jitter   Not every packet takes the same route to the destination, so some will be more delayed than others if they travel through a slower or busier network connection. The variation in packet delay is called *jitter*, and this can have a nastily negative impact on programs that communicate in real time.

Out-of-Order Delivery   Out-of-order delivery is also a result of packets taking different paths through the network to their destinations. The application at the receiving end needs to put them back together in the right order for the message to be completed. So if there are significant delays, or the packets are reassembled out of order, users will probably notice degradation of an application's quality.

QoS can ensure that applications with a required level of predictability will receive the necessary bandwidth to work properly. Clearly, on networks with excess bandwidth, this is not a factor, but the more limited your bandwidth is, the more important a concept like this becomes!

Traffic Characteristics

In today's networks, you will find a mix of data, voice, and video traffic. Each traffic type has different properties.

Figure 22.12 shows the traffic characteristics found in today's network for data, voice, and video.

FIGURE 22.12   Traffic characteristics

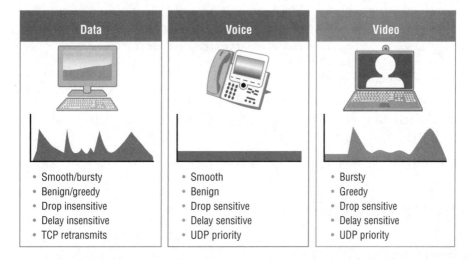

Data traffic is not real-time traffic, and includes data packets comprising of bursty (or unpredictable) traffic and widely varying packet arrival times.

The following are data characteristics on a network, as shown in Figure 22.12:

- Smooth/bursty

- Benign/greedy

- Drop insensitive

- Delay insensitive

- TCP retransmits

Data traffic doesn't really require special handling in today's network, especially if TCP is used. Voice traffic is real-time traffic with constant, predictable bandwidth and known packet arrival times.

The following are voice characteristics on a network:

- Smooth traffic

- Benign

- Drop insensitive

- Delay sensate insensitive

- UDP priority

One-way voice traffic needs the following:

- Latency of less than or equal to 150 milliseconds

- Jitter of less than or equal to 30 milliseconds

- Loss of less than or equal to 1%
- Bandwidth of only 30–128k Kbps

There are several types of video traffic, and a lot of the traffic on the Internet today is video traffic, with Netflix, Hulu, etc. Video traffic can include streaming video, real-time interactive video, and video conferences.

One-way video traffic needs the following:

- Latency of less than or equal to 200–400 milliseconds
- Jitter of less than or equal to 30–50 milliseconds
- Loss of less than or equal to 0.1%–1%
- Bandwidth of 384 Kbps to 20 Mbps or greater

Trust Boundary

The trust boundary is a point in the network where packet markings (which identify traffic such as voice, video, or data) are not necessarily trusted. You can create, remove, or rewrite markings at that point. The borders of a trust domain are the network locations where packet markings are accepted and acted upon. Figure 22.13 shows some typical trust boundaries.

FIGURE 22.13   Trust boundaries

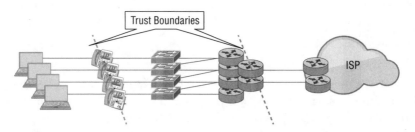

The figure shows that IP phones and router interfaces are typically trusted, but beyond those points are not. Here are some things you need to remember for the exam objectives:

Untrusted domain   This is the part of the network that you are not managing, such as PC, printers, etc.

Trusted domain   This is part of the network with only administrator-managed devices such as switches, routers, etc.

Trust boundary   This is where packets are classified and marked. For example, the trust boundary would be IP phones and the boundary between the ISP and enterprise network. In an enterprise campus network, the trust boundary is almost always at the edge switch.

Traffic at the trust boundary is classified and marked before being forwarded to the trusted domain. Markings on traffic coming from an untrusted domain are usually ignored to prevent end-user-controlled markings from taking unfair advantage of the network QoS configuration.

QoS Mechanisms

In this section we'll be covering these important mechanisms:

- Classification and marking tools
- Policing, shaping, and re-marking tools
- Congestion management (or scheduling) tools
- Link-specific tools

So let's take a deeper look at each mechanism now.

Classification and Marking

A classifier is an IOS tool that inspects packets within a field to identify the type of traffic that they are carrying. This is so that QoS can determine which traffic class they belong to and determine how they should be treated. It's important that this isn't a constant cycle for traffic because it does take up time and resources. Traffic is then directed to a policy-enforcement mechanism, referred to as policing, for its specific type.

Policy enforcement mechanisms include marking, queuing, policing, and shaping, and there are various layer 2 and layer 3 fields in a frame and packet for marking traffic. You are definitely going to have to understand these marking techniques to meet the objectives, so here we go:

Class of Service (CoS)   An Ethernet frame marking at layer 2, which contains 3 bits. This is called the Priority Code Point (PCP) within an Ethernet frame header when VLAN tagged frames as defined by IEEE 802.1Q are used.

Type of Service (ToS)   ToS comprises of 8 bits, 3 of which are designated as the IP precedence field in an IPv4 packet header. The IPv6 header field is called Traffic Class.

Differentiated Services Code Point (DSCP or DiffServ)   One of the methods we can use for classifying and managing network traffic and providing quality of service (QoS) on modern IP networks is DSCP. This technology uses a 6-bit differentiated services code point in the 8-bit Differentiated Services field (DS field) in the IP header for packet classification. DSCP allows for the creation of traffic classes that can be used to assign priorities. While IP precedence is the old way to mark ToS, DSCP is the new way. DSCP is backward compatible with IP precedence.

Layer 3 packet marking with IP precedence and DSCP is the most widely deployed marking option because layer 3 packet markings have end-to-end significance.

Class Selector   Class Selector uses the same 3 bits of the field as IP precedence and is used to indicate a 3-bit subset of DSCP values.

Traffic Identifier (TID)   TID, used in wireless frames, describe a 3-bit field in the QoS control field in 802.11. It's very similar to CoS, so just remember CoS is wired Ethernet and TID is wireless.

Classification Marking Tools

As discussed in the previous section, classification of traffic determines which type of traffic the packets or frames belong to, which then allows you to apply policies to it by marking, shaping, and policing. Always try to mark traffic as close to the trust boundary as possible.

To classify traffic, we generally use three ways:

Markings   This looks at header informant on existing layer 2 or 3 settings, and classification is based on existing markings.

Addressing   This classification technique looks at header information using source and destinations of interfaces, layer 2 and 3 addresses, and layer 4 port numbers. You can group traffic with devices using IP and traffic by type using port numbers.

Application signatures   This is the way to look at the information in the payload, and this classification technique is called deep packet inspection.

Let's dive deeper into deep packet inspection by discussing something called Network Based Application Recognition (NBAR).

NBAR is a classifier that provides deep-packet inspection on layer 4 to 7 on a packet, however, know that using NBAR is the most CPU intensive technique compared to using addresses (IP or ports) or access control lists (ACLs).

Since it's not always possible to identify applications by looking at just layers 3 and 4, NBAR looks deep into the packet payload and compares the payload content against its signature database called a Packet Description Language Model (PDLM).

There are two different modes of operation used with NBAR:

Passive mode   Using passive mode will give you real-time statistics on applications by protocol or interface as well as the bit rate, packet, and byte counts.

Active mode   Classifies applications for traffic marking so that QoS policies can be applied.

Policing, Shaping, and Re-Marking

Okay—now that we've identified and marked traffic, it's time to put some action on our packet. We do this with bandwidth assignments, policing, shaping, queuing, or dropping. For example, if some traffic exceeds bandwidth, it might be delayed, dropped, or even re-marked in order to avoid congestion.

Policers and shapers are two tools that identify and respond to traffic problems and are both rate limiters. Figure 22.14 shows how they differ.

FIGURE 22.14   Policing and shaping rate limiters

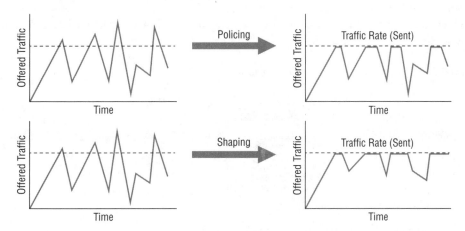

Policers and shapers identify traffic violations in a similar manner, but they differ in their response:

Policers   Since the policers make instant decisions you want to deploy them on the ingress if possible. This is because you want to drop traffic as soon as you receive it if it's going to be dropped anyway. Even so, you can still place them on an egress to control the amount of traffic per class. When traffic is exceeded, policers don't delay it, which means they do not introduce jitter or delay, they just check the traffic and can drop it or re-mark it. Just know that this means there's a higher drop probability, it can cause a significant amount of TCP resends.

Shapers   Shapers are usually deployed between an enterprise network, on the egress side, and the service provider network to make sure you stay within the carrier's contract rate. If the traffic does exceed the rate, it will get policed by the provider and dropped. This allows the traffic to meet the SLA and means there will be fewer TCP resends than with policers. Be aware that shaping does introduce jitter and delay.

Just remember that policers drop traffic and shapers delay it. Policers have significant TCP resends and shapers do not. Shapers introduce delay and jitter, but policers do not.

Tools for Managing Congestion

This section and the next section on congestion avoidance will cover congestion issues. If traffic exceeds network resource (always), the traffic gets queued, which is basically the temporary storage of backed-up packets. You perform queuing in order to avoid dropping packets. This isn't a bad thing. It's actually a good thing or all traffic would immediately be dropped if packets couldn't get processed immediately. However, traffic classes like

VoIP would actually be better off just being immediately dropped unless you can somehow guarantee delay-free bandwidth for that traffic.

When congestion occurs, the congestion management tools are activated. There are two types, as shown in Figure 22.15.

FIGURE 22.15 Congestion management

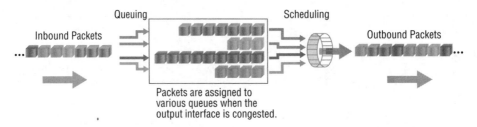

Let's take a closer look at congestion management:

Queuing (or buffering) Buffering is the logic of ordering packets in output buffers. It is activated only when congestion occurs. When queues fill up, packets can be reordered so that the higher-priority packets can be sent out of the exit interface sooner than the lower-priority ones.

Scheduling This is the process of deciding which packet should be sent out next and occurs whether or not there is congestion on the link.

Staying with scheduling for another minute, know that there are some schedule mechanisms that exist you really need to be familiar with. We'll go over those, and then I'll head back over to a detailed look at queuing:

Strict priority scheduling Low-priority queues are only serviced once the high-priority queues are empty. This is great if you are the one sending high-priority traffic, but it's possible that low-priority queues will never be processed. We call this traffic or queue starvation.

Round-robin scheduling This is a rather fair technique because queues are serviced in a set sequence. You won't have starving queues here, but real-time traffic suffers greatly.

Weighted fair scheduling By weighing the queues, the scheduling process will service some queues more often than others, which is an upgrade over round-robin. You won't have any starvation here either, but unlike with round-robin, you can give priority to real-time traffic. It does not, however, provide bandwidth guarantees.

Okay, let's run back over and finish queueing. Queuing typically is a layer 3 process, but some queueing can occur at layer 2 or even layer 1. Interestingly, if a layer 2 queue fills up, the data can be pushed into layer 3 queues, and at layer 1 (called the transmit ring or TX-ring queue), when that fills up, the data will be pushed to layer 2 and 3 queues. This is when QoS becomes active on the device.

There are many different queuing mechanisms, with only two typically used today, but let's take a look at the legacy queuing methods first:

First in, first out (FIFO)   A single queue with packets being processed in the exact order in which they arrived.

Priority queuing (PQ)   This is not really a good queuing method because lower-priority queues are served only when the higher-priority queues are empty. There are only four queues, and low-priority traffic many never be sent.

Custom queueing (CQ)   With up to 16 queues and round-robin scheduling, CQ prevents low-level queue starvation and provides traffic guarantees. But it doesn't provide strict priority for real-time traffic, so your VoIP traffic could end up being dropped.

Weighted fair queuing (WFQ)   This was actually a pretty popular way of queuing for a long time because it divided up the bandwidth by the number of flows, which provided bandwidth for all applications. This was great for real-time traffic, but it doesn't offer any guarantees for a particular flow.

Now that you know about all the not so good queuing methods to use, let's take a look at the two newer queuing mechanisms that are recommended for today's rich-media networks, detailed in Figure 22.16).

FIGURE 22.16   Queuing mechanisms

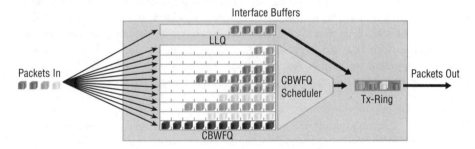

The two new and improved queuing mechanisms you should now use in today's network are class-based weighted fair queuing and low latency queuing:

Class-based weighted fair queuing (CBWFQ)   Provides fairness and bandwidth guarantees for all traffic, but it does not provide latency guarantees and is typically only used for data traffic management.

Low latency queuing (LLQ):   LLQ is really the same thing as CBWFQ but with stricter priorities for real-time traffic. LLQ is great for both data and real-time traffic because it provides both latency and bandwidth guarantees.

In Figure 22.16, you can see the LLQ queuing mechanism, which is suitable for networks with real-time traffic. If you remove the low-latency queue (at the top), you're then left with CBWFQ, which is only used for data-traffic networks.

Tools for Congestion Avoidance

TCP changed our networking world when it introduced sliding windows as a flow-control mechanism in the mid-1990s. Flow control is a way for the receiving device to control the amount of traffic from a transmitting device.

If a problem occurred during a data transmission (always), the previous flow control methods used by TCP and other layer 4 protocols like SPX, that we used before sliding windows, the transmission rate would be in half, and left there at the same rate, or lower, for the duration of the connection. This was certainly a point of contention with users!

TCP actually does cut transmission rates drastically if a flow control issue occurs, but it increases the transmission rate once the missing segments are resolved or the packets are finally processed. Because of this behavior, and although it was awesome at the time, this method can result in what we call tail drop. Tail drop is definitely suboptimal for today's networks because using it, we're not utilizing the bandwidth effectively.

Just to clarify, tail drop refers to the dropping of packets as they arrive when the queues on the receiving interface are full. This is a waste of precious bandwidth since TCP will just keep resending the data until it's happy again (meaning an ACK has been received). So now this brings up another new term, *TCP global synchronization*, where senders will reduce their transmission rate at the same time when packet loss occurs.

Congestion avoidance starts dropping packets before a queue fills, and it drops the packets by using traffic weights instead just randomness. Cisco uses something called weighted random early detection (WRED), which is a queuing method that ensures that high-precedence traffic has lower loss rates than other traffic during congestion. This allows more important traffic, like VoIP, to be prioritized and dropped over what you'd consider less important traffic such as, for example, a connection to Facebook.

Queuing algorithms manage the front of the queue and congestion mechanisms manage the back of the queue.

Figure 22.17 demonstrates how congestion avoidance works.

FIGURE 22.17   Congestion avoidance

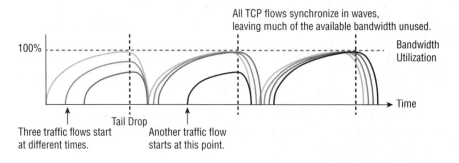

If three traffic flows start at different times, as shown in the example in Figure 22.17, and congestion occurs, using TCP could first cause tail drop, which drops the traffic as soon as it is received if the buffers are full. At that point TCP would start another traffic flow, synchronizing the TCP flows in waves, which would then leave much of the bandwidth unused.

Summary

This all-new chapter was totally focused on the CCNA objectives for intelligent networks. I started the chapter by covering switch stacking using StackWise and then moved on to discuss the important realm of cloud computing and what effect it has on the enterprise network.

Although this chapter had a lot of material, I stuck really close to the objectives on the more difficult subjects to help you tune in specifically to the content that's important for the CCNA, including the following: Software Defined Networking (SDN), application programming interfaces (APIs), Cisco's Application Policy Infrastructure Controller Enterprise Module (APIC-EM), Intelligent WAN, and finally, quality of service (QoS).

Exam Essentials

Understand switch stacking and StackWise.   You can connect up to nine individual switches together to create a StackWise.

Understand basic cloud technology.   Understand cloud services such as SaaS and others and how virtualization works.

Have a deep understanding of QoS.   You must understand QoS, specifically marking; device trust; prioritization for voice, video, and data; shaping; policing; and congestion management in detail.

Understand APIC-EM and the path trace.   Read through the APIC-EM section as well as the APIC-EM path trace section, which cover the CCNA objectives fully.

Understand SDN.   Understand how a controller works, and especially the control and data plane, as well as the northbound and southbound APIs.

Written Lab 22

You can find the answers to this lab in Appendix A, "Answers to Written Labs."
    Write the answers to the following questions:

1.   Which QoS mechanism is a 6-bit value that is used to describe the meaning of the layer 3 IPv4 ToS field?

2.   Southbound SDN interfaces are used between which two planes?

3.   Which QoS mechanism is a term that is used to describe a 3-bit field in the QoS control field of wireless frames?

4.   What are the three general ways to classify traffic?

5.   CoS is a layer 2 QoS _____?

6.   A session is using more bandwidth than allocated. Which QoS mechanism will drop the traffic?

7.   What are the three SDN layers?

8.   What are two **examples** of newer queuing mechanisms that are recommended for rich-media **networks**?

9.   What is a layer 4 to 7 deep-packet inspection classifier that is more CPU intensive than marking?

10.   _____ APIs are responsible for the communication between the SDN controller and the services running over the network.

Review Questions

The following questions are designed to test your understanding of this chapter's material. For more information on how to get additional questions, please see www.lammle.com/ccna.

You can find the answers to these questions in Appendix B, "Answers to Review Questions."

1. Which of the following is a congestion-avoidance mechanism?

   A. LMI

   B. WRED

   C. QPM

   D. QoS

2. Which of the following are true regarding StackWise? (Choose two.)

   A. A StackWise interconnect cable is used to connect the switches to create a bidirectional, closed-loop path.

   B. A StackWise interconnect cable is used to connect the switches to create a unidirectional, closed-loop path.

   C. StackWise can connect up to nine individual switches joined in a single logical switching unit.

   D. StackWise can connect up to nine individual switches joined into multiple logical switching units and managed by one IP address.

3. Which of the following is the best definition of cloud computing?

   A. UCS data center

   B. Computing model with all your data at the service provider

   C. On-demand computing model

   D. Computing model with all your data in your local data center

4. Which three features are properties and one-way requirements for voice traffic? (Choose three.)

   A. Bursty voice traffic.

   B. Smooth voice traffic.

   C. Latency should be below 400 ms.

   D. Latency should be below 150 ms.

   E. Bandwidth is roughly between 30 and 128 kbps.

   F. Bandwidth is roughly between 0.5 and 20 Mbps.

5. On which SDN architecture layer does Cisco APIC-EM reside?

    A. Data

    B. Control

    C. Presentation

    D. Application

6. In which cloud service model is the customer responsible for managing the operating system, software, platforms, and applications?

    A. IaaS

    B. SaaS

    C. PaaS

    D. APIC-EM

7. Which statement about QoS trust boundaries or domains is true?

    A. The trust boundary is always a router.

    B. PCs, printers, and tablets are usually part of a trusted domain.

    C. An IP phone is a common trust boundary.

    D. Routing will not work unless the service provider and the enterprise network are one single trust domain.

8. Which statement about IWAN is correct?

    A. The IWAN allows transport-independent connectivity.

    B. The IWAN allows only static routing.

    C. The IWAN does not provide application visibility because only encrypted traffic is transported.

    D. The IWAN needs special encrypting devices to provide an acceptable security level.

9. Which advanced classification tool can be used to classify data applications?

    A. NBAR

    B. MPLS

    C. APIC-EM

    D. ToS

10. The DSCP field constitutes how many bits in the IP header?

    A. 3 bits

    B. 4 bits

    C. 6 bits

    D. 8 bits

11. Between which two planes are SDN southbound interfaces used?

    A. Control

    B. Data

    C. Routing

    D. Application

12. Which option is a layer 2 QoS marking?

    A. EXP

    B. QoS group

    C. DSCP

    D. CoS

13. You are starting to use SDN in your network. What does this mean?

    A. You no longer have to work anymore, but you'll get paid more.

    B. You'll need to upgrade all your applications.

    C. You'll need to get rid of all Cisco switches.

    D. You now have more time to react faster when you receive a new business requirement.

14. Which QoS mechanism will drop traffic if a session uses more than the allotted bandwidth?

    A. Congestion management

    B. Shaping

    C. Policing

    D. Marking

15. Which three layers are part of the SDN architecture? (Choose three.)

    A. Network

    B. Data Link

    C. Control

    D. Data

    E. Transport

    F. Application

16. Which of the following is NOT true about APIC-EM ACL analysis?

    A. Fast comparison of ACLs between devices to visualize difference and identify misconfigurations

    B. Inspection, interrogation, and analysis of network access control policies

    C. Ability to provide layer 4 to layer 7 deep-packet inspection

    D. Ability to trace application-specific paths between end devices to quickly identify ACLs and other problem areas

17. Which two of the following are not part of APIC-EM?

    A. Southbound APIs are used for communication between the controllers and network devices.

    B. Northbound APIs are used for communication between the controllers and network devices.

    C. OnePK is Cisco proprietary.

    D. The control plane is responsible for the forwarding of frames or packets.

18. When stacking switches, which is true? (Choose two.)

    A. The stack is managed as multiple objects and has a single management IP address.

    B. The stack is managed as a single object and has a single management IP address.

    C. The master switch is chosen when you configure the first switch's master algorithm to on.

    D. The master switch is elected from one of the stack member switches.

19. Which of the following services provides the operating system and the network?

    A. IaaS

    B. PaaS

    C. SaaS

    D. None of the above

20. Which of the following services provides the required software, the operating system, and the network?

    A. IaaS

    B. PaaS

    C. SaaS

    D. None of the above

21. Which of the following is NOT a benefit of cloud computing for a cloud user?

    A. On-demand, self-service resource provisioning

    B. Centralized appearance of resources

    C. Local backups

    D. Highly available, horizontally scaled application architectures

Appendix A

Answers to Written Labs

Chapter 1: Internetworking

Written Lab 1.1: OSI Questions

1. The Application layer is responsible for finding the network resources broadcast from a server and adding flow control and error control (if the application developer chooses).

2. The Physical layer takes frames from the Data Link layer and encodes the 1s and 0s into a digital or analog (Ethernet or wireless) signal for transmission on the network medium.

3. The Network layer provides routing through an internetwork and logical addressing.

4. The Presentation layer makes sure that data is in a readable format for the Application layer.

5. The Session layer sets up, maintains, and terminates sessions between applications.

6. PDUs at the Data Link layer are called frames and provide physical addressing plus other options to place packets on the network medium.

7. The Transport layer uses virtual circuits to create a reliable connection between two hosts.

8. The Network layer provides logical addressing, typically IP addressing and routing.

9. The Physical layer is responsible for the electrical and mechanical connections between devices.

10. The Data Link layer is responsible for the framing of data packets.

11. The Session layer creates sessions between different hosts' applications.

12. The Data Link layer frames packets received from the Network layer.

13. The Transport layer segments user data.

14. The Network layer creates packets out of segments handed down from the Transport layer.

15. The Physical layer is responsible for transporting 1s and 0s (bits) in a digital signal.

16. Segments, packets, frames, bits

17. Transport

18. Data Link

19. Network

20. 48 bits (6 bytes) expressed as a hexadecimal number

Written Lab 1.2: Defining the OSI Layers and Devices

Description	Device or OSI Layer
This device sends and receives information about the Network layer.	Router
This layer creates a virtual circuit before transmitting between two end stations.	Transport
This device uses hardware addresses to filter a network.	Bridge or switch
Ethernet is defined at these layers.	Data Link and Physical
This layer supports flow control, sequencing, and acknowledgments.	Transport
This device can measure the distance to a remote network.	Router
Logical addressing is used at this layer.	Network
Hardware addresses are defined at this layer.	Data Link (MAC sub-layer)
This device creates one collision domain and one broadcast domain.	Hub
This device creates many smaller collision domains, but the network is still one large broadcast domain.	Switch or bridge
This device can never run full-duplex.	Hub
This device breaks up collision domains and broadcast domains.	Router

Written Lab 1.3: Identifying Collision and Broadcast Domains

A. Hub: One collision domain, one broadcast domain

B. Bridge: Two collision domains, one broadcast domain

C. Switch: Four collision domains, one broadcast domain

D. Router: Three collision domains, three broadcast domains

Chapter 2: Ethernet Networking and Data Encapsulation

Written Lab 2.1: Binary/Decimal/Hexadecimal Conversion

1.

Decimal	128	64	32	16	8	4	2	1	Binary
192	1	1	0	0	0	0	0	0	11000000
168	1	0	1	0	1	0	0	0	10101000
10	0	0	0	0	1	0	1	0	00001010
15	0	0	0	0	1	1	1	1	00001111
Decimal	128	64	32	16	8	4	2	1	Binary
172	1	0	1	0	1	1	0	0	10101100
16	0	0	0	1	0	0	0	0	00010000
20	0	0	0	1	0	1	0	0	00010100
55	0	0	1	1	0	1	1	1	00110111
Decimal	128	64	32	16	8	4	2	1	Binary
10	0	0	0	0	1	0	1	0	00001010
11	0	0	0	0	1	0	1	1	00001011
12	0	0	0	0	1	1	0	0	00001100
99	0	1	1	0	0	0	1	1	01100011

2.

Binary	128	64	32	16	8	4	2	1	Decimal
11001100	1	1	0	0	1	1	0	0	204
00110011	0	0	1	1	0	0	1	1	51
10101010	1	0	1	0	1	0	1	0	170
01010101	0	1	0	1	0	1	0	1	85

Binary	128	64	32	16	8	4	2	1	Decimal
11000110	1	1	0	0	0	1	1	0	198
11010011	1	1	0	1	0	0	1	1	211
00111001	0	0	1	1	1	0	0	1	57
11010001	1	1	0	1	0	0	0	1	209
Binary	128	64	32	16	8	4	2	1	Decimal
10000100	1	0	0	0	0	1	0	0	132
11010010	1	1	0	1	0	0	1	0	210
10111000	1	0	1	1	1	0	0	0	184
10100110	1	0	1	0	0	1	1	0	166

3.

Binary	128	64	32	16	8	4	2	1	Hexadecimal
11011000	1	1	0	1	1	0	0	0	D8
00011011	0	0	0	1	1	0	1	1	1B
00111101	0	0	1	1	1	1	0	1	3D
01110110	0	1	1	1	0	1	1	0	76
Binary	128	6	32	16	8	4	2	1	Hexadecimal
11001010	1	1	0	0	1	0	1	0	CA
11110101	1	1	1	1	0	1	0	1	F5
10000011	1	0	0	0	0	0	1	1	83
11101011	1	1	1	0	1	0	1	1	EB
Binary	128	64	32	16	8	4	2	1	Hexadecimal
10000100	1	0	0	0	0	1	0	0	84
11010010	1	1	0	1	0	0	1	0	D2
01000011	0	1	0	0	0	0	1	1	43
10110011	1	0	1	1	0	0	1	1	B3

Written Lab 2.2: CSMA/CD Operations

When a collision occurs on an Ethernet LAN, the following happens:

1. A jam signal informs all devices that a collision occurred.

2. The collision invokes a random backoff algorithm.

3. Each device on the Ethernet segment stops transmitting for a short time until the timers expire.

4. All hosts have equal priority to transmit after the timers have expired.

Written Lab 2.3: Cabling

1. Crossover

2. Straight-through

3. Crossover

4. Crossover

5. Straight-through

6. Crossover

7. Crossover

8. Rolled

Written Lab 2.4: Encapsulation

At a transmitting device, the data encapsulation method works like this:

1. User information is converted to data for transmission on the network.

2. Data is converted to segments, and a reliable connection is set up between the transmitting and receiving hosts.

3. Segments are converted to packets or datagrams, and a logical address is placed in the header so each packet can be routed through an internetwork.

4. Packets or datagrams are converted to frames for transmission on the local network. Hardware (Ethernet) addresses are used to uniquely identify hosts on a local network segment.

5. Frames are converted to bits, and a digital encoding and clocking scheme is used.

Chapter 3: Introduction to TCP/IP

Written Lab 3.1: TCP/IP

1. 192 through 223, 110*xxxxx*

2. Host-to-Host or Transport

3. 1 through 126

4. Loopback or diagnostics

5. Turn all host bits off.

6. Turn all host bits on.

7. 10.0.0.0 through 10.255.255.255

8. 172.16.0.0 through 172.31.255.255

9. 192.168.0.0 through 192.168.255.255

10. 0 through 9 and *A*, *B*, *C*, *D*, *E*, and *F*

Written Lab 3.2: Mapping Applications to the DoD Model

1. Internet

2. Process/Application

3. Process/Application

4. Process/Application

5. Process/Application

6. Internet

7. Process/Application

8. Host-to-host/Transport

9. Process/Application

10. Host-to-host/Transport

11. Process/Application

12. Internet

13. Internet

14. Internet

15. Process/Application

16. Process/Application

17. Process/Application

Chapter 4: Easy Subnetting

Written Lab 4.1: Written Subnet Practice #1

1. 192.168.100.25/30. A /30 is 255.255.255.252. The valid subnet is 192.168.100.24, broadcast is 192.168.100.27, and valid hosts are 192.168.100.25 and 26.

2. 192.168.100.37/28. A /28 is 255.255.255.240. The fourth octet is a block size of 16. Just count by 16s until you pass 37. 0, 16, 32, 48. The host is in the 32 subnet, with a broadcast address of 47. Valid hosts 33–46.

3. A /27 is 255.255.255.224. The fourth octet is a block size of 32. Count by 32s until you pass the host address of 66. 0, 32, 64, 96. The host is in the 64 subnet, and the broadcast address is 95. Valid host range is 65–94.

4. 192.168.100.17/29. A /29 is 255.255.255.248. The fourth octet is a block size of 8. 0, 8, 16, 24. The host is in the 16 subnet, broadcast of 23. Valid hosts 17–22.

5. 192.168.100.99/26. A /26 is 255.255.255.192. The fourth octet has a block size of 64. 0, 64, 128. The host is in the 64 subnet, broadcast of 127. Valid hosts 65–126.

6. 192.168.100.99/25. A /25 is 255.255.255.128. The fourth octet is a block size of 128. 0, 128. The host is in the 0 subnet, broadcast of 127. Valid hosts 1–126.

7. A default Class B is 255.255.0.0. A Class B 255.255.255.0 mask is 256 subnets, each with 254 hosts. We need fewer subnets. If we used 255.255.240.0, this provides 16 subnets. Let's add one more subnet bit. 255.255.248.0. This is 5 bits of subnetting, which provides 32 subnets. This is our best answer, a /21.

8. A /29 is 255.255.255.248. This is a block size of 8 in the fourth octet. 0, 8, 16. The host is in the 8 subnet, broadcast is 15.

9. A /29 is 255.255.255.248, which is 5 subnet bits and 3 host bits. This is only 6 hosts per subnet.

10. A /23 is 255.255.254.0. The third octet is a block size of 2. 0, 2, 4. The subnet is in the 16.2.0 subnet; the broadcast address is 16.3.255.

Written Lab 4.2: Written Subnet Practice #2

Classful Address	Subnet Mask	Number of Hosts per Subnet ($2^x - 2$)
/16	255.255.0.0	65,534
/17	255.255.128.0	32,766
/18	255.255.192.0	16,382
/19	255.255.224.0	8,190
/20	255.255.240.0	4,094
/21	255.255.248.0	2,046
/22	255.255.252.0	1,022
/23	255.255.254.0	510
/24	255.255.255.0	254
/25	255.255.255.128	126
/26	255.255.255.192	62
/27	255.255.255.224	30
/28	255.255.255.240	14
/29	255.255.255.248	6
/30	255.255.255.252	2

Written Lab 4.3: Written Subnet Practice #3

Decimal IP Address	Address Class	Number of Subnet and Host Bits	Number of Subnets ($2x$)	Number of Hosts ($2x - 2$)
10.25.66.154/23	A	15/9	32,768	510
172.31.254.12/24	B	8/8	256	254
192.168.20.123/28	C	4/4	16	14
63.24.89.21/18	A	10/14	1,024	16,382
128.1.1.254/20	B	4/12	16	4,094
208.100.54.209/30	C	6/2	64	2

Chapter 5: VLSMs, Summarization and Troubleshooting TCP/IP

1. 192.168.0.0/20

2. 172.144.0.0 255.240.0.0

3. 192.168.32.0 255.255.224.0

4. 192.168.96.0 255.255.240.0

5. 66.66.0.0 255.255.240.0

6. 192.168.0.0/17

7. 172.16.0.0 255.255.248.0

8. 192.168.128.0 255.255.192.0

9. 53.60.96.0 255.255.224.0

10. 172.16.0.0 255.255.192.0

Chapter 6: Cisco's Internetworking Operating System (IOS)

Written Lab 6: Cisco IOS

1. Router(config)#**clock rate 1000000**

2. Switch#**config t**
    switch config)# **line vty 0 15**
    switch(config-line)# **no login**

3. Switch#**config t**
    Switch(config)# **int f0/1**
    Switch(config-if)# **no shutdown**

4. Switch#**erase startup-config**

5. Switch#**config t**
    Switch(config)#**line console 0**

```
Switch(config-line)#password todd
Switch(config-line)#login
```

6. Switch#**config t**
    `Switch(config)# enable secret cisco`

7. Router#**show controllers serial 0/2**

8. Switch#**show terminal**

9. Switch#**reload**

10. Switch#**config t**
    `Switch(config)#hostname Sales`

Chapter 7: Managing a Cisco Internetwork

Written Lab 7.1: IOS Management

1. `copy start run`

2. `show cdp neighbor detail` or `show cdp entry *`

3. `show cdp neighbor`

4. Ctrl+Shift+6, then X

5. `show sessions`

6. Either `copy tftp run` or `copy start run`

7. NTP

8. `ip helper-address`

9. `ntp server` *ip_address* `version 4`

10. `show ntp status`

Written Lab 7.2: Router Memory

1. Flash memory

2. ROM

3. NVRAM

4. ROM

5. RAM

6. RAM

7. ROM

8. ROM

9. RAM

10. RAM

Chapter 8: Managing Cisco Devices

Written Lab 8.1: IOS Management

1. `copy flash tftp`

2. 0x2101

3. 0x2102

4. 0x2100

5. UDI

6. 0x2142

7. `boot system`

8. POST test

9. `copy tftp flash`

10. `show license`

Chapter 9: IP Routing

1. `router(config)#`**`ip route 172.16.10.0 255.255.255.0 172.16.20.1 150`**

2. It will use the gateway interface MAC at L2 and the actual destination IP at L3.

3. `router(config)#`**`ip route 0.0.0.0 0.0.0.0 172.16.40.1`**

4. Stub network

5. Router#**show ip route**

6. Exit interface

7. False. The MAC address would be the local router interface, not the remote host.

8. True

9. router(config)#**router rip**
   router(config-router)#**passive-interface S1**

10. True

Chapter 10: Layer 2 Switching

1. show mac address-table

2. Flood the frame out all ports except the port on which it was received

3. Address learning, forward/filter decisions, and loop avoidance

4. It will add the source MAC address in the forward/filter table and associate it with the port on which the frame was received.

5. Maximum 1, violation shutdown

6. Restrict and shutdown

7. Restrict

8. The addition of dynamically learned addresses to the running-configuration

9. Show port-security interface fastethernet 0/12 and show running-config

10. False

Chapter 11: VLANs and InterVLAN Routing

1. False! You do not provide an IP address under any physical port.

2. STP

3. Broadcast

4. VLAN 1 is the default VLAN and cannot be changed, renamed, or deleted. VLANs 1002–1005 are reserved, and VLANs 1006–4094 are extended VLANs and can only be configured if you are in VTP transparent mode. You can only configure VLANs 2–1001 by default.

5. `switchport trunk encapsulation dot1q`

6. Trunking sends information about all or many VLANs across a single link.

7. 1000 (2 to 1001). VLAN 1 is the default VLAN and cannot be changed, renamed, or deleted. VLANs 1002–1005 are reserved, and VLANs 1006–4094 are extended VLANs and can only be configured if you are in VTP transparent mode.

8. True

9. Access link

10. `switchport trunk native vlan 4`

Chapter 12: Security

1. `access-list 10 deny 172.16.0.0 0.0.255.255`
    `access-list 10 permit any`

2. `ip access-group 10 out`

3. `access-list 10 deny host 192.168.15.5`
    `access-list 10 permit any`

4. `show access-lists`

5. IDS, IPS

6. `access-list 110 deny tcp host`
    `172.16.10.1 host  172.16.30.5 eq 23`
    `access-list 110 permit ip any any`

7. `line vty 0 4`
    `access-class 110 in`

8. `ip access-list standard No172Net`
    `deny 172.16.0.0 0.0.255.255`
    `permit any`

9. `ip access-group No172Net out`

10. `show ip interfaces`

Chapter 13: Network Address Translation (NAT)

1. Port Address Translation (PAT), also called NAT Overload

2. `debug ip nat`

3. `show ip nat translations`

4. `clear ip nat translations *`

5. Before

6. After

7. `show ip nat statistics`

8. The `ip nat inside` and `ip nat outside` commands

9. Dynamic NAT

10. `prefix-length`

Chapter 14: Internet Protocol Version 6 (IPv6)

Written Lab 14.1: IPv6 Foundation

1. 128 and 129

2. 33-33-FF-17-FC-0F

3. Link-local

4. Link-local

5. Multicast

6. Anycast

7. OSPFv3

8. ::1

9. FE80::/10

10. FF02::2

Written Lab 14.2: EUI-64 Format

1. 2001:db8:1:1:090c:abff:fecd:1234

2. 2001:db8:1:1:040c:32ff:fef1:a4d2

3. 2001:db8:1:1:12:abff:fecd:1234

4. 2001:db8:1:1:0f01:3aff:fe2f:1234

5. 2001:db8:1:1:080c:abff:feac:caba

Chapter 15: Enhanced Switched Technologies

Written Lab 15

1. PAgP

2. show spanning-tree summary

3. 802.1w

4. STP

5. BPDU Guard

6. (config-if)#**spanning-tree portfast**

7. Switch#**show etherchannel port-channel**

8. Switch(config)#**spanning-tree vlan 3 root primary**

9. show spanning-tree, then follow the root port that connects to the root bridge using CDP, or show spanning-tree summary.

10. Active and passive

Chapter 16: Network Device Management and Security

Written Lab 16

1. INFORM

2. GET

3. TRAP

4. SET

5. WALK

6. If the active router fails, the standby router takes over with a different virtual IP address, and different to the one configured as the default-gateway address for end devices, so your hosts stop working which defeats the purpose of a FHRP.

7. You'll start receiving duplicate IP address warnings.

8. You'll start receiving duplicate IP address warnings.

9. In version 1, HSRP messages are sent to the multicast IP address 224.0.0.2 and UDP port 1985. HSRP version 2 uses the multicast IP address 224.0.0.102 and UDP port 1985.

10. RADIUS and TACACS+, with TACACS+ being proprietary.

Chapter 17: Enhanced IGRP

Written Lab 17

1. `ipv6 router eigrp` *as*

2. FF02::A

3. False

4. The routers will not form an adjacency.

5. Passive interface

6. A backup route, stored in the topology table

Chapter 18: Open Shortest Path First (OSPF)

Written Lab 18

1. `router ospf 101`

2. `show ip ospf`

3. `show ip ospf interface`

4. `show ip ospf neighbor`

5. `show ip route ospf`

6. Cost (bandwidth)

7. Areas don't match. The routers are not in same subnet. RIDs are the same. Hello and Dead timers don't match.

8. `show ip ospf database`

9. 110

10. 10 and 40

Chapter 19: Multi-Area OSPF

Written Lab 19

1. Type 5 or Type 7

2. 2WAY

3. Type 3, and possibly Type 4 and 5

4. When all LSAs have synchronized with a neighbor on a point-to-point link

5. True

6. EXCHANGE

7. Type 1

8. `ipv6 ospf 1 area 0`

9. OSPFv2 and v3 use the same items when forming an adjacency; Hello and Dead timers, subnet info, and area ID all must match. Authentication must also match if configured.

10. `show ip protocols` and `show ipv6 protocols`

Chapter 20: Troubleshooting IP, IPv6, and VLANs

Written Lab 20

1. The INCMP is an incomplete message, which means a neighbor solicitation message has been sent but the neighbor message has not yet been received.

2. `switchport trunk native vlan 66`

3. Access, auto, desirable, nonegotiate, and trunk (on)

4. Verify that the default gateway is correct. Verify that name resolution settings are correct. Verify that there are no ACLs blocking traffic.

5. `ping ::1`

Chapter 21: Wide Area Networks

Written Lab 21

1. True

2. False

3. BGP

4. `show ip bgp neighbor`

5. `show run interface tunnel` *tunnel_number*

6. False

7. PPPoE or PPPoA

8. HDLC, LCP, and NCP

9. VPLS, VPWS

10. Layer 2 MPLS VPN, Layer 3 MPLS VPN

Chapter 22: Evolution of Intelligent Networks

Written Lab 22

1. DSCP

2. Control, data

3. TID

4. Markings, addressing, and application signatures

5. Marking

6. Policing

7. Data, control, application

8. CBWFQ, LLW

9. NBAR

10. Northbound

Appendix B

Answers to Review Questions

Chapter 1: Internetworking

1. A. The device shown is a hub and hubs place all ports in the same broadcast domain and the same collision domain.

2. B. The contents of a protocol data unit (PDU) depend on the PDU because they are created in a specific order and their contents are based on that order. A packet will contain IP addresses but not MAC addresses because MAC addresses are not present until the PDU becomes a frame.

3. C. You should select a router to connect the two groups. When computers are in different subnets, as these two groups are, you will require a device that can make decisions based on IP addresses. Routers operate at layer 3 of the Open Systems Interconnect (OSI) model and make data-forwarding decisions based on layer 3 networking information, which are IP addresses. They create routing tables that guide them in forwarding traffic out of the proper interface to the proper subnet.

4. C. Replacing the hub with a switch would reduce collisions and retransmissions, which would have the most impact on reducing congestion.

5. Answer:

Layer	Description
Transport	Bits
Data Link	Segment
Physical	Packet
Network	Frame

The given layers of the OSI model use the PDUs shown in the above diagram.

6. B. Wireless LAN Controllers are used to manage anywhere from a few access points to thousands. The AP's are completely managed from the controller and are considered lightweight or dumb AP's as they have no configuration on the AP itself.

7. B. You should use a switch to accomplish the task in this scenario. A switch is used to provide dedicated bandwidth to each node by eliminating the possibility of collisions on the switch port where the node resides. Switches work at layer 2 in the Open Systems Interconnection (OSI) model and perform the function of separating collision domains.

8.

Answer:

Transport	End-to-end connection
Physical	Conversion to bits
Data Link	Framing
Network	Routing

The listed layers of the OSI model have the functions shown in the diagram above.

9. C. Firewalls are used to connect our trusted internal network such as the DMZ, to the untrusted outside network—typically the internet.

10. D. The Application layer is responsible for identifying and establishing the availability of the intended communication partner and determining whether sufficient resources for the intended communication exist.

11. A, D. The Transport layer segments data into smaller pieces for transport. Each segment is assigned a sequence number so that the receiving device can reassemble the data on arrival. The Network layer (layer 3) has two key responsibilities. First, this layer controls the logical addressing of devices. Second, the Network layer determines the best path to a particular destination network and routes the data appropriately.

12. C. The IEEE Ethernet Data Link layer has two sublayers, the Media Access Control (MAC) layer and the Logical Link Control (LLC) layer.

13. C. Wireless AP's are very popular today and will be going away about the same time that rock n' roll does. The idea behind these devices (which are layer 2 bridge devices) is to connect wireless products to the wired Ethernet network. The wireless AP will create a single collision domain and is typically its own dedicated broadcast domain as well.

14. A. Hubs operate on the Physical Layer as they have no intelligence and send all traffic in all directions.

15. C. While it is true that the OSI model's primary purpose is to allow different vendors' networks to interoperate, there is no requirement that vendors follow the model.

16. A. Routers by default do NOT forward broadcasts.

17. C. Switches create separate collision domains within a single broadcast domain. Routers provide a separate broadcast domain for each interface.

18. B. The all-hub network at the bottom is one collision domain; the bridge network on top equals three collision domains. Add in the switch network of five collision domains—one for each switch port—and you get a total of nine.

19. A. The top three layers define how the applications within the end stations will communicate with each other as well as with users.

20. A. The following network devices operate at all seven layers of the OSI model: network management stations (NMSs), gateways (not default gateways), servers, and network hosts.

Chapter 2: Ethernet Networking and Data Encapsulation

1. D. The organizationally unique identifier (OUI) is assigned by the IEEE to an organization composed of 24 bits, or 3 bytes, which in turn assigns a globally administered address also comprising 24 bits, or 3 bytes, that's supposedly unique to each and every adapter it manufactures.

2. A. Backoff on an Ethernet network is the retransmission delay that's enforced when a collision occurs. When that happens, a host will only resume transmission after the forced time delay has expired. Keep in mind that after the backoff has elapsed, all stations have equal priority to transmit data.

3. A. When using a hub, all ports are in the same collision domain, which will introduce collisions as shown between devices connected to the same hub.

4. B. FCS is a field at the end of the frame that's used to store the cyclic redundancy check (CRC) answer. The CRC is a mathematical algorithm that's based on the data in the frame and run when each frame is built. When a receiving host receives the frame and runs the CRC, the answer should be the same. If not, the frame is discarded, assuming errors have occurred.

5. C. Half-duplex Ethernet networking uses a protocol called Carrier Sense Multiple Access with Collision Detection (CSMA/CD), which helps devices share the bandwidth evenly while preventing two devices from transmitting simultaneously on the same network medium.

6. A, E. Physical addresses or MAC addresses are used to identify devices at layer 2. MAC addresses are only used to communicate on the same network. To communicate on different network, we have to use layer 3 addresses (IP addresses).

7. D. The cable shown is a straight-through cable, which is used between dissimilar devices.

8. C, D. An Ethernet network is a shared environment, so all devices have the right to access the medium. If more than one device transmits simultaneously, the signals collide and cannot reach the destination.If a device detects another device is sending, it will wait for a specified amount of time before attempting to transmit.

   When there is no traffic detected, a device will transmit its message. While this transmission is occurring, the device continues to listen for traffic or collisions on the LAN. After the message is sent, the device returns to its default listening mode.

9. B. In creating the gigabit crossover cable, you'd still cross 1 to 3 and 2 to 6, but you would add 4 to 7 and 5 to 8.

10. D. When you set up the connection, use these settings:

- Bits per sec: 9600
- Data bits: 8
- Parity: None
- Stop bits: 1
- Flow control: None

11. D. When set to 0, this bit represents a globally administered address, as specified by the IEEE, but when it's a 1, it represents a locally governed and administered address.

12. B. You can use a rolled Ethernet cable to connect a host EIA-TIA 232 interface to a router console serial communication (COM) port.

13. B. The collision will invoke a backoff algorithm on all systems, not just the ones involved in the collision.

14. A. There are no collisions in full-duplex mode.

15. B. The connection between the two switches requires a crossover and the connection from the hosts to the switches requires a straight-through.

16. The given cable types are matched with their standards in the following table.

IEEE 802.3u	100Base-Tx
IEEE 802.3	10Base-T
IEEE 802.3ab	1000Base-T
IEEE 802.3z	1000Base-SX

17. B. Although rolled cable isn't used to connect any Ethernet connections together, you can use a rolled Ethernet cable to connect a host EIA-TIA 232 interface to a router console serial communication (COM) port.

18. B. If you're using TCP, the virtual circuit is defined by the source and destination port number plus the source and destination IP address and called a *socket*.

19. A. The hex value 1c is converted as 28 in decimal.

20. A. Fiber-optic cables are the only ones that have a core surrounded by a material called cladding.

Chapter 3: Introduction to TCP/IP

1.   C. If a DHCP conflict is detected, either by the server sending a ping and getting a response or by a host using a gratuitous ARP (arp'ing for its own IP address and seeing if a host responds), then the server will hold that address and not use it again until it is fixed by an administrator.

2.   B. Secure Shell (SSH) protocol sets up a secure session that's similar to Telnet over a standard TCP/IP connection and is employed for doing things like logging into systems, running programs on remote systems, and moving files from one system to another.

3.   C. A host uses something called a gratuitous ARP to help avoid a possible duplicate address. The DHCP client sends an ARP broadcast out on the local LAN or VLAN using its newly assigned address to help solve conflicts before they occur.

4.   B. Address Resolution Protocol (ARP) is used to find the hardware address from a known IP address.

5.   A, C, D. The listed answers are from the OSI model and the question asked about the TCP/IP protocol stack (DoD model). Yes, it is normal for the objectives to have this type of question. However, let's just look for what is wrong. First, the Session layer is not in the TCP/IP model; neither are the Data Link and Physical layers. This leaves us with the Transport layer (Host-to-Host in the DoD model), Internet layer (Network layer in the OSI), and Application layer (Application/Process in the DoD). Remember, the CCENT objectives can list the layers as OSI layers or DoD layers at any time, regardless of what the question is asking.

6.   C. A Class C network address has only 8 bits for defining hosts: $2^8 - 2 = 256$.

7.   A, B. A client that sends out a DHCP Discover message in order to receive an IP address sends out a broadcast at both layer 2 and layer 3. The layer 2 broadcast is all Fs in hex, or FF:FF:FF:FF:FF:FF. The layer 3 broadcast is 255.255.255.255, which means any networks and all hosts. DHCP is connectionless, which means it uses User Datagram Protocol (UDP) at the Transport layer, also called the Host-to-Host layer.

8.   B. Although Telnet does use TCP and IP (TCP/IP), the question specifically asks about layer 4, and IP works at layer 3. Telnet uses TCP at layer 4.

9.   RFC 1918. These addresses can be used on a private network, but they're not routable through the Internet.

10.   B, D, E. SMTP, FTP, and HTTP use TCP.

11.   C. Class C addresses devote 24 bits to the network portion and 8 bits to the host portion.

12.   C. The range of multicast addresses starts with 224.0.0.0 and goes through 239.255.255.255.

13.   C. First, you should know easily that only TCP and UDP work at the Transport layer, so now you have a 50/50 shot. However, since the header has sequencing, acknowledgment, and window numbers, the answer can only be TCP.

14. A. Both FTP and Telnet use TCP at the Transport layer; however, they both are Application layer protocols, so the Application layer is the best answer for this question.

15. C. The four layers of the DoD model are Application/Process, Host-to-Host, Internet, and Network Access. The Internet layer is equivalent to the Network layer of the OSI model.

16. C, E. The Class A private address range is 10.0.0.0 through 10.255.255.255. The Class B private address range is 172.16.0.0 through 172.31.255.255, and the Class C private address range is 192.168.0.0 through 192.168.255.255.

17. B. The four layers of the TCP/IP stack (also called the DoD model) are Application/Process, Host-to-Host (also called Transport on the objectives), Internet, and Network Access/Link. The Host-to-Host layer is equivalent to the Transport layer of the OSI model.

18. B, C. ICMP is used for diagnostics and destination unreachable messages. ICMP is encapsulated within IP datagrams, and because it is used for diagnostics, it will provide hosts with information about network problems.

19. C. The range of a Class B network address is 128–191. This makes our binary range 10*xxxxxx*.

20.

Answer
DHCPDiscover
DHCPOffer
DHCPRequest
DHCPAck

The steps are as shown in the answer diagram.

Chapter 4: Easy Subnetting

1. D. A /27 (255.255.255.224) is 3 bits on and 5 bits off. This provides 8 subnets, each with 30 hosts. Does it matter if this mask is used with a Class A, B, or C network address? Not at all. The number of subnet bits would never change.

2. D. A 240 mask is 4 subnet bits and provides 16 subnets, each with 14 hosts. We need more subnets, so let's add subnet bits. One more subnet bit would be a 248 mask. This provides 5 subnet bits (32 subnets) with 3 host bits (6 hosts per subnet). This is the best answer.

3. C. This is a pretty simple question. A /28 is 255.255.255.240, which means that our block size is 16 in the fourth octet. 0, 16, 32, 48, 64, 80, etc. The host is in the 64 subnet.

4. C. A CIDR address of /19 is 255.255.224.0. This is a Class B address, so that is only 3 subnet bits, but it provides 13 host bits, or 8 subnets, each with 8,190 hosts.

5. B, D. The mask 255.255.254.0 (/23) used with a Class A address means that there are 15 subnet bits and 9 host bits. The block size in the third octet is 2 (256 – 254). So this makes the subnets in the interesting octet 0, 2, 4, 6, etc., all the way to 254. The host 10.16.3.65 is in the 2.0 subnet. The next subnet is 4.0, so the broadcast address for the 2.0 subnet is 3.255. The valid host addresses are 2.1 through 3.254.

6. D. A /30, regardless of the class of address, has a 252 in the fourth octet. This means we have a block size of 4 and our subnets are 0, 4, 8, 12, 16, etc. Address 14 is obviously in the 12 subnet.

7. D. A point-to-point link uses only two hosts. A /30, or 255.255.255.252, mask provides two hosts per subnet.

8. C. A /21 is 255.255.248.0, which means we have a block size of 8 in the third octet, so we just count by 8 until we reach 66. The subnet in this question is 64.0. The next subnet is 72.0, so the broadcast address of the 64 subnet is 71.255.

9. A. A /29 (255.255.255.248), regardless of the class of address, has only 3 host bits. Six is the maximum number of hosts on this LAN, including the router interface.

10. C. A /29 is 255.255.255.248, which is a block size of 8 in the fourth octet. The subnets are 0, 8, 16, 24, 32, 40, etc. 192.168.19.24 is the 24 subnet, and since 32 is the next subnet, the broadcast address for the 24 subnet is 31. 192.168.19.26 is the only correct answer.

11. A. A /29 (255.255.255.248) has a block size of 8 in the fourth octet. This means the subnets are 0, 8, 16, 24, etc. 10 is in the 8 subnet. The next subnet is 16, so 15 is the broadcast address.

12. B. You need 5 subnets, each with at least 16 hosts. The mask 255.255.255.240 provides 16 subnets with 14 hosts—this will not work. The mask 255.255.255.224 provides 8 subnets, each with 30 hosts. This is the best answer.

13. C. First, you cannot answer this question if you can't subnet. The 192.168.10.62 with a mask of 255.255.255.192 is a block size of 64 in the fourth octet. The host 192.168.10.62 is in the zero subnet, and the error occurred because `ip subnet-zero` is not enabled on the router.

14. A. A /25 mask is 255.255.255.128. Used with a Class B network, the third and fourth octets are used for subnetting with a total of 9 subnet bits, 8 bits in the third octet and 1 bit in the fourth octet. Since there is only 1 bit in the fourth octet, the bit is either off or on—which is a value of 0 or 128. The host in the question is in the 0 subnet, which has a broadcast address of 127 since 112.128 is the next subnet.

15. A. A /28 is a 255.255.255.240 mask. Let's count to the ninth subnet (we need to find the broadcast address of the eighth subnet, so we need to count to the ninth subnet). Starting at 16 (remember, the question stated that we will not use subnet zero, so we start at 16, not 0), we have 16, 32, 48, 64, 80, 96, 112, 128, 144, etc. The eighth subnet is 128 and the next subnet is 144, so our broadcast address of the 128 subnet is 143. This makes the host range 129–142. 142 is the last valid host.

16. C. A /28 is a 255.255.255.240 mask. The first subnet is 16 (remember that the question stated not to use subnet zero) and the next subnet is 32, so our broadcast address is 31. This makes our host range 17–30. 30 is the last valid host.

17. B. We need 9 host bits to answer this question, which is a /23.

18. E. A Class B network ID with a /22 mask is 255.255.252.0, with a block size of 4 in the third octet. The network address in the question is in subnet 172.16.16.0 with a broadcast address of 172.16.19.255. Only option E has the correct subnet mask listed, and 172.16.18.255 is a valid host.

19. D, E. The router's IP address on the E0 interface is 172.16.2.1/23, which is 255.255.254.0. This makes the third octet a block size of 2. The router's interface is in the 2.0 subnet, and the broadcast address is 3.255 because the next subnet is 4.0. The valid host range is 2.1 through 3.254. The router is using the first valid host address in the range.

20. A. For this example, the network range is 172.16.16.1 to 172.16.31.254, the network address is 172.16.16.0, and the broadcast IP address is 172.16.31.255.

Chapter 5: VLSMs, Summarization, and Troubleshooting TCP/IP

1. D. A point-to-point link uses only two hosts. A /30, or 255.255.255.252, mask provides two hosts per subnet.

2. C. Using a /28 mask, there are 4 bits available for hosts. Two-to-the-fourth power minus 2 = 14, or block size –2.

3. D. For 6 hosts we need to leave 3 bits in the host portion since 2 to the third power = 8 and 8 minus 2 is 6. With 3 bits for the host portion, that leaves 29 bits for the mask, or /29.

4. C. To use VLSM, the routing protocols in use possess the capability to transmit subnet mask information.

5. D. In a question like this, you need to look for an interesting octet where you can combine networks. In this example, the third octet has all our subnets, so we just need to find our block size now. If we used a block of 8 starting at 172.16.0.0/19, then we cover 172.16.0.0 through 172.16.7.255. However, if we used 172.16.0.0/20, then we'd cover a block of 16, which would be from 172.16.0.0 through 172.16.15.255, which is the best answer.

6. C. The IP address of the station and the gateway are not in the same network. Since the address of the gateway is correct on the station, it is *most likely* the IP address of the station is incorrect.

7. B. With an incorrect gateway, Host A will not be able to communicate with the router or beyond the router but will be able to communicate within the subnet.

8. A. Pinging the remote computer would fail if any of the other steps fail.

9. C. When a ping to the local host IP address fails, you can assume the NIC is not functional.

10. C, D. If a ping to the local host succeeds, you can rule out IP stack or NIC failure.

11. E. A /29 mask yields only 6 addresses, so none of the networks could use it.

12. A. The most likely problem if you can ping a computer by IP address but not by name is a failure of DNS.

13. D. When you issue the ping command, you are using the ICMP protocol.

14. B. The traceroute command displays the networks traversed on a path to a network destination.

15. C. The ping command tests connectivity to another station. The full command is shown below.

```
C:\>ping 172.16.10.2
Pinging 172.16.10.2 with 32 bytes of data:
Reply from 172.16.10.2: bytes=32 time<1ms TTL=128
Reply from 172.16.10.2: bytes=32 time<1ms TTL=128
Reply from 172.16.10.2: bytes=32 time<1ms TTL=128
Reply from 172.16.10.2: bytes=32 time<1ms TTL=128
Ping statistics for 172.16.10.2:
    Packets: Sent = 4, Received = 4, Lost = 0 (0% loss),
Approximate round trip times in milli-seconds:
    Minimum = 0ms, Maximum = 0ms, Average = 0ms
```

16.

traceroute	Displays the list of routers on a path to a network destination
arp -a	Displays IP-to-MAC-address mappings on a Windows PC
show ip arp	Displays the ARP table on a Cisco router
ipconfig /all	Shows you the PC network configuration

The commands use the functions described in the answer table.

17. C. The interesting octet in this example is the second octet, and it is a block size of four starting at 10.0.0.0. By using a 255.252.0.0 mask, we are telling the summary to use a block size of four in the second octet. This will cover 10.0.0.0 through 10.3.255.255. This is the best answer.

18. A. The command that displays the ARP table on a Cisco router is show ip arp.

19. C. The /all switch must be added to the ipconfig command on a PC to verify DNS configuration.

20. C. If you start at 192.168.128.0 and go through 192.168.159.0, you can see this is a block of 32 in the third octet. Since the network address is always the first one in the range, the summary address is 192.168.128.0. What mask provides a block of 32 in the third octet? The answer is 255.255.224.0, or /19.

Chapter 6: Cisco's Internetworking Operating System (IOS)

1. D. Typically, we'd see the input errors and CRC statistics increase with a duplex error, but it could be another Physical layer issue such as the cable might be receiving excessive interference or the network interface cards might have a failure. Typically, you can tell if it is interference when the CRC and input errors output grow but the collision counters do not, which is the case with this question.

2. C. Once the IOS is loaded and up and running, the startup-config will be copied from NVRAM into RAM and from then on, referred to as the running-config.

3. C, D. To configure SSH on your router, you need to set the username command, the ip domain-name, login local, and the transport input ssh under the VTY lines and the crypto key command. However, SSH version 2 is suggested but not required.

4. C. The show controllers serial 0/0 command will show you whether either a DTE or DCE cable is connected to the interface. If it is a DCE connection, you need to add clocking with the clock rate command.

5.

Mode	Definition
User EXEC mode	Commands that affect the entire system
Privileged EXEC mode	Commands that affect interfaces/processes only
Global configuration mode	Interactive configuration dialog
Specific configuration modes	Provides access to all other router commands
Setup mode	Limited to basic monitoring commands

User exec mode is limited to basic monitoring commands; privileged exec mode provides access to all other router commands. Specific configuration modes include the commands that affect a specific interface or process, while global configuration mode allows commands that affect the entire system. Setup mode is where you access the interactive configuration dialog.

6. B. The bandwidth shown is 100000 kbits a second, which is a FastEthernet port, or 100 Mbs.

7. B. From global configuration mode, use the line vty 0 4 command to set all five default VTY lines. However, you would typically always set all lines, not just the defaults.

8. C. The enable secret password is case sensitive, so the second option is wrong. To set the enable secret password, use the enable secret *password* command from global configuration mode. This password is automatically encrypted.

9. C. The banner motd sets a message of the day for administrators when they login to a switch or router.

10. C. The prompts offered as options indicate the following modes:

Switch(config)# is global configuration mode.
Switch> is user mode.
Switch# is privileged mode.
Switch(config-if)# is interface configuration mode.

11. D. To copy the running-config to NVRAM so that it will be used if the router is restarted, use the copy running-config startup-config command in privileged mode (copy run start for short).

12. D. To allow a VTY (Telnet) session into your router, you must set the VTY password. Option C is wrong because it is setting the password on the wrong router. Notice that you have to set the password before you set the login command.

13. C. Wireless AP's are very popular today and will be going away about the same time that rock n' roll does. The idea behind these devices (which are layer 2 bridge devices) is to connect wireless products to the wired Ethernet network. The wireless AP will create a single collision domain and is typically its own dedicated broadcast domain as well.

14. B. If an interface is shut down, the show interface command will show the interface as administratively down. (It is possible that no cable is attached, but you can't tell that from this message.)

15. C. With the show interfaces command, you can view the configurable parameters, get statistics for the interfaces on the switch, check for input and CRC errors, and verify if the interfaces are shut down.

16. C. If you delete the startup-config and reload the switch, the device will automatically enter setup mode. You can also type **setup** from privileged mode at any time.

17. D. You can view the interface statistics from user mode, but the command is show interface fastethernet 0/0.

18. B. The % ambiguous command error means that there is more than one possible show command that starts with *r*. Use a question mark to find the correct command.

19. B, D. The commands show interfaces and show ip interface will show you the layer 1 and 2 status and the IP addresses of your router's interfaces.

20. A. If you see that a serial interface and the protocol are both down, then you have a Physical layer problem. If you see `serial1 is up`, `line protocol is down`, then you are not receiving (Data Link) keepalives from the remote end.

Chapter 7: Managing a Cisco Internetwork

1. B. The IEEE created a new standardized discovery protocol called 802.1AB for Station and Media Access Control Connectivity Discovery. We'll just call it Link Layer Discovery Protocol (LLDP).

2. C. The `show processes` (or `show processes cpu`) is a good tool for determining a given router's CPU utilization. When it is high, it is not a good time to execute a debug command.

3. B. The command `traceroute` (`trace` for short), which can be issued from user mode or privileged mode, is used to find the path a packet takes through an internetwork and will also show you where the packet stops because of an error on a router.

4. C. Since the configuration looks correct, you probably didn't screw up the copy job. However, when you perform a copy from a network host to a router, the interfaces are automatically shut down and need to be manually enabled with the `no shutdown` command.

5. D. Specifying the address of the DHCP server allows the router to relay broadcast traffic destined for a DHCP server to that server.

6. C. Before you start to configure the router, you should erase the NVRAM with the `erase startup-config` command and then reload the router using the `reload` command.

7. C. This command can be run on both routers and switches and it displays detailed information about each device connected to the device you're running the command on, including the IP address.

8. C. The Port ID column describes the interfaces on the remote device end of the connection.

9. B. Syslog levels range from 0–7, and level 7 (known as Debugging or local7) is the default if you were to use the `logging ip_address` command from global config.

10. C. If you save a configuration and reload the router and it comes up either in setup mode or as a blank configuration, chances are the configuration register setting is incorrect.

11. D. To keep open one or more Telnet sessions, use the Ctrl+Shift+6 and then X keystroke combination.

12. B, D. The best answers, the ones you need to remember, are that either an access control list is filtering the Telnet session or the VTY password is not set on the remote device.

13. A, D. The show hosts command provides information on temporary DNS entries and permanent name-to-address mappings created using the ip host command.

14. A, B, D. The tracert command is a Windows command and will not work on a router or switch! IOS uses the traceroute command.

15. D. By default, Cisco IOS devices use facility local7. Moreover, most Cisco devices provide options to change the facility level from their default value.

16. C. To see console messages through your Telnet session, you must enter the terminal monitor command.

17. C, D, F. There are significantly more syslog messages available within IOS as compared to SNMP Trap messages. System logging is a method of collecting messages from devices to a server running a syslog daemon. Logging to a central syslog server helps in aggregation of logs and alerts.

18. E. Although option A is certainly the "best" answer, unfortunately option E will work just fine and your boss would probably prefer you to use the show cdp neighbors detail command.

19. D. To enable a device to be an NTP client, use the ntp server *IP_address* version *number* command at global configuration mode. That's all there is to it! Assuming your NTP server is working of course.

20. B, D, F. If you specify a level with the "logging trap *level*" command, that level and all the higher levels will be logged. For example, by using the logging trap 3 command, emergencies, alerts, critical, and error messages will be logged. Only three of these were listed as possible options.

Chapter 8: Managing Cisco Devices

1. B. The default configuration setting is 0x2102, which tells the router to load the IOS from flash and the configuration from NVRAM. 0x2142 tells the router to bypass the configuration in NVRAM so that you can perform password recovery.

2. E. To copy the IOS to a backup host, which is stored in flash memory by default, use the copy flash tftp command.

3. B. To install a new license on an ISR G2 router, use the license install url command.

4. C. The configuration register provides the boot commands, and 0x2101 tells the router to boot the mini-IOS, if found, and not to load a file from flash memory. Many newer routers do not have a mini-IOS, so as an alternative, the router would end up in ROM monitor mode if the mini-IOS is not found. However, option C is the best answer for this question.

5. B. The show flash command will provide you with the current IOS name and size and the size of flash memory.

6. C. Before you start to configure the router, you should erase the NVRAM with the `erase startup-config` command and then reload the router using the `reload` command.

7. D. The command `copy tftp flash` will allow you to copy a new IOS into flash memory on your router.

8. C. The best answer is `show version`, which shows you the IOS file running currently on your router. The `show flash` command shows you the contents of flash memory, not which file is running.

9. C. All Cisco routers have a default configuration register setting of 0x2102, which tells the router to load the IOS from flash memory and the configuration from NVRAM.

10. C. If you save a configuration and reload the router and it comes up either in setup mode or as a blank configuration, chances are the configuration register setting is incorrect.

11. D. The `license boot module` command installs a Right-To-Use license feature on a router.

12. A. The `show license` command determines the licenses that are active on your system. It also displays a group of lines for each feature in the currently running IOS image along with several status variables related to software activation and licensing, both licensed and unlicensed features.

13. B. The `show license feature` command allows you to view the technology package licenses and feature licenses that are supported on your router along with several status variables related to software activation and licensing, both licensed and unlicensed features.

14. C. The `show license udi` command displays the unique device identifier (UDI) of the router, which comprises the product ID (PID) and serial number of the router.

15. D. The `show version` command displays various pieces of information about the current IOS version, including the licensing details at the end of the command's output.

16. C. The `license save flash` command allows you to back up your license to flash memory.

17. C. The `show version` command provides you with the current configuration register setting.

18. C, D. The two steps to remove a license are to first disable the technology package and then clear the license.

19. B, D, E. Before you back up an IOS image to a laptop directly connected to a router's Ethernet port, make sure that the TFTP server software is running on your laptop, that the Ethernet cable is a "crossover," and that the laptop is in the same subnet as the router's Ethernet port, and then you can use the `copy flash tftp` command from your laptop.

20. C. The default configuration setting of 0x2102 tells the router to look in NVRAM for the boot sequence.

Chapter 9: IP Routing

1. `show ip route`

   The `ip route` command is used to display the routing table of a router.

2. B. In the new 15 IOS code, Cisco defines a different route called a local route. Each has a /32 prefix defining a route just for the one address, which is the router's interface.

3. A, B. Although option D almost seems right, it is not; the mask option is the mask used on the remote network, not the source network. Since there is no number at the end of the static route, it is using the default administrative distance of 1.

4. C, F. The switches are not used as either a default gateway or other destination. Switches have nothing to do with routing. It is very important to remember that the destination MAC address will always be the router's interface. The destination address of a frame, from HostA, will be the MAC address of the Fa0/0 interface of RouterA. The destination address of a packet will be the IP address of the network interface card (NIC) of the HTTPS server. The destination port number in the segment header will have a value of 443 (HTTPS).

5. B. This mapping was learned dynamically, which means it was learned through ARP.

6. B. Hybrid protocols use aspects of both distance vector and link state—for example, EIGRP. Be advised, however, that Cisco typically just calls EIGRP an advanced distance-vector routing protocol. Do not be misled by the way the question is worded. Yes, I know that MAC addresses are not in a packet. You must read the question to understand of what it is really asking.

7. A. Since the destination MAC address is different at each hop, it must keep changing. The IP address, which is used for the routing process, does not.

8. B, E. Classful routing means that all hosts in the internetwork use the same mask and that only default masks are in use. Classless routing means that you can use variable length subnet masks (VLSMs).

9. B, C. The distance-vector routing protocol sends its complete routing table out of all active interfaces at periodic time intervals. Link-state routing protocols send updates containing the state of their own links to all routers in the internetwork.

10. C. This is how most people see routers, and certainly they could do this type of plain ol' packet switching in 1990 when Cisco released their very first router and traffic was seriously slow, but not in today's networks! This process involves looking up every destination in the routing table and finding the exit interface for every packet.

11. A, C. The S* shows that this is a candidate for default route and that it was configured manually.

12. B. RIP has an administrative distance (AD) of 120, while EIGRP has an administrative distance of 90, so the router will discard any route with a higher AD than 90 to that same network.

13. D. Recovery from a lost route requires manual intervention by a human to replace the lost route.

14. A. RIPv1 and RIPv2 only use the lowest hop count to determine the best path to a remote network.

15. A. Since the routing table shows no route to the 192.168.22.0 network, the router will discard the packet and send an ICMP destination unreachable message out of interface FastEthernet 0/0, which is the source LAN from which the packet originated.

16. C. Static routes have an administrative distance of 1 by default. Unless you change this, a static route will always be used over any other dynamically learned route. EIGRP has an administrative distance of 90, and RIP has an administrative distance of 120, by default.

17. C. BGP is the only EGP listed.

18. A, B, C. Recovery from a lost route requires manual intervention by a human to replace the lost route. The advantages are less overhead on the router and network as well as more security.

19. C. The show ip interface brief command displays a concise summary of the interfaces.

20. B. The 150 at the end changes the default administrative distance (AD) of 1 to 150.

Chapter 10: Layer 2 Switching

1. A. Layer 2 switches and bridges are faster than routers because they don't take up time looking at the Network Layer header information. They do make use of the Data Link layer information.

2. mac address-table static aaaa.bbbb.cccc vlan 1 int fa0/7

You can set a static MAC address in the MAC address table, and when done, it will appear as a static entry in the table.

3. B, D, E. Since the MAC address is not present in the table, it will send the frame out of all ports in the same VLAN with the exception of the port on which it was received.

4. show mac address-table

This command displays the forward filter table, also called a Content Addressable Memory (CAM) table.

5.

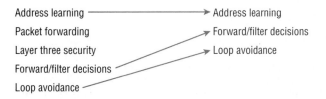

The three functions are address learning, forward/filter decisions, and loop avoidance.

6. A, D. In the output shown, you can see that the port is in Secure-shutdown mode and the light for the port would be amber. To enable the port again, you'd need to do the following:

```
S3(config-if)#shutdown
S3(config-if)#no shutdown
```

7. `switchport port-security maximum 2`

The maximum setting of 2 means only two MAC addresses can be used on that port; if the user tries to add another host on that segment, the switch port will take the action specified. In the `port-security violation` command.

8. B. The `switchport port-security` command enables port security, which is a prerequisite for the other commands to function.

9. B. Gateway redundancy is not an issue addressed by STP.

10. A. If no loop avoidance schemes are put in place, the switches will flood broadcasts endlessly throughout the internetwork. This is sometimes referred to as a broadcast storm.

11. B, C. Shutdown and protect mode will alert you via SNMP that a violation has occurred on a port.

12. Spanning Tree Protocol (STP) STP is a switching loop avoidance scheme use by switches.

13. `ip default-gateway`

If you want to manage your switches from outside your LAN, you need to set a default gateway on the switches, just as you would with a host.

14. C. The IP address is configured under a logical interface, called a management domain or VLAN 1.

15. B. The `show port-security interface` command displays the current port security and status of a switch port, as in this sample output:

```
Switch# show port-security interface fastethernet0/1
Port Security: Enabled
Port status: SecureUp
Violation mode: Shutdown
Maximum MAC Addresses: 2
Total MAC Addresses: 2
Configured MAC Addresses: 2
Aging Time: 30 mins
Aging Type: Inactivity
SecureStatic address aging: Enabled
Security Violation count: 0
```

16. `switchport port-security mac-address sticky`

Issuing the `switchport port-security mac-address sticky` command will allow a switch to save a dynamically learned MAC address in the running-configuration of the switch, which prevents the administrator from having to document or configure specific MAC addresses.

17. B, D. To limit connections to a specific host, you should configure the MAC address of the host as a static entry associated with the port, although be aware that this host can still connect to any other port, but no other port can connect to F0/3, in this example. Another solution would be to configure port security to accept traffic only from the MAC address of the host. By default, an unlimited number of MAC addresses can be learned on a single switch port, whether it is configured as an access port or a trunk port. Switch ports can be secured by defining one or more specific MAC addresses that should be allowed to connect and by defining violation policies (such as disabling the port) to be enacted if additional hosts try to gain a connection.

18. D. The command statically defines the MAC address of 00c0.35F0.8301 as an allowed host on the switch port. By default, an unlimited number of MAC addresses can be learned on a single switch port, whether it is configured as an access port or a trunk port. Switch ports can be secured by defining one or more specific MAC addresses that should be allowed to connect, and violation policies (such as disabling the port) if additional hosts try to gain a connection.

19. D. You would not make the port a trunk. In this example, this switchport is a member of one VLAN. However, you can configure port security on a trunk port, but again, that's not valid for this question.

20. `switchport port-security violation shutdown`

This command is used to set the reaction of the switch to a port violation of shutdown.

Chapter 11: VLANs and InterVLAN Routing

1. D. Here's a list of ways VLANs simplify network management:
  - Network adds, moves, and changes are achieved with ease by just configuring a port into the appropriate VLAN.
  - A group of users that need an unusually high level of security can be put into its own VLAN so that users outside of the VLAN can't communicate with them.
  - As a logical grouping of users by function, VLANs can be considered independent from their physical or geographic locations.
  - VLANs greatly enhance network security if implemented correctly.
  - VLANs increase the number of broadcast domains while decreasing their size.

2. `ip routing`

Routing must be enabled on the layer 3 switch.

3. C. VLANs can span across multiple switches by using trunk links, which carry traffic for multiple VLANs.

4. B. While in all other cases access ports can be a member of only one VLAN, most switches will allow you to add a second VLAN to an access port on a switch port for your voice traffic; it's called the voice VLAN. The voice VLAN used to be called the auxiliary VLAN, which allowed it to be overlaid on top of the data VLAN, enabling both types of traffic through the same port.

5. A. Yes, you have to do a `no shutdown` on the VLAN interface.

6. C. Unlike ISL which encapsulates the frame with control information, 802.1q inserts an 802.1q field along with tag control information.

7. D. Instead of using a router interface for each VLAN, you can use one FastEthernet interface and run ISL or 802.1q trunking. This allows all VLANs to communicate through one interface. Cisco calls this a "router on a stick."

8. `switchport access vlan 2`

This command is executed under the interface (switch port) that is being placed in the VLAN.

9. `show vlan`

After you create the VLANs that you want, you can use the `show vlan` command to check them out.

10. B. The `encapsulation` command specifying the VLAN for the subinterface must be present under both subinterfaces.

11. A. With a multilayer switch, enable IP routing and create one logical interface for each VLAN using the `interface vlan number` command and you're now doing inter-VLAN routing on the backplane of the switch!

12. A. Ports Fa0/15–18 are not present in any VLANs. They are trunk ports.

13. C. Untagged frames are members of the native VLAN, which by default is VLAN 1.

14. `sh interfaces fastEthernet 0/15 switchport`

This `show interfaces interface switchport` command shows us the administrative mode of dynamic desirable and that the port is a trunk port, DTP was used to negotiate the frame tagging method of ISL, and the native VLAN is the default of 1.

15. C. A VLAN is a broadcast domain on a layer 2 switch. You need a separate address space (subnet) for each VLAN. There are four VLANs, so that means four broadcast domains/subnets.

16. B. The host's default gateway should be set to the IP address of the subinterface that is associated with the VLAN of which the host is a member, in this case VLAN 2.

17. C. Frame tagging is used when VLAN traffic travels over a trunk link. Trunk links carry frames for multiple VLANs. Therefore, frame tags are used for identification of frames from different VLANs.

18. `vlan 2`

To configure VLANs on a Cisco Catalyst switch, use the global config `vlan` command.

19. B. 802.1q uses the native VLAN.

20. `switchport nonegotiate`

You can use this command only when the interface switchport mode is access or trunk. You must manually configure the neighboring interface as a trunk interface to establish a trunk link.

Chapter 12: Security

1. D. It's compared with lines of the access list only until a match is made. Once the packet matches the condition on a line of the access list, the packet is acted upon and no further comparisons take place.

2. C. The range of 192.168.160.0 to 192.168.191.0 is a block size of 32. The network address is 192.168.160.0 and the mask would be 255.255.224.0, which for an access list must be a wildcard format of 0.0.31.255. The 31 is used for a block size of 32. The wildcard is always one less than the block size.

3. C. Using a named access list just replaces the number used when applying the list to the router's interface. `ip access-group Blocksales in` is correct.

4. B. The list must specify TCP as the Transport layer protocol and use a correct wildcard mask (in this case 0.0.0.255), and it must specify the destination port (80). It also should specify any as the set of computers allowed to have this access.

5. A. The first thing to check in a question like this is the access-list number. Right away, you can see that the second option is wrong because it is using a standard IP access-list number. The second thing to check is the protocol. If you are filtering by upper-layer protocol, then you must be using either UDP or TCP; this eliminates the fourth option. The third and last answers have the wrong syntax.

6. C. Of the available choices, only the `show ip interface` command will tell you which interfaces have access lists applied. `show access-lists` will not show you which interfaces have an access list applied.

7.

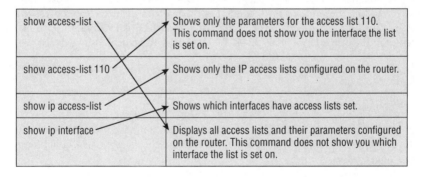

The command `show access-list` displays all access lists and their parameters configured on the router; it does not show you which interface the list is set on. `show access-list 110` shows only the parameters for the access list 110 and, again, does not tell you which interface the list is set on. `show ip access-list` reveals only the IP access lists configured on the router. Finally, `show ip interface` shows which interfaces have access lists set.

The functions of each command are as shown in the solution graphic.

8. C. The extended access list ranges are 100–199 and 2000–2699, so the access-list number of 100 is valid. Telnet uses TCP, so the protocol TCP is valid. Now you just need to look for the source and destination address. Only the third option has the correct sequence of parameters. Option B may work, but the question specifically states "only" to network 192.168.10.0, and the wildcard in option B is too broad.

9. D. Extended IP access lists use numbers 100–199 and 2000–2699 and filter based on source and destination IP address, protocol number, and port number. The last option is correct because of the second line that specifies permit ip any any. (I used 0.0.0.0 255.255.255.255, which is the same as the any option.) The third option does not have this, so it would deny access but not allow everything else.

10. D. First, you must know that a /20 is 255.255.240.0, which is a block size of 16 in the third octet. Counting by 16s, this makes our subnet 48 in the third octet, and the wildcard for the third octet would be 15 since the wildcard is always one less than the block size.

11. B. To find the wildcard (inverse) version of this mask, the zero and one bits are simply reversed as follows:

11111111.11111111.11111111.11100000 (27 one bits, or /27)

00000000.00000000.00000000.00011111 (wildcard/inverse mask)

12. A. First, you must know that a /19 is 255.255.224.0, which is a block size of 32 in the third octet. Counting by 32s, this makes our subnet 192 in the third octet, and the wildcard for the third octet would be 31 since the wildcard is always one less than the block size.

13. B, D. The scope of an access list is determined by the wildcard mask and the network address to which it is applied. For example, in this case the starting point of the list of addresses affected by the mask is the network ID 192.111.16.32. The wildcard mask is 0.0.0.31. Adding the value of the last octet in the mask to the network address (32 + 31 = 63) tells you where the effects of the access list ends, which is 199.111.16.63. Therefore, all addresses in the range 199.111.16.32–199.111.16.63 will be denied by this list.

14. C. To place an access list on an interface, use the ip access-group command in interface configuration mode.

15. B. With no permit statement, the ACL will deny all traffic.

16. D. If you add an access list to an interface and you do not have at least one permit statement, then you will effectively shut down the interface because of the implicit deny any at the end of every list.

17. C. Telnet access to the router is restricted by using either a standard or extended IP access list inbound on the VTY lines of the router. The command access-class is used to apply the access list to the VTY lines.

18. C. A Cisco router has rules regarding the placement of access lists on a router interface. You can place one access list per direction for each layer 3 protocol configured on an interface.

19. C. The most common attack on a network today is a denial of service (DoS) because it is the easiest attack to achieve.

20. C. Implementing intrusion detection services and intrusion prevention services will help notify you and stop attacks in real time.

Chapter 13: Network Address Translation (NAT)

1. A, C, E. NAT is not perfect and can cause some issues in some networks, but most networks work just fine. NAT can cause delays and troubleshooting problems, and some applications just won't work.

2. B, D, F. NAT is not perfect, but there are some advantages. It conserves global addresses, which allow us to add millions of hosts to the Internet without "real" IP addresses. This provides flexibility in our corporate networks. NAT can also allow you to use the same subnet more than once in the same network without overlapping networks.

3. C. The command `debug ip nat` will show you in real time the translations occurring on your router.

4. A. The command `show ip nat translations` will show you the translation table containing all the active NAT entries.

5. D. The command `clear ip nat translations *` will clear all the active NAT entries in your translation table.

6. B. The `show ip nat statistics` command displays a summary of the NAT configuration as well as counts of active translation types, hits to an existing mapping, misses (an attempt to create a mapping), and expired translations.

7. B. The command `ip nat pool` *name* creates the pool that hosts can use to get onto the global Internet. What makes option B correct is that the range 171.16.10.65 through 171.16.10.94 includes 30 hosts, but the mask has to match 30 hosts as well, and that mask is 255.255.255.224. Option C is wrong because there is a lowercase t in the pool name. Pool names are case sensitive.

8. A, C, E. You can configure NAT three ways on a Cisco router: static, dynamic, and NAT Overload (PAT).

9. B. Instead of the `netmask` command, you can use the `prefix-length` *length* statement.

10. C. In order for NAT to provide translation services, you must have `ip nat inside` and `ip nat outside` configured on your router's interfaces.

11. A, B, D. The most popular use of NAT is if you want to connect to the Internet and you don't want hosts to have global (real) IP addresses, but options B and D are correct as well.

12. C. An inside global address is considered to be the IP address of the host on the private network after translation.

13. A. An inside local address is considered to be the IP address of the host on the private network before translation.

14. D. What we need to figure out for this question is only the inside global pool. Basically we start at 1.1.128.1 and end at 1.1.135.174; our block size is 8 in the third octet, or /21. Always look for your block size and the interesting octet and you can find your answer every time.

15. B. Once you create your pool, the command `ip nat inside source` must be used to say which inside locals are allowed to use the pool. In this question we need to see if access-list 100 is configured correctly, if at all, so `show access-list` is the best answer.

16. A. You must configure your interfaces before NAT will provide any translations. On the inside network interfaces, you would use the command `ip nat inside`. On the outside network interfaces, you will use the command `ip nat outside`.

17. B. You must configure your interfaces before NAT will provide any translations. On the inside networks you would use the command `ip nat inside`. On the outside network interfaces, you will use the command `ip nat outside`.

18. C. Another term for Port Address Translation is *NAT Overload* because that is the keyword used to enable port address translation.

19. B. Fast-switching is used on Cisco routers to create a type of route cache in order to quickly forward packets through a router without having to parse the routing table for every packet. As packets are processed-switched (looked up in the routing table), this information is stored in the cache for later use if needed for faster routing processing.

20. B. Once you create a pool for the inside locals to use to get out to the global Internet, you must configure the command to allow them access to the pool. The `ip nat inside source list` *number pool-name* `overload` command has the correct sequence for this question.

Chapter 14: Internet Protocol Version 6 (IPv6)

1. D. The modified EUI-64 format interface identifier is derived from the 48-bit link-layer (MAC) address by inserting the hexadecimal number FFFE between the upper 3 bytes (OUI field) and the lower 3 bytes (serial number) of the link layer address.

2. D. An IPv6 address is represented as eight groups of four hexadecimal digits, each group representing 16 bits (two octets). The groups are separated by colons (:). Option A has two double colons, B doesn't have 8 fields, and option C has invalid hex characters.

3. A, B, C. This question is easier to answer if you just take out the wrong options. First, the loopback is only ::1, so that makes option D wrong. Link local is FE80::/10, not /8 and there are no broadcasts..

4. A, C, D. Several methods are used in terms of migration, including tunneling, translators, and dual-stack. Tunnels are used to carry one protocol inside another, while translators simply translate IPv6 packets into IPv4 packets. Dual-stack uses a combination of both native IPv4 and IPv6. With dual-stack, devices are able to run IPv4 and IPv6 together, and if IPv6 communication is possible, that is the preferred protocol. Hosts can simultaneously reach IPv4 and IPv6 content.

5. A, B. ICMPv6 router advertisements use type 134 and must be at least 64 bits in length.

6. B, E, F. Anycast addresses identify multiple interfaces, which is somewhat similar to multi-cast addresses; however, the big difference is that the anycast packet is only delivered to one address, the first one it finds defined in terms of routing distance. This address can also be called one-to-one-of-many, or one-to-nearest.

7. C. The loopback address with IPv4 is 127.0.0.1. With IPv6, that address is ::1.

8. B, C, E. An important feature of IPv6 is that it allows the plug-and-play option to the network devices by allowing them to configure themselves independently. It is possible to plug a node into an IPv6 network without requiring any human intervention. IPv6 does not implement traditional IP broadcasts.

9. A, D. The loopback address is ::1, link-local starts with FE80::/10, site-local addresses start with FEC0::/10, global addresses start with 200::/3, and multicast addresses start with FF00::/8.

10. C. A router solicitation is sent out using the all-routers multicast address of FF02::2. The router can send a router advertisement to all hosts using the FF02::1 multicast address.

11. A, E. IPv6 does not use broadcasts, and autoconfiguration is a feature of IPV6 that allows for hosts to automatically obtain an IPv6 address.

12. A. The NDP neighbor advertisement (NA) contains the MAC address. A neighbor solicita-tion (NS) was initially sent asking for the MAC address.

13. B. IPv6 anycast addresses are used for one-to-nearest communication, meaning an anycast address is used by a device to send data to one specific recipient (interface) that is the closest out of a group of recipients (interfaces).

14. B, D. To shorten the written length of an IPv6 address, successive fields of zeros may be replaced by double colons. In trying to shorten the address further, leading zeros may also be removed. Just as with IPv4, a single device's interface can have more than one address; with IPv6 there are more types of addresses and the same rule applies. There can be link-local, global unicast, multicast, and anycast addresses all assigned to the same interface.

15. A, B, C. The Internet Header Length field was removed because it is no longer required. Unlike the variable-length IPv4 header, the IPv6 header is fixed at 40 bytes. Fragmentation is processed differently in IPv6 and does not need the Flags field in the basic IPv4 header.

In IPv6, routers no longer process fragmentation; the host is responsible for fragmentation. The Header Checksum field at the IP layer was removed because most Data Link layer technologies already perform checksum and error control, which forces formerly optional upper-layer checksums (UDP, for example) to become mandatory.

16. B. There are no broadcasts with IPv6. Unicast, multicast, anycast, global, and link-local unicast are used.

17. D. This question asked how many bits in a field, not how many bits in an IPv6 address. There are 16 bits (four hex characters) in an IPv6 field and there are eight fields.

18. A, D. Global addresses start with 2000::/3, link-locals start with FE80::/10, loopback is ::1, and unspecified is just two colons (::). Each interface will have a loopback address automatically configured.

19. B, C. If you verify your IP configuration on your host, you'll see that you have multiple IPv6 addresses, including a loopback address. The last 64 bits represent the dynamically created interface ID, and leading zeros are not mandatory in a 16-bit IPv6 field.

20. C. To enable IPv6 routing on the Cisco router, use the following command from global config:

```
ipv6 unicast-routing
```

If this command is not recognized, your version of IOS does not support IPv6.

Chapter 15: Enhanced Switched Technologies

1. B, D. The switch is not the root bridge for VLAN 1 or the output would tell us exactly that. The root bridge for VLAN 1 is off of interface G1/2 with a cost of 4, meaning it is directly connected. Use the command show cdp nei to find your root bridge at this point. Also, the switch is running RSTP (802.1w), not STP.

2. D. Option A seems like the best answer, and had switches not been configured with the primary and secondary command, then the switch configured with priority 4096 would have been root. However, since the primary and secondary both had a priority of 16384, then the tertiary switch would be a switch with a higher priority in this case.

3. A, D. It is important that you can find your root bridge, and the show spanning-tree command will help you do this. To quickly find out which VLANs your switch is the root bridge for, use the show spanning-tree summary command.

4. A. 802.1w is the also called Rapid Spanning Tree Protocol. It is not enabled by default on Cisco switches, but it is a better STP to run because it has all the fixes that the Cisco extensions provide with 802.1d. Remember, Cisco runs RSTP PVST+, not just RSTP.

5. B. The Spanning Tree Protocol is used to stop switching loops in a layer 2 switched network with redundant paths.

6. C. Convergence occurs when all ports on bridges and switches have transitioned to either the forwarding or blocking states. No data is forwarded until convergence is complete. Before data can be forwarded again, all devices must be updated.

7. C, E. There are two types of EtherChannel: Cisco's PAgP and the IEEE's LACP. They are basically the same, and there is little difference to configuring them. For PAgP, use auto or desirable mode, and with LACP use passive or active. These modes decide which method you are using, and they must be configured the same on both sides of the EtherChannel bundle.

8. A, B, F. RSTP helps with convergence issues that plague traditional STP. Rapid PVST+ is based on the 802.1w standard in the same way that PVST+ is based on 802.1d. The operation of Rapid PVST+ is simply a separate instance of 802.1w for each VLAN.

9. D. BPDU Guard is used when a port is configured for PortFast, or it should be used, because if that port receives a BPDU from another switch, BPDU Guard will shut that port down to stop a loop from occurring.

10. C. To allow for the PVST+ to operate, there's a field inserted into the BPDU to accommodate the extended system ID so that PVST+ can have a root bridge configured on a per-STP instance. The extended system ID (VLAN ID) is a 12-bit field, and we can even see what this field is carrying via the show spanning-tree command output.

11. C. PortFast and BPDU Guard allow a port to transition to the forwarding state quickly, which is great for a switch port but not for load balancing. You can somewhat load balance with RSTP, but that is out of the scope of our objectives, and although you can use PPP to configure multilink (bundle links), this is performed on asynchronous or synchronous serial links. Cisco's EtherChannel can bundle up to eight ports between switches.

12. D. If the Spanning Tree Protocol is not running on your switches and you connect them together with redundant links, you will have broadcast storms and multiple frame copies being received by the same destination device.

13. B, C, E. All the ports on both sides of every link must be configured exactly the same or it will not work. Speed, duplex, and allowed VLANs must match.

14. D, F. There are two types of EtherChannel: Cisco's PAgP and the IEEE's LACP. They are basically the same, and there is little difference to configure them. For PAgP, use the auto or desirable mode, and with LACP use the passive or active mode. These modes decide which method you are using, and they must be configured the same on both sides of the EtherChannel bundle.

15. D. You can't answer this question if you don't know who the root bridge is. SC has a bridge priority of 4,096, so that is the root bridge. The cost for SB was 4, with the direct link, but that link went down. If SB goes through SA to SC, the cost would be 4 + 19, or 23. If SB goes to SA to SD to SC, the cost is 4 + 4 + 4 = 12.

16. A, D. To configure EtherChannel, create the port channel from global configuration mode, and then assign the group number on each interface using the active mode to enable LACP. Just configuring the channel-group command under your interfaces will enable the bundle, but options A and D are the best Cisco objective answers.

17. A, D. You can set the priority to any value from 0 through 61,440 in increments of 4,096. Setting it to zero (0) means that the switch will always be a root as long as it has a lower MAC than another switch with its bridge ID also set to 0. You can also force a switch to be a root for a VLAN with the spanning-tree vlan vlan primary command.

18. A. By using per-VLAN spanning tree, the root bridge can be placed in the center of where all the resources are for a particular VLAN, which enables optimal path determination.

19. A, C, D, E. Each 802.1d port transitions through blocking, listening, learning, and finally forwarding after 50 seconds, by default. RSTP uses discarding, learning, and forwarding only.

20. A, C, D, E, F. The roles a switch port can play in STP are root, non-root, designated, non-designated, forwarding, and blocking. Discarding is used in RSTP, and disabled could be a role, but it's not listed as a possible answer.

Chapter 16: Network Device Management and Security

1. B. You can enter the ACL directly in the SNMP configuration to provide security, using either a number or a name.

2. C. 100. By setting a higher number then the default on a router, you are making that router the active router. Setting preempt would assure that if the active router went down, it would become the active router again when it comes back up.

3. D. To enable the AAA commands on a router or switch, use the global configuration command aaa new-model.

4. A, C. To mitigate access layer threats, use port security, DHCP snooping, dynamic ARP inspection, and identity based networking.

5. D. DHCP snooping validates DHCP messages, builds and maintains the DHCP snooping binding database, and rate-limits DHCP traffic for trusted and untrusted source.

6. A, D. TACACS+ uses TCP, is Cisco proprietary, and offers multiprotocol support as well as separated AAA services.

7. B. Unlike with TACACS+, separating AAA services is not an option when configuring RADIUS.

8. A, D. With a read-only community string, no changes can be made to the router. However, SNMPv2c can use GETBULK to create and return multiple requests at once.

9. C. The idea of a first hop redundancy protocol is to provide redundancy for a default gateway.

10. A, B. A router interface can be in many states with HSRP; the states are shown in Table 2.1.

11. A. Only option A has the correct sequence to enable HSRP on an interface.

12. D. This is a question that I used in a lot of job interviews on prospects. The show standby command is your friend when dealing with HSRP.

13. D. There is nothing wrong with leaving the priorities at the defaults of 100. The first router up will be the active router.

14. C. In version 1, HSRP messages are sent to the multicast IP address 224.0.0.2 and UDP port 1985. HSRP version 2 uses the multicast IP address 224.0.0.102 and UDP port 1985.

15. B, C. If HSRP1 is configured to preempt, then it will become active because of the higher priority; if not, HSRP2 will stay the active router.

16. C. In version 1, HSRP messages are sent to the multicast IP address 224.0.0.2 and UDP port 1985. HSRP version 2 uses and the multicast IP address 224.0.0.102 and UDP port 1985.

17. C, D. SNMPv2c introduced the GETBULK and INFORM SNMP messages but didn't have any different security than SNMPv1. SNMPv3 uses TCP and provides encryption and authentication.

18. D. The correct answer is option D. Take your newly created RADIUS group and use it for authentication, and be sure to use the keyword local at the end.

19. B. DAI, used with DHCP snooping, tracks IP-to-MAC bindings from DHCP transactions to protect against ARP poisoning. DHCP snooping is required in order to build the MAC-to-IP bindings for DAI validation.

20. A, D, E. There are three roles involved in using client/server access control for identity-based networking on wired and wireless hosts: The client, also referred to as a supplicant, is software that runs on a client and is 802.1x compliant. The authenticator is typically a switch that controls physical access to the network and is a proxy between the client and the authentication server. The authentication server (RADIUS) is a server that authenticates each client before it can access any services.

Chapter 17: Enhanced IGRP

1. B. Only the EIGRP routes will be placed in the routing table because it has the lowest administrative distance (AD), and that is always used before metrics.

2. A, C. EIGRP maintains three tables in RAM: neighbor, topology, and routing. The neighbor and topology tables are built and maintained with the use of Hello and update packets.

3. B. EIGRP does use reported distance, or advertised distance (AD), to tell neighbor routers the cost to get to a remote network. This router will send the FD to the neighbor router and the neighbor router will add the cost to get to this router plus the AD to find the true FD.

4. E. Successor routes are going to be in the routing table since they are the best path to a remote network. However, the topology table has a link to each and every network, so the best answer is topology table and routing table. Any secondary route to a remote network is considered a feasible successor, and those routes are found only in the topology table and used as backup routes in case of primary route failure.

5. C. Any secondary route to a remote network is considered a feasible successor, and those routes are found only in the topology table and used as backup routes in case of primary route failure. You can see the topology table with the `show ip eigrp topology` command.

6. B, C, E. EIGRP and EIGRPv6 routers can use the same RID, unlike OSPF, and this can be set with the `eigrp router-id` command. Also a `variance` can be set to provide unequal-cost load balancing, along with the `maximum-paths` command to set the amount of load-balanced paths.

7. C. There were two successor routes, so by default, EIGRP was load-balancing out s0/0 and s0/1. When s0/0 goes down, EIGRP will just keep forwarding traffic out the second link s0/1. s0/0 will be removed from the routing table.

8. D. To enable EIGRPv6 on a router interface, use the command `ipv6 eigrp as` on individual interfaces that will be part of the EIGRPv6 process.

9. C. The path to network 10.10.50.0 out serial0/0 is more than two times the current FD, so I used a `variance 3` command to load-balance unequal-cost links three times the FD.

10. B, C. First, a maximum hop count of 16 only is associated with RIP, and EIGRP never broadcasts, so we can eliminate A and D as options. Feasible successors are backup routes and stored in the topology table, so that is correct, and if no feasible successor is located, the EIGRP will flood its neighbors asking for a new path to network 10.10.10.0.

11. D. The `show ip eigrp neighbors` command allows you to check the IP addresses as well as the retransmit interval and queue counts for the neighbors that have established an adjacency.

12. C, E. For EIGRP to form an adjacency with a neighbor, the AS numbers must match, and the metric K values must match as well. Also, option F could cause the problem; we can see if it is causing a problem from the output given.

13. A, D. Successor routes are the routes picked from the topology table as the best route to a remote network, so these are the routes that IP uses in the routing table to forward traffic to a remote destination. The topology table contains any route that is not as good as the successor route and is considered a feasible successor, or backup route. Remember that all routes are in the topology table, even successor routes.

14. A, B. Option A will work because the router will change the network statement to 10.0.0.0 since EIGRP uses classful addresses by default. Therefore, it isn't technically a wrong answer, but please understand why it is correct for this question. The 10.255.255.64/27 subnet address can be configured with wildcards just as we use with OSPF and ACLs. The /27 is a block of 32, so the wildcard in the fourth octet will be 31. The wildcard of 0.0.0.0 is wrong because this is a network address, not a host address, and the 0.0.0.15 is wrong because that is only a block of 16 and would only work if the mask was a /28.

15. C. To troubleshoot adjacencies, you need to check the AS numbers, the K values, networks, passive interfaces, and ACLs.

16. C. EIGRP and EIGRPv6 will load-balance across 4 equal-cost paths by default but can be configured to load-balance across equal- and unequal-cost paths, up to 32 with IOS 15.0 code.

17. B, E. EIGRP must be enabled with an AS number from global configuration mode with the `ipv6 router eigrp as` command if you need to set the RID or other global parameters. Instead of configuring EIGRP with the network command as with EIGRP, EIGRPv6 is configured on a per-interface basis with the `ipv6 eigrp as` command.

18. C. There isn't a lot to go on from with the output, but that might make this easier than if there were a whole page of output. Since s0/0/2 has the lowest FD and AD, that would become the successor route. For a route to become a feasible successor, its reported distance must be lower than the feasible distance of the current successor route, so C is our best answer based on what we can see.

19. C. The network in the diagram is considered a discontiguous network because you have one classful address subnetted and separated by another classful address. Only RIPv2, OSPF, and EIGRP can work with discontiguous networks, but RIPv2 and EIGRP won't work by default (except for routers running the new 15.0 code). You must use the `no auto-summary` command under the routing protocol configuration. There is a passive interface on RouterB, but this is not on an interface between RouterA and RouterB and won't stop an adjacency.

20. A, B, C, D. Here are the documented issues that Cisco says to check when you have an adjacency issue:

- Interfaces between the devices are down.
- The two routers have mismatching EIGRP autonomous system numbers.
- Proper interfaces are not enabled for the EIGRP process.
- An interface is configured as passive.
- K values are mismatched.
- EIGRP authentication is misconfigured.

Chapter 18: Open Shortest Path First (OSPF)

1. B. Only the EIGRP routes will be placed in the routing table because it has the lowest administrative distance (AD), and that is always used before metrics.

2. A, B, C. Any router that is a member of two areas must be an area border router or ABR.

3. A, C. The process ID for OSPF on a router is only locally significant, and you can use the same number on each router, or each router can have a different number—it just doesn't matter. The numbers you can use are from 1 to 65,535. Don't get this confused with area numbers, which can be from 0 to 4.2 billion.

4. B. The router ID (RID) is an IP address used to identify the router. It need not and should not match.

5. C. The router ID (RID) is an IP address used to identify the router. Cisco chooses the router ID by using the highest IP address of all configured loopback interfaces. If no loopback interfaces are configured with addresses, OSPF will choose the highest IP address of all active physical interfaces.

6. A. The administrator typed in the wrong wildcard mask configuration. The wildcard should have been 0.0.0.255 or even 0.255.255.255.

7. A. A dash (-) in the State column indicates no DR election, because they are not required on a point-to-point link such as a serial connection.

8. D. By default, the administrative distance of OSPF is 110.

9. A. Hello packets are addressed to multicast address 224.0.0.5.

10. A. The show ip ospf neighbor command displays all interface-related neighbor information. This output shows the DR and BDR (unless your router is the DR or BDR), the RID of all directly connected neighbors, and the IP address and name of the directly connected interface.

11. A. 224.0.0.6 is used on broadcast networks to reach the DR and BDR.

12. D. The Hello and Dead timers must be set the same on two routers on the same link or they will not form an adjacency (relationship). The default timers for OSPF are 10 seconds for the Hello timer and 40 seconds for the Dead timer.

13.

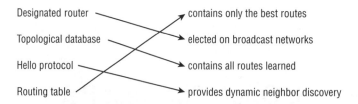

A designated router is elected on broadcast networks. Each OSPF router maintains an identical database describing the AS topology. A Hello protocol provides dynamic neighbor discovery. A routing table contains only the best routes.

14. passive-interface fastEthernet 0/1

The command passive-interface fastEthernet 0/1 will disable OSPF on the specified interface only.

15. B, G. To enable OSPF, you must first start OSPF using a process ID. The number is irrelevant; just choose a number from 1 to 65,535 and you're good to go. After you start the OSPF process, you must configure interfaces on which to activate OSPF using the network command with wildcards and specification of an area. Option F is wrong because there must be a space after the parameter area and before you list the area number.

16. A. The default OSPF interface priority is 1, and the highest interface priority determines the designated router (DR) for a subnet. The output indicates that the router with a router ID of 192.168.45.2 is currently the backup designated router (BDR) for the segment, which indicates that another router became the DR. It can be then be assumed that the DR router has an interface priority higher than 2. (The router serving the DR function is not present in the truncated sample output.)

17. A, B, C. OSPF is created in a hierarchical design, not a flat design like RIP. This decreases routing overhead, speeds up convergence, and confines network instability to a single area of the network.

18. `show ip ospf interface`

The `show ip ospf interface` command displays all interface-related OSPF information. Data is displayed about OSPF information for all OSPF-enabled interfaces or for specified interfaces.

19. A. LSA packets are used to update and maintain the topological database.

20. B. At the moment of OSPF process startup, the highest IP address on any active interface will be the router ID (RID) of the router. If you have a loopback interface configured (logical interface), then that will override the interface IP address and become the RID of the router automatically.

Chapter 19: Multi-Area OSPF

1. A, B, D. As the size of a single-area OSPF network grows, so does the size of the routing table and OSPF database that have to be maintained. Also, if there is a change in network topology, the OSPF algorithm has to be rerun for the entire network.

2. B. An autonomous system boundary router (ASBR) is any OSPF router that is connected to an external routing process (another AS). An ABR, on the other hand, connects one (or more) OSPF areas together to area 0.

3. B, D, E. In order for two OSPF routers to create an adjacency, the Hello and Dead timers must match, and they must both be configured into the same area as well as being in the same subnet. Also, if authentication is configured, that info must match as well.

4. C. The process starts by sending out Hello packets. Every listening router will then add the originating router to the neighbor database. The responding routers will reply with all of their Hello information so that the originating router can add them to its own neighbor table. At this point, we will have reached the 2WAY state—only certain routers will advance beyond this to establish adjacencies.

5.   D. If you have multiple links to the same network, you can change the default cost of a link so OSPF will prefer that link over another with the `ip ospf cost` *cost* command.

6.   B. In the FULL state, all LSA information is synchronized among adjacent neighbors. OSPF routing can begin only after the FULL state has been reached. The FULL state occurs after the LOADING state finishes.

7.   B, D, E. Configuring OSPFv3 is pretty simple, as long as you know what interfaces you are using on your router. There are no network statements; OSPFv3 is configured on a per-interface basis. OSPFv2 and OSPFv3 both use a 32-bit RID, and if you have an IPv4 address configured on at least one interface, you do not need to manually set a RID when configuring EIGRPv3.

8.   B. When OSPF adjacency is formed, a router goes through several state changes before it becomes fully adjacent with its neighbor. The states are (in order) DOWN, ATTEMPT, INIT, 2WAY, EXSTART, EXCHANGE, LOADING, and FULL.

9.   B. Referred to as a network link advertisement (NLA), Type 2 LSAs are generated by designated routers (DRs). Remember that a designated router is elected to represent other routers in its network, and it establishes adjacencies with them. The DR uses a Type 2 LSA to send out information about the state of other routers that are part of the same network.

10.   C. Referred to as summary link advertisements (SLAs), Type 3 LSAs are generated by area border routers. These ABRs send Type 3 LSAs toward the area external to the one where they were generated. The Type 3 LSA advertises networks, and these LSAs advertise inter-area routes to the backbone area (area 0).

11.   D. To see all LSAs a router has learned from its neighbors, you need to see the OSPF LSDB, and you can see this with the `show ip ospf database` command.

12.   B. Based on the information in the question, the cost from R1 to R2 is 4, the cost from R2 to R3 is 15, and the cost from R3 to R5 is 4. 15 + 4 + 4 = 23. Pretty simple.

13.   B, D. Since R3 is connected to area 1 and R1 is connected to area 2 and area 0, the routes advertised from R3 would show as OI, or inter-area routes.

14.   A, D, E, F, G. For two OSPF routers to form an adjacency, they must be in the same area, must be in the same subnet, and the authentication information must match, if configured. You need to also check if an ACL is set and if a passive interface is configured, and every OSPF router must use a different RID.

15.   C. The IOS command `show ip ospf neighbor` shows neighbor router information, such as neighbor ID and the state of adjacency with the neighboring router.

16.   D. The command `show ip ospf` *interface* on a default broadcast multi-access network will show you DRs and BDRs on that network.

17.   A, C, D, F. It's hard to tell from this single output what is causing the problem with the adjacency, but we need to check the ACL 10 to see what that is doing, verify that the routers are in the same area and in the same subnet, and see if passive interface is configured with the interface we're using.

18. B, D, G. The default reference bandwidth is 100 by default, and you can change it under the OSPF process with the `auto-cost reference bandwidth` *number* command, but if you do, you need to configure this command on all routers in your AS.

19. A, D. An OSPF RID will be used as source of Type 1 LSA, and the router will chose the highest loopback interface as its OSPF router ID (if available).

20. B, C. With single area OSPF you'd use only a couple LSA types, which can save on bandwidth. Also, you wouldn't need virtual links, which is a configuration that allows you to connect an area to another area that is not area 0.

Chapter 20: Troubleshooting IP, IPv6, and VLANs

1. D. Positive confirmation has been received confirming that the path to the neighbor is functioning correctly. REACH is good!

2. B. The most common cause of interface errors is a mismatched duplex mode between two ends of an Ethernet link. If they have mismatched duplex settings, you'll receive a legion of errors, which cause nasty slow performance issues, intermittent connectivity, and massive collisions—even total loss of communication!

3. D. You can verify the DTP status of an interface with the `sh dtp interface` *interface* command.

4. A. No DTP frames are generated from the interface. Nonegotiate can be used only if the neighbor interface is manually set as trunk or access.

5. D. The command `show ipv6 neighbors` provides the ARP cache on a router.

6. B. The state is STALE when the interface has not communicated within the neighbor reachable time frame. The next time the neighbor communicates, the state will change back to REACH.

7. B. There is no IPv6 default gateway, which will be the link-local address of the router interface, sent to the host as a router advertisement. Until this host receives the router address, the host will communicate with IPv6 only on the local subnet.

8. D. This host is using IPv4 to communicate on the network, and without an IPv6 global address, the host will be able to communicate to only remote networks with IPv4. The IPv4 address and default gateway are not configured into the same subnet.

9. B, C. The commands `show interface trunk` and `show interface` *interface* `switchport` will show you statistics of ports, which includes native VLAN information.

10. A. Most Cisco switches ship with a default port mode of auto, meaning that they will automatically trunk if they connect to a port that is on or desirable. Remember that not all switches are shipped as mode auto, but many are, and you need to set one side to either on or desirable in order to trunk between switches.

Chapter 21: Wide Area Networks

1. C. The command debug ppp authentication will show you the authentication process that PPP uses across point-to-point connections.

2. B, D. Since BGP does not automatically discover neighbors like other routing protocols do, you have to explicitly configure them using the neighbor peer-ip-address remote-as peer-as-number command.

3. D. BGP uses TCP as the transport mechanism, which provides reliable connection-oriented delivery. BGP uses TCP port 179. Two routers that are using BGP form a TCP connection with one another. These two BGP routers are called "peer routers," or "neighbors."

4. D. The show ip bgp neighbor command is used to see the hold time on two BGP peers.

5. B. The 0.0.0.0 in the next hop field output of the show ip bgp command means that the network was locally entered on the router with the network command into BGP.

6. A, D. GRE tunnels have the following characteristics: GRE uses a protocol-type field in the GRE header so any layer 3 protocol can be used through the tunnel, GRE is stateless and has no flow control, GRE offers no security, and GRE creates additional overhead for tunneled packets—at least 24 bytes.

7. C. If you receive this flapping message when you configure your GRE tunnel, this means that you used your tunnel interface address instead of the tunnel destination address.

8. D. The show running-config interface tunnel 0 command will show you the configuration of the interface, not the status of the tunnel.

9. C. PPP uses PAP and CHAP as authentication protocols. PAP is clear text, CHAP uses an MD5 hash.

10. C. PPPoE encapsulates PPP frames in Ethernet frames and uses common PPP features like authentication, encryption, and compression. PPPoA is used for ATM.

11. C, D. S0/0/0 is up, meaning the s0/0/0 is talking to the CSU/DSU, so that isn't the problem. If the authentication failed or the other end has a different encapsulation than either one of those reasons would be why a data link is not established.

12. C. The show interfaces command shows the configuration settings and the interface status as well as the IP address and tunnel source and destination address.

13. B, C, D. This is just a basic WAN question to test your understanding of connections. PPP does not need to be used, so option A is not valid. You can use any type of connection to

connect to a customer site, so option B is a valid answer. You can also use any type of connection to get to the Frame Relay switch, as long as the ISP supports it, and T1 is valid, so option C is okay. Ethernet as a WAN can be used with Ethernet over MPLS (EoMPLS); however, you don't need to configure a DLCI unless you're using Frame Relay, so E is not a valid answer for this question.

14. B. All web browsers support Secure Sockets Layer (SSL), and SSL VPNs are known as Web VPNs. Remote users can use their browser to create an encrypted connection and they don't need to install any software. GRE doesn't encrypt the data.

15. E. This is an easy question because the Remote router is using the default HDLC serial encapsulation and the Corp router is using the PPP serial encapsulation. You should go to the Remote router and set that encapsulation to PPP or change the Corp router back to the default of HDLC by typing no encapsulation under the interface.

16. A, C, E. VPNs can provide very good security by using advanced encryption and authentication protocols, which will help protect your network from unauthorized access. By connecting the corporate remote offices to their closest Internet provider and then creating a VPN tunnel with encryption and authentication, you'll gain a huge savings over opting for traditional leased point-to-point lines. VPNs scale very well to quickly bring up new offices or have mobile users connect securely while traveling or when connecting from home. VPNs are very compatible with broadband technologies.

17. A, D. Internet providers who have an existing Layer 2 network may choose to use layer 2 VPNs instead of the other common layer 3 MPLS VPN. Virtual Pricate Lan Switch (VPLS) and Virtual Private Wire Service (VPWS) are two technologies that provide layer 2 MPLS VPNs.

18. D. IPsec is an industry-wide standard suite of protocols and algorithms that allows for secure data transmission over an IP-based network that functions at the layer 3 Network layer of the OSI model.

19. C. A VPN allows or describes the creation of private networks across the Internet, enabling privacy and tunneling of TCP/IP protocols. A VPN can be set up across any type of link.

20. B, C. Layer 2 MPLS VPNs and the more popular Layer 3 MPLS VPN are service provided to customers and managed by the provider.

Chapter 22: Evolution of Intelligent Networks

1. B. Dropping packets as they arrive is called tail drop. Selective dropping of packets during the time queues are filling up is called congestion avoidance (CA). Cisco uses weighted random early detection (WRED) as a CA scheme to monitor the buffer depth and performs early discards (drops) on random packets when the minimum defined queue threshold is exceeded.

2. A, C. You unite switches into a single logical unit using special stack interconnect cables that create a bidirectional closed-loop path. The network topology and routing information are updated continuously through the stack interconnect.

3. C. A more efficient use of resources has a cost benefit because less physical equipment means less cost. What minimizes the spending is the fact that the customer pays only for the services or infrastructure that the customer uses.

4. B, D, E. Voice traffic is real-time traffic and comprises constant and predictable bandwidth and packet arrival times. One-way requirements incudes latency < 150 ms, jitter <30 ms, and loss < 1%, and bandwidth needs to be 30 to 128 Kbps.

5. B. The control plane represents the core layer of the SDN architecture and is where the Cisco APIC-EM resides.

6. A. Infrastructure as a Service (IaaS) provides only the network and delivers the computer infrastructure (platform virtualization environment).

7. C. A trust boundary is where packets are classified and marked. IP phones and the boundary between the ISP and enterprise network are common examples of trust boundaries.

8. A. The IWAN provides transport-independent connectivity, intelligent path control, application optimization, and highly secure connectivity.

9. A. NBAR is a layer 4 to layer 7 deep-packet inspection classifier. NBAR is more CPU intensive than marking and uses the existing markings, addresses, or ACLs.

10. C. DSCP is a set of 6-bit values that are used to describe the meaning of the layer 3 IPv4 ToS field. While IP precedence is the old way to mark ToS, DSCP is the new way and is backward compatible with IP precedence.

11. A, B. Southbound APIs (or device-to-control-plane interfaces) are used for communication between the controllers and network devices, which puts these interfaces between the control and data planes.

12. D. Class of Service (CoS) is a term to describe designated fields in a frame or packet header. How devices treat packets in your network depends on the field values. CoS is usually used with Ethernet frames and contains 3 bits.

13. D. Although option A is the best answer by far, it is unfortunately false. You will save time working on autonomous devices, which in turn will allow you more time to work on new business requirements.

14. C. When traffic exceeds the allocated rate, the policer can take one of two actions. It can either drop traffic or re-mark it to another class of service. The new class usually has a higher drop probability.

15. C, D, F. The SDN architecture slightly differs from the architecture of traditional networks. It comprises three stacked layers: data, control, and application.

16. C. NBAR is a layer 4 to layer 7 deep-packet inspection classifier.

17. B, D. Southbound APIs (or device-to-control-plane interfaces) are used for communication between the controllers and network devices. Northbound APIs, or northbound interfaces, are responsible for the communication between the SDN controller and the services running over the network. With onePK, Cisco attempting to provide a high-level proprietary API that allows you to inspect or modify the network element configuration without hardware upgrades. The data plane is responsible for the forwarding of frames or packets.

18. B, D. Each stack of switches has a single IP address and is managed as a single object. This single IP management applies to activities such as fault detection, VLAN creation and modification, security, and QoS controls. Each stack has only one configuration file, which is distributed to each member in the stack. When you add a new switch to the stack, the master switch automatically configures the unit with the currently running IOS image and the configuration of the stack. You do not have to do anything to bring up the switch before it is ready to operate.

19. B. Platform as a Service (PaaS) provides the operating system and the network by delivering a computing platform and solution stack.

20. C. Software as a Service (SaaS) provides the required software, operating system, and network by providing ready-to-use applications or software.

21. C. All data that the cloud stores will always be available. This availability means that users do not need to back up their data. Before the cloud, users could lose important documents because of an accidental deletion, misplacement, or computer breakdown.

Appendix C

Disabling and Configuring Network Services

By default, the Cisco IOS runs some services that are unnecessary to its normal operation, and if you don't disable them, they can be easy targets for denial-of-service (DoS) attacks and break-in attempts.

DoS attacks are the most common attacks because they are the easiest to perform. Using software and/or hardware tools such as an intrusion detection system (IDS) and intrusion prevention system (IPS) tools can both warn and stop these simple, but harmful, attacks. However, if we can't implement IDS/IPS, there are some basic commands we can use on our router to make them more safe. Keep in mind, though, that nothing will make you completely safe in today's networks.

Let's take a look at the basic services we should disable on our routers.

Blocking SNMP Packets

The Cisco IOS default configurations permit remote access from any source, so unless you're either way too trusting or insane, it should be totally obvious to you that those configurations need a bit of attention. You've got to restrict them. If you don't, the router will be a pretty easy target for an attacker who wants to log in to it. This is where access lists come into the game—they can really protect you.

If you place the following command on the serial0/0 interface of the perimeter router, it'll stop any SNMP packets from entering the router or the DMZ. (You'd also need to have a permit command along with this list to really make it work, but this is just an example.)

```
Lab_B(config)#access-list 110 deny udp any any eq snmp
Lab_B(config)#interface s0/0
Lab_B(config-if)#access-group 110 in
```

Disabling Echo

In case you don't know this already, small services are servers (daemons) running in the router that are quite useful for diagnostics. And here we go again—by default, the Cisco router has a series of diagnostic ports enabled for certain UDP and TCP services, including echo, chargen, and discard.

When a host attaches to those ports, a small amount of CPU is consumed to service these requests. All a single attacking device needs to do is send a whole slew of requests with different, random, phony source IP addresses to overwhelm the router, making it slow down or even fail. You can use the no version of these commands to stop a chargen attack:

```
Lab_B(config)#no service tcp-small-servers
Lab_B(config)#no service udp-small-servers
```

Finger is a utility program designed to allow users of Unix hosts on the Internet to get information about each other:

```
Lab_B(config)#no service finger
```

This matters because the finger command can be used to find information about all users on the network and/or the router. It's also why you should disable it. The finger command is the remote equivalent to issuing the show users command on the router.

Here are the TCP small services:

Echo Echoes back whatever you type. Type the command **telnet x.x.x.x echo ?** to see the options.

Chargen Generates a stream of ASCII data. Type the command **telnet x.x.x.x chargen ?** to see the options.

Discard Throws away whatever you type. Type the command **telnet x.x.x.x discard ?** to see the options.

Daytime Returns the system date and time, if correct. It is correct if you are running NTP or have set the date and time manually from the EXEC level. Type the command **telnet x.x.x.x daytime ?** to see the options.

The UDP small services are as follows:

Echo Echoes the payload of the datagram you send.

Discard Silently pitches the datagram you send.

Chargen Pitches the datagram you send and responds with a 72-character string of ASCII characters terminated with a CR+LF.

Turning off BootP and Auto-Config

Again, by default, the Cisco router also offers the BootP service as well as remote auto-configuration. To disable these functions on your Cisco router, use the following commands:

```
Lab_B(config)#no ip boot server
Lab_B(config)#no service config
```

Disabling the HTTP Interface

The ip http server command may be useful for configuring and monitoring the router, but the cleartext nature of HTTP can obviously be a security risk. To disable the HTTP process on your router, use the following command:

```
Lab_B(config)#no ip http server
```

To enable an HTTP server on a router for AAA, use the global configuration command ip http server.

Disabling IP Source Routing

The IP header source-route option allows the source IP host to set a packet's route through the IP network. With IP source routing enabled, packets containing the source-route option are forwarded to the router addresses specified in the header. Use the following command to disable any processing of packets with source-routing header options:

```
Lab_B(config)#no ip source-route
```

Disabling Proxy ARP

Proxy ARP is the technique in which one host—usually a router—answers ARP requests intended for another machine. By "faking" its identity, the router accepts responsibility for getting those packets to the "real" destination. Proxy ARP can help machines on a subnet reach remote subnets without configuring routing or a default gateway. The following command disables proxy ARP:

```
Lab_B(config)#interface fa0/0
Lab_B(config-if)#no ip proxy-arp
```

Apply this command to all your router's LAN interfaces.

Disabling Redirect Messages

ICMP redirect messages are used by routers to notify hosts on the data link that a better route is available for a particular destination. To disable the redirect messages so bad people can't draw out your network topology with this information, use the following command:

```
Lab_B(config)#interface s0/0
Lab_B(config-if)#no ip redirects
```

Apply this command to all your router's interfaces. However, just understand that if this is configured, legitimate user traffic may end up taking a suboptimal route. Use caution when disabling this command.

Disabling the Generation of ICMP Unreachable Messages

The no ip unreachables command prevents the perimeter router from divulging topology information by telling external hosts which subnets are not configured. This command is used on a router's interface that is connected to an outside network:

```
Lab_B(config)#interface s0/0
Lab_B(config-if)#no ip unreachables
```

Again, apply this to all the interfaces of your router that connect to the outside world.

Disabling Multicast Route Caching

The multicast route cache lists multicast routing cache entries. These packets can be read, and so they create a security problem. To disable the multicast route caching, use the following command:

```
Lab_B(config)#interface s0/0
Lab_B(config-if)#no ip mroute-cache
```

Apply this command to all the interfaces of the router. However, use caution when disabling this command because it may slow legitimate multicast traffic.

Disabling the Maintenance Operation Protocol (MOP)

The Maintenance Operation Protocol (MOP) works at the Data Link and Network layers in the DECnet protocol suite and is used for utility services like uploading and downloading system software, remote testing, and problem diagnosis. So, who uses DECnet? Anyone with their hands up? I didn't think so. To disable this service, use the following command:

```
Lab_B(config)#interface s0/0
Lab_B(config-if)#no mop enabled
```

Apply this command to all the interfaces of the router.

Turning Off the X.25 PAD Service

Packet assembler/disassembler (PAD) connects asynchronous devices like terminals and computers to public/private X.25 networks. Since every computer in the world is pretty much IP savvy, and X.25 has gone the way of the dodo bird, there is no reason to leave this service running. Use the following command to disable the PAD service:

```
Lab_B(config)#no service pad
```

Enabling the Nagle TCP Congestion Algorithm

The Nagle TCP congestion algorithm is useful for small packet congestion, but if you're using a higher setting than the default MTU of 1,500 bytes, it can create an above-average traffic load. To enable this service, use the following command:

```
Lab_B(config)#service nagle
```

It is important to understand that the Nagle congestion service can break X Window connections to an X server, so don't use it if you're using X Window.

Logging Every Event

Used as a syslog server, the Cisco ACS server can log events for you to verify. Use the `logging trap debugging` or `logging trap` *level* command and the `logging` *ip_address* command to turn this feature on:

```
Lab_B(config)#logging trap debugging
Lab_B(config)#logging 192.168.254.251
Lab_B(config)#exit
Lab_B#sh logging
Syslog logging: enabled (0 messages dropped, 0 flushes, 0 overruns)
    Console logging: level debugging, 15 messages logged
    Monitor logging: level debugging, 0 messages logged
    Buffer logging: disabled
    Trap logging: level debugging, 19 message lines logged
        Logging to 192.168.254.251, 1 message lines logged
```

The show logging command provides you with statistics of the logging configuration on the router.

Disabling Cisco Discovery Protocol

Cisco Discovery Protocol (CDP) does just that—it's a Cisco proprietary protocol that discovers directly connected Cisco devices on the network. But because it's a Data Link layer protocol, it can't find Cisco devices on the other side of a router. Plus, by default, Cisco switches don't forward CDP packets, so you can't see Cisco devices attached to any other port on a switch.

When you are bringing up your network for the first time, CDP can be a really helpful protocol for verifying it. But since you're going to be thorough and document your network, you don't need the CDP after that. And because CDP does discover Cisco routers and switches on your network, you should disable it. You do that in global configuration mode, which turns off CDP completely for your router or switch:

```
Lab_B(config)#no cdp run
```

Or, you can turn off CDP on each individual interface using the following command:

```
Lab_B(config-if)#no cdp enable
```

Disabling the Default Forwarded UDP Protocols

When you use the ip helper-address command as follows on an interface, your router will forward UDP broadcasts to the listed server or servers:

```
Lab_B(config)#interface f0/0
Lab_B(config-if)#ip helper-address 192.168.254.251
```

You would generally use the ip helper-address command when you want to forward DHCP client requests to a DHCP server. The problem is that not only does this forward port 67 (BootP server request), it forwards seven other ports by default as well. To disable the unused ports, use the following commands:

```
Lab_B(config)#no ip forward-protocol udp 69
Lab_B(config)#no ip forward-protocol udp 53
Lab_B(config)#no ip forward-protocol udp 37
Lab_B(config)#no ip forward-protocol udp 137
```

```
Lab_B(config)#no ip forward-protocol udp 138
Lab_B(config)#no ip forward-protocol udp 68
Lab_B(config)#no ip forward-protocol udp 49
```

Now, only the BootP server request (67) will be forwarded to the DHCP server. If you want to forward a certain port—say, TACACS+, for example—use the following command:

```
Lab_B(config)#ip forward-protocol udp 49
```

Cisco's *auto secure*

Okay, so ACLs seem like a lot of work and so does turning off all those services I just discussed. But you do want to secure your router with ACLs, especially on your interface connected to the Internet. However, you are just not sure what the best approach should be, or maybe you just don't want to miss happy hour with your buddies because you're creating ACLs and turning off default services all night long.

Either way, Cisco has a solution that is a good start, and it's darn easy to implement. The command is called auto secure, and you just run it from privileged mode as shown:

```
R1#auto secure
                --- AutoSecure Configuration ---

*** AutoSecure configuration enhances the security of
the router, but it will not make it absolutely resistant
to all security attacks ***

AutoSecure will modify the configuration of your device.
All configuration changes will be shown. For a detailed
explanation of how the configuration changes enhance
security and any possible side effects, please refer to Cisco.com
for Autosecure documentation.
At any prompt you may enter '?' for help.
Use ctrl-c to abort this session at any prompt.

Gathering information about the router for AutoSecure
Is this router connected to internet? [no]: yes
Enter the number of interfaces facing the internet [1]: [enter]
Interface          IP-Address      OK? Method Status                Protocol
FastEthernet0/0    10.10.10.1      YES NVRAM  up                    up
Serial0/0          1.1.1.1         YES NVRAM  down                  down
FastEthernet0/1    unassigned      YES NVRAM  administratively down down
Serial0/1          unassigned      YES NVRAM  administratively down down
Enter the interface name that is facing the internet: serial0/0
```

Securing Management plane services...

Disabling service finger
Disabling service pad
Disabling udp & tcp small servers
Enabling service password encryption
Enabling service tcp-keepalives-in
Enabling service tcp-keepalives-out
Disabling the cdp protocol

Disabling the bootp server
Disabling the http server
Disabling the finger service
Disabling source routing
Disabling gratuitous arp

Here is a sample Security Banner to be shown
at every access to device. Modify it to suit your
enterprise requirements.

Authorized Access only
   This system is the property of So-&-So-Enterprise.
   UNAUTHORIZED ACCESS TO THIS DEVICE IS PROHIBITED.
   You must have explicit permission to access this
   device. All activities performed on this device
   are logged. Any violations of access policy will result
   in disciplinary action.

Enter the security banner {Put the banner between
k and k, where k is any character}:
#
If you are not part of the www.globalnettc.com domain, disconnect now!
#
Enable secret is either not configured or
 is the same as enable password
Enter the new enable secret: *[password not shown]*
% Password too short - must be at least 6 characters. Password configuration
failed
Enter the new enable secret: *[password not shown]*
Confirm the enable secret : *[password not shown]*
Enter the new enable password: *[password not shown]*
Confirm the enable password: *[password not shown]*
Configuration of local user database
Enter the username: **Todd**

```
Enter the password: [password not shown]
Confirm the password: [password not shown]
Configuring AAA local authentication
Configuring Console, Aux and VTY lines for
local authentication, exec-timeout, and transport
Securing device against Login Attacks
Configure the following parameters
Blocking Period when Login Attack detected: ?
% A decimal number between 1 and 32767.
Blocking Period when Login Attack detected: 100
Maximum Login failures with the device: 5
Maximum time period for crossing the failed login attempts: 10
Configure SSH server? [yes]: [enter to take default of yes]
Enter the domain-name: lammle.com
Configuring interface specific AutoSecure services
Disabling the following ip services on all interfaces:

 no ip redirects
 no ip proxy-arp
 no ip unreachables
 no ip directed-broadcast
 no ip mask-reply
Disabling mop on Ethernet interfaces

Securing Forwarding plane services...

Enabling CEF (This might impact the memory requirements for your platform)
Enabling unicast rpf on all interfaces connected
to internet

Configure CBAC Firewall feature? [yes/no]:
Configure CBAC Firewall feature? [yes/no]: no
Tcp intercept feature is used prevent tcp syn attack
on the servers in the network. Create autosec_tcp_intercept_list
to form the list of servers to which the tcp traffic is to
be observed

Enable tcp intercept feature? [yes/no]: yes
```

And that's it—all the services I mentioned earlier are disabled, plus some! By saving the configuration that the auto secure command created, you can then take a look at your running-config to see your new configuration. It's a long one!

Although it is tempting to run out to happy hour right now, you still need to verify your security and add your internal access-list configurations to your intranet.

Index

^ (caret), 215
? (question mark), 213–216, 257
/ (slash notation), CIDR, 138, 140, 142, 150–154
2WAY neighbor state, 792
2x - 2 formula, 143–144
3DES (Triple DES), 919
3G/4G (cellular), WANs and, 891
6-to-4 tunneling, 555
10Base-T, 45
10GBase-T, 57
15.0 IOS code, 341–342
100Base-FX, 45
100Base-TX, 45
802.1AB standard, 297
802.1d, 584
802.1q standard, 453
802.1s (MSTP), 610
802.1w, 584
802.3 standard, 56
802.3ab standard, 56
802.3an standard, 57
802.3u standard, 56
802.3z standard, 56–57
1000Base-CX, 45
1000Base-LX, 57
1000Base-SX, 57
1000Base-T, 56, 62
1000Base-ZX, 57

A

AAA (authentication, authorization, and
    accounting), 650
aaa new-model command, 654
ABR (area border router), 748, 784
access control lists. *See* ACLs
access layer, 650–651
    port security, 651
    threats, mitigation, 651
access layer, Cisco hierarchical model, 72
access links, 450
access points, 11–12, 44
access ports, 449–451
access-class command, 497
access-class in command, 496–497
ACLs (access control lists)
    auto secure command, 628–630
    extended, 486, 847–849

example one, 501–503
example three, 504–505
example two, 503
IPv6, 858–861
remarks, 507–508
general guidelines, 487–488
implicit deny, 486–487, 501, 511
inbound, 487
monitoring, 508–510
named, 486–487, 505–507, 509–510
    configurations, 213
    sequence numbers, 509
NBAR and, 966
outbound, 487
show ip interface command, 861
standard, 486, 489–490
    example, 492–496
    remarks, 507–508
    VTY access, controlling, 496–497
    wildcard masking, 490–492
Active mode (NBAR), 966
AD (administrative distance), 391–392
address learning, 413–415
Address Resolution Protocol. *See* ARP
addresses
    global, 850
    IPv6, temporary, 856
    link local, 850
    multicast, LSA, 752
adjacency, OSPF, 749
administrative configurations, Cisco IOS, 218–219
    banners, 219–221
    descriptions, 229–231
    hostnames, 219
    passwords
        encrypting, 227–229
        setting, 221–227
advanced distance-vector protocols, 392, 682
AES (Advanced Encryption Standard), 919
aggregate rates, 48
AH (Authenticated Header) security protocol,
    918
algorithms, DUAL (Diffusing Update Algorithm),
    689
all 1s broadcast, 120
alternate port, 605
answers
    review questions, 998–1035
    written labs, 978–991

any command, 492–493, 502
anycast addresses, 550, 554
APIC-EM (Application Policy Infrastructure
    Controller Enterprise Module), 948, 971
    network devices, 958
    path tracing and, 959–960
    REST and, 958
    SBI API, 958
    screen, 958–959
    SDN stack and, 957
APIPA (Automatic Private IP Addressing), 98–99
APIs (application programming interfaces), 948
    NBI (northbound interface), 956–957
    SBI (southbound interface), 955–956
        NETCONF, 956
        onePK, 956
        OpenFlow, 956
        OpFlex, 956
    SDN (Software Defined Networking), 955
        application plane, 954
        control plane, 954
        data plane, 954
Application layer, OSI reference model, 17
APs. *See* access points
architecture
    hierarchical, 13–14
    layered, 13–14
ARP (Address Resolution Protocol), 114–116
    gratuitous ARP, 98
    proxy ARP, disabling, 624
    in routing process, 362
arp -a command, 191, 362
ARPA (Advanced Research Project's Agency), 87
ARPAnet, 87
AS (autonomous system), 390, 692
    BGP and, 928
    EGP and, 925
AS external link advertisements, 790
ASA (Adaptive Security Appliance), 12
ASA firewalls, 958
ASBR (autonomous system boundary router), 748, 784
ASICs (application-specific integrated circuits), 27
ASR routers, 958
asymmetric encryption, 919
ATM (Asynchronous Transfer Mode), WANs and,
    891
ATTEMPT neighbor state, 792
authentication
    external, 653–655
    identity-based networking, 652
    LCP, 899
    PPP
        CHAP, 901
        configuration, 901–902, 936–937
        debugging, 904
        PAP, 901

RADIUS, 653
    configuring, 654
TACACS+, 654
    configuring, 655
authenticator, identity-based networking, 652
auto secure command, 628–630
autoconfiguration, IPv6
    stateful, 559
    stateless, 556–559
auto-detect mechanism, 48–49
auto-summary, 394
auxiliary passwords, 225
auxiliary VLANs, 450
AWS (Amazon Web Services), 953

B

backup and restore
    Cisco configuration, 277–280
    Cisco IOS, 331–337
    Cisco IOS licenses, 347
    device configuration, 276–280
    erasing backup configuration, 242
backup port, 605
bandwidth
    OSPF metrics, 753
    serial transmission, 895
    WANs
        DS0 (digital signal 0), 886
        E1, 887
        OC-3, 887
        OC-12, 887
        OC-48, 887
        OC-192, 887
        T1, 886
        T3, 887
bandwidth command, 239–240
banners, 219–221
baselines, SNMP, 93
BDR (backup designated router), OSPF, 750
BGP (Border Gateway Protocol), 390, 882, 925
    ASs and, 928
    attributes, 928
    eBGP (external BGP) neighbors, 928–929
    iBGP (internal BGP) neighbors, 928–929
    IGPs (interior gateway protocols), 928
    network structure, 928
    OSPF comparison, 926–927
binary numbers/conversion, 50–52
binding, 14
block sizes, 140
    Class A addresses, 165–166
    Class B addresses, 163
    Class C addresses, 144, 146, 149, 152–154
    VLSM networks, 179–186

blocked port, 605
boot command, 327
boot field, 325–326
boot sequence, 275–276
boot system command, 327–328
boot system flash:ios-file command, 335
boot system rom command, 328
boot system tftp command, 328
BootP
    versus DHCP, 96
    disabling, 623
bootstrap, 274–276
BPDU (Bridge Protocol Data Unit), 604
    lab, 640
BPDU Guard, 627–629
    configuration, 640
bridges, 6, 8–11
    at Data Link layer, 27–29
    hardware-based, 27
    ID, 604
        modifying, 618–623
        verifying, 618–623
    ports, 604–605
    transparent bridging, 28
broadcast domains, 5–11, 25, 28, 44–45
broadcast storms, 6, 28, 421–422
broadcasts, 123
    all 1s broadcasts, 120
    ARP, 114–116
    control, 447–448
    DHCP, 97–98
    layer 2 broadcasts, 124
    layer 3 broadcasts, 124–125
    multicast addresses, 126
    NBMA, 750
    OSPF, multi-access, 750
    unicast addresses, 125
BSD (Berkeley Software Distribution), 87
buffering, 20
bus topology, 30
bytes, 50–53

C

cabling, 59
    crossover, 60–62
    fiber optic, 64–66
    HFC (hybrid fiber-coaxial), 890
    rolled, 62–64
    smart-serial, 894–895
    straight-through, 59–60
    WANs, serial transmissions, 894–895
call setup, 19–20
CAM (Content Addressable Memory) filter tables,
    412–414, 416, 424, 431–432, 436

cd command, 338
CDP (Cisco Discovery Protocol), 289–290
    disabling, 627
    holdtime information, 290–291
    neighbor information, 291–294
    network topology, documenting, 295–297
    timers, 290–291
cdp holdtime command, 290–291
cdp timer command, 290–291
CDPCP (Cisco Discovery Protocol Control Protocol),
    899
CEF (Cisco Express Forwarding), 367
channel-group command, 630
CHAP (Challenge Handshake Authentication
    Protocol), 901
chargen services, 622–623
CIDR (Classless Inter-Domain Routing), 140–142,
    152–154
circuit switching
    MPLS and, 888
    WANs and, 888
Cisco
    Catalyst switches, configuring, 422–423
        boot process review, 423–424
        IP address requirement, 424
        port security, 417, 428–430
        S1, 424–425
        S2, 426–427
        S3, 427–428
        verifying configuration, 430–433
    device connections, 207–208
    hierarchical model, 69–72
Cisco, OIDs, 657
Cisco 2960 switch, 207–208
Cisco 3560 switch, 207–208
Cisco Discovery Protocol. *See* CDP
Cisco Express Forwarding (CEF), 367
Cisco IFS, 337–341
Cisco IOS
    administrative configurations, 218–219
        banners, 219–221
        descriptions, 229–231
        hostnames, 219
        passwords
            encrypting, 227–229
            setting, 221–227
    backup and restore, 331–337
    command-line interface, 209
        editing/help features, 213–218
        entering, 210
        global configuration mode, 210, 213
        interface configuration mode, 212
        privileged exec mode, 210
        prompts, 211–213
        router modes, 210
        setup mode, 209, 213, 240, 242, 256
        user exec mode, 210, 213, 220

DHCP, verifying, 282–283
global configuration mode
    auxiliary passwords, configuring, 225
    statistics, viewing, 230–231
interface configuration, 231–240
IOS 15.0 code, 341–342
licensing, 341–348
overview, 206–207
responsibilities, 207
user interface, 206–209
Cisco Product License Registration portal, 343
Class A networks, 118, 120–121
default subnet mask, 139
reserved IP address space, 122–123
subnetting, 163–166
valid host IDs, 121
Class B networks, 118–119, 121
default subnet mask, 139
reserved IP address space, 122–123
subnetting, 154–163
valid host IDs, 121
Class C networks, 118–119, 121–122
default subnet mask, 139
reserved IP address space, 122–123
subnetting, 142–154
valid host IDs, 122
Class D networks, 118
address range, 119
Class E networks, 118
address range, 119
classful networks, 177
subnetting (*See* subnetting)
versus VLSM classless networks, 186
classful routing, 176–177, 393
classless networks, 176–178
classless routing, 393
clear counters command, 250
clear ip nat translations command,
    529, 531
CLI. *See* command-line interface, Cisco IOS
clients
identity-based networking, 652
redundancy issues, 659–661
clock rate command, 238–239
cloud computing, 971
benefits, 951
centralization, 951–953
consolidation, 951–953
IaaS (Infrastructure as a Service), 952
PaaS (Platform as a Service), 952–953
SaaS (Software as a Service), 952–953
service models, 952–953
CO (central office), WANs, 886
collision domains, 5–11, 43–44
collisions, 247–252

command-line interface, Cisco IOS
editing/help features, 213–218
entering, 210
global configuration mode, 210, 213
interface configuration mode, 212
privileged exec mode, 210, 213
prompts, 211–213
router modes, 210
setup mode, 209, 213, 240, 242, 256
user exec mode, 210, 213, 220
commands
aaa new-model, 654
boot system, 327–328
channel-group, 630
global, 210, 212
interface port-channel, 630
interface range, 588
interfaces interface switchport, 864
ipconfig, 834
major, 212
neighbors, 710
netsh interface ipv6 show neighbor, 856
network, 727
no bandwidth, 702
passive-interface, 696–697
ppp multilink group, 910
route print, 834
router bgp AS, 930
router eigrp, 690
router-id, 764–765
service password-encryption, 902
show interface, 898, 903
show interface trunk, 596–597
show interfaces, 924
show interfaces multilink1, 910
show interfaces trunk, 586
show ip bgp, 933
show ip bgp neighbors, 933–934
show ip bgp summary, 931–932
show ip eigrp events, 714
show ip eigrp interface, 710
show ip eigrp interface detail, 711
show ip eigrp interfaces, 709, 716
show ip eigrp neighbors, 709, 716
show ip eigrp topology, 709, 716
show ip eigrp traffic, 709, 713
show ip interface, 861
show ip interface brief, 923–924
show ip ospf, 766–767, 797–798
show ip ospf database, 767–768, 796,
    802–804
show ip ospf interface, 768–769, 796,
    798–800
show ip ospf neighbor, 769–770, 796–797
show ip protocols, 705, 709, 770–771, 796, 801

show ip route, 703, 796, 801–802
show ip route eigrp, 709
show ppp multilink, 910
show protocols, 717
show run, 902
show running-config, 898
show vlan, 585–586, 863
show vlan brief, 863
show vlan id 200, 586
show vtp status, 598
snmp-server, 658
subcommands, 212
switch access vlan, 866
switchport mode access, 588, 590
switchport mode dynamic auto, 590
switchport mode dynamic desirable, 590
switchport mode trunk, 589–591
switchport nonegotiate, 591
traceroute, 836
username, 902
vlan, 584
communication modes, 18
compression, LCP and, 900
config t command, 381
config-register command, 329–330
configuration
    GRE tunnels, 921–923
    MLP, 907–908
    OSPF, verification, 765–771
    register, 275, 324
        bits, 324–326
        boot system commands, 327–328
        current values, 326–327
        password recovery, 328–331
configured VLANs, 450
congestion, LAN traffic, 6–7, 9, 20
connectionless network services, 19
connection-oriented communication, 19–21
connections, Cisco devices, 207–208
connectivity
    IP network, 833–843
        ACLs, extended, 847–849
        SLAs, 843–845
        SPAN and, 845–846
    IWANs, 893–894
Consistency Checks, 602
console passwords, 223–224
console ports, 207–208
control plan, 954
copy command, 338, 340–341
copy flash tftp command, 332–334
copy run start command, 276
copy running-config command, 241
copy running-config startup-config command,
    240–241, 258, 277–278, 331

copy running-config tftp command, 277–278
copy source-url destination-url command, 337
copy startup-config tftp command, 277
copy tftp running-config command, 279
copy tftp startup-config command, 279
core layer, Cisco hierarchical model, 71
Corp router, 758–759
CoS (Class of Service), 965
CPE (customer premises equipment), 885
    DSL and, 890
CRCs (cyclic redundancy checks), 251
crossover cable, 60–62
CSMA/CD (Carrier Sense Multiple Access with
    Collision Detection), 45–47
CST (Common Spanning Tree), 610–611
CSU/DSU (channel service unit/data service unit), 29,
    886, 895–896
CWS (Cloud Web Security), 894

D

DA (Destination Address), 54–55
DAD (duplicate address detection), 563–565
DAI (Dynamic ARP inspection), 652
    DHCP snooping and, 651
DARPA, 87
data encapsulation. See encapsulation
Data field
    Ethernet frame, 55
    IP header, 110
data frames, 26, 54, 415–417, 452
Data Link layer, OSI reference model, 26–29. See
    also layer 2 devices
    Ethernet addressing, 49–54
    Ethernet frames, 54–55
data packets, Network layer, 24
data plane, 953
databases, synchronization
    DD packets, 786
    LSR packets, 786
    LSU packets, 786
DCE (data communication equipment), 895–896
DD (Database Description) packets, 786
debug all command, 308–309
debug command, 308–310
debug ip icmp command, 309–310
debug ip nat command, 529, 531
debugging, 308–310
    PPP authentication, 904
DEC (Digital Equipment Corporation), 584
decimal numbering, 50–53
de-encapsulation, 67
default routing, 387–390
default-information originate command, 398

delete command, 338–340
delimiting character, 220
demarcation point, WANs, 886
DES (Data Encryption Standard), 919
description command, 229–230
designated port, 604
Destination Address field, IPv6 header, 560
Destination IP address field, IP header, 110
Destination unreachable message, ICMP, 112
device connections, 207–208
device-to-control-plane interfaces, 955–956
DHCP (Dynamic Host Configuration Protocol),
    96–98
    configuring, 280–283, 380–381
    conflicts, 98
    relays, 281–282
    snooping, 651
DHCPv6, 559
dir command, 338
disable command, 210
disabling network services, 622
    auto-config, 623
    BootP, 623
    Cisco Discovery Protocol, 627
    default forwarded UDP protocols, 627–628
    HTTP interface, 624
    ICMP unreachable messages, 625
    IP source routing, 624
    Maintenance Operation Protocol, 625
    multicast route caching, 625
    proxy ARP, 624
    redirect messages, 624–625
    small services, 622–623
    X.25 PAD, 626
discard services, 622–623
disconnect command, 301, 497
distance-vector protocols, 400
distance-vector routing protocols, 392
distribution layer, Cisco hierarchical model, 71–72
DIX (Digital, Intel, and Xerox), 55
DMVPN (Dynamic Multipoint Virtual Private
    Network), 921
DMZ (demilitarized zone), 485
DNS (Domain Name Service), 95–96
DNS servers
    resolving hostnames, 304–305
    vs. host tables, 305
do command, 230–231
DoD (Department of Defense)
    ARPA (Advanced Research Project's Agency),
        87
    model, 87–89
        Host-to-Host layer, 87–89, 99–108
        Internet layer, 87–89, 108–116
        Process/Application layer, 87–89

Domain Name Service. See DNS
domains, trusted/untrusted, 964
DoS (denial of service) attacks, 488–489, 622
DOWN neighbor state, 792
DR (designated router), OSPF, 749
DS0 (digital signal 0), WAN bandwidth and, 886
DSCP/DiffServ (Differentiated Services Code Point),
    965
DSL (Digital Subscriber Line), 882
    WANs and, 890
DSLAM (Digital Subscriber Line Access
    Multiplexer), 890
DTE (data terminal equipment), 895–896
DTE-DCE-DTE WAN connection, 895–896
DTP (Dynamic Trunk Protocol), 458–459, 462–463,
    586
    VLANs, 589–591
DUAL (Diffusing Update Algorithm), 683, 686, 689,
    732
    EIGRPv6 and, 727
dual-stack, 555
duplex
    full-duplex, 47–49
    half-duplex, 18, 47–49
    interface configuration mode, 232–234
duplex mode, mismatched, 838
dynamic NAT (Network Address Translation), 524,
    527–528
dynamic routing, 359, 390–392

E

E1, WAN bandwidth and, 887
EBGP (external BGP), 928–929
    BGP process, 930
    configuration, 929–931
    layout, 929
    neighbor relationships, 930
    verification
        show ip bgp command, 933
        show ip bgp neighbors command, 933–934
        show ip bgp summary command, 931–932
echo services, disabling, 622–623
editing features, Cisco IOS, 213–218
EGPs (exterior gateway protocols), 390, 925
    local network advertisement, 930–931
EIA (Electronic Industries Alliance), 56
EIGRP (Enhanced Interior Gateway Routing
    Protocol), 392, 584, 682, 746, 928
    bandwith, 697
    configuration, 690–693
    default administrative distance, 391
    delay, 697
    distance-vector updates, 682

DUAL (Diffusing Update Algorithm) and, 689
exam essentials, 733
FD (feasible distance) and, 685
FS (feasible successor) and, 687
hellos, 684
hop count, 699
labs
    configuration, 734–735
    verification, 735
load, 697
load balancing, unequal-cost, 705–707
MTU (maximum transmission unit), 697
multicast addresses, 126
neighbors
    discovery, 683–688
    tables, 684
packets
    ACK, 689
    Hello, 688
    Query, 688
    Reply, 688
    Update, 688
paths, maximum, 699
RD/AD (reported/advertised distance)
    and, 684
reliability, 697
routes, 689–690
    selecting, 699–704
RTP (Reliable Transport Protocol) and,
    688–689
split horizon, 707–709
successors, 687
topology table, 686
traffic control, 696–697
troubleshooting, 715–725
    CCNA exam and, 725–727
    commands, 709
verification, 709–715
VLSM support, 693–696
EIGRPv6, 727–732
    configuration, 735–736
    verification, 735–736
Electronic Industries Alliance (EIA), 56
enable command, 210, 221–222
enable passwords, 263
    encrypting, 227–229
    setting, 221–222
enable secret passwords, 221–222, 227, 257
encapsulation, 66–69, 465
    de-encapsulation, 67
    PPP, 936–937
encapsulation command, 465
encryption
    asymmetric, 919
    private keys, 919

RADIUS, 653–654
symmetric, 919
VPNs, 919
enterprise-managed VPNs, 915–917
erase command, 338
erase start command, 375–376
erase startup-config command, 242, 279–280,
    312
error detection, LCP, 900
error-disabled state, port security, 418–419, 430
errors, 251–252
ESP (Encapsulating Security Payload) security
    protocol, 918–919
EtherChannel, 629–630
    configuration, 641–642
    lab, 641–642
    LACP and, 630
    layer 3, 633–634
    PAgP and, 630
    port channels, 629–630
        configuration, 630–634
        verifying, 630–634
    verifying, 641–642
        lab, 641–642
Ethernet, 42–43
    addressing, 49–53
    broadcast domains, 44–45
    cabling, 59–66
    collision domains, 8, 43–44
    CSMA/CD, 45–47
    at Data Link layer, 49–55
    duplex mode, mismatched, 838
    frames, 54–55
    full-duplex, 47–49
    half-duplex, 47–49
    IEEE standards, 55–57
    Metro Ethernet, 882
    multicast mapping over, 564–565
    at Physical layer, 55–57
    PPPoE (Point-to-Point Protocol over Ethernet),
        882
EUI-64 addresses, 556–559
evaluation licenses, 342, 344–347
EXCHANGE neighbor state, 793
exec banners, 219–221
EXEC session, 207
exit command, 301
EXSTART neighbor state, 792
extended ACLs (access control lists), 497–501
    example one, 501–503
    example three, 504–505
    example two, 503
    remarks, 507–508
exterior gateway protocols (EGPs), 390
extranet VPNs, 915

F

fast switching, 367
FastEthernet interface, 248
fault-tolerant solutions, 662
FCS (Frame Check Sequence), 55, 251, 363–366
FD (feasible distance), 685
FHRPs (first hop redundancy protocols), 661–662
fiber-optic cabling, 64–66
finger command, 623
firewalls, 12
first hop, 661–662
Flags field, IP header, 109
flash memory, 275–276
    booting from, 327–328
    verifying, 332–333
flat networks, 445
flow control, 20–22
Flow Label field, IPv6 header, 560
format command, 338
forward/filter tables, 413–417, 431
forwarding port, 605
FQDN (fully qualified domain name), 95–96
Fragment offset field, IP header, 109
frame flooding, 421
Frame Relay, WANs and, 889
frame tagging, 451–452, 472
frames, 54–55
    data frames, 26, 54, 415–417, 452
    de-encapsulation, 67–69
    latency, 27
    MAC frame format, 54
    multiple frame copies, 421
    untagged, 468
FS (feasible successor), 687
FTP (File Transfer Protocol), 90–92
FULL neighbor state, 793
full-duplex, 18, 47–49
fully meshed topology, 884

G

gateway of last resort, 387
GETBULK, 93
GGP (Gateway to Gateway Protocol), 925
giants, 251
Gigabit UTP transmission, 62
G/L bit, 50
GLBP (Gateway Load Balancing Protocol), 662
global addresses, 850
    NAT, 524–525
global commands, 210, 212
global configuration file, Cisco IOS, 221–222
global configuration mode, Cisco IOS, 210, 213
    auxiliary passwords, configuring, 225
    statistics, viewing, 230–231

global unicast addresses, 553
go indicator, Transport layer, 21
GRA over IPsec, 920–921
gratuitous ARP, 98
GRE (Generic Routing Encapsulation), 882
    tunnels, 919–920
        configuration, 921–923, 935, 938–940
        DMVPN, 921
        GRA over IPsec, 920–921
        IPSec VTI, 921
        verification, 923–925

H

half-duplex, 18, 47–49
hardware addressing, 49
hardware broadcasts, 124
HDLC (High-Level Data-Link Control) protocol,
        882, 896–899, 934
    configuration, 937–938
    monitoring, 937–938
    WANs and, 889
Header checksum field, IP header, 110
Header length field, IP header, 109
Hello protocol, OSPF, 750–752, 790–791
Hello/Dead interval, 791
help, Cisco IOS, 213–218
hexadecimal
    addressing, 52–53
    architecture, 13–14
    IP addressing scheme, 117–122
    model, Cisco, 69–72
HFC (hybrid fiber-coaxial) networks, 890
hold timer, 684
holdtime information, Cisco Discovery Protocol,
        290–291
Hop Limit field, IPv6 header, 560
hops, 392
host tables
    building, 302–304
    vs. DNS servers, 305
hostname command, 219
hostnames. *See also* DNS
    administrative configuration, Cisco IOS, 219
    resolving, 302–305
    setting, 257, 265
Host-to-Host layer, DoD model, 87–89, 99–108
    TCP, 99–101
    UDP, 101–104
HSRP (Hot Standby Router Protocol), 650, 662–664
    configuration, 669–673
    group roles, 667–668
    interface tracking, 668–669
    load balancing, 673–674
    timers, 665–667
    troubleshooting, 674–675

verification, 669–673
virtual MAC address, 664–665
HSSDC (High Speed Serial Data Connector), 56
HTTP (Hypertext Transfer Protocol), 93–94
    disabling, 624
HTTPS (Hypertext Transfer Protocol Secure), 94
hub-and-spoke topology, 883–884
hubs, 5–11
    at Physical layer, 29–30
    vs. switches, 28–29
hybrid routing protocols, 682
hybrid topology, 30–31

I

IaaS (Infrastructure as a Service), 952
iBGP (internal BGP), 928–929
ICMP (Internet Control Message Protocol), 111–114
    Destination unreachable message, 112
    echo request, 833
    ICMPv6, 561–565
    redirect messages, disabling, 624–625
    in routing process, 362
    unreachable messages, disabling, 625
ICMPv6
    addresses
        DELAY, 855
        INCMP (incomplete), 855
        PROBE, 855
        REACH (reachable), 855
        STALE, 855
    NA (neighbor advertisement), 852
    NDP (Neighbor Discovery) and, 851–858
    NS (neighbor solicitation), 852
    RA (router advertisement), 851
    RS (router solicitation), 851
    uses, 850
Identification field, IP header, 109
identity-based networking, 652
IEEE
    802.1AB standard, 297
    802.1d standard, 610
    802.1q standard, 453
    802.1w standard, 610
    802.3 standard, 56
    802.3ab standard, 56
    802.3an standard, 57
    802.3u standard, 56
    802.3z standard, 56–57
IETF (Internet Engineering Task Force), 654
IGMP function. *See* ICMPv6
IGPs (interior gateway protocols), 390, 928
IGRP (Interior Gateway Routing Protocol), 928
INIT neighbor state, 792
input errors, 839
input queue, drops, 839

intelligent networks, 948
Intelligent Path Control, 893–894
Intelligent WAN, 948
inter-area routes, 789
interesting octet, 165
interface command, 211–212
interface configuration
    deleting, 242
    enabling/disabling interfaces, 234–235
    IP addresses, 235–236
    pipe output modifier, 236–237
    saving, 240–242
    serial interface commands, 237–240
    verifying, 242–255
interface configuration mode, 212
interface port-channel command, 630
interface range command, 459–460, 588
interface vlan number command, 472
interfaces. *See also* APIs (application programming
        interfaces)
    device-to-control-plane, 955–956
    loopback, configuration, 763–765
    OSPF, configuration, 774–775
    split horizon, 707–709
interfaces interface switchport command,
        864
Internet layer, DoD model, 87–89, 108–116
    ARP, 114–116
    ICMP, 111–114
    IP, 108–111
Internetwork Operating System (IOS). *See* Cisco IOS
internetworking. *See also* networks/networking
    overview, 4–13
    reference models, 13–14
IOS (Internetwork Operating System). *See* Cisco IOS
ip address address mask command, 235
ip address command, 235–236
IP addresses
    Class A networks, 120–121
    Class B networks, 121
    Class C networks, 121–122
    hierarchical scheme, 117–122
    mismatched, 906–907
    network addresses, 117–120
    private, 122–123
    reserved, 119–120, 122–123
    resolving hostnames, 302–305
    subnetting, 136–137
        CIDR, 140–142
        Class A addresses, 163–166
        Class B addresses, 154–163
        Class C addresses, 142–154
        creating subnets, 138
        ip subnet zero command, 142
        subnet masks, 138–139
    troubleshooting, 189–196
    virtual, 661–662

IP Base licensing, 342–344
ip default-gateway command, 428
ip domain-lookup command, 304–305
ip domain-name command, 304–305
IP header, 109–111
ip helper-address command, 282
ip host command, 313
ip http server command, 624
ip name-server command, 304–305
ip nat command, 527
ip nat inside command, 527
ip nat inside source command, 527
ip nat outside command, 527
ip nat pool command, 532–533
ip nat translation max-entries command, 530
ip nat translation timeout command, 531
ip route command, 383–384, 386
IP routing. *See* routing
ip subnet zero command, 142, 166
ipconfig /all command, 192
ipconfig command, 834
IPCP (Internet Protocol Control Protocol), 899
IPsec
    AH (Authenticated Header) security protocol,
        918
    ESP (Encapsulating Security Payload) security
        protocol, 918–919
    transforms, 918
IPSec VTI, 921
IPv4, 123–124, 546–548, 559–561
    layer 2 broadcasts, 124
    layer 3 broadcasts, 124–125
    loopback addresses, 123
    multicast addresses, 124, 126
    unicast addresses, 125
IPv6
    ACLs, extended, 858–861
    addresses, 551, 553
        headers, 559–561
        manual assignment, 555–556
        shortened expressions, 551–552
        special, 554–555
        temporary, 856
        types, 552–554
    benefits and uses, 549–551
    configuring, 566–572
    IMCPv6, 561–565
    reasons for, 549
    routing protocols, 565–566
    stateful autoconfiguration, 559
    stateless autoconfiguration, 556–559
ipv6 address autoconfig command, 559
ipv6 address command, 555–556
ipv6 enable command, 556
IPv6 header, 560–561

ipv6 unicast-routing command, 555
ISDN (Integrated Services Digital Network), WANs
        and, 889
ISL (Inter-Switch Link), 452–453
ISPs and Classless Inter-Domain Routing, 140–142
ISR (Integrated Services Router), 208, 221, 232–234
IVR (Inter-VLAN Routing), 444, 455–456, 471–472
IWAN (Intelligent WAN), 891–894, 960–961
    application optimization, 961
    connectivity
        security, 961
        transport-independent, 961
    intelligent path control, 961

K

K values, 698–699

L

LA router, 759–762
lab answers, 978–991
LACP (Link Aggregation Control Protocol), 630
LANs (local area networks), 5. *See also* Ethernet;
        networks/networking
    Pinging, 836–838
    traffic congestion, 6–7, 9, 20
    virtual (*See* VLANs)
    WAN comparison, 882–883
late collisions, 252
latency, 27
layer 2 devices. *See also* Data Link layer, OSI
        reference model
    broadcast storms, 28
    broadcasts, 124
    switching
        address learning, 413–415
        advantages, 412–413
        boot process review, 423–424
        forward/filter tables, 413–417, 431
        IP address requirement, 424
        loop avoidance, 420–422
        port security, 417–420, 428–430
        S1 configuration example, 424–425
        S2 configuration example, 426–427
        S3 configuration example, 427–428
        verifying configuration, 430–433
    transparent bridging, 28
layer 3 devices, 8, 24, 28. *See also* Network layer,
        OSI reference model; routers
    broadcasts, 97, 116, 124–125
    inter-VLAN communication, 454–456
    router interface configuration information,
        252–253

layer 3 EtherChannel, 633–634
layered architecture, 13–14
layers, OSI reference model, 15–17. *See also* specific
    layers
LCP (Link Control Protocol), 898–900, 934
leased lines, 887–888
Length field, Ethernet frame, 54
license boot module command, 344–345, 348
license install command, 343–344, 348
license save command, 347
licensing, IOS, 341–348
line aux command, 225
line command, 212, 222
line console command, 223
line vty command, 224–225
line-activation banners, 219–221
Link Layer Discovery Protocol (LLDP), 297–298
link-local addresses, 553, 556, 850
links, OSPF, 749
link-state protocols, 400
link-state routing protocols, 392
LLDP (Link Layer Discovery Protocol), 297–298
lldp receive command, 298
lldp run command, 298
lldp transmit command, 298
LLDP-MED (Media Endpoint Discovery), 297
load balancing
    HSRP, 673–674
    MLP, 908
    third-party balancers, 958
    unequal-cost, 705–707
LOADING neighbor state, 793
local addresses, NAT, 524–525
local loop, WANs, 886
local routes, 360
log command, 501
logging command, 285–288, 312
logging host ip_address command, 287
logging IP_address command, 287
logging ip_address command, 626
logging sync command, 374
logging trap debugging command, 626
logging trap level command, 626
logical topologies, 27, 30
login banners, 219–221
login command, 222–223
logout command, 210
longest match rule, 359–361
loop avoidance, 420–422
loopback addresses
    IPv4, 123
    pinging, 835
loopback interfaces, 244
    OSPF, configuration, 763–765
loops, WAN local loop, 886

LSA (Link State Advertisement), 784
    flooding, 752
    multicast addresses, 752
    OSFP, 750
    Type 1 LSA, 788
    Type 2 LSA, 789
    Type 3 LSA, 789–790
    Type 4 LSA, 790
    Type 5 LSA, 790
LSR (Link-State Request) packets, 786
LSU (Link-State Update) packets, 786

M

MAC (Media Address Control) addresses, 49–50
    Proxy ARP, 660
    virtual, 661–662
MAC frame format, 54–55
major commands, 212
MANs (metropolitan area networks), 891
many-to-many NAT (Network Address Translation),
    524, 527–528
MD5 verification, 335
mesh topology, 30–31
Metro Ethernet, 882
    WANs and, 891
MIB (management information base), 655–657
Mills, David, 94
MILNET, 87
mini-IOS, 275
mkdir command, 338
MLP (Multilink PPP), 900, 907–908
    configuration, 908–910
    load balancing, 908
    redundancy, 908
    verification, 910–911
MOP (Maintenance Operation Protocol), disabling,
    625
more command, 338
MOTD (message of the day) banners, 219–220
MPLS (MultiProtocol Label Switching), 882, 888
    VPNs
        Layer 3, 917
        VPLS, 916
        VPWS, 916
    WANs and, 890–891
        deployment, 891–892
MTU (maximum transmission unit), 697
multi-area network OSPF, 785–786
    adjacency, requirements, 786–787
    configuration
        basic, 793–795
        labs, 821–823
    exam essentials, 819–820

verification
  labs, 821–823
  show ip ospf command, 797–798
  show ip ospf database command, 796,
    802–804
  show ip ospf interface command, 796,
    798–800
  show ip ospf neighbor command, 796
  show ip protocols command, 796, 801
  show ip route command, 796, 801–802
multicast addresses, 554, 564
  LSA, 752
multicast route caching, disabling, 625
multimode fibers, 65–66

N

NA (neighbor advertisement), 563–564, 852
Nagle TCP congestion algorithm, 626
named access lists, 486–487, 505–510
  configurations, 213
  sequence numbers, 509
NAT (Network Address Translation)
  advantages/disadvantages, 523
  dynamic (many-to-many), 524
  overloading (one-to-many), 524, 526, 528–529
  static (one-to-one), 524, 526–527
  troubleshooting, 529–534
  verifying configuration, 529
  when to use, 522–523
NAT Overload, 524, 526, 528–529
native VLANs, 452–453, 458, 464–465
NBAR (Network Based Application Recognition),
  966
NBI (northbound interface) APIs, 956–957
NBMA (nonbroadcast multi-access), OSPF, 750
NCP (Network Control Protocol), 87, 900, 934
  CDPCP and, 899
  IPCP and, 899
ND (neighbor discovery), 562–565
NDP (Neighbor Discovery), ICMPv6 and, 851–858
neighbors
  adjacency and, 800
  discovery, 683–688, 727
  NDP (Neighbor Discovery), 851–858
  OSPF, 749
    Hello protocol, 791
    states, 791–793
  tables, 684, 686
neighbors command, 710
neighborship database, OSFP, 750
NETCONF, SBI APIs, 956
netsh interface ipv6 show neighbor command,
  856

network addresses, 117–120
network command, 393, 727
Network layer, OSI reference model, 24–25. *See also*
  layer 3 devices
Network Time Protocol. *See* NTP
networks
  identity-based networking, 652
  intelligent (*See* intelligent networks)
  programmability, 953–954
networks/networking. *See also* internetworking
  debugging, 308–310
  reliable, 19
  segmentation, 6
  services, disabling
    auto-config, 623
    BootP, 623
    CDP (Cisco Discovery Protocol), 627
    default forwarded UDP protocols, 627–628
    HTTP interface, 624
    ICMP unreachable messages, 625
    IP source routing, 624
    MOP, 625
    multicast route caching, 625
    proxy ARP, 624
    redirect messages, 624–625
    small services, 622–623
    X.25 PAD, 626
  topologies
    Data Link layer, OSI model, 26
    documenting with CDP, 295–297
    logical, 27, 30
    Physical layer, OSI model, 29–31
  troubleshooting connectivity, 306–308
Next Header field, IPv6 header, 560
next hop, 383–385
Nexus data center switches, 958
NGFW (Next Generation Firewalls), 12
NGIPS (Next Generation IPS), 12
nibbles, 50–53, 324
NLA (network link advertisement), 789
NMS (network management station), 16, 650
  SNMP and, 655–656
no bandwidth command, 702
no banner login command, 220
no cdp enable command, 627
no cdp run command, 291
no debug command, 309
no ip boot server command, 623
no ip domain-lookup command, 304, 374
no ip forward-protocol udp command,
  627–628
no ip host command, 303–304
no ip http server command, 624
no ip mroute-cache command, 625
no ip proxy-arp command, 624

no ip redirects command, 624
no ip source-route command, 624
no ip unreachables command, 625
no license boot module command, 347
no lldp run command, 298
no login command, 225
no mop enabled command, 625
no service command, 623
no service config command, 623
no service finger command, 623
no service pad command, 626
no service tcp-small-servers command, 623
no service udp-small-servers command, 623
no shutdown command, 234–235, 249, 279, 374
no switchport trunk native vlan command, 464–465
non-designated port, 604–605
non-root bridges, 604
nonvolatile RAM. *See* NVRAM
not ready indicator, Transport layer, 21
NS (neighbor solicitation), 563–564, 852
NTP (Network Time Protocol), 94–95, 288–289
ntp master command, 289
ntp server command, 288–289
NVRAM (nonvolatile RAM), 209, 240, 275
    Cisco configuration backups, 277–278
    Cisco configuration restores, 279
    configuration register, 324–331
    router and switch boot sequence, 276
nvram:startup-config, 338

O

OC-3, WAN bandwidth and, 887
OC-12, WAN bandwidth and, 887
OC-48, WAN bandwidth and, 887
OC-192, WAN bandwidth and, 887
OIDs (Organizational IDs), 656
onePK, SBI APIs, 956
one-to-many NAT, 524, 528–529
one-to-one NAT, 524, 527
OpenFlow, SBI APIs, 956
OpFlex, SBI APIs, 956
optical fiber converters, WANs, 886
Options field, IP header, 110
OSI reference model, 13–17
    advantages, 14
    Application layer, 17
    Data Link layer, 26–29
    Network layer, 24–25
    Physical layer, 29–31
    Presentation layer, 18
    Session layer, 18
    Transport layer, 18–23

OSPF (Open Shortest Path First), 584, 746, 928
    adjacency, 749
    BDR (backup designated router), 750
    benefits, 748
    BGP comparison, 926–927
    broadcast
        multi-access, 750
        NBMA, 750
    configuration
        enabling OSPF, 753–754
        verification, 765–771
    Corp router, 758–759
    costs, 753
    database synchronization
        DD packets, 786
        LSR packets, 786
        LSU packets, 786
    default administrative distance, 391
    DR (designated router), 749
    exam essentials, 772–773
    Hello protocol, 750–752, 790–791
    LA router, 759–762
    labs
        enabling process, 773–774
        interface configuration, 774–775
        verifying operation, 775
    links, 749
    loopback interfaces, 762–763
        configuration, 763–765
    LSA (Link State Advertisement), 750
        flooding, 752
    metrics, 753
    multi-area network, 785–786
        adjacency, 786–787
        configuration, 793–795, 821–823
        exam essentials, 819–820
        verification, 796–804, 821–823
    neighbors, 749
        states, 791–793
    neighborship database, 750
    OSPF areas, 750
        configuration, 754–762
    OSPFv3, 565, 570, 814–816
        labs, 824–825
        verification, 816–819
    overview, 746–748
    point-to-multipoint, 751
    point-to-point, 751
    RID (router ID), 749
    RIP comparison, 747
    routers, roles, 787–788
    scalability, 784–786
    SF router, 759
    single-area network, 785
    SPF tree, calculations, 752

topological database, 750
troubleshooting, 804–812
    simple, 812–814
OUI (organizationally unique identifier), 49–50, 73
outbound ACLs (access control lists), 487
out-of-band communication, 207
output errors, 248–252, 839
output queue, drops, 839
outside global addresses, 525–527, 530
outside local addresses, 524–525, 530
overhead, 19
overloading NAT configuration, 524, 528–529

P

PaaS (Platform as a Service), 952–953
packet switching
    MPLS and, 888
    WANs and, 888
packets
    collision domains, 8
    comparing to ACLs, 486
    Data Link layer, 26–27
    dropped, 962
    errors, 962
    forwarding process, 366–367
    jitter, 962
    Network layer, 24–25
    out-of-order delivery, 962
    packet filtering, 8
    packet switching, 8
PAD (packet assembler/disassembler), disabling, 626
PAgP (Port Aggregation Protocol), 630
PAK (product authorization key), 343–344
PAP (Password Authentication Protocol), 901
partially meshed topology, 884–885
Passive mode (NBAR), 966
passive state, routes, 713
passive-interface command, 397, 696–697
passwords
    auxiliary passwords, 225
    console passwords, 223–224
    enable passwords, 221–222, 263
    enable secret passwords, 221–222, 227, 257
    encrypting, 227–229
    recovering, 328–331
    user-mode, 222
        configuring, 212, 222, 224–225
        for Telnet access, 224–225
PAT (Port Address Translation), 524, 526, 528–529
path cost, 604
Path Selection, 893–894
path selection, 8

path tracing, APIC-EM and, 959–960
Payload Length field, IPv6 header, 560
PDLM (Packet Description Language Model), 966
PDUs (protocol data units), 66–69
perimeter routers, 484–485
permit any command, 487
Physical layer, OSI reference model, 29–31
    Ethernet at, 55–57
    hubs, 29–30
    topologies, 30–31
physical topologies, 27, 29–31
ping command, 190–191, 306–307, 388
Ping program, 833–837
    LAN, 836–838
    loopback address, 835
pipe, 236–237
point-to-multipoint, OSPF, 751
point-to-point
    leased lines, 887–888
    OSPF, 751
Port Address Translation (PAT), 524, 526, 528–529
port channels, 630
    configuration, 630–634
    EtherChannel, 629–630
    verifying, 630–634
port cost, 604
port VLAN ID (PVID), 452
PortFast, 625–627
    configuration, 640
    lab, 640
ports
    access ports, 449–451
    console ports, 207–208
    security, 417–420, 651
        dynamic MAC addresses, 417, 428, 431
        error-disabled state, 418–419, 430
        static MAC addresses, 419–420, 428–431
        sticky, 419
        violation actions, 417–420, 429–430
port-security command, 418
positive acknowledgment with retransmission, 23
POST (power-on self-test), 209, 274–275
powers of 2, 139–140
PPP (Point-to-Point Protocol), 882, 934
    authentication
        CHAP, 901
        configuration, 901–902
        debugging, 904
        PAP, 901
    configuration
        authentication, 901–902, 936–937
        encapsulation, 936–937
        routers, 901
    EIA/TIA-232-C, 899
    IP addresses, mismatched, 906–907

ISDN, 899
LCP (Link Control Protocol), 898
   configuration, 899–900
MLP (Multilink PPP), 907–908
   configuring, 908–910
   verifying, 910–911
PPP callback, 900
PPPoE, 911
   configuration, 912–913
serial links, 895
   HDLC and, 896–897, 899
   PPP and, 898
   troubleshooting, 902–907
   verification, 902–907
sessions
   authentication phase, 900
   link-establishment phase, 900
   network layer protocol phase, 900
troubleshooting, 934
V.24, 899
V.35, 899
WANs and, 889
   mismatched encapsulations, 905–906
ppp multilink group command, 910
PPPoE (Point-to-Point Protocol over Ethernet), 882
   ADSL and, 911
   configuration, 912–913
   WANs and, 890
preamble field, Ethernet frame, 54
prefix routing, 393
Presentation layer, OSI reference model, 18
Priority field, IP header, 109
private IP addresses, 122–123
privileged exec mode, Cisco IOS, 210, 213
process switching, 367
Process/Application layer, DoD model, 87–99
   APIPA, 98–99
   DHCP, 96–98
   DNS, 95–96
   FTP, 90–92
   HTTP, 93–94
   HTTPS, 94
   NTP, 94–95
   SNMP, 93
   SSH, 90
   Telnet, 89–90
   TFTP, 91–92
programmability in enterprise network, 953–954
prompts, Cisco IOS, 211–213
Protocol field, IP header, 110–111
protocols
   advanced distance-vector protocols, 682
   AH (Authenticated Header), 918
   BGP (Border Gateway Protocol), 882, 925
      ASs and, 928

      attributes, 928
      eBGP (external BGP) neighbors, 928–929
      iBGP (internal BGP) neighbors, 928–929
      IGPs (interior gateway protocols), 928
      network structure, 928
      OSPF comparison, 926–927
   CDPCP (Cisco Discovery Protocol Control
      Protocol), 899
   CHAP (Challenge Handshake Authentication
      Protocol), 901
   DTP (Dynamic Trunk Protocol), 586
      VLANs, 589–591
   EGP (exterior gateway protocol), 925
      local network advertisement, 930–931
   EIGRP (Enhanced Interior Gateway Routing
      Protocol), 584, 682, 746, 928
      bandwith, 697
      configuration, 690–693
      delay, 697
      distance-vector updates, 682
      DUAL (Diffusing Update Algorithm) and, 689
      exam essentials, 733
      FD (feasible distance) and, 685
      FS (feasible successor) and, 687
      hellos, 684
      hop count, 699
      labs, 734–735
      load, 697
      load balancing, unequal-cost, 705–707
      MTU (maximum transmission unit), 697
      neighbors, 683–688
      packets, 688–689
      paths, maximum, 699
      RD/AD (reported/advertised distance) and,
        684
      reliability, 697
      routes, 689–690, 699–704
      RTP (Reliable Transport Protocol) and,
        688–689
      split horizon, 707–709
      successors, 687
      topology table, 686
      traffic control, 696–697
      troubleshooting, 709, 715–727
      verification, 709–715
      VLSM support, 693–696
   ESP (Encapsulating Security Payload), 918–919
   exterior gateway protocols, 390
   FHRPs (first hop redundancy protocols),
      661–662
   GGP (Gateway to Gateway Protocol), 925
   GLBP (Gateway Load Balancing Protocol), 662
   HDLC (High-Level Data-Link Control) protocol,
      882, 896–899, 934
      configuration, 937–938

monitoring, 937–938
WANs and, 889
HSRP (Hot Standby Router Protocol), 650, 662
hybrid routing protocols, 682
IGPs (interior gateway protocols), 928
IGRP (Interior Gateway Routing Protocol), 928
interior gateway protocols, 390
IPCP (Internet Protocol Control Protocol), 899
LACP (Link Aggregation Control Protocol), 630
LCP (Link Control Protocol), 898
configuration, 899–900
MPLS (MultiProtocol Label Switching), 882
NCP (Network Control Protocol), 900
PAgP (Port Aggregation Protocol), 630
PPP (Point-to-Point Protocol), 882, 934
authentication, 901–902, 904
configuration, 901–902, 936–937
EIA/TIA-232-C, 899
IP addresses, mismatched, 906–907
ISDN, 899
LCP (Link Control Protocol), 898–900
MLP (Multilink PPP), 907–911
PPP callback, 900
PPPoE, 911–913
serial links, 895–899, 902–907
sessions, 900
troubleshooting, 934
V.24, 899
V.35, 899
WANs and, 889, 905–906
PPPoE (Point-to-Point Protocol over Ethernet),
882
Proxy ARP (Proxy Address Resolution Protocol),
660
routing protocols
EIGRP, 584
OSPF, 584
RIP, 584
RSTP (Rapid Spanning Tree Protocol), 613–615
RTP (Reliable Transport Protocol), 683, 688–689
SNMP (Simple Network Management Protocol),
650
STP (Spanning Tree Protocol), 584
TCP (Transmission Control Protocol), 970–971
thin protocols, 101
tunneling
GRE, 917
L2F, 917
L2TP, 917
PPTP, 917
unreliable protocols, 102
VRRP (Virtual Router Redundancy Protocol), 662
VTP (VLAN Trunking Protocol), 585
provider-managed VPNs, 915–917
proxy ARP, disabling, 624

Proxy ARP (Proxy Address Resolution Protocol), 660
pruning, 596–597
PVID (port VLAN ID), 452
PVST+ (Per-VLAN Spanning Tree+), 611–617
pwd command, 338–339

Q

QoS (quality of service), 948, 971
CBWFQ (class-based weighted fair queuing), 969
classification, 965–966
Class Selector, 966
CoS (Class of Service), 965
DSCP/DiffServ (Differentiated Services Code
Point), 965
marking tools, 966
TID (Traffic Identifier), 966
tools, 966
ToS (Type of Service), 965
delays and, 962
LLQ (low latency queuing), 969
packets
dropped, 962
errors, 962
jitter, 962
out-of-order delivery, 962
policers, 966–967
shapers, 966–967
traffic
buffering, 968
congestion avoidance, 970–971
congestion management, 967–969
CQ (custom queuing), 969
data traffic, 963
FIFO, 969
PQ (priority queuing), 969
queuing, 968
scheduling, 968
video traffic, 963–964
voice traffic, 963–964
WFQ (weighted fair queuing), 969

R

RA (router advertisement), 558–559, 563–564, 851
RADIUS (Remote Authentication Dial-In User
Service), 654
exam essentials, 675
identity-based networking, 652
RAM (random access memory), 275
Rapid PVST+, 610
RD/AD (reported/advertised distance), 684
ready indicator, Transport layer, 21

recovering passwords, 328–331
redistribution, 397
redundancy
    client redundancy, 659–661
    GLBP (Gateway Load Balancing Protocol), 662
    HSRP (Hot Standby Router Protocol), 662
    MLP, 908
    VRRP (Virtual Router Redundancy Protocol), 662
redundant links, 420–422
reference models, 13–14
    OSI (*See* OSI reference model)
reliable data transport, 20–21
    positive acknowledgment with retransmission, 23
reliable multicast, 688
reliable networking, 19
reload command, 280, 331
remote-access VPNs, 915
resolving hostnames, 302–305
review question answers, 998–1035
RFC 791, 109
RFC 1256, 111
RFC 1918, 122
RFC 3232, 104
RID (router ID), 749, 790
    setting, 762
Right-To-Use (RTU) licensing, 342, 344–347
ring topology, 30
RIP (Routing Information Protocol), 392–393, 584, 928
    configuring RIP routing, 393–396
    default administrative distance, 391
    EIGRP and, 682
    OSPF comparison, 747
    preventing propagations, 396–398
RIPv2, 393–398
RJ45 cabling, 56–57, 63–64
RLA (router link advertisement), 788
rmdir command, 338
ROAS (router on a stick), 455–456, 465
rolled cable, 62–64
ROM (read-only memory), 274–275
ROM monitor, 275, 329
rommon prompt, 335–336
root bridges, 603–604, 637
    configuration, 638–640
    selecting, 609–610
    verification, 638–640
root port, 604
route aggregation. *See* summarization
route print command, 834
route update packets, Network layer, 24
routed protocols, 24
    vs. routing protocols, 358
router bgp AS command, 930

router eigrp command, 690
router on a stick (ROAS), 455–456, 465
router rip command, 393
router-id command, 764–765
routers. *See also* layer 3 devices
    administrative functions, configuring, 218–219
        banners, 219–221
        hostnames, 219
        interface descriptions, 229–231
        passwords, 221–229
    advantages, 8
    backup and recovery, 276–280
    boot sequence, 275–276
    Corp, 758–759
    first hop, 661–662
    interface configuration, 231–240
        deleting configuration, 242
        enabling/disabling interface, 234–235
        IP addresses, 235–236
        pipe output modifier, 236–237
        saving configuration, 240–242
        serial interface commands, 237–240
        verifying configuration, 242–255
    internal components, 274–275
    internal packet-forwarding process, 366–367
    LA, 759–762
    modes, Cisco IOS, 210
    perimeter routers, 484–485
    roles, OSPF, 787–788
    router solicitation (RS), 557–559, 563–564
    SF, 759
routes, passive, 713
routing, 832–833
    basics, 359–361
    classful, 393
    classless, 393
    configuring, 372–390
        default routing, 387–390
        DHCP, 380–381
        RIP routing, 392–398
        router one, 373–375
        router three, 379–380
        router two, 375–379
    dynamic, 359, 390–392
    prefix, 393
    process, 361–372
    protocols, 24
        AD (administrative distance), 391–392
        advanced distance-vector, 392
        configurations, 213–214
        distance-vector, 392, 400
        EIGRP, 584
        IPv6, 565–566
        link-state, 392
        OSPF, 584

redistribution, 397
RIP, 584
summarization, 186–189
vs. routed protocols, 358
static, 359, 382–387
tables, 8, 24–25
administrative distance, 391–392
gateway of last resort, 387–388
metric, 385
next hop, 383–385
routing protocol code, 375
RS (router solicitation), 557–559, 563–564, 851
RSTP (Rapid Spanning Tree Protocol), 613–615
RTO (Retransmission Time Out) field, 710
RTP (Reliable Transport Protocol), 683, 688–689, 732
RTU (Right-To-Use) licensing, 342, 344–347
running-config file, 240–242, 276–279
RXBOOT, 275, 326

S

SA (Source Address), 54–55
SaaS (Software as a Service), 952–953
SAL (service abstraction layer), 958
SBI (southbound interface) APIs, 955–956
APIC-EM, 958
NETCONF, 956
onePK, 956
Openflow, 956
OpFlex, 956
scalability
OSPF, 784–786
VLANs, 448–449
SDN (Software Defined Networking), 948, 955, 971
APIC-EM and, 957
application plane, 954
control plane, 954
data plane, 954
security
access control lists (*See* ACLs)
DoS (denial of service) attacks, 488–489, 622
firewalls, 12
port security, 417–420
dynamic MAC addresses, 417, 428, 431
error-disabled state, 418–419, 430
static MAC addresses, 419–420, 428–431
sticky, 419
violation actions, 417–420, 429–430
SSH (Secure Shell), 225–227
trusted networks, 485
untrusted networks, 485
VLANs, 448
sequence numbers, 509

serial links, 895
HDLC and, 896–897, 899
PPP and, 898
troubleshooting, 902–907
verification, 902–907
serial transmission, 894–895
service nagle command, 626
service password-encryption command, 228–229, 902
service timestamps log datetime msec command, 288
Session layer, OSI reference model, 18
session multiplexing, 23, 108
setup command, 209
setup mode, Cisco IOS, 209, 213, 240, 242, 256
SF router, 759
SFD (Start Frame Delimiter), 54
SFPs (Small Form-Factor Pluggables), 66
shortest-path-first (SPF) protocols, 392
show access-list 110 command, 498–505, 508
show access-list command, 508–509, 511
show cdp command, 290
show cdp entry command, 294
show cdp neighbors command, 291–294, 296–297, 312
show cdp neighbors detail command, 292–294, 297
show controllers command, 254–255, 379
show controllers int command, 239
show file command, 338–339, 341
show flash command, 332–333
show history command, 217
show hosts command, 302–303, 313
show interface command, 229–230, 246–252, 430–431, 898, 903
show interface description command, 229–230
show interface trunk command, 596–597
show interfaces command, 234, 306, 924
show interfaces interface switchport command, 458–461
show interfaces multilink1 command, 910
show interfaces trunk command, 586
show ip access-list command, 508
show ip arp command, 191, 364, 428
show ip bgp command, 933
show ip bgp neighbors command, 933–934
show ip bgp summary command, 931–932
show ip dhcp binding command, 282, 389
show ip dhcp conflict command, 283, 390
show ip dhcp pool command, 283, 389–390
show ip dhcp server statistics command, 283
show ip eigrp events command, 714
show ip eigrp interface command, 709–710, 716
show ip eigrp interface detail command, 711
show ip eigrp neighbors command, 709, 716

show ip eigrp topology command, 709, 716
show ip eigrp traffic command, 709, 713
show ip int brief command, 377–378, 393–395
show ip interface brief command, 231–234, 253, 431, 923–924
show ip interface command, 252–253, 367, 508, 510–511, 861
show ip nat statistics command, 530–531
show ip nat translations command, 529–530
show ip ospf command, 766–767, 797–798
show ip ospf database command, 767–768, 796, 802–804
show ip ospf interface command, 768–769, 796, 798–800
show ip ospf neighbor command, 769–770, 796–797
show ip protocols command, 705, 709, 770–771, 796, 801
show ip route command, 360–361, 375, 378, 399, 703, 796, 801–802
show ip route eigrp command, 709
show ipv6 int brief command, 570–571
show license command, 345, 348
show license feature command, 346, 348
show license UDI command, 342
show logging command, 286, 627
show mac address-table command, 416, 431–433
show ntp command, 289
show ntp status command, 289
show port-security interface command, 429, 434
show ppp multilink command, 910
show processes command, 310–311
show protocols command, 253–254
show protocols command, 717
show run | begin int command, 377
show run command, 902
show running-config command, 227–230, 234–235, 241–242, 258, 277, 430, 434, 464, 506, 508, 898
show sessions command, 300–301, 313
show startup-config command, 241–242, 277
show terminal command, 217–218
show users command, 301, 497
show version command, 257, 326–327, 346–348
show vlan brief command, 863
show vlan command, 457–458, 585–586, 863
show vlan id 200 command, 586
show vtp status command, 598
SHTTP, 94
shutdown command, 234
simplex mode, 18
single-area OSPF, 785
single-mode fibers, 65–66
site-to-site VPNs, 915

SLA (summary link advertisement), 789–790
    troubleshooting and, 843–845
slash notation (/), CIDR, 140, 142, 152–154
small services, disabling, 623
smart-serial cabling, 894–895
SNMP (Simple Network Management Protocol), 93, 622, 650, 655–656
    configuring, 657–659
    exam essentials, 675
    GET, 657
    INFORM, 657
    MIB (management information base), 656–657
    read/write options, 659
    SET, 657
    TRAP, 657
    WALK, 657
snmp-server command, 658
solicited-node address, 562–564
Source Address field, IPv6 header, 560
Source IP address field, IP header, 110
SPAN, troubleshooting and, 845–846
special addresses, IPv6, 554–555
speed and duplex settings, 838
SPF (shortest-path-first) protocols, 392
SPF tree, calculations, 752
split horizon, 707–709
SPT (Spanning Tree Protocol), 413
squeeze command, 338
SRTT (smooth round-trip timer), 684
SSH (Secure Shell), 90–91, 225–227
StackWise, 948–949, 971
    benefits, 949–950
    features, 949
    unit, creating, 949–950
standard ACLs (access control lists), 486, 489–490
    example, 492–496
    remarks, 507–508
    VTY access, controlling, 496–497
    wildcard masking, 490–492
star topology, 30, 883–884
startup-config file, 209, 213, 240–242, 256
state transitions, 29
stateful autoconfiguration, IPv6, 559
stateless autoconfiguration, IPv6, 556–559
static NAT (Network Address Translation), 524, 527
static routing, 359, 382–387
    with IPv6, 565–566
sticky command, 419
STP (Spanning Tree Protocol), 413, 584, 602–603
    802.1s (MSTP), 610
    BPDU (Bridge Protocol Data Unit), 604
        lab, 640
    bridge ID, 604
    convergence and, 606
    CST (Common Spanning Tree), 610–611

failures, 623–625
IEEE 802.1d, 610
IEEE 802.1w, 610, 612–618
link costs and, 606–607
non-root bridges, 604
operations, 607–609
    root bridge selection, 609–610
path cost, 604
port cost, 604
PortFast, lab, 640
PVST+ (Per-VLAN Spanning Tree+), 610
Rapid PVST+, 610
root bridge, 603–604, 637
    lab, 638–640
states
    blocking, 605
    disabled, 605
    forwarding, 606
    learning, 605
    listening, 605
switched networks, 603
verification, 637
    lab, 637–638
straight-through cable, 59–60
subcommands, 212
subnetting, 136–137
    CIDR, 140–142
    Class A addresses, 163–166
    Class B addresses, 154–163
    Class C addresses, 142–154
    creating subnets, 138
    ip subnet zero command, 142, 166
    subnet masks, 138–139
    VLSMs, 176–178
        implementing, 179–186
        network design, 178
successor route, 687
summarization, 186–189
SVIs (switched virtual interfaces), 455–456, 471, 476
switch access vlan command, 866
switch fabric, 452
switch ports, assigning to VLANs, 587–589
switch stacking, 948, 971. *See also* StackWise
switched networks, 603
    STP and, 603
    switching loops and, 603
switches
    administrative functions, configuring, 218–219
        banners, 219–221
        hostnames, 219
        interface descriptions, 229–231
        passwords, 221–229
    backup and recovery, 276–280
    boot sequence, 275–176
    Catalyst switches, configuring, 422–423
        boot process review, 423–424
        IP address requirement, 424

port security, 417, 428–430
    S1, 424–425
    S2, 426–427
    S3, 427–428
    verifying configuration, 430–433
functions, 413
    address learning, 413–415
    forward/filter decisions, 413, 415–417
    loop avoidance, 413, 420–422
interface configuration, 231–240
    deleting configuration, 242
    enabling/disabling interface, 234–235
    IP addresses, 235–236
    pipe output modifier, 236–237
    saving configuration, 240–242
    serial interface commands, 237–240
    verifying configuration, 242–255
internal components, 274–275
Nexus data center, 958
redundant links, 420–422
SPAN and, 845–846
vs. hubs, 28–29
switchport access command, 460
switchport command, 459–460
switchport mode access command, 460, 462–463,
    588, 590
switchport mode dynamic auto command, 462, 590
switchport mode dynamic desirable command,
    462, 590
switchport mode trunk command, 461–462,
    589–591
switchport nonegotiate command, 462, 591
switchport port-security command, 418–420,
    429–430, 434
switchport port-security mac-address
    command, 418, 420, 428
symmetric encryption, 919
syslog, 283–288
system:running-config, 338

T

T1, WAN bandwidth and, 886
T3, WAN bandwidth and, 887
tables
    neighbor tables, 684, 686
    topology tables, 686
TAC (Technical Assistance Center), 698
TACACS+ (Terminal Access Controller Access
    Control System), 654
    configuring, 655
    exam essentials, 675
TCP (Transmission Control Protocol), 18–19,
    99–100, 970–971
    key concepts, 103–104
    port numbers, 104–107

segment format, 100–101
session multiplexing, 108
small services, 623
TCP global synchronization, 970–971
TCP/IP, 86, 89
    DoD model, 87–89
        Host-to-Host layer, 87–89, 99–108
        Internet layer, 87–89, 108–116
        Process/Application layer, 87–89
    history of, 87
Telnet, 89–90, 298–299
    checking connections, 300–301
    checking users, 301
    closing sessions, 301
    connecting multiple devices, 300
    troubleshooting and, 841–842
    user-mode passwords, 224–225
telnet command, 298–299
TFTP (Trivial File Transfer Protocol), 91–92
threats, access layer, mitigation, 651
TIA (Telecommunications Industry Association), 56
timers
    hold timer, 684
    SRTT (smooth round-trip timer), 684
TLV (Type-Length Value), 602
toll network, WANs, 886
topological database, OSFP, 750
topology
    fully meshed, 884
    hub-and-spoke, 883–884
    partially meshed, 884–885
    star, 883–884
    tables, 686
ToS (Type of Service), 965
traceroute command, 836
tracert command, 191, 197, 306–307
traffic
    buffering, 968
    congestion, 6–7, 9, 20
    congestion avoidance, 970–971
    congestion management, 967–969
    CQ (custom queuing), 969
    data traffic, 963
    FIFO, 969
    PQ (priority queuing), 969
    queuing, 968
    scheduling, 968
    trust boundaries, 965
    video traffic, 963–964
    voice traffic, 963–964
    WFQ (weighted fair queuing), 969
    WRED and, 970
Traffic Class field, IPv6 header, 560
Transmission Control Protocol. *See* TCP
Transmission Control Protocol/Internet Protocol. *See*
    TCP/IP
transparent bridging, 28

Transport layer, OSI reference model, 18–23
    connection-oriented communication, 19–20
    flow control, 20–21
    session multiplexing, 23, 108
    windowing, 22
troubleshooting
    collisions, 247–252
    commands, EIGRP, 709
    EIGRP, 725–727
        examples, 715–725
    errors, 251–252
    HSRP, 674–675
    IP addresses, 189–196
    IP network connectivity, 833–843
        ACLs, extended, 847–849
        SLAs, 843–845
        SPAN, 845–846
    IPv6 network connectivity, 850
        ICMPv6 and, 850–858
    NAT, 529–534
    OSPF, 812–814
    serial links, 902–907
    syslog, 283–288
    VLANs (virtual LANs), 862
        CAM table, 862
        scenario, 862–867
        trunk troubleshooting, 867–874
trunk links, 450–452
trunk ports, 450, 461–465
    VLANs
        allowed, 591–592
        configuration, 589–591
        modifying, 592–593
trunk troubleshooting, VLANs, 867–874
trunking
    advantages, 451
    disabling, 463
    DTP (Dynamic Trunking Protocol), 458–459,
        462–463
    IEEE 802.1q, 453
    ISL (Inter-Switch Link), 452–453
    VTP (VLAN Trunking Protocol), 457, 463
trust boundaries, 964–965
trusted domains, 964
trusted networks, 485
tunneling, 54
    6-to-4 tunneling, 555
    and NAT, 523
    protocols
        GRE, 917
        L2F, 917
        L2TP, 917
        PPTP, 917
twinax, 56
Type 1 LSA, 788–789
Type 2, 789
Type 3, 789–790

Type 4 LSA, 790
Type 5 LSA, 790
Type field, Ethernet frame, 54–55
Type of Service field, IP header, 109

U

UDP (User Datagram Protocol), 18–19, 101–104
    disabling default forwarded protocols, 627–628
    key concepts, 103–104
    segment format, 102–103
    session multiplexing, 108
    small services, 623
U/L bit, 50
undebug all command, 309
unequal-cost load balancing, 705–707
unicast addresses, 125, 550, 552–553
unique local addresses, 553
universal images, 342
unreliable protocols, 102
unshielded twisted-pair cabling, 56, 59, 62, 64
untagged frames, 468
untrusted domains, 964
untrusted networks, 485
upgrades
    copy command, 334–337
    using Cisco IFS, 338–341
    verifying flash memory, 332–333
upstream routing, 465
URL (Uniform Resource Locator), 94
user exec mode, Cisco IOS, 210, 213, 220
user interface, Cisco IOS, 206–209
user-mode passwords, 222, 224
    configuring, 212, 222, 224–225
    encrypting, 227–229
    for Telnet access, 224–225
username command, 902
UTP. *See* unshielded twisted-pair cabling
UTP Gigabit, 62

V

V.35 interface, 7
variable length subnet masks. *See* VLSMs
verification
    EBGP
        show ip bgp command, 933
        show ip bgp neighbors command, 933–934
        show ip bgp summary command, 931–932
    GRE tunnels, 923–925
    MLP, 907–908
    multi-area network OSPF
        show ip ospf command, 797–798
        show ip ospf database command, 796, 802–804

        show ip ospf interface command, 796, 798–800
        show ip ospf neighbor command, 796–797
        show ip protocols command, 796, 801
        show ip route command, 796, 801–802
    serial links, 902–907
Version field
    IP header, 109
    IPv6 header, 560
Version-Dependent Transparent Mode, 602
violation actions, port security, 417–420, 429–430
violation shutdown command, 430
virtual accounts, 348
virtual addresses, 661–662
virtual local area networks. *See* VLANs
vlan command, 456–457, 584
VLANs (virtual LANs), 444–447
    access ports, 449–451
    broadcast control, 447–448
    configuring
        S1 switch, 584–585
    configuring, 456–459
        assigning switch ports, 459–461
        inter-VLAN routing, 465–462
        trunk ports, 461–465
    database, modes, 595–596
    flexibility, 448–449
    frame tagging, 451–452, 472
    identification methods, 452–453
    IVR (Inter-VLAN Routing), 444, 455–456, 471–472
    native, 452–453, 458, 464–465
    routing between, 454–456
    scalability, 448–449
    security, 448
    switch ports, assigning, 587–589
    troubleshooting, 862
        CAM table, 862
        scenario, 862–867
        trunk troubleshooting, 867–874
    trunk ports
        allowed, 591–592
        configuration, 589–591
        modifying, 592–593
    voice VLANs, 450
    VPNs and, 913–914
    VTP (VLAN Trunking Protocol), 457, 463
VLSMs (variable length subnet masks), 176–178
    benefits, 197
    BGP and, 928
    EIGRP and, 693–696
    implementing VLSM networks, 179–186
    network design, 178
    VLSM tables, 179–183
voice access ports, 450, 459
voice VLANs, 450

VPLS (virtual private LAN switching service), 916
VPNs (virtual private networks), 882, 913–914, 935
  compatibility, 914
  cost, 914
  encryption, 919
  enterprise-managed, 915–917
  extranet, 915
  MPLS, 916–917
  provider-managed, 915–917
  remote-access, 915
  scalability, 914
  security, 914
  site-to-site, 915
  VPLS (virtual private LAN switching service), 916
  VPWS (virtual private wire service), 916
VPWS (virtual private wire service), 916
VRRP (Virtual Router Redundancy Protocol), 662
VSAT (Very Small Aperture Terminal), WANs and, 891
VTP (VLAN Trunking Protocol), 457, 463, 585, 593–594
  configuration, 597–598
  considerations, 595
  domains, 599
  modes, 594, 600
    client, 595
    server, 595
    transparent, 596
  pruning, 596–597
  troubleshooting, 598–602
VTP transparent mode, 594

W

WANs (wide area networks), 7, 882. *See also* Intelligent WAN
  3G/4G (cellular), 891
  ATM (Asynchronous Transfer Mode), 891
  bandwidth
    DS0 (digital signal 0), 886
    E1, 887
    OC-3, 887
    OC-12, 887
    OC-48, 887
    OC-192, 887
    T1, 886
    T3, 887
  branches, 892
  cable, HFC, 890
  CO (central office), 886
  connection types, 935
    circuit-switched, 887–888
    dedicated, 887–888
    packet-switched, 887–888
  CPE (customer premises equipment), 885
  CSU/DSU (channel service unit/data service unit), 886, 895–896
  DCE (data communication equipment), 895–896
  demarcation point, 886
  deploying, 891–892
  DSL (digital subscriber line), 890
  DTE (data terminal equipment), 895–896
  DTE-DCE-DTE connection, 895–896
  encapsulations, mismatched, 905–906
  Frame Relay, 889
  HDLC (High-Level Data-Link Control), 889, 896–898
  IP addresses, mismatched, 906–907
  ISDN (Integrated Services Digital Network), 889
  LAN comparison, 882–883
  local loop, 886
  Metro Ethernet, 891
  MPLS (MultiProtocol Label Switching), 890–891
  optical fiber converters, 886
  PPP (Point-to-Point Protocol), 889
    authentication, 901
    EIA/TIA-232-C, 899
    ISDN, 899
    LCP (Link Control Protocol), 898–900
    session establishment, 900
    V.24, 899
    V.35, 899
  PPPoE (Point-to-Point Protocol over Ethernet), 890
  serial transmission, 894–895
  support, 888–891
  telcos, 883
  toll network, 886
  topology
    fully meshed, 884
    hub-and-spoke, 883–884
    partially meshed, 884–885
    star, 883–884
  VLANs and, 913
  VPNs and, 913–914
  VSAT (Very Small Aperture Terminal), 891
web addresses, 94
wildcard masking, 490–492
windowing, 22
wireless access points, 44
wireless controllers, 12
wireless hot spots, 3G/4G, 891
workgroup layer, Cisco hierarchical model, 71–72
WRED (weighted random early detection), traffic and, 970

X-Y-Z

Xmodem protocol, 336–337

Yeager, William, 206

Comprehensive Online Learning Environment

Register on Sybex.com to gain access to the comprehensive online interactive learning environment and test bank to help you study for your CCNA Routing and Switching exams.

The online test bank includes the following:

- **Assessment Test** to help you focus your study to specific objectives
- **Chapter Tests** to reinforce what you've learned
- **Practice Exams** to test your knowledge of the material
- **Digital Flashcards** to reinforce your learning and provide last-minute test prep before the exam
- **Searchable Glossary** to define the key terms you'll need to know for the exam
- **eBooks in Multiple Formats** for you to read on your favorite device
- **21 hours of CCENT/CCNA instruction and 1 FREE Switch lab** from the subject matter experts at ITProTV

Go to `http://www.wiley.com/go/sybextestprep` to register and gain access to this comprehensive study tool package.

30% off On-Demand IT Video Training from ITProTV

ITProTV and Sybex have partnered to provide 30% off a Premium annual or monthly membership. ITProTV provides a unique, custom learning environment for IT professionals and students alike, looking to validate their skills through vendor certifications. On-demand courses provide over 1,000 hours of video training with new courses being added every month, while labs and practice exams provide additional hands-on experience. For more information on this offer and to start your membership today, visit `http://itpro.tv/sybex30/`.